RESEARCH HANDBOOK ON THE PROTECTION OF INTELLECTUAL PROPERTY UNDER WTO RULES

RESEARCH HANDBOOKS ON THE WTO

This timely series of *Research Handbooks* analyses the interface between international economic law and other disciplines at the centre of current debate about the role and impact of the WTO. Each volume is edited by a prominent expert at the heart of this debate and brings together original contributions from an internationally recognisable cast of leading scholars and practitioners.

These *Handbooks* will be essential reference tools for academic researchers and doctoral students as well as for policy-makers and practising lawyers.

Future titles will include:

Research Handbook on Environment, Health and the WTO
Edited by Geert Van Calster

Research Handbook on the WTO Agriculture Agreement
Edited by Joseph McMahon and Melaku Desta

Research Handbook on the Protection of Intellectual Property under WTO Rules

Intellectual Property in the WTO
Volume I

Edited by

Carlos M. Correa

Director, Center for Interdisciplinary Studies of Industrial Property and Economics, University of Buenos Aires, Argentina

RESEARCH HANDBOOKS ON THE WTO

Edward Elgar
Cheltenham, UK • Northampton, MA, USA

Published by
Edward Elgar Publishing Limited
The Lypiatts
15 Lansdown Road
Cheltenham
Glos GL50 2JA
UK

Edward Elgar Publishing, Inc.
William Pratt House
9 Dewey Court
Northampton
Massachusetts 01060
USA

A catalogue record for this book
is available from the British Library

Library of Congress Control Number: 2009941129

Mixed Sources
Product group from well-managed
forests and other controlled sources
www.fsc.org Cert no. SA-COC-1565
© 1996 Forest Stewardship Council
FSC

ISBN 978 1 84720 904 7 (cased)

Printed and bound by MPG Books Group, UK

Contents

PART II SUBSTANTIVE RIGHTS

Contributors

Denis Borges Barbosa, LL.B and J.S.D in International Law (State U. Rio de Janeiro), LL.M (Columbia), LL.M in Business Law (UGF), is a former Attorney General of the Brazilian National Institute of Industrial Property, and is a lawyer and Professor of Intellectual Property Law at the Graduate Division of the Catholic University of Rio de Janeiro and at the Master Degree Program of the Brazilian PTO.

Charles Clift is an independent consultant.

Beatriz Conde Gallego is Research Fellow at the Max Planck Institute for Intellectual Property, Competition and Tax Law, Munich.

Carlos M. Correa is Director of the Centre for Interdisciplinary Studies of Industrial Property and Economics at the University of Buenos Aires, Argentina.

Kasturi Das is Associate Professor at the Centre for WTO Studies, Indian Institute of Foreign Trade, New Delhi, India.

Carolyn Deere-Birkbeck is a Senior Researcher at the Global Economic Governance Programme at University College, Oxford where she is the Director of the Global Trade Governance Project.

Graeme B. Dinwoodie is Professor of Law at the Chicago-Kent College of Law and Chair in Intellectual Property Law at Queen Mary College, University of London.

Rochelle C. Dreyfuss is the Pauline Newman Professor of Law at the New York University School of Law.

Graham Dutfield is Professor of International Governance in the School of Law at the University of Leeds, UK.

Luis Mariano Genovesi, LL.M (The George Washington University) is Professor of Commercial Law in the Law Faculty at the Universidad de Buenos Aires.

Thomas Hoeren is the Director of the Institute for Information, Telecommunications and Media Law (ITM) in Münster and a judge at the Court of Appeal of Düsseldorf, Germany.

P. Bernt Hugenholtz is Professor of Law at the University of Amsterdam and Director of the Institute for Information Law (IViR). He has acted as an advisor to WIPO, the European Commission, the European Parliament and the Dutch Ministry of Justice.

Annette Kur is Senior Research Fellow at the Max Planck Institute for Intellectual Property, Competition and Tax Law, Munich.

Florian Leverve is Doctoral Associate at Queen Mary, University of London.

Owen Morgan teaches intellectual property in the Department of Commercial Law in the University of Auckland Business School. He is a Research Associate of the Intellectual Property Research Institute of Australia (IPRIA).

Lois Muraguri is a lawyer working as a research fellow in life sciences and development at the Innogen ESRC centre for social and economic research on innovation in genomics.

Ruth L. Okediji is the William L. Prosser Professor of Law at the University of Minnesota Law School.

Kevin Outterson is Associate Professor at the Boston University School of Law.

Dwijen Rangnekar is the Research Councils UK Academic Fellow and Assistant Professor of Law at the School of Law and the Centre for the Study of Globalisation and Regionalisation at the University of Warwick, Coventry, UK.

Jerome H. Reichman is the Bunyan S. Womble Professor of Law at the Duke University School of Law, Durham, NC.

Pedro Roffe is Senior Fellow at the International Centre for Trade and Sustainable Development, Project on Intellectual Property and Sustainable Development.

Xavier Seuba, PhD (Law), is Public International Law Lecturer at the Universiteit Pompeu Fabra, Barcelona.

Christoph Spennemann is a Legal Expert in the Intellectual Property Team, Policy Implementation Section, Division on Investment and Enterprise, UNCTAD.

S.K. Verma is Professor of Law at the University of Delhi, India.

Johanna von Braun is a Postdoctoral Fellow at the Intellectual Property Law Research Unit, University of Cape Town.

Peter K. Yu holds the Kern Family Chair in Intellectual Property Law and is the founding director of the Intellectual Property Law Center at Drake University Law School. He is also a Wenlan Scholar Chair Professor at Zhongnan University of Economics and Law in Wuhan, China and a visiting professor of law at the University of Hong Kong Faculty of Law.

Preface

Carlos M. Correa

The World Trade Organization (WTO) has become, with the adoption of the TRIPS (Trade-related Aspects of Intellectual Property Rights) Agreement, the principal standard-setting organization in the area of intellectual property rights (IPRs). The Agreement sets forth minimum standards in most areas of IPRs, which have demanded massive changes in national legislation, particularly in developing countries. Few agreements in the WTO system have created so much controversy. Several issues relating to the implementation and interpretation of the TRIPS provisions have given rise to disputes. A Ministerial Declaration has been necessary to clarify the relationship between the TRIPS Agreement and public health (Doha, 2001), which eventually led to an amendment to the Agreement, currently subject to ratification.

The TRIPS Agreement has generated an enormous amount of academic work, as well as numerous analyses by international organizations and civil society groups. There are already a number of books, reports and articles that cover different aspects of the TRIPS Agreement and that provide commentaries on the Agreement's provisions. Many of these analyses, however, do not explore in depth the fundamental issues raised by the treaty, or aim to discuss the impact of such provisions rather than to better understand the content and scope of the imposed obligations in the light of the WTO system as a whole.

This book aims to contribute to filling some of these gaps.

A basic objective of this *Handbook* is to provide a source of high quality original reference material for research, teaching and professional practice on WTO-related issues concerning intellectual property protection. Although it is not intended to be used as a textbook, it would be useful for advanced and postgraduate students as reference points, as well as for scholars and policy-makers. While there has been no attempt to deal with all areas covered by the TRIPS Agreement, the book includes analyses of most of the themes concerning the substantive standards of protection provided for in the Agreement.[1]

A group of distinguished scholars and practitioners have contributed

[1] In a separate volume, issues relating to enforcement and dispute settlement

the various chapters that make up this volume. In inviting these authors to contribute, an attempt was made to include scholars and experts from developed and developing countries, as well as to gather both authors with a long experience and also those representing a new generation of talented analysts in the field of intellectual property.

This volume contains 21 chapters divided into two parts. Part I examines the history of the TRIPS Agreement, including its origins and the political context in which it was negotiated. It elaborates on the principles and objectives that underlie the Agreement's interpretation, explains some of the general standards applicable to all the areas covered by the Agreement, and provides studies on the interaction between the Agreement and other areas of law, namely human rights and competition policy. This part also contains an analysis of the relationship between World Intellectual Property Organization (WIPO) treaties and the TRIPS Agreement and offers readers an account of post-TRIPS developments in the context of free trade agreements.

Part II deals with substantive obligations assumed by WTO Members in specific areas. Three chapters are devoted to key issues concerning copyright and related rights – with particular emphasis on the exceptions and limitations currently discussed within the framework of the WIPO – one chapter on trademarks, two on geographical indications, three on issues related to patents, including compulsory licensing for facilitating access to medicines, and a chapter on an often overlooked issue, the protection of integrated circuits.

I am immensely thankful to the contributors for their willingness to be a part of this initiative and for the informed and rigorous analyses they have provided. I am sure readers will appreciate their efforts and the quality of the materials gathered in this volume.

Carlos M. Correa

---

are addressed, including an analysis of WTO jurisprudence on the TRIPS Agreement.

PART I

HISTORY, INTERPRETATION AND PRINCIPLES

1 Why IPR issues were brought to GATT: a historical perspective on the origins of TRIPS

Charles Clift

Introduction

Intellectual property rights have been with us a long time, at least since the 15th century when the practice spread from Florence to Venice and then to other countries in Northern Europe and to North America by the 17th century. Historically, the institution of patents and copyrights as used to stimulate invention and creativity by protecting for varying lengths of time the invention or creation from imitation or copying. Typically, these rights were also used or misused as a form of patronage by the handing out of monopolies on the sale of particular products, not necessarily new inventions, to favoured individuals. In England, these rights were embodied in 'letters patent'. The Statute of Monopolies (1623) sought to put an end to the misuse of the system by allowing the grant of a 14-year monopoly only for new inventions.

As the system spread, it also became clear that the grant of patents and copyright, although national in scope, had international implications. Countries had an interest in providing rights to their own nationals while denying them to others. The USA, along with many other countries, practised such discrimination in the 19th century. Less advanced countries spent much effort fighting to acquire technology from more advanced countries, and the more advanced countries spent much effort fighting to prevent other countries acquiring their technologies – their patent and copyright laws being one weapon in their respective armouries.

The need for some kind of international cooperation became evident when foreign exhibitors refused to attend the International Exhibition of Inventions in Vienna in 1873 because they were afraid their ideas would be stolen and exploited commercially in other countries. This led to the 1883 Paris Convention for the Protection of Industrial Property, which established the principle of national treatment (that is, although the nature of national patent laws might vary, foreigners should be accorded the same rights as nationals). In 1886, the Berne Convention for the Protection of Literary and Artistic Works was also agreed. The Paris and Berne Conventions, while recognising the desirability of reciprocity, also allowed considerable flexibility in the design of IP regimes. Two of the industrialised founding members of the Paris Convention, the Netherlands and Switzerland, had at the time no patent system in place.

Adherence to these international conventions covering intellectual property, and others that followed, was voluntary. Moreover, there were no mechanisms in place to enforce their provisions. Many countries were slow to comply with the provisions they had signed up to. By 1970, 75 countries had adhered to the Paris Convention and 58 to Berne.

The GATT

In 1948, the General Agreement on Tariffs and Trade (GATT) was founded, with the principal objective of promoting international trade and, in its initial years, primarily through the progressive reduction of tariffs. In the 1960s, the 'Kennedy Round' somewhat extended the agenda, including the conclusion of an 'Antidumping Agreement'. The Tokyo Round during the 1970s was the first major attempt to tackle non-tariff trade barriers. A series of agreements on non-tariff barriers emerged from the negotiations.

As trade liberalisation and tariff reduction proceeded under the aegis of the GATT, attention turned to the impact of other policies on trade. In particular, the highly protective agricultural subsidy and pricing regimes adopted by many countries attracted attention. Similarly, the role of foreign investment and the importance of the trade in services had increased significantly since the formation of the GATT. Meanwhile, outside GATT, a restrictive agreement, the Multifibre Arrangement, had been instituted to limit the growing impact of developing countries' textile exports on developed country producers. Intellectual property protection, although hardly featuring in the Tokyo Round, was another non-tariff issue to which the attention of some nations increasingly turned.

A result of this increasingly complex agenda for trade reform was a desire, particularly on the part of developed countries, to address these 'trade-related' issues simultaneously in the next GATT round, which was finally launched at Punta del Este, Uruguay in 1986. In addition, there was a widespread concern amongst some countries that the dispute settlement system under GATT was deficient. Moreover, the GATT non-tariff agreements negotiated in the Tokyo Round (such as on anti-dumping and government procurement) were voluntary (so-called 'plurilateral agreements') and only a proportion of GATT members participated in them. As we shall see, the objective set in Punta del Este to convert all aspects of GATT accords to a single undertaking (meaning all members of GATT would be bound by all the separate agreements reached in the Uruguay Round) was of great significance in the negotiations that led to the Trade-related Aspects of Intellectual Property Rights (TRIPS) Agreement.

Trade and intellectual property

The origins of the introduction of intellectual property into the GATT agenda lay principally in the efforts of the USA, later supported by the European Economic Community (EEC), to conclude an 'Agreement on Measures to Discourage the Importation of Counterfeit Goods' (L/4817, 31 July 1979).[1] This measure had been initially promoted by the International Anti-counterfeiting Coalition, an organisation of multinational companies based in the USA, created in 1979. This initiative in 1979 came too late in the Tokyo Round to have a chance of gaining sufficient support. It also needs to be noted that its sole purpose was to address the trade in falsely trademarked goods, reflecting the proper meaning of counterfeit in intellectual property terminology. The proposals made no suggestions concerning national rules on assigning trademarks, or any other forms of intellectual property.

For the story of how the full range of intellectual property rights came to be included in the agenda for the Uruguay Round in 1986, we need to consider the evolution of intellectual property rights legislation and discourse in the USA, because it was the USA which was the principal proponent in the deliberations in GATT leading up to Punta del Este.

US legislation

As early as 1930, Section 337 of the USA Tariff Act provided remedies under US law against the importation of goods that constituted unfair competition, including infringing the rights of intellectual property holders in the USA. The 1974 Trade Act transferred from the President to the International Trade Commission responsibility for adjudication, and imposed a 12-month deadline for claims to be adjudicated. Like the anti-counterfeiting proposals introduced in the Tokyo Round, these measures only addressed the symptom of the perceived problem (that is, the import of infringing goods), but could not address the inadequacies in law and enforcement that gave rise to the export of infringing goods from source countries. To address this issue, the 1974 Act prescribed in Section 301 that the President could deny benefits, or impose duties on countries' exports, where they unjustifiably restricted US commerce. It also established an advisory role for US private sector interests by setting

---

[1] All GATT negotiating documents referred to are available via the WTO GATT Documents website page: www.wto.org/english/docs_e/gattdocs_e.htm.

up the Advisory Committee for Trade Policy and Negotiations (ACTPN) to ensure that trade policy and trade negotiation objectives adequately reflected US commercial and economic interests. In parallel, the Act provided a legislative charter for the Special Trade Representative (originally established by President Kennedy) as part of the Executive Office of the President and made it responsible for the trade agreements programmes under the Tariff Act of 1930, the Trade Expansion Act of 1962, and the Trade Act of 1974.

In 1979 new legislation converted the Special Trade Representative to the Office of the United States Trade Representative (USTR), which was assigned overall responsibility for developing and coordinating the implementation of US trade policy and made responsible for asserting and protecting 'the rights of the United States under all bilateral and multilateral international trade and commodity agreements' (USTR, n.d.).

It is apparent, even at this relatively early stage, that in the eyes of the US government, trade policy was seen as a potentially potent instrument to be used to improve the climate for US trade and investment, including attempting to influence the domestic policy regimes in other countries, in particular developing ones. Moreover, the 1974 legislation institutionalised the practice whereby the principal influence on US trade policy was the business sector, and the equation of US trade interests with the demands of that sector. This replaced the previously rather ad hoc influence on trade policy of the kind that continued to prevail in European countries, which had a more arm's length relationship with business interests. Viewed from this perspective, the idea that trade policy could be used multilaterally as well as bilaterally to influence domestic policy regimes in developing countries was hardly a novel one in the US.

The ACTPN, which was chaired from 1981 by Edmund Pratt, CEO of Pfizer, and included John Opel, CEO of IBM, proved influential, both in its impact on US trade policy and in mobilising business, Congressional and policymaker support for changes they wanted to see. Pratt and the ACTPN argued strongly that developing countries should adopt minimum standards of intellectual property protection worldwide. Initially, they focused their efforts on the World Intellectual Property Organization (WIPO), which was the UN agency now responsible for administering the Paris and Berne Conventions. However, this effort foundered because of the opposition of developing countries. Whereas the latter wanted to 'weaken' the rules embodied in Paris and Berne, the developed countries wanted to strengthen them, establish minimum standards and devise effective means of enforcement. Negotiations on revising the Paris Convention broke down comprehensively in 1984. It became clear to the developed countries and the ACTPN that WIPO, with its inbuilt developing country majority, and absence of effective enforcement mechanisms, could not be the vehicle for enhancing intellectual property standards globally (Deveraux et al., 2006, p. 47).

It was for these reasons that the ACTPN, in the time leading up to the launch of the Uruguay Round, focused its attention on getting the business community and the USTR to include intellectual property rights fully in the forthcoming negotiations. An important aspect of this challenging task, given the opposition of most developing countries, and the apparent relative indifference of many developed countries, was to strengthen US ability to influence other countries. As a result of pressure from the business community, particularly the copyright-based industries, Congress passed the Trade Act of 1984. This strengthened Section 301 of the 1974 Act and provides the USTR with authority to take action if unreasonable, unjustifiable, or discriminatory foreign government practices restrict US commerce, including ineffective protection of intellectual property rights. In any Section 301 investigation, the USTR must first consult with the foreign government under investigation. If the consultations are unsuccessful, enforcement actions may be taken under Section 301. These may include suspending concessions given under trade agreements, imposing duties or other remedies.

In 1984 the International Intellectual Property Alliance (IIPA) was formed to represent the interests of the US copyright-based industries, principally the film, recording and publishing industries. Its objective was to press Congress and the Administration to recognise the critical importance to the US of trade in protected goods, and to help create the tools necessary for US 'trade negotiators to convince foreign nations to take action against massive and debilitating piracy and counterfeiting' (Sell, 2003, pp. 84–5). In 1985, IIPA published a report on the 'Piracy of US Copyrighted Works in Ten Selected Countries' which estimated total US losses in these ten countries at $1.3 billion annually (Stewart, 1993, p. 2254). Partly as a result, the USTR launched the first self-initiated Section 301 IPR action against Korea for failing to protect copyright of US products (as well as patents), which resulted in 1986 in reforms to Korean law to provide protection (IIPA, 2004).

The continued lobbying of the IIPA and other industry groups resulted in further amendments to the Trade Act in 1988 to create 'Special 301'. These amendments devolved power from the President to USTR in order to reduce the risk that other foreign policy considerations would enter into decisions on trade sanctions. Under the Act, USTR annually identifies those countries that deny adequate IPR protection or fair access for IP-protected products. Countries that have the most 'onerous or egregious' policies and the greatest adverse impact (actual or potential) on US products must be designated as 'Priority Foreign Countries'. These countries are potentially subject to an investigation unless they are entering into good faith negotiations or making significant progress in bilateral or multilateral negotiations to provide adequate and effective protection of IPR.

As a result of the Act, each year USTR publishes a Special 301 report which classifies offending countries on a 'Priority Watch List' and 'Watch List'. Placement on the Priority Watch List or Watch List indicates particular problems in relation to IPR protection, enforcement or market access. Countries placed on the Priority Watch List are the focus of increased bilateral attention concerning the problem areas.

Thus, pressure from industry resulted in powerful legislation which was seen as a prerequisite for effective action against countries held to be protecting IP ineffectually. Beginning in 1984, Section 301 was increasingly used to target prime offenders. In 1985, South Korea was targeted in respect of both its patent and copyright laws and enforcement and as a result revised its patent and copyright laws. In 1987, Brazil was listed for lack of protection for pharmaceutical products and 100 per cent tariffs on $39 million of Brazilian pharmaceuticals were imposed. In the end, sanctions were dropped as a result of a Brazilian promise to introduce patent protection, although this was only implemented in 1996.

Leading up to the Uruguay Round

Preparatory discussions on the format of what became the Uruguay Round began in November 1985. By that time, business interests in the US and the US government were mobilising support to include the full range of their concerns about foreign intellectual property protection in the Uruguay Round. The US view was clearly stated in the discussions of the Preparatory Committee in February 1986:

> Given the need for GATT to respond to problems in the trading environment as they arose, his delegation viewed as a key agenda item for a new round the better protection of intellectual property rights, including patents, trademarks, trade dress, copyright, mask works, trade secrets. Better protection would promote innovation, encourage more rapid transfer of the newest technologies and increase foreign exchange earnings by promoting investment. It was therefore to the advantage of both developed and developing countries. GATT action in this area should complement current efforts at the national and international levels and, if necessary, go beyond existing international conventions. GATT had the appropriate legal and institutional framework to deal with the problems, including the machinery for ensuring transparency, notification, consultation, and dispute settlement, which were missing in other international fora. (REP.COM(86)SR/3, 1986)

The statement made clear that not only was it considered appropriate to include the full gamut of intellectual property issues in the new Round, but also that such measures might go beyond existing conventions. It also highlighted, by implication, that the GATT had a potentially superior framework for enforcement which was missing in the existing IP Conventions.

By contrast, the European Community was non-committal about both inclusion in the Round and the case for superseding WIPO:

> The Community looked to the GATT to reach agreement on broadly acceptable rules dealing with trade aspects of counterfeit. Negotiations could be without prejudice to the complementary work being carried on elsewhere, for example in the World Intellectual Property Organization (WIPO). The more general problem of protection of intellectual property aroused significant interest, but his delegation felt that it merited further discussion before a decision could be reached on how best to deal with it in the context of a new round. (ibid.)

In response, developing countries, including Brazil, Argentina and India, argued that the case had not been made for introducing a discussion on counterfeiting, let alone on intellectual property rights more generally, into the GATT. They argued that WIPO was the body with the appropriate competence and that introducing these matters into the GATT would detract from other discussions on important matters that were integral to the trade liberalisation agenda.

In March 1986, Pratt and Opel set up the Intellectual Property Committee (IPC), composed of a dozen CEOs, with the objective of mobilising support for the inclusion of IPRs in the Uruguay Round. The IPC made it a priority to get the business communities in Europe and Japan on side in order that they might influence their governments' positions in the Round.

As a result of these efforts, the following text was agreed in the Ministerial Declaration that launched the Round in September 1986:

> **Trade-related aspects of intellectual property rights, including trade in counterfeit goods**
>
> In order to reduce the distortions and impediments to international trade, and taking into account the need to promote effective and adequate protection of intellectual property rights, and to ensure that measures and procedures to enforce intellectual property rights do not themselves become barriers to legitimate trade, the negotiations shall aim to clarify GATT provisions and elaborate as appropriate new rules and disciplines.
>
> Negotiations shall aim to develop a multilateral framework of principles, rules and disciplines dealing with international trade in counterfeit goods, taking into account work already undertaken in the GATT.
>
> These negotiations shall be without prejudice to other complementary

> initiatives that may be taken in the World Intellectual Property Organization and elsewhere to deal with these matters. (MIN.DEC, 1986)

This text is, as is often the case with negotiated language, ambiguous. Developing countries opposed to the inclusion of IPRs in the Round tended to regard the first paragraph as being no more than introductory to the second, so that the debate essentially remained about counterfeit goods; and they were reassured by the reference to WIPO in the third. By contrast, the US could interpret the first paragraph, with its reference to 'new rules and disciplines' in relation to intellectual property rights, as the most important one, and the second as a subsidiary aspect, albeit also significant.

Symbolic of the change in emphasis that had been achieved, was the evolution of the title between the February Preparatory Meeting when the record of the relevant discussion was headed: 'Trade in Counterfeit Goods and Other Aspects of Intellectual Property'. By the Ministerial Declaration in September, intellectual property rights had moved to centre stage, albeit trade-related. The final title of the TRIPS Agreement, of course, excludes the subsidiary clause on counterfeit goods altogether. Throughout the subsequent negotiations the exact meaning of trade-related IPRs was continuously debated. It was possible to argue equally plausibly that either almost all or almost none of the IPR agenda was trade-related – since there were no accepted criteria for determining what trade-related entailed. And it was in the interest of the developed countries to argue the former case in order to legitimise the inclusion of IPR issues in GATT, and of the developing country opponents to argue the latter to keep them out of GATT.

The negotiations

The Uruguay Round negotiations began with the establishment of 14 negotiating groups, including one on Trade-related Aspects of Intellectual Property Rights, including Trade in Counterfeit Goods. In January 1987 Ministers agreed a negotiating structure and negotiating plans for each of these groups. The plans for the TRIPS Group focused on the collection of information relevant to the Negotiating Objective, including on existing agreements and the problems experienced with respect to the subject matter. Further, it was envisaged that delegations could make suggestions and table specific texts with a view to establishing a common basis for negotiation. This gave scope for delegations, supported by the Secretariat, to build their expertise in this complex area, which was new to the GATT. It also provided opportunities for countries with their own expertise to submit texts in the form of a possible agreement, thus giving them the advantage of defining the agenda and scope of subsequent negotiations.

In the first phase of negotiations almost all of the running, as regards documentation submitted to the negotiating group, was made by the developed countries. Initially, they submitted notes on 'trade problems associated with intellectual property rights' – submissions came from the European Communities, the US, Japan, the Nordic countries and Switzerland. In these submissions, developed countries set out a wide-ranging agenda of ways in which inadequate protection and enforcement of intellectual property rights distorted international trade. The US Submission concluded:

> The foregoing indicates that deficiencies in protection of intellectual property rights distort trade in goods and services and reduce the value of concessions negotiated in previous rounds of trade negotiations. The main problems identified by U.S. companies include: 1) total lack of patent, trademark or copyright laws; 2) narrow scope of protection under intellectual property laws resulting in failure to protect entire categories of products or works; 3) terms of protection that are too short to permit an innovator time to test a product, market it and achieve an adequate return on investment; 4) misuse of compulsory licensing programs, especially for patents; 5) inadequate and ineffective enforcement provisions; and 6) the inability of intellectual property laws and regulations to keep pace with technological innovations.
>
> The GATT Articles do not address the distortions of trade and impairment of concessions that arise from inadequate and ineffective protection of intellectual property rights. The negotiating group should, therefore, adopt additional disciplines in an Agreement on protection and enforcement of intellectual property rights. To that end, the United States intends to table texts that propose measures to improve protection and enforcement of patents, trademarks, trade dress, copyrights, mask works, and trade secrets. (MTN.GNG/NG11/W/7, 1987)

These were followed later in the year and in 1988 by a similar set of papers from the same group of countries, making suggestions on achieving the negotiating objective. The US argued for a GATT agreement on intellectual property rights, although, oddly, it appeared to envisage the possibility that such an agreement might be plurilateral – only binding on parties to the Agreement, not all GATT members.

However, what was noticeable in the early stages of the negotiation was the absence of substantive written input from developing countries. Submissions were made by Mexico and Brazil in 1987, but neither were substantive comments on the negotiating agenda. Developing countries therefore largely confined themselves to oral presentations which argued that the wide-ranging agenda proposed by developed countries was not appropriate to the GATT, that all these issues were properly dealt with in WIPO, or other relevant international organizations, and that devoting time to this issue would distract attention from the more important trade issues that had to be negotiated (for example, on textiles). But this was sniping from the sidelines – the refusal to engage in substantive discussions allowed the developed countries to build and take forward a comprehensive agenda of their own, which was not directly challenged in the absence of alternative proposals coming from developing countries. The dilemma was a familiar one – to argue ineffectually from outside or to get the best deal possible by actively engaging with an agenda not of one's own making.

It was not until the end of 1988 that developing countries made their first substantive written contributions to the negotiations and these, unlike in the case of the developed countries, were not coordinated. In September 1988, Thailand suggested that the 'scope of negotiations should be confined to issues relating to the enforcement of intellectual property rights at the border only'. In Thailand's view, those countries 'proposing wider coverage including the establishment of international norms and standards. . . [based] on their own national interest and standards clearly go beyond the intents and spirit of the Ministerial Declaration on this issue' (MTN.GNG/NG11/W/27, 1988).

In October, Brazil made its first substantive written contribution, over two years after the launch of the Round. It argued that the mandate of the Group was to discuss 'trade-related aspects of intellectual property rights in the context of the promotion of trade and development'. In Brazil's view, the problem was not the inadequate protection of intellectual property rights, but rather that 'rigid and excessive protection of IPRs impedes the access to latest technological developments, restricting, therefore, the participation of developing countries to international trade'. Excessive IPR protection meant that countries could not 'freely acquire and adapt foreign technology, nor freely import new processes and products'. A flexible IPR system was 'essential for developing countries in need of new technologies'. Thus, if the main objective of the Uruguay Round was the promotion of growth and development, the Negotiating Group should focus on the problems caused by excessive IPR protection in relation to international trade (MTN.GNG/NG11/W/30, 1988).

Meanwhile, outside the negotiating room, the US continued to press its 301 case against Brazil. Brazil noted in the meeting of the Group in October 1988:

> 27 . . . . that on 20 October 1988 unilateral restrictions had been applied by the United States to Brazilian exports as a retaliatory action in connection with an intellectual property issue. This type of action seriously inhibited Brazilian participation in the work of the Group, since no country could be expected to participate in negotiations while experiencing pressures on the substance of its position. The action of the United States Government was a blatant infringement of GATT rules and was thus contrary to the standstill commitment of

> the Declaration of Punta del Este. The United States action was an attempt to coerce Brazil to change its intellectual property legislation. However, Brazil's legislation was fully consistent with the relevant intellectual property conventions. Furthermore, it represented an attempt by the United States to improve its negotiating position in the Uruguay Round, specifically in this Group.
> 28. The representative of the United States said that the measures had been taken with regret and as a last resort after all alternative ways of defending legitimate United States interests had been exhausted. The United States was prepared to lift the measures as soon as Brazil responded fully to United States concerns. The United States further believed that the adoption of effective patent protection was in Brazil's own interest.
> 29. A number of participants expressed their support for the Brazilian statement and their concern for the effect of the United States action on the multilateral negotiating process. (MTN.GNG/NG11/10, 1988)

In the course of the negotiations, the US initiated actions against the following GATT members for alleged intellectual property violations under Section 301:

- Brazil 1987 and 1993 (Section 301 investigations), 1989–92 (priority watch), 1993 (priority foreign country);
- Argentina 1988 (Section 301 investigation), 1993 (priority watch);
- Thailand 1989, 1990 (priority watch), 1991–3 (priority foreign country) and 1992 (Section 301 investigation);
- India 1989, 1990 (priority watch), 1991–3 (priority foreign country), 1991 (Section 301 investigation);
- Taiwan 1989, 1993 (priority watch), 1992 (priority foreign country);
- Saudi Arabia 1989, 1993 (priority watch);
- Mexico 1989 (priority watch);
- South Korea 1989, 1992–3 (priority watch);
- Hungary 1992–3 (priority watch);
- Poland 1992–3 (priority watch);
- Philippines 1992 (priority watch);
- Turkey 1992–3 (priority watch) (Stewart, 1999, pp. 495–509).

This strategy of influencing the negotiations was a perfectly open one on the part of the US government. In fact, it was mandated, as alluded to above, by the 1988 amendments to the Trade Act. An official US government publication on the first Special 301 Annual Report in 1989 made clear that a country's negotiating stance in the Uruguay Round was a relevant factor in determining its 301 status. Although South Korea was placed on priority watch, its 'constructive role' in the TRIPS negotiations was noted, as was Thailand's position in supporting 'negotiation on a broad agenda of topics'. The United States wanted 'to encourage Mexico to play a more constructive role in the Uruguay Round negotiations'. It noted also that although neither Brazil nor India had been constructive in the Uruguay Round negotiations, 'they did not block the decision in April 1989 to allow the negotiations to go forward on the basis of a comprehensive negotiating agenda'. The publication concluded:

> Special 301, in its first year of operation, has already encouraged higher levels of IPR protection among our trading partners. It also can be credited with assisting U.S. negotiators to achieve a comprehensive negotiating agenda for the Uruguay Round TRIPs negotiations during the April Mid-Term review. The work does not stop here. Special 301 is a tool the United States can use indefinitely to work for upgraded protection of IPR – both bilaterally and multilaterally. (Main, 1989)

In April 1989, as noted above, the mid-term review of the negotiations did result in a considerable broadening of the agenda in the negotiations. With various qualifications to placate reluctant developing countries (for example, paras 3, 4(e) and 5 below), Ministers agreed on a very broad agenda for the content of the negotiations (4(a) to 4 (d)):

> 3. . . . that the outcome of the negotiations is not prejudged and that these negotiations are without prejudice to the views of participants concerning the institutional aspects of the international implementation of the results of the negotiations in this area, which is to be decided pursuant to the final paragraph of the Punta del Este Declaration.
> 4. . . . that negotiations on this subject shall continue in the Uruguay Round and shall encompass the following issues:
> (a) the applicability of the basic principles of the GATT and of relevant international intellectual property agreements or conventions;
> (b) the provision of adequate standards and principles concerning the availability, scope and use of trade-related intellectual property rights;
> (c) the provision of effective and appropriate means for the enforcement of trade-related intellectual property rights, taking into account differences in national legal systems;
> (d) the provision of effective and expeditious procedures for the multilateral prevention and settlement of disputes between governments, including the applicability of GATT procedures;
> (e) transitional arrangements aiming at the fullest participation in the results of the negotiations.
> 5. . . . that in the negotiations consideration will be given to concerns raised by participants related to the underlying public policy objectives of their national systems for the protection of intellectual property, including developmental and technological objectives.

The Mid-term Review marked a watershed in the TRIPS negotiations. In spite of the concessions to the opponents, including not prejudging whether the outcome of negotiations was included in GATT or elsewhere, the agenda set out is very much wider, and also more concrete, than the oblique commitments in the Punta del Este Declaration 'to clarify GATT provisions and elaborate as appropriate new rules and disciplines'. Nevertheless, both India and Brazil welcomed the compromise. Brazil expressed its 'willingness to have a frank discussion and arrive at a balanced compromise' and it hoped 'that the coming deliberations would confirm a new spirit of cooperation, in which the just and legitimate aspirations of developing countries for a system that allowed for access to technology and real economic development to the benefit of all partners, would be met'. India was 'gratified that a way had been found to bridge the gap between the differing views of participants'. Although its view remained that the Punta del Este Declaration 'did not include consideration of standards and principles for intellectual property rights', nevertheless 'India had agreed to allow the multilateral process to move forward with the objective of strengthening the multilateral system' (MTN.TNC/10, 1989).

However an Indian participant, familiar with the progress and outcomes of negotiations, regards the outcome of the Mid-term Review as a significant victory for the US and other developed countries. She felt the various concessions offered were comparatively worthless compared to what developed countries had gained, that developing countries had given away too much without extracting concessions in return either within TRIPS or in other areas of negotiation. She attributed this to poor negotiating tactics and fear of US trade reprisals (Watal, 2001, pp. 27–8).

Thus, after the Mid-term Review, the march towards an agreement became almost inevitable. Developing countries had committed to a more active role in negotiations which their heart was not in. The attitude of India reflected this slightly schizophrenic approach to the negotiations.

In July 1989, India contributed for the first time a document setting out its views, far more substantial than Brazil's October 1988 paper, but getting on for three years after the start of the Round. This was the first substantive contribution by a developing country setting out in a coherent manner the case against TRIPS. But it came after about 20 contributions made at each stage by the developed country groupings.

It began by saying that India believed (very like Brazil in its earlier submission) that 'only the restrictive and anti-competitive practices of the owners of intellectual property rights . . . can be considered to be trade-related because they alone distort or impede international trade'. Nevertheless, it looked at other aspects of intellectual property rights 'since they have been raised in the various submissions made to the Negotiating Group and in order to place them in the wider developmental and technological context to which they properly belong'.

India argued that current international conventions governing intellectual property rights incorporated 'as a central philosophy, the freedom of members to attune their intellectual property protection to their own needs and conditions'. In discussing patents, it argued there 'should be no attempt at harmonization of the patent laws of the industrialized and developing countries nor should there be any imposition on developing countries of standards and principles that may be relevant to industrialized countries, but are inappropriate to developing countries'. More specifically, the submission argued that compulsory licensing should be allowed liberally to remedy a variety of problems from failure to work the patent (that is, to manufacture it domestically) to public interest needs, and in sectors of critical importance, such as food or pharmaceuticals, a 'licence of right' should be freely available (that is, automatic permission for third parties to exploit the patent on payment of a royalty). It also proposed a specific list of areas to be excluded from patentability, including, for instance, food and agriculture and pharmaceuticals, and argued strongly for process, rather than product, patents, noting that many developed countries had relied on process patents as one of the foundations of the development of their chemical and pharmaceutical industries. It also argued that the patent term in developing countries should be significantly lower than in developed countries.

Having given its views on intellectual property, India concluded that it would 'not be appropriate to establish within the framework of the General Agreement on Tariffs and Trade any new rules and disciplines pertaining to standards and principles concerning the availability, scope and use of intellectual property rights' (MTN.GNG/NG11/W/37, 1989).

In September 1989 India submitted another paper on the applicability of the basic principles of the GATT and of relevant international intellectual agreements. Again it reiterated 'that the protection of intellectual property rights has no direct or significant relationship to international trade'. There could be 'no linkage between the basic principles relating to intellectual property rights and the GATT system'. In examining the basic principles of the GATT, it concluded that the only principles relevant to intellectual property were those relating to transparency and differential treatment for developing countries. It did not think this surprising because whereas GATT was about liberalization of trade in goods, the intellectual property system sought to confer exclusive rights. In analysing existing intellectual property agreements, particularly the Paris Convention, it emphasised the freedom afforded for each country to determine the scope and level of intellectual property protection according to its own interests and the right to use compulsory licensing to prevent abuses, such as failure to work (MTN.GNG/NG11/W/39, 1989).

Other developing countries that submitted contributions at this time included Peru (MTN.GNG/NG11/W/45, 1989) and Korea (MTN.GNG/NG11/W/48, 1989), both of whom emphasised the need to have a balanced approach and to keep in mind public policy objectives. Peru argued for a much more flexible system than Korea, no doubt partly because of the pressure that had been exerted on the latter since the early 1980s to reform its intellectual property system. Thus Peru argued for the exclusion of pharmaceutical products from patentability, while Korea noted explicitly that they should be eligible for patentability.

In December 1989 Brazil contributed another paper. This reiterated its previously stated position on the relationship between trade and intellectual property. Nevertheless, Brazil (as in the case also of Peru and Korea) did explicitly engage with the agenda in paragraph 4 of the mid-term mandate, setting out its position on patents, trademarks, trade secrets, copyright and enforcement. Thus, while there was no meeting of minds with developed countries, these exchanges mark the point where developing countries began actively to engage with the agenda determined by the developed countries (MTN.GNG/NG11/W/57, 1989).

In the first half of 1990, the developed countries went straight to submitting draft texts of a TRIPS agreement in the language of a treaty. The European Communities kicked off the proceedings in March (MTN.GNG/NG11/W/68, 1990). This was followed by the United States (MTN.GNG/NG11/W/70, 1990), in a very similar format and with much common language. Switzerland (MTN.GNG/NG11/W/73, 1990) and Japan (MTN.GNG/NG11/W/74, 1990) also submitted proposals. It is claimed that these proposals drew significantly from a document produced in 1988 by the IPC and the European and Japanese business associations: 'Basic Framework of GATT Provisions on Intellectual Property: Statement of Views of the European, Japanese and United States Business Communities' (Sell, 2003, pp. 107–108).

Alongside these, a group of 12 developing countries (Argentina, Brazil, Chile, China, Colombia, Cuba, Egypt, India, Nigeria, Peru, Tanzania and Uruguay) also submitted a draft text of an agreement. In reality, this submission was far thinner and more general than the detailed texts submitted by the developed countries. It was not, for the most part, a genuine alternative text that could be actively negotiated, and its frame of reference (emphasising the need to restrict the rights of intellectual property owners in the public interest) was too far removed from that of the developed country submissions to provide much room for constructive engagement (MTN.GNG/NG11/W/71, 1990).

Following these submissions, the Chairman of the Negotiating Group incorporated them into a draft text, in two parts. Part A was a draft agreement following the structure of the original European and US draft texts, envisaging a single TRIPS Agreement covering all aspects of intellectual property rights and their enforcement. Differences between developed countries were incorporated in square bracketed alternatives. Alongside this was a Part B, including a draft agreement on counterfeit and pirated goods intended to be incorporated in a new GATT agreement, and another section covering intellectual property rights, but to be implemented outside GATT in keeping with developing countries' preference for implementation under the auspices of WIPO, with its weaker enforcement mechanisms (Gervais, 2003, pp. 18–19).

There followed in the rest of 1990 an intensive series of formal and informal discussions leading in December 1990 to the 'Brussels Draft' (MTN.TNC/W/35/Rev.1, 1990). In reality, the ministerial negotiations in Brussels in December broke down, but over the issue of agriculture rather than intellectual property. Discussions resumed in the second half of 1991, culminating in December 1991 in the famous 'Dunkel draft', named after the Director-General of GATT, encompassing all negotiating areas, including TRIPS. This draft contained no square brackets and, in respect of TRIPS, is in large part identical to the final TRIPS text (MTN.TNC/W/FA, 1991).

Issues in negotiations

The final rounds of the negotiations raised issues for both developed and developing countries, and between them. On the one hand, there were areas where developed country intellectual property laws were difficult to reconcile. The USA had a problem with inheriting in TRIPS the concept of moral rights in the Berne Convention (that is, the right of authors to maintain their ability to prevent distortion or modification of their works, even after their economic rights had been transferred). In the final text, these Berne rights were excluded. Other differences between developed countries had to be resolved in respect of performers' rights, computer software and databases, collective licensing and rights relating to renting of videos and CDs. In respect of patents, the US was able to maintain its system of 'first to invent', as against every other country's 'first to file' system.

One interesting dispute related to compulsory licensing. In the Brussels draft, parties could impose compulsory licensing without prior consultation with the patent owner only in the circumstances of 'national emergency or other circumstances of extreme urgency'. Because of the US laws relating to government use of patents, particularly relevant in the sphere of defence, these circumstances were extended in the Dunkel draft to cases of 'non-commercial public use', with a rider to absolve governments from unknowingly using a patent before invoking government use. A largely unintended effect of this was to permit governments to invoke government use in the case of health-related patents where the product was to be used in government-provided health programmes in developing countries, which in recent years has become a bone of contention when Brazil and Thailand, amongst other countries, relied on these provisions.

The protection of geographical indications, strongly promoted by the European Communities, split both developing and developed countries. So also did the issue of exhaustion, which hinged on whether or not countries should be permitted to allow imports of products protected under intellectual property rights from other countries. In both cases, compromises not entirely satisfactory to both sides were reached.

There were several issues where the divide was principally between developed and developing countries. These included patentable subject matter, where most developed countries wanted plants and animals to be broadly patentable, whereas developing countries supported by the European Communities wanted broad exceptions to patentability in this area. The final text, which provided for plants and animals to be excluded from patentability (with exceptions for micro-organisms and non-biological and microbiological processes), built on the existing language of the European Patent Convention.

Up until the final round of negotiations the US government, firmly supported by industry lobbyists, objected strongly to the transition periods allowed for least developed and developing countries to comply with TRIPS, and in particular the ten-year transition period allowed to countries currently not providing patentability to pharmaceutical products or agricultural chemicals.

The pharmaceutical industry also argued that the impact of the transition period was compounded by the failure to allow 'pipeline' protection of pharmaceuticals. The US proposed that exclusive marketing rights should be available from the coming into force of the TRIPS agreement, if a patent had been granted in a member country on or after the start of the Uruguay Round in 1986. This offered the possibility of patent protection for existing products and thus a much faster global introduction of patented products. A similar 'pipeline' arrangement had been negotiated in the recently concluded North American Free Trade Agreement to accelerate the introduction of patented products into Mexico. In the event, the position of the Dunkel draft was maintained, whereby exclusive marketing rights could only be provided for products where a patent was first filed on or after 1 January 1995 (or after 1 January 1994 if a foreign priority were claimed in accordance with the Paris Convention).

Conclusions

The negotiation of the TRIPS Agreement is a case study in how business interests can effectively influence the outcome of an international intergovernmental negotiation. Several factors were important:

- the close relationship between the US knowledge-based business community and the US government;
- the formation of effective lobbying groups in the recording, software, chemical, pharmaceutical and other industries (see Chapter 2 by Carolyn Deere-Birkbeck for more detail on these groups);
- reaching out by US business groups to their colleagues in Europe and Japan;
- the strengthening of US trade law to allow unilateral pressure to be exerted on countries judged by the US as failing to protect intellectual property adequately. This helped both as a stick to bring developing countries to the table, and also as a carrot in that a multilateral agreement in the WTO might be preferable to continued US bilateral pressure;
- the lack of coherence amongst developing countries, and a failure to mount effective counterproposals to the developed country agenda.

Above all, a necessary condition for the successful negotiation of the agreement was the multifaceted nature of the Uruguay Round negotiations. What developed countries gained, and developing countries lost, on TRIPS could be set against potential gains for developing countries in other areas of negotiations such as textiles or agriculture (the cause of the breakdown in negotiations in Brussels in 1991). Such tradeoffs were impossible to make in single issue negotiations, such as took place in WIPO prior to the Uruguay Round. Moreover, the fact that the overall agreement was a 'single undertaking' where no part could be separately negotiated, and whereby 'nothing is agreed until everything is agreed', increased pressure on participants to accept difficult texts even where, in a different negotiating setting, these would have been deal breakers.

Thus developing countries in the end agreed to a TRIPS agreement which their major spokesmen had initially argued strongly should not form part of a multilateral trade agreement at all. Moreover this agreement also exceeded, in its depth and breadth, the early expectations of its business proponents in the mid-1980s. Clayton Yeutter, the US Trade Representative in 1985–8, noted that 'many trade experts questioned whether an agreement that contained minimum substantive standards for intellectual property could be negotiated in an international trade body' (Gorlin, 1999, p. i). In the event, in spite of reservations on the part of some business interests about parts of the agreement, the overall industry consensus was that TRIPS was a major success. In particular, there was now a much stronger enforcement mechanism under the WTO, which had not existed in the Berne, Paris or other intellectual property agreements.

References

Devereaux, C., Lawrence, R. and Watkins, M. (2006), *Case Studies in US Trade Negotiation Volume 1: Making the Rules*, Washington, DC: Institute for International Economics.

Gervais, D. (2003), *The TRIPS Agreement: Drafting History and Analysis*, London: Sweet and Maxwell.

Gorlin, J. (1999), *An Analysis of the Pharmaceutical-related Provisions of the WTO TRIPS (Intellectual Property) Agreement*, London: Intellectual Property Institute.

IIPA (2004), *Milestones of the International Intellectual Property Alliance: Twenty Years of Global Copyright Reform (1984–2004)*, www.iipa.com/pdf/IIPA_Milestones_20_years_100704b.pdf.

Main, A. (1989), 'Pursuing U.S. goals bilaterally: intellectual property and "special 301"', *Business America*, http://findarticles.com/p/articles/mi_m1052/is_n19_v110.

Sell, S. (2003), *Private Power, Public Law: The Globalization of Intellectual Property Rights*, Cambridge, UK: Cambridge University Press.

Stewart, T. (ed.) (1993), *The GATT Uruguay Round: A Negotiating History (1986–1992) Volume II: Commentary*, Boston: Kluwer.

Stewart, T. (ed.) (1999), *The GATT Uruguay Round: A Negotiating History (1986–1994) Volume IV: The End Game*, The Hague: Kluwer.

USTR (n.d.), www.ustr.gov/Who_We_Are/History_of_the_United_States_Trade_Representative.html.

Watal, J. (2001), *Intellectual Property Rights in the WTO and Developing Countries*, The Hague: Kluwer Law International.

2 Developing countries in the global IP system before TRIPS: the political context for the TRIPS negotiations

Carolyn Deere-Birkbeck

The history of the global intellectual property (IP) system set the political backdrop for developing country responses to the TRIPS (Trade-related Aspects of Intellectual Property Rights) negotiations and the Agreement they produced. This chapter reviews the origins of the political stand-off between developed and developing countries during the TRIPS negotiations. It traces developing country participation in the international IP system through three phases: the colonial era, the post-colonial era, and then the lead-up to TRIPS negotiations during the Uruguay Round. The chapter concludes with a synopsis of how these historical tensions influenced the politics of the TRIPS negotiations, the Agreement that emerged, and the implementation process (see Chapter 1 by Charles Clift for a fuller analysis of the TRIPS negotiation process).

1. The colonial era: variation and external control

In most developing countries, Western conceptions of privately held rights over intellectual assets have no local cultural or legal roots.[1] For many countries, pre-colonial commercial legal arrangements with European powers marked their first encounter with Western practices related to IP.[2] Subsequently, formal IP laws in developing countries emerged largely from colonial administration.[3] The trajectory of IP laws was, however, not uniform across the developing world. Most notably, the experience of a number of countries in the Americas was distinct from that of many countries in Africa, Asia, and the Pacific.

In Latin America and the Caribbean (LAC), the establishment of

---

1 For background on indigenous, traditional, and community-based approaches to law and the management of intellectual assets, see Dutfield (2004). Ruth Gana (1995) provides a useful overview of how European philosophy influenced the development of IP laws in developing countries. Also see Alford (1993).

2 For a discussion of the European legal influence in Africa before colonialism, see Adewoye (1977: 33–5), Ehrensaft (1972), and Priestly (1969).

3 Okediji (2003: 323).

national IP laws began in the wake of independence from the Spanish and Portuguese in the early nineteenth century. Several countries in the Americas promulgated formal IP laws far earlier than other developing countries and indeed earlier than many developed countries. In 1809, Brazil followed England, the United States, and France, to become the fourth country to adopt an industrial property law. As with most national laws, Brazil adopted the French Civil Code enacted by Napoleon in 1804 (also known as the Napoleonic Code) as the foundation for IP laws. In 1832, the first Mexican industrial property law was passed (replacing Mexico's first ordinance on industrial property established in 1820 by a Spanish court decree). By the 1850s, eight Latin American countries had formal IP laws, several decades before some developed countries took similar action.[4]

In Africa, Asia, and the Pacific, the formal introduction of IP laws began later in the nineteenth century, and was undertaken by European colonial powers. Spurred on by the 1884 Congress of Berlin, the colonizers moved swiftly to impose new laws, authorities, and institutions throughout their respective territories to regulate their dealings with local populations and their own citizens.[5] In so doing, the major colonial powers, especially France and Great Britain, laid the foundations for an enduring influence on legal development in developing countries and on how law was perceived and understood.[6]

In most of its possessions, the British Empire introduced the whole body of its prevailing law, sometimes supplemented by local ordinances.[7] Under British colonial rule, India acquired a patent law in 1856, long before many European countries. In the early twentieth century, the United Kingdom transplanted its 1911 Copyright Act throughout its Empire, including in East Africa, Malaysia, and Nigeria.[8] In the 1930s, for instance, the Federated Malay States, North Borneo, and Sarawak adopted laws based on the same British Copyright Act under pressure from British publishers and collecting societies concerned about the copying of their works.[9]

---

4 The dates of the first IP laws in these countries were as follows: Cuba (1833), Chile (1844), Venezuela (1842), Paraguay (1845), Colombia (1848), and Argentina (1846). These first countries were followed in the early twentieth century by El Salvador (1901), Honduras (1902), Panama (1905), Dominican Republic (1907), and Bolivia (1916). For further discussion, see Roffe (2007) and Patel (1974).

5 Okediji (2003: 321).

6 Roberts and Mann (1991: 5).

7 Roberts and Mann (1991: 11–24).

8 Gana (1996: 447). Also see Allot (1976) and Geller (1994).

9 Tee (1994).

France also applied its own IP laws to its colonies.[10] While political debates in France impacted upon how some of its laws applied in its colonies, French IP law remained dominant throughout the colonial period. Until 1962, French laws governed patent rights in the majority of francophone African countries, and the French National Institute for Intellectual Property (INPI) served as the central IP authority. In the Philippines, Spanish rule saw the introduction of Spanish patent law. When the United States assumed control of the Philippines in 1898, the US Patent and Trademarks Office examined its patent applications according to US law. The trajectory of Korean patent law was similarly externally driven. Under Japanese occupation, Korea's patent law was replaced by Japan's law in 1910. Then, under US military administration, US patent law was transplanted to Korea in 1946. In countries under the influence of the former Soviet Union after the Second World War, such as Vietnam, Soviet laws served as the model for IP laws.[11]

Across the developing world, colonial IP laws embodied concepts alien to many traditional and indigenous approaches to the stewardship of ideas, knowledge, and innovation, and did little to incorporate them.[12] For colonial powers keen to 'civilize' new subjects, the imposition of their laws was considered a precondition for progress.[13] Colonial administrators held 'customary' or 'traditional' laws of their dominions in low regard, particularly because they did not serve the commercial interests of colonizers determined to extract as much wealth from the colonies as they could.[14] While the approach colonial powers took to existing customary laws differed, they were equally disinclined to tailor laws to build innovation and technological capacity in their colonies. Colonial legal systems also failed to build either local IP expertise or an IP 'culture' among their subjects. In francophone Africa, for instance, France supplied legal experts and expertise from the *métropole*, devoting little attention to training colonial subjects in matters of legal administration in general and far less in the area of IP. While the British had a greater emphasis on socializing the legal profession in its colonies and generating an English legal culture, this practice rarely extended to the realm of IP, which remained largely administered from London. India was a notable exception in that colonial administrators did take measures to foster the development of a cadre of local IP experts.

---

10 Betts and Asiwaju (1985: 321).
11 Tran (2003).
12 See Endeshaw (1996: 151), and Okediji (2003: 335, nn. 373 and 374).
13 Endeshaw (1996: 150).
14 Okediji (2003: 322–3).

The first contact of developing countries with *international* IP law began in the late nineteenth century with the forging of the first multilateral IP agreements,[15] namely the 1883 International Convention for the Protection of Industrial Property (the Paris Convention)[16] and the 1886 Berne Convention for the Protection of Literary and Artistic Works (the Berne Convention).[17] Together, these two treaties were designed to enhance the degree of protection that IP holders enjoyed in foreign jurisdictions[18] and to replace the loose network of reciprocal IP arrangements that European powers had previously included in some of their bilateral commercial treaties.[19] The cornerstone of both the Paris and Berne Conventions was and remains the principle of National Treatment, which provides that signatory countries shall extend to foreign nationals the same advantages, rights, and legal remedies against infringement as enjoyed by their own nationals. In 1893, the secretariats of the Berne and Paris Conventions were merged to form the United International Bureaux for Intellectual Property Protection (BIRPI), the predecessor of the World Intellectual Property Organization (WIPO).

Only a handful of developing countries were among the original signatories of the Berne and Paris Conventions and fewer participated in their negotiation.[20] Of the twelve countries that participated in the original Berne negotiations (two as observers), only three countries now classified as developing were present, namely Haiti, Liberia, and Tunisia. In the case of the Paris Convention, only Brazil, Ecuador, El Salvador, and Guatemala were founding members of the Union, along with Tunisia, which became a member through adherence as a French protectorate.[21] Notably, almost half of the original signatories to the Paris Convention

---

15 For a history of the first international IP treaties, see Anderfelt (1971), Beier (1984), Coulter (1991), and Gaultier (1997).

16 The Paris Convention addresses the protection of patents and trademarks (commonly referred to together as 'industrial property'), setting some minimum standards for each. See WIPO (1983).

17 See Ricketson (1987).

18 Matthews (2002: 11) and May (2003: 6).

19 European countries sometimes included reciprocal commitments to respect IP in their bilateral commercial treaties. The scope of protection provided was limited and often discriminatory. See Culbertson (1930: 26).

20 The Berne and Paris Conventions began with fourteen and eleven signatories respectively.

21 Other developing countries that joined the Paris Union in its first decades were the Dominican Republic (1890), Mexico (1903), Cuba (1904), Morocco (1917), Lebanon (1924), Syria (1924), and South Africa (1947). See Patel (1974: 13–14).

lacked national patent regimes at the time of their ratification, including Ecuador, El Salvador, and Guatemala, Serbia, Switzerland, and the Netherlands.[22] The three former countries left the Paris Union in 1886, 1887, and 1895 respectively, only rejoining more than 100 years later with the adoption of TRIPS.

The reach of the Berne and Paris Conventions gradually extended across the developing world, primarily through the accessions of the major colonial powers (France, Germany, Italy, Belgium, Spain, and the United Kingdom).[23] Using Article 19 of the Berne Convention (the so-called colonial clause), European powers included their vast colonial holdings of territories, colonies, and protectorates in the terms of their respective accessions.[24] In 1914, the addition of a further two colonial powers to the Berne system, Portugal and the Netherlands, further extended the global reach of international IP law.[25] Only two countries from the Americas joined the Berne Convention: Brazil in 1922 and Canada in 1928. Instead, a distinct inter-American approach to IP protection emerged among Latin American and Caribbean countries and the United States.[26] Several inter-American treaties on copyright were adopted between 1889 and 1946 (namely, the Montevideo, Mexico, Rio, Buenos Aires, Caracas, Havana, and Washington Conventions).[27] Meanwhile, two further international IP treaties came into force: the 1891 Madrid Agreement concerning the international registration of trademarks and the 1925 Hague Agreement on the international deposit of industrial designs.

2. The Post-colonial era: reform and resistance

2.1. Variation in post-colonial reforms

With decolonization in the 1950s and 1960s, the diversity of approaches to IP law among developing countries continued. Despite independence, most developing countries maintained strong policy and legal links with their formal colonizers, particularly those countries that emerged from colonization with weak and fragile governments.

In many newly sovereign countries, IP laws promulgated after independence still closely resembled earlier colonial laws or those of former

---

22 Roffe and Vea (2008) and Schiff (1971).
23 Okediji (2003) and Ricketson (1987).
24 Okediji (2003: 324) and Ricketson (1987: 79).
25 The UK accession, for example, included 'all the colonies and possessions of Her Britannic Majesty'. See Ricketson (1987: 79).
26 Ladas (1938).
27 Totcharova (2006).

colonial powers. Most former British colonies and dominions, for instance, enacted copyright laws based on the same 1911 British Copyright Act that had served as the foundation for their colonial laws.[28] In Lesotho, for instance, Britain's 1919 Patents, Trade Marks, and Designs Protection Proclamation operated until 1989. In most anglophone African countries, governments reregistered patents already approved in the United Kingdom, often irrespective of whether such patents were consistent with their new national patent laws.[29] In francophone Africa, many countries adopted copyright laws that replicated those of France at the time and in some cases simply kept prior French laws in place.[30] Despite obtaining independence in 1968, Mauritius continued to rely on the French Trade Marks Act (1968) and Patents Act (1975) for over twenty years. Upon acquiring independence in 1947, the Philippines created an independent patent system, but modelled it on US patent law.[31]

Across Africa, regional arrangements facilitated the enduring influence of former colonial powers on IP laws. In September 1962, twelve francophone African countries signed the Libreville Agreement which established a regional framework for industrial protection largely based on French legislation and created the African and Malagasy Patent Rights Authority (OAMPI).[32] The Agreement was updated in 1977, at which time OAMPI became the African Intellectual Property Organization (OAPI), but French influence on the legal provisions in the Agreement and on national copyright laws continued.[33]

Anglophone African countries followed suit in the 1970s. A regional seminar on patents and copyright held in Nairobi recommended the pooling of national resources on industrial property and the creation of a regional organization. In 1973, WIPO and the United Nations Economic Commission for Africa (UNECA) moved this agenda forward, responding to a formal request from anglophone African countries for assistance.[34] Following meetings at the UNECA headquarters in Ethiopia and

---

28 Kongolo (2000: 269–70).

29 Ibid.

30 Cazenave (1989) and Endeshaw (1996). In Chad, for instance, national regulation of copyright is still governed directly by French law. Chad also belongs to a regional IP agreement, the Bangui Agreement, which includes a complementary regional legal framework for copyright protection.

31 Astudillo (1999).

32 See Cazenave (1989). Chapter 7 provides a detailed account of the history of IP protection in Francophone Africa.

33 Ibid.

34 This history draws from ARIPO's website at http://www.aripo.wipo.net/background.html.

at WIPO in Geneva, a draft agreement on the creation of the Industrial Property Organization for English-speaking Africa (ESARIPO) was prepared and adopted in 1976 by a diplomatic conference in Lusaka, Zambia. The UNECA and WIPO served jointly as the Secretariat of ESARIPO until 1981 when the organization established an independent Secretariat. In 1985, ESARIPO members amended the Lusaka Agreement to open membership to all African countries and became the African Regional Industrial Property Organization (ARIPO). While the OAPI system serves as the equivalent of a regional IP law for most aspects of IP and derives primarily from French IP laws, the ARIPO system coexists with the national IP laws in its member states and draws primarily from British IP law. The scope of ARIPO's activities subsequently expanded from industrial property to include traditional knowledge, copyright, genetic resources, and expressions of folklore knowledge, prompting a further name change to the African Regional Intellectual Property Organization (ARIPO).

By contrast, in some Asian countries, the decolonization era coincided with efforts to substantially revise IP laws. In the Americas, the decolonization era also coincided with reforms to long-standing IP laws. Convinced that governments must play a central role in advancing national development, these countries adopted policies with an eye to building domestic industrial capacity and shifting their comparative advantage in the international economy.[35] Common strategies deployed by Argentina, Brazil, Colombia, Mexico, and Peru included import controls to protect domestic markets, subsidies to channel investment into new sectors, regulations on foreign investment to spur backwards linkages and technology transfer, and the reform of IP regimes to make modern technologies cheaper and foreign innovations more widely available. Specific IP reforms included restrictions on the private rights of (largely foreign) patent holders and licensing practices that were more favourable to local producers.[36]

The approach adopted by the Andean Community, established in 1969 by Chile, Colombia, Bolivia, Ecuador, and Peru, exemplified the 'reformist' agenda.[37] United by a joint commitment to industrial development

---

[35] The contribution of state-led approaches to development remains intensely disputed as does the question of the appropriate lessons to draw for contemporary development strategy. See Amsden and Hikino (1994), Amsden (2001), Wade (2003), and World Bank (1988–9).

[36] Sell (1998: 80–5) provides a summary of these efforts. For a broader view of IP policies in Latin America at the time, see Correa (1981) and Roffe (2007).

[37] The Andean Community of Nations (ANCOM) was called the Andean Pact

and deeper regional integration, the Andean countries adopted common rules on foreign direct investment (FDI), IP (including licences and royalties), and technology transfer.[38] The Andean Community's Decision 24, adopted in 1970, was the centrepiece of this approach.[39] The Decision set forth a series of performance requirements for foreign investors and stipulated that all contracts covering technology imports, patents, and trademarks be submitted to member states for examination and approval. In Colombia, for instance, the criteria for evaluating technology contracts included consideration of the potential effects on the national balance of payments and employment.[40] A significant additional element of the Andean approach was that members were barred from unilaterally forging IP agreements with third countries or with international organizations (IOs) that were considered contrary to the common IP policies.[41] The practical implication was that no individual Andean country could join the Paris Union while Decision 24 was in force.[42]

Meanwhile in Asia, the newly independent Indian government sought advice from two national expert committees on appropriate reforms to its colonial patent system.[43] The Patent Enquiry Committee (1948–50) concluded that, 'the Indian patent system has failed in its main purpose, namely to stimulate inventions among Indians and to encourage the development and exploitation of new inventions for industrial purposes in the country so as to secure the benefits thereof to the largest section of the public'.[44] Later, the Ayyangar Committee (1957–9) noted that 80 to 90 per cent of patents in India were held by foreigners. The Committee argued that this ownership pattern limited the affordability of goods in India, while enabling foreigners to gain monopolistic control of the local market.[45] On the advice of these two committees, India reformed its IP laws to better address its specific social priorities (for example, increased access to medicines at lower prices), economic realities (for example, low domestic capacity for research and development (R&D)), and national development

---

until the 1969 signing of the Cartagena Agreement. Chile withdrew from ANCOM in 1976. Venezuela joined in 1980, but then withdrew in 2006.

38 See Abbott (1975), Adler (1987), and Remiche (1982).

39 Another element of the ANCOM framework was a foreign investment code that limited foreign ownership and control of domestic enterprises.

40 Baranson (1981).

41 Roffe and Vea (2008).

42 This Decision was repealed in 1991. By 1999, all of the Andean countries had joined the Paris Union.

43 Vedaraman (1972: 43).

44 Government of India (1949).

45 Ayyangar (1959).

priorities (for example, building national industrial capacity, fostering R&D in areas of national significance, and rural development).[46]

The reformist efforts by some developing countries to tailor IP laws to national priorities were exemplified by their approach to IP protection for pharmaceuticals. In 1970, India adopted a new Patent Law which allowed patents on the methods or processes related to new medicines but not on medicines themselves. The new law also limited the term of patents in areas of social concern, such as food and health, to seven years (in contrast to fourteen years for other inventions), including for pharmaceutical processes. This law then became the legal foundation for India's generic drug industry.[47] Brazil, Mexico, and Argentina similarly lowered standards of patent protection to stimulate local production of generic medicines. From 1971 to 1996, Brazil did not, for example, permit patents on chemical products or on pharmaceutical and nutritional processes and products.[48]

Importantly, the revised IP laws of the 'reformist' developing countries did not diverge radically from prevailing practice in developed countries. Indeed, IP standards among developed countries also varied considerably at that time.[49] Through legislative or procedural means, many developed countries favoured domestic IP owners over foreigners.[50] There was diversity in the scope and term of IP rights and also in the range of exceptions to patentability. Notably, in the 1970s, no other country in the world beyond the United States granted protection for pharmaceutical products. The IP policies of reformist developing countries were nonetheless unpopular, particularly among pharmaceutical cartels in developed countries which had hitherto dominated the international market for medicines.[51]

2.2. The rise of developing country voices for reform of international IP rules

With the end of the colonial era, the growth in the number of sovereign developing countries resulted in an expanding membership of international IP agreements. Developing country membership of the Paris Union grew from three to fifteen between 1900 and 1958, and then to forty-four

---

46 Ramanna (2005).
47 Roffe (2000).
48 Gontijo (2005).
49 Roffe (1974).
50 May (2003: 6–8) and Matthews (2002: 11).
51 Drahos (2002: 5). In the 1960s, for example, Mexico's success in the manufacture of steroids contributed to the decline of European producers' dominance in that area. See Gereffi (1983).

by 1973.[52] African countries were the swiftest to join the international IP system. Egypt, Morocco, and Tunisia, for instance, became members of the Paris Union before 1960, followed by a further twenty-two African country members by 1975. Membership of the Berne Convention also grew. BIRPI moved swiftly to facilitate a system whereby newly independent states in Africa and Asia that were no longer bound by Berne's colonial clause could issue 'declarations of continued adherence'.[53] Through such declarations, and also sometimes by virtue of customary law, the Berne Convention continued to apply in many countries on the same terms as in the pre-independence accession of the former colonial power. The automatism and formalism of this process forestalled careful reflection among new signatories as to the alignment of these agreements with their national interests.[54] Reflecting on the accession of eleven francophone African countries to the Berne Convention between 1962 and 1964, one critic argues persuasively that in the aftermath of independence, these countries were 'so totally dependent economically and culturally upon France (and Belgium) and so inexperienced in copyright matters that their adherence was, in effect, politically dictated by the "mother country"'.[55]

The response of developing countries to the international IP system in the post-colonial era also varied by region. A range of larger developing countries delayed their adherence to the international IP conventions. In the Americas, governments were sceptical of the merits of international IP agreements and proceeded cautiously.[56] Bangladesh, China, India, Malaysia, Pakistan, Korea, Sudan, and Thailand all joined the Paris Union only in the 1980s. India became a member in 1998 and Pakistan in 2004. In 1970, only eight countries from Latin America and the Caribbean were members of the Paris Union: Argentina, Brazil, Cuba, the Dominican Republic, Haiti, Mexico, Trinidad and Tobago, and Uruguay. The majority of developing countries in the Americas postponed adherence to the Paris Convention until the 1990s after the adoption of TRIPS.

In addition, most Latin American countries declined to join the Berne

---

52 In 2007, the Paris Union had over 170 members, including 115 developing countries (not including Eastern European states or those in the Commonwealth of Independent States).

53 Okediji (2003) and Ricketson (1987: 799–806).

54 Ruth Okediji (2003: 323) emphasizes that the ongoing application of the Berne Convention in former colonies was considered 'presumptively appropriate, necessary and legitimate'. She argues that the prevailing view at the time was that independent statehood gave rise to obligations of ongoing adherence, in large part to protect the interests of citizens of other countries.

55 Lazar (1971: 12).

56 Roffe and Vea (2008).

Convention in part because they already adhered to inter-American treaties regulating copyright. Further, like some of the newly independent states no longer bound by the Berne Convention, they were reluctant to join what they perceived as a developed country grouping, which demanded standards they considered too high. In 1970, only Argentina, Brazil, Mexico, and Uruguay from LAC were members of the Berne Convention (most joined only post-TRIPS).[57] Instead, at that time, most LAC countries became signatories of the United Nations Educational, Scientific and Cultural Organization's (UNESCO) 1952 Universal Copyright Convention (UCC).[58] The UCC emerged as a less protective but more attractive alternative to Berne, bringing developing countries together with the Soviet Union and the United States,[59] neither of which intended to adhere to the Berne Convention but were interested in an international system for copyright protection.[60]

Meanwhile, to advance specific commercial interests, developed countries pushed for a growing number of international IP agreements. Between 1957 and 1961, four new international treaties were concluded, covering issues including the classification of marks and the protection of geographical indications, performances and broadcasts, and plant varieties. In 1957, for instance, France hosted the first preparatory meetings for a new treaty to protect new plant varieties at the prompting of commercial plant breeders and the International Chamber of Commerce (ICC). (Beginning in the 1920s and 1930s, several European countries had already introduced distinct *sui generis* legislation separate from patent law, for the protection of so-called breeders' rights).[61] The result of international talks emerged in 1961 in Paris, when six European countries founded the International Convention for the Protection of New Varieties of Plants, which in turn established an International Union (UPOV).[62] The Convention provides exclusive property rights to breeders of new plant varieties for a given period of time and came into force in 1968. The UPOV

---

57 Roffe (2007).

58 Anderfelt (1971).

59 The United States became bound by the Berne Convention only in 1989.

60 The UCC specifies, for instance, that the standard copyright term should be the life of the author plus (at least) twenty-five years, whereas the Berne Convention calls for a copyright term of the life of the author plus fifty years.

61 For historical analysis of UPOV, see Andersen (2006: 13) and Fowler (1994: 14).

62 UPOV is an independent intergovernmental organization. Pursuant to an agreement concluded between WIPO and UPOV, the Director General of WIPO is the Secretary General of UPOV, and WIPO provides administrative services to UPOV.

Convention was subsequently revised several times, each time strengthening the protection available to plant breeders.[63]

From the 1960s onward, the Andean countries, Argentina, and Brazil led the assertion of a distinct developing country voice on international IP regulation. In 1961, Brazil tabled a first proposal on patents and developing countries at the UN General Assembly. The proposal resulted in a General Assembly Resolution calling on the UN Secretary General to prepare a study that would include analysis of the effects of patents on developing country economies and a survey of patent legislation.[64] Concerned about the progressive strengthening of the Paris Convention since its inception,[65] Brazil's goal was to use the Resolution and subsequent UN report to push for revisions to the Convention that would better address the special needs of developing countries.[66]

Developing countries were also active in promoting reforms of international copyright treaties in the 1960s. Led by India, they argued that their ability to improve mass education was limited by publishing cartels and the high royalties and licensing fees demanded by developed country copyright holders. This concern culminated in a campaign to revise the Berne Convention and the UCC to increase their access to information, literature, and artistic works.[67]

This growing activism provoked concern in BIRPI and among its developed country members that developing countries might challenge the agency's primacy on international IP issues and push for other parts of the international system, such as the UN Economic and Social Council (ECOSOC), to play a greater role.[68] In 1962, keen to attract a greater number of developing countries in what was largely a 'developed country club', BIRPI's members established a Committee of Governmental Experts charged with considering structural and administrative reforms that would facilitate its transformation into a fully-fledged International Organization and its incorporation into the UN system.[69]

In 1964, the UN published its response to the 1961 Resolution,

---

63 The latest revision, the 1991 Act, came into force in 1998.

64 UN General Assembly (1961). Also see Kunz-Hallstein (1979).

65 Roffe (2007).

66 The resolution called for the UN Secretary General's report to consider the advisability of holding an international conference to examine problems related to patents and the special needs of developing countries.

67 Drahos (2002: 4). For a history of these efforts, see Johnson (1970–1), Olian (1974), Ricketson (1987), and Yu (2004). For a critical perspective on the Berne Convention, see Story (2003).

68 Ladas (1975), and Musungu and Dutfield (2003).

69 Bogsch (1992), and Musungu and Dutfield (2003: 4).

highlighting a range of challenges for developing countries with respect to the patent system.[70] The report demurred on the question of holding an international conference to examine problems related to patents. Developing countries nonetheless continued to push for reform of the major IP conventions.[71]

In 1966, the nine developing countries[72] attending discussions on the reform of BIRPI successfully ensured that membership of the proposed new organization would not require accession to either of its two core conventions (Paris and Berne).[73] In 1967, the Convention establishing the World Intellectual Property Organization (WIPO) was approved at the Stockholm Diplomatic Conference. At the same meeting, after much wrangling between developed and developing countries, a Protocol was added to both the Berne Convention and the UCC, extending selected special rights to developing countries to limit the rights of authors and publishers in the area of translation and reproduction.[74] Concerns from copyright holders in developed countries, however, prevented the ratification of the new Protocol. A further four years of intense negotiations yielded a less ambitious Appendix to the Berne Convention (the so-called Paris revisions) which grants developing countries special permissions to issue compulsory licences for the translation and reproduction of copyrighted works, but establishes more restrictive conditions than the original Protocol.[75] Subsequent use of the Appendix by developing countries was constrained by the complicated procedures it established for issuing compulsory licences.[76]

---

[70] UNDESA (1964).

[71] Patel (1974).

[72] In total, thirty-nine member states participated in the second meeting of the Committee of Governmental Experts in 1966. See Patel (1974).

[73] Many developing countries postponed their accession to the Paris Union, for instance, until the 1990s after the entry into force of TRIPS (e.g., India and the Andean countries).

[74] The Stockholm Protocol enabled developing countries to make special reservations to the Berne Convention in respect of translations, reproduction, broadcasting, and educational use of copyrighted works. Under the Protocol, the translation rights of an author would expire if they were not used for ten years in a particular developing country. The Protocol also permitted developing countries to grant compulsory licences for purposes related to teaching, study, and research, and for translation rights where these had not been used for three years. In addition, developing countries could grant non-exclusive licences for the reproduction for educational or cultural purposes of works if they were not published in that country within three years of publication in the country of origin. See Johnson (1970–1).

[75] See Tocups (1982), Story (2003), and UNESCO (1973).

[76] Okediji (2003: 328) observes that the Appendix is ‘generally acknowledged

Meanwhile, the call for reform of the Paris Convention intensified.[77] In the 1970s, nationals of developing countries held only around 1 per cent of the world's 3.5 million patents.[78] As net technology-importing countries, developing countries contended that the granting of monopoly IP rights in their markets favoured the commercial strategies of foreign enterprises over national interests.[79] Indeed, the evidence showed that 80 per cent of patents granted worldwide at that time were owned by major corporations from five industrialized countries.[80] Further, over 80 per cent of the patents in force in developing countries were held by foreigners and registered on the basis of research conducted elsewhere.[81] Developing countries thus argued that international patent rules were intrinsically unbalanced in favour of developed countries.[82] They also questioned the purported links between stronger IP protection and increased domestic innovation, noting that even where patents were granted in their countries, 'a very small number were actually used in domestic production'.[83] In addition, they contended that monopoly IP rights frustrated competition and made many technologies unaffordable in their markets.

At the United Nations, the developing country appeal for more development-friendly international regimes extended far beyond the IP arena. In 1964, they had already achieved the establishment of the United Nations Conference on Trade and Development (UNCTAD). In addition, they succeeded in pushing for the incorporation of the principle of special and differential treatment, and other provisions designed to favour developing countries, in the General Agreement on Tariffs and Trade (GATT).[84] In 1970, developing countries achieved a UN General Assembly Resolution on

---

as a failure in terms of its utility to and use by developing countries'. Between 1971 and 1998, only eight developing countries declared their intention to use the Appendix. There were no further declarations until 2004–6 when a further eleven countries notified WIPO that they intended to avail themselves of rights provided in the Appendix. Notifications aside, subsequent efforts to make actual, practical use of these rights were scarce.

77 For a review of developing country engagement at BIRPI and WIPO, see May (2006).

78 Patel (1989: 978, 980).

79 Roffe and Tesfachew (2001: 381).

80 O'Brien (1974: 30).

81 O'Brien (1974: 30) observes that these patents bore 'no relation whatsoever to the flow of domestic inventive activity'.

82 Drahos (2002).

83 Ibid.

84 For discussion of the emergence of UNCTAD and Part IV of the GATT, see Gardner (1964), Rothstein (1979), Wells (1969), Whalley (1989), Williams (1991), and Zartman (1987).

an 'International Development Strategy for the Second UN Development Decade',[85] which included a call for a programme to promote technology transfer, including a 'review of the international conventions on patents'.[86] In 1972, Latin American countries pushed the case for reform at a regional conference on science and technology organized by the Organization of American States (OAS) in Brazil.[87] In the resulting 'Consensus of Brasilia', governments claimed that IP regimes had 'become inadequate and have been exploited by technology exporters to impose consumption patterns and obtain production, distribution, and trade privileges'.[88] The same year, developing countries called on UNCTAD for an update of the UN's 1964 patent study to further improve understanding of the role of the international patent system in technology transfer. In 1973, in a report to ECOSOC on the relationship between WIPO and the UN, the WIPO Director General reported his view that 'it would probably be more practical to concentrate on new international instruments which could be better geared to the solution of some problems of transfer of technology, restrictive business practices, etc.'.[89] Citing the 1971 Paris revisions to the Berne Convention as a precedent, however, the Director General did nonetheless concede that 'if a revision of existing conventions would appear more desirable, and feasible, such revision, even if substantial, would be possible'.[90]

The year 1973 also marked the consolidation of developing country efforts to incorporate their reformist agenda for the international IP system into a broader call for fairer international economic relations. Developing countries launched their agenda for a New International Economic Order (NIEO) at the 1973 Summit Conference of Non-aligned Nations held in Algiers. In 1974, when the global oil crisis shifted the power dynamics at the UN in their favour, developing countries seized the opportunity to secure the General Assembly's adoption of a 'Declaration and Program of Action on the NIEO',[91] as well as the UN Charter of Economic Rights and Duties of States.[92]

The NIEO agenda included specific proposals to promote international cooperation in science and technology, industrialization of developing

---

85 UN General Assembly (1970).

86 For further background on this Resolution, see Patel (1974).

87 White (1975).

88 Cited in Seidel (1974).

89 WIPO (1973).

90 Ibid.

91 For a history of the NIEO and surrounding discussion, see Bhagwati (1977), Cox (1979), Krasner (1985), Murphy (1984), and Rothstein (1979).

92 UN General Assembly (1974).

countries, and fairer terms for technology transfer. Reflecting their concern about the unequal global distribution of technology ownership, developing countries achieved statements in the UN Charter affirming that '[e]very State has the right to benefit from the advances and developments in science and technology for the acceleration of its economic and social development' and that all countries should cooperate to develop 'internationally accepted guidelines or regulations for the transfer of technology'.[93]

To further advance their agenda on technology transfer, developing countries worked in the 1970s to empower several parts of the UN system, including UNCTAD, ECOSOC, and the UN Industrial Development Organization (UNIDO). At UNCTAD, developing countries pushed for a Code of Conduct on the Transfer of Technology (CCTT) to promote technology transfer on more advantageous terms.[94] Developing countries also called for a UN Code of Conduct on Transnational Corporations (TNCs) to better regulate the monopoly power of transnational corporations and boost their contribution to national development.[95] While the calls for these Codes ultimately failed, developing countries used the negotiations to question the scope of rights, including IP rights, extended to foreign individuals and companies active within their borders.[96] In addition, throughout the negotiations for the 1982 UN Convention on the Law of the Sea, developing countries argued for commitments to technology transfer on fair and reasonable terms and conditions.[97]

By 1974, WIPO had concluded an agreement with the UN, thereby establishing itself as a UN-specialized agency and securing recognition for being the primary UN actor in the area of IP.[98] Developing countries used the agreement as an opportunity to make WIPO's mandate and activities more strongly informed by the development agenda they had advanced in the UN system. The original 1967 Convention establishing WIPO had emphasized the desire of members to encourage 'creative activity' by promoting 'the protection of intellectual property throughout the world', and

---

93 Ibid.

94 A Code was drafted but never adopted. See UNCTAD (1985).

95 The developing country agenda in this respect was clearly reflected in a 1973 UNCTAD Resolution affirming the sovereign right of countries 'to take the necessary measures to ensure that foreign capital operates in accordance with the national development needs of the countries concerned, including measures to limit the repatriation of profits'. See UNCTAD (1973).

96 The provisions of the Code and its political history are analysed by Conrood (1977) and Sell (1998).

97 Oxman (1982).

98 Anderfelt (1971), Bogsch (1992), May (2006), and Musungu and Dutfield (2003).

by modernizing and improving the efficiency of the administration of its conventions. WIPO's 1974 Agreement with the UN assigns WIPO broader responsibilities, namely 'for promoting creative intellectual activity and for facilitating the transfer of technology related to industrial property to the developing countries in order to accelerate economic, social, and cultural development'.[99]

In 1975, UNCTAD released its report on the role of the international patent system in the transfer of technology to developing countries.[100] Compared to the 1964 UN patent study, this report advanced more assertive conclusions on the need for the revision of international conventions.[101] While WIPO was involved in the study, largely to show it could respond to development concerns, its leadership remained cautious about the need for reform. Developing countries used the 1975 UN General Assembly to advance a resolution calling for the reform of the Paris Convention to ensure that it met the 'special needs of developing countries'.[102] Soon thereafter, WIPO established an Ad Hoc Group of Governmental Experts on the Revision of the Paris Convention. In 1977, WIPO's members adopted a Declaration of Objectives to set the framework for the subsequent Diplomatic Conference.[103] The Declaration emphasized that industrial property systems should help advance the industrialization of developing countries, including by improving access to technology, the terms of technology transfer, the actual working of inventions in developing countries, and greater inventive activity within their borders.[104] When governments formally began the review process in 1980, the Paris Union became a 'battleground' between developed and developing countries.[105]

3. The Counter-offensive for Stronger IP Protection

In the 1980s, a developed country counter-offensive to strengthen international IP protection began to build momentum. As concerns about waning competitiveness grew, developed country governments attached increasing importance to the strategic role of technology and the protection of intangible assets for their economic growth and trade prospects.[106]

---

99 See WIPO (1975).
100 UN (1975).
101 UNDESA (1964).
102 UN General Assembly (1975).
103 WIPO (1979).
104 Ibid.
105 Drahos (2002: 166).
106 For analyses of this period, see Kastenmeier and Beier (1989), Hartridge and Subramanium (1989), Roffe and Tesfachew (2001: 390), and Sell (2003: 75).

In the United States, over 25 per cent of exports in the 1980s contained a high IP component (chemicals, books, movies, records, electrical equipment, and computers) compared to 10 per cent in the post-war period.[107] While rapid advances in information and communication technologies had increased opportunities for international trade in knowledge-based goods, they also multiplied the possibilities for imitation, copying, and unauthorized use of technologies. Together, these factors altered the economic dynamics of the so-called content and R&D-based industries.[108] US corporations drew attention to a range of challenges posed by weak protection of IP within and beyond national borders, claiming that stronger rights were central to their business models both at home and abroad.[109] Initially, the United States and Europe focused on threats from each other and from the growing industrial strength of the Japanese economy. The spotlight then turned to the domestic IP policies of new competitors perceived to endanger returns from trade and investment in IP-related goods and services.[110] As the US trade deficit burgeoned, competition from cheaper products from the newly industrializing countries in East and Southeast Asia, such as Korea and Taiwan, became a core concern.[111]

Facing cuts to their profit margins, export markets, and also domestic market shares, US industries complained that foreign competitors were 'free-riding' on their R&D investments. They called on the US government to help halt imitation and reverse engineering abroad. Like-minded leaders of major US corporations then mobilized to consolidate a US agenda for a trade-based conception of IP rights and to integrate IP into international trade policies. Key actors in this effort included the International Intellectual Property Alliance, the Pharmaceutical Manufacturers Association, the Chemical Manufacturers Association, the National Agricultural Chemicals Association, the Motor Equipment Manufacturers Association, the Auto Exports Council, the International Anti-counterfeiting Coalition, and the Semiconductor Industry Association.[112] The industry push to link trade and IP was facilitated by reforms to US trade law and USTR, which gave US corporations even greater access to, and influence on, the US trade policymaking process.[113] The international IP agenda of the US government was firmly captured by large IP producers and exporters (even

107 See Office of Technology Assessment (1986).
108 May (2000: 81–5).
109 Drahos (2002: 5), Dutfield (2003), and Sell (2003).
110 Trebilcock and Howse (2001: 307).
111 Bergsten (1973) provides a clear summary of the core concerns.
112 Sell (2003).
113 Ibid.

as debates continued in US Congress about the appropriate balance in national IP laws and policies).[114]

A core concern of developed country multinationals was that IP laws and practices in developing countries favoured domestic IP holders over foreigners and offered little effective protection to non-national IP holders.[115] Pharmaceutical companies facing competitive threats from cheaper generic versions of medicines complained about the narrow scope and short term of patent protection in many developing countries, lack of transparency in the patent-granting process, and limited legal security in respect of the enforcement of patent rights.[116] Together, representatives of companies from many different sectors alleged that developing countries lacked vigilance in preventing the production of counterfeit goods and the unauthorized use of trademarks.[117] Companies in the entertainment industry charged that developing countries were too tolerant of piracy of sound recordings and video, citing losses of billions of dollars per year.[118]

US and European multinational companies were particularly frustrated by the diversity in the strength and duration of IP rights around the world. Of the ninety-eight developed and developing country members of the Paris Convention, forty-nine excluded pharmaceutical products from protection, forty-five excluded animal varieties, forty-four excluded methods of treatment, forty-four excluded plant varieties, forty-two excluded biological processes for producing animal or plant varieties, thirty-five excluded food products, thirty-two excluded computer programs, and twenty-two excluded chemical products.[119] Many developing countries still had in place some or all of the patent exceptions that most developed countries had abandoned ten to twenty years earlier. Countries such as India, China, and Vietnam, for instance, exempted pharmaceutical products, food products, *and* chemicals from patentability.[120] Importantly, the picture varied among developing countries. A large proportion of the poorest developing countries, particularly those which had inherited IP laws from their colonizers, did not incorporate many of the IP exceptions, exclusions, and limitations found elsewhere. A core priority of large multinational companies was to ensure that the steps that countries such as India, Brazil, Argentina, and Mexico had

---

114 Subramanian (1991).

115 May (2000: 6–8) and Matthews (2002: 11).

116 IPC (1988). The IPC also raised concerns about safety risks associated with imitations of some products.

117 Trebilcock and Howse (2001).

118 Sell (2003).

119 WIPO (1988).

120 Dutfield (2000).

taken to lower IP protection would not set a precedent for other countries to follow.

Existing international IP agreements offered frustrated multinational companies little recourse. Many developing countries had not yet acceded to the various WIPO conventions, which in any case were widely acknowledged to be 'toothless'.[121] While developing countries hoped to use revisions to WIPO's Paris Convention to 'reclaim some of the flexibilities lost in the numerous and substantial revisions' since 1883 (such as the diminishing scope for countries to use compulsory licensing and revoke patents), developed countries wanted the revision process to further strengthen the rights of patent holders.[122] During the negotiations held between 1981 and 1983, 'developing countries were as intent on lowering the international minimum standards of patent protection as the developed countries were resolved to elevate the same standards'.[123] Especially contentious were developing country proposals to strengthen their ability to use compulsory licences.[124] The United States considered such proposals to be 'tantamount to expropriation'[125] of the rights of US IP holders (despite the fact that the US government itself made use of compulsory licences in several areas it considered critical to the national interest).[126] Developing countries achieved little headway. Their efforts were further frustrated when the WIPO Director General introduced a proposal to address issues of concern to developed countries through a Complementary Agreement to the Paris Convention, thereby countering the push for reform of the main convention. An Expert Group appointed to consider WIPO's proposal expanded its mandate to include consideration of increased substantive standards for some aspects of patent protection (for example, the minimum duration of rights, the scope of patentability, and enforcement).[127] In 1991, a

---

[121] May (2000: 6). While the various treaties administered by WIPO contain general obligations with respect to implementation, they lack strong enforcement mechanisms for the settlement of disputes regarding the protection offered to non-nationals. See Beier and Schicker (1996). Stewart (1993) notes that the WIPO Conventions do nonetheless offer countries the possibility of accepting the jurisdiction of the International Court of Justice. WIPO has also appointed special informal committees of experts to address particular disagreements about the functioning of its Conventions.

[122] Roffe and Vea (2008: 13). Also see Kunz-Hallstein (1979).

[123] Reichman and Hasenzahl (2003: 12).

[124] For further analysis of these debates, see Yu (2008).

[125] This statement by Michael Kirk, former head of the international division at the US Office of Patents and Trademarks (USPTO), is cited in Lewis (1982). Also see Mills (1985).

[126] Reichman and Hasenzahl (2003).

[127] Salmon (2003).

Diplomatic Conference for the proposed Complementary Agreement was convened in The Hague. Ultimately a North–South stalement, combined with important differences among developed countries (on issues such as 'first to file' versus 'first to invent'), stalled this set of negotiations.[128]

4 The push for TRIPS

In the early 1980s, the United States and the European Union intensified the process of bolstering their respective trade laws, equipping themselves with new unilateral tools to push for stronger IP protection in developing countries.[129] Using a combination of both sticks (unilateral trade threats) and carrots (promises of new market access for products of interest to developing countries), they worked to strengthen IP protection at the national level in developing countries.

Having lost confidence in WIPO as the prime forum for negotiation of international IP rules and improving their enforcement, US officials had already begun to pursue other tools for strengthening international IP regulation.[130] By the mid-1980s, US officials were working alongside multinational companies to pressure developing countries to agree to inclusion of IP rules in the GATT regime (see Chapter 1 by Charles Clift), where they assessed that the prospects for obtaining stronger international IP standards were highest. (Developed countries had hitherto called upon the GATT system to address only IP matters specifically related to international trade in counterfeit goods.)[131]

Compared to WIPO and other UN fora, developing countries were poorly organized in the GATT context. The GATT negotiation process also gave the United States the possibility to make progress on its international IP agenda a condition for movement on developing country market access priorities. Further, the inclusion of a multilateral IP agreement in the GATT system would enable the United States to use trade remedies to push for stronger IP enforcement.[132]

Not surprisingly, developing countries opposed the move to include

---

128 Salmon (2003: 433). Also see Gervais (2002).

129 In 1974, the United States had already augmented Section 337 (Unfair Trade Practices and Intellectual Property Rights) of its trade law to allow for unilateral action against foreign products produced in ways that violated the IP rights that US individuals or firms hold under US law.

130 Sell (2003).

131 In 1978, the EU and US jointly submitted a draft proposal on anti-counterfeiting measures during Tokyo Round negotiations. In 1982, the United States followed up by circulating a further draft revised proposal. See UNCTAD-ICTSD (2005).

132 Abbott (1989), and Braithwaite and Drahos (2000: 61–4).

IP in the Uruguay Round. When the United States raised IP issues in a GATT expert meeting in 1985, Brazil and India perceived the move as a frontal attack on their efforts to reform international and national IP rules. They insisted that the GATT's purview be limited to trade in goods and argued that WIPO was a more appropriate and competent forum for multilateral IP negotiations.[133]

Despite the mounting pressures, key developing countries continued to resist. Even as many developing countries were shifting, albeit often reluctantly, from import substitution to more liberal, export-oriented economic strategies, the push for TRIPS was considered a step too far. The TRIPS agenda, like the structural adjustment reforms advanced by the World Bank and International Monetary Fund (IMF) in the 1980s and 1990s, was perceived as a serious threat to national industrial policies and development.[134] In January 1989, the Group of 77 developing countries (G77) issued a collective statement in which they described the GATT IP negotiations as an attempt to use IP protection 'as a mere device and instrument for promoting the trade competitive interests of developed countries and their TNCs'.[135] They further argued that developed countries were advancing 'protectionist' IP policies in order to 'safeguard and increase their dominant positions in the world market'.[136] This trend, they contested, would lead progressively 'to the concentration of technological and economic power in the hands of the industrialized countries and in favour of their TNCs and state-owned monopolies', thus perpetuating 'the technological gap between the technological haves and have-nots'.[137]

In the second half of 1989, the negotiations gathered speed. Developed countries submitted several draft negotiating proposals to the GATT Secretariat (first the Europeans, then the United States, Switzerland, and Japan). A core group of fourteen developing countries conceded they would have no choice but to participate more fully in the TRIPS discussions (Argentina, Brazil, Chile, Colombia, Cuba, Egypt, India, Nigeria, Peru, Tanzania, and Uruguay later joined by Pakistan and Zimbabwe).[138]

---

[133] Drahos (2002, 2004: 19).

[134] Wade (2003).

[135] Cited in Raghavan (1989).

[136] Ibid.

[137] Ibid.

[138] Drahos (2002: 774) argues persuasively that developing countries 'had simply run out of alternatives and options [. . .]. If they did not negotiate multilaterally they would each have to face the U.S. alone. [. . .] Furthermore, if they resisted the U.S. multilaterally they could expect to be on the receiving end of a 301 action'.

Together, they submitted a detailed proposal designed to divert attention away from substantive standards on IP and to contain the scope of any eventual agreement by focusing on two issues: principles for the use of IP rights, and trade in counterfeit and pirated goods. On the first issue, developing countries emphasized the importance of the public policy objectives underlying national IP systems, the necessity of recognizing such objectives at the international level, and the need to specify some basic principles that could elucidate the application of any standards established in the TRIPS Agreement. Given their diverse needs and levels of development, developing countries used the proposal to insist upon the need to respect and safeguard national legal systems and traditions on IP. In addition, the proposal included detailed perspectives on the appropriate scope of patents, compulsory licensing, and the control of anti-competitive practices.[139]

Developing countries faced increasing difficulty in countering the pro-TRIPS agenda. With the support of the GATT Secretariat, developed countries pushed ahead with an intensive series of bilateral discussions, small group consultations, and informal group processes.[140] Around fifteen developing countries were involved in some aspects of these discussions. Only a few countries, notably India, Argentina, and Brazil, were a tenacious presence in the highly technical and legally complex negotiations.[141] Most developing country delegations were comprised of generalist officials from national trade ministries or Permanent Missions in Geneva rather than IP specialists. Most negotiators thus lacked the legal mastery of the technical details and implications necessary to engage substantively in discussion.[142] 'Negotiation fatigue'[143] overwhelmed many developing country delegations and even the leading negotiators 'came to feel they were wasting their time'.[144]

The United States was not dissuaded. Supported by industry lobbyists, the US government worked to enlist the support of European countries

---

139 Gervais (1998: 15) and UNCTAD-ICTSD (2005).

140 This included the '10 + 10 group' (meaning ten developed countries plus ten developing countries). The size and membership of the 10 + 10 group varied according to the IP issue under discussion. The most active developing countries were Argentina, Brazil, Chile, Colombia, Egypt, Hong Kong, India, Indonesia, Malaysia, Mexico, Peru, Singapore, South Korea, and Thailand. This list included some that had not been part of the earlier negotiations and excluded several of those that had been (most notably from Africa). See Matthews (2002: 38). Also see Drahos (2004) and Gorlin (1999).

141 Drahos (2002: 11), Gervais (1998: 15), and Matthews (2002: 44).

142 Balasubramanium (2000).

143 This term was coined by Braithwaite and Drahos (2000: 197).

144 Drahos (2002: 11).

and Japan,[145] as well as a network of economists and legal scholars willing to build the case as to why stronger IP protection would be good for development. The argument they advanced was that IP protection would help developing countries attract FDI, promote technology transfer, stimulate domestic innovation, and increase their global competitiveness.[146] In Geneva, the United States and the European Union insisted that the inclusion of IP on the Uruguay Round agenda was a necessary concession for launching new trade negotiations.[147]

To break the North–South stand-off, developed countries and leading corporations launched an economic and diplomatic offensive that ultimately forced developing countries to concede to the TRIPS Agreement.[148] The deal was sealed with the introduction of the 'single undertaking' as a device to help close the Uruguay Round. Developing countries were cornered. In order to gain long-sought improvements in market access for their textiles and agricultural products, they were forced to concede to TRIPS despite their opposition.[149]

Conclusion

This chapter has traced the evolution of tensions between developed and developing countries on matters related to IP regulation, illustrating how these set the context for the TRIPS negotiations and influenced them. The first formal encounters between developing countries, Western concepts of IP, and international IP rules began during the colonial era. As colonial powers imposed their respective legal regimes in their colonies, variation in the IP regimes of developing countries emerged. A second phase began in the post-colonial era. In the late 1960s, a distinct reformist discourse on international IP regulation arose, led by countries in the Americas and India in favour of reforms that would advance their industrialization and boost their access to technologies and knowledge. While there were regional differences in the approach developing countries took to IP regulation, most national IP systems continued to be dominated by foreign commercial priorities. Local expertise and institutional capacity to manage IP systems were generally weak.

The chapter shows that developing country activism to revise national and international IP laws spurred a developed country counter-offensive on

---

145 Drahos (2002: 6).

146 Ryan (1998).

147 This history has been detailed at length by Drahos (2002, 2004).

148 For a more extensive review of this period, see Drahos (2002, 2004), Ryan (1998), Sell (1998), Matthews (2002) and Deere (2008).

149 Braithwaite and Drahos (2000: 197).

IP in the mid-1980s, which ultimately led to the inclusion of IP in the multilateral trade agenda. While developing countries as a group opposed the TRIPS agenda, less than 20 of the 106 developing country WTO members that are now bound by the TRIPS Agreement were actively involved in the negotiations. Given the limited expertise of most developing country officials on the particularities of IP law, even those developing countries that did engage in the negotiations made limited inputs into the technical aspects of the discussion and concentrated mainly on containing the Agreement's scope. Upon signing the Agreement, most developing countries thus had poor understanding of its provisions and implications.

Only as the push for TRIPS implementation intensified did many developing countries take stock of the extent of their commitments. Disputes over the terms of the TRIPS deal set the scene for intense battles over the Agreement's implementation. Dissatisfaction with TRIPS spurred ongoing debate between developed and developing countries on the terms of the bargain, and laid the foundations for a dynamic interaction between efforts to alter the TRIPS deal and influence the process of its implementation.[150]

References

Abbott, F. (1975) 'Bargaining Power and Strategy in the Foreign Investment Process: A Current Andean Code Analysis,' *Syracuse Journal of International Law and Commerce*, 3, 2: 319–62.

Abbott, F. (1989) 'Protecting First World Assets in the Third World: Intellectual Property Negotiations in the GATT Multilateral Framework,' *Vanderbilt Journal of Transnational Law*, 22, 4: 689–745.

Adewoye, O. (1977) *The Judicial System in Southern Nigeria: 1854–1954*, London: Longman.

Adler, E. (1987) *The Power of Ideology: The Quest for Technological Autonomy in Argentina and Brazil*, Berkeley: University of California Press.

Alford, W. (1993) 'Don't Stop Thinking About . . . Yesterday: Why There Was No Indigenous Counterpart to Intellectual Property Law in Imperial China,' *Journal of Chinese Law*, 7, 3: 7–34.

Allot, A. (1976) 'The Development of East African Legal Systems During the Colonial Period,' in *History of East Africa*, edited by D. Low and A. Smith, Oxford: Clarendon, 348–82.

Amsden, A. (2001) *The Rise of 'the Rest': Challenges to the West from Late-Industrializing Economies*, New York: Oxford University Press.

Amsden, A. and Hikino, T. (1994) 'Staying Behind, Stumbling Back, Sneaking Up and Soaring Ahead: Late Industrialization in Historical Perspective,' in *Convergence of Productivity: Cross-national Studies and Historical Evidence*, edited by W. Baumol, R. Nelson, and E. Wolff, Oxford: Oxford University Press, Part IV, Section 11.

Anderfelt, U. (1971) *International Patent Legislation and Developing Countries*, The Hague: Martinus Nijhoff.

Andersen, R. (2006), *Governing Agrobiodiversity: Plant Genetics and Developing Countries*, Aldershot: Ashgate Press.

Astudillo, E. (1999) 'Intellectual Property Regime of the Philippines,' in *Intellectual Property*

150 Deere (2008).

Protection in Asia, 2nd edn., edited by A. Wineburg, Charlottesville, VA: Lexis Law Publishing.
Ayyangar, R. (1959) *Report on the Revision of the Patent Law*, New Delhi: Government of India Press.
Balasubramanium, K. (2000) 'Implications of the TRIPS Agreement for Pharmaceuticals: Consumers' Perspectives,' paper presented at the *ASEAN Workshop on the TRIPS Agreement and Its Impact on Pharmaceuticals*, Jakarta: Sponsored by the Association of Southeast Asian Nations (ASEAN), 2–4 May.
Baranson, J. (1981) *North-South Technology Transfer: Financing and Institution Building*, Mt. Airy, MD: Lomond Publications.
Beier, F. (1984) 'One Hundred Years of International Cooperation: The Role of the Paris Convention in the Past, Present and Future,' *International Review of Industrial Property and Copyright Law*, 15, 1: 1–20.
Beier, F. and Schicker, G. (1996) *From GATT to TRIPS: The Agreement on Trade Related Aspects of Intellectual Property Rights*, Studies in Industrial Property and Copyright Law, New York: Weinheim Press.
Bergsten, F. (1973) 'The Threat from the Third World,' *Foreign Policy*, 11, Summer: 102–24.
Betts, R. and Asiwaju, M. (1985) 'Methods and Institutions of European Domination,' in *African Under Colonial Domination 1880–1935*, edited by A. Adu Boahen, Berkeley, CA: University of California Press, 312–31.
Bhagwati, J.N. (1977) *The New International Economic Order: The North-South Debate*, Cambridge, MA: MIT Press.
Bogsch, A. (1992) *The First Twenty Five Years of the World Intellectual Property Organization from 1967 to 1992, WIPO Document 881 (E),* Geneva: World Intellectual Property Organization (WIPO).
Braithwaite, J. and Drahos, P. (2000) *Global Business Regulation*, Cambridge: Cambridge University Press.
Cazenave, B. (1989) 'The African Intellectual Property Organisation (OAPI): From Libreville to Bangui,' *Industrial Property: Monthly Review*, 19: 8–9.
Conrood, S. (1977) 'The United Nations Code of Conduct for Transnational Corporations,' *Harvard International Law Journal*, 18, 3: 209–27.
Correa, C. (1981) 'Transfer of Technology in Latin America: A Decade of Control,' *Journal of World Trade Law*, 15, 1: 388–409.
Coulter, M. (1991) *Property in Ideas: The Patent Question in Mid-Victorian Britain*, Kirksville: Thomas Jefferson University Press.
Cox, R. (1979) 'Ideologies and the NIEO,' *International Organization*, 31, 2: 257–80.
Culbertson, W. (1930) 'Commercial Treaties,' *Encyclopaedia of the Social Sciences, Volume 4*, edited by E. Seligman and A. Johnson, New York: Macmillan.
Deere, C. (2008) 'What to Look For in a New WIPO Director-General,' *Intellectual Property Watch*, 12 February.
Drahos, P. (2002) 'Negotiating Intellectual Property Rights: Between Coercion and Dialogue,' in *Global Intellectual Property Rights: Knowledge, Access and Development*, edited by P. Drahos and R. Mayne, Basingstoke: Palgrave and Oxfam, 161–82.
Drahos, P. (2004) *Who Owns the Knowledge Economy? Political Organising Behind TRIPS,* Dorset: The Corner House.
Dutfield, G. (2000) *Intellectual Property Rights, Trade and Biodiversity*, London: Earthscan.
Dutfield, G. (2003) *Intellectual Property and the Life Sciences Industries: A Twentieth Century History*, Aldershot: Dartmouth Publishing Company.
Dutfield, G. (2004), *Intellectual Property, Biogenetic Resources, and Traditional Knowledge*, London: Earthscan Publications.
Ehrensaft, P. (1972) 'The Political Economy of Informal Empire in Pre-colonial Nigeria, 1807–84,' *Canadian Journal of African Studies*, 6, 3: 451–90.
Endeshaw, A. (1996) *Intellectual Property Policy for Non-industrial Countries*, Aldershot, UK: Ashgate.

Fowler, C. (1994) *Unnatural Selection: Technology, Politics and Plant Evolution*, Yverdon, Switzerland: Gordon and Breach Science Publishers.
Gana, R. (1995), 'Has Creativity Died in the Third World? Some Implications of the Internationalization of Intellectual Property', *Denver Journal of International Law and Policy*, 24: 109.
Gana, R. (1996) 'Two Steps Forward: Reconciling Nigeria's Accession to the Berne Convention and the TRIPS Agreement,' *International Review of Industrial Property and Copyright Law*, 27, 4: 446–89.
Gardner, R. (1964) 'GATT and the United Nations Conference on Trade and Development,' *International Organization*, 18, 4: 685–704.
Gaultier, G. (1997) *The History of AIPPI: AIPPI and the Development of Industrial Property Protection 1897–1997*, Basel: Association Internationale pour la Protection de la Propriété Intellectuelle (AIPPI) Foundation.
Geller, P. (1994) 'Legal Transplants in International Copyright: Some Problems of Method,' *UCLA Pacific Basin Law Journal*, 13, 1: 199–230.
Gereffi, G. (1983) *The Pharmaceutical Industry and Dependency in the Third World*, Princeton, NJ: Princeton University Press.
Gervais, D. (1998) *The TRIPS Agreement: Drafting History and Analysis*, London: Sweet and Maxwell.
Gervais, D. (2002) 'The Internationalisation of Intellectual Property: New Challenges from the Very Old and the Very New,' *Fordham Intellectual Property Media and Entertainment Journal*, 12, 4: 929–90.
Gontijo, C. (2005) 'Changing the Patent System: From the Paris Convention to the TRIPS Agreement – The Position of Brazil,' *Global Issue Papers*, Berlin: Heinrich-Böll Stiftung.
Gorlin, J. (1999) *An Analysis of the Pharmaceutical-Related Provisions of the WTO TRIPS (Intellectual Property) Agreement*, London: Intellectual Property Institute (IPI).
Hartridge, D. and Subramanium, A. (1989) 'Intellectual Property Rights: The Issues in GATT,' *Vanderbilt Journal of Transnational Law*, 22, 4: 893–910.
IPC (1988) 'Basic Framework of GATT Provisions on Intellectual Property,' *Statement of Views of the European, Japanese and United States Business Communities*, Washington DC Intellectual Property Committee (IPC).
Johnson, C. (1970–1) 'The Origins of the Stockholm Protocol,' *Bulletin of the Copyright Society of the USA*, 18, 91: 103–4.
Kastenmeier, R. and Beier, D. (1989) 'International Trade and Intellectual Property: Promise, Risks, and Reality,' *Vanderbilt Journal of Transnational Law*, 22, 2: 285–307.
Kongolo, T. (2000), 'The African Intellectual Property Organizations: The Necessity of Adopting One Uniform System for All Africa,' *The Journal of World Intellectual Property*, 3, 2: 265–88.
Krasner, S.D. (1985) *Structural Conflict: The Third World Against Global Liberalism*, Berkeley: London: University of California Press.
Kunz-Hallstein, P. (1979) 'The Revision of the International System of Patent Protection in the Interests of Developing Countries,' *International Review of Industrial Property and Copyright Law*, 10, 6: 649–70.
Ladas, S. (1938) *The International Protection of Literary and Artistic Property*, New York: Macmillan.
Ladas, S. (1975) *Patents, Trademarks, and Related Rights: National and International Protection*, Cambridge: Harvard University Press.
Lazar, A. (1971) 'Developing Countries and Authors' Rights in International Copyright,' *Copyright Law Symposium*, 19, 1: 1–42.
Lewis, P. (1982) 'U.S. and the Third World at Odds Over Patents,' *The New York Times*, 5 October.
Matthews, D. (2002) *Globalising Intellectual Property Rights: The TRIPS Agreement*, London: Routledge.
May, C. (2000) *A Global Political Economy of Intellectual Property Rights: The New Enclosures?*, London: Routledge.

May, C. (2003) 'Why IPRs Are a Global Political Issue,' *European Intellectual Property Review*, 25, 1: 1–5.
May, C. (2006), *The World Intellectual Property Organization: Resurgence and the Development Agenda*, Oxford: Routledge.
Mills, D. (1985) 'Patents and the Exploitation of Technology Transferred to Developing Countries (in Particular, Those of Africa),' *Industrial Property,* 24: 120–26.
Murphy, C. (1984) *Emergence of the NIEO Ideology*, Boulder, CO: Westview Press.
Musungu, S. and Dutfield, G. (2003), 'Multilateral Agreements and a TRIPS-Plus world: The World Intellectual Property Organisation,' *TRIPS Issues Paper 3*, Geneva/Ottawa: Quaker United Nations Office (QUNO) and Quaker International Affairs Program (QIAP).
O'Brien, P. (1974) 'Developing Countries and the Patent System: An Economic Appraisal,' *World Development,* 2, 9: 27–36.
Office of Technology Assessment (1986) *Intellectual Property Rights in an Age of Electronics and Information*, Washington DC: U.S. Government Printing Office
Okediji, R. (2003), 'The International Relations of Intellectual Property: Narratives of Developing Country Participation in the Global Intellectual Property System,' *Singapore Journal of International & Comparative Law*, 7: 315.
Olian, I. (1974) 'International Copyright and the Needs of Developing Countries: The Awakening at Stockholm and Paris,' *Cornell Journal of International Law,* 7, 2: 3–26.
Oxman, B. (1982) 'The Law of the Sea: The Tenth Session,' *The American Journal of International Law,* 76, 1: 1–23.
Patel, S. (1974) 'The Patent System and the Third World,' *World Development*, 2, 9: 3–14.
Patel, S. (1989) 'Intellectual Property Rights in the Uruguay Round: A Disaster for the South?,' Economic and Political Weekly, 6 May.
Priestly, M. (1969) *West African Trade and Coast Society: A Family Study*, Oxford: Oxford University Press.
Raghavan, C. (1989) 'Technology: G77 Assail TRIPS Moves, Urge Finalisation of Code,' *Daily News Report, South-North Development Monitor (SUNS)*, Geneva, 23 January.
Ramanna, A. (2005) 'Shifts in India's Policy on Intellectual Property: The Role of Ideas, Coercion and Changing Interests,' in *Death of a Patent System*, edited by P. Drahos and U. Suthersanen, London: Lawtext Press, 150–74.
Reichman, J. and Hasenzahl, C. (2003) 'Non-voluntary Licensing of Patented Inventions: Historical Perspective, Legal Framework under TRIPS, and an Overview of the Practice in Canada and the United States of America', *IPRs and Sustainable Development Series Issue Paper 5,* Geneva: UN Conference on Trade and Development (UNCTAD) and International Centre for Trade and Sustainable Development (ICTSD).
Remiche, B. (1982) *Le rôle du système des brevets dans le développement: Le cas des pays andins*, Paris: Libraires Techniques.
Ricketson, S. (1987) *The Berne Convention for the Protection of Literary and Artistic Works: 1886–1986*, London: Kluwer Centre for Commercial Law Studies.
Roberts, R. and Mann, K. (1991*) Law in Colonial Africa*, Portsmouth, NH and London: Heinemann and James Curry.
Roffe, P. (1974) 'Abuses of Patent Monopoly: A Legal Appraisal,' *World Development*, 2, 9: 15–26.
Roffe, P. (2000) 'The Political Economy of Intellectual Property Rights: A Historical Perspective,' in *Governance, Development and Globalization*, edited by J. Foudez, M. Footer, and J. Norton, London: Blackstone Press, 396–413.
Roffe, P. and Tesfachew, T. (2001) 'The Unfinished Agenda,' in *International Technology Transfer*, edited by S. Patel, P. Roffe and A. Yusuf, London: Kluwer Law International, 381–404.
Roffe, P. (2007) *América Latina y la Nueva Arquitectura Internacional de la Propiedad Intellectual: De los ADPIC-TRIPS a los Nuevois Tratados de Libre Comercio*, Buenos Aires: Editorial La Ley Facultdad de Derecho, Universidad de Buenos Aires.
Roffe, P. and Vea, G. (2008) 'The WIPO Development Agenda in a Historical and Political

Context,' in *The Development Agenda: Global Intellectual Property and Developing Countries*, edited by N. Netanel, Oxford: Oxford University Press.
Rothstein, R. (1979) *Global Bargaining: UNCTAD and the Quest for a New International Economic Order*, Princeton, NJ: Princeton University Press.
Ryan, M. (1998) *Knowledge Diplomacy: Global Competition and the Politics of Intellectual Property*, Washington DC: Brookings Institution Press.
Salmon, P. (2003) 'Cooperation Between WIPO and the WTO,' *St. John's Journal of Legal Commentary*, 17: 263–74.
Schiff, E. (1971) *Industrialization Without National Patents: The Netherlands, 1869–1912; Switzerland, 1850–1907*, Princeton: Princeton University Press.
Seidel, R. (1974) *Toward an Andean Common Market for Science and Technology*, Ithaca, NY: Cornell University Press.
Sell, S. (1998) *Power and Ideas: North-South Politics of Intellectual Property and Antitrust*, SUNY Series in Global Politics, Albany, NY: State University of New York Press.
Sell, S. (2003) *Private Power, Public Law: The Globalisation of Intellectual Property Rights*, Cambridge: Cambridge University Press.
Stewart, T. (1993) *The GATT Uruguay Round: A Negotiating History, 1986–1992*, Boston, MA: Kluwer Law and Taxation Publishers.
Story, A. (2003) 'Burn Berne: Why the Leading International Copyright Convention Must Be Repealed,' *Houston Law Review*, 40, 3: 763–802.
Subramanian, A. (1991) 'The International Economics of Intellectual Property Right Protection: A Welfare-Theoretic Trade Policy Analysis,' *World Development*, 19, 8: 945–56.
Tee, K.L. (1994) *Copyright Law in Malaysia*, Malaysia: Butterworths Asia.
Tocups, N. (1982) 'The Development of Special Provisions in International Copyright Law for the Benefit of Developing Countries,' *Journal of the Copyright Society of the USA*, 28, 2: 402–50.
Totcharova, P. (2006) *UNESCO Copyright Activities*, Paris: United Nations Educational, Scientific and Cultural Organization (UNESCO).
Tran, T. (2003) 'Public Interests and the Protection of Intellectual Property Holder Rights in the TRIPS Agreement and the Socialist Republic of Vietnam,' *Monday Business Briefing*, 9 December.
Trebilcock, M. and Howse, R. (2001) *The Regulation of International Trade*, 2nd edn., London: Routledge.
UN (1975) *The Role of the Patent System in the Transfer of Technology to Developing Countries*, Report prepared jointly by the UN Department of Economic and Social Affairs (UNDESA), the United Nations Conference on Trade and Development (UNCTAD) Secretariat and the International Bureau of the World Intellectual Property Organization (WIPO), E. 75.II.D.6, Geneva: United Nations (UN).
UNCTAD (1973) Third Session, Volume 1, Resolution 56 (111), Publication E.73.II.D.4, Geneva: United Nations Conference on Trade and Development (UNCTAD).
UNCTAD (1985) Draft International Code of Conduct on the Transfer of Technology, Geneva: United Nations Conference on Trade and Development (UNCTAD).
UNCTAD-ICTSD (2005) *Resource Book on TRIPS and Development*, Cambridge: Cambridge University Press.
UNDESA (1964) *The Role of Patents in the Transfer of Technology to Developing Countries*, Report of the Secretary General 65.II.B.I, New York and Geneva: United Nations Publication.
UNESCO (1973) *Records of the Conference for the Revision of the Universal Copyright Convention*, Paris: United Nations Educational, Scientific and Cultural Organization (UNESCO).
UN General Assembly (1961) *Resolution 1713 (XVI) on the Role of Patents in the Transfer of Technology to Underdeveloped Countries, 19 December*, New York: United Nations (UN).
UN General Assembly (1970) *Resolution 2626 (XXV) on an International Development Strategy for the Second United Nations Development Decade, 24 October*, New York: United Nations (UN).

UN General Assembly (1974) *Resolution 3281 (XXIX) on Charter of Economic Rights and Duties of States, 12 December*, New York: United Nations (UN).
UN General Assembly (1975) *Resolution 3362 (S-VII), para 3, Section III, Development and International Economic Cooperation, 19 September*, Geneva: United Nations (UN).
Vedaraman, S. (1972) 'The New Indian Patents Law,' *International Review of Industrial Property and Copyright Law*, 3: 39–54.
Wade, R. (2003) 'What Strategies Are Viable for Developing Countries Today? The World Trade Organisation and the Shrinking of "Development Space,"' *Review of International Political Economy*, 10, 4: 621–44.
Wells, S. (1969) 'Developing Countries, GATT and UNCTAD,' *International Affairs*, 45, 1: 64–79.
Whalley, J. (1989) *Developing Countries and the Global Trading System*, London: Macmillan.
White, E. (1975) 'La cuestión de la propriedad industrial en américa latina y su papel en el proceso de desarrollo e integración económica: un examen de las actuales tendencias legislativas, con especial referencia al tratamiento de las patentas,' paper presented at the *Institute for the Integration of Latin America of the Inter-American Development Bank, as a contribution to the Expert Meeting on the Role of the Patent System,* Geneva: sponsored by the United Nations Conference on Trade and Development (UNCTAD), 20 August.
Williams, M. (1991), *Third World Co-operation: The Group of 77 in UNCTAD*, London: Pinter.
WIPO (1973) Report of WIPO Director General to ECOSOC on Relations between the UN and WIPO, Geneva: World Intellectual Property Organization (WIPO).
WIPO (1975) *Agreement Between the United Nations and the World Intellectual Property Organization*, WIPO Publication 111, Geneva: World Intellectual Property Organization (WIPO).
WIPO (1979) *Diplomatic Conference for the Revision of the Paris Convention: Basic Proposals,* PR/DC/3, 25 June, Geneva: World Intellectual Property Organization (WIPO).
WIPO (1983) *The Paris Convention for the Protection of Intellectual Property from 1883 to 1983*, Geneva: World Intellectual Property Organization (WIPO).
WIPO (1988) *Existence, Scope and Form of Generally Internationally Accepted and Applied Standards/Norms for the Protection of Intellectual Property,* WO/INF/29, September, Geneva: World Intellectual Property Organization (WIPO).
World Bank (1988/1989) *World Development Report: Knowledge for Development,* Washington DC: World Bank and Oxford University Press.
Yu, P. (2004) 'Currents and Crosscurrents in the International Intellectual Property Regime,' *Loyola of Los Angeles Law Review*, 38: 323–443.
Yu, P. (2008) 'A Tale of Two Development Agendas,' *Ohio Northern University Law Review*, 34.
Zartman, W. (1971) *The Politics of Trade Negotiations Between Africa and the European Economic Community: The Weak Confront the Strong*, Princeton, NJ: Princeton University Press.
Zartman, W. (ed.) (1987) *Positive Sum: Improving North-South Negotiations*, New Brunswick, NJ: Transaction Books.

3 Minimum standards vs. harmonization in the TRIPS context: the nature of obligations under TRIPS and modes of implementation at the national level in monist and dualist systems

*Denis Borges Barbosa**

Article 1 Nature and Scope of Obligations
1. (a) Members shall give effect to the provisions of this Agreement. (b) Members may, but shall not be obliged to, implement in their law more extensive protection than is required by this Agreement, provided that such protection does not contravene the provisions of this Agreement. (c) Members shall be free to determine the appropriate method of implementing the provisions of this Agreement within their own legal system and practice.

The effect of TRIPS provisions

Some international legal instruments are created to be inductive, not prescriptive. Indicating areas or principles to which its parties agree, those inductive instruments (sometimes described as *soft law*[1]) simply declare the extent of such agreement, or purport to propitiate voluntary actions by the signatories. By stating in its very first provision that 'Members shall give effect to the provisions of this Agreement', TRIPS dispels any doubts about its prescriptive nature.

The legal duty that requires that the TRIPS Agreement shall be made effective results not only from the specific consent from the member states to do so, but also from a general rule of international law:

> The requirement to implement an international agreement is implicit in the obligation to perform it in good faith. The obligation to perform in good faith ('pacta sunt servanda') is established by Article 26 of the Vienna Convention

* The author must thank Professor David Vaver for his the attentive review of and suggestions offered on this study.

[1] Defined as '[r]ules of conduct that are laid down in instruments which have not been attributed legally binding force as such, but nevertheless may have certain – indirect – legal effects, and that are aimed at and may produce practical effects', Linda Senden, 'Soft Law, Self-regulation and Co-regulation in European Law: Where do they meet?', *EJCL*, Vol. 9, 1.1.2005.

> on the Law of Treaties (VCLT), which substantially codifies customary international law. Article 1.1 of TRIPS provides that Members will 'give effect to the provisions' of the Agreement, restating the basic international legal obligation.[2]

The good faith requirement mandates a duty to implement the obligations conceived at international level, irrespective of any domestic legal constraints.[3] Is it really so?

No doubt, the accepted view is that there is an inherent duty to follow the commitments a State freely enters into,[4] and even the precepts of domestic law are no excuse for non-compliance.[5] Commentators have indicated the ethical, and therefore intrinsically mandatory, nature of such commitments.

In EC case C-149-96,[6] a different perspective on the essence of the *jus cogens* in connection with trade-related treaties was, however, considered. The issue was the impact of WTO rules upon the internal legal system of Portugal, and the European Court of Justice noticed:

> 35. It should also be remembered that according to the general rules of international law there must be bona fide performance of every agreement. Although each contracting party is responsible for executing fully the commitments which it has undertaken it is nevertheless free to determine the legal means appropriate for attaining that end in its legal system, unless the agreement,

---

[2] UNCTAD–ICTSD, *Resource Book on Trips and Development*, New York and Cambridge: Cambridge University Press, 2005, p. 17. Carlos Correa, *Trade Related Aspects of Intellectual Property Rights*, Oxford: Oxford University Press, 2007, p. 22, also notes that in the Vienna Treaty Preamble it states that this principle is 'universally recognized'.

[3] Richard Gardiner, *Treaty Interpretation*, Oxford: Oxford University Press, 2008, p. 148.

[4] Ian Brownlie, *Principles of Public International Law*, Oxford: Clarendon Press, 1990, p. 12. Nguyen Quoc Dinh, *Droit International Public*, 5th edition, Paris: LGDJ, 1995 (updated by P. Daillier and A. Pellet), p. 216.

[5] According to the Alabama Claims case of 1872, C.C. Beaman (1871), *The National and Private Alabama Claims and their Final and Amicable Settlement*, Washington: W.H. Moore., reprinted in the Michigan Historical Reprint Series, ISBN 1418129801. 'The American case also contended that Great Britain could not escape liability by reason of alleged deficiencies in internal legislation enacted for the purpose of enabling the government to fulfill its international duties'. The tribunal held that 'the government of Her Britannic Majesty can not justify itself for a failure in due diligence on the insufficiency of the legal means of action which it possessed'. The case is particularly interesting as one of the arbiters was the Brazilian diplomat and law professor Viscount of Itajubá.

[6] Found at http://eur-lex.europa.eu/LexUriServ/LexUriServ.do?uri=CELEX:61996J0149:EN:HTML.

> interpreted in the light of its subject-matter and purpose, itself specifies those means (Kupferberg, paragraph 18).
> 36. While it is true that the WTO agreements, as the Portuguese Government observes, differ significantly from the provisions of GATT 1947, in particular by reason of the strengthening of the system of safeguards and the mechanism for resolving disputes, the system resulting from those agreements nevertheless accords considerable importance to negotiation between the parties.
> 37. Although the main purpose of the mechanism for resolving disputes is in principle, according to Article 3(7) of the Understanding on Rules and Procedures Governing the Settlement of Disputes (Annex 2 to the WTO), to secure the withdrawal of the measures in question if they are found to be inconsistent with the WTO rules, that understanding provides that where the immediate withdrawal of the measures is impracticable compensation may be granted on an interim basis pending the withdrawal of the inconsistent measure.
> 38. According to Article 22(1) of that Understanding, compensation is a temporary measure available in the event that the recommendations and rulings of the dispute settlement body provided for in Article 2(1) of that Understanding are not implemented within a reasonable period of time, and Article 22(1) shows a preference for full implementation of a recommendation to bring a measure into conformity with the WTO agreements in question.
> 39. However, Article 22(2) provides that if the member concerned fails to fulfill its obligation to implement the said recommendations and rulings within a reasonable period of time, it is, if so requested, and on the expiry of a reasonable period at the latest, to enter into negotiations with any party having invoked the dispute settlement procedures, with a view to finding mutually acceptable compensation.
> 40. Consequently, to require the judicial organs to refrain from applying the rules of domestic law which are inconsistent with the WTO agreements would have the consequence of depriving the legislative or executive organs of the contracting parties of the possibility afforded by Article 22 of that memorandum of entering into negotiated arrangements even on a temporary basis.

In other words, the Court pointed out that in the WTO agreements, the good faith principle does not require specific performance, but is compatible with an obligation to pay *compensation* to preclude a punitive result from compliance – at least temporarily. The norms are certainly coactive, and compliance is preferable to substitutive performance[7] but no ethical imperative compulsion attaches to it. As the Portugal case states, the imme-

[7] As states DSU 22(1): '1. Compensation and the suspension of concessions or other obligations are temporary measures available in the event that the recommendations and rulings are not implemented within a reasonable period of time. However, neither compensation nor the suspension of concessions or other obligations is preferred to full implementation of a recommendation to bring a measure into conformity with the covered agreements. Compensation is voluntary and, if granted, shall be consistent with the covered agreements.'

diate unconditional judicialization of TRIPS in the member state courts would withdraw from them this faculty of substitutive performance.

Subsequent facts confirm the European Court's reading. Enforcement of Dispute Settlement Understanding (DSU) has been held to be never punitive, but only strictly compensatory,[8] and compensation substitutes for specific performance at least, as anticipated in the Portugal case, on a temporary but sometimes indefinite basis.[9] The peculiar nature of TRIPS, as compared with the prior GATT 1947, does not alter this conclusion.[10]

Rules that are not conceived to be applied to private parties

A second but extremely important characteristic of TRIPS is also rarely noticed: even if a member state gives effect to some of its specific provisions, such action cannot affect rights and obligations between private parties, by the very nature of the precept embodied in the international rule.

As Bodenhausen noticed, referring to the Paris Convention, but substantially to every treaty:[11]

> As to the principal rules of the Convention, a distinction must be made between four different categories of rules which it contains:
> 1. First, the Convention contains provisions of international public law regulating rights and obligations of the member States and establishing the organs of

---

[8] Decision by the Arbitrators on EC – Bananas III (US) (Article 22.6 – EC), para. 6.3. See also Decision by the Arbitrators in EC – Hormones (Article 22.6 – Canada), para. 39.

[9] O'Connor, Bernard and Djordjevic, Margareta, 'Practical Aspects of Monetary Compensation: The US – Copyright Case (March 2005). *Journal of International Economic Law*, 8(1), 2005, 127–42. Available at SSRN: http://ssrn.com/abstract=915558.

[10] Judson Osterhoudt Berkey, The European Court of Justice and Direct Effect for the Gatt: A Question Worth Revisiting, Harvard Law School, found at http://www.jeanmonnetprogram.org/papers/98/98-3-.html – visited 9/5/2009. ('The reasons for being cautious about drawing comparisons between the direct effect granted to the other international agreements and direct effect for the GATT 47 apply to the new GATT as well. The GATT 47 preamble, which is still the preamble to the GATT today, conveys the message that the GATT system is designed merely to provide a forum for engaging in multilateral negotiations directed at trade liberalization. And while it is true that the GATT system has produced some agreements requiring harmonization, most noticeably the Uruguay Round Agreements on Antidumping, Subsidies, and Trade Related Aspects of Intellectual Property (TRIPS), it is also true that those agreements require national law provisions protecting individual rights.')

[11] G.H.C. Bodenhausen. *Paris Convention for the Protection of Industrial Property*, Geneva: BIRPI, 1968, p. 10.

> the Union created by the Convention, as well as provisions of an administrative character. (. . .)
> 2. Secondly, the Convention contains provisions which require or permit the member States to legislate within the field of industrial property. (. . .)
> 3. A third category of provisions of the Convention relates to substantive law in the field of industrial property regarding rights and obligations of private parties but only to the extent of requiring the domestic law of the member States to be applied to these parties. (. . .)
> 4. Finally, a fourth category of provisions of the Convention contains rules of substantive law regarding rights and obligations of private parties, rules however which do not merely refer to the application of domestic laws, but the contents of which may directly govern the situation at issue.

Bodenhausen´s analysis could also be focused on the addressee of the rule: the member state as a public international law person, the member state in its capacity of issuer of internal law, and the private party either as obligated under internal law, or as beneficiary of the rules of the treaty itself, 'the contents of which may directly govern the situation at issue'.

It must be noticed that this distinction is a *prius* to the fact that the member state's internal legal order is subject to monist or dualist doctrines, on which we shall now focus. Even entirely monist systems would be prevented from giving direct effect to a provision that empowers its legislative chambers to legislate within certain limits, or to apply some general principles to given purposes. There would be no prescription liable to be applicable to private parties.

An example is extracted from the WIPO Copyright Treaty article 6:

> (2) Nothing in this Treaty shall affect the freedom of Contracting Parties to determine the conditions, if any, under which the exhaustion of the right in paragraph (1) applies after the first sale or other transfer of ownership of the original or a copy of the work with the authorization of the author.

Or the classic example mentioned by Bodenhausen:

> Article 10bis
> Unfair Competition
> (1) The countries of the Union are bound to assure to nationals of such countries effective protection against unfair competition.

As the same author mentions:

> Paragraph (10) merely contains *an obligation for the member states* (. . ..) In most countries, it will hardly be possible to assure *effective* protection against unfair competition by means other than *legislation*, but it was admitted at several Revision Conferences that member states are not obliged to introduce *special* legislation to this effect if their existing legislation (. . .) suffices to assure effective protection against unfair competition.

Or, turning now to TRIPS,

> Article 25
> Requirements for Protection
> 1. Members shall provide for the protection of independently created industrial designs that are new or original. Members may provide that designs are not new or original if they do not significantly differ from known designs or combinations of known design features. Members may provide that such protection shall not extend to designs dictated essentially by technical or functional considerations.

As was noted,

> To the extent they comply with the protection requirements under Article 25.1, Members can opt for either protection through copyright or *sui generis* design protection, depending on the local industrial needs. (. . .) A WTO Member is also free to adopt both ways of *sui generis* protection, as illustrated by the Japanese example: in addition to its registered design law, Japan now protects unregistered designs under an unfair competition regime, based on liability principles.[12]

Obviously the empowerment of the member state's legislature preempts direct application among private parties, irrespective of monism or dualism. A designer is not enabled by article 25 to concoct privately his protection between copyright or unfair competition, at will, preventing the legislator from making his own choice.[13]

Effectiveness and actual implementation of TRIPS

The Bodenhausen analysis has, however, a peculiar application in the case of TRIPS. A considerable body of case law and most commentators[14] have

---

[12] UNCTAD-ICTSD, op. cit., p. 330.

[13] Nuno Pires de Carvalho, *The TRIPS Regime of Trademarks and Designs*, Frederick (USA): Kluwer Law International, 2006, pp. 71–83. 'Some obligations, such as those of Article 3 I, may be directly transposed into national law by according the Agreement direct applicability. But other obligations may not, because they just offer broad parameters and thus require further definitions. For instance, Article 32 says that "[a]n opportunity for judicial review of any decision to revoke or forfeit a patent shall be available." In the absence of a corresponding provision at the national level clarifying at least the nature of that review and the competent appellate court (or administrative body), Article 32 is not operative'.

[14] See Frédérique Berrod, 'La Cour de Justice refuse l'invocabilité des accords OMC: essai de régulation de la mondialisation – A propos de l'arrêt de la Cour de Justice du 23 novembre 1999, Portugal c/ Conseil, (accords textiles avec le Pakistan et l'Inde)', [2000] *R. T. D. Eur*. 36(3) 419. Ronald A. Brand, 'Direct Effect of International Economic Law in the United States and the European Union', [1997] *Nw. J. Int'l L. & Bus*. 556. James J. Callaghan 'Analysis of the European Court of Justice's Decision on

ascertained that the whole agreement, to the extent that it pertains to IP law, is to be classified as type 2 under Bodenhausen's categories, namely, TRIPS is to be held as 'contain[ing] provisions which require or permit the member States to legislate within the field of intellectual property'.

Footnote 14 (*cont.*)
Competence in the World Trade Organization: Who Will Call the Shots in the Areas of Services and Intellectual Property in the European Union?', [1996] *Loy. L.A. Int'l & Competition. L. Rev.* (18) 497. Alexander A. Caviedes 'International Copyright Law: Should the European Union Dictate its Development?', [1998] *B. U. Int'l L.J.* (16) 165. William Cook, 'Judicial Review of the EPO and the Direct Effect of TRIPS in the European Community', [1997] *Eur. Intel. Propert. Rev.* 19(7) 367. Paul Craig and Gráinne de Búrca, *EU Law – Text, Cases and Materials*, 2nd edition, Oxford: Oxford University Press, 1998. G.A. Desmedt, 'European Court Rules on TRIPS Agreement', *Journal of International Economic Law*, 1(4), pp. 679–82, [1998]. Sigrid Dörmer, 'Dispute Settlement and New Developments Within the Framework of TRIPS – An Interim Review', [2000] *Int'l Rev. Ind. Prop. & Copyright L.* (31) 1. Josef Drexl, 'The TRIPS Agreement and the EC: What Comes Next after Joint Competence?', in Friedrich-Karl Beier and Gerhard Schricker (eds), *From GATT to TRIPS – The Agreement on Trade-Related Aspects of Intellectual Property Rights*, Munich: Weinheim, [1996]; New York: VCH, viii, 495pp, [c1996]. Piet Eeckhout, 'Judicial Enforcement of WTO Law in the European Union – Some Further Reflections', *Journal of International Economic Law*, 5(1), March 2002, 91–110. Carlos D. Esposito, 'The Role of the European Court of Justice in the Direct Applicability and Direct Effect of WTO Law, with a Dantesque Metaphor', [1998] *Berkeley J. Int'l L.* (16) 138. Meinhard Hilf, 'The Role of National Courts in International Trade Relations', [1997] *Mich. J. Int'l L.* (18) 321. Meinhard Hilf and Ernst-Ulrich Petersmann, *National Constitutions and International Economic Law*, Deventer Kluwer, Holland [1993]. Judith Hippler Bello, 'The WTO Dispute Settlement Understanding: Less is More', [1996] *Amer. J. Int'l L.* (90) 416. John H. Jackson, 'The WTO Dispute Settlement Understanding – Misunderstandings on the Nature of Legal Obligations', [1997] *Amer. J. Int'l L.* (91) 60. Jan Kuilwijk Kees, 'The European Court of Justice and the GATT Dilemma: Public Interest versus Individual Rights?', [1996] Nexed Editions. Philip Lee and Brian Kennedy, 'The Potential Direct Effect of GATT 1994 in European Community Law', 30 *Journal of World Trade*, 67 (No. 1), 1996. Mark Miller, 'The TRIPS Agreement and Direct Effect in European Community Law: You Can Look . . . But Can You Touch?', [1999] *Notre Dame L. Rev.* (74) 59. Pierre Pescatore, 'Opinion 1/94 on "Conclusion" of the WTO Agreement: Is There an Escape From a Programmed Disaster?, [1999] *C.M.L. Rev.* (36) 387. Gil Carlos Rodriguez Iglesias, 'Le pouvoir judiciaire de la Communauté Européenne au stade actuel de l'évolution de l'Union', Winston Churchill Conference, 7th Session of the Academy of European Law, European University Institute, Florence, 1 July 1996, Jean Monnet, Geert A. Zonnekeyn, 'Mixed Feelings about the Hermès Judgment', [1999] *Int'l Trade L. & Reg.* 5(1) 20. Geert A. Zonnekeyn, 'The Status of WTO Law in the EC Legal Order, The Final Curtain?', [2000] *JWT* 34(3) 111. Antônio Augusto Cançado Trindade, 'Direito Internacional e Direito Interno: Sua Interação na Proteção dos Direitos Humano's, found at http://www.dhnet.org.br/direitos/militantes/cancadotrindade/cancado_cd.htm.

This conclusion derives in considerable portion from the third clause of TRIPS 1.1: 'Members shall be free to determine the appropriate method of implementing the provisions of this Agreement within their own legal system and practice'. The addressee of the rule is the member state;[15] it is bound and simultaneously empowered to implement TRIPS in its internal legal order.[16]

Further reasons seem to indicate that direct application would be inappropriate. A specific proposal[17] to have a fully self-executing TRIPS was

---

[15] Judson Osterhoudt Berkey, idem, eadem. ('The GATT, however, ultimately is an agreement regulating the rights and obligations of its members not individuals. The preamble to the GATT states that the members, as sovereign states, recognize "that their relations in the field of trade and economic endeavor should be conducted with a view to raising standards of living, ensuring full employment and a large and steadily growing volume of real income and effective demand, developing the full use of the resources of the world and expanding the production and exchange of goods." These are goals which can only be achieved and evaluated on a macroeconomic basis with respect to the members themselves and not on a microeconomic basis with respect to individuals. This emphasis on the GATT members as opposed to individuals is inherent in several of the GATT's founding principles. For example, non-discrimination within the GATT means non-discrimination between members and not non-discrimination between individual traders in different members. In fact, it would be impossible to ensure that discrimination did not occur between individual traders across GATT members because natural differences in the factor endowments and technology of the different members automatically produce differences in the competitive positions of these traders. Without these differences in factor endowments and technology, international trade would not produce economic welfare gains at all.')

[16] A.M. Ávila, J.A.D. Castilla Urrutia and M.A. Mier, *Regulación del Comercio Internacional tras la Ronda Uruguay*, Madrid: Tecnos, 1996, p. 192, ('Es un Acuerdo de resultados, ya que los Estados miembros tendrán libertad para adoptar los medios racionales que estimen convenientes y que sean conformes con sus propios ordenamientos jur'dicos'). Carlos M. Correa, *Acuerdo TRIPS*, Buenos Aires: Ciudad Argentina, 1996, 'Las disposiciones del Acuerdo están dirigidas a los Estados y no modifican directamente la situación jur'dica de las partes privadas, quienes no podrán reclamar derechos en virtud del Acuerdo hasta y la medida que el mismo sea receptado por la legislación nacional'.

[17] It should be noted that Switzerland led an initiative halfway through the Uruguay Round to require each GATT member to give the GATT direct effect, or some equivalent status, in their national law. As Kuijper, supra its note 11, at 65, notes, this 'would have assured equality between the parties in respect of "internal enforcement" of the GATT'. (See Kuijper, Pieter Jan, 'The New WTO Dispute Settlement System – The Impact on the European Community', 29, *Journal of World Trade*, 49(6), 1995.) The fact that this was not included in the final Uruguay Round Agreement seems to indicate that the GATT members as a whole still do not desire a direct effect for the GATT; Judson Osterhoudt Berkey, 'The European Court of Justice and Direct Effect for the Gatt: A Question Worth

discussed during the Uruguay Round and dismissed.[18] TRIPS article 63.2 requires periodical reports of such implementation, which would be superfluous if the IP provisions were self-executing.[19] The various DSU decisions on TRIPS have also required the defendant member state to change its law to conform to the provided standards.

At regional or local level, this principle has been widely accepted. A number of decisions of the ECJ exclude direct application of WTO elementary treaties beyond the constrained scope of the Portugal case already mentioned.[20] Thus, the *Parfums Christian Dior* decision states:[21]

Footnote 17 (*cont.*)
Revisiting', Harvard Law School, available at http://www.jeanmonnetprogram.org/papers/98/98-3-.html.

[18] Armin von Bogdandy, 'Case note on Hermès', [1999] *C.M.L. Rev.* (36) 663, at 668, ('there are strong arguments for and against direct applicability' [but there is] 'almost unanimous political opposition to the direct application of the WTO law').

[19] For instance, see the report submitted at the TRIPS Council, Doc. IP/C/8, 6 November 1996: '(a) Article 63.2 1) At its meeting in November 1995, the Council adopted the following decisions to give effect to the obligation to notify implementing legislation under Article 63.2: Procedures for Notification of, and Possible Establishment of a Common Register of, National Laws and Regulations under Article 63.2 (document IP/C/2); Format for Listing of "Other Laws and Regulations" to be Notified under Article 63.2 (document IP/C/4); and Checklist of Issues on Enforcement (document IP/C/5). 2) These procedures require that, as of the time that a Member is obliged to start applying a provision of the TRIPS Agreement, the corresponding laws and regulations shall be notified without delay. A very substantial volume of legislation has been notified under these procedures. As of the date of this report, 30 Members have notified some or all of their implementing legislation. Most of the material to be notified by Members whose legislation, in the area of copyright and related rights, was the subject of review at the Council's July meeting (see paragraph 14 below) has been notified; three other countries have notified some of their legislation while indicating that this is without prejudice to their transition period under the provisions of Article 65; and 11 Members have notified legislation relating to the implementation of Article 70.8 and, in some cases, Article 70.9 of the TRIPS Agreement'.

[20] For instance, the cases decided on 16 June 1998 (Hermès) and 14 December 2000 (*Dior* v. *Tuk* and *Assco* v. *Lahyer*), and specifically on the application of TRIPS art. 50, 13 September 2001, case C-89/99 (Hoge Raad der Nederlanden, Schieving-Nijstad), Of. Journal noc C 303, 27 October 2001, pp. 0002–0003. See also Judgment of the Court of 9 October 2001, *Kingdom of the Netherlands v. European Parliament and Council of the European Union*, at http://eur-lex.europa.eu/smartapi/cgi/sga_doc?smartapi!celexplus!prod!CELEXnumdoc&numdoc=61998J0377&lg=EN.

[21] Decision of 14 December 2000, joint cases C-300/98 and C-392/98 (Parfums Christian Dior), found at http://eur-lex.europa.eu/LexUriServ/LexUriServ.do?uri=CELEX:61998J0300:EN:HTML. See especially '44. For the same reasons as those set out by the Court in paragraphs 42 to 46 of the judgment in Portugal v

> 1. Where the judicial authorities of the Member States are called upon to order provisional measures for the protection of intellectual property rights falling within the scope of the Agreement on Trade-Related Aspects of Intellectual Property Rights (the TRIPS Agreement), as set out in Annex 1 C to the Agreement establishing the World Trade Organisation, approved on behalf of the Community, as regards matters within its competence, by Council Decision 94/800/EC of 22 December 1994, and a case is brought before the Court of Justice in accordance with the provisions of the EC Treaty, in particular Article 177 thereof (now Article 234 EC), the Court of Justice has jurisdiction to interpret Article 50 of the TRIPS Agreement.
> 2. In a field to which the TRIPS Agreement applies and in respect of which the Community has already legislated, the judicial authorities of the Member States are required by virtue of Community law, when called upon to apply national rules with a view to ordering provisional measures for the protection of rights falling within such a field, to do so as far as possible in the light of the wording and purpose of Article 50 of the TRIPS Agreement.
>
> In a field in which the Community has not yet legislated and which consequently falls within the competence of the Member States, the protection of intellectual property rights, and measures adopted for that purpose by the judicial authorities, do not fall within the scope of Community law. Accordingly, Community law neither requires nor forbids that the legal order of a Member State should accord to individuals the right to rely directly on the rule laid down by Article 50(6) of the TRIPS Agreement or that it should oblige the courts to apply that rule of their own motion.
> 3. Article 50 of the TRIPS Agreement leaves to the Contracting Parties, within the framework of their own legal systems, the task of specifying whether the right to sue under general provisions of national law concerning wrongful acts, in particular unlawful competition, in order to protect an industrial design against copying is to be classified as an intellectual property right within the meaning of Article 50(1) of the TRIPS Agreement.

Commentators note that the ECJ ruled in this case that, in principle, individuals may not rely directly on Article 50, but must resort to their national law.[22] This understanding transcends European law: 'So the question of whether a party to a dispute before courts of a WTO member can

---

Council, the provisions of TRIPS, an annex to the WTO Agreement, are not such as to create rights upon which individuals may rely directly before the courts by virtue of Community law'.

[22] De Bandt, Van Hecke, Lagae & Loesch De Brauw Blackstone Westbroek Gianni, Origoni, Grippo & Partners Linklaters, Issue 19, November 2000, Intellectual Property News ('Does article 50(6) TRIPS have direct effect?'). 'In cases concerning intellectual property rights (as defined in TRIPS) where the European Community has already legislated, the judicial authorities of the Member States are obliged to apply national rules as far as possible in the light of the wording and the purpose of Article 50(6). They must ensure that a balance is struck between the competing rights and obligations of the intellectual property right holder and the defendant'.

invoke the TRIPS provisions to protect that party's rights is answered by the domestic law of that member'.[23]

The member states are bound to bring TRIPS IP rules and principles into conformity with their respective constitutional system to make it as effective as possible.[24] If their constitutional system permits giving direct effect to TRIPS rules (and, this author notes, the rules are capable of direct effect under the Bodenhausen analysis), some direct effect would in theory be possible,[25] even though in practice it might be difficult to conceive.[26]

---

[23] T.T. Nguyen and H.H. Lidgard, 'The CFI Microsoft Judgment and TRIPS Competition Flexibilities', found at http://works.bepress.com/cgi/viewcontent.cgi?article=1000&context=hans_henrik_lidgard, visited 26 November 2008.

[24] Judson Osterhoudt Berkey, 'The European Court Of Justice and Direct Effect for the Gatt: A Question Worth Revisiting', available at http://www.jeanmonnetprogram.org/papers/papers99.html, and Ga'lle Bontinck, 'The TRIPS Agreement and The ECJ: A New Dawn? Some Comments About Joined Cases C-300/98 and C-392/98, Parfums Dior and Assco Gerüste', found at http://www.jeanmonnetprogram.org/papers/papers01.html, both visited at 17 May 2002. However, in the case *India – Patent Protection for Pharmaceutical and Agricultural Chemical Products*, Report of the Appellate Body, WT/DS50/AB/R, 19 December 1997 ('India – Mailbox'), the AB second-guessed what India had deemed to be an adequate implementation.

[25] The ECJ, in case C-431/05, decided 11 September 2007, found at http://eur-lex.europa.eu/LexUriServ/LexUriServ.do?uri=CELEX:62005J0431:EN:HTML, had concluded that it is not offensive to the EC legal system if a state decides – with due regard to its constitutional law – to apply a TRIPS rule directly: 'Having regard to the principle recalled in paragraph 34 above, it must be concluded that, since Article 33 of the TRIPS Agreement forms part of a sphere in which, at this point in the development of Community law, the Member States remain principally competent, they may choose whether or not to give direct effect to that provision'.

[26] The opinion of the Advocate General in case C-431/05 expresses this point: '93. Greater doubts arise in the recognition of horizontal direct effect, because of the lack of a maximum limit. The end of the period of protection for those special rights affects not only their holder but, in particular, third parties and the public domain, which in this respect represents the general interest. Competitors and also the appropriate registration authority have to know when protection of that patent comes to an end in the national legal order. 94. If the legislature does not exercise that power, it is impossible to pinpoint, merely from the wording of Article 33, the precise moment at which the term of the lawfully granted monopoly ends. In particular, to decide that it is sufficient to take the minimum option of 20 years would amount to assuming a power belonging to the legislature and it could not be raised against third parties. 95. Consequently, Article 33 of the TRIPS Agreement, because it is subject to the power of the national legislature to fix the exact duration of the protection granted to patents in its own legal order, does not have direct effect'. However, Vietnam has stated in their legislative act incorporating TRIPS in 2007 that direct effect would be effected; Article 6 of the Vietnam National

Some notable domestic cases have also refused direct application, in the UK[27] and in Germany.[28] But the main argument against direct application is the WTO jurisprudence itself:[29]

> 7.72 Under the doctrine of direct effect, which has been found to exist most notably in the legal order of the EC but also in certain free trade area agreements, obligations addressed to States are construed as creating legally enforceable rights and obligations for individuals. Neither the GATT nor the WTO has so far been interpreted by GATT/WTO institutions as a legal order producing direct effect.[30] Following this approach, the GATT/WTO did *not* create a new

---

Assembly's Law No. 41/2005/QH11 of 14 June 2005 on signing, accessing, and implementing international treaties.

[27] High Court of Justice for England and Wales, dated 20 December 1996 in the case of Lenzing AG's European Patent (UK), [1997] R.P.C., 245, see pp. 267 f, available at http://www.bailii.org/ew/cases/EWHC/Admin/1996/390.html ('67. I think the point really merits no further consideration, but it is only fair that I go into some of the arguments further. First then I think it worthy of note that the language of TRIPS is not that of a Treaty intended by the signatories to have direct effect: "Members shall give effect to the provisions of this Agreement . . . . Members shall be free to determine the appropriate method of implementing the provisions of this Agreement within their own legal system and practice" – see Article 1(1). And as I have said it is accepted that other signatories do not consider it to have such effect.') '76. I do not see any of this as altering the fundamental character of the WTO and TRIPS as merely an agreement between nations. In the end there is still great flexibility. Moreover the very nature of the machinery imposed, urging members towards compliance, is inconsistent with the notion that the Treaty itself is self-executing by way of conferring private rights on citizens. Mr. Hoskins who argued the TRIPS point so splendidly, said that TRIPS is "far more binding" than GATT 1947. But ultimately it is not binding and I have no doubt that the distinctions of procedure he relies upon are distinctions without a difference.') ('I conclude that the WTO and TRIPS is not capable of having direct effect and that the point is so self-evident as to fall within the acte claire doctrine').

[28] P. Katzenberger, 'TRIPS and copyright law' in F. Beier and G. Schricker (eds), *From GATT to TRIPS – The Agreement on Trade-Related Aspects of Intellectual Property Rights*, Munich: IIC Studies, Max Planck Institute for Foreign and International Patent, Copyright and Competition Law, 1996, p. 73.

[29] Report of the Panel of 22 December 1999, United States – Sections 301–310 of the Trade Act of 1974, 99/5454, WT/DS152/Re.h.

[30] [Original Footnote] We make this statement as a matter of fact, without implying any judgment on the issue. We note that whether there are circumstances where obligations in any of the WTO agreements addressed to Members would create rights for individuals which national courts must protect, remains an open question, in particular in respect of obligations following the exhaustion of DSU procedures in a specific dispute (see Eeckhout, P., The Domestic Legal Status of the WTO Agreement: Interconnecting Legal Systems, Common Market Law Review, 1997, p. 11; Berkey, J., The European Court of Justice and Direct Effect for the GATT: A Question Worth Revisiting, European Journal of International

> legal order the subjects of which comprise both contracting parties or Members and their nationals.

Also in the Patent Protection for Pharmaceutical and Agricultural Chemical Products case[31]

> 34. (. . .) The Panel also referred to certain GATT 1947 panel reports[32] as authority for this principle. The Panel noted that whereas the 'disciplines formed under GATT 1947 (so-called GATT *acquis*) were primarily directed at the treatment of the goods of other countries', 'the concept of the protection of legitimate expectations' in relation to the *TRIPS Agreement* applies to 'the competitive relationship between a Member's own nationals and those of other Members (rather than between domestically produced goods and the goods of other Members, as in the goods area)'.[33] (. . .)
> 48. For these reasons, we do not agree with the Panel that the legitimate expectations of Members *and* private rights holders concerning conditions of competition must always be taken into account in interpreting the *TRIPS Agreement*.

The monist-dualist legend

In one of the most ingrained themes of international law scholars, international and domestic laws are deemed to interact either in a unitary environment, where the two kinds may conflict, or in two different spheres altogether, where no direct conflict between the two strata is possible. The first doctrine is called monism, the second dualism.[34] As Nguyen and Lidgard note:

Footnote 30 (*cont.*)
Law, 1998, p. 626). The fact that WTO institutions have not to date construed any obligations as producing direct effect does not necessarily preclude that in the legal system of any given Member, following internal constitutional principles, some obligations will be found to give rights to individuals. Our statement of fact does not prejudge any decisions by national courts on this issue.

[31] AB-1997-5 Report of the Appellate Body, p. 2. WT/DS50/AB/R, found at http://homepages.law.asu.edu/~dkarjala/InternationalIP/WTO-IndiaAppPan.doc.

[32] [Original Footnote] In particular: Panel Report, Italian Discrimination Against Imported Agricultural Machinery, adopted 23 October 1958, BISD 7S/60, paras. 12–13; Panel Report, United States – Taxes on Petroleum and Certain Imported Substances, adopted 17 June 1987, BISD 34S/136, para. 5.22; and Panel Report, United States – Section 337 of the Tariff Act of 1930, adopted 7 November 1989, BISD 36S/345, para. 5.13.

[33] [Original Footnote] Panel Report, para. 7.21.

[34] Nguyen Quoc Dinh, *Droit International Public*, 5th. edition, Paris: LGDJ, 1995 (updated by P. Daillier and M. Pellet), pp. 93–5. Monists also disagree on which stratum – in an occasional conflict – has the upper hand: the international or the domestic.

In a country with a monist approach, such as most of the civil law tradition countries, international agreements are incorporated directly into domestic law, i.e. they are self-executing. In a country with a dualist approach, such as most common law countries, international agreements become national law only after passing further national legislation, i.e. they are not recognized as self-executing.[35]

Different WTO member states profess to subscribe to one or other doctrine, while some seem to choose an intermediate path. The United States and Brazil[36] are held to be middle-of-the road countries, as direct effect is possible, but subsequent laws may alter the rule originally provided by the international stratum. In most Latin American countries, a monist system prevails (again, when such an effect is possible under Bodenhausen´s criteria).[37]

The United States, moreover, has introduced a domestic rule specifically barring direct application of the Uruguay Round treaties, so that 'no provision of any of the Uruguay Round Agreements, nor the application of any such provision to any person or circumstance, that is inconsistent with any law of the United States shall have effect'.[38] The same provision limits causes of action regarding the direct application of the Round to the United States as a public law person, thereby excluding private parties

---

[35] [Original footnote] Martin Dixon, International Law, Oxford University Press, 2007, pp. 88–90 & 94–97; Xin Zhang, Direct Effects of the WTO Agreements: National Survey, 2 Int.T.L.R 35 (2003); Thomas Cottier & Krista N. Schefer, The Relationship between World Trade Organization Law, National and Regional Law, 1 J. Int'l Eco. L. 83 (1998).

[36] Brazil is a 'moderate dualist' country (Brazilian Supreme Court Decision ADIn 1480-DF of 1997 (by applying the principle *ex posterior derogat priori*), but also accepts the application of the crieteria of *lex specialiter*, 'A eventual precedência dos tratados ou convenções internacionais sobre as regras infraconstitucionais de direito interno somente se justificará quando a situação de antinomia com o ordenamento doméstico impuser, para a solução do conflito, a aplicação alternativa do critério cronológico ("lex posterior derogat priori") ou, quando cab'vel, do critério da especialidade'.

[37] Carlos M. Correa, *Trade Related Aspects of Intellectual Property Rights: Commentary on the TRIPS Agreement*, Oxford: Oxford University Press, 2007, p. 22, (herein below referred to as 'Commentary'): 'As to the direct effect of TRIPS, including enforcement, see the decision of the Argentinian Supreme Court "Unilever NVc Instituto Nacional de La Propriedad Intelectual s/denegatória de Patentes", CS, octubre 24, 2000. in KORS Jorge. Patentes de Invención Diez anos de jurisprudência – Comentários e fallos. Buenos Aires: La Ley, 2004, p. 13'.

[38] Section 102(a)(1) of the Uruguay Round Agreements Act, Pub. L. 103-465, 108 Stat. 4809 (1994).

from initiating any litigation against the government. This limitation has been accepted by the courts.[39]

As Nuno Carvalho notes:

> Actually, several WTO Members have included in their implementing laws provisions according to which in the event a conflict arises between national law and international treaties, the latter shall prevail. This solution may not be very helpful as far as provisions like Article 32 and Article 34.1 of the TRIPS Agreement are concerned, but nonetheless it may increase the level of consistency of national laws with TRIPS provisions to the extent that such provisions constitute a clear guideline for national courts.[40]

A further point should, however, be noted. What happens where the municipal law is simply silent on the compliance of some specific aspect of TRIPS? If the legal system is monist *and* the provision is one that allows for direct application, TRIPS may apply to the whole legal context. Thus, compliance will have to be assessed in the light of the actual practice of administrative and judicial bodies, and weighing the legal system as a whole.[41]

On the other hand, even in situations where a non-monist (dualist or any other intermediate) system is silent as to the incorporation of a TRIPS element, compliance should be recognized if existing rules can be interpreted as if the treaty was in effect incorporated, under the doctrine of 'consistent interpretation'.[42] This interpretation may eventually make it

---

[39] *In re Rath*, 402 F.3d 1207, 1209 note 2 (Fed. Cir. 2005); *ITC v. Punchgini*, 482 F.3d 135, 161–2 (2nd Cir. 2007).

[40] Nuno Carvalho, op. cit.

[41] Carlos Correa, Commentary.

[42] 'The doctrine of consistent interpretation in the EU does not only mean that secondary Community law (regulations, directives and decisions) should be interpreted in conformity with primary Community law, but also that the interpretation of Community law of any level should be adapted to the international obligations of the Community irrespective of whether these obligations have direct effect or not. Consistent interpretation can be regarded as lesser level of intrusion of international law in the domestic legal system. The limit of this doctrine occurs when the domestic rule at stake cannot be construed in accordance with the relevant international law provisions, the system becomes disarticulated unless the direct effect doctrine is applied. This will result in the overruling of the domestic provision inconsistent with the international provision that the State has accepted. By giving direct effect to that provision the court will prevent that the State engages its international responsibility for breaching international law', Jonathan Curci, 'The Question of Direct Effect of International Treaties: a US–EU Comparative Approach of the WTO Treaties', found at http://zope0.itcilo.org/masters/turin-ip/2005/turin-ip-new/Documents/Documents2005/internationalip/Directeffect/preview_popup, visited 3 December 2008.

easier to hold in favour of the compatibility of TRIPS-compliant norms with the member state's constitutional restraints.[43]

Minimum standards

Once the issue that TRIPS article 1.1 requires effective implementation is resolved, a second question must be dealt with. To what extent should the requirements contained in TRIPS IP elements be made effective? The second clause of article 1.1 states: 'Members may, but shall not be obliged to, implement in their law more extensive protection than is required by this Agreement, provided that such protection does not contravene the provisions of this Agreement'.[44]

It is quite a common assertion that TRIPS is a 'minimum standards' treaty. A subtler alternative purports to see the prescriptions just as its backbone.[45]

---

[43] This author has taken the view that under Brazilian Law the TRIPS elements that were not directly incorporated into the local system should be taken as an interpretative tool of the local law, whenever (a) the municipal law does not oppose such interpretation or (b) the municipal law, even when more extensive than TRIPS requires as minimum standards, is liable to defy the substantive process of law standards posed by the Constitution; see *Uma Introdução à Propriedade Intelectual*, 2nd edition, Lumen Juris, 2003. The rationale is that a rule generally accepted by the international community as reasonable seems adequate to guide a due process analysis. On the issue of 'consistent interpretation', see T Cottier, 'The Impact of the TRIPS Agreement on Private Practice and Litigation', in J. Cameron and K. Campbell (eds), *Dispute Resolution in the World Trade Organization*, London: Cameron May Ltd., International Law Publishers, 1998, p. 124. See also the Designers Guild case in the House of Lords: *http://www.bailii.org/uk/cases/UKHL/2000/58.html* in Lord Hoffmann's speech at heading 6, where he refers to TRIPS as reinforcing the local law that copyright does not extend to ideas.

[44] The Paris Convention always allowed for limited, more-than-minimum standards agreements among its member states, according to its Article 19 – Special Agreements: 'It is understood that the countries of the Union reserve the right to make separately between themselves special agreements for the protection of industrial property, in so far as these agreements do not contravene the provisions of this Convention'. The Berne Convention also provides in the same sense: Article 20 of the Berne Convention (1971) reads: 'The Governments of the countries of the Union reserve the right to enter into special agreements among themselves, in so far as such agreements grant to authors more extensive rights than those granted by the Convention, or contain other provisions not contrary to this Convention [. . .]'.

[45] Laurence R. Helfer, 'Adjudicating Copyright Claims under the TRIPS Agreement: The Case for a European Human Rights Analogy', 39 *Harv. Int'l L.J.* 357, 360 (1998) ('TRIPS is at its core a "minimum standards" agreement.'). The classical analysis by J.H. Reichman, 'Universal Minimum Standards of Intellectual Property Protection under the TRIPS Component of the WTO Agreement', 29

Prior intellectual property multilateral treaties certainly also had a minimum standards content.[46] The Paris Convention has some very clear prescriptive standards: no member state to the Paris Convention can ever declare a patent void on account of the mere importation of the item patented, as provided for in article V of the 1883 text – and this is certainly a 'minimum standard'.[47] As to the Berne Convention, the prescriptive content was certainly much wider than in its sister instrument.[48]

No members of the Berne or Paris Convention were allowed to make reservations to such 'minimum standards' provisions. Signing any such convention meant accepting those prescriptions as an international obligation. However, acceptance would not necessarily result in immediate changes in the domestic laws, if such changes were needed.[49] For instance,

---

Footnote 45 (*cont.*)
International Lawyer 345 (1995), p. 347, also seems to indicate the minimum standards issue as the crucial aspect of the then recent treaty: 'The absorption of classical intellectual property law into international economic law will gradually establish universal minimum standards governing the relations between innovators and second comers in an integrated world market'.

46 Other commentators do not discern such minima in the Paris Convention, for example, UNCTAD–ICTSD, *Resource Book on TRIPS and Development*, New York and Cambridge: Cambridge University Press, 2005, p. 19: "While the Berne Convention established minimum standards of copyright protection, the Paris Convention did not define the principal substantive standards of patent protection, essentially leaving this to each state party'.

47 However, if this specific agreement should be recognized as 'core', so probably should the national treatment rule. J.H. Reichman, 'Universal Minimum': 'While some international minimum standards and the rule of national treatment apply to all these institutions, the Paris Convention entrusted the protection of industrial creations primarily to "the various kinds of industrial patents recognized by the laws of the countries of the Union.'

48 J.H. Reichman, 'Charting the Collapse of the Patent-Copyright Dichotomy: Premises for a Restructured International Intellectual Property System', *Cardozo Arts & Ent. L.J.* 475 (1995), 'Article 1 of the Berne Convention established "a Union for the protection of the rights of authors in their literary and artistic works." Such works, categorized at length in Article 2(1), should receive automatic and mandatory protection in the domestic copyright laws of the member states'.

49 Many of those prescriptions, however, presaged a change of domestic laws, at least in those countries accepting pure or moderate monist systems. The original wording of article IV, for instance, created directly a priority right for any beneficiary of the treaty, in such a self-contained style that it dispensed with further normative implementation, except for an extreme dualist system. On the other hand, Art. 10-*bis* of the Paris Convention was not directly prescriptive, as it just required the member states to legislate in order to protect fair competition, under a set of standards; no straight right was created for the beneficiaries themselves, but only an obligation to the member state.

Brazil deferred compliance with its obligation to create a system for opposing unfair competition for decades after the signature of the Paris Convention text that required such minimum standard (article 10-*bis*).[50] This delay was possible because there was no international system of legal coercion to expedite the implementation of such obligations.[51]

Moreover, the member states could (and many actually did) reject the new versions of the old Convention, which included minimum standards deemed inconvenient to their national purposes, without any adverse legal or practical consequences. Brazil objected to the new 1934 rule that prohibited revocation of patent on account of lack of usage, except in cases where a compulsory licence had been granted earlier, and such grant was ineffectual; the prior 1925 version was the last applicable for Brazil up to 1991. Hundreds of patents were lost for lack of usage since 1934, and no violation of Brazil's international obligations could be argued.[52]

The most obvious difference between the WTO agreement and its predecessors, therefore, is that 'minimum standards' are implemented through the Dispute Settlement system peculiar to the new treaty, which has actual coercive power.[53] Canada and India have been obliged to conform their domestic laws to TRIPS at a very early stage of the new rules, through an adjudication and economic sanction system unknown under the older Conventions.

---

[50] However, when Brazil signed the original 1883 text, the Brazilian delegate to the negotiations of the original Convention reported that all required changes in domestic law were already enacted (especially the article 5 item mentioned above).

[51] Arguably, resort to the Hague International Court and to arbitration could be requested by any aggrieved member state to the Paris Convention; however, those methods were not imposed as *jus cogens*.

[52] Although it was argued that protection of the interests of the US patent-holders in Brazil was being prejudiced by such Convention-sanctioned rule, during the exercises of unilateral economic pressure carried out by the United States under Section 301 of its Trade Act during the late 1980s, as a non-violation nullification argument under GATT 1947. A GATT panel was set in 1969, but the issue was solved by agreement.

[53] Graeme B. Dinwoodie, 'Detaching Trademark', *Houston Review*, 41(3), 2004, p. 886. Available at SSRN: http://ssrn.com/abstract=616661, 'Even if the Paris Convention had contained a far greater number of provisions aimed at substantive harmonization, other structural aspects of the system would have limited its effectiveness in modifying the territoriality of trademark laws. First, the Convention articulated minimum levels of substantive protection: states were free to grant higher levels of protection. 58 Thus, expanding the number of obligations would not necessarily have effected substantial harmonization. Second, the treaty imposed obligations on member states; private parties were left largely to rely on faithful national implementation of member state obligations without, pre-TRIPS, much formal compliance pressure applied to recalcitrant states'.

The impact of the 'minimum standards' issue in TRIPS was realized through the single undertaking requirement;[54] instead of bargaining just-intellectual property issues as happened before, parties to the WTO discussed access to markets comprising physical goods, investment and services (in the case of some of these issues, to different extents). As a 'whole bunch' bargain, sanctioned by cross-retaliation, multilaterally imposed coercion, the 'minimum standards' issue took on an entirely new light.[55]

The 'minimum standards' concept is not, therefore, a new legal category, peculiar to TRIPS. The problem is *which minimum standards* were included in the 1994 Agreement.

At the inception of the Paris Convention in 1884, its minimum standards were agreed at higher levels than those prevailing in all of its original signatories.[56] French industrialists reacted bitterly against the new rule that allowed patent-holders to import the protected object without losing their monopoly; a hasty Revision Conference was set for 1886, where resistance to the new minimum standards was openly voiced.

However, as noted, minimum standards were not the core of the Paris Convention. Frenchmen in 1886 were especially affected by the fact that whereas France granted patents and was therefore subjected to the import of products patented in France as an exclusive right of the patent-holder,

---

[54] Pedro Roffe, 'Bringing Minimum Intellectual Property Standards', found at http://www.idrc.ca/en/ev-119947-201-1-DO_TOPIC.html, visited on 21 October 2008. 'This became possible because the Uruguay Round, although dealing with many different areas, was conducted on the basis that the final deal would be a single undertaking – which meant that countries had to accept all elements of the packets agreed (such as agriculture, services and textiles), even if they really only wanted some of them'.

[55] 'One hundred and seventeen nations, including all NICs and thus Brazil, signed the TRIPS Agreement allowing intellectual property rights to be enforced by trade sanctions. Although many of them had reservations about strengthening intellectual property rights, signing the TRIPS Agreement was a condition for participating in the WTO, which was then viewed as an essential component for them to take part in the international wave of trade and prosperity of a globalized world. By situating the TRIPS Agreement within the framework of multilateral trade relations, the Agreement benefits from the increased incentive for nations to enforce intellectual property rights through the threat of trade sanctions. The TRIPS Agreement envisages that the threat of trade sanctions will propel the forward motion of respect and protection of IPRs worldwide', 'Patent Bargains in NICs: The Case of Brazil', found at http://repositories.cdlib.org/cgi/viewcontent.cgi?article=1125&context=bple, visited 5 December 2008.

[56] F. Savignon and Y. Plasseraud, *Paris 1883 – Genèse du Droit Unioniste des Brevets*, Paris: LITEC, 1983, pp. 212–55.

Holland, Switzerland, Romania and Serbia had no patents whatsoever. The Paris Convention does not have a minimum standard requiring the issuance of any patents, provided that nationals and foreigners were treated in the exact same manner (foreigners, however, could be granted further perks besides mere equal treatment[57]).

The minimum standards as the essence of TRIPS

The common perception therefore is that TRIPS is 'the' minimum standards IP agreement. In the Canada Generics case, the panel so ruled:

> 6.87 Article 1.1 confirms that the *TRIPS Agreement* is a minimum standards agreement in respect of intellectual property rights. Under Article 1.1, Members may, but are not obligated to, implement a more stringent standard for the protection of intellectual property rights so long as such measures do not contravene any of the provisions of the *TRIPS Agreement*. (. . .)

These minimum standards comprise three different tiers:

(a) the prior treaty level as stated in TRIPS article 2, comprising the Paris Convention, Berne Convention, Rome Convention and the Treaty on Intellectual Property in Respect of Integrated Circuits (the 'basic treaties'),[58]
(b) some less-than-prior level, as in the case of TRIPS Article 9 (moral rights), where parties may comply with the WTO at a lesser level than that stated in prior treaties;[59] and

---

[57] The text of the Convention states that its beneficiaries shall enjoy the same treatment as the nationals of the member state, 'all without prejudice to the rights specially provided for by this Convention'. For example, the Convention's article VIII requirements on commercial names impose nationwide protection and do not subject name owners to registration; under the Brazilian Civil Code, commercial name protection only covers specific states (not the whole country) and is dependent on registration of the corporation itself. Case law has asserted that on this point the foreign beneficiaries of the Convention have nationwide protection, irrespective of corporate registration, which is a more extensive right than locals enjoy.

[58] Article 2 – Intellectual Property Conventions – 1. In respect of Parts II, III and IV of this Agreement, Members shall comply with Articles 1 through 12, and Article 19, of the Paris Convention (1967). 2. Nothing in Parts I to IV of this Agreement shall derogate from existing obligations that Members may have to each other under the Paris Convention, the Berne Convention, the Rome Convention and the Treaty on Intellectual Property in Respect of Integrated Circuits.

[59] Article 9 – Relation to the Berne Convention – 1. Members shall comply with Articles 1 through 21 of the Berne Convention (1971) and the Appendix thereto. However, Members shall not have rights or obligations under this Agreement in

(c) any prescriptive obligation imposed by TRIPS over the prior treaty level.

This cumulative level must be attained by implementing the provisions through the means discussed in the other sections of this chapter.

Going beyond the minimum: domestic context

Being *minimum*, these standards may be exceeded by the member state autonomously in its internal legal order, provided that such further protection does not contravene the provisions of the Agreement.[60] Why would a country *voluntarily*[61] exceed such a base?

Two considerations might be pertinent: either domestic IP requirements would justify this more extensive protection, or else non-IP considerations would lead the country to impose extra requirements. As a result of the 'single undertaking' rule, many countries would accept the basic standards that have no domestic demand, in order to achieve other targets in the wider range of the Uruguay Round agreements. The same reason would lead such countries to accept more extensive protection in the context of post-TRIPS bilateral or restricted agreements. The compatibility of this interest with TRIPS will be analysed below.

NON-PERMISSIBLE UNILATERAL ENHANCEMENTS

More extensive protection is not always permissible, as the pertinent clause requires that any enhanced standard 'does not contravene the provisions of this Agreement'.

More extensive protection may contravene TRIPS, for instance, by

---

Footnote 59 (*cont.*)
respect of the rights conferred under Article 6bis of that Convention or of the rights derived therefrom.

[60] How would this further protection go against TRIPS? As mentioned in an other section of this chapter, it could refuse such enhanced protection to non-nationals, violating the National Treatment rule. Or else (as pointed out by Nuno Carvalho), granting extended patent protection to pharmaceuticals, but denying it to aerospatcial technologies, violating the TRIPS article 27 rule against discriminating among technology areas. Some authors note that the limits to enhanced protection are the provisions and not the principles of TRIPS; however, there are some principles clearly embodied in provisions, such as, for example, articles 7 and 8 of TRIPS.

[61] The issue of whether enhanced protection (that is, an implementation of rights more favourable to title holders or creators) is actually voluntary is quite complex. Indirect pressure and biased technical assistance may lead to uncoerced but tainted decisions. See S. Sell, *Private Power, Public Law: The Globalization of Intellectual Property Rights*, Cambridge: Cambridge University Press, 2003, pp. 151–2.

colliding with its maximum standards. A very specific aspect of TRIPS is that it contains rules consisting of *maximum* standards, and therefore does not admit more extensive protection:

> Nevertheless, existing TRIPS standards may conflict with TRIPS-plus standards in bilateral agreements in cases in which the former do not only define minimum, but also maximum standards. Although it seems, according to Art. 1.1 TRIPS, that such maximum standards are inherently foreign to the concept of the TRIPS, the Agreement nevertheless prohibits 'more intensive protection' in its provisions on enforcement of Part III to the extent that it fixes general procedural provisions to the benefit of any party to IP litigation. In some instances, the Agreement even explicitly provides for procedural rights of the defendant, like with regard to the level of legal certainty as a requirement for provisional measures (Art. 50.3 TRIPS) and the rights of the alleged infringer to be informed and to be heard within a reasonable time after provisional measures have been adopted *inaudita altera parte* (Art. 50.4 TRIPS). Most strikingly, Art. 48 TRIPS provides for a right to indemnification of the defendant in case of an abuse of enforcement procedures.[62]

It can also be incompatible with the limitations contained in the basic treaties, as Carlos Correa remarks:[63]

> Another situation of a 'more extensive' protection that contravenes the TRIPS Agreement can arise in the case of 'revalidation', 'confirmation', or 'importation' patents; that is, patents that are granted on the basis of foreign patent grants, without consideration of the novelty requirement. This kind of patent was introduced as a means to facilitate the importation of technologies in some patent laws and treaties[64] of the nineteenth century, and survived in some countries (e.g. Argentina, Chile) until recently. The more extensive protection conferred by these patents conflicts with Article 4bis of the Paris Convention for the Protection of Industrial Property,[65] as interpreted more than half a century ago in relation to Article 29 of the French law of 1844.[66] The inconsistency of revalidation patents with the TRIPS Agreement was also found by the Argentine Supreme Court,[67] which declared that they were incompatible with the Paris Convention and the principles of the TRIPS Agreement.[68]

---

62 Drexl, op. cit.

63 Commentary, op. cit.

64 [Original footnote] See eg The Montevideo Treaty on Patents, signed on 16 January 1889.

65 [Original footnote] As discussed below, this Convention was incorporated into the TRIPS Agreement.

66 [Original footnote] See A Casalonga, Traité Technique et pratique des brevets d'invention (1949: Paris), pp 273, 296.

67 [Original footnote] See Unilever NV v Instituto Nacional de Propiedad Industrial s/denegatória de patente, reproduced in El Derecho, 2 August 2001.

68 [Original footnote] Bodenhausen argued that the principle of independence of the Paris Convention did not apply with regard to special patents like

Also incompatible with TRIPS would be those protections that, albeit in excess of a minimum standard, oppose principles and rules intrinsic to the agreement. For example, an enhanced patent term that is not extended to foreign filings would contravene the National Treatment principle. Less stringent patent examination criteria for software inventions would infringe the non-discrimination rule of Article 27.1.[69]

As to the limitations that might be provided by the *objectives* and *Principles* covered by the preambulary texts and Articles 7 and 8 of TRIPS, see the specific section below.

TRIPS minimum standards and subsequent agreements

Let us now consider the case of concessions made by member states, and their relationship to the state's international obligations. May member states provide, through later international agreements, more extensive protection than what are stated as minimum standards under article 1.1? The issue will be investigated through the posing of some further questions.

The first is: does the more extensive protection cover just unilaterally adopted or bilaterally adopted protection as well? The second question is: are multilaterally negotiated obligations that are more extensive than the minimum standard compatible with Article 1.1?

It is not suggested that TRIPS would prevent protection beyond its minimum level:

> The basic observation is very straightforward: TRIPS does not prohibit WTO Members to conclude among themselves treaties containing obligations that go beyond the standards of TRIPS. Although there is no clear provision specifically dealing with the relationship with other agreements, several TRIPS provisions indicate TRIPS conformity of TRIPS-plus standards in agreements among individual WTO members.[70]

But there is no obligation whatsoever to go further than what was negotiated in TRIPS as an acceptable level. Nuno Carvalho has extensively dealt with these issues:

Footnote 68 (*cont.*)
'revalidation' patents. This argument, however, is unconvincing as the principle is to be applied, according to the Convention, in an 'unrestricted sense' (G Bodenhausen, Guide to the Application of the Paris Convention of Industrial Property as revised at Stockholm in 1967 (1991: Geneva, WIPO) pp 208–9).

[69] As related in Document WT/DS 153/ 1 of 7 December 1998, Canada denounced the Special Protection Certificate provided for Regulations EEC No. 1768/92 and EEC No. 1610/96, as incompatible with Article 27.1 of the TRIPS Agreement, as it assured discriminatory advantages to the pharmaceutical sector.

[70] Drexl, op. cit.

> The answer to these questions is in the conjunction of Article 1.1 with Article 71.2 of the TRIPS Agreement. On the one hand, Article 1.1 seems to indicate that Members may not be obliged (by other WTO Members, naturally) to implement in their domestic laws 'TRIPS plus' standards. On the other hand, Article 71.2 implies that the TRIPS Agreement does not stand in the way of multilateral agreements that adopt higher standards of protection.[71] Let us not forget that the Paris Convention does contain a number of 'TRIPS plus' commitments, which the TRIPS Agreement has not derogated from, in accordance with Article 2.2. The consequence of those two provisions is that WTO Members may be obliged by other WTO Members to follow standards of protection that are higher than those imposed by the TRIPS Agreement when those standards are adopted multilaterally and accepted under the mechanism of Article 71. But they may not be obliged to comply with extended protection adopted under bilateral, regional or plurilateral agreements.

The same author stresses, however, a most important characteristic of TRIPS, not generally considered by mainstream commentators:

> The reason is that Article 1.1, at the same time it establishes obligations, also constitutes a safeguard for small trading partners, which, without the protection of that provision, could not have the negotiating power to seek adequate and balanced trade deals in a non-multilateral environment.
>
> Therefore, other than in a multilateral setting, WTO Members shall not be obliged to comply with more extensive protection than that accorded by the TRIPS Agreement. This does not mean that bilateral FTAs (or regional or plurilateral agreements) containing 'TRIPS plus' standards are necessarily TRIPS-inconsistent, provided compliance is left to the discretion of each of the contracting parties. The use by one of the parties of a non-multilateral mechanism of pressure (either built-in in the FTA in question or not) for obliging the other to follow those standards is a violation of Article 1.1 as well as a non-violation situation, as explained above.[72] In other words, the TRIPS Agreement represents a safeguard, a mechanism of protection against unilateral trade pressure.[73]

---

71 [Original footnote] Article 71.2 refers to agreements 'accepted by all Members of the WTO'. This strict requirement is imposed merely for the purposes of adopting a fast-track approval of an amendment to the TRIPS Agreement. Where such unanimity does not exist, amendments will be subject to the normal rules under Article X of the WTO Agreement.

72 [Original footnote] A detailed analysis of the patent-related provisions included in a number of FTAs can be found in Nuno Pires de Carvalho, Patent Policy and Law Making in the Early 21st Century: Learning the Past, Teaching the Future, paper presented at the seminar on 'Patents in Europe and North America – Past and Present', held on April 26, 2004, at the Ironbridge Gorge Museum (Museum of Iron), Coalbrookdale, Telford, Shopshire, UK. Information on the Seminar is available on the website of the Queen Mary Intellectual Property Research Institute, at <www.qmipri.org>.

73 Nuno Carvalho, op. cit., also notes: 'The expression "shall not be obliged" has an impact on Article 67, because it prohibits developed country Members to

Therefore, more extensive protection, whether unilateral, bilateral or multilateral, is not *necessarily* contrary to TRIPS, provided that its effects, even though granted in bilateral agreements, are universal,[74] benefiting all WTO members through the Most Favored Nation device typical of the GATT structure.[75]

The question of the voluntary nature of these agreements (like the analogous issue of voluntariness of unilateral enhancements) is crucial under international law.[76] Much may be said about the unilateral pressures that

---

Footnote 73 (*cont.*)
require recipient Members to adopt standards beyond the minimum levels set forth by the Agreement as a condition for providing technical and financial assistance as regards the implementation of TRIPS obligations'.

[74] Josef Drexl, 'The Evolution of TRIPS: Towards Flexible Multilateralism', in J. Kors, and B. Remiche, *ADPIC, première décennie: droits d'auteur et accès à l'information. Perspective latino-americaine. L'Accord ADPIC: dix ans après.* Belgica: Larcier, 2007, pp. 13–45. 'Although there is no clear provision specifically dealing with the relationship with other agreements, several TRIPS provisions indicate TRIPS conformity of TRIPS-plus standards in agreements among individual WTO members. The first indication can be drawn from the principle of minimum protection. Following the example of the Paris and Berne Conventions, Art. 1.1 TRIPS provides that WTO members "may, but shall not be obliged to, implement in their law more extensive protection". Of course, this freedom to provide more extensive protection may also be exercised by entering in additional treaties – multilateral, regional or bilateral ones – that provide for such TRIPS-plus standards. Secondly, application of the most-favoured-nation principle to the protection of IPRs presupposes the effectiveness of agreements between individual WTO members from which advantages granted by a WTO member to the nationals of any other countries may typically arise in the sense of Art. 4 TRIPS. By only exempting international agreements entered into force prior to the entry into force of the TRIPS Agreement from the MFN obligation, Art. 4(d) TRIPS makes clear that later agreements have to be considered potential connecting factors of MFN application. Hence, TRIPS-plus standards in other agreements are not only applicable in the light of TRIPS. According to Art. 4 TRIPS they even become multilateral TRIPS standards in favour of those WTO members that are not party to the individual agreement'.

[75] John Jackson, *Legal Problems of International Economic Relations*, St. Paul, Minnesota, West Publishing, 1986, p. 483: 'The national treatment, like the MFN obligation, is a rule of "nondiscrimination". In the case of MFN, however, the obligation prohibits discrimination between goods from different exporting countries. The national treatment clause, on the other hand, attempts to impose the principle of nondiscrimination as between goods which are domestically produced, and goods which are imported. It is, needless to say, a central feature of international trade rules and policy.'

[76] Nuno Carvalho, op. cit.: 'As explained before, concessions extracted under unilateral pressure and threats are TRIPS-inconsistent, under Article 1.1. But concessions voluntarily made must be extended to other WTO Members, under

preceded the enactment of TRIPS,[77] arising from unilateral international sanctions of various kinds. Some of the legal instruments that provided the basis for such action [78] remain in force, and may arguably be used to induce formally voluntary, but in fact forced, concessions from weaker parties.[79] However, economic or political pressure by itself would not be

Article 4'. Article 51 of the Vienna Treaty denies validity to treaties extracted under actual duress.

77 Theoretically, involuntary concessions would be against the DSU principle: 'Understanding leaves no doubt that it is intended to strengthen the multilateral trading system. In an article clearly signaling this intent, entitled "Strengthening of the Multilateral System," the ministers impose upon the member states a requirement to seek "recourse to, and abide by, the rules and procedures of this Understanding," when seeking redress of a "violation of obligations or other nullification or impairment of benefits under the covered agreements". Article 23 goes on to specify that the members "shall . . . not make a determination to the effect that a violation has occurred . . . except through recourse to dispute settlement in accordance with the rules and procedures of this Understanding. . ." In short, the Understanding leaves no doubt that freelance, unilateral, or even unauthorized bilateral dispute resolution is not acceptable', as described by Michael Young, 'Dispute Resolution in the Uruguayan Round – Lawyers triumph over diplomats', 29 *Int'l. Lawyer* 389 (1995). In what would seem to be a prudent conclusion, Prof. Young remarked: 'However, the Understanding does not forbid the parties from resolving a dispute by means other than a panel decision. Negotiations and consultations are still allowed, indeed encouraged. The Understanding specifically invites the parties to resolve disputes through mutual agreement. It also adopts, virtually intact, the provisions of the Improvements of 1989 regarding negotiation, consultation, good offices, conciliation, and mediation'.

78 Holger Hestermeyer, *Human Rights and the WTO*, Oxford: Oxford University Press, 2007, pp. 39–41 notices some of the most conspicuous acts of unilateral pressure in the years preceding the inception of the TRIPS Agreement. This author, as an official of the Brazilian government during the years 1986–88, has participated both in the exercises that led to the application of a suspension of SGP benefits as a result of US Section 301 procedures and, simultaneously, in the TRIPS negotiations, and may witness to the close relationship of such procedures.

79 However, after its 2003 DSU case, the Section 201 affair, the US has not shown any resolve to abstain from using the full power of unilateral sanctions against their partners, with or without WTO support: 'the U.S. President emphasized and vowed, "We will continue to pursue [our] economic policies", as well as "our commitment to enforcing our trade laws", right after the U.S. had lost in the "Section 201" Disputes and was forced to temporarily terminate the abused U.S. "safeguard measures" of unilateralism. Similar to the USTR's declaration right after the end of "Section 301" Disputes in December 1999, the U.S. President's proclamation right after the end of "Section 201" Disputes in December 2003 actually announced to the world: We, the U.S.A., will continue to pursue our policies of economic hegemony, and continue to conduct such activities still under the camouflage of defending U.S. "sovereignty", safeguarding U.S. interests, and enforcing U.S. laws. Therefore, even though the U.S. lost in the recent "Section

considered as a *legal* reason to invalidate such agreements,[80] although in cases where flawed consent is not a legal issue, defective bargaining power is certainly a crucial aspect of any public policy analysis.[81]

The next issue is, thus, whether *voluntary* arrangements between non-multilateral parties may exceed those TRIPS requirements that provide *minimum,* not maximum, level of protection.

Balancing principles as a moderator to enhancement[82]

There is a reasonable argument to be made that the power of member states to provide enhanced protection beyond the minimum level provided by TRIPS may be constrained by other principles contained in the Agreement, besides those already mentioned. No member country can protect IP to a level so strong, that it actually disrupts the trade flows.[83]

Most important in this context are the principles incorporated into TRIPS through the preamble and articles 7 and 8.1:

> Article 7 – Objectives
> The protection and enforcement of intellectual property rights should contribute to the promotion of technological innovation and to the transfer and

---

Footnote 79 (*cont.*)
201" Disputes, its hegemonic chronic continue to recur at any time'. An Chen, 'The Three Big Rounds of U.S. Unilateralism versus WTO Multilateralism during the last decade', found at http://www.southcentre.org/publications/workingpapers/paper22/wp22.pdf.

80 W. Heintschel von Heinegg, in K. Ipsen (ed.) *Völkerrecht*, 4th edition, Munich: Beck, 1999; Brownlie, op. cit, p. 590.

81 Bruno Meyerhof Salama, Daniel Benoliel, Patent Bargains in NICs: The Case of Brazil, found at http://repositories.cdlib.org/bple/alacde/052408-1,visited 22/12/2009.

82 This section borrows extensively from Denis Borges Barbosa, Margaret Chon and André Moncayo, 'Slouching Towards Development in International Intellectual Property', 2007 *Mich. St. L. Rev*. 71, 110 (2007).

83 Carlos Correa, Commentary. . .: 'The TRIPS Agreement, unlike pre-existing conventions on IPRs, was negotiated and adopted as a component of the multilateral trading system. Despite the Preamble's opening provision indicating that IPRs should not "become barriers to legitimate trade", the proponents of the Agreement focused on the trade distortion created by the lack of effective protection (eg, as a result of counterfeiting). But they overlooked the extent to which higher levels of IPR protection may create barriers to legitimate trade. For instance, if parallel imports are restrained, international trade in legitimate products may be prevented. When low standards of patentability are allowed, barriers against imports of products that should otherwise freely circulate may be created. In view of these possible effects, governments negotiating the TRIPS Agreement should have considered establishing upper, and not only lower limits on the levels of IPR protection'.

dissemination of technology, to the mutual advantage of producers and users of technological knowledge and in a manner conducive to social and economic welfare, and to a balance of rights and obligations.
Article 8 – Principles

1. Members may, in formulating or amending their laws and regulations, adopt measures necessary to protect public health and nutrition, and to promote the public interest in sectors of vital importance to their socio-economic and technological development, provided that such measures are consistent with the provisions of this Agreement.

The issue at stake here was described thus:[84]

According to the UNCTAD Resource Book on TRIPS,[85]
'IPRs have been designed to benefit society by providing incentives to introduce new inventions and creations. Article 7 makes it clear that IPRS are not an end in themselves. It sets out the objectives that member countries should be able to reach through the protection and enforcement of such rights. The wording of Article 7 ("The protection . . . should contribute. . . ") suggests that such a protection does not automatically lead to the effects described therein. In introducing IPR protection, countries should frame the applicable rules so as to promote technological innovation and the transfer and dissemination of technology "in a manner conducive to social and economic welfare".'

The article should therefore be read as an *interpretative* tool before everything,[86] in a way conducive to the technology transfer; but it stresses especially the *balanced* nature[87] of the overall agreement.[88]

The effect of those articles (and, to some extent, the preambulary wording) is to impose a balanced reading of the prescriptive content of

---

[84] Denis Borges Barbosa, 'TRIPS art. 7 and 8, FTAs and Trademarks' 9 March 2006. Available at SSRN: http://ssrn.com/abstract=889107.

[85] [Original footnote] UNCTAD-ICTSID Resource Book on TRIPS and Development, Cambridge, 2005.

[86] [Original footnote] Id. Eadem, 'Article 7 provides guidance for the interpreter of the Agreement, emphasizing that it is designed to strike a balance among desirable objectives. It provides support for efforts to encourage technology transfer, with reference also to Articles 66 and 67'.

[87] [Original footnote] Certain authors emphasize, however, that this balancing would prevent and exclude the constitutional re-balance at the moment of the internment of the norms of TRIPS. He has, there, however, an underlying certainty of a dualism, with prevalence of the international norm.

[88] [Original footnote] Id. Ead. 'In litigation concerning intellectual property rights, courts commonly seek the underlying objectives of the national legislator, asking the purpose behind establishing a particular right. Article 7 makes clear that TRIPS negotiators did not mean to abandon a balanced perspective on the role of intellectual property in society. TRIPS is not intended only to protect the interests of right holders. It is intended to strike a balance that more widely promotes social and economic welfare'.

TRIPS, to provide a necessary moderating influence on the extent to which enhanced protection might be admissible. Prior WTO jurisprudence was not entirely friendly to balance:

> In the first few years after the adoption of TRIPS, the WTO's Dispute Settlement Body (DSB) considered two complaints regarding domestic standards of patent protection that were alleged to violate international trade law obligations. Their resolution has proved illuminating. Both decisions proceed from the assumption that TRIPS is primarily concerned with protecting intellectual property even though the Agreement plainly recognises the objective of protecting and enforcing exclusive rights in IP for the purpose of contributing to the promotion of technological innovation and to the transfer and dissemination of technology, to the mutual advantage of producers and users of technological knowledge and in a manner conducive to social and economic welfare, and to a balance of rights and obligations.
>
> In *India Patent Protection for Pharmaceutical and Agricultural Chemical Products*, the DSB's Appellate Body had to consider whether India had complied with its obligations under TRIPS in respect of a means for the filing of patent applications for pharmaceutical and agricultural chemical products. It was common cause that India's obligations to provide minimum standards of patent protection would become effective only ten years after the adoption of TRIPS (i.e., in 2005).
>
> India unsuccessfully defended the original complaint lodged by the US (and largely supported by the European Union) before a DSB panel. It was largely unsuccessful in its attempt to overturn the panel decision on appeal. The Appellate Body decision tempered some of the more disagreeable aspects of the panel's findings. But its reasoning views the main object and purpose of TRIPS as the need to promote effective and adequate protection of intellectual property rights. In its view, TRIPS is simply about the protection of IP.
>
> The principle of balance suffered a similar fate in *Canada Patent Protection of Pharmaceutical Products*. In that case, a DSB panel had to deal with three issues. First, does TRIPS permit the production and stockpiling of pharmaceutical products prior to patent expiry? Second, does the agreement allow for generic manufacturers to start and complete the drug regulatory process prior to patent expiry? Third, can pharmaceutical products be treated differently from inventions in other fields of technology?
>
> Importantly, not one of the provisions of Canadian patent law under attack would have allowed for the introduction of generic competition during the life of a pharmaceutical patent. Collectively, they merely sought to eliminate delays in bringing generic medicines to market upon patent expiry. In other words, the provisions would have allowed for generic competition immediately upon patent expiry, because drugs would have already been registered and produced in advance.
>
> In its decision, the WTO panel declared the stockpiling provision to be in violation of TRIPS. It upheld the early registration of pharmaceutical products. And it sidestepped the differential treatment question. On the surface, the outcome appeared almost acceptable. The direct consequences for Canada were fairly minimal. This was because the loss of the right to stockpile meant

little more than that generic drugs produced in Canada reached the market about three weeks later.

Yet the position was critically different for countries with weaker generic manufacturing capacity. And it would be shortsighted to view the decision solely from the point of view of its impact on Canada. The panel's interpretation of the general exceptions clause (whose existence signifies the need for a mechanism to resolve legitimate, competing policy interests) provides cause for general concern. Seemingly heedless of the principle of balance that lies at the core of patent protection, the panel considered the TRIPS provision Canada invoked to justify its statute solely in the light of how much the rights holder might lose, not in how much society might gain, from a given exception. It never asked what scope the exception might require to achieve the social purposes at issue.[89]

Overcoming precedent jurisprudence

Therefore, the idea of a balancing role of articles 7 and 8 has not received full support in the WTO case law. The WTO Appellate Body's analysis in *Canada – Patent Protection of Pharmaceutical Products, Complaint by the European Communities and their Member States* (hereinafter *Canada – Patent Protection of Pharmaceutical Products*) is not definitive, as even the Appellate Body itself recognized at the time:

101. [W]e note that our findings in this appeal do not in any way prejudge the applicability of Article 7 or Article 8 of the *TRIPS Agreement* in possible future cases with respect to measures to promote the policy objectives of the WTO Members that are set out in those Articles. Those Articles still await appropriate interpretation.[90]

Achieving a proper balance within TRIPS necessarily involves assessing how the pertinent adjudicatory bodies are interpreting the relevant legal texts. For all practical purposes, the most relevant bodies in this context are those established by WTO.[91]

Therefore, we shall analyse the evolving nature of WTO case law and suggest applicable principles, in connection with general principles of treaty interpretation, including the Vienna Convention on the Law of Treaties (VCLT), applicable jurisprudence of the International

---

[89] Edwin Cameron (Supreme Court of Appeal, Bloemfontein, South Africa), 'Patents and Public Health: Principle, Politics and Paradox', Inaugural British Academy Law Lecture held at the University of Edinburgh, Tuesday 19 October 2004, http://www.law.ed.ac.uk/ahrc/script-ed/issue4/Cameron.pdf.

[90] World Trade Organization, Appellate Body Report, Canada – Term of Patent Protection, ¶ 101, WT/DS170/AB/R, 18 September 2000.

[91] National and regional courts such as the ECJ are obviously also relevant sources of international law.

Court of Justice (ICJ), as well as the WTO Dispute Settlement Understanding (DSU) and the Dispute Settlement Body (DSB) of the WTO.

Furthermore, although not a dispute settlement decision, the Ministerial Conference in Singapore emphasized the importance of the Preamble in the Declaration adopted on 13 December 1996: 'For nearly 50 years Members have sought to fulfil, first in the GATT and now in the WTO, the objectives reflected in the preamble to the WTO Agreement of conducting our trade relations with a view to raising standards of living worldwide'.[92] We shall also explore the general process of interpreting international texts, including the role of principles versus rules.

The principle of In Claris Non Fit Interpretatio versus the principle of integration

Thus far, the WTO case law reveals a restrictive interpretive approach towards the TRIPS agreement. Many have been critical of this approach, which is based on an aggressively textual[93] and one-sided view of the objectives and principles of TRIPS.[94] For example, Robert Howse states:

> The recent decision of a WTO panel, in the Canadian *Generic Medicines* case, however, ignores [Article 7's] words about balance and mutual advantage [and may] . . . have very harmful impacts, particularly on developing countries . . . Even though it was dealing with an explicit 'exceptions' provision, comprehensible only if there are legitimate, competing policy interests, the Panel was only interested in how much the rights holder might lose, not in how much society might gain, from a given exception. It never asked what scope the exception might require to achieve the social purpose at issue.[95]

---

[92] World Trade Organization, Singapore Ministerial Declaration of 13 December 1996, ¶ 2, WT/MIN(96)/DEC, 36 ILM 218 (1997). See also Petersmann, supra (emphasizing general principles of justice). The whole WTO Treaty receives some impact of developmental purposes; see Mitsuo Matsushita, Thomas J. Schoenbaum and Petros C. Mavroidis, *The World Trade Organization, Law Practice and Policy*, 2nd edition, Oxford: Oxford University Press, 2006, p. 777, for a full listing of those provisions.

[93] Joseph H.H. Weiler, 'The Rule of Lawyers and the Ethos of Diplomats: Reflections on the Internal and External Legitimacy of WTO Dispute Settlement', 35 J. *World Trade* 191, 206 (2001) (observing the 'almost obsessive attempts of the Appellate Body to characterize . . . interpretations of the Agreement as "textual"').

[94] See Cameron, op. cit.

[95] Robert Howse, 'The Canadian Generic Medicines Panel: A Dangerous Precedent in Dangerous Times', 3 *J. World Intell. Prop.* 493–96 (2002).

The general framework for treaty interpretation is governed by articles 31[96] and 32[97] of the Vienna Convention on the Law of Treaties. The International Court of Justice displays special reliance upon such interpretative principles,[98] as indeed do domestic and regional courts. Within

---

[96] Vienna Convention on the Law of Treaties article 31, 23 May 1969, 1155 UNTS 331; 8 ILM 679 (1969). Article 31 reads:

> General rule of interpretation
> 1. A treaty shall be interpreted in good faith in accordance with the ordinary meaning to be given to the terms of the treaty in their context and in the light of its object and purpose.
> 2. The context for the purpose of the interpretation of a treaty shall comprise, in addition to the text, including its preamble and annexes:
> (a) any agreement relating to the treaty which was made between all the parties in connection with the conclusion of the treaty;
> (b) any instrument which was made by one or more parties in connection with the conclusion of the treaty and accepted by the other parties as an instrument related to the treaty.
> 3. There shall be taken into account, together with the context:
> (a) any subsequent agreement between the parties regarding the interpretation of the treaty or the application of its provisions;
> (b) any subsequent practice in the application of the treaty which establishes the agreement of the parties regarding its interpretation;
> (c) any relevant rules of international law applicable in the relations between the parties.
> 4. A special meaning shall be given to a term if it is established that the parties so intended. Id.

[97] Vienna Convention on the Law of Treaties article 32, 23 May 1969, 1155 UNTS 331; 8 ILM 679 (1969). Article 32 reads:

> Supplementary means of interpretation
> Recourse may be had to supplementary means of interpretation, including the preparatory work of the treaty and the circumstances of its conclusion, in order to confirm the meaning resulting from the application of article 31, or to determine the meaning when the interpretation according to article 31:
> (a) leaves the meaning ambiguous or obscure; or
> (b) leads to a result which is manifestly absurd or unreasonable.

[98] In doing so, it seeks in the first place to determine the usual and natural meaning of the words in their context, without, however, sticking too closely to the particular rules applicable under the procedural law of any legal system, and in that regard frequently refers to article 31 of the VCLT. '[A]n international instrument has to be interpreted and applied within the framework of the entire legal system prevailing at the time of the interpretation'. The International Court of Justice 92 (5th edition, 2004), available at http://www.icj-cij.org/icjwww/igeneralinformation/ibleubook.pdf (citing Legal Consequences for States of the Continued Presence of South Africa in Namibia, Advisory Opinion, 1971 ICJ 21 (June 1971)).

the WTO's explicit decision-making framework, article 3.2 of the DSU[99] refers to the 'customary rules of interpretation of public international law', which is understood as those rules incorporated in the VCLT. For example, the WTO panel in *India – Patent Protection for Pharmaceutical and Agricultural Chemical Products* explicitly relied on GATT *acquis*, customary rules of interpretation of public international law and, specifically, article 31 of the VCLT.[100]

However, the WTO's Appellate Body has generally given high priority to the WTO text. For example, in *United States – Import Prohibition of Certain Shrimp and Shrimp Products*, the Appellate Body stated:

> The Panel did not follow all of the steps of applying the 'customary rules of interpretation of public international law' as required by Article 3.2 of the DSU. As we have emphasized numerous times, these rules call for an examination of the ordinary meaning of the words of a treaty, read in their context, and in the light of the object and purpose of the treaty involved. A treaty interpreter must begin with, and focus upon, the text of the particular provision to be interpreted. . . . Where the meaning imparted by the text itself is equivocal or inconclusive, or where confirmation of the correctness of the reading of the text itself is desired, light from the object and purpose of the treaty as a whole may usefully be sought.[101]

---

[99] Understanding on Rules and Procedures Governing the Settlement of Disputes article 3(2), Annex 2 to Marrakesh Agreement Establishing the World Trade Organization, 15 April 1994, available at http://www.wto.org/English/docs_e/legal_e/28_dsu.pdf. Art. 3(2) states that

> [t]he dispute settlement system of the WTO is a central element in providing security and predictability to the multilateral trading system. The Members recognize that it serves to preserve the rights and obligations of Members under the covered agreements, and to clarify the existing provisions of those agreements in accordance with customary rules of interpretation of public international law. Recommendations and rulings of the DSB cannot add to or diminish the rights and obligations provided in the covered agreements.

[100] Panel Report, *India – Patent Protection for Pharmaceutical and Agricultural Chemical Products*, WT/DS79/R (24 August 1998). The basic methodology is set out in Panel Report, United States – Anti-Dumping Measures on Certain Hot-Rolled Steel Products from Japan, ¶ 7.27, WT/DS184/R (28 February 2001).

> As the Appellate Body has repeatedly stated, panels are to consider the interpretation of the WTO Agreements, including the AD Agreement, in accordance with the principles set out in the Vienna Convention on the Law of Treaties (the 'Vienna Convention'). Thus, we look to the ordinary meaning of the provision in question, in its context, and in light of its object and purpose. Finally, we may consider the preparatory work (the negotiating history) of the provision, should this be necessary or appropriate in light of the conclusions we reach based on the text of the provision.

[101] Appellate Body Report, *United States – Import Prohibition of Certain Shrimp and Shrimp Products*, ¶ 114, WT/DS58/AB/R (12 October 1998) (citations omitted).

As applied in the TRIPS context, the WTO dispute settlement panel in *Canada – Patent Protection of Pharmaceutical Products* reiterated this principle of *in claris non fit interpretatio*:[102]

> Thus, the correct approach was to focus first on the text of the provisions to be interpreted read in its context and to discern from this the intention of the parties to an agreement. It was only if this left a doubt that it was appropriate to seek enlightenment from the object and purpose of the agreement.[103]

This panel opposed the use of the object and purpose of TRIPS, as also stated in its preamble, as interpretative tools to the document.

> Canada claimed to be interpreting Article 30 of the TRIPS Agreement *in context* when it invoked the first recital to the Preamble and Articles 1.1 and 7 of the TRIPS Agreement. It was clear that the whole text of an agreement, including the preamble, formed part of the context of a provision of that agreement. However, the above provisions were not in reality being invoked by Canada as *context* to discern the ordinary meaning of the terms used in Article 30, but as expressions of *object and purpose*. The arguments drawn from these provisions by Canada all related to the supposed object and purpose of the TRIPS Agreement and not to contextual guidance as to the meaning of the terms of Article 30 thereof.[104]

---

[102] 'In clarity there is no room for interpretation' (translated from the Latin). In connection with this rule, it might be remarked that clarity presumes community of ground between legislator and interpreter to a very considerable degree, which time and cultural elements can easily deny. For instance, authors have indicated that the clear interpretation of TRIPS article 27.1 at its inception excluded business methods as patentable matter; but soon after the WTO initial term, changes in US case law brought this matter into the patent laws; the fact that other members would not follow this understanding should not attract undue discrimination charges (perhaps the contrary should be held to be true, from a societal point of view). As to the scope of the non-discrimination rule of TRIPS article 27, see Denis B. Barbosa, 'O princ'pio de não-discriminação em propriedade intelectual', in *Usucapião de Patentes e Outros Estudos de Propriedade Industrial*, Rio de Janeiro Lumen Juris, 2006. Legal culture may also influence the clarity standard: for instance, common-law practitioners could be attracted to an historical interpretation, always politically useful when interpreting the actual bargain among the contracting parties, but not accepted as primary means of interpretation in Continental legal systems and (by the way) article 32 of the Vienna Convention. This article reserves such means to a supplementary level, only applicable when the use of the non-historical interpretation leaves the meaning ambiguous or obscure, or leads to a result which is manifestly absurd or unreasonable.

[103] Panel Report, *Canada – Patent Protection of Pharmaceutical Products*, Complaint by the European Communities and their Member States, at 51, WT/DS114/R (17 March 2000).

[104] Id. at 51–2.

The *Canada – Patent Protection of Pharmaceutical Products* panel's interpretative method does not conform to mainstream treaty interpretation, which includes the principle of integration: the whole treaty must be read as a whole, rather than placing focus on a single provision, however clearly that provision may appear to shine in isolation.[105] Indeed, a counter-example exists within the intellectual property jurisprudence of the WTO: a different panel interpreting TRIPS, the *United States – Section 110(5) of the U.S. Copyright Act* panel, adopted this integration principle, stating 'that the text of the treaty must of course be read as a whole. One cannot simply concentrate on a paragraph, an article, a section, a chapter or a part.'[106]

The whole treaty includes, perhaps especially, the stated objects and purposes of the document. An essential part of a treaty is its preamble.[107] As to the relevance of external sources, the treaty segment under inspection should be read together with the whole body of relevant international law, both at the moment of the inception of the treaty and at the moment when the interpretation is performed.[108] This principle of integration is as important as the principle of prioritizing text, so heavily relied upon by the *Canada – Patent Protection of Pharmaceutical Products* panel. It would be proper, therefore, to classify the panel decision as an incomplete ground upon which to build a robust TRIPS reading.

This integration principle can be detected in some other WTO decisions. In construing the WTO Marrakesh Agreement, the Appellate Body report in *Brazil – Desiccated Coconut* invoked the Preamble to the Agreement in

---

[105] Ian Brownlie, *Principles of Public International Law*, 6th edition, Oxford: Oxford University Press, 2003, p. 604.

[106] Panel Report, *United States – Section 110(5) of the US Copyright Act*, at 17, n. 49, WT/DS160/R (15 June 2000). As David Vaver notes in its remarks on the draft of this study: 'There is a recent example of this technique in domestic copyright interpretation, involving what constitutes an "assignment" in England where the transaction occurs in Switzerland between Swiss entities: a literal, logical interpretation by the trial judge was reversed by the appeal court, taking into account the whole context of the statute including materials outside its four walls'. See *Thorn Security Ltd v. Siemens Schweiz AG* [2008] EWCA Civ 1161, found at http://www.bailii.org/ew/cases/EWCA/Civ/2008/1161.

[107] Gervais, op.cit., supra note 98, at p. 80.

The preamble to the TRIPS Agreement is an essential part of it. Under 'GATT law', preambles are on occasion relied upon to a considerable extent by panels when the wording of a provision is not clear or where it is susceptible to divergent interpretations. . . . The preamble, together with footnotes, should be considered as an integral part of the agreement, a condensed expression of its underlying principles.

[108] Brownlie, supra note 105, at p. 604.

the context of the integrated WTO system that replaced the old GATT 1947.[109] Dispute settlement panels have made the same inclusive interpretive gesture in other circumstances (leaving aside the cases concerning environmental issues).[110]

The integration principle provides for a supra-textual reading of the treaties, which is not extraneous to WTO case law.[111] It considers both the treaty as a whole, including its teleological markings (like preambles),[112]

---

[109] Appellate Body Report, *Brazil – Measures Affecting Desiccated Coconut*, at p. 18, WT/DS22/AB/R (21 February 1997).

The authors of the new WTO regime intended to put an end to the fragmentation that had characterized the previous system. This can be seen from the preamble to the WTO Agreement which states, in pertinent part:

> Resolved, therefore, to develop an integrated, more viable and durable multilateral trading system encompassing the General Agreement on Tariffs and Trade, the results of past trade liberalization efforts, and all of the results of the Uruguay Round of Multilateral Trade Negotiations.

[110] Panel Report, *India – Quantitative Restrictions on Imports of Agricultural, Textile and Industrial Products*, ¶ 7.2, WT/DS90/R (6 April 1999) (at the outset, we recall that the Preamble to the WTO Agreement recognizes both (i) the desirability of expanding international trade in goods and services and (ii) the need for positive efforts designed to ensure that developing countries secure a share in international trade commensurate with the needs of their economic development. In implementing these goals, WTO rules promote trade liberalization, but recognize the need for specific exceptions from the general rules to address special concerns, including those of developing countries); see also Panel Report, *Brazil – Export Financing Programme for Aircraft – Recourse by Canada to Article 21.5 of the DSU*, ¶ 6.47 n.49, WT/DS46/RW (9 May 2000) ('The preamble to the WTO Agreement recognizes "that there is need for positive efforts designed to ensure that developing countries, and especially the least-developed among them, secure a share in the growth in international trade commensurate with the needs of their economic development."').

[111] See Appellate Body Report, *United States – Standards for Reformulated and Conventional Gasoline*, at p. 17, WT/DS2/AB/R (29 April 1996) ('Gasoline') ('[T]he General Agreement is not to be read in clinical isolation from public international law.'). A critical analysis of the interpretative usages of the adjudicatory bodies of OMC can be found in Evandro Menezes de Carvalho, 'The Juridical Discourse of the World Trade Organization: The Method of Interpretation of the Appellate Body's Reports', *Global Jurist Topics*, 7(1), article 4 (2007), available at http://www.bepress.com/cgi/viewcontent.cgi?article=1211&content=gj.

[112] Panel Report, *United States – Section 110(5) of the US Copyright Act*, WT/DS160/R (15 June 2000); see also Appellate Body report, *United States – Import Prohibition of Certain Shrimp and Shrimp Products*, WT/DS58/AB/R (12 October 1998) ('A treaty interpreter must begin with, and focus upon, the text of the particular provision to be interpreted. It is in the words constituting that provision, read in their context, that the object and purpose of the states parties to the treaty must

and even other treaties.[113] Like the overall WTO Agreement itself, TRIPS should not be read in 'clinical isolation' from public international law.[114]

Constructing legal principles out of Articles 7 and 8 of TRIPS

One barrier to incorporating balance as a concept within TRIPS is that the WTO dispute settlement bodies so far have not fully captured the valence of articles 7 and 8.[115] Thus, we recommend the application of two inter-

---

Footnote 112 (*cont.*)

first be sought. Where the meaning imparted by the text itself is equivocal or inconclusive, or where confirmation of the correctness of the reading of the text itself is desired, light from the object and purpose of the treaty as a whole may usually be sought.'). In Panel Report, *United States – Sections 301–310 of the trade Act of 1974*, ¶ 7.22, WT/DS152/R (22 December 1999), the Panel concluded that the elements of Article 31 of the VCLT 'are to be viewed as one holistic rule of interpretation rather than a sequence of separate tests to be applied in a hierarchical order'. The same was stated in Panel Report, *European Communities – Measures Affecting Asbestos and Asbestos-Containing Products*, ¶ 8.46, WT/DS135/R (18 September 2000), providing that 'to the extent that Article 31 of the Vienna Convention contains a single rule of interpretation and not a number of alternative rules, the various criteria in the Article should be considered as forming part of a whole'.

113 Under the standards of ICJ of what should be the context (the framework of the entire legal system prevailing at the time of the interpretation), even some particular instances of soft law would be relevant rules of international law applicable in the relations between the parties. This is not a secondary instance of interpretation (as perhaps the rulings in the *Shrimp-Turtles* and *Canada Pharmaceuticals* cases might be felt to indicate), but should be consulted together with the context where a primary reading is to be affected.

114 See generally Gabrielle Marceau, 'A Call for Coherence in International Law: Praises for the Prohibition against "Clinical Isolation" in WTO Dispute Settlement', 33 *J. World Trade* 87–152 (1999) (arguing in favour of incorporating non-WTO law in WTO DSU decisions). The integration of TRIPS into the overall WTO structure also raises an extremely important issue: the balancing of interests that, as shall be seen below, is a crucial aspect of TRIPS application and enforcement, is a complex operation where trade interests and specific IP-related interests shall be considered in some specific cases. However, to the extent that access to technology, expressive creations and commercial image instruments are essential to a certain notion of development, a complete nullification of societal values related to intellectual property rights and obligations would seem contrary to the core TRIPS law, particularly as interpreted by the member states in the Doha Round exercises.

115 As Ruth Okediji stated, '[a] particularly revealing aspect of these [relevant TRIPS] disputes is the way each of the Panels and the Appellate Body have ducked the thorny question of how to apply the preambular statements and the broad themes of Article 7 and 8 to evaluate the substantive obligations of the TRIPS Agreement', Ruth L. Okediji, 'Public Welfare and the Role of the WTO: Reconsidering the TRIPS Agreement', 17 *Emory Int'l L. Rev.* 819, 914 (2003).

pretive principles to their jurisprudence: (1) an 'evolutive interpretative' approach that considers the changing context for interpretation of relevant treaty provisions; and (2) a 'vectorial' approach that acknowledges and weighs competing principles that animate the agreements.

1. From Rules to Principles: The Principle of Evolutive Interpretation

International law jurist Maristela Basso has articulated a principle of evolutive interpretation[116] consistent with the interpretative practice of the ICJ.[117] As stated earlier, the Vienna Convention on the Law of Treaties provides a basis for considering subsequent agreements and practices of the parties in treaty interpretation.[118] In the case of TRIPS, the combination of articles 7 and 8, and 71.1 of TRIPS, led to the enactment of paragraph 6 of the Doha Declaration.[119] This so-called paragraph 6 solution subsequently evolved into a non-soft law norm – proposed Article 31-*bis*.[120]

Although this author would not subscribe to the 'hortatory' qualification, note also here Margaret Chon, 'Intellectual Property and the Development Divide', 27 *Cardozo L. Rev.* 2821, 2828 (2006); supra its note 5, at 2843 ('A key impediment, however, is that the language referencing development in TRIPS [Article 8] is not mandatory, but rather hortatory and that the language is placed within parts of the treaty that are not in the main treaty body. This issue (rather than the substantive content of development) has preoccupied the few legal scholars who have addressed these terms').

[116] Maristela Basso, *O Direito Internacional Da Propriedade Intelectual*, Porte Alegre, Livraria do Advogado edition, 2000, p. 76.

[117] *Case Concerning Kasikili/Sedudu Island (Botswana/Namibia)*, 13 December 1999, (Parra-Aranguren, J., dissenting), http://www.icj-cij.org/icjwww/idocket/ibona/ibonaframe.htm (last visited 5 April 2007). As a general rule of interpretation, Article 31, paragraph 3(b), of the 1969 Vienna Convention on the Law of Treaties provides that account shall be taken, together with the context, of 'any subsequent practice in the application of the treaty which establishes the agreement of the parties regarding its interpretation.'). Vienna Convention on the Law of Treaties article 31(b), 23 May 1969, 1155 UNTS 331, 340.

[118] Vienna Convention on the Law of Treaties arts. 31(3)(a) and 31(3)(b), 23 May 1969, 1155 UNTS 331, 8 ILM 679 (1969).

[119] Doha Declaration, supra its note 116, at ¶ 6; See also Doha Public Health Declaration, supra its note 115, at ¶4 (affirming 'WTO Members' right to protect public health and, in particular, to promote access to medicines for all') (emphasis added).

[120] See Council for TRIPS, Implementation of Paragraph 11 of the General Council Decision of August 2003 on the Implementation of Paragraph 6 of the Doha Declaration on the TRIPS Agreement and Public Health, IP/C/41 (6 December 2005).

Under the evolutive interpretation principle, the Doha Declaration itself arguably supersedes the *Canada Patent Protection of Pharmaceutical Products* panel's limited interpretation of articles 7 and 8. The Doha Declaration states that work in the TRIPS Council on these reviews or any other implementation issue should also look at the relationship between the TRIPS Agreement and the UN Convention on Biodiversity; the protection of traditional knowledge and folklore; and other relevant new developments that member governments raise in the review of the TRIPS Agreement.[121] It adds that the TRIPS Agreements objectives (article 7) and principles (article 8) should guide the TRIPS Council's work on these topics, and must take development fully into account.[122]

The Doha Declaration, Doha Ministerial Declaration and General Council Decision are obvious applications of the balancing approach anticipated by articles 7 and 8 and the preambular text. These balancing exercises were undertaken by the very source holding the *jus tractuum* (the treaty power) – that is, the member states themselves, in a manner provided by the WTO and TRIPS rules. Thus it is an authentic interpretation by authoritative law-making bodies that clearly integrates development within IP norm interpretation.[123]

Furthermore, these agreements directly indicate that some of the exceptions provided by the TRIPS text (especially article 31) are to be employed as tools to enforce the development and public interest values indicated by article 8. Finally, the Doha Declaration and General Council decision regarding IP dispel the starkly one-sided interpretation of TRIPS in *Canada Patent Protection of Pharmaceutical Products*, according to which TRIPS was only intended to enhance the protection of the IP rights holder.

An evolutive interpretation principle is further guided by the changing context provided by the new WIPO Development Agenda, which unmistakably links the language of article 7 to development norms within WIPO's IP mandate. While not an agreement of the WTO member states regarding the interpretation of TRIPS, this language is nonetheless relevant as a type of 'practice' of certain member states (overlapping among the WTO and WIPO) because of the close relationship of the WTO to WIPO.

---

121 Doha Declaration, supra its note 116, at ¶ 19.

122 Id. Eadem.

123 Richard Gardiner, Treaty Interpretation, op. cit, p. 159 mentions that balancing of interests may be held to be a *good faith* requirement under Vienna Treaty article 31, offering as an example of this interpretative tool the AB decision in the *Shrimp-Turtle* case, Doc. WT/DS58/AB/R, 12 October 1998, paras 158–9.

2. From Rules to Principles: The Principle of Vectorial Interpretation

2.1 Defining the vectorial approach The Preamble, along with articles 7 and 8 of TRIPS, are to be understood as norms of different function and character from the strictly prescriptive provisions of the same text (for instance, the rule of a minimum term for patents). The former are in the nature of principles, whereas the latter are formulated as rules.[124] Principles serve a different function from rules. They lead away

---

[124] Luis Roberto Barroso, *Interpretação e Aplicação da Constituição, Fundamentos de uma dogmática Constitucional Transformadora*, Rio de Janeiro Editora Saraiva, 5th edition, 2003, p. 232 (As Barroso, the most celebrated Brazilian Constitutional Law author, explains:

> The qualitative distinction between rule and principle is one of the pillars of the modern Constitutional Law, indispensable for overcoming the legal positivism where the concept of Law was restricted to rules. The Constitution turns into an open system, comprising rules and principles, permeable to legal values beyond the positivism, where the ideas of justice and of accomplishment of the basic rights play a central role. The change of paradigm in this matter must render special tribute to the systematization of Ronald Dworkin. Its elaboration concerning the different roles played by rules and principles gained universal course and now is the conventional knowledge in the field.
>
> Rules are normative proposals formulated under form of all or nothing . . .
>
> Principles contain, normally, a higher valorative load, an ethical bedding, a relevant policy decision, and indicate a certain direction to follow. It occurs that it may exist, in a pluralist sequence, other principles that shelter diverse decisions, values or fundaments, even opposed among themselves. The collision of principles, therefore, is not only possible, as it is part of the logic of the system, which has a dialectic nature. Therefore its incidence cannot be treated in terms of all or nothing, of validity or invalidity. A dimension of weight or importance must be recognized to the principles. Considering the elements of the concrete case, the interpreter will have to make biased choices, when coping with inevitable antagonisms, as the ones that exist between the freedom of speech and the right of privacy, the free initiative and the state intervention, the right of property and its social function. The application of the principles is effected predominantly by means of balancing. (citations omitted; translated by Denis Borges Barbosa).

For a comprehensive analysis of the application of the opposition between principle and rules in the context of International and Comparative Law, see Jacob Dolinger, *Evolution of Principles for Resolving Conflicts in the Field of Contracts and Torts*, Académie De Droit International, Recueil Des Cours, Kluwer Law International, Den Hague, 2000.

from a positivist approach towards a normative approach of treaty interpretation.[125]

Within a treaty, principles can be inferred (as in the anti-dumping case mentioned above) or explicitly read from the preambulatory and principle-specific clauses. This is especially the case with respect to TRIPS article 8 (labelled 'Principles', so as to dispel any doubts as to its nature). But article 7, together with some crucial preambulatory text,[126] also has a purpose. Moncayo von Hase has emphasized the active interpretation resulting from a purpose-centred – or teleological – approach.[127]

Another important aspect of a principle-based approach is that principles are not applied in the abstract, but rather to the facts of a specific case, in which choices are implemented upon chosen value-grounds. This fact-specific analysis, coupled with a balancing of principles, contrasts with a more positivist interpretative approach.[128] Such an approach has

---

[125] Robert Alexy, *Teor'a de los derechos fundamentales*, Centro de Estudios Constitucionales, Madrid, 1993, p. 81.

[126] The first recital indicates two potentially opposing interests to be balanced: intellectual property vs. trade ('Desiring to reduce distortions and impediments to international trade, and taking into account the need to promote effective and adequate protection of intellectual property rights, and to ensure that measures and procedures to enforce intellectual property rights do not themselves become barriers to legitimate trade', TRIPS, at pmbl.). The third and fourth recitals draw an opposition between private interests to be given due regard ('Recognizing that intellectual property rights are private rights', TRIPS, note 3, at pmbl.) and public interests to be similarly endorsed ('Recognizing the underlying public policy objectives of national systems for the protection of intellectual property, including developmental and technological objectives', TRIPS, at pmbl.). The fifth recital is a clear and strong expression of a substantive equality mandate towards the least developed countries.

[127] Andrés Moncayo von Hase, 'La protección de las invenciones en América Latin durante los a–os 2001–2002, Incidencia del ADPIC en las legislaciones latinoamericanas', available at http://www.ml.ua.es/webprom/Jornadas/documentos/Moncayo-Invenciones.pdf.

[128] James Gathii, 'Fairness as Fidelity to Making the WTO Fully Responsive to All its Members, in The American Society of International Law: Proceedings of the 97th Annual Meeting' 163 (2003), available at http://papers.ssrn.com/sol3/papers.cfm?abstract_id=594485&high=%20james%20Gathii ('WTO Appellate Body (AB) in the initial Shrimp-Turtle case (Shrimp-Turtle I) held, in interpreting the meaning of Article 3.1 of the SPS Agreement, that where there is a choice in construing a treaty provision, the principle of in *dubio mitius* – "the less onerous meaning to the party which assumes the obligation, or which interferes less with the territorial and personal supremacy of a party, or involves less general restrictions upon the parties" – is to be preferred. The AB therefore concluded: "We cannot lightly assume that sovereign states intended to impose upon themselves the more onerous, rather than the less burdensome obligation."' (footnotes omitted)).

in fact occurred in some cases, where the equities of a particular case and the consequences of choosing one outcome over another was part of the process of adjudication.

By contrast, the adjudicating body in *Canada – Patent Protection of Pharmaceutical Products* decided to ignore such interpretative mechanisms, as though they were irrelevant to the specific case under its review.[129] The panel decided to focus on just one of the interests to be balanced: the purpose of TRIPS as to IP rights was held to be to 'reinforce the protection of these rights'. Therefore, this decision is viewed by many as an example of an unbalanced, hypertextual, ultra-positivist ruling.[130]

We propose a vectorial approach to interpretation. This approach would incorporate the purposes of TRIPS, as expressed in its preambulary language and articles 7 and 8. It would also pay more heed to the principle of integration, as described in the previous section, as well as to foundational treaty principles where conflicting values may be at issue on the particular facts of a dispute. Thus, the objectives and principles of TRIPS should play a central role in the interpretation of the entire agreement.

2.2 Towards a vectorial reading of TRIPS TRIPS principles command a vectorial reading. The norms expressed in the Preamble and articles 7 and 8 indicate opposing interests to be given due respect and reconciliation. A vectorial reading presupposes that different interests receive their due. The resulting finding of law never excludes any of the interests at stake but, very much to the contrary, strives to give to each its proper legal consideration according to the classical rule of *sui cuique tribuere*.

One-sidedness in a vectorial system means wiping out the competing interest, which amounts to a violation of the system. Therefore, vectorial analysis is not satisfied by a starkly unilateral interpretation of TRIPS, or

---

[129] More precisely, the panel decided to focus on just one of the interests to be balanced: the purpose of TRIPS as to intellectual property rights was held to 'reinforce the protection of these rights'. Panel Report, *Canada – Patent Protection of Pharmaceutical Products*, Complaint by the European Communities and their Member States, at 52, WT/DS114/R (17 March 2000).

[130] Robert Howse, supra its note 138, at 502. By denying the balancing norm of articles 7 and 8 just to enhance the interests of the right holders, the panel was excluding the effect of a provision of the text. Appellate Body Report, *United States – Standards for Reformulated and Conventional Gasoline*, at 17, WT/DS2/AB, (29 April 1996) ('One of the corollaries of the "general rule of interpretation" in the Vienna Convention is that interpretation must give meaning and effect to all the terms of a treaty. An interpreter is not free to adopt a reading that would result in reducing whole clauses or paragraphs of a treaty to redundancy or inutility.').

even by the overall WTO context: as the much quoted *Gasoline* case states, the General Agreement cannot be read in clinical isolation.[131]

An effective vectorial approach assumes that all competing interests are to be given some degree of subjective fungibility, that is, any party may be held to the same rigours of the law (putting every party in Rawls's 'original position'),[132] extended to the global community approaching a new planet.[133] Whether using a vectorial approach in international law is safe or wise is a very serious question.

Developing and developed country interests are not fully fungible, at least in the short term,[134] and the long-term view is not the province of adjudicatory bodies. These are real problems. But fact is that the WTO Agreements include vectorial norms, as well as the rule of *pacta sunt servanda*.

Articles 7 and 8 are, beyond any doubt, interpretative tools with respect to the meaning of the TRIPS agreement.[135] Crucial for developing countries in the TRIPS negotiations was the perceived vectorial role of articles 7 and 8. A stated target for developing countries during TRIPS negotiations

---

[131] United States Standards for Reformulated and Conventional Gasoline, WT/DS2/AB/R, p. 16, para 17.

[132] See generally John Rawls, *A Theory of Justice*, Harvard University Press, Cambridge, Massachusetts 1999.

[133] Gathii, supra note 128, at p. 159.

> Egalitarian liberals invoke a Rawlsian framework according to which benefits and burdens in the trading regime ought to be distributed in accordance initially with an equality principle that would treat all members of the WTO similarly and without distinction. However, egalitarian liberals emphasize the importance of John Rawls's difference principle, according to which, in the distribution of benefits and burdens, concern for the most vulnerable members of the trading regime should be taken into account. One thread that runs through this approach is that fairness is regarded as a condition of moral equality and, for some of its advocates, a precondition for economic justice. (Id. quoting John Rawls, *A Theory of Justice*, 1971, pp. 4, 14–15).

[134] When some portion of the parties is probably immune from that fungibility – as TRIPS assumes that the least developed countries for the time being are – a rule of substantive equality is a requirement of justice, or (in a rather utilitarian perspective) of long term efficiency. Chon notes, 'As Carlos Correa has stated, "When the [knowledge] products are essential for life – as with food and pharmaceuticals – allocative efficiency becomes an important objective on both economic and equity grounds." In other words, equality tilts the balance towards static efficiency and away from dynamic efficiency arguments, at least for resource-poor areas of the world. A failure to understand that will lead to policy impasses.' Chon, supra its note 5, at p. 2891.

[135] Moncayo von Hase, 'La proteccion', supra note 127.

was to achieve a balancing of interests.[136] Written submissions of a more general nature presenting views on these questions were circulated by Thailand,[137] Mexico[138] and Brazil.[139]

The Brazilian position is relevant in this context. The Brazilian paper emphasized the need to keep in view both the trade-related and developmental aspects of intellectual property rights. It distinguished the discussion in the developing countries' working group from the more legal discussion being held by the developed countries.

> It advocated priority attention in the Group to:
> i) The extent to which rigid and excessive protection of intellectual property rights impedes access to the latest technological developments, restricting therefore the participation of developing countries in international trade. In this

---

[136] See TRIPS Negotiating Document, MTN.GNG/NG11/W/32/Rev.1 (29 September 1989).

[137] Statement by Thailand at the Meeting of 12–14 September 1988, MTN. GNG/NG11/W/27 (12 September 1988).

> The Thai statement . . . emphasi[zed] that the two fundamental goals pursued by governments when granting intellectual property protection are the stimulation or encouragement of intellectual property creation and the accord of proper and legitimate protection of the public interest; the former must not put an undue burden on or adversely affect the latter.

TRIPS Negotiating Document, ¶ 5, MTN.GNG/NG11/W/32/Rev.1 (29 September 1989).

[138] Statement by the Delegation of Mexico at the Meeting of 17, 18, and 21 October 1988, MTN.GNG/NG11/W/28 (19 October 1988).

> The statement by Mexico . . . [stated] that the negotiating objective regarding the improvement of intellectual property rights should not become a barrier to access by developing countries to technologies produced in developed countries. Any results obtained in the Group would therefore necessarily have to include more flexible elements for the use of such technology by developing countries, since countries with different levels of development cannot respond in the same way to each of the trade and intellectual property aspects. Mexico also advocates examination of Articles IX, XX and XXIII of the General Agreement and says that the provisions of the General Agreement should not be used to modify legal regimes governing intellectual property rights, but should aim, in the best of cases, at recommendations to reduce distortions in international trade and barriers to that trade which may derive from the application and protection of intellectual property rights.

TRIPS negotiating document, ¶ 5, MTN.GNG/NG11/W/32/Rev.1 (29 September 1989).

[139] Submission from Brazil, MTN.GNG/NG11/W/30 (30 October 1988).

> context, it emphasizes the importance of specific exclusions from the protection of intellectual property rights.
> ii) The extent to which abusive use of intellectual property rights gives rise to restrictions and distortions in international trade. Practices which have this effect should be subject to adequate multilateral discipline.
> iii) The risks that a rigid system of protection of intellectual property rights implies for international trade. Attentive consideration should be given to cases where the protection and enforcement of intellectual property rights become a barrier or harassment to legitimate trade, including where it is used as an excuse to implement protectionist and discriminatory measures.[140]

The language of article 7 does not limit itself to technological IPRs, as the final clause indicates: 'The protection and enforcement of intellectual property rights should contribute . . . to *a balance of rights and obligations*'.[141] The idea of balancing is obviously a vectorial device. Thus, the necessary balancing to the rights of intellectual property holders, as it is developed in the legal discourse in many countries, appears explicitly in TRIPS article 7. It prevents the protection of the interests of the intellectual property rights holders to the exclusion of other 'rights and obligations'.

Article 8 of TRIPS foresees that each country can legislate, within the scope of TRIPS, 'to protect the public health and nutrition and to promote the public interest in sectors of vital importance for its socioeconomic and technological development',[142] The retention of state sovereignty or traditional 'police powers' in these areas relative to other measures in the TRIPS Agreement, combined with the procedural rule that the alleging party has the burden of proof, point to an effective article 8 default procedural presumption in a vectorial analysis.

Article 8 also has substantive as well as procedural dimensions. 'Public health . . . and interest in sectors of vital importance'[143] are obviously interest categories of higher value in any legal system; once the content

---

140 TRIPS negotiating document, ¶ 5, MTN.GNG/NG11/W/32/Rev.1 (29 September 1989).

141 TRIPS, article 7 (emphasis added).

142 TRIPS, article 8.1 ('Members may, in formulating or amending their laws and regulations, adopt measures necessary to protect public health and nutrition, and to promote the public interest in sectors of vital importance to their socio-economic and technological development, provided that such measures are consistent with the provisions of this Agreement'). Incidentally, the provision is, by allowing the national law to promote the public interest in sectors of vital importance to their socio-economic and technological development, almost a littera ad litteram reproduction of the wording of art. 5. XXIX of the Brazilian Constitution of 1988.

143 TRIPS, supra note 3, article 8.1.

of such measures are not *prima facie* a means of arbitrary or unjustifiable discrimination between countries where the same conditions prevail, or a disguised restriction on international trade, a vectorial interpretative approach should give great weight to the built-in flexibilities of TRIPS to address domestic development concerns.[144]

2.3 Re-interpreting case law through the vectorial approach In the first few years after the adoption of TRIPS, the WTO Dispute Settlement Body (DSB) considered two complaints regarding domestic standards of patent protection alleged to have violated international trade law obligations. Despite the explicit language of articles 7 and 8, as well as the negotiating history of those articles, both decisions proceed from the assumption that TRIPS is primarily concerned with protecting intellectual property, even though TRIPS plainly indicates a vectorial approach.

In *India Patent Protection for Pharmaceutical and Agricultural Chemical Products*, the WTO Appellate Body considered whether India had complied with its obligations under TRIPS in respect of the means for filing patent applications on pharmaceutical, agricultural, and chemical products. India's obligations to provide minimum standards of patent protection would become effective only ten years after the adoption of TRIPS

---

[144] The conclusion of article 8 is an important consideration: '[P]rovided that they are consistent with the provisions of this Agreement'. Id. at article 8.2. A similar provision can be found at the 1947 GATT article XX(b). GATT 1947 allows for such measures as non-violative, provided that they are not applied in a manner that constitutes a means of arbitrary or unjustifiable discrimination between countries where the same conditions prevail, or a disguised restriction on international trade. Article 8.1 simply provides that necessary measures must be 'consistent with' the Agreement. As the UNCTAD *Resource Book* notes:

> Since language of a treaty is presumed not to be surplus, it would appear that Article 8.1 is to be read as a statement of TRIPS interpretative principle: it advises that Members were expected to have the discretion to adopt internal measures they consider necessary to protect public health and nutrition, and to promote the public interest in sectors of vital importance to their socio-economic and technological development. The constraint is that the measures they adopt should not violate the terms of the agreement. This suggests that measures adopted by Members to address public health, nutrition and matters of vital socio-economic importance should be presumed to be consistent with TRIPS, and that any Member, seeking to challenge the exercise of discretion should bear the burden of proving inconsistency. Discretion to adopt measures is built into the agreement. Challengers should bear the burden of establishing that discretion has been abused.

UNCTAD–ICTSD, supra note 2, pp. 126–27.

(that is, in 2005). India unsuccessfully defended the original complaint lodged by the US (and largely supported by the European Union) before a DSB panel.

It was largely unsuccessful in its attempt to overturn the panel decision on appeal. The Appellate Body decision tempered some of the more disagreeable aspects of the panel's findings, but its reasoning viewed the main object and purpose of TRIPS as the need to promote effective and adequate protection of intellectual property rights. In its view, TRIPS is simply about the protection of intellectual property.[145]

As discussed above, balance suffered a similar fate in *Canada Patent Protection of Pharmaceutical Products*, where the panel adopted the European Communities' argument that three conditions of TRIPS article 30 should not be construed against the objectives and purposes stated in TRIPS articles 7 and 8. In so doing, the panel rejected Canada's position that 'these purposes call for a liberal interpretation of the three conditions . . . so that governments would have the necessary flexibility to adjust patent rights to maintain the desired balance with other important national policies'.[146] The panel ultimately stated that doing so would constitute 'a renegotiation of the basic balance of the Agreement'.[147]

By contrast, under a vectorial interpretation, the application of each provision of TRIPS by the member states would be analysed by reference to the principles identified in the preamble and articles 7 and 8. Rather than assuming that the balance has already been struck with respect to each separate part of the treaty, an adjudicative body would recalibrate the balance of principles with respect to each treaty provision as applied to the specific legal issue in dispute.

Moreover, any particular dispute would be considered under the principle of evolutive interpretation, discussed earlier. That is, interpretation of treaty text should be considered in light of subsequent agreements regarding its interpretation. As discussed, the overall interpretative context for development provisions within TRIPS has changed dramatically with the

---

145 Report of the Panel, *India – Patent Protection for Pharmaceutical and Agricultural Chemical Products*, WT/DS50/6 (16 October 1997); Appellate Body Report, *India – Patent Protection for Pharmaceutical and Agricultural Chemical Products*, WT/DS50/AB/R (19 December 1997).

146 Report of the Panel, *Canada – Patent Protection of Pharmaceutical Products*, Complaint by the European Communities and their member states, ¶ 7.24, WT/DS114/R (17 March 2000).

147 Id. ¶ 7.26.

advent of the Doha Declaration, etc.[148] A vectorial interpretation would encompass these developments.[149]

In a recent study from very much the same perspective as the one offered by Barbosa, Chon and Von Hase, Grosse Ruse notes:[150]

> In para.4 and 5 (a) of the Doha Declaration on TRIPS and Public Health, WTO Members pointed to an alternative way of operationalising Art.8:1 TRIPS: By interpreting and implementing all individual TRIPS provisions in light of the balancing objective of Art.7 and the public interest principle in Art.8:1 TRIPS. Supported by the general principles of treaty interpretation in international law, all TRIPS provisions which embody broad and open language allow for an implementation which gives due respect to public interest considerations. Giving effect to the latter therefore is much more dependent on a smart reliance on discretion and policy space that follows from the openness of individual provisions – combined with the use of general principles and objectives in the process of implementation. It implies a greater role and sophistication on the side of the interpreter/implementer. In my view, the individual provisions regulating exceptions and limitations (as well as other TRIPS norms) are sufficiently open for this purpose – even though existing WTO Panel jurisprudence has certainly not realised this goal.

How balance actually works

As noted by Cynthia Ho:[151]

---

148 As to the legal effects of the Doha Declaration, see Steve Charnovitz, 'The Legal Status of the Doha Declarations', 5 *J. Int'L EC. Law* 207 (March 2002); Carlos Correa, 'Implications of the Doha Declaration on TRIPS and Public Health, Health Economics and Drugs', EDM Series No. 12, at 45 (2002), available at http://www.who.int/medicines/areas/policy/WHO_EDM_PAR_2002.3.pdf; James Gathii, 'The Legal Status of the Doha Declaration on TRIPS and Public Health under the Vienna Convention on the Law of Treaties', 15 *Harv. J L & TECH.* 291 (2002); Carmen Otero Garcia-Castrillon, 'An Approach to the WTO Ministerial Declaration on the TRIPS Agreement and Public Health', 5 *J Int'L Econ. L* 212 (2002).

149 Frederick M. Abbott, 'Compulsory Licensing for Public Health Needs: The TRIPS Agenda at the WTO after the Doha Declaration on Public Health', http://www.quno.org/geneva/pdf/economic/Occassional/Compulsory-Licensing.pdf: 'In deciding on an interpretation of the TRIPS Agreement, the TRIPS Council and General Council (and the Ministerial Conference) are not bound by interpretations of the TRIPS Agreement that a panel or the Appellate Body may have developed in the context of a case previously decided between Members'.

150 Henning Grosse Ruse-Khan, 'A Comparative Analysis of Policy Space in WTO Law' (26 November 2008), Max Planck Papers on Intellectual Property, Competition & Tax Law Research Paper No. 08-02. Available at SSRN: http://ssrn.com/abstract=1309526.

151 Cynthia M. Ho, 'On Breaking Patents: Separating Strands of Fact from Fiction under Trips', found at http://works.bepress.com/cynthia_ho/1/, visited 5 December 2008.

> While articles 7 and 8 seem to clearly suggest some type of balance, how that balance is to be achieved in any given case is less clear.[152] One scholar suggests that because there are multiple objectives, disputes over the appropriate interpretation of open-ended TRIPS provisions should give deference to national law when there is no clear international norm since TRIPS only provides minimum standards.[153]

The present study, however, does not propose any special balancing techniques to be applied to the TRIPS vectorial devices; the *ad hoc* approach developed by the Constitutional jurisdictions of many countries over the years seems to be perfectly adequate to implement a vectorial reading of the IP principles incorporated in the WTO agreement.

Exogenous rules as constraints

It could also be argued that some constraints could come from other sources, including, to a certain extent, precepts of international law not self-contained in TRIPS or the WTO Agreements as a whole. Some commentators discuss the notion that non-WTO rules, for instance, those related to human rights, could have some importance is curbing excessive IP protection.[154] Some other multilateral IP treaties would most certainly be brought to the attention in any dispute arising under TRIPS, for instance, the 1996 WIPO treaties on copyright and related matters and those agreements related to plant variety protection.

Another important area that calls for interaction with the TRIPS norms is the UN Convention on Biological Diversity;[155] the interaction of the

---

152 [Original footnote] See, e.g., CORREA, 2007, supra note 42, at 102 (noting that although a WTO panel has stated that articles 7 and 8 are important, it failed to elaborate on the specifics). On the other hand, some have tried to assert that these provisions are simply hortatory and of no value. E.g., Id. at 93 [References are made to Correa, Commentary. . .].

153 [Original footnote] Susy Frankel, WTO Application of the Customary Rules of Interpretation of Public International Law to Intellectual Property, 46 VA J INT'L L 365, 393–94 (2005–06).

154 Hestermeyer, op. cit., pp. 208–29, enters into a long discussion of this argument. According to his views, direct cognizance of non-WTO rules remains improbable under DSU rules. However, it would not seem impossible that non-WTO rules could be brought to the context of TRIPS, at least as a means of clarifying the meaning of some of its provisions. Incidentally, human rights could also justify constraints on flexibilities: according to the European Court of Human Rights, in the case *Smith Kline & French Laboratories Ltd. v. the Netherlands*, corporations could object to granting the compulsory licences provided for under TRIPS article. 31, on the grounds of their [corporate] human rights. See http://ec.europa.eu/enterprise/pharmaceuticals/caselaw/caselaw_en.htm.

155 According to paragraph 19 of the 2001 Doha Declaration, the TRIPS

two agreements is acknowledged by both the WTO and the Convention's bodies and extensive work has been under way to effectively conciliate the respective norms. Even before such exercises result in changes in the WTO treaties, it is reasonable to expect that a special deference should be given to such interaction, should any intersecting case be submitted to a DSU procedure.

Another complex of exogenous rules that could certainly impact on TRIPS context is the Multilateral Environmental Agreements.[156]

Whereas a more orthodox view of WTO jurisprudence would counsel a prudent utilization of such exogenous rules as applicable to the TRIPS context, it is necessary to indicate some less conservative views in this regard. For instance, in a recent study, Christopher Jon Arup calls upon the authority of a number of IP and international law commentators to advance the idea of a more pluralist interpretation:

> So, while some might strive to ensure that TRIPS is a self-contained source of law, its many soft spots mean that other texts and processes will enjoy a sphere of operation too. Those other legal sources are to be found both inside and outside the WTO. In the broadest view of the field, they include local custom, informal understandings, marketplace transactions, national constitutions and legislation, state and municipal government laws, administrative and judicial rulings, bilateral and regional agreements between governments, trans-national epistemic, advocacy and regulatory networks and official international organisations and treaties.[157]

Council is supposed to look at the relationship between the TRIPS Agreement and the UN Convention on Biological Diversity, as well as into the protection of traditional knowledge and folklore. The same item stresses that such an exercise should be guided by the TRIPS Agreement's objectives (article 7) and principles (article 8), taking development issues into account. See Doc. WTO IP/C/W/368/Rev.1, revised 8 February 2006 and http://www.cbd.int/incentives/int-trade.shtml.

[156] 'Though it is very unlikely that two WTO members participating in a MEA would decide to resort to WTO dispute settlement system to challenge a trade measure taken by the other member pursuant to the MEA, potential threat may materialize mainly for the reason that most MEAs do not have a robust compliance mechanism or dispute settlement system as the one in the WTO. Therefore, to avoid such disputes gravitating to the WTO in the future, trade agreements and environment agreements should be mutually supportive and complementary in order to ensure smooth operation of both the WTO and the MEAs', as read in http://awto.wtocenter.org.tw/Upload/20060424Session5_3.doc, visited 16 December 2008.

[157] Christopher Jon Arup, 'TRIPS as Competitive and Cooperative Interpretation' (13 August 2008). Monash University Department of Business Law & Taxation Research Paper No. 15. Available at SSRN: http://ssrn.com/abstract=1224282. Another representative of the same doctrinal trend, broadening the scope of international law sources related to the TRIPS environment

While this perspective may indicate a future trend of international adjudication, especially considering that the WHO and other fora have now dedicated some focus to intellectual property matters, present WTO case law would not be expected to follow such a pattern.

Freedom to incorporate and indefinite terms

The last clause of Article 1.1 states that 'Members shall be free to determine the appropriate method of implementing the provisions of this Agreement within their own legal system and practice'.

Freedom to choose how to implement TRIPS signifies that the treaty does not impose any means that may be extraneous to the legal system *and* practice of the member state. On the one hand, this freedom is very much limited to the actual system and practice patterns in such a way that an extravagant implementation, which would act exclusively to the detriment of the interests advanced by TRIPS, would detract from this rule. On the other hand, it would be unreasonable to require that only practices and legal instruments already used *before* the TRIPS applicable term are acceptable, as there might be no practice whatsoever to follow, for example, where the member state had never granted pharmaceutical patents.[158]

Implementation also means that IP notions not contained in the TRIPS glossary (or the definitions provided by the basic treaties) must be given the meaning applicable within the respective legal system and practice. 'Invention', for instance, is a non-defined term within the international instruments, and legal systems and practice have significantly differed;[159]

Footnote 157 (*cont.*)
may be found in Graeme B. Dinwoodie, 'The International Intellectual Property System: Treaties, Norms, National Courts, and Private Ordering' (1 December 2007). Graeme B. Dinwoodie, 'The International Intellectual Property System: Treaties, Norms, National Courts, and Private Ordering', in Daniel Gervais (ed.), *Intellectual Property, Trade and Development: Strategies to Optimize Economic Development in a Trips Plus Era*, Oxford: Oxford University Press, 2007, 61–114; Chicago-Kent Intellectual Property & Technology Research Paper No. 08-007. Available at SSRN: http://ssrn.com/abstract=1306608.

[158] See, in connection with the duplication of the examination of pharmaceutical patents by two separate agencies, WTO document WT/TPR/M/75, of 6 December 2000, para. 76, WTO document IP/Q3/BRAIl, of 24 February 2004, at p. 20, and WTO document WT/TPR/M/ 140/ Add. l, of 15 February 2005, at p. 96.

[159] Carlos Correa, 'IP Rights, WTO and Developing Countries', found at http://findarticles.com/p/articles/mi_qa3780/is_200204/ai_n9023190, last visited on 3 December 2008: 'WTO Member countries have retained the right to define the concept of invention in their national laws, or through administrative and judicial practice'.

'prior art' is a somewhat non-fixed term, even though quite a precise concept in the context of PCT.[160]

'Practice' is by itself an amorphous term; an *extra* or *ultra legem* practice may lack the legal certainty required for adequately implementing TRIPS, as indicated in *India – Patent Protection for Pharmaceutical and Agricultural Chemical Products*.[161] In systems where the law issues to some extent from judicial practice, judge-made law may also lack certainty, even if backed by a thousand-year tradition.[162]

The freedom to choose implementation has a further limitation, namely, that the interpretation of a member state of its own legal system may be second-guessed by the judicative bodies of WTO, down to the minutiae of each comma.[163] Therefore, the freedom to implement TRIPS recalls the Latin paradox *libertas obediente*: members are free to obey the stringent rules deduced from the nature of things.

While much more could be said on the darker view of article 1.1, some commentators have been less pessimistic:

> An important implication of the approach adopted in Article 1.1 is that the TRIPS Agreement cannot be seen as a uniform law, but rather as a set of

---

[160] Carlos Correa, Commentary: 'The flexibility of the TRIPS Agreement was also articulated by the US but in relation to a substantive standard, in responding to a questioning about the standard applied under 35 USC Section l02(a), which provides for a relative requirement of novelty regarding inventions disclosed outside the US in a non-written form. The US held that in the TRIPS Agreement there was "no prescription as to how WTO Members define what inventions are to be considered 'new' within their domestic systems" and, hence, that its legislation was "perfectly consistent with the provisions of the TRIPS Agreement" (Doc. IP/Q3/USN1, 1 May 1998)'.

[161] WTO document WT/DS50/R, 5 September 1997, Panel Report, modified by the AB Report, adopted on 16 January 1998, para. 7.35.: 'There is no denying that economic operators – in this case potential patent applicants – are influenced by the legal insecurity created by the continued existence of mandatory legislation that requires the rejection of product patent applications in respect of pharmaceutical and agricultural chemical products. [. . .] The existence of the legislation per se is not a problem under the TRIPS Agreement. However, in the absence of clear assurance that applications for pharmaceutical and agricultural chemical product patents will not be rejected and that novelty and priority will be preserved despite the wording of the Patents Act, the legal insecurity remains.'

[162] WTO document IP/Q2/GBR/1, of 13 October 1997, at pp. 2–3. However, in 26 WT/DS 160/R, 15 June 2000 (at 6.108), the panel accepted as sufficient certainty: 'there is no need to identify explicitly each and every possible situation to which the exception could apply, provided that the scope of the exception is known and particularised. This guarantees a sufficient degree of legal certainty'.

[163] European Communities I, supra note 102, at paras 7.41 and 7.42.

elements that IPR national laws must observe, thereby leaving Members total discretion to deal with matters not specifically addressed in the Agreement, as well as significant room for interpreting and implementing its provisions in accordance with the Members' policy objectives and legal systems.[164]

Harmonization as restraints of flexibility

Attaining TRIPS minimum standards is a way of approaching a uniform IP regime throughout WTO membership.[165] It is another form of harmonization of IP laws, like the exercises conducted under the auspices of WIPO in the 1980s with that avowed purpose. Harmonization of laws, and IP laws in particular, has both many enthusiasts and also many detractors.[166]

Surprising as it may appear, compared to later exercises such as the Substantive Treaty on the Law of Patents or trilateral cooperation among patent offices,[167] TRIPS is not an extreme harmonization treaty. This fact

---

164 Correa, Commentary, p. 22–30.

165 C. Correa and S. Musungu, 'The WIPO Patent Agenda: The Risks for Developing Countries', Working Paper No. 12, Geneva: South Centre, 2002.

166 For a reflection on the advantages and risks of harmonization, see Graham Dutfield and Uma Suthersanen, 'Harmonisation or Differentiation in Intellectual Property Protection? The Lessons of History', found at http://www.informaworld.com/index/713630429.pdf, visited 5 December 2008. Peter K. Yu 'The Harmonization Game: What Basketball Can Teach about Intellectual Property and International Trade', *Fordham International Law Journal*, Vol. 26, http://ssrn.com/abstract=341242; Commission on Intellectual Property Rights (2002), *Integrating Intellectual Property Rights and Development Policy*, London: Report of the Commission on Intellectual Property Rights; G. Dutfield (lead author) (2003), *Intellectual Property Rights: Implications for Development*, UNCTAD and ICTSD.

167 Philip W. Grubb, 'The Trilateral Cooperation', *Journal of Intellectual Property Law & Practice*, 2007, 2(6): 397–401; doi:10.1093/jiplp/jpm054: 'Many readers will already be familiar with the multilateral international treaties such as the Paris Convention and the Patent Cooperation Treaty that form the basis for the present worldwide patent system. There are other important treaties, for example, the Patent Law Treaty (PLT) dealing with formal requirements for patent applications and the Substantive PLT (SPLT). However, the PLT is as yet in force in only 14 countries, and the SPLT is still being discussed by the World Intellectual Property Organization (WIPO), with little or no progress being made. Potentially more important than either the PLT or the SPLT is something that is not a multinational treaty at all, but a relatively informal trilateral cooperation (TC) between the world's three most important patent offices – the United States Patent and Trademark Office (USPTO), the European Patent Office (EPO), and the Japan Patent Office (JPO). (. . .) The issue of harmonization of substantive patent law has been discussed within WIPO for more than 20 years by the Standing Committee on the Law of Patents (SCP), and the whole issue is presently on ice, following an open forum meeting in March 2006 which has been described as a "one-sided political rant on all sorts of matters to do vaguely with patents"'.

has eventually created some misgivings among believers in a stronger IP global system.[168] As Reichman and Dreyfuss[169] have noted:

> Yet the Agreement, which did not attempt to create a uniform or deeply harmonized global patent regime, left ample room for national variations and approaches, which are often collectively deemed 'the TRIPS flexibilities'.

Our purpose here is not to discuss the general inequalities associated with harmonization exercises,[170] but simply to indicate the extent that implementation of TRIPS, by creating unnecessary enhanced protection, may impede the balancing and adapting virtues of TRIPS flexibilities.

For those like this author, who experienced the TRIPS negotiations as the possible demise of most developing countries' interests, the ensemble of original TRIPS flexibilities, when added to those provided by the Doha

---

[168] 'Indeed, TRIPS may be outliving its purpose for those corporations that successfully lobbied for an IP agreement in the Uruguay Round and the governments that took up their demands', as Dutfield and Suthersanen, op. cit., state. Not surprisingly as an unmitigated enthusiast for IP strength, Sherwood sees no evil in limitless harmonization: R. Sherwood, 'Why a Uniform Intellectual Property System makes Sense for the World', in M.B. Wallerstein, M.E. Mogee and R.A. Schoen, *Global Dimensions of Intellectual Property Rights in Science and Technology*, Washington, DC: National Academy Press, 1993.

[169] Jerome H. Reichman and Rochelle Dreyfuss, 'Harmonization without Consensus: Critical Reflections on Drafting a Substantive Patent Law Treaty', *Duke Law Journal*, 57(1), 2007; NYU Law and Economics Research Paper No. 07-43; Duke Law School Legal Studies Paper No. 178; Duke Science, Technology & Innovation Paper No. 22. Available at SSRN: http://ssrn.com/abstract=1028331.

[170] 'It is not self-evident that harmonising the international IP rules and making them as responsive as possible to technological evolution is bad for developing countries just because they further the interests of transnational corporations. But making the rules identical and legally binding whether you are a very rich country with enormous balance of payments surpluses in IP protected goods, services and technologies, or a poor country with highly burdensome trade deficits seems to be tremendously expensive and risky for the latter type of country', Dutfield and Suthersanen, op. cit. However, Keith Maskus, 'Intellectual Property Rights in the Global Economy', found at http://bookstore.petersoninstitute.org/book-store/99.html, visited 5 December 2008, distinguishes between the effects of harmonization according to the level of competitiveness of TRIPS developing member states. Reichman and Dreyfuss are much less optimistic about rapid harmonization: 'A further round of harmonization will likely aggravate these and other unresolved problems without producing any offsetting user rights or concessions for these countries. On the contrary, the dynamics of TRIPS and the post-TRIPS trade agreements teach that even a development-sensitive negotiation process is likely to produce an instrument that furthers the interests of developed countries at the expense of poorer, less powerful participants'.

Round, constitutes quite a reasonable set of rules – as compared with subsequent bilateral treaties and impending multilateral proposals.[171]

Flexibilities comprise, for instance, the different periods granted to developing countries to enforce TRIPS and, particularly, pharmaceutical patents (articles 65 and 66), which Brazil and Argentina, among other countries, waived at least partially. One may also list the parallel importation of items acquired abroad from, or with the consent of, the holder of an IP right; various cases of use of the object of an IP right without the consent of its holder (for example, those provided under the compulsory licensing provisions of articles 31 and 31(a)), including governmental noncommercial use (as provided in the United States by 28 USC § 1498); and the ensemble of limitations provided, for instance, under article 30. To a lesser degree, TRIPS article 27.2, by listing what can be excluded from the scope of patents, might also be included among the flexibilities.

A number of developing countries failed to utilize the whole scope of available flexibilities when incorporating TRIPS.[172] Brazil, in particular, did not take full advantage of any of the flexibilities when enacting its TRIPS-compliant laws. Even though this relinquishing of flexibilities cannot be considered harmonization (as many developed countries retain more access to allowed flexibilities than does Brazil), the pursuance of additional minimum levels through new international agreements may prove costly for member states' abilities to attend to their peculiar needs.[173]

Going back to required standards

Would excessive compliance, if recognized as such, be amendable by member states, in order to regain the full benefits of TRIPS? Article 65.5

---

171 Denis Borges Barbosa, 'TRIPS e a experiência brasileira', in Marcelo Dias Varella (ed.). *Propriedade Intelectual e Desenvolvimento*, São Paulo: Lex Editora, 2004, pp. 129–65, found at http://denisbarbosa.addr.com/trips2004.doc.

172 P. Thorpe, 'Study on the Implementation of the TRIPS Agreement by Developing Countries', Study Paper No 7, London: CIPR, 2001. B.K. Keyla, *Review of National Patent Legislations of India, Indonesia, Sri Lanka & Thailand*, New Delhi: National Working Group on Patent Laws, 2003. M. Oliveira, J.A.Z. Bermudez and G. Velasquez, 'Has the Implementation of the TRIPS Agreement in Latin America and the Caribbean Produced Intellectual Property Legislation that Favours Public Health? Bulletin of the World Health Organization, 2004; 82:815-21, 2004.

173 Reichman and Dreyfuss, op. cit.: 'any form of deep harmonization through the SPLT that is likely to win the support of the developed countries seems certain to erode whatever flexibilities the developing countries still retain under the TRIPS Agreement and under subsequently negotiated TRIPS-plus Free Trade Agreements (including their Most Favoured Nation implications)'.

only prevents a 'rolling back' to prior non-TRIPS-compliant levels during the transitional periods provided under articles 65 and 66:

> This is essentially a provision which prevents WTO Members from 'rolling back' during the transition period, i.e., from providing a reduced degree of IP protection in their domestic laws. On the other hand, this provision also makes sure that, if under a bilateral arrangement some developing countries choose to go 'TRIPS plus', the Agreement does not prevent them from rolling back to the common TRIPS standards. This issue would exclusively be governed by the respective bilateral agreement.[174]

Therefore, after the transitional periods expire, any eventual mistakes committed by member states (for example, in cases where enhanced protection has not demonstrated the beneficial effects they expected), could be corrected by rolling back such protection to the level of the pertinent minimum standard, and this retroaction would not violate directly TRIPS.

However, some caution may be in order here, as those other member states that demonstrate their *reasonable expectations* that the surplus IP protection provided by the rolling-back member would not be readjusted to lesser grounds could be motivated to try *non-violation* claims to prevent the retroaction.[175]

---

[174] UNCTAD-ICTSID, op. cit., p. 715. The same opinion is expressed by Nuno Carvalho, op. cit., p. 751. Other standstill clause seems to have been included in the TRIPS section on Geographical Indications, as article 24.3 freezes the TRIPS-plus levels already assured by some countries, as noted by Dwijen Rangnekar in 'Geographical Indications: A Review of Proposals at the TRIPS Council: Extending Article 23 to Products other than Wines and Spirits', found at http://ictsd.net/downloads/2008/06/cs_rangnekar.pdf, visited 6 December 2008.

[175] See Tuan N. Samahon, 'TRIPS Copyright Dispute Settlement after the Transition and Moratorium: Nonviolation and Situation Complaints against Developing Countries', found at http://www.allbusiness.com/legal/3589056-1.html, visited 6 December 2008. Article 23(1)(b) defines non-violation as that which nullifies or impairs TRIPS objectives resulting from the 'application by another contracting party of any measure, whether or not it conflicts with the provisions of this Agreement.' (. . .) (1) affirmative government action, such as an offending member state's application of a measure offsetting any trade benefit it had conceded; (2) the complaining member state's justified reliance on the non-occurrence of the applied measure or event; and (3) actual injury. In claiming that the offending state applied a nullifying or impairing measure, the injured state must point to a specific measure applied by the offending state. In addition, the application of the measure must have not been 'reasonably anticipated at the time that specific rights and obligations of market access were negotiated'.

Conclusion

TRIPS obligations are to be made effective in the internal order of each member state, according to its own system of incorporating international norms, in the best way possible. The unavailability of domestic means to make such norms fully applicable is no excuse to the effectiveness requirement.

However, not all TRIPS norms are intended to be applied directly in the legal order of any country, even in those cases where the country's legal system accepts in theory incorporation of international rules without the mediation of a domestic law. Among TRIPS norms are

(a) *principle* norms, which direct how application and incorporation should be done in such a way as to obtain the *maximum optimization* of WTO purposes;
(b) *rules*, which embody precepts directly addressed to parties.

In some egregious cases, the addressees of the precepts are not private parties, but the member states themselves, who must choose (through their own peculiar law-making procedures) among the permissible variations provided by TRIPS (patents must last for *at least* 20 years. . .) some rule to be incorporated and applied in the relations among private parties.

Both when exercising this choice and otherwise internally implementing TRIPS, member states are subject to three limitations:

(a) domestic laws (or subsequent international commitments) cannot provide less protection to IP interests than what TRIPS states as being the minimum protection (being those levels already provided by the basic treaties, as modified by TRIPS itself);
(b) domestic laws and further applicable international norms cannot exceed the protection of IP interests beyond the maximum levels admissible under TRIPS, either by a rule (for example, article 50.3 TRIPS) or by a principle (for example, National Treatment);
(c) whenever TRIPS allows for a member state's choice, such choice must be directed by the TRIPS objects and purposes as criteria of reasonableness and equilibrium between IP and non-IP interests.

While the first analysis is currently occurring, including in WTO jurisprudence, the second and third analyses deserve more attentive consideration. The joint application of the three limitations provides member states with public policy space to conform their domestic laws to their peculiar needs.

One special type of TRIPS provision is precisely intended to allow for 'national variations and approaches, which are often collectively deemed "the TRIPS flexibilities"'. Such provisions are not constrained by other base-level considerations, only by the limits and conditions imposed by their special norms.

This allowance for national diversity follows the tradition provided by the Paris Convention, albeit in a more restrictive ambiance. Harmonization or other forms of establishing less idiomatic IP national regimes deny to national public policies the full benefits of TRIPS, the real extent of which were enlightened by succeeding international commitments comprising IP rules.

While limitations on the choices member states may make apply to their unilateral decisions, they also constrain the will of member states engaging in IP-related international commitments with third parties. In this context especially, balancing of interests may provide motives to renounce choosing just minimum standards or other allowed spaces, including flexibilities. This author's contention, however, is that there is some mandatory balancing among IP and non-IP considerations which prevents unbounded levels of protection of IP interests.

The body comprising TRIPS maximum standards and a bare level of equilibrium between IP and non-IP interests does not seem disposable by even willing member states either in domestic or international commitments. The effective denial of essential public health and nutrition interests are examples of non-negotiable elements whenever TRIPS is implemented, but other non-IP essential interests would possibly result from the application of TRIPS objective and purposes.

A further contention is that this balancing process – which precludes effective annihilation of any of the interests at stake – is a prescriptive norm of TRIPS, and its application remains within the scope of DSU procedure as a strict 'covered agreements' issue.

4 Enhancing global innovation policy: the role of WIPO and its Conventions in interpreting the TRIPS Agreement

*Graeme B. Dinwoodie and Rochelle C. Dreyfuss**

1 Introduction

In recent years, it has become clear that the TRIPS regime is in trouble.[1] Although lawmaking in the World Trade Organization (WTO) has essentially stalled,[2] there is a continuing need to recalibrate the rules applicable to knowledge production. For developing countries, entry into the WTO was a compromise. When intellectual property lawmaking was centered in the World Intellectual Property Organization (WIPO), these nations resisted attempts to increase the level of protection. That changed, however, with the inclusion of intellectual property in negotiations over trade: in return for access to markets in the developed world, developing countries were required to enact and enforce new intellectual property laws.[3] While the TRIPS Agreement tried to ease their conversion to greater protection, the transitional provisions it included proved to be largely illusory: the time periods for compliance were too short; the promises of technology transfer and technical assistance, inadequately realized.[4] Paradoxically, for some developing

* The authors have published a more detailed account of the issues discussed in this chapter see 'Designing a Global Intellectual Property System Responsive to Change: The WTO, WIPO, and Beyond', 46 *Hous. L. Rev.* 1187 (2009).

1 Agreement on Trade-related Aspects of Intellectual Property Rights (1994), Marrakesh Agreement Establishing the World Trade Organization [hereinafter WTO Agreement], Annex 1C, Legal Instruments – Results of the Uruguay Round, 33 ILM 1197 (hereinafter TRIPS Agreement or TRIPS).

2 Stephen Castle and Mark Landler, 'After 7 Years, Talks Collapse on World Trade', *New York Times*, July 30, 2008, at A1 col. 1.

3 Christopher May and Susan K. Sell, *Intellectual Property Rights: A Critical History,* United States, Lynne Rienner Publishers, Inc. (2006).

4 See TRIPS Agreement, arts. 66–7; see also Duncan Matthews and V. Munoz-Tellez, 'Bilateral Technical Assistance and TRIPS: the United States, Japan and the European Communities in Comparative Perspective' [2006] 9 *Journal of World Intellectual Property* 629–53.

countries, the WTO regime can also be insufficiently protective: TRIPS rights are structured for the types of knowledge goods generated in the North, but do not cover the traditional knowledge, folklore, and natural endowments that constitute much of the informational wealth of the South. To be sure, the Doha Declaration and subsequent actions dealt with a few of the concerns of developing countries,[5] but unless more radical accommodations are found, many WTO members may languish in a social and economic backwater, paying high prices for information products without the ability to fully exploit their own creative capacities.[6]

For developed nations, the problems are not very different, for there too TRIPS now offers both too much and too little protection. The Agreement was, after all, crafted for a particular era – an era that largely predated Internet commerce in trademarked goods, distribution of digitized copyrighted materials, and the informatics revolution within the patent industries. The explosion in global marketing puts pressure on the territoriality principle embedded in TRIPS,[7] arguably leading to underprotection, particularly of works distributed electronically. At the same time, however, the emergence of new intellectual opportunities and enterprises alters the economics of information production. TRIPS' strong commitment to a particular vision of proprietary rights – and, on the patents side, to technological neutrality – makes it difficult to revise the law to deal with such matters as the thickets of rights created in the software and biotechnological sectors, with open source innovation, and with new opportunities for serial and collaborative production.[8]

In theory, the problems facing WTO members could be resolved through new lawmaking. This could take a number of forms. For instance, a 'bottom up' approach would give states greater flexibility to adopt local laws to deal with the different problems they each encounter. As common solutions emerge, the Agreement could be modified to reflect these developments. Alternatively, solutions could originate at

---

[5] See infra text accompanying note 116.

[6] Rochelle Cooper Dreyfuss, 'Fostering Dynamic Innovation, Development and Trade: Intellectual Property as a Case Study in Global Administrative Law', *Acta Juridica* (pp. 237–82, 2009); M. Chon, 'Intellectual Property and the Development Divide' (2006) 27 *Cardozo L. Rev.* 2821; J.H. Reichman, 'From Free Riders to Fair Followers: Global Competition under the TRIPS Agreement' (1997) 29 *NYU J. Int'l L. and Pol.* 11.

[7] G.B. Dinwoodie, 'Trademarks and Territory: Detaching Trademark Law from the Nation-State', 41 *Hous. L. Rev.* 885 (2004).

[8] G.B. Dinwoodie and R.C. Dreyfuss, 'Intellectual Property Law and the Public Domain of Science' (2004) 7(2) *J. Int'l Econ. L.* 431.

the international level; after codification into the Agreement, they would then 'trickle down' as member states transposed their new obligations into domestic law. For a variety of reasons, however, neither of these approaches has materialized. In part, the problem is simply stasis in the WTO. In part, there is a disconnect between the WTO's objective of enhancing economic welfare through free trade and the values embodied in intellectual property law.[9] For example, because of concerns over how liberalizing the rules on compulsory licensing would affect the market, even the one concrete achievement of the Doha Round – assuring developing countries access to essential medicines – has yet to be fully implemented.[10]

As many have noted, the WTO's adjudicatory system has compensated somewhat for the lack of activity in the Ministerial Conference and the General Council.[11] But for a number of reasons, it is not a substitute for a well-functioning 'legislative body'. It cannot replicate the top-down approach of an international agreement on substantive norms because, under the Understanding for Dispute Settlement (DSU),[12] the decisions by the Dispute Resolution Board (DSB) may not 'diminish the rights and obligations provided in the covered agreements'.[13] And the institutional character of the DSB does not encourage disregard of this formal limit on judicial activism.[14] These constraints, both formal and institutional,

---

[9] Graeme B. Dinwoodie, 'The International Intellectual Property System: Treaties, Norms, National Courts and Private Ordering' in D. Gervais (ed.) *Intellectual Property, Trade and Development: Normative and Institutional Aspects*, Oxford: Oxford University Press 2007 p. 61; R.C. Dreyfuss and A.F. Lowenfeld, 'two Achievements of the Uruguay Round: Putting TRIPS and Dispute Settlement Together', 37 *Va. J. Int'l L.* 275 (1997).

[10] Anthony Taubman, 'Rethinking TRIPS: "Adequate Remuneration" for Non-voluntary Patent Licensing', 11 *J. Int'l Econ.* L. 927 (2008); Daniel Gervais, *The TRIPS Agreement: Drafting History and Analysis*, London, UK: Sweet & Maxwell 3rd edition, 2008, pp. 395–401.

[11] See, for example, Tomer Broude, *International Governance in the WTO: Judicial Boundaries and Political Capitulation*, London, UK: Cameron – Man Ltd. 2004; R.H. Steinberg, 'Judicial Lawmaking at the WTO: Discursive, Constitutional, and Political Constraints' (2004) 98 *Am. J. Int'l L.* 247, 254; C.D. Ehlerman and L. Ehring, 'Decision-making in the World Trade Organization' (2005) 8 *J. Int'l Econ L* 51.

[12] Understanding on Rules and Procedures Governing the Settlement of Disputes (April 15, 1994), [WTO Agreement], Annex 2, Legal Instruments – Results of the Uruguay Round, 33 ILM 1125 (1994) [hereinafter DSU].

[13] DSU, art. 3.2. The TRIPS Council's role in lawmaking is similarly circumscribed, WTO Agreement, art. IX.

[14] See Graeme B. Dinwoodie, 'A New Copyright Order: Why National Courts should Create Global Norms', 149 *U. Pa. L. Rev.* 469, 505–18 (2000).

appear to allow the DSB to complement a bottom-up approach because the TRIPS Agreement ostensibly leaves members with substantial room to maneuver.[15] Members can, for example, increase the level of domestic protection.[16] But as we have explained in other writing, the DSB has interpreted TRIPS flexibilities so narrowly that member states cannot otherwise adapt their laws to new circumstances.[17]

There are other confounding factors. Both developing and developed countries are showing signs of giving up on the WTO. Some countries have begun to use bilateral agreements to enhance the level of protection.[18] Others are engaging in 'regime shifting'.[19] Claims to the knowledge embedded in natural resources are moving to negotiations over the Convention on Biological Diversity;[20] some intellectual property issues have been restructured as human rights claims;[21] and a new criminal enforcement regime is under contemplation.[22] In part, the focus has even shifted back, *from* the WTO *to* WIPO. Although, in theory, regulatory competition could enrich international innovation policy, the early indication is that asymmetries in bargaining power, coupled with the overlap in lawmaking authority, are leading to a suboptimal global regime: thickets

---

[15] J. H. Reichman, 'Universal Minimum Standards of Intellectual Property Protection under the TRIPS Component of the WTO Agreement', in C.M. Correa and A.A. Yusuf (eds), *Intellectual Property and International Trade – The TRIPS Agreement* 1998.

[16] New Zealand, for example, offers enhanced protection for the Maori culture. See Graeme W. Austin, 'Valuing "Domestic Self-Determination" in International Intellectual Property', 77 *Chi.-Kent L. Rev.* 1155 (2002).

[17] See Dinwoodie and Dreyfuss, supra note 8; G.B. Dinwoodie and R.C. Dreyfuss, 'TRIPS and the Dynamics of International Property Lawmaking' (2004) 36 *Case Western Reserve J. Int'l L.* 95 (hereinafter Dynamics); G.B. Dinwoodie and R.C. Dreyfuss, 'Diversifying without Discriminating: Complying with the Mandates of the TRIPS Agreement' (2007) 13 *Michigan Telecommunication and Technology L. Rev.* 445 (hereinafter Diversifying).

[18] Timothy P. Trainer, 'Intellectual Property Enforcement: A Reality Gap (Insufficient Assistance, Ineffective Implementation)?', 8 J. *Marshall Rev. Intell. Prop*. L. 47 (2008).

[19] Laurence R. Helfer, 'Regime Shifting: The TRIPS Agreement and New Dynamics of International Intellectual Property Lawmaking', 29 *Yale J. Int'l L.* 1, 20–22 (2004).

[20] Convention on Biological Diversity, June 5, 1992, Art. 15(1), 31 ILM 818, 823 (1992).

[21] Laurence R. Helfer, 'The New Innovation Frontier? Intellectual Property and the European Court of Human Rights', 49 *Harv. Int'l L.J.* 1 (2008).

[22] Office of the United States Trade Representative, Anti-Counterfeiting Trade Agreement (ACTA): Request for Public Comments, 73 Fed. Reg. 8910 (February 15, 2008); Trainer, supra note 18.

of rights,[23] conflicting demands,[24] disputes that perpetually cycle,[25] and uncertainties created by institutional cacophony.[26]

The move to WIPO is, however, intriguing. WIPO and its predecessor, the United International Bureaux for the Protection of Intellectual Property (BIRPI), were established to consolidate the international intellectual property regime and WIPO agreed that as part of its mission, it would consider the impact of intellectual property protection on the developing world.[27] Although WIPO's early attempts at resolving the problems of the South largely faltered, it recently renewed its commitment to a 'Development Agenda', and has even taken up questions about overprotection in the North.[28] WIPO has a governance structure that potentially permits more diverse input than the WTO and greater flexibility in voting. It has restructured its norm development processes to enable it to respond expeditiously to new issues though the adoption of soft law instruments.[29] As a result, it is also not suffering as badly from the lawmaking problems confounding the WTO. Post-TRIPS, it has held conferences and issued influential reports on emerging issues;[30]

---

[23] Sabrina Safrin, 'Hyperownership in a Time of Biotechnological Promise: The International Conflict to Control the Building Blocks of Life', 98 *Am. J. Int'l L.* 641, 646–58 (2004) (describing overlap between rights protected by TRIPS and the CBD).

[24] See, for example, *European Communities – Protection of Trademarks and Geographic Indication for Agricultural Products and Foodstuffs*, WT/DS174/R (Panel Report, 2005) [hereinafter *EC-GI*].

[25] See, for example, *Anheuser-Busch v. Budejovicky Budvar NP*, [1984] FSR 413 (CA) (UK); *Anheuser-Busch Inc. v. Portugal*, App. No. 73049/01, 45 Eur. H.R. Rep. 36 [830] (Grand Chamber 2007); T-225/06 *Budějovický Budvar v OHMI – Anheuser-Busch* (BUD) (ECJ – Court of First Instance 2008).

[26] See European Communities – Regime for the Importation, Sale and Distribution of Bananas – Recourse to Arbitration by the European Communities under Article 22.6 of the DSU (Decision of the Arbitrators, March 24, 2006) (suggesting that it was not within the jurisdiction of WTO arbitrators to assess whether measures authorized under the WTO Agreements might result in noncompliance with obligations under WIPO Conventions).

[27] D.J. Halbert, 'The World Intellectual Property Organization: Past, Present and Future' (2007) 54 *J. Copyright Society USA* 253, 263.

[28] An excellent overview is provided by Neil Weinstock Netanel (ed.), *The Development Agenda: Global Intellectual Property and Developing Countries*, Oxford: Oxford University Press, 2009. See, for example, Provisional Committee on Proposals Related to a WIPO Development Agenda ('PCDA'), Fourth Session (11–15 June 2007) available at http://www.wipo.int/ip-development/en/agenda/pcda07_session4.html.

[29] See Dinwoodie, supra note 9, at 80–84.

[30] See, for example, Standing Committee on The Law of Trademarks, Industrial

it has also successfully concluded negotiations over several new intellectual property instruments.[31] Significantly, the TRIPS Agreement contemplates a formal tie with WIPO, the two organizations have entered into an agreement 'to establish a mutually supportive relationship',[32] and enjoy a host of informal connections.[33] In theory, then, WIPO could serve as a vehicle for keeping WTO law responsive to the changing demands of both producers and consumers of innovation, and to the varied needs of the WTO's membership. With WIPO's greater receptivity to emerging issues and the WTO's capacity to enforce compliance, certain of the impasses caused by regime shifting would hopefully abate, along with the other problems caused by overlapping regulatory authority.

Greater input from WIPO would be beneficial for another reason as well. Because the focus of the WTO is trade, the TRIPS Agreement tends to view intellectual property very much as a commodity. Lost in the drafting process was the sense that intellectual property embodies cultural values, that it encompasses the building blocks of education and future technological development, or that it protects goods essential to social welfare.[34] Although WIPO's stated mission is to '*promote* the protection

---

Designs and Geographical Indications, Use of Trademarks on The Internet: Issues Paper (3rd Session), Sct/3/4, available at http://www.wipo.int/edocs/mdocs/sct/en/sct_3/sct_3_4.pdf; Joint Recommendation Concerning Provisions on the Protection of Well-known Marks, adopted by the Assembly of the Paris Union for the Protection of Industrial Property and General Assembly of the World Intellectual Property Organization, WIPO Doc. 833(E) (September 1999); WIPO, *Final Report of the WIPO Internet Domain Name Process* (April 30, 1999), available at http://wipo2.wipo.int/process1/report/finalreport.html.

[31] Examples include the WIPO Performances and Phonograms Treaty (adopted on May 20, 2002) 36 ILM 76, the WIPO Copyright Treaty (adopted on March 6, 2002) 36 ILM 65, the Trademark Law Treaty, 2037 UNTS I-35236, the Revised Trademark Law Treaty and a new (Geneva) Act of the Hague Agreement on the Deposit of Industrial Designs.

[32] Articles 63 and 68 of TRIPS; Agreement between the World Intellectual Property Organization and the World Trade Organization (22 December 1995), available at http://www.wipo.int/treaties/en/agreement/pdf/trtdocs_wo030.pdf ('WTO/WIPO Agreement'), Preamble.

[33] Indeed, the panels of the DSB that have produced reports on intellectual property disputes have included former high-ranking officials of WIPO, such as Mihaly Ficsor, who served on the panel that resolved a patent dispute involving Canada; see *Canada – Patent Protection of Pharmaceutical Products*, WT/DS114/R (Panel Report, 2000) [hereinafter *Canada – Pharmaceutical Products*].

[34] Henning Grosse Ruse-Khan, 'A Comparative Analysis of Policy Space in the WTO' in A. Kur and M. Levin (eds), *Intellectual Property Rights in Transition*, Cheltenham, UK and Northampton, USA: Edward Elgar Publishing 2010.

of intellectual property throughout the world',[35] its institutional structure, which requires member states to enter into intellectual property agreements without the possibility of side-payments in the form of concessions on unrelated matters, has always forced it to strike a balance between access and proprietary interests.[36] Furthermore, in most intellectual property areas, its instruments set standards that are less comprehensive than TRIPS. Thus, they give members far more flexibility to shape their own creative environments. In short, the organization, along with the agreements it administers, bring to the table an intellectual property sensibility that is currently lacking in the WTO.

Unfortunately, however, the nature of the lawmaking relationship between these two organizations has yet to be fully elucidated. There are other agreements within the WTO framework that rely explicitly on the expertise of non-WTO organizations: they reference standards enunciated by international bodies with relevant expertise,[37] mandate consultations with groups having overlapping jurisdiction,[38] or establish joint oversight in areas where there are potential conflicts.[39] In contrast, the relationship with WIPO is opaque. Although TRIPS incorporates several WIPO instruments, it is not evident whether (or how) the WTO should be taking account of WIPO's view of these commitments.[40] Nor is it clear how (or when) new developments within these conventions should affect WTO

---

[35] Convention Establishing the World Intellectual Property Organization, July 14, 1967, 21 UST 1749, 848 UNTS 3 [hereinafter WIPO Convention], Preamble and arts. 3–4 (emphasis added).

[36] See, for example, Pamela Samuelson, 'The U.S. Digital Agenda at WIPO', 37 *Va. J. Int'l L.* 369 (1997); Standing Committee on Copyright and Related Rights, WIPO Study on Limitations and Exceptions of Copyright and Related Rights in the Digital Environment, at 14, SCCR/9/7 (April 5, 2003) (prepared by Sam Ricketson).

[37] See Joost Pauwelyn, *Conflict of Norms in Public International Law: How WTO Law Relates to other Rules of International Law*, Cambridge: Cambridge University Press, 2003, pp. 348–50, citing SPS art. 3.2, which refers to standards established by the Codex Alimentarius Commission, the International Office of Epoizootics, and the Secretariat of the International Plant Protection Convention; the Subsidies Agreement, which refers implicitly to actions undertaken by the OECD, and TBT, arts. 2.4 and 2.5, which make general references to standards developed by international organizations.

[38] Pauwelyn, supra note 37, at 347, citing the relationship between the WTO Treaty and rules of the International Monetary Fund, see; for example, GATT art. XV:2, providing for consultations with the IMF.

[39] Pauwelyn, supra note 37, at 350, citing the Declaration on Trade and Environment, which is part of the 1994 Final Act.

[40] See, for example, William R. Cornish, 'Genevan Bootstraps', 19 *Eur. Intell. Prop. Rev.* 336 (1997).

obligations.[41] The Agreement permits the TRIPS Council to 'consult with and seek information from any source it deems appropriate' to carry out its obligations,[42] but the current WTO/WIPO Agreement is limited to legal and technical assistance – to providing the WTO with copies and translations of domestic legislation and to assisting WTO members in meeting their obligations.[43]

This chapter takes up the question of how the WTO can best make use of WIPO's experience and expertise in intellectual property matters. After examining how the intellectual property cases decided to date have relied on the text and negotiating histories of, and other materials relevant to, WIPO conventions to elucidate TRIPS norms, we suggest some revisions to interpretive approaches pursued by the dispute settlement panels to date. We point out methodologies that would leaven and cabin the trade perspective, and thus allow the WTO to capitalize on WIPO's experience and on WIPO developments that cope with the dynamic nature of intellectual property and the changing landscape of knowledge production. We conclude with some thoughts on how far such reliance on WIPO – and, by analogy, on the work of other international organizations – can take the enterprise of squaring TRIPS obligations with current concerns.[44]

2. The role of WIPO and its Conventions in interpreting TRIPS: the story so far

It is one thing to recognize that WIPO could help the WTO internalize and update intellectual property norms. Developing effective mechanisms for importing intellectual property values into TRIPS is quite another matter. Aside from the many intentional differences between the agreements, there are also discontinuities, inconsistencies, and divergent capacities to deal with changing circumstances. Transposing provisions from one context into another is fraught with error-making possibilities. Furthermore, there are no authoritative interpretations of the WIPO instruments.[45] Neither

---

[41] See, for example, Neil W. Netanel, 'The Next Round: The Impact of the WIPO Copyright Treaty on TRIPS Dispute Settlement', 37 *Va. J. Int'l L.* 441 (1997).

[42] TRIPS, art. 68. Earlier drafts of the Agreement contemplated a larger role for intellectual property experts; Draft of July 23, 1990, W/76, Gervais, supra note 10, at 541.

[43] WTO/WIPO Agreement, supra note 32, arts. 2 and 4.

[44] The World Health Organization, for example, is also considering the question of development and essential medicines; see Jack Lerner, 'Intellectual Property and Development at WHO and WIPO', 34 *Am. J.L. & Med.* 257 (2008).

[45] In theory, obligations under the Berne and Paris Conventions can be enforced in the International Court of Justice Paris Convention, art. 28(1); Berne Convention, art. 33(1), but no cases have been brought there. Nor is WIPO in

Berne nor Paris even specifies what interpretive sources are appropriate. TRIPS refers to 'customary principles of international law'[46] – generally taken to mean the Vienna Convention on the Law of Treaties.[47] But, formally, the Vienna Convention discusses prior and subsequent treaties; it does not deal with agreements incorporated by reference.[48] The following section explores the problems created by incorporation and how they have been resolved to date.

2.1 Relying on incorporated provisions

In theory, the incorporation of WIPO measures into the TRIPS Agreement should be straightforward and lead to a successful amalgamation of intellectual property values with trade objectives. TRIPS articles 2.1 and 9.1 state that WTO members must comply with the principal articles of the Paris and Berne Conventions. At the same time, TRIPS makes clear how far incorporation extends; article 9.1 dis-incorporates Berne article 6*bis* (which addresses moral rights); and article 2.2 states that there is nothing in the substantive provisions of the TRIPS Agreement that derogates from the obligations incurred under the Paris, Berne, or Rome Conventions, or the treaty on integrated circuits.

Havana Club[49] illustrates how the incorporation strategy can work to preserve the balances struck by the WIPO conventions. In that case, the EC challenged a provision of US law denying protection to the owners of Cuban trademarks and trade names, on the ground that the property had been confiscated. Relying on art. 6*quinquies* of the Paris Convention (the '*telle quelle*' provision), the EC argued that once a trademark qualified for registration in its country of origin, registration in another member state

---

Footnote 45 (*cont.*)
a position to offer strictly authoritative readings of its own conventions. See Cornish, supra note 40, at 336. In practice, WTO dispute settlement panels have made extensive use of leading works on the WIPO conventions, such as Ricketson on the Berrne Convention, and Bodenhausen on the Paris Convention, the latter of which was authored by a leading WIPO official and published by BIRPI.

[46] DSU, art. 3.2.

[47] Vienna Convention on the Law of Treaties, UN Doc. A/Conf. 39/27, 8 ILM 679 (1969) (entered into force January 27, 1980); see also Steven P. Croley and John H. Jackson, 'WTO Dispute Procedures, Standard of Review, and Deference to National Governments', 90 *Am. J. Int'l L.* 193, 200 (1996).

[48] For further discussion of these issues, see Susy Frankel, 'WTO Application of "The Customary Rules of Interpretation of Public International Law" to Intellectual Property', 46 Va. J. Int'l L. 365 (2006).

[49] *United States – Section 211 of the Omnibus Appropriations Act of 1998*, WT/DS176/AB/R (WTO Appellate Body, 2001) [hereinafter *Havana Club*].

could not be denied for any reason other than those expressly recognized in Article 6*quinquies*. In contrast, the United States took the position that *telle quelle* restricted only the ability of the second state to deny registration based upon the mark's visual form. The Appellate Body examined the language of the disputed Paris Convention provision and its context, including the Final Protocol of 1883 – which it regarded as 'an integral part of that Convention'[50] – as well as the Washington Revision Conference of 1911. It also consulted a well-known treatise on the Paris Convention.[51] In the end, it concluded that 'the drafters of the Paris Convention did not intend' the result propounded by the EC, either when the Convention was first concluded or in its subsequent revisions.[52] In other words, even under Paris and TRIPS obligations, states remain substantially free to regulate the registration of trademarks under national law, so long as there is no interference with their form.[53]

The opinion is at least as significant for what the Appellate Body did not do as for what it did. The EC had criticized the Panel that initially resolved the dispute for resorting directly to the negotiation history of the Paris Convention instead of relying first on the rules of the Vienna Convention,[54] which, per article 32, would have required an ambiguity before resort could be made to background materials.[55] Had the Appellate Body adopted this circuitous approach, the meaning of the TRIPS Agreement would have been determined in the first instance through a

---

[50] Id., ¶ 145.

[51] Id., ¶ 138; G.H.C Bodenhausen, *Guide to the Application of the Paris Convention for the Protection of Industrial Property as revised at Stockholm in 1967*, United International Bureaux for the Protection of Intellectual Property, (1968, reprinted 1991). *China – Measures Affecting the Protection and Enforcement of Intellectual Property Rights*, WT/DS362/R (Panel Report 2009) [hereinafter *China – Enforcement*] is to similar effect, citing a broad array of treatises and other works to determine the nature of Berne rights; see, e.g., ¶7.126. Of course, it is not unusual for international tribunals to make greater use of treatise writers. See Ian Brownlie, *Principles of Public International Law*, 7th edition (2008).

[52] *Havana Club*, supra note 49, at ¶ 141; see generally, ¶¶ 130–48.

[53] But see Paris Convention for the Protection of Industrial Property, arts. 6*bis*, 6*ter*, March 20, 1883, revised July 14, 1967, 21 UST 1583, 828 UNTS 305 (requiring member states to deny trademark rights in certain claimed marks).

[54] *Havana Club*, supra note 49, at ¶ 19.

[55] Cf. *United States – Section 110(5) of the US Copyright Act*, WT/DS160/R, ¶ 6.41 (Panel Report, 2000) [hereinafter *US – 110(5)*] ('We note that Article 30 of the Vienna Convention on the application of successive treaties is not relevant in this respect, because all provisions of the TRIPS Agreement – including the incorporated Articles 1–21 of the Berne Convention (1971) – entered into force at the same point in time').

trade lens: had a term appeared unambiguous when seen from that perspective, that trade-oriented meaning would have automatically prevailed, regardless of its impact on creative production.[56] By instead allowing decision-makers to consider the Paris Convention directly, this approach ensured that the sensibilities of intellectual property were brought into play. Since intellectual property is aimed at striking a balance between the demands of right holders and other national interests, the Appellate Body's direct approach to the Paris Convention leaves WTO members with greater latitude to tailor their law to their domestic intellectual agendas (so long, of course, as their policies are consistent with the trade objectives of the WTO agreements).[57]

2.2 Dealing with potential discrepancies between TRIPS and the incorporated conventions

The simplicity of this direct approach can, however, be deceptive. For one, there are situations where TRIPS sets out a rule that, while attempting to incorporate the WIPO instruments, appears inconsistent with them.[58] But even here, DSB adjudicators have often found techniques that valorize intellectual property values. To stay with the trademark example, *Havana Club* identified several potential discontinuities between TRIPS and the Paris Convention. First, article 2 of TRIPS explicitly incorporates article 8 of the Paris Convention, which requires the protection of trade names. However, because article 1 of TRIPS limits the scope of the Agreement to the subject matter listed in sections 1 through 7 of Part II – none of

---

56 Moreover, most of the panelists serving on dispute panels and on the Appellate Body are trained as experts in trade law, not intellectual property law.

57 *India – Patent Protection for Pharmaceutical and Agricultural Chemical Products*, WT/DS50/AB/R (Appellate Body, 1997) [hereinafter *India – Pharmaceuticals*], which concerned the transition provisions of the Agreement, similarly leaves states with maximal flexibility. The Appellate Body rejected claims that India's obligations should be augmented by the expectations of other WTO members, ¶¶ 45–8. Furthermore, it held that '[m]embers . . . are free to determine how best to meet their obligations under the TRIPS Agreement within the context of their own legal systems', ¶ 59. See also *China – Enforcement*, ¶¶ 7.240–7.374, where the Panel recognized China's substantial discretion to order border measures that balanced right holders' interests and public needs; and id. at ¶ 5.95 (noting that art. 41.5 gives members substantial discretion over implementation of law enforcement measures) and ¶ 7.602 (noting that so long as China has criminal enforcement measures in place, it survives a facial challenge).

58 We deal separately below with cases where TRIPS clearly and intentionally imposes greater obligations on member states. TRIPS was a Berne-plus and Paris-plus convention, so these are to be expected. See infra text accompanying notes 91–105.

which explicitly includes trade names – the *Havana Club* Panel took the position (argued by the United States) that trade name disputes could not be brought in the WTO.[59] The Appellate Body reversed. Relying on article 32 of the Vienna Convention to interpret the TRIPS Agreement,[60] it accorded primacy to the WIPO instrument: 'To adopt the Panel's approach would be to deprive Article 8 of the Paris Convention . . . of any and all meaning and effect'.

A second question – on ownership – presented something of the opposite question. The EC contended that the TRIPS Agreement's references to the 'undertakings' of trademark holders set out rules on ownership, even though the Paris Convention did not appear to cover the matter.[61] Clearly, the TRIPS Agreement does contain instances where it expressly augments or elaborates on the obligations of the earlier WIPO conventions. Here, in contrast, the EC's contention would have required the Panel to imply an enhancement that was not clear on the face of TRIPS. This time, notwithstanding that the claim appeared to rest on the meaning of TRIPS alone, the Panel looked first at the Paris Convention, asking whether it addressed the ownership question. To find out, it sent a letter to the International Bureau of WIPO requesting 'factual information . . . relevant to the dispute, in particular the negotiating history and subsequent developments'.[62] In response, the Director-General stated that nothing in the Paris Convention covered ownership and the Panel (apparently) assumed that this resolved the question.[63] While the Appellate Body in fact examined the TRIPS provisions relied upon by the EC, in the end, it too came to the conclusion that TRIPS did not disturb the decision by the negotiators of the Paris Convention to leave the question of ownership to member states.[64]

As yet, there are no Appellate Body decisions on the relationship between the TRIPS Agreement and the Berne Convention, which imposes many more substantive requirements than does Paris. However, the Panel Report in the *US – 110(5)* case suggests that here too, efforts will be made to interpret TRIPS in a manner that preserves the flexibilities inherent in the antecedent intellectual property conventions.[65] The issue in that case

---

59 *United States – Section 211 of the Omnibus Appropriations Act of 1998*, WT/DS176/R ¶ 8.27 (Panel Report, 2001) [hereinafter *Havana Club Panel*].

60 *Havana Club*, supra note 49, ¶¶ 333–41.

61 See, for example, TRIPS art. 15.1.

62 *Havana Club Panel*, supra note 59, ¶ 6.1.

63 See *Havana Club*, supra note 49, ¶ 189 (describing the Panel's disposition).

64 Id., ¶¶ 190–95.

65 *United States – Section 110(5) of the US Copyright Act*, WT/DS160/R (Panel Report, 2000) [hereinafter *US – 110(5)*].

was whether the United States, which permitted certain establishments to make unauthorized usages of musical broadcasts, had violated its obligations under articles 11 and 11*bis*, the broadcast and rebroadcast provisions of the Berne Convention. Looking at the Berne Convention directly,[66] the Panel endeavored to determine what these provisions required. It examined members' practices before 1948, when the provision was proposed, the General Report, which was issued contemporaneously with the proposal, and the work of the diplomatic conferences at which the provision was adopted.[67] The Panel noted that throughout this time, members tolerated 'minor exceptions' – limited unauthorized performances of copyrighted materials. Relying on article 31(3)(b) of the Vienna Convention, it concluded:

> In our view, state practice as reflected in the national copyright laws of Berne Union members before and after 1948, 1967 and 1971, as well as of WTO Members before and after the date that the TRIPS Agreement became applicable to them, confirms our conclusion [that] the minor exceptions doctrine [forms a part of the context of arts. 11 and 11*bis*].[68]

Using the negotiation history of the TRIPS Agreement – including a document the Negotiating Group asked the International Bureau of WIPO to prepare in order to 'to facilitate an understanding of the existence, scope and form of generally internationally accepted and applied standards/norms for the protection of intellectual property'[69] – the Panel reasoned that absent an indication in the TRIPS Agreement that it intended to eliminate the minor exceptions doctrine, the 'entire Berne *acquis*' was incorporated into the TRIPS Agreement.[70] The Panel concluded that it was important to 'adopt the meaning that reconciles the texts of different treaties and avoids a conflict between them'.[71]

These different analyses can be read to suggest that where a complaint is in essence an effort to enforce an intellectual property norm found in a WIPO Convention through the opportunity for dispute settlement system found in the WTO framework, panels will respect the intellectual property

---

66 Id., ¶ 6.11 ('We note that Article 30 of the Vienna Convention on the application of successive treaties is not relevant in this respect, because all provisions of the TRIPS Agreement – including the incorporated Articles 1–21 of the Berne Convention (1971) – entered into force at the same point in time').

67 Id., ¶ 6.53–6.54.

68 Id., ¶ 6.55.

69 Id., ¶ 6.64.

70 Id., ¶ 6.62–6.66.

71 Id., ¶ 6.66.

origins of the dispute. That is to say, although TRIPS claims to be about trade-related aspects of intellectual property, a large part of the rationale for its inclusion in the WTO regime is that the effective enforcement machinery of trade law provides a mechanism for hardening (WIPO-generated) intellectual property norms.

2.3 Use of WIPO conventions by analogy

In some cases, WIPO treaties utilize terminology similar to that used in the TRIPS Agreement. Where the meaning in the WIPO instrument is clear, it can sometimes be consulted to infuse the TRIPS Agreement with an intellectual property perspective. The *EC – GI* case provides an example. One issue in that case was whether the EC's rules on protecting geographic indications violated the national treatment provision of the TRIPS Agreement by applying different rules to geographic indications pointing to territories outside the EU. The EC argued that the differential rules did not amount to a discrimination based on 'nationality' because certain foreign nationals had, in fact, acquired protection under the challenged EC Regulation.[72] The Panel rejected the argument on the ground that these rights were derived through subsidiaries based in the EC. To buttress its conclusion that TRIPS treated discrimination according to residence and that the place of establishment was a close substitute for residence (and therefore essentially a proxy for nationality), the Panel looked at how the terms were used in other, pre-existing, intellectual property instruments.[73]

Relying on WIPO conventions in this manner is, however, fraught with possibilities for mistake. Importantly, the *EC – GI* Panel relied on the connection because it was consistent with the purposes of the TRIPS Agreement.[74] Elsewhere in its report, the Panel rejected efforts to incorporate from the Paris Convention definitions of terms used but undefined in TRIPS.[75] The Panel thus showed some sensitivity to when (and when not) to use analogous terms in the pre-existing conventions. Attention must also be paid to the historical context in which the various agreements were negotiated. Otherwise, the attempted analogy can seriously misfire.

One example of this type of miscalculation can be seen from the way in which TRIPS' own attempts to achieve a measure of balance have been interpreted. Thus, each of the principal intellectual property areas

---

[72] *EC – GI*, at ¶ 7.197.

[73] Id., at ¶ 7.198.

[74] Id., at ¶ 7.199.

[75] Id., at ¶ 7.170 (meaning of 'interested party' for purposes of arts. 22–23 of TRIPS).

covered by the TRIPS Agreement includes a provision on 'exceptions'.[76] Although they are all different, their formats are similar: a multi- (usually three-) part test that allows members to limit intellectual property rights so long as they do not overly conflict with normal exploitation of the protected work or unreasonably prejudice the legitimate interests of the right holder.[77] Except for the copyright test, all permit adjudicators to also consider the interests of third parties. There have been three Panel decisions interpreting the exceptions, the aforementioned *US – 110(5)*; *Canada – Pharmaceuticals*,[78] which challenged Canada's decision to permit generic drug makers to test pharmaceuticals and stockpile them prior to patent expiration; and the part of the *EC – GI* dispute, in which the United States claimed that the EC's protection for geographic indications impinged on trademark rights.

In each case, adjudicators left members with leeway to reconcile *conflicting* TRIPS obligations (that is, the conflict between GIs and trademarks, which are both protected by TRIPS) and to prevent right holders from benefiting from exclusive terms *in excess* of those mandated by TRIPS (that is, to exploit the de facto exclusivity available to pharmaceutical companies by reason of the need for premarket clearance). At the same time, however, the decisions severely hamper the states' ability to accommodate national interests in any manner that constitutes a true exception – that is, *a genuine intrusion* into a TRIPS obligation. The Panels ignored the domestic rationales for the challenged legislation,[79] they considered the various parts of the tests cumulatively (which meant that the interests of third parties were not reached),[80] and they largely refused to interpret terms like 'normal', 'legitimate', 'prejudice', and 'unreasonable'

---

[76] TRIPS arts. 9 (copyrights), 17 (trademarks), 26.2 (industrial designs), and 30 (patents). The patent provisions of the Agreement also permit exclusions from protection for certain important public purposes, arts. 27.2 and 27.3. Article 31 gives states a modicum of authority to offer compulsory licenses.

[77] The trademark provision is only a two-part test because it does not consider exploitation of the work. There are differences in wording among the three provisions.

[78] *Canada – Patent Protection of Pharmaceutical Products*, supra note 33.

[79] For example, the copyright exception test, like the Berne Convention, uses the term 'special'. That could have been used to examine the justification for the measure; instead it was taken to mean 'clearly defined', *US – 110(5)*, ¶¶ 6.107–6.110. On options for examining the justifications, see Graeme B. Dinwoodie, 'The Development and Incorporation of International Norms in the Formation of Copyright Law', 62 *Ohio State L.J.* 733, 751 n. 73 (2001); Dinwoodie and Dreyfuss, 'Dynamics', supra note 17.

[80] See, for example, id., at ¶ 7.20; *Canada – Pharmaceuticals*, at ¶ 7.21.

normatively.[81] Instead, adjudicators did little more than mechanically count the number of rights within the bundle affected by the challenged provision, or the number of situations where the exception was applicable. Every right received equal weight, no matter how small the impact on the right holders' market.[82] Markets the right holder had never utilized were counted equivalently with those that it had. Economic effects were regarded as paramount and estimates of loss were extremely generous.[83] At the end of the day, Canada and the United States were not permitted to make allowances for user interests.

What appears to have happened is that the Panels relied too heavily on the provenance of these tests. All are based on a three-part exceptions test found in article 9(2) of the Berne Convention,[84] and the Panels may have assumed that since the tests derived from a WIPO instrument, they would automatically balance user and producer interests appropriately. Apparently, the Panels did not appreciate how radically the context changed when these provisions were adapted for TRIPS. The Berne Convention test was formulated to protect only the *reproduction* right. Since for most works, copyright holders make the bulk of their profits through control over reproduction, it is not surprising that Berne might be read to impose firm limits on interferences with the exploitation of that

---

[81] See, for example, Jane C. Ginsburg, 'Toward Supranational Copyright Law? The WTO Panel Decision and the "Three Step Test" for Copyright Exemptions', 187 *Revue Internationale du Droit d'Auteur* 17 (2001). To be sure, the *Canada – Pharmaceuticals* Panel considered the practises of other states to determine the patent holder's legitimate interests; it was not persuaded that they demonstrated a consensus position, ¶¶ 7.78–7.82.

[82] To be sure, the *Canada – Pharmaceuticals* Panel rejected the idea of simply counting rights, ¶ 7.32. But it refused to consider whether some rights are more important than others, ¶ 7.33, and in fact did appear to do no more than count rights, ¶ 7.34.

[83] For example, the *US – 110(5)* Panel found that EC copyright holders could lose as much as $53.65 million per year; later, an arbitrator found the amount was only €1,219,900 per year (this at a time when a dollar and a euro were close to parity), *Recourse to Arbitration under Article 25 of the DSU, Award of the Arbitrators, United States – Section 110(5) of the US Copyright Act*, 5.1, WT/DS160/ARB25/1 (November 11, 2001).

[84] Article 9(2) of the Berne Convention provides:

> It shall be a matter for legislation in the countries of the Union to permit the reproduction of such works in certain special cases, provided that such reproduction does not conflict with a normal exploitation of the work and does not unreasonably prejudice the legitimate interests of the author.

See Gervais, supra note 10, at 237, 332, and 380.

right.[85] The Panels failed to consider the ramification of transposing the measure into TRIPS, where it applies to all user activities, all markets, and to all of the principal intellectual property regimes. The language of Berne 9(2) was altered and tailored to each regime; the Panels might have accorded some significance to those changes.

The opportunity to consider this issue actually arose in the *US – 110(5)* case, where the EC asked the Panel to consider how TRIPS article 13, the copyright test, applied to rights – like the rebroadcast right – which were not within the ambit of Berne's exceptions test.[86] Consistent with the desire to reflect prior intellectual property conventions discussed above, the Panel rather easily concluded that the 'TRIPS Agreement need not lead to different standards from those applicable under the Berne Convention'.[87] However, in arriving at that conclusion, it considered only half the question. As framed by the EC, the issue was whether TRIPS should be read to *narrow* the ambit of exceptions. The Panel never seriously addressed the question whether TRIPS had *adapted* the exceptions to deal with new situations. Had the Panel done so, it might well have reached a different conclusion. After all, it claimed that it was reconciling article 13 with the minor exceptions doctrine.[88] Yet, the minor exceptions that it identified – use of music by religious, military, and educational institutions[89] – were surely uses the right holders could have otherwise exploited. Had the Panel done the thought experiment of applying its interpretation of article 13 to these uses, it might have seen the fallacy in its analysis and realized that when individual rights are considered in isolation, without giving any thought to their significance within the copyright 'bundle' or to the impact of a use on the *total* potential revenue of the right holder, members are strait-jacketed. Rather than grandfathering in existing practices, the Panel might have understood the need to develop normative positions on what constitutes normal exploitation, unreasonable prejudice, and legitimate expectations.[90] Instead, the Panel decision was a rather bare vindication of

---

[85] Sam Ricketson and Jane C. Ginsburg, *International Copyright and Neighbouring Rights: The Berne Convention and Beyond*, (2nd edition), ¶ 11,01 Oxford: Oxford University Press, 2006.

[86] *US – 110(5)*, ¶ pp.6.72–6.78.

[87] Id., ¶ 6.81.

[88] Id., ¶ 6.90.

[89] Id., ¶ 6.36 (mentioning religious ceremonies, military bands and the needs of child and adult education).

[90] The *Canada – Pharmaceuticals* case is somewhat similar. The Panel in that case also canvassed the laws of other countries. Although it held that 'the subsequent acts by individual countries did not constitute "practice in the application of the treaty which establishes the agreement of the parties regarding its

intellectual property rights as nothing more than commodities to be traded. The Panel *looked* to antecedent intellectual property sources, but it did not *understand* the richer complexity of those intellectual property norms.

2.4 Coping with TRIPS standards expressly different from the WIPO conventions

Although the previous sections demonstrated that relying on WIPO instruments will often serve as a way to preserve intellectual property values, more intractable problems arise in situations in which TRIPS expressly adds to the requirements of the WIPO agreements. This is especially true with regard to patents, where the Paris Convention did little more than facilitate seriatim patent applications and establish limits on certain types of compulsory licenses.[91] In contrast, the TRIPS Agreement requires protection of inventive developments in all fields of technology, sets a minimum term of protection and minimum rights, and further restricts compulsory licensing.[92] Even for copyright and trademarks, TRIPS goes beyond the WIPO instruments. For trademarks, the subject matter of protection is elucidated and the scope of trademark rights is expanded;[93] the provisions on copyright and related rights mandate new protection for computer programs and rentals, phonograms, and performances.[94] Furthermore, TRIPS establishes obligations regarding other forms of intellectual property, including geographic indications,[95] industrial designs,[96] and trade secrets.[97] In all these areas, TRIPS also adds norms of enforcement.[98]

The Appellate Body's decision in the *Canada – Patent Term* case illustrates what can occur when a dispute concerns one of these new areas, where by definition there is no ready WIPO source to which a panel can refer.[99] In that case, the United States claimed that Canada had violated article 33 of the TRIPS Agreement by failing to extend the terms of

---

interpretation" within the meaning of Article 31.3(b) of the Vienna Convention', ¶ 7.47, it did appear to consider them when determining the legitimate interests of right holders, ¶ pp. 7.78–7.79.

91 Paris Convention, arts. 2, 4, and 5.

92 TRIPS Agreement, arts. 27–31.

93 Id., arts. 15–21.

94 Id., arts. 10–14.

95 Id., arts. 22–4.

96 Id., arts. 25–6.

97 Id., art. 39.

98 Id., arts. 41–61.

99 *Canada – Term of Patent Protection*, WT/DS170/AB/R (Appellate Body, 2000) [hereinafter *Canada – Patent Term*].

patents that had issued before the Agreement had entered into force, but which continued to subsist afterwards. Canada claimed that article 70, which required the protection of existing subject matter, was not relevant to 'acts' that transpired before the Agreement applied – including the 'act' of awarding a patent for a specific term of years.

Had the issue of retroactivity arisen in a WIPO negotiation, the problem might have been conceptualized as balancing accessibility interests against the claims of those holding pending patents. Since these right holders had sunk all their investments under the prior regime, in reliance on the rewards that would be generated during an (arguably) shorter time period, the negotiators might well have decided not to require the retroactive extension of patent terms.[100] But the Paris Convention did not deal with patent duration. Accordingly, its negotiators never had occasion to consider the retroactivity issue.[101] The Appellate Body was thus left with nothing but definitions in the intellectual property component of a trade agreement. It duly consulted the Paris Convention as well as a WIPO treatise[102] to determine the meaning of 'acts'. But without apparently weighing the interests involved, it concluded that the length of the term was a 'right' and not the result of the 'act' of granting a patent; it thus held the TRIPS term to apply retroactively.[103] The adjudicators were equally undeferential to Canada's own weighing of the interests: the Panel rejected Canada's argument that its term (17 years from issuance, as opposed to TRIPS' 20 years from filing) was effectively compliant with TRIPS.[104] Canada was thus left with no flexibility to protect the public from windfall gains by right holders.[105]

---

[100] Had the negotiators focused on the type of patents mainly at issue in *Canada – Patent Term*, that is an especially likely result as the patents that were of particular concern covered pharmaceuticals; see Canada Department of Foreign Affairs and International Trade, Backgrounder, WTO Appellate Body Report on US Challenge of Canada's Patent Term, http://w01.international.gc.ca/MinPub/PublicationContentOnly.asp?publication_id=378064&Language=E&MODE=CONTENTONLY&Local=False.

[101] Significantly, the Berne Convention does contain a provision on the retroactivity issue; see art. 18: it is a complex provision, which makes retroactivity turn on whether the work remains protected in its country of origin.

[102] *Introduction to Intellectual Property, Theory and Practice* (Kluwer Law International Ltd., 1997), *Canada – Patent Term*, ¶ 54 n. 40.

[103] Id., ¶¶ 56–60.

[104] Id., at ¶¶ 80–101.

[105] Article 28 of the Vienna Convention, which sets out a rule of non-retroactivity with respect to acts and facts predating a treaty, might have also furnished the Appellate Body with a vehicle for giving Canada the flexibility to strike this balance on its own. However, the adjudicators instead used art. 28 to reject

2.5 Using Post-TRIPS WIPO developments to inform TRIPS

There is yet another reason why the full range of relevant intellectual property values cannot be integrated into TRIPS merely through the incorporation of the WIPO instruments: as we noted at the outset, social, economic and technological situations change. The WIPO conventions that we have discussed thus far were adopted prior to the conclusion of TRIPS. But new rights are needed to respond to evolving technological conditions (such as the delocalization of digitized works), and new exceptions are necessary to accommodate new practices (such as open innovation). Furthermore, as developing nations begin to cope with intellectual property protection, they are finding approaches to interest-balancing that are different from the methods traditionally utilized by the developed world.[106] While TRIPS leaves members free to increase the level of their own domestic protection, many of these developments require a collective response. Under current conditions, these responses are taking place outside the WTO, including in WIPO. This raises the question whether new (or newly modified) WIPO instruments should also be factored into the interpretation of the TRIPS Agreement.

To many commentators, the answer is clearly no. Article 31 of the Vienna Convention permits the use of a treaty or rule of international law to interpret another agreement, but only when all of the parties have agreed to both measures or accept that there is an interpretive relationship between them. Since the parties to the WTO are not all signatories of the WIPO instruments, strict application of the Vienna Convention would suggest that evolution in WIPO cannot affect TRIPS; that the only way to change the rights and obligations in TRIPS is to renegotiate it.[107]

But another response is conceivable. While membership in the WIPO agreements and the WTO are not coextensive, there are very few countries that do not belong to both. For example, most of the states that are in WIPO but not the WTO are absent for purely political reasons.[108]

Canada's position, by reasoning that a rule that refers to a 'situation which ceased to exist' could not apply to subsisting patents. *Canada – Patent Term*, ¶¶ 72–9.

[106] Indian patent law is a good example; see, for example, India Patents Act, No. 39 of 1970, § 3(d) (Universal 2005) (raising inventive step); Shamnad Basheer, "Policy Style" Reasoning at the Indian Patent Office', [2005] *IPQ* 309.

[107] Pauwelyn, supra note 37, at 265. The Panel in the *Canada – Pharmaceuticals* case was similarly reluctant to consider subsequent practices by many of the parties to inform the meaning of TRIPS; see text at note 131, infra.

[108] The only WTO members that are not officially in WIPO are the EC, whose members joined WIPO individually; Hong Kong, Macao, and Taiwan, where there are political obstacles, and the Solomon Islands. Vanuatu has observer status at the WTO and is not a member of WIPO.

Furthermore, because the WIPO agreements constitute the backbone of TRIPS, the relationship between these instruments was evident to all WTO members. Neil Netanel, who addressed this question in the copyright context, thus concluded that, at least with respect to copyright agreements negotiated almost contemporaneously with TRIPS, new developments should be taken into account:

> TRIPS drafters must have been well aware [that] the Berne Convention is a dynamic instrument . . . and [that] the rapid development of copyright-related technology require[s] an ongoing process of interpretation and reinterpretation within the framework that Berne sets forth.[109]

Under Netanel's approach, WIPO's elucidations of the terms of the instruments it administers would be immediately incorporated into TRIPS, either because WTO members should be regarded as having agreed to an evolving interpretation of the Agreement or because each new interpretation represents a 'subsequent agreement between the parties' within article 31(3)(a) of the Vienna Convention.

At least one Panel seems to have agreed. In the *US – 110(5)* case, the United States argued that the WIPO Copyright Treaty (WCT), which was largely designed to deal with the special problem of protecting works in a digital era, along with the statements made during the negotiation of the WCT, shed meaning on the exceptions test in the TRIPS Agreement.[110] Although the Panel was careful to note that the WCT (which, at the time, had very few signatories) did not constitute a subsequent agreement with the meaning of article 31(3), 'the wording of the WCT, and in particular of the Agreed Statement thereto, nonetheless supports, as far as the Berne Convention is concerned, that the Berne Union members are permitted to provide minor exceptions to the rights provided under Articles 11 and 11*bis*. . .'.[111] The Panel went on to say that since the WCT was unanimously concluded at a diplomatic conference attended by 127 countries, most of which also participated in TRIPS negotiations, 'it is relevant to seek contextual guidance . . . in the WCT. . .'.[112]

3. Interpretive approaches and relevant sources

The impasse in WTO lawmaking, coupled with the relatively few intellectual property cases adjudicated by the DSB – and in particular, by the

---

109 Netanel, supra note 41, at 471–2.
110 *US – 110(5)*, ¶ 6.67.
111 Id., ¶ 6.69.
112 Id., ¶ 6.70.

Appellate Body – present both a problem and an opportunity. Until WTO lawmaking becomes more robust, nations must cope with the uncertainty of not knowing whether their laws comply with their international obligations. In turn, they must deal with a distorted political economy.[113] Because TRIPS is a minimum standards regime, those interested in strong intellectual property protection can cite TRIPS in support of their legislative agendas and can use TRIPS to block moves intended to safeguard the public interest. At the same time, however, the fluidity of the current regime makes this a good time to ponder the interpretive approaches that are best able to maintain a productive creative environment in the face of changing needs. As we suggested in Section 2, generous and informed use of the intellectual property expertise at WIPO might helpfully be part of the solution. But encouraging panels to put TRIPS in its historical (Berne/Paris-derived) context will not be enough in and of itself, as existing panel reports show. Extant WIPO conventions are but one source of guidance for panels. As the WTO thinks through the problem of interpreting the Agreement in new contexts and incorporating intellectual property values into a trade framework, it will hopefully address the following issues.

3.1 The role of TRIPS' principles and objectives in interpretation

One problem that emerges clearly from studying the existing case law is that a strategy for balancing interests and responding to change that relies solely on the bare text of the incorporated WIPO conventions is likely to fail. Despite the valiant efforts of the Appellate Body in *Havana Club* (and in other cases as well[114]) to preserve flexibility for member states by relying on WIPO conventions for guidance, there are too many inconsistencies, differences, and transpositional errors for this strategy to fully succeed.

Significantly, however, TRIPS furnishes its own guidance, quite apart from the multi-part exceptions tests discussed earlier. The Objectives of the TRIPS Agreement are stated in article 7 as the use of intellectual property rights to promote innovation 'to the mutual advantage of producers and users' in a manner 'conducive to social and economic welfare'. Furthermore, article 8 (Principles) permits members to adopt measures that protect public heath and promote sectors of vital interest to their economies and to technological development (so long as they are

---

[113] For example, Indian law aimed at preventing evergreening has been heavily criticized on TRIPS-compatibility grounds; see Tushar Dhara, 'India Unplugged: Thoughts on the Gleevac Controversy', http://arthedains.com/indiaunplugged/2008/03/14/87/ (March 14, 2008).

[114] See note 57, supra, discussing *India – Pharmaceuticals*. Panels have been similarly conciliatory, as the *China – Enforcement* case demonstrates, id.

consistent with the Agreement). So far, these provisions have not played an important interpretive role. Indeed, the *Canada – Pharmaceuticals* Panel essentially wrote them off, rejecting the claim that they should be used to determine whether Canada's policies on behalf of generic competition fall within the patents exception provision. While the Panel agreed that the sentiments expressed in the Objectives and Principles had to be 'borne in mind', it also warned against using these provisions to alter the deal struck in the Uruguay Round.[115]

That reluctance to impose a purposive gloss must change. The Doha Declaration on the TRIPS Agreement and Public Health specifically stated that 'each provision of the TRIPS Agreement shall be read in the light of the object and purpose of the Agreement as expressed, in particular, in its objectives and principles'.[116] The status of the Declaration is not entirely clear.[117] What is clear, however, is that the commitments expressed in the Objectives and Principles would go a long way toward providing the normative dimension to the exceptions test that was absent in both the *US – 110(5)* and the *Canada – Pharmaceuticals* cases.[118] A perspective informed by these provisions would be similarly useful in considering other issues, such as the structural relations between the various parts of the Agreement (an issue which arose, with unsatisfying results, in *Canada – Pharmaceuticals*[119]), and the role that should be played by a state's stated rationale for enacting a challenged action.[120]

3.2 TRIPS as a trade agreement

In addition to a more nuanced intellectual property perspective, and a more purposive reading of the TRIPS agreement, adjudicators could

---

[115] *Canada – Pharmaceutical Products,* ¶ 7.26; see also *India – Patent Protection for Pharmaceutical and Agricultural Chemical Products*, WT/DS50/AB/R (December 19, 1997).

[116] Declaration on the TRIPS Agreement and Public Health, adopted on 14 November 2001, WT/MIN(01)DEC/2, at http://www.wto.org/english/thewto_e/minist_e/min01_e/mindecl_trips_e.htm (November 20, 2001).

[117] See Robert Howse, 'Mainstreaming the Right to Development into International Trade Law and Policy at the World Trade Organization', E/CN/4Sub.2/2004/27 (June 9, 2004), available at http://documents-dds-ny.un.org/doc/UNDOC/GEN/G04/145/22/pdf/G0414522.pdf?OpenElement, at ¶ 37; Pauwelyn, supra note 37, at 47.

[118] Gervais, supra note 10, at 206–07.

[119] In that case, the Panel subjected Canada's research exemption, which had been held valid under the three-part exceptions test, to a separate analysis under art. 27.1, which requires technological neutrality, ¶ 6.69.

[120] See Dinwoodie, supra note 79, at 751.

also better preserve the balance needed in intellectual property law by viewing the TRIPS Agreement with its trade-related character consciously in mind. Currently adjudicators tend to look mainly at how states treat intellectual property within their borders, largely ignoring effects on international trade. Admittedly, the drafters of TRIPS were heavily focused on local infringement. Negotiations over intellectual property moved to the WTO because WIPO was viewed as hostile to raising domestic levels of intellectual property protection and because the WTO provided a way to pay off developing countries for accepting stronger obligations.[121] Nonetheless, the fact remains that the Agreement is denominated *Trade Related* Aspects of Intellectual Property. Since dispute resolution is only applicable to intellectual property by virtue of its nexus to trade, the DSB could enable the states to better tailor their intellectual property laws to local interests if it focused its attention on the extent to which challenged actions specifically encumber or distort trade.[122]

For example, in *China – Enforcement,* on the issue of whether China was taking strong enough action to remove infringing goods from the channels of commerce, the Panel used a single reference in article 51 (on border measures) to claim that members' obligations extend only to preventing the *importation* of infringing goods.[123] Even though other provisions in the Agreement explicitly refer to *exportation*,[124] and the Decision of the General Council implementing the Doha Declaration paid particular attention to exports,[125] the *China – Enforcement* Panel found that states have no duty to prevent their territories from becoming information havens – hubs for international infringement operations. This is not surprising in light of the WTO's origins, which focused on barriers to the *entry* of goods into members' markets. However, those concerned with trade in intellectual property need to be concerned about flows in both directions.

A contrast between the *US – 110(5)* case and the stockpiling portion of *Canada – Pharmaceuticals* provides a further illustration of how requiring

---

[121] S.K. Sell, *Private Power, Public Law: The Globalization of Intellectual Property Rights*, Cambridge: Cambridge University Press, 2003.

[122] Frankel, supra note 48.

[123] *China – Enforcement*, ¶ 7.224.

[124] See, for example, TRIPS arts. 51 (allowing members to control goods destined for exportation) and 59 (creating a duty to 'not allow the re-exportation of infringing goods').

[125] Decision of the General Council on Implementation of paragraph 6 of the Doha Declaration on the TRIPS Agreement and public health, WT/L/540 and Corr.1 ¶ 4 (30 August 2003), available at http://www.wto.org/english/tratop_e/trips_e/implem_para6_e.htm.

a trade nexus might affect the extent to which the TRIPS Agreement circumscribes national intellectual property lawmaking. Although the complainant won each of the cases, the challenged measures were factually different. The United States had been permitting rebroadcasts of music in small establishments *within the United States.* Since there was no possibility of re-rebroadcast abroad, the potential loss of trade was extremely limited. It consisted only of the (somewhat tenuous) claim that without the exemption, the establishments in question would have paid licensing fees for the relevant rebroadcasts. In contrast, Canada was apparently permitting generic drug companies to stockpile drugs for sale *around the world*; thus, Canada's laws really affected trade in goods, not just the distribution of global wealth.

Perhaps the cases should have come out as they did, but had the adjudicators mandated that closer attention be paid to impacts on world trade, they would have left states with more room to maneuver. In particular, emerging economies would benefit from such an approach. They could provide their populations with easier access to educational materials and training opportunities by raising the inventive step, taking novel approaches to the scope of intellectual property rights, or adopting new defenses to infringement. Because their manufacturing capacities are modest, the activities thus permitted would be unlikely to affect world trade in a meaningful way.[126] Accordingly, they might not be regarded as TRIPS violations, even if substantially similar actions by developed countries would be.[127]

To put this another way, instead of using trade as a lens through which to filter the scope of international obligations imposed by the eponymous TRIPS Agreement, the Appellate Body and the panels have largely subsumed the international intellectual property system as a whole within the trade apparatus. Thus, as noted above, the treatment by panels of discrepancies between TRIPS and WIPO conventions suggests that it is well understood that intellectual property was incorporated into the WTO system in order to take advantage of the latter's enforcement machinery.

---

[126] Cf. *Recourse to Arbitration under Article 25 of the DSU, Award of the Arbitrators, United States – Section 110(5) of the US Copyright Act*, WT/DS160/ARB25/1 (November 11, 2001) (suggesting that *harm* may vary according to the historical state of the market); see also Richard Owens, 'TRIPS and the Fairness in Music Arbitration: The Repercussions', 25 *Eur. Intell. Prop. Rev.* 49 (2003) (criticizing this reading).

[127] Rochelle C. Dreyfuss, '*Fostering Dynamic Innovation, Development and Trade: Intellectual Property as a Case Study in Global Administrative Law*', Capetown: Dreyfuss, supra note 6 forthcoming.

But this was a purely strategic move. For reasons we have discussed elsewhere, the coupling of intellectual and property and trade is an uneasy one. The relationship is undertheorized in the literature (partly because intellectual property was treated exceptionally under Article XX(d) of the old GATT regime) and neither the Appellate Body nor TRIP panels have fully explored the interaction.

3.3 Relying on multiple sources

Our short survey of the TRIPS cases reveals that the panels and Appellate Body have on occasion taken an eclectic approach to the materials they use to interpret the TRIPS Agreement. For example, the adjudicators in *Havana Club* and the *US – 110(5)* cases consulted the 1883 Final Protocol to the Paris Convention, materials from the 1911 Paris Revision Conference, the General Report and materials of the diplomatic conferences leading to the inclusion of broadcast rights in the Berne Convention, as well as learned treatises interpreting the conventions.[128] To be sure, some reports place undue reliance on the dictionary; and references to WIPO materials without proper regard for history and context can undermine the intellectual property values at stake. Unfamiliar materials must be handled with care. However, we do not wish to discourage openness on the part of the dispute settlement body to a wide variety of sources. In particular, under the Vienna Convention, practices of states might be relevant to the meaning of TRIPS.[129] So too might other bilateral and multilateral international agreements. WTO panels should view these sources of law broadly to ensure the most intellectual property-sensitive reading of the TRIPS Agreement. And they should be willing to innovate procedurally to optimize their awareness and appreciation of these broader materials; here again WIPO has an important role to play.

3.3.1. National Practices

Article 31(3)(b) of the Vienna Convention permits interpretation to be shaped by subsequent practises by the parties that reflect on the agreement's meaning. Too rigid a dichotomy between post-WIPO and post-TRIPS events could, however, potentially complicate the use of state practice. Panels have readily accepted that state practises initiated prior to the adoption of the TRIPS Agreement shed direct light on how WIPO members viewed their Berne and Paris obligations. For example, the *US – 110(5)* Panel made considerable use of exceptions found in different

---

[128] See text at notes 50–51, 67, and 102, supra.

[129] See Vienna Convention on the Law of Treaties, art. 31.3.

national laws and implicitly authorized by the 'minor exceptions' doctrine that it held to be part of the Berne *acquis*.[130] But events post-TRIPS might also speak to a country's understanding of either its TRIPS obligations or underlying Paris/Berne obligations. Nonetheless, in *Canada – Pharmaceuticals,* the Panel was quite ambivalent about the use of state practises: indeed, the Panel did appear to consider them in determining the legitimate expectations of rights holders.[131]

However, in *EC – GI*, the Panel's decision on whether the protection the EC offered geographic indications was unduly interfering with trademarks was importantly informed by the ways in which the EC had dealt with potential interferences in the recent past, and by the paucity of confusing simultaneous registrations.[132] Such regard might not, as a formal matter, satisfy the definition of state practise within the meaning of the Vienna Convention.[133] But such flexibility toward the relevance of state practises will be useful in ensuring that the context of how international norms operate locally is fully taken into account by panels. Among other things, this validates the freedom expressed in article 1.1 to implement international obligations in ways appropriate to the national regime in question. Just as the *US – 110(5)* Panel resisted a dogmatic approach to the relevance of post-TRIPS developments as subsequent agreements within the meaning of the Vienna Convention, so too panels should be willing to look to a range of national practises (both before and after the TRIPS Agreement) to inform a coherent understanding of the international intellectual property regime as a whole.

As helpful as these national sources are, their use without regard to full historical context is not without problems. First, there is no reason to believe that the parties to the Paris and Berne Convention fully utilized the flexibilities available to them under those instruments. Indeed, the opposite is clearly true: developed countries have long had trademark and

---

[130] See text at notes 64–7.

[131] See text at note 68, supra. However, the *Canada – Pharmaceuticals* Panel expressed skepticism about relying on the laws of individual countries.

[132] *EC – GI*, ¶¶ 7.573 (on the Budvar issue), 7.667–7.679 (on how the EC handled applications) and 7.674 (on instances of potential confusion). In its analysis of the trademarks exception test, the *EC–GI* Panel also drew significant support from the example of an acceptable practise that was included in the text of the provision. Id., ¶ 7.655, citing the example of fair use of descriptive terms, which is found in TRIPS art. 17. When TRIPS lawmaking resumes, drafters should keep in mind how useful it is to provide adjudicators with such examples.

[133] Elsewhere in its report, the Panel also did look at implemented laws operating in other countries, which more formally satisfies the understanding of state practise in the Vienna Convention. See *EC–GI*, at ¶ 7.642.

patent laws that vastly exceed the requirements of the Paris Convention. Accordingly, while laws that predated TRIPS may identify practises that are allowable, no inference can be made about whether other measures should also be considered permissible.[134] The same is true of learned treatises: they may shed light on practises that states were using or had contemplated, but omissions do not constitute evidence that a practise is inconsistent with WIPO obligations.

Second, care must be taken lest national norms adopted in a few countries are quickly consolidated at the international level, precluding reversal of any national experiments deemed unsuccessful. In recent years, the United States (and to some extent, other developed countries) have embarked on a series of bilateral trade agreements, often with developing countries, which are intended to raise the level of intellectual property protection above the requirements of the TRIPS Agreement. Many fall on the heels of WIPO efforts to expand the Paris or Berne Conventions to cover new regimes, and they appear to be intended to convert WIPO's 'soft law' into genuine obligations.[135] In effect, however, these agreements are pay-offs: they give one country greater access to the other's markets in exchange for raising the level of protection. While many of them may be in the contracting parties' mutual trading interests, they should not be viewed as evidence of how the WIPO instruments or the TRIPS Agreement should be interpreted. Nations that have not received the quid pro quo should not be required to nonetheless accord higher levels of protection to intellectual products.[136]

Third, it is important to ensure that grandfathering – the practise of relying on pre-TRIPS practises and materials – does not end up privileging developed countries, which had evolved a considerable repertoire of practises under the Paris and Berne Conventions, over developing countries that are so new to intellectual property that they have never considered how to adjust their implementing legislation to their national interest. This problem of privileging the approaches of the developed world could be ameliorated simply by incorporating this historical understanding into

---

[134] This is also important when panels look to commercial practises in particular states. See Dinwoodie, supra note 105, at 758.

[135] Anselm Kamperman Sanders, 'Intellectual Property, Free Trade Agreements And Economic Development', 23 *Ga. St. U. L. Rev.* 893 (2007); Peter K. Yu, 'TRIPS and its Discontents', 10 *Marq. Intell. Prop. L. Rev.* 369 (2006).

[136] See Susy Frankel, 'The Legitimacy and Purposes of FTAs', in Ross P. Buckley, Vai lo Lo and Lawrence Boulle (eds), *Challenges to Multilateral Trade: The Impact of Bilateral, Preferential and Regional Agreements*, Kluwer Law International BV, 2008, pp. 185, 186–7.

any analysis of state practise, or adapting the role of state practise as an interpretative device to require consensus across countries of different development.[137]

It is important to be sensitive to post-TRIPS practises for positive reasons too. As developing countries attempt to accommodate their contemporary national interests to TRIPS' mandate, new solutions might be developed. For example, India has pioneered a new interpretation of the inventiveness requirement.[138] Should similar economies adopt the same strategy, the emerging consensus might be taken into account in interpreting the TRIPS' reference to the 'inventive step'.[139] Similarly, widespread adoption of rules like Germany's on the scope of gene patents[140] might be interpreted as a response to upstream patenting, rather than as an attempt to treat the biotechnology sector specially, in violation of the nondiscrimination proviso of the TRIPS Agreement.[141] The Panel in *US – 110(5)* appeared alert to the danger of viewing international norms statically, and specifically noted that minor exceptions were not '"frozen" in 1967', when broadcasting rights were added to the Berne Convention.[142] Being willing to consider national practises across time allows dispute settlement panels to decide cases based on the most refined conceptualization of available policy levers and in ways relevant to new social and technological developments.

3.3.2. Subsequent WIPO material

The most straightforward way to keep TRIPS current with changes in the innovation landscape is to take post-TRIPS developments in international intellectual property lawmaking into account in interpreting the Agreement. Article 31(3)(a) of the Vienna Convention allows resort to subsequent agreements among all of the parties and as we saw, the *US – 110(5)* Panel relied on the WCT to interpret the copyright exceptions test of the TRIPS Agreement.[143] It remains to be seen whether the Appellate Body will agree to this approach and if it does, how much further it

---

137 Cf. Laurence R. Helfer, 'Adjudicating Copyright Claims under the TRIPS Agreement: The Case for a European Human Rights Analogy', 39 *Harv. Int'l L.J.* 357, 431 (1998).

138 India Patents Act, No. 39 of 1970, § 3(d) (Universal 2005); TRIPS art. 27.1.

139 TRIPS art. 27.1.

140 Id; German Patent Statute, PatG § 1a (4).

141 TRIPS, art. 27.1.

142 *US – 110(5)*, at ¶ 6.59.

143 See text at notes 110–112, supra.

would take it.[144] The *US – 110(5)* Panel was careful to note that the WCT was concluded only a year after TRIPS;[145] negotiators could not have anticipated agreements made much later. The WCT is also a completed treaty (although it had not entered into force at the time the Panel consulted it). More informal WIPO actions, such as the Reports of Standing Committees, Model Laws, or the advice given by WIPO technical advisors to WTO members, present a very different situation. Finally, the WCT is an easy case because it deals with the same type of works that are covered by TRIPS and it supplements (increases) the level of intellectual property protection. Far more tenuous would be the incorporation of instruments that recognize rights in new kinds of subject matter – databases, folklore, genetic endowments, or traditional knowledge – or agreements (such as the potential findings of the WIPO Development Agenda) that mandate a level of protection below that which TRIPS explicitly requires.[146]

Nonetheless, a strong case can be made for consulting many of these materials.

Certainly, contemporaneity with TRIPS should not be dispositive. Indeed, the more distant from TRIPS, the more likely the measure will reflect members' efforts to cope with new developments in TRIPS-consistent ways. If one understands the interpretive project as avoiding the obsolescence of the system of international intellectual property rather than an historical inquiry designed to divine what they thought appropriate in 1994, this argument is even stronger.[147] While many WIPO measures are not formal agreements, neither was the WCT at the time it was cited in

---

144 Interestingly, in the *Havana Club* case, the Appellate Body was apparently willing to consider a somewhat subsequent development, namely the letter that WIPO wrote in response to the questions put to it by the Panel; see text at note 62, supra.

145 *US – 110(5),* at ¶ 6.70.

146 The Singapore Treaty on the Law of Trademarks, March 27, 2006, S. Treaty Doc. No. 110–2, available at http://www.wipo.int/export/sites/www/treaties/en/ip/singapore/pdf/singapore_treaty.pdf, which updates WIPO's Trademark Law Treaty, is another example of a relatively easy case. The treaty was the product of extensive working sessions by the WIPO Standing Committee on the Law of Trademarks, Geographical Indications and Industrial Designs (SCT). Among other things, it settles the question whether three-dimensional marks are protectable; Rule 3(b)(4), which was a longstanding issue under art. 15.1 of the TRIPS Agreement; see, for example, *Philips Elec. BV v. Remington Consumer Prods*, [1998] RPC 283 (Ch. D. 1997) (UK).

147 Cf. Stephen Breyer, *Active Liberty*, Vintage Books, Random House, USA, 2005, p. 25, (noting that 'we the people' in the US Constitution did not mean 'we the people in 1787').

US – 110(5).[148] Even when WIPO instruments are not destined to become formally binding, they represent the work of experts in the field and are open to input from state delegations. As such, they are somewhat akin to the internationally developed standards that other WTO framework agreements expressly take into account.[149] These materials demonstrate how the terms in the TRIPS Agreement are construed in new contexts, and what interested parties see as appropriate ways to resolve novel issues.[150]

Of course, not every document issued by WIPO is subject to the kind of vetting that produces a balanced instrument and many are not the product of genuine consensus among the WIPO membership (let alone the WTO). These issues should, however, go to the weight these materials are given in the interpretive process.[151] The nature of the measure – be it report, model laws or resolution – should be taken into account, along with such matters as the degree of transparency accorded to interested parties (including civil society); the diversity of the input; the extent to which state delegations participated; how states, commentators, and practitioners reacted to the instrument; and how many WIPO members formally adopted the conclusions (and under what circumstances). Thus, for example, the *China – Enforcement* Panel, when determining what counted as 'commercial scale' for determining whether China had breached its enforcement obligations, consulted how that term was used by the WIPO Committee of Experts on Measures Against Counterfeiting and Piracy and the Draft Model Provisions for National Laws set out in a Memorandum by the International Bureau of WIPO.[152] However, it ultimately decided not to use the explanatory material accompanying these materials because there had been no agreement on them. According to the Panel, they should not be 'elevate[d] to the status of the proper interpretation of a treaty text that was negotiated in another forum and that was finally agreed'.[153] The Panel did not specify what sort of agreement it was looking for; were the WTO to consider the factors we have enumerated in determining how much deference to accord this material, there would be an interesting side benefit:

---

[148] *US – 110(5)*, ¶ 6.68. Admittedly, the parties to the dispute had both ratified it, but the Vienna Convention is usually interpreted as requiring agreement by the parties to the *agreement* at issue, not the dispute.

[149] See note 37, supra.

[150] Pauwelyn, supra note 37, at 257–63.

[151] See Graeme B. Dinwoodie, 'Copyright Lawmaking Authority: An (Inter) Nationalist Perspective on the Treaty Clause', 30 *Colum. J. L. & Arts* 355, 386–91 (2007) (suggesting similar considerations in weight to be given to international instruments in domestic constitutional analysis).

[152] *China–Enforcement*, ¶ 7.562.

[153] Id., ¶ 7.567.

WIPO negotiators would have a new incentive to make their deliberations more open and participatory.[154] Interpretive canons of this sort thus not only allow for updating of international norms, they can also alter the political economy and institutional economy in more structural ways.[155]

Skepticism is also appropriate for WIPO measures that recommend protection for new kinds of subject matter, such as databases, traditional knowledge, or publicity rights. While national intellectual property laws tend to be interpreted capaciously in order to encourage revolutionary advances,[156] the legitimacy of international instruments is strongly dependent on genuine agreement among the parties. There will be some close calls where the work of WIPO could be helpful in determining whether TRIPS covers the new subject matter; patent protection for software is an example.[157] But new kinds of intellectual property are likely to require new minimum standards. Thus, even when there is substantial activity in WIPO, extending coverage to new fields is best done through formal revision of TRIPS rather than through more ad hoc actions, such as adjudication.

So far, most WIPO developments tend to be in the direction of interpreting agreements to maximize intellectual property holders' rights. That should change with WIPO's new Development Agenda. If it does, then similar considerations should apply: in disputes over how TRIPS structures the balance between consumer and producer interests (or how much authority it leaves to member states), recommendations that are the product of expert views, that were subject to transparent procedures, are well supported by members, and clearly within the scope of WIPO's core expertise, ought to be consulted. Where there is evidence of disagreement

---

[154] An example is furnished by the World Intellectual Property Organization, Joint Recommendation Concerning Provisions on the Protection of Well-Known Marks, 833(E) (September 20–29, 1999), available at http://www.wipo.int/about-ip/en/development_iplaw/pub833.htm. One part of this report tackled the problem of defining a well-known mark. Because it achieved consensus, under this approach, it should be utilized by the DSU when interpreting the TRIPS Agreement. Another part, on dilution protection, was hotly contested; see Memorandum of the Director on the Joint Recommendation, A/34/13 ¶ 8 (August 4, 1999), available at http://www.wipo.int/meetings/en/doc_details.jsp?doc_id=1101. Accordingly, it should not be used to inform the meaning of the TRIPS Agreement.

[155] Cf. Dinwoodie and Dreyfuss, 'Dynamics', supra note 17 (discussing the effect a more flexible approach to national forms of implementation could have on the political structure of WTO member states).

[156] See, for example, *Diamond v. Chakrabarty*, 447 US 303 (1980).

[157] See Dreyfuss and Lowenfeld, supra note 9, at 284–97; Patent Cooperation Treaty, Rules 39.1 and 67.1, 28 UST. 7645, 1160 UNTS. 231 (1970).

or overreaching, or where the WIPO measure involves new types of rights, the WIPO instrument should not be used to construe TRIPS' meaning and move international intellectual property forward too quickly.

3.3.3 Other International Developments

Expanding the sources to which panels might refer is part of a larger effort to understand the international intellectual property system as a broad regime with a number of constituent parts. The international intellectual property system has always been highly textured. In the past, it required regard for national developments and a web of bilateral agreements.[158] The current system is even more complicated, for the many moving parts are now multinational in nature, compelling attention to more varied international sources. Thus, the WTO should also consider referencing the efforts of other international organizations. For example, the WTO ought to regard the work of the World Health Organization as highly relevant to deciding when state actions improving access to medicines are compatible with TRIPS. It should take the actions of the Convention on Biological Diversity into account on issues regarding rights in agricultural knowledge. Because intellectual property often raises human rights issues, the work of the UN Millennium Project and the Commission on Human Rights would likewise interject important principles into TRIPS decision-making. 'Mainstreaming'[159] these values into TRIPS will not only provide a normative dimension currently missing from trade law, it will also make the decisions of the WTO more acceptable to a broad array of constituents. This enriched perspective would help panels to engage in the normative analysis that they declare relevant to decision-making but seem unable (or unwilling) to do. And, to the extent that conformity with international norms should – as we believe – depend in part upon the relationship between a national law and its stated purpose, these sources should help panels to assess the policy justifications for different approaches.

3.3.4 Devices for Ensuring Input

Collectively, these arguments represent a call for deciding international intellectual property cases on the basis of a richer factual and normative record. How is this to be achieved within the WTO dispute settlement machinery? It appears that the Appellate Body approves of the practise, initiated by the *Havana Club* Panel, of asking the International Bureau of WIPO for relevant information on the negotiation history and

---

[158] See Ricketson and Ginsburg, supra note 85, at §§ 1.29–1.42.

[159] The term is Howse's, supra note 117.

subsequent developments.[160] This practise apparently follows one that the TRIPS negotiators used themselves; indeed, the document that the TRIPS Negotiating Group asked the International Bureau of WIPO to prepare was itself used in the *US – 110(5)* case.[161] As we saw, WIPO does not have a seat at the table in the meetings of the TRIPS Council; asking it to provide its views during dispute resolution interjects a measure of intellectual property sensibilities into the WTO lawmaking process.

It may, however, be possible to build on these practices in ways that are helpful in addressing a pervasive problem; how to maintain the currency of international intellectual property law. As we suggested above, consulting only sources about the Paris and Berne Conventions that existed at the end of the Uruguay Round does not provide a mechanism for adapting the TRIPS Agreement to new circumstances. One idea is to continue to ask for input from WIPO's International Bureau, but to broaden the request to include not only 'factual information' about pre-TRIPS practices,[162] but also its opinions on implementation options and how to handle new problems. The technical assistance that WIPO is currently providing to TRIPS members gives it a window on the problems confronting developing countries and a unique position from which to devise TRIPS-consistent solutions. Pursuant to TRIPS article 67, nations in the North are required to offer help to the countries of the South in implementing their laws; as previously noted, the WTO has an agreement with WIPO to assist in this process. While there are continuing suspicions about the nature of the help thus offered (including claims that the North is using this duty to impose on emerging economies laws more appropriate for the developed than the developing world), both WIPO and the WTO have embarked on Development Agendas. If the organizations are true to the spirit of article 67, the advice given should include information about the flexibilities in the Agreement, and the steps these countries could take to promote their domestic interests. The practices resulting from this collaboration ought then to be regarded as strong evidence of the meaning of the TRIPS Agreement.[163] (More radically, perhaps, WIPO could provide advice directly to adjudicators, playing a role not unlike the Advocate-General in the European Court of Justice.[164])

---

[160] See text at note 62.
[161] See text at note 69.
[162] See text at note 62, supra.
[163] Howse, supra note 117.
[164] See Kim Van der Borght, 'The Review of the WTO Understanding on Dispute Settlement: Some Reflections on the Current Debate', 14 *Am. U. Int'l L. Rev.* 1223, 1230–32 (1999).

Either of these ideas would, of course, confer on WIPO broader authority than currently exists. And despite recent movements to embrace the Development Agenda, many groups remain skeptical of investing too much power in WIPO. But it might be possible to lift traditional restraints on the form of WIPO involvement if other institutional checks are put in place to ensure balance. If there are concerns about whether WIPO adequately represents the collective views of its members, then the WTO could predicate its willingness to solicit WIPO's opinion on the transparency of WIPO's deliberative process.

Conclusion

Much ink has been spilled on how to interpret WTO agreements. However, as we and others have noted, TRIPS presents many special problems. Trade law is largely negative in nature (it sets limits on what countries can do). It is highly technical in effect and aims at producing a result – lowering trade barriers – that is, from a global perspective, regarded as an unmitigated benefit. In contrast, TRIPS imposes positive rights (it requires states to enact new law). Because these rights touch on critical spheres, such as health, safety, culture, and political life, the thrust of TRIPS – maximizing protection – is not always the optimal result. To make matters worse, TRIPS does not include robust protection for national interests. The 'general exceptions' clause that safeguards the impact of other parts of the WTO agreements on the welfare of member states does not appear to apply to TRIPS and multiple Panel decisions have eroded the value of the flexibilities that TRIPS expressly mentions.[165]

WIPO holds considerable potential for helping the WTO mitigate these concerns. It has long experience in intellectual property matters and in accommodating the various interests of the creative community and those who consume its products. By relying on WIPO's instruments and expertise, the WTO could incorporate intellectual property values into its lawmaking process. We are aware that some readers will find it odd that we recommend relying on WIPO as a source for a more balanced approach to intellectual property protection; that some will think it easier to amend TRIPS (for example by adding user rights[166]) than to put faith in

[165] General Agreement on Tariffs and Trade 1994 art. XX, April 15, 1994, WTO Agreement, supra note 2, 1867 UNTS 187, 33 ILM 1153 (1994) [hereinafter GATT]. See Ruse-Khan, supra note 34; Dinwoodie and Dreyfuss, 'Dynamics', supra note 17; Pauwelyn, supra note 37, 159–61.

[166] See P. Bernt Hugenholtz and Ruth L. Okediji, 'Conceiving an International Instrument on Limitations and Exceptions To Copyright, Final Report' (March 6, 2008), http://www.ivir.nl/publications/hugenholtz/limitations_exceptions_copyright.

an organization whose primary goal is not to balance interests, but rather to promote intellectual property rights.[167] While we share these concerns, we believe that WIPO brings to the table an intellectual property sensibility that the WTO currently lacks. WIPO's Development Agenda also suggests that its approach to intellectual property is changing in a manner conducive to a more sophisticated analysis of the role these rights play in the economy. Besides, with so many organizations working on issues that relate to intellectual property, the time has come to conceptualize their interaction. There is no better place to begin than with the relationship between WIPO and the WTO.

pdf; Annette Kur and Henning Grosse Ruse-Khan, 'Enough is Enough – The Notion of Binding Ceilings in Intellectual Property Protection', 9-01 Max Planck Papers on Intellectual Property, Competition & Tax Law Research, available at http://ssrn.com/abstrat =1326429; Graeme B. Dinwoodie, 'The International Intellectual Property Law System: New Actors, New Institutions, New Sources', 8 *Am. Soc'y Int'l L.* Proc. 213, 219 (2004); Rochelle C. Dreyfuss, 'TRIPS – Round II: Should Users Strike Back?', 71 *U. Chi, L. Rev.* 21 (2004).

[167] Ruth Okediji, in particular, has made a strong case for giving a hierarchically superior role to the WTO, based on the theory that it is too late for it to 'successfully diverst itself of its own institutional culture' as a promoter of strong intellectual property rights; 'WIPO-WTO Relations and the Future of Global Intellectual Property Norms' (2008), available at www.ssrn.com/abstract=1338902.

5 The objectives and principles of the TRIPS Agreement

*Peter K. Yu**

Introduction

The Agreement on Trade-related Aspects of Intellectual Property Rights (TRIPS Agreement) is one of the more controversial international intellectual property agreements that have entered into force. Its negotiations were highly contentious, and the perspectives of developed and less developed countries on the role of intellectual property protection and enforcement remain far apart.

In recent years, less developed countries – including both developing and least developed countries – have expressed their deep dissatisfaction with the way the TRIPS Agreement has been interpreted and implemented. They are also frustrated by the ongoing demands by developed countries for protections that are in excess of what they promised during the TRIPS negotiations – often through new bilateral and regional trade and investment agreements. As they claim, the Agreement as interpreted by their developed trading partners and the additional TRIPS-plus demands ignore their local needs, national interests, technological capabilities, institutional capacities, and public health conditions.[1] These concerns and frustrations eventually led to the establishment of a set of development agendas at the World Trade Organization (WTO), the World Intellectual Property Organization (WIPO), and other international fora.[2]

Although the TRIPS Agreement's one-size-fits-all – or, more precisely, super-size-fits-all – approach is highly problematic, the Agreement includes a number of flexibilities to facilitate development and to protect the public interest. To safeguard these flexibilities, Articles 7 and 8 provide explicit and important objectives and principles that play impor-

---

 This chapter was abridged and adapted from Yu, Peter K. (2009), 'The objectives and principles of the TRIPS agreement', *Houston Law Review*, **46**(4): 979.

[1] Yu, Peter K. (2007), 'The international enclosure movement', *Indiana Law Journal*, **82**(4): 827–907, 828.

[2] Yu, Peter K. (2009), 'A tale of two development agendas', *Ohio Northern University Law Review*, **35**(2): 465–573.

tant roles in the interpretation and implementation of the Agreement. This chapter explores the origins of these two provisions and the roles they can play in promoting the development goals of less developed countries.

The chapter begins by tracing the development of Articles 7 and 8 of the TRIPS Agreement. By recounting their historical origins and subsequent developments, it shows that, even though only a small amount of the treaty language proposed by less developed countries was included in the final text of the Agreement, the choice of such language in Articles 7 and 8 may provide less developed countries with important tools for restoring the balance of the international intellectual property system.

The chapter then examines the normative content of Articles 7 and 8 of the TRIPS Agreement. It highlights the interpretations made by WTO panels and the Appellate Body and the implications of the two declarations adopted during the Fourth WTO Ministerial Conference in Doha (Doha Ministerial). The chapter concludes by exploring the multiple roles Articles 7 and 8 can play in facilitating a more flexible interpretation and implementation of the TRIPS Agreement. It also explains how less developed countries can use these provisions to preserve the hard-earned bargains they won through the TRIPS negotiations.

Origins and development

The TRIPS negotiations

The negotiations of the TRIPS Agreement began with the Ministerial Conference of the General Agreement on Tariffs and Trade (GATT) in Punta del Este, Uruguay. Held in September 1986, the conference took place at a critical point in time when the negotiations between developed and less developed countries over the revision of the Paris Convention for the Protection of Industrial Property (Paris Convention) were deadlocked at WIPO.[3] During that ministerial conference, the GATT contracting parties set out their negotiating objectives for the new Uruguay Round, which included the establishment of a new multilateral intellectual property agreement.

In the beginning, many less developed countries naively believed they could use the text of the Punta del Este Declaration to 'limit the negotiations primarily on trade in counterfeit goods and other such trade-related

[3] Yu, Peter K. (2004), 'Currents and crosscurrents in the international intellectual property regime', *Loyola of Los Angeles Law Review*, **38**(1): 323–443, 357–8.

aspects'.[4] As these countries claimed, the GATT mandate did not allow for the discussion of substantive issues on intellectual property rights. Led by Brazil and India, these countries insisted that only WIPO had the institutional competence to discuss those issues. However, as Jayashree Watal, a former negotiator for India, pointed out, 'This was a misreading not only of the text but also of the writing on the wall. Clearly, the negotiations were aimed not only at clarifying GATT provisions but elaborating, "as appropriate", new rules and disciplines.'[5]

By the early 1990s, virtually all negotiating parties accepted as inevitable the inclusion of minimum standards for intellectual property protection and enforcement in the GATT framework.[6] Such a change of attitude was largely the result of the United States' aggressive strategies toward the hardliner opposition countries, its successful 'divide and conquer' tactics, the economic crises confronting many of these countries, and the successful lobbying of the European Communities, Japan, and the United States by global intellectual property industries.[7] By the time Canada proposed to create a new multilateral trade organization in October 1990, its proposal, along with the less developed countries' fears of being excluded from such an organization, 'effectively ended the debate on the earlier developing country position of WIPO as the appropriate forum for lodging the results of the TRIPS negotiations'.[8]

What remained in the negotiations were the details of these new standards and how these standards were to be incorporated into the new Agreement without adversely affecting the protections already put in place by the extant international intellectual property conventions. To expedite the negotiation process, and to bring the positions of developed and less developed countries closer to each other, the GATT Secretariat and Lars Anell, chairman of the TRIPS Negotiating Group, prepared what was commonly referred to as the Anell Draft. This draft was later formalized as the Chairman's

---

4 Watal, Jayashree (2001), *Intellectual Property Rights in the WTO and Developing Countries*, The Hague and Boston: Kluwer Law International, p. 21.

5 *Id.*

6 Yusuf, Abdulqawi A. (2008), 'TRIPS: Background, principles and general provisions', in Carlos M. Correa and Abdulqawi A. Yusuf (eds), *Intellectual Property and International Trade: The TRIPS Agreement*, 2nd edn, Alphen aan den Rijn: Kluwer Law International, pp. 3–21, 9.

7 Sell, Susan K. (2003), *Private Power, Public Law: The Globalization of Intellectual Property Rights*, Cambridge and New York: Cambridge University Press; Watal, supra note 4, at 19; Yu, Peter K. (2008), 'Access to medicines, BRICS alliances, and collective action', *American Journal of Law & Medicine*, **34**(2): 345–94, 365; Yu, supra note 3, at 412–3.

8 Watal, supra note 4, at 34.

Report to the Group of Negotiation on Goods. As Daniel Gervais, who was working at the Secretariat at the time of negotiations, recounted in detail:

> In the first few months of 1990, a number of industrialized countries tabled, with little advance notice, draft legal texts of what they saw as the future TRIPS Agreement. Prior to the tabling of these texts, the discussions had focused on identifying existing norms and possible trade-related gaps therein, but the emerging outline of a possible TRIPS result had essentially been at the level of principles, not legal texts. The draft legal texts, which emanated from the European Community, the United States, Japan, Switzerland, and Australia, foreshadowed a detailed agreement covering all IP rights then in existence, even the seldom used *sui generis* protection for computer chips. The proposals also included detailed provisions on the enforcement of those rights before national courts and customs authorities and a provision bringing future TRIPS disputes under the General Agreement on Tariffs and Trade ('GATT')/WTO dispute-settlement umbrella. These proposals were far from obvious in light of the limited mandate of the TRIPS negotiating group.
>
> As a reaction, more than a dozen developing countries proposed another 'legal' text, much more limited in scope, with few specific normative aspects. They insisted on the need to maintain flexibility to implement economic and social development objectives. In retrospect, some developing countries may feel that the Uruguay Round Secretariat did them a disservice by preparing a 'composite' text, which melded all industrialized countries' proposals into what became the 'A' proposal, while the developing countries' text became the 'B' text. The final Agreement mirrored the 'A' text. As such, it essentially embodied norms that had been accepted by industrialized countries. The concerns of developing countries were reflected in large part in two provisions – Articles 7 and 8.[9]

The Chairman's Report was later followed up by the text included in the Dunkel Draft – a 'take it or leave it' final draft of the TRIPS Agreement advanced by Arthur Dunkel, GATT's Director General. That draft constituted the Secretariat's best judgment of what would be acceptable to all of the negotiating parties.[10] Although Dunkel's approach, and the linkage between trade and intellectual property, was and remains controversial, his approach proved to be effective. The negotiations concluded quickly. In April 1994, the TRIPS Agreement was adopted with very minor changes as Annex 1C of the Marrakesh Agreement Establishing the World Trade Organization.[11]

---

9 Gervais, Daniel J. (2005), 'Intellectual property, trade & development: The state of play', *Fordham Law Review*, **74**(2): 505–35, 507–8.

10 Gervais, Daniel (2003), *The TRIPS Agreement: Drafting History and Analysis*, 2nd edn, London: Sweet & Maxwell, pp. 24–5; Watal, supra note 4, at 37–40.

11 Watal, supra note 4, at 40–1; Gervais, Daniel J. (2007), 'The TRIPS agreement and the Doha round: History and impact on economic development', in Peter K. Yu (ed.), *Intellectual Property and Information Wealth: Issues and Practices in the Digital Age*, Westport, Conn.: Praeger Publishers, vol. 4, pp. 23–72, 29.

The WTO panel's clarification

Since the TRIPS Agreement entered into force on January 1, 1995, WTO member states have explored the use of Articles 7 and 8 to support their positions. The divergence of these positions was well reflected in *Canada – Patent Protection of Pharmaceutical Products.*[12] In this dispute, the European Communities challenged the regulatory review and stockpiling exceptions in Canadian patent law for violation of the TRIPS Agreement. Calling attention to Articles 7 and 8 of the Agreement, Canada contended that these provisions 'call for a liberal interpretation of the three conditions stated in Article 30 of the Agreement, so that governments would have the necessary flexibility to adjust patent rights to maintain the desired balance with other important national policies'. As the WTO panel recounted:

> In the view of Canada, [the clause 'in a manner conducive to social and economic welfare, and to a balance of rights and obligations' in] Article 7 . . . declares that one of the key goals of the TRIPS Agreement was a balance between the intellectual property rights created by the Agreement and other important socio-economic policies of WTO Member governments. Article 8 elaborates the socio-economic policies in question, with particular attention to health and nutritional policies.

Although the European Communities 'did not dispute the stated goal of achieving a balance within the intellectual property rights system between important national policies', it took a very different view of Articles 7 and 8. As the panel continued:

> [I]n the view of the EC, Articles 7 and 8 are statements that describe the balancing of goals that *had already taken place* in negotiating the final texts of the TRIPS Agreement. According to the EC, to view Article 30 as an authorization for governments to 'renegotiate' the overall balance of the Agreement would involve a double counting of such socio-economic policies. In particular, the EC pointed to the last phrase of Article 8.1 requiring that government measures to protect important socio-economic policies be consistent with the obligations of the TRIPS Agreement. The EC also referred to the provisions of first consideration of the Preamble and Article 1.1 as demonstrating that the basic purpose of the TRIPS Agreement was to lay down minimum requirements for the protection and enforcement of intellectual property rights.

In the end, the panel found Canada's position a little more convincing and struck a compromise between the two positions by allowing

---

[12] World Trade Organization (2000), *Canada – Patent Protection of Pharmaceutical Products*, Panel Report, WT/DS114/R.

for 'certain adjustments', while preventing 'a renegotiation of the basic balance of the Agreement'. As the panel declared:

> Article 30's very existence amounts to a recognition that the definition of patent rights contained in Article 28 would need certain adjustments. On the other hand, the three limiting conditions attached to Article 30 testify strongly that the negotiators of the Agreement did not intend Article 30 to bring about what would be equivalent to a renegotiation of the basic balance of the Agreement. Obviously, the exact scope of Article 30's authority will depend on the specific meaning given to its limiting conditions. The words of those conditions must be examined with particular care on this point. Both the goals and the limitations stated in Articles 7 and 8.1 must obviously be borne in mind when doing so as well as those of other provisions of the TRIPS Agreement which indicate its object and purposes.

Some commentators were disappointed by the panel's finding, which they argued would perpetuate the unfairness of the TRIPS Agreement and take away the member states' needed discretion in developing their public policies.[13] Although these reactions are understandable, judicial activism and loose interpretation in WTO decisions can cut both ways. If the panel allowed a party to use Articles 7 and 8 to renegotiate the basic balance of the TRIPS Agreement, later panels would have to allow other parties to do the same. In the end, it is questionable whether a more activist approach would help less developed countries more than it would hurt them (considering the fact that developed countries hitherto have brought most of the complaints filed with the WTO Dispute Settlement Body).[14]

It is, nevertheless, worth noting that neither the WTO panels nor the Appellate Body has made any definitive interpretation and application of Articles 7 and 8 of the TRIPS Agreement. As Carlos Correa pointed out, the panel in *Canada – Patent Protection of Pharmaceutical Products* 'avoided elaboration of the content and implications of Articles 7 and 8.1, despite the specific reference that the parties made thereto in their submission'.[15]

---

[13] Barbosa, Denis Borges, Margaret Chon and Andres Moncayo von Hase (2007), 'Slouching towards development in international intellectual property', *Michigan State Law Review*, **2007**(1): 71–141, 113; Howse, Robert (2002), 'The Canadian Generic Medicines panel: A dangerous precedent in dangerous times', *Journal of World Intellectual Property*, **3**(4): 493–507; Okediji, Ruth L. (2003), 'Public welfare and the role of the WTO: Reconsidering the TRIPS agreement', *Emory International Law Review*, **17**(2): 819–918, 915.

[14] Davey, William J. (2005), 'The WTO dispute settlement system: The first ten years', *Journal of International Economic Law*, **8**(1): 17–50, 17.

[15] Correa, Carlos M. (2007), *Trade Related Aspects of Intellectual Property Rights: A Commentary on the TRIPS Agreement*, Oxford and New York: Oxford University Press, p. 102.

In a later case, *Canada – Term of Patent Protection*, the Appellate Body also acknowledged that it has yet to determine 'the applicability of Article 7 or Article 8 of the TRIPS Agreement in possible future cases with respect to measures to promote the policy objectives of the WTO Members that are set out in those Articles'.[16] According to the Apellate Body, and that '[t]hose Articles still await appropriate interpretation'.

The Doha fortifications

During the Doha Ministerial, WTO member states adopted two very important documents: (1) the Doha Ministerial Declaration (Ministerial Declaration) and (2) the Declaration on the TRIPS Agreement and Public Health (Doha Declaration). Both documents strongly reinforced the objectives and principles set forth in Articles 7 and 8 of the TRIPS Agreement.

Paragraph 19 of the Ministerial Declaration concerned the work program conducted by the TRIPS Council, including 'the review of Article 27.3(b) [of the TRIPS Agreement], the review of the implementation of the TRIPS Agreement under Article 71.1 and the work foreseen pursuant to paragraph 12 of this declaration', which focused on implementation-related issues and concerns. The Declaration explicitly 'instruct[ed] the Council . . . to examine, *inter alia*, the relationship between the TRIPS Agreement and the Convention on Biological Diversity, the protection of traditional knowledge and folklore, and other relevant new developments raised by members pursuant to Article 71.1'. The Declaration also stated that '[i]n undertaking [the work outlined in this paragraph], the TRIPS Council shall be guided by the objectives and principles set out in Articles 7 and 8 of the TRIPS Agreement and shall take fully into account the development dimension'.

Compared to the Ministerial Declaration, the Doha Declaration focused more specifically on the interplay between intellectual property protection and the protection of public health. The first two paragraphs of the Declaration explicitly 'recognize[d] the gravity of the public health problems afflicting many developing and least-developed countries, especially those resulting from HIV/AIDS, tuberculosis, malaria and other epidemics . . . [and] stress[ed] the need for the [TRIPS Agreement] to be part of the wider national and international action to address these problems'.

Paragraph 4 of the Declaration then stated that member states 'agree that the TRIPS Agreement does not and should not prevent members

---

16 World Trade Organization (2000), *Canada – Term of Patent Protection*, Appellate Body Report, WT/DS170/AB/R, para. 101.

from taking measures to protect public health'. The paragraph further noted that the TRIPS Agreement 'can and should be interpreted and implemented in a manner supportive of WTO members' right to protect public health and, in particular, to promote access to medicines for all'. Finally, the Declaration underscored the various 'flexibilities' reserved to all WTO member states under the TRIPS Agreement.

Taken together, the two declarations have put in a special light the relationship between the TRIPS Agreement and the protection of public health. Nevertheless, their legal effect on Articles 7 and 8 remains unclear. As Professor Correa pointed out:

> There are different possible interpretations for [paragraph 4 of the Doha Declaration]. On the one hand, it may be viewed as a statement of fact rather than a rebalancing of the Agreement. On the other, it may be regarded as an indication that in cases where there is conflict, IPRs should not be an obstacle to the realization of public health.[17]

Those who view the Declaration as a statement of fact are unlikely to impute to Articles 7 and 8 any new or elevated legal status. In fact, one could make a strong argument that the Doha Declaration was a *mere* restatement of Article 31(1) of the Vienna Convention on the Law of Treaties (Vienna Convention), which stipulates that '[a] treaty shall be interpreted in good faith in accordance with the ordinary meaning to be given to the terms of the treaty . . . *in the light of its object and purpose*'. Since the WTO panels and the Appellate Body began their operations, they have embraced the provision as part of the customary rules of interpretation as required by the Understanding on Rules and Procedures Governing the Settlement of Disputes (Dispute Settlement Understanding). Moreover, it is important not to overstate the impact of the Doha negotiations. As Susy Frankel noted:

> Doha may have rightfully curtailed attempts to suggest meanings other than that each Member may determine what is a 'national emergency,' but the idea that the declaration provides any clarity to the already clear words appears to be a politically convenient overstatement that turns a blind eye to the principles of treaty interpretation.[18]

By contrast, those who consider the Declaration an attempt to rebalance the TRIPS Agreement are likely to point to the fact that the trade

---

[17] Correa, supra note 15, at 105.

[18] Frankel, Susy (2006), 'WTO application of "the customary rules of interpretation of public international law" to intellectual property', *Virginia Journal of International Law*, **46**(2): 365–431, 401.

ministers of the WTO member states, via the Doha Declaration, 'agree[d] that the TRIPS Agreement does not and should not prevent members from taking measures to protect public health'. Notably, paragraph 4 of the Declaration did not repeat the phrase 'adopt measures *necessary* to protect public health' as used in Article 8(1) of the TRIPS Agreement. The necessity requirement was conspicuously omitted.

If such an omission is insufficient, paragraph 4 uses the word 'agree', while the other paragraphs of the Declaration use words such as 'recognize', 'stress', 'affirm', and 'reaffirm'. As noted in the *UNCTAD-ICTSD Resource Book on TRIPS and Development* (*TRIPS Resource Book*):

> The first important point regarding this paragraph is that it is stated in the form of an agreement (i.e., 'we agree'). Since this statement was adopted by consensus of the Ministers, and since the operative language is in the form of an agreement, this may be interpreted as a 'decision' of the Members under Article IX.1 of the WTO Agreement. Although paragraph 4 is not an 'interpretation' in the formal sense since it was not based on a recommendation of the TRIPS Council pursuant to Article IX:2 of the WTO Agreement, a decision that states a meaning of the Agreement should be considered as a very close approximation of an interpretation and, from a functional standpoint, may be indistinguishable.[19]

Indeed, the word choice in this paragraph is identical to that of paragraph 7 of the Declaration – the provision that extended the deadline for least developed countries to protect pharmaceuticals to January 1, 2016. Because those two paragraphs are the *only* paragraphs in the whole declaration that use the word 'agree', paragraph 4 should be given the same legal effect. After all, there is no denial that the WTO member states have reached an *agreement* over the extension of the deadline for least developed countries in paragraph 7.

Regardless of whether the Doha Declaration restates or renegotiates the balance in the TRIPS Agreement, the explicit inclusion of Articles 7 and 8 in the Ministerial Declaration is likely to have a significant impact on the work of the TRIPS Council. This is particularly true when paragraph 19 of the Ministerial Declaration is read together with paragraph 4 of the Doha Declaration. The two Doha documents are also likely to have additional impact on decisions reached by WTO panels and the Appellate Body. As Professor Gervais noted:

> The importance accorded to these Articles in the Doha negotiations . . . may lead a panel to take a longer look at how these provisions should be interpreted

---

[19] UNCTAD-ICTSD (2005), *Resource Book on TRIPS and Development*, Cambridge: Cambridge University Press, p. 131.

> in the context of the Agreement as a whole, especially with respect to the need for 'balance'. A possible practical impact of the Doha insistence of Arts 7 and 8 may serve as a basis for the interpretation of certain provisions of the Agreement.[20]

Moreover, Article 31(3) of the Vienna Convention states that '[t]here shall be taken into account, together with the context . . . any subsequent agreement between the parties regarding the interpretation of the treaty or the application of its provisions'. Although one could argue whether the Doha documents would constitute a subsequent agreement, WTO panels and the Appellate Body are likely to take the documents into account as subsequent developments. After all, as Professor Frankel pointed out, the WTO panel in *United States – Section 110(5) of the US Copyright Act* considered the WIPO Copyright Treaty as a subsequent development even though it has neither come into force nor been ratified by either party.[21] Based on an extension of that logic, one could make a strong argument that the Doha documents should constitute a subsequent agreement.

Normative content

Article 7

Article 7 delineates the objectives of the TRIPS Agreement. The article provides:

> The protection and enforcement of intellectual property rights *should* contribute to the promotion of technological innovation and to the transfer and dissemination of technology, to the mutual advantage of producers and users of technological knowledge and in a manner conducive to social and economic welfare, and to a balance of rights and obligations.

While the first three objectives – technological innovation, transfer and dissemination of technology, and the production and use of technological knowledge – focus mainly on technological development and may not affect all forms of intellectual property rights, the latter two have a much broader focus and cover virtually all forms of intellectual property rights.

The origin and focus of these objectives become clearer when they are viewed in light of the negotiating history of Article 7. In the beginning of the TRIPS negotiations, the discussion focused primarily on the interests of developed countries – that is, to promote the contributions of authors and inventors. As Frederick Abbott pointed out, the promotion of these

---

[20] Gervais, supra note 10, at 120.
[21] Frankel, supra note 18, at 413–14.

contributions can be seen as the protection of 'First World assets' – assets that were of marginal interest to the less developed world.[22]

Although less developed countries initially resisted the inclusion of new substantive standards for the protection and enforcement of intellectual property rights in GATT, they soon realized that they were fighting a losing battle. As a result, they began to insist on linking intellectual property protection to the promotion of social, economic, and technological development.[23] Deeply aware of their weakness in generating new science and technology, they feared that stronger intellectual property protection 'would give too much power to title-holders and limit access to, and transfer of, technology to those countries'[24] – and, in GATT parlance, would result in distortions or impediments to trade in legitimate goods. They were also worried that their interests would be relegated to secondary status, if those interests were respected at all.[25]

When the European Communities submitted their draft text in March 1990, which was followed by the United States two months later, less developed countries had no choice but to respond by advancing their own text.[26] As Abdulqawi Yusuf recounted, some of the provisions in this text 'were either directly based on or inspired by those of the Draft International Code of Conduct on the Transfer of Technology which was negotiated under the auspices of UNCTAD but was never adopted as an international instrument'.[27] Article 2 of the draft, which provides the normative principles, states:

> (1) *Parties recognize that intellectual property rights are granted not only in acknowledgement of the contributions of inventors and creators, but also to* assist in the diffusion of technological knowledge and its dissemination to those who could benefit from it in a manner conducive to social and economic welfare and agree that this balance of rights and obligations inherent in all systems of intellectual property rights should be observed.

---

22 Abbott, Frederick M. (1989), 'Protecting first world assets in the third world: intellectual property negotiations in the GATT multilateral framework', *Vanderbilt Journal of Transnational Law*, **22**(4): 689–745.

23 Yusuf, supra note 6, at 10.

24 Correa, supra note 15, at 91.

25 UNCTAD-ICTSD, supra note 19, at 119.

26 TRIPS Negotiating Group (1990), 'Draft agreement on trade-related aspects of intellectual property rights', MTN.GNG/NG11/W/68; TRIPS Negotiating Group (1990), 'Draft agreement on the trade-related aspects of intellectual property rights: Communication from the United States', MTN.GNG/NG11/W/70; TRIPS Negotiating Group (1990), 'Communication from Argentina, Brazil, Chile, China, Colombia, Cuba, Egypt, India, Nigeria, Peru, Tanzania and Uruguay', MTN.GNG/NG11/W/71.

27 Yusuf, supra note 6, at 10 n. 18.

> (2) In formulating or amending their national laws and regulations on IPRs, Parties have the right to adopt appropriate measures to protect public morality, national security, public health and nutrition, or to promote public interest in sectors of vital importance to their socio-economic and technological development.
> (3) Parties agree that the protection and enforcement of intellectual property rights should contribute to the promotion of technological innovation and enhance the international transfer of technology to the mutual advantage of producers and users of technological knowledge.
> (4) Each Party will take the measures it deems appropriate with a view to preventing the abuse of intellectual property rights or the resort to practices which unreasonably restrain trade or adversely affect the international transfer of technology. Parties undertake to consult each other and to co-operate in this regard. (Emphasis added)

The text was eventually adopted as Articles 7 and 8 of the TRIPS Agreement. While subparagraphs (1) and (3) found their way to Article 7, the rest became Article 8. The italicized text, which was omitted in the final version of Article 7, made clear the concerns of the less developed world. Those concerns also explain why the first three objectives of Article 7 focus significantly on technology-related intellectual property rights. As Professor Correa surmised:

> This imbalance [in the focus] is possibly attributable to developing countries' preoccupation about the impact of higher standards of IPR protection on the access to innovations and the products and services derived therefrom. Negotiations on issues not directly related to access to and use of technology were overall less controversial between the North and the South, while they often created considerable tensions between developed countries themselves.[28]

It is worth noting that the first provision of the B text supplied the last two objectives, while the third provision provided the first three objectives.

From the standpoint of treaty interpretation, it is important to point out that Article 7 is a 'should' provision, as compared to a 'shall' provision.[29] Although this word choice has led some industry groups and commentators to argue that the provision is merely hortatory,[30] the location of the provision should not be ignored. In fact, according to Professor Gervais,

---

[28] Correa, supra note 15, at 92.

[29] Gervais, supra note 10, at 116.

[30] Correa, supra note 15, at 93; Gorlin, Jacques J. (1999), *An Analysis of the Pharmaceutical-Related Provisions of the WTO TRIPs (Intellectual Property) Agreement*, London: Intellectual Property Institute, p. 16; Chon, Margaret (2006), 'Intellectual property and the development divide', *Cardozo Law Review*, **27**(6): 2821–912, 2843.

'[t]he fact that a provision of this nature is contained in the body of the agreement, and not in the preamble, would seem to heighten its status'.[31] His view is further supported by the Appellate Body in *United States – Standards for Reformulated and Conventional Gasoline*, which stated that treaty interpreters should 'take adequate account of the words actually used by [the covered agreement]'.[32]

Moreover, the TRIPS Agreement represents a compromise between the two texts advanced by the developed and less developed worlds. While the objectives and principles in the A text found their way to the *Preamble*, the B text provided the *language* for Articles 7 and 8 of the TRIPS Agreement (as well as the Preamble). As the *TRIPS Resource Book* reminded us:

> It is significant that the developing country proposal for objectives and principles became operative provisions of TRIPS (i.e., Articles 7 and 8), while the largely developed country proposals set out in the Annex were reflected in the more general statement of intent (i.e., the Preamble). Because articles of a treaty are intended to establish rights and obligations, Articles 7 and 8 should carry greater weight in the process of implementation and interpretation.[33]

Thus, the strongest argument developed countries and their intellectual property industries could make based on the plain meaning of the Agreement and the context provided by the TRIPS negotiation history is that Article 7 'may not be used to reduce the scope of "shall" or equivalents thereof in other Articles', assuming that the Doha documents did not elevate its legal status.[34] However, because Article 7 is included in the text of the Agreement, it should be given greater weight than the treaty's preambular provisions. After all, the latter were primarily 'designed to establish a definitive record of the intention or purpose of the parties in entering into the agreement'.[35]

From the standpoint of policy development, Article 7 is also rather important. Highlighting the many public interest objectives of the TRIPS Agreement, the provision 'makes it clear that IPRs are not an end in themselves'.[36] As less developed countries declared in their submission to the TRIPS Council before the Doha Ministerial: '*Article 7* . . . clearly estab-

---

[31] Gervais, supra note 10, at 116; Correa, supra note 15, at 93.

[32] World Trade Organization (1996), *United States – Standards for Reformulated and Conventional Gasoline*, Appellate Body Report, WT/DS2/AB/R, part III.B.

[33] UNCTAD-ICTSD, supra note 19, at 123–24.

[34] Gervais, supra note 10, at 116.

[35] UNCTAD-ICTSD, supra note 19, at 2.

[36] *Id.* at 125–6.

lishes that *the protection and enforcement of intellectual property rights do not exist in a vacuum.* They are supposed to benefit society as a whole and do not aim at the mere protection of private rights.'[37]

Likewise, the final report of the UK Commission on Intellectual Property Rights states that intellectual property rights should be regarded 'as instruments of public policy which confer economic privileges on individuals or institutions solely for the purposes of contributing to the greater public good' and that the conferred privileges should be 'a means to an end, not an end in itself'.[38] Such an emphasis is important, 'because interest groups', the Commission claimed, 'often lose sight of the basic mission of the WTO which, as stated in the preamble of the WTO Agreement, is to promote trade and economic development, not to protect the interests of particular private IPR-holding interest groups'.

The use of the word 'should' in Article 7 further reminds member states that stronger intellectual property protection does not necessarily lead to more innovation, dissemination of knowledge, or the transfer of technology.[39] To date, economists have provided an abundance of empirical studies to demonstrate the ambiguous relationship intellectual property protection has with economic development, technology transfer, and foreign direct investment (FDI).[40] For example, Claudio Frischtak states that a country's overall investment climate is often more influential on FDI decisions than the strength of intellectual property protection it offers.[41] Carsten Fink and Keith Maskus observed that '[a] poor country hoping to attract inward FDI would be better advised to improve its overall investment climate and business infrastructure than to strengthen its patent regime sharply, an action that would have little effect on its

---

[37] Council for Trade-Related Aspects of Intellectual Property Rights (2001), 'Submission by the African Group, Barbados, Bolivia, Brazil, Cuba, Dominican Republic, Ecuador, Honduras, India, Indonesia, Jamaica, Pakistan, Paraguay, Philippines, Peru, Sri Lanka, Thailand and Venezuela', IP/C/W/296, para. 18.

[38] Commission on Intellectual Property Rights (2002), *Integrating Intellectual Property Rights and Development Policy: Report of the Commission on Intellectual Property Rights*, London: Commission on Intellectual Property Rights, p. 6.

[39] Correa, supra note 15, at 97.

[40] Yu, Peter K. (2007), 'Intellectual property, economic development, and the China puzzle', in Daniel J. Gervais (ed.), *Intellectual Property, Trade and Development: Strategies to Optimize Economic Development in a TRIPS Plus Era*, Oxford: Oxford University Press, pp. 173–220, 176–80.

[41] Frischtak, Claudio R. (1993), 'Harmonization versus differentiation in intellectual property right regimes', in Mitchel B. Wallerstein, Mary Ellen Mogee and Roberta A. Schoen (eds), *Global Dimensions of Intellectual Property Rights in Science and Technology*, Washington, DC: National Academy Press, pp. 89–106, 99–100.

own'.[42] Professor Maskus further stated that, if stronger intellectual property protection always led to more FDI, 'recent FDI flows to developing economies would have gone largely to sub-Saharan Africa and Eastern Europe . . . [rather than] China, Brazil, and other high-growth, large-market developing economies with weak IPRs'.[43]

Furthermore, the five objectives in Article 7 provide useful guidance to those involved in implementing the TRIPS Agreement. For example, the first three objectives – technological innovation, the transfer and dissemination of technology, and the production and use of technological knowledge – provide support to those provisions of the TRIPS Agreement that outline the obligations of developed countries to promote technology transfer, technical cooperation, and legal assistance in developing and least developed countries.[44] Article 66 of the TRIPS Agreement states that '[d]eveloped country Members shall provide incentives to enterprises and institutions in their territories for the purpose of promoting and encouraging technology transfer to least-developed country Members in order to enable them to create a sound and viable technological base'. Titled technical cooperation, Article 67 further provides:

> In order to facilitate the implementation of this Agreement, developed country Members shall provide, on request and on mutually agreed terms and conditions, technical and financial cooperation in favour of developing and least-developed country Members. Such cooperation shall include assistance in the preparation of laws and regulations on the protection and enforcement of intellectual property rights as well as on the prevention of their abuse, and shall include support regarding the establishment or reinforcement of domestic offices and agencies relevant to these matters, including the training of personnel.

The third objective highlights the *equal* importance of both producers and users of technological knowledge. It therefore makes a strong case that exceptions and limitations in the TRIPS Agreement should be treated as important as the rights provided in the Agreement – an argument commentators have made with respect to exceptions and limitations

---

[42] Fink, Carsten and Keith E. Maskus (2005), 'Why we study intellectual property rights and what we have learned', in Carsten Fink and Keith E. Maskus (eds), *Intellectual Property and Development: Lessons from Recent Economic Research*, Washington, DC: World Bank, pp. 1–15, 7.

[43] Maskus, Keith E. (1998), 'The role of intellectual property rights in encouraging foreign direct investment and technology transfer', *Duke Journal of Comparative and International Law*, **9**(1): 109–61, 129.

[44] UNCTAD-ICTSD, supra note 19, at 126.

in the domestic intellectual property system.[45] To some extent, Article 7 paves the way for the development of future exceptions and limitations, which can be used to restore the balance of the international intellectual property system. This objective is particularly important to less developed countries, which 'are largely users of technologies produced abroad'.[46] Because these countries tend to have many more consumers than producers, Article 7 will greatly benefit them when users are broadly 'interpreted as encompassing final consumers as well as producers of goods and services that utilize technological knowledge'.[47]

The last two objectives underscore the needs to take account of the member state's 'social and economic welfare' and its need to develop 'a balance of rights and obligations'. As the *TRIPS Resource Book* declared: 'Article 7 makes clear that TRIPS negotiators did not mean to abandon a balanced perspective on the role of intellectual property in society. TRIPS is not intended only to protect the interests of rights holders. It is intended to strike a balance that more widely promotes social and economic welfare.'[48]

Although there is a tendency for policymakers to strike a balance within the TRIPS regime, Article 7 mentions broadly '[t]he protection and enforcement of intellectual property rights'. The provision therefore anticipates further balancing within the larger international trading system. As the WTO panel declared in *United States – Section 110(5) of the US Copyright Act*, 'the agreements covered by the WTO form a single, integrated legal system'.[49] Because '[t]he proper balance of rights and obligations is an overriding objective of the WTO system',[50] the objectives and principles of the TRIPS Agreement need to be considered in relation to this particular objective.

While it is important to strike a balance within the TRIPS regime, maintaining balance outside the WTO is also very important. As I have noted elsewhere, the spillover effects of intellectual property protection and the increased fragmentation of the international treaty system have necessitated the development of not only *endogenous* limits to intellectual

---

45 Boyle, James (1996), *Shamans, Software and Spleens: Law and the Construction of the Information Society*, Cambridge, Mass.: Harvard University Press, p. 138.

46 UNCTAD-ICTSD, supra note 19, at 126.

47 Correa, supra note 15, at 99.

48 UNCTAD-ICTSD, supra note 19, at 126.

49 World Trade Organization (2000), *United States – Section 110(5) of the US Copyright Act*, Panel Report, WT/DS/160/R, para. 6.185.

50 Correa, supra note 15, at 92.

property protection, but also *exogenous* limits that can be found in related regimes, such as those concerning human rights, public health, biological diversity, food and agriculture, and information and communications.[51] As the complexity of the international intellectual property regime continues to increase, the need to better understand the interactions between intellectual property rights and rights in other areas becomes even greater.

Article 8(1)

Article 8 provides the interpretative or normative principle of the TRIPS Agreement. It echoes the Agreement's Preamble by recognizing 'the special needs of the least-developed country Members in respect of *maximum flexibility* in the domestic implementation of laws and regulations in order to enable them to create a sound and viable technological base'. In addition, the provision, together with Article 7, 'confirms the broad and unfettered discretion that Members have to pursue public policy objectives'.[52] As the *TRIPS Resource Book* noted, the provision 'advises that Members were expected to have the discretion to adopt internal measures they consider necessary to protect public health and nutrition, and to promote the public interest in sectors of vital importance to their socio-economic and technological development'.[53]

Article 8(1) lays out the public interest principle in the TRIPS Agreement.[54] The provision states: 'Members may, in formulating or amending their laws and regulations, adopt measures necessary to protect public health and nutrition, and to promote the public interest in sectors of vital importance to their socio-economic and technological development, provided that such measures are consistent with the provisions of this Agreement'. As Professor Correa pointed out, these measures include both measures inside and outside the intellectual property regime:

> Article 8.1 broadly recognizes Members' rights 'in formulating or amending their laws and regulations'. . . . [I]t does not only refer to laws and regulations on IPRs but to measures adopted in other fields, for instance, those that restrict the manufacture or commercialization of IPR-protected goods. Issues

---

[51] Yu, Peter K. (2009), 'The political economy of data protection', *Chicago-Kent Law Review*, **84**: forthcoming.

[52] Correa, supra note 15, at 108; Deere, Carolyn (2009), *The Implementation Game: The TRIPS Agreement and the Global Politics of Intellectual Property Reform in Developing Countries*, Oxford and New York: Oxford University Press, p. 64; UNCTAD-ICTSD, supra note 19, at 546; Yusuf, supra note 6, at 13.

[53] UNCTAD-ICTSD, supra note 19, at 126–7.

[54] Yusuf, supra note 6, at 13–5.

> concerning the application of Article 8.1 may, hence, arise in two contexts, one fully within the IPR realm, and another one outside it, but with implications on the protection of IPRs.[55]

Although the original proposal in the less developed countries' B text included additional measures to protect 'public morality' and 'national security', those two areas were omitted in the final version of Article 8. These measures, nonetheless, are covered elsewhere in the TRIPS Agreement. Article 27(2) of the TRIPS Agreement allows member states to exclude certain inventions from patentability provided that the prevention of the commercial exploitation of those inventions 'is necessary *to protect ordre public or morality*, including to protect human, animal or plant life or health or to avoid serious prejudice to the environment' (emphasis added). Article 73 further enables member states to pursue their essential security interests and to fulfill obligations under the United Nations Charter in relation to the maintenance of international peace and security.

Article 8(1) is important to less developed countries, because it provides justifications for special exceptions that promote the public interest in sectors of vital importance to socio-economic and technological development. Notably, the provision uses the term 'public interest', which can be easily contrasted with the narrower term '*ordre public*' in Article 27(2) of the TRIPS Agreement. Because the Appellate Body reminds us that the interpretation of a provision should 'take adequate account of the words actually used' there,[56] this distinction is likely to be significant.

Moreover, as Professor Correa pointed out, the term 'public interest' is likely to be more subjective than, say, the term '*ordre public*'.[57] According to Gillian Davies, whose work Professor Correa cited for elaboration:

> Whether a particular act is 'in the public interest' . . . is probably not subject to any objective tests. Inherent in the noble motive of the public good is the notion that, in certain circumstances, the needs of the majority override those of the individual, and that the citizen should relinquish any thoughts of self-interest in favor of the common good of society as a whole.[58]

---

[55] Correa, supra note 15, at 104.

[56] World Trade Organization (1996), *United States – Standards for Reformulated and Conventional Gasoline*, Appellate Body Report, WT/DS2/AB/R, part III.B.

[57] Correa, supra note 15, at 105–6.

[58] Davies, Gillian (2002), *Copyright and the Public Interest*, London: Sweet & Maxwell, p. 4.

Also of interest in Article 8(1) are the ambiguities over what constitute the necessary measures for 'promot[ing] the public interest in sectors of vital importance to their socio-economic and technological development'. The TRIPS Agreement does not offer any definition of the relevant sectors. In fact, '[s]ectors of vital importance may vary from country to country and region to region, and the provision is not limited to implementation by developing countries'.[59]

For instance, these sectors can be defined based on their specialization – for example, the pharmaceutical industry versus the automotive industry. The only major constraint seems to be Article 27(1) of the TRIPS Agreement, which prohibits discrimination based on 'the place of invention, the field of technology and whether products are imported or locally produced'. The sectors can also be defined based on the size of the sectors or their stage of development – for example, infant industry or small and mid-sized enterprises. In those scenarios, Article 27(1) will not even present a barrier, except in situations when there is *de facto* discrimination based on the composition of the affected industries.

In his new treatise on the TRIPS Agreement, Professor Correa went even further to argue that each member state should be able to decide what constitute these sectors based on their needs, goals, and interests.[60] As he explained:

> On the one hand, 'sectors' may refer to economic activities at different levels of aggregation (eg agriculture, maize production), as well as to certain groups of economic agents (eg, small and medium enterprises). Although the adjective 'vital importance' would seem to limit the scope of the provision to specially significant sectors, which sector is important or not is also subject to determination by the concerned Member in the light of its 'socio-economic and technological development'.
>
> . . . [T]he concept of 'social-economic and technological development' is broad enough to encompass any sector, socially, economically, or technologically relevant. Thus, the importance of a sector may be measured by its contribution to GNP; but it may be also socially important, despite a low contribution thereto.

According to Professor Correa, permissible actions may include 'measures excluding foreign direct investment in certain sectors, and the regulation of royalty rates and other conditions in licensing agreements'.[61] As he reminded us, '[t]hese regulations were applied by many developing (and

---

59 UNCTAD-ICTSD, supra note 19, at 127.
60 Correa, supra note 15, at 106.
61 *Id.* at 105.

some developed) countries during the 1970s and 1980s but were gradually abandoned in the context of more liberal policies towards foreign direct investment'.

With the rapid development experienced by complex economies, such as Brazil, China, India, and South Africa, what constitute sectors of vital importance may take on new complexities. Unlike the United States and most members of the European Communities, these economies have the distinctive characteristics of having wide internal divergences in their socio-economic conditions and technological capabilities. It is therefore difficult to determine what constitute the relevant sectors in those countries. As I have suggested in the past, China may prefer stronger protection of intellectual property rights in entertainment, software, semiconductors, and selected areas of biotechnology,[62] even though it may remain reluctant to increase protection for pharmaceuticals, chemicals, fertilizers, seeds, and foodstuffs – due to its huge population, continued economic dependence on agriculture, and concerns about public health and its people's overall well-being.

Although Article 8(1) can be interpreted broadly to promote the development goals of less developed countries, the provision contains two major constraints, both of which were added at the request of developed countries in the last stages of the negotiation.[63] The first constraint concerns the necessity requirement, which is somewhat similar to the one found in Article XX of the GATT.[64] By limiting the flexibilities available in the TRIPS Agreement, this requirement threatens to impede the public policy goals of many less developed countries.

For example, without taking into account the language in paragraph 4 of the Doha Declaration, Article 8 of the TRIPS Agreement does not allow member states to adopt *any* measures they deem useful to protect public health and nutrition. Rather, the provision states explicitly that they can only adopt measures that are *necessary* for those purposes. In fact, they may not even adopt measures that *they consider necessary* for those purposes. As Wesley Cann explained:

> the use of the term 'necessary,' as opposed to the language 'it considers necessary' employed in the Article 73 security exception, would seem to indicate that the imposition of these measures are not within the absolute discretion of the

---

[62] Yu, Peter K. (2007), 'International enclosure, the regime complex, and intellectual property schizophrenia', *Michigan State Law Review*, **2007**(1): 1–33, 25–6.

[63] Gervais, supra note 10, at 121; Yusuf, supra note 6, at 14.

[64] Correa, supra note 15, at 106.

> invoking Member, but are instead subject to potential WTO review in regard to their validity.[65]

Even worse, the provision requires the measures to be 'consistent with the provisions of [the TRIPS] Agreement'. This second constraint greatly erodes the pro-development aspect of Article 8. As Professor Gervais noted:

> It is . . . tempting to conclude that this Article may serve as a basis for broader exceptions than [Article 7]. That is not the case, however. Both paras of Art. 8 are limited by the use of the phrase 'consistent with the provisions of this Agreement' . . . . Given the phrase added by negotiators, it would be difficult to justify an exception not foreseen under the Agreement, unless it is an exception to a right not protected under other provisions of the TRIPS Agreement or those of other international instruments incorporated in TRIPS.[66]

Fortunately for less developed countries, whether one fails the TRIPS-consistency requirement will depend on the overall interpretation of the TRIPS Agreement. When Articles 7 and 8 are read together, a careful and effective interpretation of Article 7 may help remove the potential inconsistency with the TRIPS Agreement. Also of great importance is a skillful use of the Preamble, which arguably can be viewed as a 'condensed expression of [the] underlying principles' of the TRIPS Agreement.[67] As Professor Correa pointed out, consistency with the TRIPS Agreement 'should be assessed in the light of Article 7 and of the Preamble, that is, taking the balance of rights and obligations and the social and economic welfare into account'.[68] Abdulqawi Yusuf went even further: '[E]ven though certain public interest measures may be inconsistent with some of the specific standards laid down in the TRIPS Agreement, it is their overall consistency with the agreement that should be taken into account'.[69]

The developed countries' push for the addition of these requirements is understandable. From their standpoint, both requirements are greatly needed to ensure that the protections offered by the TRIPS Agreement will not be undercut by measures adopted under the pretexts of protecting health and nutrition or promoting socio-economic and technological

---

[65] Cann, Wesley A. Jr. (2004), 'On the relationship between intellectual property rights and the need of less-developed countries for access to pharmaceuticals: creating a legal duty to supply under a theory of progressive global constitutionalism', *University of Pennsylvania Journal of International Economic Law*, **25**(3): 755–944, 808.

[66] Gervais, supra note 10, at 121–2.

[67] *Id.* at 80.

[68] Correa, supra note 15, at 104.

[69] Yusuf, supra note 6, at 14.

development.[70] Unfortunately for the less developed world, the added requirements in Article 8(1) have created the perverse effect of privileging intellectual property protection over other arguably more important socio-economic goals, such as providing access to essential medicines to combat HIV/AIDS, tuberculosis, malaria and other epidemics. Such an effect is undoubtedly one of the Agreement's more harmful unintended consequences. To some extent, the added requirements and the less developed countries' willingness to accept the modifications during the TRIPS negotiations reflect the countries' then-limited understanding of the dramatic adverse spillover effects of strong international intellectual property protection.[71] Nevertheless, even if these countries were aware of these effects, they would have been unlikely to 'withstand the considerable political resources that the developed countries' negotiators brought to bear to secure the TRIPS agreement'.[72]

It is also problematic that the safeguards available in the TRIPS Agreement are more restrictive than those available under Article XX of the GATT. As noted in the *TRIPS Resource Book*:

> TRIPS does not contain a general safeguard measure comparable to Article XX of the GATT 1994 or Article XIV of the GATS. For those other Multilateral Trade Agreements (MTAs), the necessity to protect human life or health may take priority over the generally applicable rules of the agreement, subject only to general principles of non-discrimination. Yet when it comes to intellectual property, the 'exceptions' are circumscribed with various procedural or compensatory encumbrances, making their use more difficult.[73]

---

[70] Ullrich, Hanns (2004), 'Expansionist intellectual property protection and reductionist competition rules: A TRIPS Perspective', *Journal of International Economic Law*, **7**(2): 401–30, 410.

[71] Yu, supra note 3, at 419.

[72] May, Christopher (2007), *The World Intellectual Property Organization: Resurgence and the Development Agenda*, London and New York: Routledge, p. 30.

[73] UNCTAD-ICTSD, supra note 19, at 132. Although commentators have explored whether the general exceptions in article XX of the GATT are permitted under the TRIPS Agreement, commentators have expressed skepticism over such application. Gervais, supra note 10, at 122. The WTO panel decision in *European Communities – Protection of Trademarks and Geographical Indications for Agricultural Products and Foodstuffs* also seems to have confirmed this skeptical position. World Trade Organization (2005), *European Communities – Protection of Trademarks and Geographical Indications for Agricultural Products and Foodstuffs*, Panel Report, WT/DS174/R. As the panel declared, 'there is no hierarchy between the TRIPS Agreement and GATT 1994, which appear in separate annexes to the WTO Agreement. The ordinary meaning of the texts of the TRIPS Agreement and GATT 1994, as well as Article II:2 of the WTO Agreement, taken together,

It is therefore no surprise that concern over the restrictiveness of these safeguards in the public health area in part precipitated the Doha negotiations,[74] which sought to renegotiate the ways safeguards are handled in the TRIPS Agreement. Viewed against this background, the Ministerial Declaration and the Doha Declaration may have given Article 8 a 'higher legal status not only for the negotiations but in interpreting the Agreement in the context of, e.g., dispute-settlement procedures'.[75] It is, indeed, significant that they omitted the necessity requirement. Such omission is likely to create interesting discussion concerning the interpretation and implementation of the TRIPS Agreement.

Article 8(2)
Article 8(2) provides: 'Appropriate measures, provided that they are consistent with the provisions of this Agreement, may be needed to prevent the abuse of intellectual property rights by rights holders or the resort to practices which unreasonably restrain trade or adversely affect the international transfer of technology'. The structure of this provision is similar to that of Article 8(1), and the provision resembles its predecessor in including the TRIPS-consistency requirement.

To some extent, Article 8(2) is somewhat redundant. Virtually all the public policy objectives mentioned in the provision have already been addressed elsewhere in the Agreement. For example, Article 30 allows member states to 'provide limited exceptions to the exclusive rights conferred by a patent' on the condition that such exceptions satisfy the three-step test – that is, they are '[1] limited . . . [2] do not unreasonably conflict with a normal exploitation of the patent and [3] do not unreasonably prejudice the legitimate interests of the patent owner, taking account of the legitimate interests of third parties'. Article 31(k) enumerates special conditions for members to issue compulsory licenses in an effort 'to remedy a practice determined after judicial or administrative process to be anti-competitive'. That provision also allows for '[t]he need to correct anti-competitive practices . . . [to] be taken into account in determining the amount of remuneration in such cases'. In addition, Article 40 permits member states to take appropriate measures to curb 'an abuse of intellectual property rights having an adverse effect on competition in the relevant market'.

While the provision no doubt offers added support to these provisions,

---

Footnote 73 (*cont.*)
indicates that obligations under the TRIPS Agreement and GATT 1994 can co-exist and that one does not override the other.'

[74] Correa, supra note 15, at 108.

[75] Gervais, supra note 10, at 120.

it is likely to have limited legal effect. Article 8, for example, is unlikely to provide the legal basis for 'justify[ing] an exception not foreseen under the Agreement, unless it is an exception to a right not protected under other provisions of the TRIPS Agreement or those of other international instruments incorporated in TRIPS'.[76] It is therefore no surprise that Professor Gervais has described Article 8 as 'essentially a policy statement that explains the rationale for measures taken under Arts 30, 31 and 40'.[77]

Nevertheless, Article 8(2) is important for both historical reasons and symbolic effect. The provision serves as a conspicuous reminder of what less developed countries initially considered within the mandate of the GATT negotiations.[78] As India noted in a detailed intervention during a meeting of the TRIPS Negotiating Group, 'it was only the restrictive and anti-competitive practices of the owners of the IPRs that could be considered to be trade-related because they alone distorted or impeded international trade'.[79] Notably, India 'did not regard the other aspects of IPRs [discussed in the Group at that time] to be trade-related', that is, not within the mandate set up by the Punta del Este Declaration.[80]

A similar structure was followed in the B text, which was divided into two parts. As Adronico Adede noted, '[b]y presenting the proposed text of a TRIPS agreement into two parts, the developing countries wanted . . . to signal their determination to emphasize the part dealing with trade in counterfeit goods while minimizing the part relating to substantive standards on IPRs'.[81] Notably, Articles 7 and 8 were taken from the first part of the B text, which focused on what less developed countries considered to be trade-related intellectual property matters.

Multiple uses of Articles 7 and 8

Articles 7 and 8, which outline the objectives and principles of the TRIPS Agreement, constitute 'a central piece for the implementation and interpretation of the TRIPS Agreement'.[82] These objectives and principles

---

[76] *Id.* at 121–2.

[77] *Id.* at 121. The *TRIPS Resource Book*, however, disagreed with Professor Gervais and observed that 'Article 8.2 states a "principle", which is different from a mere "policy statement"'. UNCTAD-ICTSD, supra note 19, at 546.

[78] UNCTAD-ICTSD, supra note 19, at 127.

[79] *Id.* at 121.

[80] *Id.*

[81] Adede, Adronico Oduogo (2003), 'Origins and history of the TRIPS negotiations', in Christophe Bellmann, Graham Dutfield and Ricardo Meléndez-Ortiz (eds), *Trading in Knowledge: Development Perspectives on TRIPS, Trade and Sustainability*, London and Sterling, VA: Earthscan Publications, pp. 23–35, 28.

[82] Correa, supra note 15, at 108.

become even more important, due to the revolutionary nature of the TRIPS Agreement, which has transformed the international intellectual property system from an inter-national patchwork system to a global supranational code.[83] As elaborated in the *TRIPS Resource Book*:

> Since TRIPS brought the regulation of intellectual property rights into the GATT, and now WTO, multilateral trading system for the first time, there is no pre-TRIPS situation in respect to the objectives and principles of the Agreement. In other words, the objectives and principles of . . . TRIPS are unique to the Agreement. . . . Neither the Paris nor Berne Convention included provisions analogous to Articles 7 and 8. That is, there are no provisions that act to establish an overarching set of principles regarding the interpretation and implementation of the agreement.[84]

Because the pre-TRIPS international intellectual property conventions do not contain 'provisions that act to establish an overarching set of principles regarding the interpretation and implementation of the agreement',[85] one could argue that 'the elaboration of objectives and principles in Articles 7 and 8 may well be viewed as a means to establish a balancing of interests at the multilateral level to substitute for the balancing traditionally undertaken at the national level'.[86] To some extent, the two provisions codify the multilateral norms concerning the protection of the public interest in intellectual property law.[87] As such, they 'qualify the scope of harmonization [of intellectual property standards] at the national level'.[88]

This section discusses the role Articles 7 and 8 can play in facilitating a more flexible interpretation and implementation of the TRIPS Agreement. It focuses, in particular, on five ways in which the provisions can be put into effective use: (1) as a guiding light for the interpretation and implementation of the Agreement; (2) as a shield against aggressive expansion of intellectual property rights and demands for TRIPS-plus protections; (3) as a sword to challenge the lack of balance in the international intellectual property system; (4) as a bridge to connect the TRIPS regime with intel-

---

[83] Geller, Paul Edward (1998), 'From patchwork to network: Strategies for international intellectual property in flux', *Duke Journal of Comparative and International Law*, **9**(1): 69–90; Ginsburg, Jane C. (2000), 'International copyright: From a "bundle" of national copyright laws to a supranational code?', *Journal of the Copyright Society of the USA*, **47**(1): 265–89; Yu, supra note 3, at 354–75.

[84] UNCTAD-ICTSD, supra note 19, at 119.

[85] *Id.*

[86] *Id.*; Yusuf, supra note 6, at 10.

[87] Yusuf, supra note 6, at 12.

[88] *Id.* at 14.

lectual property and other related international regimes; and (5) as a seed for the development of new international intellectual property norms.

Guiding light

Among the five different uses, the use of the provisions to clarify the TRIPS Agreement is the most obvious. Such a use is strongly supported by the WTO documents. Article 3(2) of the Dispute Settlement Understanding states that provisions of the covered agreements are to be clarified 'in accordance with customary rules of interpretation of public international law', including those stipulated in the Vienna Convention. Since *United States – Standards for Reformulated and Conventional Gasoline*, the first case decided by a WTO panel, the WTO panels and the Appellate Body have both embraced Article 31 of the Vienna Convention as a general rule of interpretation. As the panel declared in its report:

> In resolving this interpretative issue the Panel referred, in conformity with Article 3.2 of the Understanding on Rules and Procedures Governing the Settlement of Disputes, to the Vienna Convention on the Law of Treaties, which states in Article 31 that 'a treaty shall be interpreted in good faith in accordance with the ordinary meaning to be given to the terms of the treaty in their context and in the light of its object and purpose'.[89]

The panel's position was subsequently endorsed by the Appellate Body, which described Article 31 of the Vienna Convention as 'a fundamental rule of treaty interpretation'.[90] In the TRIPS context, this rule of interpretation was first applied in *India – Patent Protection for Pharmaceutical and Agricultural Chemical Products*,[91] which concerned India's failure to provide a mailbox system as required by Article 70(8) of the TRIPS Agreement.

Article 31(1) of the Vienna Convention stipulates that '[a] treaty shall be interpreted in good faith in accordance with the ordinary meaning to be given to the terms of the treaty . . . *in the light of its object and purpose*'. Because Articles 7 and 8 were the designated provisions for determining the objectives and principles of the TRIPS Agreement, the Vienna

---

89 World Trade Organization (1996), *United States – Standards for Reformulated and Conventional Gasoline*, Panel Report, WT/DS2/R, para. 6.7.

90 World Trade Organization (1996), *United States – Standards for Reformulated and Conventional Gasoline*, Appellate Body Report, WT/DS2/AB/R, part III.B.

91 World Trade Organization (1997), *India – Patent Protection for Pharmaceutical and Agricultural Chemical Products*, Panel Report, WT/DS50/R, para. 7.18.

Convention requires that the Agreement be interpreted in the light of these two provisions. As Professor Correa reminded us, '[i]f the Agreement itself contains a definition of its purpose, as Article 7 does, panels and the Appellate Body cannot ignore it or create their own definition in interpreting other provisions of the Agreement'.[92]

Although Articles 7 and 8 have been used only sparingly in WTO panel decisions, the panels thus far have referred favorably to the provisions. In *Canada – Patent Protection of Pharmaceutical Products*, for example, the panel declared: 'Both the goals and the limitations stated in Articles 7 and 8.1 must obviously be borne in mind when [examining the words of the limiting conditions in Article 30] as well as those of other provisions of the TRIPS Agreement which indicate its object and purposes'.[93] This panel decision was particularly important because it was issued before the adoption of the Doha Declaration. As Professor Abbott pointed out:

> In late 1999, the political pressures resulting from aggressive US and EC policies on TRIPS were building up, but public antipathy towards that conduct had not yet manifested itself at the level surrounding the Medicines Act trial in South Africa. The Doha Declaration on the TRIPS Agreement and Public Health was about two years off.[94]

During the Doha negotiations, Articles 7 and 8 were 'singled out' for their special importance.[95] Paragraph 19 of the Ministerial Declaration stated explicitly that the work of the TRIPS Council 'shall be guided by the objectives and principles set out in Articles 7 and 8 of the TRIPS Agreement and shall take fully into account the development dimension'. Although the legal effect of this document remains unclear, the document 'may lead a panel to take a longer look at how these provisions should be interpreted in the context of the Agreement as a whole, especially with respect to the need for "balance"'.[96]

Articles 7 and 8 become even more important in light of the many ambiguities built into the TRIPS Agreement. Because Articles 7 and 8 memorialize the hard-fought bargains less developed countries have won through the TRIPS negotiations, these provisions provide policymakers, WTO

---

92 Correa, supra note 15, at 93.

93 World Trade Organization (2000), *Canada – Patent Protection of Pharmaceutical Products*, Panel Report, WT/DS114/R, para. 7.26.

94 Abbott, Frederick M. (2003), 'Bob Hudec as chair of the *Canada – Generic Pharmaceuticals* panel – The WTO gets something right', *Journal of International Economic Law*, **6**(3): 733–7, 736.

95 Gervais, supra note 10, at 120.

96 *Id.*

panels, and the Appellate Body with objective clues as to how ambiguous words in the TRIPS Agreement are to be interpreted. 'The context provided by Articles 7 and 8 may [also] be of particular importance to correctly interpret the extent of several obligations and exceptions under the TRIPS Agreement, such as the concepts of "third party" and "legitimate interests" in Article 30, "unfair commercial use" under Article 39.3, and "abuse" in Articles 40 and 50.3, among others'.[97]

Consider, for example, the word 'review' in Article 27(3)(b) of the TRIPS Agreement, which concerns the patentability of diagnostic, therapeutic, and surgical methods and plants and animals other than microorganisms. As Professor Correa pointed out, 'there has been no agreement in the Council for TRIPS on the meaning of "review"'.[98] While developed countries interpreted the word to mean 'review of implementation', less developed countries interpreted the word to suggest the possibility for 'revising' the Agreement to meet their needs and interests.

Likewise, Sisule Musungu reminded us of the different ways to conceptualize the transitional periods built into the TRIPS Agreement and extended through the Doha Declaration:

> While giving extra time due to administrative and financial constraints was one aim, the central objective of the LDCs [least developed countries] transition period under the TRIPS Agreement is different. Article 66.1 of TRIPS read together with the Preamble of the TRIPS Agreement and its objectives under Article 77 [sic] envisage the purpose and objectives of the LDCs transition period to be to respond and address: the special needs and requirements of these countries; and the need for maximum flexibility to help these countries create a sound and viable technological base.[99]

Indeed, Jayashree Watal described these ambiguous words and phrases as 'constructive ambiguities'.[100] These ambiguities are constructive, because they can be strategically interpreted and deployed to provide less developed countries with additional 'wiggle room' to implement their obligations under the TRIPS Agreement.[101] These 'constructive ambiguities' therefore

---

97 Correa, supra note 15, at 94–5.

98 Correa, Carlos M. (2000), *Intellectual Property Rights, The WTO and Developing Countries: The TRIPS Agreement and Policy Options*, London and New York: Zed Books, p. 211.

99 Musungu, Sisule (2007), 'A conceptual framework for priority identification and delivery of IP technical assistance for LDCs during the extended transition period under the TRIPS agreement', Quaker United Nations Office Issue Paper No. 7, p. 5.

100 Watal, supra note 4, at 7.

101 Reichman, J.H., (1997), 'From free riders to fair followers: Global

provide less developed countries with a bulwark against the continuous expansion of intellectual property rights.[102] If strategically used, they will allow less developed countries to actively push for interpretations that meet their needs, interests, and goals. They will also preserve the much-needed policy space that has been appropriately reserved to them during the TRIPS negotiations. In Watal's view, a constructive resolution of these ambiguities may even provide less developed countries with a 'means of "clawing" back much of what was lost in the negotiating battles in TRIPS'.[103]

Politically, Articles 7 and 8 are also important, because they legitimize the TRIPS Agreement. They confirm that the Agreement was a bargain struck between developed and less developed countries over a multi-year negotiation process. Because the two provisions were directly taken from the less developed countries' B text with limited modification and those provisions are the very few provisions taken from this text,[104] the taken language should be considered highly important. If such language is ignored, it would be very hard to make a good-faith argument that the TRIPS Agreement was a *legitimate* bargain between developed and less developed countries. As Abdulqawi Yusuf reminded us:

> To the extent that the operative provisions of the TRIPS text principally reflected the positions of the developed countries and established higher standards of protection for IPRs, it would appear that the developing countries found comfort and consolation in the clear statement of the objectives they proposed in the preambular clauses as well as in Article 7, together with the recognition of some of the principles they suggested in Article 8.[105]

There is a tendency for policymakers in developed countries and the global intellectual property industries to demand concessions in exchange for proposals that further the development dimension of the TRIPS Agreement. However, these *demandeurs* tend to overlook the fact that the TRIPS Agreement is now in a deepening crisis. Its legitimacy has been called into question by the high standards of protection and enforcement that ignore the needs, interests, and goals of the less developed member states.[106] If the Agreement is to regain its legitimacy, the less developed

---

Footnote 101 (*cont.*)
competition under the TRIPS agreement', *New York University Journal of International Law and Politics*, **29**(1): 11–93, 28.

102 Watal, supra note 4, at 7.
103 *Id.*
104 Gervais, supra note 9, at 30.
105 Yusuf, supra note 6, at 12.
106 Sell, supra note 7, at 173.

countries' side of the bargain, including the objectives and principles set forth in Articles 7 and 8, ought to be kept.

Finally, Articles 7 and 8 are important, because WTO panels and the Appellate Body are often 'tempted to introduce their own policy views on IPRs'.[107] For example, in determining the normal exploitation of intellectual property rights, the panels have taken views that focus narrowly on the right holder's economic interests. As Professor Correa lamented in relation to *Canada – Patent Protection of Pharmaceutical Products*:

> The panels' view, while emphasizing stimulation to innovation, fails to consider other equally essential objectives of the patent grants. Like other IPRs, patents are granted in the public interest, and not merely to allow the patent owners to obtain the 'economic returns anticipated from a patent's grant of market exclusivity'. The diffusion of knowledge and its continuous improvement are equally important objectives of that system.
>
> If the commercial interests of the patent owner were the only ones to be considered, the interpretation of the Agreement would in practice defeat its intended objectives.[108]

Likewise, Ruth Okediji expressed her disappointment over the decisions of the WTO panels and the Appellate Body:

> A particularly revealing aspect of these disputes is the way each of the Panels and the Appellate Body have ducked the thorny question of how to apply the preambular statements and the broad themes of Article 7 and 8 to evaluate the substantive obligations of the TRIPS Agreement. While tribunals can use strict construction to constrict or expand the requirements of TRIPS, the vagueness of these general qualifications in Articles 7 and 8 will likely lead to a one-way ratchet of rights. In each of these cases, the dispute panels have invariably emphasized the market preserve of intellectual property owners as a dominant factor in determining whether a TRIPS violation had occurred. Further, the cases suggest that the panels, in focusing on the purpose and objective of the TRIPS agreement, and the context of the negotiations, have interpreted the provisions almost solely in light of the economic expectations of the private right holders.[109]

As Graeme Dinwoodie reminded us, 'the incorporation of intellectual property agreements within trade mechanisms might (if trade concerns become paramount) deprive intellectual property policymaking of the rich palette of human values that historically has influenced its formulation'.[110]

---

[107] Correa, supra note 15, at 94.

[108] *Id.*

[109] Okediji, supra note 13, at 914–5.

[110] Dinwoodie, Graeme B. (2002), 'The architecture of the international intellectual property system', *Chicago-Kent Law Review*, **77**(3): 993–1014, 1004.

In sum, Articles 7 and 8 provide important tools to ensure that the WTO panels focus on the compromise struck between developed and less developed countries during the TRIPS negotiations.[111] Even if they were to ignore such a bargain, the two provisions provide the needed textual evidence for the Appellate Body to correct such misinterpretations.

Shield

Related to the first use, and partly as its outcome, is the second – the use of Articles 7 and 8 as a shield to defend a member state's use of flexibilities that have been built into the TRIPS Agreement. The use of these provisions for defensive purposes is particularly important in light of the fact that developed countries have been the predominant users of the WTO dispute settlement process.[112] Such use is even more important, considering the fact that WTO panel decisions may ultimately affect the tone and direction of future negotiations between developed and less developed countries – whether the negotiations are at the bilateral, regional, or multilateral levels. As Gregory Shaffer explained in the WTO context:

> Participation in WTO political and judicial processes are complementary. The shadow of WTO judicial processes shape bilateral negotiations, just as political processes and contexts inform judicial decisions. If developing countries can clarify their public goods priorities and coordinate their strategies, then they will more effectively advance their interests in bargaining conducted in WTO law's shadow, and in WTO legal complaints heard in the shadow of bargaining. They, in turn, will be better prepared to exploit the 'flexibilities' of the TRIPS Agreement, tailoring their intellectual property laws accordingly, and will gain confidence in their ability to ward off US and EC threats against their policy choices.[113]

The previous section discusses the use of Articles 7 and 8 to clarify the ambiguous provisions of the TRIPS Agreement. While it is important to seek clarifications in a member state's efforts to implement the Agreement, there are situations in which the provisions are open to many different interpretations. As Professor Frankel pointed out:

> Using [Articles 7 and 8] to help interpret the object and purpose is only a starting point. There are inherent difficulties in that the articles seek to capture competing objectives and purposes, and they represent a compromise between

---

[111] Yu, Peter K. (2006), 'TRIPs and its discontents', *Marquette Intellectual Property Law Review*, **10**(2): 369–410, 371–73.

[112] Davey, supra note 14, at 17.

[113] Shaffer, Gregory (2004), 'Recognizing public goods in WTO dispute settlement: Who participates? Who decides? The case of TRIPS and pharmaceutical patent protection', *Journal of International Economic Law*, **7**(2): 459–82, 476–7.

> the disparate views of those entering the agreement. What amounts to 'promotion of technological innovation and to the transfer and dissemination of technology' is, by its nature, open to some debate and the viewpoint of any WTO member is likely to relate to its economic position.[114]

As a result, it is important for less developed countries to interpret the provisions in a way that would highlight the social aspect, development dimension, and public policy goals of the TRIPS Agreement.

Unfortunately, such interpretation has been made difficult by a lack of institutional capacity and a growing orientation toward treaty compliance, not to mention a misplaced and misleadingly simplistic hope that greater compliance with the treaty will result in an increase in foreign direct investment, technology transfer, inward trade flows, and human capital.[115] To help restore the balance of the international intellectual property system, the TRIPS Agreement therefore needs to be interpreted through a pro-development lens,[116] with an emphasis on the objectives and principles set forth in Articles 7 and 8 of the TRIPS Agreement and the flexibilities expressly recognized in those provisions.

If such interpretations are to be developed, a better understanding of the development implications of the TRIPS Agreement is in order. It is also essential to develop model laws, policies, and best practices that are 'development friendly' and that take account of the needs, interests, and goals of less developed countries. Because these models can serve as good starting points for international negotiations, they are particularly useful as a response to the growing use of TRIPS-plus bilateral and regional trade agreements. The models can also help less developed countries build the much-needed experience and human capital to tailor their laws and policies to their specific local conditions.

Articles 7 and 8 can be used to help develop these models in three ways. First, as Jerome Reichman pointed out in the context of promoting access to essential medicines, the safeguards implicit in Articles 7 and 8 can be used to 'convince the Council for TRIPS . . . to recommend narrowly described waivers to meet specified circumstances for a limited period of time'.[117] In the alternative, less developed countries can use those

---

114 Frankel, supra note 18, at 393.

115 Deere, supra note 52, at 242; Maskus, Keith E. and Jerome H. Reichman (2005), 'The globalization of private knowledge goods and the privatization of global public goods', in Keith E. Maskus and Jerome H. Reichman (eds), *International Public Goods and Transfer of Technology under a Globalized Intellectual Property Regime*, Cambridge and New York: Cambridge University Press, pp. 3–45, 18.

116 Yu, supra note 111, at 387–9.

117 Reichman, J.H. (2000), 'The TRIPS agreement comes of age: Conflict

provisions in the WTO dispute settlement process to provide defense for their needed public health measures. As Professor Reichman explained:

> [D]eveloping country defendants responding to complaints of nullification and impairment under Article 64 might invoke the application of Articles 7 and 8(1) to meet unforeseen conditions of hardship. This defense, if properly grounded and supported by factual evidence, could persuade the Appellate Body either to admit the existence of a tacit doctrine of frustration built into the aforementioned articles or to buttress those articles by reaching out to the general doctrine of frustration recognized in the Vienna Convention on the Law of Treaties.

In an earlier article, Professor Reichman also suggested that, under the appropriate circumstances, the safeguard provisions implicit in the objectives set out in Article 7 of the TRIPS Agreement and the public interest exceptions expressly recognized in Article 8 'may legitimize ad hoc exceptions and limitations required by overriding national development needs or for reasons of national health, welfare or security'.[118]

Second, as Professor Gervais pointed out, 'the reference to social and economic welfare and to a balance of rights and obligations could serve to justify exceptions to exclusive rights where the right holder has failed to participate in social and economic development or, in other words, has used his rights without performing his obligations'.[119] Although exceptions and limitations in the copyright and patent systems are generally examined through the three-step test laid out in Articles 13 and 30 of the TRIPS Agreement, it is important to keep in mind the Appellate Body's reminder in *Canada – Patent Protection of Pharmaceutical Products*. As the Appellate Body stated, the Vienna Convention requires those interpreting and implementing the TRIPS Agreement to bear in mind the goals and limitations stated in Articles 7 and 8(1) when they examined the limiting conditions outlined in the three-step test.[120]

To date, commentators have generally focused on the use of Articles 7 and 8 to promote access to essential medicines in less developed countries. However, the two provisions can be used in many other areas. For example, Professor Okediji described how the provisions can be used to justify the validity of the fair use privilege in US copyright law under the

---

Footnote 117 (*cont.*)
or cooperation with the developing countries', *Case Western Reserve Journal of International Law*, **32**(3): 441–70, 461.

118 Reichman, supra note 101, at 35.

119 Gervais, supra note 10, at 116.

120 World Trade Organization (2000), *Canada – Patent Protection of Pharmaceutical Products*, WT/DS114/R, para. 7.26.

TRIPS Agreement.[121] Srividhya Ragavan also explored the use of the provisions to determine whether a member state has provided an effective *sui generis* system to protect plant varieties.[122] Utilizing Article 7 of the TRIPS Agreement, Marco Ricolfi further pointed out that

> efforts currently under way to make the patent system mutually supportive with the objective of preserving and fostering biodiversity can be better visualized under the heading of 'social welfare,' because this notion implies a respect for the autonomy of the (also non-IP) values of indigenous communities that may well defy the flatness of the *calculus felicificus* at which economists are so adept.[123]

Third, the two provisions are likely to be of increasing importance when countries began to file nonviolation complaints – complaints of nullification or impairment of benefits despite a lack of substantive violations. During the Seventh WTO Ministerial Conference in Geneva, WTO members agreed to extend the moratorium on these complaints until the next ministerial conference. Although nonviolation complaints are unlikely to present problems for less developed countries in the near future, problems may arise if the moratorium is finally lifted.

Thus far, the WTO panels and the Appellate Body have expressed their preference for a narrow definition of a right holder's normal exploitation of intellectual property rights. Based on this logic, a member state's normal expectations concerning the protection and enforcement of those rights will also be narrowly interpreted, with a strong emphasis on economic interests. Because '[t]he peculiarity of the notion of non-violation is that it does not, like many other international treaties, focus on the *legality* of an action, but rather on the *protection of expectations* arising from reciprocal tariff and market access concessions (in the GATT context) or from a Member's specific commitments (in the GATS context)',[124] Articles 7 and 8 are needed to ensure that the WTO panels and the Appellate Body properly divine these expectations.

As Professor Gervais pointed out, based on Article 7, 'any country

---

121 Okediji, Ruth (2000), 'Toward an international fair use doctrine', *Columbia Journal of Transnational Law*, **39**(1): 75–175, 167–8.

122 Ragavan, Srividhya and Jamie Mayer O'Shields (2007), 'Has India addressed its farmers' woes? A story of plant protection issues', *Georgetown International Environmental Law Review*, **20**(1): 97–127.

123 Marco Ricolfi (2006), 'Is there an antitrust antidote against IP overprotection within TRIPs?', *Marquette Intellectual Property Law Review*, **10**(2): 305–67, 325–6.

124 UNCTAD-ICTSD, supra note 19, at 655.

wishing to establish a violation of TRIPS or a nullification or impairment would be well advised to carefully provide in its submissions the data to deal with' the argument that the right holder has failed to participate in social and economic development or has used its rights without performing the accompanying obligations.[125] Likewise, Professor Correa noted:

> Article 8.1 is likely to be important in limiting the potential range of non-violation nullification or impairment causes, if allowed in the context of the TRIPS Agreement, as it makes clear that a wide range of public policy measures eventually changing the balance of concessions should be reasonably expected. Given the broad powers recognized to Members under Article 8.1, a Member challenging a measure adopted by another Member in pursuance of public policy objectives should have the initial burden of proof of inconsistency with the provisions of the TRIPS Agreement.[126]

Sword

While the provisions can be used as a shield to protect less developed countries, it remains questionable whether these provisions can also be used as a sword to challenge the existing provisions in developed countries or to enlarge the countries' policy space in the intellectual property area. Within the WTO dispute settlement process, the use of Articles 7 and 8 as the legal basis for any *affirmative* challenge is likely to be remote. Because Article 7 is only a 'should' provision, it does not provide the usual strength of a 'shall' provision.[127] Moreover, given the strong views taken by the European Communities and the United States during the negotiation process, WTO panels and the Appellate Body are likely to distinguish those two provisions from the operative or substantive provisions. Compared to Article 7, Article 8 is even weaker. Both Articles 8(1) and 8(2) use the word 'may' and are heavily constrained by the TRIPS-consistency requirement. Article 8(1) is further weakened by an additional necessity requirement.

In one of the leading treatises on the TRIPS Agreement, Professor Gervais suggests that Article 7 'could be invoked to limit an obligation to protect or enforce a given intellectual property right where no promotion of intellectual innovation and/or transfer or dissemination of technology can be proven'.[128] Although a textual analysis of the provision supports his suggestion, it is rather difficult for a complainant to provide such proof in reality. One may still remember the famous remark of economist Fritz Machlup in his critical examination of the US patent system:

---

[125] Gervais, supra note 10, at 116–7.

[126] Correa, supra note 15, at 108.

[127] Gervais, supra note 10, at 116.

[128] *Id.*

> If we did not have a patent system, it would be irresponsible, on the basis of our present knowledge of its economic consequences to recommend instituting one. But since we have had a patent system for a long time, it would be irresponsible, on the basis of our present knowledge, to recommend abolishing it.[129]

Moreover, the WTO panels and the Appellate Body have adopted a strict textual approach and have practiced judicial restraint.[130] As the Appellate Body made clear in *India – Patent Protection for Pharmaceutical and Agricultural Chemical Products*, the principles of interpretation set out in Article 31 of the Vienna Convention 'neither require nor condone the imputation into a treaty of words that are not there or the importation into a treaty of concepts that were not intended'.[131] Thus far, WTO panels and the Appellate Body have been interpreting the TRIPS Agreement narrowly, showing great deference to the Vienna Convention, the plain meaning of the text, the context of the TRIPS negotiations, and subsequent developments in the intellectual property field.

Notwithstanding these limitations, Articles 7 and 8 can be used as offensive tools in six different ways. First, although the provisions may not provide the legal basis for challenging intellectual property laws and policies in developed countries in the WTO dispute settlement process, both provisions can be used to strengthen other operative provisions that promote social and economic welfare or that help preserve the balance of the intellectual property system.

Articles 66 and 67 of the TRIPS Agreement, for example, require developed countries to provide technical cooperation to least developed countries. Although less developed countries were concerned that Article 66 is 'couched in "best endeavour" terms',[132] paragraph 11.2 of the Doha Ministerial Decision of 14 November 2001, which covers implementation-related issues and concerns, reaffirmed the mandatory nature of the provision. The decision further required the TRIPS Council to 'put in place a

---

[129] Machlup, Fritz (1958), *An Economic Review of the Patent System*, Study No. 15 of the Subcommittee on Patents Trademark and Copyright of the Senate Committee on the Judiciary, Washington, DC: Government Printing Office, p. 80.

[130] Barbosa, Chon and von Hase, supra note 13, at 99; Okediji, supra note 13, at 889; Reichman, Jerome H. (1998), 'Securing compliance with the TRIPS agreement after *US v. India*', *Journal of International Economic Law*, **1**(4): 585–601, 594–6; Weiler, J.H.H. (2001), 'The rule of lawyers and the ethos of diplomats: Reflections on the internal and external legitimacy of WTO dispute settlement', *Journal of World Trade*, **35**(2): 191–207, 206.

[131] World Trade Organization (1997), *India – Patent Protection for Pharmaceutical and Agricultural Chemical Products*, Appellate Body Report, WT/DS50/AB/R.

[132] Correa, supra note 15, at 98.

mechanism for ensuring the monitoring and full implementation of the obligations in question'. With fortifications from Articles 7 and 8, Articles 66 and 67 are likely to become even more robust and effective.

In the patent area, Articles 7 and 8 can help strengthen the limitations and exceptions in Articles 27 and 31. Articles 27(2) and 27(3), for example, stipulate the standards for excluding inventions from patentability. Article 27(3) also preserves the flexibility for member states to design protection for plant varieties. Article 31 lays down the various conditions under which member states can use patented products without the right holders' authorization. The two provisions can also help clarify the limiting conditions in Article 30, which provides a three-step test for evaluating limitations and exceptions in the patent field. As shown in *Canada – Patent Protection of Pharmaceutical Products*, the WTO panel has used Articles 7 and 8 to clarify the limiting conditions stated in the three-step test.[133]

Second, Articles 7 and 8 may be used to promote the development of maximum standards as well as exceptions and limitations at the TRIPS Council meetings. Paragraph 19 of the Ministerial Declaration instructed the TRIPS Council to take into account 'the objectives and principles set out in Articles 7 and 8 of the TRIPS Agreement and . . . the development dimension'. While the legal effect of this declaration remains suspect in future challenges before the WTO Dispute Settlement Body, Articles 7 and 8 are likely to receive more attention in the TRIPS Council, which was specifically instructed to take account of those provisions. There is a difference between judicial adjudication on the one hand and political persuasion or diplomatic negotiation on the other. More importantly, the two provisions provide the needed principles and rhetoric that often prevail in international negotiations.[134] Echoing loudly the demands of less developed countries, they also provide a strategic reminder of the bargain these countries have struck during the TRIPS negotiations.

In addition, Articles 7 and 8 may feature prominently in the review processes established by the TRIPS Council, WTO bodies, and other international organizations. For example, '[a] number of developing countries have [already] indicated that the implementation of Article 7 should be examined in the Council for TRIPS in the context of determining whether TRIPS is fulfilling the objective of contributing to the dissemination and transfer of technology'.[135] Outside the WTO, Articles 7 and 8 will

---

133 World Trade Organization (2000), *Canada – Patent Protection of Pharmaceutical Products*, Panel Report, WT/DS114/R, para. 7.26.

134 Gervais, supra note 9, at 508.

135 UNCTAD-ICTSD, supra note 19, at 132.

also make clear the intended objectives of the TRIPS Agreement. In doing so, they promote coherency within the international treaty system while at the same time providing a yardstick for international organizations to determine for themselves whether the Agreement has been properly implemented.

Third, Articles 7 and 8 can be used as a *sword* in non-violation complaints just as they can be used as a *shield*. Although less developed countries have been rather concerned that they might be on the receiving end of these complaints once the moratorium is lifted, they can also use these complaints to challenge measures in developed countries that alter the balance of the TRIPS regime. In such challenges, Articles 7 and 8 will provide the helpful textual basis to show how the measures have upset the balance of the international intellectual property system, the reasonable expectations these countries had when the TRIPS negotiations entered into effect, and whether their reliance on such expectations is justified.

Fourth, Articles 7 and 8 may help identify the right holders' obligations stipulated explicitly or implicitly in the TRIPS Agreement. These obligations are essential to maintaining the balance of the international intellectual property system – a key objective of the TRIPS Agreement. While the Agreement clearly delineates the substantive rights of intellectual property holders in each member state, it fails to outline clearly the right holders' obligations. As the High Commissioner for Human Rights declared in her report:

> [W]hile the Agreement identifies the need to balance rights with obligations, it gives no guidance on how to achieve this balance. On the one hand, the Agreement sets out in considerable detail the content of intellectual property *rights* – the requirements for the grant of rights, the duration of protection, the modes of enforcement. On the other hand, the Agreement only alludes to the *responsibilities* of IP holders that should balance those rights in accordance with its own objectives. The prevention of anti-competitive practices and the abuse of rights, the promotion of technology transfer, special and differential treatment for least developed countries are merely referred to – but unlike the rights it sets out, the Agreement does not establish the content of these responsibilities, or how they should be implemented.[136]

It is therefore no surprise that the United Nations Sub-commission on the Protection and Promotion of Human Rights reminded governments

---

[136] United Nations Economic and Social Council, Sub-commission on the Promotion and Protection of Human Rights (2001), *The Impact of the Agreement on Trade-related Aspects of Intellectual Property Rights on Human Rights: Report of the High Commissioner*, E/CN.4/Sub.2/2001/13, para. 23.

'of the primacy of human rights obligations over economic policies and agreements'.[137] Meanwhile, a new authoritative interpretation of the International Covenant on Economic, Social and Cultural Rights also states clearly that 'intellectual property is a social product . . . [with] a social function' and that 'the private interests of authors should not be unduly favoured and the public interest in enjoying broad access to their productions should be given due consideration'.[138]

These emphases on and reminders of international human rights obligations are important, because the WTO member states all have international obligations outside the intellectual property area. As noted in the *TRIPS Resource Book*:

> Human rights instruments, such as the International Covenant on Economic, Social and Cultural Rights, support a number of the same objectives and principles as Articles 7 and 8. The various agreements of the International Labour Organization, and the charter of the World Health Organization, support the development-oriented objectives and principles of TRIPS. In the implementation of TRIPS and in any dispute settlement proceedings it will be useful to establish the supportive links between the objectives and principles stated in Articles 7 and 8, and the objectives and principles of other international instruments.[139]

In fact, the use of the word 'should' and the references to the 'social and economic welfare' and 'a balance of rights and obligations' in Article 7 provide a strong reminder of the many obligations imposed by the International Covenant on Economic, Social and Cultural Rights, such as the right to life, the right to food, the right to health, the right to education, the right to self-determination, the right to freedom of expression, the right to cultural participation and development, and the right to the benefits of scientific progress. Those references also pave the way for the development of substantive obligations with the TRIPS regime.

In recent years, commentators have widely discussed the need to build obligations, responsibilities, maximum standards, and affirmative rights into the intellectual property system. For example, Jacqueline Lipton pointed out that, when laws borrowed from traditional property theory

---

137 Sub-commission on Human Rights (2000), *Intellectual Property Rights and Human Rights*, Res. 2000/7, E/CN.4/Sub.2/RES/2000/7, para. 3.

138 Committee on Economic, Social and Cultural Rights (2006), *General Comment No. 17: The Right of Everyone to Benefit from the Protection of the Moral and Material Interests Resulting from Any Scientific, Literary or Artistic Production of Which He is the Author (Article 15, Paragraph 1(c), of the Covenant)*, E/C.12/GC/17, para. 35.

139 UNCTAD-ICTSD, supra note 19, at 130.

are applied in the information property context, there is a tendency to overlook the fact that 'traditional Property rights entail significant concurrent obligations or responsibilities imposed on the proprietary owner as an incident of their Property ownership'.[140] Scholars have also advanced proposals to develop affirmative user rights to facilitate public access to protected materials.[141] Many of those proposals seek to benefit user groups that are acknowledged implicitly in Article 7, including 'libraries, educational institutions, research institutes, or non-governmental organizations[, all of whom] were noticeably absent during TRIPS negotiations'.[142]

Fifth, the identification in Article 7 of promoting 'social and economic welfare' and 'a balance of rights and obligations' as the key objectives of the TRIPS Agreement provides a strong textual basis for less developed countries and intergovernmental organizations to demand the establishment of impact studies on development, which have been widely endorsed in the areas of human rights, public health, and biological diversity.[143] After all, welfare and balance cannot be determined *in vacuo*. The recently adopted WIPO Development Agenda also includes a number of recommendations concerning assessment, evaluation, and impact studies. These studies are particularly important as intellectual property protection expands to create spillover effects in other policy areas. In fact, it would be good policy to conduct impact studies to undertake a holistic evaluation of the ramifications of all new intellectual property standards before their adoption.[144]

Finally, Articles 7 and 8 can be used to help reframe the existing intellectual property debate. Although legal scholars have widely ignored the importance of such framing and reframing, their importance has been recently picked up by commentators outside the legal discipline or by those having interdisciplinary research interests. If carefully developed, a constructive frame can effectively convince the WTO member states, the TRIPS Council, WTO panels, and the Appellate Body to become more receptive to the demands, or perhaps pleas, of less developed countries.[145] As John Braithwaite and Peter Drahos noted in the public health context: 'Had TRIPS been framed as a public health issue, the anxiety of mass publics in the US and other Western states might have become

---

140 Lipton, Jacqueline, 'Information property: Rights and responsibilities', *Florida Law Review*, **56**(1): 135–94, 148 (2004).
141 Yu, supra note 111, at 396–401.
142 Okediji, supra note 13, at 858.
143 Yu, supra note 1, at 901.
144 Yu, supra note 51.
145 Yu, supra note 7, at 377–8.

a factor in destabilizing the consensus that US business elites had built around TRIPS'.[146] Likewise, Susan Sell reminded us that 'grants talk' is preferable to 'rights talk' from the standpoint of international development, because it 'highlights the fact that what may be granted may be taken away when such grants conflict with other important goals' and is likely to discourage policymakers from focusing on the entitlement of the rights holders.[147]

Bridge

Articles 7 and 8 can serve as a useful bridge that connects the TRIPS regime with those other regimes that may be implicated by the protection and enforcement of intellectual property rights. Paragraph 19 of the Ministerial Declaration, for example, stated explicitly that the TRIPS Council should be guided by Articles 7 and 8 in its examination of 'the relationship between the TRIPS Agreement and the Convention on Biological Diversity [and] the protection of traditional knowledge and folklore'. Such protection, after all, can be covered in many different regimes – most notably, the biodiversity regime and the food and agriculture regime.

Likewise, the language of Article 7 has recently been incorporated into a recommendation adopted as part of the WIPO Development Agenda. As Recommendation 45 states specifically:

> To approach intellectual property enforcement in the context of broader societal interests and especially development-oriented concerns, with a view that 'the protection and enforcement of intellectual property rights should contribute to the promotion of technological innovation and to the transfer and dissemination of technology, to the mutual advantage of producers and users of technological knowledge and in a manner conducive to social and economic welfare, and to a balance of rights and obligations', in accordance with Article 7 of the TRIPS Agreement.

Articles 7 and 8 of the TRIPS Agreement, therefore, are important for maintaining the balance not just in the TRIPS regime, but also in the global innovation system.

Today, international law has become highly fragmented,[148] and the continuous proliferation of international fora and the widespread use

---

146 Braithwaite, John and Peter Drahos (2000), *Global Business Regulation*, Cambridge and New York: Cambridge University Press, p. 576.

147 Sell, supra note 7, at 146.

148 Benvenisti, Eyal and George W. Downs (2007), 'The empire's new clothes: Political economy and the fragmentation of international law', *Stanford Law Review*, **60**(2): 595–631.

of regime-shifting maneuvers have led to the development of intellectual property-related norms in many different international fora.[149] This development has resulted in the creation of what I have described as the 'international intellectual property regime complex' – a larger conglomerate regime that includes not only the traditional area of intellectual property laws and policies, but also the overlapping areas in related regimes or fora.[150]

Thus, while it remains important to strengthen safeguards in the international intellectual property system, or develop the so-called ceilings of or maximum standards for intellectual property protection and enforcement, it is equally important to develop support in other international instruments that can be used to enhance the impact of Articles 7 and 8 within the TRIPS Agreement. With the support of these additional standards, Articles 7 and 8 may more effectively 'persuade the [WTO panels and the Appellate Body] to recognize and give effect to developmental priorities'.[151] In fact, it may be 'useful in the context of dispute settlement to cross-reference developmental objectives and principles of the appropriate agreements'.[152] After all, the Preamble of the TRIPS Agreement states the drafters' intention to '[r]ecogniz[e] the underlying public policy objectives of national systems for the protection of intellectual property, including developmental and technological objectives'.

This approach makes a lot of sense. As Professor Correa pointed out, '[i]ntellectual property cannot be regarded in isolation from broader national policies, such as competition and development policies. In order to contribute to national objectives, the intellectual property system must be integrated into such policies'.[153] Likewise, Graeme Austin noted:

> To the extent that intellectual property policies and values can be identified, it might be more helpful to regard them as aspects of much broader issues of public policy. Policies that help ensure that populations get fed, enjoy the benefits of literacy, are healthy, have viable agricultural bases, and can participate in technological and cultural development – these seem to be the kinds of policies that should have priority in any analysis of the values that intellectual property laws are meant to serve.[154]

---

149 Braithwaite and Drahos, supra note 146, at 564–71; May, supra note 72, at 66; Helfer, Laurence R. (2004), 'Regime shifting: The TRIPs agreement and new dynamics of international intellectual property lawmaking', *Yale Journal of International Law*, **29**(1): 1–83.

150 Yu, supra note 62, at 13–21.

151 UNCTAD-ICTSD, supra note 19, at 130.

152 *Id.*

153 Correa, supra note 15, at 12.

154 Austin, Graeme W. (2002), 'Valuing "domestic self-determination" in inter-

Most recently, Henning Ruse-Khan also suggested the use of 'the WTO-overarching objective of sustainable development as a principle for reconciling economic, social and environmental interests which applies to all WTO Agreements', including the TRIPS Agreement.[155]

Like these commentators, the WTO Dispute Settlement Body has acknowledged the overlap between intellectual property protection and protection under other international regimes. In its first dispute, *United States – Standards for Reformulated and Conventional Gasoline*, the Appellate Body declared that 'the General Agreement [which consists of agreements in many different areas] is not to be read in clinical isolation from public international law'.[156] In *India – Patent Protection for Pharmaceutical and Agricultural Chemical Products*, the WTO panel also recognized that the TRIPS Agreement 'is an integral part of the WTO system, which itself builds upon the experience of over nearly half a century' under the GATT.[157] Moreover, in *United States – Import Prohibition on Certain Shrimp and Shrimp Turtle Products*, the Appellate Body 'moved firmly away from the notion of the WTO as a "self-contained" legal regime'.[158]

Seed

Articles 7 and 8 can be used as a seed for the development of new norms both *within* and *without* the international intellectual property regime.[159] They can supply the needed language or provide direction for the development of these new norms. They also help remind the treaty drafters of the nature, scope, and objectives of intellectual property norms.

In designing the *internal* norms, Articles 7 and 8 can be used in two ways.

Footnote 154 (*cont.*)
national intellectual property jurisprudence', *Chicago-Kent Law Review*, **77**(3): 1155–211, 1193.

[155] Ruse-Khan, Henning Grosse (2008), 'A comparative analysis of policy space in WTO law', Max Planck Institute for Intellectual Property Competition and Tax Law, Research Paper No. 08–02.

[156] World Trade Organization (1996), *United States – Standards for Reformulated and Conventional Gasoline*, Appellate Body Report, WT/DS2/AB/R, part III.B.

[157] World Trade Organization (1997), *India – Patent Protection for Pharmaceutical and Agricultural Chemical Products*, Panel Report, WT/DS50/R, para. 7.19.

[158] UNCTAD-ICTSD, *supra* note 19, at 30 (citing World Trade Organization (1998), *United States – Import Prohibition on Certain Shrimp and Shrimp Turtle Products*, Appellate Body Report, WT/DS58/AB/R).

[159] These norms may take the form of substantive rules or standards, procedural safeguards, or even equitable remedies.

First, by stating the objectives and principles of the TRIPS Agreement, the two provisions highlight the concerns of less developed countries as well as those areas that need greater balancing. For example, Article 8 mentions public health and restraint on trade. Those provisions therefore underscore the important interfaces between intellectual property protection and the protection of public health or between intellectual property protection and regulation of anticompetitive and restrictive business practices.[160]

Second, Articles 7 and 8 provide objective evidence for determining whether an international political consensus exists. The provisions therefore outline the boundaries of the TRIPS regime. Delineating these boundaries clearly is particularly important, as countries increasingly induce others to transplant laws through bilateral, regional, and multilateral efforts. As Abdulqawi Yusuf aptly suggests, the objectives set forth in Article 7 of the TRIPS Agreement also 'provide the overall criteria against which the adequacy and effectiveness of national legislation for the protection and enforcement of IPRs should be measured'.[161]

Although countries that comply with their TRIPS obligations can be hardly described as offering ineffective or inadequate protection – at least according to the TRIPS Agreement[162] – the United States Trade Representative can take Section 301 actions on countries that fail to provide 'adequate and effective protection of intellectual property rights *notwithstanding the fact that [they] may be in compliance with the specific obligations of the Agreement on Trade-Related Aspects of Intellectual Property Rights*'. It is, therefore, no surprise that Canada has been put on the Section 301 watch list perennially, along with countries that are, from the US perspective, more likely to have laws in violation of the TRIPS Agreement, such as Brazil, China, India, Russia, and Ukraine.

While the previous three sections focus primarily on developments within the TRIPS regime, that regime is only part of the larger international intellectual property system. In fact, shortly after the Agreement entered into force, WIPO quickly adopted the WIPO Copyright Treaty and the WIPO Performances and Phonograms Treaty. The organization also developed soft-law recommendations on the protection of well-known marks and marks on the Internet. As Professor Dinwoodie observed:

> the sudden emergence of the WTO as part of the international intellectual property lawmaking process seemed to energize WIPO, resulting in the conclusion

---

160 Ricolfi, supra note 123, at 326.
161 Yusuf, supra note 6, at 13.
162 Correa, supra note 15, at 1–2.

> of several new treaties in copyright, patent and trademark law, as well as the reorganization . . . designed to make WIPO fit for the twenty-first century.[163]

In the past few years, WIPO has explored the development of a Substantive Patent Law Treaty and the WIPO Treaty on the Protection of Broadcasting Organisations. Nevertheless, it has faced significant opposition in both areas.

Articles 7 and 8 are equally helpful in developing *external* norms. While some of these norms may be complementary to or compatible with existing internal norms, others may be what commentators have called 'counterregime norms'.[164] As Laurence Helfer defined, counterregime norms are 'binding treaty rules and nonbinding soft law standards that seek to alter the prevailing legal landscape'.[165] Once developed, these norms can help set up maximum standards for intellectual property protection. They may also be further internalized within the intellectual property regime as 'revisionist norms'.[166] As the impact of intellectual property protection continues to spill over into other areas, such as agriculture, health, the environment, education, culture, competition, free speech, privacy, democracy, and the rule of law, these revisionist norms will only become more important.[167]

Although many commentators still perceive international organizations, such as WIPO and the WTO, as self-interested players,[168] these organizations are beginning to cooperate with each other more – regardless of whether they do it willingly or reluctantly. Article 68 of the TRIPS Agreement states specifically that the Council for TRIPS 'may consult with and seek information from any source it deems appropriate' in carrying out its functions and 'shall seek to establish, within one year of its first meeting, appropriate arrangements for cooperation with bodies

---

163 Dinwoodie, supra note 110, at 1005.

164 Helfer, supra note 149, at 58–9.

165 *Id.* at 14.

166 Helfer, Laurence R. (2004), 'Mediating interactions in an expanding international intellectual property regime', *Case Western Reserve Journal of International Law*, **36**(1): 123–36, 127.

167 Abbott, Frederick M. (2003), 'Non-violation nullification or impairment causes of action under the TRIPS agreement and the fifth ministerial conference: A warning and reminder', Quaker United Nations Office Occasional Paper No. 11, p. 2.

168 May, supra note 72, at 59; Abbott, Frederick M. (2000), 'Distributed governance at the WTO-WIPO: An evolving model for open-architecture integrated governance', *Journal of International Economic Law*, **3**(1): 63–81, 72; Dinwoodie, supra note 110, at 1001.

of [WIPO]'. The Agreement between the World Intellectual Property Organization and the World Trade Organization also calls for cooperation between the WTO and WIPO in the notification of, provision of access to, and translation of national legislation; the communication of national emblems and transmittal of objections pursuant to Article 6*ter* of the Paris Convention; and legal-technical assistance and technical cooperation.

Indeed, as intellectual property protection expands and as issue areas and international regimes continue to overlap with each other, there will be an increasing and more active flow of language, concepts, standards, measures, and safeguards from one regime to another. While the WTO panels and the Appellate Body remain faithful to the application of the Vienna Convention, they have increasingly looked to treaties in the WIPO or other fora to resolve ambiguities in the TRIPS Agreement. The converse can also be true. It would be, indeed, no surprise if drafters in other fora or interpreters of non-intellectual property treaties look to Articles 7 and 8 to help resolve ambiguities in existing treaties, alleviate tension between and among the various treaties, or even to provide a starting point for new treaties and initiatives.

Conclusion

Since their creation and limited application in the early days of the WTO, Articles 7 and 8 have attracted growing attention from policymakers, commentators, intergovernmental organizations, and nongovernmental organizations. Legally, the two provisions play important roles in the interpretation and implementation of the TRIPS Agreement. Economically, they facilitate innovation, technology transfer, and knowledge production, while at the same time promoting social and economic welfare and development goals. Politically, they provide the much-needed balance to make the Agreement a legitimate bargain between developed and less developed countries. Structurally, the two provisions bridge the gap between the TRIPS regime and other international regimes. Globally, they have sowed the seeds for the development of new international norms both within and without the TRIPS regime. Although most of the draft language proposed by less developed countries did not make its way to the TRIPS Agreement, the choice of such language for Articles 7 and 8 is more than consolation. In fact, it may be a blessing in disguise! Whether the two provisions can become a true blessing, however, will depend on whether the WTO member states can use them effectively, to their advantage, and to the fullest possible extent.

6 Mainstreaming the TRIPS and human rights interactions

Xavier Seuba

1. Introduction

In the year 2000, the United Nations Sub-commission on Human Rights affirmed that 'actual or potential conflicts exist between the implementation of the TRIPS Agreement and the realisation of economic, social and cultural rights'. Among those conflicts, the Sub-commission singled out 'impediments to the transfer of technology to developing countries, the consequences for the enjoyment of the right to food of plant variety rights and the patenting of genetically modified organisms, "bio-piracy" and the reduction of communities' (especially indigenous communities) control over their own genetic and natural resources and cultural values, and restrictions of access to patented pharmaceuticals'.[1] According to the Sub-commission, said problems were caused because 'the implementation of the TRIPS Agreement does not adequately reflect the fundamental nature and indivisibility of all human rights, including the right of everyone to enjoy the benefits of scientific progress and its applications, the right to health, the right to food and the right to self-determination'.[2] Since then, numerous United Nations human rights bodies, national courts and States have emphasized similar concerns, and the relationship between the TRIPS Agreement and the international human rights legal system has been studied in greater depth.

The relationship between the TRIPS Agreement and international human rights law must be studied in two broad frameworks, namely, that concerning the more general relation between intellectual property law and human rights law, and the other related to the interaction between public international law and World Trade Organization (WTO) law. It is the combination of the two that gives adequate answers to specific cases, such as those pointed out by the Sub-commission on Human Rights.

---

1 Sub-commission on the Protection and Promotion of Human Rights, *Intellectual property rights and human rights,* 17 August 2000, E/CN.4/Sub.2/RES/2000/7, Preamble.

2 *Ibid.*, par. 2.

Although this chapter will address both relations,[3] especial emphasis will be devoted to the effects on the TRIPS and human rights relationships of the WTO legal system anchorage in public international law. It will be held that thanks to the room for manoeuvre existing in the TRIPS, said anchorage permits most of the *potential* problems envisaged by the UN Sub-Commission on Human Rights to be solved through interpretation. On the other hand, as far as *actual* conflicts are concerned, it will be argued that although responses can be found in public international law rules on conflict of treaties, the gravity of problems arising out of TRIPS *plus* and *extra* provisions indicates that much more than solutions based on legal technique is needed.

2. Intellectual property and its relationship with human rights

2.1. General appraisal

In the last fifteen years, two traditionally unrelated legal regimes – human rights law and intellectual property law – started a controversial dialogue. On the one hand, the remarkable international strengthening of intellectual property law has raised numerous difficulties when trying to fulfil human rights obligations. The TRIPS Agreement and subsequent treaties raising TRIPS obligations have been considered responsible for the majority of these problems. On the other hand, the clarification of the scope of numerous economic, social and cultural rights has facilitated the identification of the specific impediments that certain levels of intellectual property protection imply for the fulfilment of human rights. In this second regard, there has been significant effort on the part of human rights treaties monitoring organs, scholars and civil society organizations to identify those specific problems and set them out in precise legal terms. The factors that have contributed to outlining the link between both regimes have been, therefore, the specification of what is owed to people carried out by international human rights law, added to the curtailment of the tools necessary to provide it provoked by intellectual property law.

An important part of the discussion surrounding intellectual property protection has as a background the very basis that sustains said protection. The positive public nature of knowledge[4] – that is, its public

---

[3] A more detailed study on the general interaction between intellectual property law and human rights law can be found in X. Seuba, 'Human Rights and Intellectual Property Rights', in C.M. Correa and A.A. Yusuff (eds), *Intellectual Property and International Trade: The TRIPS Agreement*, second edition, Dordrecht: Kluwer International Law, 2007, pp. 387–419.

[4] J. Stiglitz, 'Knowledge as a Global Public Good', in I. Kaul, I. Grunberg

good status – has led the justification of the private appropriation of innovation's exploitation through intellectual property. In this sense, the protection of creativity via property is the response to a specific utilitarian thinking, which justifies the protection of products resulting from human creativity and inventiveness as a way to stimulate art and science.[5] Presently, instrumentalism is seen as the ultimate justification of intellectual property protection. A protection that, at least in the industrial property field, should led to the promotion of socially useful technical innovations. Moreover, as Professor Drahos affirms, instrumentalism sees property as an institutional mechanism that has to serve moral values,[6] an understanding which precludes intellectual property from any absolute status and makes its protection conditional upon serving those values.

The link between intellectual property and moral values and social functions is an important one in order to establish a positive relationship between intellectual property regulation and the human rights legal order. By itself, intellectual property is devoid of values. However, human rights law provides rules which synthesize the value judgements lacking in the intellectual property regime, and establishes the limits of intellectual property rights protection should human rights fulfilment problems arise. It can be said that intellectual property protection must serve the objective of human well-being, to which human rights instruments give legal expression.[7] In this sense, human rights serve two functions regarding intellectual property. First, they inform the shaping of the intellectual property regime and, second, once the system is established, they inform the interpretation of specific issues arising from its application.[8]

Footnote 4 (*cont.*)
and M. Stern (eds), *Global Public Goods in the 20th Century: International Cooperation in the 20th Century*, Oxford: Oxford University Press, 1999.

5 For instance, article I, section 8, of the United States Constitution vests the Congress with the power to 'promote the Progress of Science and useful Arts, by securing for limited Times to Authors and Inventors the exclusive Right to their respective Writings and Discoveries'. Internationally, it is worth mentioning article 7 of the TRIPS Agreement, which notes that 'protection and enforcement of intellectual property rights should contribute to the promotion of technological innovation'.

6 *Ibid.*, p. 214.

7 Committee on Economic, Social and Cultural Rights (CESCR), *Follow-up to the day of general Discussion on article 15.1.c),* 26/11/2001, E/C.12/2001/15, par. 4.

8 United Nations High Commissioner for Human Rights, *The impact of the Agreement on Trade-Related Aspects of Intellectual Property Rights on Human Rights*, 27 June 2001, E/CN.4/Sub.2/2001/13, par. 15.

2.2. *Intellectual property rights relationship with first, second and third generation human rights*

The above-quoted reference of the Sub-commission on Human Rights to the TRIPS Agreement's effects on human rights protection is certainly short. The Sub-commission only alluded to the so-called second generation human rights, which includes economic, social, and cultural rights. However, intellectual property rights, and therefore the TRIPS Agreement itself, are also related to first and third generation human rights. The first generation includes the most classical human rights, that is, civil and political rights, while third generation human rights refer to so-called solidarity rights, which are related to economic and social aspirations. If we were to follow the well-known French Revolution proclamation, 'Liberté, Égalité, Fraternité', first generation human rights would refer to *liberty*, second generation would correspond to *equality* and third generation would be related to *fraternity*.

Regarding the interactions between intellectual property rights and the rights pertaining to first generation human rights, the most notorious relationships are with the right to privacy, the right to receive information and the right to life. As far as the right to privacy is concerned, in the context of the initiative to enforce the highest intellectual property standards – which has several fronts, such as the ACTA initiative and the enforcement provisions contained in free trade agreements (FTA) promoted by the European Community (EC) and the United States (US) – concerns have been raised regarding third persons' private data that title holders may order the infringer to inform on alleged intellectual property violations. TRIPS article 47 already set up a demanding standard regarding information that can be demanded from the infringer. However, the scope of article 47 is much more limited when compared to that enshrined in the new standards. Moreover, article 47 lays down the condition to not ask for information that would be out of proportion to the seriousness of the infringement, which, together with the fact that article 47 represents a shared view among WTO Members, makes article 47 in itself less controversial from a human rights point of view. Also, in the context of the interaction between the right to privacy and intellectual property rights, the challenge of peer-to-peer systems on copyright grounds raises concerns from the right to privacy point of view. These concerns, added to ones arising from curtailment of the right to a fair trial, become even worse when analysing the techniques deployed to identify private and non-commercial interest users of peer-to-peer systems.[9]

[9] See F. Coudert and E. Werkers, 'In The Aftermath of the Promusicae

On the other hand, a more positive link can be found between the right to receive information and some obligations arising from intellectual property treaties. TRIPS article 29, for instance, permits the request for clear and complete information for the patented invention to be carried out, and allows requiring the disclosure of the best way to carry out the invention. Both extremes can be instrumental in the fulfilment of the right of access to information. Among the roles attached to patents is the informative one, because granting a patent also implies detailing the state of the art. In order to fulfil this function, authorities must examine information supporting an applicant's claims so that it is complete and describes the best mode to perform the invention. The disclosure of said supporting information will be instrumental to both spreading knowledge and promoting further innovation. Moreover, and in addition to more technical information referred to the patentable invention, the right to access to information – together with TRIPS articles 27.1 and 29, and also the Convention on Biological Diversity – should be explored as a suitable basis to ask for presently controversial information, such as the source and origin of genetic resources which have been isolated or slightly modified in order to obtain patents for dubious 'innovations'. In any case, the relationship between the right to freedom of expression – which includes the right to seek, receive and impart information[10] – and certain intellectual property rights categories, such as copyrights, can also be controversial.[11]

Another example among first generation rights is related to the right to life, a right which is presently understood as a positive and inclusive one. In this sense, the right to life not only prohibits the intentional deprivation of someone's life but also commands States to adopt positive measures, particularly to 'eliminate malnutrition and epidemics'.[12] The restrictive effects of patent protection on seeds provision and access to medicines can, therefore, be analysed taking the right to life as reference. In this same context, another particularly worrying case is that concern-

---

Footnote 9 (*cont.*)
Case: How to Strike the Balance?', *International Journal of Law and Information Technology*, 25 October 2008, doi:10.1093/ijlit/ean015.

[10] *Vid.* International Covenant on Civil and Political Rights art. 19.2.

[11] As the English Court of Appeal held, 'the Court is bound . . . to apply the Copyright, Patents and Designs Act in a manner that accommodates the right of freedom of expression'. *The Right Honourable Paddy Ashdown MP PC v. Telegraph Group Ltd.*, 2001, EWCA Civ. 1142 (Eng. CA), p. 45.

[12] Human Rights Committee, General Comment no. 6, Article 6 (Sixteenth session, 1982), Compilation of General Comments and General Recommendations Adopted by Human Rights Treaty Bodies, UN Doc. HRI/GEN/1/Rev.6 at 127 (2003), par. 4.

ing the protection of test data submitted to obtain market authorization of certain regulated products, that is, pharmaceuticals and agrochemicals. In opposition to its traditional protection against unfair competition, a certain interpretation of TRIPS article 39 as well as numerous US and EC FTA provisions compel the granting of periods of exclusivity to said data. These exclusivity periods, which may last from between five to eleven years, either impede the production of bioequivalent drugs or oblige the repetition of clinical tests on human beings. These tests are unnecessary and therefore arbitrary, endanger participants' lives and can be related to the most classical meaning of the right to life, that is to say, the prohibition on arbitrarily depriving someone of their life.

Up until now, most attention has been devoted to the effects of the TRIPS Agreement on second generation human rights. In this context, the potential negative effects of said agreement on the rights to health care, food and education, deserve special attention. Take for instance the conditions set forth in the TRIPS regarding patents, which limit the capacity of States to implement pharmaceutical policies adjusted to their public health needs and economic reality. Remarkably, among these conditions, the obligation to grant patents for products and processes in all fields of technology appears, thereby extinguishing the traditional and widely used power to bar the protection of pharmaceutical products via patents. As far as food security and hence the right to food are concerned, it has been observed that the TRIPS régime for the protection of micro-organisms and plant varieties may limit the freedom that farmers enjoyed to exchange and sell seeds and may also lead to the harvesting of a reduced diversity of genetically uniform crops, the latter entailing the impoverishment of diet and a greater vulnerability of crops to devastating plagues. Although, in accordance with TRIPS article 27.3(b), a *sui generis* system for the protection of plant varieties may be adopted, the vast majority of developing countries are adopting the International Convention for the Protection of New Varieties of Plants. The UPOV Convention entails the problems alluded to above[13] and its ratification is made mandatory in numerous FTAs, thereby endangering the livelihood of farmers from developing countries.

The main international treaty enshrining the above-mentioned second generation rights is the International Covenant on Economic, Social and Cultural Rights (ICESCR). Its supervising Committee has pointed out

---

[13] UPOV Convention, as amended in 1991, restricts but does not prohibit what is referred to as 'farmers' privileges', that is, they can replant the seeds obtained from previous crops; however, their exchange or commercial sale, albeit small scale, is prohibited. See Gaia Foundation–GRAIN, *Ten reasons why not to join UPOV,* Global Trade and Biodiversity in Conflict Series, Issue 2, 1999.

that States have a duty to prevent the protection of intellectual property resulting in 'unreasonably high costs for access to medicines, plant seeds or other means of food production, or to schoolbooks and learning materials'.[14] As aforementioned, potential conflicts do in fact exist between the TRIPS Agreement and several ICESCR articles, namely article 11.1 on 'the right of everyone to an adequate standard of living for himself and his family, including adequate food', article 12 on the right to the highest attainable standard of health, which includes medical assistance and treatment in the event of sickness, and articles 13 and 14, on the right to education, which includes the universal and free nature of education.

Regarding third generation rights, particular attention must be devoted to the right to development. States have the right to formulate national development policies that aim at improving the well-being of their population,[15] and all peoples may, for their own ends, freely dispose of their natural wealth and resources.[16] In spite of being a right marked by the vagueness of the obligations derived from the same, the right to development certainly implies the right to choose the model of development and to rule out methods and policies which hinder people's progress. Prior to the TRIPS, States were free to decide what level of protection they would give to whatever applications of technology they saw as relevant to their development needs.[17] Nevertheless, and despite of the recognition in the TRIPS Preamble of 'the underlying public policy objectives of national systems for the protection of intellectual property, including developmental and technological objectives', the TRIPS Agreement's imposed obligation to provide protection in all fields of technology has a direct impact on the ability of States to decide on their development strategies. It is indeed true that States' access to the WTO and therefore to the TRIPS is voluntary, but at least two comments must be made in this respect. On the one hand, when almost no other option exists, the voluntary nature of an act must be seriously qualified. On the other hand, the TRIPS Agreement references to the transfer of technology have been marginalized, these

---

[14] CESCR, *General Comment No. 17, The right of everyone to benefit from the protection of the moral and material interests resulting from any scientific, literary or artistic production of which he is the author (article 15 paragraph 1c) of the Covenant,* E/C.12/GC/17, 12 January 2006, par. 35.

[15] Declaration on the Right to Development, article 2.3. See also article 1.2, which states that the human right to development also implies the full realization of the right to self-determination, which includes the right to full sovereignty over all their natural wealth and resources.

[16] Article 1.2 of the International Covenant on Economic, Social and Cultural Rights.

[17] United Nations High Commissioner of Human Rights, op. cit., p. 24.

provisions being the ones that could balance developed and developing countries' rights and obligations so that the right to development has a real chance of being fulfilled.

2.3. *Is there any 'human right to intellectual property'?*

In response to the criticism directed at the current intellectual property rights system and its management, certain think tanks and authors have resorted to human rights arguments to defend said system and management.[18] They have claimed that intellectual property rights are not merely a tool to foster innovation, but also human rights that protect their products. Accordingly, all intellectual property categories would not only be instrumental in fostering innovation and safeguarding a certain return for the right holder, but would also be human rights *per se*. Legally speaking, this is an untenable argument.

The right to culture enshrined in ICESCR article 15 foresees the right to enjoy the benefits of scientific progress, receive material and moral benefits resulting from one's creativity, and the freedom of scientific research and creative activity. The introduction in article 15 of the protection of authors' interests was made at the last moment of the ICESCR *travaux préparatoires*[19] and was aimed at safeguarding the personal link between innovators and their works,[20] with the exclusion of legal persons.[21] Certainly, the latter is a relevant exclusion when analysing who is backing the promotion of a human rights validation of intellectual property protection.

There are radical differences of nature, scope and content between human rights and intellectual property rights. Merely summarizing them, it must be stated that human rights are attributed to people and collectives, whereas intellectual property rights can be attributed to legal entities; human rights are inherent in the human being, while intellectual property rights are granted with an instrumental end; the former have

---

18 See T. Giovannetti and M. Matthews, 'Intellectual Property Rights and Human Rights', *Ideas,* no. 34, 2005; VVAA, *Are Intellectual Property Rights Human Rights?,* Washington, DC: The Federalist Society, 2006.

19 M. Green, *Drafting history of the Article 15 (1) (c) of the International Covenant on Economic, Social, and Cultural Rights*, Background paper presented to the Day of General Discussion on the Article 15 (1) (c) held by the Committee on Economic, Social, and Cultural Rights in cooperation with the World Intellectual Property Organization, 9 October 2000, E/C.12/2000/15.

20 CESCR, *General Comment No. 17*, op. cit., par. 2.

21 Only the 'author', namely the creator, of scientific, literary or artistic productions can be the beneficiary of the protection of article 15.1(c). CESCR, *General Comment No. 17*, op. cit., par. 7 and 17.

no time constraints and are inalienable, while the latter are assignable and revocable.[22] Additionally, it must be noted that several intellectual property rights categories bear no relationship whatsoever with human rights. The required personal link might be clear in certain cases, such as copyright, but it is equally non-existent in many cases, such as trademarks and geographical indications. Moreover, the adequate protection of material and moral benefits deriving from human creativity would, on the one hand, demand arrangements not foreseen by contemporary intellectual property regimes, such as specific legal institutions to protect traditional knowledge[23] and, on the other hand, would allow the implementation not only of the conventional type of intellectual property rights systems, but also any other system that protects the personal link and the material interests in an invention.

What is more, States are free to decide the level and type of protection, something that will depend both on the real connection existing between the innovation and its inventor and other prevailing economic and human rights considerations. In this context, States are only under an obligation to grant the material benefits to allow the author or inventor to attain an adequate standard of living.[24] This point of departure allows for a wide margin of consideration of private and social interests implicit in intellectual property regimes, the determination of which shall depend on each country's circumstances and the satisfaction of human rights. In this last regard, article 15.1(c), which lays down the right to receive the material and moral benefits resulting from one's creativity, is subject to limitations in the public interest[25] and must be balanced with other rights,[26] it being necessary to ensure that its protection does not hinder the State's ability to comply with its core obligations in relation to other human rights.[27]

---

[22] See CESCR, *General Comment No. 17*, op. cit., par. 1–2, and *Follow-up to the day of general discussion on article 15.1.c),* op. cit., par. 6. P. Drahos, 'The Universality of Intellectual Property Rights: Origins and Development', op. cit., pp. 31–2. A.R. Chapman, 'A Human Rights Perspective on Intellectual Property', op. cit., p. 128. United Nations High Commissioner for Human Rights, op. cit., par. 14.

[23] See P. Cullet, 'Human Rights and Intellectual Property Rights: Need for a New Perspective', *International Affairs*, 79(1), p. 6. *General Comment No. 17,* op. cit., par. 32.

[24] CESCR, *General Comment No. 17,* op. cit., par. 15.

[25] Sub-commission on the Protection and Promotion of Human Rights, op. cit., par. 1.

[26] CESCR, *General Comment No. 17*, op. cit., par. 22.

[27] '[A]ny intellectual property regime that makes it more difficult for a State party to comply with its core obligations in relation to health, food, education,

So, in short, human rights and intellectual property rights are two different legal regimes, legal persons have no human rights entitlements, receiving moral and material benefits derived from human creativity is part of a broader right to culture and its implications must be addressed in that context, most intellectual property categories are insufficient or irrelevant to safeguarding authors' and inventors' rights if a human rights perspective is adopted, and, additionally, other human rights prevail over the granting of the material benefits derived from authors' and inventors' creativity.

3. TRIPS Agreement and human rights law interactions

It is possible to envisage three main interactions between the TRIPS Agreement and human rights law. First, in many cases the TRIPS Agreement offers different options and it is up to States to choose the one that best fits their interests. Although in most cases none of these options implies a violation of human rights obligations *per se*, the outcomes are not insignificant from a human rights point of view. In this sense, it is possible to have to resort to human rights to inform policy choices. Second, in other frequent cases, the TRIPS Agreement contains vague terms which need clarification. In a similar vein, many of the so-called TRIPS flexibilities, especially when they are enforced, are disputed and different interpretations on their real extent do exist. As will be further explained, this is an interesting case for the so-called systemic interpretation, which compels resort to public international law norms not contained in the WTO legal system in order to clarify vague terms and differing interpretations. Third, a situation where the fulfilment of a TRIPS obligation violates a specific human right is also possible. This case, which is much clearer in agreements enshrining TRIPS *plus* and *extra* obligations, presents the most difficult response if human rights obligations are to prevail not only formally, but also in practice.

---

especially, or any other right set out in the Covenant, is inconsistent with the legally binding obligations of the State party', Cf. CESCR, *Follow-up to the day of general discussion on article 15.1.c),* op. cit., par. 12. This is more relevant, if possible, on examination of the essential content of the right to the material and moral benefits resulting from inventors and authors creativity, which includes the obligation 'to strike an adequate balance between the effective protection of the moral and material interests of authors and States parties' obligations in relation to the rights to food, health and education, as well as the rights to take part in cultural life and to enjoy the benefits of scientific progress and its applications, or any other right recognized in the Covenant.' CESCR, *General Comment No. 17*, op. cit., par. 39. e).

3.1. Human rights as guide and trigger

It is frequently stated that the TRIPS Agreement is a treaty of minimums. Even though true, this affirmation requires qualification, because the TRIPS certainly lays down standards that can be subsequently raised, but this minimum is made up of numerous demanding obligations. Having said that, it is also true that the TRIPS often sets up a regime that allows States to choose from among diverse intellectual property policies and to apply certain intellectual property figures whenever they deem it necessary. As far as policies are concerned, TRIPS openness can be observed for instance in the patentability criteria and in the exhaustion of rights regime. In the first case, countries can adjust the level of privatization of public goods when deciding the standards to be applied in the assessment of novelty, innovative step and industrial application. The case of India is well-known in this regard. In the second case, countries decide the level of market segmentation of intellectual property-protected goods, which implies choosing among the national, regional or international exhaustion of rights doctrine. Regarding intellectual property figures and measures, TRIPS permits institutions such as the Bolar exception and non-voluntary licences. In both cases, these are pro-competition tools that try to balance the rights-holder's exclusive rights with public interests, such as rapid access to patent-protected medicines when they go out of patent, or access to patent-protected goods on public policy grounds or to remedy anti-competitive practices.

Both the implementation of said policy options and the application of the aforementioned pro-competition institutions depend on a State's will. When making their decision on whether one or another is the best means to achieve public policy goals, States might take into account other factors, such as their commitments in the human rights field. Those commitments, if properly invoked, may also reinforce the arguments of States and the legitimacy of their policies. In fact, a recent and not yet well-studied phenomenon is the invoking of human rights arguments by States themselves when deciding on intellectual property matters. That is to say, some States have changed their traditional defensive behaviour in the human rights field – which made them permanent defendants – and have adopted a completely different approach. The relative openness of the TRIPS Agreement facilitates things in this regard, because it is up to States to decide on numerous matters and their decisions might be influenced by human rights obligations.

Non-voluntary licences were previously mentioned as one of those TRIPS tools helpful at integrating public interest in intellectual property management. In recent years, several States have invoked human rights when granting compulsory licences. They were certainly not obliged to do so because, in fact, TRIPS article 31 is quite broad with regard to the reasons that can be invoked when granting a compulsory licence. However, those States invoking human rights were acting in the intellectual property rights field motivated by compelling human rights arguments and deemed it important to state so explicitly. The first case that can be tracked is that of Indonesia. In 2004, the Indonesian presidential decree authorizing the Ministry of Health to designate a producer to exploit government use licences granted on lamivudine and neviraprine-patented products,[28] referred to the National Health Act. This reference is interesting because the Indonesian National Health Act is built upon the human right to health, which is alluded to either directly or indirectly on several occasions. The Preamble, for instance, links Indonesian development with Indonesians' good health, and articles 2 and 3, which enshrine the Act's objectives and principles, quote superior humanity values. It is in article 4 where the right to health is found, whereas subsequent articles 6, 7 and 9 lay down the Indonesian State obligations with regard to individual and collective health.

Much clearer cases were those of Thailand and Brazil, countries which expressly invoked human rights when granting compulsory licences on patented products. Between the end of 2006 and the beginning of 2007, Thailand granted three compulsory licences, two of them for two antiretroviral drugs[29] and another for a cardiovascular disease medicine.[30] At the end of 2007, the process to grant compulsory licences was opened again for four oncological products. When making use of its power to grant compulsory licences,[31] the Ministry of Health expressly invoked the Thai Constitution and the National Health Security Act.[32] These texts oblige the government to assure each Thai access to medicines contained in the

---

[28] Government of Indonesia, *Decree of the President Republic of Indonesia no. 83 2004 regarding exploitation of patent on antiretroviral drugs by the Government*; Government of Indonesia. These licences were followed by an additional one for efavirenz; see *Decree of the President Republic of Indonesia no. 6 2007, amending Decree number 83 year 2004 regarding exploitation of patent on antiretroviral drugs by the Government*. See http://lists.essential.org/pipermail/ip-health/2004-December/007233.html (6/2007).

[29] Efavirenz (Stocrin) and lipinavir and ritonavir combination (Kaletra).

[30] Clopidogrel (Plavix).

[31] Patent Act B.E. 2522, as amended by the Patent Act (No. 2) B.E 253, and the Patent Act (No. 3) B.E. 2542, article 51.

[32] Ministry of Public Health–National Health Security Office, *The 10 burning questions on the Government Use of Patents on the four anti-cancer drugs in Thailand*, Bangkok: Ministry of Public Health–National Health Security Office, 2008, p. 12.

national essential medicines list. Thai Constitution, Section 51, recognizes the right to health care, which must be enjoyed without discrimination and free of charge for those lacking economic resources. The same article obliges the efficient organization of sanitary services and the prevention and eradication of diseases. The Thai Constitution was the driving force leading to the adoption of the National Health Security Act, the outstanding provision of which is the obligation to guarantee universal access to health care.

In July 2007, Brazil granted a compulsory licence for efavirenz, an antiretroviral included in the World Health Organization Essential Medicines List. In Brazil, in order to grant a compulsory licence, a previous 'declaration of interest' must be issued. Most of President Lula's declaration of interest for the efavirenz licence referred to Brazilian obligations regarding human rights and access to medicines. From that declaration, it could be clearly inferred that human rights obligations were the ones leading and justifying the granting of such a compulsory licence. More precisely, the declaration referred to the fact that the right to health had been enshrined in the Universal Declaration of Human Rights article 25, ICESCR article 12 and San Salvador Protocol to the American Convention on Human Rights article 10. The declaration of interest recalled that in 1992, said right had been incorporated into the national legal framework, and made a double reference to the Brazilian Constitution. On the one hand, the declaration made reference to Brazilian Constitution article 196, on the right to health, and on the other hand, it also quoted article 5, which states that property has a social function, a role that intellectual property must also perform.[33]

3.2. Human rights as an interpretation tool: the systemic interpretation

Contradictory interpretation have been attributed to numerous TRIPS articles. This can be partially explained by the fact that the TRIPS Agreement was a compromise between very different understandings and almost irreconcilable positions on matters such as the role that intellectual property performs in several respects (for instance, innovation, transfer of technology and investment) and the level of protection it deserves. In order to conclude the treaty, and with it all the WTO 'package deal', numerous articles were drafted ambiguously and, as a result, its application is open to differing interpretations. The TRIPS terminology illustrates the ambiguity and flexibility alluded to and, for instance, the TRIPS

[33] Ministerio da Saúde, Portaria No. 886, 24 April 2007, No. 79 – *DOU* de 25/04/07, pp. 3–4.

contains open terms such as 'effective', 'reasonable', 'normal', 'fair and equitable' and 'adequate'; it also includes terms the meaning of which can be found outside the field of intellectual property, this being the case with 'morals' and 'public health'; and it also contains legal terms which have a specific meaning in other legal branches, such as 'unfair competition' or even the 'most favoured nation treatment' standard. In most cases, either a literal or teleological interpretation – the latter achieved by invoking the Preamble and articles 7 and 8 of the TRIPS Agreement – will suffice to resolve potential doubts. Nonetheless, if this is not possible, other public international law norms may be invoked in the search for clarification.

WTO law is part of public international law and it is closely linked with the rest of the international legal order. This is why the WTO Appellate Body statement that WTO agreements are not 'to be read in clinical isolation from public international law'[34] has been quoted so many times. In fact, WTO adjudicative organs frequently revert to non-WTO norms on different grounds. First, they resort to other public international law rules pursuant to the norm that compels them to clarify the agreements in accordance with public international law's customary norms of interpretation. Second, they also resort to non-WTO norms in the application of general public international law norms for the management of their own WTO 'primary norms'. Third, the referral to other international norms is also explained by the fact that WTO agreements themselves allude to other international treaties. Finally, WTO adjudicative organs have also taken certain public international law norms as relevant 'facts' when ruling on a specific controversy.[35]

For some, the reference contained in WTO Dispute Settlement Understanding (DSU) articles 3.2 and 19 to preserving WTO Members' rights and obligations would preclude any consideration of non-WTO norms. To sustain that view, it is argued that any reference to external agreements would alter said rights and obligations. However, in this regard, the distinction between jurisdiction (*ratione materiae* competence) and applicable law (norms to apply or to be taken into account)[36] is of fundamental importance. In this sense, it is admitted that the jurisdiction of the WTO Dispute Settlement Body (DSB) adjudicative organs is constrained to assess the existence of any WTO rights and obligations'

---

34 *United States – Gasoline,* WT/DS2/AB/R, 29/4/1996, section III. *B).*

35 X. Fernández Pons, *La Organización Mundial del Comercio y el Derecho internacional,* Madrid and Barcelona: Marcial Pons, 2006, p. 515.

36 L. Bartels, 'Applicable Law in WTO Dispute Settlement Proceedings', *Journal of World Trade*, 35(3), 2001, p. 518.

nullification or impairment.[37] Consequently, WTO adjudicative bodies jurisdiction is limited to claims under the WTO covered agreements, thus panels and Appellate Body *ratione materiae* competence is limited to establishing the existence of a violation of any WTO agreement.[38] Nevertheless, the question of the applicable law is different and undoubtedly more disputed.

According to Pauwelyn, DSU articles 3.2 and 19.2 do not impede the incorporation of non-WTO norms when ruling on a case, even if a solution against WTO agreements is inferred from those external norms. He sustains that said articles refer to interpretation but not to the applicable law, thus its sense is found in the prohibition on creating new rights or obligations without limiting the jurisdiction or the applicable law.[39] There are more restrained and probably more pragmatic theses in between Pauwelyn and those other authors that deny any role to non-WTO norms.[40] Zapatero, for instance, holds that the WTO dispute settlement system enshrines a set of positive and negative principles referred to as teleology:[41] principles that tend to preserve WTO Members' rights and obligations as a specific goal of the system.[42] According to Zapatero and Bartels, although the applicable norm does not limit the incorporation of other public international law norms, it operates as a bottleneck that makes said incorporation rather difficult.[43] The limit, in any case, would

---

[37] Something well illustrated by DSU article 7, which mandates WTO adjudicative organs to examine disputes in the light of the covered agreement. See also articles 1, 3.2, 3.4, 3.5 and 11.

[38] J. Pauwelyn, *Conflict of Norms in Public International Law: How WTO Law Relates to other Rules of International Law*, Cambridge: Cambridge University Press, 2003, p. 444.

[39] J. Pauwelyn, 'The Application of Non-WTO Rules of International Law in WTO Dispute Settlement', in P.F.J. Macrory, A.E. Appleton and M.G. Plummer, *The World Trade Organization: Legal, Economic and Political Analysis,* New York: Springer, 2005, p. 1422; J. Pauwelyn, *Conflict of Norms* op. cit., p. 353.

[40] According to J.P. Trachtman, the WTO dispute resolution panels and the Appellate Body are limited to the application of WTO substantive law and other conventional international law. J.P. Trachtman, 'The Domain of the WTO Dispute Resolution', *Harvard International Law Journal,* 40, Spring, 1999, pp. 347–48.

[41] Said principles allow us to distinguish between positive obligations (resolving in accordance with covered agreements, preserve rights and obligations, keep an adequate equilibrium) and negative obligations (not nullify resulting advantages, not impair benefits accruing under the covered agreements, not impede the achievement of goals and not add to or diminish the rights and obligations).

[42] P. Zapatero Miguel, *Derecho del comercio global,* Madrid: Thomson-Civitas, 2003, pp. 63–6.

[43] *Ibid.*, p. 76. Also, L. Bartels, op. cit., pp. 499, 507; G. Marceau, 'Conflicts of Norms and Conflicts of Jurisdictions: The Relationship between the WTO

be found in not contradicting the covered agreements, either by adding to or diminishing the rights and obligations set forth therein.[44]

The key element in this discussion is the Vienna Convention on the Law of Treaties (Vienna Convention) article 31.3(c). This article is among the norms referred to by DSU article 3.2, which mandates interpreting WTO agreements in accordance with public international law's customary norms of interpretation. Article 31.3(c) lays down that, when interpreting a treaty, and together with the context, any relevant rules of international law applicable in the relationships between the parties shall be taken into account. This has been the basis supporting the incorporation of – among others – environmental law and human rights treaties in the pursuit of clarification of WTO agreements.

It has been stated that the referral to those customary norms shows the will to anchor WTO system in the public international law general system.[45] This being true, it has to be duly taken into account that article 3.2 merely gives a role to other public international law norms as far as interpretation is concerned.[46] It is not, therefore, a sound avenue to incorporate contradicting obligations and, despite being important, its limitations are also quite clear. As such, article 31.3(c) will only come into play whenever a certain norm is ambiguous, when a term has a specific meaning in customary international law or when terms are open and need further references to other public international law norms to specify their meaning.[47] In this context, a WTO panel affirmed that when the application of article 31 – which contains the so-called 'general rule of interpretation – gives several possible interpretations as a result, the interpreter will

---

Agreement and MEAs and other Treaties', *Journal of World Trade*, 35(6), 2001, pp. 1103–04.

44 In this sense, P. Mengozzi, 'The Present State of Research Carried out by the English-speaking Section of the Centre for Studies and Research', Centre d'étude et de recherche de droit international et des relations internationals, Académie de droit international de La Haye, *L'Organisation Mondiale du commerce,* The Hague: Martinus Nijhoff Publishers, 1997, p. 71. As the Appellate Body affirmed, neither panels nor the Appellate Body itself can add or subtract rights and obligations set forth in WTO agreements. See Appellate Body, *India – Patents*, op. cit., section V.

45 P. Mengozzi, 'The Present State of Research', op. cit., p. 69.

46 E. Canal-Forgues, 'Sur l'interpretation dans le droit de l'OMC', *Revue Général de Droit International Public*, 2001(1), p. 13.

47 D. French, 'Treaty Interpretation and the Incorporation of Extraneous Legal Rules', *International and Comaparative Law Quarterly*, 55, April 2006, pp. 303–4; C. McLachlan, 'The Principle of Systemic Integration and Article 31(3)(c) of the Vienna Convention', *International and Comparative Law Quarterly,* 54, April 2005, p. 312.

be obliged to choose the one that better matches other applicable norms of public international law.[48]

The above-mentioned may be a useful framework in order to have recourse to human rights norms when ruling on complex cases. The following could be a good example. In 2008 and 2009, the implementation of EC Council Regulation 1383/2003 resulted in numerous seizures of in-transit medicines that were non-patented either in the exporting or importing countries. Doubts have been raised as to whether those measures and the Regulation itself were compatible with WTO law. It has been argued that when assessing EC Regulation and seizures compatibility with WTO law, attention must be paid to the GATT, TRIPS and subsequent WTO agreements. If a WTO panel was asked to judge, it would be compelled to answer if the power granted to WTO Members to adopt higher levels of intellectual property protection had been implemented in a manner that restricted the trade on legitimate products, violating the territoriality principle inherent in intellectual property law and impeding the protection of public health.[49] The case would be an interesting one and surely doubts would arise among panel members. States confronting European seizures and regulations surely would bring up the public health problems caused by said actions and regulation. Probably, they would have a very strong argument to make by invoking the Doha Declaration on the TRIPS Agreement and public health. However, if that did not suffice and panel members were still insecure, pursuant to DSU article 3.2 they would be compelled to apply Vienna Convention on the Law of Treaties article 31, and, therefore, article 31.3(c). As a consequence, the whole human rights framework could come into play, especially the human right to health. This right, as enshrined in ICESCR article 12, not only obliges States to adopt internal measures but also to 'provide international assistance and cooperation' with a view to achieving the realization of the right to health. Due to its restricting effects on access to medicines, EC border measures mandating the seizure of legitimate in-transit generic medicines would work against said ICESCR obligation, something that could, therefore, permit the WTO panel to rule against those measures and even the Regulation itself.

---

[48] Panel Report, *European Communities – Measures Affecting the Approval and Marketing of Biotech Products (EC-Biotech)*, 21/11/2006, WT/DS291/R, WT/DS292/R, WT/DS293/R, par. 7.69.

[49] See. X. Seuba, *Border Measures Concerning Goods Allegedly Infringing Intellectual Property Rights: The Seizures of Generic Medicines in Transit*, Geneva: ICTSD, 2009.

3.3. Human rights and TRIPS conflicts

More difficult is the situation where a real conflict exists, that is to say, a situation where interpretation does not suffice and the fulfilment of a norm contained in one treaty has effects on the fulfilment of another obligation set forth in a distinct treaty. It could be argued that a reading of the TRIPS Agreement that interprets to the maximum possible extent the flexibilities contained therein gives as an answer that no conflict exists between the TRIPS Agreement and human rights. However, this reading would certainly omit several important facts and would run the risk of becoming a fruitless academic exercise.

Among the 'facts' that cannot be omitted, particular attention must be devoted to the existing serious disagreements as to the real extent of several TRIPS legal provisions, including some TRIPS flexibilities. In this regard, it has already been mentioned that human rights can be decisive in securing a TRIPS Agreement interpretation that is consistent with superior social and human interests, placing those superior interests above intellectual property protection. However, albeit being a thriving interaction, its incipient exercise indicates that it must be further explored, for instance by invoking it more frequently in the controversies sent to the DSB.

On the other hand, it is also true that it is no longer possible to address the TRIPS and human rights interactions without also mentioning the numerous TRIPS *plus* and *extra* obligations. These provisions, either by strengthening obligations laid down in the TRIPS or by adding new obligations to the TRIPS framework, have in just a decade broken the intellectual property and public goods fragile equilibrium set forth in the TRIPS. The seriousness and gravity of the TRIPS *plus* and *extra* secured obligations makes resorting to norms on treaty conflict unavoidable. However, thinking that implementation of technical rules such as the ones on conflict of treaties is going to completely change the complex, stringent and deliberate regimes set forth in FTAs may be a naïve stance. Although the application of treaty conflict rules is a worthwhile exercise and results in positive outcomes from the human rights point of view, it rather seems more adequate to consider the promotion of TRIPS *plus* and *extra* provisions as a political problem which requires much more than responses based on legal technique. Having said that, the basics to be taken into account when addressing the potential conflicts between human rights and TRIPS, TRIPS *plus* and TRIPS *extra* norms are set out below.

Article 30 of the Vienna Convention sets forth the basic rules on the application of successive treaties dealing with the same subject matter. It envisages the possibility that treaties themselves incorporate conflict clauses (30.2) and codifies the chronological criteria (*lex posterior derogat priori)* with regard to treaty provisions that are incompatible with posterior obligations whenever the parties to the treaties in conflict are the same. However, difficulties appear when parties to two conflicting treaties do not coincide. In this last situation, the *lex posterior* rule is applied only between parties that coincide in both treaties (30.4(a)), but for the rest, the treaty where States do coincide will be applied, irrespective of its temporal precedence (30.4(b)). This framework is completed with the customary *lex specialis* rule, which prescribes the precedence of the norm that is more detailed and right to the point. Moreover, it should be noted that *ius cogens* norms will always prevail over any other contradictory norm.

The easiest situation to address is precisely the latter, namely the one involving a *ius cogens* norm. In public international law, *ius cogens* norms are the sole ones to which a hierarchical status has been granted, and all conflicts with said norms are *inherent* conflicts which have the most drastic outcomes, specifically the nullity of both the contradicting norm and treaty. Nevertheless, only a few human rights have the *ius cogens* status, among them, prohibition of torture and the right to life. Arguments can be made in the sense that the right to life and the right to not suffer an inhuman or degrading treatment are affected by certain levels of intellectual property protection.[50] However, in such argumentation and in both cases, the positive dimension of said rights is the one implied, that is to say, not the prohibition of doing something but the obligation to act in the socio-economic field. The current conception and content of *ius cogens* norms makes the incorporation of that positive dimension of the right to life and the right to not suffer inhuman treatment difficult. In principle, this means that arguments based on the *ius cogens* status of human rights whose fulfilment is affected by intellectual property standards will hardly prosper. Notwithstanding said difficulties, the *ius cogens* notion is not devoid of a certain evolutionary nature, and it may be worth challenging its limits on a regular basis.

After ruling out the application of the consequences attached to the infringement of *ius cogens* norms, Vienna Convention article 30 must come into play. A first question to be addressed is its heading, namely the limitation of article 30 rules to successive treaties dealing with the *same subject matter*. Thus, first of all, for some, the claim that different subject matter can be found questions the effectiveness of said criteria.[51] If this were

---

[50] See International Law Commission, *Articles on Responsibility of States for Internationally Wrongful Acts: Report of the International Law Commission on the Work of its Fifty-third Session*, UN GAOR, 56th Sess. Supp. no. 10, UN Doc. A/56/10 (2001), pp. 202, 282–4.

[51] A clear deviation from the 'same subject matter' condition can be found in the affirmation by the US that 'the WTO is not a successive treaty relating to

the case, most of the interactions between norms pertaining to different international legal regimens – for instance, conflicts between human rights and trade treaties – would be beyond the reach of article 30. By contrast, a more accepted thesis, and the one supported by the International Law Commission, holds that 'the test of whether two treaties deal with the "same subject matter" is resolved through the assessment of whether the fulfilment of the obligation under one treaty affects the fulfilment of the obligation of another'.[52] Therefore, whenever it is possible to demonstrate that the fulfilment of an obligation under an intellectual property treaty affects the fulfilment of the obligation contained in a human rights treaty, that condition will be satisfied.

Having established the applicability of Vienna Convention article 30, the conflict characteristics – mainly the States involved and the date of ratification of the affected treaties – will determine which of the article 30 rules may be invoked. As of March 2009, 159 States were Members of the ICESCR, whereas 153 States were WTO members and were, therefore, obliged to apply the TRIPS Agreement. It is also important to be aware that all European States have ratified the ICESCR, but not the US, which nevertheless signed it and is hence obliged, pursuant to Vienna Convention article 18, to not defeat the ICESCR object and purpose.[53] In any case, the rule is quite clear: if both states coincide in the treaties concerned, the latter prevails, whereas should States not coincide, only the one in which they do concur will be applied. In practical terms, both situations would seem – in principle and in most cases – to imply that either the TRIPS Agreement or the TRIPS *plus* or *extra* provisions would prevail over a provision contained in the ICESCR. This is so because either the IESCR is a treaty of which most of the States have been Members since the 1980s, while involved intellectual property provisions are set forth in much more recent treaties or because relevant States when assessing the TRIPS,

---

the same subject matter as the NAFTA. The NAFTA is a free trade agreement establishing preferential treatment among the NAFTA parties. The WTO is a multilateral trade agreement providing for multilateral trading rules'. *Tariffs applied by Canada to certain US-origin agricultural products,* 1 December 1996, CDA-95-2008-01, par. 87.

[52] International Law Commission, *Fragmentation of international law: difficulties arising from the diversification and expansion of international law, report of the Study Group of the International Law Commission*, A/CN.4/L.682, 13 April 2006, p. 130.

[53] This latter would be important if a more detailed analysis on the precise situation of the US as far as the ICESCR and TRIPS interactions was undertaken. Article 18 and the signatory status of US would come into play, together with the Vienna Convention articles on *inter se* agreements.

TRIPS *plus* and TRIPS *extra* problems have not ratified the ICESCR. However, this outcome must be seriously qualified, to the extent that it is the opposite.

It is widely accepted that human rights treaties have special features that lead them to deviate from some general international law rules. Its objective nature, the speciality of its reservations regime, the debate surrounding its *ius cogens* status, and the qualification of human rights as *erga omnes* obligations, all refer to the special relationship that exists between international human rights law and public international law.[54] As such, for example, the demand for *effective protection* characteristic of human rights treaties led Roucounas to maintain that the *lex posterior* and *lex specialis* rules are of reduced application when dealing with human rights.[55] In this context, it is important to notice one specific feature of human rights treaties. These conventions set forth obligations of an objective nature, that is to say, they exclude reciprocity and Member States are obliged to comply with treaty obligations regardless of other Members' infringements. This objective nature, which is related to the creation of a community of interests among Member States, implies that treaty provisions are designed not to protect State's interests but human beings' fundamental rights.[56] Moreover, human rights conventions are 'integral' treaties, treaties which are to be distinguished from those laying down either synalagmatic or interdependent obligations. In this regard, the International Law Commission has confirmed that 'a human rights convention, for its part, is an absolute or "integral" treaty. The obligations it imposes are independent of any expectation of reciprocity or performance on the part of other parties of their obligations'.[57]

---

[54] The European Court of Human Rights, when ruling upon a case regarding a reservation to a human rights treaty, denied said reservation and distinguished the human rights regime concerning reservations from the general public international law one. It affirmed that 'fundamental difference in the role and purpose of the respective tribunals [i.e. the International Court of Justice and the European Court of Human Rights], coupled with the existence of a practice of unconditional acceptance [. . .] provides a compelling basis for distinguishing Convention practice from that of the International Court'. *Loizidou v. Turkey*, Preliminary Objections, 23 March 1995, ECHR A/No. 310, par. 67.

[55] E. Roucounas, 'Engagements Parallèles et Contradictories', *Recueil des Cours*, 206, (1987-VI), p. 197.

[56] See European Court of Human Rights, *Ireland v. The United Kingdom,* Petition 5310/71, 18/1/1978. In a similar vein, *The Effect of Reservations*, OC-2/82; American Court on Human Rights, *Restrictions to the Death Penalty*, OC-3/83, Corte Interamericana de Derechos Humanos, *Series A*, No. 3, pp. 76 and 77, par. 50

[57] International Law Commission, *Fragmentation of international law*, op. cit., p. 161.

The interaction between, on the one hand, the special nature of human rights treaties and obligations, and on the other hand, Vienna Convention article 30 rules of conflict results in a complex problem. As has been said, in most cases, the mere application of conflict rules would result in the prevalence of intellectual property rules as either posterior rules or the only ones applicable to both parties. But this outcome would not exempt parties from the obligation to continue the application of the human rights treaty obligations with regard to other Member States not involved in the conflict. However, setting aside other considerations, from a purely technical point of view, it is impossible to fulfil both obligations entirely. In this sense, a certain State cannot infringe the fulfilment of a human rights treaty merely with respect to a single State and nevertheless continue its application with respect to others. Due to the fact that human rights obligations imply respecting, protecting and fulfilling the human rights of those persons under the jurisdiction of the treaty Member State, it is impossible to respect said duty partially. Because of the integral nature of human rights treaties, and the *erga omnes* consideration of the obligations set forth therein, the nature of the breach would be of such a character as to radically change the position of all the other States to which the obligation is owed.

The International Law Commission has affirmed that integral obligations, and more precisely human rights obligations, enjoy some kind of precedence over merely transactional instruments. Of particular importance is that the International Law Commission affirms that the abovementioned treaty conflict rules find their limit precisely when integral obligations come into play.[58] In this sense, it is confirmed that human rights treaties cannot be operated through the same techniques as 'ordinary' treaties creating bilateral relationships. As far as the consequences attached to the violation of *erga omnes* and integral obligations are concerned, these are particularly serious: it will not be possible to invoke those violating obligations and other States will be compelled to not recognize the resulting situation.[59] Hence, this would result in the non-application of TRIPS, TRIPS *plus* and TRIPS *extra* obligations whenever they were against human rights norms.

---

[58] According to the Commission, 'Although such clauses (conflict clauses) are undoubtedly useful, there is a limit to what they can achieve. They cannot, for instance, affect the rights of third parties or interfere with the operation of *jus cogens* or other hierarchical principles (such as those having to do with integral or interdependent obligations)'. International Law Commission, *Fragmentation of international law*, op. cit., p. 137.

[59] See for instance *Legal Consequences of the Construction of a Wall in the Occupied Palestinian Territory*, Advisory Opinion, ICJ Reports 2004, par. 159.

This drastic outcome can be addressed from two different stances, either qualifying it or confirming it. On the one hand, it can be argued that norms of public international law dealing with treaty conflict are short and do not adequately address the complexity of contemporary interactions between legal regimes. So, albeit technically correct, said outcome would respond to this inadequacy. On the other hand, it is also possible to sustain that the international community does in fact recognize the precedence of human rights norms and the above-mentioned results are those that are really desired. The *pro-homine* and evolutionary principles inherent in the international human rights regime, and the fundamental principle to respect human dignity that cuts across the whole public international law legal system both sustain the second proposal.

Due to its serious consequences, the application of this latter thesis would certainly be helped by explicit mentions in its favour regarding specific intellectual property and human rights interactions. A good example can be found in the context of the right to health and intellectual property interaction. In response to doubts and controversies arising from the consequences of the TRIPS Agreement on the right to health, WTO Members adopted the Doha Declaration, which stated that the TRIPS Agreement should be 'implemented in a manner supportive of WTO Members' right to protect public health' and that the said Agreement 'does not and should prevent Members from taking measures to protect public health'. The Doha Declaration thus makes clear the existence of a 'right to protect public health' and said protection is above that of intellectual property. As a consequence, it has been held that 'the Doha Declaration is implicitly a human rights instrument',[60] and some constitutional courts have already invoked it to confirm the supremacy of human rights obligations.[61] From a human rights point of view, and also in the pursuit of clarity and coherence with WTO Members' declared principles and values, similar statements would be necessary regarding, at least, the right to food, the right to education and the right to development.

4. Conclusions

The relation between intellectual property law and human rights law, together with the interaction between public international law and WTO

---

[60] F.M. Abbot, 'The "Rule of Reason" and the Right to Health: Integrating Human Rights and Competition Principles in the Context of TRIPS', in T. Cottier, J. Pauwelyn and E. Burgi Bonanomi (eds), *Human Rights and International Trade*, Oxford: Oxford University Press, 2005, p. 283.

[61] *Azanca Alhel' Meza Garc'a,* Sentencia del Tribunal Constitucional de Perú, EXP No. 2945-2003 AA/TC.

law, determines the specific outcomes of the TRIPS Agreement and human rights law relationship. As far as the relation between intellectual property law and human rights law is concerned, it is important to highlight that human rights law provides rules which synthesize the value judgements lacking in the intellectual property regime, and establishes the limits of intellectual property rights protection. In this context, it is necessary to emphasize that not only human rights pertaining to second generation human rights, but also those belonging to first and third generation human rights might be affected by certain intellectual property standards. Although most of the research has been conducted on the effects that intellectual property protection has on social, economic and cultural rights, the continuous rise of intellectual property protection makes it necessary to further expand said analysis to the consequences on civil, political and solidarity rights. Finally, intents to treat intellectual property rights as a form of human rights protection are not defensible from a legal standpoint and respond rather to a vested interests strategy.

Three broad interactions can be identified between the TRIPS Agreement and human rights law. First, human rights law might act as a guide and trigger for the adoption of certain measures and policies foreseen in the TRIPS. In this sense, particularly noteworthy is the explicit invocation by several States of its obligations in the human rights field when adopting TRIPS-related measures. Second, WTO adjudicative bodies resort to other public international law rules on different grounds, pursuant to the norm that compels them to clarify the agreements in accordance with public international law customary norms of interpretation. This is the adequate path to integrate treaties and obligations pertaining to international human rights law when ruling on TRIPS-related cases. In this context, human rights obligations might become relevant if TRIPS provisions are ambiguous, include terms with a specific meaning in customary international law or foresee terms which are open and need further references to other public international law norms. Third, the most difficult situation to address is the one where a real conflict exists between human rights norms and obligations contained either in the TRIPS or in treaties establishing TRIPS *plus* and *extra* obligations. Public international law norms on conflict of treaties, together with the specific features of international human rights law as a legal regime, permit upholding the precedence of human rights norms. However, both a jurisdictional problem and the feasibility itself of implementing said outcome make it necessary to state explicitly said precedence with regard to the different areas of potential conflict. In this sense, the Doha Declaration is a good example to be exported to areas such as education, food and development.

7 The TRIPS Agreement and intellectual property rights exhaustion

Luis Mariano Genovesi

The principle of exhaustion of intellectual property rights (IPR), in its classic version, holds that once the owner of the IPR places the product protected by the IPR on the market, the IPR owner cannot use the right granted by the IPR against any person who acquires the product from the IPR owner or from another person with the consent of the IPR owner. This principle, which can also be applied to products put on the market by any authorized person – for instance, under a compulsory licence – limits the power of the IPR owner, and allows persons to use, offer to sell or sell a product embodying an IPR without fear that the IPR owner might enforce the IPR against them.

At its origins during the second half of the 19th century, the *exhaustion* of IPR theory addressed domestic sales made by the IPR owner or its licensee.[1] Nevertheless, incipient international trade allowed a third person who had acquired a product embodying the invention in a foreign country to import and sell products which were similar or identical to

[1] Prominent European scholars attribute paternity of the *exhaustion doctrine* to Josef Kohler, or at least that he established the foundations for this theory in Germany. See Ulrich Schatz, *The Exhaustion of the Patent Rights in the Common Market*, 2 IIC 3 (1971); R. Singer, *L'epuisement du droit du breveté et les regles allemandes, in* 1ère RENCONTRE DE PROPRIÉTÉ INDUSTRIELLE L'EPUISEMENT DU DROIT DU BREVETÉ 17, 18 (Centre d'Etudes Internationales de la Propriete Industrielle ed., Librairies Techniques 1971); Amiram Benyamini, *Patent Infringement in the European Community*, 13 IIC STUDIES IN INDUSTRIAL PROPERTY AND COPYRIGHT LAW 281 (1993). Kohler was certainly the one who exposed the theory in Europe for the first time, but he borrowed some concepts from France and the United States. Schatz assumed that Kohler found inspiration in French law because he was 'well acquainted with the comparative law method, and, in particular, with the French law'. However, it seems that Kohler was also inspired by US case law and commentators. In fact, Kohler cited in several footnotes of section 178 of HANDBUCH DES DEUTSCHEN PATENTRECHTS – where he developed his theory about the *connection of forms of exploitation* – the US courts' decisions in *Adams v. Burque, Holiday v. Mattheson, Perrigo v. Spaulding,* and *Wilder v. Kent*, which he read from Myer's recompilation and from the *Official Gazette of the United States Patent Office*.

those marketed domestically by the patentee or licensee. Thus, the question was whether it was admissible to extend these doctrines crafted for domestic sales to international sales.

A direct consequence of the extension of the *exhaustion doctrine* to international sales is so-called *parallel imports* or *grey markets products*. *Parallel imports* have two distinguishing features. First, they are lawfully put on the market in the place of export – the foreign country – by the IPR owner or with its consent.[2] Second, a different person than the IPR owner makes an importation 'in parallel to the authorized distribution network'.[3]

The distinction among national, regional and international exhaustion takes into account the territory in which the product covered by the IPR has been placed. National exhaustion occurs when the product is placed in the territory of the country that confers the IPR; regional exhaustion means that the IPR is exhausted when the product is put in the territory of a regional trade agreement, for instance the European Union; and international exhaustion happens when the product is put in the stream of commerce in any country.

1. The World Trade Organization's provisions on Intellectual Property Rights exhaustion

The issue of international exhaustion of IPR was one of the most critical issues during the negotiations of the Uruguay Round, which concluded with the establishment of the World Trade Organization (WTO) in 1994.[4] The WTO has two sources dealing with this topic: specific provisions about exhaustion in Articles 6, 28 and 51 of the TRIPS; and the general framework regarding trade of goods in GATT 1994, particularly Articles III(4), XI(1), and XX(d).

1.1. Agreement on Trade-Related Aspects of Intellectual Property Rights

During the Uruguay Round negotiations, there was strong disagreement about IPR exhaustion.[5] Some countries, like Switzerland and the United States, wanted the future TRIPS Agreement to establish a territorial exhaustion principle, and others – that is, Australia, Brazil, India, New Zealand, etc – wanted an international exhaustion regime.[6] Eventually,

---

2 WARWICK A. ROTHNIE, PARALLEL IMPORTS 1 (SWEET & MAXWELL 1993).

3 *Id.*

4 DANIEL GERVAIS, THE TRIPS AGREEMENT: DRAFTING HISTORY AND ANALYSIS 112 (Sweet & Maxwell, 2nd edition 2003) (1997).

5 *Id.*

6 *Id.*

a compromise solution was reached and the issue of the exhaustion of IPR was practically left out of the legal framework of the TRIPS Agreement.[7]

Article 6 provides that '[f]or the purposes of dispute settlement under this Agreement, subject to the provisions of Articles 3 and 4, nothing in this Agreement shall be used to address the issue of the exhaustion of intellectual property rights'. Article 6 is *an agreement to disagree* and concerns procedural aspects of IPR exhaustion, not a substantive rule.[8]

It is implied in Article 6 that Members keep freedom to choose between national, international or regional exhaustion, although they must fulfil their obligations regarding national treatment (Article 3) and most-favoured-nation treatment (Article 4).[9] In addition, its plain language states that IPR exhaustion cannot be invoked before the dispute settlement procedure as a direct violation of the TRIPS Agreement.[10]

The particular issue of patent rights exhaustion received special treatment in the TRIPS Agreement. Article 28.1(a) provides that, when the patent covers a product, the owner has the right to exclude third parties from acts of making, using, offering for sale, selling, or importing the product. The provision has a footnote that qualifies it, and states that '[t]his right, like all other rights conferred under this Agreement in respect of the use, sale, importation or other distribution of goods, is subject to the provisions of Article 6'. Thus, the patent holder has the right to prevent third parties from importing a product protected by a patent, but a Member can limit this right by adopting an international exhaustion rule.

The *Declaration on the TRIPS Agreement and Public Health*[11] supports and confirms this interpretation. In fact, it declares that 'the effect of the provisions in the the TRIPS Agreement that are relevant to the exhaustion of intellectual property rights is to leave each Member free to establish its own regime for such exhaustion without challenge, subject to the MFN and national treatment provisions of Articles 3 and 4'.[12]

Finally, Article 51 also refers to IPR exhaustion by establishing that

---

[7] ALBERTO CASADO CERVIÑO & BEGOÑA CERRO PRADA, GATT Y PROPIEDAD INDUSTRIAL 87 (Tecnos 1994).

[8] William J. Davey and Werne Zdouc, *The Triangle of TRIPS, GATT and GATS*, *in* INTELLECTUAL PROPERTY: TRADE, COMPETITION, AND SUSTAINABLE DEVELOPMENT 53, 69 (Thomas Cottier and Petros C. Mavroidis eds., The University of Michigan Press 2003).

[9] *Id.*

[10] *See* CARLOS CORREA, ACUERDO TRIPS 47 (Ediciones Ciudad Argentina 1996); GERVAIS, *supra* note 4, at 113.

[11] World Trade Organization, Ministerial Declaration of 14 November 2001, WT/MIN(01)/DEC/1, 41 ILM 746 (2002).

[12] *Id.*

WTO Members shall adopt judicial or administrative procedures to allow IPR owners to require the suspension of the release by customs of counterfeit trademark or pirated copyright goods. Members may also apply this provision to other IPR, including patents. However, Article 51 also has a footnote which clarifies that '[i]t is understood that there shall be no obligation to apply such procedures to imports of goods put on the market in another country by or with the consent of the right holder'. Thus, Members may but are not obliged to suspend the release of imported goods when the IPR owner or a third party with its consent put the product in the market of another country. It is implied that if a Member establishes an international exhaustion of IPR regime, this Member does not have any obligation to apply border measures to goods marketed abroad by the IPR owner or with its consent.

1.2. The General Agreement on Tariffs and Trade of 1994

There are three provisions in GATT 1994[13] that may impact upon the issue of international exhaustion of IPR: the principle of national treatment and non-discrimination for imported goods, the prohibition of quantitative restrictions or measures of equivalent effect against importations, and an exception that allows the application of quantitative restrictions if they are necessary to protect, among other things, patent rights.

Article III:4 of GATT 1994 establishes the principle of national treatment or non-discrimination against imported goods:

> [t]he products of the territory of any contracting party imported into the territory of any other contracting party shall be accorded *treatment no less favourable* than that accorded to like products of national origin in respect of all laws, regulations and requirements affecting their internal sale, offering for sale, purchase, transportation, distribution or use. The provisions of this paragraph shall not prevent the application of differential internal transportation charges which are based exclusively on the economic operation of the means of transport and not on the nationality of the product.[14]

Under a regime of national exhaustion, the IPR owner cannot prevent the circulation of the product once that IPR owner has put the product in circulation in the national market, but the IPR owner could prevent the

---

[13] GATT 1994 is integrated by the provisions of the General Agreement on Tariffs and Trade of 1947 (General Agreement on Tariffs and Trade, October 30, 1947, 61 Stat. A-11, 55 UNTS 194) [hereinafter GATT 1947], certain instruments concluded under the umbrella of GATT 1947, and several understandings resulting from the Uruguay Round. Therefore, Articles III, XI and XX as well as all the other provisions of GATT 1947 are identical in GATT 1994.

[14] GATT 1994, Article III(4) (emphasis added).

circulation of an identical or similar product that the IPR owner marketed abroad. Therefore, the imported products would receive a *treatment less favourable* than national products, and consequently, a regime of national exhaustion of IPR may be considered inconsistent with Article III(4) of GATT 1994.

Article XI(1) and Article XX(d) are also relevant to this issue. The former forbids quantitative restrictions or measures of equivalent effect:

> [n]o prohibitions or restrictions other than duties, taxes or other charges, whether made effective through quotas, import or export licences or other measures, shall be instituted or maintained by any contracting party on the importation of any product of the territory of any other contracting party or on the exportation or sale for export of any product destined for the territory of any other contracting party.

Nevertheless, Article XX(d) is a safeguard that allows Members to maintain otherwise inconsistent measures in order to protect IPR:[15]

> Subject to the requirement that such measures are not applied in a manner which would constitute a means of arbitrary or unjustifiable discrimination between countries where the same conditions prevail, or a disguised restriction on international trade, nothing in this Agreement shall be construed to prevent the adoption or enforcement by any contracting party of measures:
>
> . . .
>
> (*d*) necessary to secure compliance with laws or regulations which are not inconsistent with the provisions of this Agreement, including those relating to . . . the protection of patents, trademarks and copyrights, and the prevention of deceptive practices.[16]

Before the conclusion of the Uruguay Round and commenting GATT 1947 and the ongoing TRIPS Agreement negotiations, Yusuf and Moncayo von Hase argued that the application of the national exhaustion of IPR and the consequent prevention of parallel imports were measures that had an effect equivalent to a quantitative restriction.[17] They also considered that although some degree of discrimination may be admitted under Article XX(d), 'it is difficult to see how a territorial regime of exhaustion

---

[15] Frederick M. Abbott, *First Report (Final) to the Committee on International Trade Law of the International Law Association on the Subject of Parallel Importation*, 1 J. INT'L ECON. L. 607 (1998).

[16] GATT 1994, Article XX(d).

[17] Abdulqawi A. Yusuf and Andrés Moncayo von Hase, *Intellectual Property Protection and International Trade – Exhaustion of Rights Revisited*, *in* 16(1) WORLD COMPETITION 116, 129 (1992).

would meet the "necessity" test of that provision'.[18] They pointed out that a national exhaustion regime is not *necessary* to secure the protection of intellectual property rights because when a title-holder sells a product embodying an IPR or grants a licence, it receives either a direct sale or royalties payment and, therefore, '[it] is no longer justified to have its exclusive rights extended over the entire distribution process'.[19]

Professor Abbott agreed with this approach. He considered that the rules restricting parallel importations were non-tariff barriers to trade inconsistent with Article XI(1), and that the prohibition of such importation is not justified under Article XX(d), because parallel import goods are placed on markets with the consent of rights holders, thus that prohibition is not *necessary* to protect IPR.[20]

In addition, the parallelism between Articles XI(1) and XX(d) of GATT 1994 and Articles 30 and 36 of the EC Treaty stands out, and it has led some authors to affirm that they 'perform largely the same functions' in regulating restrictions.[21] Thus, it is also suggested that the rationale underlying the ECJ's doctrine of regional exhaustion should be applied within the WTO framework, and laws preventing international exhaustion of IPR should be considered inconsistent with GATT 1947.[22]

In conclusion, the principles of national treatment and prohibition of quantitative restrictions on imported goods of GATT 1994 – even if interpreted in isolation from other WTO agreements, particularly the TRIPS Agreement – seem to foreclose a regime of national exhaustion of IPR.

1.3. The TRIPS Agreement provisions prevail over GATT 1994

The summarized rules relating to IPR exhaustion show a conflict between the TRIPS Agreement and GATT 1994. The germ of this contradiction is that GATT 1994 governs the circulation of *physical* goods, and the TRIPS Agreement the protection of *intangible* creations. Thus, goods embodying intellectual property rights are subject to a dual regulation that may lead to conflicts and deep contradictions.

The tension between the TRIPS Agreement and GATT 1994 regarding parallel imports is not the only conflict among WTO agreements and understandings. While neither the TRIPS Agreement nor GATT 1994

---

18 *Id.* at 128–9.

19 *Id.* at 129.

20 Abbott, *supra* note 15.

21 Tomás de las Heras Lorenzo, elagotamiento del derecho de marca, 462, 464 (Editorial Montecorvo 1994).

22 *Id.*; see also Abdulqawi A. Yusuf and Andrés Moncayo von Hase, *supra* note 17, at 129.

have specific or general provisions to solve this conflict, other WTO agreements have special rules.[23] For instance, Article XVI(3) of the Agreement Establishing the WTO stipulates that it has supremacy over other WTO agreements; or the General Interpretative Note to Annex 1A that states that the understandings and agreements listed in this annex prevail over the general provisions of GATT 1994.[24]

In the absence of specific provisions, the interpreter must apply the general rules of interpretation set out by Article 31 of the Vienna Convention. Article 31 states that a treaty shall be interpreted in good faith, taking into account the ordinary meaning of the terms, in their context and illuminated by the object and purpose of the treaty.

Subsumed within the principle of *good faith* is the principle of effective treaty interpretation for which '[a] treaty should not be interpreted in such a manner as to lead to a result which is manifestly absurd or unreasonable'.[25] Specifically, the Appellate Body of the Dispute Settlement Body (DSB) of WTO ruled that 'one of the corollaries of the "general rule of interpretation" in the Vienna Convention is that interpretation must give meaning and effect to all the terms of a treaty. An interpreter is not free to adopt a reading that would result in reducing whole clauses or paragraphs of a treaty to redundancy or inutility'.[26]

Applying the principle of effective treaty interpretation, if GATT 1994 prevails over Article 6 of the TRIPS Agreement, this provision is redundant and inutile. Conversely, if Article 6 of the TRIPS Agreement has priority, Articles III(4), XI(1) and XX(d) of GATT 1994 are still effective.[27]

To conclude, Articles 6 and 28 – with its footnote – of the TRIPS Agreement govern exhaustion of IPR, and the provisions of GATT 1994 are default rules that apply to situations other than IPR exhaustion and for which the TRIPS Agreement does not have a specific rule.

2. The United States – Argentina consultations

On May 6, 1999 and May 30, 2000, the United States requested consultations with Argentina under the Understanding on Rules and Procedures

---

23 William J. Davey and Werne Zdouc, *supra* note 8, at 59.

24 *Id.*

25 Ian Mc Taggart Sinclair, The Vienna Convention on the Law of Treaties 120 (Manchester University Press, 2nd edition 1984) (1973).

26 Appellate Body Report, *United States – Standards for Reformulated and Conventional Gasoline*, p. 21, WT/DS2/AB/R (April 29, 1996).

27 The same outcome is reached if the canon *lex especialis derogat lex generalis* is applied. Article 6 of the TRIPS Agreement is *lex especialis* and GATT 1994 is *lex generalis*. Thus, Article 6 of the TRIPS Agreement should prevail over GATT 1994.

Governing the Settlement of Disputes (DSU) of the WTO. The United States alleged that several provisions of the Argentinean Patent Law[28] and the Confidentiality Law were inconsistent with the TRIPS Agreement;[29] in particular, some provisions relating to compulsory licences, exclusive marketing rights, product by process patent protection, shifting of the burden of proof in process patent infringement cases, preliminary injunctions, patentability of micro-organisms and other subject matter, transitional patents, and protection of test data against unfair commercial use.

After nine rounds of consultations between May 1999 and April 2002, the United States and Argentina ended this process with a mutually agreed solution (the 'Mutually Agreed Solution'), and notified to the DSB that 'they reached an agreement on all of the matters raised by the United States'.[30]

Parallel imports and international exhaustion of patent rights were not mentioned in the requests of consultations, but the Mutually Agreed Solution included a section regarding this issue. This point was introduced during the negotiations by the United States[31] alleging that Article 36, paragraph (c) of the Argentinean Patent Act, which establishes the principle of international exhaustion of the patent rights, was inconsistent with the TRIPS Agreement.[32]

The Mutually Agreed Solution states that the parties agreed that the

---

[28] Law No. 24.481, September 20, 1995, [28,232] B.O. 1.

[29] Request for Consultations by the United States, Argentina – Patent Protection for Pharmaceuticals and Test Data Protection for Agricultural Chemicals, WT/DS171/1, (May 10, 1999); and Request for Consultations by the United States, Argentina – Certain Measures on the Protection of Patents and Test Data, WT/DS196/1, (June 6, 2000).

[30] Notification of Mutually Agreed Solution According to the Conditions Set Forth in the Agreement, Argentina – Patent Protection for Pharmaceuticals and Test Data Protection for Agricultural Chemicals (WT/DS171), Argentina – Certain Measures on the Protection of Patents and Test Data (WT/DS/196), WT/DS/171/3 WT/DS/196/4 (June 20, 2002) [hereinafter Notification of Mutually Agreed Solution].

[31] See Daya Shanker, *Argentina – US Mutually Agreed Solution, Economic Crisis in Argentina and Failure of the WTO Dispute Settlement System*, 44 IDEA 565, 577 (2004).

[32] Article 36(c) of the Argentinean Patent Act states that '[t]he right granted by any patent shall not have any effect against: . . . c) any person that acquires, uses, imports or commercializes in any way the products patented or obtained by the patented process, once that said product has been legally placed in the market of any country. It shall be understood that the marketing is legal when it conforms to the Agreement on Trade-Related Intellectual Property Rights, Part III, Section IV, TRIPS/GATT Agreement.'

relevant provisions of the Argentinean Patent Law and regulations regarding exhaustion were consistent with Argentina's obligations under the TRIPS Agreement.[33]

As was pointed out *supra*, Article 6 of the TRIPS Agreement declares that for the purposes of dispute settlement under this Agreement, nothing in the TRIPS Agreement can be used to address the issue of the exhaustion of intellectual property rights. In addition, Article 3(5) of the DSU establishes that all solutions to matters formally raised under consultations shall be consistent with the covered agreements.[34] However, the United States and Argentina addressed the issue of international patent rights exhaustion, violating both provisions.[35]

---

[33] In the text attached to the Notification of Mutually Agreed Solution, the parties state that

> The Governments of the United States and Argentina have analyzed article 36(c) of Law No. 24.481 and article 36 of Decree 260/96 in light of the provisions of Articles 6 and 28.1 of the TRIPS Agreement. Pursuant to this analysis, Argentina has confirmed that, according to its law and regulations, the owner of a patent granted in the Argentinean Republic shall have the right to prevent third parties not having the owner's consent from the acts of making, using, offering for sale, selling or importing the patented product in the territory of Argentina. However, a voluntary licensee in Argentina authorized by the Argentinean patent owner to import the patented product may import the product if he proves the product has been put on the market in a foreign country by the owner of the Argentinean patent or by a third party authorized for its commercialization. On this basis, Argentina and the United States agree that article 36(c) of Law No. 24.481, read in conjunction with article 36 of Decree 260/96, is consistent with Argentina's obligations under the TRIPS Agreement.

Id.

[34] Article 3(5) DSU:

> All solutions to matters formally raised under the consultation and dispute settlement provisions of the covered agreements, including arbitration awards, shall be consistent with those agreements and shall not nullify or impair benefits accruing to any Member under those agreements, nor impede the attainment of any objective of those agreements.

[35] Shanker suggested that it was the Argentinean economic crisis at the beginning of the century that led Argentina to accept consultations that included the issue of patent rights exhaustion. Shanker, *supra* note 31, at 615. However, the United States grounded its request on Article 28 of the Agreement and it seems that Argentina preferred to settle the controversy, taking into account that the general outcome of the consultations was favourable to its interest, without making any concession in relation to the principle of exhaustion as contained in its legislation.

In conclusion, the consultations between the United States and Argentina involved negotiations regarding international exhaustion of patent rights. They concluded that the Argentinean Law was consistent with the TRIPS Agreement. Indeed, if Argentina had adopted a regimen of national or regional patent rights exhaustion, the result would have been the same, because Articles 6 and 28 – with its footnote – of the TRIPS Agreement grant WTO Members the freedom to adopt the regimen of patent exhaustion of their choice.

8 Intellectual property rights and competition policy

Beatriz Conde Gallego

1. Introduction: International trade, IPRs and competition

By conceiving the Agreement on Trade Related Aspects of Intellectual Property Rights (TRIPS) as an integral part of the WTO trading system, intellectual property rights (IPRs) and international trade have been definitively linked. Whereas previous chapters of this *Handbook* have dealt with different aspects of the relationship between IP protection and international trade liberalisation,[1] this chapter adds another dimension, namely the competition dimension. In order to approach the complex issues at the interface between international trade, IPRs and competition, it is worth looking first at the two binomials IP protection/competition and international trade/competition separately.

IP protection and competition It may at first sight be somehow surprising to find competition-related elements in an international instrument which has as its purpose the protection of IPRs. The inclusion of competition-related rules in the TRIPS Agreement was to a certain extent a concession to the developing countries which, once it was clear that the TRIPS Agreement would cover issues beyond counterfeiting and piracy, insisted on having competition rules as a component of TRIPS.[2] Indeed, the request by developing countries for competition rules largely reflects their understanding of IPRs as a danger to competition.[3] Despite the negotiat-

---

[1] See, for example, Chapter 1 of Volume II; Frankel, Susy (2010), 'The applicability of GATT jurisprudence to the interpretation of the TRIPS Agreement', in Correa, Carlos M. (ed.), *Research Handbook on the Interpretation and Enforcement of Intellectual Property under WTO Rules: Intellectual Property in the WTO Volume II*, Cheltenham, UK and Northampton, MA, US: Edward Elgar.

[2] UNCTAD-ICTSD (2004), *Resource Book on TRIPS and Development*, Cambridge: Cambridge University Press, at 543. On the negotiating history of TRIPS, see among others, Evans, Gail E. (1994), 'Intellectual Property as a Trade Issue – The Making of the Agreement on Trade-related Aspects of Intellectual Property Rights', *World Competition*, **18** (2), 137–80.

[3] See, for instance, the summary of the views expressed in the Report (1998)

ing history, supplementing the TRIPS Agreement with – even rudimentary – competition rules would still have been unavoidable if one considers the fundamental relationship between IP protection and competition.

Behind all this, there is a presumption that more innovation is good for society. Although there is still much economic discussion on the relationship between competition and innovation,[4] it is now widely accepted that competition and open markets provide better incentives for innovation than a monopoly.[5] On the one hand, competition among firms seeking to develop new products or processes encourages innovation. On the other hand, competition among firms producing an existing product encourages them to reduce costs, to improve quality or to develop better products. Put differently, innovation helps firms to escape competition. While this is true, it is also right that firms would not invest – or would invest less – in innovation if they had to fear fierce competition after having innovated. At this point, IPRs come into play. By allowing the right holder to exclusively exploit the protected subject matter – or in other words, to exclude competition by imitation – the IP-system enables him to recoup the gains of his investment and compels competing undertakings to develop new and improved products. By doing so, the IP-system furthers competition by substitution and contributes to dynamic competition, that is, to promoting innovation. Yet, the incentives to innovate arising from the IP-system are only effective if it is guaranteed that first, firms feel pressure to innovate and second, that competitors may come up with new products that can substitute for the product protected by the IPRs. This is primarily the task of competition law.

IPRs and competition law are thus complementary in achieving the goal of promoting innovation.[6] From this it does not follow, however,

---

of the Working Group on the Interaction between Trade and Competition Policy, WT/WGTCP/2, 8 December 1998, available at www.wto.org/english/tratop_e/comp_e/wgtcp_docs_e.htm, at para. 114. There are also authoritative voices in developed countries which emphasise the negative effects of IPRs on competition; see Stiglitz, Joseph E. (2003), *The Roaring Nineties: A New History of the World's Most Prosperous Decade*, New York: W.W. Norton & Company, at 208: 'market economies only lead to efficient outcomes when there is competition and intellectual property rights undermine the very basis of competition'.

4 For an excellent overview of how the economic literature analysing the relationship between competition and innovation has developed, see Baker, Jonathan B. (2007), 'Beyond Schumpeter vs. Arrow: How Antitrust Fosters Innovation', *Antitrust Law Journal*, **74** (3), 577 *et seq.*

5 *Ibid.*, at 587. See also Lemley, Mark A. (2007), 'A New Balance between IP and Antitrust', *Southwestern Journal of Law and Trade in the Americas*, **13**, at 13.

6 This is the view now supported in the European Union and the United

that the relationship between both bodies of law is free from tensions. On the contrary, frictions can arise at two different levels. On an abstract level, finding the right balance between ensuring an effective competitive environment that compels firms to innovate and protecting companies' *ex ante* incentives to innovate by allowing them to benefit from their innovations is a difficult task. Moreover, IPRs, like any other right, may be abused. Competition concerns may come up where a right holder uses his IPRs to gain unwarranted market power or otherwise in a manner that restrains competition. Thus, on a (more) concrete level, competition law may set limits on what the IP right holder may do with its right. Whereas the TRIPS Agreement may be interpreted as containing principles that help to strike the former balance,[7] the competition-related provisions of TRIPS clearly focus on this latter aspect of the relationship between IPRs and competition.

Competition and international trade The necessity of accompanying the process of trade liberalisation with competition rules is not only well shown by the example of European market integration, as one of the main purposes of the competition rules of the EC Treaty is to prevent already abolished governmental trade barriers from being re-erected by private undertakings. As early as 1948, Chapter V (Article 46) of the stillborn Havana Charter on an International Trade Organization addressed the problem of business practices adversely affecting international trade.[8] Private firms may restrain

---

Footnote 6 (*cont.*)
States. See for the European Union, European Commission (2004), 'Commission Notice – Guidelines on the Application of Article 81 to Technology Transfer Agreements', OJ 2004 No. C 101, para. 7: 'Innovation constitutes an essential and dynamic component of an open and competitive market economy. Intellectual property rights promote dynamic competition by encouraging undertakings to invest by developing new or improved products and processes. So does competition by putting pressure on undertakings to innovate. Therefore, both intellectual property rights and competition are necessary to promote innovation and ensure a competitive exploitation thereof.' For the United States, see Department of Justice and Federal Trade Commission (2007), 'Antitrust Enforcement and Intellectual Property Rights: Promoting Innovation and Competition', www.usdoj.gov/atr/public/hearings/ip/222655.pdf, p. 2: 'Consequently, antitrust and intellectual property are properly perceived as complementary bodies of law that work together to bring innovation to consumers: [. . .]'.

[7] See the analysis of the TRIPS general principles made by Ricolfi, Marco (2006), 'Is there an Antitrust Antidote against IP Overprotection within TRIPS?', *Marquette Intellectual Property Law Review*, **10** (1), at 321 *et seq.*

[8] Havana Charter for an International Trade Organization, United Nations Conference on Trade and Employment held at Havana from 21 November 1947 to

competition and trade in a variety of ways. The WTO Working Group on the Interaction between Trade and Competition Policy[9] identified three types of trade-related restraints on competition: (1) private market barriers; (2) international cartels and (3) anticompetitive practices directed at foreign markets, in particular export cartels.[10] Though the Working Group did not specifically consider the effects of private practices in connection with IPRs, it is obvious that IP-related anticompetitive practices may also negatively affect international trade. In fact, IP-related conduct may well be subsumed under the three categories mentioned above.[11]

The interface between competition law and international trade can also be approached from a different perspective. As states have publicly committed themselves to liberal trade and thus narrowed the scope for unilateral trade measures, they may use competition law as an alternative 'weapon' to protect their domestic industries.[12] In view of the manifold interest of the participants in international trade, it is thus conceivable that national competition authorities might apply – or refuse to apply – their law in a way that best serves the interests of their own nationals. To mention just a few examples: the reluctance of the Japanese competition authority to apply the competition rules to exclusive dealing agreements in the photographic film and paper market was seen by the United States as a protectionist strategy to shield the Japanese market from foreign competition.[13] On the contrary, there are enough grounds to suspect

---

24 March 1948, Final Act and Related Documents. The full text of the Charter is available at www.wto.int/english/docs_e/legal_e/havana_e.pdf.

[9] As a result of the Ministerial Conference in Singapore (1996), the Working Group on the Interaction between Trade and Competition Policy (WGTCP) was established to study different aspects of this issue; see WTO (1996), 'Singapore Ministerial Declaration of 13 December 1996', WT/MIN(96)/DEC, available at www.wto.org/english/thewto_e/minist_e/min96_e/min96_e.htm.

[10] WTO (1998), 'Report (1998) of the Working Group on the Interaction between Trade and Competition Policy to the General Council', WT/WGTCP/2, 8 December 1998, available at www.wto.org/english/tratop_e/comp_e/wgtcp_docs_e.htm.

[11] For a detailed analysis of trade-related anticompetitive practices in licensing agreements, see Conde Gallego, Beatriz (2003), *Handelsbezogene Aspekte des Lizenzkartellrechts*, Berne: Stämpfli Verlag, at 77 *et seq*. See also *infra* Section 2.2.1.

[12] On this argument, see Hawk, Barry E. (1996), 'Overview', in OECD (ed.), *Antitrust and Market Access – The Scope and Coverage of Competition Laws and Implications for Trade*, Paris: OECD Publishing, at pp. 9 *et seq*; Iacobucci, Edward (1997), 'The Interdependence of Trade and Competition Policies', *World Competition*, **21** (2), at 18.

[13] The Kodak/Fuji case was the object of a WTO panel decision; see WTO (1998), 'Japan – Measures Affecting Consumer Photographic Film and Paper', WT/DS44/R, 31 March 1998. Though this case is often referred to as an example

that behind the initial prohibition by the European Commission on the merger of Boeing and McDonnell Douglas was also the intent to protect the European champion Airbus.[14] Furthermore, even if states do not use competition rules in such a strategic way, the ability of national competition laws to deal with international trade and competition problems is to a large extent determined by the fact that neither international free trade nor the protection of competition in international or foreign markets is among the goals of national competition regimes.

It is not the purpose of this chapter to go through these issues in detail.[15] Nevertheless, as we shall see, the TRIPS Agreement relies on the competition laws of its members to combat IP-related restraints of competition. Thus, the question remains whether this is the right approach to achieve this goal effectively.

This brief overview has shown that there are many problematic and open issues at the interface between IPRs, international trade and competition law. Trying to address all of them in the present chapter would be too ambitious. In particular, there is increasing support in academic circles for a competition-oriented scrutiny of the TRIPS provisions. Behind this, there is an awareness that the expansionist tendencies of IP laws observed

---

Footnote 13 (*cont.*)
of the limits of WTO law in dealing with private anticompetitive practices, it best exemplifies those cases in which a competition authority may refrain from enforcing its competition law when only foreign competition is perceived as being restricted, even though as a consequence, the intensity of competition in its own market is also being reduced.

[14] On this point, see Fox, Eleanor M. (1998), 'World Antitrust: A Principled Blueprint', in Großfeld, Bernard, et al. (eds), *Festschrift für Wolfgang Fikentscher zum 70. Geburtstag*, Tübingen: Mohr Siebeck, at 860.

[15] The debate on the necessity of international competition rules has been to a large extent damped as a consequence of the decision of the General Council in August 2004 that the interaction between trade and competition would no longer form part of the work programme set out in the Doha Ministerial Declaration; see WTO (2004), 'Doha Work Programme – Decision Adopted by the General Council on 1 August 2004', WT/L/579, 2 August 2004, p. 3. The discussion produced considerable writing in the late 1990s and earlier 2000s; see among others, Amato, F. (2001), 'International Antitrust: What Future?', *World Competition*, **24** (4), 451–73; Drexl, Josef (ed.) (2003), *The Future of Transnational Antitrust – From Comparative to Common Competition Law*, Berne: Stämpfli; Fox, Eleanor M. (2000), 'Antitrust and Regulatory Fedaralism: Races Up, Down, and Sideways', *New York University Law Review*, **75**, 1781–807; García Bercero, Ignacio and Stefan D. Amarasinha (2001), 'Moving the Trade and Competition Debate Forward', *Journal of International Economic Law*, **4** (3), 481–506; Tarullo, Daniel K., 'Norms and Institutions in Global Competition Policy', *American Journal of International Law*, 94, 478–504.

during the last decade may bring the whole IP-system out of balance by not taking sufficient account of the competition rationale underlying it. Such an analysis would certainly exceed the scope of this contribution. Rather, the purpose of this chapter is to focus on competition law itself and to analyse the role the TRIPS Agreement ascribes to it. To do that, the remainder of the chapter is structured as follows: Section 2 considers first the current competition-related provisions contained in the TRIPS Agreement. This analysis will show that TRIPS Agreement leaves WTO Members considerable room for manoeuvre to design their own IP-related competition rules. The object of Section 3 is to examine which role the TRIPS objectives may play in the design and application of these rules. Section 4 explores how a decentralised application of national IP-related competition rules could be improved with the aim of achieving these goals. Finally, Section 5 contains some concluding remarks.

2. Competition-related provisions of the TRIPS Agreement

Article 8(2), Article 31(k) and Article 40 are normally referred to as the relevant competition-related rules of the TRIPS Agreement.[16] In the following, the structure, scope of application and nature of these provisions will be examined.

2.1. Article 8(2) TRIPS

Under the heading of 'Principles', Article 8(2) TRIPS provides that 'appropriate measures, provided that they are consistent with the provisions of this Agreement, may be needed to prevent the abuse of intellectual property rights by right holders or the resort to practices which unreasonably restrain trade or adversely affect the international transfer of technology'. Article 8(2), which has to be read in connection with the first paragraph of the provision,[17] states the general framework within which Members may make exceptions to the implementation and enforcement of the TRIPS

---

[16] See, for example, UNCTAD-ICTSD (2004), *supra* note 2, at 541; OECD (1999), 'Competition Elements in International Trade Agreements: A Post-Uruguay Round Overview of WTO Agreements', COM/TD/DAFFE/CLP(98)26/FINAL, 28 January 1999, available at www.olis.oecd.org/olis/1998doc.nsf/linkto/com-td-daffe-clp(98)26-final, at 14 *et seq.* Other authors would also consider Article 67 TRIPS as competition-related, as the technical and financial cooperation duties of developed members towards developing and least developed members also extend to the preparation of laws and regulations on the prevention of abuse of intellectual property rights; see Ricolfi, Marco (2006), *supra* note 7, at 312–13.

[17] Article 8(1) stipulates: 'Members may, in formulating or amending their laws and regulations, adopt measures necessary to protect public health and nutrition, and to promote the public interest in sectors of vital importance to their

minimum standards of protection. Whereas the measures to be adopted under Article 8(1) are generally of a positive nature, those referred to in Article 8(2) are of a preventive or defensive nature.[18]

Though the competition-relation of Article 8(2) is commonly taken for granted, the scope of application of this provision is, however, broader than covering only anticompetitive practices. Indeed, it is only by closely looking at it that the competition-link may be established. Before analysing in more detail the types of IP-related conduct that may be controlled, two general remarks should be made. First, notwithstanding the clear focus of Article 8 on technology-related IP rights, the general reference to IP right holders means that practices concerning all kind of IP rights dealt with in TRIPS are covered by this provision.[19] Second, Article 8(2), unlike Article 40 which explicitly refers to practices in contractual licenses, generally speaks about 'abuse' and 'practices'. Consequently, both the contractual exploitation of the right as well as unilateral conduct by the IP right holder may be the subject of control.

Article 8(2) enables WTO Members to address three types of behaviour by IP right holders, namely (1) abuses of IPRs, (2) practices which unreasonably restrain trade and (3) practices which adversely affect the international transfer of technology. With regard to the latter, their inclusion goes back to the work of the UNCTAD in the framework of preparing an international Code of Conduct for the Transfer of Technology[20] and reflects the concerns of developing countries on the necessity of safeguarding the dissemination of technology. As Article 40 explicitly states, anticompetitive practices in licensing agreements may also have an adverse effect on the transfer of technology.[21] However, on this point, Article 8(2) is interpreted

---

Footnote 17 (*cont.*)
socio-economic and technological development, provided that such measures are consistent with the provisions of this Agreement'.

[18] Yusuf, Abdulqawi A. (2008), 'TRIPS: Background, Principles and General Provisions', in Correa, Carlos M. and Abdulqawi A. Yusuf (eds), *Intellectual Property and International Trade – The TRIPS Agreement*, Alphen aan den Rijn, The Netherlands: Kluwer Law International, at 13.

[19] UNCTAD-ICTSD (2004), *supra* note 2, at 547.

[20] Heinemann, Andreas (2002), *Immaterialgüterschutz in der Wettbewerbsordnung – Eine grundlageorientierte Untersuchung zum Kartellrecht des geistigen Eigentums*, Tübingen: Mohr Siebeck, at p. 587. On the Code of Technology Transfer, see generally, Patel, Surendra J., Pedro Roffe and Abdulqawi A. Yusuf (eds) (2001), *International Technology Transfer – The Origins and the Aftermath of the United Nations Negotiations on a Draft Code of Conduct*, The Hague: Kluwer Law International.

[21] See *infra* Section 2.2.1.

as enabling the control of practices restricting the international transfer of technology even if they are not deemed to be anticompetitive.[22]

The allusion in Article 8(2) to practices which unreasonably restrain trade is generally understood as a reference to anticompetitive practices.[23] The similarity in the wording of this provision and the one in Section 1 of the Sherman Act, which prohibits every contract, trust or conspiracy in restraint of trade, may certainly suggest this conclusion. Nevertheless, there are reasons for not equating restrictive trade practices with anticompetitive practices too readily.[24] Thus, the TRIPS Agreement is conceived as an integral part of the WTO multilateral trading system, which has as one of its objectives the substantial reduction of tariffs and other trade barriers.[25] In this context, the TRIPS Preamble highlights the '[desire] to reduce distortions and impediments to international trade' as one of the main goals of the Agreement. Any reference to restrictive trade practices in the TRIPS Agreement should be interpreted in this broader context. Moreover, since Article 40(1) refers to those licensing practices which restrain competition *and* may have an adverse effect on trade, it clearly seems to differentiate between both concepts. As was mentioned before in the introductions, IP-related anticompetitive practices may often result in impeding trade. Yet not every conduct which may objectively restrain trade must also be qualified as anticompetitive. This is well shown, for instance, by territorial restrictions (with an international element) in vertical agreements, including licensing agreements, whose effects on competition are largely ambivalent.[26] While a competition analysis may conclude that the pro-competitive effects of such a restriction outweigh the anticompetitive ones and may thus not be objected to, viewed from a trade perspective such a (pro-competitive) restriction may still bar market access.[27] Whether

---

[22] UNCTAD-ICTSD (2004), *supra* note 2, at 549; Correa, Carlos M. (2007), *Trade Related Aspects of Intellectual Property Rights – A Commentary on the TRIPS Agreement*, Oxford: Oxford University Press, at p. 112; Ricolfi, Marco (2006), *supra* note 7, at 342.

[23] UNCTAD-ICTSD (2004), *supra* note 2, at 548.

[24] In this sense, see also Brand, Oliver (2007), 'Artikel 8 – Grundsätze', in Busche, Jan and Peter-Tobias Stoll (eds), *TRIPs – Internationales und europäisches Recht des geistigen Eigentums*, München: CHV, at 183.

[25] Preamble of the Agreement Establishing the World Trade Organisation at Marrakesh, 15 April 1994, reproduced at www.wto.org/english/docs_e/legal_e/04-wto.pdf.

[26] For a detailed analysis, see Jofer, Florian (2004), 'Verrikalvereinbarungen als Begelungs problematik des internationalen Handels- und Kartellrechts'.

[27] On this point see Marsden, Philip (1998), 'The Impropriety of WTO "Market Access" Rules on Vertical Restrains', *World Competition*, **21** (6), at 9 *et seq*.

in the light of its positive effects on competition such a practice constitutes an *unreasonable* restraint of trade is a different question.

The third kind of behaviour by IP right holders that Article 8(2) is able to control relates to abuses of intellectual property rights. Again, the notion of an abuse of IPRs goes beyond purely IP-related anticompetitive practices. It presupposes neither the existence of market dominance on the part of the right holder,[28] nor an anticompetitive use of the right.[29] Article 5(A) of the Paris Convention, which is usually brought up in this context,[30] mentions the failure to work an invention within a given period of time that is not justified by legitimate reasons as an example of an abuse of the patent right. Apart from stating a concrete example of what may constitute an abuse, this provision, however, gives only limited guidance in shedding light on the concept of abuse. Thus, it follows from it that an abuse consists in an illegitimate use of the right. In this context, it has been further argued that an abuse would be a use of the right that defeats its purpose, and that it is for the WTO Members to define the concept of abuse through the adoption of appropriate measures.[31] Even though there is nothing to object to in the first part of this affirmation, such a broad statement needs to be concretised. Moreover, without negating that WTO Members retain a great degree of flexibility over the determination of what constitutes an abuse, the TRIPS Agreement does however set out the framework within which Members may do this.

In this regard, Article 7 TRIPS conceives the protection of IPRs not as a goal in itself but rather as a means to achieve further ends.[32] According to this provision, intellectual property protection should contribute to the promotion of technological innovation, to the transfer and dissemination of technology and to the mutual advantage of producers and users of technological knowledge, all this in a manner conducive to social and economic welfare and to a balance of rights and obligations. Whereas the goal of promoting innovation underlines the classical rationale for granting IP protection, the reference in this article to the transfer and dissemination of technology, and to the interests of users of IP-protected goods, clearly points towards access considerations. Hence, the TRIPS Agreement is

---

[28] Thus, the notion of abuse in Article 8(2) is not to be confused with the European concept of an abuse of a *dominant position*.

[29] Brand, Oliver (2007), *supra* note 24, at 182; UNCTAD-ICTSD (2004), *supra* note 2, at 548; Correa, Carlos M. (2007), *supra* note 22, at 111.

[30] See Correa, Carlos M. (2007), *supra* note 22, at 111 and Yusuf, Abdulqawi A. (2008), *supra* note 18, at 15.

[31] UNCTAD-ICTSD (2004), *supra* note 2, at 548.

[32] See Ricolfi, Marco (2006), *supra* note 7, at 323 *et seq.*

not only concerned with the production of knowledge, but also with its diffusion and with the fact that this knowledge gets used. Moreover, as users of IP-protected goods are both end users as well as producers of goods and services that incorporate an existing invention while developing it, the TRIPS Agreement is also very much concerned with the continuous improvement of existing knowledge and as a precondition for this, with preserving access to this knowledge by third parties. Coming back to the concept of abuse, a use of the IP right that runs counter to the goals of promoting the diffusion of knowledge and of preserving access to it would definitively defeat its purpose. Likewise, as was pointed out above in the introduction, IP protection can only effectively contribute to the goal of promoting innovation if the operability of the mechanism of dynamic competition is guaranteed. Thus, a use of the IP right directed at restricting or excluding the possibility of competing firms to offer substitutive goods would also qualify as an abuse of the right.

The foregoing analysis of the scope of application of Article 8(2) has shown that this provision allows WTO Members to adopt measures to meet non-specific competition concerns like safeguarding international trade in IP-protected goods as well as the international transfer of technology – or in broader terms, of knowledge – from undue restrictions. On the other side, competitive concerns play a major role in determining what constitutes an abuse of an IPR. This is particularly the case when assessing the behaviour of the IP right holder in the light of the objective of promoting innovation, both original and follow-on innovation. Two conclusions may be drawn from this analysis. On one side, Article 8(2) opens the door for WTO Members to take account of competitive concerns by relying on measures other than antitrust measures. The decompilation exception provided for in Article 6 of the European Directive on the legal protection of computer programs[33] and the current European Commission's proposal for a repairs clause in the context of the design protection of spare parts[34] may be cited as examples thereof.[35] On the other side, IP-related

---

[33] Council Directive 91/250/EEC of 14 May 1991 on the legal protection of computer programs, OJ 1991 No. L 122, p. 42.

[34] Proposal of 14 September 2004 for a Directive of the European Parliament and of the Council amending Directive 98/71/EC on the legal protection of designs, COM(2004) 582 final, available at http://eur-lex.europa.eu/LexUriServ/LexUriServ.do?uri=COM:2004:0582:FIN:EN:PDF. On this specific topic, see Kur, Annette (2008), 'Limiting IP protection for Competition Policy Reasons – A Case Study Base on EU Spare-parts-design Discussion', in Drexl, Josef (ed.), *Research Handbook on Intellectual Property and Competition Law,* Cheltenham, UK and Northampton, MA, US: Edward Elgar, 313–45.

[35] For further examples of pro-competitive IP-legislation see Correa, Carlos

competition rules of WTO Members may well be designed to give consideration to non-specific competition concerns such as the negative impact of a certain practice on the transfer of technology.

Measures adopted in the framework of Article 8(2) are subject to some limitations. Namely, they must be both 'consistent with other provisions of the [TRIPS] Agreement' and 'appropriate'. Whereas the appropriateness requirement hints at the necessity that national measures be proportional to the purpose of preventing abusive or restrictive behaviour of the IP right holder and thus imposes a negatively defined limitation on the remedial action of WTO Members,[36] the interpretation of the consistency requirement proves to be more difficult. As already stated, Article 8(2) lays down the framework within which WTO Members may make exceptions to the implementation and enforcement of TRIPS minimum standards of protection. Subjecting these exceptions to the observation of precisely those provisions, an exception of which is to be made, is somehow contradictory.[37] Also from a public international law perspective, the consistency requirement in a way states the obvious as Article 26 of the Vienna Convention[38] explicitly provides that 'every treaty in force is binding upon the parties to it and must be performed in good faith'.[39] The adoption of national measures in the context of Article 8(2) that would cancel out the content of other TRIPS provisions and would run counter to their purpose and spirit could hardly be deemed as a performance in good faith. A brief look at the negotiating history of this provision may help to give the requirement of consistency some functional meaning. Thus, as already

---

Footnote 35 (*cont.*)
M. (2001), 'Pro-competitive Measures under the TRIPS Agreement to Promote Technology Diffusion in Developing Countries', *Journal of World Intellectual Property*, **4** (4), at 483 *et seq.*

[36] UNCTAD-ICTSD (2004), *supra* note 2, at 553. In this respect, the wording of Article 8(2) does not differ much from other WTO provisions that allow for exceptions to WTO obligations, see Nguyen, Tu T. (2008), 'Competition Rules in the TRIPS Agreement – The CFI's Ruling in Microsoft v. Commission and Implications for Developing Countries', *International Review of Intellectual Property and Competition Law*, **39** (5), at 565.

[37] In this sense, see also Heinemann, Andreas (1996), 'Antitrust Law of Intellectual Property in the TRIPS Agreement of the World Trade Organization', in Beier, Friedrich-Karl and Gerhard Schricker (eds), *From GATT to TRIPS – The Agreement on Trade-related Aspects of Intellectual Property Rights*, Weinheim: VCH, at 242.

[38] Vienna Convention on the Law of Treaties, done at Vienna on 23 May 1969, United Nations, Treaty Series, vol. 1155, p. 331, also available at http://untreaty.un.org/ilc/texts/instruments/english/conventions/1_1_1969.pdf.

[39] See Odman, Ayse (2000), 'Using TRIPS to Make the Innovation Process Work', *Journal of World Intellectual Property*, **3** (3), at 350.

mentioned, Article 8(2) was introduced on the insistence of (some major) developing countries which were concerned about the possible negative effects of introducing broad standards of IP protection. While stating a concession to the interests of developing countries, industrialized countries also made sure that the system of IP protection established in the TRIPS Agreement would be maintained as such.[40] The consistency clause therefore fulfils a clarifying function: Article 8(2) merely allows the prevention of individual excesses within the system.[41] As far as national competition rules are concerned, the consistency requirement thus precludes an excessive application of these rules that would outlaw uses and forms of IPRs guaranteed by the TRIPS Agreement.[42]

Finally, as to the nature of Article 8(2), this provision is permissive rather than mandatory in character. Article 8(2) enables WTO Members to take measures to prevent abusive and restrictive behaviour by the right holder. Yet, they are not obliged to do so.[43] Accordingly, if a WTO Member abstains from adopting legislation – and in particular IP-related competition rules – to control this kind of practice, this policy option would, in principle, be unobjectionable and could not be the subject of a complaint under the WTO Dispute Settlement Understanding.[44, 45] Moreover, other

---

40 Note that the corresponding provision of the Anell Draft of July 1990 did not include such a consistency requirement. Conversely, the Brussels Ministerial Text of December 1990 used the formula: 'appropriate measures, provided that they do not derogate from the obligations arising under this Agreement [. . .]'. Both documents are available at www.wto.org/english/docs_e/gattdocs_e.htm under the documents symbols MTN.GNG/NG11/W/76 and MTN.TNC/W/35/Rev. 1, respectively. The final text seems to be a compromise between these two texts, as the wording 'consistent with the provisions of this Agreement' arguably leaves a broader scope for national measures adopted in the context of Article 8(2).

41 Heinemann, Andreas (1996), *supra* note 37, at 243.

42 See UNCTAD-ICTSD (2004), *supra* note 2, at 551 *et seq* (with some abstract examples of non-compliance with the consistency requirement). See also Ullrich, Hanns (2004), 'Expansionist Intellectual Property Protection and Reductionist Competition Rules: A TRIPS Perspective', *Journal of International Economic Law*, **7** (2), at 410.

43 At least concerning Article 8(2), there seems to be agreement on this point. See, for example, UNCTAD-ICTSD (2004), *supra* note 2, at 546. More contentious is the character of Article 40; see *infra* Section 2.2.1.

44 Understanding on Rules and Procedures Governing the Settlement of Disputes, Annex 2 of the Agreement Establishing the World Trade Organization. The text is available at www.wto.org/english/docs_e/legal_e/28-dsu.pdf.

45 Ricolfi, Marco (2006), *supra* note 7, at 316. In this context, it has been argued that the failure of a WTO Member to address IP-related anticompetitive practices would amount to an abuse of this Member's rights, see Odman, Ayse (2000), *supra* note 39, at 364 *et seq*.

than with regard to the IP standards of protection, in the field of IP-related competition law and policy no harmonization has been intended by the TRIPS Agreement. WTO Members thus retain full sovereignty in the formulation and application of their competition rules on IPRs,[46] the only substantial limitation being that they are TRIPS-consistent.

2.2. *Article 40 TRIPS*

The general principle stated in Article 8(2) is further concretised in Article 40 which specifically deals with anticompetitive practices in contractual licences. Article 40 is structured in four paragraphs, the first two dealing with aspects of substantive law, the final two providing for procedural rules for cross-border violations of competition law.

2.2.1. Substantive law

Article 40(1) contains the consensual recognition of WTO Members that 'some licensing practices or conditions pertaining to intellectual property rights which restrain competition may have adverse effects on trade and may impede the transfer and dissemination of technology'. As a logical implication of this recognition, Article 40(2) provides further that Members are not prevented 'from specifying in their legislation licensing practices or conditions that may in particular cases constitute an abuse of intellectual property rights having an adverse effect on competition in the relevant market' and that they may 'adopt, consistently with the other provision of the Agreement, appropriate measures to control such practices [. . .]'.

The interpretation of Article 40(1) and (2) poses a number of challenging questions as to its scope of application and nature. Thus, it is not entirely clear what is to be understood under the terms 'licensing practices or conditions'. Furthermore, the explicit reference in the first part of this provision to the adverse effects on trade and on the transfer and dissemination of technology is fully omitted in the second paragraph. Beside the need to shed some light on these ambiguities, the interrelation between the two paragraphs should also be explored. In addition, it has been argued that other than Article 8(2), Article 40 may be read as containing a minimum obligation for WTO Members to act. This, in turn, raises the question of the relationship between Article 8(2) and Article 40. Before

---

[46] Again, there seems to be wide consensus on this conclusion; see Abbott, Frederick M. (2004), 'Are the Competition Rules in the WTO TRIPS Agreement Adequate?', *Journal of International Economic Law*, **7** (3), at 692; Ricolfi, Marco (2006), *supra* note 7, at 316 *et seq.*; Ullrich, Hanns (2004), *supra* note 42, at 408; UNCTAD-ICTSD (2004), *supra* note 2, at 546.

addressing these issues in more detail, some general considerations regarding the significance of this provision, as well as of those of its aspects that remain widely undisputed, should be made.

Article 40 is by far the most detailed competition-related provision of the TRIPS Agreement. Its inclusion in the TRIPS Agreement stands in the same direct tradition as the competition chapter of the Draft International Code of Conduct on Transfer of Technology and corroborates the observation that, in an international context, intellectual property protection and competition law have traditionally been considered in the framework of policies promoting the transfer of technology from developed to developing countries.[47] While the latter countries have largely seen the technological and economic development of the recipient country as the benchmark for the control of restrictive clauses in licensing agreements, industrialised countries have traditionally put the emphasis on the notion of restraint of competition.[48] The TRIPS Agreement in its Article 40 clearly adopts a competition approach to the control of licences. Thus, the 'restraint [of] competition' and the 'adverse effect on competition' are the central elements in the definition of the practices covered by this provision. In this context, it is worth remarking that licensing agreements are increasingly[49] seen as being essentially pro-competitive as they contribute to the dissemination of technology and knowledge, permit the exploitation of intellectual assets by firms which may have a greater comparative advantage, enable efficient production, and offer a significant source of revenue for the right holder, therefore increasing the right holder's incentives to invest in further innovation.[50] A competition law analysis of licensing agreements

---

[47] Drexl, Josef (2008), 'Intellectual Property and Competition: Sketching a Competition-oriented Reform of TRIPs', in Bakardjieva, Antonina, Ulf Bernitz, Bengt Domej, Annette Kur and Per Jonas Nordell (eds), *Festkrift Marianne Levin*, Stockholm: Norstedts Juridik, at 261.

[48] On different approaches followed during the negotiations of the International Code of Conduct on Transfer of Technology, see Miller, Debra L. and Joel Davidow (2001), 'Antitrust at the United Nations: A Tale of Two Codes', in Patel, Surendra J., Pedro Roffe and Abdulqawi A. Yusuf (eds), *supra* note 20, at 77 *et seq*. See also Roffe, Pedro and Christoph Spennemann (2008), 'Control of Anti-competitive Practices in Contractual Licences under the TRIPS Agreement', in Correa, Carlos M. and Abdulqawi A. Yusuf (eds), *supra* note 18, at 308 *et seq*.

[49] The competition law assessment of licensing agreements has evolved parallel to the general relationship between IPRs and competition law. For an overview of this development in Germany, Europe and the United States, see Ullrich, Hanns (1996), 'Lizenzkartellrecht auf dem Weg zur Mitte', *Gewerblicher Rechtsschutz und Urheberrecht Internationaler Teil*, 555–68.

[50] OECD (1998), 'Competition Policy and Intellectual Property Rights',

will balance these pro-competitive effects with the negative effects on competition resulting from particular clauses of the licence contract.[51]

Article 40 applies to the licensing of all kinds of IPRs. Even though the practices exemplified under Article 40(2) are commonly found in patent and know-how licensing agreements, a systematic interpretation of Article 40, which complements the provisions of Part II of the TRIPS Agreement dealing with the 'standards concerning the availability, scope and use of intellectual property rights', supports this conclusion.[52] Likewise, both bilateral and multilateral licensing agreements like cross-licensing or patent pools are covered by the term 'contractual licenses'.[53]

More controversial, however, is the question of whether Article 40 also encompasses unilateral behaviour relating to licences. In this regard, it has been argued that the wording 'practices or conditions' has to be understood broadly in the sense of including not only contractual clauses, but all circumstances surrounding the grant and execution of licences, thus including situations of refusal to license or discriminatory conduct by right holders.[54] In the view of this author, such a broad interpretation of Article 40 to also cover unilateral behaviour on the part of the right holder

---

Footnote 50 (*cont.*)
DAFFE/CLP(98)18, 21 September 1998, available at www.oecd.org/dataoecd/34/57/1920398.pdf, at p. 8; UNCTAD (1999), 'A Preliminary Report on How Competition Policy Addresses the Exercise of Intellectual Property Rights', TD/B/COM.2/CLP/10, 30 March 1999, available at www.unctad.org/en/docs/c2clp99d10.pdf, at No. 12. See also the guidelines on intellectual property and competition law of leading industrialised countries: European Commission (2004), *supra* note 6, at No. 9; Department of Justice and Federal Trade Commission (1995), 'Antitrust Guidelines for the Licensing of Intellectual Property', 6 April 1995, available at www.usdoj.gov/atr/public/guidelines/0558.htm, at 2.3.; Competition Bureau (Canada) (2000), Intellectual Property Enforcement Guidelines, available at http://strategis.ic.gc.ca/pics/ct/ipege.pdf, p. 6.

[51] Note that while a 'case-by-case' – or 'rule of reason' approach to the control of licences seems to better take account of the positive effects resulting from licensing agreements, a balancing exercise, whose outcome would be that a certain practice almost always restrain competition, underlies also the option for *per se* rules (prohibitions). Thus, by referring at this point to this general balancing exercise under a competition law analysis, no pre-decision has been taken on the concrete methodological approach to the control of licences. Indeed, most competition laws rely on a combination of both case-by-case and *per se* rules.

[52] UNCTAD-ICTSD (2004), *supra* note 2, at 556.

[53] UNCTAD-ICTSD (2004), *supra* note 2, at 556 *et seq*.

[54] See UNCTAD-ICTSD (2004), *supra* note 2, at 556. Supporting this view, Correa, Carlos M. (2007), *supra* note 22, at 399; Roffe, Pedro and Christoph Spennemann (2008), *supra* note 48, at 317.

overstretches the scope of application of this provision.[55] Thus, as the title of Section 8 explicitly states, Article 40 is concerned with the 'control of anticompetitive practices *in* contractual licences'. Consequently, Article 40 seems to focus on the content of licence contracts. The negotiating history of Article 40[56] and the illustrative practices listed in Article 40(2) underpin this conclusion. Moreover, while it is true that in some cases the anticompetitive character of the licensing agreement derives from the abusive exercise of market power by the right holder and that the competition rules governing restrictive agreement and abuses of market power may overlap,[57] it is also true that the rationale underlying both sets of rules is a different one. Underlying the broader interpretation of Article 40 is certainly the idea that this provision, as an empowering rule for WTO Members in the field of competition, should not be unnecessarily constricted. Even though there is nothing to object in this, there is no necessity to resort to Article 40, as Article 8(2) may actually offer WTO Members broader scope for the control of IP-related abusive behaviour.

Other than Article 8(2), Article 40 makes the negative effects of a certain practice on competition the necessary condition for WTO Members to control it. At this stage, a closer look at Article 40(1) and (2) is required. As pointed out above, despite the close connection between paragraphs (1) and (2), there are remarkable differences between them which may go beyond the mere choice of wording. Hence, in Article 40(1), WTO Members recognise that certain anticompetitive licensing practices may have an adverse effect on trade and technology transfer. The specific link between the restriction of competition and the negative effects on trade and the transfer of technology is to be understood in the sense that the harm arising from these licensing practices must result from a restraint of competition, and must consist of either[58] a negative impact on trade or an impediment to the transfer and dissemination of technology.[59] Article

---

[55] Excluding unilateral behaviour from the scope of application of Article 40, see also Ricolfi, Marco (2006), *supra* note 7, at 311.

[56] Article 43 of the so-called Brussels Draft (MTN.TNC/W/35/Rev. 1; see *supra* note 40), on which the final text of Article 40 is based, contained an exhaustive list of fourteen practices and conditions that could be deemed to be abusive or anticompetitive, all of them directly related to specific licence clauses.

[57] Take, for instance, exploitative licensing terms or the case of a conditional licensing, where the imposition of certain excessive clauses results in a desistance of the licence.

[58] It has been convincingly argued that despite the express language of Article 40(1) ('and'), these two negative criteria should apply alternatively rather than cumulatively, see UNCTAD-ICTSD (2004), *supra* note 2, at 557.

[59] UNCTAD-ICTSD (2004), *supra* note 2, at 557.

40(2), on its the other hand, affirms the Members' sovereign power to establish and define rules to prevent and control 'licensing practices and conditions that may in particular cases constitute an abuse of intellectual property rights having an adverse effect on competition in the relevant market'. As noted, no reference is made to the impact on trade and technology transfer in this part of the provision.

When trying to shed light on the meaning, scope and relationship between the two paragraphs of Article 40, commentators point out that Article 40(2) is more narrowly worded than Article 40(1).[60] In the view of this author, the opposite is true. Article 40(1) focuses on two specific kinds of anticompetitive licensing practices, namely those which are trade restrictive and those which hinder the transfer and dissemination of technology. As to the first category, one may think, for instance, of territorial restrictions and export prohibitions inserted in licensing agreements, of exclusivity clauses that have the effect of blocking foreign market access, of quantitative restrictions resulting in an impediment of parallel trade, or of a segmentation of national markets on the basis of a net of licensing contracts. Without denying that these sorts of practices should be at the centre of any international instrument which like the TRIPS Agreement is concerned with the trade relations of intellectual property rights, it is also right that they only involve one kind of possible negative effects. Significantly, any of the practices exemplified in Article 40(2) – exclusive grant-back conditions, no challenge clauses and coercive package licensing – have a clear trade-related element. With regard to the second type of anticompetitive licensing practices covered by Article 40(1), the explicit reference to technology excludes from the outset the consideration of anticompetitive practices in licensing agreements which do not have a technological subject matter. As a basis for the regulatory power of WTO Members in the field of competition rules relating to licensing agreements, Article 40(1) is definitively too narrow. Not so Article 40(2). Like Article 40(1), Article 40(2) further qualifies those anticompetitive practices that Members may address. Unlike Article 40(1), it does this by referring to the broader concept of the 'abuse of intellectual property rights'. If, as proposed in this chapter, the notion of abuse is to be interpreted and concretised in the light of the objectives set out in Article 7,[61] it becomes clear that Article 40(2) states a broad framework for national rules preventing anticompetitive licensing practices

[60] Brand, Oliver (2007), 'Artikel 40 – Vertragliche Lizenzen', in Busche, Jan and Peter-Tobias Stoll (eds), *supra* note 24, at 586; UNCTAD-ICTSD (2004), *supra* note 2, at 558.

[61] See *supra* Section 2.1.

which may not only restrain trade with IP-protected products and impede the transfer of technology, but also and more generally run counter to the goal of promoting innovation and of diffusing knowledge and preserving access to it. In this context, it is Article 40(1) that must be read in the light of Article 40(2),[62] as its recognition provides a consensual instance of what constitutes an abuse of intellectual property rights.

The analysis of Article 40 up to now has shown that this provision is narrower in scope than Article 8(2) both with regard to the kind of IP-related behaviour covered as well as to the approach followed, since the anticompetitive character of the IP-related behaviour is made the necessary connecting factor for regulating it. Because of the different language employed by these two provisions ('may be needed' and 'Members agree'), it has been argued that Article 40 is also of a different nature than Article 8(2) in the sense that it may be understood as containing a minimum obligation for WTO Members to act.[63] To substantiate this position, the argument has been brought forward that 'if Members have indeed agreed that certain licensing practices should be addressed, it is difficult to see why TRIPS would allow Members to remain inactive with respect to such practices, since these run directly contrary to the objectives of Article 7'.[64] Whereas it is true that the wording of Article 40(1) seems to be more compelling, the second part of this argument would equally apply to the kind of IP behaviour considered in Article 8(2). Thus, abuses of IPRs and practices which unreasonably restrain trade and adversely affect the international transfer of technology, even if not pursued in a licensing context, would also directly offend the basis and objectives of the TRIPS Agreement. Furthermore, though Article 40 specifically addresses practices on which an international agreement had been long sought by developing countries, it has been repeatedly stated that the competition-related rules of TRIPS were regarded as a concession to the interests of developing countries in as much as they recognise the Members' sovereignty to regulate in this area. It would therefore go too far to transform them, by way of interpretation, into positive obligations for the Members.[65]

---

62 Suggesting the opposite reading, see UNCTAD-ICTSD (2004), *supra* note 2, 558.

63 UNCTAD-ICTSD (2004), *supra* note 2, 555.

64 Ibid.

65 See Ullrich, Hanns (2004), supra note 42, at 408. See also Gervais, Daniel (2003), 'The TRIPS Agreement – Drafting History and Analysis', London: Sweet & Maxwell, at 281; Heinemann, Andreas (1996), *supra* note 37, at 245.

2.2.2. Procedural rules

Of a mandatory nature are, on the contrary, the procedural rules contained in Article 40(3) and (4). They provide for a consultation and cooperation procedure regarding the enforcement of competition measures relating to anticompetitive practices in licensing agreements. Concretely, Article 40(3) states that each WTO Member shall enter, upon request, into consultations with any other Member which has cause to believe that an intellectual property right owner that is a national or domiciliary of the requested Member is undertaking anticompetitive licensing practices in violation of the requesting Member's law and which wishes to secure compliance with such legislation. Further, the requested Member has not only the obligation to enter into such consultations, but also has an obligation to supply publicly available non-confidential information.[66] For its part, Article 40(4) contemplates the case where nationals or domiciliaries of a Member State are subject to competition law proceedings in another Member state related to anticompetitive licensing practices. This latter Member shall, upon request, grant the former Member an opportunity for consultation under the same conditions foreseen in Article 40(3).[67]

The obligations imposed by these two provisions are, however, of a rather limited scope. First, they only relate to one kind of IP-related anticompetitive practices, namely to those related to the licensing of IPRs.[68] Secondly, Members remain free as to whether or not they take any action, as well as regarding their ultimate decision. Thus, the requesting Member is free to abandon the enforcement proceedings subsequent to the request. Likewise, it has no obligation to take account of the effects of the proceedings and measures on other Members' competition policy and markets. Also, the requested Member is free to decide whether or not to open proceedings, if as a consequence of the request, it turns out that the licensing practices also comes under its jurisdiction.[69] Consequently, the procedural duties established in TRIPS are far from the negative and positive comity obligations known from bilateral cooperation agreements in the field of competition law.[70] Yet, their significance has to be seen first and foremost in the fact that they constitute a *novum* in a multilateral trade agreement

---

[66] The disclosure of other, non-publicly available and confidential information is subject to the national rules of the requested Member.

[67] The concrete interpretation of Article 40(4), however, remains far from clear. For a detailed analysis, see UNCTAD-ICTSD (2004), *supra* note 2, 564.

[68] See Heinemann, Andreas (1996), *supra* note 37, at 247.

[69] UNCTAD-ICTSD (2004), *supra* note 2, 562 *et seq.*

[70] An overview of the agreements entered into by the EC is available at http://ec.europa.eu/competition/international/bilateral/. A list of US antitrust coopera-

and that they reflect the will of WTO Members to provide mechanisms for the effective control of anticompetitive IP-related conduct.

2.3. Article 31(k) TRIPS

References to anticompetitive practices are also found in Article 31(k) of the TRIPS Agreement. Article 31 has to be read in conjunction with Article 28, regulating the rights conferred by a patent, and Article 30, allowing exceptions to the rights conferred by a patent in the form of a general clause. Under the heading of 'other use without authorization of the right holder', Article 31 deals with the instrument of compulsory licensing. Rather than specifying or limiting the grounds on which WTO Members may grant compulsory licences, it sets out the conditions that they must fulfil if granted.[71]

In this context, Article 31(k) subjects the granting of a compulsory licence that is directed at remedying practices which have been rendered anticompetitive after a judicial or administrative process to less stringent conditions. Concretely, it is neither necessary to enter into prior negotiations with the patent holder in order to obtain an authorisation (Article 31(b)) nor that the license is granted predominantly for the supply of the domestic market (Article 31(f)). In addition, although Article 31 does not eliminate the requirement of compensation for compulsory licences issued to remedy anticompetitive practices, the level of compensation may be adjusted to reflect the need to remedy past misconduct and to affirmatively promote the entry of new competitors.[72]

Even if limited to the field of patents,[73] Article 31(k) confirms that a compulsory licence may well be a remedy provided for the competition rules. Moreover, by subjecting limitations of IPRs for competition reasons to less strict conditions than limitations imposed for other reasons, it

---

tion agreements is also available at http://www.usdoj.gov/atr/public/international/int_arrangements.htm.

[71] UNCTAD-ICTSD (2004), *supra* note 2, 468.

[72] UNCTAD-ICTSD (2004), *supra* note 2, 476.

[73] Ironically, most of the competition law cases in which a compulsory licence has or would have been a possible remedy have dealt with IPRs other than patents. See, for example, Europe Case 238/87, *Volvo*, [1988] ECR 6211; Joined Cases C-241/91P and C-242/91P, *RTE and ITP v. Commission ('Magill')*, [1995] ECR I-743; Case C-418/01, *IMS Health*, [2004] ECR I-5039; Case T-201/04, *Microsoft v. Commission*, [2007] ECR II-3601. For the USA, *Data General Corp. v. Grumman Systems Support Corp.*, 36 F.3d 1147 (1st Cir. 1994); *In re Independent Service Organizations Antitrust Litigation (CSU v. Xerox)*, 203 F.3d 1322 (Fed. Cir. 2000).

becomes clear that the TRIPS Agreement accords a high status to the protection of competition.[74]

3. Designing IP-related competition rules in the light of TRIPS' objectives

From the analysis above, it has been clear that the TRIPS Agreement relies on the national competition rules of the Members to prevent and combat abuses within the IP-system. By doing so, the TRIPS Agreement offers them an open and flexible framework for the formulation of their competition rules with regard to IPRs.[75] Though referring to anticompetitive practices and abuses, the TRIPS Agreement remains silent on what is to be considered anticompetitive. In this regard, it has been pointed out that TRIPS assumes and recognises concepts as defined in the domestic law of the Members.[76] While this is true, it would be wrong to deny the TRIPS Agreement any guiding function in the design of IP-related competition rules. This is due to the fact that measures referred to in Articles 8(2) and 40 are conceived as instruments to safeguard the proper functioning of the IP-system and ultimately the attainment of those goals that the community of WTO Members have consensually agreed the IP-system should fulfil. Hence, when framing their IP-related competition rules, WTO Members should have these goals in mind.

3.1. IP-related competition rules and the goal of promoting innovation

Requiring that IP-competition rules are designed in the light of the objective of promoting innovation should, in principle, pose no major acceptance problems as current trends in developed countries approach the interface between IPRs and competition precisely from this perspective. Indeed, the theory of complementarity mentioned above[77] relies on the

---

[74] See Heinemann, Andreas (1996), *supra* note 37, at 244.

[75] See Abbott, Frederick M. (2004), *supra* note 46, at 691 *et seq*.; Anderson, Robert (2008), 'Competition Policy and Intellectual Property in the WTO: More Guidance Needed?', in Drexl, Josef (ed.), *supra* note 34, at 457; Cottier, Thomas (2007), 'The Doha Waiver and its Effects on the Nature of the TRIPS System and on Competition Law – The Impact of Human Rights', in Govaere, Inge and Hanns Ullrich (eds), *Intellectual Property, Public Policy and International Trade*, Brussels: Peter Lang, at 189; Janis, Mark D. (2005), '"Minimal" Standards for Patent-related Antitrust Law under TRIPS', in Maskus, Keith E. and Jerome H. Reichman, *International Public Goods and Transfer of Technology under a Globalized Intellectual Property Regime*, Cambridge: Cambridge University Press, at 775; Ricolfi, Marco (2006), *supra* note 7, at 333 *et seq.*

[76] Cottier, Thomas (2007), *supra* note 75, at 189.

[77] See *supra* 1, footnote 6 and relating text.

idea that both IPRs and competition law contribute to efficient markets, not only in terms of allocative efficiency, but also of dynamic (innovative) efficiency. Innovation-related restrictions are, therefore, at the centre of the sophisticated IP-competition rules already developed in many industrialised countries. In this context, the evaluation of an IP-related behaviour – be it contractual restrictions imposed in the framework of licensing and related agreements or be it the unilateral exercise of IPRs by dominant right holders – under these competition rules does not only consider its innovation-enhancing potential vis-à-vis its anticompetitive effects,[78] but also the negative impact that a competition law-based intervention would have on the incentives to invest and innovate arising from the IP-system.[79] Without contesting the correctness of such an approach, putting too much emphasis on the necessity of safeguarding the right holder's incentives to innovate, however, runs the risk of displacing the focus from the objective of protecting the competitive process that ultimately promotes innovation.

To analyse the relationship between the incentives to innovate provided by IPRs and those arising from competition a recent article by Jonathan B. Baker proves to be most helpful.[80] Building upon previous economic literature, Baker identifies four economic principles relating to innovation and competition:[81] first, when firms see themselves in a race to innovate,

---

[78] See for instance European Commission (2004), *supra* note 6, at paras 17 and 146.

[79] See Department of Justice and Federal Trade Commission (2007), *supra* note 6, at 2: '[. . .], the Agencies must apply antitrust principles to identify illegal collusive or exclusionary conduct while at the same time supporting the incentives to innovate created by intellectual property rights. Condemning efficient activity involving intellectual property rights could undermine that incentive to innovate, [. . .].' In the more concrete context of evaluating refusals to supply, including refusals to license, the European Commission will 'consider claims by the dominant undertaking that a refusal to supply [*to license*] is necessary to allow the dominant undertaking to realise an adequate return on the investments required to develop its inputs business, thus generating incentives to continue to invest in the future [. . .]. The Commission will also consider claims by the dominant undertaking that its own innovation will be negatively affected by the obligation to supply [*to license*], or by the structural changes in the market conditions that imposing such an obligation will bring about, [. . .].'; see European Commission (2008), Guidance on the Commission's Enforcement Priorities in Applying Article 82 EC Treaty to Abusive Exclusionary Conduct by Dominant Undertakings, 3 December 2008, available at http://ec.europa.eu/competition/antitrust/art82/guidance.pdf., at para. 88 [remarks added by the author].

[80] Baker, Jonathan B. (2007), *supra* note 4.

[81] *Ibid.*, at 579 *et seq.*

they will try harder to win. Thus, competition in innovation itself encourages innovation. Second, pre-innovation product market competition promotes innovation as firms will invest in innovation to escape current competition. Third, if firms anticipate great post-innovation product market competition they may have no incentive to invest in innovation since they cannot be sure that they will benefit from their new ideas. As instruments that enable firms to appropriate the results of their investments in research and development, IPRs implement the idea behind this economic principle. And fourth, the so-called pre-emption incentive would explain why a firm will have an extra incentive to innovate if in doing so it can discourage potential rivals from investing in innovation.

Whereas the first economic principle argues for resolute competition law enforcement against conduct that directly reduces competition in innovation,[82] the complex interplay between the second and third principles, which point in opposite directions with regard to product market competition,[83] seems at first sight to call for cautious – or even for an absence of – competition law enforcement against conduct involving IPRs, since action targeted at promoting product market competition could result in a reduction of the incentives to invest and innovate that arise from those rights. In this respect, it has been stated that a competition law-based obligation on the right holder to license his right – certainly the most drastic measure to introduce or promote product market competition – would have profound adverse effects on the incentives to invest in R&D, to innovate, and to seek intellectual property protection.[84]

Though it is by no means the intention of this author to play down the importance of the necessity of preserving IPRs' incentives to innovate, some considerations in this respect should be made. Hence, in the first place, the assumption that the prospect of facing post-innovation product market competition negatively affects the incentive of a future right holder to invest in innovation can in general not be supported. Surely, by transforming what otherwise would be a public good into an economic good,[85] IPRs enable the right holder to obtain a reward for what is, in most cases,

---

82 *Ibid.*, at 592.

83 *Ibid.*, at 588.

84 Ahlborn, Christian, Vincenzo Denicolò, Damien Geradin and Jorge Padilla (2006), 'DG Comp's Discussion Paper on Article 82: Implications of the Proposed Framework and Antitrust Rules for Dynamically Competitive Industries', 31 March 2006, available at http://ec.europa.eu/competition/antitrust/art82/057.pdf, at 42.

85 See Maskus, Keith E. and Jerome H. Reichman (2005), 'The Globalization of Private Knowledge Goods and the Privatization of Global Public Goods', in Maskus, Keith E. and Jerome H. Reichman (eds), *supra* note 75, at 16.

risky and costly investment in research. This said, IPRs award neither a guarantee of a full reward nor fixed compensation. Rather, the IP-system assumes that the return that can be realised in a particular market reflects the value of the innovation to society. It is thus the market and not the IPR itself which determines the return on the innovation.[86] That the market in which the right holder reaps his reward in the majority of cases is a competitive one is reflected in today's widely accepted observation that an IPR does not in itself create a dominant position or, in US terminology, confer monopoly power.[87] Consequently, the incentives system created by IPRs does not only cope well with post-innovation competition, but it may even presuppose the existence of such competition.[88]

From this, it also follows that competition rules that aim at protecting product market competition by keeping markets open for new and better products that can substitute for the ones protected by IPRs are perfectly in line with the rationale of the IP-system.[89] Even if this observation is valid for all kind of IP-related markets,[90] information technology markets are

---

[86] See Ullrich, Hanns and Andreas Heinemann (2007), 'Die Anwendung der Wettbewerbsregeln auf die Verwertung von Schutzrechten und sonstigen Kenntnissen', in Immenga, Ulrich and Ernst-Joachim Mestmäcker (eds), *Wettbewerbsrecht, EG/Teil 2*, Munich: C.H. Beck, at 119.

[87] See Joined Cases C-241/91P and C-242/91P, *RTE and ITP v. Commission ('Magill')*, [1995] ECR I-743, para. 46; *Illinois ToolsWorks et al. v. Independent Ink*, 126 S. Ct. 1281 (2006), at 7. On the relationship between legal exclusivity and market power and dominance, see Drexl, Josef (2008), 'The Relationship between Legal Exclusivity and Economic Market Power – Links and Limits', in Govaere, Inge and Hanns Ullrich (eds), *Intellectual Property, Market Power and the Public Interest*, Brussels: P.I.E. Peter Lang, 13–33.

[88] In this regard, the German Federal Supreme Court in a decision dealing with the effects of a standard wisely stated: '[. . .]. In this case, the standard makes it difficult or impossible *for the patent-based solution to fulfil the spirit and purpose of patent protection by proving itself in competition with different technical solutions.* [. . .]' (emphasis added). German Federal Supreme Court (Bundesgerichtshof), judgment of 13 July 2004, Case K ZR 40/02, *Standard-Spundfass*, English translation published in *International Review of Intellectual Property and Competition Law*, **36**, 741.

[89] For an in-depth analysis of IP-related markets in the light of the theory of contestable markets, see Heinemann, Andreas (2008), 'The contestability of IP-protected markets', in Drexl, Josef (ed.), *supra* note 34, 54–79.

[90] Notably, the patent system contains a wide range of features to safeguard both subsequent and substitutive innovation on the part of competing firms. For an exhaustive analysis of these 'pro-competitive antibodies' see Ghidini, Gustavo (2006), *Intellectual Property and Competition Law – The Innovation Nexus*, Cheltenham, UK and Northampton, MA, US: Edward Elgar, 13 *et seq.* Nevertheless, patents are increasingly used in a way to exclude or to render difficult the market entry of competing products. For a recent study of patent strategies

perhaps the ones which pose the most challenging issues when it comes to the goal of preserving the openness of markets and the mechanism of dynamic competition. Thus, these markets are, among other specific features, characterised by the presence of strong network effects and a tendency to standardisation.[91] Competition in network markets is fierce as long as the market has not tipped in favour of a given technology. At this early stage, firms compete for the whole market, since once a given technology has reached a critical mass and the market has tipped in favour of this technology, competing technologies will have to exit the market. Because of the strong competitive pressure that firms faced during this first stage of a network race, they will have enough incentives to innovate even in the absence of IP protection.[92] On the contrary, once the market has tipped and a given technology has become the standard, consumers are locked into the network standard. The market structure becomes durable. Unlike in conventional markets, where consumers can more or less easily switch to an alternative technology that serves the same purpose, in network markets they have little alternative to an incumbent standard technology.[93] At the same time, due to the network effects, it is more difficult for competing firms to invent around an IPR that controls a network standard. Whereas in conventional markets the difficulty to invent around an IPR reflects the innovative potential of a technology and its value to society, in network markets there is not necessarily a correlation between the innovative achievement and the returns the market offers for it.[94] Even trivial innovations result in awarding the right holder the whole market. Furthermore, the competitive pressure and the incentives to innovate are weaker in network markets after the tipping of the market. On the one hand, as a result of the lock-in effect, the owner of the incumbent standard will have little incentive to improve it. Though competing firms may have

---

Footnote 90 (*cont.*)
in the pharmaceutical sector see European Commission (2008), Pharmaceutical Sector Inquiry – Preliminary Report (DG Competition Staff Working Paper), 28 November 2008, available at http://ec.europa.eu/competition/sectors/pharmaceuticals/inquiry/preliminary_report.pdf.

[91] See Ahlborn, Christian, Vincenzo Denicolò, Damien Geradin and Jorge Padilla (2006), supra note 84, at 12 *et seq*. See also Heinemann, Andreas (2003), 'Antitrust Law and the Internet', in Drexl, Josef (ed.), *supra* note 15, at 131 *et seq*.

[92] On this aspect, see the exhaustive analysis of the effects of IPRs in network markets conducted by Mackenrodt, Mark-Oliver (2008), 'Assessing the Effects of Intellectual Property Rights in Network Standards', in Drexl, Josef (ed.), *supra* note 34, at 92 *et seq*.

[93] Mackenrodt, Mark-Oliver (2008), *supra* note 92, at 100.

[94] *Ibid.*, at 101.

a higher incentive to develop the standard, if the latter is protected by IPRs, the right holder may exclude them from improving it.[95] On the other hand, with regard to those innovations that do not directly relate to the standard itself but rather to product features that do not form part of the standard, their market success will require access to the network standard. Again, IPRs may help to enforce incompatibility and to reduce the competitive pressure coming from these follow-on innovations.[96]

The specific market mechanisms at work in network markets may well justify a competition law-based duty to give access to an IP-protected standard. As shown, as soon as a standard has conquered the market, the mechanism of competition by substitution upon which the IP-system ultimately relies is basically distorted. Substitution of the protected subject matter is, in most cases, not a viable option for competing firms. To be sure, the extent to which network effects act as barriers to entry may vary. However, even if this aspect has to be taken into account, opening up the standard by requiring the right holder to grant a licence or to afford compatibility may in many cases be the only option to restore the mechanism of dynamic competition in the market. In this respect, multilateral standardisation procedures precisely aim at maintaining enough competitive pressure in a standardised market by ensuring that no market participant is excluded by an IPR on the standard. The same principle should also apply to *de facto* standards. Hence, a duty to open the standard for other market participants (and at the same time, potential sources of innovation) may help to overcome the weak competitive pressure that the holder of a standard faces once the market has tipped and the lower incentives to innovate resulting there from. While a duty to license would admittedly reduce the returns the right holder may extract from the market and would arguably have a negative impact on his future innovative efforts, it is not so clear that the overall incentives to innovate would be reduced. Thus, first, as shown above, in network markets there is not necessarily a correlation between the innovative achievement and the return the market offers for it. If, because of the specific market conditions that exclude competition by substitution, the right holder were to get the whole market, the exclusivity afforded by the IPR would clearly over-compensate. When deciding whether a duty to license is justified, the innovative features of the standard should therefore be carefully considered. A duty to license would rather be justified if the innovation is obvious and if the 'winner' standard is only slightly different from those alternative standards against which it

95 *Ibid.*, at 98.
96 *Ibid.*

had competed.[97] Second, and more importantly, restricting the exclusivity of IPRs in situations in which competition by substitution is not possible should be understood as an attempt to correct an 'anomalous' situation that is not covered by the rationale of IPRs and should therefore leave the overall incentives arising from the IP-system untouched.

Undoubtedly, the case of network markets states an extreme example both with regard to the foreclosing effects of IPRs as well as with regard to the remedial action needed. Also, the case law and the enforcement practice of competition authorities in this area remain far from settled.[98] Nevertheless, it best serves to illustrate how an innovation-enhancing design and application of IP-related competition rules should very much focus on protecting the competitive mechanism on which the IP-incentive system relies, even if this paradoxically results in the exclusivity of the IPR being restricted.

3.2. IP-related competition rules and the promotion of social goals: protecting access and distribution

As pointed out above,[99] the introduction of international minimum standards of IP-protection by the TRIPS Agreement should not only contribute to the – in the words of Article 7 – promotion of technological innovation, but also should promote the diffusion of knowledge and contribute to the social and economic development of WTO Members.[100] As also shown,

---

[97] On this argument see Mackenrodt, Mark-Oliver (2008), *supra* note 92, 101. For the same reasons, this author would also favour patent protection instead of copyright protection for network standards.

[98] Although it is undisputed that the right of exclusion inherent in IPRs includes the right to refuse a licence and that this right may be limited only in exceptional circumstances, the approaches followed to determine when a refusal to license constitutes an abuse as a matter of competition law largely differ. For an analysis of the case law relating to refusals to license in the USA and in Europe, see Conde Gallego, Beatriz (2008), 'Unilateral Refusal to License *Indispensable* Intellectual Property Rights – US and EU approaches', in Drexl, Josef (ed.), *supra* note 34, 215–38. Also Drexl, Josef (2008), 'Abuse of Market Dominance and IP Law – Recent Developments in Europe', *Global Law Review*, 119–28 for an additional examination of the case law in selected European countries.

[99] See *supra* Section 2.1.

[100] Furthermore, given that the TRIPS Agreement is part of the WTO Agreement, the overall objectives stated in the Preamble of the WTO Agreement, such as the objective of sustainable development, also concern the TRIPS Agreement. In this context, the Appellate Body has interpreted the concept of sustainable development as 'integrating economic and social development and environmental protection' and sees its role in '[adding] colour, texture and shading to [the] interpretation of the Agreements annexed to the WTO Agreement'; see

competition rules have an important role to play in promoting innovation by protecting the competitive mechanism of the IP-system against distortions. The question of whether, and if so, which role IP-related competition rules may play in the achievement of these other distributional and social goals is the object of the following analysis.

To begin with, it should be recalled that there is an inherent tension between the goal of enhancing the production of technology and other knowledge goods and the goal of maximising access thereof. Whereas in the long run the interest of promoting innovation and creativity and the interest of allowing people to access and use innovations and creations are in a rather mutually supportive relation, in the short run, namely during the term of protection, national and international IP policymakers are confronted with the difficult task of drawing a line between protection and the public domain. This task becomes even more challenging when access to what Keith Maskus and Jerome Reichman call 'critical public goods'[101] is at stake. The issue of patent protection for essential medicines illustrates this. Thus, on the one hand, it is particularly important from a social point of view to maintain the incentives provided by the patent system in generating new essential drugs. On the other side, precisely because of the social value of these drugs, there is a tremendous interest for them to be accessible for all and as soon as possible. This dilemma would, however, equally arise with regard to other public goods such as education[102] or nutrition,[103] to give only a few examples.

Although the balance between these two public interests should, in principle, be struck within the IP-system itself,[104] the TRIPS Agreement explicitly

---

United States – Import Prohibition of Certain Shrimp and Shrimp Products, Appellate Body Report WT/DS58/AB/R (12 October 2008), at para. 129 (footnote 107) and para. 153, respectively.

[101] Maskus, Keith E. and Jerome H. Reichman (2005), 'Preface', in Maskus, Keith E. and Jerome H. Reichman (eds), *supra* note 75, at xiii.

[102] See Okediji, Ruth L. (2005), 'Sustainable Access to Copyrighted Digital Information Works in Developing Countries', in Maskus, Keith E. and Jerome H. Reichman (eds), *supra* note 75, at 142 *et seq.*

[103] See Breining-Kaufmann, Christine (2005), 'The Right to Food and Trade in Agriculture', in Cottier, Thomas, Joost Pauwelyn and Elisabeth Bürgi Bonanomi (eds), *Human Rights and International Trade*, Oxford: Oxford University Press, at 354 *et seq*; Edwardson, Shelley (2005), 'Reconciling TRIPS and the Right to Food', in *ibid.*, at 382 *et seq.*

[104] In this sense, see Dreier, Thomas (2001), 'Balancing Propietary and Public Domain Interests: Inside or Outside of Propietary Rights', in Dreyfuss, Rochelle C., Diane L. Zimmerman and Harry First (eds), *Expanding the Boundaries of Intellectual Property – Innovation Policy for the Knowledge Society*, Oxford: Oxford University Press, at 303 *et seq.* (analysing different instruments both within

recognises that there may also be a need to resort to measures outside the system. Hence, Article 8(1) TRIPS leaves WTO Members great discretion to adopt measures necessary to protect vital public interests, provided, however, that such measures are consistent with the provisions of the TRIPS Agreement.[105] To what extent competition rules fall within the measures allowed for in Article 8(1) is, however, not that clear. Thus, Article 8(1) refers generally to measures that may be taken in the public interest irrespective of the right holder's particular conduct. Competition law, however, focuses on the conduct of market operators which may distort competition in the market. Nevertheless, even if a resort to Article 8(1) might prove to be difficult,[106] this does not mean that the possibility of serving public interests associated with access to IP-protected goods by means of competition law is not allowed for in the TRIPS Agreement. On the contrary, as analysed above, WTO Members may well rely on Article 8(2) TRIPS to prevent or control problematic conduct on the part of the right holder whenever the problematic nature of the conduct results from a negative impact on the transfer of technology, or more generally, from the fact that the key objective of promoting access to and dissemination of knowledge is being impaired.

Yet, even though the TRIPS Agreement would not get in the way of such a distribution-oriented application of competition law, it is still questionable whether it would be supported by the rationale of competition

---

Footnote 104 (*cont.*)
and outside IPRs to accommodate conflicting interest in the field of copyright). For a further example of how the public interest may be accommodated within the IP-system, see the so-called Doha Waiver, see WTO (2001), 'Declaration on the TRIPS Agreement and Public Health', WT/MIN(01)/DEC/2, 14 November 2001, available at http://www.wto.org/english/thewto_e/minist_e/min01_e/mindecl_trips_e.htm as well as WTO (2003), 'Decision of the General Council of 30 August 2003 on the Implementation of Paragraph 6 of the Doha Declaration of the TRIPS Agreement and Public Health', WT/L/540 and Corr.1, 1 September 2003, available at http://www.wto.org/english/tratop_e/trips_e/implem_para6_e.htm.

[105] For a comparative analysis of Article 8(1) TRIPS, see Grosse Ruse-Khan, Henning (2008), 'A Comparative Analysis of Policy Space in WTO Law', Max Planck Papers on Intellectual Property, Competition and Tax Law Research No. 08-02, available at http://ssrn.com/abstract=1309526 (arguing that unlike other similar provisions in WTO law that allow Members to give effect to public interests on the domestic level, the TRIPS-consistency test introduced in Article 8(1) has effectively prevented this provision from functioning as a self-standing right to override individual TRIPS obligations).

[106] See, however, Berger, Jonathan (2006), 'Advancing Public Health by Other Means: Using Competition Policy', in Roffe, Pedro, Geoff Tansey and David Vivas-Eugui (eds), *Negotiating Health – Intellectual Property and Access to Medicines*, London and Sterling, VA, USA: Earthscan, at 184.

law and policy itself. The answer to this question very much depends on the goals ascribed to competition law in general and to IP-related competition rules in particular. To be sure, an in-depth analysis of this issue would largely exceed the scope of this chapter. Alone the European debate on the role of EC competition law in the framework of a *more economic approach* demonstrates that even in jurisdictions with a long history of competition law this question is not yet settled.[107] What may be affirmed, however, is that at least in these jurisdictions competition law and policy have moved – mainly under the influence of the Chicago School's and Post-Chicago School's theories – from focusing on broader political and social goals to putting an emphasis on the economic goals of competition law.[108] In this respect, there is consensus among economists that competition law should promote economic welfare in the sense of economic efficiency.[109] From a static perspective, economic efficiency is achieved in a situation in which limited existing resources are optimally allocated according to the preferences of consumers. As compared to a monopoly, competition leads markets to produce more of a given good at a lower price.[110] The concept of economic efficiency, however, does not exhaust in this kind of allocative (static) efficiency. Rather, dynamic efficiency, that is, the extent to which a firm develops new products and forms of production,[111] is nowadays considered to be of utmost importance for economic welfare. The trade-off between promoting allocative efficiency by contesting anti-competitive behaviour that leads to higher prices and lower output and promoting dynamic efficiency by safeguarding firms' incentives to innovate is at the core of each competition law. In a way, this trade-off largely corresponds to the one underlying the design of IPRs. As observed in the previous paragraph, the cautious approach towards IP-related anticompetitive conduct in developed countries reflects the fear that competition law and policy end in hindering innovation. Thus, the focus lies clearly

---

107 See for example Drexl, Josef (2009), 'Competition Law as Part of the European Constitution', in von Bogdandy, Armin and Jürgen Bast (eds), *Principles of European Constitutional Law*, Portland, USA: Hart Publishing.

108 For an analysis of this development in the US antitrust law, see First, Harry (2002), 'Antitrust Goals: The Theories of Antitrust in the United States and Japan', in Jones, Clifford A. and Mitsuo Matsushita (eds), *Competition Policy in the Global Trading System*, The Hague, London and New York: Kluwer International Law, at 176 *et seq*.

109 Drexl, Josef (2009), *supra* note 107.

110 See Motta, Massimo (2004), *Competition Policy: Theory and Practice*, Cambridge: Cambridge University Press, at 40.

111 *Ibid.*, at 55.

on the dynamic component of economic efficiency.[112] As critically noted by Hanns Ullrich, competition law and policy in leading industrialised nations have moved from promoting competition to becoming an innovation policy which largely deems restraints of competition to be part of the innovation process.[113]

However, the fact that trends in developed countries favour an application of competition law that gives priority to dynamic efficiency over static efficiency considerations does not mean that this has to be the sole paradigm. Rather, the static–dynamic efficiency trade-off very much depends on the socio-economic conditions of countries in which competition laws are adopted and applied.[114] Whereas an innovation-oriented competition policy serves the interests of industrialised countries, and maybe of those sufficiently technologically advanced countries which may wish to join the innovation race, it may be at odds with the interests of developing countries. In this context, it should be remembered that intellectual property protection in developing countries very often leads to higher prices for protected goods without substantially contributing to domestic innovation. The dilemma faced by the legislator and the competition law enforcer in developed countries of promoting static competition without chilling innovation does not arise, or at least not in the same terms, in developing countries.[115] Moreover, even if considered from a global perspective, given the limited willingness and capacity to pay in low-income countries, the decision of a developing country to focus rather on the goal of keeping prices down and increasing consumers' choices would in a vast number of cases have only little impact on the innovation incentives of right holders

---

[112] In this sense, see the unequivocal statement of the European Commission made at the time the competition rules governing the technology transfer were being revised: 'In reviewing the current rules and devising a future regime, account has to be taken of the fact that innovation in new products and new technologies are the ultimate source of substantial and major competition over time. Undue emphasis on short-term allocative efficiency may therefore create a socially unfavourable trade-off between static and dynamic efficiency.' Commission Evaluation Report on the Transfer of Technology Block Exemption Regulation No. 240/96, COM(2001) 786 final, 20 December 2001, at para. 190, available at http://eur-lex.europa.eu/LexUriServ/LexUriServ.do?uri=COM:2001:0786:FIN:EN:PDF.

[113] Ullrich, Hanns (2004), *supra* note 42, at 420 *et seq*. (424).

[114] In this sense, see also Correa, Carlos M. (2007), 'Intellectual Property and Competition Law: Exploration of Some Issues of Relevance to Developing Countries', ICTSD IPRs and Sustainable Development Programme Issue Paper No. 21, International Centre for Trade and Sustainable Development, at p. 6, available at http://www.iprsonline.org/resources/docs/corea_Oct07.pdf.

[115] See also Berger, Jonathan (2006), *supra* note 106, at 187.

in the developed world.[116] Under these premises, it is conceivable that competition law is used to mitigate the effects of IPRs on static efficiency. A classical example of this would be to combat excessive prices emerging from the exercise of IPRs. Despite the controversial character of such a measure,[117] the successful South African experience[118] shows that this may indeed be a valid policy option for developing countries. Thus, in the first place, developed countries' optimistic view of and confidence in market forces have not necessarily to be shared by developing countries, where public and private entry barriers are still high and the number of potential competitors low. Second, without contesting the necessity of also challenging exclusionary abuses, the focus on exploitative abuses and on excessive prices in particular – especially when they relate, as in the South African case, to essential products – had the strategic advantage of eliciting broad public support, a support that may be of vital importance for competition authorities in developing countries.[119]

Within the framework of guaranteeing access to essential IP-protected goods, particularly in the context of access to medicines, the issue of a competition law-based compulsory licence has also been discussed. Compared with an 'ordinary' compulsory licence granted under Article 31 TRIPS, a competition law-based compulsory licence had the advantage

---

116 Similarly Drexl, Josef (2005), 'The critical role of competition law in preserving public goods in conflict with intellectual property rights', in Maskus, Keith E. and Jerome H. Reichman (eds), *supra* note 75, at 720 (arguing for the necessity to consider the economics of local markets when limiting IPRs for public policy reasons).

117 Thus, although competition laws in developed nations may explicitly allow this kind of exploitative abuse to be addressed (see, for example, Article 82(a) EC), controlling prices under competition law is generally considered to be a 'bad policy'; see Motta, Massimo (2004), *supra* note 110, at 69. Rather than intervening with the price mechanism, competition authorities should be much more concerned with keeping markets open by preventing dominant firms from establishing entry barriers in an anticompetitive way.

118 In September 2002, Hazel Tau, together with a number of civil society organizations lodged a complaint against the two pharmaceutical companies GlaxoSmithKline and Boehringer Ingelheim, alleging that they had among other things violated Article 8(a) of the South African Competition Act which prohibits dominant companies from 'charg[ing] an excessive price to the detriment of consumers' by charging excessive prices for their patent protected anti-retroviral medicines. After more than one year of investigations, the Competition Commission had found sufficient evidence to substantiate this complaint; see 'Competition Commission Finds GSK and BI in Contravention of the Competition Act', 16 October 2003, available at http://www.tac.org.za/newsletter/2003/ns16_10_2003.htm. For a detailed analysis of the facts of the case, see Berger, Jonathan (2006), *supra* note 106, at 197 *et seq*.

119 On this point, see also Berger, Jonathan (2006), *supra* note 106, at 198.

that it would neither be necessary to enter into prior negotiations with the patent holder nor would it be required that the licence is granted predominantly for the supply of the local market.[120] Also an exception could be made from the duty to provide an adequate remuneration. Yet, the application of Article 31(k) TRIPS presupposes the existence of an anticompetitive practice. Though a compulsory licence could be a remedy in cases of abusive pricing, it is normally in the context of refusals to supply and license that it is drawn on as a remedy. As already mentioned, the case law in developed nations, as to whether and under which conditions a refusal to supply and/or license may trigger competition law liability, is not yet settled. As a matter of principle, the right to refuse a licence is seen as part of the right of exclusion inherent in IPRs. By contrast with the case law in the United States, the European Courts have recognized that this right may be limited in those exceptional circumstances in which access to the IPR is indispensable to compete in a secondary market, and where the refusal to license results in precluding the appearance of a new product for which there is potential consumer demand and it is not objectively justified.[121] Behind this jurisprudence lies the idea that competition law-based limitations of IPRs should be constrained to those cases in which the right holder's conduct runs contrary to the objective of promoting innovation, by, for example, preventing the development of an innovative product. This, in turn, corroborates the above-mentioned tendency in these countries of conceiving competition law and policy as a further form of innovation policy. Although cases of this kind may be thought of in the context of promoting access to essential goods,[122] a compulsory licence is normally requested in order to replicate the IP-protected goods. From this, it follows that if legislators and competition law enforcers in developing countries would like to make use of the instrument of a compulsory licence, a different reasoning should be put forward.

In principle, a compulsory licence under competition law could also be justified by pointing to static efficiency considerations. Hence, the refusal to

---

[120] See *supra* in Section 2.3: the analysis of Article 31(k) TRIPS.

[121] See ECJ, Joined Cases C-241/91P and C-242/91P, *RTE and ITP v. Commission ('Magill')*, [1995] ECR I-743 and Case C-418/01, *IMS Health*, [2004] ECR I-5039. CFI, Case T-201/04, *Microsoft v. Commission*, [2007] ECR II-3601.

[122] In this sense, see the illustrative example put forward by Berger, Jonathan (2006), *supra* note 106, at 192: generic manufactures may be able to develop and offer simplified and equally effective treatments for chronic HIV-patients (so-called ARV FDCs). In countries where anti-retroviral medicines are subject to patent protection, they would be dependent on the grant of a licence in order to do that.

license by the right holder would result in higher prices and lower output for consumers. However, the TRIPS-consistency of such an approach is highly doubtful. Thus, in the first place, the possibility of the right holder extracting higher prices from the market is not only provided for by the exclusivity of the right, but is also fully in line with competition law, provided that the price is not the result of an anticompetitive agreement or otherwise abusive. Second, it would amount to considering the mere refusal to license as an anticompetitive abuse. As already noted, the right to refuse a licence is seen as part of the right of exclusion inherent in IPRs and constitutes an exercise of the IPR expressly safeguarded by the TRIPS Agreement. Against this background, the proposal has been made to inform the design and application of competition law by human rights considerations.[123] Consequently, a refusal by a (dominant) right holder to grant a licence or to sell IP-protected essential medicines would negatively affect the human right to health. Although the argument has mainly been made in the context of access to medicines, it would equally apply when other economic, social and cultural basic rights, such as the right to food, are at stake. Competition law would be applied in these cases neither with the aim of promoting innovation nor of promoting an efficient allocation of resources, but rather to ensure that all can benefit from innovation and creativity in fields of essential importance for human development. Taking account of the widespread developmental elements in the TRIPS Agreement, and in particular in the Preamble as well as in Articles 7 and 8, such an approach would certainly fall within the scope of manoeuvre left to the WTO Members in the field of competition law.[124] Also from the perspective of competition law itself, focusing on the distributional and social impact of a certain conduct would definitively not contradict its rationale. Thus, although we are now used to think of competition law in terms of economic efficiency, the significance of competition law should by no means be reduced to these terms. The relatively long history of competition law in developed countries shows that it has been applied to serve other than mere economic goals.[125] Competition law may also be understood as

---

[123] See principally Abbott, Frederick M., 'The "Rule of Reason" and the Right to Health: Integrating Human Rights and Competition Principles in the Context of TRIPS', in Cottier, Thomas, Joost Pauwelyn and Elisabeth Bürgi Bonanomi (eds), *supra* note 103, at 287 *et seq.* and Cottier, Thomas (2007), *supra* note 75, at 193 *et seq.*

[124] See also Ricolfi, Marco (2006), *supra* note 7, at 353 (considering a competition-law approach to refusals to license based on 'fairness' considerations).

[125] See Fox, Eleanor M. (1986), 'Monopolization and Dominance in the United States and the European Community: Efficiency, Opportunity and Fairness', *Notre Dame Law Review*, **61**, at 981 *et seq.*

a social institution.[126] It would somehow be false-faced to deny developing countries uses of competition law which developed countries have in the past relied on. Moreover, the protection of universal human rights is an issue that concerns all nations.[127] To be sure, the design and application of competition law in pursuit of broader public interests bears clear risks. It would not only pose a challenge for young competition authorities in developing countries. It could also run the risk of being overstretched and resulting in a prohibition of efficiency-enhancing IP-related conduct. Requiring that public interests are defined in the light of and with the aim of giving effect to fundamental human rights could, however, help to minimise those risks.

To sum up the foregoing analysis, a competition law approach to IPRs that puts the emphasis on anticompetitive practices and abuses that result in a loss of allocative efficiency would be covered by the flexibilities provided by the TRIPS Agreement in this field. Surely, to be TRIPS-consistent, competition law enforcers should be aware of not condemning the normal exercise of IPRs, but rather individual excesses. In the context of controlling the pricing practices of IP right holders, for example, account should be taken of the fact that the exclusivity of the right may provide for higher prices of IP-protected goods without this amounting to an abuse or being the result of an anticompetitive practice. IP right holders should be able to include in the price the costs of their innovative and creative endeavours. In this context, one additional consideration should be made. Thus, given the fact that markets in developing countries may be largely irrelevant to the incentives to innovate of right holders in industrialised nations, a price that would not ordinarily be alleged to be excessive in Europe or in the United States might still contravene domestic prohibitions against excessive prices.[128] Moreover, where fundamental human rights are affected, there should be no doubt that both the TRIPS Agreement and the rationale of competition law support an application of competition law vis-à-vis IPRs that aims at maximising access to IP-protected goods by relying on considerations of distributional justice.

4. Promoting TRIPS' objectives by means of national competition rules?

The foregoing analysis has shown that the TRIPS Agreement does not only leave Members a great deal of room for manoeuvre to formulate their IP-related competition rules, but that Members may use this flexibility

---

126 Drexl, Josef (2005), *supra* note 116, at 719 (focusing, however, on the positive distributional aspects of a consumer-welfare standard).

127 Emphasising this, see Cottier, Thomas (2007), *supra* note 75, at 194.

128 Berger, Jonathan (2006), *supra* note 106, at 189.

to meet different needs. Hence, a use of competition law to combat IP-related restraints of competition that inhibit innovation would be covered by the rationale of the TRIPS Agreement just as much as an application of competition law aimed at enhancing access to and dissemination of IP-protected goods. From this perspective, the decision taken by the TRIPS negotiators of allowing Members to contest IP-related anticompetitive conduct without explicitly defining the content of such prohibitions seems to be the right one. Unlike in other fields of competition law in which broad consensus on the pernicious effects of certain anticompetitive practices exists,[129] the application of competition law to IPRs is highly complex and hotly debated, even between jurisdictions following a similar approach to the relationship between IPRs and competition law. From this perspective, a harmonisation exercise in this field would be hardly feasible. Most importantly, however, introducing international substantive standards on IP-related competition law would necessarily result in constricting the leeway of WTO Members.

Yet, the fact that an international harmonisation of IP-related competition standards may not be desirable does not mean that the system may not and should not be improved. In the first place, consideration could be given to transforming the voluntary IP-related rules of TRIPS into positive obligations. WTO Members would thus be obliged to introduce and apply competition rules to anticompetitive practices of IP right holders.[130] Certainly, the rationale for mandatory competition rules in TRIPS would be explained by the outstanding importance of competition law as an element to balance and safeguard the proper functioning of the IP-system. However, given that anticompetitive practices often escape the jurisdictional reach of substantive competition laws, making TRIPS' competition rules mandatory would only be the first and necessary step.

As a general principle of administrative law, national competition authorities are allowed to act against restrictions of competition only to the extent to which substantive competition law applies to those practices. To date most states follow the so-called effects doctrine.[131] According to this

---

129 See, for instance, OECD (1998), 'Recommendation of the Council Concerning Action Against Hard Core Cartels', OECD-Doc. C(98)35/FINAL, 25 March 1998, available at http://webdomino1.oecd.org/horizontal/oecdacts.nsf/linkto/C(98)35.

130 See also in this sense the proposal for an amendment of Article 8(2) TRIPS and the introduction of a new Article 8(b) in TRIPS elaborated by the project 'Intellectual Property Rights in Transition' (IPT), available at http://www.atrip.org/upload/files/activities/Parma2006/Kur%20synopsis.pdf.

131 Also those nations which like the United Kingdom and Australia still rely

principle, national competition law applies to anticompetitive practices which have effect within the national territory, even if they result from activity outside this area. Conversely, domestic anticompetitive activity which is entirely or mainly directed at foreign markets falls outside the scope of application of national competition laws. Whereas by relying on the effects doctrine the targeted country may apply its competition law against those practices, the shortcomings of extraterritorial competition law enforcement become evident, however, when contemplating the fact that the exercise of state force may only be asserted within the state's borders. A competition agency seeking to apply its law extraterritorially would have to rely on the willingness of the firms involved and, particularly, on the cooperation of foreign competition agencies. As a consequence, as long as the application of national competition laws is made dependent on the existence of anticompetitive effects on the domestic market, private restraints targeted at foreign markets would not be fought by the most suitable competition agency. Moreover, the negative consequences of the effects doctrine are more strongly perceived in developing countries, since, on the one hand, they are often the target of foreign anticompetitive conduct, and on the other hand, they may not rely on functioning competition law systems to protect their own markets. Yet, the problem of the non-enforcement of domestic competition law against practices restricting competition in foreign markets has deeper roots than the effects doctrine. It is based on the very aim of national competition law, namely the protection of the national economic order from restraints of competition. Thus, if national competition is to be merely concerned about preserving national competition, the effects doctrine certainly appears best to meet its *ratio legis*. The protection of domestic competition as the sole goal of competition law, however, is not predetermined. Rather, states are by no means precluded from taking the protection of international competition as an additional goal for their competition laws.

Building on this idea, Josef Drexl has proposed the adoption of a principle of non-discrimination, according to which WTO Members should be prohibited from protecting competition in foreign markets less strin-

---

Footnote 131 (*cont.*)
on the territoriality principle use cumulative connecting factors based on subjective and objective territoriality, thus narrowing the differences with countries which apply the effects doctrine. For an exhaustive overview, see Schwarzt, Ivo E. and Jürgen Basedow (1995), 'Restrictions of Competition', in Lipstein, Kurt (ed.), *International Encyclopedia of Comparative Law*, volume III, chapter 35, sections 8–88, Tübingen: Mohr Siebeck.

gently than competition in domestic markets.[132] Though such a principle is conceived in the much broader framework of designing principles for a WTO competition law, it likewise had implications for the treatment of IP-related practices. Thus, for example, contractual clauses that were prohibited in purely domestic licensing agreements had to be equally banned in cross-border licensing agreements.[133] A similar rule would apply in the field of unilateral abuses of market power. Besides contributing to protect competition in international and foreign markets, it is expected that the application of such a non-discrimination rule would result in industrialized countries lending a helping hand to the protection of competition in developing countries.[134] Still, there are some caveats to this latter argument. Thus, a principle which obliges WTO Members to apply the same standards of competition law in IP-related cases irrespectively of whether the restraint affects the domestic market or only the market of another WTO Member may not be that effective considering the different approaches and priorities WTO Members pursue when they apply their competition rules to IPRs. The example put forward by Thomas Cottier when exploring the role of competition law to guarantee access to essential medicines helps to illustrate this point.[135] Accordingly, neither the European prohibition of abusing a dominant position nor the US law on monopolisation would capture the conduct of one of their dominant right holders that refuses to license its patent on a new and highly efficient drug to generic manufacture in an emerging country which, in turn, seeks to export it to a developing country. While the proposed non-discrimination principle would indeed allow for considering the negative effects of a domestic conduct on a foreign market, in evaluating these effects under the national competition law adequate consideration should be given to the specific

---

132 Drexl, Josef (2004), 'International Competition Policy after Cancún: Placing a Singapore Issue on the WTO Development Agenda', *World Competition*, **27** (3), at 450 *et seq*. See also Article 2, Sec. 2(b) of the Draft International Antitrust Code (DIAC): 'Each Party to the Agreement shall apply all rules and principles applicable to national antitrust cases [. . .] to all interstate antitrust cases'. The DIAC is a draft proposal of a full-fledged international competition law intended as a GATT/WTO Plurilateral Agreement. An English version of the Draft is available at Fikentscher, Wolfgang and Ulrich Immenga (eds) (2005), *Draft International Antitrust Code, Kommentierter Entwurf eines internationalen Wettbewerbsrechts mit ergänzenden Beiträgen*, Baden-Baden: Nomos Verlag.

133 See Drexl, Josef (2003), 'International Competition Law – A Missing Link between TRIPs and Transfer of Technology', available at http://www.iprsonline.org/resources/competition.htm, at 13 *et seq*.

134 *Ibid.*, at 14.

135 See Cottier, Thomas (2007), *supra* note 75, at 188.

socio-economic conditions of the affected country.[136] As a consequence, this would imply that when applying their IP-related competition rules to conduct targeted at developing countries, industrialised nations should not only be concerned with the protection of innovation, but should also very much consider the distributional impact of such conduct.

Finally, once the competition-related rules of the TRIPS Agreement had been made mandatory, the GATT/WTO dispute settlement system should also be used – provided that the necessary adaptations to the specific features of competition law have been made – to guarantee an efficient decentralised application of competition law by the national competition agencies. Accordingly, national agencies would, upon request of any other national agency that has cause to believe that an IP right holder who is a national of or domicilied in the requested Member is undertaking prohibited anticompetitive practices, have to investigate the case and to proceed against the right holder. Whereas Article 40(3) and (4) TRIPS already contain similar rules on cooperation between national competition agencies,[137] they are limited to anticompetitive licensing practices. Furthermore, the requested Member is not obliged to take action and retains full freedom of ultimate decision. Under the proposed rules, however, the requested agency would have to consider the case and apply its law. In case the Member in question did not comply with the request, the requesting Member should have the right to bring the case before a GATT/WTO dispute resolution panel. Likewise, the right of appeal should be available if excessive competition law enforcement resulted in the erosion of the intellectual property protection granted by TRIPS. After the examination of the case by the WTO panel and possibly also by the Standing Appellate Body, the inactive or 'hyperactive' national competition agency could be required to take appropriate measures to remove the restraint or revoke the measures taken, respectively. Ultimately, as a remedy, trade sanctions could be imposed under Article 22 of the Dispute Settlement Understanding.

5. Concluding remarks

Though rather embryonic, the competition-related rules contained in the TRIPS Agreement play an essential role in guaranteeing the proper functioning of the IP-system. The TRIPS Agreement relies on the national competition laws of the WTO Members to combat abuses within the

---

[136] More generally, Josef Drexl (2004), *supra* note 132, at 451 derives from the principle of non-discrimination the obligation of evaluating the effects of conduct on global welfare.

[137] See *supra* Section 2.2.2.

system. By doing so, it offers them an open and flexible framework for the formulation of their IP-related competition rules. Yet, at the same time, the standard against which national rules have to be measured is clearly set up in TRIPS. Thus, the competition laws of WTO Members should help to attain the TRIPS' objectives. Both, innovation-oriented and distribution-oriented competition rules are therefore covered by TRIPS.

Competition rules have an important role to play in promoting innovation by protecting the competitive mechanism of the IP-system against distortions. Concretely, they have to ensure that markets remain open for new and better products that can substitute for the IP-protected ones. While an innovation-oriented approach to competition law best serves the interests of industrialised nations, developing countries may well make use of competition law to ensure that anticompetitive practices of right holders do not unduly restrict access to and dissemination of protected goods. To attain this objective, however, it may not be sufficient to focus on the negative effects of anticompetitive practices on allocative efficiency. Rather, the application of competition law should be based on considerations of distributive justice. Again, at least where it comes to access to essential IP-protected goods, such an approach would not only be supported by the TRIPS Agreement, but would also be perfectly in line with the rationale of competition law.

Finally, in order to be fully effective, the competition rules of TRIPS should be made mandatory. Whereas an international harmonisation of IP-competition rules would neither be feasible nor desirable, WTO Members should accept an obligation to non-discriminate between restraints of competition affecting the domestic market and those affecting foreign markets. In evaluating the effects of a practice on a foreign market, account should be taken of the specific socio-economic conditions of that country. As a consequence, this would imply that when applying their IP-related competition rules to conduct targeted at developing countries, industrialised nations should not only be concerned with the protection of innovation, but should also very much consider the distributional impact of such conduct. By contrast, developing countries should be aware of and contemplate in their assessment the negative impact of an antitrust intervention not only on the domestic incentives to innovate, but also on foreign – mainly industrialised – markets.

9 Intellectual property rights in free trade agreements: moving beyond TRIPS minimum standards

Pedro Roffe, Christoph Spennemann and Johanna von Braun

Introduction

Regional and bilateral free trade agreements (FTAs)[1] and their relationship with the World Trade Organization (WTO) Agreement on Trade-related Aspects of Intellectual Property Rights (TRIPS Agreement) are the main focus of this chapter.

In exploring these matters we examine, first, how the latter Agreement marks the starting point of a major shift with respect to the pre-existing intellectual property (IP) landscape by both breaking with the traditional evolution of the international system and by opening the way to new and expansive developments in the international protection and enforcement of intellectual property rights (IPRs).

The chapter then analyses the main features of FTAs negotiated after the conclusion of the TRIPS Agreement and their implications for developing countries. Particular attention is paid throughout the chapter to a number of public interest-related policy matters, where the FTAs increase and expand the minimum standards of protection and enforcement established under TRIPS, with particular attention to issues such as public health, the protection of life forms and of traditional knowledge, access to knowledge in general and to the new obligations on enforcement and dispute settlement. The final section draws some overall conclusions around these recent developments and their implications.

We begin with an examination of the main features of the TRIPS Agreement and of the policy space afforded to countries with respect to its implementation.[2]

---

1 Free trade initiatives adopt different names. For simplicity we encompass all these arrangements under the broad label of 'FTAs'.

2 Parts of this chapter draw on work and publications the authors have been involved with in recent years and these are referred to throughout the chapter.

The TRIPS Agreement

Main features

One of the most important consequences of the TRIPS Agreement is the formal incorporation of IP into the international trading system. This means, among other things, that the main pillars of the system – national treatment and most favoured nation treatment (MFN) – apply to the IP relations between WTO Members. The full incorporation of IP into the international trading system leads to the application of the WTO's Dispute Settlement Understanding (DSU) of the TRIPS Agreement. The application of the DSU could justify measures of commercial retaliation, including cross-retaliation in the event of non-compliance with TRIPS obligations.[3] This 'linkage' issue[4] allows Member States to retaliate in fields such as agricultural tariffs, which are of crucial importance to developing countries, for lack of compliance with IP obligations.

Apart from these systemic developments, the TRIPS Agreement constitutes a milestone in the process of harmonization of IP standards. Before TRIPS, countries could differentiate on the patentability of industrial or technological sectors and choose whether to protect processes and/or products. For example, at the time of the Uruguay Round negotiations, almost half of national patent laws, including those of a range of developed countries, excluded pharmaceutical products from patent protection. Food-related products were also among the sectors most frequently excluded from patent protection. Countries could not only exclude certain fields of technology, but could also determine the nature and duration of the rights granted.[5]

In contrast to the dispersed nature of legal instruments dealing with IP, the TRIPS Agreement includes, in one single instrument, all the major IP disciplines and sets minimum standards for their protection. These

---

[3] According to the WTO Dispute Settlement Understanding (DSU), retaliation may take place in the same sector as the one where the TRIPS violation has occurred (Article 22.3(a)). A 'sector' in this context is synonymous with a category of IP covered under the TRIPS Agreement, see Article 22.3(f)(iii) of the DSU. If the complainant considers that retaliation within the same sector is not practicable, it may seek the suspension of concessions in a different sector of the same agreement, and eventually even suspend concessions under a different agreement ('cross-retaliation'). See Article 22.3(b), (c), DSU.

[4] For further reading on the linking of IPRs to other WTO negotiation subjects, see Bhagwati (2002).

[5] See WIPO, document HL/CE/IV/INF/1, prepared for the consideration of the Committee of Experts on the harmonization of certain aspects of laws protecting inventions, fourth meeting, 14 October 1987.

minimum standards are supplemented by the substantive provisions of, among others, the classical IP treaties of the 19th century, the Paris[6] and Berne[7] Conventions, that are explicitly imported into TRIPS.[8]

The TRIPS Agreement minimum standards relate to copyright and related rights, trademarks, geographical indications, industrial designs, patents, layout-designs of integrated circuits and undisclosed information. As observed, in the pre-TRIPS landscape, countries had the freedom to modulate the manner in which protection was fashioned for each of the IP disciplines. Under TRIPS, countries are obliged to accept at least these minimum standards, but, as will be discussed below, may adopt more extensive protection, as is actually the case with respect to those countries parties to FTAs that in general cover the same subject matters dealt with in TRIPS.

Among the substantive minimum standards for all categories of IP covered by the Agreement, probably the most far-reaching changes brought about by TRIPS concern patents and undisclosed information. In all the other areas covered by the Agreement, TRIPS primarily imported and developed the main standards covered already in pre-existing World Intellectual Property Organization (WIPO)-administered treaties. The FTAs expand further on these matters.

With respect to patent protection, the TRIPS Agreement includes a number of important obligations for Members that limit the legislative freedom they enjoyed prior to TRIPS. For example, the Agreement states that patents shall be available and patent rights exercised without discrimination as to the place of invention, the field of technology and whether products are imported or locally produced. Whilst stating this principle of non-discrimination with respect to the patentability of inventions in all fields of technology, the Agreement leaves WTO Members the flexibility, within the broad parameters of the provisions of TRIPS, to characterize what an invention is for the purpose of granting a patent. This is, in a way, a manifestation of the remaining legislative freedom available under the TRIPS Agreement, and is commonly referred to as TRIPS 'flexibilities'.[9] Article 27.1 of TRIPS provides that patents shall be available for any inventions, whether products or processes, in all fields of technology, provided that they are new, involve an inventive step and are capable of industrial application.[10]

---

6 See http://www.wipo.int/treaties/en/ip/paris/trtdocs_wo020.html.

7 See http://www.wipo.int/treaties/en/ip/berne/trtdocs_wo001.html.

8 See Article 2, TRIPS.

9 See, in general, UNCTAD-ICTSD (2005).

10 For these purposes, the terms 'inventive step' and 'capable of industrial

As far as undisclosed information is concerned, the TRIPS Agreement (Article 39.3) contains general principles on the need to protect this information against unfair commercial use, with respect to data submitted to governments or governmental agencies as a condition of approving the marketing of pharmaceutical or of agricultural chemical products which utilize new chemical entities. This second aspect, as discussed in this chapter, has largely been expanded in FTAs.

Another major feature of the TRIPS Agreement is the incorporation of disciplines related to the enforcement of rights. WTO Members are obliged not only to recognize and protect those rights but also to establish mechanisms that secure, through administrative, civil and criminal procedures, including border measures, the appropriate means for the domestic enforcement of those rights.[11] These minimum standards are again largely expanded by the FTAs.

The policy choices and the flexibilities of the Agreement

Despite this considerable move toward harmonization of IPRs, the TRIPS Agreement provides WTO Members with a number of important policy choices. Above all, it leaves Members the freedom of implementation of its provisions, in the sense that Members are free to determine the appropriate method of incorporating its provisions into domestic law, within their own legal system and practice.[12] This reflects the notion that the Agreement recognizes flexibilities and discretion in the implementation of its minimum standards. In many respects, this question of flexibilities has permeated the evolution of the TRIPS Agreement and has been one the main bones of contention among WTO Members. The matter reached a climax in discussions on the relationship between public health and IPRs that led to the adoption of the Doha Declaration on TRIPS and Public Health in 2001.[13]

Flexibilities are mainly expressed in the lack of specific definitions of particular concepts that can then be properly incorporated in national laws according to local circumstances. For instance, the lack of definition, under TRIPS and some FTAs, of what constitutes a patentable invention and how to further define the criteria for patentability, may have a major

---

application' may be deemed by a Member to be synonymous with the terms 'non-obvious' and 'useful', respectively.

[11] See Part IV of the Agreement dealing with the Acquisition and Maintenance of Intellectual Property Rights and Related Inter-partes procedures.

[12] See Article 1, TRIPS.

[13] See WTO document WT/MIN(01)/DEC/2, 20 November 2001 at http://www.wto.org/english/thewto_e/minist_e/min01_e/mindecl_trips _e.htm.

impact on where countries draw the line between private exclusive rights and the public domain. Applying stricter standards of patentability risks blocking follow-on innovation through monopolization of knowledge that ought to be more freely available.

On its part, exceptions and limitations to private rights also play an important role in the design of a balanced innovation policy. They can take a number of forms and they respond to different rationales (Scotchmer 2005: p. 114). Under most patent laws, exclusive rights may not be exercised with regard to certain acts considered legitimate, for example in relation to non-commercial acts (for example, private use or experimental use) (Garrison 2006).[14] This means that under certain specified circumstances, there may be exceptions to the exclusive rights. In general, the TRIPS Agreement limits the establishment of such exceptions to those that 'do not unreasonably conflict with a normal exploitation of the patent and do not unreasonably prejudice the legitimate interests of the patent owner, taking account of the legitimate interests of third parties' (Art. 30). A common limitation on the exclusive rights conferred by a patent is the possibility of using the patent without the patent holder's authorization in certain events and under conditions established in national regimes. These are commonly known as compulsory licences permitted under TRIPS, a subject to which we return below.

The FTAs, in general, replicate the conditions of TRIPS for the establishment of further exceptions and limitations. In the case of copyright, limitations and exceptions could in theory include those related to the promotion of competition in a given technology to permit interoperability, so that two or more systems can interact (for example, a computer functioning with software from other companies) or to the efforts of educational institutions to utilize the most effective technological means to communicate with and train students (Okediji 2004: p. 27). In the case of patents (as well as in all categories of IP), typical limitations might include the treatment of the exhaustion of rights and the regulatory exception in the case of pharmaceutical products to allow for the marketing approval of generics before the expiration of a patent, in order that it can reach the market without delay upon expiration of the patent.

The issue of flexibilities in IP policy making is not only relevant to developing countries, but equally for developed countries' innovation

---

[14] Note that according to Article 9 of the Swiss Patent Act, a patented substance may be used by researchers even for commercial purposes, provided such use results in new knowledge on the patented product. See <http://www.admin.ch/ch/f/rs/232_14/> for a French version of the Swiss Patent Act.

policies, which also depend on an appropriate balance between private rights and knowledge dissemination. In the literature, concerns have been raised that further limitations in this direction, such as through multilateral harmonization efforts as in the case of substantive patent harmonization, may cause considerable harm to the national innovation systems of those countries that are currently their main *demandeurs* (Reichman and Dreyfuss 2007).

The flexibilities in TRIPS relevant to public health

As pointed out, the issue of policy space and the appropriate use of flexibilities became particularly controversial in the case of public health issues. In this connection, it is appropriate to recall that the TRIPS Agreement leaves, in general, WTO Members some discretion for the design of their national patent laws, namely by leaving Members the freedom to define whether they will apply strict criteria of patentability. This is, for example, an important tool for preserving a large public domain for follow-on research and the promotion of competing products to help bring down prices. The Agreement establishes no obligation to make patents available for new (or second) uses of known patented products.[15] This may avoid the 'evergreening' of patents by seeking an additional full patent term for the same or similar products.[16] Furthermore, the TRIPS Agreement does not affect the authority for curbing prices of patented products. It also legitimizes the control of possible abuses in the use of the exclusive rights through competition laws and policies, in particular in IP licensing agreements.[17] As pointed out earlier, the Agreement also allows for exceptions to the exclusive rights conferred by a patent.[18] One relevant exception in

---

15 For instance, Sildenafil (Viagra) was first patented by Pfizer to treat heart disease. After finding out that it also served to treat impotence, Pfizer filed a second patent for this new use of the same drug. This second patent has been invalidated in some countries because of lack of novelty or because it was found obvious. See http://www.lockeliddell.com/files/News/ab9ebdd4-621f-4432-a383-1cae37df9ea1/Presentation/NewsAttachment/c5a9d67e-bdd9-4c7e-97e9-1d6efb6314dc/Andrews_Pfizers%20Viagra%20Patent.pdf and http://mb.rxlist.com/rxboard/viagra.pl?noframes;read=183.

16 For example, this flexibility is affected in the US–Oman FTA, where each party expressly 'confirms that it shall make patents available for any new uses for, or new methods of using, a known product, including new uses and new methods for the treatment of particular medical conditions' (Article 15.8.1(b)). See http://www.ustr.gov/assets/Trade_Agreements/Bilateral/Oman_FTA/Final_Text/asset_upload_file715_8809.pdf.

17 See Articles 8.2, 40, TRIPS Agreement.

18 See Article 30, TRIPS Agreement.

the public health field is the early working or regulatory ('Bolar') exception. In the same line, TRIPS permits Members to freely determine the substantive grounds for the issuance of compulsory licences[19] and authorizes them to determine their own system of IPR exhaustion that might facilitate parallel imports of low-priced drugs.[20] Finally, the Agreement, in dealing with test data submitted to regulatory authorities for marketing approval purposes, leaves each Member to determine the appropriate form of protection.[21]

These types of flexibilities were reaffirmed in the Doha Declaration on Public Health of 2001 by reinstating the right of WTO Members 'to use, to the full, the provisions in the TRIPS Agreement, which provide flexibility for this purpose'.[22]

In addition, the WTO General Council Decision of 30 August 2003 on the Implementation of Paragraph 6 of the Doha Declaration on the TRIPS Agreement and Public Health[23] extended the TRIPS flexibilities with regard to compulsory licensing. The 30 August Decision facilitates the exportation of cheaper generic drugs produced under compulsory licence to countries without sufficient domestic pharmaceutical manufacturing capacities. The Decision in Paragraph 6 waives the exporting country's obligation under TRIPS Article 31(f) to use drugs produced under compulsory licence predominantly for the supply of its own domestic market.[24] It also waives the obligation of the importing Member under Article 31(h) to pay an adequate remuneration to the patent holder, where remuneration for the same product has already been paid in the exporting Member.[25] Finally, the decision provides some important incentives to pharmaceutical producers located within a regional trade agreement, at least half of the membership of which is made up of least developed countries (LDCs).[26] In essence, these producers are not subject to the generally applicable limitation that the compulsory licence in the exporting country will only authorize production of the amount necessary to meet the needs of the eligible importing Member.[27]

---

19 See Article 31, TRIPS Agreement.

20 See Article 6, TRIPS Agreement.

21 Another view in the literature has questioned this flexible interpretation of Article 39.3 of the TRIPS Agreement; see Kampf (2002), p.120.

22 See paragraph 4 *in fine* of the Declaration on the TRIPS Agreement and Public Health.

23 WTO document WT/L/540 of 2 September 2003.

24 See paragraph 2 of the Decision.

25 See paragraph 3, second sentence of the Decision.

26 See paragraph 6(i) of the Decision.

27 In spite of its existence for over five years, the mechanisms have only

We turn next to the FTAs, negotiated either by the USA, or the European Union (EU) and the European Free Trade Association (EFTA) that even though adopting different terms and emphases on IP and following different patterns, tend to pursue a trend towards an expansion of the minimum standards of protection and enforcement of the TRIPS Agreement.

Bilateral and regional free trade initiatives

To a different degree and intensity, major trading powers have pursued in recent years selected free trade initiatives with developing countries with the view of intensifying and deepening the WTO agreements. With respect to IP, these agreements have been characterized as TRIPS-plus arrangements. While the main aim of FTAs is increased market access, these agreements contain a number of trade-related rules, including investment, services and government procurement and follow the concept of a single undertaking as in the case of the Marrakesh WTO Final Act.

While developing countries tend to be the *demandeurs* of bilateral trade deals with developed countries mainly to gain better access to their more affluent markets, it is developed countries that push for the incorporation of IP chapters into these agreements. Similar to the acceptance of the TRIPS Agreement as a quid pro quo for the benefits of WTO membership,[28] many government officials seem to acknowledge that the IP provisions in the FTAs respond to a trade-off in exchange for trade concessions in areas more closed to their national commercial interests. In the case of developed countries, the driving forces behind the incorporation of comprehensive and robust IP provisions in bilateral free trade agreements have been those industrial sectors highly dependent on IP protection and interested in sustaining their technological comparative advantages (Sell 2003; Matthews 2002; Drahos and Braithwaite 2002). The political economy of why governments enter into these agreements responds to a number of sovereign considerations that are beyond the scope of analysis of this chapter (Roffe, von Braun and Vivas-Eugui 2007).

---

recently been successfully implemented for the first time. In a process that took over four years to put together, Canada's Apotex started to export Apo-TriAvir, a triple-combination HIV/AIDS drug, to Rwanda in 2008. Public health advocates blame above all the complex nature of making use of the mechanisms for its scarce use (*Bridges* 2008).

[28] For further reading on why developing countries ultimately signed on to the TRIPS Agreement as part of the WTO package, see Bhagwati (1991), Stewart (1999) and Ryan (1998).

FTAs negotiated with the EU and EFTA

Unlike the FTAs negotiated by the USA, IP provisions in the FTAs signed with the EU and EFTA do not follow a particular model. By and large there is an emphasis on reinforcing the existing international IP architecture by committing the parties to become party to a number of multilateral IP-related agreements (Santa Cruz 2007). For example, in the case of the Agreement between Chile and the EU, the parties have 'to accede to and ensure an adequate and effective implementation of the obligations arising from' a number of WIPO-administered treaties[29] and of making 'every effort to ratify and ensure an adequate and effective implementation of the obligations arising from' multilateral conventions.[30] The ratification of these agreements is reinforced by the overarching obligation prescribed in the EU agreements of ensuring adequate and effective protection to IPRs in accordance with the highest international standards, including effective means of enforcing such rights provided for in international treaties (Roffe and Santa Cruz 2006).

Traditionally, the most significant IP-related provisions in the EU agreements relate to specific arrangements on the trade in wines and spirits. These arrangements include provisions on the reciprocal protection of geographical indications (GIs) related to wines and spirits, and the protection of traditional expressions (of both parties). The special arrangements on wines include protection of 'homonymous signs', as allowed in TRIPS.[31]

---

[29] For example: the World Intellectual Property Organization Copyright Treaty (WCT), 1996; the World Intellectual Property Organization Performances and Phonograms Treaty (WPPT), 1996; the Patent Cooperation Treaty of 19 June 1970; Washington Act amended in 1979 and modified in 1984; the Nice Agreement Concerning the International Classification of Goods and Services for the Purposes of the Registration of Marks of 15 June 1957, Geneva Act 1977, amended in 1979; the Strasbourg Agreement Concerning the International Patent Classification of 1971, amended in 1979; the Convention for the Protection of Producers of Phonograms against the Unauthorized Reproduction of their Phonograms, Geneva, 1971; the Locarno Agreement establishing the International Classification for Industrial Designs, 1968, amended in 1979; the Budapest Treaty on the International Recognition of the Deposit of Microorganisms for the Purposes of Patent Procedure, of April 28 1977, amended in 1980; and the Trademark Law Treaty, 1994.

[30] For example: the Protocol to the Madrid Agreement Concerning the International Registration of Marks; the Madrid Agreement concerning the International Registration of Marks; Stockholm Act 1967, as amended in 1979; and the Vienna Agreement establishing an International Classification of Figurative Elements of Marks, 1973, amended in 1985.

[31] 'In the case of homonymous geographical indications for wines, protection

The EFTA model, again, follows very closely the EU approach (Roffe and Santa Cruz 2006), but expands the protection in the case of pharmaceutical products to data provided to national authorities on the safety and efficacy of those products by way of exclusive protection for an adequate number of years or by adequate compensation. But again, the FTAs are not identical. For example, as noted, they all contain references to agreements that parties should adhere to, but follow different schemes to achieve the same objective. For example, in the FTA between EFTA and Tunisia it is stipulated that the latter 'will do its outmost to accede to the international conventions concerning IPRs to which EFTA States are Parties' (Abdel Latif 2009).

In broad terms, and compared to the FTAs sponsored by the USA, those with EFTA and the EU have been less comprehensive. However, the EU has recently launched a series of negotiations that include stronger IP chapters with a number of countries, including new Economic Partnership Agreements (EPAs) with six regional groupings of the African, Caribbean and Pacific (ACP) states (Santa Cruz 2007) and with members of the Andean Community (Seuba 2008) and Central American countries, which put greater emphasis on IP provisions, particularly with respect to enforcement measures.

FTAs negotiated with the USA

The FTAs where the USA is a party have a more expansive and detailed coverage than those sponsored by the EU. They are guided by the following main objectives: (i) the adequate and effective protection of IPRs by ensuring accelerated and full implementation of TRIPS obligations and that the provisions of any trade agreement reflect a standard of protection similar to that found in US law; (ii) strong protection for new and emerging technologies and new methods of transmitting and distributing products embodying IP; (iii) elimination of discrimination with respect to matters affecting the availability, acquisition, scope, maintenance, use, and enforcement of IPRs; (iv) that the standards of protection and enforcement keep pace with technological developments, and in particular ensuring that right holders have the legal and technological means to

---

shall be accorded to each indication, subject to the provisions of paragraph 4 of Article 22. Each Member shall determine the practical conditions under which the homonymous indications in question will be differentiated from each other, taking into account the need to ensure equitable treatment of the producers concerned and that consumers are not misled'. Article 23.3, TRIPS. For a detailed analysis of the EU's approach to GIs protection in FTAs, see Vivas-Eugui and Spennemann (2007).

control the use of their works through the Internet and other global communication media, and to prevent the unauthorized use of their works; (v) the provision of strong enforcement of IPRs, including through accessible, expeditious, and effective civil, administrative, and criminal enforcement mechanisms and provisional measures and requirements related to border measures; and (vi) the creation of an additional WTO-based dispute settlement mechanism applicable also to IP-related matters, including non-violation complaints.[32]

As in the case of TRIPS, the breadth and scope of the agreements sponsored by the USA, relate to all major IP disciplines. The IP chapters, as in all FTAs of the latest generation, are an integral part of the general agreement that include, in a single undertaking, a number of trade disciplines and general chapters dealing with the settlement of disputes and the administration of the Agreement, including the monitoring of its implementation. The IP chapters have been the subject of fierce controversies and they have been structured around a negotiation template, which has evolved since the North American Free Trade Agreement (NAFTA) negotiations of 1993.[33] As a result, while the structure and specific contents vary in the choice of words, they follow a common pattern that has changed over time but comprises, in general, the following subject matters: all-purpose provisions (such as the entry into force of the agreements, a general reference to the international IP architecture and the ratification of a number of WIPO-administered conventions,[34] and transparency of laws and administrative regulations); trademarks; GIs; domain names on the Internet; obligations pertaining to copyright and related rights; protection of encrypted program-carrying satellite signals; patents; measures related to certain regulated products (pharmaceutical and chemical products); and enforcement of IPRs.

It should be noted that the US IP template experienced important changes in May 2007 as a result of a bipartisan understanding with respect to the ratification of the FTAs negotiated by the US Administration with Colombia, Panama and Peru resulting, among other things, in changes in the IP provisions related to pharmaceutical products, discussed below in this chapter.

---

32 See, among others, Section 2102 of the Trade Promotion Authority, Trade Act of 2002.

33 See, http://www.nafta-sec-alena.org/DefaultSite/index_e.aspx?DetailID= 78.

34 The coverage of agreements, with differences in the timing of the ratification, follows the EU scheme closely. See above.

The controversies

As suggested, the FTAs have raised a number of controversies particularly because they have added a new layer of complexities to the many challenges that most developing countries face with respect to the minimum standards of the TRIPS Agreement. Concerns have been expressed that the TRIPS-plus provisions in these agreements reduce the opportunities to use the flexibilities outlined above.

The main critical questions that have been raised with respect to the added layer of protection put forward by FTAs are the following:

- In the case of patents and regulated products: the compensatory extensions of the patent duration for administrative delays in the granting of the patents or in the marketing approval of products; the limitations that can be placed on the use of public policy instruments such as compulsory licensing and parallel imports; the restrictive use of exceptions and limitations; the relaxation of the patentability criteria allowing for new uses, the protection of business models and extending patent protection to software programmes; the exclusive rights-based protection of undisclosed data; the linkage between patent protection and marketing approval; the compatibility of the IP chapters with the Doha Declaration on TRIPS and Public Health.
- With respect to copyright and related rights: extension of the duration of rights (in general from the life of the author plus 50 years under TRIPS to 70 years); the expansion of the protection to the digital environment; the application of effective technological measures and management rights; the more restrictive use of exceptions and limitations; the responsibility of service providers.
- In the case of biotechnology and traditional knowledge: protection of life forms via patents; the compatibility with the Convention on Biological Diversity (CBD) and the lack of provisions dealing with the disclosure of origin of new inventions; the protection of plant varieties via the International Union for the Protection of New Varieties of Plant (UPOV) 1991.
- With respect to enforcement of IPRs: their expansion mode affecting the balance reached in TRIPS by, among other things, making civil or administrative offences of a criminal character and expanding the control of border measures.

One of the critical aspects of the TRIPS-plus nature of these provisions is that they pre-empt or affect positions that countries might pursue or sustain in multilateral negotiation fora. In other words, the bilateral track – legitimatized by the TRIPS Agreement – might be detrimental to advances that could be made through the multilateral system. Advocates of FTAs argue, on the other side, that the IP provisions are a mere elaboration of the TRIPS minimum standards in the case, for example, of the more detailed provisions on the protection of pharmaceutical products. The argument is also made that FTAs are the only possible path to advance positions that otherwise are not achievable through the multilateral system that has become cumbersome and time-consuming.

However, few could dispute that the IP provisions have been one of the most contentious aspects of the negotiations of the FTAs. The general critique made to the FTAs is that while these agreements build on the TRIPS minimum standards, they tend to affect the general balance of the Agreement by overemphasizing the protection aspects of IP, while reducing policy spaces otherwise available for the protection of the broader public interest. This general observation is discussed with greater detail with respect to developing countries' public policy objectives in areas such as access to medicines, genetic resources, access to knowledge and enforcement issues.

Health and access to medicines

As reiterated in this chapter, the relationship of IPRs, particularly patents, with public health policies and access to medicines, in general, has been one of the most controversial multilateral trade-related topics of recent years. With the adoption of the Doha Declaration on the TRIPS Agreement and Public Health, the WTO General Council Decision for the implementation of Paragraph 6 of that Declaration[35] and the subsequent amendment of the TRIPS Agreement, the focus of the debate has shifted away from the multilateral level to the regional and bilateral front and the impact of recent FTAs (Roffe and Spennemann 2006; Abbott and Reichman 2007). As a result, the World Health Organization (WHO) has been increasingly engaged in questions related to IP and health, particularly through the work and final report of its Commission on Intellectual Property Rights, Innovation and Public Health,[36] and the follow-up work of its Intergovernmental Working Group on Public Health, Innovation and Intellectual Property (IGWG).[37]

---

[35] Implementation of Paragraph 6 of the Doha Declaration of the TRIPS Agreement and Public Health, WT/L/540, September 2003.

[36] See: http://www.who.int/intellectualproperty/en/.

[37] The IGWG was established by the World Health Assembly in 2006, by Resolution 59.24, which set 'an intergovernmental working group open to all interested Member States to draw up a global strategy and plan of action in order to provide a medium-term framework based on the recommendations of the Commission' [on Intellectual Property Rights, Innovation and Public health]; the

As far as substance is concerned, the FTAs have consolidated a new form of protection to traditional patent rights, namely exclusive rights for pharmaceutical test data submitted to regulatory authorities with the purpose of gaining marketing approval. TRIPS mandates the protection of data submitted for the registration of medicines against unfair commercial use of that information (thus allowing other fair and reasonable uses), while the FTAs have expanded this protection, barring almost any use of that information unless there is consent from the right holder.

The classical balance between private and public interests has been most affected in the health sector. This has led prominent actors to voice concern that the set of provisions in FTAs that go beyond the TRIPS minimum standards may have a serious impact on countries' public health policies. Nobel Prize laureate Joseph Stiglitz has observed with respect to the FTA with Morocco: 'The new agreement, many Moroccans fear, will make generic drugs needed in the fight against AIDS even less accessible in their country than they are in the United States' (Stiglitz 2004).

A number of US congressmen have also reacted strongly to these developments:

> . . . In the 2002 Trade Promotion Authority Act, Congress directed the Administrative branch to adhere to the Doha Declaration as a 'principal negotiating objective' in U.S. trade negotiations. Regrettably, recent . . . FTAs appear to undermine this commitment with provisions that strip away flexibilities to which countries are entitled under TRIPS. The FTAs provisions also appear to upset an important balance between innovation and access by elevating intellectual property at the expense of public health. The end result is that they threaten to restrict access to life-saving medicines and create conditions where poor countries could wait even longer than the Unites States for affordable generic medicines.[38]

As explained below, the bipartisan understanding between US Congress and the Administration has sought to address such apprehensions.

It should be highlighted that concerns raised by the expansive exclusive rights on pharmaceutical products are not limited to access issues, but extend to the building of technological capacities in developing countries. Overly broad exclusive rights may threaten the ability of local innovators, especially in developing countries, to engage in research and development

---

'Global strategy and plan of action on public health, innovation and intellectual property' were subsequently adopted by the 61st World Health Assembly in May 2008. The document can be found at: http://www.who.int/gb/ebwha/pdf_files/A61/A61_R21-en.pdf.

[38] Public letter dated 12 March 2007 addressed to the USA Trade Representative, signed by 12 members of the USA Congress.

(R&D) through reverse engineering and the creation of functional generic equivalents and improvements (Jaszi 2004: p. 8). Extended exclusive rights might discourage potential generic investors from investing in existing local production plants in developing countries, thus denying important opportunities for technology transfer to local producers of pharmaceuticals (UNCTAD forthcoming). Thus, FTA provisions, where implemented without due regard to their potential impact on innovation, may seriously hamper developing countries' efforts at technological catching-up.

The FTAs and the flexibilities in the case of pharmaceutical products
Free trade agreements include provisions on patents and regulated products that go beyond the minimum standards established by the TRIPS Agreement. This is particularly the case of FTAs sponsored by the USA and by EFTA (with respect to provisions dealing with data exclusivity). The main TRIPS-plus provisions in this respect deal with patent extensions, the patentability criteria, compulsory licences, parallel imports, the regulatory exception, data exclusivity and linking drug approval to patent status. The following sections provide further details on these provisions.

Patent extensions
Under Article 33 of the TRIPS Agreement, the minimum term of patent protection is 20 years from the filing date. However, particularly in the case of regulated products such as medicines, the period during which the patentee may actually take advantage of his monopoly rights may be affected by administrative delays in the actual grant of the patent and finally in the marketing approval process of the medicine. This is the apparent rationale behind the FTA provisions that require an extension of the patent term in case the regulatory approval process delays the marketing of the patented product or process, and in cases where the granting of the patent has suffered administrative delays not attributable to the patent applicant.

Such an outright extension of the patent term has been criticized for indiscriminately postponing the entry of competing medicines into the market. As will be discussed below, the US Congress elected in 2006 has addressed this trend in the case of some of the new FTAs by altering the template followed since NAFTA and adopted until the US-Central America-Dominican Republic Free Trade Agreement (CAFTA-DR) Agreement (Roffe 2004).

Patentability criteria and their potential impact on access to affordable medicines
In contrast to the TRIPS Agreement, most of the US FTAs contain a definition of what constitutes 'industrial application', referring to the US

law concept of 'utility' in the sense that the invention operates according to its intended purpose (Morin 2004). This is the case with the recent FTAs with CAFTA-DR, Morocco, Peru, Colombia, and Panama.[39] This type of provision might preclude countries from adopting narrower definitions, like the concept of 'industrial applicability' as defined, for example, in European countries.[40]

Contrary to the concept of 'industrial applicability', the 'utility' approach could open the opportunity for the patentability of business models. As opposed to copyright, patents would protect the right holder against independent creators of comparable business models. This may prove to be a considerable disincentive for generic competitors with regard to the development of efficient business methods.[41] With respect to the patenting of pharmaceutical research tools, it should be noted that the revised 2001 Patent and Trademark Office (PTO) Utility Examination Guidelines have toughened the utility standard by requiring credible, specific and substantial utility, particularly with respect to biotechnological inventions (Thomas 2005: pp. 68–70). Research tools that may be used for a variety of different undefined purposes, such as expressed sequence tags (ESTs)[42] and single nucleotide polymorphisms (SNPs),[43] do not meet these tighter utility requirements.[44] This being said, the concern remains that provisions in FTAs referring to 'utility' may be interpreted in a less restrictive manner, especially in jurisdictions less familiar with the specific treatment

---

39 For example, Article 16.9.11 of the US–Peru FTA states: 'Each Party shall provide that a claimed invention is industrially applicable if it has a specific, substantial, and credible utility'. See also Article 15.9.11 of the Morocco FTA with the USA.

40 Article 57 of the European Patent Convention: 'Industrial application: An invention shall be considered as susceptible of industrial application if it can be made or used in any kind of industry, including agriculture'. See http://www.european-patent-office.org/legal/epc/e/ar57.html.

41 See Reichman and Dreyfuss (2007), p. 22, in the context of the information technology sector.

42 An EST is a tiny portion of an entire gene that can be used to help identify unknown genes and to map their positions within a genome, in a quick and inexpensive fashion. See http://www.ncbi.nlm.nih.gov/About/primer/est.html.

43 SNPs are variations of a DNA sequence. Variations in the DNA sequences of humans can affect how humans develop diseases, respond to pathogens, chemicals, drugs, etc. As a consequence, SNPs are of great value to biomedical research and in developing pharmacy products.

44 See *In re Fisher*, 421 F.3d 1365, 1373 (Fed. Cir. 2005), where the USA Federal Circuit rejected the patentability of ESTs if disclosure of their use is not more specific than broadly referring to the isolation of protein-encoded genes for the purpose of performing further research.

of the utility test in US domestic patent practice (Jaszi 2004: footnote 19; Abbott 2006). The broad patenting of research tools would create considerable obstacles for the development of competing products and domestic technological capacity as such.

In addition to the potential misapplication of unknown patentability standards, FTA partners of the USA may face serious challenges to domestic innovation and access to medicines as triggered by the 'evergreening' of existing patents. The FTAs with Australia, Bahrain and Morocco provide for the obligation to make patents available for 'any new uses or methods of using a known product'.[45] This might constitute a limitation of WTO Members' freedom to assess the patentability of a product, resulting in additional terms of patent protection for an already protected substance, thus keeping it unavailable for generic competition.[46]

Compulsory licences

As noted, the TRIPS Agreement leaves Member countries free to determine the substantive ground for the issuance of a compulsory licence. However, FTAs signed between the USA with, respectively, Australia, Jordan, Singapore and Vietnam limit the grounds for the use of compulsory licences to cases of anti-trust remedies, public non-commercial use and national emergencies or other circumstances of extreme urgency.[47] This excludes the grant of compulsory licences on other essential grounds, such as the promotion of innovation and research in case of one patent blocking the exploitation of another one ('dependent patents', TRIPS Article 31(l)) or in case of the unavailability, due to a patent, of an essential research tool for the development of new products. In the literature, concern has been expressed regarding the impact of such limitations on countries' technological development prospects (Jaszi 2004: p. 10).

This is not the case for the FTAs signed with Latin American countries that do not contain express limitations on the use of compulsory licences and at the same time include side letters[48] referring to the 'WTO health

---

[45] See, for example, Article 15.9.2 of the USA–Morocco FTA (http://www.ustr.gov/assets/Trade_Agreements/Bilateral/Morocco_FTA/FInal_Text/asset_upload_file797_3849.pdf).

[46] For further reading on the importance of patentability criteria for maintaining public health standards in the examination of pharmaceutical patents, see Correa (2006b).

[47] See, for example, Article 4, paragraph 20 of the USA–Jordan FTA.

[48] Side letters are documents signed by the parties to the main agreement, with the purpose of clarifying certain aspects of the text. Technically, they should have the same legal status as the main text. See a USTR document from July 2007 clarifying several aspects of an understanding contained in a side letter to CAFTA at

solution'. The FTA with Chile, for its part, expressly refers to the terms of the Doha Declaration on TRIPS and Public Health in a Preamble to its IP chapter, a practice that was not afterwards followed in subsequent US FTA negotiations. It was only most recently reintroduced when the reference to the Doha Declaration made its way back into the main text of the US FTA with Peru.[49] Nevertheless, the actual use of this reference, for example to enable the unrestricted use of a compulsory licence in the context of existing FTAs, has never been tested.

Parallel imports

The doctrine of exhaustion addresses the issue of when the IPR holder's control over the distribution of a specific good ceases. This cessation of control is critical to the functioning of any market economy because it facilitates the circulation of goods. The basic idea is that once the right holder has been able to obtain an economic return from the first sale or placing a good on the market, the purchaser or transferee of the good is entitled to use and dispose of it without further restriction. Without an exhaustion doctrine, the original IPR holder would continue exercising control over the sale, transfer or use of a good or service after the first sale. This has a particular impact on pharmaceutical products, where prices for the same products vary substantially among different countries. From the standpoint of the international trading system, the issue is whether the exhaustion operates on a national, regional or international basis.[50]

Exhaustion was one of the most difficult issues that arose during the negotiation of TRIPS (Gervais 1998, p. 61). The compromise at that time was that each WTO Member would be entitled to adopt its own exhaustion policy and rules. This agreement was framed in Article 6, precluding

---

http://www.ustr.gov/assets/Trade_Agreements/Bilateral/CAFTA/Briefing_Book/asset_upload_file650_13202.pdf. However, their status has never been tested in case of conflict and some scholars have expressed doubt about their legal status. See, for example, Roffe, von Braun and Vivas-Eugui (2007).

[49] See original negotiation text of US FTA with Peru, Article 16.13 (Understandings regarding certain public health measures). With the revised text of the FTA as a result of US revised trade policy, the understanding was made redundant.

[50] A country may choose to recognize that the exhaustion of an IPR occurs when a good is first sold or marketed anywhere outside its own borders (international exhaustion). If exhaustion occurs when a good or service is first sold or marketed outside a country, the IPR holder within the country may not oppose a given importation on the basis of its IPR. The importation of a good for which exhaustion of an IPR has occurred abroad is commonly referred to as 'parallel importation'.

anything in TRIPS from being used to address the exhaustion of rights in dispute settlement, subject to the TRIPS provisions on national and MFN treatment. This understanding was reaffirmed in the Doha Declaration on TRIPS and Public Health, which stated that in recognizing the flexibilities built into the Agreement, each WTO Member is free to establish its own regime on exhaustion of IPRs (UNCTAD-ICTSD 2005: pp. 92–4; Watal 2001: pp. 294–5).

Some FTAs signed by the USA (Australia, Morocco and Singapore) expressly acknowledge the patent holder's right to prevent parallel imports through the use of contracts or other means.[51] This approach was openly criticized in a US House of Representatives report (2005) prepared for Representative Henry Waxman:

> . . . making this policy permanent in trade agreements prevents countries that do not currently restrict parallel importation from reconsidering their national policies. Even in the United States there is great support for a form of parallel importation: both the House and the Senate have measures that would allow the importation of lower-priced patented drugs from Canada. The trade agreement language would make it difficult for the United States or other nations with current restrictions on importation to revisit their national policies.

This apparent limitation on the freedom of countries to import goods, for which IPRs have been exhausted, has not found a place in the FTAs signed with Latin American countries and in more recent FTAs signed with Bahrain, Oman and the Republic of Korea (GAO 2007: 32). One reason for this has been increasing domestic pressure from individual Members of Congress to facilitate the purchase of cheaper medication from third countries.[52]

---

[51] See, for example, Chapter 15, Article 15.9.4 of the USA–Morocco FTA, and Chapter 17, Article 17.9.4 of the USA–Australia FTA.

[52] The withdrawal of parallel import from the IPRs template is primarily a result of US domestic political concern. Members of Congress have repeatedly expressed their concern that including parallel import in FTAs could potentially undermine a possible future option of importing cheaper drugs from Canada. Indeed, in 2002 a proposal was passed in the then Democrat-controlled Senate that aimed to clear the way to allow prescription drug importation from Canada. However, the Administration signalled it would not move the proposal forward. See Pear (2002). Discussions on including parallel imports then re-emerged during the US–Australia FTA negotiations, where US Members of Congress expressed concerns over domestic implications of parallel import provisions in FTAs. Of particular prominence was a bill tabled by Representative Northup (R-KY), named 'Protecting Free Trade in Pharmaceuticals Act of 2005'. The bill suggested an amendment to the Trade Promotion Authority (TPA) that called, among other things, for the avoidance of provisions in trade agreements that restrict the access

Data exclusivity

With respect to data exclusivity, the TRIPS Agreement prescribes that:

> when requiring, as a condition of approving the marketing of pharmaceutical or of agricultural chemical products which utilize new chemical entities, the submission of undisclosed test or other data, the origination of which involves a considerable effort, shall protect such data against unfair commercial use. In addition, Members shall protect such data against disclosure, except where necessary to protect the public, or unless steps are taken to ensure that the data are protected against unfair commercial use.[53]

In many jurisdictions, including the USA or the EU, once a product has passed domestic drug regulatory approval, copies or generic versions of the same product do not have to submit additional clinical test data, but only have to demonstrate that their product is of the same biochemical composition as (that is, bioequivalent to) the originator product. The protection of test data (that is, data exclusivity) prevents drug regulatory authorities in one way or another from relying on such data for the approval of generic products for a limited amount of time. The pharmaceutical 'research-based industry' argues that the protection of data submitted for the registration of medicines is of fundamental importance. The rationale is that the manufacturer has invested, often heavily, in the research necessary to develop the relevant data,[54] and where patent law fails to provide protection (for example, because the active component was shortly to be off-patent, or because the drug was based on a combination of known substances used in a novel manner, which may not satisfy domestic patentability requirements), the protection of such data would provide the only barrier against a generic competitor rapidly producing and registering an exact copy of the drug. From a public health perspective, however, the early entry of generic competition is also considered an important policy objective, whose realization is facilitated by regulations that allow health authorities to rely on existing test data to approve subsequent applications for generic products (UNCTAD-ICTSD 2005: p. 538; Correa 2007: pp. 373–92). It is thus argued that patent protection is the adequate incentive for investments into the marketing of a pharmaceutical product, and that data exclusivity just adds another unnecessary and

---

of consumers in the United States to pharmaceutical imports. (See: (GovTrack.us, 2005). While the bill was never passed, after the US–Australia FTA and US–Morocco FTA, parallel importation was not included in the final text of any FTA thereafter. (Source: interview as part of thesis research, von Braun (2008).)

53 See Article 39.3.

54 It is argued that the estimated clinical costs per approved new drug exceed 50 per cent of its total development costs. See Meitinger (2005), p.123.

unjustified layer of protection that prolongs the entry of generic competition. From a systemic point of view, voices in the literature have criticized the protection of clinical test data through patent-like exclusive rights, despite the fact that a clinical data file is not the result of human ingenuity and inventiveness, but of time and money-consuming, repetitive actions, which should be encouraged through other legal regimes such as non-exclusive compensatory liability systems.[55]

The original intention of the main advocates of TRIPS in the Uruguay Round was a more clear-cut system of protection of test data than what was finally embraced in Article 39.3 of TRIPS. For example, in a submission made by the USA during the Uruguay Round negotiations in 1990, which was joined by the EC and Switzerland, it was proposed that:

> Contracting parties which require that trade secrets be submitted to carry out governmental functions, shall not use the trade secret for the commercial or competitive benefit of the government or of any person other than the right holder except with right holder's consent, on payment of the reasonable value of the use, or if a reasonable period of exclusive use is given to the right holder. (Cited by Watal 2001: p. 198)

However, as no agreement could be found among the negotiating parties, the final version of the TRIPS Agreement was deliberately less precise and in many respects rather ambiguous. It established instead that undisclosed information should be protected against unfair competition, leaving the appropriate implementation of this provision strategically vague. While an express provision for data exclusivity had originally been made in earlier versions of the TRIPS Agreement, these provisions were removed from the final text of the Agreement.[56] An exclusive protection of test data for at least five years from the date of approval of the pharmaceutical product was first introduced in FTAs in NAFTA and has been further elaborated and included in FTAs concluded by the USA with a number of developing countries. The EFTA countries, however, have recently followed a more flexible approach, allowing for the option to protect undisclosed data through exclusivity or compensation.[57]

---

[55] Jerome H. Reichman (2009) *Rethinking the Role of Clinical Trial Data in International Intellectual Property Laws: The Case for a Public Goods Approach*, Marquette Intellectual Property Law Review, 13 (1).

[56] See the Brussels Draft of the TRIPS Agreement, as quoted in UNCTAD-ICTSD (2005), p. 525; see also accompanying text on p. 526, ibid.

[57] For example, the agreement with the Republic of Korea provides: 'The Parties shall protect undisclosed information in accordance with Article 39 of the TRIPS Agreement. The Parties shall prevent applicants for marketing approval for pharmaceutical and agricultural chemical products from relying on

The US FTAs have introduced a new regime of data exclusivity, providing that once a firm has submitted original data on a pharmaceutical product, regulatory authorities shall not permit competing producers to rely on that data for a period of five years from the date of marketing approval (ten years in the case of agricultural chemical products).[58] This provision effectively requires generic producers to come up with their own test data, which very often is not economically feasible and/or may be considered unethical.[59] It thus provides the data originator with a further period of exclusivity. It is important to note that this exclusivity may apply to non-patented pharmaceutical or agrochemical products, thus creating a new form of monopoly not required by TRIPS (Abbott 2004: p. 7).[60]

The CAFTA-DR agreement, as well as those originally signed with Colombia, Panama and Peru, expressly maintains the possibility of requesting marketing approval at any time during the five-year period. Where the data originator requests domestic approval at the end of the five-year exclusivity period generated by his earlier request abroad, another term of protection of five years will be triggered, extending protection effectively to ten years (15 in the case of agrochemicals) (Correa 2006a: p. 89; Abbott 2004: p. 7). As discussed below, in the case of the revised FTAs signed by the USA with Colombia, Panama and Peru, respectively, important changes have been introduced to address these criticisms.

Linking drug approval to patent status

While the above observations may concern non-patented pharmaceutical and agrochemical products, most of the FTAs also contain an additional provision that can have an important impact with respect to patented pharmaceutical and agrochemical products. For instance, CAFTA-DR provides that:

---

undisclosed test or other undisclosed data, the origination of which involves a considerable effort, submitted by the first applicant to the competent authority for marketing approval for pharmaceutical and agricultural chemical products, utilizing new chemical entities, for an adequate number of years from the date of approval, except where approval is sought for original products. Any Party may instead allow in their national legislation applicants to rely on such data if the first applicant is adequately compensated'.

58 See, for example, Chapter 15, Article 15.10.1(a) of CAFTA.

59 See World Medical Association Declaration of Helsinki: http://www.wma.net/e/policy/b3.htm.

60 The same author observes that such exclusivity renders illegal the actual marketing of generic drugs produced under a compulsory or public non-commercial use licence (p. 8). This is so because the linkage requirement makes the validity of marketing approvals dependent on the authorization of the patent holder.

> Where a Party permits, as a condition of approving the marketing of a pharmaceutical product, persons, other than the person originally submitting safety or efficacy information, to rely on evidence or information concerning the safety and efficacy of a product that was previously approved, such as evidence of prior marketing approval in the Party or in another territory, that Party:
> (a) shall implement measures in its marketing approval process to prevent such other persons from marketing a product covered by a patent claiming the product or its approved use during the term of that patent, unless by consent or acquiescence of the patent owner; and
> (b) if the Party permits a third person to request marketing approval of a product during the term of a patent identified as claiming the product or its approved use, it shall provide that the patent owner be informed of such request and the identity of any such other person.[61]

In other words, the decision by regulatory authorities to grant marketing approval to third parties is subject to the acquiescence of the patent holder, thereby, linking the separate realms of drug regulation and patent law. Such a requirement, it has been argued, would effectively transform the regulatory agencies into patent enforcement authorities. Besides the difficulties created for regulatory authorities to determine the validity of patents, this provision has been interpreted as potentially precluding governments' options for using compulsory licences to increase the availability of low-priced pharmaceutical products (Abbott 2004: p. 8). Since marketing approval is independent of patent law, the third party authorized to produce a patented product under compulsory licence would arguably depend on the patentee's consent or acquiescence for the actual marketing of the product (UNCTAD-ICTSD 2005: p. 537). Chile, in its recently revised legislation, has used a liberal implementation of the linkage provision by clearly spelling out that the exclusivity of the data shall not be an obstacle in cases of compulsory licences, national emergencies and in cases when the data is based on a registry or authorization in a foreign country of more than one year.[62]

---

61 See Article 15.10.3(a), CAFTA-DR.

62 Under Article 91, Chile's Law 19039 on Industrial Property of 1991 as amended in January 2007, protection for undisclosed information will not be granted or continued in the following cases: (a) The data right holder has engaged in acts of anticompetitive behaviour; (b) for reasons of public health, national security, non-commercial public use, national emergency; (c) the pharmaceutical product is subject of a compulsory license; (d) the product has not been commercialized in Chile within 12 months from the date of registry or sanitary approval in the country; (e) the product has a registry or authorization in a foreign country of more than 12 months. (It should be noted that the text of the FTA with Chile is not identical to other FTAs (Roffe 2004).) The USA and the EFTA countries have challenged the treatment of this matter in the Chilean law. In the case of the USA,

Peru in its implementation of the FTA with the USA has resorted to a similar approach.[63]

Recent developments in US policies

The US Congressional elections of 2006 led to a remarkable change in domestic trade policy. Four bilateral trade agreements negotiated and signed by the Executive, respectively, with the Republic of Korea, Panama, Peru and Colombia were still subject to ratification by Congress at the time of the elections[64] (von Braun 2008). In early May 2007, Congressional leaders reached a compromise with the Administration on issues related to IP, labour standards and the environment with respect to three of the FTAs pending for ratification by Congress (Peru, Colombia, Panama). The texts of the FTAs negotiated with Colombia, Panama and Peru were subsequently amended and soon thereafter the Peruvian FTA was tabled in Congress and passed by both House and Senate.[65]

The original IP chapters of the FTAs with Colombia, Panama and Peru included similar provisions as those contained in the agreements already in force. With respect to IP and access to medicines, the new deal required changes in four areas, namely, patent extensions, data exclusivity, the patent-data protection linkage and reference to the Doha Declaration (Roffe and Vivas 2007).

Patent extensions In the revised version of the FTAs, each party 'may' extend the term of a patent for a pharmaceutical product to compensate for unreasonable delays in the patent – or marketing-approval process. In other words, the mandatory obligation to compensate for those delays laid out in the original negotiated version of the FTA, as in the case of already

---

it has prompted the USTR to place Chile on the Priority Watch List of its latest annual report (Roffe 2007).

63 See Article 4, Decreto Legislativo 1074 of 28 June 2008.

64 Also outstanding at that time was the continuation of the WTO Doha Development Round, as was the extension/renewal of the domestic Trade Promotion Authority that essentially allows the Executive to negotiate foreign trade agreements on behalf of Congress.

65 The FTA with Peru is expected to enter into force in February 2009. At the time of writing, the FTA with Korea had been stalled in Congress due to trade-related issues such as US beef imports into Korea. The FTAs with Panama and Colombia have not been tabled for a vote in Congress for reasons unrelated to trade issues. In the case of Panama, a senior government official is sought for criminal offences in the US; whereas in the case of Colombia, domestic human rights abuses against labour unionists have been used as a justification for essentially stalling the ratification process for the indefinite future.

concluded FTAs, is transformed into an option for the parties. The revised text gives parties the option to compensate for unreasonable delays in the issuance of a patent for a pharmaceutical product by restoring the patent term or patent rights. In all the above circumstances, however, the Parties need to make a best effort to process patent and marketing approval applications expeditiously with a view to avoiding unreasonable delays. It is important to note that this flexibility applies only to the case of pharmaceutical products. In the event of patents not related to pharmaceutical products, the patent extensions, as in the case of FTAs in force, remain mandatory.[66] In the case of Peru, the country exercised this option and pharmaceutical patents on products and processes are exempted from the provisions dealing with restoration terms for unjustifiable administrative delays.[67]

Data exclusivity In the case of Peru, for example, the changes introduced include the notion that the protection of undisclosed test or other data should not exceed 'a reasonable period of time'. The relevant provision clarifies that for this purpose, such a timeframe shall normally mean five years, taking into account the nature of the data and the degree of effort and expenditure required to produce the data. The provision further clarifies that Parties shall be allowed to implement abbreviated approval procedures for such products on the basis of bioequivalence or bioavailability studies.[68] The revised text of the Peru FTA is indeed much more flexible than its original negotiated version, which did not condition the five-year protection rule on the quality of the data and the economic investments made in producing them. Contrary to, for example, the CAFTA-DR, the revised text leaves room for a balanced domestic implementation of the norms, including, for example, a protection for less than five years when the origination of such data has not involved considerable efforts and expenditures.

In another important departure also related to data exclusivity, the text

---

66 'With respect to any pharmaceutical product that is covered by a patent, each Party may make available a restoration of the patent term or patent rights to compensate the patent owner for unreasonable curtailment of the effective patent term resulting from the marketing approval process related to the first commercial marketing of the product in that Party. Any restoration under this subparagraph shall confer all of the exclusive rights of a patent subject to the same limitations and exceptions applicable to the original patent' (Article 16.9.6(c), revised FTA with Peru).

67 See Peru, Decreto Legislativo 1075, Article 32 of 28 June 2008.

68 Article 16.10.2(b), Peru–USA FTA and implementing legislation (Decreto Legislativo 1072, Article 5).

of the revised Peru FTA provides that the reasonable period of exclusive use shall begin when the drug was first approved in the US (a so-called 'concurrent period'), provided that Peru grants the approval of the compound within six months of an application:

> Where a Party relies on a marketing approval granted by the other Party, and grants approval within six months of the filing of a complete application for marketing approval filed in the Party, the reasonable period of exclusive use of the data submitted in connection with obtaining the approval relied on shall begin with the date of the first marketing approval relied on. (Peru FTA, Article 16.10.2(c))

This new mechanism provides an incentive for rapid marketing approval in exchange for a period of protection that starts in the country where the drug was first approved, generating a shorter period of effective protection. This important change responds to criticisms addressed to the original version of the FTA, which allowed for a priority period of five years within which the innovator could claim exclusivity in the other country. Such a priority right could generate, as pointed out above in the case of CAFTA-DR, a de facto extension of the period of protection of up to ten years. As also noted, Chile in its FTA implementation legislation provides that the protection of data cannot be granted when the product has a registry or authorization in a foreign country of more than 12 months.

Linking drug approval to patent status As discussed above, another major controversial provision in existing FTAs is the obligation not to grant marketing approval to any third party prior to the expiration of the patent term without the consent or acquiescence of the patent owner. As noted, this has been seen as an unnecessary burden on sanitary authorities, as it would require them to determine whether a private right exists on a particular pharmaceutical product. In the case of Colombia, Panama and Peru, the amended FTAs make such 'linkage' optional, and in particular do not require that sanitary authorities withhold approval of a generic until they can certify that no patent would be violated if the generic were marketed.

Instead, the revised FTAs require Parties to provide procedures and remedies (judicial or administrative proceedings, including injunctions or equivalent effective provisional measures) for adjudicating expeditiously any patent infringement of validity or dispute that arises with respect to a product for which marketing approval is sought.[69] The revised texts

---

[69] 'Each Party shall provide: (a) procedures, such as judicial or administrative proceedings, and remedies, such as preliminary injunctions or equivalent provisional measures, for the expeditious adjudication of disputes concerning the

also require greater transparency in these processes, calling on parties to the FTA to make available: (a) an expeditious procedure to challenge the validity or applicability of the patent (so as to break the 'link', where applicable) and (b) effective rewards for a successful challenge to the validity or applicability of the patent.[70] In other words, the revised FTAs try to balance the rights of patent holders with opportunities for generic producers to challenge patented products that might prevent competing products from entering the market.

Integration of the Doha Declaration As stated above, most of the FTAs recently negotiated by the USA, including the original agreements with Peru, Colombia and Panama, contained side letters with reference to the health solution of Paragraph 6 of the Doha Declaration, which allows countries with insufficient or no manufacturing capacity to make effective use of compulsory licences. The FTAs revised by Congress, departing from the earlier ones, call on the parties, in the actual text of the FTAs and not in side letters, to affirm their commitments to the Declaration, particularly emphasizing that the provisions on data exclusivity should be subordinated to the right of a party to take measures to protect public health. The revised texts further oblige the parties to respect existing waivers granted by WTO Members regarding provisions of the TRIPS Agreement.[71] These changes put both the Doha Declaration and existing waivers at the same level as other provisions in the FTAs, thus facilitating pro-public health interpretation of the provisions on regulated products, as well as other sections of the FTA.

The above-mentioned developments suggest an interesting shift in policies towards IP in the USA. The revised FTAs provide clarifications on a number of ambiguous aspects of the FTAs and leave space for innovative implementation of the agreements. Moreover, the amended deals

---

Footnote 69 (*cont.*)
validity or infringement of a patent with respect to patent claims that cover an approved pharmaceutical product or its approved method of use; (b) a transparent system to provide notice to a patent holder that another person is seeking to market an approved pharmaceutical product during the term of a patent covering the product or its approved method of use; and (c) sufficient time and opportunity for a patent holder to seek, prior to the marketing of an allegedly infringing product, available remedies for an infringing product' (Peru, Article 16.10.3).

[70] According to the revised version of the FTA with Peru, a party may comply with this clause by providing a period of marketing exclusivity for the first applicant to successfully challenge the validity or applicability of the patent (footnote 18 of chapter 16 of the FTA).

[71] In the case of the FTA with Peru, see Article 16.13.

emphasize public health-related flexibilities much more clearly than did the original texts as negotiated by Peru, Panama and Colombia. It is important to note, however, that in spite of the integration of developing country public health objectives into the new FTA text, these changes were not brought about through the bargaining power of developing country negotiators in spite of the tireless efforts of their public health negotiators. Instead, they resulted from the continued work of national and international public health advocates, coupled with a handful of Members of the US Congress, that were able to link these revisions into a wider movement of trade policy change. It is likely also that without the momentum created by the labour and environment movement to design a new trade agenda for the USA, the IP chapter would not have been changed (von Braun 2008).

However, important questions remain open for debate as we advance in understanding of this new shift: how will the revised FTAs affect third parties? Can weaker partners such as those of CAFTA-DR request a renegotiation in line with changes made to Colombia, Peru and Panama under the influence of the US Congress? Can countries be exposed to unilateral sanctions by third countries (that is, non-parties to the FTAs in question) for non-compliance with the 'linkage' obligation, when in the recent agreements the linkage is no longer mandatory?

The protection of life forms and the treatment of traditional knowledge

TRIPS describes inventions that Members may exclude from patentability while, at the same time, specifically obliging them to protect micro-organisms and certain biotechnological processes:

> Members may also exclude from patentability . . . plants and animals other than micro-organisms, and essentially biological processes for the production of plants or animals other than non-biological and microbiological processes. However, Members shall provide for the protection of plant varieties either by patents or by an effective sui generis system or by any combination thereof. The provisions of this subparagraph shall be reviewed four years after the date of entry into force of the WTO Agreement. (Article 27.3 (b))

In the context of this ongoing review process, a number of developing countries have restated their discomfort with the implications of this provision, particularly reiterating the need to reconcile TRIPS with the relevant provisions of the Convention on Biological Diversity (CBD) of 1994, particularly with respect to the principles of prior informed consent and access and benefit sharing. The African Group in the WTO has consistently raised concerns about the implications of this provision of the Agreement on life forms. In their view, patents should not be granted on micro-organisms, on non-biological and microbiological processes for the production of plants and animals, because this 'is contrary to the fabric of their society and culture, and would want to invoke these exceptions in this regard'.[72]

Thus, TRIPS allows for the exclusion from patentability of 'plants and animals' in general. Consequently, Members may exclude plants as such (including transgenic plants), plant varieties (including hybrids), as well as plant cells, seeds and other plant materials. They may also exclude animals (including transgenic) and animal races.

In brief, TRIPS (Article 27.3 (b)) suggests that Members need to afford patent protection for the following: micro-organisms, non-biological processes and microbiological processes. Furthermore, Members need to provide protection to plant varieties either by patents, an effective sui-generis system or by any combination of the two. At the same time, TRIPS suggests that Members may exclude from patent protection: plants, animals, essentially biological processes for the production of plants or animals and plant varieties. With respect to plant varieties, the options are relatively clear. The reference to patents is straightforward, due to the detailed treatment of them in TRIPS. By contrast, the reference to an 'effective sui generis system' is not so obvious. It might suggest the breeder's rights regime, as established in the UPOV Convention, but the text very deliberately did not refer to UPOV. The possibility is open to combine the patent system with a breeders' rights regime, or to develop other 'effective sui-generis' forms of protection.[73]

The patentability of micro-organisms and microbiological processes may raise similar concerns as the patenting of research tools in the pharmaceutical area. Access to patented or otherwise protected biological material may be rendered more difficult, especially for stakeholders from developing countries who lack the financial means to pay licensing fees. In addition, products developed on the basis of biotechnology are often subject to various exclusive rights held by a multitude of IP owners. A good example is the development of 'Golden Rice', which utilized a variety of about 70 intellectual property rights and/or inventions belonging to 32 different companies and universities:

---

[72] 'Note by the WTO Secretariat. The relationship between the TRIPS Agreement and the Convention on Biological Diversity: Summary of issues raised and points made', IP/C/W/369/Rev.1, 9 March 2006, paragraphs 28–9.

[73] For a non-exclusive approach to the implementation of Article 27.3(b), TRIPS Agreement, see Reichman and Lewis (2005), suggesting the protection of traditional knowledge and its use to promote small-scale innovation through a compensatory liability regime. For national examples of implementation, see Dhar (2002), referring to Indian and Namibian legislation.

> To enable those who will acquire Golden Rice and/or its technology 'freedom to operate' (being a humanitarian product), the developers needed to obtain free licenses. Whilst one acknowledges that Golden Rice would possibly have not been developed that quickly if the patented inventions were not publicly available or kept secret, negotiating through this maze or 'thicket' of patents was tasking. In the case of Golden Rice, public pressure and the use of a private partner proved to be vital.[74]

FTAs: the UPOV approach and the patenting of life forms

As discussed earlier, in recent FTAs negotiated by the USA, EU and EFTA with a variety of developing countries, the 1991 Act of the UPOV Convention is listed as one of the international treaties that parties should subscribe to in the near future as the modality of protection for plant varieties. The TRIPS Agreement (Article 27.3.(b)), as suggested, obliges countries to prescribe protection of plant varieties but offers various options including an effective sui generis system of protection.

UPOV's plant breeders' rights regimes have been criticized on the grounds that they better respond to conditions prevailing in industrialized countries and thereby risk undermining the food security of communities in developing countries (UNCTAD-ICTSD 2003: p. 105). According to activists in the NGO community, this may occur as a result of:

> encouraging cultivation of a narrow range of genetically-uniform crops, including non-food cash crops, with the possible consequences that people's diets will become nutritionally poorer and crops will be more vulnerable to outbreaks of devastating diseases; limiting the freedom of farmers to acquire seeds they wish to plant without payment to breeders, and thereby impoverishing them further; restricting the free circulation of plant genetic resources, which is generally considered essential for the development of new plant varieties; increasing the market power of seed suppliers, pushing up the prices and enabling international firms to capture a larger segment of the profits from farming than poor farmers themselves. (Oxfam 2007: pp. 12–13)

UPOV provides a framework for the protection of plant varieties. The Convention was first signed in 1961 and revised in 1972, 1978 and 1991. It entered into force in 1968. It established the International Union for the Protection of New Varieties of Plants, based in Geneva and associated with WIPO. There are two versions of the Convention: UPOV 1978 and UPOV 1991. In both versions, the breeders' right may be subject to two exceptions: the 'breeders' exemption' and the 'farmers' privilege'. The rights of breeders both to use protected varieties as an initial source of variation for the creation of new varieties and to market these varieties

---

74 UNCTAD-WIPO-CBD Secretariat (2007), paragraph 139.

without authorization from the original breeder (the 'breeder exemption') is covered in both versions of the Convention. The FTAs oblige countries to opt for the 1991 version of UPOV, which is seen as less flexible and more stringent than its previous incarnations.

The two versions of the Convention differ in many respects. For example, the 1991 version states that the original breeder's right also extends to varieties that are essentially derived from the protected one. The intention is that follow-on breeders should not be able to acquire protection too easily for minor modifications of extant varieties. This provision is also intended to ensure that patent rights and breeders rights operate harmoniously. Another important difference between the two acts is that in the 1978 version, species eligible for plant breeder's rights cannot be patented, whereas in the 1991 version the possibility of double protection is permitted.

Further, in the 1978 version there is no reference to the right of farmers to re-sow seed harvested from protected varieties for their own use (often referred to as the 'farmers' privilege'). Thus countries that are members of the 1978 version are free, but not obliged, to uphold the farmers' privilege. In this respect, the 1991 version is more specific. Whereas the scope of the breeders' right includes production or reproduction and conditioning for the purpose of propagation, governments can use their discretion to decide whether to uphold farmers' rights. The Convention (Article 15) provides for an optional exception that allows parties 'within reasonable limits and subject to the safeguarding of the legitimate interests of the breeder, [to] restrict the breeder's right in relation to any variety in order to permit farmers to use for propagating purposes, on their own holdings, the product of the harvest which they have obtained by planting, on their own holdings, the protected variety or a[n essentially derived] variety'. This means that Parties under UPOV 1991 can continue to uphold the farmers' privilege as long as their national plant variety system provides for it. If the national legislation does not feature provisions on the farmers' privilege, this presumably means there is no such privilege and that farmers cannot re-sow harvested seed even on their own farms.

Finally, contrary to UPOV 1978, it is no longer possible for farmers under UPOV 1991 to sell protected varieties to third parties, without permission of the original breeder (Article 15.2 UPOV 1991) (UNCTAD-ICTSD 2003: pp. 52–4).

Countries party to FTAs signed with the USA undertake further commitments to make efforts to introduce legislation concerning the patenting of plants which is not, as we have seen, mandatory under TRIPS. For example, the FTA between Chile and the USA provides for a 'best endeavour' clause for both parties – meaning in practice for Chile – to undertake reasonable efforts, through a transparent and participatory process, to develop and propose legislation – within four years of the entry into force of the agreement – to provide patent protection for plants which are new, involve an inventive step, and are capable of industrial application.[75] In the CAFTA-DR Agreement, plants and animals may be excluded from patentability, but any party that does not provide patent protection for plants by the date of entry into force of the agreement shall undertake all reasonable efforts to make such patent protection available.[76] In addition, according to the same FTA, any party that provides patent protection for plants and animals as of, or after, the date of entry into force of the agreement shall maintain such protection.[77] This means a practical derogation of the TRIPS flexibility by 'locking-in' countries to maintain such protection without alteration. The same approach is followed in the most recently concluded FTAs with Colombia, Panama and Peru.[78] Contrary to this best endeavour clause, in the case of the FTA between the USA and Morocco, the parties assume the obligation to grant patents to inventions on animals and plants.[79]

Revocation of patents and disclosure requirements

Another standard provision in US FTAs that goes beyond TRIPS is that patents can only be revoked or cancelled on grounds that would have justified a refusal to grant the patent initially. Apparently, then, the only causes for revocation or cancellation of a patent would be that the patent was not new, did not entail an inventive step or was not industrially applicable. FTAs such as those negotiated with CAFTA-DR and Peru add other considerations for revocation, such as fraud, inequitable conduct or misrepresentation.[80]

A related question might arise as to whether parties may incorporate substantial requirements at the domestic level on the disclosure of origin of genetic resources and associated traditional knowledge (TK). The FTAs, while being a departure from the TRIPS Agreement, are built on

---

75 Chile–USA, Article 17.9.2.
76 CAFTA-DR, Article 15.9.2.
77 Ibid.
78 Peru–USA, Article 16.9.2.
79 Morocco–USA, Article 15.9.2.
80 'Without prejudice to Article 5.A (3) of the Paris Convention, each Party shall provide that a patent may be revoked or nullified only on grounds that would have justified a refusal to grant the patent according to its laws. However, a Party may also provide that fraud, misrepresentation, or inequitable conduct may be the basis for revoking, nullifying, or holding a patent unenforceable' (Peru, Article 16.9.4).

the latter main principles that do not limit Members to place certain conditions on the disclosure of inventions. As such, the disclosure of origin at the domestic level is, in principle, TRIPS compliant. Indeed, the Swiss government has amended its patent law precisely to include such a requirement.[81] Oxfam has expressed the view that in the FTAs with CAFTA-DR, Peru and Colombia, 'governments will no longer be able to reject a patent application because a firm fails to indicate the origin of a plant or show proof of consent for its use from a local community' (Oxfam 2007: p. 14). This assertion finds its basis in two provisions of the FTAs. The two related provisions found in the FTA with Peru state:

> Each Party shall provide that a disclosure of a claimed invention shall be considered to be sufficiently clear and complete if it provides information that allows the invention to be carried out by a person skilled in the art, without undue experimentation, as of the filing date and may require the applicant to indicate the best mode for carrying out the invention known to the inventor as of the filing date (16.9.9).
>
> With the aim of ensuring that the claimed invention is sufficiently described, each Party shall provide that a claimed invention is sufficiently supported by its disclosure if the disclosure reasonably conveys to a person skilled in the art that the applicant was in possession of the claimed invention as of the filing date (16.9.10).

The extent to which these FTA provisions would inhibit the possibility of introducing disclosure requirements at the domestic level remains a matter of interpretation. But if that were their effect, as Oxfam suggests, there would be large political ramifications, especially for a country like Peru that has been one of the main proponents of amending TRIPS to accommodate a disclosure requirement of origin to combat biopiracy and the misappropriation of TK and finally make TRIPS fully consistent with CBD.[82]

Side letters on the protection of traditional knowledge and biodiversity

Side letters have been included in FTAs negotiated by the USA with Colombia[83] and Peru,[84] respectively, recognizing 'the potential contribu-

---

[81] See Article 49 a II of the Swiss Patent Act as entered into force on 1 July 2008 (French language version available at http://www.admin.ch/ch/f/rs/232_14/).

[82] See *Bridges Weekly* (2008), 'Where does TRIPS Go from Here?', 12 (27), 7 August.

[83] See USTR at http://www.ustr.gov/assets/Trade_Agreements/Bilateral/Colombia_FTA/Final_Text/asset_upload_file953_10182.pdf.

[84] See http://www.ustr.gov/assets/Trade_Agreements/Bilateral/Peru_TPA/Final_Texts/asset_upload_file719_9535.pdf.

tion of traditional knowledge and biodiversity to cultural, economic, and social development'. The side letters reaffirm the importance of obtaining prior informed consent and the equitable sharing of benefits as provided in the CBD even if the USA is not a party to the latter Convention. The parties also recognize the importance of promoting quality patent examination to ensure the conditions of patentability are satisfied. Furthermore, the side letters acknowledge the need for best endeavours to seek ways to share information that may have a bearing on the patentability of inventions based on traditional knowledge or genetic resources, by providing: 'publicly accessible databases that contain relevant information; and an opportunity to cite, in writing, to the appropriate examining authority prior art that may have a bearing on patentability'.

The side letters on biodiversity were at a point in time highlighted by the negotiators as constituting a major success in the negotiating process by receiving from the USA, for the first time, a formal recognition of the importance of preserving biodiversity and respecting TK. This apparent success responded to many criticisms made by civil society groups to the FTA negotiations and the official claim made by Colombia and Peru that if concessions were to be made on IP, positive commitments should be made in exchange on biodiversity and TK. In the case of Peru, this was particularly important, because, as outlined above, the country has been an active advocate of the reform of TRIPS by incorporating a new Article 29*bis* in the Agreement. However, the side letters underline that

> access to genetic resources or traditional knowledge, as well as the equitable sharing of benefits that may result from use of those resources or that knowledge, can be adequately addressed through contracts that reflect mutually agreed terms between user and providers.

As a result, the side letters reaffirm a position that the USA has taken in the related multilateral fora on this issue, namely to favour a contract-based approach to the protection of TK and genetic resources instead of relevant national law or international agreements. In this sense, critics have questioned the merits of this kind of side agreement (von Braun 2008).

This brief examination of the TRIPS-plus provisions in FTAs on the relationship between IP and the protection of life forms and the treatment of genetic resources and traditional knowledge suggests that the FTAs sponsored by the USA might prejudge the outcome of current multilateral processes, particularly in WTO, on how to deal with the proper implementation of Article 27.3(b). As examined, the FTAs take positions on issues still under consideration in WTO as well as in WIPO in the deliberations of its Intergovernmental Committee on Intellectual Property and Genetic Resources, Traditional Knowledge and Folklore (IGC).

The EU

Apart from the common view with respect to adherence to UPOV 1991, the EU appears to follow a different approach in some of the above matters. In its current negotiations on EPAs with regional groupings of the ACP countries it has proposed to make reference to the compatibility between TRIPS and the CBD. According to a proposal that surfaced at the end of 2006, it underlines 'the importance of acceding to the CBD and agree that, in line with Article 46.2 of the Cotonou Agreement, the patent provisions of this Title and the CBD shall be implemented in a mutually supportive way'.[85] The issue is closely related to outstanding discussions in the WTO on the relation between the TRIPS Agreement and the CBD, and more specifically on whether there is a conflict between the two treaties or whether they can be interpreted in a mutually supportive way. The EU has also incorporated in its proposals a direct reference to the CBD principle:

> Subject to their national legislation the Parties respect, preserve and maintain knowledge, innovations and practices of indigenous and local communities embodying traditional lifestyles relevant for the conservation and sustainable use of biological diversity and promote their wider application with the approval and involvement of the holders of such knowledge, innovations and practices and encourage the equitable sharing of the benefits arising from the utilization of such knowledge, innovations and practices.[86]

The FTAs and the issue of circumvention of technological measures: their potential impact on access to knowledge

As noted, the FTAs deepen the process of harmonization started in TRIPS and therefore makes provisions more stringent and precise compared to the latter Agreement. This is particularly relevant in the field of copyright and related rights, where the FTAs provide for strict rules against the circumvention of technological protection measures (TPMs) used by authors, performers and the producers of phonograms to protect their works, performances and phonograms protected by copyright and related rights. This is also the case with respect to adequate and effective legal remedies to protect rights management information.[87]

---

[85] See proposal to CARIFORUM countries at http://www.bilaterals.org/IMG/doc/EC_non-paper_on_IPRs_text_for_EPA.doc.

[86] Ibid.

[87] According to the FTA with Peru, rights management information means:

The provisions on TPMs go beyond the WIPO Internet treaties of 1996 (the WIPO Copyright Treaty and the WIPO Performances and Phonograms Treaty), which state only that parties 'shall provide adequate legal protection and effective legal remedies' against the circumvention of TPMs,[88] leaving it to each party to decide the way in which it will implement the provisions and whether it will apply civil and/or criminal sanctions to infringers. It should be noted that the WIPO Internet treaties are not incorporated in the TRIPS system and by themselves they are already a manifestation of a multilateral effort to go beyond the minimum requirements of TRIPS.

The FTAs, in general, contain detailed rules aimed at providing adequate legal protection and effective legal remedies to fight against the circumvention of effective technological measures.[89] In a common provision of the CAFTA-DR Agreement – to be found in all FTAs signed with the USA – parties are committed to provide that any person who:

> (i) circumvents without authority any effective technological measure that controls access to a protected work, performance, phonogram or other subject matter;
> (ii) manufactures, imports, distributes, offers to the public, provides, or otherwise traffic in devices, products, or components, or offers to the public or provides services, that:
> are promoted, advertised, or marketed for the purpose of circumvention of any effective technological measure; or
> have only a limited commercially significant purpose or use other than to circumvent any effective technological measure; or
> are primarily designed, produced, or performed for the purpose of enabling or facilitating the circumvention of any effective technological measure,
> shall be liable . . . Each Party shall provide for criminal procedures and penalties to be applied when any person, other than a non-profit library, archive, educational institution, or public non-commercial broadcasting entity, is found

---

(i) information that identifies a work, performance, or phonogram; the author of the work, the performer of the performance, or the producer of the phonogram; or the owner of any right in the work, performance, or phonogram; (ii) information about the terms and conditions of the use of the work, performance, or phonogram; or (iii) any numbers or codes that represent such information, when any of these items is attached to a copy of the work, performance, or phonogram or appears in connection with the communication or making available of a work, performance, or phonogram, to the public (Article 16.7.5(c)).

[88] WCT, Article 11; WPPT, Article 18.

[89] 'Effective technological measure means any technology, device, or component that, in the normal course of its operation, controls access to a work, performance, phonogram, or any other protected material, or that protects any copyright or any rights related to copyright, and cannot, in the usual case, be circumvented accidentally' (Article 17.7.5(f), US–Chile FTA).

> to have engaged wilfully and for purposes of commercial advantage or private financial gain in any of the foregoing activities. (Article 15.5.7(a))

The terminology of the TPM provisions found in the FTAs draws from the controversial US Digital Millennium Copyright Act (DMCA),[90] which was 'nominally intended to bring US law into compliance with the 1996 WIPO Treaties on copyright and the Internet, but in fact went well beyond what those treaties required' (Lemley et al. 2000: p. 89). These strong provisions make it a civil and criminal offence to tamper with embedded anti-piracy measures that control access to works and phonograms. They also provide for civil liability, and, when done wilfully and for prohibited commercial purposes, criminal liability for the manufacture, import, distribution, sale or rental of devices, products or components that serve the purpose of circumventing TPMs that control access and the exclusive rights in a work or phonogram.[91]

Critics of the TPM provisions of the DMCA argue that they impede lawful uses of works, such as making a copy of a music CD to listen to on a computer, making a backup copy of a computer program or copying small parts of a DVD movie for the purpose of teaching or criticism. TPMs have also been used to bar the manufacture of competing products, to suppress speech, to limit the first sale doctrine and to fragment markets, such as through regional codes on DVDs.[92] Moreover, the use of TPMs restricts access to works that have already fallen into the public domain. The incidence of these provisions in FTAs has been criticized precisely for limiting access to information technology:

> . . . a series of bilateral trade agreements negotiated by the USA have included DMCA like provisions, and thus made these inordinately high standards a de facto model for global implementation of the WCT [WIPO Copyright Treaty]. The combined effect of private law mechanisms such as torts and contract law, and public law regulation through copyright and other specialized regimes like the DMCA, will lead inevitably to increased difficulty in access to content. In a situation where access to hardware is already an important hindrance to developing countries, adding another layer of impediments, and inevitably raising costs, is problematic for the interests of developing countries in utilizing information technology. (Okediji 2004: p. 24)

---

90 USC. Title 17 § 1201.

91 'The DMCA was a bit of law intended to back up the protection of [this] code designed to protect copyrighted material. It was, we could say, *legal code* intended to buttress *software code* which itself was intended to support the *legal code of copyright*.' Lessig (2004).

92 Electronic Frontier Foundation, Unintended Consequences: Seven Years under the DMCA, April 2006. See http://www.eff.org/IP/DMCA/?f=unintended_consequences.html#Section5.

In the case of the FTAs, limited exemptions are permitted. They include in most cases, activities carried out by government employees, agents, or contractors for law enforcement, intelligence, national defence, essential security, or similar governmental purposes.[93]

In order to overcome some of the difficulties posed by the FTAs to the legitimate use of traditional copyright exceptions and fair use norms, a number of proposals have been advanced in the literature, such as the development of 'smart DRM' (digital rights management) technologies with the inbuilt capacity to recognize and accommodate traditional copyright exceptions, and the negotiation of an international agreement restricting the use of DRMs in cases where digital objects carry a high proportion of public interest-relevant information (Jaszi 2004). Another proposal focuses on remedial action to be taken by domestic courts when dealing with anti-circumvention provisions. Depending on the domestic design of anti-circumvention regimes, courts should, according to this suggestion, enable information users to notify copyright owners of their intent to make public good uses of technologically protected copyrighted works, triggering the rights owners' responsibility to take down the TPMs or otherwise make lawful uses possible (Reichman, Dinwoodie and Samuelson 2007).

FTAs and the enforcement of IP and the settlement of disputes

The US approach

In general, the enforcement provisions of the FTAs negotiated with the USA follow the same structure as the TRIPS Agreement. Accordingly, they contain provisions dealing with General Obligations; Civil and Administrative Procedures; Provisional Measures; Border Measures; and Criminal Procedures. For the USA,[94] probably the most important achievement in this area has been to make mandatory many of the discretionary remedies included under TRIPS. An important novelty of the FTAs, as far as TRIPS and the WIPO Internet Treaties are concerned, is that they provide for 'Limitations on Liability of Internet Service Providers'.

Inspired by TRIPS, the FTAs provide that there is no need to create a special enforcement system for IPRs, distinct from that existent for law enforcement in general. Nor is there an obligation to assign special

---

[93] For example, see FTA with Morocco (Article 15.5.9 (b)) and CAFTA-DR (article 15.5.8 (b)).

[94] Note that the IFAC-3 Chile Report (2003) states (p. 17) that the agreement makes some 'significant advances' towards deterring further infringements, and clarifies and builds upon existing TRIPS standards.

resources for the enforcement of IPRs, different from that for the law in general, but this shall not excuse a party from compliance with the provisions on enforcement of the FTA,[95] which by itself already constitutes a TRIPS-plus standard.

Among the general provisions on enforcement, FTAs provide for one important legal copyright presumption:

> In civil, administrative, and criminal proceedings involving copyright or related rights, each Party shall provide that:
> [. . .]
> It shall be presumed, in the absence of proof to the contrary, that the copyright or related right subsists in such subject matter. (CAFTA-DR, Article 15.11.5 (b))

This provision shifts the balance between copyright and the public domain in the sense that everything should be considered protected (copyrighted), except for subject matter that has evidently fallen into the public domain. In other words, the burden of proof of demonstrating that a work is not protected falls on the general public that uses original works and not on the author. Thus, under this provision the burden of proof regarding infringement or lack of infringement is reversed, falling on the defendant. In a similar provision in the FTA with Chile, parties are, however, free to provide that the presumption will only be valid on two conditions: that the work appears on its face to be original and that it bears a publication date not more than 70 years prior to the date of the alleged infringement.[96] The 70 years from publication term is the equivalent to the term of protection granted to legal persons.

The FTAs further provide (Article 17.11.8(a) in the case of Chile) that damages should be paid by the infringer to compensate for the injuries suffered by the right holder, without qualifying the nature of the infringement. The equivalent provision in the TRIPS Agreement[97] limits damages to a contravention of the rights by an infringer who 'knowingly, or with reasonable grounds to know, engaged in infringing activity'. Therefore, innocent infringement according to TRIPS may be excluded; however, it is not apparent whether that possibility is open in the FTAs.

As far as border measures are concerned, the FTAs again go beyond TRIPS, particularly in one aspect. The latter Agreement provides for border measures, including ex officio actions, only for the importation of

---

[95] See last sentence of Article 17.11.2(b) FTA with Chile and Article 16.11.4, FTA with Peru.

[96] Chile–USA, Article 17.11.6(b).

[97] Article 45.1, TRIPS.

counterfeit trademarks or pirated goods. The application of border measures to goods being exported and to goods in transit[98] is optional. The FTAs are again TRIPS-plus in the sense that they provide for ex officio measures for goods being imported, as well as for those destined for export or moving in transit.[99]

The FTAs expand the provisions in TRIPS on criminal measures. According to the latter, for example, criminal measures apply to cases of wilful trademark counterfeiting or copyright piracy on a commercial scale. The FTAs go beyond TRIPS in that they broaden the scope of what is considered a wilful infringement on a commercial scale:

> Each Party shall provide for criminal procedures and penalties to be applied at least in cases of willful trademark counterfeiting or copyright or related rights piracy on a commercial scale. Willful copyright or related rights piracy on a commercial scale includes:
> significant willful copyright or related rights infringements that have no direct or indirect motivation of financial gain;
> willful infringements for purposes of commercial advantage or private financial gain.
> Each Party shall treat willful importation or exportation of counterfeit or pirated goods as unlawful activities subject to criminal penalties to the same extent as the trafficking or distribution of such goods in domestic commerce. (FTA with Peru, Article 16.11.26)

This obligation disregards the quantitative 'commercial scale' requirement in TRIPS and replaces it with the notion of a 'commercial advantage or financial gain' element, which focuses more on the purpose of the infringement, even if it is not made at a commercial scale.

Other cases of provisions that go beyond TRIPS in the FTAs related to criminal procedures provide for detailed rules on seizure, forfeiture and destruction of infringing goods and elements used in the infringements. Finally, the FTAs provide that in cases of copyright piracy and trademark counterfeiting, the appropriate authorities could exercise legal action ex officio without the need for a formal complaint.[100]

As pointed out, the FTAs include specific rules on liability of and limitation of the liability of services providers (ISPs) for infringing content that is transmitted or stored in their networks when they perform certain functions, such as hosting, caching or linking.[101]

---

98 Footnote 13,TRIPS.

99 See Article 16.11.23, FTA with Peru.

100 Ditto, Article 16.11.11.

101 See, for example, Article 17.11.29 (US–Australia FTA), Article 16.9.22 (US–Singapore FTA) and Article 15.11.27, CAFTA.

Finally, with respect to the settlement of disputes mechanism, the FTAs allow the parties to choose the forum in which a dispute should be settled when a matter arises under the FTAs or under another trade agreement (that is, the WTO) to which they are parties. The complaining party has the right to choose the forum. In that case, the selected forum shall be used to the exclusion of the others.

The expansive nature of the FTAs' settlement of disputes mechanism include the possibility of the parties bringing cases related to: (a) the avoidance or settlement of all disputes between the parties regarding the interpretation or application of the Agreement; (b) whenever a party considers that a measure adopted by the other party is inconsistent with the obligations contained in the FTA or the party has failed to carry out its obligations; and (c) whenever a party considers that a measure of the other party causes nullification or impairment.[102]

Thus, the FTAs allow the parties to bring not only cases that address inconsistencies with the obligations of the parties, but also cases described in the WTO system as non-violation complaint situations.[103] Affected parties bringing non-violation cases might eventually argue in the case of IP that certain public policies restricting market access of protected products deprive rights holders of certain expectations arising from the FTAs' substantive rules. For example, the recourse to price controls, particularly in the area of pharmaceutical products, could be considered as impairing marketing expectations on the part of foreign patent holders. Also, the use by governments of flexibilities such as the issue of a compulsory licence or even the narrow design of patentability criteria might become the target of non-violation complaints. This could be extended, in theory, to public policy choices pursued through internal taxes, packaging and labelling requirements, consumer protection rules and environmental standards that might be perceived as causing nullification or impairment.

In the case of TRIPS and in the current state of play in WTO, non-violation complaints enjoy a virtual moratorium in the sense that they are not fully operational.[104] The FTAs, as suggested, in a clear manifestation of their TRIPS-plus nature make operational this type of situation in the context of their settlement of disputes mechanisms.

---

102 For a more detailed discussion of non-violation complaints under the Chile–USA FTA, see Roffe (2004), pp. 47–8.

103 See UNCTAD-ICTSD (2005), p. 680.

104 Ibid., pp. 673–6, with an overview of various interpretations.

The EU approach

While the above observations apply to FTAs signed with the USA, it is important to note that the EU has also recently stepped up bilateral efforts to strengthen IP enforcement in third country trading partners. In the context of its negotiations with the ACP states on follow-up agreements ('European Partnership Agreements', EPAs) to the Cotonou Agreement, the EU has made a number of proposals related to new provisions on IPRs in the ACP region. Among these, the draft EPA text for the Economic Community of West African States (ECOWAS) countries contains some detailed provisions on IP, including on enforcement.

Overall, concern has been voiced regarding a 'one-size-fits-all' approach by the EU's EPA/ECOWAS proposals related to enforcement, without due regard to different levels of development of partner countries. These have been characterized as triggering a number of challenges for the affected developing countries, namely: loss of flexibility to determine appropriate methods of implementation in light of its own legal practice and socio-economic imperatives; a disconnect between the object and purpose of the Cotonou Agreement and the proposed provisions; lack of safeguards and balancing mechanisms to protect the rights and freedoms of third parties, including abuse of procedures; creation of liability for intermediaries; far-reaching and disproportional evidence-gathering capabilities; permitting damages based on the consideration of extraneous factors; expansion of IPR enforcement to free trade zones and specific targeting of goods for re-export that are not intended to enter into the channels of trade of the country (Musungu 2008).

Concluding observations

Our examination of trends related to the minimum standards of protection in TRIPS as exemplified by the recently concluded FTAs call for the following general observations.

The public domain

Historically, IP systems have been constructed around the need for public policies in terms of exclusive rights to secure and reward innovators and creators for their contributions to society. Society prospers, culturally and economically, through innovation and the creation of new ideas.[105]

---

[105] This concept is well expressed in the Constitution of the United States: 'The Congress shall have the power to promote the Progress of Science and useful Arts, by securing for limited Times to Authors and Inventors the exclusive Right to their respective Writings and Discoveries'. US Constitution, Article 1, Section 8, Clause 8.

Implicit in this conception is that the exclusive rights granted to authors and innovators should be premised on encouraging future authors and innovators to use those contributions to further technological and cultural progress (Jaszi 2004: pp. 2, 3). Thus, the dissemination of knowledge has been at the heart of the IP system. This was well captured in the TRIPS Agreement as part of its objectives and principles:

> The protection and enforcement of intellectual property rights should contribute to the promotion of technological innovation and to the transfer and dissemination of technology, to the mutual advantage of producers and users of technological knowledge and in a manner conducive to social and economic welfare, and to a balance of rights and obligations. (Article 7)

Accordingly, the IP system should contribute to the dissemination of knowledge and to improved forms of transfer of technology. Access and dissemination of knowledge could thus be considered as the quid pro quo in exchange for monopoly rights. However, one could question whether the bargain between society at large (benefiting from the knowledge produced and disseminated by IP) and the right holders (extracting rents from their time-limited monopoly) is indeed being promoted by FTA initiatives.

Society is highly dependent on the dissemination of knowledge goods. For example, the activities of researchers, follow-on entrepreneurs, libraries, educational institutions, publishers and the media rely heavily on a robust public domain and on the delimitation of the boundaries of exclusive property rights through the establishment of exceptions and limitations to those rights. In this respect, overprotection as implied in the FTAs may reduce the scope of the public domain. For example, limiting the use of exceptions and limitations, the expansion of means to monitor and the extensive use of digital technological protection measures (TPMs), although useful to protect works, may also have unintended consequences. It has thus been argued that the proliferation of exclusive rights could raise fundamental roadblocks for the national and global provision of public goods, including scientific research, education, health care, biodiversity and environmental protection (Maskus and Reichman 2004: p. 7).

One important assumption of the IP system is that once the exclusive temporal rights of authors and inventors expired, they fall into the public domain. The process of expanding these rights and the continuing extension of their duration, either by the unilateral action of states or under the influence of the FTAs, beyond the minimum required by TRIPS, could have adverse effects on the public domain and on follow-on innovation.

Additionally, the system is constructed on the premise that certain things are not protected because the burden on society would be too heavy and general access to the respective subject matter should be provided at all times. The boundaries of protection are defined by the scope of protection, protected subject matter and rights granted. For example, according to TRIPS in the case of copyright, the scope 'shall extend to expressions and not to ideas, procedures, methods of operation or mathematical concepts as such'.[106] In the case of patents, scientific theories or discoveries are ineligible for protection in many countries, unless they are used in the context of a concrete technical application. Even then, certain requirements of novelty, inventive step, and industrial applicability must be fulfilled in order to benefit from the minimum statutory 20 years of protection. In the case of trademarks, certain words may never be protected (generic terms), while descriptive terms may not be protected, unless a secondary meaning can be proven. In the case of the protection of undisclosed information, TRIPS provides for the protection against unfair commercial use of investments made on test data required for approving the marketing of pharmaceutical and agricultural chemical products, but only if a 'considerable effort' has been made (Roffe and Santa Cruz 2006).

In brief, despite its importance for technological innovation and cultural progress, the public domain has been seriously affected by an expansion of private rights, both under the TRIPS Agreement and even more so under the new generation of FTAs. It has been observed in the literature that a fundamental tension is emerging 'between the public purposes of intellectual property and the tendency toward the commodification (and attendant rationing) of more and more forms of basic information.' (Jaszi 2004: p.2). This tendency toward commodification has upset the balance between private rights and the free dissemination of knowledge.

Standardization of IP disciplines

The TRIPS Agreement minimum standards have resulted in a more uniform treatment of IPR principles, such as minimum terms of protection, eligibility criteria for protection, and the obligation to make product patents available to all fields of technology. It is especially this latter obligation, coupled with strengthened modes of enforcement as prescribed in FTAs, which makes the reverse engineering of patented products more difficult. Reverse engineering has been a common form of imitating and upgrading technological skills in both developed and developing countries. Firms employed this technique to further industrialization by legitimately copying products and processes. In the pre-TRIPS era, when the IP system was laxer and more flexible, reverse engineering was easier to

---

106 TRIPS, Article 9.2.

achieve (Kim 2003). In addition, the obligation to make product patents available to all fields of technology terminates some developing countries' practice of excluding pharmaceutical products from patent protection, as provided under the Indian patent law until 2005 (and by many OECD countries well into the 1970s) (UNCTAD-ICTSD 2003).

Another important feature brought about by the standardization of IP rules under TRIPS and the FTAs is the expanded description of the exclusive rights conferred by IPRs. For example, in the case of patents they include the right to prevent third parties, who do not have the right holder's consent, from the acts of: making, using, offering for sale, selling, or importing for these purposes, the product (in the case of a product patent) or the product obtained directly by a patented process, as well as the use of that process (in the case of a process patent). The Agreement adds that the term of protection shall not end before the expiration of a period of 20 years counted from the filing date. As we have examined, in recent FTAs, the 20-year term may be extended further to take into account delays in the administrative grant of a patent or delays resulting from the marketing approval process of a pharmaceutical product or an agrochemical product.

Creation of new exclusive rights, expansion of protectable subject matters, the patentability criteria, and stricter IP enforcement mechanisms

The new IP architecture as expressed under the TRIPS Agreement and its FTAs' follow-up has resulted in the creation of new exclusive rights, such as the exclusive protection of agrochemical and pharmaceutical test data, exclusive rights of plant breeders, copyright for performers, as well as Internet-based rights to prevent the circumvention of technological protection measures.

The TRIPS Agreement makes copyright protection available to computer programs, and subjects micro-organisms to patent protection. FTAs, in general, include best endeavour commitments to make patent protection available to animals and plants. This expansion of the IP system to new frontiers, covering new subject matter, could again encroach upon the public domain, that is, technologies or knowledge not covered by IPRs or whose protection has expired and which is therefore available to interested parties, thus making access and dissemination of knowledge more difficult, and, in other cases, raising concerns about food security and biodiversity.

As suggested, FTAs also lead to the weakening of the patentability criteria, especially with respect to the third criterion, namely that of 'industrial application'. The importance of a balanced definition of 'industrial application' for the success of a country's industrial policy, in particular for developing countries, has been widely discussed among innovation scholars

(Commission on Intellectual Property Rights, 2002: chapter 6). As Rebecca Eisenberg writes, the industrial application criterion should be seen as '. . . a timing device, helping to identify when an invention is ripe for patent protection' (as quoted in FTC 2003: p. 199). While the TRIPS Agreement allows Member States to apply a strict interpretation of this requirement, that is, only to allow patent protection for products and processes that have advanced sufficiently in the R&D process to have in and of themselves market value, some FTAs oblige signatory parties to adapt to the US interpretation of the criteria, which only has to be 'useful'. While this concept has recently been restricted in its application under US patent law, developing countries may not necessarily follow such new interpretation, but instead approve the patenting of research tools or products at early development stages, thus potentially complicating downstream R&D.

Furthermore, as noted in this chapter, in some of the FTAs, parties are obliged to allow for 'new use', or second use patents,[107] which, depending on the national interpretation of 'novelty' and 'inventive step', could also lead to a new application of such criteria. TRIPS does not oblige Member States to protect the new application of existing products, as a result of which some Member States specifically exclude them from patent protection. Others may allow for 'new use' patents but only in cases where their application is truly 'novel' and 'inventive' to anybody skilled in the art. Integrating the protection of 'new uses' in the FTA might prevent Member States from making such policy choices.

Lowering the standards of patentability works against the recommendations for developing countries of the Commission on Intellectual Property Rights:

> [t]he underlying principle should be to aim for strict standards of patentability and narrow scope of allowed claims, with the objective of: limiting the scope of subject matter that can be patented; applying standards such that only patents which meet strict requirements for patentability are granted and that the breadth of each patent is commensurate with the inventive contribution and the disclosure made; facilitating competition by restricting the ability of the patentees to prohibit others from building on or designing around patented inventions; providing extensive safeguards to ensure that patent rights are not exploited inappropriately. (Commission on Intellectual Property Rights, 2002: p. 21)

Finally, as underlined in this chapter, the FTAs expand in an important manner what was already achieved in the TRIPS Agreement with respect to enforcement mechanisms. This is particularly the case of the FTAs

---

[107] Such as in the cases of the US FTAs with Australia, Bahrain, and Morocco.

sponsored by the USA, but, as pointed out, it is also the recent tendency of the EU in their new generation of FTAs. The expanded treatment of enforcement issues and settlement of disputes, such as, for example, the applicability of non-violation and situation complaints to IP-related disputes, is another form of diluting the core balance of the system.

Conclusion

Overall, this chapter has shown that with respect to the policy areas reviewed, the TRIPS Agreement and especially the FTAs have shifted the balance in favour of private rights holders. Their impact in reducing access to essential inventions, such as medicines or educational material, narrowing down the public domain of essential information needed for the development of technological capacities, creative works, and further reducing a pro-competitive environment should be a source of concern to policy makers, especially, but not only, in developing countries. To maintain some of the above-mentioned policy spaces, policy makers need to make use of the flexibilities that have remained in place, for example through the application of strict patentability criteria or the innovative and constructive implementation of FTAs in national laws. Proposals in the literature illustrate the potential to accommodate public interest concerns even within the most delicate legislative framework. Policy makers not only in developing countries should seek to identify common interest denominators, based on the understanding that for the promotion of innovation, there is an optimal level of IP protection, beyond which ever-increasing exclusive rights will prove counterproductive to society at large.[108]

It is the view of the authors that the FTAs pose major challenges to developing countries, further compounded by pressure exercised in the implementation process with a view to maximizing the standards established in those agreements. Nevertheless, it is also our view that the FTAs should be taken as an opportunity to modernize the domestic IP architecture by investing strongly in institutions and human resources in order to build systems of protection and enforcement around appropriate checks and balances that serve domestic policy objectives. Indeed, examples of the latter can be found particularly in those developed countries promoting strong IP chapters in FTAs. Developing countries should be encouraged and assisted in establishing a balanced system of protection and enforcement at the national level that takes into account those checks and balances.

---

[108] See, for example, the Swiss Patent Office's new approach to the innovation–protection interface, as illustrated by Thumm (2006).

References

Abbott, Frederick M. (2004), 'The Doha Declaration on the TRIPS Agreement and Public Health and the Contradictory Trend in Bilateral and Regional Free Trade Agreements', QUNO Occasional Paper 14, QUNO, Geneva, available at: http://www.quno.org/geneva/pdf/economic/Occasional/TRIPS-Public-Health-FTAs.pdf.

Abbott, Frederick M (2005), 'The WTO Medicines Decision: The Political Economy of World Pharmaceutical Trade and the Protection of Public Health', *American Journal of International Law*, 99: 317–58.

Abbott, Frederick M. (2006), 'Intellectual Property Provisions of Bilateral and Regional Trade Agreements of the United States in Light of U.S. Federal Law', UNCTAD-ICTSD Issue Paper no.12, Geneva, available at: http://www.iprsonline.org/resources/docs/Abbott%20-%20US%20bilateral%20and%20regional%20trade%20agreements%20-%20Blue%2012.pdf.

Abbott, Frederick M., Cottier, Thomas and Gurry, Francis (2007), *International Intellectual Property in an Integrated World Economy*, New York: Wolters Kluwer, Law & Business.

Abbott, Frederick M. and Reichman, Jerome H. (2007), 'The Doha Round's Public Health Legacy: Strategies for the Production and Diffusion of Patented Medicines under the Amended TRIPS Provisions', *Journal of International Economic Law*, 10: 921–87.

Abdel Latif, Ahmed (2009), 'A Perspective on Reform in Arab Countries', in ICTSD, *Intellectual Property and Sustainable Development: Development Agendas in a Changing World*, Cheltenham, UK and Northampton, MA, USA: Edward Elgar.

AFP (2008), 'South Korea Resumes Controversial US Beef Imports', 29 April 2008, http://www.bilaterals.org/article.php3?id_article=12254&var_recherche=beef+korea.

Barton, John (2006), 'The Future of the Intellectual Property System and Consequent Negotiation Topics', in ICTSD, *Views on the Future of the Intellectual Property System*, http://www.iprsonline.org/ictsd/docs/Views%20Future%20IP%20System.pdf.

Bhagwati, Jagdish (1991), *The World Trading System at Risk*, Princeton: Princeton University Press.

Bhagwati, Jagdish (2002), 'Afterword: The Question of Linkage', *American Journal of International Law*, 96: 126–34.

Bridges Monthly (2007), 'Thailand Continues the Battle for Cheaper Drugs', *Bridges Monthly*, February–March, ICTSD, Geneva.

Bridges Weekly (2008), 'Where does TRIPS go from here?', *Bridges Weekly Trade News Digest*, 12 (27).

Bridges Weekly (2008), 'First Generic Drugs En Route to Africa under 5-Year-old WTO Deal', *Bridges Weekly Trade News Digest*, 12 (31), 25 September.

Commission on Intellectual Property Rights (2002) 'Integrating Intellectual Property Rights and Development Policy', Report, London, http://www.iprcommission.org/.

Correa, Carlos (2006a), 'Protecting Test Data for Pharmaceutical and Agrochemical Products under Free Trade Agreements', in P. Roffe, D. Vivas-Eugui and G. Tansey (eds), *Negotiating Health: Intellectual Property and Access to Essential Medicines*, London, Sterling VA: Earthscan.

Correa, Carlos (2006b), 'Guidelines for the Examination of Pharmaceutical Patents: Developing a Public Health Perspective', WHO-ICTSD-UNCTAD, Working Paper, http://ictsd.net/downloads/2008/04/correa_pharmaceutical-patents-guidelines.pdf.

Correa, Carlos (2007), *Trade Related Aspects of Intellectual Property Rights: A Commentary on the TRIPS Agreement*, Oxford: Oxford University Press.

Dhar, Biswajit (2002), 'Sui Generis Systems for Plant Variety Protection: Options under TRIPS', A Discussion Paper, QUNO, Geneva.

Disney, Helen and Pugatch, Meir Perez (2007), 'Commentary – The Patent Reform Act – Divided We Are, United We Stand', *Know IP – The Stockholm Network's Monthly IPR Journal*, 3 (6), August, 1–4.

Drahos, Peter and Braithwaite, John (2002), *Information Feudalism – Who Owns the Knowledge Economy?*, New York: New Press.

Electronic Frontier Foundation (2006), 'Unintended Consequences: Seven Years under the DMCA', see: http://www.eff.org/IP/DMCA/?f=unintended_consequences.html#Section5.
Fink, Carsten and Reichenmiller, Patrick (2005), 'Tightening TRIPS: The Intellectual Property Provisions of Recent US Free Trade Agreements', Trade Note 20, The World Bank Group, Geneva.
FTC (2003), 'To Promote Innovation: The Proper Balance of Competition and Patent Law and Policy', Washington, DC: Federal Trade Commission, http://www.ftc.gov/os/2003/10/innovationrpt.pdf.
GAO (United States Government Accountability Office) (2007), 'Intellectual Property: US Trade Policy Guidance on WTO Declaration on Access to Medicines May Need Clarification', GAO-07-1198, September, http://www.gao.gov/new.items/d071198.pdf.
Garrison, Christopher (2006), 'Exceptions to Patent Rights in Developing Countries', UNCTAD-ICTSD Issue Paper no.17, ICTSD, Geneva, www.iprsonline.org/unctadictsd/projectoutouts.htm.
Gervais, Daniel (1998), *The TRIPS Agreement: Drafting History and Analysis*, London: Sweet & Maxwell.
GovTrack.US (2005) H.R. 3583 – 109th Congress (2005): Protecting Free Trade in Pharmaceuticals Act of 2005. GovTrack.us (database of federal legislation).
IFAC 3 (2003), The U.S.-Chile Free Trade Agreement (FTA) – The Intellectual Property Provisions; Report of the Industry Functional Advisory Committee on Intellectual Property Rights for Trade Policy Matters (IFAC-3)', see: http://www.ustr.gov/assets/Trade_Agreements/Bilateral/Chile_FTA/Reports/asset_upload_file799_4936.pdf.
Jaszi, Peter (2004), 'Rights in Basic Information: A General Perspective', original paper submitted at the UNCTAD-ICTSD Dialogue on Moving the IP Agenda Forward: Preserving Public Goods in Health, Education and Learning (draft available at http://www.iprsonline.org/unctadictsd/bellagio/docs/Jaszi_Bellagio4.pdf). A revised version in Meléndez-Ortiz, R. and Roffe, P. (2010), *Intellectual Property and Sustainable Development: Development Agendas in a Changing World*, Cheltenham, UK and Northampton, MA, USA: Edward: Elgar.
Kampf, Roger (2002), 'Patents versus Patients?', *Archiv des Völkerrechts*, 40 (1), March: 90–134.
Kim, Limsu (2003), 'Technology Transfer and Intellectual Property Rights: Lessons from Korea's Experience', UNCTAD-ICTSD Issue Paper no. 2, http://www.iprsonline.org/resources/docs/Kim%20-%20ToT%20and%20IPRs%20-%20Blue%202.pdf.
Landes, William M., and Posner, Richard M. (2003), *The Economic Structure of Intellectual Property Law*, Cambridge, MA: Harvard University Press.
Lemley, M., Menell, P.S., Merges, R. and Samuelson, P. (2000), *Software and Internet Law*, New York: Aspen Law & Business.
Lessig, Lawrence (2004), *Free Culture: How Big Media Uses Technology and the Law to Lock Down Culture and Control Creativity*, New York: The Penguin Press, 2004, available at: http://www.free-culture.cc/freecontent/.
Maskus, Keith E. (2000), *Intellectual Property Rights in the Global Economy*, Washington, DC: Institute for International Economics.
Maskus, Keith E. (2006), 'Reforming US Patent Policy: Getting the Incentives Right', Council on Foreign Relations, CSR No. 19, November.
Maskus, Keith E. and Reichman, Jerome (2004), 'The Globalization of Private Knowledge Goods and the Privatization of Global Public Goods', *Journal of International Economic Law*, 7: 279–320, June.
Maskus, Keith E. and Reichman, Jerome eds. (2005), *International Public Goods and Transfer of Technology: Under a Globalized Intellectual Property Regime*, Cambridge: Cambridge University Press.
Matthews, Duncan (2002), *Globalising Intellectual Property Rights*, London: Routledge.
Meitinger, Ingo (2005), 'Implementation of Test Data Protection According to Article 39.3 TRIPS: The Search for a Fair Interpretation of the Term "Unfair Commercial Use"', *Journal of World Intellectual Property*, 8 (2), March: 123–39.

Merges, R., Menell, P.S. and Lemley, M. (2000), *Intellectual Property in the New Technological Age*, New York: Aspen Law and Business.
Morin, Jean-Frederick (2004), 'The future of Patentability in International Law according to the CAFTA', *Bridges*, Geneva, March.
Musungu, Sisule (2008), 'Developing a Positive Agenda on IP Enforcement in EPAs: Lessons for the CEMAC Region from the EC-CARIFORUM EPA, ICTSD and ACDIC', available at: http://www.iprsonline.org/ictsd/Dialogues/2008-04-28/Musungu_Paper.pdf.
Okediji, Ruth (2004), 'The International Copyright System: Limitations, Exceptions and Public Interest Considerations for Developing Countries', UNCTAD-ICTSD Issue Paper no.15, Geneva, available at: www.iprsonline.org/unctadictsd/projectoutouts.htm.
Oxfam International (2007), 'Signing Away the Future: How Trade and Investment Agreements between Rich and Poor Countries Undermine Development', Briefing Paper 101, http://www.oxfam.org.uk/what_we_do/issues/trade/downloads/bp101_ftas.pdf.
Pear, R. (2002), 'Plan to Import Drugs from Canada Passes in Senate, but Bush Declines to Carry it Out', *New York Times*, 18 July.
Reichman, Jerome H. (2006), 'Compulsory Licensing of Patented Inventions: Comparing United States Law and Practice with Options under the TRIPS Agreement', paper presented to the American Association of Law Schools Mid-year Workshop on Intellectual Property, Vancouver, Canada, 14 June.
Reichman, Jerome H. (2009), *Rethinking the Role of Clinical Trial Data in International Intellectual Property Laws: The Case for a Public Goods Approach*, Marquette Intellectual Property Law Review, 13 (1).
Reichman, Jerome H. and Dreyfuss, Rochelle Cooper (2007), 'Harmonization without Consensus: Critical Reflections on Drafting A Substantive Patent Law Treaty', *Duke Law Journal*, 57 (1); NYU Law and Economics Research Paper No. 07-43; Duke Law School Legal Studies Paper No. 178; Duke Science, Technology and Innovation Paper No. 22. Available at SSRN: http://ssrn.com/abstract=1028331.
Reichman, Jerome H., Dinwoodie, Graeme B. and Samuelson, Pamela (2007), 'A Reverse Notice and Takedown Regime to Enable Public Good Uses of Technically Protected Copyrighted Works', Social Science Research Network (SSRN), at http://papers.ssrn.com/sol3/papers.cfm?abstract_id=1007817.
Reichman, Jerome H. and Hasenzahl, Catherine H. (2003), 'Nonvoluntary Licensing of Patented Inventions: Historical Perspective, Legal Framework under TRIPS and an Overview of the Practice in Canada and the United States of America', UNCTAD-ICTSD Issue Paper No. 5, Geneva; available at http://www.iprsonline.org/resources/docs/Reichman%20-%20Non-voluntary%20Licensing%20-%20Blue%205.pdf.
Reichman, Jerome H. and Lewis, Tracy (2005), 'Using Liability Rules to Stimulate Local Innovation in Developing Countries: Application to Traditional Knowledge', in Maskus, Keith E. and Jerome Reichman (eds), *International Public Goods and Transfer of Technology: Under a Globalized Intellectual Property Regime*, Cambridge: Cambridge University Press.
Roffe, Pedro (2004), 'Bilateral Agreements and a TRIPS-plus World: The Chile-US Free Trade Agreement', TRIPS Issues paper 4, QIAP, Ottawa, available in English and Spanish at www.qiap.ca/ o en www.quno.org/.
Roffe, Pedro (2006), *Intellectual Property Provisions in Bilateral and Regional Trade Agreements: The Challenges of Implementation*, Geneva: CIEL.
Roffe, Pedro (2007), 'Chile and the Priority Watch List: Some Considerations', *Bridges Monthly*, no. 11/2, p.18, ICTSD, Geneva, available at: www.ictsd.org/monthly/.
Roffe, Pedro and Santa Cruz, Maximiliano (2006), 'Lo derechos de propiedad intellectual en los acuerdos de libre comercio celebrados por paises de America Latina con paises desarrollados', CEPAL, Serie Comercial Internacional No. 70.
Roffe, Pedro and Spennemann, Christoph (2006), 'The Impact of FTAs on Public Health Policies and TRIPS Flexibilities', *International Journal Intellectual Property Management*, 1 (1/2).

Roffe, Pedro and Vivas, David (2007), 'A Shift in Intellectual Property Policy in US FTAs?', *Bridges Monthly*, 11 (5), August, ICTSD, Geneva.

Roffe, Pedro, von Braun, Johanna and Vivas-Eugui, David (2007), 'A New Generation of Regional and Bilateral Trade Agreements: Lessons from the US-CAFTA-DR', in Blouin, Chantal, Heymann, Jody and Drager, Nick (eds), *Trade and Health, Seeking Common Ground: Integrating Health Objectives and International Trade Policies*, Montreal, Canada: McGill-Queen's University Press.

Ryan, Michael. P. (1998), *Knowledge Diplomacy: Global Competition and the Politics of Intellectual Property*, Washington, DC: Brookings Institution Press.

Santa Cruz, Maximiliano (2007), 'Intellectual Property Provisions in European Union Trade Agreements: Implications for Developing Countries', ICTSD Issue Paper no. 20, ICTSD, Geneva, available at: www.iprsonline.org/unctadictsd/projectoutouts.htm.

Scotchmer, Suzanne (2005), *Innovation and Incentives*, Cambridge, MA: The MIT Press.

Sell, Susan (2003), *Private Power, Public Law: The Globalization of Intellectual Property Rights*, Cambridge: Cambridge University Press.

Seuba, Xavier (2008), 'Health Protection in the New Association Agreement between the Andean Community (or some of its Members) and the European Community in light of its Provisions concerning Intellectual Property and Recent Experiences', HAI and AIS publication.

Stewart, T.P. (ed.) (1999), *The GATT Uruguay Round: A Negotiating History – Volume IV: The Endgame*, Deventer, Boston: Kluwer Law International.

Stiglitz, Joseph (2004), 'New Trade Pacts Betray the Poorest Partners', *New York Times*, 10 July.

Thomas, John R. (2005), *Pharmaceutical Patent Law*, Washington, DC: BNA Books.

Thumm, Nikolaus (2006), 'Reasonable Patent Protection with a Statutory Research Exemption', in: IPR Helpdesk Bulletin, No. 29, September–October, www.ipr-helpdesk.org.

UNCTAD (forthcoming), *Using Intellectual Property Rights to Stimulate Pharmaceutical Production in Developing Countries: A Reference Guide*, United Nations, New York and Geneva.

UNCTAD-ICTSD (2003), 'Intellectual Property Rights: Implications for Development, Policy Discussion Paper', Geneva, available at: www.iprsonline.org/unctadictsd/projectoutouts.htm.

UNCTAD-ICTSD (2005), *Resource Book on TRIPS and Development*, Cambridge: Cambridge University Press, available at: www.iprsonline.org/unctadictsd/projectoutouts.htm.

UNCTAD–WIPO–CBD Secretariat (2007), 'The Role of Intellectual Property Rights in Technology Transfer in the Context of the Convention on Biological Diversity: A Technical Study' (tabled at the 10–12 September 2007 meeting of the CBD Expert Group on Technology Transfer in Geneva.).

United States House of Representatives (2005), 'Trade Agreements and Access to Medications under the Bush Administration, Committee on Government Reform', Minority Staff Special Investigations Division, prepared for Representative Henry A. Waxman, June, Washington, DC, available at www.reform.house.gov/min.

Vivas-Eugui, David and Spennemann, Christoph (2007), 'The Evolving Regime for Geographical Indications in WTO and in Free Trade Agreements', in Correa, Carlos M. and Yusuf, Abdulqawi (eds), *Intellectual Property and International Trade: The TRIPS Agreement*, The Netherlands: Kluwer Law International.

von Braun, Johanna (2008), 'Do Public Policy Objectives Have a Space in the Negotiation of Bilateral Free Trade Agreements? A Study of Multi-level Diplomacy and the Making of Intellectual Property Law', Draft Thesis document, unpublished, available on request from author.

Watal, Jayashree (2001), *Intellectual Property Rights in the WTO and Developing Countries*, The Netherlands: Kluwer Law International.

PART II

SUBSTANTIVE RIGHTS

10 Limits, limitations and exceptions to copyright under the TRIPS Agreement

*P. Bernt Hugenholtz**

1. Introduction

Copyright is not absolute, but a right that is confined by a subtle structure of limits and limitations. In the ideal copyright system, these limits and limitations are essential balancing tools, precisely calibrated to allow users of copyright works sufficient freedoms to interact with these works without unduly undermining copyright's incentive function to act as the 'engine of free expression'. While the general limits of copyright define the subject matter, scope of protection and duration of the exclusive rights, the statutory limitations (or 'limitations and exceptions' as they are frequently called) accommodate more specifically a variety of cultural, social, informational, economic and political needs and purposes.

In national law, limitations and exception come in many shapes and sizes, varying from the precisely circumscribed exceptions commonly found in countries of the *droit d'auteur* tradition to the more flexible 'fair dealing' or 'fair use' style provisions of the Anglo-American *copyright* tradition. At the international level, not much in terms of copyright limitations is harmonized. While incorporating the Berne Convention's minimum standards (art. 1-21 BC), the Agreement on Trade-related Aspects of Intellectual Property (TRIPS), deals with copyright limitations in a single, rather loosely worded norm: the 'three-step test' (art. 13 TRIPS), which will be discussed at some length below. The general objectives and principles of the Agreement set out in articles 7 and 8 TRIPS provide a measure of encouragement to those seeking balance within the international system of intellectual property. Art. 7 TRIPS in particular informs World Trade Organization (WTO) member states that '[t]he protection and enforcement of intellectual property rights should contribute to [. . .] a balance of rights and obligations.'

However, the integration of copyright norms into the framework of

* This chapter is based on Part II of the study 'Conceiving an International Instrument on Limitations and Exceptions to Copyright' (P. Bernt Hugenholtz and R. Okediji), which was sponsored by the Open Society Institute (OSI); the study is available at http://www.ivir.nl/publicaties/hugenholtz/finalreport2008.pdf.

international trade law by way of the TRIPS Agreement, is not without consequence. Whereas the 'original' version of the three-step test (art. 9.2 of the Berne Convention (BC)) focused on protecting the interests of authors, art. 13 TRIPS accentuates the rights and interests of 'right holders'. This has arguably somewhat limited the freedom of national lawmakers to provide for compensated limitations (for example, in the form of levies).[1] More generally, the paradigm of international trade law appears to be less suitable to accommodating the myriad variants of the public interest that justify limitations and exceptions to copyright, particularly those informed by cultural policies and human rights considerations. Nonetheless, as this chapter will reveal in more detail, effectively, despite over a century of international norm setting in the field of copyright, limitations have largely remained 'unregulated space'.

In addition to their normal calibrating function, limitations and exceptions to copyright also have a role to play in accommodating the needs of developing countries. Not surprisingly, limitations and exceptions to copyright have take centre stage in the ongoing international debate concerning intellectual property and development. The issue of limitations to copyright figures prominently on the agenda of international lawmakers today. It is one of many items shortlisted for action by the Committee on Development and Intellectual Property (CDIP) at the World Intellectual Property Organization (WIPO), which was established to implement the WIPO Development Agenda.[2] More recently, at the WIPO Standing Committee on Copyright and Related Rights (SCCR),[3] a proposal by the Chilean government to initiate what might eventually become an international instrument on copyright limitations to cater for the needs of the visually impaired received broad support and will remain on the agenda of the SCCR, despite reservations by some developed countries.

This chapter explores the 'wiggle room'[4] that the TRIPS Agreement,

---

1 See discussion relating to footnote 75.

2 See World Intellectual Property Organization (WIPO), Committee on Intellectual Property and Development (CDIP), First Session, Summary by the Chair, March 3–7, 2008, available at http://www.wipo.int/edocs/mdocs/mdocs/en/cdip_1/cdip_1_summary.doc.

3 See WIPO, Standing Committee on Copyright and Related Rights (SCCR), Sixteenth Session, Conclusions of the Sixteenth Session of the SCCR, March 10–12, 2008, available at http://www.wipo.int/edocs/mdocs/sccr/en/sccr_16/sccr_16_conclusions.doc; Seventeenth Session, Conclusions of the Seventeenth Session of the SCCR, November 5–7, 2008, available at http://www.wipo.int/edocs/mdocs/copyright/en/sccr_17/sccr_17_www_112533.pdf.

4 The term is taken from J.H. Reichman, *From Free Riders to Fair Followers:*

and the norms of the Berne Convention incorporated into TRIPS, leave to the contracting States to set limits to copyright. It assesses the latitude left by these Conventions to Member States to limit exclusive rights of copyright right holders either by tailoring subject matter or economic rights or by way of limitations and exceptions. Once established, this latitude immediately defines the breadth and scope of any limits to copyright that might form the content of an international instrument on limitations and exceptions. As will be demonstrated in Section 2, since the conventional minimum rights are incomplete and rarely precisely defined, while remaining largely immune to the application of the three-step test, this offers contracting States considerable flexibilities. This section goes on to discuss the handful of more precisely circumscribed limitations found in the Berne Convention which contracting Parties are free to implement. Section 3 thereafter turns to the 'three-step test', which governs limitations and exceptions to the minimum rights of the TRIPS Agreement. Section 4 offers conclusions.

2. Flexibilities under TRIPs

In search of flexibilities, it is important to understand the mechanics of the copyright system. Statutory limitations and exceptions are but one, albeit very important, way of creating balance inside copyright. The tool-box of copyright law consists of several other balancing instruments as well, including, for example, the concept of a 'work of authorship', which features a requirement of 'originality'; the idea/expression dichotomy, which delineates the border between protected subject matter and the public domain; the delineation of economic rights of the right holder, such as the right of reproduction and the right of communication to the public; general limits to copyright, such as the exhaustion rule (first-sale doctrine) and the term of protection; and, finally, limitations and exceptions (L&Es) proper. In addition, outside the copyright tool-box, certain limits to copyright can be directly based on fundamental rights and freedoms, such as freedom of expression and the right to privacy, and others in competition law, such as the use of compulsory licences.

From this perspective, it immediately becomes apparent that copyright limitations are not, necessarily, 'exceptions'. Notwithstanding the limits imposed upon national legislators by art. 13 TRIPS, the principle of narrow construction of copyright exemptions, so often found in copyright treatises and case law, is ill-conceived. Even in those countries where *droit*

Global Competition under the TRIPS Agreement, 29 NYU J INT'L L. & POL. 11, 29 (1997).

d'auteur principles of natural law form the solid bedrock of copyright law and jurisprudence, the notion that the law must preserve a balance between protecting the rights of authors and safeguarding fundamental user freedoms is now generally accepted. In defining this balance, copyright limitations are mere (but essential) instruments, not exceptions to a rule.[5]

Minimum standards

Characteristic of the international copyright regime is a structure of minimum standards, which qualified right holders may invoke before the national courts of the contracting States. These minimum standards need not apply in a purely national context. States have remained autonomous as regards works in their country of origin (art. 5.3 BC, art. 1.3 TRIPS). At least theoretically, this has left contracting States complete freedom to derogate from the conventional minimum rights as they see fit. Although such derogations do occasionally exist, as a rule, contracting States will shy away from discriminating against their own nationals.

The main minimum standards set by the Berne Convention, as incorporated into the TRIPS Agreement by way of art. 9.1, concern: (1) protected subject matter ('works of authorship'); (2) economic (patrimonial) rights; and (3) limitations and exceptions subject to the 'three-step test'. Each of these categories comes with certain implicitly or expressly provided limits, which shall be explored in the following subsection.

Limits to protected subject matter

The notion of a 'work of authorship', codified in art. 2(1) BC, includes an implicit requirement of 'originality',[6] which rules out, for instance, mere factual accounts. This is, in itself, an important limit, which delineates the borderline between protected creations and the public domain. This is illustrated by art. 2(8) BC, which excludes from copyright protection 'news of the day or miscellaneous facts having the character of mere items of press information'. Similarly, art. 10(2) TRIPS states that copyright in compi-

---

5 See P.B. Hugenholtz, *Fierce Creatures. Copyright Exemptions: Towards Extinction?*, keynote speech, IFLA/IMPRIMATUR Conference, *Rights, Limitations and Exceptions: Striking a Proper Balance*, Amsterdam, 30–31 October 1997, available at http://www.ivir.nl/publications/hugenholtz/PBH-Fierce Creatures.doc.

6 See Sam Ricketson and Jane Ginsburg, International Copyright and Neighboring Rights: The Berne Convention and Beyond (Oxford: Oxford University Press, 2006), 405.

lations of data 'shall not extend to the data or material itself'.[7] A related balancing tool is the idea/expression (content/form) dichotomy, codified in art. 9(2) TRIPS and art. 2 WIPO Copyright Treaty (WCT). Accordingly, copyright protection extends 'to expressions and not to ideas, procedures, methods of operation or mathematical concepts as such'.

Note that art. 2(8) BC, arts 9(2) and 10(2) TRIPS and arts 2 and 5 WCT are phrased as *mandatory* exclusions from copyright protection. The reasons for these exclusions are, however, not clear from the historic record. Are these objects excluded from copyright protection as a matter of public policy, expressing principles of free speech or freedom of competition? Or are they simply reminders of the general rule that copyright protects original expression?[8] If the former interpretation is correct, one could read into these exclusions an actual obligation upon contracting States not to protect these objects. If the latter is correct, the net effect of these exclusions would be more limited; for example, a Union 'author' of news items could not invoke minimum protection in another Union country.[9]

In addition, art. 2(4) BC permits States to exclude from copyright protection government works, an expression of freedom of information principles underlying any functioning democracy.

Limits to economic rights

The definition of the economic rights in the Conventions offers additional 'wiggle room'. The BC enumerates the minimum rights in a rather haphazard fashion, reflecting the history of the Convention; rights were added incrementally as new modes of exploitation became mainstream. Additional minimum standards are set by TRIPS and the WCT. But not all economic rights normally found in national laws have found their way into the international copyright acquis. A display right, for instance, is not recognized in any of the three main Conventions, while a right of commercial rental of films and software may not be required depending on market conditions (art. 11 TRIPS and art. 7-WCT) and an artist's resale right has voluntary status only (art. 14*ter* BC). Such unregulated or optional rights may therefore be subjected to unlimited limitations and exceptions.

But even a minimum right seemingly carved in stone, such as the right of reproduction, may leave contracting States latitude for limitation. While

---

7 Art. 5 of the WIPO Copyright Treaty (WCT) contains a similar rule.

8 See Ricketson & Ginsburg, *supra* n-6, at 498–501.

9 See Ricketson & Ginsburg, *supra* n-6, at 499.

art. 9(1) BC prescribes the 'exclusive right of authorizing the reproduction of . . . works, in any manner or form', and the Agreed Statements to the WCT confirm its application in the digital environment,[10] neither instrument defines the act of 'reproduction' as such. Scholars have convincingly argued that reproduction is basically a normative, not a technical notion, and should therefore be interpreted in the light of its objective.[11] This line of reasoning leaves room, for instance, for a statutory carve-out permitting acts of economically insignificant temporary copying.[12] Arguably, such carve-outs need not be subjected to the three-step test.[13]

Further flexibilities can be derived from the notion of 'public', which determines the scope of several other economic rights codified in the Berne Convention, some of which were eventually absorbed by the general right of communication to the public that was introduced in art. 8 WCT.[14] Indeed, many countries have already taken advantage of such flexibilities

---

10 See WCT, *supra* n. 3, Agreed statements concerning art. 1(4):

> The reproduction right, as set out in Article 9 of the Berne Convention, and the exceptions permitted thereunder, fully apply in the digital environment, in particular to the use of works in digital form. It is understood that the storage of a protected work in digital form in an electronic medium constitutes a reproduction within the meaning of Article 9 of the Berne Convention.

11 See Legal Advisory Board, Reply to the Green Paper on Copyright and Related Rights in the Information Society, Brussels, September 1995, available at http://ec.europa.eu/archives/ISPO/legal/en/ipr/reply/reply.html; see also generally P. Bernt Hugenholtz, *Adapting Copyright to the Information Superhighway*, in P. BERNT HUGENHOLTZ (ed.), THE FUTURE OF COPYRIGHT IN A DIGITAL ENVIRONMENT (Kluwer Law International, 1996) 81–102.

12 See, for example, article 13a of the Dutch Copyright Act (unofficial translation by Ministry of Justice of the Netherlands, available at http://www.ivir.nl/legislation/nl/copyrightact1912_unofficial.pdf):

> The reproduction of a literary, scientific or artistic work will not include temporary reproduction of a passing or incidental nature and forming an essential part of a technical procedure whose sole purpose is to enable a) the passing on by an intermediary through a network between third parties, or b) a lawful use and if it contains no independent economic value.

13 Note, however, that insofar as such carve-outs from the economic rights would fall under the diffuse rubric of 'minor reservations', they might still fall within the ambit of the three-step test. See discussion below.

14 These rights include the right of public performance 'by any means or process' (BC art. 11); the public recitation, including the public communication thereof (BC art. 11*ter*); the public performance of cinematographic adaptations (BC art. 14(1)); the rights of broadcasting, rebroadcasting, cable distribution, and public communication by loudspeaker (BC art. 11*bis*).

by permitting certain de minimis acts of public performance or communication to the public by way of legally defining the contours of these acts around such minimal uses. Examples abound. For instance, many European countries define 'public' performance in such a way as to rule out performances within a circle of family or friends. In some countries, carve-outs go considerably further. For example, art. 17(3)(b) of the Austrian Copyright Act permits retransmission of works over community antenna systems (small cable networks) reaching fewer than 500 households.[15]

The Berne Convention also warrants an exclusive right to make transformative uses, in the form of translations (art. 8), adaptations, arrangements and other alterations (art. 12), and cinematographic adaptations (art. 14(1)). Again, in the absence of clear definitions, these provisions leave some room for de facto limitations, for instance by determining in national statutory law or case law the criteria for copyright infringement (that is, the scope of the adaptation right).

The exhaustion rule (or first-sale doctrine) found in most national laws, and permitted under art. 6 TRIPS and art. 6.2 WCT, is another boundary of copyright. The same can be said of the limited term (duration) of copyright (art. 7 BC and art. 12 TRIPs[16]). Note that although the standard Berne minimum of 50 years p.m.a. is regularly exceeded by countries offering 'life plus seventy', the Berne minimum is in itself subject to several exceptions.[17]

Specific limitations and exceptions in the BC

The Berne Convention recognizes two types of limitations: compensated limitations and uncompensated limitations. Uncompensated limitations usually mirror uses or practices that are not considered part of the legitimate scope of the author's proprietary grant. Compensated limitations usually suggest that the copyright owner is not entitled to control whether the work is used, but is entitled to remuneration. The difference between the two categories is important, especially in relation to the three-step test

---

[15] See A.P. Groen, *De Minimis-Regelingen in het Auteursrecht*, Report to WODC (Ministry of Justice of the Netherlands), 2007.

[16] For works in which copyright is initially vested in a corporate entity, minimum terms expire fifty years from first publication or creation (art. 12 TRIPS).

[17] The standard minimum term may be reduced to fifty years from first communication to the public or from creation for cinematographic works. Contracting States may also offer shorter terms of twenty-five years from creation for photographic works and works of applied art. However, art. 9 of the WCT reinstates the normal BC term for photographic works by ruling out the application of art. 7(4) BC.

discussed below. Assuming for the moment that compensated limitations are not immune to three-step test scrutiny, the existence of a statutory compensation scheme may avoid causing 'unreasonable prejudice' to authors or right holders and thereby makes it easier for limitations of the latter category to satisfy the third step of the test.[18]

Uncompensated limitations in the Berne Convention include provisions permitting public speeches (art. 2*bis*(2)), quotations (art. 10(1)), uses for teaching purposes (art. 10(2)), press usage (art. 10*bis*(1)), reporting of current events (art. 10*bis*(2)) and ephemeral recordings by broadcasting organizations (art. 11*bis*(3)).[19] Many of these provisions simply state the purpose of the permitted use and leave a considerable measure of freedom to contracting States for implementation at the national level. In some cases (for example, arts. 10(1) and 10(2)), the norms of the Berne Convention refer to 'fair practice', a notion which arguably leaves room for an interpretation that takes account of local conditions,[20] thus creating additional flexibilities.

Note that art. 10(1) BC is phrased as a *mandatory* user freedom: 'It shall be permissible to make quotations . . . '. While mandatory limitations are not uncommon in international instruments in the general realm of intellectual property, this is the only instance of a mandatory limitation in an international copyright treaty.[21] The reason for this special status, most likely, again lies in the exception's rationale: freedom of expression. Moreover, a right to quote might be considered an essential prerogative for the authors, who traditionally occupy centre stage in the Berne Convention.

In addition to the specific limitations enumerated in the Convention, art. 9(2) allows unspecified limitations to the right of reproduction, subject to the 'three-step test', which is discussed below. The TRIPS Agreement and the WCT do not contain any additional specific limitations to the rights newly introduced by these Conventions; both Treaties extend the rule of the 'three-step test' to all rights covered by the respective treaties. Note, however, that the contracting Parties to the WCT expressly underscored

---

[18] See discussion below.

[19] See S. Ricketson, *WIPO Study on Limitations and Exceptions of Copyright and Related Rights in the Digital Environment*, WIPO Doc. SCCR/9/7, April 5, 2003, pp. 11–20, available at http://www.wipo.int/edocs/mdocs/copyright/en/sccr_9/sccr_9_7.pdf (last visited March 3, 2008). For a summary of these limitations, see Appendix A to this report.

[20] Ricketson, *supra* n. 19, at 13.

[21] Note that the BC, TRIPS and the WCT do provide for certain mandatory *exclusions* of protected subject matter. See discussion above.

the importance of retaining a balance in copyright, as is clear from its preamble,[22] which may serve as a guideline to interpretation of the norms of the WCT, and arguably the Berne Convention as well.

In addition to the limitations and exceptions discussed above, the Berne Convention allows, in a few well-circumscribed situations, for statutory (compulsory) licensing, as in the case of the recording of musical works (art. 13(1)) and broadcasting and cable retransmission (art. 11bis(2)). In such cases, right holders have a right to equitable remuneration.

Moreover, as the record of the Stockholm Conference reveals, certain exceptions to particular rights, although not expressed in the international instruments, might nevertheless be implied. [23] These so-called *minor reservations* (or 'minor exceptions') fall into two categories: (i) those in relation to performing, recitation, broadcasting, recording and cinematographic rights, and (ii) those in relation to translations. As their name 'minor reservations' indicates, these implied limitations usually concern de minimis uses, such as use of works during religious ceremonies, or use by military bands. During the Brussels and Stockholm Conferences on the Revision of the Berne Convention, the delegations invoked the 'minor reservations' doctrine to justify the maintenance in their national laws of existing exceptions of minor importance.[24]

Finally, for developing nations, there exist additional flexibilities in the Berne Appendix. However, due to the complexity of its provisions and the administrative burden that it imposes on its users, the Appendix has largely remained unused.[25]

3. The 'three-step test'

At the 1967 Stockholm Conference, the so-called three-step test of art. 9(2) was introduced in international copyright law as a companion to the formal recognition of the general right of reproduction in art. 9(1) of

---

[22] See Berne Convention, pmbl. ¶5 ('*Recognizing* the need to maintain a balance between the rights of authors and the larger public interest, particularly education, research and access to information, as reflected in the Berne Convention . . . .' (emphasis in original).

[23] Ricketson, *supra* n. 19, at 33; see also Report of the Panel, US – Section 110(5) Copyright Act, 15 June 2000, WTO Doc. WT/DS/160/R, §§6.33 et seq. (*hereinafter* US – Section 110(5) Report).

[24] M. Senftleben, Copyright, Limitations and the Three-Step Test (The Hague: Kluwer, 2004), 198–201.

[25] See R.L. Okediji, *Welfare and Digital Copyright in International Perspective*, in J. H. Reichman and K. Maskus (eds), International Public Goods and Transfer of Technology Under a Globalized Intellectual Property Regime (Cambridge: Cambridge University Press, 2005).

the Berne Convention. The three-step test reappeared in art. 13 TRIPS and subsequently in art. 10 WCT. Under art. 13 TRIPs, member States shall confine limitations and exceptions (1) to 'certain special cases', (2) 'which do not conflict with a normal exploitation of the work', and (3) 'do not unreasonably prejudice the legitimate interests of the right holder'. Increasingly, variants of the test also appear in various regional instruments, such as the European harmonization directives, or in bilateral treaties, such as the US-Australia FTA (art. 17.4(10)).

The evolution of the three-step test into the overriding norm of international copyright law through its incorporation in the TRIPS Agreement has attracted criticism from scholars and stakeholders alike.[26] The three-step test allegedly negates the balance between exclusivity and access that should be inherent in any mature copyright system. Its primary focus, as with the entire structure of minimum rights, is on protecting rights of authors or, in the case of TRIPS, 'right holders', not the interests of society or the general public. Cumulative application of the three steps, as its wording requires, heavily tilts the balance in favour of the right holders. The test also fails to take into account the justified needs of developing nations.

Fortunately, as the following analysis will reveal, despite its firm wording, the three-step test does still provide WTO members with flexibilities, and leaves sufficient room for States to enter into an instrument on L&Es with meaningful substantive content.

Scope and function of the three-step test

During its transformation from a norm of international copyright to a norm of international trade law, the focus of the test has shifted from the interests of *the author* to those of the *right holder*. This paradigm shift is not without consequences; it brings to the foreground the commercial interests of intermediaries ('right holders'), while downplaying the interests of the authors. But as Professor Gervais has noted, the trade-law gloss that TRIPS has put on the three-step test may have actually created some extra space for limitations and exceptions. Whereas under the classic

---

[26] See inter alia R. Cooper Dreyfuss, *TRIPS – Round II: Should Users Strike Back?*, 71 University of Chicago Law Review 21; R. Cooper Dreyfuss & G. Dinwoodie, *TRIPS and the Dynamics of Intellectual Property Lawmaking*, 36 *Case W. Res. J. Int'l L.* 95; Ruth Okediji, *TRIPS Dispute Settlement and the Sources of (International) Copyright Law*, 49 JCPS 585 (Winter 2001); South Centre, The TRIPS Agreement: A Guide for the South, Geneva, November 1997, *available at* http://www.southcentre.org/publications/trips/tripsagreement.pdf (last visited March 5, 2008).

authors' rights paradigm, 'prejudice' (step 3) is likely to be measured in terms of 'just reward', reflecting notions of natural justice traditionally associated with authors' rights, the same notion read through the lens of TRIPS is more likely to be assessed in terms of the actual damage criterion usually associated with trade law.[27]

The three-step test of TRIPS has found its way, via art. 10 WCT, into art. 5(5) of the European Copyright (Information Society) Directive of 2001.[28] Articles 6(3) of the EC Computer Programs Directive, 10(3) of the EC Rental Right Directive and 6(3) of the EC Database Directive were already modelled on the three-step test. Thus, the three-step test has become a norm of Community law, qualifying it for interpretation by the European Court of Justice. Moreover, following its incorporation into the Information Society Directive, and despite general agreement among European scholars that the test is a norm addressed to the legislatures,[29] not the citizens, of the Member States, several Member States, including the Czech Republic, France, Greece, Hungary, Italy, Luxembourg, Malta, Poland, Portugal and Slovakia, have seen fit to transpose the norm directly into their national laws. In these countries, the three-step test now constitutes a directly applicable rule of substantive law as regards the interpretation of limitations. Other Member States, such as Austria, Belgium, Finland, Germany, the Netherlands and the United Kingdom, have remained faithful to the test's original function as a meta-norm addressed to national legislatures. But even in Member States where no transposition of the three-step test has occurred, national courts, compelled to interpret national law in conformity with Community law, now regularly refer to the three-step test in their decisions.[30] Note that China

---

[27] D. Gervais, *Making Copyright Whole: A Principle Approach to Copyright Exceptions and Limitations* (unpublished manuscript on file with the author).

[28] See Directive 2001/29/EC of the European Parliament and of the Council of 22 May 2001 on the harmonisation of certain aspects of copyright and related rights in the information society, OJ L 167, June 22, 2001, art. 5.5 (hereinafter Directive 2001/29/EC) ('The exceptions and limitations provided for in paragraphs 1, 2, 3 and 4 shall only be applied in certain special cases which do not conflict with a normal exploitation of the work or other subject-matter and do not unreasonably prejudice the legitimate interests of the rightholder.').

[29] See, S. Dusollier, *L'Encadrement des Exceptions au Droit d'Auteur par le Test des Trois Etapes*, [2005] IRDI 212; K. Koelman, *Fixing the Three-step Test*, [2006] EIPR 407; C. Geiger, *From Berne to National Law, via the Copyright Directive: the Dangerous Mutations of the Three-step Test*, [2007] EIPR 486.

[30] See, for example, *De Nederlandse Dagbladpers v. the Netherlands*, District Court of the Hague (Rechtbanks' Gravenhage), 2 March 2005, [2005] Computerrecht 143 (state-operated electronic press-clipping service for government officials not

had already incorporated the three-step into national legislation in its copyright law of 2002.[31] More recently, following the US-Australia FTA, the Australian legislature has done the same.[32]

The three-step test is often portrayed as imposing a 'limit to limitations'. This is indeed what its language suggests. In this vein, the WTO Panel in the *IMRO* (Irish Music Rights Organisation) case, which pitted the European Union against the United States in a conflict concerning the interpretation of the so-called 'business exemption' (Section 110(5) of the US Copyright Act), notes at the outset of its opinion 'that [TRIPS] Article 13 cannot have more than a narrow or limited operation. Its tenor, consistent as it is with the provisions of Article 9(2) of the Berne Convention (1971), discloses that it was not intended to provide for exceptions or limitations except for those of a limited nature.'[33] However, the history of the three-step test tells a somewhat different story. As the drafting history of the Stockholm Revision of the BC reveals, art. 9.2 is more akin to a grandfathering clause; a purposefully vague reflection of a compromise among States of different copyright traditions,[34] which confirms that the broad array of – often broadly worded – statutory limitations that existed at the national levels in 1967[35] is in conformity with BC minimum standards. The same might be said in respect of art. 13 of the TRIPS Agreement adopted in 1994.[36]

What are 'limitations and exceptions'?

While art. 9(2) BC, art. 13 TRIPS and art. 10 WCT expressly refer to 'limitations and exceptions' as the object of the three-step test, surprisingly

---

Footnote 30 (*cont.*)
deemed to fall under news-reporting exception, because such use would conflict with normal exploitation of newspaper articles).

[31] Art. 21, Copyright Act of China. See generally G. Shoukang, *New Chinese Copyright Act*, [2000] 31 IIC 526–30.

[32] Section 200 AB, Australia Copyright Act, as amended by the Copyright Amendment Act 2006, Act. No. 158, 2006.

[33] See, US – Section 110(5) Report, *supra* n. 23, § 6.97. Note that this case is commonly referred to as *IMRO*, because it originates from a complaint on the Irish Music Rights Organisation.

[34] C. Geiger, *The Role of the Three-step Test in the Adaptation of Copyright Law to the Information Society*, UNESCO e-Copyright Bulletin, January–March 2007, p. 3, available at http://unesdoc.unesco.org/images/0015/001578/157848e.pdf.

[35] For an exemplary, see inventory of limitations and exception existing in national law in a number of contracting States (for example, Germany, Netherlands, France, United Kingdom and India) prior to the 1967 Stockholm Conference. See also M. Senftleben, *supra* n. 24, 52–81.

[36] *See* Senftleben, *supra* n. 24, at 87.

little has been written, even in the *IMRO* WTO Panel Report, on what actually constitutes 'limitations and exceptions'. In all likelihood, the term applies first and foremost to statutory limitations that curtail the rights of right holders in specific circumstances to cater for the interests of specific user groups or the public at large. Given the structure of the three Conventions, the three-step test need not be applied to codifications of the subject matter of copyright or of the minimum rights as such. According to some scholars, the term also does not encompass provisions that restrict the *exercise* of economic rights, such as provisions mandating the collective exercise of rights found in a variety of European directives and national laws.[37] An example is art. 9(1) of the EC Satellite and Cable Directive, which requires that rights of cable retransmission be exercised solely through collecting societies.[38] Although the practical effect of such a rule is similar to that of a statutory or compulsory licence providing for a right of remuneration, it is technically not a limitation, since the exclusive economic right remains intact and can still be enforced on behalf of right holders by designated collecting societies.

Whether the compensated limitations permitted under the Berne Convention qualify as 'limitations and exceptions' subject to the three-step test under art. 13 TRIPS, is an unsettled question.[39] But even if they are, such compensated limitations are more likely to pass the test given the fact that prescribing compensation to authors or right holders is generally recognized as a crucial factor in assessing 'unreasonable prejudice' under the third step.

Surely, the term 'limitations and exceptions' – and by implication the three-step test – cannot apply to exercises of State discretion that are done

---

[37] See, for example, S. von Lewinski, *Mandatory Collective Administration of Exclusive Rights – A Case Study on its Compatibility with International and EC Copyright Law*, UNESCO e-Copyright Bulletin, January–March 2004, p. 5, available at http://unesdoc.unesco.org/images/0013/001396/139656e.pdf; Geiger, *supra* n. 34, at 9–12. Cf. for example, M. Ficsor, *Collective Management of Copyright and Related Rights at a Triple Crossroads: Should it Remain Voluntary or May it be 'Extended' or Made Mandatory?*, UNESCO e-Copyright Bulletin, October–December 2003, p. 4, *available at* http://portal.unesco.org/culture/en/files/14935/10657988721Ficsor_Eng.pdf/Ficsor%2BEng.pdf.

[38] Council Directive 93/83/EEC of 27 September 1993 on the coordination of certain rules concerning copyright and rights related to copyright applicable to satellite broadcasting and cable retransmission, OJ L 248/15, 6 October 1993, art. 9(1); See P.B. Hugenholtz, Copyright without Frontiers: is there a Future for the Satellite and Cable Directive? in: DIE ZUKUNFT DER FERNSEHRICHTLINIE / THE FUTURE OF THE 'TELEVISION WITHOUT FRONTIERS' DIRECTIVE (Baden-Baden: Nomos Verlag, 2005), 65–73.

[39] Gervais, *supra* n. 27.

pursuant to public policy external to copyright issues, such as freedom of expression and competition law, since this would imply a hierarchy of copyright over other domains of law, which would effectively render the copyright system immune against such external sources. However, as case law from the highest courts reveals, such a hierarchy does not exist.[40]

Scope of the three-step test

The mother of all three-step tests, art. 9(2) BC, applies only to the right of reproduction guaranteed in art. 9(1) BC. Other economic rights guaranteed under the Convention come either with corresponding specific limitations (for example, quotation), or none at all. In the latter case, the 'minor exceptions' doctrine may apply. Given the structure of the Berne Convention, the three-step test arguably does not extend to a State exercise of discretion pursuant to those articles where such discretion has explicitly been granted, such as arts 2*bis*, 10 and 10*bis*. Thus, States may freely enact legislation with respect to the subjects covered in these provisions without the restrictions of the three-step test.[41]

Art. 13 TRIPS takes the test an important step further. It now applies to all economic rights guaranteed by TRIPS as minimum standards. These include not only the rights newly recognized in TRIPS, such as the right of rental (art. 11 TRIPS), but also the panoply of rights of the Berne acquis as incorporated into TRIPS (art. 9(1)TRIPS).[42] Likewise, art. 13 TRIPS most likely applies not only to express limitations but also to the 'minor reservations' implied in the Berne Convention.[43]

What is still unclear, however, is whether art. 13 TRIPS would permit three-step test compliant exceptions and limitations that are not allowed under the Berne Convention on account of Berne's more limited 'minor reservations' doctrine. This was one of several preliminary issues raised

---

[40] See, for example, P. Bernt Hugenholtz, *Copyright and Freedom of Expression in Europe*, in ROCHELLE C. DREYFUSS, DIANE L. ZIMMERMAN & HARRY FIRST (eds), EXPANDING THE BOUNDARIES OF INTELLECTUAL PROPERTY. INNOVATION POLICY FOR THE KNOWLEDGE SOCIETY (Oxford: Oxford University Press, 2001), 343–63 (demonstrating that European courts regularly subject copyright claims to external freedom expression norms); L. Guibault (ALAI 1998), 46–48 (external limiting of copyright by competition law well established in various national and supranational courts). See also infra Section 3.

[41] WIPO Standing Committee on Copyright and Related Rights, WIPO Study on Limitations and Exceptions of Copyright and Related Rights in the Digital Environment, 9th Session, June 23–7, 2003, WIPO Doc. SCCR/9/7 (April 5, 2003) (hereinafter WIPO Study), at 21; RICKETSON & GINSBURG, *supra* n. 6, at 763.

[42] US – Section 110(5) Report, *supra* n. 23, §6.80.

[43] US – Section 110(5) Report, *supra* n. 23, §6.81.

in the *IMRO* case. According to the European Community, this would effectively undermine the Berne acquis and therefore create a conflict with art. 20 BC and art. 2(2) TRIPS.[44] On the other hand, according to the United States, '[t]he text of Article 13 is straightforward and applies to "limitations or exceptions to exclusive rights". Not *some* limitations, not limitations to *some* exclusive rights.'[45] In the end, the WTO Panel did not have to resolve the issue, because the contentious provision of the US Copyright Act was judged by the Panel to be in direct conflict with TRIPS art. 13.[46]

Art. 10 WCT appears to be stricter and has a more pronounced dual function than art. 13 TRIPS. Art. 10(1) WCT concerns the rights newly granted in arts 6, 7 and 8 of the WCT. Like art. 9(2) BC, art. 10(1) WCT can therefore be directly invoked as a basis for national limitations. But art. WCT 10(2) serves a different function. It obligates States contracting to the WCT, which are bound to comply with the substantive provisions of the BC by virtue of art. 1(4), to subject any limitations thereto, arguably including the so-called 'minor reservations',[47] to the three-step test. Thus, like art. 13 TRIPS, art. 10(2) of the WCT applies to limitations and exceptions to all the economic rights already recognized by Berne. The potential impact of art. 10(2) WCT on Berne limitations, however, is neutralized by the Agreed statements concerning art. 10:[48]

> It is understood that the provisions of Article 10 permit Contracting Parties to carry forward and appropriately extend into the digital environment limitations and exceptions in their national laws, which have been considered acceptable under the Berne Convention. Similarly, these provisions should be understood to permit Contracting Parties to devise new exceptions and limitations that are appropriate in the digital networked environment. It is also understood that Article 10 (2) of the WCT neither reduces nor extends the scope of applicability of the limitations and exceptions permitted by the Berne Convention.[49]

Following a literal reading of the test, as enshrined in various international treaties, the three steps of the test must apply cumulatively. This is indeed the general opinion of the WTO Panel in the *IMRO* decision:

---

44 US – Section 110(5) Report, *supra* n. 23, §§6.76–6.77. Cf. D. Gervais, The TRIPS Agreement: Drafting History and Analysis (London: Sweet & Maxwell, 1998), 89 (arguing that TRIPS art. 13 'does not create new exceptions').

45 US – Section 110(5) Report, *supra* n. 23, §6.79.

46 US – Section 110(5) Report, *supra* n. 23, §6.82.

47 US – Section 110(5) Report, *supra* n. 23, §6.69.

48 Senftleben, in: Th. Dreier and P. Bernt Hugenholtz (eds) (2006), *Concise European Copyright Law*, WCT, art. 10, note 6(b) Kluwer Law International.

49 WCT, *supra* n. 3, Agreed statements concerning Article 10.

'Failure to comply with any one of the three conditions results in the Article 13 exception being disallowed'.[50] By necessity, such cumulative application implies that at least the first and second steps be applied in a liberal manner, so as to leave some relevance to the third and final step.[51] A narrow construction of these initial steps would otherwise rob the third test of most of its meaning. For this reason, Dr Geiger has advocated reading the test in reverse, that is, starting with the third test and working backwards from there. Such a reading is likely to accentuate the normative considerations built into the third (then first) step of the test. Indeed, nothing in the wording of the three-step test would prevent a legislator, international court or a WTO panel from following this approach.[52]

Another approach, which admittedly takes more liberties with the wording of the provision, would be to perceive the norms reflected in the three steps as a trio of factors to be taken into account by legislators or courts – much like the four factors of fair use in section 107 of the US Copyright Act.[53] This approach has the obvious advantage of offering greater flexibility. A limitation might score low on, for instance, the first or second step, but could still be admitted by scoring high on the third test. Indeed, such a 'holistic' approach would do more justice to the proportionality test that in essence underlies the three-step test.[54]

The three steps in some detail

No authoritative interpretation of the three-step test has ever been given under the Berne Convention.[55] However, national courts have applied, or at least referred to, the three-step test on many occasions, even before the incorporation of the test in European jurisdictions. The interpretation and application of the test by national courts varies considerably. For instance, while some European courts have judged statutory limitations that allow unauthorized digital 'press clipping' to be compliant with the three-step test, others – in almost identical cases – have not.[56]

In 2000, art. 13 TRIPS was interpreted in considerable detail in

---

50 US – Section 110(5) Report, *supra* n. 23, §6.87.

51 See, for example, SENFTLEBEN, *supra* n. 24, at 244.

52 Geiger, *supra* n. 34, at 18.

53 K.J. Koelman, *Fixing the Three-Step Test*, EIPR 2006; Geiger, *supra* n. 34, at 19.

54 SENFTLEBEN, *supra* n. 24, at 243.

55 Such an interpretation could have been given only by the International Court of Justice, see art. 33 BC; RICKETSON & GINSBURG, *supra* n. 6, at 1152.

56 See Geiger, *supra* n. 29, at 489 (discussing individual national cases).

the *IMRO* case.[57] Another Panel has interpreted the test's patent law corollary – TRIPS art. 30 – in similar detail.[58] While both Panel Reports contain valuable analyses of the three-step test and of its place and function in the international law of intellectual property, it should be borne in mind that the WTO Panels are not courts and that the legal framework within which they operate is the law of international trade, not of copyright. Thus, WTO Panels are likely to be relatively insensitive to arguments based on fundamental rights and freedoms or (other) non-economic (for example, cultural or educational) public interests, even if art. 7 TRIPS mandates that the protection of intellectual property rights be 'conducive to social and economic welfare, and to a balance of rights and obligations'.[59] Also, it is unlikely for a variety of reasons that decisions of WTO Panels qualify as definitive interpretations of the relevant norms in question.[60] In sum, WTO Panel decisions ought to have only limited precedent value for international courts, such as the International Court of Justice, which is competent to interpret the BC and the WCT, or national courts interpreting national norms of copyright law.

Step 1: Special Cases

Under the first prong of the three-step test, limitations and exceptions must be confined to 'certain special cases'. Although one might argue that any purpose-specific limitation complies with this requirement almost by definition, making the first step basically superfluous,[61] the *IMRO* Panel Report does contain exhaustive discussion of this threshold criterion. The word 'certain' implies, according to the Panel, that, as a matter of legal certainty, a limitation must be well-defined. However, this does not rule

---

57 See US – Section 110(5) Report, *supra* n. 23.

58 WTO Panel Report, Canada-Patent Protection of Pharmaceutical Products, April 7, 2000, WTO Doc. WT/DS114/R. See also Panel Reports for the trademark-related cases WT/DS174/R and DS2890/R (*US and Australia v. EU*). For a comparison of all three panel decisions, see M. Senftleben, *Towards a Horizontal Standard for Limiting Intellectual Property Rights? – WTO Panel Reports Shed Light on the Three-step Test in Copyright Law and Related Rights in Patent and Trademark Law*, IIC 2006/4, at 407.

59 See Ruth L. Okediji, *Toward an International Fair Use Doctrine*, 39 Colum. J. Transnat'l L. 75 (2000). See also R. Cooper Dreyfuss, *TRIPS-Round II: Should Users Strike Back?*, 71 U. Chi. L. Rev. 21, 22 (2004).

60 Senftleben, *supra* n. 24, at 107–108.

61 Daniel J. Gervais, *Towards a New Core International Copyright Norm: The Reverse Three-step Test*, 9 Marq. Intell. Prop. L. Rev. 1 (2005).

out broadly phrased limitations, such as the fair use exemption in the United States, as a matter of principle:[62]

> ... there is no need to identify explicitly each and every possible situation to which the exception could apply, provided that the scope of the exception is known and particularised. This guarantees a sufficient degree of legal certainty.[63]

The Panel subsequently interpreted the term 'special' as meaning something akin to exceptional. 'In other words, an exception or limitation should be narrow in quantitative as well as a qualitative sense.'[64] The Panel thus rejected the interpretation advanced by several scholars, that 'special' has normative meaning (that is, that the purpose of the exempted use be objectively justifiable).[65] However, according to the Panel, the term 'special' does not imply that policy objectives pursued by the limitation or exception at issue need to be objectively justified, as was argued by the EC in the case.

> In our view, the first condition of Article 13 requires that a limitation or exception in national legislation should be clearly defined and should be narrow in its scope and reach. On the other hand, a limitation or exception may be compatible with the first condition even if it pursues a special purpose whose underlying legitimacy in a normative sense cannot be discerned. The wording of Article 13's first condition does not imply passing a judgment on the legitimacy of the exceptions in dispute.[66]

In other words, it is left to the discretion of WTO members to determine the need for and the objectives of exceptions and limitations as they see fit.

Step 2: No Conflict with Normal Exploitation

The second step is arguably more critical, and the WTO Panel's interpretation thereof certainly more controversial. The Panel's reading of 'normal exploitation' is essentially economical, and consequently restrictive:

> We believe that an exception or limitation to an exclusive right in domestic legislation rises to the level of a conflict with a normal exploitation of the work (i.e., the copyright or rather the whole bundle of exclusive rights conferred by the ownership of the copyright), if uses, that in principle are covered by that

---

62 Several scholars have questioned whether the fair use doctrine complies with (the first part of) the three-step test. See Ricketson, *supra* n. 19, at 68–769; Okediji, *supra* n. 59, at 148; Senftleben, *supra* n. 24, at 162.

63 US – Section 110(5) Report, *supra* n. 23, §6.108.

64 US – Section 110(5) Report, *supra* n. 23, §6.109.

65 Ricketson, *supra* n. 19; Senftleben, *supra* n. 24, at 137 et seq.

66 US – Section 110(5) Report, *supra* n. 23, §6.112.

> right but exempted under the exception or limitation, enter into economic competition with the ways that right holders normally extract economic value from that right to the work (i.e., the copyright) and thereby deprive them of significant or tangible commercial gains.[67]

According to the Panel, the term 'normal' has two connotations (§6.166). Normal exploitation is, firstly, all that a right holder may – empirically – expect from exploiting the work. This interpretation obviously suffers from a certain circularity, as right holders will not expect income from rights that are subjected to exceptions. Accordingly, normal exploitation also relates to 'those forms of exploitation which, with a certain degree of likelihood and plausibility, could acquire considerable economic or practical importance' (§6.180). In other words, normal exploitation includes what right holders *may* expect from potential or future markets (§6.184). But yet again, there is an element of circularity in this interpretation. As more refined ways of exercising economic rights on a micro-level become economically feasible,[68] the field of 'normal exploitation' increases, and the discretion of States to introduce or maintain limitations is gradually whittled away. Fortunately, the Panel does admit that right holders are not protected in their expectation that they may exploit their economic rights to their fullest possible extent, that is, to the very last drop. Or else, no limitations would survive the test and the three-step test would become an empty shell (§6.167).

To avoid a circularity of reasoning that would effectively eclipse exceptions and limitations, Dr Senftleben has proposed to revisit the preparatory works of the Stockholm Conference. According to the Conference record, normal exploitation would encompass 'all forms of exploiting a work, which have, or are likely to acquire, considerable economic or practical importance'.[69] The WTO Panel appears to subscribe to this historic reading by opining:

> Thus it appears that one way of measuring the normative connotation of normal exploitation is to consider, in addition to those forms of exploitation that currently generate significant or tangible revenue, those forms of exploitation which, with a certain degree of likelihood and plausibility, could acquire considerable economic or practical importance.[70]

---

[67] US – Section 110(5) Report, *supra* n. 23, §6.183.

[68] US – Section 110(5) Report, *supra* n. 23, §6.187 ('What is a normal exploitation in the market-place may evolve as a result of technological developments or changing consumer preferences.').

[69] SENFTLEBEN, *supra* n. 24, at 177 et seq.; Dusollier, *supra* n. 29, at 219.

[70] US – Section 110(5) Report, *supra* n. 23, §6.180.

In other words, there is a conflict with the second step if the exempted use would rob the right holder of a real or potential source of income that is substantive.

Although the Panel refers to this second connotation as 'normative', it does not factor in any truly normative considerations in the second step. In this respect, the Panel decision differs markedly from the Panel decision in the Canadian patent term case. In its analysis of the criterion of normal exploitation in art. 30 TRIPS, the WTO Patent Panel standardized right holders' expectations by reference to the policy objectives underlying patent protection. Exploitation of patents is normal only insofar as it is 'essential to the achievement of the goals of patent policy'.[71]

STEP 3: NO UNREASONABLE PREJUDICE TO AUTHORS/RIGHT HOLDERS

In contrast to the second step, the third step seems to leave legislatures considerable flexibility. What the *IMRO* Panel has opined on the third step repeats much of its dictum on the second step; it appears the Panel has confused the final two steps.[72] There appears to be considerable wiggle room in the terms 'prejudice', 'unreasonable' and 'legitimate'. As to 'prejudice', the Panel opined:

> . . . a certain amount of 'prejudice' has to be presumed justified as 'not unreasonable'. In our view, prejudice to the legitimate interests of right holders reaches an unreasonable level if an exception or limitation causes or has the potential to cause an unreasonable loss of income to the copyright owner.[73]

At the 1967 Stockholm Conference, a principle was established that the payment of *equitable remuneration* could be taken into account in the context of the third criterion.[74] In other words, the third step (further) restricts the availability of *uncompensated* exceptions.[75] Note, once again, that the wording of the third step in art. 13 TRIPS refers to the interests of the 'right holder', not of the 'author'. While, arguably, a relatively far-reaching limitation may be compatible with art. 9(2) BC by combining it with a statutory scheme promising compensation to authors (for example, by way of levies), such a solution might fall short of TRIPS art. 13, since right holders might have more to gain from keeping their economic rights intact than from receiving compensation.

---

71 Senftleben, *supra* n. 58, at 424.
72 Gervais, *supra* n. 27.
73 US – Section 110(5) Report, *supra* n. 23, §6.229.
74 SENFTLEBEN, *supra* n. 24, at 237.
75 Gervais, *supra* n. 27.

The terms 'legitimate' and 'reasonable' at last inject a measure of normative meaning into the three-step test.[76] Both terms allow an, in principle infinite, variety of public interests to be factored into the three-step equation.[77] By the same token, these terms allow fundamental rights and freedoms, such as the right to privacy (which might, for example, justify a freedom to make private copies) or freedom of expression (which could justify an entire spectrum of excepted uses), to be factored into the three-step test.

Final remarks

Scholars tend to read different meanings into the three-step test. While classic copyright doctrine underscores its function as imposing limits on the 'erosion' of copyright by limitations and exceptions, more progressive scholars perceive the three-step test as no more than a 'proportionality test' allowing national legislatures a relatively broad measure of discretion in codifying limitations and exceptions, while balancing the interests of right holders against those of users and society at large.[78] Read in such a constructive and dynamic fashion, the three-step test becomes a clause not merely limiting limitations, but empowering contracting States to enact them, subject to the proportionality test that forms its core and that fully takes into account, inter alia, fundamental rights and freedoms and the general public interest.[79] According to Dr Senftleben:

> The three-step test thus is both a limiting and enabling clause alike. It is a proportionality test which enables the weighing of the different interests involved at the national level so as to strike a proper balance between rights and limitations.[80]

Further flexibilities could be created by identifying current State practices in respect of limitations and exceptions, which might serve as a valuable aid in interpreting art. 13 TRIPS in a dynamic way.[81] For example,

---

76 Gervais, *supra* n. 61, at 17.

77 Note that the WTO Panels in the corresponding patent and trademark law cases expressly referred to the interests of 'third parties', as a factor determining legitimacy. WTO Panel Reports, *supra* n. 58.

78 See 'Declaration: A Balanced Interpretation of the "Three-Step Test" in Copyright Law', drafted by the Max Planck Institute and Queen Mary University in collaboration with a large number of mostly European scholars, available at http://www.law.qmul.ac.uk/events/docs/Declaration%20Three-Step%20Test.pdf.

79 See, for example, Geiger, *supra* n. 29, at 490–91.

80 Senftleben, *supra* n. 48, at note 1(b).

81 See art. 31(3) of the Vienna Agreement; SENFTLEBEN, *supra* n. 24, at 101.

if a considerable number of WTO members considers limitation X to be compliant with the test, then such consensus can hardly be ignored by a WTO panel. Similarly, official language in preambles, agreed statements and the like accompanying post-TRIPS agreements, such as the WCT, could retroactively infuse meaning into the norms of the BC as incorporated into TRIPS and the three-step test. In this context, the importance of the Agreed Statements concerning art. 10 of the WCT can hardly be overstated.[82]

The preceding analysis leads to the conclusion that limitations and exceptions that (1) are not overly broad, (2) do not rob right holders of a real or potential source of income that is substantive, and (3) do not do disproportional harm to the right holders, will pass the test. The test does not prescribe a template for any preferred system of national limitations and exceptions. The test most likely permits both discrete European-style limitations and broader fair-use-style exemptions, or possibly a combination of both.[83]

4. Conclusion

In conclusion, despite an unmistakable 'ratcheting up' of levels of copyright protection at the international, regional and bilateral levels, ample flexibilities appear to be left to the members of the WTO to preserve existing limitations or introduce new ones. Despite over a century of international norm setting in the field of copyright, limitations and exceptions have largely remained 'unregulated space'.[84]

Indeed, nothing in the international acquis would prevent members of the WTO from entering into a special agreement listing in an exhaustive or enumerative manner those copyright limitations that are permitted within the confines of the three-step test.[85] One could imagine such an instrument as containing a preamble and a number of provisions, divided into several chapters, for example: (1) *Exclusions from protection* (excluding, for instance, facts, ideas, laws and government works); (2) *Limits to economic*

---

[82] Dusollier, *supra* n. 29, at 214.

[83] M. Senftleben, *Beperkingen à la Carte: Waarom de Auteursrechtrichtlijn Ruimte Laat voor Fair Use*, AMI 2003/1, at 10 (arguing that the EC Copyright Directive, despite its positivist provenance, permits a broadly worded, fair-use style limitation within the confines of the three-step test).

[84] Gervais, *supra* n. 27.

[85] See P. Bernt Hugenholtz and R. Okediji, 'Conceiving an International Instrument on Limitations and Exceptions to Copyright', study sponsored by the Open Society Institute (OSI), *available at* http://www.ivir.nl/publicaties/hugenholtz/finalreport2008.pdf (discussing various modalities of an international instrument on limitations and exceptions).

rights (permitting, for instance, exhaustion and various non-public acts of communication); and (3) *Limitations and exceptions proper*. As concluded earlier, only the norms listed in the latter part would have to comply with the three-step test. Here the EU Information Society Directive of 2001[86] inspires a pragmatic, albeit not very elegant, solution. Like the Directive, an international instrument on limitations and exceptions could provide a list of (mandatory and optional) limitations, and conclude with a general obligation for contracting States to subject any transpositions thereof to the three-step test.[87] A preamble might then offer guidance to the contracting States in interpreting the test.[88]

For an exemplary catalogue of limitations and exceptions that are presumably compliant with the international acquis, one need to look no further than the twenty-odd limitations and exceptions enumerated in the Information Society Directive. The Directive introduces an exhaustive list containing a single mandatory limitation (permitting transient copying incidental to digital communications, including caching and browsing) and twenty-one optional limitations, all subject to the 'three-step-test'.[89] The limitations officially authorized by the EC legislature concern not only such generally accepted uses as reprography (that is, photocopying), private copying (subject to 'fair compensation'), archival and ephemeral copying, educational uses, use in news reporting and quotation, but also more esoteric uses, such as use in religious celebrations, use for the purpose of 'caricature, parody or pastiche', 'use in connection with the demonstration or repair of equipment', etc. Interestingly, and in deviation from the European style of precisely circumscribed limitations, the list also permits an open-worded limitation allowing the 'incidental inclusion of work . . . in other material'.[90]

As recent European experience with the Directive shows, codification of a catalogue of exceptions in a supranational instrument may help national States to reassess their national needs and priorities in terms of copyright limitations. Despite the optional character of nearly all of the limitations and exceptions codified in the Directive, during the process of national

---

86 Art. 5 Directive 2001/29/EC.

87 See art. 5.5 Directive 2001/29/EC ('The exceptions and limitations provided for [. . .] shall only be applied in certain special cases which do not conflict with a normal exploitation of the work or other subject-matter and do not unreasonably prejudice the legitimate interests of the rightholder.').

88 In following this approach, however, care should be taken to avoid a proliferation of the test into the norms of national law. See Geiger, *supra* n. 29.

89 Art. 5 Directive 2001/29/EC.

90 Art. 5(3)(i) Directive 2001/29/EC.

transposition, many Member States have added exceptions from the list to their national repertoire.[91] Thus the Directive's enumeration has effectively served as a confidence-building measure at the national levels. The Directive's chapter on limitations and exceptions is, however, also proof of the drawback of an *optional* approach towards limitations and exceptions. Of the 27 Member States of the European Union, not a single State has seen fit to implement *all* the limitations and exceptions permitted under the Directive.[92]

---

[91] See L. Guibault, G. Westkamp, T. Rieber-Mohn et al., *Study on the Implementation and Effect in Member States' Laws of Directive 2001/29/EC on the Harmonisation of Certain Aspects of Copyright and Related Rights in the Information Society*, Report to the European Commission, DG Internal Market, February 2007, available at http://www.ivir.nl/publications/guibault/Infosoc_report_2007.pdf. See in particular Part II: G. Westkamp, *The Implementation of Directive 2001/29/EC in the Member States*, available at http://www.ivir.nl/publications/guibault/InfoSoc_Study_2007.pdf.

[92] Guibault et al., *supra* n. 91.

11 Copyright in TRIPS and beyond: the WIPO Internet Treaties

*Ruth L. Okediji**

Introduction

The World Intellectual Property Organization (WIPO) Copyright Treaty[1] (WCT) and the WIPO Performances and Phonograms Treaty[2] (WPPT) (collectively, the WIPO Internet Treaties) entered into force in 2002,[3] officially ushering global copyright law into the information age. Both the WCT and WPPT formally acknowledged the 'profound' impact of information and communication technologies on the creation and use of literary and artistic works, and on the production and use of performances and phonograms. The legal framework established by the Treaties was directed at facilitating 'adequate solutions to questions raised by new economic, social, cultural and technological developments'.[4] Yet it can hardly be contested that the social and cultural developments to which the Treaties refer did not emanate from the cultural or economic conditions (much less technological developments) of countries in the global South.

---

* This chapter is based on an earlier article, *The Regulation of Creativity under the WIPO Internet Treaties*, 77 *Fordham Law Review*, 2379 (2009). I am grateful for comments from participants at the Fordham Symposium on When Worlds Collide: Intellectual Property at the Interface between Systems of Knowledge Creation, April 2009.

[1] World Intellectual Property Organization [WIPO] Copyright Treaty, December 20, 1996, S. Treaty Doc. No. 105–17, 36 ILM 65 (1997) [hereinafter WCT].

[2] WIPO Performances and Phonograms Treaty, December 20, 1996, S. Treaty Doc. No. 105–17, 36 ILM 76 (1997) [hereinafter WPPT].

[3] For a treaty to enter into force means it has become binding between the parties that have ratified or acceded to it. Both treaties required thirty states to ratify or accede before they entered into force. See WPPT, *supra* note 2, Art. 29; WCT, *supra* note 1, art. 21. The WCT entered into force on March 6, 2002; the WPPT followed suit on May 20, 2002. The WCT had seventy parties as of March 22, 2009. WIPO, Contracting Parties – WCT, http://www.wipo.int/treaties/en/ShowResults.jsp?lang=en&treaty_id=16 (last visited March 22, 2009) [hereinafter WCT Contracting Parties]. As of the same date, the WPPT had sixty-eight signatories. WIPO, Contracting Parties – WPPT, http://www.wipo.int/ treaties/en/ShowResults.jsp?lang=en&treaty_id=20 (last visited March 22, 2009).

[4] *See* WPPT, *supra* note 2, pmbl.; WCT, *supra* note 1, pmbl.

Instead, in tandem with the TRIPS Agreement,[5] the WIPO Internet Treaties were crafted on two fundamental pillars: (1) a commitment to shield copyright proprietary interests from the extraordinary capacity to reproduce, alter and distribute created works through digital networks; and (2) a commitment to entrench an enhanced capacity for copyright owners to generate rent and control the terms of use of knowledge-based goods. Accordingly, despite the distinct institutional systems in which the WIPO Internet Treaties and TRIPS Agreement were negotiated, the fundamental assumptions that underlie both these regimes are firmly aligned in support of a specific vision of global copyright regulation.

Like prior copyright treaties, the WCT and the WPPT hinge on the contested utilitarianism that defines modern international copyright law, namely, that proprietary incentives are a primary requirement for knowledge creation.[6] Digital technologies have disrupted long-settled canons of this classic copyright defense in fundamental ways.[7] First, these technologies have made it possible to overcome characteristic public goods limitations by perfecting authorial control over terms of access to creative works. As firmly established business models failed to capture rent through the full range of exploitation made possible by digital technologies, copyright owners through the Internet Treaties sought a presumptive fiat over the architecture that made use and distribution over digital networks a pervasive feature of contemporary social interaction. Second, and more recently, the momentous rise of social networking tools occasioned an acute shift in the cultural and market realities confronting content proprietors. In particular, the rise of Web 2.0 forcefully demonstrated claims long recognized and championed by cultural anthropologists, literary historians, and a growing cadre of copyright scholars – namely that creative expression is motivated by a complex set of factors to which copyright law should be attuned, and that access to protected works is an indispensable part of the copyright bargain designed to encourage and reward the creative enterprise. Innovation, in both its historical and contemporary technological context relies significantly on access to an established body of knowledge whether codified in the copyright system as 'works of authorship' or excluded from it by a range of copyright principles that serve as conduits to a robust public domain.

---

[5] Agreement on Trade-Related Aspects of Intellectual Property Rights, April 15, 1994, Marrakesh Agreement Establishing the World Trade Organization, Annex 1C, 1869 UNTS 299; 33 ILM 1197 (1994).

[6] WCT, *supra* note 1, pmbl., para. 4.

[7] See, for example, Yochai Benkler, The Wealth of Networks: How Social Production Transforms Markets and Freedom (2006); James Boyle, The Public Domain: Enclosing the Commons of the Mind 54–159 (2008).

Despite the unrestrained versatility of creative exercise in the digital arena, the WIPO Internet Treaties have fallen considerably short in what was to be their central mission to provide a relevant and credible source of norms to facilitate knowledge creation in the global digital context. Academic commentary describing the perceived victories of the treaty negotiations for copyright's age-old balancing act between incentives and access initially led to euphoric headlines such as *Africa 1 Hollywood 0*,[8] which hailed an outcome that many agreed recognized public-oriented considerations in the design of global copyright.[9] In the midst of the celebration over what did *not* happen in Geneva, given the ambitious agenda of copyright proprietors,[10] there was express acknowledgement that what hung in the balance was the future of consumer interaction with new digital technologies and, specifically, how copyright law would mold that future.[11]

In retrospect, it seems presumptuous to have arrogated such centripetal power to copyright doctrine when the treaties were intentionally far less concerned with enabling new modes of creative enterprise than preserving the existing presumptions in favor of authorial prerogative.[12] Section 1

---

[8] See John Browning, *Africa 1 Hollywood 0*, WIRED, March 1997, at 61; see also Pamela Samuelson, *Big Media Beaten Back*, WIRED, March 1997, at 61 [hereinafter Samuelson, *Big Media*]; Pamela Samuelson, *The Copyright Grab*, WIRED, January 1996, at 134 [hereinafter Samuelson, *The Copyright Grab*].

[9] See Pamela Samuelson, *The U.S. Digital Agenda at WIPO*, 37 VA. J. INT'L L. 369, 370–71 (1997) (noting that, as concluded, the treaties 'are more compatible with traditional principles of U.S. copyright law than was the high-protectionist agenda that U.S. officials initially sought to promote in Geneva'); see also David Nimmer, *A Tale of Two Treaties: Dateline: Geneva – December 1996*, 22 COLUM.–VLA JL & ARTS 1, 1 (1997) ('It was the best of times, it was the worst of times. It was a far, far better copyright treaty than any the world had ever attempted before. It began with Great Expectations; by the end, the participants felt, if not quite like *Les Misérables*, at least as if they had emerged from a Bleak House.').

[10] See Samuelson, *supra* note 9, at 370–71.

[11] *Id.* at 372 (describing the negotiations as 'a battle about the future of copyright in the global information society' (citing Mihály Ficsor, *Towards a Global Solution: The Digital Agenda of the Berne Protocol and the New Instrument*, in THE FUTURE OF COPYRIGHT IN A DIGITAL ENVIRONMENT 111, 118–22 (P. Bernt Hugenholtz ed., 1996); Bruce Lehman, *Intellectual Property and the National and Global Information Infrastructures*, in THE FUTURE OF COPYRIGHT IN A DIGITAL ENVIRONMENT, *supra*, at 103, 103–09)); Browning, *supra* note 8, at 63 ('[The conference] did not give copyright holders many of the new legal powers they asked for – mostly because delegates feared that they would use those powers to force the future into the mold of the past, and so rob the Net of its potential to create change.').

[12] See WORLD INTELLECTUAL PROP. ORG., WIPO INTELLECTUAL PROPERTY

of this chapter briefly reviews the environment from which the WIPO Internet Treaties emerged, focusing specifically on the status of the treaties as special agreements under Article 20 of the Berne Convention for the Protection of Literary and Artistic Works (Berne Convention).[13] I discuss how this designation foreshadowed some of the ensuing developments in international copyright law, specifically by extending a worn paradigm of copyright relations between authors and users that fails to account for the dynamic and iterative nature of the creative enterprise in the digital age, including the significance of digital copyright rules on scientific research.[14]

Section 2 analyzes the new rights introduced by the WCT and evaluates their import for traditional copyright concerns regarding access to knowledge goods. I suggest that, far from harmonizing copyright law with respect to rights in the digital arena, the WCT instead introduced a greater deference to national copyright laws that the Berne Convention had long sought to diminish with respect to traditional copyright. Although initially such deference produced national legislative outcomes that inordinately undermined knowledge creation and the corresponding public interest therein, there is a deepening and unrelenting call for global action,[15] and some positive national responses,[16] that could address the access and

---

Footnote 12 (*cont.*)
HANDBOOK: POLICY, LAW AND USE §§ 5.222–5.227, at 271–2 [hereinafter WIPO HANDBOOK], available at http://www.wipo.int/export/sites/www/about-ip/en/iprm/pdf/ch5.pdf. 'During the preparatory work, an agreement emerged that the transmission of works on the Internet and in similar networks should be the object of an exclusive right of authorization of the author or other copyright owner, with appropriate exceptions.' *Id.* at 271.

[13] Berne Convention for the Protection of Literary and Artistic Works, September 9, 1886, as revised at Paris on July 24, 1971, and amended on September 29, 1979, 25 UST 1341, 828 UNTS 221 [hereinafter Berne Convention].

[14] See generally Reto M. Hilty, *Five Lessons about Copyright in the Information Society: Reaction of the Scientific Community to Over-protection and What Policy Makers Should Learn*, 53 J. COPYRIGHT SOC'Y USA 103 (2006); Jerome H. Reichman & Paul F. Uhlir, *A Contractually Reconstructed Research Commons for Scientific Data in a Highly Protectionist Intellectual Property Environment*, LAW & CONTEMP. PROBS. Winter/Spring 2003, at 315.

[15] See, for example, Keith E. Maskus & Jerome H. Reichman, *The Globalization of Private Knowledge Goods and the Privatization of Global Public Goods*, in INTERNATIONAL PUBLIC GOODS & TRANSFER OF TECHNOLOGY UNDER A GLOBALIZED INTELLECTUAL PROPERTY REGIME 3 (Keith Maskus and Jerome Reichman eds., 2005); Jerome H. Reichman, Graeme Dinwoodie & Pamela Samuelson, *A Reverse Notice and Takedown Regime to Enable Public Interest Uses of Technically Protected Copyrighted Works*, 22 BERKELEY TECH. LJ 981 (2007).

[16] See, for example, *Commission Green Paper on Copyright in the Knowledge Economy*, at 3, 4–6, COM (2008) 466/3, available at http://ec.europa.eu/

innovation deficit associated with an unbalanced international copyright regime.

Section 3 briefly surveys domestic implementation of the WCT based on a WIPO study and explores how national trends in this regard have ineffectively addressed the spectrum of use attendant on digital works, information networks, and their relationship to the commercial success of new technologies. As I argue, the social and legal recognition of new forms of creativity expressed through digital technologies offers an important opportunity to reconsider how international copyright law might accommodate a dynamic collage of incentives to support the innovative process across geographical, cultural, and technological boundaries.[17] What seems unambiguous within the current framework, however, is that the legal premise for which access-based considerations could be developed within the TRIPS Agreement has been inhibited by the unprecedented emphasis on private enforcement mechanisms embodied in the WIPO Internet Treaties.

1. TRIPS, authorship, and consumerism

1.1. Copyright and technology: antecedents on the road to Geneva

Copyright and technology have long shared an intimate relationship, and it is routine to describe copyright law as the product of technological change.[18]

---

internal_market/copyright/docs/ copyright-infso/greenpaper_en.pdf (last visited March 28, 2009) (setting forth a number of issues connected with the role of copyright in the digital age in order to 'foster a debate on how knowledge for research, science and education can best be disseminated in the online environment').

[17] See, for example, Julie E. Cohen, *Creativity and Culture in Copyright Theory*, 40 UC Davis L. Rev. 1151, 1178–92 (2007); Paul E. Geller, *Beyond the Copyright Crisis: Principles for Change*, 55 J. Copyright Soc'y USA 165, 170 (2008) (accentuating 'the truism that culture is enriched as it is fed back for each of us autonomously to elaborate').

[18] See, for example, *Sony Corp. of Am. v. Universal City Studios, Inc.*, 464 US 417, 430 (1984) ('From its beginning, the law of copyright has developed in response to significant changes in technology. Indeed, it was the invention of a new form of copying equipment – the printing press – that gave rise to the original need for copyright protection.' (footnote omitted)); HR Rep. No. 104-554, at 6 (1996) ('The Copyright Act was last generally revised in 1976, in response to the many technological changes that had occurred since the enactment of the 1909 Act. Since 1976, Congress regularly has had to address new issues, especially those raised by new technologies or new methods of exploitation.'); HR Rep. No. 101-735, at 7 (1990) ('Even though the 1976 Copyright Act was carefully drafted to be flexible enough to be applied to future innovations, technology has a habit of outstripping even the most flexible statutes. Copyright is, in large part, a response to new technology.');

From the printed word to maps, charts, and functional objects that today comprise, for example, architectural works,[19] copyright has mediated the relationship between authors and their works on the one hand, between users and copyrighted works on the other, and between the two *inter se*. In the classic copyright story, 'authors' and 'users' are protagonists who occupy distinct spaces and react to copyright differently. Accordingly, the law speaks to one or the other, but never to both simultaneously or with the same concerns.[20] Authors are to be protected by copyright as the fountain of creative expression by which social welfare will be enhanced; users are to be at once benefited by having access to protected works, but also constrained by copyright in order to preserve the incentives that pervade the utilitarian scheme. For much of its history, then, a presumptive cloak woven from notions of an authorial process in which literary works emerge solely from the mind of a single person called an 'author', rather than a 'user', has hung heavily on the copyright frame and powerfully shaped considerations of copyright's allocation of proprietary rights.[21]

The image of copyright law's audience as passive recipients and/or inert absorbers of content also mirrored the long-standing dominant view

---

Footnote 18 (*cont.*)
PAUL GOLDSTEIN, COPYRIGHT'S HIGHWAY: FROM GUTENBERG TO THE CELESTIAL JUKEBOX 21 (Stanford University Press, rev. ed. 2003) (1994) (noting that copyright has always been 'technology's child'); Douglas Reid Weimer, *Digital Audio Recording Technology: Challenges to American Copyright Law*, 22 ST. MARY'S LJ 455, 491 (1990) ('Over the years, American copyright law has evolved in order to respond to societal and technological changes.').

[19] See John B. Fowles, *The Utility of a Bright-line Rule in Copyright Law: Freeing Judges from Aesthetic Controversy and Conceptual Separability in* Leicester v. Warner Bros., 12 UCLA ENT. L. REV. 301, 308 n. 41 (2005) (tracing evolution and expansion of the subjects of copyright protection to the inclusion of architectural works).

[20] For criticism of this binary approach and arguments in favor of a more developed construction of the consumer in copyright law, see Joseph P. Liu, *Copyright Law's Theory of the Consumer*, 44 BCL REV. 397 (2003).

[21] For criticisms of this view of the individual 'romantic' author, see, for example, Peter Jaszi, *On the Author Effect: Contemporary Copyright and Collective Creativity*, 10 CARDOZO ARTS & ENT. LJ 293, 302, 319–20 (1992) [hereinafter Jaszi, *On the Author Effect*]; Peter Jaszi, *Toward a Theory of Copyright: The Metamorphoses of 'Authorship'*, 1991 DUKE LJ 455, 458–60; Jessica Litman, *The Public Domain*, 39 EMORY LJ 965, 965–6 (1990) ('Our copyright law is based on the charming notion that authors create something from nothing, that works owe their origin to the authors who produce them.' (citing MELVILLE B. NIMMER & DAVID NIMMER, NIMMER ON COPYRIGHT §§ 1.06[A], 201[A], at 2–8.1 (1989)); Martha Woodmansee, *On the Author Effect: Recovering Collectivity*, 10 CARDOZO ARTS & ENT. LJ 279, 288–92 (1992)).

of copyright relations between developed and developing countries. In orthodox accounts of global copyright relations, the demands of developing countries for access and use of copyrighted works have been analyzed primarily in terms of the priorities associated with conditions conducive for economic development, and not with the core principle that recognizes access to knowledge goods as a basic requisite of the creative process. As a result, stronger copyright rights in the global setting have become synonymous with 'economic growth' and 'development' while matters associated with how to stimulate access to knowledge goods for purposes of enhancing creative production have been marginalized in the legal doctrines that inform international copyright law. This impoverished vision of copyright regulation became the subject of increasing scholarly criticism with respect to developing countries[22] as well as domestically in some developed countries,[23] just as the emergence of digital technology revealed in concrete, practical terms the inadequacy of a conceptual framework in which stronger copyright protection was presumed to beget greater creativity.

The consumer electronics revolution of the late 1980s, which presaged the digital revolution, altered how *consumers* could access and experience creative works on a scale akin perhaps to how the printing press changed how *owners* could control access to and copying of literary works. By the late 1990s, the ubiquity of the Internet over the mundane and the sublime aspects of daily life engendered symmetry between owners and users of digital works, concurrently empowering the capacity of both groups to reach markets with protected works in unprecedented fashion. Owners and consumers were equally disrupted from their settled expectations surrounding the production, distribution, and experience of the creative enterprise;[24] but, very quickly, owners seized upon the imprimatur of

---

[22] See, for example, Ruth L. Okediji, *Sustainable Access to Copyrighted Digital Information Works in Developing Countries*, in Maskus and Reichman, *supra* note 15.

[23] See, for example, Julie E. Cohen, *Creativity and Culture in Copyright Theory*, 40 UC Davis L. Rev. 1151, 1179 (2007) (noting the 'conventional dichotomies between author and consumer, author and imitator, author and improver, and author and critic that pervade the copyright literature'). See also generally Jaszi, *On the Author Effect*, *supra* note 21 (summarizing various critiques of the author concept); Litman, *supra* note 21; Liu, *supra* note 20.

[24] Digital media are leading industries and consumers 'to abandon the central reality of modern economic life – the market exchange of property between sellers and buyers'. Jeremy Rifkin, The Age of Access: The New Culture of Hypercapitalism, Where All of Life Is a Paid-For Experience 4 (2000); see also Paul Ganley, *Digital Copyright and the New Creative Dynamics*, 12 Int'l JL & Info. Tech. 282, 302–03 (2004) ('Consumers seem eager to immerse themselves in a

copyright title to assert priority in considerations of what new rights might be needed to fully exploit the new media to distribute works, while also controlling access and use.[25] Underlying the presumption of authorial ascendancy was a more complex set of ideals that viewed the digital arena as no more than another technological stage that justified copyright status with regard to treating owners as the only indispensable actors in formulating the copyright bargain. It was in this immediate context that the rationale for the WIPO Internet Treaties began to emerge.

Within the context of the Agreement on Trade-related Aspects of Intellectual Property Rights (TRIPS) important limits on the scope of copyright protection had already been introduced, in some cases for the first time in international copyright history. For example, Article 7 of the Agreement described the objectives of intellectual property protection in stark utilitarian terms, stating that protection and enforcement of rights should 'contribute to the promotion of technological innovation and to the transfer and dissemination of technology, to the mutual advantage of producers and users of technological knowledge and in a manner conducive to social and economic welfare, and to a balance of rights and obligations'. This constitutes a seminal articulation of a purpose-driven copyright agreement – one in which the creative ends of the specific rights recognized were explicitly identified in the formal treaty text. Further, Article 7 represents the first

---

Footnote 24 (*cont.*)
digital entertainment market whilst the industry clings to antiquated conceptions of the copy and redundant distribution channels.'); Michael P. Matesky II, Note, *The Digital Millennium Copyright Act and Non-infringing Use: Can Mandatory Labeling of Digital Media Products Keep the Sky From Falling?*, 80 CHI.–KENT L. REV. 515, 516 (2005) (noting impact of technology on consumers' expectations about fair use).

25 See WORKING GROUP ON INTELLECTUAL PROP. RIGHTS, INFO. INFRASTRUCTURE TASK FORCE, INTELLECTUAL PROPERTY AND THE NATIONAL INFORMATION INFRASTRUCTURE: A PRELIMINARY DRAFT OF THE REPORT OF THE WORKING GROUP ON INTELLECTUAL PROPERTY RIGHTS pt. II (1994), available at http://palimpsest.stanford.edu/bytopic/intprop/ipwg/ (describing how technology can be used to control distribution of, and access to, protected works); WORKING GROUP ON INTELLECTUAL PROP. RIGHTS, INFO. INFRASTRUCTURE TASK FORCE, INTELLECTUAL PROPERTY AND THE NATIONAL INFORMATION INFRASTRUCTURE: THE REPORT OF THE WORKING GROUP ON INTELLECTUAL PROPERTY RIGHTS 177 (1995), available at http://www.uspto.gov/go/com/doc/ipnii/ipnii.pdf ('Concurrently, copyright owners are developing and implementing technical solutions to facilitate the delivery of protected works in an easy, consumer-friendly yet reliable and secure way. These solutions enable copyright owners not only to protect their works against unauthorized access, reproduction, manipulation, distribution, performance or display, but also serve to assure the integrity of these works and to address copyright management and licensing concerns.').

instance in which the international framework identified the 'advantage of users' as a goal of the system, and on terms correlated with the advantage of owners. As other commentators have pointed out, Article 7 contains no positive obligation to address users' interests as such. Nonetheless, this provision identifies the welfare objectives of intellectual property protection as a norm consistent with the goals of the global system. As such, it offers a principled basis for assessing the extent to which national laws can be designed to satisfy the competing claims of content proprietors, creators, consumers of knowledge goods and the public interest at large.[26]

In addition, the TRIPS Agreement codified the idea/expression dichotomy,[27] eliminated mandatory protection for moral rights[28] and declined to extend protection to non-original compilations of data.[29] These limitations in the TRIPS Agreement represent important milestones in the evolution of international copyright norms. Not only are these significant deviations from the highly protectionist ethos of the Berne Convention, but the doctrinal limitations also represent an attempt to insulate the public domain from encroachment by global copyright mandate. Rather than build on this promising set of constraints, the WIPO Internet Treaties reflect, instead, the highly protectionist ethos associated with the Uruguay Round trade context. The prospect of mass-scale copying of digital works resurrected the passive image of copyright's audience with ever greater force and inflexibility. The increased autonomy, privacy, secrecy, and ease with which copyrighted works could be used or enjoyed generated immense angst in the entertainment industry, particularly over the security of traditional copyright rights in a digital environment.[30] The author-consumer/consumer-author spectrum was suppressed in the

---

26 See, for example, TRIPS Agreement, Art. 8 (1) ('Members may, in formulating or amending their laws and regulations, adopt measures necessary to protect public health and nutrition, and to promote the public interest in sectors of vital importance to their socio-economic and technological development, provided that such measures are consistent with the provisions of this Agreement.').

27 See Art. 9(2).

28 See Art. 9(1).

29 See Art. 10 (2).

30 See, for example, Lucy Cradduck & Adrian Mccullagh, *Designing Copyright TPM: A Mutant Digital Copyright*, 13 INT'L JL & INFO. TECH. 155, 165 (2005) (describing industry fears over unauthorized distribution via the Internet); Matt Richtel, *Surfing for Music*, POPULAR SCI., September 1, 1999, at 70 (noting that 'Web music' threatens the industry's business model); Yoshiko Hara & Junko Yoshida, *Code Hack Prompts Delay of DVD-Audio Launch*, ELECTRONIC ENGINEERING TIMES, December 3, 1999, available at http://www.eetimes.com/showArticle.jhtml?articleID=18303366 (describing the 'immediate threat' of copying digital audio DVD disks).

ensuing forceful discourse over how best to serve the public interest in view of the capacity inherent in digital networks to engender untold nefarious activities with respect to creative works.

Domestic efforts in the United States to retool copyright for the digital environment focused almost entirely on how digital technologies could facilitate greater rent from *uses* of copyrighted works, not on how copyright law might be recalibrated to stimulate creative output, effective dissemination, and user participation in the creative process. Initial proposals were radical at best and outrageously audacious – calling for control by the copyright owner over all digital reproductions of works transmitted over the Internet, even those reproduced in temporary form;[31] elimination of the first-sale doctrine;[32] elimination of fair use when licensing of the work is possible;[33] and giving control to owners over every digital transmission.[34] In addition, there were proposals for technological protection and anticircumvention measures to secure the expanded menu of proposed rights.[35] None of the aspirations or limitations codified in the TRIPS Agreement bore weight on the deliberations for absolute control of knowledge goods by proprietors on the international copyright highway.

As is well known, the avid efforts to secure large-scale transformation of copyright law for the digital age were not initially successful on the US domestic front,[36] and ultimately the terrain for this great contest became

---

31 See Samuelson, *The Copyright Grab*, *supra* note 8, at 136.

32 See *id.*

33 See *id.*

34 See *id.*

35 See *id.*

36 See Meeka Jun & Steven D. Rosenboro, *The WIPO Treaties: The International Battle over Copyright Cyberturf*, ENT. & SPORTS LAW., Fall 1997, at 8, 8 ('The [National Information Infrastructure (NII)] Task Force's proposed Copyright Protection Act of 1995 (the NII Act) was fiercely opposed by Internet service providers, telecommunications companies, software manufacturers, the academic community and consumer advocacy groups who were concerned that the NII's restrictive policies would stymie the growth of the net. As a result of their lobbying efforts, the NII Act failed to graduate from the Senate committee level, despite strong support from the Clinton Administration.'); see also Stephen Fraser, *The Copyright Battle: Emerging International Rules and Roadblocks on the Global Information Infrastructure*, 15 J. MARSHALL J. COMPUTER & INFO. L. 759, 782–83 (1997) (noting the Clinton administration's failure to obtain new rights holders' protections in Congress); Maureen Ryan, *Cyberspace as Public Space: A Public Trust Paradigm for Copyright in a Digital World*, 79 OR. L. REV. 647, 671 (2000) ('Having failed to obtain Congressional enactment of the White Paper's proposed legislation to expand the copyright rights of digital content providers, the Clinton Administration reintroduced key elements of the failed legislation as treaty proposals at the December 1996 World Intellectual Property Organization

WIPO. There, with the concerted and coordinated efforts of civil society groups, Internet Service Providers (ISPs), coalitions of scholars, research institutes, and libraries, an ambitious effort to convert all the gains of the digital environment into surplus rent for copyright owners was successfully rolled back – at least for that moment in time. As the years have unfolded, and Free Trade Agreements have been pervasively employed to more directly expand copyright interests beyond TRIPS obligations, prospects for a multilateral approach to public interest goals for international copyright have become less viable, and the vision of TRIPS Article 7 less credible as a means to best secure the public gains possible through balanced access to creative works.

1.2. The legal design context for the WIPO Internet Treaties

In international copyright parlance, the WIPO Internet Treaties are 'special agreements' pursuant to Article 20 of the Berne Convention.[37] Under this article, Berne member states can enter into copyright agreements only if 'such agreements grant to authors more extensive rights than those granted by the Convention, or contain other provisions not contrary to [the] Convention'.[38] This provision was intended to reflect the existing network of bilateral economic relations between member states, which had been extensive prior to the negotiations for the Berne Convention and which was likely to continue despite the nascent multilateral cooperation evidenced by the convention.[39] Given the minimalist approach to international copyright protection that characterized the Berne Convention

---

(WIPO) conference in Geneva.' (citing James Boyle, *A Politics of Intellectual Property: Environmentalism for the Net?*, 47 DUKE LJ 87, 101 (1997)); Samuelson, *supra* note 9, at 410–11; Hannibal Travis, Comment, *Pirates of the Information Infrastructure: Blackstonian Copyright and the First Amendment*, 15 BERKELEY TECH. LJ 777, 833 (2000) (same).

37 JÖRG REINBOTHE & SILKE VON LEWINSKI, THE WIPO TREATIES 1996. THE COPYRIGHT TREATY AND THE WIPO PERFORMANCES AND PHONOGRAMS TREATY: COMMENTARY AND LEGAL ANALYSIS 3 (2002) at 3 (stating that the WCT is a special agreement under Berne); *id.* at 242–3 (stating that, although the WPPT does not explicitly claim to be a special agreement, it should be considered one); see also MIHÁLY FICSOR, THE LAW OF COPYRIGHT AND THE INTERNET: THE 1996 WIPO TREATIES, THEIR INTERPRETATION AND IMPLEMENTATION 591 (2002) (same).

38 Berne Convention, *supra* note 13, Art. 20.

39 See SAM RICKETSON, THE BERNE CONVENTION FOR THE PROTECTION OF LITERARY AND ARTISTIC WORKS: 1886–1986, at 25–38 (1987) (describing these relations). For a brief discussion of various periods of bilateralism in international intellectual regulation from a US perspective, see Ruth L. Okediji, *Back to Bilateralism? Pendulum Swings in International Intellectual Property Protection*, 1 U. OTTAWA L. & TECH. J. 125, 131–46 (2004).

negotiations,[40] countries did not intend to foreclose the possibility of bilateral agreements with higher levels of copyright protection on a reciprocal basis than was afforded by Berne. Accordingly, the Berne Act[41] incorporated two provisions to secure the negotiated multilateral baseline for copyright protection. The first was an additional article that preserved the legitimacy of existing agreements between member states that already contained rights stronger than those agreed to in the Berne Convention or that were 'not contrary to [the] Convention'.[42] The second provision, contained in Article 15, reiterated the same standard for application to future agreements between Berne signatories, namely, that bilateral 'special arrangements' could prospectively be concluded between member states, but only so long as such arrangements conferred stronger rights or terms not contrary to the provisions in the Berne Convention.

For the most part, the strategic and structural importance of these two provisions has been overlooked by scholars and commentators.[43] The addition of these clauses to the design of the multilateral copyright framework effectively foreclosed any legitimate possibility of reimagining international copyright as anything but an ever-increasing strengthening of authors' rights.[44] As a result of these provisions, several countries denounced bilateral agreements that offered less protection than the Berne Convention.[45] By 1928, the Berne Convention had been revised twice,

---

[40] See Ruth Okediji, *Toward an International Fair Use Doctrine*, 39 COLUM. J. TRANSNAT'L L. 75, 104 (2000) (describing why the Berne Convention initially set minimal levels of protection).

[41] Berne Convention for the Protection of Literary and Artistic Works, September 9, 1886, 828 UNTS 221. The Berne Act was the first iteration of the Convention.

[42] RICKETSON, *supra* note 39, at 683–85 (providing the text of the Additional Article of September 9, 1886).

[43] But see Okediji, *supra* note 39; Ruth L. Okediji, *The International Copyright System: Limitations, Exceptions and Public Interest Considerations for Developing Countries* (Int'l Ctr. for Trade & Sustainable Dev. (ICTSD) Issue Paper No. 15, 2006), available at http://www.unctad.org/en/docs/iteipc200610_en.pdf.

[44] See Keith Aoki, *Considering Multiple and Overlapping Sovereignties: Liberalism, Libertarianism, National Sovereignty, 'Global' Intellectual Property, and the Internet*, 5 IND. J. GLOBAL LEGAL STUD. 443, 463 (1998) ('In turn, this [ratcheting] up of domestic standards of intellectual property protection has the potential to change [the Agreement on Trade Related Aspects of Intellectual Property Rights (TRIPS)] into an agreement that underwrites an international copyright grab by United States intellectual property industries.'); Peter Drahos, *Securing the Future of Intellectual Property: Intellectual Property Owners and their Nodally Coordinated Enforcement Pyramid*, 36 CASE W. RES. J. INT'L L. 53, 55 (2004) (describing the 'intellectual property ratchet').

[45] See RICKETSON, *supra* note 39, at 683–84.

with the Berlin Revision of 1908 contributing significantly to a unified codification of international copyright to which most European countries acceded. During the Paris Conference of 1971, with increased substantive harmonization of the Berne Convention, the two provisions were merged into a single provision codified as Article 20.[46] It provides,

> The Governments of the countries of the Union reserve the right to enter into special agreements among themselves, in so far as such agreements grant to authors more extensive rights than those granted by the Convention, or contain other provisions not contrary to this Convention. The provisions of existing agreements which satisfy these conditions shall remain applicable.[47]

Two initial observations should be made here. First, the willingness of states to denounce existing treaty obligations reflects both the moral and political strength of the negotiated commitments under the Berne Convention, particularly given the absence of an enforcement mechanism to secure compliance.[48] Second, the success of the Berne Convention established an intractable momentum toward consolidation of a strong, harmonized multilateral accord for global copyright protection. I have pointed out elsewhere that the laments about a 'one-way ratchet' for intellectual property (IP) rights that have followed the conclusion of TRIPS are not only belated, but also underestimate the deliberate architecture of international copyright. The fact is that the legal design of the Berne Convention purposefully exerts a maximalist force over multilateral copyright regulation[49] by, in effect, defining legitimate treaty activities in the copyright realm as only those that unambiguously enhance the rights of authors and owners. This could not have been the case under the TRIPS Agreement, given the explicit delimitation of the Agreement as an international trade treaty.

In addition to requiring that 'special agreements' do not offer less protection than the minimum established by the Berne Convention, Article 20 may also impose significant limitations on a state's ability to negotiate treaties over issues not addressed within the Berne Convention. Professor Sam Ricketson has opined that the right to make or maintain 'special agreements' under Article 20 depends upon a threshold assessment of whether

---

46 *Id.*

47 Berne Convention, *supra* note 13, Art. 20.

48 Although disputes could be brought before the International Court of Justice (ICJ), the compulsory jurisdiction of the court was resisted by many countries. Accordingly, during the Stockholm Revisions, a new provision making jurisdiction of the court optional was added to the Berne Convention. *See id.* Art. 33.

49 See Okediji, *supra* note 43, at 4–9.

the agreement contravenes the provisions of the convention.[50] Thus, agreements dealing with matters ancillary to copyright, such as the regulation of collecting societies, addressing new subject matter for copyright protection, or a protocol on limitations and exceptions, are all arguably subject to the scrutiny of Article 20.[51] Indeed, even the act of negotiating an agreement inconsistent with Article 20 could arguably be a violation of the Berne Convention,[52] as would agreements between members to suspend the operation of the Berne Convention between them,[53] and agreements to modify the obligations of the Berne Convention, or in other ways end run the level of protection afforded under its terms.[54] The result, at least in theory, is that the rights and obligations of the Berne Convention cannot be constricted by mutual agreement between member states or by the operation of international law under the Vienna Convention on the Law of Treaties (Vienna Convention).[55] This view of Article 20, if persuasive, would suggest that in addition to its substantive minima, the Berne Convention also exerts an implicit jurisdictional authority over subject matter beyond the bounds of traditional copyright as reflected in the WIPO Internet Treaties. Thus, notwithstanding the ameliorative outcome of the WIPO Internet Treaty negotiations,[56] it could be argued that the Treaties can only be interpreted to strengthen existing global rights for owners even in the face of the Agreed Statements which make clear the efforts to establish access principles in the digital arena.

The ritualistic invocation of Article 20 in the WIPO Internet Treaties reflects a long-standing pathological exclusion of copyright (and intellectual

---

[50] See RICKETSON, *supra* note 39, at 685–9.

[51] *Id.*

[52] *Id.*

[53] *Id.* at 687.

[54] *Id.* at 685–9.

[55] See Vienna Convention on the Law of Treaties Art. 30(3)–(4), May 23, 1969, 1155 UNTS 331 [hereinafter Vienna Convention] (providing that subsequent treaties on the same subject matter between the same parties prevail over earlier treaties to the extent they are incompatible); see also RICKETSON, *supra* note 39, at 687 ('[A]rticle 20 continues to oblige states not to enter into agreements which modify, rather than extend, protection. . . . [I]t goes without saying that this prevents parties to the Convention [from] agreeing to suspend, even temporarily, the operation of the Convention as between themselves. This is an important point, as the general rule of international law appears to be that parties to a multilateral treaty may do this, unless such a suspension is prohibited by that treaty. Article 20 is clearly such a prohibition.' (citing Vienna Convention, *supra*, art. 58; IAN M. SINCLAIR, THE VIENNA CONVENTION ON THE LAW OF TREATIES 185 (2nd ed. 1984))).

[56] See Nimmer, *supra* note 9, at 1; Samuelson, *supra* note 9, at 435–6.

property generally) from general principles of public international law. Simply put, the constraints of Article 20 are unnecessary in light of obligations under the Vienna Convention, which has mechanisms designed to (1) ensure that states adhere to existing treaty obligations[57] and (2) deal with conflicting treaty obligations.[58] By maintaining Article 20 as the sole authorizing premise for presumptively Berne-consistent copyright agreements, whether or not WIPO-originated, and by further extending its reach to para-copyright subjects, the WIPO Internet Treaties do not go far enough to offer an opportunity to evaluate the normative effect of global copyright principles in the digital age and, more importantly, to assess how the design of the Berne Convention can more explicitly reflect copyright's long-standing commitment to various aspects of the public interest.

2. In copyright's lineage?: the new rights of the WCT

With the Berne Convention as its starting point, the project of devising a copyright for the information age was circumscribed by two inalterable propositions. The first was obvious: the analogue version of copyright had to be translated into the digital environment.[59] Consistent with the history of copyright's development, the project had to extend beyond a technical translation of extant rights to include accommodation of the new opportunities for use and dissemination of works through digital networks.[60] Notably absent were explicit considerations of what digital technologies could enable with respect to authorship and how information communications networks would make possible new modes of authorship and new genres of creative expression.[61] Indeed, other than noting the 'outstanding significance of copyright protection as an incentive for literary and artistic creation',[62] neither the WCT nor the WPPT reflect the complexity of creative endeavor in an online environment,[63] nor, as increasingly dynamic uses

---

57 See Vienna Convention, *supra* note 55, Arts. 26–7, 31, 41–6, 54–64.

58 See *id.* Art. 30.

59 WCT, *supra* note 1, pmbl., paras. 1, 2.

60 *Id.* pmbl., paras. 2, 3, 5.

61 See Michael Cieply, *Show Series to Originate on MySpace*, NY TIMES, September 13, 2007, at C1 (referring to an Internet site designed to encourage fans' creative work); John Markoff, *Mashups are Breaking the Mold at Microsoft*, NY TIMES, February 10, 2008, at BU4.

62 WCT, *supra* note 1, pmbl., para. 4.

63 See *Panel III: Fair Use: Its Application, Limitations and Future*, 17 FORDHAM INTELL. PROP. MEDIA & ENT. LJ 1017, 1039–40 (2007) ('Likewise, people are sharing and creating together, Wikipedia being the clearest example of this. Wiki as a productivity tool of digital natives is well known. And then, lots of people re-aggregating other people's content, so finding what is the best of the digital natives'

of social networking sites show, do the agreements even portend the myriad of ways users interact with and within digital space.[64] Consequently, the framing principles of the two treaties suggest immediately that the preservation of incentives to create, represented solely by the right to control uses of a protected work, remained the core justification and focus of the new digital regime. This focus greatly impoverished the WIPO Internet Treaties by justifying their relevance in terms that vastly underestimated the versatility of the digital environment and the implausibility of excluding consumers, qua users, as part of the global copyright bargain.

2.1. The new rights: an overview

With respect to the WCT, Article 1 formally establishes its status as a 'special agreement' within the meaning of Article 20 of the Berne Convention.[65] Article 1 retains the distinctiveness of the Berne regime[66] and, unlike the Berne Convention itself, does not provide a formal link to other copyright conventions.[67] However, Article 1's invocation of the

---

Footnote 63 (*cont.*)
content that they have created in the Web 2.0 space and then re-aggregating it.' (footnote omitted) (remarks of John G. Palfrey Jr., Executive Director, The Berkman Center for Internet and Society, Harvard Law School)); see also Lisa Veasman, Note, *'Piggy Backing' on the Web 2.0 Internet: Copyright Liability and Web 2.0 Mashups*, 30 Hastings Comm. & Ent. LJ 311, 314–15 (2008).

[64] See Maria Aspan, *Promotion is Not Just Another Brick in the Wall*, NY Times, July 13, 2007, at C5 ('"Social networking has spawned a lot of people creating personal content" . . . ' (quoting Ann Lewnes, Senior Vice President for Corporate Marketing and Communications, Adobe Systems Inc.)); Julie Bosman, *Agencies are Watching as Ads Go Online*, NY Times, August 15, 2006, at C6 (describing user-generated advertisements, using some copyrighted material); Scott Kirsner, *All the World's a Stage (That Includes the Internet)*, NY Times, February 15, 2007, at C7 (describing how amateurs are gradually getting paid for creative work on the Internet); Noah Robischon, *Little Films on Little Screens (But Both Seem Set to Grow)*, NY Times, March 18, 2007, at AR11.

[65] See WCT, *supra* note 1, Art. 1(1) ('This Treaty is a special agreement within the meaning of Article 20 of the Berne Convention for the Protection of Literary and Artistic Works, as regards Contracting Parties that are countries of the Union established by that Convention.').

[66] See *id.* ('This Treaty shall not have any connection with treaties other than the Berne Convention, nor shall it prejudice any rights and obligations under any other treaties.'); *id.* Art. 1(2) ('Nothing in this Treaty shall derogate from existing obligations that Contracting Parties have to each other under the Berne Convention for the Protection of Literary and Artistic Works.').

[67] Compare WCT, *supra* note 1, Art. 1, *with* Berne Convention, *supra* note 13, Art. 20. For analysis of the relationship of the Berne Convention to the Universal Copyright Convention (UCC), see Ralph Oman, *The United States and the Berne Union: An Extended Courtship*, 3 JL & Tech. 71, 75–6 (1988); Kelsey

Paris Act as the relevant Berne Convention text to which the treaty is to be applied and the inexplicable obligation to comply with the Berne Appendix,[68] strongly indicates a conscious attempt by the negotiators to ensure coordination and continuity between the WCT and the TRIPS Agreement.[69] Technically, such coordination should not extend the reach of TRIPS' interpretations to the WCT. However, the commonality of subject matter and close proximity of the negotiations raise a compelling argument for ensuring consistency between the obligations required by the two agreements.[70] Indeed, part of the WCT's goal is to provide clarity

---

Martin Mott, *The Relationship between the Berne Convention and the Universal Copyright Convention: Historical Background and Development of Article XVII of the U.C.C. and its Appendix Declaration*, 11 PAT. TRADEMARK & COPYRIGHT J. RES. & EDUC. 306, 307 (1967). TRIPS has rendered the UCC largely irrelevant. See Ruth L. Okediji, *The International Relations of Intellectual Property: Narratives of Developing Country Participation in the Global Intellectual Property System*, 7 SINGAPORE J. INT'L & COMP. L. 315, 333 (2003) ('Despite the United States' recent rejoining of [the United Nations Educational, Scientific and Cultural Organization (UNESCO)], and the formal persistence of the UCC as an instrument of international law, the incorporation of substantive provisions of the Berne Convention into the TRIPS Agreement has, for all intents and purposes, relegated the UCC to the periphery of international copyright protection.' (citing Sean D. Murphy, *United States' Return to UNESCO*, 97 AM. J. INT'L L. 977 (2003)).

68 See Mihály Ficsor, *The WIPO 'Internet Treaties': The United States as the Driver: The United States as the Main Source of Obstruction – As Seen by an Anti-revolutionary Central European*, 6 J. MARSHALL REV. INTELL. PROP. L. 17, 32 (2006) ('The options offered in the Appendix to the Berne Convention are out-of-date in the era of more perfect and efficient forms of reprographic reproduction and the widespread use of digital technology and the Internet.'); see also WIPO, *Report on the Online Forum on Intellectual Property in the Information Society*, June 1–15, 2005, at 25, WIPO Doc. WIPO/CRRS/INF/1 (September 19, 2005) ('Copyright-protected content can also be made available under certain exceptions and limitations to rights in national laws and, in limited circumstances under the Appendix to the Berne Convention, under compulsory licensing of certain rights.'). For a more detailed analysis of the Appendix's provisions, see Salah Basalamah, *Compulsory Licensing for Translation: An Instrument of Development?*, 40 IDEA 503, 511–22 (2000).

69 See Agreement on Trade-related Aspects of Intellectual Property Rights Arts. 9(1), 10(1), 14(3), 14(6), April 15, 1994, Marrakesh Agreement Establishing the World Trade Organization, Annex 1C, Legal Instruments – Results of the Uruguay Round, 1869 UNTS 299 (1994) [hereinafter TRIPS Agreement].

70 See Vienna Convention, *supra* note 55, arts. 30, 31(3); WIPO, *The Advantages of Adherence to the WIPO Copyright Treaty (WCT) and the WIPO Performances and Phonograms Treaty (WPPT)*, at 8–9 (December 20, 1996) [hereinafter WIPO, *Advantages of Adherence*], available at http://www.wipo.int/copyright/es/activities/wct_wppt/pdf/ advantages_wct_wppt.pdf ('The WCT and WPPT each contain several provisions that impose obligations derived from, and

to Berne Convention obligations;[71] accordingly, even if a WCT provision cannot be formally invoked for enforcement before a World Trade Organization (WTO) TRIPS dispute panel, it is certainly the case under international law that WCT provisions can and will provide sources of interpretation to TRIPS obligations.[72] This point is particularly applicable to those Berne Convention provisions that have been directly incorporated into the WCT.[73]

With regard to clarifying existing Berne Convention rules, Articles 2, 4 and 5 of the WCT affirm several key principles of copyright law in the international sphere. Most notable is the idea/expression dichotomy,[74] which, although recognized in most jurisdictions,[75] had not been an explicit provision in the Berne Convention.[76] Similarly, the treatment of computer programs as literary works[77] and the protection of original databases[78] were explicitly incorporated into the WCT as already recognized in the TRIPS Agreement.[79] By and large, these acknowledgments of

---

Footnote 70 (*cont.*)
similar to, those in the TRIPS Agreement . . . . The WCT and WPPT serve to update the TRIPS obligations, creating a modern and comprehensive framework of rights for the digital age.').

71 WCT, *supra* note 1, pmbl., para. 2 ('*Recognizing* the need to introduce new international rules and clarify the interpretation of certain existing rules . . . .').

72 See, for example, Vienna Convention, *supra* note 55, arts. 30, 31(3). For a fuller analysis of the relationship between the WCT and the TRIPS Agreement, see generally WIPO, *Implications of the TRIPS Agreement on Treaties Administered by WIPO*, at 164, WIPO Publ'n No. 464(E) (1996); Neil W. Netanel, *The Next Round: The Impact of the WIPO Copyright Treaty on TRIPS Dispute Settlement*, 37 VA. J. INT'L L. 441 (1997).

73 See WCT, *supra* note 1, art. 3 (incorporating Articles 2 through 6 of the Berne Convention directly).

74 See *id.* Art. 2 (setting forth the scope of copyright protection). The idea/expression dichotomy was first explicitly incorporated in the international copyright system in the TRIPS Agreement. See TRIPS Agreement, *supra* note 69, Art. 9(2).

75 JAL STERLING, WORLD COPYRIGHT LAW 221 & n. 10 (2nd ed. 2003) (noting that while the idea/expression dichotomy is a distinctly US doctrine and not explicitly incorporated in the laws of major European countries, it has influenced judicial decisions in those countries).

76 Instead, the Convention had articulated a definition of 'literary and artistic works' and restricted protection for factual works, which together effectively accomplished the delimiting purpose of the idea/expression dichotomy. See Berne Convention, *supra* note 13, Art. 2.

77 See WCT, *supra* note 1, Art. 4.

78 See *id.* Art. 5.

79 See TRIPS Agreement, *supra* note 69, Art. 10.

rights that already existed as a form of international common law do not portend significant shifts in the digital context.[80]

In terms of *new* rights to reflect the impact of digital technologies on the fundamental economics of copyright's core right of reproduction, the WCT recognizes an exclusive right of 'making available to the public' originals or copies of works through sales or other means.[81] It also recognizes the exclusive right of authors of computer programs, cinematographic works, and works embodied in phonograms to authorize commercial rental to the public of originals or copies of their works.[82] For these new rights, the term 'copies' means only 'copies that can be put into circulation as tangible objects' to ensure that transient reproductions, such as those automatically generated by computers in Random Access Memory (RAM) modules, are not swept under the ambit of these provisions.[83] The WCT also established an exclusive right of communication to the public. Contained in Article 8, the right of communication to the public covers both print and digital works and includes language that constrains the means and ends of user access to protected works. Owners have the exclusive right to make their works available to the public 'in such a way that members of the public may access these works from a place and at a time individually chosen by them'.[84] The strong presence of ISPs and other representatives of the telecommunications industry during the WIPO negotiations[85] ensured that merely providing technologies or a physical place to access digital content would not run afoul of the new right.[86]

---

[80] Indeed, the Agreed Statements to Articles 4 and 5 make clear that the WCT is consistent with sister provisions in the Berne Convention and the TRIPS Agreement. See WCT, *supra* note 1, Art. 4 n. 3, Art. 5 n. 4.

[81] See *id.* Art. 6.

[82] See *id.* Art. 7.

[83] See *id.* Art.6 n. 5 (Agreed Statements concerning Arts. 6–7).

[84] See *id.* Art. 8.

[85] See Ficsor, *supra* note 68, at 22 (discussing coalition building during negotiations on the WIPO Internet Treaties and highlighting the important role 'telecommunication companies, Internet service providers, other information technology industries, entertainment equipment, and recording material manufacturers' played in the successful conclusion of the treaties); Reichman, Dinwoodie and Samuelson, supra note 15, at 1058 (2007) ('By the end of the multilateral negotiations held at Geneva in 1996, the intense struggle among stakeholders representing content providers, the telecommunications industry, online service providers, and the educational and scientific communities produced a workable compromise in the WCT.').

[86] See WCT, *supra* note 1, Art. 8 n. 8. During the WCT negotiations, a strong consensus emerged against strict liability for Internet Service Providers (ISPs) for copyright infringement. See Samuelson, *supra* note 9, at 382–92 (discussing the WIPO negotiations on ISP liability).

With the benefit of hindsight, this tenuous compromise between content and service providers did not resolve the question of whose presumptive privileges – owners' or users' – should prevail in controlling public engagement with digital content and, more importantly, who should bear the brunt of controlling unauthorized access and use.[87] Despite the basic principle established by WCT Article 8, content providers in Europe have sought tirelessly to direct legislative attention and efforts to mandate greater action by service providers to control users' online activities,[88] while the Digital Millennium Copyright Act (DMCA)[89] in the United States provides a calibrated process or 'dance' in which content owners and ISPs play a role in addressing violations of copyright rights.[90] Weary legislators recently appear to see the inefficacy of new laws, instead highlighting the desirability of privately negotiated industry agreements.[91] The claim that 'both the WCT and WPPT address the challenges posed by today's digital technologies, in particular the dissemination of protected material over digital networks such as the Internet',[92] now seems quite hollow in light of the increasing complexity of claims arising from new uses, new users, and new works.

---

[87] See Doreen Carvajal, *Net Firms as the New Cybercops?: Critics Wary of Errant Online Users*, INT'L HERALD TRIB. (Paris), April 14, 2008, at 1.

[88] See, for example, *U.K. Urged to Follow France Lead on Piracy*, INT'L HERALD TRIB. (London), February 13, 2008, at 13.

[89] WIPO Copyright and Performances and Phonograms Treaties Implementation Act of 1998, Pub. L. No. 105-304, 112 Stat. 2860 (codified as amended in scattered sections of 5, 17, 28, and 35 USC).

[90] See 17 USC § 512 (2006); see also Reichman et al., *supra* note 85, at 989–94 (describing the legislative history of the DMCA ISP safe-harbors and concluding that they have 'generally been efficacious in run-of-the-mill copyright infringement cases involving users and their ISPs' (citing Heidi Pearlman Salow, *Liability Immunity for Internet Service Providers – How Is It Working?*, 6 J. TECH. L. & POL'Y 31, 49–50 (2001); Christian C.M. Beams, Note, *The Copyright Dilemma Involving Online Service Providers: Problem Solved . . . for Now*, 51 FED. COMM. LJ 823, 846 (1999))).

[91] See, for example, Nikki Tait, *EU to Rule Out New Piracy Laws*, FIN. TIMES (London), May 13, 2008, at 5; Dugie Standeford, *EU Internal Market Chief: Counterfeiting and Piracy Need Industry-led Solutions*, INTELL. PROP. WATCH, May 14, 2008, http://www.ip-watch.org/weblog/2008/05/14/eu-internal-market-chief-counterfeiting-and-piracy-need-industry-led-solutions/.

[92] See WIPO Permanent Comm. on Cooperation for Dev. Related to Intellectual Prop., *The Digital Agenda: Implementation of the WIPO Copyright Treaty (WCT) and the WIPO Performances and Phonograms Treaty (WPPT)*, at 2, WIPO Doc. PCIPD/3/9 (July 2002) [hereinafter WIPO, *The Digital Agenda*], available at http://www.wipo.int/edocs/mdocs/ mdocs/en/pcipd_3/pcipd_3_9.pdf.

2.2. National push-back?: the case of the United States

Recent decisions in the United States addressing the right of distribution highlight the marginal role of the WCT in defining user interests in the face of the traditional copyright balance. In *Capital Records, Inc. v. Thomas*,[93] for example, the US District Court for the District of Minnesota considered the issue of whether making sound recordings available for distribution on a peer-to-peer network qualifies as 'distribution' under the 1976 Copyright Act. Rejecting the plaintiffs' claim, the court held that actual dissemination of copyrighted works, rather than making them available for dissemination through a file-sharing application, is required to establish the infringement of the distribution right under US law. Utilizing Articles 6(1) and 8 of the WCT and Articles 12(1) and 14 of the WPPT, the plaintiffs argued that the provisions of the Copyright Act should be interpreted in light of the United States' international treaty obligations and therefore should be held to incorporate an exclusive making-available right.[94] Refusing to follow this reasoning, the court noted that since the WIPO Internet Treaties are not self-executing, 'the fact that [they] protect a making-available right does not create an enforceable making-available right' under US law.[95] Rather, according to the court, 'the contents of the WIPO treaties are only relevant insofar as [a provision of the Copyright Act] is ambiguous and there is a reasonable interpretation . . . that aligns with the United States' treaty obligations'.[96]

Similarly, in *Elektra Entertainment Group, Inc. v. Barker*,[97] the US District Court for the Southern District of New York rejected the plaintiffs' call for recognition of a making-available right as 'not grounded' in the provisions of the Copyright Act.[98] As in *Thomas*, the court distinguished the construction of the distribution right in the digital context and refused to follow the decision of the US Court of Appeals for the Fourth Circuit in *Hotaling v. Church of Jesus Christ of Latter-Day Saints*,[99] which recognized an enforceable making-available right in the offline environment.[100] Furthermore, the court rejected the plaintiffs' argument that the

---

93 579 F. Supp. 2d 1210 (D. Minn. 2008).

94 *Id.* at 1225–6.

95 *Id.* at 1226.

96 *Id.*

97 551 F. Supp. 2d 234 (SDNY 2008).

98 *Id.* at 243.

99 118 F.3d 199 (4th Cir. 1997).

100 *Barker*, 551 F. Supp. 2d at 243–4 (citing *Hotaling*, 118 F.3d at 201); see also *London-Sire Records, Inc. v. Doe* 1, 542 F. Supp. 2d 153, 166–9 (D. Mass. 2008) (holding that infringement of the right to distribute requires the actual dissemination of copyrighted works); *In re Napster, Inc. Copyright Litig.*, 377 F. Supp. 2d

provisions of the WIPO Internet Treaties should control the interpretation of the US Copyright Act, noting that the treaties 'create no private right of action on their own'.[101]

In another example of recent attempts by US courts to recalibrate the presumptions that underlie the use of content in the online environment, the court in *Lenz v. Universal Music Corp.*[102] held that the DMCA requires a content owner to have a good faith belief that the use of content is not fair use. The plaintiff argued that fair use is a user's right protected by the Copyright Act, a privilege that the defendants reframed as merely a defense.[103] The court ruled that '[t]he purpose of [the DMCA] is to prevent the abuse of takedown notices', and '[a] good faith consideration of whether a particular use is fair use is consistent with the purpose of the statute'.[104] Further, the court observed that '[r]equiring owners to consider fair use will help "ensure [] that the efficiency of the Internet will continue to improve and that the variety and quality of services on the Internet will expand" without compromising "the movies, music, software and literary works that are the fruit of American creative genius"'.[105]

As these cases illustrate, the challenge of digital content ownership is aggravated by the proliferation of consumer technologies and social networking sites, which routinely enable repeated access to and use of digital content such that consumers hardly expect interference with their ability to control, access, and manage an array of works created, shifted, and shared across a versatile set of personal, portable technologies. It is not merely the easy availability of content-laden consumer goods that propels an assumption among users that access, use, and sharing are the prevailing norms of the digital environment, but, more significantly, the fact that the social (and increasingly economic) currency of the digital age is explicitly dependent on the network features that characterize most new technologies. So powerful is the salience of interactive platforms as prototypical of the digital age that even the recent struggle over a single platform for high-definition videos must, at least in part, be understood as implicitly rooted in the compulsion to create technologies that

---

Footnote 100 (*cont.*)
796, 802–05 (ND Cal. 2005) (noting that to establish a violation of the distribution right, the plaintiff must show proof of either actual dissemination of a copyrighted work or an offer to distribute).

101 *Barker*, 551 F. Supp. 2d at 242 n. 7.

102 572 F. Supp. 2d 1150 (ND Cal. 2008).

103 *Id.* at 1154.

104 *Id.* at 1156.

105 *Id.* (quoting S. Rep. No. 105-190, at 2 (1998)).

allow users to employ existing content *and* leverage it across multiple contexts.[106]

2.3. *Privatizing the search for copyright balance*

Despite the express effort to use the WIPO Internet Treaties to 'gap fill' the Berne Convention (which did not contain an exclusive right of communication to the public),[107] the indomitable role of users in enhancing the value of the online world through content creation has in fact produced various efforts to mediate a private compromise between content owners and ISPs. The most salient example is the recent collaboration between leading media and content providers that produced a set of guidelines dealing with so-called User Generated Content (UGC).[108] In addition to legislative fatigue, the orientation toward privately negotiated norms to govern the iterative process of creativity in the online world reflects the futility of treating users as external to the creative enterprise, and opens up the possibility of entrenching access principles as a constituent part of the economic models that drive copyright regulation.[109] In this regard, the WIPO Internet Treaties remain imprecise and thus largely irrelevant to the dominant copyright questions facing acceding states today. In obligating states to enhance protection for content providers, but failing to presage the vital role of users in the creative process, the treaties opened up a significant unregulated space in which the major actors – content providers and ISPs – must contend for the creative surplus of the public at large that will help determine the extent of the economic value derived from new technologies.[110]

---

[106] Marc Saltzman, *New Features Coming for Blu-ray Format: High-def DVD Players Go to the Next Level with Interactive Net Access*, USA TODAY, March 19, 2008, at 4B (describing various new features on Blu-ray machines that allow users to share audio or video content).

[107] See WIPO HANDBOOK, *supra* note 12, §§ 5.223, 5.225, at 271–2.

[108] See User Generated Content Principles, Principles for User Generated Content Services: Foster Innovation. Encourage Creativity. Thwart Infringement., www.ugcprinciples.com (last visited March 22, 2009).

[109] In line with this point, a recent study estimated that, as of 2006, companies benefiting from fair use represented one-sixth of the US gross domestic product (GDP). See THOMAS ROGERS & ANDREW SZAMOSSZEGI, CAPITAL TRADE, INC., FAIR USE IN THE U.S. ECONOMY: ECONOMIC CONTRIBUTION OF INDUSTRIES RELYING ON FAIR USE 6 (2007).

[110] See Andrew M. Ballard, *Transparency, Trust Said Needed to Develop Effective Marketplace for IP*, 75 PAT. TRADEMARK & COPYRIGHT J. (BNA) 447 (2008); see also Austin Modine, *YouTube Blocks Music Videos in UK*, REGISTER, March 9, 2009, available at http://www.theregister.co.uk/2009/03/09/youtube_blocks_music_vids_in_uk/ (describing the recent dispute between YouTube and the UK Performing Rights Society, which resulted in the blocking of most

It would be an overstatement to suggest that the new WCT rights significantly added to the portfolio of claims held by copyright owners. Arguably, existing Berne Convention rights such as the right of reproduction and the right of distribution could have been used to address concerns about granting copyright owners the authority to determine how and when their works could be accessed and used in the online environment.[111] There certainly is no question that the driving principle of the WCT was to give authors the right to control access to and use of their works on digital networks.[112] However, the new rights were in some ways prematurely recognized given the lack of agreement among states as to the specific form of the right to control digital transmissions and public access to protected works.[113] Today, even within the European Union, a consistent approach to the WCT rights has been frustrated by the failure to acknowledge the role of access rights in construing the precise acts for which a user might have violated the author's legitimate entitlement.[114] Similarly, in the United States, as noted earlier, several federal district courts have rejected rights holders' requests for relief and ruled that 'making available to the public' is not a right recognized under US copyright law.[115]

Footnote 110 (*cont.*)
YouTube music videos from UK viewers); Tim Arango, *Rights Clash on YouTube, and Videos Disappear*, NY TIMES, March 22, 2009, at BU1 (describing a similar dispute between YouTube and the Time Warner Music Group).

[111] See Mihály Ficsor, *The Spring 1997 Horace S. Manges Lecture – Copyright for the Digital Era: The WIPO 'Internet' Treaties*, 21 COLUM.–VLA J.L. & ARTS 197, 207–14 (1997) (noting the inherent limitations in such an approach).

[112] See WIPO HANDBOOK, *supra* note 12, §§ 5.222–5.227, at 271–2.

[113] See Ficsor, *supra* note 111, at 207–10.

[114] Guido Westkamp, *Transient Copying and Public Communications: The Creeping Evolution of Use and Access Rights in European Copyright Law*, 36 GEO. WASH. INT'L L. REV. 1057, 1074–79 (2004).

[115] See, for example, *Atl. Recording Corp. v. Howell*, 554 F. Supp. 2d 976, 983 (D. Ariz. 2008) (noting that '[t]he majority of district courts have rejected the . . . "making available" theory because [it] is inconsistent with the Copyright Act' and holding that merely making a work available on a peer-to-peer network does not constitute copyright infringement); *Elektra Entm't Group, Inc. v. Barker*, 551 F. Supp. 2d 234, 243–5 (SDNY 2008); *Atl. Recording Corp. v. Brennan*, 534 F. Supp. 2d 278, 281–2 (D. Conn. 2008) (describing the 'making available' theory as 'problematic'); *In re Napster, Inc. Copyright Litig.*, 377 F. Supp. 2d 796, 802–05 (ND Cal. 2005) (declining to recognize a 'making available' theory of copyright infringement because it is contrary to the weight of authority and 'inconsistent with the text and legislative history of the Copyright Act of 1976'); *Arista Records, Inc. v. MP3Board, Inc.*, No. 00 Civ. 4660(SHS), 2002 WL 1997918, at *4 (SDNY August 29, 2002); see also Steven Seidenberg, *International 'Making Available' Right Becoming Less Available in US Law*, INTELL. PROP. WATCH, May 28, 2008,

The standards ultimately agreed to in the WIPO Internet Treaties leave open a range of design possibilities at the national level,[116] a flexibility that, while desirable politically, also cuts against the chief benefits of a global accord on the scope of digital copyright rights. But, in the end, as already discussed, any of the early debates over the scope and form of the WCT rights fell short of addressing the fundamental question of how digital networks and the value that users bring to the table can be harvested to generate the social and economic value that indispensably fuels the digital economy.[117]

3. Disabling development in the digital age

3.1. Deference and disharmony

By far, the most significant additions to copyright's traditional legacy are the new rights concerning technological measures[118] and rights management information.[119] Articles 11 and 12 of the WCT are the primary examples of new international rights introduced to 'provide adequate solutions to the questions raised by new . . . technological developments'.[120] Article 11 of the WCT expresses the well-known provision requiring protection for anticircumvention measures used by copyright owners in conjunction with the exercise of their legitimate rights. Article 12 is a corollary to this new right, providing for the protection of rights management information. Both of these provisions have been the most controversial aspects of the WCT. The US implementation of these provisions, which adopts an extreme version in the DMCA,[121] has been extended to the multilateral trade environment through a network of Free Trade Agreements (FTAs), which require countries to ratify the WIPO Internet Treaties.[122] Indeed,

---

http://www.ip-watch.org / weblog / 2008 / 05 / 28 / international-making-available-right-becoming-less-available-in-us-law/.

[116] See generally Urs Gasser, *Legal Frameworks and Technological Protection of Digital Content: Moving Forward Towards a Best Practice Model*, 17 FORDHAM INTELL. PROP. MEDIA & ENT. L.J. 39 (2006).

[117] But see Reichman et al., *supra* note 85 (proposing a 'reverse notice and takedown' scheme to address public interest uses).

[118] See WPPT, *supra* note 2, Art. 18; WCT, *supra* note 1, Art. 11.

[119] See WPPT, *supra* note 2, Art. 19; WCT, *supra* note 1, Art. 12.

[120] See WCT, *supra* note 1, pmbl., para. 2.

[121] See *supra* note 89.

[122] See Anupam Chander, *Exporting DMCA Lockouts*, 54 CLEV. ST. L. REV. 205, 212–16 (2006); see also Dominican Republic-Central America–United States Free Trade Agreement Art. 15.5.7, August 5, 2004, 119 Stat. 462 [hereinafter CAFTA-DR], available at http://www.ustr.gov/assets/Trade_Agreements/Bilateral/CAFTA/CAFTA-DR_Final_Texts/ asset_upload_file934_3935.pdf.

in particularly pernicious forms, some FTAs go as far as to spell out the precise language of obligations, which typically mirrors the language of the DMCA.[123] Since the Berne Convention authorizes protection stronger than any minimum terms set forth in the treaty or related special agreements, this globalization of the DMCA is, in theory, compatible with the Berne framework. However, neither adoption of the DMCA model nor ratification of the WIPO Internet Treaties has established a global harmonized baseline for technological protection measures (TPMs) or anticircumvention legislation.[124] The WCT thus accomplished a remarkable feat: a global treaty was negotiated not to harmonize various national approaches to a particular copyright issue, but rather to create a framework in which states could choose to live in disharmony – to provide specific rights within their domestic copyright laws without any concomitant obligations to attend to the often touted benefits of harmonization. The WCT goes even further. Beyond encouraging states to exercise national policy prerogatives in implementing its obligations, the WCT also contemplates that such implementation can be accomplished using non-copyright regimes such as unfair competition laws,[125] which are non-existent in most DCs and LDCs.

3.2. National implementation of the WCT/WPPT

In 2003, WIPO conducted a survey of thirty-nine member states that had acceded to or ratified either or both the WCT and the WPPT prior to April

---

[123] See, for example, CAFTA-DR, *supra* note 122, Arts. 15.5.7–.8.

[124] Gasser, *supra* note 116, at 65–93 (discussing various design options).

[125] See, for example, Jane C. Ginsburg, *Legal Protection of Technological Measures Protecting Works of Authorship: International Obligations and the US Experience*, 29 Colum. JL & Arts 11, 20 & n. 40 (2005) ('It is worth noting that the WCT does not require that protections for technological measures be enacted as part of national copyright laws; that certainly is one route, but so too are sui generis laws or inclusion of protections within the scope of more general laws, such as those addressing unfair competition. . . . For example, Japan has divided coverage of technological measures between the copyright law and the unfair competition law. Australia has done this solely within the provisions of its 1968 Copyright Act but makes them the subject of separate rights of action that may be brought by the copyright owner.' (citations omitted)); see also WIPO Standing Committee on Copyright & Related Rights, *Survey on Implementation Provisions of the WCT and the WPPT*, WIPO Doc. SCCR/9/6 (April 25, 2003) [hereinafter WIPO, *Implementation Survey*], available at http://www.wipo.int/edocs/mdocs/copyright/en/sccr_9/sccr_9_6.pdf (providing an overview of the methods individual member states have utilized to implement the WIPO Internet Treaties and highlighting the diversity among them).

1, 2003.[126] Of the countries surveyed, only Japan and the United States are considered 'developed' countries.[127] Today, the WCT has seventy contracting parties, more than half of which joined the WCT in 2002 and the majority of which are DCs and LDCs.[128] If judged solely by the acceding countries, the WIPO Internet Treaties reflect a drastic change from the concert of countries that negotiated the Berne Convention over a century ago. Where the Berne Convention countries were all European with fairly similar levels of socioeconomic development, the WCT contracting parties were mainly DCs and LDCs whose combined gross domestic product (GDP) represents a mere fraction of that of their developed country counterparts.[129]

The survey results reflect significant consistency between developed countries and developing countries in the implementation of the WIPO Internet Treaties' provisions in national laws, including limitations and exceptions.[130] This may quickly be attributed to WIPO's role in providing technical assistance in implementing the treaties in the latter group of countries. However, national implementation of anticircumvention measures and the obligation to protect rights management information were highly inconsistent.[131] Countries that provided protection against anticircumvention did so using a variety of legal means, ranging from criminal law to unfair competition law.[132] In some laws, only acts of circumvention

---

[126] The countries surveyed were Albania, Argentina, Belarus, Bulgaria, Burkina Faso, Chile, Colombia, Costa Rica, Croatia, Czech Republic, Ecuador, El Salvador, Gabon, Georgia, Guatemala, Honduras, Hungary, Indonesia, Jamaica, Japan, Kyrgyzstan, Latvia, Lithuania, Mali, Mexico, Mongolia, Republic of Moldova, Nicaragua, Panama, Paraguay, Peru, Philippines, Romania, Saint Lucia, Senegal, Slovakia, Slovenia, Ukraine, and the United States. See WIPO, *Implementation Survey*, *supra* note 125.

[127] See *id.*

[128] See WCT Contracting Parties, *supra* note 3.

[129] As revealed by analysis of World Bank data, in 2007, the combined real GDP of developing countries (DCs) and least-developed countries (LDCs) party to the WCT was roughly 20 percent of the combined real GDP of developed WCT members. See World Bank, World Development Indicators 14–16 (2007).

[130] See WIPO, *Implementation Survey*, *supra* note 125, at 2–3.

[131] See *id.* at 3; see also Richard Li-Dar Wang, *DMCA Anti-circumvention Provisions in a Different Light: Perspectives from Transnational Observation of Five Jurisdictions*, 34 AIPLA QJ 217, 219 (2006).

[132] Compare, for example, WIPO, *Implementation Survey*, *supra* note 125, at 395–6 (reproducing relevant provisions of the Jamaican Copyright Act employing criminal sanctions to address anticircumvention), with *id.* at 438–9 (reproducing relevant provisions of the Japanese Unfair Competition Prevention Law employing unfair competition principles to address same).

were prohibited, while preparatory acts or making equipment available were prohibited in others.[133] Similar variations were evident in the implementation of Article 12 relating to digital rights management (DRM).[134]

As mentioned earlier, the variety of implementation models with respect to Articles 11 and 12 reflects the essential flexibility in the global obligations contained in the WCT[135] and an unusual deference to the national design of digital copyright. Despite a standard that could be tilted solely in favor of owners, national laws in developed countries can and have implemented these obligations in ways that reflect deliberate policy choices and nuances that calibrate a variety of domestic interests at stake.[136] The core principle of anticircumvention, for example, designed to secure the economic interests (primarily) of owners, should yield not only to the reality of coordinated technologies that conform to modern lifestyles, but also to changed expectations of users about what such technology presumptively entitles them to do.[137]

Without question, US implementation of the anticircumvention and DRM obligations[138] has engendered significant controversy both domestically and globally,[139] and considerable attention has been directed at the

---

[133] Compare, for example, *id.* at 902–03 (reproducing relevant provisions of US copyright law prohibiting only actual circumvention), with *id.* at 610 (reproducing relevant provisions of the Paraguayan Copyright Act prohibiting the act of making equipment available).

[134] Compare, for example, *id.* at 821 (reproducing relevant provisions of the Copyright and Related Rights Act of Slovenia requiring that Rights Management Information (RMI) be embodied in a copy of the work), with *id.* at 199 (reproducing relevant provisions of the Copyright Act of the Czech Republic not requiring that RMI be embodied in a copy of a work).

[135] Samuelson, *supra* note 9, at 414–15; Thomas C. Vinje, *A Brave New World of Technical Protection Systems: Will there Still be Room for Copyright?*, 18 Eur. Intell. Prop. Rev. 431, 431–2 (1996) (noting differences between the WCT and US implementation of its provisions).

[136] Gasser, *supra* note 116, at 66–93; Wang, *supra* note 131, at 230–35 (comparing scope of protection of anticircumvention provisions in Japan, Australia, the European Union, and the United States).

[137] See WIPO, *Technological Protection Measures: The Intersection of Technology, Law and Commercial Licenses*, at 4, WIPO Doc. WCT-WPPT/IMP/3 (December 3, 1999) (prepared by Dean S. Marks & Bruce H. Turnbull), available at http://www.wipo.int/ edocs/mdocs/copyright/en/wct_wppt_imp/wct_wppt_imp_3.pdf.

[138] See 17 USC § 1201(a)(1)(A) (2006).

[139] See, for example, June M. Besek, *Anti-circumvention Laws and Copyright: A Report from the Kernochan Center for Law, Media and the Arts*, 27 Colum. JL & Arts 385, 467–9 (2004); David Nimmer, *Back from the Future: A Proleptic Review of the Digital Millennium Copyright Act*, 16 Berkeley Tech. LJ 855, 867 (2001);

negative effects of the DMCA in the domestic US market. The impact of TPMs on access to digital content has also been noted by WIPO as being of great concern to DCs and LDCs.[140] As I explore briefly in the following section, the extent of these concerns is noteworthy because, in the current global economic context, these countries have little to gain from the WIPO Internet Treaties and, by many accounts, have much to lose by the design choices made during domestic implementation of the treaties in developed countries. Importantly (or perhaps ironically), developing countries who typically agitate for less substantive harmonization and greater domestic flexibility in IP matters, have now received it in an area in which the exercise of such flexibility has little meaning for development policy goals.

3.3. Participation by developing and least-developed countries in the WCT and WPPT framework

With China's accession to the WCT,[141] the vast majority of the world's population has become subject to the digital copyright regime. Despite its application to a global audience whose citizens live well below the global poverty level, the stark reality is that digital copyright has yet to fully impact most citizens of DCs and LDCs. The premature ratification of the WIPO Internet Treaties is thus troubling where these regions are concerned. Over 18 percent of the countries that ratified the WCT are in Africa.[142] Africa is

---

Pamela Samuelson, *Intellectual Property and the Digital Economy: Why the Anti-circumvention Regulations Need to Be Revised*, 14 BERKELEY TECH. LJ 519, 534–7 (1999). See also generally Ian Brown, *The Evolution of Anti-circumvention Law*, 20 INT'L REV. L. COMPUTERS & TECH. 239 (2006).

[140] See WIPO General Assembly, *Proposal by Argentina and Brazil for the Establishment of a Development Agenda for WIPO*, at 3, WIPO Doc. WO/GA/31/11 (August 27, 2004) [hereinafter WIPO, *Development Agenda Proposal*], available at http://www.wipo.int/edocs/mdocs/govbody/en/wo_ga_31/wo_ga_31_11.pdf ('The ongoing controversy surrounding the use of technological protection measures in the digital environment is also of great concern. The provisions of any treaties in this field must be balanced and clearly take on board the interests of consumers and the public at large. It is important to safeguard the exceptions and limitations existing in the domestic laws of Member States. In order to tap into the development potential offered by the digital environment, it is important to bear in mind the relevance of open access models for the promotion of innovation and creativity.').

[141] See WIPO, WCT Notification No. 66, WIPO Copyright Treaty: Accession by the People's Republic of China (March 9, 2007), http://www.wipo.int/edocs/notdocs/en/wct/ treaty_wct_66.html. The WCT entered into force in China on June 9, 2007. *Id.*

[142] See WCT Contracting Parties, *supra* note 3.

estimated to hold 14.2 percent of the world's population,[143] but only 5.6 percent of the population has access to the Internet.[144] Asia represents 60.5 percent of the world's population,[145] but only 17.2 percent of the population has Internet access.[146] In Latin America and the Caribbean, which comprise 8.6 percent of the world's population,[147] only 28.6 percent of the population has Internet access.[148] For all practical purposes, then, the vast majority of the population in these countries cannot make any significant use of digital works, and, arguably, the WIPO Internet Treaties are even less relevant to these countries than traditional copyright agreements.

If, as I argued earlier, the Treaties do not enhance incentives for creativity in general, and if infrastructure needs render them mostly immaterial for most of the world's population, in what ways have copyright goals been meaningfully advanced either for users or owners *anywhere* by the proliferation of digital copyright obligations? More importantly, why was it important for DCs and LDCs to ratify the Treaties?[149] Since the entry into force of both Treaties, not a single DC or LDC has had reason to experiment with their provisions domestically, nor have the domestic laws implementing the treaties ever been invoked before a domestic court. This observation of limited national experience is certainly not limited to the WIPO Internet Treaties, but it does point to the extreme improbability that DCs and LDCs can exercise effective design choices at the national level. Even if so, there is a question whether such investments can be justified in the absence of sophisticated institutions to develop and sustain a public-interest balance in the deployment of TPMs locally. Nevertheless, three main reasons can be identified for extending the WIPO Internet Treaties to developing countries.

3.3.1. The Importance of Making Good on Claimed Benefits

Assimilating DCs and LDCs into the global copyright system is a familiar component of the path dependency characteristic of global copyright lawmaking. Since the Stockholm Protocol, which first formally acknowledged

---

143 See Population Reference Bureau, 2007 World Population Data Sheet 7 (2007), available at http://www.prb.org/pdf07/07WPDS_Eng.pdf.

144 See Internet World Stats, World Internet Usage Statistics News and World Population Stats, http://www.internetworldstats.com/stats.htm (last visited March 22, 2009).

145 See Population Reference Bureau, *supra* note 143, at 8.

146 See Internet World Stats, *supra* note 144.

147 See Population Reference Bureau, *supra* note 143, at 8.

148 See Internet World Stats, *supra* note 144.

149 See *Tracking Pirates in Cyberspace*, 24 Loy. LA Ent. L. Rev. 73, 76 (2004) (remarks of Peter Harter, Managing Principal, The Farrington Group).

special needs of DCs,[150] no other revision of the Berne Convention or associated special treaty has purposively sought to identify the impact of new provisions on the development needs and aspirations of the global South beyond general statements regarding the 'balance' evidenced by the formal language of the treaties.[151] Instead, the justifications for 'globalizing copyright' have sought to impute benefits deeply linked to and dependent on the existence of capital markets and institutional actors to copyright regulation in the impoverished and unstable economies of much of the Southern Hemisphere. In the context of the WIPO Internet Treaties, DC and LDC participation has been specifically justified in ways that echo disputed, untested, and at times inapplicable (but as yet historically pervasive) rationalizations for the internationalization of IP more generally. These include, most notably, benefits of technology transfer, foreign direct investment, stimulation of domestic creativity and innovation, and general development progress. However, none of these claims has been proven in the experience of most DCs and LDCs, and there is some consensus that the relationship between IP and development is much more complex than the claims suggest. Indeed, it is instructive to compare official justifications for DC and LDC participation in the WIPO Internet Treaties with concerns articulated by these countries in the proposal for a WIPO Development Agenda. With respect to the possibility of foreign technology transfers, the proposal states,

> The transfer of technology has been identified as an objective that intellectual property protection should be supportive of and not run counter to, as stated in Articles 7 and 8 of the TRIPS Agreement. Yet, many of the developing

---

[150] See RICKETSON, *supra* note 39, at 593–623.

[151] References to 'balance' and 'flexibilities' have recently become a staple part of IP *lingua franca*, including within WIPO, which has historically emphasized the benefits of IP protection for development. See, for example, WIPO Standing Committee on Copyright & Related Rights, *WIPO Study on Limitations and Exceptions of Copyright and Related Rights in the Digital Environment*, WIPO Doc. SCCR/9/7 (April 5, 2003) (prepared by Sam Ricketson), available at http://www.wipo.int/edocs/mdocs/copyright/en/sccr_9/sccr_9_7.pdf. But formal statements alone cannot alleviate the burden of IP enforcement in DCs and LDCs, nor alter the troubling practise of offering technical assistance to these countries primarily for enforcing rights, not limitations and exceptions – which are the mechanisms of the so-called balance reflected in the treaties. See, for example, WIPO Permanent Committee on Cooperation for Development Related to Intellectual Properly, *WIPO's Legal and Technical Assistance to Developing Countries for the Implementation of the TRIPS Agreement from January 1, 1996, to June 30, 2000*, WIPO Doc. WIPO/TRIPS/2000/1 (August 1, 2000), available at http://www.wipo.int/meetings/en/doc_details.jsp?doc_id=33295.

> countries and LDCs that have taken up higher IP obligations in recent years simply lack the necessary infrastructure and institutional capacity to absorb such technology.
>
> Even in developing countries that may have a degree of absorptive technological capacity, higher standards of intellectual property protection have failed to foster the transfer of technology through foreign direct investment and licensing. In effect, corrective measures are needed to address the inability of existing IP agreements and treaties to promote a real transfer of technology to developing countries and LDCs.[152]

Yet, according to a WIPO document outlining the advantages of adherence to the WCT and WPPT,[153] digital copyright protection

> will encourage investment in the country, both domestic and foreign, by providing greater certainty to businesses that their property can be safely disseminated there.
>
> . . . .
>
> The level of intellectual property protection and enforcement is very much a factor in industry's decisions to invest in any particular country. Companies evaluate the likelihood that they will sell enough legitimate copies of the products – in light of local intellectual property protection. It does not make sense for investors to put money into a market where they will not recover their investment and generate a reasonable profit. For copyrighted products, this depends almost entirely on the level of copyright protection. Adherence to the treaties makes a strong statement of the country's commitment to copyright protection and readiness to respond to technological change.[154]

Another stated advantage of the WIPO Internet Treaties includes the protection in developed countries of works by local creators and enterprises from DCs and LDCs, which ensures 'that [these] creators and enterprises enjoy the economic rewards from outside the country'.[155] Yet, recently, a major Indian filmmaker noted the failure of US authorities to crack down on US sales of home videos of movies made in India.[156] Indeed, it is hardly likely that enforcement of foreign rights in developed countries represents any meaningful concern for authorities in those countries.[157] Further, claims that 'jobs all over the world' are created by copyright industries,

---

152 WIPO, *Development Agenda Proposal*, *supra* note 140, Annex, at 3.

153 See generally WIPO, *Advantages of Adherence*, *supra* note 70.

154 *Id.* at 7.

155 *Id.* at 4.

156 See Tony Dutra, *Indian Film Maker Faults Failure to Address Counterfeit Movie Sales in U.S.*, 75 PAT. TRADEMARK & COPYRIGHT J. (BNA) 680, 680–81 (2008).

157 *Id.* at 681 (noting Indian film producer's hopes that cooperation between the Indian film industry and the Motion Picture Association of America (MPAA)

'not just for developed countries, but also for developing countries and for many related economic sectors that contribute to manufacturing, sales and service of these products'[158] simply are not borne out by existing empirical evidence or the conclusions of leading economists.[159] Neither is the claim that copyright industries can make significant contributions to the economies of developing countries. In short, other than the enactment of implementing legislation, there is no evidence of local engagement with the WIPO Internet Treaties in DCs and LDCs, much less any evidence to verify these assertions. Even with respect to benefits that might inure to developed countries, such as the enhancement of technology markets and e-commerce, the stated official justifications are simply facile. Technology markets in IP have been stymied for a variety of reasons that include a reliance on the right to exclude use as a dominant model.[160] In Europe, where considerable substantive harmonization has occurred since the 1990s, there remain considerable challenges to the development of a robust internal market for online works.[161]

---

could help address the issue of enforcement of foreign rights in the United States).

[158] WIPO, *The Digital Agenda*, *supra* note 92, at 5; see also WIPO, *Advantages of Adherence*, *supra* note 70, at 6.

[159] See, for example, Edwin Mansfield, *Unauthorized Use of Intellectual Property: Effects on Investment, Technology Transfer, and Innovation*, in Mitchel B. Wallerstein, Mary E. Mogee and Robin E. Schoen (eds), GLOBAL DIMENSIONS OF INTELLECTUAL PROPERTY RIGHTS IN SCIENCE AND TECHNOLOGY 107, 122–4 (1993); Keith E. Maskus & Denise Eby Konan, *Trade-related Intellectual Property Rights: Issues and Exploratory Results*, in Alan V. Deardorff & Robert M. Stern (eds), ANALYTICAL AND NEGOTIATING ISSUES IN THE GLOBAL TRADING SYSTEM 401, 414–15 (1994). See generally KEITH E. MASKUS, INTELLECTUAL PROPERTY RIGHTS IN THE GLOBAL ECONOMY (2000).

[160] See, for example, Michael L. Katz & Howard A. Shelanski, *Mergers and Innovation*, 74 ANTITRUST LJ 1, 2 (2007) (discussing the difficulties antitrust regulators face in technology markets due 'to the uncertain fit between the market conditions that produce innovation and the market conditions to which antitrust policy generally aspires, and, in part, to uncertainty about how innovation might affect market structure and performance'); Keith E. Maskus, *Using the International Trading System to Foster Technology Transfer for Economic Development*, 2005 MICH. ST. L. REV. 219, 234–5 (noting that a principal factor inhibiting international technology-transfer markets is market power of owners of technical information rooted in, among other things, the exercise of IP rights); Kathryn McMahon, *Interoperability: 'Indispensability' and 'Special Responsibility' in High Technology Markets*, 9 TUL. J. TECH. & INTELL. PROP. 123, 171 (2007) (discussing the detrimental effects of 'abusive and exclusionary conduct' in high technology markets); see also Ballard, *supra* note 110, at 448.

[161] See generally Tilman Lüder, *The Next Ten Years in E.U. Copyright: Making Markets Work*, 18 FORDHAM INTELL. PROP. MEDIA & ENT. LJ 1 (2007).

3.3.2. The Accountability Deficit

Claims that strong protection for intellectual property will ineluctably produce positive development gains in the global South systematically underestimate and undervalue the importance of access to knowledge and technology as part of a necessary global bargain to facilitate consumer creativity and contribute to development aspirations. Likewise, resting the development challenge solely at the feet of a flawed global copyright system falls far short of confronting the significant infrastructural shortcomings of many developing countries which makes harnessing intellectual property rights (balanced or not) for development a truly difficult task. Nevertheless, the fact that developing countries are somehow successfully persuaded to ratify major intellectual property treaties suggests that there is some capacity at the global institutional level to influence the direction of copyright regulation in the global South. Arguments presented systematically by private actors, developed countries, and even WIPO[162] that new rights and regimes offer development benefits to developing countries require regulatory space to address, on a global front, the access needs that are most relevant to leveraging technology for development gains in areas ranging from bulk access to educational materials to distance learning.[163] There should be corresponding accountability by WIPO and developed countries for the negative effects of heightened copyright standards and, importantly, attention directed at redressing the lack of corresponding minimum limitations and exceptions in the global copyright scheme that now includes the WIPO Internet Treaties. This lack of accountability for the claims that, when leveraged, have historically encouraged developing country ratification of intellectual property treaties, have contributed to a political and institutional global culture in which the needs of these countries are often framed as illegitimate attempts to undermine the economic value of knowledge-based goods. If such value is not dispersed among all signatory countries, there can be nothing illegitimate about demands that the system be examined to determine its impact on the aspirations of the majority of treaty members.

3.3.3. Considerations of Private Enforcement

To the extent consumers in the global South are far less vulnerable to the enforcement processes of developed countries, the legitimacy and efficacy

---

[162] See Tove Iren S. Gerhardsen & William New, *WIPO Copyright Advice Deemed Misleading to Developing Countries*, Intell. Prop. Watch, February 20, 2006, http://www.ip-watch.org/weblog/index.php?p=221.

[163] *Id.*; see also Margaret Chon, *Intellectual Property 'From Below': Copyright and Capability for Education*, 40 UC Davis L. Rev. 803, 840–42 (2007).

of technological controls become far more important to content providers whose reliance on private enforcement will likely be far greater across territorial lines. Ratification of the WIPO Internet Treaties by DCs and LDCs was thus important not necessarily to obligate these countries to new copyright standards as such, but, instead, as a means for content providers to circumvent reliance on domestic institutions in those countries in enforcing their rights – whether or not such rights are consistent with the domestic choices of treaty implementation. Put differently, the technological protection controls legitimized in the WIPO Internet Treaties not only trivialize the possibility that users in the global South might actually engender value in the global networks, but could also render the dominance of national copyright laws a nullity.

3.4. The importance of accounting for the future

As with the developed countries, the WIPO Internet Treaties simultaneously offer too little for users in developing countries. The sheer populational advantage of the global South is increasingly being leveraged by the new models of interaction, entrepreneurship, and creativity that pervade the digital realm.[164] Over 80 percent of estimated Internet users live outside of the United States and 50 percent of the online advertising market is also non-US.[165] Between 2006 and 2007, use of social networking sites in the Middle East and Africa increased by almost 70 percent, and in Asia Pacific by 50 percent.[166] In international fora, demands by developing countries that global copyright regulation must reflect and be accountable to broader economic and social goals have engendered new action programs and initiatives,[167] while an active and engaged civil society network steadfastly resists the unfettered expansion of intellectual property rights more generally.

The tendency of global copyright regulation to marginalize the public-interest priorities that make copyright law both necessary and relevant is evident in the compromises that yielded the WIPO Internet Treaties. After more than a decade, neither developed nor developing countries appear to have benefited uniquely from the hard-fought battle over the appropriate role of copyright in the digital age; instead, there appears to

---

164 See Jon Swartz, *Social-Networking Sites Going Global*, USA Today, February 11, 2008, at 3B.

165 *Id.*

166 *Id.*

167 See, for example, WIPO, *Development Agenda Proposal*, *supra* note 140, Annex, at 1.

be only increasing regulatory space for private lawmaking to occur[168] as the best means to appropriate copyright's goals within the contested arena of global digital networks. This might suggest that the real danger of the WIPO Internet Treaties is not that they strengthen private copyright interests, but that they make public copyright regulation less meaningful. At best, it would appear that the WIPO Internet Treaties offered too little too early and, consequently, serve a more technocratic and political – rather than substantive and legal – role in the future of digital copyright.

Conclusion

In its classic utilitarian posture, copyright was not designed as the exclusive repository of authorial interests.[169] Instead, copyright law mediated internal tensions between the creative experiences of authors writing over the shoulders of giants,[170] and of readers or other kinds of users whose interaction with the objects of copyright protection generated a diffuse but important social value. The TRIPS Agreement, despite its strong minimal standards of global protection and enforcement, recognized the careful balance necessary to promote creativity and dissemination in a global innovation system. The new rights introduced by the WIPO Internet Treaties threaten to redirect the social value of the copyright system away from diffusion to containment. Ultimately, however, these rights cannot alter or overcome the creative engagement and force of users worldwide whose interests are critical to the capacity of owners and technology suppliers to appropriate value from new technological developments.

---

168 On some important issues regarding private norms in international copyright law, see generally Graeme B. Dinwoodie, *Private Ordering and the Creation of International Copyright Norms: The Role of Public Structuring*, 160 J. Institutional & Theoretical Econ. 161, 173–4 (2004).

169 See H. Comm. on the Judiciary, 87th Cong., Report of the Register of Copyrights on the General Revision of the U.S. Copyright Law 5 (Comm. Print 1961) ('The ultimate purpose of copyright legislation is to foster the growth of learning and culture for the public welfare, and the grant of exclusive rights to authors for a limited time is a means to that end.'); Pierre N. Leval, *Toward a Fair Use Standard*, 103 Harv. L. Rev. 1105, 1107 (1990) (noting that the goal of copyright law is 'to stimulate activity and progress in the arts for the intellectual enrichment of the public').

170 See Letter from Sir Isaac Newton to Robert Hooke (February 5, 1676). For the history of this quotation, which was apparently in general use during Isaac Newton's time, see Robert K. Merton, On the Shoulders of Giants: A Shandean Postscript (1965).

12 The protection of 'related rights' in TRIPS and the WIPO Performances and Phonograms Treaty

Owen Morgan

Introduction

This chapter discusses the international intellectual property rights of members of three key groups within the entertainment industry, namely, broadcasters, producers of phonograms and performers. The first two provide investment and entrepreneurial drive, while performers are, of course, an essential element in the industry. The intellectual property rights of the three are commonly grouped together and referred to as 'neighbouring rights' or 'related rights'.[1]

Article 5 of the Agreement on Trade-related Aspects of Intellectual Property Rights, Annex 1C to the Agreement Establishing the World Trade Organization, done at Marrakesh on April 15, 1994 ('TRIPS') states that 'The protection and enforcement of intellectual property rights should contribute to the promotion of technological innovation and to the transfer and dissemination of technology'. This was a surprisingly forward-thinking statement because the period since TRIPS was concluded has been one of sustained technological advance. The entertainment industry, which employs the technology of sound recording and broadcasting, is an industry that has been marked by significant technological development. The value of the investment in the entertainment industry has meant that investors, rights holders and potential rights holders have sought to increase the level of protection afforded to their investments and the United States government, for one, has regarded their efforts favourably.[2]

---

1 '"Neighbouring rights" is a term that in its narrow sense covers the rights of performers, producers of phonograms and broadcasting organizations, that is, the beneficiaries under the Rome Convention. In a wider sense, the term covers a range of rights in subject matter such as cinematographic films, photographs and typographical arrangements.' Jehoram, H. (1990), 'The Relationship between Copyright and Neighbouring Rights' *Revue Internationale du Droit d'Auteur* (144), 81, 83.

2 In 2003, the United States IP industries comprised nearly 20 per cent

TRIPS has been instrumental in the development and the implementation of international protection of the investment in phonograms and in broadcasting and the protection of the rights of performers whose performances are embodied in phonograms and broadcasts.[3] It provides protection that is international in scope because Members of the World Trade Agreement ('WTO') are obliged to ensure protection for the rights of other nationals within their national borders. This has resulted in a codification of those rights and, in respect of some states, the introduction of the rights.[4] Soon after TRIPS was concluded in 1994, the World Intellectual Property Organization ('WIPO') treaties – the WIPO Copyright Treaty ('WCT') and the WIPO Performances and Phonograms Treaty ('WPPT') – were adopted on December 20, 1996 and they built on the basis that was established by TRIPS. The WPPT can now be regarded as the international benchmark for related rights.

In the literature of intellectual property, it is common to see the combined term, 'copyright and neighbouring rights'. The term 'related rights' is also used in the same way, as in 'copyright and related rights'. In brief, the terms – 'neighbouring rights' and 'related rights' – are used to refer to the rights that are regarded as being neighbours to or are related to copyright, although they are often or usually comprised in the copyright legislation. TRIPS uses the term 'related rights' and for that reason it will be used throughout this chapter.[5]

The chapter will begin by discussing the nature of related rights. It will then provide an analysis of the relevant TRIPS standards and the standards introduced by the WPPT. It will also include, where necessary, reference to provisions of the International Convention for the Protection of Performers, Producers of Phonograms and Broadcasting Organizations done at Rome on October 26, 1961 ('the Rome Convention'). The chapter

---

Footnote 2 (*cont.*)
of the US private industry's contribution to GDP. Siwek, S. (2005) *Engines of Growth: Economic Contributions of the US Intellectual Property Industries* (Commissioned by NBC Universal) 6; available at: http://www.nbcuni.com/About_NBC_Universal/Intellectual_Property/pdf/Engines_of_Growth.pdf, visited December 11, 2008.

[3] It is one of the issues of intellectual property law that the terminology reflects an older era. While the term phonogram may have been common once, it is no longer a term in common use in the marketplace. In the law of related rights, a phonogram is understood to be a sound recording.

[4] A number of countries, particularly those in the common law jurisdictions (for example, New Zealand), did not have protection for performers prior to acceding to the WTO Agreement.

[5] The heading of Section 1 of Part II of TRIPS is 'Copyright and Related Rights'.

will conclude with a consideration of the post-WPPT era and the various developments that have occurred in terms of the extension of TRIPS and TRIPS-plus standards.

The concept of related rights

The concept of related rights is best understood after reviewing the distinction between the rationales for copyright protection under the copyright system and the author's rights system. The focus of the copyright system is on the utility of copyright for society, on the benefit that the public will secure from the production of works; whereas the focus of the author's rights system is on the protection of the author and his or her works as a matter of justice, that is, because it is right to do so. Although the differences between the two systems have narrowed in recent times, the differing rationales justify the differing approaches taken to the protection of the rights of phonogram producers, broadcasters and performers, the main rights holders under a regime of related rights.

The Anglo-American common law system of copyright is based on the grant of copyright as a form of economic inducement for works to be created and to be disseminated to the public. The economic incentive theory assumes that the promise of exclusive rights will encourage authors to create and publish works for the benefit of the public and for producers to invest in the process of production and dissemination. It has been described as a 'utilitarian approach'.[6] The copyright system requires a minimal level of originality; it also requires that works and other subject matter must be fixed in order for them to be protected. Phonogram producers and broadcasters are able to seek protection under the copyright system because the concept of copyright in the states that have implemented a copyright system of rights is wide enough to encompass the protection of the legal persons, as opposed to the natural persons, that invest in the production of works that are intended to be disseminated to the public. This flexibility allows for the protection of works that are created for or on behalf of others and for the protection of those persons who invest in the production of such works.

By contrast, the author's rights system of the states of continental Europe is based on the belief that the author is entitled, irrespective of the utility of his or her creation, to control the output of his or her labour that constitutes the reflection of his or her personality. Under the natural right theory, works that spring from the intellect of the author are the expression

---

[6] Von Lewinski, S. (2008), *International Copyright Law and Policy*, Oxford: Oxford University Press, para 3.12, 38.

or projection of the author's personality.[7] The author is deemed to have a natural right to control the use to which the works are put. He or she is the true right holder. There is an emphasis in the author's right system, absent until recently from the copyright system, on protecting an author's works against actions that might be prejudicial to his or her moral rights. Another distinction is that the level of creativity required in order to justify the award of exclusive rights is higher in the author's rights system than in the copyright system.

Under the author's rights system, only works that can be described as products of the author's intellect are protected by copyright, a condition that might not be achieved by works such as broadcasts, phonograms or performances which are the products of investment by producers and other investors. As a result, valuable works may not be protected as such under the author's rights system, although they may be protected under the copyright system. 'In order to nevertheless protect such products that were considered valuable and in need of protection, author's rights countries developed the notion of "neighbouring rights".'[8] It is worth noting that the term 'neighbouring rights' is more descriptive than 'related rights' and it is more immediately obvious to what it refers. 'Rights neighbouring to copyright by definition are rights which are not copyrights themselves. They provide a strengthened protection against certain acts of unfair competition which can very loosely be associated with copyright infringements. Therefore they are situated "in the vicinity of copyright".'[9] This concept of rights that are neighbours to or are related to copyright allows the author's rights states to provide protection for broadcasters and phonogram producers without distorting their system of copyright, although the level of protection for related rights is normally less than that provided for the exclusive rights of copyright.

TRIPS

The fundamental purpose of an international system of related rights is to implement the protection of rights holders in states other than their state of origin; protection is available only in the states that have acceded to the relevant international instrument. The instruments are intended to cover circumstances that are truly international in nature and their provisions acquire the force of law in contracting states only when they are incorporated into

---

7 Jehoram, above n 1, 81, 87; Gaudel, D. (1980), 'The Eternally Excommunicated – The Situation of Performers in France' *Revue Internationale du Droit D'Auteur* (103), 92, 128.

8 Von Lewinski, above n 6, paras 3.35, 46.

9 Jehoram, above n 1, 81, 83.

national law. They do not prescribe the protection that contracting states should provide for their own citizens. They provide only the minimum level of rights, although the scope of protection will finally be determined by the national legislation of the state in which protection is sought.

The three most important instruments that provide for the international protection of related rights holders are: the Rome Convention (which preceded TRIPS); TRIPS; and the WPPT (which was concluded after TRIPS). As an Annex to the WTO Agreement, TRIPS is binding on all WTO Members. It established an international system for the protection of intellectual property, including minimum rights for performers, producers of phonograms and broadcasters as a means of reducing 'distortions and impediments to international trade'.[10] Although TRIPS added nothing substantive to the development of the law of related rights, its significance is that it has a high level of international acceptance.[11]

Article 14 of TRIPS is a code of the minimum rights to be accorded to performers, producers of phonograms and broadcasting organizations. The rights are to last for a period of up to fifty years from the year in which the fixation was made or the performance took place. The concept of national treatment is an essential element of TRIPS and Members are obliged to treat the nationals of other Members in the same way as they treat their own nationals, at least to the level of minimum protection provided in TRIPS.[12] Members are, of course, permitted to implement more extensive protection than is required by TRIPS itself.[13]

The relationship of TRIPS with the Rome Convention

The conclusion of the Rome Convention in 1961 was a major event in the development of an international system of related rights. TRIPS followed that Convention closely. Although there is no direct linkage between the three instruments that deal with related rights, certain provisions of the Rome Convention are incorporated by reference only into TRIPS and

---

10 Article II(2) of the WTO Agreement provides: 'The agreements and associated legal instruments included in Annexes 1, 2 and 3 (hereinafter referred to as "Multilateral Trade Agreements") are integral parts of this Agreement, binding on all Members'. See also Article 1(1) of the TRIPS Agreement which begins, 'Members shall give effect to the provisions of this Agreement'. The first sentence of the Preamble to the TRIPS Agreement begins: 'Desiring to reduce distortions and impediments to international trade . . . .'

11 As of July 23, 2008 there were 153 Members of the World Trade Organization. See: http://www.wto.org/english/thewto_e/whatis_e/tif_e/org6_e.htm, visited December 11, 2008.

12 Article 1(3) and Article 3(1) of TRIPS.

13 Article 1(1) of TRIPS.

the WPPT – probably because of the relatively few number of states that had acceded to the Convention by 1994. Nevertheless, two important principles that formed the basis of the Rome Convention can also be found in TRIPS. These are: (i) The principle of national treatment – if a rights holder is a national of a state that has acceded to the Convention, his or her works will be protected in other states that have also acceded to the Convention. (ii) The principle of a minimum level of protection for foreign rights holders, although it is always open to states, whether or not they are not parties to the Convention, to provide protection at a higher level than the conventional minima.[14]

National treatment

One of the basic problems that the framers of international instruments must overcome is whether those instruments can establish uniform protection on an international basis. The problem of the varying levels of protection is balanced to some extent by the principle of national treatment. Where the obligation to offer the same rights to foreigners as a state offers to its own nationals is adjusted in this way, it expands the scope of protection provided to foreign rights holders. It ensures that, as between contracting states, a national of State A has a guaranteed minimum level of protection in State B, whatever the level of protection for domestic rights holders that is provided in State B. National treatment therefore accommodates differences in national laws and helps ensure a basic level of protection.

The protection of foreign rights holders involves two issues: (i) Who are the people protected and what are the international circumstances under which protection should be granted to them (bearing in mind that the international instruments protect rights holders only in international circumstances)? (ii) What is the nature and extent of this protection?[15] The answers to those questions are to be found in the provisions in the international instruments that identify the beneficiaries of protection (the rights holders who meet the criteria of eligibility – performers, producers of phonograms and broadcasting organizations) and in the application of the principle of national treatment.

The people protected and the circumstances under which they are protected are determined by reference to the criteria of eligibility. The latter

---

[14] Criticism has been strong of the level of protection provided in the Rome Convention for foreign performers. For example: Masouye, P. (1985), 'The Rome Convention: Realities and Prospects' Copyright 296.

[15] Report of the Rapporteur-General (1968), Records of the Diplomatic Conference on the International Protection of Performers, Producers of Phonograms and Broadcasting Organizations, Geneva: WIPO, 38.

are also known as the 'points of attachment'. They are the conditions that must be satisfied if a foreign rights holder is to be granted national treatment. The provisions that embody those criteria are crucial to the protection of foreign rights holders. They should be read together with the definitions in the relevant treaties of the provisions that provide for national treatment. The criteria of eligibility under TRIPS are set out in Article 1(3) which incorporates the criteria of the Rome Convention which are, in turn, variously found in Articles 4, 5 and 6 of the Rome Convention. A performer is protected under TRIPS if: the performance takes place in another WTO Member State; or the performance is incorporated in a phonogram which is protected under Article 5 of the Rome Convention; or, if the performance is unfixed, it is protected if carried by a broadcast protected by Article 6 of the Rome Convention.[16] A phonogram producer is protected if: the producer is a national of another WTO Member State; or the first fixation was made in another WTO Member State; or the phonogram was first published in another WTO Member State.[17] A broadcasting organization is protected if: its headquarters is situated in another WTO Member State; or the broadcast was transmitted in another WTO Member State.[18]

The rights holders of other contracting states who meet the relevant criteria of eligibility must also meet the relevant definitions. The significance of the definition of the beneficiaries of protection is that, together with the criteria of eligibility, they determine who is protected under the international instruments. It is implicit in the Rome Convention and TRIPS, and explicit in the WPPT, that contracting states should have regard to that definition when interpreting the criteria of eligibility.[19] Unlike the Rome Convention and the WPPT, TRIPS does not include a definition section; however, it is appropriate to look to the definitions in the Convention.[20] Article 3 of the Convention includes definitions for 'performers', 'phonogram', 'producers of phonograms', and 'broadcasting'.[21]

---

16 See Article 4 of the Rome Convention.

17 See Article 5 of the Rome Convention.

18 See Article 6 of the Rome Convention.

19 The final sentence of Article 3(2) of the WPPT provides: 'In respect of these criteria of eligibility, Contracting Parties shall apply the relevant definitions of Article 2 of this Treaty'.

20 As noted above, Article 1(3) of TRIPS provides that 'the nationals of other Members' are the persons who meet the criteria for protection under the Rome Convention. As those persons must also meet the definitions in the Convention, it is appropriate to apply the definitions in the Convention when interpreting Article 14 of TRIPS.

21 The definitions in Article 3 of the Rome Convention include: '(a) "performers"

In line with the major intellectual property conventions, national treatment is therefore a cornerstone of TRIPS.[22] The relevant provisions are Articles 1(3) and 3(1) which follow the same pattern as the Rome Convention.[23] Read together, these two Articles incorporate a general requirement that Members of the WTO must provide to the nationals of other Members the level of protection provided for in TRIPS.

Minimum protection: primary rights

The related rights provisions are comprised in Article 14 of TRIPS. The following section describes the scope of protection afforded to rights holders by the primary economic rights under TRIPS. The term 'primary economic rights' is used because the rights described are the rights that were first granted. The expression also distinguishes them from the rights described in the next section, the 'extended rights'; in that context, 'extended' is used to denote rights that take the protection beyond the primary rights.

PERFORMERS

The main protection for performers is set out in Article 14(1). The obligation to provide a minimum level of protection to performers is drafted in the form of a general goal or purpose, rather than an exclusive right, just as it is in Article 7(1) of the Rome Convention. Performers are to have

---

Footnote 21 (*cont.*)
means actors, singers, musicians, dancers, and other persons who act, sing, deliver, declaim, play in, or otherwise perform literary or artistic works;' '(b) "phonogram" means any exclusively aural fixation of sounds of a performance or of other sounds;' '(c) "producer of phonogram" means the person who, or the legal entity which, first fixes the sounds of a performance or other sounds;' '(f) "broadcasting" means the transmission by wireless means for public reception of sounds or of images and sounds;'.

[22] Associated with the principle of national treatment is the principle of most-favoured-nation treatment. Article 4, which provides for the principle of most-favoured-nation in TRIPS, is a provision that does not have a counterpart in other intellectual property instruments. 'Its purpose is to ensure uniformity of the multilateral trade environment. Its principal relevance in this framework would be where an advantage, favour (e.g. as regards registration, deposit or fees) has been granted bilaterally and is not subject to the national treatment clause.' D. Gervais (1998), The TRIPS Agreement: Drafting History and Analysis, London: Sweet & Maxwell, para 2.30.

[23] The requirement in Article 3(1) that the protection be no less favourable than that provided for a Member's own nationals recognizes that it is possible, however unlikely it would be in practice, that a Member would provide the nationals of other Members with treatment that is more favourable than the treatment it accords its own performers.

'the possibility of preventing' certain acts when those acts are undertaken without the performer's authorization. The legal means that would enable performers to prevent these acts are not spelt out; they have deliberately been left to national legislation.[24]

The first of these acts is 'the fixation of their unfixed performance and the reproduction of such fixation'. The protection provided in TRIPS is narrower than the corresponding provision of the Rome Convention in that the fixation must be made on a phonogram whereas the Rome Convention contemplates fixation in any medium. However, in other respects, Article 14(1) of TRIPS corresponds to Article 7(1)(b) of the Rome Convention. Although 'phonogram' is not defined in TRIPS, the heading to Article 14 reads 'Protection of Performers, Producers of Phonograms (Sound Recordings) and Broadcasting Organizations'. For the purposes of Article 14, a phonogram is therefore a sound recording and the protection granted by TRIPS in fixations of performances relates only to sound recordings.[25]

Article 14(1) goes on to provide that performers also have the possibility of preventing 'the broadcasting by wireless means and the communication to the public of their live performance'. The words used are similar to those used in the Rome Convention, but are not exactly the same. Broadcasting under Article 14(1) is explicitly a transmission by wireless means but, like the Rome Convention, communication to the public is not defined. It is logical to assume that a distinction between wired and wireless technology applies and that communication to the public involves transmission by wire. The concept of a live performance is also contentious. It is clearly an unfixed performance, but an unfixed performance may also be one that has been broadcast or communicated to the public. The effect of the provision concerned with broadcasting and communication to the public provision is therefore the same as in the Rome Convention. A performance that is

---

24 This drafting was adopted at Rome to enable the United Kingdom to retain criminal sanctions as the means of protecting performers and still comply with the Rome Convention. Report of the Rapporteur-General, above n 15, 43. Masouye suggests that other options include employment law, unfair competition, unjust enrichment and the provision of an exclusive right: Masouye, C. (Wallace, W. trans) (1981), *Guide to the Rome Convention and to the Phonograms Convention*, Geneva: WIPO, para 7.4.

25 The International Bureau of WIPO arrived at the same conclusion as to the meaning of phonogram. As TRIPS includes, by reference, some provisions of the Rome Convention that use the term phonogram, in their view, this indicates that the definition in the Rome Convention applies. International Bureau of WIPO (1997), *Implications of the TRIPS Agreement on Treaties Administered by WIPO*, Geneva: WIPO, para 56.

broadcast by one organization and then rebroadcast by another organization is no longer a live performance and is therefore not protected, either by TRIPS or by Article 7 of the Rome Convention.[26]

The other notable point about the right of broadcasting and communication to the public is that it encompasses both 'live' audio and 'live' audiovisual performances. The other rights granted under Article 14 are restricted to performances fixed on phonograms.

Producers of phonograms

Article 14(2) of the TRIPS Agreement provides phonogram producers with an exclusive right 'to authorise or prohibit the direct or indirect reproduction of their phonograms'. Article 14(2) is identical to Article 10 of the Rome Convention and the interpretation of the latter provision can be referred to for guidance.[27] 'Direct reproduction' includes reproduction by using the matrix, that is, directly from the phonogram; while 'indirect reproduction' includes recording a broadcast which includes the phonogram.[28]

Broadcasting organizations

'Article 14(3) of the TRIPS Agreement reflects its nature as a compromise between the countries that favoured and opposed protection for broadcasts.'[29] The first sentence of Article 14(3) largely corresponds to Article 13 of the Rome Convention. It provides that broadcasting organizations shall have the exclusive right to 'the fixation, the reproduction of fixations, and the rebroadcasting of by wireless means of broadcasts, as well as the communication to the public of television broadcasts of the same'. However, the ability of broadcasters to enjoy this bundle of rights is jeopardized by the second sentence of Article 14(3) which enables Members to meet their obligations under the Article by providing 'owners of the copyright in the subject matter of the broadcasts with the possibility of preventing such acts'. Many states, particularly those that adhere to the copyright system, protect the contents of broadcasts by way of copyright and, therefore, do not have to grant special rights to broadcasting organizations. This does not mean that broadcasters are

---

[26] The International Bureau of WIPO agree that the effect is the same as Article 7(1)(a). However, their view is that the provision in TRIPS does not include any reference to rebroadcasting, and therefore it can be assumed that it is not covered in Article 14(1): above n 25, [59].

[27] Masouye, above n 24, paras 10.1–10.6.

[28] Masouye, above n 24, para 10.2.

[29] Von Lewinski, above n 6, para 10.96, 300.

necessarily disadvantaged, just that protection is afforded by a different regime.

Minimum protection: extended rights

The term 'extended rights' is used herein to refer to those rights that take protection beyond the primary rights discussed in the previous section. The extended rights may take the form of both economic rights and moral rights; however, the only extended right in TRIPS is the right of rental in Article 14(4).

Article 14(4) applies the provisions of Article 11 of TRIPS to phonogram producers who are thereby to be provided with 'the right to authorize or to prohibit the commercial rental to the public of originals or copies of their copyright works.' It has been suggested that this right can be excluded by a Member 'whose legislation already provides for a system of equitable remuneration, provided that the commercial rental of phonograms does not give rise to the material impairment of the exclusive rights of reproduction of the right holders'.[30]

The more interesting issue raised by this provision is whether performers can be the beneficiaries of the grant of an exclusive right of rental in phonograms. This option arises because Article 14(4) refers to 'producers of phonograms and any other right holders in phonograms'. Unfortunately, the drafting of Article 14(4) leaves it unclear whether Members are obliged to provide performers with a rental right and the scope of such a right is also unclear. The provision is so uncertain that failure to provide a rental right is unlikely to be regarded as a breach of a Member's obligations under TRIPS. On this interpretation, Members can determine for themselves whether to provide performers with an exclusive right of rental and Members will choose the interpretation that best fits their national circumstances.

Limitations and exceptions and reservations

The international instruments permit limitations and exceptions to the protection that they provide to the rights holders and those limitations and exceptions have a significant role to play balancing the rights of owners against the demands of users, something Hugenholtz has called 'fine-tuning'.[31] The boundaries of the rights granted under the international

---

30 Bercovitz, A. 'Copyright and Related Rights' in Correa, C. & Yusuf, A. (2008) *Intellectual Property and International Trade: The TRIPS Agreement*, The Netherlands: Walters Kluwer, 140.

31 Hugenholtz, P. (1997), 'Rights, Limitations and Exceptions: Striking a Proper Balance', Paper presented at IFLA/IMPRIMATUR Conference, Amsterdam, October 30–31, 1997, 4.

instruments are set by those limitations and exceptions by specifying that certain uses are outside the control of the rights holder. The international instruments also permit contracting states to make reservations. A reservation enables a state that wishes to become a party to a treaty to declare that it will exclude or modify the operation of certain provisions of the treaty and declare the extent to which they will exclude or modify those provisions. If a state does not make a reservation in respect of a provision, then it must implement that provision in full.

Two provisions in TRIPS deal with exceptions. There is a specific provision in Article 14(6) that establishes a further link with the Rome Convention. It permits any Member to 'provide for conditions, limitations, exceptions and reservations to the extent permitted by the Rome Convention' in respect of the rights conferred under paragraphs 1, 2 and 3 of Article 14. The exceptions and reservations permitted by Articles 15 and 16 of the Rome Convention have therefore been incorporated into TRIPS in relation to the rights in TRIPS that parallel the rights granted by the Rome Convention. It would also seem that the limitation on compulsory licensing of the rights granted in Article 7(1) of the Convention carries over to the rights granted in Article 14(1) of TRIPS. The reservations permitted by Article 16(1)(a) of the Rome Convention are not relevant in a discussion of TRIPS because they relate to equitable remuneration for secondary uses which is not included under TRIPS.

There is also a provision of general application in TRIPS which is derived from Article 9(2) of the Berne Convention. Article 13 of TRIPS implements a three-step test that requires that Members 'confine limitations or exceptions to exclusive rights to certain special cases which do not conflict with a normal exploitation of the work and do not unreasonably prejudice the legitimate interests of the right holder'. Although the three-step test in TRIPS extends horizontally to 'exclusive rights' without exception, the effect of this provision on performers' rights will be limited.[32] The rights granted to performers in Article 14(1) are not exclusive rights and, in any event, they are subject to the specific application of Article 14(6). It would be surprising if Article 13 required that exceptions permitted under Article 14(6) should also be measured against the three-step test. Of the rights granted to performers by TRIPS, only the rental right is an exclusive right (if one accepts the argument discussed above that performers are entitled

---

[32] How much further Article 13 of TRIPS extended the three-step test was apparently debated at some length at the Geneva Diplomatic Conference: Cresswell, C. (1997), 'Copyright Protection Enters the Digital Age: The New WIPO Treaties' (15) *Copyright Reporter* 4, 16.

to a rental right by Article 11 of TRIPS). As the rental right is not included in the Rome Convention, any exceptions that a Member makes to a right of rental for performers must meet the requirements of the three-step test.

In respect of reservations, Article 14(6) applies to reservations permitted by the Rome Convention. The general provision as to reservations to rights other than those governed by the Rome Convention is Article 72 of TRIPS. It prohibits a Member from entering a reservation in respect of any provision of TRIPS without the consent of other Members.

Duration

There are two aspects to the duration of intellectual property rights. The first and most important is the term of the right, that is, how long does it last? Because certain provisions place a time limit on the exercise of the rights that are granted to rights holders, they act as limitations on the exercise of those rights and are part of the balance between owners of the works and users. The second aspect of duration is the application in time of the right; in other words, from what point in time does the right take effect? For the sake of clarity and certainty, a definite date from which intellectual property rights take effect is required. Associated with the latter question is the issue of retroactivity: is the subject matter protected in relation to activities that took place before the right was established in law? It is important to be clear as to the application of those rights backwards in time.

The term of protection provided in TRIPS to performers and producers of phonograms is more generous than the term provided in the Rome Convention. Article 14(5) of TRIPS provides for a term of protection that 'shall last at least until the end of a period of 50 years computed from the end of the calendar year in which the fixation was made or the performance took place'. As well, the starting point for the computation of the term of protection is stated more precisely in this provision than it is in the Rome Convention.

TRIPS is also more generous to performers and producers of phonograms because it provides for the retroactive application of its provisions. Article 14(6) applies the provisions of Article 18 of the Berne Convention, *mutatis mutandis*, to the rights of performers and producers of phonograms. Article 18(1) of the Berne Convention sets out the general principle of retroactivity; it provides protection for works that existed at the time the Convention came into force and in respect of which the term of protection had not expired. Applying that principle to TRIPS, performers and phonogram producers have rights in phonograms that existed when TRIPS became applicable and in respect of which the fifty-year term of protection had not expired.[33] The conditions referred to in paragraphs (2), (3) and (4) of Article 18 of the Berne Convention will also apply.[34] TRIPS does not, however, give rise to obligations in respect of acts that occurred before TRIPS became applicable; the latter is explicit in Article 70(1).

TRIPS is less generous towards broadcasting organizations. Article 14(5) provides that the term of protection remains the same as in the Rome Convention, namely, twenty years 'from the end of the calendar year in which the broadcast took place'. Moreover, the provisions of Article 18 of the Berne Convention are applied only to performers and phonogram producers: broadcasting organizations are not included in this provision.[35]

The WIPO Performances and Phonograms Treaty

In conjunction with the WCT, the rights that the WPPT provides are intended to take account of the new digital environment. There are a number of extended rights that take the related rights regime to a new level. The WPPT includes a number of provisions that extend the obligations provided for under the Rome Convention and TRIPS. It also includes provisions for rights that were not included under those instruments. However, the content of the WPPT also reduces its impact. Where the other two international instruments provided for three rights holders, under the WPPT, there are only two rights holders – broadcasting organizations are not protected under the WPPT. As well, performers' rights are restricted to performances fixed in audiovisual media, otherwise the WPPT covers much the same ground as the Rome Convention and TRIPS.

The format of the WPPT is that there are provisions that are applicable to performers only; other provisions that are applicable to producers of phonograms only; and there are provisions that apply to both performers and producers of phonograms.

The relationship of the WPPT with the Rome Convention and TRIPS

The WPPT is the third of the three international instruments that, taken together, have established an international system of related rights that sets out the rights and obligations to be incorporated into the national law of contracting states. As noted above, there is no direct linkage

---

33 This provision is reinforced by Article 70(2) of TRIPS.

34 Article 18(2) bars protection being granted anew if protection has lapsed in the country in which it was originally protected. Article 18(3) provides that contracting states may implement transitional measures to safeguard acquired rights. Article 18(4) provides for new accessions and other events that are likely to bring this Article into operation.

35 Article 14(6) of TRIPS.

between the three instruments, although certain provisions of the Rome Convention are incorporated by reference into the other two and the WPPT replicates some of the wording from the Convention. The independence of the WPPT is stated in Article 1(3) of that Treaty, and there are non-derogation clauses in respect of existing obligations under the Rome Convention in Article 2(2) of TRIPS and in Article 1(1) of the WPPT.[36] Like TRIPS, the WPPT was intended to build on the Rome Convention. It likewise includes the principles of national treatment and minimum protection.

National treatment

Article 3 of the WPPT follows the TRIPS style of drafting in the manner in which it provides protection to performers and producers of phonograms who are the nationals of other Contracting Parties. This provision is followed by the incorporation by reference of the criteria of eligibility provided under the Rome Convention. Contracting Parties are also required to apply the relevant definitions in Article 2 of the WPPT which have been updated since the Convention was concluded.[37] (The relevant definitions are those of: 'performers', 'publication', 'fixation', 'producer of phonograms' and 'phonograms'.[38])

---

[36] Article 2(2) of TRIPS provides: 'Nothing in Parts I to IV of this Agreement shall derogate from existing obligations that Members may have to each other under the Paris Convention, the Berne Convention, the Rome Convention and the Treaty on Intellectual Property in Respect of Integrated Circuits'. Article 1(1) of the WPPT provides: 'Nothing in this Treaty shall derogate from existing obligations that Contracting Parties have to each other under the International Convention for the Protection of Performers, Producers of Phonograms and Broadcasting Organisations done in Rome, October 26, 1961 (hereinafter the "Rome Convention")'.

[37] For example, the definition of 'performers' in Article 2(a) of the WPPT was expanded to include performers who perform 'expressions of folklore'.

[38] The definitions in Article 2 of the WPPT include: '(a) "performers" are actors, singers, musicians, dancers and other persons who act, sing, deliver, declaim, play in, interpret, or otherwise perform literary or artistic works or expressions of folklore;' '(b) "phonogram" means the fixation of the sounds of a performance or of other sounds, or of a representation of sounds, other than in the form of a fixation incorporated in a cinematographic or other audiovisual work;' '(c) "fixation" means the embodiment of sounds, or of the representations thereof, from which they can be perceived, reproduced or communicated through a device;' '(d) "producer of a phonogram" means the person, or the legal entity, who or which takes the initiative and has the responsibility for the first fixation of the sounds of a performance or other sounds, or the representation of sounds;' '(e) "publication" of a fixed performance or a phonogram means the offering of copies of the fixed performance or the phonogram to the public, with the consent

In the WPPT, national treatment does not extend beyond the obligation in Article 4(1) to provide protection in respect of the exclusive rights and the right to equitable remuneration provided in the treaty. Article 4(2) further reduces that obligation on the basis of the use that is made of the reservation provision in Article 15(3).[39] The decision not to include a provision making national treatment subject to the limitations and exceptions in the treaty itself means that the WPPT differs from Article 2(2) of the Rome Convention and Article 3(1) of TRIPS. It is a matter of interpretation by individual states of their obligations under the WPPT as to whether they will limit national treatment in accordance with the limitations and exceptions that they have made to the exclusive rights in the WPPT.

Minimum protection: primary rights

PERFORMERS

In respect of unfixed performances, the WPPT grants three economic rights: the right of broadcasting; the right of communication to the public;[40] and the right of fixation. Article 6 states that performers are to 'enjoy the exclusive right of authorising'; it is an exclusive right and therefore differs from Article 7 of the Rome Convention and Article 14(1) of TRIPS, which both refer to the 'possibility of preventing'. Performers are also given an exclusive right of reproduction in fixed performances – a right to authorize the direct or indirect reproduction of the performance, as fixed in a phonogram, in any manner or form. However, Article 7 of the WPPT is restricted to fixations in phonograms; audiovisual fixations such as cinematograph films are excluded. For performers, this is an unfortunate reduction in the protection provided in the WPPT as compared to the protection provided in TRIPS, as the latter does not differentiate between audio and audiovisual fixations.

Footnote 38 (*cont.*)
of the rightholder, and provided that copies are offered to the public in reasonable quantity'.

[39] In practical terms, the effect of Article 4 is that states that have implemented, or intend to implement, remuneration schemes in respect of analog sound recordings will not have to allow the nationals of the United States to participate in those schemes. The United States has a remuneration scheme that is limited to copying by digital media: Martin, R. (1997), 'The WIPO Performances and Phonograms Treaty: Will the US Whistle a New Tune?' *Journal of the Copyright Society of the USA* 157, 167.

[40] 'Communication to the public' is defined in Article 2 of the WPPT as 'the transmission to the public by any medium, otherwise than by broadcasting, of sounds of a performance, or the representations of sounds fixed in a phonogram'.

Article 15 of the WPPT is a common provision in that it provides that both 'performers and producers of phonograms shall enjoy the right to a single equitable remuneration'.[41] In general, it corresponds to Article 12 of the Rome Convention. Although it includes indirect as well as direct uses of phonograms, the right is explicitly granted to performers and producers of phonograms and the provision cannot be interpreted as permitting payment to either party alone. However, performers have not been given a guarantee under the WPPT that they will receive equitable remuneration. A right to equitable remuneration for the secondary use of phonograms and of performances fixed in phonograms is merely a right to receive remuneration for that use. A right holder does not have the right to authorize or prohibit the use of the phonogram or the performances for broadcasting or communication to the public. It does not matter that members of the public do not receive the broadcast or the communication to the public.

PRODUCERS OF PHONOGRAMS

The exclusive right of reproduction provided for phonogram producers by Article 11 of the WPPT is drafted in similar words to Article 14(2) of TRIPS and both that provision and Article 10 of the Rome Convention are relevant when interpreting Article 11.[42] Article 11 of the WPPT goes further than the provisions in the earlier instruments by clarifying that reproduction may take place 'in any manner or form', although this interpretation could be read into the provisions of the Rome Convention and TRIPS. As noted above, producers of phonograms share with performers the right to equitable remuneration.

Minimum protection: extended rights

The extended rights in the WPPT take the form of both economic rights and moral rights. The economic rights discussed in this section are the right of distribution, the right of rental and the right of making available. The extended economic rights granted to performers and to producers of phonograms are drafted in very similar terms. The moral rights provided for performers are the right of attribution and the right of integrity. In the section below, performers' rights are discussed in more detail than the rights provided for phonogram producers.

---

[41] There is a right of remuneration in Article 12 of the Rome Convention, but it was adopted only after a lengthy debate. There is no right of equitable remuneration in TRIPS.

[42] Article 10 of the Rome Convention provides a right of reproduction for producers of phonograms, see Masouye above, n 24, paras 10.1–10.6.

PERFORMERS

The right of distribution contained in Article 8(1) enables the right holder to set conditions concerning the distribution of copies of a performance, fixed in a phonogram, generally by sale or other transfer of ownership. The right is closely related to the right of reproduction because there is little or no value in the commercial world in having the right to make copies of a performance without also having the right to distribute those copies: 'In practice, it flows from the right of reproduction'.[43] There is no definition of distribution in the international instruments.[44] The right of distribution makes performers' rights directly applicable to decisions about the marketing of a performance. It is obvious that a performer's opinion of the best way to distribute a performance and the phonogram in which it is fixed may not match the assessment made by the producer or the investors in the performance. The right of distribution can and should be subject to contractual arrangements between performer and producer.

Article 8(2) enables Contracting Parties to provide for the exhaustion of rights after the first sale or transfer of ownership of the copy. Because exhaustion of rights was such a divisive issue at the Geneva Diplomatic Conference, at which the WPPT was concluded, the treaty does not oblige Contracting States to choose between national, regional or international exhaustion.

The next extended economic right granted to performers is the right of rental – the right to authorize commercial rental to the public of copies of a performance fixed in a phonogram. Article 9 is modelled on the provisions of Article 14(4) of TRIPS. The rental right granted to performers under the WPPT is an exclusive right. It is also clear from Article 9 that the rental right survives after the distribution of the phonograms in which performances are fixed; Article 9 is therefore an exception to the exhaustion principle. There are, however, a number of limitations. Article 9(1) specifically refers to commercial transactions and therefore excludes the public lending right. The exclusive right is also limited to 'the original and copies of performances' fixed in phonograms. This restriction is consistent with the other articles in the WPPT dealing with fixations of performances. Performers should be more concerned with the other limitation, namely, the protected performances are qualified by the words: 'as determined in the national law of Contracting Parties'. (This qualification is not included in Article 13 of the

---

43 Masouye above, n 24, para 9.4.

44 In the WIPO *Glossary of Terms of the Law of Copyright and Neighbouring Rights*, the 'distribution of a work' is defined as: 'Generally understood as offering copies of a work to the general public or any section thereof, mainly through appropriate commercial channels'.

WPPT, which provides for a right of rental for producers of phonograms.) It has been suggested that the effect of this qualifying phrase is to render the obligation to grant a rental right to performers 'less than absolute', based on matters raised in the debate over the place of the rental right in the WCT.[45]

A further limitation on the effect of the rental right is Article 9(2), which is similar to Article 14(4) of TRIPS. Accordingly, if a Contracting Pary falls into the category set out in paragraph (2), it need not have regard to paragraph (1) if it can satisfy the material impairment test. The end result is that the apparently exclusive right of rental can be watered down to a right of remuneration. However, if a state chooses to provide a right of rental after acceding to the WPPT, it must provide an exclusive right.

The right of making available in Article 10 is the right to authorize the making available to the public of copies of a performance fixed in a phonogram by way of sale or other transfer of ownership. It is the third of the extended performers' rights in the WPPT. The right of making available has its origin in the development of digital technology. It is designed to meet the challenge of introducing new rules on an international basis to provide performers and producers of phonograms with effective and uniform protection.

Article 10 of the WPPT protects performers against the unauthorized exploitation of their performances in an interactive digital environment. The delegates to the Geneva Diplomatic Conference recognized the difficulties of fitting issues associated with the on-demand delivery of electronic copies into the coverage of the traditional rights. The problem of devising a right acceptable to the international community led to a compromise solution which came be known as the 'umbrella solution'.[46] In brief, an umbrella provision is one that leaves to national law the decision as to the legal qualification or the characterization of the rights covered in the provision. Article 10 provides performers with an exclusive right. However, Contracting Parties are free to implement the obligation in the legal terminology that they choose. Although the WPPT was concerned with issues around modern technology, it maintains the restriction of the protection to performances fixed in phonograms. The term 'making available' is not defined, but the right covers the grant of access to performances that are not embodied in a tangible article. It is to be distinguished from the right of distribution that relates to performances fixed in a tangible form.

The WPPT also provides for moral rights for performers. Article 5 of the

---

45 Cresswell, above n 32, 13.

46 Ficsor, M. (2002), *The Law of Copyright and the Internet*, Oxford: Oxford University Press, 148.

WPPT follows Article 6*bis* of the Berne Convention, although the moral rights granted are restricted to live aural performances or performances fixed in phonograms. They are the right to be identified as the performer and the right to object to any distortion, mutilation or other modification that would be prejudicial to his or her reputation (the right of integrity of the performance). The rights are independent of the economic rights, although they are maintained after the performer's death until the expiry of the economic rights.

Producers of phonograms

The economic rights provided for producers of phonograms are very similar to the performers' economic rights. The right of distribution is the first of these rights and is expressed in the same terms in Article 11, *mutatis mutandis*, as the performers' distribution right. However, it is more valuable to the producers of phonograms than it is to performers. After all, it is the producer who has made the investment in a performance that is fixed on a phonogram who will be called on to make decisions as to the best avenues for the distribution of the performance. It can be expected that a producer will seek to obtain the transfer to itself of the distribution right. The provision relating to the exhaustion of the distribution right is virtually identical to that in respect of the exhaustion of the performers' right.

As the producers' right of rental in Article 13 of the WPPT is in very similar words to the performers' right of rental, the comments made above concerning Article 9 are generally applicable here. It should be remembered that there is no qualification as national law. Of course, the rental of phonograms is now such a minor commercial enterprise that the right of rental is of little consequence for either performers or producers of phonograms.

Of more importance to the rights holders is the right of making available that protects them against unauthorized exploitation of their performances and their phonograms in an interactive digital environment. This right is provided to phonogram producers in Article 14 of the WPPT. This is another provision that is virtually identical to the provision made for performers and the general comments made above are applicable here.

Limitations and exceptions and reservations

In the WPPT, the general approach to the provision of limitations and exceptions in the form of the three-step test has been adopted in preference to the practice of enumerating unqualified exceptions. However, this does not prevent a contracting state from adopting an enumerative approach in national legislation. The treaty includes two general provisions as to exceptions and limitations, taking one from the Rome Convention and the other from the Berne Convention. Article 16(1) replicates the first sentence of Article 15(2) of the Rome Convention.[47] Although it does vary from the Rome Convention model in one respect: it does not include the restriction on compulsory licensing contained in Article 15(2) of the Convention. However, any compulsory licensing scheme that affected the rights granted in the WPPT would either have to be provided for in respect of the corresponding right in copyright, or it would have to meet the three-step test in paragraph (2) of Article 16.

For the second general provision, the WPPT adopted the three-step test in the Berne Convention. On one interpretation of Article 16, the two paragraphs are cumulative. On this interpretation, Article 16(1) is unnecessary because any exceptions made to the rights granted under the Treaty, whether they parallel exceptions to the protection of literary or artistic works or not, must meet the three-step test. This is the view taken by the International Bureau of WIPO.[48] There is another interpretation that contracting states may prefer. On this other interpretation, paragraphs (1) and (2) of Article 16 are quite distinct and paragraph (2) does not govern paragraph (1), even though paragraph (2) functions as a general limit on the exceptions that may be made to the rights granted by the WPPT.[49] States that accede to the WPPT have the option of adopting the interpretation that best suits their circumstances.

The inclusion of the three-step test in Article 16 has restricted the level of limitations that can be placed on the rights granted in the WPPT. The exception for private use, for example, is now subject to the three-step test. This will be seen to benefit performers and, perhaps, the producers responsible for exploiting their performances.

---

[47] Article 16(1) of the WPPT states: 'Contracting Parties may, in their national legislation, provide for the same kinds of limitations or exceptions with regard to the protection of performers and producers of phonograms as they provide for, in their national legislation, in connection with the protection of copyright in literary and artistic works'. Article 16(2) of the WPPT states: 'Contracting Parties shall confine any limitations of or exceptions to rights provided for in this Treaty to certain special cases which do not conflict with a normal exploitation of the performance or phonogram and do not unreasonably prejudice the legitimate interests of the performer or of the producer of the phonogram'.

[48] 'It is obvious that any limitations and exceptions – existing or new – in the digital environment are only applicable if they are acceptable under the "three-step test" indicated in Article 16(2) of the Treaty.' See International Bureau of WIPO, 'New Trends in the Protection of Copyright and Neighbouring Rights: The WIPO Performances and Phonograms Treaty (1996)' WIPO/CR/GE/97/4b (Introductory Seminar on Copyright and Neighbouring Rights, Geneva, October 8 to 10, 1997) 7.

[49] Morgan, O. (2002), *International Protection of Performers' Rights*, Oxford: Hart Publishing, 212.

As far as reservations are concerned, Article 21 of the WPPT follows the example of the Rome Convention by permitting reservations only to the right of remuneration. One observer commented on this provision: 'One wonders how effective a performances and phonograms treaty is if a country does not have to grant performance rights to performers and can still be a party to it'.[50]

Duration

The WPPT provides that performers shall enjoy economic rights and moral rights, and the duration of those rights is dealt with separately. Producers of phonograms enjoy only economic rights.

ECONOMIC RIGHTS

The duration of performers' economic rights is dealt with in Article 17(1) and in Article 22. The duration of the rights provided for the producers of phonograms is dealt with in Article 17(2) and Article 22. The WPPT follows TRIPS in providing that the duration of the economic rights of performers and phonogram producers is fifty years. In stipulating the point from which the term of protection is calculated, the WPPT specifies that the term is calculated from the end of the year in which the performance is fixed in a phonogram; and, in respect of producers, the phonogram was published or the fixation of the phonogram was made. This is in the looser wording of the Rome Convention rather than the slightly tighter wording adopted in TRIPS.[51]

Article 22(1) provides for the retroactive protection of performers in respect of both economic and moral rights and for the retrospective protection of phonogram prodcuers. The difference between the provisions in the WPPT and TRIPS is that the WPPT does not include an express provision of non-retroactivity that parallels Article 70(1) of TRIPS. Nevertheless, it is unlikely that the rights provided under the WPPT would be seen as applying to acts that took place before a state acceded to the Treaty.[52]

MORAL RIGHTS

Article 5(2) of the WPPT prescribes the duration of performers' moral rights. It is modelled on Article 6*bis*(2) of the Berne Convention. The

---

50 Martin, above n 39, 181.

51 Compare Article 14 of the Rome Convention with Article 14(5) of TRIPS.

52 World Intellectual Property Organization (1997), *Implications of the TRIPS Agreement on Treaties Administered by WIPO*, above n 25, 231.

term of protection for moral rights, including the time of application, is the same as for economic rights. The words used in Article 5(2) – 'at least until the expiry of the economic rights' – suggest that contracting states can extend the term of moral rights in national legislation beyond that granted to economic rights. There is also an internal exception in Article 5(2) that parallels Article 6*bis*(2) of the Berne Convention, namely, that Contracting Parties whose laws do not provide for the protection after the performer's death of the moral rights set out in Article 5(1) may restrict their protection after the death of the performer to 'some' of those rights. As only two moral rights (the right of attribution or the right of integrity) are made obligatory in Article 5(1), this provision must mean that the duration of either of those rights may be limited to the life of the performer. The retroactive application of moral rights is dealt with further in Article 22(2), which may be implemented notwithstanding the operation of Article 22(1). By virtue of Article 22(2), Contracting Parties are permitted to limit the application of the moral rights provisions to performances that took place after the WPPT entered into force for each individual state. The restriction of the application of the moral rights provisions may have been a gesture of conciliation to those delegations to the Geneva Diplomatic Conference that opposed moral rights.

The situation post-WPPT

Events that have taken place since the WPPT was adopted have meant that the standards and norms established in that treaty have become the new benchmark for the global protection of related rights – at least for performers and phonogram producers. A number of states have acceded to the WPPT, although there are not as many as there are Members of the WTO.[53] However, the TRIPS-plus standards in the WPPT have been adopted more widely than may be immediately apparent. This is because of the ratcheting up of intellectual property standards that has taken place outside the ambit of the multilateral treaties.[54] The movement to establish a more comprehensive intellectual property regime on a global scale has taken place largely as a consequence of the movement by the United States and the European Union back to the negotiation of bilateral treaties that

---

[53] As of July 23, 2008 there were 153 members of the World Trade Organization. See: http://www.wto.org/english/thewto_e/whatis_e/tif_e/org6_e.htm, visited December 11, 2008. As of December 11, 2008 there were 67 Contracting Parties to the WPPT. See: http://www.wipo.int/treaties/en/ShowResults.jsp?lang=en&treaty_id=20, visited December 11, 2008.

[54] Drahos, P. (2004) 'Intellectual Property and Pharmaceutical Markets: A Nodal Governance Approach' *Temple Law Review*, 401, 406.

enable them to impose their intellectual property requirements as part of an overall trade package. The period has also been marked by the failure to conclude the two proposed WIPO treaties that covered aspects of related rights.

The WIPO Audiovisual Performances Treaty

Under the regime established by the Rome Convention and by TRIPS, the protection of audiovisual performances is limited. The problem for performers was exacerbated at the Geneva Diplomatic Conference. A deadlock over audiovisual performances developed that threatened the Conference and the deadlock was overcome only by excluding audiovisual performances from the scope of protection under the treaty. The WPPT was successfully concluded even though it denied virtually all protection to audiovisual performers. Under the WPPT, the rights of performers in audiovisual performances are limited to a right to prevent the first fixation of such performances.[55]

Nevertheless, the need for international protection for audiovisual performances was acknowledged and, after a series of meetings of the WIPO Standing Committee on Copyright and Related Rights ('SCCR'), a Diplomatic Conference on the Protection of Audiovisual Performances was convened in Geneva from December 7 to 20, 2000. If an international instrument had been agreed, it would have brought audiovisual performers, at the international level, up to the same level of protection accorded to audio performers.

The draft treaty largely repeated, *mutatis mutandis*, the provisions of the WPPT. The major difference was that the draft treaty made express provision for the transfer of the economic rights. A number of alternatives were put forward. They included the alternative sponsored by the United States that provided for a rebuttable presumption of transfer of the rights in specific fixations. The European Union preferred the alternative of having no transfer provision – in other words, to leave the inclusion of a transfer provision up to the individual states. Provisional agreement was reached at the Conference on most of the provisions, but agreement could not be reached on the fundamental issue of the transfer of the economic rights. The Diplomatic Conference closed without adopting the new treaty.[56]

---

55 Article 6 of the WPPT.

56 For an analysis of the WAPT, see: Morgan, above n 49, Chapter 13; and, Morgan, O. (2002), 'The Problem of the International Protection of Audiovisual Performances' *IIC – International Review of Industrial Property and Copyright Law* 33.

Unfortunately, the prospects for meaningful protection of audiovisual performances are not great. The failure to conclude a new treaty at a conference devoted to the interests of performers was a disturbing outcome. Until then, the trend at WIPO had been to provide an increasing level of protection for performers on an international basis. The unsuccessful conference established an unfortunate precedent for audiovisual performers and for others who seek new forms of intellectual property protection. No decision has been taken to reconvene the Diplomatic Conference and there has not been any meaningful progress made at WIPO. Although the WIPO General Assembly which took place from September 24 to October 3 2007 decided that the issue should remain on the Agenda of the Assembly and the delegates to the Sixteenth Session of the SCCR in 2008 expressed willingness for further discussions, the future of the draft audiovisual treaty is uncertain.[57]

The WIPO Treaty on the Protection of Broadcasting Organizations

Broadcasting organizations were included as beneficiaries of protection in both the Rome Convention and in TRIPS, but they were not included as such in the WPPT. 'One of the reasons is certainly that it emerged from the call to better protect phonograms and their producers at the international level; performers, whose performances are often incorporated into phonograms, were natural allies for protection. Broadcasting organizations, however, are no such natural allies; rather, their interests are often in conflict with those of phonogram producers and performers. Consequently, their inclusion could have complicated negotiations on the WPPT.'[58] However, there was support for extending protection for broadcasters and this was initially framed as a proposal for a new WIPO treaty that would give broadcasters an exclusive right in their signals; in other words, it would update the protection of broadcasters provided under the earlier related rights instruments.

If protection had been limited to a minimal improvement of the protection in TRIPS and the WPPT, it may have been possible to achieve consensus and to agree to a new related rights treaty. However, apart from the lack of natural allies for broadcasters (which meant that it was difficult for broadcasters to achieve their aims), there was always likely to be a problem over the scope of protection that broadcasters demanded. The chance that broadcasters would obtain international protection that would encompass

---

[57] Conclusions of the Sixteenth Session of the SCCR prepared by the Chair, Sixteenth Session of the SCCR, Geneva, March 10–12, 2008.

[58] Von Lewinski, above, n 6, para 19.01, 511.

the content of their broadcasts meant that copyright owners felt that their rights were threatened and the control of the use of their works was no longer complete. Apart from authors, other related rights holders, including phonogram producers and performers, were involved. A concern was raised that the available royalties for the use of the content would have to be distributed more thinly in order to be shared with another group of beneficiaries.[59] The matter was further complicated when it was proposed that protection should be extended to apply to technologies that were not encompassed by the earlier instruments, including webcasting.

Following a number of meetings of the SCCR, the General Assembly of WIPO finally agreed to convene a diplomatic conference with the purpose of concluding a new WIPO treaty – the proposed WIPO Treaty on the Protection of Broadcasting Organizations ('Broadcasters' Treaty') – although opposition to any form of extended protection for broadcasters remained widespread and deep-seated. The protection contained in the proposed treaty was therefore limited to the broadcasting and cablecasting organizations; however, the draft text of the treaty to be put to the proposed diplomatic conference could not be agreed and the conference did not take place. The broadcasters' treaty has been maintained on the agenda of the SCCR on the basis that 'many delegations showed their interest towards the conclusion of a treaty'.[60]

Although delegations to WIPO agreed that it was important to keep the business of the broadcasters' treaty on the agenda, there remain fundamental disagreements on the objectives, the scope and the objects of protection under the treaty. The likelihood of a diplomatic conference in the near future, let alone a treaty providing extended rights to broadcasters, is remote. The Chairman of the SCCR has recommended two options for assessment by Member States of WIPO; but also recommended that if it was not possible to make progress on a treaty, 'the SCCR should end these discussions through an express decision in order to avoid further spending of time, energy and resources to no avail'.[61]

---

59 For a perspective opposing the draft broadcasters' treaty, see Public Knowledge, 'WIPO Broadcasters Treaty' http://www.publicknowledge.org/issues/wipobroadcasters visited December 28, 2008.

60 Conclusions of the Sixteenth Session of the SCCR prepared by the Chair (2008), Sixteenth Session of the SCCR, Geneva, March 10–12, 2008.

61 Chairman of the SCCR (2008), 'Informal Paper', *The WIPO Treaty on the Protection of Broadcasting Organizations*, Standing Committee on Copyright and Related Rights, Seventeenth Session, Geneva, November 3–7, 2008, SCCR/17/INF/1, para 48.

Harmonization of intellectual property rights and the influence of free trade agreements

The forces of globalization have driven developed and developing economies alike to reform their intellectual property regimes to provide the same level of protection for the nationals of the United States and the European Union as they enjoy in their home states. Since the WTO Agreement was concluded, the standards and norms that govern intellectual property have become increasingly numerous, complex and robust and that trend has continued.[62] The push to lift the levels of intellectual property protection has been most obviously fuelled by large corporations anxious to protect their investments. Organizations such as the International Intellectual Property Alliance have exerted, and continue to exert, a considerable influence on the United States government policy.[63] A consequence for the trading partners of the United States has been the need to respond to pressure to implement higher levels of intellectual property to protect the interests of United States corporations.

Harmonization of intellectual property rights has been associated with lifting the levels of global intellectual property protection. It is a means adopted by stronger nations of imposing higher standards of intellectual property on nations in a poorer bargaining position. Bilateral free trade agreements illustrate the pressure that is exerted to lift those levels. The result is that protection for the intellectual property interests of the stronger nations is implemented whether that protection meets the needs of the weaker states and whether or not it fetters the ability of those weaker states to protect their own nationals and their interests. Harmonization frequently involves the imposition of norms and standards by a stronger state or group of states on a weaker state or group of states. Smaller states have little bargaining power and they will often link themselves to other powers to achieve their aims. The only means of resistance for these states to the demands of the major economies for greater intellectual property protection is to delay acceding to multilateral treaties until pressure from their major trading partners forces them to do so. However, even this strategy may be denied to them. Recent free trade agreements that the United States has concluded with its trading partners contain an obligation to comply with the requirements of the WPPT. For example, paragraph 4 of Article 17.1 of the Australia-United States Free Trade Agreement requires the Parties to the Agreement to ratify or accede to the WPPT. In this way,

---

[62] As an example of the more stringent standards, criminal offence provisions are increasingly common in intellectual property legislation.

[63] See www.iipa.com.

certain TRIPS plus standards have become incorporated in the national law of states that might not have otherwise acceded to them.

When multilateral agreements, such as TRIPS or the WIPO treaties, are concluded, they may mandate protection for new rights, whether or not there has been any pressure for these new rights from within the states that were now obliged by those instruments to implement them, with detrimental effects. 'The absence of any comparable legal regime in developing countries meant that they were required to grant monopoly rights to IP holders without any meaningful or credible instruments to regulate the exercise of these rights. Given the huge disparities existing across the world, it could be questioned whether IP harmonization benefited developing countries.'[64]

The recent failure to conclude WIPO treaties – first, for the protection of audiovisual performers and, more recently, for the protection of broadcasters – suggests that the difficulty of achieving consensus amongst competing national interests has resulted in the multilateral agreement losing favour as a means of implementing the harmonization of intellectual property at a higher level.

Conclusion

The purpose of this chapter was to examine the TRIPS standards as they apply to related rights and to examine how the adoption of the WPPT has led to TRIPS plus standards in the national law of the states that have acceded to the treaty for the benefit of the nationals of states other than the states in which protection is sought. The technology of exploitation has presented broadcasters, phonogram producers and performers with problems that must be addressed on an international basis. TRIPS and, more particularly, the WPPT were concluded with a view to ensuring protection in an era of technological development.

The discussion in this chapter has shown that the three international instruments that make up the international regime of related rights have not advanced that much since the conclusion of the Rome Convention in 1961. It is true that the WPPT has introduced extended rights for both performers and producers of phonograms; however, this is offset by the lack of protection for audiovisual performances and broadcasting organizations. The reality is that the international related rights regime provides protection that is flawed – in particular, in terms of how truly global its

---

64 Statement of the Delegation of India (2004), *Report of the WIPO General Assembly*, Thirty-first (15th Extraordinary) Session Geneva, September 27 to October 5, 2004, W0/GA/31/15, para 201.

application really is; whether its application is even; and, whether it provides complete coverage for all potential rights holders.

Recent developments suggest that is unlikely that these flaws will be addressed at WIPO. These developments include the twin failures to conclude WIPO treaties protecting first, the interests of audiovisual performers and, second, the interests of broadcasting organizations. Alongside the failure to conclude new multilateral WIPO treaties has been the return by various states, in particular, the United States, to a system of bilateral trade treaties that include and encompass TRIPS-plus standards for related rights. The harmonization of intellectual property standards means that those norms and standards will continue to be ratcheted up. However, this will more likely occur as a result of bilateral negotiations that result in trading agreements than negotiations that result in new multilateral treaties concluded at WIPO or perhaps in the re-negotiation of TRIPS as part of a new WTO Agreement. States that are considering the need to implement TRIPS-plus standards should therefore carefully consider the demands of their trading partners.

13 Marks for goods or services (trademarks*)

Annette Kur

1. Introduction

1.1 The position of trademarks in the intellectual property system

It is basically undisputed that trademarks occupy a special place within the spectrum of intellectual property rights. Unlike inventions or original works, distinctive signs are not considered as achievements that are worthy of protection as such; the ground for protection lies rather in their 'origin function', that is, in the ability of marks to convey information about the commercial origin of the goods or services to which they relate. It is further undisputed that the origin function of signs makes them an indispensable element of a competitive environment: it would be practically impossible otherwise to repeat purchases that were satisfactory, and avoid those that were not. Hence, trademarks enable entrepreneurs to reap the fruits of their commercial efforts, and thereby encourage further investment in the quality and variety of goods or services offered. This in turn benefits consumers, who also profit from the massive reduction in search costs.[1] Vice versa, it follows that competition is distorted if marks are used by others in a way that misleads about the commercial origin of the goods.

Although those assumptions are basically correct, the picture is considerably more nuanced in reality. Trademarks can be, and often are, much more than just a tool for conveying information about the commercial origin of goods or services. Supported by considerable and sophisticated marketing efforts, trademarks can turn into much-coveted symbols of lifestyle or specific attitudes. Instead or in addition to informing about commercial origin and quality, they themselves may be used by those who buy, wear or consume the goods to which the mark is attached in order to signal

* In the following, the term 'trademarks' is understood as covering trademarks in a narrow sense as well as service marks. Where service marks are specifically addressed by the Agreement on Trade-related Aspects of Intellectual Property Rights (TRIPS), this will be pointed out expressly.

1 See in particular Landes, W.M. and R.A. Posner (1987), 'Trademark Law: An Economic Perspective', 30 *J. L. & Econ.* 265.

social status, or affiliation with certain peer groups, etc. Once a mark has attained that force of attraction, it becomes a business asset whose value is basically independent from the goods or services for which it is, or was originally, used.

Viewed from a consumer policy perspective, as well as under the aspect of efficient competition, the phenomenon is not without risks.[2] Owing to their capacity to symbolize and communicate extra-objective qualities (lifestyle, prestige, etc.), the psychological dimension of trademarks and hence their market power can be enormous. This may result in high consumer prices and lead to misallocation of resources; it may also enhance entry barriers for newcomers, impair market transparency, boost companies' leveraging power, and so on.[3] Such effects give rise to concern even in affluent societies, and they pose even thornier issues in countries where the majority of the population lives under economic conditions which barely allow the most basic needs to be satisfied.[4]

1.2 International trademark law before and after TRIPS

Substantive international trademark law in the pre-TRIPS era was regulated by the Paris Convention (1883, last revised in Stockholm, 1967). Pursuant to the basic rule anchored in Art. 6, trademarks protected in different countries are independent of each other, with protection being confined to each territory. Art. 2 Paris Convention obliges each Member State to grant equal protection to nationals of other Paris Union Members ('national treatment'). In addition to that, provisions such as Art. 6 bis (protection for well-known marks) and Art. 6 quinquies (the *telle quelle* privilege to be invoked in regard of trademarks validly registered in the holder's country of origin[5]) ensure specific protection for foreign nationals

---

[2] For the downside of strong trademarks and the societal concerns to which they give rise, see *UNCTAD-ICTSD Resource Book on TRIPS and Development* (2005), Cambridge University Press (in the following cited as *UNCTAD-ICTSG Resource Book* (2005)), p. 266.

[3] The most outspoken criticism against this development is found in the American literature. From an earlier time, but still quite relevant, see Brown, R.S. (1948), 'Advertising and the Public Interest: Legal Protection of Trade Symbols', 57 *Yale L.J.* 1165. More recently, see, for example, Litman, J (1999), 'Breakfast with Batman: The Public Interest in the Advertising Age', 108 *Yale L.J.* 1717, 1725–31.

[4] On that point see also infra (comments on Art. 20).

[5] '*Telle quelle*' means 'as is': a mark invoking Art. 6 quinquies must be accepted for registration in the same form also in other Paris Union countries, unless it can be rejected on one of the grounds for refusal listed in part B of the provisions. For more details, see below.

in situations typically occurring in cross-border trade, thereby possibly granting stronger – or more easily accessible – protection than what would follow from the application of domestic rules. Otherwise, the substantive trademark law rules in the Paris Convention are relatively sparse.[6]

The Madrid system for international registration of trademarks, consisting of the Madrid Agreement (1891) and the Madrid Protocol (1989), constitutes another important element of international trademark law. Being solely aimed at providing an administrative framework facilitating the acquisition of marks in a plurality of countries, the Madrid system does not deal at all with issues of substantive law.

The third international treaty system to be mentioned here is the Trademark Law Treaty (TLT) that entered into force in 1994, that is, simultaneously with TRIPS. The TLT is mainly focused on registration proceedings, but unlike the Madrid system, it does compel members to observe certain substantive requirements in their domestic law, such as certain limits to the formal requirements that are imposed on (foreign) applicants.

In the aftermath of TRIPS, international trademark law has been developing further in several aspects. In part, this resulted from legal challenges posed by the use of signs in the digital context. Unauthorized use of trademarks as domain names (often referred to as 'cybersquatting') led to the establishment of the Uniform Dispute Resolution System adopted by ICANN[7] and administered inter alia by the World Intellectual Property Organization (WIPO) Mediation and Arbitration Center.[8] Furthermore, WIPO provided the forum for the elaboration of soft law instruments in the form of 'Joint Recommendations'. Three such instruments were passed by unanimous decisions of the WIPO and Paris Assemblies, dealing with well-known marks (1999), registration of licences (2000) and use of signs on the internet (2001). The latter rules sought to establish the principle that if trademarks or other signs are used in content that is made available over the Internet, an infringement of domestic marks will only be found if the conflicting sign has 'commercial effect' in the relevant territory.

Finally, also under the auspices of WIPO, the TLT was revised in 2006 and entered into force in March 2009 as the 'Singapore Treaty'. Its

---

[6] Further mention should be made of Art. 4 (Union priority, six months after first filing), Art. 5 C (qualification of the use reqirement) and Art. 6 ter (exclusion from protection of flags, state emblems, and hallmarks).

[7] For further information on ICANN, see http://www.icann.org/en/about/, last visited 3 April 2009.

[8] For further information on the Uniform Domain Name Resolution Policy, see http://www.wipo.int/amc/en/domains/, visited 3 April 2009.

contents are basically the same as in the 1994 version; however, it was complemented by the rules on recordal of licences which were originally promulgated as Joint Recommendations (2000).

In addition to developments at the multinational level, trademark law usually also figures as a subject of bilateral free trade agreements. Most frequently, it is stipulated in such agreements that parties adhere to the Madrid Protocol on international registration of marks, and/or commit themselves to observe the WIPO Joint Recommendations.

1.3 Trademark provisions in TRIPS

Compared with other parts of the TRIPS Agreement, in particular patents, the negotiations in the Uruguay Round concerning trademarks were relatively uncontroversial.[9] It was and is widely uncontested that trademarks serve a useful function for entrepreneurs and consumers, by offering an easy way for the latter to trace the commercial source of goods or services, and thereby to reduce search costs. Also, no fundamental objection was raised against the primary aim pursued by the industrialized countries to oblige Members to enact measures necessary to combat trade in counterfeit goods.[10] However, whereas some countries endorsed the position that the Agreement should go no further than that,[11] TRIPS does not stop at imposing rules destined to outlaw counterfeiting in the narrow sense, but has created, for the first time in the history of international trademark law, an entire framework of provisions embracing acquisition, scope and use of marks.

Apart from the discussions concerning the ambit of the trademark provisions as such, the basically antagonistic positions of the industrialized and developing countries were articulated most strongly with regard to Art. 20, the provision dealing with regulations imposed on the manner in which use should be made of a mark (for more details, see below). The only other issue which would eventually have given rise to even stronger controversies – national versus global exhaustion of rights after first sale

---

9 For a detailed account of the history of the trademark provisions in TRIPS, see *UNCTAD/ICTSD Resource Book* (2005), pp. 218 et seq.

10 *UNCTAD/ICTSD Resource Book* (2005), pp. 216, 217.

11 See, for instance, the joint proposal submitted by Argentina, Brazil, Chile, China, Colombia, Cuba, Egypt, India, Nigeria, Peru, Tanzania and Uruguay (MTN.GNG/NG11/W/71, 14 May 1990) (in the following cited as: joint developing country proposal (1990)), which in its core provision on trademarks stipulated only that owners of valid marks should be protected against a likelihood of confusion caused by the use of identical or similar signs for the same or similar goods or services, leaving everything else to national legislation.

– had been removed from the agenda[12] by excluding exhaustion from the range of topics that were judiciable under the WTO Dispute Settlement regime (Art. 6 TRIPS).[13]

Like the negotiations themselves, the implementation of the TRIPS trademark provisions has triggered relatively few open controversies. Apart from Art. 20, which continues to pose problems, not least with regard to health-related measures affecting the use of marks,[14] most discussions related to the protection of well-known marks. The concerns raised were motivated not only by the breadth of the provision, in particular regarding protection vis-à-vis dissimilar goods, but even more so by the difficulties inherent in the determination of whether a mark was to be regarded as 'well-known'.[15]

2. The TRIPS trademark section – substantive contents

2.1 Overview

By virtue of Art. 2.1 TRIPS, the Paris Convention (1967) still establishes the minimum level of international trademark protection. In addition, TRIPS Arts. 15–21 provide for a number of extensions to that groundwork. Art. 15 contains a definition of protectable subject matter and addresses the acquisition of rights through use. Art. 16 delineates the rights conferred by a mark and expands the notion of protection granted to well-known marks to situations when no (direct) confusion is caused. Art. 17 deals with limitations, by enunciating a reduced (two-prong) version of the three-step test to be found in other sections of TRIPS. Art. 18 sets forth a minimum protection term of seven years for trademark registrations, which must be capable of being prolonged infinitely. Art. 19 elaborates on the use requirement as a condition for maintenance of rights, Art. 20 bans provisions by which the use of marks would be unreasonably encumbered, and Art. 21, finally, prohibits compulsory licenses and declares it to be a matter of common understanding that trademarks may be assigned with or without the business in which they are used.

Apart from the trademark section proper, rules from other parts of

---

12 The proposal submitted by Brazil (MTN.GNG/NG11/W/57, 11 December 1989) (in the following cited as Brazilian proposal (1989)) had included the clause that 'the principle of international exhaustion should be applied in the case of parallel imports'. The same was stipulated in the joint developing country proposal (1990).

13 Correa, Carlos (2007), *Trade Related Aspects of Intellectual Property Rights*, Oxford University Press (cited in the following as Correa (2007), *TRIPS*), p. 78.

14 See comments on Art. 20 (below).

15 See comments on Art. 16.2 and 3 (below).

TRIPS are also of immediate interest for this field, such as in particular Art. 62 (registration procedures) and, of course, the enforcement rules in TRIPS Part III (Arts. 41–61). However, as the relevance of those provisions goes beyond trademark law, they will not be considered in any detail in this chapter.

2.2 Article 15 – protectable subject matter

2.2.1 Capability to distinguish

Art. 15.1, 1st sentence, sets forth the principle that 'any sign. . ., capable of distinguishing the goods or services of one undertaking from those of other undertakings, shall be capable of constituting a trademark'.[16] The definition thereby underlines the distinguishing function of marks as constituting the core element of the protected subject matter.[17]

The relevance of that point was highlighted in the WTO Panel report dealing with the complaint of the USA (and Australia) against the EU regime of protection for geographical indications (*EC – GIs*).[18] The Panel emphasized that Art. 15.1, in addition to defining the essential requirement for trademark protection, also expressed the core interest of the trademark holder 'in preserving the distinctiveness, or capacity to distinguish, of its trademark so that it can perform [its essential] function'.[19] That way, account would also be taken of the proprietor's interest 'in the economic value of its mark arising from the reputation it enjoys and the quality it denotes'.[20]

---

[16] A similar provision, modelled on the (at that time) pending European trademark legislation – the 1989 Trade Mark Directive (TMD) and the 1994 Community Trade Mark Regulation (CTMR) – is found in the proposal by the European Communities of (MTN.GNG/NG11/W/26, 7 July 1988) (in the following cited as EC proposal (1988)). The additional requirement of 'graphical representability', which is found in the relevant provisions of European trademark law, is dropped in the consolidated text drafted by chairman Anell (MTN.GNG/NG11/W/76, 23 July 1990) (cited in the following as Anell draft).

[17] This appears to be universally accepted; see, for instance, Art. 4 CTMR; Sec. 2 Lanham Act (15 USC Sec. 1052: trademarks eligible for registration in the principal register); Sec. 45 Lanham Act (15 USC Sec. 1127: definition of a trademark).

[18] *European Communities – Trademarks and Geographical Indications* (*EC – GIs*), WTO Panel report WT/DS174/R, 15 March 2005.

[19] *EC – GIs*, at para. 7.644; Senftleben, M. (2006), 'Towards a Horizontal Standard for Limiting Intellectual Property Rights? – WTO Panel Reports Shed Light on the Three-step Test in Copyright Law and Related Tests in Patent and Trademark Law', 37 *IIC*, 407–38, at 431.

[20] *EC – GIs*, *id.*

In addition to stating the basic principle, forms of signs that are eligible for registration are listed in Art. 15.1, 2nd sentence, in an exemplary manner ('in particular words, including personal names, letters, numerals, figurative elements and combinations of colours as well as any combination of such signs'). As indicated by the words 'in particular', the list is not exclusive, meaning that other forms of marks are likewise eligible, if they meet the general requirement of capability to distinguish.[21] This is of practical relevance, for example, for three-dimensional shapes ('trade dress') and colours per se. Although not expressly listed, such signs are generally considered as being capable of conveying a message about the commercial origin of goods (or services), and hence do constitute protectable subject matter. In principle, the same applies to more unusual forms of signs, such as smells, tastes, and sounds.[22] However, Art. 15.1(1), last sentence, allows members to exclude marks from protection that are not 'visually perceptible',[23] thus permitting such signs from being barred from registration in spite of their potentially distinguishing character.[24]

2.2.2 (Further) grounds for refusal

Art. 15.1, 2nd sentence, further allows the exclusion from registration of signs that are not inherently distinctive, making registrability dependent on a showing of distinctiveness acquired through use. This is of relevance when distinctive character is assessed, and eventually found to be lacking, on a case-by-case basis – for instance, when registration is denied of clearly

---

[21] See Correa *TRIPS* (2007), p. 176 footnote 13, with reference to Appellate Body report, *United States – Sec. 211 Omnibus Appropriations Act of 1998* (*US – Omnibus Appropriations Act*), 2 January 2002, WT/DS176/AB/R, para 145.

[22] Further forms of signs could be added here, for example, haptic marks ('feel marks'); see German Federal Supreme Court, BGH GRUR 2007, 148, 149/150 or movements, OHIM Appeal Board decision R0772/2001-1 (door movement of a vehicle).

[23] It needs to be noted here that the notion of what is 'visually perceptible' differs from the requirement of 'graphical representability', which is set out as a condition for registration, for example, in European trademark law (see above, reference to Art. 4 CTMR). While, for example, sounds (in particular musical tunes) are capable of graphical representation (see ECJ case C-283/01 – *Shield mark v. Kist*), they cannot be perceived visually and may therefore remain excluded from registration.

[24] It is another question whether protection must be granted to such signs on the basis of unfair competition (Art. 10 bis Paris Convention). See Correa, *TRIPS* (2007), p. 176 footnote 13 with reference to WIPO (1988), *Background Reading Material on Intellectual Property* Geneva, p. 145.

descriptive wordmarks, such as 'mild blend' for coffee.[25] In addition, it arguably also furnishes a justification for excluding entire classes of signs (for example, signs consisting of the shapes of products,[26] abstract colours,[27] or surnames[28]), without consideration of the individual sign at stake.[29]

By stipulating that members may make registration dependent on acquired distinctiveness, Art. 15.1, 2nd sentence, appears to submit that such an option *must exist* in any case. On the basis of that understanding, legal regimes that do not permit (subsequent) registration of inherently indistinctive signs on the basis of acquired distinctiveness would be in violation of TRIPS.[30]

The interpretation of Art. 15.1 is further informed by the second paragraph, where it is pointed out that countries may deny registration for other reasons than those mentioned in the first paragraph, 'provided that they do not derogate from the provisions of the Paris Convention (1967)'. Most importantly, the reference implies an obligation to observe the so-called *telle quelle* principle embedded in Art. 6 quinquies Paris Convention. Member States are obliged thereby to accept a trademark validly registered in the applicant's country of origin in the same form as the original registration. The ambit of that provision was contentious for some time; in particular, it was unclear whether it only relates to the form of trademarks or to other constitutive elements as well, like prior use[31] or the requirement to carry out a relevant business[32].

---

[25] More examples, also for marks that are 'suggestive' and 'arbitrary' and may therefore be considered as inherently distinctive, are given in the *UNCTAD-ICTSD Resource Book* (2005), p. 230.

[26] This is the case in US law; see *Wal-Mart Stores Inc. v. Samara Bros, Inc.*, 529 US 205, 120 S.Ct. 1339.

[27] For US law, see *Qualitex Co. v. Jacobson Products Co., Inc.*, 514 US 159 (1995).

[28] See Sec. 2 Lanham Act (15 USC Sec. 1052(2)(4)).

[29] Contrary to US law, where access to the principal register is barred for the forms of signs previously mentioned unless secondary meaning can be established, European trademark law excludes no class of sign per se, requiring a showing of secondary meaning only on the basis of a case-by-case assessment.

[30] This poses a problem not least for functional shapes which are regularly excluded from protection irrespective of the secondary meaning they may have acquired; see below (footnote 37).

[31] The issue was relevant in particular in US law, where it led to the introduction of the possibility of registering trademarks based on intent to use (ITU) instead of actual use, so as not to be obliged to grant privileges to foreign registrants on the basis of the *telle quelle* principle; see below, footnote 40.

[32] This was assumed by the German Federal Supreme Court (BGH) under previous German law; see BGH GRUR 1989, 525, 526 – LITAFLEX.

The issue was addressed by the WTO Appellate Body in *Havana Club* (*USA – Omnibus Appropriation Act*),[33] which dealt with the obstacle posed by US legislation against the acquisition, transfer and use of marks that had been registered in Cuba and were expropriated in the course of the Cuban revolution.[34] Inter alia, the argument had been made in that case by the EU that, based on the fact that the trademark 'Havana Club' was validly registered in Cuba, where the holder of the mark was established, he and his successor in title could invoke the *telle quelle* rule with regard to registration in the USA. However, the Panel, as well as the Appellate Body, opined[35] that Art. 6 quinquies is only concerned with the form of marks and does not extend to other issues, such as whether a person qualifies as trademark owner.[36]

Vice versa, it follows that Art. 6 quinquies does set the standard to be observed when the form of a mark constitutes an obstacle for protection. Where that is the case, an application invoking the *telle quelle* principle may only be rejected on the grounds listed in Art. 6 quinquies, part B. These grounds are: (1) existence of prior rights, (2) lack of distinctiveness, descriptive character, or the fact that the sign has become customary in bona fide trade, and finally (3) conflict with public order or accepted principles of morality, in particular when the mark is deceptive. Furthermore, Art. 6 quinquies, part C, prescribes that when deciding upon distinctiveness, Members must take into account all circumstances of the case, including the duration of use that has been made of the sign.[37]

---

[33] Above, footnote 21.

[34] For a detailed account of the conflict and the WTO panel's reasoning see *UNCTAD-ICTSD Resource Book* (2005), pp. 249 et seq.

[35] *USA – Omnibus Appropriations Act* (above, footnote 21), paras 155 *et seq.*; Correa (2007), *TRIPS*, p. 179, citing the relevant passage of the Appellate Body report.

[36] It should be noted in this context that Art. 15 TRIPS also does not specify anything about ownership; members are therefore free to regulate the matter, as long as they comply with other parts of the Agreement, in particular Arts. 3 and 4. For instance, countries may require that the applicant of a mark carries out relevant business (that is, produces or distributes the goods in question). However, while such a requirement would not clash with Art. 15 or other rules in TRIPS, it has been banned by Art. 3(7)(iii) TLT 1994 (Art.3(4)(ii) Singapore Treaty 2006); see Kur, A. (1996), 'TRIPS and Trademark Law', in G. Schricker and F.-K. Beier (eds.), *From GATT to TRIPS*, Verlag Chemie, p. 103; Correa, *TRIPS* (2007), p. 180.

[37] This confirms that showing of distinctiveness acquired through use must always be an option; it cannot be precluded for good (see above). This creates an issue inter alia for TRIPS Members, precluding the possibility of account being taken of acquired distinctiveness or secondary meaning – as most countries do with regard to 'functional' signs; see Art. 7(1)(e) in connection with Art.

Further to Art. 6 quinquies, the reference made in Art. 15.1, 2nd sentence, to the Paris Convention concerns Art. 6 ter, the provision prohibiting registration of flags and other state symbols, and also Art. 6 bis, which protects well-known marks against registration or use by third parties (see below).

2.2.3 Protection of service marks

From the wording of Art. 15.1, first sentence, in conjunction with the second sentence, it follows that service marks must be eligible for registration. This marks a step forward from Art. 6 sexies Paris Convention, where it had only been stipulated that service marks must be *protected*, thus leaving it to Member States whether they wanted to comply with that requirement by way of registration or other means, for example, by granting protection on the basis of unfair competition rules. In practice, however, by the time of the enactment of TRIPS, the possibility for registration of service marks was nearly universally accepted anyhow, so that the express anchoring of that option in TRIPS is rather of a declaratory character.

2.2.4 Use as a condition for registration

In contrast to most other trademark systems[38], the acquisition of trademark rights in US law depends on use of the sign in commerce. As a matter of principle, Art. 15.3 TRIPS confirms the compatibility of that approach with international law.[39] However, it is also set out that actual use, that is, showing that the sign is already used in commerce, may not be imposed as a condition for filing a valid application. Furthermore, an application for

---

7(3) CTMR (likewise: Art. 3(1)(e) European Trade Mark Directive – TMD); 15 USC Sec. 1052(e)(5). It is necessary in those cases to motivate the exclusion by reasons complying with the overall scheme of Art. 6 quinquies B and C, in particular by relying on the *ordre public* character of those rules: arguably, trademark protection for purely functional signs would severely conflict with competition concerns and would thus clash with the very foundations of the trademark system.

[38] Indeed, at present, the USA seems to be the only country left where use is basically still required as a valid prerequisite for acquiring trademark protection. By contrast, other legislations require use of a mark as a condition for maintenance of trademark rights; see below Art. 19.

[39] In the initial US 'Suggestion for Achieving the negotiating Objective' (MTN.GNG/NG11/W/14, 14 November 1987) (cited in the following as US proposal (1987)), it had been stipulated that 'exclusive rights should derive from use or registration'. The EC proposal (1988) also referred to both ways of acquisition, but had already added that actual use should not be a requirement for registration; the same was set forth in the Brazilian proposal (1989).

registration may not be denied merely on the ground that no use has been made of the trademark within three years after the filing.

US law complies with Art. 15.3 by admitting applications based on a declaration of intent to use.[40] Actual use must then be established within six months after the issue of the Statement of Allowance, that is, after termination of substantive examination. That period can be extended for an additional six months upon application; thereafter, further extensions are possible upon showing of proper reasons, adding up to a maximum period of 24 months.[41] Although, in their sum, those time segments will usually lead to a longer duration of the entire period allowed for showing of actual use than the three years stipulated in TRIPS, it remains critical that only for the first 12 months after the issue of the Statement of Allowance, the time frame for showing actual use is granted automatically or is extended simply upon application, whereas thereafter, further extension requires specific justification. However, whereas an argument can be made that this runs counter to the wording of Art. 15.3 TRIPS, the issue is largely moot, as it does not affect foreign right holders basing their applications on a valid registration in their country of origin. For such applications, Sec. 44(e) Lanham Act (15 USC 1126(e)) partly derogates from the requirements under national law. Whereas applications under Art. 44 (e) do have to be accompanied by a statement of intent to use, they are not subject to the timeframes for establishing actual use that the Lanham Act sets out for national registrations.[42]

For applications filed under Sec. 1 (b) and 44 (e) Lanham Act alike, registration will only be effected after actual use has been made. Furthermore, actual use is a precondition for asserting rights against alleged infringers. Before that date, the position of trademark applicants is safeguarded

---

40 Sec. 1(b) Lanham Act (15 USC 1051(b)). The rule was introduced into US trademark legislation by a reform bill enacted in 1988. The motivation for that amendment had been that (some) US courts and authorities had found that owners of trademarks validly registered in their country of origin were entitled, on the basis of Art. 6 quinquies Paris Convention, to claim acceptance of their applications 'as is', without having to establish prior use; see in particular *en banc* decision by the Trademark Trial and Appeal Board (TTAB) *Crocker Nat'l Bank v. Canadian Imperial Bank of Commerce*, 223 USPQ 909; on the legislative history, see Pegram, J. (1989), 'Section 44 Revision: After the 1988 Act', 79 *TMR* 220–37.

41 Sec. 1(d) Lanham Act (15 USC 1051(d)).

42 This detail was overlooked in Kur (1996), 'TRIPS and Trademark Law', p. 103. Strictly speaking, however, the provisions remain critical, if TRIPS is understood as giving rise to an obligation to bring one's law into full conformity with the substantive rules set out therein, that is, irrespective of whether foreign nationals are offered more favourable treatment.

(only) by the fact that registration confers priority vis-à-vis subsequent acts by which others seek to acquire rights in the same mark. As TRIPS only stipulates that applications are not rejected, without specifying that registration must be fully accomplished, that regulation appears to be compatible with Art. 15.

2.2.5 'Nature of the goods' as an obstacle for registration

Art. 15.4 reiterates, and extends to service marks, the principle embodied in Art. 7 of the Paris Convention that the nature of the product to which a trademark is applied shall in no way constitute an obstacle to registration of the mark. The fact that Art. 15.4 repeats the Paris Convention provision (almost) literally, and does not merely extend its application to service marks by reference to Art. 7, appears to highlight the importance attached to this principle.

The aim of Art. 7 Paris Convention is to secure the option for trademark registration even if a mark relates to products that are not, or not yet, allowed on the market in the respective country. In the commentary to the Paris Convention by Bodenhausen,[43] the example is mentioned of a medicament for which the regulatory process of market permission has not been concluded; nevertheless, the holder shall be entitled to have the mark registered, in order to safeguard his priority position vis-à-vis subsequent registrants.[44] According to Bodenhausen, the same would apply if a product is not permitted on the market at all.[45] It would follow that states which, for instance, ban the sale of alcohol completely, would still have to accept that trademarks are registered for such goods.

It has been pointed out that this marks a difference vis-à-vis the corresponding rule in patent law, where it is possible to refuse patents for inventions 'the prevention within their territory of the commercial exploitation of which is necessary to protect *ordre public* or morality' (Art. 27.2).[46] However, patents cannot be denied for the sole reason that commercial exploitation is prohibited by law, meaning that the reservations must be of particular gravity. Under that consideration, the question appears to be largely moot for trademarks, because it is hardly conceivable that applications would be filed for products or services which are banned

---

43 Bodenhausen, G.H.C. (1968), *Paris Convention* (commentary), (1971).

44 Bodenhausen (1971), *Paris Convention*, commentary on Art. 7, sub (b).

45 Bodenhausen, *id.*

46 Correa, *TRIPS* (2007), p. 182, referring to Kingston, W. (2004), 'Why Harmonization is a Trojan Horse', 2004 EIPR, p. 460, who argues that the same possibility as in patent law should apply regarding registration of trademarks which are contrary to public order and morality.

for particularly aggravating reasons (such as hard drugs like heroin or human trafficking). However, if that should nevertheless occur, it ought indeed not to be required of TRIPS members to accept such marks for registration.[47]

It is understood that Art. 15.4, just like Art. 7 Paris Convention, cannot and does not preclude account being taken of the nature of products or services when the deceptive or 'immoral' character of a mark is evaluated. Thus, it is only by considering that a trademark, such as, for instance, 'Cotonnelle',[48] is intended to designate clothes made from Polyester, or that a picture mark showing a woman holding a small child on her lap shall be used for cigarettes, that the respective grounds for refusal can be properly appreciated.[49] It is more doubtful, however, whether the same applies if a mark as such does not contain any potentially misleading or offensive message, but nevertheless would give reason for concern when applied in connection with specific products. The issue has given rise to debates when legislation was proposed in certain countries which would have prohibited the registration of trademarks for tobacco products, if the same marks were already used for other goods.[50] The aim of that legislation was to prevent hazardous goods from taking advantage of the positive associations a mark may have acquired in other product sectors.

As it is not the mark, but solely its connection with specific products, which would motivate the rejection, it appears quite likely that Art. 15.4 would indeed pose an obstacle to such far-reaching prohibitions.[51] On the other hand, this leaves unrestricted the freedom of legislatures to regulate or prohibit advertising measures for products considered as noxious, and it also does not hinder the imposition of other marketing-related requirements such as printing of warning texts on packages etc.[52]

---

47 The argument could of course be made that the same ought to apply where, depending on the societal order, manufacturing and/or trade in alcoholic beverages is subject to similar unequivocal condemnation.

48 See ECJ case C-313/94 – *Graffione/Fransa* (trademark 'Cotonelle').

49 For another example, see *Jebaraj Kenneth trading as Screw You*, case R 495/2005-G (OHIM Grand Board of Appeals): trademark 'Screw You' was accepted for products usually sold in sex stores, but not for products generally distributed through regular trade channels.

50 *UNCTAD-ICTSD Research Book* (2005), p. 234.

51 Kur, A. (1996), 'The Right to Use One's Own Trade Mark: A Self-evident Issue or a New Concept in German, European and International Trade Mark Law?', 1996 *EIPR*, 198–203

52 Further on the issue of warning texts, see below, comments on Art. 20.

2.2.6 Obligation to Publish; Opposition Proceedings

Art. 15.5 stipulates that trademarks must be published[53] either before or immediately ('promptly'[54]) after the registration; furthermore, a reasonable opportunity must be afforded to apply for cancellation of the registration. In practice, many countries grant the opportunity for filing an opposition in the course of a limited period after the mark has been published – this is usually the fastest and cheapest way to clear the register of marks violating prior rights. Opposition proceedings are also mentioned in Art. 15.5, but only as an option to be considered by Member States. In this and other respects, Members are free to arrange the details of the proceedings,[55] taking into account the principles contained in Art. 62.[56]

---

[53] No particular way of publication is prescribed. However, it is submitted that it must be 'public' in the sense that it can easily be accessed by the circles to which it is addressed, be it in printed form or online.

[54] There is no further specification as to the meaning of 'promptly'. In the light of Art. 31 Vienna Convention, it would seem that it refers to publication 'without undue delay'. On the meaning of 'promptly', see also Correa (2007), *TRIPS*, p. 183; *UNCTAD-ICTSD Resource Book* (2005), p. 235.

[55] This has been confirmed by the *Appellate Body in US – Omnibus Appropriations Act* (supra, footnote 21), paras 122 et seq.; Correa (2007), *TRIPS*, p. 184.

[56] Text of Art. 62:

> 1. Members may require, as a condition of the acquisition or maintenance of the intellectual property rights provided for under Sections 2 through 6 of Part II, compliance with reasonable procedures and formalities. Such procedures and formalities shall be consistent with the provisions of this Agreement.
> 2. Where the acquisition of an intellectual property right is subject to the right being granted or registered, Members shall ensure that the procedures for grant or registration, subject to compliance with the substantive conditions for acquisition of the right, permit the granting or registration of the right within a reasonable period of time so as to avoid unwarranted curtailment of the period of protection.
> 3. Article 4 of the Paris Convention (1967) shall apply *mutatis mutandis* to service marks.
> 4. Procedures concerning the acquisition or maintenance of intellectual property rights and, where a Member's law provides for such procedures, administrative revocation and inter partes procedures such as opposition, revocation and cancellation, shall be governed by the general principles set out in paragraphs 2 and 3 of Article 41.
> 5. Final administrative decisions in any of the procedures referred to under paragraph 4 shall be subject to review by a judicial or quasi-judicial authority. However, there shall be no obligation to provide an opportunity for such

2.3 Article 16 – exclusive rights

2.3.1 Structure of the provision

Art. 16 deals with the rights conferred by a trademark. The first paragraph stipulates that a trademark holder must be entitled to enjoin third parties from making unauthorized use in commerce of the same or a similar mark, thereby creating a likelihood of confusion. In the second paragraph, the protection granted to marks that are well-known in the meaning of Art. 6 bis Paris Convention is extended slightly to apply to service marks and marks that have become well-known as a result of their promotion; in the third paragraph, the protection for well-known marks is extended further so as to comprise use of the mark for goods or services that are not similar to those for which the mark has been registered.

Whereas the first paragraph basically reiterates traditional principles deriving from the essential function of a trademark, the second and in particular the third paragraph add substantially to the standards prevailing in international law before TRIPS.

2.3.2 Paragraph 1: the basic rule

(1) Use in commerce In trademark law, infringing conduct is regularly limited to commercial activities. This principle is confirmed by Art. 16.1 TRIPS, which only relates to use made 'in commerce'. Hence, private actions – such as adorning one's own clothes (not intended for sale) with hand-sewn labels such as 'Dior' or 'Chanel' – would not have to be considered as infringing.[57] While those examples appear as rather theoretical, the issue becomes relevant when end-consumers knowingly buy counterfeit goods for their own private use. Countries reinforcing their efforts to bolster the fight against counterfeiting increasingly tend to criminalize such private actions, in order to 'dry out' the market for counterfeits. Art.

Footnote 56 (*cont.*)
review of decisions in cases of unsuccessful opposition or administrative revocation, provided that the grounds for such procedures can be the subject of invalidation procedures.

[57] The principle was confirmed in a decision by the German Federal Supreme Court denying liability for trademark infringement of persons who had their 'plain' Rolex watches set up with diamonds so as to resemble the – much more expensive – 'Royal Oyster' model; Federal Supreme Court, GRUR 1998, 696 – 'Rolex Watch with Diamonds'.

16.1 remains neutral about such strategies[58] – while it does not bar them, it certainly does not make them necessary.[59]

It is not easy in practice to draw the borderline between private and commercial use; this depends very much on the circumstances in each individual case. As a matter of principle, it is not necessary that commercial use is aimed at receiving direct financial gain, by selling the goods on which, or in connection with which, the mark appears. Indirect advantages can be sufficient, if they are of commercial dimensions or otherwise commercially relevant. For instance, use would generally be considered as 'commercial' if traffic is attracted to a website (where that is of interest for advertisers), or use by which a newspaper or other publication is likely to increase its sales.[60]

It is another question whether in such situations a mark is actually used 'as a mark', that is, as a sign identifying one's own goods or services. Although that requirement is not expressly mentioned anywhere, it follows from the structure and spirit of the trademark provisions in TRIPS that use other than 'as a mark' does not form part of the core exclusive rights delineated by Art. 16. This is confirmed by the fact that the provision only encompasses cases in which a 'likelihood of confusion' exists (see below). If the mark is used for other purposes than to indicate the commercial origin of one's own products, such likelihood will regularly be lacking.

---

[58] Further in this context, see Art. 60, which allows to exclude from the applicability of the provisions on border measures 'small quantities of goods of a non-commercial nature contained in travellers' personal luggage. . .'. This seems to suggest that in contrast to liability for private use under Art. 16, private imports are not excluded 'automatically', but only if Members provide for a specific exemption.

[59] As a matter of principle, Art. 61 only obliges Members to impose criminal sanctions in cases of 'wilful trademark counterfeiting . . . on a commercial scale'. As was confirmed in the WTO Panel report, *China – Measures affecting the protection and enforcement of intellectual property rights*, WT/DS/362/R (*China – Enforcement*), the underlying reason is that in general, criminal sanctions are only meant to apply to specifically 'egregious' types of infringement. This stands in stark contrast to the practice in countries criminalizing end-consumers for private use.

[60] For a different opinion, see *UNCTAD-ICTSD Resource Book* (2005), p. 236; Correa (2007), *TRIPS*, p. 186. However, this does not necessarily affect the end result, because in the cases mentioned, the use may not be such as to infringe the mark, either because the use does not jeopardize the mark's essential function ('for use as a mark', see below), or because it is admissible on the basis of an explicit limitation.

(2) Likelihood of confusion Trading off one's own products or services as those of another enterprise by using the same or a similar trademark is the most straightforward example of trademark infringement. Such cases are regularly assessed by considering the (degree of) identity or similarity of the marks on the one hand and the goods or services on the other, and by evaluating whether a likelihood of confusion arises from the combined effect of both. That way of assessment corresponds to what is set out in Art. 16.1, 1st sentence. Further to that, Art. 16.1, 2nd sentence, stipulates that likelihood of confusion must be presumed if the marks as well as the goods or services are identical, meaning that in those cases, the burden to dispel the allegation of infringement rests on the unauthorized user. However, as likelihood of confusion continues to be legally relevant in those cases,[61] the presumption may be rebutted if such a risk is obviously lacking. For instance, this would regularly be the case if only nominal or 'referential' use is made of a mark, that is, use which basically correctly identifies particular goods or services as originating from the proprietor of the right.[62] Likewise, sales of genuine goods that were imported from abroad regularly without the right holder's consent do not give rise to a likelihood of confusion, and hence do not form part of the core exclusive rights as defined by Art. 16.[63] Other than that, it is questionable whether the presumption can also be rebutted by showing that in view of the actual circumstances – in particular regarding the price and manner of sales (for example, on street markets) of fake goods – no likelihood of confusion could realistically arise. Although a strictly literal interpretation of Art. 16.1 might warrant such an understanding, it would apparently contravene the very objective of the provision, which is primarily aimed at capturing counterfeits.[64]

---

[61] This is different from some jurisdictions, for example, the European Union, where 'double identity' is regularly considered as infringing (unless the use is permissible on the basis of a limitation). A corresponding rule ('in case of the use of an identical sign for identical goods or services, a likelihood of confusion shall not be required') was contained in the EC proposal (1988), but did not become part of the final text.

[62] It is another question whether the use in such cases takes 'unfair advantage', or is detrimental to a mark's reputation. In such instances, members may provide for liability under trademark law or adjacent rules, such as unfair competition. However, such remedies are not mandatory under TRIPS.

[63] As was stated above, TRIPS does not regulate on the issue of exhaustion (see Art. 6). It is therefore left to members to decide whether or not trademark owners are entitled to oppose the use of marks in connection with parallel imports.

[64] The original intention of the EC to expressly set out in TRIPS that a likelihood does not have to be shown in cases of 'double identity' was

Apart from that, TRIPS largely leaves it to the discretion of members to concretize the standards for assessment of likelihood of confusion.[65] However, certain substantive minima must be respected: in particular, by referring to a *likelihood* of confusion, it is made clear that evidence of *actual* confusion cannot be required.

Many countries apply a wide notion of likelihood of confusion, which comprises direct as well as indirect confusion (confusion as to the identity of products/confusion as to the existence of a relationship between the commercial sources). As TRIPS does not undertake any autonomous definition, members are free to make their own choice in that regard. On the basis of that understanding, likelihood of confusion may be restricted to confusion of products or services, without including the wider notion of confusion concerning the commercial source of the goods. However, it is important to note that the option only applies to 'ordinary' marks addressed by Art. 16.1. Regarding well-known marks, it is mandatory to apply the wider concept set out in Art. 16.3 (see below).

(3) Prior rights; rights granted on the basis of use Pursuant to Art. 16.1, 3rd sentence, the exclusive rights accorded by Art. 16 shall not prejudice existing prior rights, and they shall also not affect the possibility of Members to make rights available on the basis of use. The last part of the sentence addresses systems allowing for rights to be acquired through use, in parallel with acquisition through registration: it is clarified that the latter does not have to prevail. No attempt is made to further regulate the details of how and when acquisition of rights through use takes place, that is, whether use alone is sufficient, or whether qualified requirements apply, such as showing some degree of public awareness, or use during an extended time period, etc. In that regard, Members are left to exercise their own discretion.

Apart from that, the meaning of Art. 16.1, 3rd sentence, is not unequivocal. First and foremost, it can be understood as confirming the principle that trademarks may be subject to cancellation, if they have been registered in spite of a prior right existing in the relevant country. Read in that

---

supposedly motivated by the desire to exclude any such reasoning in cases of obvious counterfeiting.

65 For instance, in US law, courts apply a multi-pronged test named after the leading case(s) followed by jurisprudence in a particular circuit, like the 'Polaroid-factors' applied by the 2nd Cir. (after *Polaroid Corp. v. Polarad Electronics Corp.*, 287 F.2d 492 (2d Cir.1961)). In EU trademark law, the leading decisions are ECJ cases C-251/95, *SABEL BV v. Puma AG* (primarily concerning similarity of marks) and C-39/97, *Canon Kabushiki Kaisha v. MGM* (concerning similarity of goods).

way, the phrase does nothing but state the obvious: it is undisputable that a prior right prevails vis-à-vis a younger mark, whether or not it has been asserted during the registration process. Additionally, the provision can be understood as clarifying that even if a prior right for certain reasons is not 'strong enough' to warrant invalidation of a younger trademark, it may still continue to (co)exist in parallel with the latter, or even to claim (limited) superiority in relation to the mark. For example, according to Art. 8.4 Community Trade Mark Regulation (CTMR), signs with 'merely local significance' cannot be invoked as grounds for refusal or cancellation of a Community Trade Mark (CTM); nevertheless, Art. 107 CTMR leaves it to the law of EU Member States whether they allow the proprietor of an earlier sign to oppose the use of the CTM in a locality where it enjoys stronger protection. Alternatively, national law may also allow both rights to be used in parallel ('honest concurrent use'). Coexistence may also ensue if two rights, which were initially used on distant markets in the same territory, are later on extended to comprise a larger area. Based on the interpretations endorsed above, none of those solutions would conflict with Art. 16.

Other than that, it has been suggested that Art. 16.1, 3rd sentence, might be understood as declaring that the rules of Art. 16.1 are not intended to have an effect on trademark rights that arose prior to the entry into force of the TRIPS Agreement,[66] whereas marks that are acquired after that date must be granted full exclusivity (unless they themselves are liable to cancellation on account of prior rights). This would mean that rules such as those referred to above would basically be in conflict with Art. 16. However, the potential repercussions of such an understanding might be mitigated by the possibility to justify regimes allowing for (limited) coexistence of trademarks with other distinctive signs on the basis of Art. 17. The WTO panel in *EU – GIs* basically accepted that kind of reasoning.[67]

The European Court of Justice (ECJ) has offered yet another interpretation of the ambiguous notion of 'prior existing rights' in Art. 16.1, 3rd sentence. The actual case concerned the conflict between the US-based firm Anheuser Busch and the Czech brewery Budějovický Budvar about the 'Budweiser' sign.[68] Inter alia, the ECJ had been asked to evaluate the

---

[66] This is due to the fact that Art. 16.1, 3rd sentence represents an ambiguity, as the term 'prior' might refer to the date of entry into force of the Agreement rather than to the effective date of the trademark registration; see *ICTSD Resource Book* (2005), p. 238; Correa (2007), *TRIPS*, p. 188.

[67] See below, comments on Art. 17.

[68] ECJ case C-245/02 – *Anheuser Busch v. Budějovický Budvar, národn' podnik*.

compatibility with Art. 16 TRIPS of the use made by Budějovický Budvar of the trade name 'Budweiser' in Finland, under consideration of the fact that Anheuser Busch had acquired trademark rights in that country after the Czech brewery had lost its own registration.[69] The ECJ concluded that although the Czech trade name had not been registered or established through use in Finland at the time when Anheuser Bush acquired its trademark, it nevertheless constituted 'a right falling within the substantive and temporal scope of [TRIPS] *which arose prior to the trade mark* with which it is alleged to conflict' in the meaning of Art. 16.1, 3rd sentence (emphasis added), and that the Czech brewery was therefore entitled 'to use a sign identical or similar to that trade mark'.[70] This seems to indicate that according to the ECJ, 'priority of existence' means priority of the sign, irrespective of the legal situation in the country where protection is sought, as long as the relevant point in time pre-dates the coming into existence of the TRIPS Agreement.[71]

2.3.3 PROTECTION OF WELL-KNOWN MARKS

(1) Protection without registration (well-known marks in the meaning of Art. 6 bis Paris Convention) Since the 1925 Revision Conference of the Hague, the Paris Convention provides for specific protection of well-known marks (Art. 6 bis). The provision was motivated by the fact that many Paris Union countries granted no, or only inadequate, protection for unregistered marks, with the result that such marks were easily subject to misappropriation. Agreement was reached that this should be prevented, at least where it is well known that the mark belongs to a business established in another Union Member State.[72] In its scope, the protection granted to well-known marks under Art. 6 bis remains within the tradi-

---

[69] The registrations of Anheuser Busch's trademarks in Finland dated from 1985 to 1992, that is, they were already held by Anheuser Busch at the time when TRIPS entered into force.

[70] C-245/02, no. 100.

[71] It appears extremely doubtful whether that position, with its implied derogation from territoriality, and hence from one of the most fundamental principles of intellectual property, is actually compatible with a 'normal understanding in good faith' of the wording used in Art. 16.

[72] The relevant part of Art. 6 bis provides as follows:

> The countries of the Union undertake, . . . to refuse or to cancel the registration, and to prohibit the use, of a trademark which constitutes a reproduction, an imitation, or a translation, liable to create confusion, of a mark considered by the competent authority of the country of registration or use to be well known

tional structures: it only applies vis-à-vis use of the same or a similar mark for the same or similar goods, if this results in a likelihood of confusion.

Some adaptations of that rule are necessitated by Art. 16.2 TRIPS. First, in parallel with the pattern reflected in Art. 15.1 and 15.4, the benefits accruing from Art. 6 bis are extended, *mutatis mutandis*, to service marks. The practical impact of that extension is probably minimal, not least because service marks frequently coincide with trade names, in regard of which registration requirements do not apply anyhow (Art. 8 Paris Convention).

Second, by referring to the *promotion* of a trademark as a potential basis for the sign having become well-known, it is clarified that actual use in the country of protection may not be required as a condition for claiming protection under 6 bis resp. 16.2 TRIPS. This complies with the majority view already held under the Paris Convention; however, as previous attempts to clarify that point have remained unsuccessful,[73] its mentioning in TRIPS is not without practical importance.[74]

Finally, as the decisive element for a sign to be considered as well-known, Art. 16.2 refers to the 'knowledge of the trademark in the relevant sector of the public'. This formulation appears to refute the view previously endorsed in several jurisdictions, that a foreign marks must attain a (high) level of public awareness in the *public at large*, that is, not only in a particular segment of the market. For trademarks which are used for specialized goods typically known only to a rather small sector of the public, the difference can be quite significant.[75] At the same time, the wording makes it clear that it is the level of knowledge within those circles which counts, and not external factors such as the intensity of use and level of protection abroad.[76]

---

in that country as being already the mark of a person entitled to the benefits of this Convention and used for identical or similar goods.

[73] The issue had been on the agenda for the 1958 Revision Conference in Lisbon, but failed to attain unanimity by one vote. See Bodenhausen, *Paris Convention* (1971), p. 91 (Art. 6 bis), in footnote 4 with reference to *Actes de Lisbonne*, pp. 659, 667.

[74] See also Correa (2007), *TRIPS*, p. 189, with reference to Cohen, S. (1993), 'GATT TRIPs and character merchandising', 1993 *Trademark Law*, June, p. 25 (emphasizing the importance of renouncing to the requirement of domestic use as a condition for protection of merchandising property).

[75] Correa (2007), *TRIPS*, p. 189.

[76] Correa (2007), *TRIPS*, p. 190; see also Kur (1996), 'TRIPS and Trademark Law', at 106, 107.

(2) Protection vis-à-vis dissimilar goods (Art. 16.3 TRIPS) The issue addressed by Art. 16.3 arose in connection with marketing strategies that became widespread during the final decades of the last century. By placing emphasis on the 'lifestyle' aspects of a brand rather than on the objective properties of the product it stands for, a mark may acquire high independent value, making it possible for the owner as well as for others to exploit its reputation even in connection with goods that are unrelated to those for which the mark was originally used. As the scope of protection granted under Art. 6 bis Paris Convention (just as in traditionally structured trademark laws) is confined to similar goods, it did not provide for an appropriate tool to deal with such situations. Art. 16.3 seeks to amend the deficiency by extending protection for well-known marks to dissimilar goods or services, if a connection between the mark and its owner is indicated thereby, and if the interests of the right holder are likely to be damaged.

Like Art. 16.2, Art. 16.3 TRIPS refers to well-known marks in the meaning of Art. 6 bis Paris Convention. However, the provision deviates from the original notion of well-known marks in a fundamental aspect: by referring twice to 'registered' marks, the text seems to indicate that members can make protection vis-à-vis dissimilar goods dependent on registration.[77] This underlines the fact that Art. 16.3 TRIPS on the one hand and Art. 6 bis Paris Convention on the other are based on completely different objectives: while the latter is concerned with misappropriation of marks in foreign countries due to lack of registration or domestic use, Art. 16.3 deals with restrictions resulting from the fact that trademarks traditionally were only meant to grant protection within a specific segment of the market. The only element those cases have in common is the requirement that the mark must be well-known, without the specifics of that threshold being established in any detail.[78]

---

[77] In view of the history of the provision, it seems plausible to assume that this is due to a drafting error: whereas previous versions of the draft text had explicitly referred to registration as a prerequisite for granting extended protection, the requirement was deleted from the final text, so that the references to 'registered marks' appear to refer to a provision which is no longer included in the text; see Kur (1996), 'TRIPs and Trademark Law', at p. 108 with reference to reports on the status of work in the negotiating group, dated 25 October 1990 and 13 October 1990. However, this was not meant to say that the reference to registration could be ignored for the purpose of interpretation; see on that point Correa (2007), *TRIPS*, pp. 192–3.

[78] The provision on extended protection appears to have been introduced into the TRIPS negotiations through the EC proposal (1988). The proposal had used the same terminology as in European trademark law, that is, it had referred to marks having a 'reputation'. As this term had never been used before on the

The substantive conditions imposed by Art. 16.3 are two-fold. First, the use of the mark must indicate a *connection* with the right holder, and second, it must be such that it will likely *damage* his or her interests. By combining those two elements, the wording of Art. 16.3 is somewhat more restrictive than statutes prohibiting dilution, or abuse of reputation, as such.[79] As the use must be of such a nature as to indicate a 'connection', Art. 16.3 still requires what might be called a 'likelihood of confusion in the widest sense'. In addition, uses from which the alleged infringer derives benefit, without at the same time damaging the value of the mark,[80] would arguably not qualify as harmful.

(3) Protection of well-known marks according to the WIPO Joint Recommendation The ramifications of the protection to be granted to well-known marks, in particular the question of how the relevant threshold should be determined, have always been an intricate issue. The matter became particularly topical in the aftermath of TRIPS, inter alia because of the political and economic situation in the relevant period. In the course of the dissolution of the former 'Eastern bloc', a number of new market economies had emerged, each enacting their own trademark laws and establishing independent registration authorities. It was not uncommon during that phase for rent-seeking firms or individuals to try, and actually succeed, in registering famous marks like 'Coca Cola' or 'Cartier', in order to extract money from foreign proprietors at the time when they tried to get a foothold on the same market. Trademark holders were alarmed, and political warnings were addressed to the governments of those countries that they were in violation of the Paris Convention (and TRIPS). In response, countries demanded secure guidelines for assessing which marks were to be considered as 'well-known'.[81]

Footnotes 78 (*cont.*)
international level, however, it was obviously found more appropriate to replace it by terminology from Art. 6 bis Paris Convention, without regard to the fact that the underlying concepts do not match.

[79] For the broader approaches taken, for example, in US and EU trademark law, see below.

[80] For example, if a person sells unauthorized merchandising goods (such as fan articles bearing the logo of football clubs etc.), this will typically (though not necessarily) indicate a connection, but it will not harm the trademark holder's interests in any other aspect than by not allowing him to derive additional profits (which should arguably not be sufficient, because it would effectively read the requirement of 'damage' out of the provision).

[81] One proposal discussed (and finally rejected) in that context was to establish national or international registries for well-known marks that could be consulted by the national trademark offices and/or interested business circles. A

This resulted in the adoption of the WIPO Joint Recommendation on Well-known Marks (JR 1999),[82] the contents of which were elaborated in the framework of the WIPO Standing Committee on the Law of Trademarks, Industrial Designs and Geographical Indications (SCT).[83]

The central provision consists of an extensive list of factors by which it shall be indicated that a mark is well-known (Art. 2.1 lit. b JR 1999).[84] Inter alia, those factors comprise the degree of knowledge or recognition of the mark in the relevant sector of the public, the duration, extent and geographical area of any use, promotion and registrations of the mark, the record of successful enforcement of rights, as well as the value of the mark. It is further stipulated that those factors are only 'guidelines to assist the competent authority to determine whether the mark is a well-known mark', and that they should not be understood as 'pre-conditions for reaching that determination' (Art. 2.1 lit. c JR 1999).

Most importantly, while Art. 6 bis Paris Convention as well as Art. 16.2 TRIPS suggest that the level of awareness *in the country of protection* is the (only) relevant aspect for determining whether a mark is well-known, the list in Art. 2.1 lit. b JR 1999 also comprises 'foreign' factors, like the

---

similar proposal was also contained in the Brazilian proposal (1988). As an option, it was suggested therein that 'well-known trademarks should be given protection in all classes, and be *kept in a special register* so as to prevent the registration of another mark' (emphasis added).

[82] The text is available at http://www.wipo.int/export/sites/www/about-ip/en/development_iplaw/doc/pub833.doc.

[83] The initiative was mainly driven by international stakeholders' associations, in particular INTA and AIPPI.

[84] (1) [Factors for Consideration] (a) . . .

(b) In particular, the competent authority shall consider information submitted to it with respect to factors from which it may be inferred that the mark is, or is not, well known, including, but not limited to, information concerning the following:

1. the degree of knowledge or recognition of the mark in the relevant sector of the public;
2. the duration, extent and geographical area of any use of the mark;
3. the duration, extent and geographical area of any promotion of the mark, including advertising or publicity and the presentation, at fairs or exhibitions, of the goods and/or services to which the mark applies;
4. the duration and geographical area of any registrations, and/or any applications for registration, of the mark, to the extent that they reflect use or recognition of the mark;
5. the record of successful enforcement of rights in the mark, in particular, the extent to which the mark was recognized as well known by competent authorities;
6. the value associated with the mark.

number of registrations abroad, or the record of 'successful enforcement' of the mark in other countries. Another element arguably resulting in a lowering of standards applying under the Paris Convention and TRIPS concerns the fact that according to Art. 2 Sec. 2 JR 1999, it shall be sufficient if a mark is well-known among one of the following groups: actual or potential consumers, *and/or* persons involved in channels of distribution of the type of goods or services to which the mark applies, *and/or* business circles dealing with those goods or services.

Art. 4 JR 1999 addresses the scope of protection to be granted to well-known marks.[85] Further to the formulation used in Art. 16.3 TRIPS,[86] the text also contains wording borrowed from US anti-dilution legislation[87] and from European trademark law.[88] It seems to be the aim of that somewhat strange mixture to ensure that countries applying the recommendation will have to consider as infringing all modes of conduct possibly conflicting with a well-known mark under any of those standards. The potential effect of that endeavour is, however, somewhat lessened by the fact that according to the same provision, countries may require, as a condition for granting extended protection, that the mark must be well-known to 'the public at large', thereby expressly derogating from the standard applying to well-known marks in general.[89]

Further TRIPS- and Paris-Plus elements in the Joint Recommendation

---

[85] In the relevant part, the provision reads:

(1) [Conflicting Marks] (a) [Use of the same or similar mark for identical or similar goods or services]
(b) Irrespective of the goods and/or services for which a mark is used . . . ,that mark shall be deemed to be in conflict with a well-known mark where the mark, or an essential part thereof, constitutes a reproduction, an imitation, a translation, or a transliteration of the well-known mark, and where at least one of the following conditions is fulfilled:
(i) the use of that mark would indicate a connection between the goods and/or services for which the mark is used, is the subject of an application for registration, or is registered, and the owner of the well-known mark, and would be likely to damage his interests;
(ii) the use of that mark is likely to impair or dilute in an unfair manner the distinctive character of the well-known mark;
(iii) the use of that mark would take unfair advantage of the distinctive character of the well-known mark.'

[86] Cf. Art. 4(1)(b)(i) JR 1999.
[87] Cf. Art. 4(1)(b)(ii) JR 1999 and Sec. 43(d) Lanham Act (prior to the 2006 amendment).
[88] Cf. Art. 4(1)(b)(iii) JR 1999 and Art. 9(1)(c) CTMR.
[89] C. Art. 4(1)(c): 'Notwithstanding Article 2(3)(a)(iii), for the purpose

concern the fact that registration, or an application for registration, of the mark may not be required, including cases when extended protection is claimed under Art. 16.3;[90] furthermore, the period during which the owner of a well-known mark must initiate cancellation proceedings in order not to forfeit his right is extended from three to five years.[91]

In sum, instead of clarifying the contents of existing international obligations, the Joint Recommendation has resulted in a lowering of the threshold and an extension of the scope of protection for well-known marks,[92] without offering more legal certainty in return.

2.4 Article 17 – exceptions

2.4.1 General remarks; structure of the provision

In addition to defining the scope of rights conferred, intellectual property laws regularly provide for defences in the form of limitations and exceptions. The same applies to trademark law: being a tool for commercial communication, it is particularly important to ensure that the assignment of exclusive rights does not unduly restrict the possibility of others commercializing their own products, or conveying factual information or exchanging opinions about the products designated by the mark. Whether and which limitations a given trademark law must comprise in order to achieve that end depends inter alia on the breadth of the area it covers: if protection under trademark law is restricted ab initio to situations in which the origin function of a mark is actually jeopardized – that is, cases when the same or a similar mark is used to identify another person's products[93] – the scope of protection will usually not extend beyond what is necessary to protect the interests of the right holder as well as those of consumers and honest competitors, so that the need to provide for further defences is relatively small. Vice versa, if a broad approach is taken towards trademark law, meaning that basically all modes of unauthorized use are considered to fall within the ambit of the proprietor's exclusive right, the need

---

of applying paragraph (1)(b)(ii) and (iii), a Member State may require that the well-known mark be well known by the public at large'.

90 Art. 2(3)(a)(i) JR 1999. The same standard applies under US law, as was clarified in the 2006 amendment of Sec. 43(c) Lanham Act.

91 Art. 4(3) JR 1999.

92 This is noteworthy not least in view of the fact that the Joint Recommendation on Well-known Marks was included in a number of Free Trade Agreements (for example, USA–Chile and USA–Singapore); Correa (2007), *TRIPS*, p. 192, note 78.

93 As a matter of principle, Art. 16 allows the restriction of trademark protection to such cases; see supra, comments on Art. 16.

for legislation to encompass a full range of adequately tailored limitations becomes particularly urgent.

Art. 17 TRIPS for the first time addresses limitations and exceptions in international trademark law. Previously, such provisions were not needed due to the fact that unlike TRIPS, the Paris Convention did not contain binding rules regarding the subject matter and scope of protection. In its wording and structure, Art. 17 reflects the pattern of the so-called three-step test,[94] which underlies the limitation clauses in copyright (Art. 13), design (Art. 26.2) and patent law (Art. 30). However, Art. 17 bears the least resemblance to the other provisions as well as to the 'original' three-step test set out in Art. 9.2 Berne Convention (RBC). Only the first step, with its reference to 'limited exceptions', conforms to the corresponding clauses in patent and industrial design law.[95] However, unlike the other provisions, no 'second step' exists which makes reference to possible conflicts with a 'normal exploitation'. Instead, the provision mentions descriptive use of marks as an example of a permissible exception. Finally, on the third step, Art. 17 stipulates that account must be taken of 'legitimate interests of the right holder and of third parties'.[96] All of this appears to signal that, in accordance with what was said above, TRIPS Members enjoy a fairly broad leeway to provide for limitations of trademark rights.

2.4.2 Article 17 in the Light of WTO Practice

Art. 17 was addressed in some length in the WTO panel report concerning the compatibility of the European protection regime for geographical indications[97] (GIs) with TRIPS (*EC – GIs*).[98] While the most important issue in that conflict concerned allegations by the USA that the principle of national treatment had not been duly respected, the question was also posed whether the fact that a prior trademark must coexist with a subsequently protected GI, instead of being entitled to claim a fully exclusive right, was clashing with Art. 16 TRIPS. With regard to that question, the panel found that in this specific case, and under the precautions set out in

---

[94] Although it actually consists only of two steps, see infra.

[95] See Arts. 30 and 26.2 TRIPS respectively. Regarding copyright, Art. 13 on the first step refers to 'certain special cases'.

[96] The wording thereby places the interests of trademark holders on the same level as those of third parties, whereas in the other versions of the test, right holders' interests appear to be given a superior position (which should not necessarily prejudice the outcome); see Correa (2007), *TRIPS*, p. 195.

[97] EC Regulation 2081/1992 (GI Regulation). After the panel report, the regulation has been enacted in amended form as EC Regulation 510/2006.

[98] Supra, footnote 18.

the EU GI Regulation, coexistence did constitute an acceptable solution, which could be justified in the light of Art 17.

In motivating its decision, the panel, on one hand, paid close attention to the previous reports dealing with copyright,[99] and in particular patent law[100]; on the other hand, it was also emphasized that Art. 17 had to be interpreted 'according to its own terms'.[101] Regarding the interpretation of 'limited exceptions', the trademark panel agreed with the patent panel in that the combination of both terms had to be understood as connoting a narrow exception, or 'small diminution' of the right in question. As an illustration, the panel considered the example of 'fair use of descriptive terms' which is given in Art. 17. It was emphasized that such use would be inherently limited 'in terms of the sign which may be used and the degree of likelihood of confusion which may result from such use'.[102] It was added that there were no quantitative restrictions regarding the number of persons, or of goods or services, by and for which such use might be made.

Finally, the panel expanded on the aspect of legitimate interests of the trademark holder that must be weighed and measured against those of 'third parties'. Like the patent and copyright panels, the trademark panel emphasized the difference between 'legal' and 'legitimate' interests, with the latter denoting (only) 'interests that are "justifiable" in the sense that they are supported by relevant legal policies or other social norms'.[103] On that basis, the legitimate interests of trademark holders were considered to be vested 'in preserving the distinctiveness, or capacity to distinguish, of its trademark'.[104] Whereas the interests of consumers were basically held to coincide with those interests,[105] the panel also took into account the interests of users of geographical indications that were protected under Art. 13 of the European GI Regulation. It was in particular with a view to the latter that the coexistence regime established by the Regulation was considered to comply with Art. 17.[106]

---

[99] Presented on 15 June 2000, WTO Document WT/DS160/R (*US – Copyright*)

[100] Presented on 17 March 2000, WTO Document WT/DS114/R (*Canada – Patents*).

[101] *EC – GIs,* para. 7.649.

[102] *EC – GIs*, para. 7.654.

[103] *EC – GIs*, para. 7.663.

[104] *EC – GIs*, para. 7.664.

[105] *EC – GIs*, paras. 7.676; 7.680.

[106] This is criticized by Senftleben (2006), 'Towards a Horizontal Standard for Limiting Intellectual Property Rights? – WTO Panel Reports Shed Light on the Three-step Test in Copyright Law and Related Tests in Patent and Trademark Law', 37 *IIC* 407, at 433.

2.4.3 Application of the test to other types of limitations

Apart from the specific conflict addressed by the WTO panel, the following clauses provide typical examples for trademark limitations:[107] the right to use one's own (personal) name in commerce;[108] use of signs in order to indicate the properties of one's products or their purpose (for example, as a spare part or accessory); use of another person's mark to comment on or inform about the goods, for example, in comparative advertising or for other purposes typically covered by freedom of speech or freedom of art. As was said above, the latter modes of use may already be exempted from trademark protection even in absence of express limitation: as they regularly do not interfere with the origin function of a mark, they may be deemed as falling outside the ambit of the exclusive right assigned to the proprietor. However, even where trademark laws take a broader approach, submitting such acts in principle to the applicability of trademark rules, it would nevertheless be fully compliant with international norms to declare them admissible on the basis of Art. 17.

As was emphasized by the *EC – GIs* panel, it is important to note with regard to those cases that it would not make sense to require that the scope of exceptions from trademark protection must be limited in a *quantitative* sense, meaning that they should apply only in a few exceptional cases. No per se limitation of that kind can arguably be held to apply regarding comparative advertisement, nor would it be appropriate to impose quantitative barriers to legitimate use by others, if a sign closely resembles or includes descriptive notions. For instance, the proprietor of the trademark 'BABY DRY' for babies' nappies (or diapers) cannot possibly expect or demand that competitors only exceptionally indicate, in their own commercial statements, that their products as well will 'keep a baby dry'.

Whereas quantitative restrictions appear as pointless, the panel also noted correctly that such exceptions are inherently limited in a qualitative manner, in the sense that they apply to specific situations. It is further submitted that in the interest of legal certainty, the conditions and confines of such limitations should be spelled out in a manner which renders their application foreseeable. This does not mean, however, that limitation provisions must necessarily take the form of conclusive, pre-fixed catalogues;

---

[107] See also Correa (2007), *TRIPS*, p. 195.

[108] Arguably, this would furnish a basis for rules such as Art. 8(4), 107 CTMR, which allow for coexistence of trademarks with prior (local) trade names, even if Art. 16.1, 3rd sentence, were to be understood strictly, in the sense that trademarks arising after TRIPS must in general enjoy full exclusivity; see on that point above, comments on Art. 16.

the legal techniques applied in that regard can be left to the discretion of Member States. For instance, while countries with a civil law tradition might prefer detailed and conclusive rules, others may opt for more flexible, open-ended clauses.[109] Also the latter would basically qualify as meeting the criteria of Art. 17, if the framework within which they operate is set out clearly enough, and if jurisprudence can be trusted to provide for precedents furnishing reliable guidelines.[110]

The last and essential point to be observed in accordance with the *EC – GIs* panel concerns the fact that, whatever form limitations and exceptions may take, it must be ensured that the use of signs which is permitted on that basis must not unreasonably prejudice the common interest of right holders and consumers to keep the core function of trademarks intact, namely the capacity of the mark to identify and distinguish the commercial origin of goods or services. Hence, where use of a sign results in a serious likelihood of consumers being misled, it can no longer be regarded as admissible. However, instead of entirely prohibiting such uses, it may be sufficient to provide for other remedies, such as requiring additional information.

Lastly, it remains to be pointed out that provisions dealing with (international or regional) exhaustion, as well as the requirement of genuine use as a condition for maintenance of a mark's validity, are usually considered as forming part of the limitations of trademark rights. However, neither is comprised by Art. 17, due to the fact that exhaustion is not judiciable under TRIPS at all, and the use requirement is addressed in a separate provision (Art. 19), which will be considered below.

2.5 Article 18 – term of protection

Trademarks are the only kind of intellectual property right which is not subject to a definite end in time. Two reasons account for this. First and foremost, the information conveyed by trademarks does not become obsolete with the passage of time: as long as the manufacturer (or his or her successor in title) continues to offer goods of the same description, consumers will need to rely on the trademark for identification purposes. Second, contrary to other IP rights, trademarks typically do not restrain full competition on the market for products (or services) as such, so that,

---

[109] The issue has given rise to much debate in copyright law; see, for example, Cohen, J.E. (1999), 'WIPO Copyright Treaty Implementation in the United States: Will Fair Use Survive?', 1999 *EIPR*, 236; for a more thorough evaluation (with a positive result), see Senftleben, Martin (2004) *Copyright, Limitations and the Three-Step Test*, Kluwer Law International, pp. 162 et seq.

[110] Senftleben, M. *id.*

unlike patent, design and copyright law, there is no need to 'restore' freedom of competition after a given time.[111]

In view of those considerations, the principle of 'eternal' protection is generally accepted as appropriately reflecting the specific character of marks. Also during the TRIPS negotiations, that point was beyond dispute. The only differences of opinion concerned the question which minimum term should apply regarding the protection period triggered by the (initial) registration and each subsequent prolongation. While the industrialized countries opted for a period of ten years,[112] the group of threshold and developing countries wanted to give national legislatures full freedom to choose the appropriate term.[113] The seven-year term now anchored in Art. 18 TRIPS appears to strike a compromise between both positions.

2.6 Article 19 – the use requirement

In the vast majority of TRIPS Member States, actual use of a mark is not required as a precondition for obtaining protection. It is therefore possible in principle that a large number of 'inactive' trademarks clog national registries and impede the adoption of attractive signs by new market entrants. In view of such detrimental effects, it has become a general requirement stipulated by trademark laws throughout the world that actual (or 'genuine') use must be made within a specified period after the registration, as a condition not for acquiring, but for *maintaining*, protection.

As the matter is of importance in particular when the proprietor of the mark is not based in the relevant country and hence might not carry out continuous business there, the use requirement constitutes a typical concern for internationally operating enterprises. A general framework of regulations was therefore set out in the Paris Convention (Art. 5 C). Art. 19 TRIPS builds on those rules, by adding and clarifying further details. Hence, while Art. 5 C.1 Paris Convention stipulates that cancellation of a mark for non-use may only take place after a 'reasonable

---

[111] The second rationale becomes questionable when products become their own marks, such as typically in the case of protection of three-dimensional shapes. See Kur, A. (2008), 'Strategic Branding: Does Trade Mark Law Provide for Sufficient Self-help and Self-healing Forces', in Govaere, Inge and Ullrich, Hanns (eds.), *Intellectual Property, Market Power and the Public Interest*, P.I.E. Peter Lang, pp. 191–217 at p. 192; also available at http://papers.ssrn.com/sol3/papers.cfm?abstract_id=1311243.

[112] However, the US proposal (1987) had suggested a term of 'no less than five years'.

[113] In the Brazilian proposal (1989) and the joint developing countries' proposal (1990); Correa (2007), *TRIPS*, p. 196.

period', Art. 19.1 TRIPS specifies this to be a period of not less than three years. Furthermore, where Art. 5 C.1 states that a right holder must be given the possibility to 'justify his inactivity', Art. 19.1 provides for more clarification by pointing out that valid reasons for non-use are to be found in circumstances arising independently of the will of the trademark holder, and by adding examples such as import restrictions on or other government requirements for the goods or services protected by the trademark.[114]

Art. 19.2 lays down that use of the mark by another person also qualifies for genuine use, if the use is subject to control by the right holder. The rule pursues similar aims as those underlying Art. 5 C.3 Paris Convention, which refers to use by enterprises acting as 'co-proprietors' of the mark. Whereas the latter constellation is rather seldom found in practice, Art. 19.2 is formulated so as to address the more common situation of marks being used by enterprises within the same company, or on the basis of licence contracts (see also below, Art. 21).

As Art. 19 only prescribes a minimum standard, Members may provide for a more generous measurement of the conditions and timeframe applied to assess genuine use. For instance, in the European Union, the relevant period has been set at five instead of three years. US law, on the other hand, does not contain a provision exactly corresponding to the use requirement. A similar function is assumed, however, by the notion of 'abandonment', which is defined in Sec. 45 Lanham Act (15 USC § 1127).[115]

2.7 Article 20 – other requirements

Of all the provisions in the trademark section of TRIPS, Art. 20 has probably been the most controversial. The provision concerns requirements posed by national law on the way in which trademarks may, or have to, be used. There is no antecedent for such a rule in the Paris Convention or in any other piece of international trademark legislation. However, the issue had raised international attention in the second half of the last century, inter alia in view of regulations such as Art. 127 of the Mexican Act on Inventions

---

114 For a more extensive interpretation of obstacles possibly furnishing valid justifications for non-use see Correa (2007), *TRIPS*, p. 197. The ECJ has made reference to Art. 19 TRIPS and the reference made therein to obstacles arising independently from the will of the right holder in case C-246/05 *Armin Häupl/Lidl Stiftung*; in paras. 43 et seq.

115 Prior to accession to WTO/TRIPS, it had been spelled out in the definition that failure to use a trademark during two consecutive years constitutes prima-facie evidence of abandonment. In order to secure full compliance with Art. 19, the time was later extended to three years.

and Trade Marks (1975), which had stipulated that the trademarks of a foreign licensor should not appear in isolation on products manufactured under licence, but only together with the mark owned by the local licensee.[116] This measure was intended to raise the awareness of the public to the fact that the goods were actually produced by local firms, so as to reduce the (psychological) advantage of foreign marks over local brands.

Similar concerns as those underlying the Mexican legislation were reflected in an opinion submitted during the RIPS negotiations by India.[117] The document set forth that the use of foreign trademarks in the domestic markets of developing countries may have adverse implications for social and economic development in those countries. The tendency to imitate the consumption patterns and lifestyle of affluent countries, which are typically ill-suited to the conditions and circumstances of developing societies, might lead to a severe misallocation of resources towards goods that are unable to satisfy the basic needs of the poor majority of the population. Moreover, it was stated that the domestic industry was hardly in a position to effectively compete with the promotional efforts of transnational corporations. In conclusion, it was declared that strong policy objectives may exist in developing countries to submit the use of foreign marks to specific regulations, and that that freedom should not be curtailed.[118] Quite obviously, this would have required to provide for a certain carve-out from the principle of equal (national) treatment, which otherwise constitutes a cornerstone of international regulation in trade as well as intellectual property. It is little wonder, therefore, that the position taken by the industrialized countries was fundamentally different from what had been suggested by India. Already in the US proposal of November 1987,[119] it

---

116 For (mainly critical) comments on that rule see Fernandez-Novoa, 1977 GRUR Int. 400 et seq., Freitag, 1978 GRUR Int. 4 et seq., Sagasser, 1984 RIW/AWD 363. The Act (which was later repealed) also contained a clause according to which licence agreements concerning use of a foreign mark must include the proviso that the foreign mark may only be used in conjunction with a mark belonging to the national licensee and being registered in Mexico.

117 Proposal of the Indian delegation (MTN.GNG/NG11/W/37, 10 July 1989). The document was supported by Brazil as well as by other developing countries.

118 In that context, reference was made to the case when products which are manufactured and sold in a developing country under a foreign trademark are of distinctly inferior quality than in their country of origin. In order to avoid such situations, it was suggested that a clause could be inserted into the trademark laws of developing countries, according to which a foreign trademark holder is obliged to give a categorical assurance that the quality of the products bearing the mark is the same as of those sold in his own country.

119 Above, footnote 39.

had been proposed to set out expressly that the use of trademarks should 'not be encumbered by special requirements'. The proposal was endorsed by other industrialized countries, and, after considerable modifications, became the basis for Art. 20 TRIPS.

The provision sets out, first, that the use of trademarks shall not be 'unjustifiably encumbered' by special requirements. That initial statement is followed by examples of what might possibly constitute such requirements, namely use with another trademark, use in a special form or use in a manner detrimental to the mark's capability to distinguish the goods or services of one undertaking from those of another. As D. Gervais has pointed out, the provision can be read in two ways: either the examples given 'are *by their nature unjustifiable* encumbrances or they are examples of cases of special requirements that may be *prima facie* unjustifiable encumbrances' (emphasis added).[120] He further suggests that 'it seems reasonable to assume that some requirements mentioned in the list could be justifiable, but the burden of proving that they are would rest on the member that introduced the requirement'.[121]

The second interpretation is indeed preferable. Whereas it might arguably comply with the black-letter text of Art. 20 to hold that the examples listed in the first sentence are *always* unjustifiable, this would hardly be compatible with a reading of the provision which is informed by the principles and objectives of TRIPS, whose importance for the interpretation of individual articles was highlighted in the Doha Declaration of 2001.[122] Only by leaving leeway for members to justify measures that might be, at first glance, in conflict with Art. 20, will it be possible to ensure that national policy objectives in sensitive sectors such as public health or nutrition can be pursued.

The issue is of practical importance primarily for the pharmaceutical sector as well as for health-hazardous products such as cigarettes etc. For cigarettes and other tobacco products, this concerns the obligation to print sometimes rather drastic health warnings onto the packages. For pharmaceuticals, the issue is debated with regard to health policy schemes obliging manufacturers of branded medicaments to prominently display the generic name – known as 'International Nonproprietary Name' (INN) – of the active substance on samples offered for sale. In particular, the latter is arguably in conflict with Art. 20, because from the perspective of

---

[120] Gervais, Daniel (2008), *The TRIPS Agreement – Drafting History and Analysis*, 3rd edition, at p. 286; Correa (2007), *TRIPS*, p. 200.

[121] Gervais, *id.*

[122] Doha Ministerial Conference, Declaration on the TRIPS Agreement and Public Health, 20 November 2001, WT/MIN(01)/DEC/2.

the public, the INN will often be regarded as 'another trademark', in connection with which the mark is used. Nevertheless, to impose such obligations may be justified, as an important element of a country's domestic health policy, depending on the circumstances. On the other hand, the restrictions implied in Art. 20 continue to be important in the sense that the aim to emphasize the generic ingredients of medicaments must not be pursued in a manner which is likely to entail a loss, or substantial impairment, of the distinguishing character of the relevant trademarks.[123] That risk might occur, for instance, if trademark holders are obliged to display the INN in a way that creates a direct link between the INN and the mark, with the INN appearing as the dominant element in the relationship. By contrast, the risk would be smaller where both indications are clearly separated from each other, and where the specific character of the INN becomes immediately apparent, for example, by adding words such as 'consists of' or 'active ingredients' etc.

The fact that TRIPS Members do enjoy certain flexibilities with regard to special regulations concerning the use of marks, without thereby prejudicing their essential distinguishing character, is also underlined by the second sentence of Art. 20. The freedom of Members is expressly acknowledged therein to stipulate that goods must bear the sign identifying the business of the actual manufacturer, along with, but without being linked to, the trademark under which the goods are marketed. This means that national legislatures may oblige trademark holders to disclose the fact that products are manufactured under licence, with the name of the licensee being laid open to the public. However, where such regulations apply, they must observe the rule of national treatment enshrined in Art. 3. Other than the Mexican legislation to which reference was made above, rules targeting only foreign companies would not be compatible with TRIPS.

In WTO practice, Article 20 was briefly addressed in a panel report dealing with Indonesia's subsidized National Car Programme.[124] Participation in the National Car Programme was restricted to 'pioneer'

---

[123] This follows from the fundamental importance of the element of distinctiveness, which has been recognized in the *EC – GI* Panel report as constituting the core interest of trademark holders as well as of consumers (see above). Keeping in mind that an interpretation of rules in the light of Art. 8.1 must not lead to results that would amount to renegotiation of TRIPS, that fundamental objective cannot be discarded.

[124] *Indonesia – Certain Measures Affecting the Automobile Industry* (*Indonesia – Cars*), Report of the Panel, WT/DS54/R, WT/DS55/R, WT/DS59/R, WT/DS64/R, 2 July 1998; *UNCTAD-ICTSD Resource Book* (2005), p. 254. The trademark issue only formed a side-aspect in the dispute, which was primarily about the Agreement on Subsidies and Countervailing Measures (SCM); in addi-

companies or joint ventures using an Indonesian-owned trademark. The USA argued that this condition violated the national treatment rule (Art. 3) on account of the preferential treatment granted in the acquisition and maintenance of rights by Indonesian enterprises. Furthermore, it was claimed that Indonesia violated Art. 20 by imposing special rules on the use of marks: by having to adopt an Indonesian trademark in order to participate in the programme, foreign companies would face a de facto obstacle to using their 'international' trademark on the Indonesian market, meaning that the overall value of that mark would be diminished. The panel rejected the complaints; it was held that the foreign company was not impeded in the acquisition, maintenance and use of its marks in general – only if it chose to participate in the programme, did it have to submit to the conditions posed.

2.8 Article 21 – licensing and assignment

The concept of marks being subject to licensing and assignment is to some extent alien to the very idea that their essential function is to indicate one particular, and basically consistent, commercial origin. Many countries were therefore reluctant in the past to accept those practices at all. Furthermore, if and when licensing and assignment of marks were allowed, legal safeguards were frequently installed as a corollary, so as to ensure that the basic tenets of trademark law were maintained, and that consumers were not misled as to the true source of the goods.

Art. 21 TRIPS marks a shift in the traditional attitude by compelling members to accept the transfer of marks without the business in which they are used. In addition to that, it is declared to constitute an accepted principle ('it is understood') that trademarks, by contrast to all other categories of intellectual property rights, shall not be subject to compulsory licences.[125] This derives from the fact that compulsory licences are basically ill-adapted to the very nature of marks: granting such licences might even amount to warranting commercial misrepresentation, if and where this would conceal the true commercial origin. Concerns about possible anticompetitive effects of trademarks or similar risks must therefore preferably be encompassed by trademark law itself.[126] This concerns in particular the possibility to deny protection in view of the need of competitors to keep

---

tion, it involved the old GATT provisions and the Agreement on Trade Related Investment measures (TRIMs).

125 The ban against compulsory licences formed part already of the US proposal (1987); likewise the EC proposal (1988).

126 More specifically on the interface between trademarks and competition law see Kur, 'Strategic Branding' (above, footnote 111).

certain signs free from monopolization;[127] in addition, competition concerns might also warrant less far-reaching consequences, such as curtailing the breadth of the scope of protection granted, or the application of specific limitations and exceptions. Apart from that, the possibility remains unrestricted to submit competition restraints resulting from contract clauses to control by the competent authorities under Art. 40 TRIPS.

Regarding licences granted on a voluntary basis, national legislatures are free to regulate the conditions, as long as this is in compliance with Art. 20 or other TRIPS rules. In particular, this leaves unimpeded the possibility for Member States to maintain or introduce rules securing that the quality standards signalled by the mark continue to be under the control and responsibility of the mark's proprietor. To this end, trademark law may stipulate, for example, that the licensor must ensure compliance by the licensee with specified quality requirements, and must implement appropriate supervisory measures for this purpose. Furthermore, Members may order that a licence must be disclosed, be it by affixing licence notices on products manufactured by a licensor,[128] and/or by prescribing that an entry must be made in a public register, in order for the licence to become legally valid.

While the possibility to demand such licence recordals is not limited as such, the type and amount of the paperwork required may be subject to certain restrictions, if countries have committed themselves to observe the rules set out in the WIPO Joint Recommendation on trademark licences (JR 2000).[129] The initiative for that endeavour was taken in response to the abundance of formalities in certain countries which arguably created conspicuous practical difficulties for foreign trademark holders in registering and thereby validating the licence contracts concluded with domestic enterprises. The text therefore sets out in a conclusive manner the requirements that may be imposed, and explicitly prohibits stipulating other or more formalities.

Although originally being of soft law character, the standards set out in JR 2000 become binding where they have been included, by way of reference, in bilateral Free Trade Agreements. In addition, it is of note that the contents of JR 2000 have been included in the Trademark Law Treaty in the course of its revision in Singapore, 2006.[130]

---

[127] A primary example for that is the obstacle for registration of functional signs; see above footnote 37.

[128] See above, comments on Art. 20.

[129] Text available at http://www.wipo.int/export/sites/www/about-ip/en/development_iplaw/pdf/pub845.pdf.

[130] After having been ratified by Australia on 16 December 2008, the Singapore Treaty entered into force on 16 March 2009.

Finally, regarding the assignment of trademarks, the fact that pursuant to Art. 21 TRIPS, trademarks may be transferred without the business to which they belong, does not mean that it is impossible to establish certain safeguards ensuring that proper account is taken of the interests of consumers in the guarantee of origin –and thereby, indirectly, of quality – believed to be vested in a mark. Hence, the rule prevailing in US trademark law that a trademark may not be assigned 'in gross', but must be underpinned by transfer of the goodwill it represents,[131] does retain its validity. The same applies, of course, to less-far reaching provisions such as Art. 17(4) CTMR, according to which the competent authority may refuse to register the transfer of a mark if it is obvious that this will result in a risk that consumers may be misled.

3. Final remarks

3.1 Substantive trademark law

The survey on TRIPS trademark provisions evokes ambiguous feelings. On the one hand, trademarks pose relatively few issues that are seriously controversial.[132] In particular where TRIPS seeks to emphasize and secure the essential function of marks as badges of origin, compliance with the provisions lies in the interest of any country striving to maintain a workable and reliable system of protection for distinctive signs. Furthermore, even where TRIPS goes beyond what is warranted under the aspect of safeguarding the essentials, most provisions offer sufficient leeway for countries to arrive at sensible results, and to pursue their own policies. In particular, it merits emphasizing here again that TRIPS does not compel Members to consider modes of use as falling within the ambit of trademark law which do not interfere with a trademark's basic origin function, in particular because they do not purport to indicate the commercial origin of the goods on which, or in connection with which, they appear. If that rule is observed strictly, most forms of informative or otherwise merely referential use remain outside the exclusive right assigned to the right holder. In addition to that – or instead of generally curtailing the ambit of trademark law – Art. 17 provides broad discretion for implementing limitations and exceptions, of which Members can and should make active use.

However, as was stated at the beginning of this chapter, it would be

---

131 Sec. 10(a)(1) Lanham Act (15 USC 1060(1)(a)).

132 The picture is completely different if the view is widened so as to include other forms of distinctive signs, in particular geographical indications, which figure among the most controversial issues in present multilateral discussions.

dangerously naïve to ignore that trademarks and the messages they convey have a capacity to permeate people's minds and transform their lifestyle, possibly to an even larger extent than any other intellectual property right. Viewed from that perspective, those elements in the trademark chapter which are particularly conducive to the strength of marks, and/or which impose limits on the possibility of Members regulating the ways in which marks may be registered or used, appear in a more critical light.

Without doubting the justification of such concerns, however, it is questionable whether more regulation, or less protection, would actually lead to substantial changes in the pervasive impact of trademarks on consumers' preferences and mindset. It can rather be submitted that the forces active in shaping and enhancing market demand are capable of functioning independently of the legal system in which they operate. But of course, even under that assumption, it makes a difference whether no choice is given to national law but to endorse developments of market reality instigated by strong commercial actors, or whether legal support may be denied for reasons of policy.

3.2 Counterfeiting and enforcement

Whereas substantive trademark law does not play a prominent role in present trade talks, the opposite is true when it comes to issues of enforcement. Trademark counterfeiting, together with copyright piracy, ranks at the very top of the political agenda. The urgency of measures cutting off or at least curbing the constant stream of counterfeit goods is underpinned by alarming figures and trends. Particular concerns are raised when large-scale counterfeiting occurs in sensitive areas, such as medicaments[133] or other safety-relevant goods.

It is beyond the scope of this chapter to investigate and comment upon those aspects. Nevertheless, the following observations should be added. It is a truism that the basic economic rationale of counterfeiting lies in the discrepancy between high fixed costs and low variable costs that is a characteristic feature of all IP goods. It is further submitted that the incentives are rising in proportion with the widening of the costs gap. One of the many factors contributing to that effect lies in the large amount of

[133] It appears generally inappropriate and even dangerous when the risks represented by fake medicaments and similarly sensitive products are used as a vehicle for promoting stronger rules for enforcement of trademark rights. Rather than placing the accent on legislation, bolstering the position of private interests, the emphasis should lie on the public interests that are severely endangered whenever ineffective or toxic substances are sold as pharmaceuticals – basically irrespective of whether such sales occur under a 'fake' or a genuine trademark.

investment spent not solely on production and innovation as such, but also on promotional activities. If successful, this results in the promoted brand accumulating a marketing potential that allows its owner to take in profit margins which are not only sufficient to recoup the investments made, but which will also render disproportionate gains. At the same time, however, such high-profile brands become primary targets for counterfeiters, who can cash in on the triple effect of increased demand, high price level and extended markets. In economic terms, it therefore makes sense to assume that counterfeiting would be less likely to occur in markets where companies reduce their costs by spending less on promotional activities, keeping prices for their goods at a level that reflects the actual costs of production and innovation, without seeking to further inflate consumer demand.

Without wanting to promote that strategy as the preferred way to curb counterfeiting at the international level, it could be of interest to observe in further discussions that piracy and counterfeiting are not just 'external' phenomena haunting intellectual property, but that to a certain extent, they have their roots within the system, and are impacted in their frequency and magnitude by the way in which the protection system is shaped, and how it is employed by its main actors. Indeed, action and reaction in this field can lead to a vicious circle: the more companies feel harassed by illegal copying, the more they will struggle to gain a market position that allows them to reap extraordinary gains, and the louder will be the demands for stronger legal protection, both of which will create more incentives for copying, and so forth.

Whether calls for enhanced sanctions and stricter enforcement can stop that trend must be doubted. It is rather to be feared that it will benefit the concentration of such activities in the hands of those who are actually determined, and muster the criminal energy, to brace any challenges, however harsh the sanctions may be. The desperate story of the fight against illegal drugs provides a sad example of that. In addition, more pressure on sanctions and enforcement is likely to produce unwanted side-effects, such as over-reactions vis-à-vis 'ordinary' infringers that may foster a generally hostile climate against intellectual property protection.

International trademark law is therefore faced with the ambitious task of conceiving of efficient and proportionate measures that rise to the challenge, without misplacing the accent and thereby risking damage for the system as a whole. This may sound hollow in the ears of those who suffer from mass copying, and it will certainly not provide short-term relief, but in the end, it may be wiser first to concentrate on broadening the basis for acceptance of the system, instead of 'hammering it down' into the minds and lives of those for whose benefit it was created in the first place.

14 Unresolved issues on geographical indications in the WTO

Kasturi Das

1. The backdrop

The protection of Geographical Indications (GIs) has, over the years, emerged as one of the most contentious intellectual property rights (IPRs) issues in the realm of the Agreement on Trade-related Aspects of Intellectual Property Rights (TRIPS) of the World Trade Organization (WTO). Interestingly, while the Uruguay Round (1986–94) negotiations were witness to a major North–South division regarding the inclusion of IPRs on the agenda, GIs was the only issue on which there was a significant North–North divide all through the Uruguay Round negotiations. In fact, the torch-bearers of the IPRs agenda in the Round, namely, the United States and the European Communities (EC),[1] were at loggerheads on this particular issue. While the EC was aggressively pushing for foolproof protection for GIs, particularly for those pertaining to wines and spirits, the United States was strictly opposed to even recognizing GIs as a separate category of IPRs, arguing instead for its inclusion only as a part of the trademarks field. Divisions also existed among other developed countries and among developing countries, exacerbating the difficulties of the negotiations further. The eventual framework of the TRIPS provisions on GIs reflected a very sensitive compromise reached during the Uruguay Round in which a higher level of protection was granted for wines and spirits[2] compared to all other categories of GIs, ostensibly for the political reason of persuading the EC to join the consensus on the Uruguay Round package, despite strong opposition on the part of many other countries. The higher protection for wines and spirits, however, was

---

1 For legal reasons, the European Union is known officially as the European Communities in WTO business. The EU is a WTO member in its own right as are each of its 27 Member States – making 28 WTO Members altogether. While the Member States coordinate their position in Brussels and Geneva, the European Commission alone speaks for the EU and its members at almost all WTO meetings and in almost all WTO affairs. For this reason, in most issues, WTO materials refer to the 'EU', or the legally official 'EC'.

2 The addition of spirits occurred at the end of the negotiations. See WTO document MTN.TNC/W/89 of 7 November 1991.

subject to certain prior use exceptions that were clearly granted to take care of the concerns raised by the United States and Australia, among others, at least to an extent. The final text of the Agreement also left room for future negotiations, clearly reflecting the difficulties encountered during the Uruguay Round in arriving at an agreed outcome on some of the important issues. In the post-Uruguay Round period, negotiations on GIs have focused on two hotly debated issues: the creation of a multilateral system of notification and registration of GIs for wines and spirits; and the 'extension' of the higher level of protection presently accorded to wines and spirits to all other categories of GIs (henceforth extension). As was to be expected, it is again the EC which is the foremost proponent of both these issues that form part of the TRIPS agenda of the Doha Round. In addition, the EC has also triggered a third stream of the debate under the agriculture agenda by tabling in the Negotiating Group on Agriculture its proposal on the 'claw-back' of a select set of GIs. For the EC, all these three routes are nothing but different procedural means to achieve the long-standing policy goal of stringent protection for GIs at the global level. This time around also the traditional opponents of a strong GI regime like the United States, Australia, Canada, among others, are leaving no stones unturned to deter the EC from fulfilling its objective. After being forced to swallow the inclusion of GIs as a separate category of IPRs under TRIPS, these staunch opponents are in no mood to let the EC get away with further strengthening of the GIs regime under the WTO. Interestingly, in sharp contrast with some of the other controversial IPRs issues in the realm of the WTO, such as access to medicine, on which there exist a clear-cut North–South division, in the case of GIs, particularly on extension, one can find developing countries joining hands with developed countries either as demandeurs or opponents, depending on their respective stakes in GIs. This, certainly, is a striking feature of the current round of negotiations on GIs in the WTO.

The aim of this chapter is to provide a concise account of the ongoing WTO negotiations on GIs and to objectively reflect on the positions adopted by the key players in the debate. However, in our view, the crux of the GIs debate in the WTO, which has been widely referred to as one between the Old World (for example, the EC, Switzerland) and the New World (for example, United States, Australia, Canada, Argentina, Chile, etc.) cannot be understood unless and until one appreciates the key reasons underlying the discordance between these two sides on this highly contentious issue. While the reasons are multi-pronged and hence can be judged from various perspectives, exhaustive coverage of all these issues is outside the scope of the present chapter. Nevertheless, at the risk of being selective, an attempt is made in Section 2 to touch upon some of the key reasons underlying the positions adopted by the Old World and the New World on GIs in the WTO and beyond. Given that the issues currently on the negotiating table have their origin in the Uruguay Round negotiations and the compromise deal on GIs that they culminated in, the current debates can be put into perspective only when assessed in the light of the negotiating history of the Uruguay Round and the resultant TRIPS provisions pertaining to GIs. Section 3 is developed with this perspective in mind. Section 4 then moves on to the current negotiations on GIs in the WTO on the three issues: multilateral register for wines and spirits; extension and claw-back. Section 5 concludes the chapter.

2. The GI row between the two 'worlds': what lies beneath?

GIs stand at the intersection of three increasingly central and hotly debated issues in international law: trade, IPRs and agricultural policy.[3] While economic concerns evidently loom large in the global row over GIs, there are also fundamental differences in the history and the ideological underpinnings pertaining to GIs between the Old World and the New. The efforts to entrench GI protection in international law also draw strength from more diffuse concerns about authenticity, heritage and locality in a rapidly integrating world. To assert the necessity of GI protection is, in part, to assert the importance of local culture and tradition in the face of ever-encroaching globalization. The GI question is, as a result, linked to larger, politically sensitive debates about the appropriate level of protection for farmers and rural communities, the degree to which international law ought to touch upon questions of culture and tradition, the necessity of IPRs and, above all, the importance of economic competition.[4] The discordance on what would constitute the most appropriate international legal regime on GIs that has surfaced in the GATT/WTO context ever since the beginning of the Uruguay Round, and also in other international forums like the World Intellectual Property Organization (WIPO) even before that, is also in a large measure attributable to the diverse approaches by which GIs have been protected domestically in various countries of the world. In fact, while GIs have long since been well-anchored in the legal systems of many European countries, for a vast majority of countries elsewhere this is indeed a relatively new concept.

The history of origin-labelled products in Europe dates back centuries if not millennia. Certain southern European countries like France, Spain,

---

[3] Raustiala and Munzer (2007), p. 338.
[4] Raustiala and Munzer (2007), p. 339.

Italy, Greece and Portugal are home to numerous renowned GIs that carry with them age-old traditions. French law first addressed GIs in 1824. Some commentators have argued that in the history of the privileges of the French wine growers, as illustrated by Bordeaux and Champagne, one finds the combination of elements of rural policy, guarantees of authenticity and the search for competitive advantage, which marks the current WTO debate about global regime on GIs. The appellation of origin concept emerged from the privileges that were enjoyed by particular wine-producing regions in France from the Middle Ages and continued almost till the end of the eighteenth century.[5] Regulation in the ancient regime was piecemeal and adapted to local political and historical privileges and conditions, rather than based on a uniform national approach. It was very much inspired by the fear of fraudulent admixtures and false attachment of names. At that time, since it was not possible to test adulteration chemically, a very high degree of specific regulation and supervision of production was required to prevent subterfuge. This obviously imposed enormous costs and resulted in regulatory constraints whose effect was anti-competitive. As Caenegem (2003b) has argued, it was only with difficulty that the notion of appellation of origin managed to emerge from this regulatory morass once the privileges were later abolished. Early twentieth-century France saw the beginning of an era of more general regulation of production and trade in foodstuffs, in general and wines, in particular. Uncertainty about the delimitation of wine-producing regions, and adjacent frauds, was finally removed by the Law of 6 May 1919 concerning *Appellations d'Origine Contrôllée* (AOC). This Law fixed the principles of delimitation of regions, defined the characteristics that the products were required to have and also stipulated the protection afforded to them. In 1935, the general system of establishment of AOCs was set up under the Law (*Loi-décret*) of 30 July under the supervision of a Committee, which became the INAO (*Institut National des Appellations d'Origine*) from 1947. Notwithstanding such initiatives, a well-protected AOC like Champagne, with all its associated goodwill, continued to remain susceptible to misappropriation by rival traders. Even if such unscrupulous traders did not make direct use of the famous AOCs on their products, they did make attempts to ride on its coat-tails by cunning subterfuge or modification of terms which sometimes allowed them to escape the law. The modern-day approach to registered GIs for wines in the EU, which is very strict and does not permit the use of the GI in combination with other terms, in translations, in the form of '. . . –style', etc., or with

---

5 For further details, refer to Caenegem (2003b).

clear disclaimers, basically originated with the aim of combating such cunning ways of misappropriation.[6]

Central to the French AOC, which has influenced the current EU system of GI protection in large measure, is the idea that particular regions bestow unique qualities on foods and wines. This is closely linked to the French word *terroir*.[7] In its increasingly active media campaigns to promote GI-denominated foods, the European Commission defined *le gout du terroir* as 'a distinct, identifiable taste reminiscent of a place, region or locality . . . Foods and beverages that evoke the term *terroir* have signature qualities that link their taste to a specific soil with particular climate conditions. Only the land, climate and expertise of the local people can produce the product that lives up to its name.'[8] Under the AOC-type of system, production is highly regulated in an endeavour to guarantee its close connection with both the human and the physical characteristics of a narrowly circumscribed region. Stringent quality and production control ensures consistency in product standards over time, to a degree at least, which is considered to be an essential prerequisite for GIs to fulfil their function of a meaningful quality signal.[9] Thus, as per this conceptual underpinning, a GI product is not only regarded as originating from a place, it is also supposed to have certain unusual, even unique qualities that the place alone can provide.[10] The European system of GI protection based on this conceptual foundation, therefore, prevents producers from

---

6 Caenegem (2003b), pp. 865–66.

7 For further details on French AOC and *terroir*, see Barham (2003).

8 Raustiala and Munzer (2007), p. 344.

9 The system of regulation and control of Champagne is considered to be the model of an *Appellation d'Origine Contrôllée* (AOC). A set of 35 rules controls every aspect of the production of Champagne: the grape varieties used; planting and pruning of vines; limited yields; harvest by hand; minimum ageing periods. The 'protected designations of origin' (PDOs) of the EU require all elements of production, processing and preparation to occur within the designated area. By contrast, the 'protected geographical indications' (PGIs) requirements are relatively more flexible: only one facet of production, processing or preparation needs to take place within the designated area.

10 In the case of Feta cheese, this interplay was said to include: 'The development of small native breeds of sheep and goats which are extremely tough and resilient, fitted for survival in an environment that offers little food in quantitative terms but, in terms of quality, is endowed with an extremely diversified flora, thus giving the finished product its own specific aroma and flavour. The interplay between the natural factors and the specific human factors, in particular the traditional production method, which requires straining without pressure, has thus given Feta cheese its remarkable international reputation' (ECJ press release on the Feta judgment: Press release No. 92/05.25 October 2005).

outside the designated region associated with a protected GI from using it. This uniqueness principle also forms a core justification for GI protection without a genericness defence, as espoused by the Old World. Going by this principle, the name of a region, when used by producers from outside the region, is unavoidably misleading because the latter products could never have the unique regional characteristics that only the original geographical area could entail. Therefore, the name of a region can, *a fortfiori*, never become a general descriptor of a category or kind of goods.

The uniqueness principle is not universally accepted, however. According to an alternative school of thought[11] that questions the European-type protection regime based on this principle, production methods may, in general, be far more significant to the characteristics of agricultural products than geographic origin. While geographic characteristics are obviously not transferable, but are rarely absolutely unique, even the most unusual methods of growing and processing crops can be copied, and skills transferred or learned.[12] Accepting this view, however, has far-reaching consequences, as it not only undermines the uniqueness principle, but also undermines the consumer-protection function of registered GIs. In other words, as per this school of thought, whereas there may be no difficulty in accepting that the law should be structured to ensure that traders correctly indicate where goods originate (actions against misrepresentation), it is harder to accept that the law should reinforce the arguably questionable perception that goods bear unique characteristics because of their place of origin (as in strong GI registration systems). Criticism of the uniqueness proposition is particularly significant in the context of the prohibition on any form of generic use of GIs that lies at the heart of the debate between the two worlds. The origin of this debate may be traced back to past waves of immigration, particularly around the turn of the nineteenth century, which brought millions of farmers and artisans from Europe to the Americas and elsewhere – commonly referred to as the New World. These immigrants brought with them their food products and,

---

[11] In case of wine, for instance, it may be the case that if grapes come from a very small denomination that is geographically homogenous and distinct, and the wine is consistently produced by idiosyncratic methods, it cannot be replicated anywhere else. This proposition is difficult to test, but it must become more doubtful the larger the denomination and the more varied the geography. For other products, the proposition may be even more doubtful. For cheese, for instance, there is unlikely to be a discernible difference between products from different regions as long as certain transferable methods are observed in the derivation and making (see Moran, 1993).

[12] Caenegem (2003a), p. 712.

more importantly, their traditional production methods and recipes. Once settled, they often recreated the products they had known back home and promoted them using the geographical names from their home countries that were associated with quality products.[13] In the New World including the United States, Canada, Australia, and some Latin American countries, among others, such place names have been treated as generic names that refer simply to certain types of products rather than the specific place of origin of that product, to the chagrin of the European countries where the regions are actually located (for example, Champagne and Chablis in France).[14] In fact, a critical difference between the legal frameworks for protecting GIs in the EU and the New World countries lies in the approach towards generic names. The legal regime for GIs protection in the United States is an appropriate case in point in this context.

The United States relies on its trademark law system for protecting GIs rather than the *sui generis* protection afforded by the EU.[15] The trademark regime, however, does not ensure protection as comprehensive as that offered by the EU-type system for a number of reasons. In trademark law, protection is determined by the strength of the mark. This in turn depends on the classification of the mark as one of the following: (i) arbitrary, (ii) descriptive, (iii) suggestive or (iv) generic. In line with this approach, the United States provides a multi-tiered approach to GIs protection that differentiates between certain terms as being generic, semi-generic or non-generic designations of geographic significance. Examples of names that have become generic terms for types of beverages are 'vermouth' and 'sake'. A semi-generic designation is one that uses a GI, but

---

13 Raustiala and Munzer (2007), p. 349.

14 Caenegem (2003a), p. 712.

15 In 1946, the current legislation over trademarks came into place as the Lanham Act. Under this act, the US Patent & Trademark Office maintains a register of trademarks, allowing the owner to enforce its rights against those infringing the mark. Section 43 of the Lanham Act titled, 'False Designations of Origin, False Descriptions, and Dilution Forbidden', offers a thorough means by which to challenge the use of a mark that misleads consumers based on GI concepts. The Bureau of Alcohol Tobacco and Firearms (BATF) regulated domestic and international GIs until a January 2003 amendment under the Homeland Security Act. The BATF was also the governmental body responsible for establishing viticultural areas in the United States and approving future ones. The BATF established over 150 American Viticultural Areas, ranging from Napa Valley to the Ohio River Valley. In January 2003, the new Alcohol and Tobacco Tax and Trade Bureau (TTB) was designated to administer the regulation of wine label content. The TTB oversees proper grape variety representations and appellation designations, and monitors the inclusion of health statements on wine labels. (Torsen, Molly 2005, pp. 30–32).

with a corrective that indicates the true place of origin of the product. An example is 'California Burgundy', which indicates that the wine has some similarity to the wine produced in Burgundy – a place in Europe – but that the wine is actually produced in California. Non-generic names are distinctive designations of specific grape wines, that is, wines that comport with the European ideal of AOCs. Some examples are Chateau Y'quem, Chateau Margaux, Pommard, Montrachet, Schloss Johannisberger and Lacryma Christi.[16]

In the United States and many other New World countries, the European GI producers are confronted with registered trademarks which contain their GI names. According to the principle of 'first in time, first in right' applicable to trademarks, it is therefore not possible for an EU producer to seek trademark registration for the geographical origin of his/her product, as it is already legally owned by another private party. Parma ham is a perfect case in point. In Italy, Parma ham denotes ham from the region of the city of Parma; but in Canada, it has long been a registered trademark for ham made by a particular Canadian company. Hence, Italian producers of 'Prosciutto di Parma' could not sell their Parma ham under that name in Canada because the trademark 'Parma Ham' was reserved for that company in Canada.[17] The Italian producers had to resort to expensive litigation, re-label their products as 'n. 1 ham' and 'compete with a lower-quality product actually labelled "Parma".'[18] Parma ham has faced similar problems in Mexico, Argentina and many other countries in the world. In such cases, European producers have only two options. Either they can launch proceedings to obtain the cancellation of the registered trademark or they can enter into negotiations with the owner of the trademark in order to buy it. Apparently, in both cases, actions launched by the EU producers have proved very costly and not always successful. Notably, as per the trademark law system, if it was found that consumers were deceived by the use of a mark on a particular good, that mark would be rendered invalid, otherwise not. This makes things difficult for the EU producers. For instance, if it was found that the consumers in the United States did not regard Dijon mustard as coming from Dijon, France and instead considered the term only as an indicator of a type of mustard, it would be hard for the EU producers of Dijon to argue that consumers were being deceived by such uses of their GI.

---

[16] Torsen (2005), p. 1431.

[17] 'A Ham and Cheese Sandwich by Any Other Name', Deutsche Welle, August 29, 2003, available at: http://www.dw-world.de/dw/article/0,1564,958339,00.html.

[18] European Commission (2003b), p. 4.

There are certain other limitations on the GI protection under trademark law that the EU producers are confronting. Most trademark laws, in general, prohibit the registration of a name with a geographical meaning. Therefore, GI names are often protected via a collective or a certification mark when such legal concepts exist. When they are not available, EU GI producers have often been forced to seek a limited protection – for their logo only – via a figurative trademark registration. In addition, experience shows that intellectual property offices outside of the EU regularly reject registration requests from EU producers on the grounds that GI names are: (i) a simple indication of the place of origin of the goods (that is, an indication of source); (ii) a description of the product, and/or (iii) a generic name. Therefore, the use of the name is considered not protectable and allows false use in relation to goods not coming from the place of origin. The difficulty for GI producers in dealing with these problems lies with the fact that the interpretation and analysis regarding the generic or descriptive character of a name varies extensively from one country to another. Moreover, in many cases, it is up to GI producers to prove that their name has not become generic in the market concerned. This is an expensive challenge.

In countries where protection is available via unfair competition and consumer protection acts, the experience shows that European producers have had to spend a considerable amount of money trying to fend off abuses on foreign markets. They had to launch costly legal actions to seek protection of their GI. In such a case, producers are often required to prove that their GI is not a generic name and that it has acquired distinctiveness. This can be done via consumer surveys which are expensive and not always conclusive. It has also been very costly for the EU GI producers to seek protection via passing-off actions. Experience shows that securing protection in that context is a difficult, expensive and a largely uncertain process.[19] It may be noted here that the rationales underlying the legal effects of notification of a GI in the proposed multilateral register for wines and spirits, as will be discussed later in this chapter, may be found in the aforesaid difficulties confronted by the EU producers in various WTO Member countries, including the New World.

Notwithstanding the roles played by historical, ideological and other non-economic factors, in our view, the key driving force in the ongoing effort to entrench GIs in international law is economic. In fact, despite its long history, GIs gained markedly greater political salience over the past few decades against the backdrop of the increasing integration in

---

[19] European Commission (2005), pp. 13–15.

the global economy. The expansion of globalization and international trade has led to the increasing consolidation of formerly discrete local and regional markets, resulting in increased competition as well as opportunities for the traditional producers of GIs. The share of the household income available for niche food products, which are often marketed through GIs, has also shown an increasing trend over the past few decades, particularly in the developed countries. Luxury goods, once limited to a tiny coterie of the wealthy, have become widely accessible. Enhanced global competition in luxury goods markets has raised the incentives for producers to claim and assert their GIs in the global market as a way of appealing to consumers fascinated by local traditions and authentic products. While globalization has raised the value of property rights in GIs, it has also made them more susceptible to misappropriation, thereby increasing the incentives for various actors to seek to create or strengthen global protection for GIs through international rules as a means to safeguard and enhance market share in these products. The overall international trend towards stronger IPRs protection, epitomized by the inclusion of IPRs as a new area under the Uruguay Round agenda, has also aided this process.[20]

An appropriate example, and one that is absolutely central to the current debate over GIs, is the case of the world wine industry. For centuries Europe, particularly France, dominated the world wine market, though the vast majority of production was meant for local consumption only. While in the 1960s less than 10 per cent of global wine production was traded internationally, in the 2000s the proportion has exceeded 25 per cent, and is rising rapidly. For the US and the EU, the two major powers in world trade, wine is now a highly traded product and is overlaid with cultural conflict: New World technique versus Old World *terroir*.[21] Large segments of the wine industry in the Member countries of the EU, particularly France, operate according to a classification system based on geographical origin (for example, Beaujolais, Bordeaux). In the global wine market, this geographic system is in direct competition with a largely New World system based on the grape variety used in the production of the wine (for example, Chardonnay, Riesling). The battle over what indicates wine quality is being vigorously contested and there are large and valuable markets at stake. It is a battle over the shaping of consumer perceptions of quality and taste of wines.[22] Not surprisingly, the French

---

[20] Raustiala and Munzer (2007), pp. 339 and 347.
[21] Raustiala and Munzer (2007), pp. 348–9.
[22] Yeung and Kerr (2008), p. 13.

are unwilling to abandon their long-established system for protecting the goodwill of their wines, particularly when the French wine industry is going through a critical phase owing to fierce competition from the New World wines that are capturing an increasing share of the global wine market and are also increasingly being imported into the EU, as well. The legal powers to restrict the use of the words 'Chianti', 'Champagne', or 'Rioja' to the products of European origin could certainly confer a significant economic advantage on the EU against competition from the New World.[23] The fierce attempt on the part of the EU to ensure GI status for all terms long since considered generic names in various New World countries needs to be assessed from this economic angle. The recuperation of geographical names currently considered to be generic is likely to bring the greatest and most immediate economic returns to the EU, as its producers would be able to reap the benefits of years (or even centuries) of expenditures on marketing, brand-building and product refinement, undertaken not only by their forebears, but also by producers from the New World who had thus far been using these terms as generic.[24] However, it is this group of producers from the New World who would have to bear the economic burden of adjustments, while at the same time losing the fruits of all their past investments and efforts towards building their brands. One notable example is Budweiser beer, made in the United States by Anheuser-Busch, but also made in the Czech Republic by Budweiser Budvar, which lays claim to the title of 'original' Budweiser beer producer. Notably, Budweiser 'US' is the number one selling beer in the world, reflecting years of adroit advertising strategy as well as significant expenditure. It would be naive to assume that Anheuser-Busch would relinquish the European name without a struggle, and the same holds true for many other corporations worldwide that find themselves in similar situations. Such conflicting interests make compromise extremely difficult.[25] In fact, such conflicting interests between the two 'worlds' made GIs a very difficult area to negotiate in the Uruguay Round, as will be discussed in detail later in this chapter. While the EU tried hard to get rid of what it considered to be the 'sins' of the past in the New World in the Uruguay Round itself, owing to vehement opposition put forward by some of the major players from the New World, such as the United States and Australia, it could not succeed in its endeavour. The end-result was a hierarchical system of protection for GIs under TRIPS, coupled with a

23 Raustiala and Munzer (2007), pp. 348–9.
24 Yeung and Kerr (2008), p. 13.
25 Barham (2003), pp. 128–9.

series of exceptions (under Article 24) that created room for continuation of prior good faith uses in the New World. These are some of the lacunae that the EU is trying to rectify in the negotiations under the ongoing Doha Round. Importantly, the attempts on the part of the EU towards further strengthening of the GIs protection under this Round is part of a larger strategy to shield its agricultural producers from increasing New World price-based competition, in the face of increasing pressure to reduce its bloated farm subsidies by reforming the Common Agricultural Policy. The EU has argued that in the Doha negotiations it was ready to make very significant concessions on agriculture by eliminating export subsidies, considerably reducing domestic trade-distorting support and agreeing to unprecedented tariff cuts. However, while the EU accepted that it would have to face increased competition, its farmers must have the opportunity to compete where they were competitive, namely in the high quality processed food sector related to the area where they were produced. This stance is in tune with the European Commission's policy of competing internationally on quality rather than quantity. Yet, the EU maintains that its efforts to compete on quality would be futile if the main vehicle of its quality products, GIs, were not adequately protected in international markets.[26] The aggressive stance taken by the EC on GIs may be better understood in the light of the fact that the EC has in its possession some 4800 registered GIs, 4200 for wines and spirits and another 600 for other categories, mainly food products.[27]

3. The Uruguay Round in retrospect

At the international level, TRIPS sets out the minimum standards of protection for GIs that WTO Members[28] are bound to comply with in their respective national legislations. However, there is a problem of hierarchy in the levels of protection based on an arbitrary categorization of goods. This is because, although TRIPS contains a single, identical definition for all GIs, irrespective of product categories, it mandates a two-level system of protection: a basic protection applicable to all GIs in general; and an additional protection applicable only to the GIs denominating wines and spirits. This is a striking feature of the TRIPS provisions on GIs, because in no other categories of IPRs covered by TRIPS is such hierarchical protection found. This, despite the fact that GIs stand on an

---

[26] For further details on the EU's stakes in GIs, see European Commission (2003b).

[27] European Commission (2003b), p. 2.

[28] The WTO had 153 Members as at 31 December 2008.

equal footing with all other IPRs.[29] While it is difficult to find any logical or legal justification for the hierarchical protection granted to GIs under TRIPS, it can be explained quite clearly in the light of the Uruguay Round negotiations. That the present form of GIs protection under TRIPS was eventually agreed upon as a sort of compromise between different Parties with conflicting opinions and interests, becomes evident if one looks closely at the drafting history of TRIPS. Starting with a brief outline of the key TRIPS provisions on GIs, this section dwells on the drafting history of these provisions in some detail.

3.1 Highlights of the TRIPS provisions on GIs

TRIPS provides the minimum standards of IPRs protection that WTO Members are obliged to comply with. Members however, are free to implement more extensive protection, provided such protection does not contravene the provisions of the Agreement. TRIPS also leaves it up to the Member countries to determine the appropriate method of implementing the provisions of the Agreement within their own legal system and practice (*Article 1.1* of TRIPS).

Section 3 of Part II of the TRIPS Agreement incorporates provisions for protection of GIs in three articles:

- Article 22 contains a definition of GIs and sets out the general standards of protection that must be available to all GIs;
- Article 23 deals with the additional protection granted to GIs for wines and spirits; and
- Article 24 lays out certain exceptions and also creates room for future negotiations in GIs.

3.1.1 Article 22: Basic Protection

Section 3 of Part II of TRIPS begins by defining GIs in *Article 22.1*, as follows:

> Geographical indications are, for the purposes of this Agreement, indications which identify a good as originating in the territory of a Member, or a region or locality in that territory, where a given quality, reputation or other characteristic of the good is essentially attributable to its geographical origin.

Implicit in the TRIPS definition is the idea that the indication must evoke the geographical origin of the good. However, it need not necessarily be a

---

[29] See WTO document: IP/C/W/247/Rev.1 dated 17 May 2001, paragraph 15.

geographical name. Any other symbol (for example, 'Feta' cheese) would suffice as long as it succeeds in evoking the geographical origin of the good. Notably, the definition categorically refers to 'good', thereby leaving out services from the scope of GI protection.[30] As per the definition, the good must necessarily possess 'a given quality', 'reputation' or 'other characteristic' essentially attributable to the designated geographical area of origin. It is important to note that, *ceteris paribus*, each one of these qualifiers is on its own merits a sufficient condition for the grant of GI protection. However, TRIPS does not define any of these qualifiers, leaving it to the discretion of WTO Members. Given such flexibilities available in the definition of the subject matter (GIs) under TRIPS, its counterparts in the national legislations of Member countries vary widely.[31]

Article 22.2 requires WTO Members to provide the legal means for interested parties to prevent the use of any means in the designation or presentation of a good that indicates or suggests that the good in question originates in a geographical area other than the true place of origin in a manner which misleads the public as to the geographical origin of the good. It further prohibits any use, which constitutes an act of unfair competition within the meaning of Article 10*bis* of the Paris Convention (1967).[32]

---

[30] Notwithstanding this, Articles 24.4 and 24.6 of TRIPS contain explicit reference to services. A close look at the negotiating history of the TRIPS Agreement, however, reveals that the preferred term in this context was 'product'. It is only in the Brussels draft dated 3 December 1990 that the term 'good' is found to replace 'product', with the simultaneous removal of the bracketed term 'services' (for further details, see Das, 2007, pp. 19–20). However, in some countries services are also included, for example in Azerbaijan, Bahrain, Croatia, Jamaica, Saint Lucia, and Singapore.

[31] For further details, refer to WTO (2001).

[32] Article 10*bis* of the Paris Convention reads as follows:

(1) The countries of the Union are bound to assure to nationals of such countries effective protection against unfair competition.
(2) Any act of competition contrary to honest practices in industrial or commercial matters constitutes an act of unfair competition.
(3) The following in particular shall be prohibited:
    1. All acts of such a nature as to create confusion by any means whatever with the establishment, the goods, or the industrial or commercial activities, of a competitor;
    2. False allegations in the course of trade of such a nature as to discredit the establishment, the goods, or the industrial or commercial activities, of a competitor;
    3. Indications or allegations the use of which in the course of trade is liable to mislead the public as to the nature, the manufacturing process, the

Article 22.3 obliges Members to refuse or invalidate the registration of a trademark, which contains or consists of a GI with respect to goods not originating in the territory purported, when this could mislead the public as to the true place of origin of the product. This provision, among a few others, has been included with the aim of tackling the conflicts that may arise between GIs and trademarks.

Article 22.4 extends the protection enshrined in the previous three paragraphs of Article 22 to a GI, which, although literally true as to the territory, region or locality in which the good originates, falsely represents to the public that the good originates in another territory. In other words, this provision relates to 'homonymous' GIs. 'Homonymous' GIs are geographical names which are spelled and pronounced alike, but which designate the geographical origin of products stemming from entirely different geographical locations. For instance, 'Rioja' is the name of a region in Spain as well as a region in Argentina and the designation is used for wines produced in both countries.[33] This kind of situation often arises in the case of former colonies. For instance, when people from one country, say France, emigrated to another country and set up a village/town there, they might have given that new village/town the name of their native village/region of origin, which may be famous for a special kind of good, say, cheese. In such a case, if the new village/town produced cheese under its name, it could (depending on the circumstances of each case, of course) falsely represent to the public the origin of the cheese.[34]

3.1.2 Article 23: additional protection for wines and spirits

In contrast to Article 22, which relates to any good, Article 23 deals exclusively with wines and spirits. Under *Article 23.1*, using a GI identifying wine/spirit for wine/spirit not originating in the place indicated by the GI is prohibited, even where the true origin of the wine/spirit concerned is indicated and/or a translation is used and/or the indication is accompanied by expressions such as 'kind', 'type', 'style', 'imitation' or the like.

Article 23.2 is, in a way, the counterpart of Article 22(3), with the difference that unlike the latter, the former allows refusal or invalidation of registration of a trademark irrespective of whether the public is being misled.

Footnote 32 (*cont.*)
characteristics, the suitability for their purpose, or the quantity, of the goods.

33 See Addor and Grazioli (2002), p. 879.
34 See Gervais (1998), p. 128.

Article 23.3 deals with the case of 'homonymous' GIs for wines (not spirits), whose use is not misleading (or deceptive) under Article 22(4) of TRIPS. In such cases, both the indications have to be protected and each Member must determine the practical conditions under which such homonymous indications will be differentiated from each other. In doing so, each Member must ensure that consumers are not misled and that the producers concerned are treated equitably.

Finally, to facilitate the protection of GIs for wines, *Article 23.4* requires negotiations to be undertaken in the TRIPS Council for 'establishment of a multilateral system of notification and registration of geographical indications for wines eligible for protection in those Members participating in the system'. The Singapore Ministerial Declaration of 1996 extended this provision to spirits as well.[35] The ongoing negotiations on the multilateral register are as per the mandate enshrined in this provision.

3.1.3 Article 24: International Negotiations and Exceptions

Article 24 of TRIPS deals with international negotiations and also includes a series of exceptions, most notably in relation to continued and similar use of GIs for wines and spirits; prior 'good faith' trademark rights; and generic designations. These exceptions and concessions were included in this article to take into account the concerns raised by some WTO Members that protection of GIs would challenge what they considered to be 'acquired rights', as will be discussed later in this chapter.

For instance, by virtue of the exception included in *Article 24.4* of TRIPS, a Member country is not obliged to prevent continued and similar use of a particular GI of another Member identifying wines or spirits where such a use takes place in connection with goods or services by any of its nationals or domiciliaries who have used that GI in a continuous manner with regard to the same or related goods or services in its territory either (a) for at least ten years preceding 15 April 1994[36] or (b) in good faith preceding that date.

In order to take care of the potential conflicts that may arise between GIs and trademarks, *Article 24.5* contains what is often called the 'grandfather clause'[37] in favour of trademarks that are identical with or similar to GIs, provided certain conditions are satisfied. This provision states that:

---

35 See WTO Document IP/C/8 dated 6 November 1996, paragraph 34.

36 This is the date of the Ministerial Meeting concluding the Uruguay Round of Multilateral Trade Negotiations.

37 The grandfather clause is the TRIPS provision which allows right holders to maintain certain acquired rights, even if TRIPS inconsistent (see Addor and Grazioli, 2002, p. 872).

> Where a trademark has been applied for or registered in good faith, or where rights to a trademark have been acquired through use in good faith either:
> (a) before the date of application of these provisions in that Member as defined in Part VI; or
> (b) before the geographical indication is protected in its country of origin;
> measures adopted to implement this Section shall not prejudice eligibility for or the validity of the registration of a trademark, or the right to use a trademark, on the basis that such a trademark is identical with, or similar to, a geographical indication.

Another exception contained in *Article 24.6* relating to generic names states that:

> Nothing in this Section shall require a Member to apply its provisions in respect of a geographical indication of any other Member with respect to goods or services for which the relevant indication is identical with the term customary in common language as the common name for such goods or services in the territory of that Member. Nothing in this Section shall require a Member to apply its provisions in respect of a geographical indication of any other Member with respect to products of the vine for which the relevant indication is identical with the customary name of a grape variety existing in the territory of that Member as of the date of entry into force of the WTO Agreement.

Article 24.8 relating to patronymic GIs upholds the right of any person to use, in the course of trade, his/her name or the name of his/her predecessor in business, except where such name is used in such a manner as to mislead the public.

As per *Article 24.1*, Members undertake 'to enter into negotiations aimed at increasing the protection of individual geographical indications under Article 23'. The provision further clarifies that the exceptions provided for in Article 24 'shall not' be used by any Member to refuse to conduct negotiations or to conclude bilateral or multilateral agreements. However, it further stipulates that in the context of such negotiations, 'Members shall be willing to consider the continued applicability of these provisions' to individual GIs under negotiation. This means that, notwithstanding the exceptions granted under Article 24, WTO Members may be required to enter into negotiations to phase out these exceptions. Notably, Article 24 exceptions, coupled with the provision for future negotiations implies that the additional protection granted to wines and spirits under Article 23 is also subject to certain exceptions, which are open to future negotiations, leaving room for bilateral or multilateral agreements among WTO Members to phase out such prior rights.

Article 24.9 relieves Members from any obligation to protect a GI, which (i) is not protected in its country of origin, or (ii) ceases to be protected in that country, or (iii) has fallen into disuse in that country. This provision underscores the need for ensuring appropriate GI protection at the national level of a WTO Member, in the absence of which other WTO Members would have no obligation whatsoever to protect the GIs of the former country within their respective territories.

3.2 Drafting history of the TRIPS provisions on GIs[38]

Prior to the advent of TRIPS, there were three main international conventions dealing with protection of geographical appellations: the Paris Convention for the Protection of Industrial Property (1883), the Madrid Agreement for the Repression of False or Deceptive Indications of Source of Goods (1891) and the Lisbon Agreement for the Protection of Appellations of Origin and their International Registration (1958).[39] However, given the restricted scope of protection afforded by these multilateral conventions and the limited number of signatory states, none of these treaties could have any significant impact on the global protection of these indicators. In the 1956 Lisbon Conference for the Revision of the Paris Convention, the EU made an attempt to include the term 'origin' in Article 10*bis,* so as to make the application of principles of unfair competition on geographical appellations explicit. However, this initiative was defeated by a single vote of the United States. Other efforts at the World Intellectual Property Organization (WIPO), such as the preparation of a multilateral treaty on GIs in 1974–5, or deliberations in the 1990s on the WIPO's Committee of Experts on geographical indicators remained unsuccessful.[40] The aggressive push by the European Communities (EC) and its Member States to include GIs in the Uruguay Round agenda may be understood in the light of their high stakes in GIs and their frustrated attempts to strengthen global protection for these appellations under the international conventions that pre-dated TRIPS.

When the Uruguay Round got under way, 14 Negotiating Groups were established under the 'Group of Negotiation on Goods', including the 'Negotiating Group on Trade-related Aspects of Intellectual Property Rights, Including Trade in Counterfeit Goods'.[41] Participants in this Negotiating Group were allowed to make 'suggestions' on various aspects of IPRs. As regards GIs, the EC and Switzerland were the countries that placed enormous emphasis on this area throughout the Uruguay Round negotiations. From the very beginning, the EC proposal emphasized

---

38 This discussion draws heavily on Das (2008a), pp. 487–93.

39 For a discussion on the relevant provisions of these agreements, see European Commission (2005), pp. 2–5.

40 For further details, refer to Rangnekar (2003), p. 15.

41 Gervais (1998), p. 12.

the major trade distortions that were arising, in their view, because of widespread misleading use of GIs, in particular the misuse of names of geographical areas located in the European territory, which represented products specific to the natural and/or human environment in which they were elaborated,[42] with special importance being attached to the GIs associated with wines. These views were consolidated in treaty language in the 'Draft Agreement on Trade-Related Aspects of Intellectual Property', which was tabled by the EC on 29 March 1990,[43] and covered all aspects of IPRs. This proposal required that 'all' GIs 'shall be protected against any use which constitutes an act of unfair competition, including use which is susceptible to mislead the public as to the true origin of the product'. The proposal also included a list of 'acts', which were to be considered as such. These were:

- any direct or indirect use in trade in respect of products not coming from the place indicated or evoked by the geographical indication in question;
- any usurpation, imitation or evocation, even where the true origin of the product is indicated or the appellation or designation is used in translation or accompanied by expressions such as 'kind', 'type', 'style', 'imitation' or the like;
- the use of any means in the designation or presentation of the product likely to suggest a link between the product and any geographical area other than the true place of origin.

Thus, while the proposal required protection against 'unfair competition' and against consumers being misled for all categories of GIs (and not only for those associated with wines), the 'acts' which it was proposed should be prohibited in practice meant stringent protection against any misappropriation of GIs. In fact, it is the second kind of 'act' that figured in the EC proposal, which visibly formed the basis of the stringent protection ultimately granted to wines and spirits under Article 23.1 of TRIPS.

The corresponding provision in the Draft Agreement tabled by Switzerland[44] required that GIs 'shall' be protected against any use which is likely to mislead the public, while including exactly the same set of (three kinds of) 'acts' as specified in the EC Draft as examples of such 'mislead-

---

[42] See WTO document MTN.GNG/NG11/14, dated 12 September 1989, paragraph 53.

[43] See WTO document MTN.GNG/NG11/W/68, dated 29 March 1990.

[44] See WTO document MTN.GNG/NG11/W/73.

ing' use. Though the Swiss proposal closely resembled that of the EC, it was stronger in two respects. First, unlike the EC proposal, it did not make any reference to 'unfair competition'. The reason was that Switzerland believed in absolute protection for GIs, with no undue 'burden of proof' being imposed on the plaintiff.[45] Second, while the EC proposal required protection against any use which is 'susceptible to mislead the public as to the true origin of the product', the Swiss proposal required protection against any use which is 'likely to mislead the public'. The Swiss viewpoint was that the misleading of the public should not be limited to matters of origin. It could relate to quality characteristics as well. According to them, basically it was the goodwill linked to a GI or an 'appellation of origin' that warranted protection.[46]

Another major difference between the Draft Agreements tabled by the EC and Switzerland was that the EC proposal specifically required that, where appropriate, protection should be granted to 'appellations of origin', in particular for products of the vine, to the extent that it was provided in the country of origin. The Swiss Draft, however, did not include any such particular reference to 'products of the vine'. It clearly reveals the difference in approach between the EC and Switzerland. Although the EC proposed a somewhat all-encompassing protection for all GIs, its interest basically lay in ensuring 'absolute' protection for wines. Switzerland, on the contrary, always maintained that 'absolute' protection was required not only for wines and other agricultural products but also for other goods as well as services.[47]

The United States, however, was grossly opposed to dealing with the case of GIs as a separate intellectual property. Rather, it wanted GIs to be protected as a part of trademark law,[48] a proposal that was supported by Canada as well.[49] Hence, the Draft Agreement tabled by the United

---

[45] WTO document MTN.GNG/NG11/21, dated 22 June 1990, paragraph 41.

[46] Ibid.

[47] See WTO document MTN.GNG/NG11/14, dated 12 September 1989, paragraph 55.

[48] See WTO document MTN.GNG/NG11/14, dated 12 September 1989, paragraph 56.

[49] The Canadian proposal also placed special emphasis on meeting the relevant provisions of the Paris Convention to ensure adequate protection for GIs, including appellations of origin. In addition to the general provisions of the Paris Convention on trademarks and the specific provision of Article 7*bis* requiring protection of collective marks, the Canadian proposal drew attention to Articles 9, 10 and 10*ter* of the Paris Convention requiring Members to provide appropriate legal remedies effectively to repress the direct or indirect use of false indications of the source of the goods or of the identity of the producer, manufacturer or merchant

States[50] merely proposed that the contracting Parties 'shall' protect GIs that certify regional origin by providing for their registration as certification or collective marks,[51] while the form of protection proposed to be provided for registered trademarks was nothing more than protection against consumer confusion and any act of unfair competition.[52] The EC, however, regarded such trademark protection as unsatisfactory due to its formal requirements, such as registration and the use requirement.[53] While the United States felt that the protection of GIs should be based on the fundamental principle of avoidance of consumer confusion, the EC was concerned about the trade problems that could arise if the only form of protection granted was that of consumers against deception.[54] In the EC's view, the use of a GI for products not originating from the source purported by the GI concerned was always a parasitical and therefore unfair act, even when no consumer deception was involved.[55]

Another alternative form of protection was proposed in the 'Draft text on Geographical Indications' tabled by Australia in June 1990.[56] This text provided for protection by requiring Parties to refuse registration or to invalidate a trademark suggesting the territory or part thereof of

---

Footnote 49 (*cont.*)
(see WTO document MTN.GNG/NG11/16, dated 4 December 1989, paragraph 19).

50 WTO document MTN.GNG/NG11/W/70, dated 11 May 1990.

51 The proposals regarding trademarks in the US Draft clarified that 'The term 'trademark' shall include service marks, collective and certification marks'.

52 Article 12 of the US Draft Agreement (WTO Document MTN.GNG/NG11/W/70, dated 11 May 1990) included the following two provisions:

> (1) The owner of a registered trademark shall have exclusive rights therein. He shall be entitled to prevent all third parties not having his consent from using in commerce identical or similar signs for goods or services which are identical or similar to those in respect of which the trademark is protected, where such use would result in a likelihood of confusion. However, in case of the use of an identical sign for identical goods or services, a likelihood of confusion shall be presumed.
> (2) The owner of a trademark shall be entitled to take action against any unauthorized use which constitutes an act of unfair competition or passing off.

53 See WTO document MTN.GNG/NG11/16, dated 4 December 1989, paragraph 53.

54 See WTO document MTN.GNG/NG11/14, dated 12 September 1989, paragraphs 56 and 60.

55 See WTO document MTN.GNG/NG11/16, dated 4 December 1989, paragraph 53.

56 WTO document MTN.GNG/NG11/W/75, dated 13 June 1990.

a Party with respect to goods not originating in that territory, when this could mislead or confuse the public, and by prohibiting the use of such an indication.[57]

Interestingly, somewhat similar provisions had already been proposed in both the EC and the Swiss drafts.[58] However, the difference lay in the fact that while Australia wanted GIs to be protected solely through refusal or invalidation of registration of such trademarks, for the EC or Switzerland, it constituted only one of a whole lot of provisions, which they had proposed for protection of GIs. Eventually, the latter approach was adopted in the TRIPS Agreement. However, while an 'unconditional' refusal or invalidation of registration of a trademark, as was proposed in the EC proposal, has been provided to trademarks associated with wines and spirits under Article 23.2 of TRIPS, for all other trademarks such actions have been made conditional on the 'misleading test', under Article 22.3, following the Swiss approach.

The EC proposal further required that appropriate measures 'shall' be taken under national law for interested parties to prevent a GI from developing into a designation of generic character as a result of the use in trade for products from a different origin, with the special mention that appellations of origin for products of the vine shall not be susceptible to develop into generic designations. The Swiss Draft also included a similar provision, but without the special reference to the 'products of the vine'.[59]

One of Australia's prime concerns with the texts on GIs submitted by the EC and Switzerland lay in the proposition that standards for the protection of GIs should require contracting Parties to protect GIs, which had a history of traditional use in many countries (such as Australia) and, as

---

[57] Gervais (1998), p. 16.

[58] The EC Draft required that 'the registration of a trademark which contains or consists of a geographical or other indication denominating or suggesting a country, region or locality with respect to goods not having this origin shall be refused or invalidated and that national laws shall provide the possibility for interested parties to oppose the use of such a trademark'. It should be noted here that unlike the Australian proposal, this proposal of the EC did not want such protection to be conditional upon the 'misleading test'. The Swiss proposal, however, was even closer to the Australian proposal as it included the 'misleading test' as well.

It required that 'The registration of a trademark which contains or consists of a geographical or other indication designating or suggesting a country, region or locality with respect to products not having this origin shall be refused or invalidated, if the use of such indication is likely to mislead the public'.

[59] The Swiss proposal reads as follows: 'Appropriate measures shall be taken so as to prevent a geographical indication from developing into a designation of a generic character as a result of its use in trade for products of a different origin'.

a result of such use, had become 'generic'. Australia maintained that such indications no longer reflected a geographical region or locality; these had rather become associated with a general set of characteristics pertaining to a particular product, or alternatively were names which, like China for porcelain, were in the common language. Australia acknowledged that there was some justification for extending the scope of protection to GIs which had acquired a reputation in relation to certain goods, not only against misleading use, but also to prevent the degeneration of such indications into 'generic names'. However, at the same time, it maintained that acquired 'prior rights' relating to an indication identical with or similar to a GI, where acquired in good faith, should be preserved by a 'grandfather clause'.[60] The Australian proposal, therefore, required that the provisions regarding protection of GIs should not apply:

- to the prejudice of holders of rights relating to an indication identical with or similar to a GI or name and used or filed in good faith before the date of entry into force of this [amendment] [Annex] in the contracting party;
- with regard to goods for which the GI or name is in the common language the common name of goods in the territory of that contracting party, or is identical with a term customary in common language.[61]

The United States' Draft also made an attempt to safeguard the interests of those who were relying on terms, which, according to the Draft, had long since become 'generic' in their countries.[62] Hence, the sole provision proposed by the United States for geographical appellations associated with wines applied only to 'non-generic' appellations:

> Contracting parties shall provide protection for non-generic appellations of origin for wine by prohibiting their use when such use would mislead the public as to the true geographic origin of the wine. To aid in providing this protection, contracting parties are encouraged to submit to other contracting parties evidence to show that each such appellation of origin is a country, state, province, territory, or similar political subdivision of a country equivalent to a state or county; or a viticultural area.

It may be noted that the United States' proposal fell far short of the EC's ambition regarding protection of appellations of origin associated

---

[60] WTO document MTN.GNG/NG11/22 dated 22 August 1990, paragraph 2.

[61] WTO document MTN.GNG/NG11/W/75, dated 13 June 1990.

[62] WTO document MTN.GNG/NG11/21, dated 22 June 1990, paragraph 12.

with wines. First, the United States proposed to make such protection conditional on the 'misleading test', instead of the 'absolute' protection proposed by the EC. Second, it proposed to protect only 'non-generic' appellations for wine.

The kind of stringent protection that has ultimately been accorded to GIs for wines and spirits under TRIPS can be regarded as adequate in safeguarding against the possibility of their degeneration into 'generic names', as was demanded by the EC. However, a similar safeguard has not been provided for all other GIs, as was proposed by Switzerland. The safeguard included in Article 24.4 of TRIPS, which relates to wines and spirits alone, seems to be influenced by the first exception proposed in the Australian proposal. The second exception proposed by Australia seems to have influenced the first sentence of Article 24.6 of TRIPS, while its second sentence is a specific insertion for products of the vine.

The foregoing discussion makes it clear that the provisions pertaining to GIs under TRIPS have taken shape as a combination of the proposals put forward by some of the key players from the Old World and the New, with their conflicting interests. The eventual framework reflects a very sensitive compromise in an area that was one of the most difficult to negotiate during the Uruguay Round. Notably, the 'Commission on Intellectual Property Rights' appointed by the British government has clearly stated in its final report that the difficulty of negotiations '. . . stemmed from clear divisions between the main proponents of the TRIPS Agreement – the US and EU. In addition, divisions also exist among other developed countries and among developing countries. The final text of the agreement reflects these divisions and, in mandating further work (in Article 24), recognises that agreement could not be reached in a number of important areas.'[63] These provisions are basically the result of tradeoffs, which were specific to the circumstances prevailing at the time of the Uruguay Round negotiations, in particular, the Brussels Ministerial Conference (1990). This was, to some extent, due to the link at that time between the negotiations on GIs and the negotiations on agriculture.[64] Given this link, the higher level of protection for wines and spirits[65] was granted solely for the political reason of persuading the EC to join the consensus on the Uruguay Round package, despite strong opposition on the part of many other countries. Notably, the aforementioned Commission on Intellectual Property Rights

---

[63] Commission on Intellectual Property Rights (2002).

[64] See WTO document: IP/C/W/204/Rev.1, dated 2 October 2000, paragraph 6.

[65] The addition of spirits occurred at the end of the negotiations. See WTO document MTN.TNC/W/89, dated 7 November 1991.

has observed that the outcome of the difficult negotiations in the field of GIs ' . . . was that the current text of TRIPS provides a basic standard of protection, and a higher standard specifically for wines and spirits'. The Commission has clearly stated that 'The inclusion of this higher standard does not refer to the unique characteristics of wines and spirits, but was rather a compromise reached in negotiations'.

Importantly, Article 24 of TRIPS is also the direct consequence of difficult negotiations between a number of wine-producing participants, notably in the EC, who wished to protect indications for wines and spirits fully, that is, without legitimizing 'past sins' for all posterity, and others (for example, Australia, the United States) who were afraid that it might affect rights more or less considered to be acquired rights in certain appellations. The result of the negotiations was only partly satisfactory for both sides, because, while protection was granted, it was not done exactly in the way proposed by the former group. Similarly, while safeguards for 'acquired rights' were included, these were neither complete nor permanent, given the scope for further negotiations and agreements regarding these issues (under Article 24.1). In fact, the only feasible option not blocking the negotiations was to agree to further talks. In this context, Article 24.1 established the principle, clearly with a view to increasing the protection. Since safeguards were added to satisfy one group, negotiators clearly stated in Article 24.1 that (a) those safeguards (that is, exceptions granted under Article 24.4 through Article 24.8) '. . . shall not be used by a Member to refuse to conduct negotiations or to conclude bilateral or multilateral agreements', but (b) that in the context of such negotiations, 'Members shall be willing to consider' the continued applicability of the safeguards for individual GIs.[66] As for the multilateral register, originally it was the EC Draft Act that proposed the establishment of an international register, presumably for all GIs.[67] However, this provision was restricted to wines only in the original legal text of TRIPS (Article 23.4). The provision was extended to spirits also in the Singapore Ministerial Declaration later in 1996.[68]

---

[66] See Gervais (1998), pp. 134–35.

[67] The EC proposal was that:

> In order to facilitate the protection of geographical indications including appellations of origin, an international register for protected indications shall be established. In appropriate cases the use of documents certifying the right to use the relevant geographical indication should be provided for.

[68] See WTO document: IP/C/8, dated 6 November 1996, Section III.

4. Ongoing negotiations on GIs in the WTO

Currently there are three GI issues on the negotiating table in the WTO: (i) creation of a multilateral system of notification and registration of wines and spirits GIs; (ii) extension of the ambit of the higher level of protection currently granted only to wines and spirits to all other GIs; and (iii) the 'claw-back' proposal on a select set of GIs put forward by the EC. While the first two issues come under the purview of TRIPS, deliberations on the last one – exclusively an EC agenda – is part of the agriculture negotiation. However, for the EC, all three issues are different but closely interlinked routes for reaching the ultimate destination of a strong GI regime at the global level. The European Commission has clearly declared that the EU has three issues of interest on GIs:

> 1. A multilateral register for geographical indications (TRIPS): The EU envisages a simple, cost-effective system of world-wide registration for geographical indications so that farmers and SMEs can protect their GIs, even if they don't have deep pockets.
> 2. The extension of the additional GI protection (TRIPS): Ensuring that not only wines & spirits but also cheeses, rices and teas can enjoy the benefit of not being copied by producers from other countries by simply indicating 'made in USA' or 'style of Roquefort'.
> 3. Ensuring market access for EU GI products (Agriculture): By asking WTO members, for a selected group of GIs, to remove prior trademarks and, if necessary, grant protection for EU GIs that were previously used or have become generic so that our GI products can gain market access.[69]

This section dwells in some detail on each of the three GI issues on the negotiating table at the WTO. Given the long-drawn-out nature of the debates and the plethora of arguments and counter-arguments that have over time been put forward by WTO Members, a complete exposition of these debates is beyond the scope of this chapter. Nevertheless, while in no way exhaustive, an attempt is being made in this section to bring to the fore some of the key aspects of these debates.

4.1 Multilateral register for wines and spirits

In order to facilitate the protection of GIs for wines, Article 23.4 of TRIPS mandates negotiations for the establishment of a multilateral system of notification and registration of GIs for wines eligible for protection in those Members participating in the system. The Singapore Ministerial Declaration of 1996 extended the scope of the provision to cover spirits as well. In the Singapore Ministerial, Article 23.4 was also identified by

---

[69] European Commission (2003b), p. 2.

the TRIPS Council as one of the built-in agenda items (that is, unfinished business of the Uruguay Round) of the TRIPS Agreement.[70] The work began in the TRIPS Council in 1997 and was subsequently subsumed by the Doha Development Agenda. According to Paragraph 18 of the Doha Ministerial Declaration (DMD), with a view to completing the work started in the TRIPS Council on the implementation of Article 23.4, Members 'agree to negotiate the establishment of a multilateral system of notification and registration of geographical indications for wines and spirits by the Fifth Session of the Ministerial Conference' (that is, the Cancún Ministerial of 2003). Thus the DMD set an earlier deadline for completing the negotiations on the register than for the rest of the Doha package. For purposes of negotiations regarding the register, an ad hoc negotiating group – the Special Session of the Council for TRIPS – was established. Legally speaking, the Special Session is distinct from the Council for TRIPS which had hitherto been dealing with all TRIPS matters and is now referred to as the 'Regular Session' of the Council for TRIPS.[71] The Special Session, however, was unable to meet the deadline stipulated by the DMD owing to widespread divergences in views. In the Hong Kong Ministerial Declaration, Ministers took note of the progress made in these negotiations and agreed to intensify them in order to complete them within the overall timeframe for the conclusion of the negotiations that were foreseen in the DMD.[72] Since then, negotiations have been taking place within the overall timeframe of the Doha Round.

However, even after years of negotiations, Members have not been able to reach a consensus on this contentious issue. The core issues have turned out to be the following two: what would be the consequences or legal effects, if any, of registration of a GI in the multilateral system; and whether participation in the system should be voluntary or mandatory, and if it is voluntary, to what extent the effects of registration would apply to non-participating Members? In addition, there are various other elements, including notification and registration; fees, costs, and administrative burdens, particularly as they impact on developing and least developed country Members, and special and differential treatment; as well as the duration of registrations and procedures for their modification and withdrawal; arrangements for review; and contact points, among others.

---

[70] See WTO document: IP/C/8 of 6 November 1996, Section III.

[71] Wasescha (2007), p. 7.

[72] See, WTO document: WT/MIN(05)/DEC of 22 December 2005, paragraph 29.

4.1.1 Highlights of the Key Proposals

There are three key positions pertaining to this debate as contained in three formal proposals.[73] At one end of the spectrum there is the EC – the prime proponent of the proposed multilateral register – pressing for a mandatory system with strong legal effect. At the other end, there is the proposal put forward by the so-called 'joint proposal group' (Argentina, Australia, Canada, Chile, Costa Rica, Dominican Republic, Ecuador, El Salvador, Honduras, Mexico, New Zealand, Nicaragua, Paraguay, Chinese Taipei and the United States, among others), which is in favour of a voluntary system with very little legal effect. The middle ground is occupied by Hong Kong-China, proposing a voluntary system with some legal effects, though more limited than those espoused by the EC. While Hong Kong–China is not a producer of wines and spirits, it has made the proposal for strong systematic interests. Its concern is that failure in this negotiating group might endanger the Doha Round as a whole.[74] As for the legal form of the register, while the EC envisages inclusion of an annex to TRIPS (Article 23.4) through an amendment, the Joint Proposal Group conceives it in the form of a TRIPS Council decision.

The *EC proposal* (ECP),[75] envisages a multilateral system for notification and registration of GIs pertaining to wines and spirits that would be applicable to all WTO Members. Each Member may 'elect' to participate in the system by notifying its GIs for registration under the system. Members choosing not to notify GIs for registration will be deemed to be 'non-participating Members'. An international administering body at the WTO level will be responsible for the notification and registration of GIs. Each participating Member shall be entitled to notify GIs that meet the definition of a GI specified in Article 22.1 of TRIPS; and is protected in its territory and has not fallen into disuse in that territory. Upon receipt, the notification shall be circulated to all WTO Members and published on the internet. Within 18 months from the date of circulation and publication, any Member may lodge a reservation with the administering body to

---

[73] The formal proposals on the three positions are contained in the following three WTO documents: TN/IP/W/11 of 14 June 2005 (EC); TN/IP/W/10 of 1 April 2005 (Joint Proposal Group) and TN/IP/W/8 of 23 April 2003 (Hong Kong, China). The key points of these three formal proposals have been compiled and put side by side in the WTO document TN/IP/W/12 of 14 September 2005.

[74] Wasescha (2007), p. 8.

[75] Discussion here is based on the official submission of the EC contained in the WTO document TN/IP/W/11 of 14 June 2005. More recently, the EC has made some alterations in its position. These new developments are discussed at a later stage in this chapter.

the effect that it considers the notified GI not to be eligible for protection in its territory. Such reservation may be based on any of the following grounds and needs to be duly substantiated: (1) the notified GI does not meet the definition of a GI specified in Article 22.1; (2) the notified GI is false-homonymous, that is, although it is literally true as to the territory, region or locality in which the goods identified by it originate, it falsely represents to the public that the goods originate in the territory of the Member lodging reservation (as per Article 22.4); or (3) the notified GI is considered a generic term for a type of wine or spirit in the territory of the challenging Member, or with respect to products of the vine, the notified GI is a generic term of a grape variety existing in the territory of the challenging Member as of the date of entry into force of the WTO Agreement (as per the Article 24.6 exception). While according to this proposal, the other two important Article 24 exceptions, namely Article 24.4 (on prior good-faith use) and Article 24.5 (on prior good-faith trademarks or the 'grandfather' clause), cannot form the basis of a reservation, these may be invoked under the domestic law of Member countries at any time (if legislation so permits). Where a reservation has been lodged in respect of a notified GI within the 18-month period, the notifying Member and the challenging Member shall, before the expiry of that period, enter into negotiations aimed at resolving the disagreement if so requested by the notifying country, in line with Article 24.1 of TRIPS. At the expiry of the 18-month period, the GI will be registered on the Multilateral Register. If there is any reservation in respect of that GI that has not been withdrawn by the challenging Member at the time of registration, the registration shall be accompanied by an annotation referring to the reservation by the particular Member. The Register shall take the form of a searchable online database, freely accessible to all Members and to the public. As for the legal effects of the registration, the EC proposal suggests that each participating Member which has not lodged a reservation in respect of a notified GI within the 18-month period or which has withdrawn such a reservation, shall provide the legal means for interested parties to use the registration of the GI as a 'rebuttable presumption of the eligibility for protection' of that GI in its territory. Furthermore, upon registration, neither participating nor non-participating Members shall refuse protection of the GI on any of the grounds that could have justified a reservation. Thus, where no opposition is being raised by a WTO Member in respect of a notified GI on any of the three grounds on which oppositions could be raised within the 18-month period or a reservation is being withdrawn, that Member would lose the possibility of denying protection to the GI concerned on those three grounds later; that is to say, an irrebuttable presumption would be created with respect to those three grounds.

Under the *Joint Proposal* (JP), participation in the Multilateral Register would be strictly voluntary. To participate, a Member shall submit a written notification to the WTO Secretariat expressing such intention. Each participating Member may notify a GI that identifies a wine or a spirit originating in its territory. The WTO Secretariat shall, following receipt of the notification, register the GI on the database of GIs for Wines and Spirits ('the database'). The database shall be searchable online, free of charge, accessible to all WTO Members and the public, and provide a means to access the original notifications. Each participating Member may, at any time, withdraw a previously notified GI by a written notification to the WTO Secretariat to that effect. The previously registered GI in question will thereupon be removed from the database. A Member may also terminate, at any time, its participation in the system by making a written notification to the WTO. Upon termination of participation in the system by a Member, all GIs previously notified by that Member will be removed from the database. In terms of the legal effect of the registration suggested by the proposal, each participating Member will 'commit to ensure' that its domestic legal procedures include the provision to consult the database when making decisions regarding registration and protection of trademarks and GIs for wines and spirits in accordance with its domestic law. Non-participating Members will be encouraged, but not obliged, to make similar consultations of the database.

The *Hong Kong, China proposal* (HKCP) attempts to span the divide between the aforesaid two extremes. In line with the JP, participation in the system is voluntary in the sense that Members should be free to participate and notify GIs protected in their territories. But like the EC proposal, registration creates certain legal effects that would be binding only upon Members choosing to participate in the system. An administering body will be responsible for notification and registration of GIs as per the HKCP. Members wishing to participate in the system may notify the administering body of any domestic GIs for wines and spirits which are protected under their domestic legislation, judicial decisions or administrative measures. After receiving notifications from participating Members, the administering body shall undertake formality examination of the notifications and ensure that documents submitted are in order, following which the GI will be recorded in the register of GIs. For each GI recorded on the Register, the administering body will issue an official copy of the certificate of registration to the relevant participating Member. The register will be made available on the WTO website for access and search by the public and the administering body will distribute a copy of the register to every participating Member on an annual basis. As for the legal effects of registration, HKCP proposes that in any domestic courts, tribunals or administrative bodies of the participating Members in any judicial, quasi-judicial or administrative proceedings related to the GI, registration of an indication on the register shall be admitted as prima-facie evidence to prove: (a) ownership of the indication; (b) that the indication satisfies the definition enshrined in Article 22.1 of TRIPS; and (c) that the indication is protected in the country of origin (that is, Article 24.9 of TRIPS does not apply). The issues will be deemed to have been proved unless evidence to the contrary is produced by the other party to the proceedings. In effect, a 'rebuttable presumption' will be created in relation to the above three issues. Importantly, HKCP provides that any participating Member may refuse protection of a GI in accordance with its domestic laws, if any of the grounds or exceptions under Articles 22 to 24 of TRIPS is found to be applicable by its domestic courts, tribunals or administrative bodies having regard to the relevant local circumstances. Thus, HKCP envisages legal effects of registration that would, in a way, be more limited than those suggested by the ECP, but more extensive than those in the JP. Moreover, evidently with the aim of reaching a compromise deal, HKCP suggests that the notification and registration system shall be subject to review after four years from establishment of the system. In particular, the question of scope of participation should be re-visited as part of the review.

4.1.2 Key Arguments on the Proposals[76]

While a range of issues have come to the fore on the deliberation in the WTO on each of the aforesaid three proposals, the following discussion briefly touches upon some of the key issues raised and views expressed by the key players.

Participation The EC has argued that a voluntary register would not meet the mandate of Article 23.4, because it denies the basic principle that any multilateral instrument should, in WTO terms, have effects in all Members. A voluntary system would not add value and hence would not 'facilitate' the protection of GIs, as mandated by Article 23.4. In response, it has been argued by the supporters of a voluntary system that the words 'in those Members participating in the system' in Article 23.4 meant that the system had to be voluntary; in other words, that there could be Members 'not' participating in the system. A system with mandatory participation would go beyond the mandate of Article 23.4 and would also

[76] For want of space, the discussion here is only selective and in no way exhaustive. For a detailed exposition of the points raised and views expressed on these proposals, refer to the WTO document TN/IP/W/12/Add.1 of 4 May 2007.

disturb the balance in TRIPS. The JP, they maintain, had a multilateral character as all Members would participate in the negotiations to establish the system, have access to the system once it was established, and if they so wished, have the opportunity to participate in the system. Such a system, they argue, would fully meet the mandate of Article 23.4 and of paragraph 18 of the Doha Declaration. By way of reaction, the EC has further argued that the reference to 'geographical indications eligible for protection in those Members participating in the system' in Article 23.4 meant that Members would only have to participate if they wished their indications to enjoy the benefits of the multilateral register. Members would be free to choose whether or not to benefit from the multilateral system by notifying and registering their GIs under it and, in that sense, to participate in the system. However, once a GI was included in the system, protection should be facilitated in all Members, because the system was supposed to be multilateral. The JP Group has, however, criticized this argument on the grounds that it meant that non-participating Members would not be able to benefit from the system but would nevertheless be obligated to protect the terms of those countries that did participate in it. Such a mandatory system would impose onerous obligations and undue burdens on developing countries, many of which would have no economic interest in participating in such a system.

Reservation and bilateral negotiations The reservation system and the corresponding bilateral negotiations, as suggested by the ECP, have attracted significant criticism from the opposite camp. According to the EC, since the system envisioned in the ECP should have legal effects and presumptions in all Members in order to fulfil the mandate, it also made sense to open the challenge procedures to all Members and give them the opportunity to examine the notifications made within a stipulated time period (that is, 18 months). This would allow Members to be able to prevent certain legal effects from unfolding in their territories by raising a reservation. The EC argues that the idea of oppositions and objections was something that was well known in international registration systems for intellectual property. The JP Group, however, argues that the ECP would upset the balance of rights and obligations established under TRIPS with regard to the protection of GIs. Article 23.4 required the implementation of a two-phase system, comprising a notification phase and a registration phase. However, the ECP provided for three additional phases, that is, examination, reservation and bilateral negotiations, which would substantially change the existing obligations under TRIPS. In contrast, the voluntary JP system did not include any of these additional phases with a view to keeping within the mandate. Under JP, both examination and opposition procedures would remain at the national level and consequently the balance of rights and obligations, as carefully negotiated in TRIPS, would not be disturbed. Moreover, the reservation system would limit Members' rights to use certain TRIPS exceptions by making them conditional on reservations and negotiations. If a Member failed to object to a notified GI within the 18-month period, it would then have waived its ability to object to that GI later and have removed the ability of its domestic producers to object to it in court proceedings later. There was nothing in TRIPS or the negotiating mandate which placed an expiry date on the rights of Members to access these exceptions, the JP Group underscores. Hence, according to them, it was an attempt on the part of the EC to renegotiate the text agreed upon in the Uruguay Round, an exercise not part of the present negotiations. Furthermore, objecting Members would have to duly substantiate the grounds for their reservations which were not a condition of using Article 24 exceptions. If a Member had placed any objections to a notification, it would then be forced into bilateral negotiations with the notifying Member. The JP group is apprehensive that these negotiations would be stacked in favour of increased protection for the notified GI, given the link in the EC proposal to Article 24.1 of TRIPS. The JP Group maintains that requiring Members' governments to pursue reservations regarding, and negotiations on, what had traditionally been private rights to be determined and enforced at the national level in each Member's individual territory would go against the well-established norm, expressly recognized in the preamble of TRIPS, that IPRs were private rights. Such bilateral negotiations between states dealing with what were private property rights would result in less legal certainty and transparency in national systems of protection, they argue. Furthermore, the reservation system would itself erode the principle of territoriality by forcing Members to be proactive in denying IP rights to GI right holders rather than providing a framework of minimum standards within which IPRs could be acquired in relation to their territories, in accordance with TRIPS. Members would be expected in negotiations to be open to trading away legal judgments made by their domestic courts or authorities and that such compulsory bilateral negotiations therefore constituted an attempt to bypass national legal systems. This would be inconsistent with the principle of territoriality, according to the JP Group.

The question has been raised by the JP Group as to why the reservation system proposed by the ECP differentiated between different types of exceptions granted under Article 24 of TRIPS, while the negotiating mandate appeared to provide no such basis. This, according to them, changed the balance of rights and obligations by unjustifiably creating a hierarchy between different exceptions. The EC, in response, has clarified that Article 24 exceptions would continue to apply under the EC proposal; some should be exercised within the 18-month reservation period, while others could be invoked at the national level at any time. It did not propose a reservation system for all exceptions, because not all exceptions were 'optional' and the nature of these exceptions was different.

The reference to Article 24.1, contained in the ECP with respect to the proposed system of bilateral negotiations, has been criticized by the JP Group on the grounds that it was illegitimate since Article 24.1 defined the aim of the bilateral negotiations to be that of 'increasing the protection of the individual geographical indications', while Article 23.4 referred to 'facilitating protection'. Article 24.1 appeared under Article 24 and not under Article 23, particularly its paragraph 4. If Members had agreed in the Uruguay Round to increase the protection of individual GIs through a register of GIs for wines and spirits, both Articles 23.4 and 24.1 would have been in the same article, which was not the case, they argue. The provisions in Articles 23.4 and 24.1 could not be combined, as intended by the EC, to justify replacing the neutral way to resolve disputes under the WTO dispute settlement system with a politically oriented dispute mechanism, the JP Group maintains. In response, the EC has argued that while Articles 23.4 and 24.1 of the TRIPS Agreement were not in the same provision, Article 23.4 referred to a register that was meant to facilitate the protection of GIs. Such protection was certainly provided for in Articles 22, 23 and 24 of TRIPS. Since Article 24.1 was part of these three provisions, surely there would be a place for that provision within the register to facilitate its application. That was why the ECP had included a reference to Article 24.1.

Consequences/legal effects of registration A number of criticisms have been put forward by the JP Group on the presumptions envisaged in both ECP and HKCP. The presumptions, they maintain, would essentially create a GI right in each WTO Member without any national examination as it would allow for a notifying country to use its country of origin protection as a basis to receive protection in another country, without having to comply with the statutory requirements of that country. Such a system could not be reconciled with the notion that IPRs were territorial, that rights had to be established and asserted under the laws of the country where protection was being sought, and that such rights typically had effects only within the territory of the Member that had granted them. Moreover, the effect of such presumptions would be to shift the burden of proof and thereby substantively alter the balance of rights and obligations under TRIPS. This reversal of the burden of proof would place GIs at a higher level than any other form of IPR under TRIPS. Such a reversal would force trademark owners and generic users to prove their right to continued use of their trademark or of a generic term, respectively, if a later-in-time GI was notified. As a matter of public policy, it was questionable why the burden should be on users of generic terms, that is, terms in the public domain, to justify their continued uses, rather than on the IP owner seeking the monopoly. Commercially, such a limitation on Article 24.6 posed particular risks in export markets. The EC proposal would give GI right holders presumptive rights in all markets without giving other legitimate users any certainty that they would have an opportunity to rebut the presumption. For those who already had rights, this reversal put a burden on them to defend the rights they thought they already had. Shifting the burden of proof away from the right holder, where it traditionally and logically belonged,[77] would impose higher costs on those producers seeking to avoid disruption of trade.

Commenting on the ECP, in particular, the JP Group argues that the substantive legal effects included in it for the participating Members were not foreseen in the current standards of TRIPS. Under TRIPS, there were carefully negotiated relationships between trademarks and GIs, with neither of them having preference over the other. The ECP, they maintain, would upset this balance by creating a presumption that a notified term should be automatically protected in all WTO Members, whether or not it was considered a GI in those Members. The EC proposal wanted to rely on Article 24.1 of TRIPS to eradicate the generic exception under Article 24.6, which was a matter to be decided by the domestic courts of each Member according to their domestic legislation, taking account of local circumstances.

The reversal of the burden of proof would transfer directly to national governments all the country-by-country costs that currently were the responsibility of individual producers. This meant that the majority of countries, particularly developing ones, would have to assume all the costs of examining the notified GIs. The GI right holders, especially those from countries with greater purchasing power, would save in litigation costs because they would be able to litigate in other countries, based solely on the protection given in their own territories. Producers from third countries would be the ones who would have to go to court to defend their rights. Hence, the JP Group believes that the system proposed by the ECP would grant supranational exclusive rights to some producers who would have an additional competitive advantage over other competitors

---

[77] It is only in Article 34 of TRIPS with regard to process patents that the reversal of the burden of proof is expressly provided for.

in third markets. The proposal entailed a supranational approach whereby one single action taken at international level would trigger immediate and automatic global effects regardless of any intent of the right holder to actively market a term in any particular country, thereby potentially foreclosing markets that otherwise would not be foreclosed. This system would therefore facilitate a type of 'automatic claiming' of a broad range of terms throughout the WTO membership. By contrast, the underlying general approach for existing international IPR systems was that a person filing an application in various countries had an interest in operating in those countries.

In response, the EC has argued that its proposal would not bypass national administrations because it gave Members' national authorities a reasonable period of time of 18 months to review an application and decide whether a GI could be protected in their territories. The EC further points out that the possibility of seeking global protection on the basis of the protection granted in the country of origin was not new to intellectual property systems. It was based on the TRIPS Agreement itself, which introduced the notion of country of origin. For example, trademarks registered in one country enjoyed certain priority rights in others. It was on the basis of the protection in the 'country of origin', that is, the country of first registration, that priority rights could be obtained in other third countries if applications were lodged within a certain period of time.

Regarding the consequences of registration under the JP, its proponents have argued that a registration itself would have no impact on the legal rights and obligations of Members in terms of the status of individual GIs. However, Members choosing to participate in the system would make a commitment to 'consult' the database when making national decisions about protecting GIs. It would be up to the Member consulting the database to determine, according to the provisions of its domestic laws and registration requirements, what evidentiary weight to give to the registration of a GI included in the database when making determinations on whether or not to protect a trademark or a GI. Nationals from Members seeking protection would still be able to apply directly to national offices. There would be no legal consequences for non-participating Members, who would, however, have free access to the database. Consistent with the principle of territoriality, all decisions about GIs, including the applicability of the Article 24 exceptions, would therefore be left with national decision-makers in IP offices. Hence, neither would the JP system upset the current balance of rights and obligations of WTO Members under TRIPS, nor would it generate burdens for developing countries. However, the EC and Switzerland have argued that the obligation to consult the register, without any mechanism to ensure that such an obligation would be respected, would not be sufficient to truly 'facilitate' the protection of GIs, as mandated by Article 23.4. It would only create an illusion of facilitation, the EC argues. Switzerland maintains that a database that simply compiled national information would be merely a source of information which would not 'facilitate' the protection of GIs in other WTO Members. The objective of 'facilitation' of protection could not be achieved without providing, as the ECP and HKCP proposals did, that a registration would have as a legal effect the presumption of validity of the registered GI in all the Members that had not opposed it. This presumption should be rebuttable at any time and on any applicable ground, Switzerland argues. The EC has argued that had the drafters of Article 23.4 had the intention of simply establishing a list of GIs, they would have clearly mandated that. In contrast to provisions in TRIPS, which explicitly indicated that some notification obligations were simply for the purposes of exchanging information, Article 23.4 went beyond that and mandated the establishment of a multilateral system for the notification and registration of GIs. Multilateral systems of registration carried certain legal effects. Therefore, it still remained for Members to ensure that any proposed legal effects actually met the mandate of facilitating the protection of GIs.

In response, the JP Group has argued that the obligation to consult the GI database was a serious and meaningful new commitment that would need to be built into Members' systems and procedures, and was one that participating Members would be expected to honour. The register would be an unprecedented source of information that would 'facilitate' protection by increasing awareness of notified GIs and would provide a useful tool in helping IP offices anywhere in the world avoid possible conflicts between trademarks and GIs.

Costs and burden The questions of the range of costs and burdens that could be entailed by the ECP and the extent to which they would be covered by the fees proposed and could be handled using existing administrative arrangements have been discussed. The JP Group has expressed the view that there were grounds for concern on these counts, since the EC system would entail costs and burdens on several counts, such as monitoring GIs notifications; examining notifications; identifying the applicable grounds for reservations and duly substantiating them; lodging reservations; entering into bilateral negotiations; monitoring trademarks and fees for trademark searches for purposes of notification of trademarks, which were normally carried out by lawyers or trademark practitioners; costs for notifying such trademarks. In addition, there would be costs for governments to set up systems to deal with a flood of applications, including those associated with the additional human resources required and their capacity building and equipment; and costs relating to enforcement, including border controls. Members would also have the obligation to set up efficient processes for the purpose of collating the representations of their traders so as to lodge reservations within the short period of 18 months. There would also be costs associated with liaising closely with traders and businesses so as to competently negotiate bilaterally on their behalf. Many of the costs, the JP Group maintains, are hidden costs that would be borne by national administrations and would not be recoverable by the fee mechanism proposed by ECP. Hence, the ECP system would be burdensome for developed and developing country Members alike. Developing countries, in particular, would face greater difficulties, for they would not be able to react appropriately to notifications under that system. The only valid alternative for developing countries, they believe, is the JP system, which would be user-friendly, accessible, simple, effective, non-costly and non-burdensome.

4.1.3 Recent Developments and State of Play

EC's 'new thinking' More recently, there have been some significant developments in the negotiations that are worth discussing in some detail. The EC, for instance, has put forward some 'new thinking', ostensibly with the aim of narrowing the gaps among different positions. In informal consultations held in November 2007, the EC shared with the participants a 'non-paper' on its 'new thinking'. While there was no formal submission on the part of the EC on this 'new thinking', it was discussed in some detail in an informal meeting of the Special Session held on 29 April 2008[78] and subsequently formed the basis of the EC's position reflected in the Chair's report on the multilateral register issued on 9 June 2008.[79] Collecting the bits and pieces of this 'new thinking' from these two sources, one can identify the following key divergences from the EC's original proposal (discussed above).

First, the EC has dropped the proposed system of lodging reservation within an 18-month period, along with the provision for subsequent bilateral negotiations. On participation, the EC still foresees the system as being mandatory: 'In accordance with paragraph 4 of Article 23 of

---

[78] For minutes of this meeting, see WTO document TN/IP/M/19 of 19 July 2008.

[79] See WTO document TN/IP/18 of 9 June 2008.

the TRIPS Agreement, the system is multilateral, that is, applicable to all WTO Members'. However, while the 2005 proposal defined participating Members as those that would notify and register GIs in the system, the 'new thinking' contains the following criterion: 'Participating Members are Members above a certain share in world trade'. The logic underlying this new definition, however, remains unclear.

As for legal effects, the 'new thinking' proposes the following:

(i) Commitment to consult the Register when making decisions on registration and protection of trademarks and GIs in accordance with domestic law.
(ii) Rebuttable presumptions that the notified GI:

- is a GI in accordance with the definition in Article 22.1 TRIPS;
- is not a generic term (Article 24.6 TRIPS);
- does not falsely represent to the public the true origin of the goods (Article 22.4 TRIPS).

It may be noted that by removing the provision for lodging reservation within an 18-month period, the EC, in its 'new thinking', has also removed the effect of creating an irrebuttable presumption on the three grounds, as included in its 2005 proposal. Though presumptions would still be created on the three grounds, all of them would be rebuttable, at any point in the future. It would no longer be necessary to take action in the WTO within a given timeframe, and any Member would be able to take decisions according to its own national system and at any time. Challenges could be made at any time in the country where protection was sought after the notification had been made. However, unless proven otherwise at any time and according to the legislation of each of the WTO Members, a notified GI would be considered valid. But a notification in the register would not ensure automatic protection for it in every WTO Member. The right holder of the GI would still have to approach a country's administration where it seeks protection and register its GI as per the domestic system of that country. However, what the EC is suggesting is that contrary to the current situation in the legal systems of many WTO Members, the domestic authorities in that country (where protection is sought) would no longer be able to ask the GI right holder to prove, say, that the GI was not generic. The onus would be upon any third party challenging the GI on the ground of genericness in that country to prove that the GI was generic. The EC further emphasized that its proposals were forward-looking and did not aim to correct history. The system proposed would have no retroactive effects: no names would have to be given up as a result of a deal, it clarified in the 29 April 2008 informal meeting of the Special Session.[80]

While the EC claimed that 'in order to maintain momentum the EC had over the years drastically reduced its level of ambition', the 'new thinking' did not find many takers, particularly in the JP group. It rather triggered another round of arguments and counter-arguments, as discussed briefly below.

Criticizing the 'new thinking' on several counts, the JP Group pointed out that the EC continued to go beyond the mandate of facilitating protection and proposed a system with mandatory participation and obligations for all Members, with a reversal of the burden of proof. With respect to the legal presumptions and their implications for the principle of territoriality, the EC's 'new thinking' did not seem to be very different from their 2005 proposal to the JP Group. The main difference between the EC's 2005 proposal and the 'new thinking' was the removal of the cumbersome state-to-state multilateral reservations and negotiations mechanism. While some members of the JP Group like Australia welcomed this reduction of excessive and inappropriate government involvement in asserting and defending GI rights under the register by no longer subjecting determinations of a GI status to political negotiations, it still argued that the reservation system was a function of the legal presumptions; hence, one could not be removed without the other; otherwise the system would in fact get worse. Whereas previously a Member could object to a notification and consequently did not have to provide the legal presumption in its law, now all participating Members would be required to implement the presumption that a foreign GI was a GI in their respective territories. While it might be possible to rebut this presumption somewhere and somehow, this remained to be elaborated, Australia argued.

Elaborating further on the implications of the legal effects, the United States argued that even under the 'new thinking', a notified term would be presumed to meet the TRIPS definition. Thus it implied that one Member's determination regarding a GI would still have a certain legal standing in the territory of other Members. Moreover, by virtue of this short-circuiting or circumvention of domestic examination and procedures, the validity of any conflicting use in the receiving country would automatically and immediately be called into question, notably before the courts. These presumptions and the reversal of the burden of proof were fundamental shifts. Furthermore, as regards the exceptions under Article 24, it believed that they were not even sacrosanct because the EC proposal put forward that a

---

80 See TN/IP/M/19 of 19 July 2008, p. 4.

notified GI would be presumed to be non-generic, and that would be a limitation. Such a system would clearly be at odds with the most basic principles underlying the TRIPS Agreement and IPR protection more generally. It would also be unworkable in its legal framework, based on trademark law, where consumer perception played a crucial role. Under the EC proposal, the act of notification would be deemed to artificially create knowledge of perceptions of consumers in the receiving Member or create a presumption that the consumers in the United States identified a particular GI with a particular good. The United States argued that the EC was asking it to create this consumer perception by statute or regulation rather than to infer it from consumers' actual experience. This was a radical shift in the concepts and in the legal foundations of the trademark field. It would significantly impact the operation of national trademark systems in a profound and far-reaching and quite unpredictable way. The United States felt that under the EC's revised concepts where the presumption would be rebuttable, there were still significant questions as to whether, at what cost to existing right holders, and through what procedures that presumption could be rebutted even within the United States system. Thus, it appeared that this process would unleash domestic litigation on a scale undetermined, and could be quite significant. Moreover, this extremely burdensome process would also have to be repeated in every Member's territory in which existing right holders sought to maintain those rights. That mandate provided neither for the expansion of the GI protection nor the encroachment upon other IP rights. They were not in any manner mandated through this negotiation to weaken or potentially negate other rights that were currently existing within the territories of WTO Members, the United States underscored.

Canada argued that while it was negotiating the bilateral wines and spirits agreement with the EC, the EC had provided a list of approximately 10 000 names that were supposedly wines and spirits GIs. For one, it was difficult and time-consuming for Canada to analyse each of these names and determine whether they were eligible for protection. More importantly, after analysis, only approximately 1500 names had qualified for consideration for protection, while the rest had to be eliminated either because they were not for a wine or a spirit; or they were not GIs; or they were not protected in their respective countries of origin. The EC was asking other Members to accept in good faith that anything notified to the system would constitute a wine and spirit GI unless proven otherwise. However, the point of concern based on the Canadian experience was that the notification of so many GIs with the addition of a rebuttable presumption, that is, a reversal of the burden of proof, would create a daunting situation for users and others dealing with the proposed system, Canada pointed out.

Run-up to the July 2008 Mini Ministerial In the informal meeting of the Special Session held on 29 April 2008, in which the EC's 'new thinking' came under scrutiny, the EC expressed the view that on the issue of a multilateral register and also extension, the potential for progress in the negotiations at the technical level had been exhausted for quite some time. Without any political guidance, discussions were going round in circles. It, therefore, sought guidance on two issues at the time of modalities of the Doha Round so that a legal draft of the register could be produced: (i) the effects of the register; and (ii) which Members would be bound by these effects. While Switzerland supported this view, it was severely criticized by various Members of the JP Group who thought much more technical work remained to be done.

The United States expressed the view that the horizontal modalities exercise should focus on agriculture, non-agricultural market access (NAMA), and services. It feared that adding other issues would seriously undercut the Round's chances of success. The EC, however, reiterated its long-standing position on linkages between GIs and the agriculture issues in the Doha negotiations and underscored that an agreement on further agriculture liberalization and improved GIs protection had to be achieved at the same time, that is, at the time of modalities.

The issue of linkages among the multilateral register and the other two TRIPS issues, namely, GI extension and TRIPS/CBD, also came up in the discussion. India, for instance, urged the need for parallelism in terms of the process between GIs and TRIPS/CBD. India was of the view that the linkages among them were well-established and that all of them should be considered together for ministerial guidance. Brazil argued that consideration of these three issues in a broader context could overcome a deadlock which, if left unresolved, could become an obstacle to progress in the horizontal modalities for the core negotiations of the Round. Switzerland also recognized these linkages and stressed that time was pressing for the GI issues – register and extension – and the TRIPS/CBD issue to make real progress for an overall result in the Doha Round.

In the subsequent negotiations prior to the July 2008 Mini Ministerial in Geneva, all three TRIPS issues got lumped together more firmly. An informal 'non-paper' dated 26 May 2008 was circulated at the WTO linking the efforts of proponents of the three key IP issues and urging that they be included in upcoming talks. The text of the 'non-paper' was as follows:

> Proponents of the TRIPS related issues under the Doha work programme (GI register, GI extension and TRIPS disclosure requirement) agree to include these issues as part of the horizontal process in order to have modality texts that reflect ministerial agreement on the key parameters for negotiating

final draft legal texts with respect to each of these issues as part of the single undertaking.[81]

The 'non-paper' was reportedly submitted by the EC and Switzerland – the key proponents of a stronger GIs regime, and Brazil and India – staunch supporters of disclosure.[82] This was indeed a significant development, because this was the first time that the proponents of both the issues joined hands to come up with a joint submission. While this strategic alliance was the outcome of some significant compromises on the part of some Members in some important respects, it meant that the 'non-paper' linking all the three TRIPS issues now had the backing of an overwhelming majority of some 110-odd WTO Members out of the total strength of 153. As far as the multilateral register was concerned, while thus far the EC proposal had some backing only from a few Members (like Switzerland), this compromise meant that the EC now managed to get the support of the vast majority of WTO Members for its agenda on the multilateral register.

Meanwhile, a small group of countries, including the United States, Canada, Chile, Korea, Australia, among others, came together to issue another 'non-paper', dated 6 June 2008, as a response to the earlier 'non-paper' by the joint demandeurs of TRIPS issues. 'We . . . wish to express our strong opposition to this proposal, and our conviction that it would substantially set back efforts to arrive at a viable way forward for the Doha negotiations', said the group of countries, who claimed to be 'united by a joint concern that the current delicate stage in the DDA negotiations should not be unnecessarily disrupted by efforts to rush, revisit, reinterpret or change' the 'existing negotiating mandates'. This group rejected the 'artificial parallelism' in the 26 May 'non-paper' by the proponents of TRIPS issues, arguing that each of the three TRIPs issues had its own terms of reference, and particular subject matter. 'Many technical issues remain, and the extent and interest of members in the content and potential outcomes for each issue varies considerably', they argued.

Against the backdrop of this heated debate, fuelled particularly by the two 'non-papers', on 9 June 2008, the WTO released two reports on TRIPS issues: the Report by Ambassador Manzoor Ahmad of Pakistan – the Chairman of the Special Session dealing with the multilateral register;[83]

---

81 http://www.ip-watch.org/weblog/index.php?p=1085.
82 http://www.ip-watch.org/weblog/index.php?p=1085.
83 See WTO document: TN/IP/18 of 9 June 2008.

and the Report by Pascal Lamy – the Director General of the WTO on the issues of GI extension and TRIPS/CBD.[84]

While the 26 May non-paper by the joint proponents of TRIPS issues was intended to be a 'draft text for inclusion' in the aforesaid two reports, the exact wording of this non-paper did not make it into either.[85] However, the DG's Report acknowledged that 'Different views have been expressed about linkages between the issues of GI extension and TRIPS/CBD and also between these issues and work elsewhere', referring to both the aforesaid non-papers. Ahmad's Report, on the other hand, declined to describe the range of views on the linkage among the three IP issues on the ground that the TRIPS/CBD and GI extension issues related to matters that went 'beyond the mandate' of the Special Session, which was limited only to issues regarding the GI registry for wines and spirits.

Ahmad's Report was basically a state-of-play kind of document that reflected various positions on the table on the GI Register. Notably, the EC's position reflected in this Report was based on its 2005 written submission as well as the 'new thinking' discussed above. On the two key issues, that is, participation and legal effects, the Report pointed out that there continued to be 'fundamental differences', notwithstanding some shift in past months. The Report also mentioned that there were different views on whether the work on the multilateral register should be addressed in the context of the modalities decision.

Draft modality text On 18 July 2008, just prior to the Mini Ministerial, the joint proponents of TRIPS issues submitted to the Trade Negotiations Committee a joint 'Draft Modalities on TRIPS Related Issues' (henceforth referred to as W/52 after the symbol of the document) that included the draft modality texts sponsored by them on each of the three IP issues.[86] The document laid out a set of substantive and procedural steps for movement towards text-based negotiations on the three IP issues, including provision for special and differential treatment. While reiterating the stand taken by the coalition in the 26 May 2008 'non-paper' regarding inclusion of all the three TRIPS issues in the horizontal modalities process, the opening paragraph of W/52 also stated that 'The central objective of the proponents remains the adoption of a procedural decision that would open up the way for negotiations on the three issues'.

---

84 See WTO document: WT/GC/W/591 and TN/C/W/50 of 9 June 2008.

85 http://www.ip-watch.org/weblog/index.php?p=1085.

86 The communication was circulated by the WTO at the request of delegations of Brazil, the EC, India and Switzerland in the form of the WTO document TN/C/W/52 of 19 July 2008.

Whether the outcome of the strategic compromise reached among the sponsors of W/52 or not, the text on the multilateral register was in some respects different from the EC's 'new thinking' elaborated above. The text read as follows:

> 1. Members agree to establish a register open to geographical indications for wines and spirits protected by any of the WTO Members as per TRIPS. Following receipt of a notification of a geographical indication, the WTO Secretariat shall register the notified geographical indication on the register. The elements of the notification will be agreed.
> 2. Each WTO Member shall provide that domestic authorities will consult the Register and take its information into account when making decisions regarding registration and protection of trademarks and geographical indications in accordance with its domestic procedures. In the framework of these procedures, and in the absence of proof to the contrary in the course of these, the Register shall be considered as a *prima facie* evidence that, in that Member, the registered geographical indication meets the definition of 'geographical indication' laid down in TRIPS Article 22.1. In the framework of these procedures, domestic authorities shall consider assertions on the genericness exception laid down in TRIPS Article 24.6 only if these are substantiated.
> 3. Text based negotiations shall be intensified, in Special Sessions of the TRIPS Council and as an integral part of the Single Undertaking, to amend the TRIPS Agreement in order to establish the Register accordingly.

Notably, unlike in the 'new thinking' by the EC, the modalities text does not make any reference to the term 'participating member' separately. However, the reference to 'Each WTO Member' in the second paragraph clearly reflects the EC's continued support for a mandatory system that would be binding upon all Members. It may also be noted that instead of using the term 'rebuttable presumption' used in the EC's 'new thinking', the modalities text uses the term '*prima facie* evidence'. However, a close look at the text seems to reveal that effectively there is not much difference. For one thing, though put in a different language, the text basically suggests that registration would create a presumption in all WTO Members that the registered GI satisfies the definition of GI as enshrined in Article 22.1. However, any WTO Member may at any time rebut this presumption provided it has got 'proof to the contrary'. As regards genericness, the text suggests that domestic authorities would be required to 'consider' an assertion in this regard, 'only if' such an assertion is substantiated, clearly by those who would make such assertion. In other words, it implies that unless any such assertion is put forward by some interested party, WTO Members would be obliged to presume that the registered term is not generic, which in effect would create a rebuttable presumption about genericness in all Members. Importantly, even as per the modality text, the burden of proof would continue to rest on the interested parties who might oppose the GI on certain grounds and not on the right holders of the GI. This would hold true for any exception enshrined in Article 24 of TRIPS and not only for genericness. The only significant difference in the modality text compared to the earlier proposals of the EC is that it has dropped from the proposed legal effects the provision pertaining to homonymy. This is a step that the EC has claimed to be part of an overall compromise on its part.

TRIPS issues in the collapsed Mini-Ministerial Notwithstanding the support of the vast majority of the WTO Membership for inclusion of all three TRIPS issues in the horizontal modalities exercise, the opposite camp, including Australia, Chile, Costa Rica, Mexico, New Zealand and the United States, among others, kept insisting that none of the IP issues should be discussed in the Mini Ministerial. When the Mini Ministerial was finally under way in Geneva, starting 21 July 2008, the focus of deliberations was squarely on the two core areas, namely agriculture and NAMA, with even services taking a back-seat. While the three IP issues were discussed by the IP negotiators, the discussions were mostly limited to 'process' matters only. In fact, these issues never got a chance to rise to the level of full negotiations at the ministerial level during a meeting that lasted for nine days.[87] Finally, in a major blow to the chances of a possible conclusion of the Doha Round by the end of 2008, the Ministerial collapsed on 29 July, purportedly owing to the discordance among some of the key players over the issue of a special safeguard mechanism (SSM) in agriculture.

Since then Doha talks resumed in September 2008, albeit slowly, and gathered momentum during November–December. With the release of new draft modalities texts on agriculture and NAMA in early December, it seemed as if the stage was almost set for another ministerial-level meeting in December aimed at reaching a breakthrough in the Round. However, this did not finally materialize.

As far as IP issues are concerned, however, there has been some movement since the resumption of talks. Efforts have continued on the part of the 110-odd co-sponsors of W/52 to keep their strategic coalition alive. Members like the EC, India, Switzerland, Turkey, Brazil, among others, have extended their support for continuation of discussions on the TRIPS issues. India, on its own behalf, has called for the W/52 document to be made the basis for negotiation, urging the Director General to continue

87 http://www.ip-watch.org/weblog/index.php?p=1184.

the process through his office. Brazil has urged that the negotiations and process across TRIPS issues 'must be intensified'.

Meanwhile, Ambassador Trevor Clarke of Barbados has become the new chair of the Special Session of TRIPS Council dealing with the multilateral register, as the former chair Ambassador Manzoor Ahmad of Pakistan returned to his capital. In the 30 October meeting of the Special Session that confirmed Ambassador Clarke as the new chair, the talks turned into a lengthy discussion over whether the mandated register negotiations could progress without simultaneous movement on two other IP issues. The co-sponsors of W/52 have continued to assert the parallelism among the three IP issues in this meeting. While Clarke expressed the view that discussion on the other two IP issues would have to be pursued elsewhere, as the mandate of the special session was currently limited only to handling the GI register, the EC voiced strong reservations about this approach. The EC argued that the GI register was linked to the other two IP issues, which must be dealt with together. The proposal in W/52 represents a relaxing of some of the stricter protection measures the EC had originally been seeking with the GI register. But these compromises are an inextricable part of a three-pillar plan, the EC maintained and hence the other two pillars – GI extension and TRIPS/CBD – must also be discussed.[88] Countries like Chile and Argentina, however, questioned the parallelism, and noted that there was no mandate for extension and TRIPS/CBD. The United States voiced the opinion that there was broad agreement on intensifying work in the special session, but was firm that the mandate of the group does not include issues beyond the register.[89] The opponents also met with the Director General in order to reinforce the view that the three TRIPS issues have different merits and mandates and it is not appropriate to deal with them together.[90]

In a meeting of the Special Session held on 4 December 2008, at which the substantive issues of the GI register proposal contained in W/52 came up for a discussion for the first time, the Joint Proposal (JP) group submitted a list of 61 'initial questions' seeking clarification on the proposal.

---

[88] The EC further pointed out that the W/52 document was a landmark not only because it was supported by nearly three-quarters of the WTO membership, but also because it represented a key compromise of groups that were not originally in agreement. It was not a coalition of like-minded countries. The document was the result of 'difficult negotiations' in which everyone had to make compromises on their original positions. There were reportedly only eight nations that were supporting both the GI issues and the CBD issues before the parallelism came to the fore.

[89] http://www.ip-watch.org/weblog/index.php?p=1294.

[90] http://www.ip-watch.org/weblog/index.php?p=1336.

Singapore also submitted a separate list of five questions for clarification, in its capacity as a non-wine-producing Member. By the next meeting on 5 December, the EC provided answers to all these questions in a marathon intervention. The JP Group, however, requested the EC for a written version of its interventions. The co-sponsors of W/52 (including the EU, India, Switzerland and others) continued to insist that all negotiations on the GI register were to be seen as part of a framework including all three IP issues.[91]

4.2 Extension of Article 23 protection to all GIs

As discussed earlier, TRIPS stipulates a hierarchical system of protection in which a basic protection is granted for all GIs under Article 22 whereas an additional protection is afforded to GIs designating wines and spirits under Article 23. The proponents of extension (such as Bulgaria, China, the Czech Republic, the EC, Hungary, India, Kenya, Liechtenstein, Mauritius, Nigeria, Pakistan, the Slovak Republic, Slovenia, Sri Lanka, Switzerland, Thailand, Turkey, among others) are demanding an extension of the ambit of Article 23 to cover all GIs irrespective of product categories. The opposing camp (comprising Argentina, Australia, Canada, Chile, Guatemala, New Zealand, the United States, Uruguay, among others) is, however, trying to resist the proposed extension by all means.

The issue of 'extension' was a part of the discussions in the Doha Ministerial held in November 2001. In particular, paragraph 18 of the Doha Ministerial Declaration (DMD) notes that the '. . . issues related to the extension of the protection of geographical indications provided for in Article 23 to products other than wines and spirits will be addressed in the Council for TRIPS pursuant to paragraph 12 of this declaration'. Notably, paragraph 12 of the DMD declares that the negotiations on 'outstanding implementation issues' shall be an integral part of the Doha Work Programme. It further states that (a) those implementation issues, on which the DMD provides a specific negotiating mandate, shall be addressed under that mandate, whereas (b) the other outstanding implementation issues shall be addressed as a matter of priority by the relevant WTO bodies, which shall report to the Trade Negotiations Committee (TNC) by the end of 2002 for appropriate action. Members have different views on the interpretation of this paragraph with regard to the issue of 'extension': proponents of extension have advanced that there is a clear mandate to launch negotiations while opponents claimed that there is no mandate in the DMD to negotiate any extension.

91 http://www.ip-watch.org/weblog/index.php?p=1351.

Paragraph 39 of the Hong Kong Ministerial Declaration (HKMD) requested the WTO Director General to intensify his consultative process on the issue of 'extension'. It further stipulated that the General Council should review progress and take any appropriate action no later than 31 July 2006. For the past several years, Deputy Director-General Rufus Yerxa has been consulting on behalf of the DG on the issue of extension pursuant to the mandate relating to outstanding implementation issues in paragraph 39 of HKMD.

The following discussion focuses on the extension debate that has turned out to be a contentious issue in the ongoing negotiations in the WTO. Putting the nuances of this debate in perspective, however, requires a close look at the implications of the two-tiered system of protection stipulated by TRIPS. An attempt in that direction is made below.

4.2.1 Implications of the Hierarchical Protection

Article 22 of TRIPS merely stipulates the general standards of protection that must be made available by WTO Members for all GIs against unfair and misleading business practices. However, there are certain genuine lacunae ingrained in the general protection enshrined in this article that may often make GIs, other than those pertaining to wines and spirits, susceptible to misappropriation, as elaborated below.

In the first place, it may be recalled that in order to be successful in a lawsuit pertaining to a passing-off action or an action relating to unfair competition against the allegedly unauthorized use of a GI, the plaintiff (that is, the right holders of the GI concerned) must show, *inter alia*, that the use of the GI by an unauthorized party is misleading and, as the case may be, that damages or a likelihood of damages result from such use. This can only be done by demonstrating that the GI in question has acquired distinctiveness or, in other words, the relevant public associates the good sold under that GI with a distinct geographical origin and/or certain qualities. Moreover, since lawsuits based on passing-off actions or unfair competition are only effective between the parties to the proceedings, the distinctiveness of a given GI must be shown every time the GI is to be enforced.[92]

Furthermore, a right holder of a GI may find it difficult to pass the 'misleading test' if the good allegedly misusing the GI contains information about its true geographical origin on its label. For instance, a producer not belonging to Switzerland may use the GI 'Swiss-made' prominently on the face of a watch, and engrave the true origin somewhere on the back of it in

---

[92] WIPO (2000), pp. 12 and 16.

a rather illegible manner. While doing so may actually allow the producer to free-ride on the renown of a famous GI, the chances are that s/he will be able to escape any legal action against such unscrupulous business practice by claiming that such a use is not misleading the consumer, since the true place of origin is mentioned on the back of the watch.

The requirement of the 'misleading test' also leads to legal uncertainty regarding the protection and enforcement of a GI at the international level. This is because it is up to the national courts and national administrative authorities to decide whether the public is being misled by a particular misuse of a GI. Since such decisions are bound to differ from one country to another, the very provision of the 'misleading test' leaves room for legal uncertainty.[93]

Article 23, however, ensures that GIs associated with wines/spirits are afforded an additional protective shield against misuse by the same category of products, that is, wines/spirits, respectively (but not in cases where they are misused by other categories of products, such as cheese or coffee). The protection of Article 23 is an extra weapon in the hands of the right holders of GIs, identifying wines and spirits, complementing the basic protection they enjoy under Article 22 (like all other categories of GIs). The ambit of the higher level of protection of Article 23 covers those cases where a GI associated with a wine/spirit is wrongfully used on wines/spirits not originating from the place identified by it. In addition, the general protection of Article 22 applies to those cases where a GI associated with a wine/spirit is misused on goods other than wine/spirit, respectively. This would be the case if, for instance, the French GI 'Champagne', identifying sparkling wine produced in the Champagne region of France, were used on say, grape juice produced in California. Since GIs identify designations with respect to a specific product category, the misuse is likely to be more attractive in the case of the same category of product compared to that of other categories of products. Hence, misuse of a GI by competitors producing the same category of product is more commonly observed and results in the greatest financial losses for the genuine right holders. It is in these more common and pertinent cases that the additional protection of Article 23 ensures effective protection for GIs identifying wines and spirits, than that provided under Article 22 of TRIPS.[94]

First, the additional protection in the case of GIs for wines and spirits implies that they need to be protected by WTO Members irrespective

---

[93] See WTO Document: IP/C/W/247/Rev.1, dated 17 May 2001, paragraph 13.

[94] Addor and Grazioli (2002), p. 882.

of whether consumers are misled or whether the use of such indications constitutes an act of unfair competition. Moreover, the use of accompanying expressions such as 'style', 'type', 'kind', 'imitation' or the like in connection with wines and spirits is prohibited under Article 23.1. Protection is also provided against the use of indications in translated forms. No such protection is available for GIs associated with other categories of goods, which do not come under the ambit of Article 23. Producers not belonging to the geographical region indicated by a GI associated with wines/spirits are also not allowed to use these indications in or as their trademarks (Article 23.2). In contrast, the refusal or invalidation of registration of a trademark for any other goods (than wines and spirits), on similar grounds, is conditional on the 'misleading test' (Article 22.3).

If Article 23 were amended to include all other GIs, it would prevent any tea company belonging to, say, Kenya from marketing its tea as 'Darjeeling tea, produce of Kenya'; or 'Kenyan Darjeeling tea'; or 'Darjeeling type tea', with the true origin of the product indicated elsewhere on the label. However, since Article 22 does not provide this kind of protection, India may find it difficult to prevent any such misuse of the reputation and goodwill associated with its renowned GI 'Darjeeling' in the international arena. The allowance of such use, however, puts the GIs at risk of becoming 'generic names' over time.

It is the aforesaid lacunae of the current TRIPS framework that the demandeurs of extension are seeking to rectify through an amendment of the agreement. The extension, if granted, would mean that: (a) the protection of Article 23 would apply, irrespective of the goods concerned, if a GI identifying a specific category of good is wrongfully used on the same category of good, whereas (b) the protection of Article 22 would apply in cases when the GI concerned is wrongfully used on a different category of good.[95]

4.2.2 Key Arguments for and against 'Extension'[96]

The demandeurs of extension question the basis of the existing differential treatment to GIs identifying goods other than wines and spirits and point out the inadequacy of protection under Article 22. They argue that the requirement of the 'misleading test' in Article 22 is tailored to suit unfair competition or consumer protection regulations, but not intellectual

---

[95] Addor and Grazioli (2002), p. 895.

[96] For want of space, the discussion here is selective and in no way exhaustive. For a detailed exposition of the arguments for and against extension, refer to the WTO document: WT/GC/W/546 and TN/C/W/25 of 18 May 2005.

property protection. Article 22, they say, allows competitors, not belonging to the geographical region purported by a GI, to easily 'usurp' a GI and free-ride on its reputation without leaving any scope for the legitimate right holders to prevent such misappropriation, as long as the true origin of the product is mentioned. Furthermore, in lieu of such illegitimate use, these GIs run the risk of becoming generic terms over time, thereby losing all their economic potential and value.[97] In contrast, Article 23 provides protection against the use of a GI with a '*délocalisant*' indicating the true origin and against use in translation or with expressions such as 'kind', 'type', 'style', 'imitation' or the like.[98] These provisions (under Article 23) not only prevent free riding but also provide an adequate protective shield against the risk of GIs becoming generic terms.

In response, the opponents argue that the perceived insufficiency of protection afforded under Article 22 is largely due to the failure of WTO Members to implement fully and appropriately its existing obligations. The ability of many Members to make use of the existing provisions of TRIPS is often constrained by their failure to protect their respective GIs domestically.[99]Article 22 protection, they maintain, is sufficient to ensure that GIs do not become generic. They are not convinced that there are chances of GIs becoming generic under a regime that fully implements the existing provisions of TRIPS. Moreover, the opponents claim that the proponents have not adequately demonstrated why such protection is insufficient. They suggest that the TRIPS Council should be provided with concrete examples of the problems Members have had, or are currently encountering, in obtaining satisfactory protection under Article 22.[100]

The opponents are apprehensive of the possible impacts of extension on producers who do not belong to the geographical region designated by a GI, but have been using the GI concerned. Such producers, they argue, might face considerable adjustment and other costs and burdens, including the marketing costs associated with developing substitute terms; changing current packaging and labelling; generating consumer awareness, among other things. The relabelling and marketing process,

---

97 WTO document TN/C/4, p. 2.

98 WTO documents: IP/C/W/353, paragraph 13; TN/C/W/14, p. 2; JOB(05)/61, p. 4.

99 WTO documents: IP/C/W/386, paragraph 6; New Zealand, IP/C/M/37/Add.1, paragraph 166; Australia, IP/C/M/38, paragraph 76.

100 WTO documents: Canada, IP/C/M/37/Add.1, paragraph 121; New Zealand, DDG consultations, 7 February 2005; Chinese Taipei, DDG consultations, 25 April 2005.

the opponents apprehend, would be complicated, because in many cases, producers would have to try and market what would appear to be 'new' products (which previously had different names), but without the benefits of those products actually having any new characteristics.[101] These costs, the opponents feel, should not be underestimated, particularly when there is a need to launch a marketing campaign in an overseas market.[102]

Opponents further argue that relabelling of goods as a result of extension would lead to consumer confusion, as consumers would no longer be able to recognize the products that they were used to purchasing. Moreover, extension would lead to a smaller number of producers making a particular product. As the supply of the named products would fall, prices would rise. Moreover, the increase in the costs to the industry to rename, relabel, and repackage would be passed on to the consumers, resulting in higher priced goods.[103] Hence, extension would leave consumers worse-off, they apprehend.

The proponents, however, are of the view that such relabelling would not be necessary because the exceptions contained in Article 24 would apply *mutatis mutandis* to the extended protection under Article 23.[104] The extension proposal was designed only for future effects and would not affect the existing uses of terms that coincided with protected GIs, as long as they were in conformity with the exceptions included under Article 24 of TRIPS.[105] If, however, such prior use had taken place in 'bad faith', with the intention to free ride on the reputation of a GI, then Article 24 exceptions would not apply. In such cases, the demandeurs of extension feel that the obligation to relabel a specific product seemed an appropriate consequence. Moreover, the long-term economic benefits of extension would, in any case, outweigh the costs of a few cases where relabelling might be necessary, according to them.[106]

As for the question of whether the extension of Article 23-level protection would lead to consumer confusion, the proponents believe that it is

---

[101] WTO documents: New Zealand, IP/C/M/38, paragraph 89; United States, DG consultations, 30 June 2003.

[102] WTO document: Australia, IP/C/M/38, paragraph 80.

[103] WTO documents: IP/C/W/386, paragraph 26; Australia, IP/C/M/38, paragraph 81.

[104] WTO documents: IP/C/W/353, paragraph 41; EC, DDG consultations, 10 March 2005; WT/GC/W/540/Rev.1 and TN/C/W/21/Rev.1, paragraph 13; JOB(03)/119, p. 2.

[105] WTO documents: IP/C/W/353, paragraph 3; Czech Republic, IP/C/M/37/Add.1, paragraph 169; JOB(05)/61, paragraph 5.

[106] WTO document: Switzerland, IP/C/M/38, paragraph 70.

not possible to understand how consumers could be confused if it had been agreed that only a product that had originated in a given geographic territory could bear a term identifying it as originating from a territory where a given quality, reputation and other characteristic of the good was essentially attributable to its geographical origin.[107]

The demandeurs accept that extension could indeed result in higher prices for products bearing GIs, which would ultimately be paid by consumers. However, they argue that consumers would not necessarily have to pay those higher prices, unlike the case of patents or copyrights, because they would be free to decide whether to buy a good with a specific GI indicating specific characteristics and qualities or to buy another good belonging to the same category, but without those specific qualities/characteristics. The prices of such goods (without the GI) could even fall as a result of extension.[108]

The proponents feel that unlike Article 22, which led to legal uncertainty, protection under Article 23, by providing greater clarity and legal certainty as to the situations in which use of a GI was lawful or not, would ensure that the legitimate users of GIs would not have to undergo costly procedures to demonstrate that the consumer was confused, involving expensive, and often inconclusive, opinion polls. The test under Article 23 was more objective and judicial decisions would be more uniform and harmonious as the final decision would not be left to the judge's appreciation on whether the public was actually misled.[109] The proponents argue that offering small producers and associations the less costly and legally secure protection of Article 23 would give them a better way to prevent the abusive use of their GIs in a foreign country than going through the difficult and burdensome procedure of 'misleading test', or the requirement to prove that there was an act of unfair competition.[110] It is further argued that basing investment and export decisions on potentially contradictory and changing judicial interpretations was a risk that producers of GI products, especially those from developing countries, could not afford. The improved legal security at the multilateral level (under Article 23) would encourage producers to use GIs as an efficient marketing tool. It would constitute an incentive for

---

107 WTO document: Hungary, IP/C/M/38, paragraph 117.

108 WTO document: Bulgaria, IP/C/M/38, paragraph 124 and DDG consultations, 25 April 2005.

109 WTO documents: IP/C/W/353, paragraph 13; TN/C/W14, p. 2; Switzerland, DDG consultations, 7 February 2005; WT/GC/W/540/Rev.1 and TN/C/W/21/Rev.1, paragraph 12.

110 WTO documents: Pakistan, IP/C/M/37/Add.1, paragraph 167; WT/GC/W/540/Rev.1 and TN/C/W/21/Rev.1, paragraph 6.

producers to market their goods internationally, thus promoting international trade.[111] Thus the benefits resulting from extension would also foster the development of local rural communities.[112]

The opponents, however, are of the view that extension would not obviate the need for producers to take action to enforce their rights and bear the associated costs. Thus, the extent to which producers would actually benefit from a higher level of protection would also depend on how far producers would be willing and able to enforce their rights.[113] Extension, they argue, could not in itself make GIs for quality products a valuable marketing tool. It was the hard work of establishing a quality product and promoting that product in the marketplace that would turn a GI from simply a place name into a valuable marketing tool.[114]

The opponents further argue that 'extension' could create an additional dichotomy between the benefits that WTO Members with many GIs would receive and the costs to be borne by Members with only a few GIs,[115] for the latter group might be obligated to protect hundreds or thousands of GIs from other Members. The demandeurs, in turn, argue that there is no evidence of this alleged 'imbalance in numbers'. Rather, there was evidence to the contrary. For instance, since 1996, Brazil, which had already implemented extension domestically, had registered or received applications for only five GIs from the EC. Paraguay, another country applying 'extension' domestically, received none. In neither country had there been any GI-related litigation. The 'imbalance in numbers' argument, according to the proponents, did not recognize the fundamental principle that GI protection within the TRIPS Agreement was an 'on-demand' protection, that is, right holders had to invoke such protection in third country courts. Right holders only went to a third country to benefit from that protection when they had the export capacity to make the investment worthwhile, and when they had an interest. Moreover, the issue of 'imbalance in numbers' was not relevant when assessing the economic benefits of an 'extended' GI pro-

---

[111] WTO documents: Switzerland, IP/C/M/38, paragraph 69; WT/GC/W/540/Rev.1 and TN/C/W/21/Rev.1, paragraph 8.

[112] WTO documents: India, DG consultations, 30 June 2003; WT/GC/W/540/Rev.1 and TN/C/W/21/Rev.1, paragraph 8.

[113] WTO document: Australia, IP/C/M/38, paragraph 78.

[114] WTO documents: New Zealand and Chile, IP/C/M/38, paragraphs 87 and 113, respectively; United States and New Zealand, DDG consultations, 7 February 2005.

[115] WTO documents: Uruguay, IP/C/M/37/Add.1, paragraph 172; IP/C/W/386, paragraphs 3–4; United States, DG consultations, 30 June 2003; Singapore, DDG consultations, 10 March 2005; Chinese Taipei, DDG consultations, 25 April 2005.

tection and resulting market opportunities. What were important were the existing and potential trade flows emanating from each individual GI, the value of which varied greatly. A single GI like 'Basmati' (rice), which generated some US $300 million in exports, for example, could be far more important than many GIs which were not used for export. The proponents further argue that if it were felt that 'imbalance in numbers' was an issue, this would suggest radical solutions when it came to trademarks or patents. For example, the USPTO (United States Patents and Trademark Office) had registered more than 2.5 million trademarks, yet no one had claimed that, because the United States was the biggest beneficiary of trademark protection, that section of the TRIPS Agreement should be abolished.[116]

Another argument put forward by the opponents, on grounds of preservation of cultural identity, is that, considering that a number of Members had received many immigrants who had brought with them their cultural traditions, including names and terms, it would be culturally insensitive for Members, predominantly those from which these people had migrated, to try to reclaim terms that had been used for decades without being contested.[117] Immigrants' customs were acquired rights, which Members could not wipe out in the course of negotiations.[118] In response, it is argued by the proponents that the continued availability of all the exceptions under Article 24, including the 'grandfather clause', would adequately take care of this important non-trade concern. According to them, Article 23.3 on 'homonymous' GIs provided additional proof that extension was not contrary to the preservation of cultural diversity.[119] It is argued by the proponents that the GIs designating goods, such as tea, coffee, rice, banana, carpet and handicrafts, and the associated cultural heritage in their own countries were also at stake and that was something they sought to protect through extension.[120]

Regarding the extent to which extension would require new or modified legislation and institutions, the proponents feel that since all Members were already obligated to provide protection to GIs according to Articles 22 and 23, extension would imply only minimum administrative changes. These might be limited to a modification of legislative provisions so that

---

116 WTO documents: EC, Hungary and Malta, IP/C/M/37/Add.1, respectively, paragraphs 142 (also citing annex, pp. 77–9), 148 and 157; EC, JOB(03)/119, p. 3; EC, DG consultations, 30 June 2003.

117 WTO document: Australia, IP/C/M/35, paragraph 146.

118 WTO document: Argentina, IP/C/M/36/Add.1, paragraph 86.

119 WTO document: Hungary, IP/C/M/37/Add.1, paragraphs 150–51.

120 WTO document: India, IP/C/M/36/Add.1, paragraph 59.

the protection of GIs for wines and spirits could be extended to GIs for all other products.[121] Therefore, the implementation of protection envisaged in Article 23 for all GIs would not necessarily require the establishment of a completely new protection system,[122] nor would it entail disproportionate costs and administrative burdens.[123]

The opponents, however, maintain that extension would require more complicated implementation than in the case of Article 22, because countries would have to institute a system that protected a wide variety of products, necessitating change in the fundamental concepts in their laws. For instance, amending the trademark and unfair competition laws to provide Article 23-level protection for all GIs would be to stand those laws on their heads.[124] This would necessitate a substantial overhaul of the entire trademark and unfair competition regime, a cost that must be acknowledged.[125]

The proponents also base their argument on the provision included in Article 24.1 of TRIPS, which requires Members to enter into negotiations aimed at increasing the protection of individual GIs under Article 23. This provision had been identified by the Singapore Ministerial Declaration (1996) as one of the built-in agenda items.[126] However, the interpretation of this provision is a highly debated issue. The opponents of extension maintain that the built-in mandate under Article 24.1 should 'only' cover an increase or extension of the protection of GIs for wines and spirits and nothing else. The advocates of extension, however, argue that this provision basically mandates negotiations to extend the additional protection of Article 23 to goods other than wines and spirits. They are of the view that in order to address all issues left for further clarification and improvement by the Uruguay Round compromise, the negotiations required by the built-in agenda of Article 24.1 should include not only the question of additional protection for GIs for wines and spirits and/or of mitigating the exceptions to protection contained in paragraphs 4 to 8 of Article 24, but should also deal with the issue of

[121] WTO documents: Switzerland, IP/C/M/38, paragraph 203; TN/C/W/14, p. 2; EC, JOB(03)/119, p. 5; WT/GC/W/540/Rev.1 and TN/C/W/21/Rev.1, paragraphs 10–11.

[122] WTO document: Switzerland, IP/C/M/38, paragraph 203.

[123] WTO documents: Switzerland, IP/C/M/38, paragraphs 204–05; WT/GC/W/540/Rev.1 and TN/C/W/21/Rev.1, paragraphs 10–11.

[124] WTO document: United States, IP/C/M/38, paragraph 175.

[125] WTO document: IP/C/W/386, paragraphs 16 and 20.

[126] See WTO document: IP/C/8, dated 6 November 1996, Section III.

increasing the protection of individual GIs to products other than wines and spirits.[127]

4.2.3 Recent Developments and State of Play

For the past several years, Deputy Director-General Rufus Yerxa has been consulting on behalf of the DG on the issue of extension as well as on the relationship between the TRIPS Agreement and the Convention on Biological Diversity (commonly referred to as the TRIPS/CBD issue) pursuant to the mandate relating to outstanding implementation issues in paragraph 39 of HKMD. Proponents of each of these issues call for TRIPS to be amended to address their respective concerns.

TRIPS/CBD has traditionally been a North-South issue under TRIPS. Developing countries, like India, Brazil, China, Peru, among others, have argued that while the patent regime introduced by TRIPS affords protection to technologies that have been developed using biological material, the rights of countries providing the material, as recognized by the CBD, are completely ignored. Notably, it is the countries of the South that are endowed with the lion's share of the biological materials and the associated traditional knowledge (TK). With a view to rectifying the aforesaid lacunae of TRIPS and ensuring implementation of both TRIPS and CBD in a mutually supportive manner, developing countries have been insisting on an amendment of TRIPS for the past several years. The original proposal[128] called for an amendment establishing an obligation for WTO Members to require patent applicants to meet the following conditions: (i) disclose the origin of biological resources and/or associated TK; (ii) provide evidence of PIC; and (iii) provide evidence of benefit sharing. The proposal further suggested that in cases where insufficient, wrongful or lack of disclosure would be discovered after the grant of a patent, the legal regime would include provisions for revocation of the patent in question.[129]

In December 2007, the proponents of GI extension and TRIPS/CBD explicitly linked these two IP issues and put forward new papers calling for both these issues to be made part of the 'single undertaking' of the Doha Round.[130] The proponents of these two issues got together to make a submission on 15 February 2008[131] on extension that included the following

127 WTO document: IP/C/W/204/Rev.1, dated 2 October 2000, paragraph 12.
128 See WTO document: WT/GC/W/564/Rev.2 of 5 July 2006.
129 Das (2008b).
130 http://www.ip-watch.org/weblog/index.php?p=859.
131 The submission was made by the European Communities, Guinea, India, Jamaica, Kenya, the Kyrgyz Republic, the Former Yugoslav Republic of

text intended to be included in the horizontal modalities decision of the Doha Round:

> Members agree to the extension of the protection of Article 23 of the TRIPS Agreement to geographical indications of all products. Negotiations shall be undertaken, in Special Sessions of the TRIPS Council and as part of the Single Undertaking, to amend the TRIPS Agreement in order to extend the protection of Article 23 of the TRIPS Agreement to geographical indications of all products as well as to apply the exceptions provided in Article 24 of the TRIPS Agreement mutatis mutandis.

As discussed earlier, these two IP issues subsequently got lumped together with the issue of multilateral register as a result of the strategic coalition among the proponents of these three issues that came up with a 'non-paper' dated 26 May 2008, demanding all three issues to be made part of the horizontal modalities of the Doha Round. This was followed by another 'non-paper' dated 6 June 2008, issued by a small group of WTO Members, including the United States, Canada, Chile, Korea, Australia, among others, which opposed the linking of all three TRIPS issues and their inclusion in the horizontal modalities exercise. The Report by the Director General released on 19 June 2008,[132] which was basically a state-of-play kind of document, acknowledged that 'Different views have been expressed about linkages between the issues of GI extension and TRIPS/CBD and also between these issues and work elsewhere', referring to both the aforesaid non-papers. On the issue of extension, the Report stated that:

> The work continues to be characterized by different views on both the merits of GI extension and on whether it was agreed at Doha that this is part of the negotiations and of the Single Undertaking. There are also different views on whether this matter should be addressed in the context of the modalities decision.

The Report further mentioned that on the one hand, there were a number of Members who supported GI extension and who wanted clear guidance on this question as part of the modalities decision, while on the other there were others who were opposed to negotiations on extension, who believe that

> . . . the case has not been made for such extension and that even basic objectives are far apart. In their view, the issue of GI extension should not be addressed in

Footnote 131 (*cont.*)
Macedonia, Madagascar, Morocco, Pakistan, Sri Lanka, Switzerland, Tanzania, Thailand and Turkey. See WTO document TN/C/W/48 of 19 February 2008.

[132] See WTO document: TN/C/W/50 of 19 June 2008.

the context of the modalities decision and the suggested draft modalities text presented by the *demandeurs* would prejudge an outcome. Some of these Members are willing to continue fact-based discussions under the present process of work as agreed in paragraph 39 of the Hong Kong Ministerial Declaration but without prejudice to the outcome and the positions of Members and provided that there is a readiness to engage meaningfully on technical matters.

On 18 July 2008, just prior to the Mini Ministerial, the joint proponents of TRIPS issues submitted to the Trade Negotiations Committee a joint 'Draft Modalities on TRIPS Related Issues' (W/52) that included the draft modality texts sponsored by them on each of the three IP issues.[133] The modality text on extension comprised the following two paragraphs:

- Members agree to the extension of the protection of Article 23 of the TRIPS Agreement to geographical indications for all products, including the extension of the Register.
- Text-based negotiations shall be undertaken, in Special Sessions of the TRIPS Council and as an integral part of the Single Undertaking, to amend the TRIPS Agreement in order to extend the protection of Article 23 of the TRIPS Agreement to geographical indications for all products as well as to apply to these the exceptions provided in Article 24 of the TRIPS Agreement *mutatis mutandis*.

In the July 2008 Mini Ministerial in Geneva that ended up in a collapse, the focus was squarely on agriculture and NAMA and the IP issues never got a chance to rise to the level of full negotiations at the ministerial level.

Since the resumption of talks in September 2008, efforts have continued on the part of the 110-odd co-sponsors of W/52 to keep their strategic coalition alive. They have continued to vouch for the parallelism among the three IP issues and the importance of including all of them in the horizontal modalities process. A group, including China, Ecuador, the EC, India, Switzerland and Thailand, on behalf of the W/52 alliance, in November called on the Director General Lamy to stress the importance to them of the two issues, namely GI extension and TRIPS/CBD, and to request a process involving dedicated consultations on the issues.[134] Such efforts, however, continue to face steadfast opposition from the opposite camp, which includes Australia, Canada, Chile, New Zealand and the United

---

[133] The communication was circulated by the WTO at the request of delegations of Brazil, the EC, India and Switzerland in the form of the WTO document TN/C/W/52 of 19 July 2008.

[134] http://www.ip-watch.org/weblog/2008/11/21/push-for-trips-changes-reaches-highest-level-at-wto-as-meetings-intensify/.

States, among others. These countries still maintain that to negotiate on GI extension or TRIPS/CBD, a significant change in mandate would be required in an already delicate Doha Round. This group called on Lamy to reinforce the view that the three TRIPS issues have different merits and mandates and it was not appropriate to deal with them together.[135]

While the issue of multilateral register saw some movement in the first week of December, the co-sponsors of W/52 (including the EU, India, Switzerland and others) continued to insist that all negotiations on the GI register were to be seen as part of a framework including all three IP issues.[136] However, among these three issues, extension, reportedly, remains the most difficult to crack, even after so many years of efforts on the part of its proponents.

4.3 'Claw-back' proposal of the European Communities

Prior to the 2003 Cancún Ministerial Conference, the EC submitted to the WTO a list of 41 geographical terms of European origin[137] that have long been used by countries of the 'New World'. The EC proposal aimed at recouping exclusivity for its producers for these terms. According to the EC, the names contained in the list were included in the EU's register of GIs and had been selected on the basis of the fact that, in many third countries, they were claimed to be generic terms and/or had been registered as trademarks by local producers. In preparing this list, the EC focused its attention on those third countries where these kinds of abuses had been most frequently observed and which were also the most important markets for these products.[138] This proposal is widely referred to as the 'claw-back' proposal because it represents a move to make many terms that are in widespread use internationally, exclusive.[139] If accepted, the

---

135 http://www.ip-watch.org/weblog/2008/11/28/wto-ip-discussion-in-question-with-possible-ministerial-on-the-horizon/.

136 http://www.ip-watch.org/weblog/index.php?p=1351.

137 The EC mentioned that the list would be completed with GIs originating in the Acceding States to the EU.

138 See European Commission (2003a).

139 'This is not about protectionism. It is about fairness. It is simply not acceptable that the EU cannot sell its genuine Italian Parma Ham in Canada because the trade mark 'Parma Ham' is reserved for a ham produced in Canada', the then EU Farm Commissioner Franz Fischler said regarding this move. The then EU Trade Commissioner Pascal Lamy added 'Geographical Indications offer the best protection to quality products which are marketed by relying on their origin and reputation and other special characteristics linked to such an origin. They reward investment in quality by our producers. Abuses in third countries undermine the reputation of EU products and create confusion for consumers.

proposal would require WTO Members to remove prior conflicting trademarks and to grant protection to EU GIs that have become generic. Such obligations would effectively erase the exceptions available under Article 24 TRIPS (paragraphs 4, 5, and 6).

The list contained the following 22 names pertaining to wines and spirits: (1) Beaujolais; (2) Bordeaux; (3) Bourgogne; (4) Chablis; (5) Champagne; (6) Chianti; (7) Cognac; (8) Grappa di Barolo, del Piemonte, di Lombardia, del Trentino, del Friuli, del Veneto, dell'Alto Adige; (9) Graves; (10) Liebfrau(en)milch; (11) Malaga; (12) Marsala; (13) Madeira; (14) Médoc; (15) Moselle; (16) Ouzo; (17) Porto; (18) Rhin; (19) Rioja; (20) Saint-Emilion; (21) Sauternes; and (22) Jerez, Xerez.

Nineteen names relating to other products in the list were: (1) Asiago; (2) Azafrán de la Mancha; (3) Comté; (4) Feta; (5) Fontina; (6) Gorgonzola; (7) Grana Padano; (8) Jijona y Turrón de Alicante; (9) Manchego; (10) Mortadella Bologna; (11) Mozzarella di Bufala Campana; (12) Parmigiano Reggiano; (13) Pecorino Romano; (14) Prosciutto di Parma; (15) Prosciutto di San Daniele; (16) Prosciutto Toscano; (17) Queijo São Jorge; (18) Reblochon; and (19) Roquefort.

The protection proposed also covered translations, such as 'Burgundy', 'Champaña', 'Coñac', 'Port', 'Sherry', 'Parmesan/o', 'Parma ham', etc. Transliterations in other alphabets, such as 'ÊÎÍÜßÊ' for Cognac, are also covered.

Interestingly, the list was submitted as a market access issue under the agriculture negotiations of the Doha Round and not in the TRIPS Council. This, despite the fact that the EC clearly acknowledged the interlinkages between the other two GIs issues in the negotiating agenda of TRIPS and this third issue. This is not a surprising stance on the part of the EC, however, given that GIs assume enormous significance in the context of the EU agriculture, as discussed earlier. Moreover, in view of the slow progress in the negotiations on the other two issues under the purview of TRIPS, the EC might have attempted to open up another window of opportunity under the agriculture agenda. Whatever it was, the move received significant criticism from some WTO Members on grounds that the negotiating mandate on agriculture set by the Doha Ministerial Declaration did not mention GIs. And quite predictably, the United States and a number of other countries expressed their strong opposition to the 'claw-back' proposal. Nevertheless, the EC has tried hard since then to keep the issue alive in the agriculture negotiations. The framework for

---

We want this to cease for the most usurped products in the world' (See European Commission, 2003a).

agriculture modalities of the Doha Round adopted by WTO Members as Annex A of the Framework Agreement of July 2004, which was stitched together after the failed Ministerial Conference in Cancún, identified GIs as an issue 'of interest but not agreed'.[140] Annex A of the Hong Kong Ministerial Declaration of 2005 dealing with agriculture again mentioned GIs as among the 'issues that remain of interest but not agreed'.[141]

Importantly, on 16 June 2006, just prior to the issuance by the WTO of the first draft modalities text on agriculture, the EC submitted a communication titled 'European Communities proposal on market access issues'[142] to the Special Session of the Committee on Agriculture in which GIs appeared on the top of its list of demands. Notably, the proposal named all three GI issues, clearly reflecting their interlinkages from the EC's perspective. The communication stated that 'geographical indications are of paramount importance for the EC due to their place in the EC's quality policy. All GI issues on the table in the various areas of negotiation should be addressed in an integrated manner with a view to achieving satisfactory results.' Notwithstanding this communication by the EC, the first draft modalities text on agriculture circulated on 22 June 2006[143] mentioned GIs within square brackets without any elaboration on the subject whatsoever. All the subsequent revised drafts on agriculture modalities[144] also maintained the same approach. While the inclusion of GIs within square brackets clearly indicates a lack of agreement as to whether it should form part of the agriculture modalities of the Doha Round, the fact that not even a single word has been said on the issue may be regarded as a signal of its lost importance in the context of the agriculture negotiations.

It may also be noted that in the context of the negotiations on the multilateral register that includes the issue of genericness in a big way, albeit thus far limited only to wines and spirits, the EC has of late underscored that its proposals are forward-looking and not intended to correct history. Having taken this position on the register issue, it would indeed be very difficult for the EC to continue to argue for the 'claw-back' proposal aimed at correcting history.

It may be noted here that while the EU has thus far not been able to make such obligations acceptable at the multilateral level, the Article 24

---

[140] See WTO document WT/L/579 of 2 August 2004, p. A-7.

[141] See WTO document WT/MIN(05)/DEC of 22 December 2005, p. A-7.

[142] See WTO document: JOB(06)/190 of 16 June 2006.

[143] See WTO document TN/AG/W/3 of 12 July 2006.

[144] See WTO documents: TN/AG/W/4 and Corr.1 of 1 August 2007; TN/AG/W/4/Rev.1 of 8 February 2008; TN/AG/W/4/Rev.2 of 19 May 2008; TN/AG/W/4/Rev.3 of 10 July 2008; and TN/AG/W/4/Rev.4 of 6 December 2008.

exceptions have increasingly become the target of its regional and bilateral agreements, such as with Australia, Chile, Mexico, South Africa, and the United States. All of these agreements relate to wines and/or spirits. The provisions included in these agreements imply a state's obligation to remove prior conflicting trademarks and to grant protection to the EU GIs that have become 'generic'.[145]

5. Concluding remarks

The origin of the long-drawn-out debate over GIs in the realm of the WTO can be traced back to the history of the Old World and the New. For some of the major players in the WTO belonging to either of these two 'Worlds', GI is an area that is intertwined with larger, politically sensitive debates about the appropriate level of protection for farmers and rural communities, the degree to which international law ought to touch upon questions of culture and tradition, the necessity of IPRs protection, the nature and scope of that protection and, above all, the economic implications of a stronger GI regime for their respective domestic interests, often with significant lobbying powers. It is such multifaceted complexities which have made compromise rather difficult for the key players from the developed world.

While there has been some movement on the multilateral register of late, in our view, it may still be difficult to arrive at a landing zone based on the modality text included in W/52 on the issue of the register, if the long list of 61 'initial questions' put forward by the Joint Proposal (JP) Group at such an advanced stage of negotiations is anything to go by. Although the EC had already responded to these questions before the WTO went for its winter holidays, it remains to be seen whether the JP Group is willing to move forward with the present text, with the register on the table. Given that even this text is highly tilted in favour of the GI right holders and is likely to result in significant financial and legal burdens on the beneficiaries of prior rights in the New World, a consensus may still be difficult to find. However, it needs to be recognized that the strategic alliance of some 110 WTO Members who are vouching for parallelism among the three TRIPS issues is a positive development from the EC's angle, at least as far as the register is concerned. While earlier it was only the EC and Switzerland backing a register with strong legal effects, now the camp has the backing of more than two-thirds of the WTO Membership. This may help the EC to achieve a favourable outcome on the register, provided of course the strategic alliance succeeds in maintaining their

---

145 For further details, see Maximiliano (2007).

unity in upholding the linkages among all three IP issues. This may also be helpful in pushing the agenda on the GI extension. This is an issue on which a number of developing countries have long since been supporting the EC. As discussed in this chapter, the hierarchical protection enshrined in TRIPS in its present form does not have any logical or legal justification whatsoever. It was nothing but a political compromise reached in the Uruguay Round. Hence, in our view, the proponents have a point in demanding a level playing field, because, Article 22-type protection indeed leaves adequate room for misappropriation of GIs other than those relating to wines and spirits. This is crucial from the point of view of some of the developing countries (such as India, China) that have in their possession a number of potential or already-protected GIs belonging to other product categories, such as handlooms, handicrafts or food/beverages other than wines/spirits. In many of these countries, GI is also regarded as an important tool for the protection of traditional knowledge and promoting rural development. Extension of Article 23 armour to all GIs can go a long way towards ensuring better protection for the GIs belonging to the countries of the South. However, it needs to be underscored here that reaping commercial benefits from GIs in the global market would require multi-pronged initiatives and efforts on the part of these countries, including identification of valuable GIs for export purposes; brand-building and promotion; and tapping appropriate marketing channels and strategies. Hence, adequate legal protection at the international level can at best be regarded as necessary but in no way sufficient to reap commercial benefits out of GIs in the global market. Many developing countries (for example, India[146]) have only recently begun to develop their national GI systems; it will take time before substantial commercial benefits arise. Meanwhile, there are difficult questions to resolve, such as delineating the geographic boundaries of a GI, defining its quality attributes and other characteristics, establishing quality control mechanisms, and collectively managing and promoting an indication. Addressing these challenges will require concerted efforts regardless of what emerges from the GI discussions in the DDA.[147]

Finally, in our view, proponents of the GI agenda from the South need to weigh the costs and benefits among the various issues of interest to them before taking any particular stance on the issue. For instance, while the

---

146 For challenges confronting the Indian GIs initiatives, refer to Das (2009), 'Early View' published at http://www3.interscience.wiley.com/journal/122381868/abstract.

147 CTA (2008), p. 13.

strategic alliance reached among the proponents of the three IP issues may be helpful for pushing the GIs agenda, it may be noted that the alliance was reached at the cost of a significant compromise on the TRIPS/CBD front on the part of the proponents of this crucial issue. While originally they were vouching for a strong legal effect in the disclosure proposal tabled by them, the modality text included in W/52 did not include this important part of the disclosure proposal. Even on the issues of prior informed consent and access and benefit sharing, W/52 only mentioned that 'Members agree to define the nature and extent of a reference to Prior Informed Consent and Access and Benefit Sharing'. This was again a significant departure from the original proposal put forward by the proponents of the disclosure requirement. Whether such compromises were worth making for some of the developing countries that evidently have a higher stake in getting a better deal on TRIPS/CBD than on GIs, remains an open question for their policy makers to ponder. Such cost-benefit analysis may turn out to be even more significant in the future course of negotiations on the Doha Round, if the proponents succeed in making all the TRIPS issues a part of the single undertaking. Because even if they succeed in getting a good deal on GIs, it is most likely to be a *quid-pro-quo* for concessions to be granted elsewhere.

References

Addor, Felix, and Alexandra Grazioli (2002), 'Geographical Indications beyond Wines and Spirits: A Roadmap for a Better Protection for Geographical Indications in the WTO TRIPS Agreement', *Journal of World Intellectual Property*, 5(6), 863–97.

Barham, Elizabeth (2003), 'Translating Terroir: The Global Challenge of French AOC Labeling', *Journal of Rural Studies*, 19, 127–38.

Caenegem, William van (2003a), 'Registered Geographical Indications: Between Intellectual Property and Rural Policy-Part I', *Journal of World Intellectual Property*, 6(5), 699–719.

Caenegem, William van (2003b), 'Registered Geographical Indications: Between Intellectual Property and Rural Policy-Part II', *Journal of World Intellectual Property*, 6(6), 861–74.

Correa, Carlos M. (2002), 'Protection of Geographical Indications in Caricom Countries', available at: http://www.crnm.org/documents/studies/Geographical%20Indications%20-%20Correa.pdf.

CTA (Technical Centre for Agricultural and Rural Cooperation ACP-EU) (2008), 'Executive Brief: WTO Negotiations on Agriculture', April.

Das, Kasturi (2006a), 'International Protection of India's Geographical Indications with Special Reference to "Darjeeling" Tea', *Journal of World Intellectual Property*, 9(5), 459–95.

Das, Kasturi (2006b), 'Protection of India's "Geographical Indications": An Overview of the Indian Legislation and the TRIPS Scenario', *Indian Journal of International Law*, 46(1), 39–73.

Das, Kasturi (2007), 'Protection of Geographical Indications: An Overview of Select Issues with Particular Reference to India', *Working Paper 8*, Centre for Trade & Development (Centad), New Delhi. Available at: http://www.centad.org/download/WorkingPaper_FinalPDF_4June07.pdf.

Das, Kasturi (2008a), 'Select Issues and Debates around Geographical Indications with Particular Reference to India', *Journal of World Trade*, 42(3), 461–507.
Das, Kasturi (2008b), 'WTO Ministerial Must Address Biopiracy Concerns', *The Economic Times,* New Delhi, India, 14 July.
Das, Kasturi (2009), 'Prospects and Challenges of Geographical Indications in India', *Journal of World Intellectual Property*, published in John Wiley 'Early View' at http://www3.interscience.wiley.com/journal/122381868/abstract.
European Commission (2003a), 'WTO Talks: EU Steps up Bid for Better Protection of Regional Quality Products', Press Release of the European Commission, Brussels, 28 August 2003, available at: http://europe.eu.int.
European Commission (2003b), 'Why Do Geographical Indications Matter to Us?', 30 July, available at: http://europa.eu.int/comm/trade/issues/sectoral /intell_property/argu_en.htm.
European Commission (2005), 'Geographical indications and TRIPS: 10 Years Later . . . : A Roadmap for EU GI Holders to get Protection in Other WTO Members'.
Fink, Carsten and Keith Maskus (2006), 'The Debate on Geographical Indications in the WTO', in Newfarmer, Richard (ed.), *Trade, Doha, and Development: A Window into the Issues*, Washington, DC: The International Bank for Reconstruction and Development/The World Bank.
Gangjee, Dev (2007), 'Say Cheese! A Sharper Image of Generic Use through the Lens of Feta', available at: http://papers.ssrn.com/sol3/papers.cfm?abstract_id=980543.
Gervais, Daniel (1998), *The TRIPS Agreement: Drafting History and Analysis*, London: Sweet & Maxwell.
Maximiliano Santa Cruz S. (2007), 'Intellectual Property Provisions in European Union Trade Agreements: Implications for Developing Countries', International Centre for Trade and Sustainable Development (ICTSD).
Moran, W. (1993), 'Rural Space as Intellectual Property', *Political Geography*, 12.
Nieuwveld, Lisa Bench (2007), 'Is This Really about What We Call our Food or Something Else? The WTO Food Name Case over the Protection of Geographical Indications', *The International Lawyer,* 41(3), 891–922.
Rangnekar, Dwijen (2003), 'Geographical Indications – A Review of Proposals at the TRIPS Council: Extending Article 23 to Products other than Wines and Spirits', International Centre for Trade and Sustainable Development (ICTSD).
Raustiala, Kal and Stephen R. Munzer (2007), 'The Global Struggle over Geographic Indications', *The European Journal on International Law*, 18(2), 337–65.
Torsen, Molly (2005), 'Apples and Oranges: French and American Models of Geographic Indications Policies Demonstrate an International Lack of Consensus', *The Trademark Reporter*, 95(6), 1415–45.
Vivas-Eugui, David, and Christophe Spennemann (2006), 'The Treatment of Geographical Indications in Recent Regional and Bilateral Free Trade Agreements', UNCTAD/ICTSD Project on Intellectual Property and Sustainable Development.
Wasescha, Thu-Lang Tran (2007), 'Geographical Indications in the International Arena: The Current Situation', WIPO/GEO/BEI/07/15 of 23 June.
World Intellectual Property Organization (WIPO) (2000), 'Standing Committee on the Law of Trademarks, Industrial Designs and Geographical Indications', Fifth Session, Geneva, 11–15 September.
World Trade Organization (WTO) (2001), Council for Trade-related Aspects of Intellectual Property Rights, 'Review under Article 24.2 of the Application of the Provisions of the Section of the TRIPS Agreement on Geographical Indications: Summary of the Responses to the Checklist of Questions', IP/C/W/253, 4 April.
Yeung, May T. and William A. Kerr (2008), 'Increasing Protection of GIs at the WTO: Clawbacks, Greenfields and Monopoly Rents', CATPRN Working Paper 2008-02, Canadian Agricultural Trade Policy Research Network (CATPRN), March.

15 No 'lemons' no more: a sketch on the 'economics' of geographical indications

Dwijen Rangnekar

Introduction

One of the most recent entrants into the growing pantheon of intellectual property rights (IPRs), Geographical Indications (GIs), continues to raise deeply fundamental questions. At one end of the spectrum are those who question their very legitimacy as IPRs (Stern 2007). In contrast, there are others who see in GIs a variety of normative possibilities like valorising the rights (actually, products) of rural communities, indigenous groups and holders of traditional knowledge (Bérard and Marchenay 1996). Even in terms of the relationship between its closest family members in the pantheon, trademarks, there are those who seek a departure from the 'language of trumps', and read in the World Trade Organization (WTO) dispute[1] on this matter a nuanced approach towards the legitimate possibility of co-existence (Gangjee 2007). The negotiations on GIs speak to some to some of these concerns as well – and go well beyond.[2] It is also the case that GIs are increasingly figuring in other forums as well, such as at the Food and Agriculture Organization (FAO) in terms of commodity prices, petty agriculture producers, at the World Intellectual Property Organization (WIPO) as one amongst other instruments to protect traditional knowledge and also at the United Nations Environment Programme (UNEP) in terms of biopiracy. GIs are often presented with these multiple policy objectives, including: protecting the environment, promoting sustainable development, securing rural livelihoods, protecting and rewarding holders of traditional knowledge and developing niche markets.

It is in this growing terrain about GIs that the chapter seeks to dwell on the negotiations concerning GI-extension. Rather than track the various submissions and juridical merits of interpreting TRIPS,[3] the

1 Discussed in Vivas-Eugui and Oliva (2010).

2 Chapter 14 of this volume by Kasturi Das provides an overview of outstanding implementation issues.

3 In this volume, Kasturi Das (ibid) provides a brief discussion of the submissions. I earlier covered this in Rangnekar (2003) and more recent

chapter seeks to step back and consider the nature of GIs and how its subject matter is constructed. In doing so, I suggest that in the normative justifications for GIs, there is an appreciation of the historical rights and reputation that accumulate to a people and place for stabilising a particular cultural repertoire. This cultural stabilisation generates a certain local specialisation, which, if we agree it is deserving of protection, then generates rights that are locally embedded; thus, generating locational immobility and denying licensing of the indication to producers located elsewhere. Like other distinctive signs, such as trademarks, GIs depend on the integrity of information channels. Unlike other distinctive signs, GIs also depend on the integrity of producers in the identified geography. It is in this prism of information and location that I locate my argument on GI-extension.

The chapter begins with a discussion on the economics of information and distinctive signs. Reflecting on how economists have approached their rationalisation of the protection of trademarks, I argue that similar precepts can be found in the case of distinctive signs like GIs. In doing so, I also reflect that the collectivity of GIs generates other concerns. The second section seeks to explicate the nature of GIs. It reflects on contributions from anthropology and geography, where ideas of localised specialisation have been used to consider the intellectual object that constitutes a GI. It is here that I suggest that the nature of locational specificity is responded to by constructing locational immobility in the rights in a GI. The final section takes the challenge of using these ideas to analyse the case for GI-extension.

The economics of information and distinctive signs

The search for information is a ubiquitous feature of our everyday lives that include the purchase (or sale) of daily groceries to finding ways to receive (or send) a money order and from deciding on which school to send one's children to or where to go for a medical procedure to deciding on an enjoyable watering hole to quench one's thirst – we seek information. As anyone's personal experience would testify, mobilising information to take these decisions is difficult, time consuming and fraught with many contingencies. We have come to rely on a variety of sources and practices which include experience, family and friends, rumour and talk, experts and elders, trade and consumer magazines, and public advisory bureaus

scholarly works are available in Silva (2005) and Raustiala and Munzer (2007).

and advertisements. Of course, the habits of practice generate and sustain their own social dynamic and networks.

Economists approaching the subject focus on the information asymmetries that exist between buyers and sellers. For instance, Stigler ([1961] 1970, p. 62) finds it 'fruitless' to explain *all* price dispersion on the basis of product heterogeneity and seeks an explanation in the 'level of ignorance' in the market. The latter is a manifestation of the information asymmetries between buyers and sellers. Consequently, if price dispersions are large relative to the costs associated with information search, a buyer would find it profitable to continue searching. To state this differently, expected savings are positively related to the level of price dispersion and thus influence consumer choice and firm investments (Akerlof 1970; Nelson 1970).

Taking the market for used cars as an example, where buyers suspect that a certain proportion of cars are 'lemons' (that is, bad cars), Akerlof (1970) focuses attention on the quality-related information asymmetries between buyers and sellers. The buyer cannot observe the quality of a used car with any significant surety, whereas the seller has more reliable information about it. In such a situation of information asymmetry, good and bad used cars would tend to sell at comparable prices. Dynamically, this leads to a situation where 'bad cars drive out good cars': the common price between good and bad cars presents sellers with perverse incentives motivating the withdrawal of good used cars. To explain, the seller does not receive a price mark-up for good used cars reflecting their superior quality in comparison with bad used cars. Consequently, as these cars are withdrawn from the market, equilibrium is achieved at lower levels of quality. For the result to hold, it is necessary that a common price exists for both types of cars and that the seller does not differentiate between good and bad used cars. Akerlof recognises that buyers form a more accurate idea of the car upon purchase and subsequent use. This indicates that information asymmetries are temporal and contingent on the nature of the good.

Taking their cue from this, other economists have classified goods on the basis of how information is accessed by and/or conveyed to consumers (Nelson 1970; Darby and Karni 1973):[4]

---

[4] It would be obvious to cultural theorists and anthropologists that patterns of purchase and use generate and sustain social networks of consumption that inhere their own institutions of trust. Durable goods and goods that foist prestige are also purchased upon deliberation that uses a variety of informational resources that act as arbiters of quality and authenticity.

- *Search goods*: These are goods where consumers develop a robust notion of quality prior to purchase through either inspection and/or research.
- *Experience goods*: These are goods where quality is known through use and experience, which then guides future consumer decisions.
- *Credence goods*: These are goods where neither prior inspection nor subsequent use is sufficient to develop a robust notion of quality.

Neither do goods fall neatly into any one of the three categories nor are individuals identical in their preferences or reception of a particular good. For example, even in the instance of a 'mundane' and everyday bag of coffee beans, there are differences. For some it could easily be a 'search good', where price is adequate in representing product attributes. For some others, it could be an experience good to the extent that other attributes (for example, flavour and aroma) are given importance. Finally, there will be a group of individuals who consider the same bag of coffee as a credence good and enquire about attributes of the production process (for example, workers' pay, use of pesticides, etc.). Cultural theorists remind us that the meaning of things to people is rarely ever unitary; not only is meaning mediated and different in different social settings, but we seek such difference. If any of this filters into economics, it is in terms of recognising multiplicity in preferences, market segments and firm strategies of product differentiation.

It is in this world of asymmetric information that social institutions like reputation, often communicated through networks and congealed in distinctive signs, acquire importance as devices signalling provenance, albeit, with all the complications of suggesting a certain quality, a certain origin and authenticity. Distinctive signs, economists argue, are signalling devices of a certain level of quality that consumers learn to expect. By maintaining this level of quality, the distinctive sign economises search costs for consumers; thus, the willingness of consumers to pay a premium (Stigler [1961] 1970, p. 79). As reputation is communicated through distinctive signs, consumers can retaliate by curtailing future purchases if quality does not meet expectations (Akerlof 1970, p. 500). Shapiro (1982) suggests that a firm's decision to invest in developing quality products is dynamic: the returns from (current) investments in producing high-quality products occur in the future, following repeated purchases on account of the firm's reputation for high-quality products. It is through repeated purchases that a link is established between a firm's current investments in maintaining quality and consumers' perceptions of the firm's reputation. It is when consumers learn about the reputation through past purchases, experience and other information channels that it becomes economically meaningful for firms to invest in producing high-quality (reputable) products. There are contesting views on the role of advertising in this respect.[5]

It is within this general frame that the economic and legal rationale for the protection of distinctive signs like trademarks is largely presented. It is the shared view in the trademark literature that two interrelated objectives underlie the protection of trademarks: protection of the investments undertaken to develop brand names and associated reputation and safeguard the informational role of trademarks as indicator of source (see Landes and Posner 1987; Economides 1988; Grossman and Shapiro 1988a, 1988b; Cornish 1999).[6] Interestingly, according to some practitioners, the primary purpose of trademark protection is to enable appropriation of investments in brand name and the informational role of trademarks (Cratchley 2000). On the other hand, there are scholars who seek a closure to this debate, and thus present a new orthodoxy in terms of search costs: 'Firms with strong trademarks . . . will command higher prices for their brands not because of market power but because the search costs associated with their brand are lower' (Landes and Posner 2003, p. 176).[7] Others seek to tread the thin line between these various functions of trademarks: 'In many markets, sellers have much better information as to the unobservable features of a commodity for sale than the buyers. . . . Unobservable features, valued by consumers, may be crucial determinants of the total value of the good. . . . However, if there is a way to identify the unobservable qualities, the consumer's choice becomes clear, and firms with a long horizon have an incentive to cater to a spectrum of tastes for variety and quality, even though these product features may be unobservable at the time of purchase' (Economides 1988, p. 526).

---

[5] In this regard, advertising, an institution that Stigler ([1961] 1970, p. 73) characterises as an 'immensely powerful instrument for the elimination of [market-based] ignorance', is of importance. No doubt, others see advertising differently. Some note the market power that advertising sustains and how it generates barriers to entry into a market (Scherer and Ross 1990) or sustains a monopolistic market structure (Chamberlin 1969, chapter 4; Schmalensee 1979). Useful narratives are also found in the work of anthropologists studying the power of brands and the contested nature in which they inhabit our everyday lifes (Coombe 1998).

[6] This should not be read as suggesting that the debate on trademark protection is settled. By way of example, Cornish opens up an enquiry into deciding the appropriate extension of legal protection of trademarks in terms of either emphasising the signalling of origin/quality or protecting investment (Cornish 1999, pp. 614–16).

[7] This is reminiscent of Schechter's characterisation of trademark's primary role as the 'creation and retention of custom, rather than the designation of source' (Schechter 1927, p. 825).

Trademarks are indicators of source enabling consumers to overcome, to some extent, the information asymmetries in the market. In this manner, trademarks are intrinsically associated with the buying and selling of products (Cornish 1999, p. 619). It is this role of 'channel of information' that allows trademarks to lower search costs, protect consumers from fraud and assist in consumer decision making.[8] However, to achieve the economies in 'search', that is, to be an efficient information channel, a trademark must meet certain conditions: the trademark must be distinct and differentiated from previously existing trademarks (Landes and Posner 2003). Article 15.1 of the TRIPs Agreement has the following definition for trademarks: 'Any sign, or any combination of signs, capable of distinguishing the goods or services of one undertaking from those of other undertakings, shall be capable of constituting a trademark'. This is a remarkably generous definition in allowing a wide variety of signifiers. More significant is the change in focus from identifying source to enabling differentiating source; thus, there is no requirement that for the sign to identify a particular undertaking as the source of goods or services. Even in terms of 'words', the possibilities include words or combination of words such as family names (for example, Ford, Chevrolet, Dodge), fanciful words that mean nothing (for example, Exxon and Kodak), and also suggestive or geographically descriptive names when they have acquired secondary meaning (for example, Mont Blanc). Also possible are images, figures, symbols, logos, monograms and insignias. However, the emphasis is on the sign (word, phrase, symbol) being *distinctive* so as to enable consumers to differentiate a firm's goods and services from those of other firms. In the absence of distinctness, closely similar signs would generate unnecessary confusion and be a waste of resources. In lieu of this, the Agreement on Trade-related Aspects of International Property Rights (TRIPS) offers trademarks a scope of protection that includes 'identical and similar signs' (Article 16).

Brand development requires investments in maintaining a certain minimum level of quality and advertising and promoting distinctive signs, names and logos. These investments are sunk or fixed costs that are substantially irreversible upon product launch and market entry (Scherer

[8] Here note that a single trademark can and is invariably used across a number of products that might fall within a category (for example, microwaves) or a broader aggregation of products (for example, home appliances). A variety of information channels exist to provide product-related information: advertising, product labels, consumer magazines, friends, etc. Trademarks, as a distinctive sign, help in linking these different information sources.

and Ross 1990, for a detailed discussion).[9] Moreover, in many product categories the evidence suggests that a substantial promotional budget is necessary – a sort of threshold level – before information reaches the consumer. The objective of these promotional efforts is to help consumers identify and differentiate the product from the vast array of similar products in the same category. Given the unobservable characteristics of the product, the identification and differentiation of the product occurs through information captured in a brand name: 'This information is not provided to the consumer in an analytic form, such as an indication of size or listing of ingredients, but rather in summary form, through a symbol which the consumer identifies with a specific combination of features. Information in an analytic form is a complement to, rather than a substitute for, trademarks' (Economides 1988, pp. 526–7). It is through its function of signalling certain quality standards that induce consumers to return and purchase new products that a 'trademark becomes an asset of the firm, embodying its accumulated goodwill' (Grossman and Shapiro 1988a, p. 60).

It is thus suggested that protecting trademarks generates incentives for firms to make investments in maintaining a certain level of quality. Apart from confusing consumers, the misappropriation of trademarks through the production of counterfeit goods is said to harm firms by diluting their reputation and market power (Grossman and Shapiro 1988a, 1988b). Here, consider the presence of counterfeit goods in a market where consumers cannot readily observe the characteristics of the good and only learn about the quality/authenticity of the good one period later. Only when the product does not match the quality claims made by the firm does the consumer feel that either the (legitimate) firm has 'shaved its quality' or that a counterfeit has been inadvertently purchased. Assuming consumer rationality, that is, they play safe, believing that a cheating firm will continue to 'shave quality', it is suggested that consumers will transfer their loyalty to another firm in the next period.

---

[9] As noted earlier, some economists recognise that advertising can act as a barrier to entry into a market. For example, in oligopolist markets, intensive advertising by incumbents reinforces existing consumer preferences and substantially raises the minimum level of promotional expenditures required by potential entrants to launch a product. The barriers to entry are on account of several reasons: (a) entrants have to incur disproportionately high advertising outlays per unit sales to win patronage, (b) economies of scale in advertising favour firms with a sizeable market presence, and (c) the absolute advertising expenditures for effective entry, that is, a threshold level, is higher when seller concentration ratios are high (Scherer and Ross 1990, pp. 430–50).

Reality is no doubt more complicated. And, unfortunately, any *doubts* about unilateral strengthening of intellectual property protection are received in prejudiced terms. Writing on copyright law, Justice Laddie expresses this evocatively: 'There is no trade union of copyright infringers. Support for any limitation on copyright is easily portrayed as support for pirates – the usual pejorative global expression for infringers. It is depicted as support for the parasites of industry' (Laddie 1996, p. 259). However, consider the situation of consumers *knowingly* purchasing a fake of a 'status good'.[10] These consumers buy-in the 'snob value' associated with the status good without paying the premium price asked by the original. Here, deception is not that of the purchaser but of observers 'who sees the good being consumed and [are] duly (but mistakenly) impressed' (Grossman and Shapiro 1988b, p. 82). The brand-owner's market power is diminished by expansion of the market of 'status goods', which also deprives consumers of the good's snob value, as prestige is contingent on a small network of exclusive consumers. However, the wider social welfare effects of faking in this instance are ambiguous and in certain instances, prohibiting the fake might result in adverse welfare results.[11]

While the discussion has largely been either in general terms of 'distinctive signs' or specifically directed at 'trademarks', it is the case that it applies equally to GIs.[12] Distinctive signs indicating geographical origin are the earliest type of trademarks, with evidence in pre-industrial periods for a variety of products like minerals, simple manufactured goods and agricultural products (Schechter 1927). Yet, ironically as Stephen Ladas notes, this avatar of IP 'was [the] last to be recognized and protected by the municipal law of different countries' (Ladas 1975, p. 658). The irony is that the normative elements of GIs have existed in the customary practices and the trading and marketing strategies of craftsmen, artisans, petty commodity producers, agriculturalists and manufacturers for a substantively long

[10] This example is from Grossman and Shapiro (1988b), who define status goods as those 'goods for which the mere use of display of a particular branded product confers prestige on their owners, apart from the utility deriving from their function' (Ibid., p. 82). The status or snob-value of these goods is a result of investments in advertising, high price, and controlled retail outlets.

[11] Grossman and Shapiro (1988b) also acknowledge that the welfare implications of stronger trademark protection, wherein counterfeiting is eliminated, are ambiguous. While there is little dispute about the benefits to trademark owners of eliminating counterfeiting, the negative impact on consumers who knowingly consume the counterfeit and on counterfeit producers raises complications.

[12] There are significant differences between the two types of distinctive signs; for a discussion see Rangnekar (2004). See Gangjee (2007) for a discussion of the WTO dispute concerning trademarks and GIs.

period of time. For instance, Egyptians are noted for stamping wine jars to indicate vintage and provenance. There is evidence in the 12th century of the use of IGOs and seals of quality to indicate city-origin by tapestry manufacturers from central Europe and clothiers in England (Schechter 1927). A variety of goods were traded under marks that indicated their geographical origin either through the depiction of local animals (panda beer), landmarks (Mt Fuji sake), buildings (Pisa silk), heraldic signs (fleur de lys butter) or well-known personalities (Mozart chocolate) (Blakeney 2001). Many of our everyday commodities are known by names that suggest a certain provenance; thus, the term china for porcelain is transparent of China and coffee is indicative of its geographical origin in Ethiopia's Kaffa province. Naturally, geographical or geographical-like distinctive signs have various connotations, as is evidenced by the kiwifruit and Bermuda shorts – both suggestive of a geography of commerce rather than a geography of origin in the GI sense. The use of place names in the case of carpets has been complicated by the influences of the 'lore of the dealer' and the displacement of the weaver (Spooner 1988). For instance, certain place names, such as Bukhara, in the mid-18th century emerge as a term of provenance indicative of the biography of carpet and its entry through trade channels into Western markets, rather than a reflection of the carpet's type (Spooner, ibid.).

Information inhabits the various signs used to mark things – and this, as cultural theorists will remind us, means different things to different people. What is the informational content of a GI? Here it is necessary to follow Ploeg (1992, p. 20) who uses the expression *art de la localité* to capture the cultural stabilisation of particular practices: '[E]very location acquired, maintained and enlargened (through among other things, the exchanges mentioned), its own cultural repertoire: its own norms and criteria that together established the local notion of "good farming"'. Thus, societies curate their surroundings and actively engage in the creative generation of their habitat and the various artefacts that constitute their surroundings. This idea that things have a *signature* reflective of place and peoples is captured in the French term *terroir*.[13]

This localised specialisation is apparent in a number of products as

[13] For a discussion on *terroir*, see Moran (1993) and Barham (2003). Political and economic geographers have used the term differently. Sack (1983, p. 59) defines *terroir* as 'the attempt to affect, influence, or control actions and interactions (of people, things, and relationships) by asserting and attempting to enforce control over a geographic area'. Moran (1993) adopts this notion to narrate a compelling account of the stratification of wine appellations in France and how this is implicated in generating and sustaining rent differentials in wine-growing areas.

Table 15.1 Distribution of Lisbon Agreement Appellations

Product	Registrations		Top Holder	
	Number	%age	Country	%age
Wines	470	61	France	81
Spirits	73	10	France	82
Agricultural Products	51	7	–	
Cheeses	50	7	France	74
Ornamental Products	33	4	Czech Republic	65
Tobacco & Cigarettes	33	4	Cuba*	100
Miscellaneous	25	3	–	
Mineral Water	17	2	Czech Republic	82
Beer and Malt	14	2	Czech Republic	93

Note: All percentages are rounded up.
* Only cigarettes

Source: Assembled from data in Escudero (2001).

evidenced by data of appellations protected under the Lisbon Agreement (Table 15.1). Cuba accounts for all the protected appellations for cigarettes and the Czech Republic for 93 per cent of the appellations in beers and malt, while France holds over 80 per cent of the wine and spirit appellations. Regional specialisation within product categories is also reflected in the EU data (Rangnekar 2004, p. 14). For that matter, this specialisation is observable at lower levels of aggregation: for example, despite widespread distribution (internationally and within nations) of the species *Vitis vinifera*, the major production areas are highly localised and each grape variety has its own distinctive geographic pattern (Moran 1993). These distinctive geographic patterns aren't illusionary as quality characteristics are strongly associated with habitat and local practices. For example, an examination of Basmati varieties that include traditional cultivars from India and Pakistan and the varieties bred by RiceTec, an American seed company, with claims of Basmati-like properties, found that the latter fail to exhibit either the genetic structure of Basmati or the full range of agronomic attributes (Bhattacharjee et al. 2002; Kamath et al. 2008). GIs can be considered as the juridical reification of these culturally settled norms of good farming and the specifications that constitute the GI are its core informational component. In this respect, Torre (2006) adopts the useful metaphor of 'social construction of compromise' to invite an analysis of the collective action dilemmas that accompany the making of and adherence to rules.

It is associations between names, things and places that come to constitute the notion of GIs. And, such associations – varying, temporal and contingent – contribute to the reputation of the name. An expression of this relationship is the case brought by the *Comité Interprofessionel du Vin de Champagne*, the consortium representing Champagne producers, to the courts of New Zealand. In passing judgment in favour of the Champagne producers, Judge Gault[14] noted that: 'Champagne is a geographical name. When used in relation to wine the primary significance it would convey to persons who know that would be as the geographical origin of the product. If the name conveys something of the characteristics of the wine it is because those familiar with wine sold by reference to the name associate those characteristics with it. . . . For suppliers the attracting force in the name constitutes a part of the goodwill of their business. [. . .] That goodwill will be damaged if someone else uses the name in relation to a product in such a manner as to deceive purchasers into believing the product has the characteristics of products normally associated with the name when it does not.' Integral to this quote are networks of reputation and information – and the next section explicates this in terms of GIs.

The construction of geographical indications

Despite the shared economic rationale and legal principles and the fact that it's all about buying and selling, there are important differences between GIs and trademarks.[15] At a fundamental level, there is the difference in terms of what is being signified. Trademarks identify the goods of an enterprise, thus suggesting provenance in terms of commercial enterprise. In contrast, 'geography is at the heart' of GIs and it is provenance in terms of a particular territory that is being signified. TRIPS defines GIs in Article 22.1 as 'indications which identify a good as originating in the territory of a Member, or a region or locality in that territory, where a given quality, reputation or other characteristic of the good is essentially attributable to its geographical origin'. Clearly, GIs are not limited to any particular enterprise and are available for use by all enterprises within the demarcated geographical area that qualify for use of the indication. Again, contrasting with trademarks, GIs should be visualised as a form of collective right that defines who can make a particular product, where the product is to be made, and what ingredients and techniques are to be used so as to satisfy 'authenticity' and 'origin'.

---

[14] *Wineworths Group Ltd. v. Comité Interprofessionel du Vin de Champagne*, 2 NZLR 327 [1991].

[15] This and the next paragraph are based on Rangnekar (2004).

It is difficult not to emphasise the nature of this collectivity. Apart from the exceptions of single enterprise GIs, there is an entire social supply chain of producers and enterprises to be considered. Specifications implicate the entire supply chain right down to raw materials and, if relevant, the land used for cultivation. Moreover, firms that are legally and economically distinct units are engaged in the production of the very same product, while also competing with each other. Firms at identical stages on the supply chain compete with each other for market shares, whereas firms that are at contiguous stages of the supply chain compete with each other for shares in the product's value. This competition matrix must be appreciated in its social setting, where firms are collectively implicated in the specifications. As such, the reputation embedded in the indication is collectively on account of and simultaneously accrues to the entire geographical region identified in the indication. This interdependence makes possible a social construction of a compromise around culturally shared 'norms of good farming'.

The construction of GIs, by definition, prohibits the possibility of assigning or licensing the indication to anyone outside the demarcated geographical territory. The scope of protection does not include the 'right to assign' an indication – a right that exists for trademarks (Article 20) and patents (Article 28.2) within the TRIPS Agreement. Some may consider this as circumscribing the scope of protection to GI-holders, whereas others, like Stern (2007), consider this as excluding GIs from the family of IPRs. However, this feature of the rights in GIs corresponds with its collective ethic and its relationship to geography. Quite simply, transferring and/or licensing a GI defeats the very essence of a GI, which requires the product to originate in a particular geography. This is the fulcrum of GIs, with the specifications spelling out the relationship to a particular geography, which then generates the indication's reputation. WIPO articulates this interweaving of information and reputation neatly: 'Geographical indications are understood by consumers to denote the origin and the quality of products. Many of them have acquired valuable reputations which, if not adequately protected, may be misrepresented by dishonest commercial operators. False use of geographical indications by unauthorised parties is detrimental to consumers and legitimate producers. The former are deceived and led into believing to buy a genuine product with specific qualities and characteristics, while they in fact get a worthless imitation. The latter suffer damage because valuable business is taken away from them and the established reputation for their products is damaged' (WIPO 2002).

Naturally, the specifications/information raise certain obligations on enterprises that seek to use the indication – they must adhere to the *art de la localité* and sustain it. In this respect, consider the predicament confronting *Newcastle Brown Ale* when, in 2005, they closed their landmark Tyne Brewery after more than 100 years of operation to expand production at an alternative site (Kerr 2005). Citing 'operational difficulties' and recognising a move to another site means that 'the specification is not any longer respected in relation to the delimited geographical area' originally stipulated, they thus requested cancellation of the GI,[16] which was accepted in 2007.[17] A similar predicament of expansion faced the producers of *Bleu de Bresse*, which was subsequently licensed for production outside the designated geographical region, though only after surrender of their rights (Rangnekar 2004, p. 18).[18] These predicaments are also suggestive of the tension between different values and how, at times, the value of commerce prevails. However, the construction of GIs, within a cultural frame of 'notions of good farming', is very different. In particular, the nature of the intellectual object is predicated on establishing 'locational specificity'; thus, the law responds by building 'locational immobility' into the rights in GIs.

One way of appreciating the locationality of GIs is to consider a set of normative justifications often articulated in terms of honouring GIs that are transparent in the French approach. The French body responsible for organising the protection of appellations, the *Institut National des Appellations d'origine* (INAO), expresses the normative justifications in terms of rights acquired by sustaining a certain practice: 'This protection constitutes a legitimate safeguard of rights acquired by generations of producers of a region who have imposed on themselves a certain number of rules and disciplines in order to put a unique and original product on the market'.[19] The honouring of these historical rights with their locational immobility is part of a wider process of cultural and endogenous

---

16 Cancellation request according to Article 12(2) and Article 17(2), 'NEWCASTLE BROWN ALE', EC No. UK/017/0372/16.08.2004, OJ C-280/13, 18 November 2006.

17 Commission Regulation (EC) No. 952/2007 of 9 August 2007 cancelling a registration of a name in the Register of protected designations of origin and protected geographical indications (Newcastle Brown Ale (PGI)), OJ L 210, 10 August 2007.

18 Caenegem (2003, p. 718) draws attention to the case of *Bleu de Bresse* and enquires as to what restricts the licensing of the indication and production elsewhere when the only requirement is sourcing a raw material from a particular geography.

19 INAO (1987), *La Protection Internationale des Appellations d'Origine des Vins et Eaux-de-Vie*, Paris: Institut National des Appellations d'origine des Vins et Eaux-de-Vie (quoted in Moran 1993).

development (Ploeg 1992), making GIs a meaningful policy intervention that enables 'people to translate their long-standing, collective, and patrimonial knowledge into livelihood and income' (Bérard and Marchenay 1996, p. 240).

There remains a duality in these normative justifications for GIs. On the one hand, it relates to sustaining a certain historical practice that relates to place and peoples (the specifications) and valorising the rights in the market place through protection of the indication (the goodwill of the indication). This duality is evident in case law at the European Court of Justice where the courts had to consider the significance of the grating of Grana Padano cheese[20] and the slicing and packing of Parma ham.[21] Even while these procedures occur close to the retail end, they are stipulated in the specifications submitted for registration under Council Regulation EC 510/2006. The court had to decide whether they constitute an exclusive right that is also directly enforceable. In both instances, the court agreed that the rules are an exclusive right that is also enforceable. It concluded that a specification 'determines both the extent of the obligations to be complied with for the purposes of using the PDO [that is, Protected Designation of Origin] and, as a corollary, the extent of the right protected against third parties by the effect of registration of the PDO'.[22] For those who adhere to the norms, the right to use the GI exists, whereas those not abiding by these norms are prohibited from using the GI. It is in this duality that Carol Rose's (1986) notion of 'limited common property' makes pertinent sense for characterising GIs: 'property held as commons amongst the member of a group, but exclusively vis-à-vis the outside world'. To clarify, adherence to the specifications sustains the informational integrity and content of the GI and prohibiting use of the indication by non-adherents ensures that neither are the information channels disturbed nor will there be a dilution of the reputation of the indication.

An attempt to extend the debate on GI-extension

One of the sore points concerning GIs, and there are many, is the hierarchy in protection on account of the differential treatment between wines and spirits through Article 23 and other goods through Article 22. Beginning with submissions to the Seattle Ministerial in 1999, a number of

---

[20] Case C-469/00, *Ravil SARL v. Bellon Import SARL and Biraghi SpA*, 2003 ECR I-05053.

[21] Case C-108/01, *Consorzio del Prosciutto di Parma and Salumificio S. Rita SpA v. Asda Stores Ltd and Hygrade Foods Ltd* 33, 2003 ECR I-05121.

[22] Case C-469/00, *Ravil SARL v. Bellon Import SARL and Biraghi SpA*, 2003 ECR I-05053 at ¶80.

WTO members from the Global South have sought to expand the scope of application of Article 23 to products other than wines and spirits and thus remove the hierarchy in Section 3 of the TRIPS Agreement.[23] This issue highlights other remarkable features of GIs in TRIPS. First, the hierarchy establishes an unlikely instance of a succeeding multilateral IP treaty (viz. TRIPS) providing a narrower scope of application and rights than its predecessor (viz. Lisbon) (Rangnekar 2003, p. 22). Second, equally unlikely, is the presence of a large number of Global South countries as *demandeurs* for stronger protection. While commentaries on GI-extension emphasise the contested nature of the debate, few have concerned themselves with paying attention to certain shared understandings. And, as Taubman (2008) recently notes, none has taken the analysis forward by offering economic analysis of the significance of the hierarchy. The remainder of the chapter concerns itself with these two challenges.

From an early stage in the debate on GI-extension there were shared perceptions.[24] For instance, both groups agreed that there is no juridical basis to or rationality in the hierarchy. While it would be obvious for *demandeurs* to argue against the differential treatment, it is remarkable to read the following candidness from countries opposing GI-extension: 'If the extension discussion were purely one of intellectual property policy, it would make sense to treat all products in the same manner legally' (WTO 2002, paragraph 3). In an associated sense, both groups of countries also agree that the peculiar structure of Section 3 on GIs is the outcome of last-minute trade-offs struck during the Brussels Ministerial (WTO 2001, paragraph 9; WTO 2000b, paragraph 6).[25] Yet, they disagree on whether there was a juridical basis within TRIPS, such as the built-in agenda of Section 3, for negotiating GI-extension or whether a fresh mandate was necessary. The mandate has since been agreed in the Doha Ministerial Declaration, where GI-extension exists as *Tiret 87* in the Compilation

---

23 By way of shorthand, this issue of demanding extension of the scope of application of Article 23 to products other than wines and spirits is referred to as 'GI-extension' and an analysis of the issues is available in Rangnekar (2003). Chapter 14 by Kasturi Das in this *Handbook* discusses this issue briefly, along with other outstanding issues concerning GIs. The curious reader is directed to the overview prepared by the WTO Secretariat paper (WTO 2005b) and to Silva (2005) and Raustiala and Munzer (2007).

24 This is obviously based on material in Rangnekar (2003).

25 For that matter, spirits were added to Article 23 (paragraphs 1 and 2) towards the end of negotiations (Gervais, 1998, p. 130). Consequently, some suggest that TRIPS provides a three-level hierarchy in the level of protection for GIs (see Escudero 2001, pp. 27–30).

of Outstanding Implementation Issues[26] and is part of the negotiations in the TRIPS Council. Subsequently, it has been reiterated in the Hong Kong Ministerial Declaration, where in paragraph 39 the WTO Director General is asked to redouble his consultative efforts on the issue of 'extension of the protection of geographical indications provided for in Article 23 of the TRIPS Agreement to products other than wines and spirits' (WTO 2005a, paragraph 39).

A more remarkable point of consensus concerns the shared appreciation of the commercial value of GIs which surprisingly goes unnoticed in the plethora of papers focusing on the 'old' world and 'new' world tussle over GIs. In an early submission, Bulgaria, with a group of *demandeurs* (in support of the GI-extension), acknowledged the 'considerable potential for commercial use . . . [as having stimulated] awareness of the need for more efficient protection of geographical indications' (WTO 2000b, paragraph 2). A more nuanced statement on the commercial value of 'distinctiveness' comes from Australia, a country opposing GI-extension (WTO 2000a, p. 2): 'tea is more valuable than undifferentiated bulk tea in the market-place if it is sold as Darjeeling tea, more valuable still if it bears the distinctive certification mark "Darjeeling – The Tea Board's Seal of Approval", and potentially yet more valuable again if it bears a distinctive trademark and is packed in distinctive packaging'. These points of consensus are perplexing only to the extent that one remains wedded to a faith in the rationality of trade negotiations and hopeful that a good argument is all it takes to complete a round of negotiations (Steinberg 2002).

In analysing the hierarchy between Article 22 and Article 23, it might make sense to explicitly state the obvious: there is a hierarchy between the two. This much is clear from the title of Article 23 – 'Additional protection for Geographical Indications for Wines and Spirits'. It would be quite disturbing to imagine the theoretical possibility of no difference, given the political and negotiating capital that has been expended in securing this hierarchy in the Uruguay Round and now in eliminating the hierarchy. The juridical element of the difference arises from the prohibitions on the use of indications for wines and spirits 'even where the true origin of the good is indicated or the geographical indication is used in translation or accompanied by expressions such as 'kind', 'type', 'style', 'imitation' or the like' (Article 23.1). Indications under Article 22 are offered protection against the misleading use of the indication (Article 22.2(a)), deceptive

[26] This compilation was set up on the basis of paragraph 13 of the Ministerial Decision on Implementation-related Issues and Concerns, adopted at Doha on 14 November 2001, WTO document WT/MIN(01)/17.

use (Article 22.4), and use which might be considered unfair competition (Article 22.2(b)).[27] It has been suggested that the difference between the provisions stems from establishing misleading use and acts of unfair competition (Addor and Grazioli 2002; Rangnekar 2003, pp. 25–7). WIPO (2000, paragraph 44) suggests that invoking these doctrines requires the mobilisation of substantial resources and the need arises each and every time that a GI is to be enforced. Lacking the 'higher level of dilution style infringement' protection that wines and spirits benefit from is the shortcoming (Evans and Blakeney 2006, pp. 581–2). There is veracity on this point which also relates to the structural logic of GIs. For an indication to be considered valid it must necessarily be perceived to be so in that jurisdiction; thus, not considered generic (Article 24.6). It is quite possible that certain indications are considered generic in some jurisdictions whilst perceived as valid indications elsewhere and of course in the home jurisdiction. Consequently, as Taubman (2008, pp. 260–65) notes, bilateral bartering has brought sectoral interests to the fore through which stronger protection for old world GIs are traded for more permissive market access for new world producers,[28] thus, precluding the functioning of either the rationality of law or acknowledging the perceptions of consumers.

Does the hierarchy really matter? The answer that is provided here is more normative in its style; though suggesting that the difference matters. The rights that are granted in GIs consist of a collective right to a sign; however, through its logistical immobility there are *de facto* implications of this right in the realm of 'things'. Consequently, the difference between Articles 22 and 23 resides in how close to the 'borders' of the sign 'a competing enterprise's sign can be located without the competing enterprise actually translocating to the identified geography. Under Article 23, to labour the point, the 'borders' to the sign are quite clear and wide: the competing enterprise's sign has to be quite distant to not be considered infringing if it has failed to translocate to the identified geography. Under Article 22, the 'borders' to the sign are permeable as translated and delocalising uses are possible even when translocation by the competing enterprise has not occurred. Now, moving from the world of signage into the world of things,

---

[27] The construction of Section 3 on GIs means that wines and spirits also benefit from this general protection, whilst exclusively benefiting from the 'additional protection'. There are other elements to the hierarchy as well. For instance, provisions for the multilateral register in Article 23.4 are directed exclusively at wines and were later extended to include spirits.

[28] In this context, he draws attention, among other things, to the 2005 US–EU bilateral treaty, which saw the upgrading of the legal status of 17 semi-generic indications into full GIs.

the issue relates to the integrity of signs as channels of information and by extension how 'things' are marked by signs. When 'things' from elsewhere start bearing confusingly similar signs, we are moving into a 'market for lemons' scenario, where quality will be compromised.

Take the market for teas as an example.[29] As noted in the previously cited submission by Australia, the market can be differentiated into a number of segments. At one level, this occurs on the basis of the type of leaf (for example, black, oolong, green and white), but it also occurs on the basis of blends (for example, English breakfast) and additives (for example, Jasmine, Earl Grey). All this apart, tea is also sold by indications of origin (for example, Darjeeling, Longjin, Ceylon), brand names of packing and blending companies (for example, Twining, Brooke Bond, Tata Tea), and retailers' own-brand (for example, Tesco, Sainsbury). Tea also bears a variety of socially generated signs indicating conditions of origin (for example, fair trade and organic). No doubt, there are examples of teas with a range of these overlapping signs.[30] Another way of putting the point is that the market for teas is substantially distributed across a number of overlapping but also separate segments – based on both characteristics and price.[31] More significantly, the collectivity of GIs means that a number of different enterprises are able to (legitimately) display the Darjeeling logo. The exclusivity is really not that exclusive and competition pretty stiff.

Competitive pressures on commodities like tea are quite compelling (Oxfam 2002). While there is no single indicative price for tea, the FAO composite international tea price has registered a decrease of over 20 per cent between 1980 and the 1990s (Intergovernmental Group on Tea 2006). A number of interrelated factors have been identified: growing export-entry of new producers (Indonesia, Vietnam, Kenya, etc.), some large exporters with minimal domestic uptake (for example, Kenya), changing consumption patterns, and stagnating demand in some key markets (for example, Russia). A continuing concern is the growing accumulation of

---

[29] The discussion on Darjeeling tea in the following paragraphs is based on Rangnekar (2009).

[30] An example that this author cherishes is the worker's cooperative EqualExchange's Organic Darjeeling Leaf Tea (http://www.equalexchange.co.uk/products/product.asp?id=70&pn=Darjeeling%20Leaf%20Tea; last visited 5 April 2009), carrying the Darjeeling GI logo, which is certified organic, and bears the World Fair Trade Organization's (IFAT) label as well.

[31] Without complicating the scenario further, it is possible to consider a bigger aggregation: the market for caffeine-based beverages and thus include coffee!

market/economic power at particular points of the supply chain by blending/packing companies, auctioneers and retailers. A World Bank study of the 1990s estimates that a mere seven transnational corporations (TNCs) control over 90 per cent of the tea market in the West (cited in Oxfam 2002). As Das (2003, p. 7) comments: 'Except for "single-estate" teas, Darjeeling tea is sold under the brand name of the foreign blender/packer'. Indicative of this accumulation of economic power towards the retail end is how the price of tea is distributed across the supply chain. One estimate is that roughly 3 per cent of the price returns to the labourer, while 15 per cent is accounted for by the plantation and factory work, and 80 per cent is absorbed by exporters, traders, blenders and retailers (Oxfam 2002).

Trade journals report that around 40000 tonnes of tea is sold as 'Darjeeling', while domestic data in India accounts for 10000 tonnes of Darjeeling tea. Surely, someone somewhere is selling something else. Starting in the 1980s, the Tea Board has sought to register its rights in Darjeeling, developing a logo in 1983 and registering it domestically and in a number of overseas jurisdictions (such as the UK, USA, Canada, Japan, Egypt and a number of European countries). With over 70 per cent of Darjeeling tea production being exported, the latter is an imperative. Domestic protection was initially through the Trade and Merchandise Mark Act, 1958, which led to protection of the 'logo' and the word 'Darjeeling'. However, with the enactment of the Geographical Indications of Goods (Registration and Protection) Act, 1999, it became possible to directly protect Geographical Indications in India and Darjeeling tea was registered in October 2004 as the first domestic GI. Various overseas registrations have been acquired, which includes certification mark no. 1632726 for the Darjeeling logo in the US, certification marks 1307518 (for the Darjeeling logo) and 2162741 (for Darjeeling word) in the UK, among others. Efforts to enforce IPRs in Darjeeling tea can be broadly categorised into two groups: (a) preventing trade in tea which is not drawn from licensed plantations or those teas which are blends of non-Darjeeling and Darjeeling teas to sell under the name and/or logo of Darjeeling and (b) action against registration or use of the term/logo Darjeeling with respect to tea and/or any other product. In 1998, the Tea Board hired an international watch agency, the Belgium-based Compumark, and retained Denton Wilde Sapte, a leading UK law firm, to help with the administration of the Darjeeling certification system worldwide. A number of actions have been initiated in the following countries: Bahrain, Belarus, Bangladesh, Canada, Estonia, France, Germany, Israel, Japan, Kuwait, Latvia, Lebanon, Lithuania, Norway, Oman, Russia, Sri Lanka, Taiwan, the UK and the USA. These include several instances of misuse and attempted registrations, domain name cancellations, and other third-party misuses of Darjeeling. In India itself, over 20 legal notices have been served and 15 oppositions have been filed. These efforts at enforcing rights do not come cheaply: in four years (1998–2002), the Tea Board spent US$200 000 on legal and registration fees and fighting infringements in overseas jurisdictions.[32] At the time of research (2007), many of the cases were still pending and where completed, the results have been mixed.

While not yet protected in any of the home jurisdiction, the problems faced by Basmati are more telling.[33] To the relevant and knowing public, Basmati is distinguished by the grain's tall and slender shape, tapering at both ends but not bulging at the belly, its distinct aroma, the chalkiness of the grain and the grain's distinct elongation on cooking. In a number of export markets, the use of the term Basmati is exclusively reserved for particular long-grain aromatic rice from certain areas of India and Pakistan. This is the case for Saudi Arabia (Bhattacharjee et al. 2002) and there is a particular testing-based system in the EU and the UK. This contrasts with the US, where Basmati (and Thai Jasmine rice) are treated as special varieties of rice (*Oryza sativa* L. scented) of no particular geographical origin (see General Regulations and Standards for Certain Agricultural Commodities, § 868.213). This classification withstood a petition filed by a coalition of civil society organisations at the US Federal Trade Commission (USFTC) and the US Department of Agriculture (USDA).[34] Thus, RiceTec – the company behind the failed patent application – has been able to domestically brand and sell a number of rice varieties with the names of Kasmati™ and Texmati™. An Internet search identifies product imagery and brand names with translated use of Basmati that evoke an association with India or Pakistan.[35] Building on an association between

---

[32] The funds come from, among other government sources, the Darjeeling Planters' Association, which has set up a dedicated 'Promotion and Protection Fund' (Rao, 2003).

[33] The narration on Basmati is based on Rangnekar and Kumar (forthcoming), where the discussion extends beyond the issue of translated use and genericity to also map out the framework for a transborder system to protect Basmati. No doubt, the challenges facing India and Pakistan if they were to collectively act on Basmati on their own are formidable.

[34] The petitions were broader in requesting similar clarification for the term 'Jasmine'. Petitions are on file with the authors.

[35] The translated use of Basmati appears to be a constant refrain in the naming of brands or varieties in the US. In addition to the examples of RiceTec's brands (discussed below), consider Calmati, a variety released by the California Rice Research Board in 1999, which is advertised as 'California's first, early, basmati [sic] type, aromatic, long-grain variety' that will 'permit grower entry into this market [and] compete in the market with basmati [sic] rice currently

the product and South Asia is part of a deliberate strategy to capitalise on the reputation of Basmati.[36] The government of India raised these issues while challenging a series of trademarks acquired by RiceTec in the UK: Texmati™ and Kasmati™ (Nair and Kumar 2005, pp. 179–84). In challenging the Texmati™ trademark, it put together a 'mosaic of evidence' that included affidavits from culinary experts and from the London Rice Brokers. RiceTec surrendered its trademark (Ibid., p. 180). The Kasmati™ trademark is more telling, as the packaging of the rice includes a caricature of the Taj Mahal and uses the phrase 'Indian-Style Basmati'.[37] Again, RiceTec opted not to contest the challenge, thus, surrendering the registration and denying the possibility of a ruling. It is not easy to predict how a US court would respond to similar evidence; however, the generic status of Basmati is presently confined to that jurisdiction only.

Returning to the hierarchy between Articles 22 and 23, the issue is of location – both in the space of signs and the space of geography. Recalling the 'logistical immobility' of GIs, any attempt to use the sign raises an obligation to adhere to the informational content of the indication. This establishes an obligation to 'locate' in the indicated geography – to the extent that the specifications require certain production processes to occur in that geography. Permitting translated uses without an obligation to translocate is the crux of the hierarchy. The examples from Darjeeling and Basmati bear on this analysis – though the problem of enforcing GIs in each instance is part of a larger problem.

Conclusion

The chapter presents another sketch on GIs by bringing together the literatures on the economics of information and distinctive signs with contributions from anthropology and geography. It considers the construction of GIs and suggests an approach that appreciates its historicity and the manner in which locational specificity has emerged. This, I argue, is

---

imported from India and Pakistan' (<http://www.carrb.com/Variety/CM-201.htm>; accessed in August 2008).

[36] There is a particular construction to this labelling practice that emerges from the ECJ decision on Feta (discussed in Rangnekar and Kumar, forthcoming). In retaining Feta's GI status, the Commission argued that 'adding text or drawings with a marked Greek connotation' is 'deliberately suggested and sought as part of a sales strategy that capitalises on the reputation of the original product . . . [which] creates a real risk of consumer confusion'. In agreeing with this view, the court observed that '[T]he Danish legislation does not refer to "feta" but to "Danish feta", which would tend to suggest that in Denmark the name "feta", by itself, has retained a Greek connotation'.

[37] For the curious, a picture is reproduced in Nair and Kumar (2005, p. 181).

reflected in the construction of the rights in GIs being embedded in place: locational immobility. Thus, the GI-extension debate concerns issues of how signs and place are reconstituted; in a sense, asking how close to a sign can another sign be located without necessarily locating in the identified geography?

It is remarkable that *demandeurs* and detractors of GI-extension agree that there is neither a juridical basis for nor rationality in the differential treatment of wines and spirits and other products. Despite this agreement, there is no consensus on how to resolve the issue. The resolution itself is, not surprisingly, embroiled in the trading of interests and obligations that configure multilateral trade negotiations. The experience of Basmati and Darjeeling, briefly narrated here, indicates the problems faced by producers seeking to enforce their GIs elsewhere. This is symptomatic of a deeper set of inequities in the global trade and legal regime. The growth of a series of socially generated appellations indicating conditions of origin seek to speak to some of these inequities. Thus, removing the hierarchy might also be a step in that direction.

References

Addor, F. and A. Grazioli (2002), 'Geographical indications beyond wines and spirits: a roadmap for a better protection for geographical indications in the WTO TRIPS Agreement', *Journal of World Intellectual Property*, **5**(6), 865–97.

Akerlof, A.G. (1970), 'The market for lemons: quality, uncertainty and the market mechanism', *Quarterly Journal of Economics*, **84** (August), 488–500.

Barham, Elizabeth (2003), 'Translating *terroir*: the global challenge of French AOC labeling', *Journal of Rural Studies*, **19**(1), 127–38.

Bérard, L. and P. Marchenay (1996), 'Tradition, regulation and intellectual property: local agricultural products and foodstuffs in France' in S.B. Brush and D. Stabinsky (eds), *Valuing Local Knowledge: Indigenous Peoples and Intellectual Property Rights*, Covelo, CA: Island Press, 230–43.

Bhattacharjee, P., Singhal, R.S. and Kulkarni, P.R. (2002), 'Basmati rice: a review', *International Journal of Food Science and Technology*, **37**, 1–12.

Blakeney, M. (2001), 'Proposals for the international regulation of geographical indications', *Journal of World Intellectual Property*, **4**(5), 629–52.

Caenegem, William van (2003), 'Registered geographical indications: between intellectual property and rural policy: Part I', *Journal of World Intellectual Property*, **6**(5), 699–719.

Chamberlin, E. (1969), *The Theory of Monopolistic Competition*, Cambridge, MA: Harvard University Press.

Coombe, Rosemary (1998), *The Cultural Life of Intellectual Properties: Authorship, Appropriation, and the Law*, Durham, NC and London: Duke University Press.

Cornish, W.R. (1999), *Intellectual Property: Patents, Copyright, Trade Marks, and Allied Rights*, London: Sweet & Maxwell.

Cratchley, Liz (2000), 'The brand owner's view', in Norma Dawson and Alison Firth (eds), *Trade Marks Perspective*, London: Sweet & Maxwell.

Darby, M. and E. Karni (1973), 'Free competition and the optimal amount of fraud', *Journal of Law and Economics*, (16), 67-88.

Das, Naba Kumar (2003), *Geographical Indications: The Experience of Indian Tea Producers – Protection of Darjeeling Tea*. Paper for Worldwide Symposium on Geographical

Indications, WIPO and USPTO, San Francisco, California, 9–11 July-WIPO/GEO/SFO/03/8. Available at http://www.wipo.int

Economides, Nicholas S. (1988), 'The economics of trademarks', *Trademark Reporter*, **78**, 523–39.

Escudero, S. (2001), *International protection of geographical indications and developing countries*, TRADE working papers no. 10, Geneva: South Centre. Available at: http://www.southcentre.org.

Evans, G.E. and Blakeney, M. (2006), 'The protection of geographical indications after Doha: Quo vadis?' *Journal of International Economic Law*, **9**(3), 575–614.

Gangjee, D. (2007) 'Quibbling siblings: conflicts between trademarks and geographical indications', *Chicago-Kent Law Review*, **82**(3), 1253–91.

Gervais, D. (1998), *The TRIPS Agreement: Drafting History and Analysis*, London, UK: Sweet & Maxwell.

Grossman, Gene M. and Carl Shapiro (1988a), 'Counterfeit-product trade', *American Economic Review*, **78**(1), 59–75.

Grossman, Gene M. and Carl Shapiro, (1988b), 'Foreign counterfeiting of status goods', *Quarterly Journal of Economics*, **103**(1), 79–100.

Intergovernmental Group on Tea (2006), *Policy Developments in the World Tea Market: Economic Impact of Maximum Residue Levels and ISO 3720 Quality Standards*, FAO's Committee on Commodity Problems, 17th Session, Nairobi, Kenya 29 November–1 December 2006, Doc. No. CCP:TE 06/5.

Kamath, S., Charles, Stephen J.K., Suresh, S., Barai, B.K., Sahoo, A.K., Radhika Reddy, K. and Bhattacharya, K.R. (2008), 'Basmati rice: its characteristics and identification', *Journal of the Science of Food and Agriculture*, **88**, 1821–31.

Kerr, Rachel (2005), 'Last orders for landmark brewery', *BBC News*, 27 May, available at http://news.bbc.co.uk/1/hi/england/tyne/4580171.stm (accessed 24 March 2009).

Ladas, S.P. (1975), *Patents, Trademarks and Related Rights: National and International Protection*, Cambridge, MA: Harvard University Press.

Laddie, H. (1996), 'Copyright: over-strength, over-regulated, over-rated', *European Intellectual Property Review*, **18**(5), 253–60.

Landes, William M. and Richard A. Posner (1987), 'Trademark law: an economic perspective', *Journal of Law and Economics*, **30**(2), 265–309.

Landes, William M. and Richard A. Posner (2003), *The Economic Structure of Intellectual Property Law*, Cambridge, MA: Harvard University Press.

Maher, M. (2001), 'On vino veritas? clarifying the use of geographic references on American wine labels', *California Law Review*, **89**(6), 1881–926.

Moran, W. (1993), 'Rural Space as intellectual property', *Political Geography*, **12**(3), 263–77.

Nair, L. and Kumar, R. (2005), *Geographical Indications: A Search for Identity*, New Delhi: LexisNexis Butterworths.

Nelson, P. (1970), 'Information and consumer behaviour', *Journal of Political Economy*, **78**(2), 311–29.

Oxfam (2002), 'The Tea Market – a Background Study', Oxfam, available at http://www.maketradefair.com/en/index.php?file=15052002135027.htm.

Ploeg, Jan Douwe van der (1992), 'The reconstitution of locality: technology and labour in modern agriculture', in T. Marsden, P. Lowe and S. Whatmore (eds), *Labour and Locality: Uneven Development and the Rural Labour Process*, London: David Fulton Publishers, 19–43.

Rangnekar, D. (2003), *Geographical Indications: A Review of Proposals at the TRIPs Council – Extending Article 23 to Products other than Wines and Spirits*, UNCTAD-ICTSD Capacity Building Project on IPRs and Sustainable Development, Geneva, Issue Paper No. 4, available at: http://www.ictsd.org/iprsonline/unctadictsd/description.htm.

Rangnekar, D. (2004), *The Socio-Economics of Geographical Indications: A Review of Empirical Evidence from Europe*, UNCTAD-ICTSD Capacity Building Project on IPRs and Sustainable Development, Geneva, Issue Paper No. 8, available at http://www.ictsd.org/iprsonline/unctadictsd/description.htm.

Rangnekar, D. (2009), 'The use and application of geographical indications: the case of Darjeeling tea', in Daniele Giovannucci, Tim Josling, William Kerr, Bernard O'Connor and May Yeung (eds), *Geographical Indications: A Guide to Global Best Practices for Developing Renowned Origins*, Geneva: International Trade Centre.
Rangnekar, D. and S. Kumar (forthcoming), 'Another look at Basmati: genericity and the problems of a transborder geographical indication', *Journal of World Intellectual Property*.
Rao, Niranjan (2003), 'Geographical indications in Indian context: a case study of Darjeeling Tea', Working Paper No. 110, ICRIER, New Delhi.
Raustiala, Kal and Stephen R. Munzer (2007), 'The global struggle over geographic indications', *The European Journal on International Law*, **18**(2), 337–65.
Rose, Carol M. (1986), 'The comedy of the commons: commerce, custom and inherently public property', *University of Chicago Law Review*, **711**, reprinted as chapter 5 in: Rose, Carol M. (1994), *Property and Persuasion: Essays on the History, Theory and Rhetoric of Ownership*, Boulder, CO: Westview Press.
Sack, Robert D. (1983), 'Human territoriality: a theory', *Annals of the Association of American Geographers*, **73**(1), 55–74.
Schechter, F. (1925), *The Historical Foundations of the Law Relating to Trademarks*, New York: Columbia University Press.
Schechter, F. (1927), 'The rationale of trademark protection', *Harvard Law Review* **40**(6), 813–33.
Scherer, F.M. and D. Ross (1990), *Industrial Market Structure and Economic Performance*, 3rd edition, Boston: Houghton Mifflin Company.
Schmalensee, R. (1979), 'On the use of economic models in antitrust: the Realemon case', *University of Pennsylvania Law Review*, **127**(4), 994–1050.
Shapiro, C. (1982), 'Consumer information, product quality and seller reputation', *Bell Journal of Economics*, **13**(1), 20–35.
Silva, Mark (2005), 'Sour grapes: the compromising effect of the United States' failure to protect foreign geographic indications of wines', *Boston College International & Comparative Law Review*, **28**(1), 197–211.
Spooner, B. (1988), 'Weavers and dealers: the authenticity of an oriental carpet', in A. Appadurai (ed.), *The Social Life of Things: Commodities in Cultural Perspective*, New York: Cambridge University Press, 195–235.
Steinberg, R.H. (2002), 'In the shadow of law or power? Consensus-based bargaining and outcomes in the GATT/WTO', *International Organization*, **56**(2), 339–74.
Stern, S. (2007), 'Are GIs IP?', *European Intellectual Property Review*, **29**(2), 39–42.
Stigler, G.J. (1961), 'The economics of information', *Journal of Political Economy*, **69**, 213–25; reprinted in D. Lamberton (ed.) (1970), *The Economics of Information*, London: Penguin.
Taubman, A. (2008), 'Thinking locally, acting globally: how trade negotiations over geographical indications improvise 'fair trade' rules', *Intellectual Property Quarterly*, **3**, 231–67.
Torre, A. (2006), 'Collective action, governance structure and organizational trust in localized systems of production: The case of the AOC organization of small producers', Entrepreneurship & Regional Development, 18(1), 55–72.
Vivas-Eugui, David and María Julia Oliva (2010), 'The WTO dispute on trademarks and geographical indications: some implications for trade policy-making and negotiations', in Carlos, M. Correa (ed.), *Research Handbook on the Interpretation and Enforcement of Intellectual Property under WTO Rules: Intellectual Property in the WTO Volume 11*, Cheltenham, UK and Northampton, MA, US: Edward Elgar.
WIPO (2000), 'Possible solutions for conflicts between trademarks and geographical indications and for conflicts between homonymous geographical indications', Standing committee on the law of trademarks, industrial designs and geographical indications, 5th session, September 11–15, SCT/5/3.
WIPO (2002), 'What is geographical indications?', available at http://www.wipo.int/about-ip/en/index.htrademarkl (accessed 4 February 2002).

WTO (2000a), Geographical indications, article 24.2 review of the application of part II, section 3: some background issues. Communication from Australia. IP/C/W/211, 19 October 2000.
WTO (2000b), Work on issues relevant for the protection of geographical indications. Communication from Bulgaria, the Czech Republic, Iceland, India, Liechtenstein, Slovenia, Sri Lanka, Switzerland and Turkey. WTO Doc. No. IP/C/W/204, 2 October 2000.
WTO (2001), Extension of the protection of geographical indications for wines and spirits to geographical indications for all products: potential costs and implications. Communication from Argentina, Australia, Canada, Chile, Guatemala, New Zealand, Paraguay and the United States. WTO Doc. No. IP/C/W/289, 2 October 2001.
WTO (2002), Implications of Article 23 Extension. Communication from Argentina, Australia, Canada, Chile, the Dominican Republic, El Salvador, Guatemala, New Zealand, Paraguay, the Philippines, Chinese Taipei and the United States. WTO Doc. No. IP/C/W/386, 8 November 2002.
WTO (2005a), Doha work programme: Ministerial Declaration, adopted on 18 December 2005, WTO Doc. No. WT/MIN(05)/DEC, 22 December 2005.
WTO (2005b), Issues related to the extension of the protection of geographical indications provided for in article 23 of the TRIPS agreement to products other than wines and spirits. Compilation of Issues Raised and Views Expressed: Note by the Secretariat, WTO Doc. No. WT/GC/W/546, 18 May 2005.

16 Exploring the flexibilities of TRIPS to promote biotechnology in developing countries[1]

Graham Dutfield, Lois Muraguri and Florian Leverve

1. Introduction

The aim of this chapter is to provide some guidance on how to design patent rules that are optimal – within the confines of what the Trade-related Aspects of Intellectual Property Rights (TRIPS) Agreement allows – in terms of enabling developing countries to participate in the much-heralded 'biotechnology revolution' and to thereby benefit their economies and populaces. It finds that totally reliable guidance is not available from any available source. Nonetheless, evidence is available to offer some general rules of thumb for avoiding patent rule-making that would *not* benefit developing world economies and populaces in the ambit of biotechnology.

According to TRIPS Article 27.1, 'patents shall be available for any inventions, whether products or processes, in all fields of technology, provided that they are new, involve an inventive step and are capable of industrial application'. Since biotechnology is obviously a field of technology, it is not possible to keep biotechnology out of the patent system altogether, whether or not to do so would be deemed as desirable. Nonetheless, it is important to understand that biotechnology is covered in the context of *exclusions* from patentability. Thus, Article 27.3(b) permits World Trade Organization (WTO) Members to exclude from patentability:

> plants and animals other than micro-organisms, and essentially biological processes for the production of plants or animals other than non-biological and microbiological processes. However, Members shall provide for the protection of plant varieties either by patents or by an effective *sui generis* system or by any

[1] This chapter is an edited version of a report produced with the support of the European Commission's sixth Framework Programme for Research as part of the project 'Impacts of the IPR Rules on Sustainable Development' (IPDEV). It does not represent the views of the European Commission, the European Union or of its Member States.

combination thereof. The provisions of this subparagraph shall be reviewed four years after the date of entry into force of the WTO Agreement.

In essence, two types of flexibility exist in Article 27.3(b).[2] These are (i) the optional subject-matter exceptions, and (ii) the possibility to define the terms in a variety of ways. Clearly, the language of this provision is complicated. But it is also subject to a wide range of interpretations, a situation that allows policy-makers to implement TRIPS in a very large number of possible ways.

The challenges that subsequently arise are threefold. The first challenge is to identify all possible ways that Article 27.3(b) can be interpreted. The second is to identify the goals that governments wish to use their biotech-related patent rules to further. This must surely be based upon assessments of the present biotech capacity of the country in question and of its future potential and realistic ambitions. The third is for government policymakers on the basis of such an assessment and a decision on the goals it wishes to pursue, to select from our 'interpretational menu', as presented in our final section, the optimal patent rules available under Article 27.3(b).

There is little doubt that countries will meet these challenges in a variety of ways. This should not surprise us. Developing countries, least developing countries and the former socialist nations together represent an enormous diversity in terms of socio-economic conditions, levels of development, and potential. Consequently, accommodation of such diversity has to be built into a study of this kind.

A few clarifications and disclaimers are in order. First, patents are one among several legal and policy measures to promote local innovation and technology transfer and may not be the most important. Second, patent subject matter scope choices are not the only way to balance the interests of all stakeholders and secure the best interests of the public. Patent systems should strike a balance so that the economic rights of inventors are sufficient to encourage invention, innovation and the dissemination of useful technical information, but not so excessive as to unduly hinder competition, stifle follow-on invention, or harm the public. Various measures are available to ensure that this balance is struck as optimally as possible. These may include:

(1) Subject-matter exceptions, such as those that may be applied to drugs, software programs, business methods, plants and animals, whether or not the standard patentability criteria can be met

---

2 More general flexibilities exist within TRIPS, but we do not discuss these.

(2) Limitations to rights, such as compulsory licensing, government use provisions, research exemption and the 'bolar' (regulatory review) exemption
(3) The patent examination, which is supposed to ensure that what is disclosed is enabling, and what is claimed does not extend beyond what is disclosed
(4) Local working requirements
(5) Pre- and post-grant opposition procedures
(6) Morality/*ordre public* objections
(7) Competition law

This chapter only deals with the first of these. This might seem to make the study rather limited in terms of what it can achieve. However, biotech patenting subject-matter flexibility is extremely broad in TRIPS and since implementation of this part of TRIPS continues to be under review at the TRIPS Council, producing evidence-based policy guidance as to how developing countries may take advantage of the flexibilities is both necessary and timely, if not long overdue.

One might add here that the existence, quality and size of the wider legal infrastructure, including patent practitioners, trained examiners, and well-functioning courts, is essential to make any patent system work. A balanced patent system in theory cannot become an optimal patent system in practice without these. But dealing with this issue falls beyond the scope of the study.

Third, this study takes no position on specific biotechnological applications that some might endorse, while others would deem them to be dangerous, immoral or otherwise inappropriate. Neither does it insist that countries should prioritise biotechnology-related research and development over other fields of technology or industrial sectors. But we do accept that biotechnology has lots of potential and ought to be promoted, and that in any case WTO members are required to make patents available for at least some biotechnological inventions. Nonetheless, we do not take it as axiomatic that what is good for the domestic biotechnology industry is necessarily good for the public.

2. Determining the biotechnological capacities and patent interests of countries

Undoubtedly, developing countries vary considerably according to the capacity of their research institutions and businesses to put the new biotechnologies to work and generate innovations of their own. Measuring biotechnology capabilities is important for a variety of reasons. For the purposes of the present study, two of these stand out: first, it is undisputed that if developing countries are to prosper, they must build the capacity to take advantage of new and emerging technologies such as biotechnology. Second, understanding what biotech capabilities exist in a given country will be instructive in designing appropriate systems and institutions that bolster domestic innovation and encourage technology transfer. These twin reasons form the foundation for this enquiry. Of course, to determine the biotechnological capacities, one needs to select workable criteria and indicators.

One can envisage a potentially useful schema for different developing countries based on (i) indicators of biotechnological activity derived *inter alia* from levels of research and development financed by productive enterprises and patenting activity, (ii) industrial performance, (iii) absorptive and innovation capacities, and (iv) biotechnology product, service and royalty and licence-fee trade balances. But we are sceptical about the quantitative methods available. We could discuss a number of these, but space limitations permit us to cover just one: patent counts, perhaps the most often cited method of measuring technological capacity in both developing and developed countries.

Although patents may seem like the most straightforward and obvious indicators of technological capacity, their use is fraught with complexity and difficulty. A study conducted in 2000 by Thompson on rankings of the most innovative companies by patent filings highlighted the difficulties in using patents as a measure of technological capacity. Foremost is the question of what patent database to use. The study accentuated that different results are obtainable depending on the patenting authority used.[3] The difficulty in applying patent statistics to rank companies is indicative of the more arduous task when the subject sample shifts from relatively straightforward organisations, such as companies, to countries. The problem is further compounded when comparing countries, especially if they happen to be at different stages of development.

The temptation to use domestic statistics when comparing patenting activity in countries is understandable. The danger is that lack of homogeneity among different national patent legislation, procedures and practice will render results inaccurate. Use of an international patent system

---

[3] See Thomson (2000) 'Rankings of the most innovative companies by patent filings'. IBM was the top company when statistics from the United States Patent and Trademark Office (USPTO) were used, while it did not feature when the Patent Corporation Treaty (PCT) and the Japan Patent Office (JPO) were used, where Siemens and Toshiba were top respectively. Siemens was top company according to European Patent Office (EPO) statistics while IBM was ninth and Toshiba did not feature in the top ten.

is generally considered more consistent over time and location.[4] Some studies have used both national and international patent systems in comparative innovative capacity studies.[5] The choice of international patent system brings us back to the initial problem. The use of a single international patent system assumes that, first, the system is equally accessible to all the target study countries; second, that fees and procedures affect everyone equally; and third that the target countries are equally keen to use the selected international patent system.

The United States Patent and Trademark Office's (USPTO's) patent statistics have been used in many studies to measure foreign countries' technological capacity.[6] For Porter and Stern, the justification is that the use of USPTO is a sign of an innovation's potential economic value, given the high costs of patenting as well as providing a high standard of technical excellence. The downside of using the USPTO is that foreign individual investors and small firms are less likely to patent abroad, especially in the US.

The World Intellectual Property Organization (WIPO) administered Patent Cooperation Treaty (PCT) system is more suitable when comparing developing countries' technological capacity. The European Patent Office (EPO) is also a candidate, but given that many applications passing through the latter are initially made through the former, using the PCT system seems easier to use for comparisons among developing countries. The assumption is that of all the international patent systems, individuals, small firms and companies in developing countries are most likely to apply for patents through the PCT system, not least because it is accessible in terms of both costs and procedure. The downside is that the system is only available to PCT members. In our case, all the study countries are PCT members, therefore this does not present a problem as such. It has also been said of the PCT system that it is biased towards high technology

---

4 Earlier work comparing inventive activity using international systems includes Dosi, G., K. Pavitt and L. Soete (1990) *The Economics of Technical Change and International Trade*. New York: New York University. See also Eaton, J. and S. Kortum (1996) 'Trade in ideas: patenting and productivity in the OECD'. *Journal of International Economics,* 40(3–4) 251–78.

5 See, for example, Porter, M.E. and Stern S. (2001) 'National innovative capacity', in World Economic Forum, *The Global Competitiveness Report 2001–2002*, New York, Oxford University Press.

6 See Pouris A. (1991) 'Identifying areas of strength in South African Technology'. *Scientometrics*, 21(1) 23–35 for a study on South Africa; Bergeron, S., Lallich, S. and C. Le Bas (1998) 'Location of innovating activities, industrial structure and techno-industrial clusters in the French economy, 1985–1990'. *Research Policy*, April 1998 on France and more recently, Porter and Stern *supra.*

industries; being concerned with biotechnology, this is not a problem for the purpose of this study. Another drawback of the PCT system is that many applications may not be new as the assessment of novelty is only made at the grant stage (although, since 2004 the IPER, International Preliminary Examination Report, has been in place). This presents the related problem of whether the statistics to use are the number of patent applications or the number of patents granted, in which case using the PCT system would be irrelevant given that the PCT system does not grant patents as such. Related to this and to the use of patent statistics generally is that not all inventions are patented and some forms of creativity, particularly in developing countries, are not patented.[7] Further, some patents are considered more valuable and important than others, leading studies such as that of Bosworth, Filiou and Longland[8] into developing weightings to rank inventions.

Another approach is that of the triadic patent family. This entails the counting of those groups of patents on the same invention that are granted by three patent-granting offices, usually the USPTO, the European Patent Office and the Japan Patent Office, which are of course the most important ones. According to Chow et al.: 'the triadic family concept aims to provide for an ever-increasing need for reliable patent statistics and high quality indicators in measuring the performance of the various nations on a comparable basis. The triadic family patent measurement is proposed on the basis that counting patents filed at different offices eliminates the problem of home bias and of ensuring that only high value added innovation should be the basis for comparison'.[9] After all, for businesses to go to the effort and expense of filing patent applications in all three offices on the same inventions, these must presumably be deemed as non-trivial inventions (to say the least).

It is clear from the foregoing discussion that relying on patent statistics alone as a measure of countries' technological capabilities is dangerous and would not yield any meaningful or accurate results. Primarily because of this, various complementary or alternative indices have been developed,

---

[7] See Jewkes, J., Sawers, D. and Stillerman, R. (1969) *The Sources of Invention*, 2nd ed., London: Macmillan, who gives various reasons why patent statistics are difficult to use (pp. 89–90).

[8] Bosworth, D., D. Filiou and M. Longland (2003) 'Measuring the "Quality" of Patents', London: UK Patent Office.

[9] Chow, K.B., K.M. Leo and S. Leong (2007) 'Singapore'. In U. Suthersanen, G. Dutfield and K.B. Boey (2007) *Innovation without Patents: Harnessing the Creative Spirit in a Diverse World.* Cheltenham, UK and Northampton, MA, USA: Edward Elgar.

but we submit that none is totally reliable. A country's technological capability is composed of a variety of sources of knowledge and innovation and is larger and more complex than any index can so far encapsulate. Many aspects of innovation are difficult to quantify and even if quantifiable, there is always the problem of lack of reliable data, particularly in developing countries. Important technology innovations in the informal sector may not be recorded and are therefore difficult to take into account in the formulation of an index, the components of which are, by their nature, definite values.

What of biotechnology? There has been significant change in biotech R&D in the past two decades. Private sector involvement in agriculture and health, both in R&D and in product and service delivery, has become more entrenched. The role of the state has similarly changed, with implications for research and delivery of research products. Above all, globalisation of knowledge, markets, regulatory and trade regimes has had pervasive implications for agriculture and health.

Hall writes that the emergence of biotechnology is evidence of the change in the broader framework conditions under which science and technology takes place. He identifies the critical features of biotechnology to include technological paradigm shifts, institutional changes, including a greater degree of ownership of knowledge and new patterns of partnerships, and science and society controversies surrounding ethical, environmental and health risks.[10]

An effort to measure biotechnology capabilities would have to take into account these defining features. Biotechnology often has high R&D content and therefore traditional input and output indicators will be our starting point. An assessment of governance issues – laws and policies – will be crucial in understanding the environment under which innovation in biotechnology flourishes. An attempt will be made to explore the synergy between organisations.

Unlike most of the composite indices discussed above, this study's approach is primarily qualitative rather than quantitative. Given the range and complexity of the data to be collected, we found it best to opt for a case study approach. We chose three developing countries where biotechnology activity takes place, albeit on varying scales of intensity, and that may be representative of other developing countries whose capacities are roughly similar. These are South Africa, Kenya and India.

---

[10] Hall, A. (2005) 'Capacity development for agricultural biotechnology in developing countries: an innovation systems view of what it is and how to develop it'. *Journal of International Development*, 17, 611–30.

3. Estimating the development-related patent interests of countries on the basis of levels of development

According to Lall, there is evidence that 'the need for IPRs varies with the level of development'. He then goes on to say that:

> Many rich countries used weak IPR protection in their early stages of industrialisation to develop local technological bases, increasing protection as they approached the leaders. Econometric cross-section evidence suggests that there is an inverted-U shaped relationship between the strength of IPRs and income levels. The intensity of IPRs first falls with rising incomes, as countries move to slack IPRs to build local capabilities by copying, then rises as they engage in more innovative effort. The turning point is $7,750 per capita in 1985 prices . . ., a fairly high level of income for the developing world.[11]

Of course, it is one thing to say that relatively advanced developing countries have preferred to weaken their intellectual property rights in order to advance their capacities to innovate through imitation-derived technological learning. It is quite another thing to assume that such a policy works just because many governments have favoured it. Nonetheless, intuitively it makes a lot of sense.

Let us then make four working assumptions to be tested in this study. Before doing so, we introduce a caveat. This is that we do not accept that the optimal patent scope[12] in terms of subject matter relates directly to indicators of income and output, such as gross national product (GNP). Optimal patent scope is more likely to be related to the capacities to absorb technological knowledge, to learn and to innovate.

The first assumption is that least-developed countries that are inactive in the field of biotechnology would benefit most from keeping as much biotechnological invention out of the patent system, assuming conveniently that the fees acquired through the processing of biotechnology patent applications are insufficient to cover the costs of examining patents and making them enforceable through the court system. Second, low-middle income developing countries may find it beneficial to expand the extent to which biotechnology inventions are patentable so as to encourage investment and technology transfer. Such inventions might

---

[11] Lall, S. with M. Albaladejo (2003) 'Indicators of the relative importance of IPRs in developing countries'. Issues Paper no. 3, UNCTAD-ICTSD Project on Intellectual Property Rights and Sustainable Development, Geneva. (Citing K.E. Maskus, *Intellectual Property Rights in the Global Economy*, Washington, DC: Institute for International Economics (2000), at pp. 95–6.)

[12] To clarify patent scope in this context does not relate to the breadth of individual patents, but to the extent of subject-matter limitations.

in many cases be difficult to copy anyway. However, they may wish to introduce certain limitations to the rights, such as a fairly broad research exemption so that emerging local firms may be able to do some imitation without fear of litigation. Third, high income and technologically advanced developing countries with a much higher capacity to imitate would benefit from reducing the extent to which biotech inventions are patentable, since the advantages of such imitation would compensate for any losses in terms of reduced investment and technology transfer. Fourth, as developing countries join the ranks of developed countries, they become sufficiently innovative that they will find it advantageous to again extend the scope of biotech patenting in line with developed world standards.

4. South Africa

South Africa has a well-developed economic and commercial sector which has been largely based on natural resources. The resources available for biotech in South Africa are limited, with the proportion of the national budget directed towards biotech much lower than in developed countries. South Africa has firmly established national priorities for utilisation of available resources, resulting in strong government influence on research direction. The government has adopted biotech as one of the areas in which to focus its research support.

Biotech in South Africa has until recently focused mainly on first-generation applications, such as those in the food industry. There are well-developed industries involved in brewing and food production, including a successful wine industry. More recently, activities around developing biotech industries, focusing on chemical, pharmaceutical, industrial and environmental biotech, have progressed rapidly particularly because of government prioritisation of biotech.

Institutional framework

Institutional actors in biotechnology R&D in South Africa include academic institutions, public research institutions, and industry. Academic institutions constitute the largest group of participants in biotechnology. They are engaged in both basic and applied research. The institutions charged with the development and regulation of biotech include the Department of Science and Technology (DST), which is the lead department in biotech. It coordinates the biotech-related research of all other departments and is a vital link to the Treasury. Medical research falls under the Department of Health, which coordinates the National Bioethics Committee and advises the Biotechnology Advisory Committee. The Department of Trade and Industry supports innovation in industry and provides funding through incentive schemes. It also plays a crucial role in the commercialisation of biotechnology. The Department of Agriculture implements the GMO Act and the Plant Breeders Act. It has a lead role in biosafety issues and advises the Biotechnology Advisory Committee. Other government departments with operations related to biotech include the Department of Environmental Affairs and Tourism, the Department of Labour and the Department of Education.

Research activity

The 2003 National Biotech Survey[13] identified 106 companies engaging in biotech-related activities; of these, 47 were core and 59 non-core.[14] The majority of the core biotech companies engage in human health. The rest are evenly distributed across the other sectors, with the exception of the 'other' category which attracts only 3 per cent of the core biotech companies.

In total, there are about 1000 projects relevant to biotechnology; these are spread over seven sectors and include projects undertaken by both public and private sector. The National Biotech Survey classified the projects as biotech, potential biotech, fundamental research and biotech services, according to their relevance to biotech. The sectoral distribution of research projects is represented below.

The largest sector is plant biotechnology, where most of the biotechnology carried out in the sector is on crop improvement, that is, insect, fungal, viral resistance and herbicide and drought tolerance. Others involve indigenous plant utilisation, fruit improvement, forest tree improvement and micro-propagation, horticultural propagation, improvement of storage properties, weed control and yield and quality enhancement. In plant biotechnology, over 590 applications involving the commercial release, importation, exportation, contained use, trials and clearance of GM crops have been received and granted by the registrar of the GMO Act, as shown below.

According to a survey conducted by Webster and Koch,[15] there is a limited number of new companies established that are solely biotechnology based. Most are small and medium-sized enterprises (SMEs). There are also a few multinational companies especially in the seed sector.

---

13 Mulder, M. and T. Henschel (2003) *National Biotech Survey 2003*, available at https://www.oecd.org/dataoecd/7/37/36036991.pdf.

14 Id. The study focused on modern biotech companies, therefore leaving out those that engage in more traditional forms of biotechnology.

15 Webster and Koch (1998) *Biotechnology Survey: A Statistical Analysis of South Africa and Sub-Saharan Africa*. CSIR Internal Report.

The majority of the 47 companies identified as 'core' in the 2003 survey comprise of either new start-ups or spin-offs from other enterprises.

With regard to geographic distribution, various studies[16] show that the majority of research stakeholders are found in the Western Cape, Gauteng, KwaZulu Natal and Free State. The regional distribution of biotech research projects and core biotech companies mirrors this.

Funding

The total funding on biotechnology R&D has been rising steadily since 1997 when it was R100 million; R200 million in 2002 and in excess of R290 million in 2003.[17] The 2001 National Biotechnology Strategy proposed the set-up of Biotechnology Regional Innovation Centres (BRICs) under the Department of Science and Technology (DST). DST committed an initial R450 million from 2004 to 2007 for biotech development.[18] The Biotechnology Partnership and Development (BioPAD) was established in 2003 as a collective response by stakeholders in biotechnology to the biotech needs of the region and continent.[19] In 2003, the government committed R250 million over two years in an effort to boost BioPAD-led commercialisation of biotechnology. It pledged to increase R&D spending from 0.27 per cent to 1 per cent of national GDP.[20] The biotechnology policy launched in 2004 looks towards forming strategic partnerships as the way forward in attracting investment.

The National Research Foundation (NRF) supports and promotes basic and applied research and innovation; it principally targets academic research and research capacity development. The Innovation Fund was established to encourage collaborative research in technology development, cross-sector and multi-disciplinary research and application-based research. It provides funding for the development of products, prototypes, proof-of-concept and initial marketing through a competitive bidding process. The Technology and Human Resource for Industry Programme (THRIP) funds research programmes involving industry partners.

Funding from the private sector is limited. The impact of BRICs and

---

16 Bioventures, Catalyst Innovation Incubator, Acorn Technologies, and eGoli BIO studies conducted as of 2003.

17 Webster and Koch (1998) *supra*; Webster and Koch (2002) *Biotechnology Sector Report: Implications of the Information Revolution for Economic Development in South Africa*. DTI Policy Support Programme; National Biotech Survey (2003) *supra*.

18 SouthAfrica info (2003) *Developing South Africa's Biotech Industry*.

19 See biopad website at http://www.biopad.org.za/.

20 Maistry, P. (2003) 'Modern biotechnology and genetic modification: bridging the gap between business and practice'.

other technology incubators established under the national strategy on private sector investment is yet to be seen. It is hoped that there will be more incentive for increased private sector investment. Consolidation of the international seed industry has led to technology being held by a small number of multinational companies.

Institutional linkages exist between South African institutions on the one hand and local and international universities on the other. These linkages are characterised by information and material exchange. There are other limited collaborations between national research institutes, international organisations, government departments, NGOs and the private sector. The need for improved institutional linkages was expressed by those interviewed.

Venture capital has not taken much root in South Africa. There are, however, some public and private sources of venture capital funding for start-up companies wishing to engage in biotechnology. These include HBD Venture Capital, Bioventures, Brait Private Equity, Support Programme for Industrial Innovation, THRIP, Industrial Development Corporation and Catalyst Innovations. Biotech firms are yet to be listed on the AltX or JSE Securities Exchange.[21]

Human resource development

There are a significant number of scientists with postgraduate qualifications. In 1998, the figure was estimated at 1200, 20 per cent of whom had PhD qualifications and 20 per cent with MSc degrees.[22] The highest concentration of the qualified individuals is found in academic institutions. Loss of graduates and staff from the system has however, lately been of concern, as qualified personnel seek greener pastures in the private sector and abroad.

The 2003 Survey identified approximately 1020 staff in biotech-related activities with biotechnology companies, showing a relatively even distribution of employees by qualification. This is probably a function of the averaging out of R&D personnel and technical/production staff in a sample that includes R&D-intensive as well as production-orientated

---

21 SouthAfrica info (2004) *SA's Budding Biotech Industry*, 5 January 2004, available at http://www.southafrica.info/ess_info/sa_glance/scitech/biotech-audit.htm. Companies need to have profits greater than R8 million before they can be listed on the stock exchange. Only 20 per cent of biotech firms have revenue in excess of R10 million.

22 Wolson, R. (2001) *Agricultural Biotechnology Assessment in Sub-Saharan Africa, Country Study: South Africa.* Report prepared for the African Centre for Technology Studies.

companies. As is to be expected, research groups are dominated by employees with at least a degree qualification, and frequently a postgraduate degree.

The Survey reports that approximately 50 per cent of companies and 81 per cent of research stakeholders that participated in the survey indicated that they had experienced shortages in human resources. The majority of research stakeholders listed skilled scientists at various levels, particularly MScs and PhDs, as being in short supply. It is expected that capacity for commercialisation of biotechnology will improve with the implementation of the national strategy through the establishment of the Regional Innovation Centres (RICs).

Administration and regulation

Until 2004, South Africa did not have a national biotech policy. National policies on areas that are related to biotechnology and biosafety such as the environment and agriculture, do not focus much attention on biotechnology and biosafety, save perhaps for the National Policy on the Conservation and Sustainable Use of Biodiversity. This expresses the need to adopt measures to regulate the use, handling, transfer and release of GMOs. The 1996 White Paper on Science and Technology underscores the role of science and technology in promoting South Africa's economy and recognises the benefits that science and technology offer in the improvement of the livelihoods of South Africans. However, it only identifies biotechnology as an area of collaboration both nationally and internationally and across various partners.

After numerous national pronouncements indicative of the political recognition of the opportunities offered by biotechnology, a national biotechnology policy was launched in September 2004. The policy[23] identifies health, agriculture, industry, mining and the environment as priority areas. The policy also identifies need related to research infrastructure for the design, testing and manufacture of drugs and vaccines. It adds that human resource development must be promoted and greater capacity and awareness of the need and potential of bioinformatics is crucial.

The National Biotechnology Strategy

In spite of South Africa's long history in use of biotechnology and the large number of biotechnology-embracing projects, various stakeholder meetings determined that the potential of third-generation biotechnology

---

[23] DST (2004) *Biotechnology Platforms: Strategic Review and Forecast*, 9 September 2004.

had not been maximised and that very few products and processes were under commercialisation. The limiting factors were identified as including the lack of infrastructure for R&D, institutional capacity, business support and management for start-up technology companies, lack of technology platforms in science and technology, coordination of policies and programmes, lack of collaboration and funding for innovative ideas. In response to this, the Department of Science and Technology embarked on a study which resulted in the drafting and gazettement of the National Biotechnology Strategy for South Africa in November 2001.[24]

The Strategy identifies gaps and suggests new institutional arrangements and specific actions to be taken by government departments. Key interventions include the creation of four Biotechnology Regional Innovation Centres (BRICs), creation of a National Bioinformatics Network to develop capacity and support services in bioinformatics, development of Biological Resource Centres to ensure the adequate protection and optimal use of biodiversity, establishment of the Biotechnology Advisory Committee to implement the strategy, coordinate R&D and address ethical issues, the establishment of a Bioethics Committee, promoting the public understanding of biotechnology and the development of a Biobank.

Working groups of experts in human health, plant improvement, animal health, industrial processes and new biotechnology platforms are currently analysing information on opportunities, key technologies and market trends under the DST Biotechnology Roadmapping Project. The emphasis is on R&D, human resource development and infrastructure needs in the named areas. The working groups consist of experts from government, industry and academic institutions.

Legal framework

There is no specific Act of Parliament regulating biotechnology in South Africa. Rather, there are various Acts regulating biotech-related activities. These include the GMO Act of 1997, which covers biosafety issues relating to GM products. Agricultural products are regulated by the Agriculture Act of 1947, while the Biodiversity and Protected Areas Acts regulate the use of biodiversity for biotechnology. In the health sector, the Medicines Control Act of 1965 governs the registration and use of medical substances, while the Human Tissue Act of 1983 regulates the use of human tissue for research.[25] The 2006 Legal Guidelines for Research in Biotechnology are

---

24 South Africa National Biotechnology Strategy (2001). www.dst.gov.za/publications/reports/dst_biotechnology_strategy.PDF.

25 The National Health Act of 2003 is set to replace the Human Tissue Act. A

intended to guide applicants through the biotech research process. The corresponding Ethical Guidelines for Research in Biotechnology deal with ethical considerations.

South Africa has five Acts of Parliament addressing intellectual property. These are the Patent, Trademark, Copyright, Registered Designs and Plant Breeders' Rights Acts. All are administered by the Department of Trade and Industry, with the exception of the Plant Breeders' Rights Act which is under the Department of Agriculture. The Patent Office is a non-examining office. For a country so advanced in innovation, at least by African standards, the intellectual property infrastructure is basic.[26] The National Biotechnology Strategy highlights the requirements for a review of the patent legislation.

Outputs and outcomes

In spite of biotechnology being in use for 25 years, few local products have been developed. The 47 companies classified as 'core' biotech companies produced about 155 products and/or services which were applied predominantly in human health, support services and plant biotech.

The creation of BRICs is intended to address this gap between research and innovation. There are currently four BRICs which specialize in different areas. The Biotechnology Partnership and Development (BioPAD) of the Gauteng region focuses on agriculture, industrial and environmental-related biotechnology. The Cape Biotech BRIC represents the Western Cape region and focuses on human health and bioprocessing. The East Coast BRIC (LIFElab) serves the KwaZulu Natal region and the East Coast. This too focuses on human health and bioprocessing. The National Innovation Centre for Plant Biotechnology (PlantBio) is the fourth BRIC and is located in KwaZulu Natal; it focuses on plant biotechnology.

The formation of the National Bioinformatics Network (NBN) is also central to the innovation, commercialisation and advancement of biotechnology in South Africa. This is based at the University of Western Cape and the University of Pretoria. The NBN provides computational power, genome interpretation facilities and networking links between the BRICs and other research institutes. The NBN also enhances the creation and development of bioinformatics skills and capacities in South Africa.

Other actors in the South Africa biotechnology landscape with activities

Footnote 25 (*cont.*)
major departure is that the former will allow therapeutic cloning, which is impermissible under the latter.

[26] Wolson (2001) *supra*.

likely to influence commercialisation and innovation include the GODISA programme, which aims at increasing economic growth and employment creation through the enhancement of technological innovation, improvement in productivity and accelerated international competitiveness of South African small, medium and micro enterprises (SMMEs). The programme supports an Innovation Support Centre, a Technology Demonstration Centre, and six Technology Incubators. Two of these – eGoli and Acorn – focus on biotechnology and aim to further commercialisation of research from the life sciences. Plans are under way for further funding of more technology incubators. Most of these initiatives are in the implementation stages and only a handful have operations spanning three years. As such, their impact on commercialisation of biotech remains to be seen. Data on this was not available. The initiatives, however, present a positive outlook for commercialisation of biotech in South Africa.

Patenting activity

Generally, scientists in South Africa have favoured publication rather than the commercial value of their work. Consequently, the level of patent output is low compared to other developing and developed countries.[27] At least 200 biotechnology-related patents were filed in the South African Patents Office by South African inventors between 1979 and 2002,[28] while 86 biotech patent applications by South African inventors were received under the PCT between 1985 and 2003. It is possible that the patent numbers do not reflect the full complement of intellectual property in South Africa given that ongoing research is yet to yield products which can be protected by intellectual property. The substantial filing fees may be a deterrent for South African biotech companies, most of which are SMEs, from seeking patents abroad.

Conclusion

Commercial biotechnology in South Africa is mainly led by small and medium-sized private firms. The government has targeted biotechnology

---

27 Generally, Cloete, E., L. Nel and J. Theron (2006) 'Biotechnology in South Africa'. *TRENDS in Biotechnology*, 24/12, 557–62; Quach, U. et al. (2006) 'Biotechnology patenting takes off in developing countries'. *International Journal of Biotechnology*, 8, 43–59; and Katnelson, A. (2004) 'South Africa fights low patent rate'. *Bioentrepreneur*, available at http://www.nature.com/bioent.

28 National Biotech Survey (2003) *supra*. This notes that the figure is an estimate given that the SA patent office does not use the International Patent Classification. The estimate figure represents those patents which the researchers presumed to be biotech patents from the titles in individual patent applications.

development as a priority research area and has increased funding to the sector. However, in spite of over two decades of research, there are few local biotech products, and the local biotech sector is largely dependent on imported technology. This is reflected in relatively low levels of local biotech innovation.

In spite of increased government funding and private investment, the sector suffers from insufficient public and private funding for research and commercialisation. The BRICs have the potential to attract funding, although their impact remains to be seen. There is a shortage of suitably skilled technical personnel and entrepreneurial and technology transfer skills.

The recent government emphasis on biotech has led to an increase in the number of biotech-related policy documents, strategies, road maps and plans which define the framework under which biotech can develop. It is expected that the new framework will rectify the general lack of cohesion in research programmes and address the gap between research and commercialisation. As for intellectual property, there is quite limited demand, with few innovations for which protection is being sought.

5. Kenya

In most of the literature, reports and surveys on biotechnology in Kenya, there is virtually no mention of biotechnology in sectors other than in agriculture. There is, however anecdotal evidence of biotechnology in the health, environment and industrial chemical sectors. As such, this report is constrained in its unintentional leanings towards agricultural biotechnology rather than biotechnology as a whole.

Plant biotechnology has been in use in Kenya since the 1960s. During the colonial period, European farmers through the then Kenya Farmers Association were employing biological nitrogen fixation biotechnology for the production of fodder legumes and soybean.[29] The early 1980s saw a rise in the use of tissue culture in the production of citrus plants and pyrethrum under a joint initiative by Kenya Agricultural Research Institute (KARI) and the University of Nairobi. In 1990, the government established the National Advisory Committee on Biotechnology Advances and their Applications, which advised that the use of modern biotech in Kenya would remain uncertain in the face of inadequate technical and regulatory capacity. By 1995, the application of tissue culture in crop improvement was commonplace in various public and private sector

---

[29] Odame, H., P. Kameri-Mbote and D. Wafula (2003) 'Governing modern agricultural biotechnology in Kenya: implications for food security', IDS Paper.

institutions. However, it was not until 2000 that modern biotechnology in crop production was used in Kenya. Currently, five transgenic crops are in various stages of the approval process by the National Biosafety Committee.

The policy and regulatory framework

Kenya's Biosafety Bill was passed in December 2008 and is currently awaiting presidential assent; a National Biotechnology Development Policy was adopted in 2006. Before then, research in biotechnology had been occurring in a policy and legal vacuum. As a gesture of goodwill, biotech scientists and researchers agreed to follow the 1998 Guidelines developed by the National Council for Science and Technology (NCST); these lacked an enabling statute and were legally unenforceable.

Policymakers have in the past made ad-hoc policy-related statements on biotechnology. This has led to fragmentation and poor communication of the biotechnology R&D agenda among various stakeholders. For example, most of the biotech initiatives reflect the interests of concerned individuals and particular institutions. There is little inter-organisational interaction and modern biotechnology activities are influenced by institutional preferences and donor funding and are not necessarily guided by or aligned with national priorities.[30]

The 1996 National Biotechnology Development Policy was a response to the fragmented and uncoordinated ad hoc attempts to address biotechnology-related issues poorly articulated in scattered provisions in different legislation. The Policy's objectives include prioritising, promoting and coordinating research in biotechnology and creating enabling frameworks for biotechnology development and commercialisation. It identifies IPRs as a 'critical aspect of biotechnology innovation' and tacitly recognises the role of IPRs in biotech-based development. The 2008 Biosafety Bill establishes the National Biosafety Authority whose function is to exercise general supervision and control over the transfer, handling and use of GMOs.

Research activity

Although Kenya seems to have a comparative advantage in biotechnology due to great genetic diversity and a significant scientific base, born of institutions that have a long tradition in research, there does not seem

---

30 Anyango, B. and P. Shiundu (1999) 'Institutional arrangements towards biotechnology policy making in Kenya'. Paper presented for Biotechnology and Public Policy Training Course, ACTS, Nairobi, Kenya.

to be much emphasis placed on actual investment in new and innovative ways of tapping benefits from biotechnology or in biotechnology research and development.

Kenya has a well-established system of national research in agriculture as well as in health. This is characterised by public goods research, use of conventional technology, and centralised and hierarchical organisation. The institutions in this national system include national research institutes, academic institutions, NGOs, producer associations and other community-based organisations. The Kenya Medical Research Institute (KEMRI) is the lead institute in health biotech, while in plant biotechnology the actors include the national agricultural research institute, the Kenya Agricultural Research Institute (KARI), universities and international agricultural research institutes (IARCs). Private sector engagement in agricultural biotechnology is taking root in Kenya. However, it is mainly multinational companies that are involved. Although there is some level of collaboration between these groups, there has not been full exploitation of organisational synergies.

In the health centre, the Centre for Biotechnology and Research Development within KEMRI is mandated to develop biotech innovations, especially diagnostic tools, vaccines and biological materials. Current areas of research include HIV/AIDs and malaria among others.[31] Anecdotal data shows that medical biotech is also conducted in the department of medicine in Moi University and at the University of Nairobi. Data showing the extent of experimentation are not, however, available.

Human resource development

Kenya has built capacity over the years in traditional biotechnology. In plant biotech, there are numerous projects involving tissue culture and marker-assisted technology, most of which are being conducted under KARI and institutions such as universities.[32]

Capacity for molecular biotechnology and risk assessment is, however, lacking in Kenya as in most African countries. Although the majority of scientists in Kenya have basic scientific knowledge in genetics and molecular biology, they lack practical experience to effectively apply their existing knowledge to modern biotechnology.[33] KEMRI has contributed to health

---

[31] KEMRI website at www.kemri.org.

[32] Traynor, P. and H. Macharia (2003) *Analysis of the Biosafety System for Biotechnology in Kenya: Application of a Conceptual Framework*. ISNAR Country Report 65. The Hague, The Netherlands: International Service for National agricultural Research.

[33] Odame H., P. Mbote and D. Wafula (2000) 'Globalisation and the

research capacity through various initiatives. These are, however, not solely targeted at biotech but at health in general. Data on approximate number of researchers working in biotechnology are not available.

The capacity of scientists is underutilised where there is lack of or low funding to provide for research grants and staff salaries. Retaining of qualified personnel is also at risk as the few highly trained scientists leave the country for better career prospects.[34]

The government and research institutions in Kenya do not have specific training strategies for building national capacity in biotechnology. There are, however, biotech-related degree programmes at three universities. The Jomo Kenyatta University of Agriculture and Technology offers various programmes on agriculture, while medical biotech courses are available at Moi University and University of Nairobi. Further data on the breakdown of the biotech-related courses and the number of enrolled students are not available.

Research institutions have incorporated their training needs within the framework of individual research programmes.[35] There are insufficient knowledgeable and trained policy-makers. Think tanks such as the African Centre for Technology Studies (ACTS) and other policy international and national NGOs have been instrumental in organising training and workshops to raise awareness in biotech among policy-makers and researchers. Capacity is lacking in biotech R&D and in auxiliary fields such as intellectual property rights.

Funding

There is limited and contradictory data on the level of funding in biotechnology. What is apparent is that research in biotechnology – mainly agriculture and health – is public sector-led with the few private sector companies involved being multinationals. A significant proportion of funding comes from bilateral donors and is of a short-term nature. Government funding for biotechnology has remained minimal. Research institutions recognise the need to explore alternative long-term financing for biotech. Appropriate policies, laws and institutional arrangements to support innovative alternatives such as venture capital are lacking.

---

international governance of modern biotechnology: the implications for food security in Kenya'. Paper prepared for a project on Globalisation and the International Governance of Modern Biotechnology under the Globalisation and Poverty Programme.

[34] BIO-EARN (2001) 'Safety in biotechnology of foods and feeds, proceedings of a BIO-EARN workshop', NCST, No. 43/2002, Nairobi, Kenya.

[35] Odame et al. (2000) *supra*.

It is worth noting that virtually all experimentation in agriculture and health biotechnology involving private companies occurs in partnership with government institutions. There is therefore an emerging pattern of public-private partnerships.

Resources such as appropriate facilities and equipment to conduct biotechnology need upgrading in Kenya. This requires financial resources at a time when public research is faced with dwindling funds. It appears that lack of funding, in addition to relevant trained personnel, is acute and there are serious constraints on laboratory capacity in Kenya.

In addition to these implementation drawbacks, other constraints include poor linkages and networks. There is a lack of adequate collaborative arrangements amongst researchers and research institutions. Biotechnology requires a multidisciplinary collaboration between researchers, lawyers, engineers, information technology experts, market researchers, business experts and other professionals. Poor infrastructure poses another problem. Biotechnology relies heavily on knowledge flows. Poor information technology – manifested in underdeveloped modern communication systems, limited access to email and internet – impedes the acquisition and exchange of necessary and relevant information vital in biotechnology.

Research output: patents

The Kenya Industrial Property Institute (KIPI) is charged with the administration of patents. KIPI does not use the International Patent Classification and therefore it is difficult to know what share of total patents belongs to biotech. Since its inception in 1991, KIPI has received about 450 patent applications from local and foreign applicants. There have been about 330 PCT applications and over 3000 applications through the African Regional Intellectual Property Organisation (ARIPO).[36]

Conclusion

Kenya is far from being a hotbed of biotechnological invention. Government commitment to biotechnology is yet to be practically expressed: there has been no budgetary commitment to biotech R&D. There is virtually no commercialisation of biotech products. *Bt* cotton, developed by KARI and Monsanto, will be the first product of modern plant biotech to be commercialised in Kenya; it is currently in the second phase of field trials and is being tested in multiple sites.

Although skilled scientists exist in traditional forms of biotechnology,

---

36 KIPI (2005) personal communication.

modern biotech suffers from limited capacity in research scientists. So while there is limited capacity to use second-generation biotechnologies, Kenya depends heavily on foreign organisations such as corporations and development agencies for technology transfer, technical support and funding. In agriculture, except for tissue culture, the local private sector is not a user of genetic engineering techniques, a situation that has not changed at all since the passage of the Industrial Property Act. It is not surprising therefore that there is virtually no investment in modern biotechnology from the local private sector. Public sector research institutes account for almost all of total research expenditure, with a significant amount of funding provided by donors. This has tended to be project specific, not always aligned to the national biotech research agenda and with no research system strengthening component. Lack of funds has resulted in limited infrastructure, with facilities like testing equipment, laboratories and machinery in dire need of an upgrade.

While the ability of Kenyan firms to copy biotech inventions by reading foreign patent specifications may be quite limited, even this possibility is precluded when the same inventions are patented in Kenya. Therefore, allowing foreign corporations to acquire patents in Kenya arguably only increases dependency, without any apparent mitigating benefits.

6. India

Institutional framework

The Indian biotech institutional framework can be traced back to the 1940s, with the establishment of the Council for Scientific and Industrial Research (CSIR). This is a government institute with a network of about 40 laboratories, 80 field stations and which employs over 22 000 personnel.[37] Of the 40 laboratories, at least seven engage in biotech research. These are the Centre for Biochemical Technology (CBT) in Delhi, the Centre for Cellular and Molecular Biology (CCMB) in Hyderabad,[38] the Indian Institute of Chemical Technology (IICT) in Hyderabad, the Central Drug Research Institute (CDRI) in Lucknow, the Institute of Microbial Technology (IMT) in Chandigarh, the Indian Institute of Chemical Biology (IICB) in Calcutta and the Central Food Technological Research Institute (CFTRI) in Mysore.[39]

---

[37] Ernst & Young (2002) *Biotechnology in India*.

[38] This was established in 1977 solely for the advancement of biotechnology.

[39] Maria, A., J. Ruet and M.-H. Zerah (2002) *Biotechnology in India*. A study commissioned by the French Embassy in India (hereafter French Embassy Report).

The institutional framework was further bolstered in the 1980s: the Sixth Five-year Plan (1980–1985) was India's first policy document covering biotechnology development.[40] CSIR was mandated to ensure coordination on an inter-agency, inter-institutional basis. One of the most important boosts to biotechnology development was the establishment of the National Biotechnology Board (NBTB) in 1982 to spearhead the development of biotech. Its primary objective was to identify priority areas in biotech development and to devise a long-term plan for biotech in India. In 1983, NBTB issued the 'Long Term Plan in Biotechnology in India', which identified as priority areas self-sufficiency in food, clothing and housing, adequate health and hygiene, provision of adequate energy and transportation, protection of the environment, employment, industrial growth and balance in international trade. The NBTB graduated to the Department of Biotechnology (DBT) in 1986. Its mandate is to promote biotechnology throughout India.

At present there are seven major agencies concerned with financing and supporting research in biotechnology. These are the Department of Science and Technology (DST), the Department of Biotechnology (DBT), the Council of Scientific and Industrial Research (CSIR), the Indian Council of Medical Research (ICMR), the Indian Council of Agriculture Research (ICAR), the University Grants Commission (UGC) and the Department of Scientific and Industrial Research (DSIR). These agencies are spread over four different government departments.[41]

Research activity

In the 1980s, programmes on biotechnology included tissue culture application for medicinal and economic plants, fermentation technology, enzyme engineering for chemicals, antibiotics and other medical product development, agricultural and forest residues and slaughterhouse wastes utilisation.[42] In addition to these first- and second-generation biotech activities, India's engagement in third-generation biotech activities such as pharmaceuticals, plant and animal biotech, aquaculture and marine biotech, and environmental biotech has grown strongly over the past

---

40 Bhargava, P. (1995) 'Biotechnology's decade of stagnation'. *Economic and Political Weekly*, 30(48).

41 DST, DBT and DSIR are under the Ministry of Science and Technology, ICMR is under the Ministry of Health, ICAR is under the Ministry of Agriculture, UGC under the Ministry of Human Resource Development. DSIR is the funding agency for CSIR and both fund biotech-related research projects.

42 Planning Commission (1981) *India, Sixth Five Year Plan Document, 1980–1985*, Government of India, New Delhi.

two decades. With India's growing global prominence in information and communications technology, bioinformatics as a sector in biotech is growing rapidly. DBT reports that it received 1325 project proposals in the 2005–2006 period, of which 805 were recommended for funding.[43]

A study conducted by Ernst & Young in 2000 found there were 800 biotech companies.[44] Fifteen per cent of these engaged in third-generation biotechnology. The study found that the biotech industry at the time employed about 10000 technical staff and generated about US$500 million in revenue per annum.

Similar studies conducted by the Biotech Consortium India Limited (BCIL) in 2001 and 2003, however, display more conservative figures, highlighting the problem of discrepancies in the biotech data available. The 2001 survey lists 176 biotech firms, while the 2003 survey lists 401 firms.[45] With 85 firms, agriculture was the largest biotech sector in 2001, representing 48 per cent of the total. Healthcare came second with about 24 per cent of the total. With its 43 firms increasing to 142 firms in 2003, healthcare was the largest sector in 2003, having a share of 35 per cent compared to agriculture's 33 per cent. Firms engaging in environmental biotech increased from 4 to 16, while 2003 figures indicate a sector not present in 2001: industrial biotechnology. These are mostly firms engaging in extraction-related activities and at 42 firms represented 10 per cent of the total biotech firms in 2003.

Most biotech firms in India are private and are predominantly small. Only about 12 biotech firms are listed on the capital market. BCIL data show that the share of small firms remained constant at about 60 per cent in 2001 and 2003. The number of large firms decreased from a share of 25 per cent to 40 per cent in 2003, while that of medium-sized firms increased from 13 per cent to about 20 per cent. There is a significant number of US and European multinationals with a manufacturing presence in India.[46]

Contract research organisations[47] have largely been responsible for the rise in the absolute number of small firms in the healthcare sector from ten

---

43 DBT Report, 2006. Available at http://dbtindia.nic.in/publication/public-main.html.

44 This includes companies engaging in first-generation biotech.

45 Only about 25 per cent of firms are common to both surveys. While this indicates that there is a high number of new firms, there is no explanation of missing firms. See Chaturvedi, S. (2005) 'Dynamics of biotechnology research and industry in India: statistics, perspectives and key policy issues', DSTI/DOC(2005)6 for an analysis of the problem of contrasting data.

46 For example, GlaxoSmithKline, Eli Lily in health and Monsanto and US Agriseeds in agriculture.

47 Chaturvedi (2005) *supra*.

in 2001 to 74 in 2003, representing the largest percentage increase across the sectors over the period. In agriculture and healthcare, medium-sized firms have increased at the same pace. In the healthcare sector, large firms have increased by about 80 per cent, suggesting the rapid entry of multinational companies.

Bioinformatics as a biotech sector is growing rapidly on the back of India's strong IT sector. The government has had a large part to play in the growth of this sector, partly by enhancing the equity of foreign companies and institutions in government-funded research centres to 51 per cent.[48] In addition, a network of at least 57 research centres linked to a high speed computer network, Biotechnology Information Systems Network (BTISnet), has been established.[49] Some state governments have also initiated efforts at strengthening bio-nanotechnology and plant genomics.

A significant proportion of biotech firms is concentrated in central and southern India. The 2002 French Embassy survey identified 18 main public research institutions, ten of which are in central and southern India. Hyderabad in Andhra Pradesh in the south stands out, with about 40 research institutes solely dedicated to biotech. Other prominent states include Karnataka, Tamil Nadu and Kerala. The western state of Maharashtra has a large biotech centre, whose base expands to other states such as Gujarat and Chandigarh.

Funding

Biotechnology is highly dependent on the availability of funds at initial stages of R&D. Access to capital for biotech firms is through government funding or private venture capital. Government support is typically targeted at government institutions and research agencies. There is little government support for private sector R&D outside that available from the Technology Development Fund, which finances CSIR-approved projects. However, some state governments have set up biotech development funds to assist private companies engaging in biotech.

In the 2005–2006 period, the biotech industry registered a revenue of US$1.07 billion, recording a growth of 36.55 per cent.[50] Leading public agencies supporting biotechnology programmes include the Indian Council of Agriculture Research (ICAR), the University Grants Commission (UGC), the Department of Scientific and Industrial Research (DSIR), the

---

[48] Suresh, N. (2003) 'Bioinformatics policy calls for 51% FDI in government labs', 17 March 2003. Available at http://www.ciol.com/content/news/repts/103031701.asp.

[49] Chaturvedi (2005) *supra.*

[50] DBT Report (2006) *supra.*

Department of Science and Technology (DST), Council of Scientific and Industrial Research (CSIR), Department of Biotechnology (DBT) and the Indian Council of Medical Research (ICMR). It should, however, be noted that apart from DBT, which deals solely in biotech, it is difficult to establish the share of funding allocated to biotech in the agencies, as allocations are not separately marked for biotech.

National budget statistics show that, apart from ICMR, DBT has registered modest growth relative to the other agencies. This may perhaps be indicative of its role in coordinating nationwide biotech research rather than direct R&D.

The national budget for the 2001–2002 fiscal year gave biotech firms a 150 per cent tax deduction for R&D in a move aimed at encouraging private sector investment in biotech. The government also promotes the establishment of biotech centres within industrial parks. The Andhra Pradesh state, in collaboration with the private sector, has built a state-of-the-art biotech park in Hyderabad. This is intended to be replicated in other states. Some of these projects are partly funded by the central and state governments as well as private investors.

Other measures to promote private sector investment and innovation include the establishment of the Small Business Innovation Research Initiative (SBIRI), a scheme launched for funding early stage pre-proof-of-concept research. Plans to expand this to fund projects which have established proof of concept and have the ability to get venture capital are under way.[51]

Private sector investment in 2002 amounted to US$10.6 billion, up from US$3.1 billion in 1999.[52] The health and medical sector accounted for 47 per cent of the total while agriculture received 32 per cent. The number of venture capital firms in India has increased greatly since 1988, when the government announced the guidelines for setting up venture capital funds. The restriction that venture capital funds could only be set up by banks and financial institutions was removed in 1995, allowing for tax exemption and therefore encouraging capital investments from overseas. The Venture Capital Funds Regulations were promulgated in 1996. At the time, only eight domestic venture capital funds were registered. In 2004, the number of funds had increased to at least 70, with US$29 billion in assets under management.

---

[51] This will be in the form of a soft loan of up to Rs. 100 000 000. DBT Report (2006).

[52] Meaning the total sum of investments made by companies in the biotech industry.

There are limitations in data collection with regard to the share of funds available to biotech. However, the data available seem to suggest that venture capital currently plays only a marginal role in funding biotech. In the French Embassy study, only four companies of the 41 interviewed received support through venture capital funds.

Interestingly, venture capital in India is dominated by public sector financial institutions, the largest of which are Industrial Credit and Investment Corporation of India (ICICI) and Small Industries Development Bank of India (SIDBI). ICICI and the Andhra Pradesh Industrial Development Corporation are the leading biotech funds. Other funds include IL&FS Venture Corporation Ltd., Industrial Development Bank of India (IDBI), and the Industrial Finance Corporation of India (IFCI). There are several other financial agencies with limited funds earmarked for biotech. Morgan Stanley is a private venture capital fund that has been active in funding biotech. However, most venture capital funds have been unwilling to invest in biotech R&D, opting rather to fund commercialisation of research already developed.[53]

Human resource development

There have been various efforts by the government to build capacity in biotech. In 1984, NBTB launched short-term training programmes to address rising demand for trained personnel in biotech. DBT promotes the development of specialised degrees at various universities at both MSc and PhD level. There are about 50 approved training programmes in various institutions.[54] In addition, there are over 60 institutions set up by the private sector offering degrees and diplomas in biotech.[55] Technician training courses, fellowships for students to go abroad, overseas associateships for qualified scientists, lecture series, awards and incentives form an integral part of human resource development in biotech in India.[56]

In 2003, there were about 160 000 people employed in biotech, 39 000 of whom were technical staff.[57] Healthcare had the largest share of employees in 2001 (47 per cent) and in 2003 (53.2 per cent). The share of technical

---

53 Ernst and Young (2002) *supra*.

54 DBT report (2006) *supra.*

55 Chaturvedi (2005) *supra,* but no data available.

56 Awards include the competitive National Bioscience Career Development Awards. There are also special programmes to increase the participation of women in science, such as the Biotechnology Golden Jubilee Park for Women, encouraging women entrepreneurs to take up biotech enterprises.

57 BCIL (2003) *Directory of Biotechnology Industries and Institutions in India*, New Delhi: BCIL. More recent figures are not available.

staff in agriculture remained constant at 30.8 per cent in 2001 and 31.3 per cent in 2003. Although this greatly increased from 18.1 per cent to 30.6 per cent in healthcare, agriculture had a greater share of technical staff in both years. Industrial biotech and environmental biotech each accounted for about 9 per cent of technical staff in 2003.

Synergies and partnerships

The BCIL was set up in 1990 with the aim of providing linkages among research institutions. Its budget comes from various Indian financial institutions as well as private firms. There have been various initiatives aimed at promoting collaboration between various institutions and agencies in the private and public sector, some of which are promoted by state governments, such as the establishment of biotech parks in Andhra Pradesh,[58] Uttar Pradesh and Karnataka. BT parks offer the infrastructure to facilitate experimentation as well as placing biotech firms in one location, thereby creating an opportunity to share not only resources but also knowledge culminating in partnerships and collaborations.

Some outstanding examples include CCMB's work with the private sector to develop India's first recombinant DNA vaccine for Hepatitis B.[59] Typically, private firms partner with CCMB by funding a particular project; CCMB does the R&D and the private sector partner handles commercialisation. Other collaborations are between multinational subsidiaries and local companies, such as an agreement between Eli Lily and Ranbaxy to market Monsanto's recombinant bovine growth hormone. Of 50 Indian private companies interviewed, there were 53 interactions involving 19 private companies and 27 public institutes. 13 companies had interactions with more than one public institute.[60]

In bioinformatics, the US accounts for about 65 per cent of India's IT exports.[61] Indian companies are looking to leverage data mining and data warehousing, with some considering establishing subsidiaries abroad and using these to nurture business relationships.[62]

---

[58] The SP Biotech Park is a joint venture between Shapoorji Pallonji & Co. Ltd. and the Andhra Pradesh government. The latter contributed 140 acres of land and owns 11 per cent of the shares. There is also a Knowledge Park in Hyderabad, a joint venture between the state government and ICICI. It sits on 200 acres of land and its primary focus is life sciences. The BT Park and the Knowledge Park form part of a larger blueprint of the Genome Valley Project

[59] With Shantha Biotechnics Ltd in Hyderabad, Ernst & Young (2002) *supra.*

[60] French Embassy Report, *supra.*

[61] Ernst & Young (2002) *supra.*

[62] Perhaps following the example set by Dr Reddy's Lab, which is listed on the New York Stock Exchange.

Administration and legislative policy
Regulation of biotech in India is characterised by a diversity of agencies; regulation is spread through four ministries – Health, Agriculture, Science and Technology and Human Resource and Development – and over eight agencies within the ministries.

The Indian Patent Act of 1970 as amended does not define 'micro-organism' and does not allow for patenting of plant or animal varieties. It does, however, allow for the patenting of biotech processes. India established biosafety guidelines in 1989 and has Biosafety and Recombinant DNA Guidelines (1990) which fall under the Environment (Protection) Act of 1986. The Guidelines for Biomedical Research were drawn up in 2000.

India does not have a national biotechnology policy, but some state governments, such as Maharashtra, Andra Pradesh, Karnataka, Tamil Nadu and Gujarat, have developed biotech policies at state level and established specific institutions to oversee biotech within their respective states.[63] The central government is in the process of developing a national ten-year strategy and action plan, which is currently in draft form. The draft biotech strategy broadly reflects that in the IT industry

Output
The biotech industry generated US$1.07 billion in the 2005–2006 fiscal year recording growth of 36.55 per cent.[64] The number of scientific articles by Indian scientists rose significantly in the same period.[65]

The Technology Information Forecasting and Assessment Council (TIFAC), the National Research Development Corporation and the various patent offices are charged with the responsibility of managing patent data. None of these uses International Patent Classification, therefore, while there are data available on the overall number of patents applied for and granted, it is difficult to establish which of these relate to biotech. This notwithstanding, figures from TIFAC estimate that there were about 2300 biotech patent applications filed in India.

---

[63] Some state governments have gone further to encourage innovation in biotech. In Andhra Pradesh, companies enjoy a sales tax of only 1 per cent on biotech products produced within the state.

[64] DBT Report (2006) *supra.*

[65] Ibid. There was also an increase in the number of publications by DBT's autonomous institutions.

Conclusion

The framework and strategy for regulating biotech in India borrows heavily from that in the IT sector. The biotech sector faces difficulty owing to the complex nature of administration. State efforts are not coordinated, as states compete with each other to become the most attractive location for biotech investment. Nevertheless, there are efforts aimed at streamlining the institutional environment. There is considerable investment in academic and industry infrastructure as well as human resource development, resulting in an impressive national network of research institutions with immense potential for growth.

Innovation in biotech in India ranges from highly intensive R&D such as the *Relicord*, a product of human stem cell research developed by Reliance Life Sciences,[66] to creative imitation, which forms the basis of the Indian pharmaceutical industry. India is both one of the largest markets for generic drugs and its pharmaceutical industry is the world's largest exporter of generic drugs, a role soon to change, given recent amendments of the Indian Patent Act to conform to TRIPS requirements.

However, the difficulty in biotech data collection and the disparity in the data available make comprehensive analysis of the biotech environment difficult. Various studies have attempted to address this, with limited success. There is no common definition of biotechnology, which means that the scope of companies from which biotech data is obtained differs across various studies.

7. Analytical presentation of the flexibilities of TRIPS Article 27.3(b)

As indicated earlier, two types of flexibility exist in Article 27.3(b). These are (i) the optional subject-matter exceptions, and (ii) the possibility to define the terms in a variety of ways. This part of the chapter discusses the potential interpretations of Article 27.3(b) of the TRIPS Agreement and their implications for the development of biotechnology. In order to do so, the following approach is adopted. An overview of the TRIPS Agreement and Article 27.3(b) addresses the possible interpretations by identifying flexibilities or ambiguities based on the architecture of the article as such, an analysis of the terms under the scientific language, the various legal interpretations and their practical industrial or technological implications, the reasoning behind the wording, and the precise and practical understanding of the terms.

To illustrate the flexibilities empirically, we also review the way WTO

---

[66] Reliance Life Sciences (2006) *Stem Cell Enriched Cord Blood Repository*. Available at http://www.relbio.com/html/sc_bloodrepository.html.

Member States have implemented and applied the wording of Article 27.3(b) in their national law, repeating how terms are interpreted in those implementations. But we start with Article 27.1.

Article 27 of TRIPS
Under Article 27.1 of TRIPS, a list of requirements is set out that clarifies what type of innovation ought to be eligible for patent protection:

> patents shall be available for any inventions, whether products or processes, in all fields of technology, provided that they are new, involve an inventive step and are capable of industrial application.

The implications of Article 27.1 are that, in the context of the application of the TRIPS, Member States shall ensure that a patent regime is available to protect any inventions that fulfil those requirements, irrespective of the technology. Thus, under TRIPS, Member States shall not discriminate as to the nature of the technology when assessing patentability.

Article 27.3(b) starts with the following wording: 'Members may also exclude from patentability'. Again, the TRIPS Agreement does not require or exclude *de facto* the protection of those subject matters, an issue left to the discretion of each Member State. The construction of Article 27.3(b) can be divided into two parts.

First, the provision 'plants and animals other than micro-organisms' specifies that plants and animals can be excluded as product patents, but such exclusion cannot be extended to micro-organisms. Following Article 27.1 TRIPS, it is then required that micro-organisms and any macro-organisms other than plants or animals be patentable subject matter. In addition, at the end of the article, it is specified that: 'Members shall provide for the protection of plant varieties either by patents or by an effective *sui generis* system or by any combination thereof'. Hence, even though Member States do not have to protect plants under their patent regime, plant varieties have to be protected. This can be achieved either under a separate regime held as 'effective' or within the patent law, or by a combination of both.

The second part of the provision addresses issues of process patents, 'essentially biological processes for the production of plants or animals other than non-biological and microbiological processes'. The construction there is more ambiguous. What are potentially excludable from patent protection are essentially biological processes, the definition of which could be understood by the end of the provision, 'other than non-biological and microbiological processes' that lead to the production of plants or animals. Therefore, it can first be understood that non-biological and microbiological processes that lead to the production of plants and animals ought to be capable of being protected. Moreover, it is only when the purpose is for the production of plants and animals that essentially biological processes can be excluded. Therefore an essentially biological process for the production of anything else than plants or animals is required to be capable of patent protection.

Furthermore, the restriction on 'plants and animals other than micro-organisms' is not being reproduced as the term micro-organism is not being repeated. So, the Member States should have discretion whether patent rights could be provided to essentially biological processes for the production of plants' and animals' micro-organisms, should there be any.

So it appears that the architecture of Article 27(3)(b) provides a certain level of flexibility as to the optional subject matter that is not so explicit and may require further clarification. Mainly, the lack of clarity of Article 27.3(b) is generated by the terms and associations used that are open to different possible interpretations, thus creating a second level of flexibility of Article 27.3(b), as previously held.

Interpreting the terms of TRIPS

Articles 31 and 32 of the Vienna Convention on the Law of Treaties provide that the terms should be interpreted 'in good faith in accordance with the ordinary meaning to be given to the terms of the treaty in their context and in the light of its object and purpose'. What should be understood as the ordinary meaning could be an accepted definition, as generally found in a dictionary. Meanwhile, such definitions might lack precision and create some grey areas. When those areas become positioned over issues of importance, then the interpretation of the terms will need further investigation.

A further means of interpretation lies in the intention of the parties to the agreement. Again, the TRIPS Agreement was enacted in order to increase trade harmonisation by focusing on standardising intellectual property rights amongst its signatory States. Substantive variations in the way the terms are being interpreted could have the consequence of compartmentalising the global market, and hence would run counter to the intentions of the TRIPS.

As identified by the Vienna Convention, the interpretation should also be made in the light of the object and purpose of the Treaty, which identify a third level of interpretation. The object and purpose of the TRIPS Agreement are to set minimum standards of intellectual property rights. In that sense, it is not required that Members include within their laws a level of protection above the minimum. The effort of harmonization is only required to the level of those standards, more extensive protection being left to the discretion of the Member.[67] Hence, the extent to which interpretation should be made by confronting other Members' law should be restricted within the minimum standard identified by the TRIPS. Meanwhile, Members are obliged to incorporate within their laws those minimum standards. In that sense, Article 27.3(b), which is an exception, should be construed narrowly. Finally, it is within the competence of the WTO Dispute Settlement Body to interpret TRIPS.[68]

Interpretations of the terms of Article 27.3(b) of TRIPS

Article 27.3(b) defines boundaries in disclosing subject matter that might be excluded, while providing restrictions on the interpretation made of such subject matter. Thus, whereas the terms might be interpreted alone, their real meaning has to be in conjunction with the other terms they are associated with.

MICRO-ORGANISMS

Micro-organism refers to organisms that are not visible to the naked eye, which should be in the range or 10^{-5} m maximum size. The term organism means a complex adaptive system of organs that influence each other in such a way that they function as a more or less stable whole and have properties of life. Generally, plant cells are in the range of 10^{-4} m, 10^{-5} m for animal cells, 10^{-6} m for bacteria or archaebacteria, and even less for viruses. Thus micro-organisms are single-cell organisms, which are most commonly bacteria or archaebacteria. Viruses are not normally classed as organisms.

As emphasised by the US[69] in a communication to the WTO, the Budapest Treaty on the International Recognition of the Deposit of Microorganisms does not provide a definition for micro-organisms; nor does TRIPS or the WIPO Committee of Experts on Biotechnological Inventions and Industrial Property. The reason for this could be found in a document prepared jointly by the European Patent Office, the Japanese Patent Office and the US Patent and Trademark Office[70] that held:

---

[67] Leskien, D. and M. Flitner (1997) *Intellectual Property Rights and Plant Genetic Resources: Options for a Sui Generis System,* Issues in Genetic Resources No 6, IPGRI, June 1997.

[68] Article 64(1) of TRIPS.

[69] IP/C/W/209 WTO.

[70] Comparative Study of Patent Practices in the Field of Biotechnology Related Mainly to Microbiological Inventions, 1988.

> None of the laws administered by any of the Offices contains a formal definition of the term 'micro-organism'. Where definitions are used in either classification, definitions or administrative guidelines, the term is defined as a non-exclusive list of organisms which are included within the scope of that term. As noted by the EPO, it does not seem expedient to introduce such a definition as the rapid evolution in the field of microbiology would necessitate its frequent updating.

The USA communication then gave their definition of micro-organisms, if any, as 'an organism not visible to the naked eye, e.g. bacterium or virus',[71] which should be sufficient in their view to distinguish them from plants and animals.

Brazil[72] also disputed the necessity to clarify the definition of micro-organisms. This was motivated by concerns about broad patents on micro-organisms, where issues of novelty, inventive step and industrial applicability were at stake, as well as potential conflict with the Convention on Biological Diversity (CBD). While those two issues have real existence and practical implications, they are not as such related to the implication of Article 27.3(b). Those are matters of basic requirements for patentability and procedures, but not issues of subject-matter exclusion as such. In addition, Article 27.3(b) is articulated in such a way that it provides the possibility for Member States to integrate in their patent regime certain exclusions, rather than actually requiring them. Hence, it seems inappropriate for it to serve as a lever against those practices. Consequently it appears that the lack of a more specific definition of micro-organisms under Article 27.3(b) is not problematic as to the identification of the subject matter, but as to the consequence of protecting certain types of micro-organisms.

Brazil's patent legislation excludes from patentability all or parts of plants and animals, except transgenic micro-organisms that satisfy the three requirements of patentability. For the purpose of this law, patentability is restricted to transgenic micro-organisms, excluding plants and animals, that express, by means of direct human intervention in their genetic composition, a characteristic normally not attainable by the species under natural conditions.[73]

An African Group communication to the WTO[74] was divergent. It argued that the distinction made did not have any scientific reasoning and its interpretation focused on the exclusion of life forms in general.

---

71 *Oxford Dictionary of Current English.*
72 IP/C/W/228 WTO.
73 Law No 9,279, 1996, Article 18, II.
74 IP/C/W/163 WTO.

In Europe and Japan, the term is understood extremely broadly. According to the European Patent Office, micro-organism 'includes not only bacteria and yeasts, but also fungi, algae, protozoa and human, animal and plant cells, i.e. all generally unicellular organisms with dimensions beneath the limits of vision which can be propagated and manipulated in a laboratory. Plasmids and viruses are also considered to fall under this definition.' Similarly, for the Japan Patent Office, micro-organism includes 'yeasts, moulds, mushrooms, bacteria, actinomycetes, unicellular algae, viruses, protozoa, etc.' and also 'undifferentiated animal or plant cells as well as animal or plant tissue cultures'.

Animals and plants (including plant varieties)

The science of taxonomy has evolved over the ages, offering an understanding of the linkages within the natural world. While it started with a general morphology approach, where appearance was the main factor of distinction, more invasive methods based on cellular biology and genetics have provided a more comprehensive and precise picture of the organisation of life and its variation.

Until the 1960s, only two kingdoms were usually referred to, namely animals and plants. Protozoa[75] and bacteria,[76] being known at that time, were respectively included in the animal and plant kingdoms. While this distinction mainly opposed what is called primary and secondary producers[77] and could easily be distinctive of plants and animals at macroscopic level, it was too limiting at the microscopic level. Indeed, more in-depth research on the microscopic world revealed life forms that were more differentiated between them than any possible differentiation between plants and animals. In 1959, R.H. Whittaker replaced the two kingdoms with five: Animalia, Plantae, Fungi, Protista and Monera.

The progress of modern genetics affected further our perception of nature's organisation. Instead of five kingdoms, it is now three domains that are being differentiated, within which over a dozen kingdoms have been recognised. The main distinction then is not really a matter of size, but is held to be within the microscopic world. The three domains, known

---

75 Micro-organisms with a cellular nucleus.

76 Micro-organisms originally identified by the lack of a cellular nucleus.

77 This distinction refers to the capacity of plants to create organic matter from inorganic matter, hence positioned at the beginning of the food chain, compared to animals that require organic matter to develop, thus occupying the second position in the food chain.

as Eukarya,[78] Eubacteria[79] and Archaea,[80] are mainly distinguished by their biochemical capabilities, cell structure, and obviously gene sequences. The plant and animal kingdoms are part of the Eukarya.

Two main issues arise from those distinctions; first, plants and animals are only a tiny fraction of the living world in term of diversity. Second, the visual distinction between micro-organism and macro-organism is not representative of fundamental differences or capabilities, that is, most of the characteristics of life are held within the microscopic world.

A general definition of the plant and animal kingdoms would be:

- *Plant kingdom*: Members of this kingdom grow out of inorganic material by photosynthesis. They lack ability to move around their environment except by growing or being transported by wind, water, or external forces. They comprise mosses, ferns, woody and non-woody flowering plants.
- *Animal kingdom*: Organisms that ingest food instead of absorbing or photosynthesising it. They also have their own means of locomotion in at least one phase of their life cycle. They comprise sponges, worms, insects, fish, amphibians, reptiles, birds and mammals.

In a strict scientific interpretation, 'plants and animals other than micro-organisms' mean that only specimens within the plant and animal kingdoms that are visible to the eye are potentially excludable from patent protection. Based on the definitions of plants and animals provided above and repeating the fact that plant cells are in the range of 10^{-4} m and 10^{-5} m for animal cells, they can thus not be classed as micro-organisms. Hence, the restriction within the plants and animals excluding of micro-organisms does not seem to have any scientific relevance, unless one is considering a different approach.

If we have to give a meaning to the opposition between plants and animals, and micro-organisms, apart from the requirement that micro-organisms be patentable subject matter, such a distinction may call for an

---

78 'An organism consisting of a cell or cells in which the genetic material is DNA in the form of chromosomes contained within a distinct nucleus' (that is, all living organisms other than the bacteria and archaea). *Concise Oxford English Dictionary*.

79 'A large group of bacteria with simple cells and rigid cell walls, comprising the "true" bacteria and cyanobacteria as distinct from archaea.' *Concise Oxford English Dictionary*.

80 'Microorganisms which are similar to bacteria in size and simplicity of structure but constitute an ancient group intermediate between the bacteria and eukaryotes.' *Concise Oxford English Dictionary*.

older interpretation of the meaning of those terms. The USPTO includes in their definition of plants other organisms such as algae and macro fungi.[81] Under a strict definition, such macro-organisms are not part of the plant or animal kingdoms.

Another approach to distinguishing between plants and animals, and micro-organisms, may also be considered under the term 'organism'. Thus, the use of the term 'micro-organism' in opposition to plants and animals could induce the requirement that only plant and animal organisms are susceptible of being excluded. While this interpretation makes no sense scientifically, it might have some practical consequences. The term organism means a complex adaptive system of organs that influence each other in such a way that they function as a more or less stable whole and have properties of life. Plants and animals are organisms when taken as a whole. Should part of a plant or an animal be considered as plant or animal in the sense of the exclusion? Following the definition of an organism, it should be assumed that only that part of a plant or an animal that is capable of propagation or development could be excluded. Hence, a gene originating from an animal or a plant cannot be considered as plants and animals, and should be capable of being patented. Whether a plant's or animal's cell including such gene must be patentable is then unclear. In addition, the question could be raised in the case of cell cultures. While they might have the capabilities to a certain extent of propagation and development, are they plants or animals within the meaning of Article 27.3(b)? What would be the situation with stem cells? Those cultures grow identical cells that tend to be independent from each other, hence might fall within the definition of a micro-organism. While those distinctions are not important for agricultural activities, they could be much more sensitive in the research aspect of biotechnology as such.

The exclusion of plants and animals seems to derive from the EPO approach. The Strasbourg Convention, 1963, which originated the Munich Convention (EPC), was concerned with the potential consequences of patent rights over certain breeding and farming activities, hence the exclusion of plant and animal variety as such under the EPC. The recent development in breeding activities is advocating the limited efficiency of the EPO approach. Indeed, it is of concern now that biotechnology allows circumventing the exclusion of plants and animals under the EPC, while their development is illustrating the current trend in breeding development. TRIPS provides a broader potential exclusion as it is not limited to varieties, hence it appears to be more integrative of new technologies

---

81 USPTO guidelines.

toward the purpose of potentially excluding a patent regime that would affect breeding activities at large. While the distinction between micro-organisms and plants or animals seems rather straightforward as to the purpose of the exclusion in the light of the final outcome, its implications becomes more problematic as to the technology behind breeding activities, as held above with biotechnology activity at the level of cells.

MICROBIOLOGICAL PROCESSES

Microbiological processes in a literal translation should stand for any processes that are being carried out by micro-organisms. It does not make much sense scientifically to differentiate between macro-organism and micro-organism in their biological activity, as most of the complexity is held within the micro realm and is usually not categorised based on such considerations. To put it another way, the most fundamental biological processes are already achieved by micro-organisms. Therefore, biological processes other than microbiological processes, in that context, should be understood as processes that could only occur in plants and animals, which should be highly dependent on matter relating to the size. Thus it identifies a subset of biological processes that are macrobiological processes.

On the contrary, in the industry, the interpretation of the term microbiological processes is focused on micro-organisms in opposition to organisms at large. Thus, under such approach, microbiological processes are restricted to those that are specific to micro-organisms and not to be found in other organisms. Hence, processes that are shared by all life forms, such as the synthesis of proteins, should then be included as biological processes. This approach adopts a different logic. In fact, micro and macrobiological processes are a subset of biological processes, thus one can oppose that the distinction between biological and microbiological processes ensures that only processes that exclusively occur in micro-organisms shall be considered as patentable subject matter, the rest being left at the discretion of the Member State.

The African Group in a communication to the WTO[82] went even further. It opposed that microbiological processes should be potentially excludable, as they were in essence biological processes. While it is scientifically true that microbiological processes are a subset of biological processes, the way Article 27.3(b) is worded does not lead to such an interpretation. Hence, it is not held that biological processes at large should be potentially excluded, but those that are not microbiological; thus a distinction is created within the wording.

---

82 IP/C/W/163 WTO.

Thus it appears that a very different approach might be taken depending on which aspect of the definition we are focusing on. If microbiological is opposed to biological, then only processes exclusive to micro-organisms will be at stake. On the contrary, if the definition assumes a wide interpretation of the term microbiological process, then only biological processes that are not found in micro-organisms are potentially excludable, thus processes that are exclusive to macro-organisms.

It has to be noted that the purpose of the TRIPS Agreement is to promote the protection of intellectual property rights – patents in the present context. Consequently, such an objective may enforce the fact that restriction may have to be interpreted in a narrow manner. This approach would favour the first interpretation that we made, which is that only processes that occur in macro-organisms may be excluded. In addition, such exclusion seems to derive from the EPC approach. The Strasbourg Convention, 1963, which originated the Munich Convention (EPC), was concerned with the potential consequences of patent rights over certain breeding and farming activities, thus focusing on processes that related to such practices.

Non-biological processes for the production of plants and animals

Biological processes are defined as any processes that occur within and by the activity of living organisms. Non-biological processes are thus any processes that are not biological processes, being those that are not accomplished as such under natural conditions. In other terms, non-biological process will include any processes that require the action of man at a certain stage to create their occurrence. It may encompass propagation by cutting, hybridisation, genetic engineering and so on.

Essentially biological processes for the production of plants or animals

What are potentially excludable from patent protection are essentially biological processes, the definition of which could be understood by the end of the provision, 'other than non-biological and microbiological processes' that leads to the production of plants or animals.

Therefore, it can first be appreciated that non-biological and microbiological processes shall be patentable subject matter, which includes those that lead to the production of plants and animals. Thus, whereas the wording under Article 27.3(b) may permit plants and animals to be excluded as patentable subject matter, certain processes for the production of plants and animals, especially those employed in biotechnology, shall be considered as patentable subject matter. Moreover, it is only when the purpose is for the production of plants and animals, that essentially biological processes can be excluded. Therefore an essentially biological process for the production of anything else than plants or animals is required to be capable of patent protection, as long as the requirements for patentability are met.

Again, biological processes are defined as any processes that are occurring within and by the activity of living organisms. The opposition with non-biological processes and microbiological processes seems confusing scientifically, as explicated above, but the purpose of the TRIPS Agreement, as well as some of the basis for such provision, seems to restrict the nature of those processes to those that can only be witnessed in macro-organisms or strictly plants and animals.

The use of the term 'essentially' holds no specific scientific meaning in that context and is only a matter of legal interpretation. It is used so as to include a legal qualitative criterion on how the exclusion should be operated. Thus, it introduces a qualitative degree on the interpretation of the exclusion. Instead of an absolute excludable subject matter, this should be understood under a substantive and qualitative approach. In other terms, if a set of processes, or a single multi-step process, which leads to the production of a plant includes a step that is biological, the exclusion should only be effective if the step is viewed as substantively essential. What makes a step substantially essential is undefined.

The possible exclusion of essentially biological processes is restricted under 'the production of plants and animals' in general. Therefore, the processes are being potentially excludable where they are in relation to the genesis of plants or animals: those should include means of selection, breeding, reproduction, propagation, regeneration and so on. Hence, it is mainly processes of propagation at large and selection from existing material that are excluded. It is the mechanistic processes that are at stake, while the acquired traits of the organism are not. While plants and animals might be excluded, a process that is not included in the definition provided above cannot be. In practical terms, this means that a process to insert a gene of interest in a plant, for example, can be patented. But if the exclusion under patent protection for plants and animals is held, the product of such process, the new plant, cannot be enforced under a patent regime. Intellectual property rights will then regulate the breeding activity rather than the agricultural practice, unless one utilises a technological lock, such as the terminator gene.

But it could be interpreted differently. Indeed, the point of view could be from the outcome in addition to the mechanistic approach to the development. The production of plants and animals would then embrace the organism at its final stage. Under that interpretation, every process that permitted such outcome will be potentially excludable. The focus there will be as to how the acquired traits are biological processes without being a microbiological process. In that case, the inclusion of a gene that originates from another macro-organism, being a feature not present in a micro-organism, could be excludable. An example could be the case of basmati rice. The identification of the gene that leads to the specific fragrance of basmati rice and its inclusion within another macro-organism could be excludable. Indeed, it is a macrobiological process that leads to the production of another macro-organism by being inserted within the latter. On the contrary, the exclusion of a trait that originated in a micro-organism would not be permissible. A practical example would be the Bt technology that transmits in plants the capacity of generating a pesticide compound which originated in a micro-organism.

The most general interpretation of the wording would read as: any processes, which are only occurring in macro-organisms, to the genesis of plants and animals in general (both macro and micro[83]), are potentially excludable from patent protection; the restriction being limited under a legal qualitative criterion. In other terms, what is being restricted are breeding methods, in a broader sense, that occur naturally in plants and animals.

Under the EPC, 'a process for the production of plants or animals is essentially biological if it consists entirely of natural phenomena such as crossing or selection'.[84] It has to be opposed with what is not 'biological' in that legal definition, which are microbiological and non-biological processes. Microbiological processes are 'any process involving or performed upon or resulting in microbiological material'.[85] Non-biological processes are generally not specified as such, but seem to relate to those that are not occurring in nature. Hence, it appears that the EPC interpretation is specifically in line with the literal interpretation made previously.

The key question arises in the interpretation of the term 'essentially'. For a process to be essentially biological in the sense of the exclusion, it requires that the substantial part of the claimed process is not within that exclusion. Hence, the fact that a process, which generally includes different steps, has one of its steps included in the restriction must not in itself be a sufficient ground for exclusion. Meanwhile, the fact that one of the steps is either a microbiological process or a non-biological process will not *de facto* make the whole process capable of being patented. Under the

---

83 In that case, the problem encountered before with cell cultures will not occur, as no distinction is made as to the resulting plant and animal size.

84 Rule 23(b)(5) EPC.

85 Rule 23(b)(6) EPC.

EPC, one should take into account the totality of human intervention. For a process not to be an essentially biological process, it will necessitate human intervention as to its capability of occurrence and the intervention should be viewed as non-trivial.[86] In a famous landmark decision of the EPO,[87] the Board analysed each technical step to assess the level of human intervention as to the outcome. Hence, the term 'essentially' should address certain discretion as to the patentability of the process, which will balance the various aspects of the process under the assessment of what appears substantial as to the outcome.

It appears that the distinction made under Article 27.3(b) is again to provide means to exclude, as patent subject matter, processes that are being used traditionally in breeding activities rather than non-traditional biotechnological processes as increasingly used in technologically advanced countries. All legal systems so far reviewed in this study seem to be concerned with basic breeding activities and appear to interpret those terms as restricting the potentially excludable subject matter to those that relate to means of reproduction or selection. Nevertheless, the distinction made previously under the scientific interpretation[88] of the terms could hold under the TRIPS and address substantial effect as to the patentability of biotechnology breeding activities.

Plant and animal varieties

The scientific approach is not very conclusive in providing a straight definition as to what a plant variety is. In botany, the following distinctions have been identified: species, subspecies, varieties, subvarieties, forms, groups and cultivars.

A species is constituted of members that are capable of interbreeding (the offspring is not sterile). A subspecies is the taxon immediately subordinate to species, which therefore has the same quality amongst its members as the one identified by a species plus another level of distinction. Its members differ morphologically and genetically from members of other subspecies. Varieties are normally mistaken with subspecies; they are used for lower degrees of distinction, if needed. A form is used to designate a minor variation within a population or region. For instance, white-flowered forms of species that usually have coloured flowers. Finally, a cultivar is a cultivated selection of a plant species that is vegetatively

---

86 EPO, Technical Board of Appeal, T 320/87.

87 Plant Transgenic Systems, EPO, Technical Board of Appeal, T 356/93.

88 Distinction made between the mechanistic approach to the production of plants and animals, and the process involved in the obtaining of certain traits of interest in the outcome.

propagated, that is, a clone, which means that its genetic pool is not affected by sexual reproduction. A good example would be a hybrid.

So it appears from the basic scientific approach that a plant variety is something between a subspecies, which is a group having a certain extent of distinctive morphological and genetic characteristics that are being reproduced within the group, which is theoretically capable of interbreeding with other subspecies, and a form, which holds all those features, but where the distinctive aspect is limited to one characteristic.

While varieties can be differentiated based on the occurrence in nature and the various levels of distinction, the term has also evolved in response to the practice of the breeding activity. Hence, based on the mode of reproduction, the means of selection and the stability of the created variety, a necessity in that field, more functional definitions were made.[89] *Autogamous fixed varieties in pure lineage* (for example, wheat, green beans, soy, tomatoes) are highly homogenous and easy to reproduce identically. *Autogamous fixed varieties* (eggplant, courgette, chilli) are slightly less stable over reproduction cycles, but still acceptable. *Allogamous homogenised fixed varieties* (carrots, onions, cabbage) originate from more heterogeneous populations and are generally selected for a specific trait. *Hybrid varieties of first generation* (wheat, colza, melon) where the parents are fixed or pure lineage; hence have an inherent stability. *Hybrid varieties of second generation* are those where the first generation is not stable enough and requires another crossing to gain in stability. *Clone varieties* (tulip, iris, rosemary, apple and peer trees, wine, potatoes . . .) are reproduced asexually, and therefore are extremely homogenous unless mutations occur. The list is non-exhaustive but is mentioned to illustrate the complexity of the term.

So, depending on the purpose for differentiating living specimens, the term can be used differently and lead to various interpretations. While considering occurring varieties, naturalists will focus on an inherent cluster of biodiversity, distinguishing factions that present certain characteristics in common. Dissimilarly, a breeder will be concerned with the creation of new stable specimens. Whereas the acquired features of the new variety are obviously the purpose of such activity, the distinction is based on the stability of the creation rather than on a comparative analysis amongst the diverse variability and clusters that could be found in the species in question.

Missing a clear-cut definition of variety, two potential interpretations can be made of the requirement under Article 27.3(b) for a *sui generis*

---

89 Group on Study and Control Variety, www.geves.fr.

protection for plant varieties. On the one hand, because of the position of variety in the taxonomy, the general scientific definition, one could argue that TRIPS does not require the protection of anything that is above or below the variety, that is, subspecies, form and cultivar for example. On the other hand, under the breeder's definition, a variety is an entity that is below the taxon of species, presents certain different features and can be reproduced in a more or less stable manner. Hence, everything that corresponds to those criteria should be capable of being protected under either a patent regime or an effective *sui generis* system.

The International Convention for the Protection of New Varieties of Plants, which is administered by the UPOV,[90] defines the term variety as follows:[91]

> 'Plant variety' means any plant grouping within a single botanical taxon of the lowest known rank, which grouping, irrespective of whether the conditions for the grant of a plant variety right are fully met, can be:
> – defined by the expression of the characteristics that results from a given genotype or combination of genotypes,
> – distinguished from any other plant grouping by the expression of at least one of the said characteristics, and
> – considered as a unit with regard to its suitability for being propagated unchanged.

This definition is reproduced literally in the Council Regulation (EC) No. 2100/94 of 27 July 1994 on Community Plant Variety Rights, Chapter I, Article 5.2, as well as under the Implementing Regulations to the Convention on the Grant of European Patents, Chapter VI Rule 23b.

Animal varieties are generally defined in science as a subgroup of species. Therefore they are theoretically capable of reproduction with other subgroups, but are differentiated with a set of characteristics that appears somehow reproduced within the same subgroup. A good example would be a dog pedigree. The distinction between animal and animal varieties is not required under TRIPS, but is being provided as it is a matter of exclusion for patentability in certain Member States such as the States signatory to the European Patent Convention.

---

[90] Union pour la Protection des Obtentions Végétales.

[91] International Convention for the Protection of New Varieties of Plants of 2 December 1961, as revised in Geneva on 10 November 1972, on 23 October 1978, and on 19 March 1991 (commonly referenced as the UPOV 1991), Chapter I, Article 1(vi).

GENES

Genes are obviously of central importance to the development and value of biotechnology. The core aspect of biotechnology is to engineer new organisms that incorporate certain traits of interest, traits that are the function of gene expression or non-expression. Article 27.3(b) of TRIPS does not mention as such the term gene in the possible exclusions. Thus, under a first appreciation, genes must be capable of being patented, reflecting the implications of Article 27.1 of TRIPS. Following the development made above, it seems that under certain interpretations, the term gene might be implied or capable of being incorporated in some of the exclusions.

They can be simply defined as the 'unit of heredity which is transferred from a parent to offspring and is held to determine some characteristic of the offspring; in particular, a distinct sequence of DNA forming part of a chromosome'.[92] Thus, by definition, they are parts of any organisms and are involved in determining the characteristics of an organisms; thus their expression have a biological role.

Under Article 27.3(b), plants and animals may be excluded from being patentable subject matter. The question may be raised as to the implications of the terms plants and animals. Are they to be conceived as whole organisms, or can the exclusion apply to parts of them? Under the latter approach, genes could then potentially be excluded under Article 27.3(b) TRIPS. On the issue whether a plant or an animal has to be considered as a whole to be excluded, it seems that more restrictive legislations will be specific in the wording of their exclusion rather than including those concerns within a definition.[93] Genes, under the EPO, JPO, USPTO, are not considered as life forms but rather as chemical compounds; however, even if they were, those patent regimes are not excluding life forms as such. It is also interesting to note that under Article 5.3 of the same Council Regulation (EC) No. 2100/94, it is held that

> A plant grouping consists of entire plants or parts of plants as far as such parts are capable of producing entire plants, both referred to hereinafter as 'variety constituents'.

Thus, it seems that under such regulation, the distinction as such between whole or parts is irrelevant; what matters is whether the subject matter is capable of producing an entire plant. This would be in line with the original reasoning behind such exception, which is to free certain breeding activity from patent protection. In the meantime, it is to be

92 *Concise Oxford English Dictionary*.

93 Andean Community Decision 486, Brazilian Patent Act, Indian Patent Act.

noted that breeding activity has evolved and is now deeply involved with technology based on the use of specific genes, thus it might still be implied in the purpose of the exclusion while adapting to modern technology.

In addition, also considered above, genes are the informational bases that define the characteristics of an organism. The information encoded is generally translated to proteins, which have a biological role. Thus, a gene as such is what governs most biological processes. So, whereas a gene as such, being a product, may not be excluded as an essentially biological process, the use made of the gene could be; especially when such traits are being selected from another plant or animal.

8. Towards optimal pro-biotech patent regimes

So can we rank developing countries according to their biotechnological capacities?

Are we capable of measuring and thereby ranking the biotechnological capacities of different developing countries so as to determine the most efficient way countries should take advantage of the flexibilities of Article 27.3(b) of TRIPS? The earlier discussion above would suggest that this is a difficult thing to do, since no 100 per cent reliable schemas or indices have yet been devised, certainly not the ones we reviewed earlier which comprise all of the well-known ones. Needless to say, perhaps, such a task is possible but requires further research.

The three developing countries that we looked at are widely acknowledged to be among the more advanced developing countries in terms of biotech capacity and potential, especially India. Indeed, India's biotech sector stands apart from almost every other developing country in its size and potential. Yet even here, the ability of India's commercial biotechnology sector to take advantage of the patent system is still quite limited at this time.

As for attracting FDI, India is becoming more successful with life science corporations setting up research and development facilities in the country. Since India's patent system is still considered by many transnational corporations to be inadequate, the existence of a large number of well-qualified and inexpensive-to-hire Indians able to do the research and the enormous growth potential of such a high-population market are likely to be far more significant factors than the patent regime, however it may be designed. That is not to say that a more expansive patent regime would not necessarily spur accelerated biotech research-oriented FDI. We have no evidence to counter such a scenario, and therefore cannot rule it out. Nonetheless, the growth of such investment has so far not been directly influenced by changes to the patent regime and has more to do with the relative cheapness of doing high quality research in India compared to Europe and North America.

The implementation menu

Regulating biotechnology, a new, complex, expensive, research-intensive and rapidly advancing field presents particular challenges for developing country policymakers. If they lack a clear idea of how – and even whether – biotechnology can benefit their economies and improve the lives of their citizens, they are in no position to design a patent system to promote welfare-enhancing biotechnological innovation. Moreover, many of these countries have no biotechnology industries to speak of, and there is every reason to be highly sceptical that such businesses will spring up just because life forms and micro- and non-biological processes can be patented. And yet, they have obligations under international intellectual property law to provide patent protection for at least some types of biotechnological invention. What is a developing country government to do?

On the basis of what we have covered so far, we present three different ways to implement Article 27.3(b). Option 1 (Table 16.1) we call the 'no exceptions option'. This more or less reflects US practice and is unlikely to be optimal for any developing country.

Option 2 (Table 16.2) is the 'all exceptions option', which incorporates all of the exceptions while construing the terminology widely or narrowly so that what must be provided is the absolute minimum that is legally acceptable and scientifically reasonable, while as much subject matter as possible is kept outside the patent system.

Option 3 (Table 16.3) is the 'some exceptions option'. It is not really a single option and the table aims merely to provide some examples of exclusions and interpretations. Between Options 1 and 2 lie a whole range of possibilities between the two extremes, and Table 16.3 provides just a few of these.

Table 16.1 Biotech patenting in TRIPS: the 'no exceptions option'

Provide
Micro-organisms (broadly defined)
Animals and plants (including plant varieties by patents and an effective *sui generis* system) and their parts including seeds, somatic cells, gametes, cells, genes
Essentially micro- and macrobiological processes
Non-biological processes
Plant varieties also (either by patents, an effective *sui generis* system or by any combination thereof)

Table 16.2 Biotech patenting in TRIPS: the 'all exceptions option'

Provide	Exclude
Micro-organisms (narrowly defined, e.g. unicellular organisms in the range of 10^{-5} m maximum size)	Whole animals and plants (including plant varieties) and their parts (including seeds, somatic cells, gametes, genes and gene products)
Microbiological processes that are specific to micro-organisms	Essentially biological processes for the production of plants or animals (even with substantial human intervention)
Non-biological processes	
Plant varieties (only by an effective *sui generis* system, e.g. modelled on UPOV 1978)	

Table 16.3 Biotech patenting in TRIPS: the 'some exceptions option'

Provide	Exclude
Micro-organisms (narrowly defined)	Whole animals and plants
Microbiological processes found in micro-organisms that are found in larger organisms too	Essentially biological processes for the production of plants or animals
Non-biological processes	
Plant varieties (only by an effective *sui generis* system, e.g. modelled on UPOV 1988 or 1991)	
Genes (as chemicals with specified function)	

In this study, we have been sceptical about the methods available for assessing the biotechnological capacities of developing countries, and we have called for more research in this area, making the case, one hopes, for why this is vitally important. However, our survey of three relatively advanced developing countries highlighted that in this recent and rapidly advancing field of technology most, if not all, of the developing world lags far behind countries like the United States, Japan and such European countries as the UK, Germany and France. Therefore, for the overwhelming majority of developing countries, the all exceptions option is for the time being the most rational basis for biotech-related patent rule-making. However, for the most advanced of the developing countries, which are beginning to innovate and seek to develop their inventions either alone or in collaboration with foreign corporations, some elements of Option 2 may now be desirable.

From policy-taking to policy-making

Historical evidence shows that well-designed intellectual property systems can benefit national economies, just as poorly designed ones can harm them. But how does one go about designing and negotiating an appropriate intellectual property system or fine-tuning an existing one? The economic and social impact of intellectual property reform is very hard to predict reliably, especially in the long term. This is particularly the case for developing countries. This is a real handicap in the present situation where countries are pressured to negotiate and implement new multilateral trade rules, bilateral or regional free trade or investment agreements, and to respond to powerful stakeholder groups – often foreign ones – demanding changes to national regimes that may not serve the interests of their citizens and other domestic stakeholders. Such difficulties in measuring impacts make it difficult for governments and their representatives to know what negotiating position to adopt on intellectual property, how best to handle complex trade issue-linkage bargains, and how far they should accommodate the demands of international business interests clamouring for change to domestic intellectual property rules.

As with other areas of business regulation, intellectual property policy-making and negotiation position formation is, or at least should be, a matter for *national* decision-making involving the collaboration of all *national* stakeholders, including owners, users and the public. Foreign interests should not be ignored, but government business regulation is about what is good for the national economy and the country's citizens. Good policy-making cannot be based solely on the implementation of obligations accepted in multilateral treaties or regional or bilateral trade agreements. Unfortunately, policy-making often seems to be done in this way, which is to say that policy-*taking* is the norm rather than policy-*making*. What we have here are political and technical challenges. So as to better overcome the challenges, technical assistance providers themselves have much to learn. In the present context, they and others claiming to be authorities on how to design biotech patent regimes sensitive to the specificities of individual countries must provide convincing objective evidence for their prescriptions. And recipient countries must of course demand such evidence.

17 Compulsory licensing of patented pharmaceutical inventions: evaluating the options

*Jerome H. Reichman**

1. How compulsory licensing survived the TRIPS Agreement of 1994

Few topics in international intellectual property law have been as controversial in recent years as the one we are about to examine. In the 1980s and early 1990s, a Diplomatic Conference attempted to revise the Paris Convention of 1883, the oldest international convention providing some protection for patented inventions outside of the domestic laws.[1] Those efforts broke down, largely because developed and developing countries could not agree on the powers that governments should retain to issue compulsory licenses or on the grounds for which these powers could be exercised.[2] The failure of this Conference, held under the auspices of the World Intellectual Property Organization (WIPO), persuaded the technology-exporting countries to link future negotiations concerning international intellectual property protection to the Multilateral Trade Negotiations, known as the Uruguay Round, which got under way in 1986.[3] The end result was Annex IC of the Agreement Establishing the

---

* An earlier version of this article appeared in 37 J. Law, Medicine and Ethics 247 (2009). The author wishes to thank Professor Kevin Outterson for his invaluable suggestions and insights. He also gratefully acknowledges the support of the National Human Genome Research Institute and the Department of Energy under Grant No. 5P50 G003391-02.

1 Paris Convention for the Protection of Industrial Property, Mar. 20, 1883, as revised at Stockholm (1967), 21 UST 1583, 828 UNTS 305 [hereinafter Paris Convention].

2 *See, e.g.,* Jerome H. Reichman with Catherine Hasenzahl, *Non-Voluntary Licensing of Patented Inventions: Historical Perspective, Legal Framework under TRIPS, and an Overview of the Practice in Canada and the U.S.A.*, UN Conf. on Trade & Devel. [UNCTAD] & Int'l Cent. Trade & Sust. Devel. [ICTSD], Project on IPRs and Sustainable Development, Issue Paper No. 5, available at http://ictsd.net/i/publications/11764/ (June 2003) [hereinafter Reichman with Hasenzahl].

3 For comprehensive accounts of this process, *see* Peter Drahos with John Braithwaite, Information Feudalism: Who Owns the Knowledge Economy? (Earthscan, 2002); Susan K. Sell, Power and Ideas: North-South Politics of Intellectual Property and Antitrust (NY State Univ. Press 1998); Susan

World Trade Organization of 1994, which incorporated a new, comprehensive and relatively elevated set of international minimum standards of patent protection into the Agreement on Trade-Related Aspects of Intellectual Property Rights (TRIPS Agreement).[4]

1.1 What the TRIPS Agreement did not give the pharmaceutical sector

Taken together, the TRIPS Agreement's standards amounted to a veritable revolution in international intellectual property law from which the research-based pharmaceutical industry emerged as one of the biggest winners. Faced with a 'take it or leave it decision', all developing-country Members of the WTO, including those with growing pharmaceutical production capabilities, such as India, Brazil and eventually China, agreed to respect relatively stringent worldwide norms of patent protection no later than 2005.[5] In return, these countries were given greater access to devel-

---

Footnote 3 (*cont.*)
K. Sell, Private Power, Public Law: The Globalization of Intellectual Property Rights (Cambridge Univ. Press, 2003); Laurence R. Helfer, *Regime Shifting: The TRIPS Agreement and New Dynamics of International Intellectual Property Lawmaking*, 29 Yale J. Int'l L. 1 (2004).

[4] *See* Agreement on Trade-Related Aspects of Intellectual Property Rights, Apr. 15, 1994, 33 ILM 81, arts. 27–34 (1994), *available at* http://www.wto.org/english/docs_e/legal_e/27-trips.pdf [hereinafter TRIPS]; Marrakesh Agreement Establishing the World Trade Organization, Apr. 15, 1994, 1867 UNTS 154; 33 ILM 1144 (1994), *available at* http://www.wto.org/english/docs_e/legal_e/legal_e.htm. The United States implemented the WTO Agreements in the Uruguay Round Agreements Act, Pub. L. No. 103-465, 108 Stat. 4809 (1994). For details, see Carlos M. Correa, *Patent Rights*, *in* Intellectual Property and International Trade – The TRIPS Agreement (C.M. Correa & A.A. Yusuf, eds, Wolfers Kluwer, 2nd ed., 2008) 227–59; Jerome H. Reichman, *Universal Minimum Standards of Intellectual Property Protection under the TRIPS Component of the WTO Agreement*, *in* Intellectual Property and International Trade – The TRIPS Agreement, *supra*, 23–78.

[5] *See* TRIPS, *supra* note 4, at arts. 65–6, 70; World Trade Organization, Declaration on the TRIPS Agreement and Public Health, Nov. 20, 2001, WT/MIN(01)/DEC/2, at para. 4, *available at* http://www.wto.org/english/thewto_e/minist_e/min01_e/mindecl_trips_e.htm [hereinafter Declaration on TRIPS]. From this date on, developing countries were required to provide at least 20 years of patent protection to a broad range of products, including pharmaceutical products, and mailboxes with pending patent applications were opened and began being processed. A few Least-developed countries (LDCs) remain exempt from protecting patents until 2013 and patents on pharmaceuticals until 2016. *See* Extension of the Transition Period Under Article 66.1 for Least-developed Country Members, Decision of the Council for TRIPS of 19 November 2005, WTO doc. IP/C/40 (Nov. 30, 2005); Extension of the Transition Period under Article 66.1 of the

oped markets for traditional manufactured goods, plus a commitment of the developed countries to stop imposing unilateral trade sanctions for allegedly inadequate protection of foreign intellectual property rights (IPRs).[6]

Ironically, if the developing countries lost the war, in the sense that their generic pharmaceutical industries could no longer freely reverse-engineer the costly products of foreign research and development under the shield of domestic laws that ignored pharmaceutical patents, they won a great battle with specific regard to the question of compulsory licenses,[7] which had triggered the drive for the TRIPS Agreement in the first place. Thanks largely to the fortitude and analytical skills of the Indian delegation,[8] the right of governments to grant compulsory licenses on virtually any ground – including public interest, abuse or anti-competitive conduct, or for non-commercial government use, among others – issued stronger and clearer from the TRIPS Agreement than had previously been the case under the Paris Convention.[9]

The TRIPS Agreement did subject the exercise of this power to certain preconditions, including a duty to notify and negotiate with the affected patentees under ordinary circumstances; but these specific conditions, among others, are waived in the case of 'national emergency or other circumstances of extreme urgency or in cases of public noncommercial [i.e., government] use'.[10] Moreover, the very existence of these conditions only magnified the legitimacy of every complying government's right to resort to compulsory licensing whenever its domestic self-interest so required.[11]

Historians may wish to note that, while international minimum standards of patent protection have gradually and progressively risen over time,

---

TRIPS Agreement for Least-developed Country Members for Certain Obligations with Respect to Pharmaceutical Products, Decision of the Council for TRIPS of 27 June 2002, WTO doc. IP/C/25 (July 1, 2002).

6 Understanding on Rules and Procedures Governing the Settlement of Disputes, Apr. 15, 1994, 33 ILM 1226, art. 23 (1994), *available at* http://www.wto.org/english/tratop_e/dispu_e/dsu_e.htm [hereinafter DSU]; *see infra* note 173 and accompanying text.

7 TRIPS, *supra* note 4, at art. 31.

8 *See* JAYASHREE WATAL, INTELLECTUAL PROPERTY RIGHTS IN THE WTO AND DEVELOPING COUNTRIES (Kluwer Law Int'l, 2001).

9 *Compare* Paris Convention, *supra* note 1, art. 5A, *with* TRIPS, *supra* note 4, art. 31; *see* Reichman with Hasenzahl, *supra* note 2.

10 TRIPS, *supra* note 4, at art. 31(b).

11 Indeed, it was the United States' inability to distinguish its routine exercise of government use licenses from other compulsory licenses that led to the breadth of article 31 in the first place. *See, e.g.*, WATAL, *supra* note 8.

in keeping with the expressed goals of the Paris Union,[12] every attempt to limit or constrain a state's power to issue compulsory licenses has invariably resulted in a strengthening of that same power at the international level.[13] Policymakers and scholars should also note that two European Union (EU) countries, France and Belgium, recently adopted new and sweeping powers to grant compulsory licenses of patented pharmaceutical inventions for public health purposes.[14]

1.1.1 The Doha Ministerial Declaration on TRIPS and Public Health

The developing countries' victory in this regard – modest as it otherwise seems in the overall context of burdensome TRIPS obligations[15] – was destined to bear even greater fruits with specific regard to pharmaceuticals. The worldwide patent standards adopted by the TRIPS Agreement threatened to disrupt future supplies of patented medicines at prices people in poor countries could afford by elevating the prices patentees would charge affluent patients in these countries.[16] In principle, developing-country governments needing drugs at prices lower than those of the patentees could issue compulsory licenses under article 31 of the TRIPS Agreement.[17] In reality, most of these countries lacked the capacity to manufacture the drugs in question, or otherwise to obtain the key active ingredients, in which case the granting of a compulsory license could amount to an empty gesture for lack of access to non-infringing generic substitutes.

Of course, Good Samaritan countries that possessed manufacturing capacity might be willing to assist a needy country by issuing compulsory

---

[12] Paris Convention, *supra* note 1, at art. 1.

[13] Reichman with Hasenzahl, *supra* note 2.

[14] Jèrôme Debrulle, Leew De Cort, & Monique Petit, *La license obligatoire belge pour raison de santé publique*, *in* Gene Patents and Public Health, 159 (Geertrui van Overwalle, ed., Bruylant, 2007) [English translation & summary at 199]; Esther van Zimmeren & Gilles Requena, *Ex-officio Licensing in the Medical Sector: The French Model, in* Gene Patents and Public Health, *supra* at 123. Switzerland has also adopted legislation allowing compulsory licenses on diagnostic processes or products to remedy anticompetitive practices. See Federal Law on Patents [Switz.] June 25, 1954, as amended Sept. 1, 2008, art. 40(c).

[15] *See* Jerome H. Reichman & Rochelle Cooper Dreyfuss, *Harmonization without Consensus: Critical Reflections on Drafting a Substantive Patent Law Treaty*, 57 Duke L. J. 85, 94–8 (2007).

[16] For the reasons, *see* Sean Flynn, Aidan Hollis, & Mike Palmedo, *An Economic Justification for Open Access to Essential Medicine Patents in Developing Countries*, 37 J.L. Med. & Ethics 184 (2009).

[17] TRIPS, *supra* note 4, art. 31.

licenses of their own, with a view to exporting supplies of the drug in question for this purpose. But that type of assistance was limited by article 31(f) of the TRIPS Agreement, which expressly required products manufactured under a compulsory license to serve 'predominantly for the supply of the domestic market' (thus limiting such exports literally to 49.9 per cent of the total output).[18] Moreover, even middle-income countries with growing manufacturing capacity, such as India and Brazil, might themselves need a drug that they could not manufacture locally, in order to temper a patentee's prices. In that case, any willing supplier to them – if one could be found in a developed country – would likewise be bound by the limitation on exports that article 31(f) imposed.

The tensions generated by these prospects for rising prices of essential medicines came to a head in the late1990s, at the very time when the developed countries wanted the developing countries to agree to yet another round of Multilateral Trade Negotiations, to be known as the Doha Round. The latter countries made removal of constraints on their public health authorities under the TRIPS Agreement a *sine qua non* of their participation in that Round. The outcome was a momentous Ministerial Declaration on the TRIPS Agreement and Public Health of 2001, which, in paragraph 4, affirmed that this Agreement 'can and should be interpreted and implemented in a manner supportive of WTO Members' rights to protect public health and, in particular, *to promote access to medicines for all*'.[19]

The Ministerial Declaration expressly reconfirmed many of the key flexibilities set out in the TRIPS Agreement,[20] including the power of WTO Members 'to grant compulsory licenses and the freedom to determine the grounds upon which such licenses are granted',[21] a freedom that the originator pharmaceutical companies had continued to question despite the clarity of the TRIPS language itself. The Declaration then expressly addressed the constraints on exports set out in article 31(f) of TRIPS. In paragraph 6, it provided a mandate for 'establishing legal machinery to enable countries lacking the capacity to manufacture generic substitutes for costly patented medicines under domestically issued compulsory licenses to obtain imports from countries able and willing to assist them without interference from the relevant patent holders'.[22]

---

18 *Id.*, art 31(f).

19 Declaration on TRIPS, *supra* note 5, at para. 4 (emphasis added).

20 Declaration on TRIPS, *supra* note 5, at paras. 4–5.

21 Declaration on TRIPS, *supra* note 5, at para. 5.b.

22 Frederick M. Abbott & Jerome H. Reichman, *The Doha Round's Public Health Legacy: Strategies for the Production and Diffusion of Patented Medicines*

1.1.2 The Waiver to, and Pending Amendment of, Article 31

This solution, which obviously improved the export opportunities for generic producers in Brazil, China, India and other emerging economies, was to be broadly applied to all 'products of the pharmaceutical sector needed to address the public health problems as recognized in paragraph 1 of [the Ministerial Declaration]'.[23] There were no limitations in that paragraph on the application of the new legal machinery either to cases of national emergency or to specific diseases or medicines.[24] This machinery would thus enable any country (that had not voluntarily waived the privilege) to issue a compulsory license for a medicine it could not produce and then to seek help from any other country having that capacity that was willing to assist it. If the latter country issued a second compulsory license, and otherwise complied with specified conditions of registration and packaging, it could produce the requested medicines entirely for export and supply the needy country, notwithstanding the language of article 31(f) of the TRIPS Agreement to the contrary.[25] While 'adequate compensation' must be paid to the patentee,[26] it will be collected once only, in the exporting country, based on conditions in the importing country.[27]

In other words, the scheme ultimately negotiated under the auspices of paragraph 6 of the Doha Ministerial Declaration envisioned a process of back-to-back compulsory licenses that would enable any country needing medicines at lower prices than those charged by local patentees to seek assistance from other countries able and willing to produce the drugs for

---

Footnote 22 (*cont.*)
under the Amended TRIPS Provisions,10(4) J. Int'l Econ. L. 921, 929 (2007); *see* Declaration on TRIPS, *supra* note 5, at para. 6; TRIPS, *supra* note 4, art. 31(f).

[23] Abbott & Reichman, *supra* note 22, at 937.

[24] For a detailed analysis of Article 31's disease scope, *see* Kevin Outterson's Chapter 19 in this volume. An earlier version of this chapter is found at: Kevin Outterson, *Should Access to Medicines and TRIPS Flexibilities be Limited to Specific Diseases?*, 34 Am. J. L. & Med. 279 (2008) [hereinafter *Access to Medicine and TRIPS*].

[25] World Trade Organization, Implementation of Paragraph 6 of the Doha Declaration on the TRIPS Agreement and Public Health, Decision of the General Council of 30 August 2003, Aug. 30, 2003, WT/L/540, *available at* http://www.wto.org/english/tratop_e/trips_e/implem_para6_e.htm [hereinafter Waiver Decision]; World Trade Organization, Amendment of the TRIPS Agreement, Dec. 6, 2005, WT/L/641, *available at* http://www.wto.org/english/tratop_e/trips_e/wtl641_e.htm [hereinafter Amendment of TRIPS]; Abbott & Reichman, *supra* note 22.

[26] TRIPS, *supra* note 4, at art. 31(h). *See generally* Antony Taubman, *Rethinking TRIPS: 'Adequate Remuneration' for Non-Voluntary Patent Licensing*, 11 J. Int'l Econ. L. 927 (2008).

[27] Abbott & Reichman, *supra* note 22, at 944.

export purposes, without interference from the patentee in either country. After protracted and difficult negotiations, this solution was initially embodied in a Waiver, known as the Decision of 30 August 2003.[28] If all goes as planned, this Waiver would be rendered permanent by virtue of a pending Amendment to the TRIPS Agreement, known as article 31*bis*.[29] The Waiver remains in effect while governments take steps to ratify the Amendment,[30] as the European Union recently did after the European Parliament endorsed the Amendment and issued instructions for its wholehearted implementation.[31] As of 2009, the Waiver process had only been used once due in part to the cumbersome procedures put in place by some governments, in addition to the core WTO process.[32]

Meanwhile, the originator pharmaceutical industry did not accept this further defeat without countervailing initiatives of its own. Besides flooding the world with misleading and self-serving interpretations of the relevant legal instruments, which continue to influence incautious government officials and even some scholars to this day, the industry persuaded the United States Trade Representative (USTR) to recapture some of the lost ground by means of Bilateral or Regional Free Trade Agreements with developing countries. While this topic lies well beyond the scope of this chapter, readers should be aware that the flexibilities concerning governmental powers to grant compulsory licenses of patented pharmaceutical medicines under the legal regime described above could be severely limited, or even largely abrogated, by the one-sided intellectual property provisions of specific FTAs.[33] Moreover, threats of retaliation and political

---

[28] Waiver Decision, *supra* note 25. *See, e.g.*, Duncan Matthews, *WTO Decision on Implementation of Paragraph 6 of the Doha Declaration on the TRIPS Agreement and Public Health: A Solution to the Access to Essential Medicines Problem?*, 7 J. INT'L ECON. L. 73 (2004).

[29] Amendment of TRIPS, *supra* note 25.

[30] Abbott & Reichman *supra* note 22, at 929.

[31] *See, e.g.,* Bryan C. Mercurio, *TRIPS, Patents, and Access to Life-saving Drugs in the Developing World,* 8 MARQ. INTELL. PROP. L. REV. 211 (2004); Abbott & Reichman, *supra* note 22, at 947.

[32] Paige E. Goodwin, *Right Idea, Wrong Result – Canada's Access to Medicines Regime*, 34 AM. J.L. & MED. 567 (2008).

[33] Bryan Mercurio, *TRIPS-plus Provisions in FTAs: Recent Trends*, *in* REGIONAL TRADE AGREEMENTS AND THE WTO LEGAL SYSTEM 215 (L. Bartels & F. Ortino, eds, 2006); Abbott & Reichman, *supra* note 22, at 958–66; Lorna Dwyer, *Patent Protection and Access to Medicine: The Colombian and Peruvian Trade Promotion Agreements*, 13 L. & BUS. REV. OF THE AMERICAS 825 (2007). For an example from a developed country, *see* Kevin Outterson, *Agony in the Antipodes: The Generic Drug Provisions in the Australia – US Free Trade Agreement*, 2 J. GENERIC MED. 316, 316–26 (2005).

pressure from USTR and other governmental agencies, including some spokesmen for intergovernmental agencies and even for the European Commission, effectively kept most governments – until recently – from actually invoking or using the legal rights they had doggedly managed to obtain at the international level.

There was, in short, a conspicuous absence of compulsory licensing in the pharmaceutical sector even after the decision of the South African authorities, in 2003, to the effect that two foreign firms had violated the domestic competition law by refusing to grant licenses for patents on essential AIDS medicines.[34] While this decision did result in the issuing of compulsory licenses (within the ambit of TRIPS Agreement article 31(k)), the heated legal battles and controversy surrounding this case, plus renewed pressures from powerful governments, may actually have diminished, rather than strengthened, the developing countries' appetites for attracting unwelcome attention by such means. This pressure was intensified by mushrooming FTAs that aimed to circumscribe their rights under TRIPS.

1.2 The legal giant escapes its chains

Beneath the surface, however, health ministries in a number of countries had quietly begun to use the threat of compulsory licenses to rein in the prices of selected medicines, particularly AIDS drugs.[35] Because negotiated deals under threat of compulsory license are often kept secret, the surface calm appeared greater than it really was. Beginning in 2006, this calm was shattered by the sudden appearance of compulsory licenses on pharmaceuticals – or public threats thereof – in both the southern and northern hemispheres. In the period 2006–2007, for example, Thailand's public health authorities issued two compulsory licenses on AIDS drugs and one on clopidogrel bisulfate (Plavix), a major cardiovascular treatment. Thailand did not issue the licenses discreetly, but with a considerable fanfare and with a list of other drugs slated for similar treatment in the future.[36] In April 2007, the President of Brazil signed an order for a compulsory license for government use of Merck's patent on the antiret-

---

[34] Flynn et al., *supra* note 16, at 191–2.

[35] Downward pressures on AIDS drugs were further exerted by private foundations (especially the Clinton Foundation) and both national (*e.g.*, PEPFAR in the US) and international aid programs.

[36] Kristina M. Lybecker & Elisabeth Fowler, *Compulsory Licensing in Canada and Thailand: Comparing Regimes to Ensure Legitimate Use of the WTO Rules*, 37 J.L. Med. & Ethics 222 (2009).

roviral drug, efavirenz (Sustiva), in a public ceremony that was broadcast around the world.[37]

All these licenses were issued under the authority of existing TRIPS provisions, that is, article 31 as it stands,[38] without regard to the Waiver. In 2007, Rwanda issued a compulsory license for AIDS drugs that it could not produce locally and applied for assistance from Canada, thus triggering the first set of back-to-back compulsory licenses under the Waiver provisions that had implemented Paragraph 6 of the Doha Ministerial Declaration.[39] In 2008, Indonesia threatened originator pharmaceutical companies with compulsory licensing and even expulsion unless they were willing to invest in local production of pharmaceuticals.[40]

Other compulsory licensing procedures that led to agreements with major pharmaceutical companies had reportedly been initiated in Malaysia (2004), Indonesia (2004), Brazil (2003 and 2007), Zambia (2004), Zimbabwe (2004), and Mozambique (2004).[41] Moreover, compulsory licenses were threatened against Roche for the use of oseltamivir (Tamiflu) in Indonesia, India, Vietnam, and South Korea, in the period 2003–2006. As a result, Roche selected partners in those countries to assist in the manufacture of sufficient supplies of Tamiflu to combat Asian influenza.[42]

Even the United States threatened Bayer with a compulsory license on ciprofloxacin (Cipro) in 2001, which the US intended to stockpile as a defense against anthrax.[43] Bayer drastically lowered its price in response.

---

[37] *See, e.g.*, Joe Cohen, *Brazil Thailand Override Big Pharma Patents*, SCIENCE, May 11, 2007, at 816; Abbott & Reichman, *supra* note 22, at 950–52 (noting that, until 2007, Brazil had reached negotiated settlements with foreign suppliers without formally issuing a compulsory license).

[38] *See* Outterson, *Access to Medicines and TRIPS, supra* note 24, at 320–21; Outterson, Chapter 19, this volume. *But see* Lybecker & Fowler, *supra* note 36 (who disagree on this point).

[39] Goodwin, *supra* note 32, at 569; Lybecker & Fowler, *supra* note 36, at 223.

[40] Sinfah Tunsarawuth, *Indonesia Mulls Compulsory Licences on Three More HIV/AIDS Drugs,* INTEL. PROP. WATCH, Nov. 26, 2007, *available at* http://www.ip-watch.org/weblog/2007/11/26/indonesia-mulls-compulsory-licences-on-three-more-hivaids-drugs/ (last accessed Mar. 3, 2009).

[41] *See* van Zimmeren & Requena, *supra* note 14, at 123, 139 n. 38; James Packard Love, *Recent Examples of Compulsory Licensing of Patents*, KEI, May 6, 2007, *available at* http://www.keionline.org/index.php?option=com_content&task=view&id=41 (last accessed Mar. 3, 2009).

[42] van Zimmeren & Requena, *supra* note 14, at 140.

[43] Love, *supra* note 41, at 3; Abbott & Reichman *supra* note 22, at 939; Jill Carroll & Ron Winslow, *Bayer Agrees to Slash Prices for Cipro Drug*, WALL ST. J.,

In the European Union, meanwhile, the French government extended an already potent system of ex-officio compulsory licensing for public health reasons to cover genetic diagnostic patents in 2004, in response to concerns about excessive prices and restrictive licensing conditions on patented diagnostic tests for breast and ovarian cancer.[44] In 2005, the Belgian government adopted even broader new measures, allowing the authorities to grant compulsory licenses in the interest of public health generally, with accelerated procedures in case of a public health crisis.[45]

These bold provisions in Belgium are even more remarkable because they do not purport to derive their authority from article 31 of TRIPS. Belgian officials claim their actions are justified under articles 8 and 30 of the TRIPS Agreement, which respectively allow 'measures necessary to protect public health' and limited exceptions to the patentee's exclusive rights under article 28.[46] In effect, the Belgian provision attempts to sidestep the conditions set out in article 31. While neither the French nor the Belgian authorities have so far issued compulsory licenses under these provisions, '[l]awyers and patent attorneys argue . . . that the presence of these mechanisms brings pressure to bear upon non-cooperative patent holders and serves as a convincing argument to settle and drag them into a licensing agreement'.[47]

On still another front, the Italian Competition Law authorities issued compulsory licenses against Merck, on certain antibiotics, for abuse of a dominant position in 2005; against Glaxo, for refusal to license a patented migraine headache drug in 2006; and against Merck again for a refusal to license a treatment for baldness in 2008.[48] Also in 2008, the European Commission began a sweeping investigation of pharmaceutical company

---

Footnote 43 (*cont.*)
Oct. 25, 2001, at A3 ('The agreement comes after a high-stakes threat by Tommy Thompson, HHS secretary, to break Bayer's patent for Cipro if he didn't get the price he wanted.'). The relevant US compulsory license statutes are 7 USC § 2404 (2000) (plant variety protection certificates necessary for the nation's fiber, food, or feed supply); 28 USC § 1498 (2000) (government use of patents); 35 USC § 203 (2000) (patents developed through the use of government research funding under the Bayh-Dole Act); and 42 USC § 2183 (2000) (atomic energy). The US compulsory license statutes do not meet all of the restrictions required by Article 31 of TRIPS. *See* TRIPS, *supra* note 4, at art. 31.

44 van Zimmeren & Requena, *supra* note 14 , at 133–4.

45 Debrulle et al., *supra* note 14, at 159, 163.

46 Debrulle et al., *supra* note 14, at 171; *but see infra* note 97.

47 van Zimmeren & Requena, *supra* note 14, at 137.

48 Love, *supra* note 41, at 10–11. For details *see* Rita Coco & Paolisa Nebbia, *Compulsory Licensing and Interim Measures in Merck: A Case for Italy or for Antitrust?*, 2 J. Intell. Prop. L. & Prac. 452 (2007).

practices[49] which, if found anticompetitive, could lead to additional compulsory licenses.

In short, the pre-existing period of calm has given rise to a proliferation of compulsory licenses in various parts of the world, which in turn has generated heated controversy in both legal and public health circles. It is against this background that, in the rest of this chapter, I will evaluate three recent articles expressing very different views on this topic.[50]

2. Contemplating the giant's footprints in the sand

For the sake of convenience, we may characterize these articles respectively as providing 'A Realistic View',[51] 'A Sympathetic Skeptic's View'[52] and a 'Hostile Sympathizer's View'.[53] I propose to examine them separately, but within the larger context sketched above.

2.1 The realists' perspective

Most economists would agree that, in a perfect world, originator pharmaceutical companies would avoid the risk of compulsory licensing by pricing their products so close to the marginal cost of production that poor people around the world could afford to buy them.[54] Assuming that

---

49 Stephen Castle & James Kanter, *European Antitrust Regulators Raid Drug Companies,* INTERNATIONAL HERALD TRIBUNE, Jan. 16, 2008 *available* at http://www.iht.com/articles/2008/01/16/business/drug.php (last accessed Mar. 7, 2009); DG COMPETITION, PHARMACEUTICAL SECTOR INQUIRY: PRELIMINARY REPORT (Nov. 28, 2008) *available at http://ec.europa.eu/competition/sectors/pharmaceuticals/inquiry/preliminary_report.pdf* (last accessed Mar. 7, 2009).

50 *See* Flynn, Hollis & Palmedo, *supra* note 16; Lybecker & Fowler, *supra* note 36; Robert C. Bird, *Developing Nations and the Compulsory License: Maximizing Access to Essential Medicines while Minimizing Investment Side Effects*, 27 J.L. MED. & ETHICS 209 (2009). These articles appeared in a Symposium Issue, guest edited by Professor Kevin Outterson, a leading authority on international public health law, which brought together a number of articles espousing rather different views of the compulsory licensing phenomenon. *See generally* Symposium on Compulsory Licenses, 27 J. L. MED. & ETHICS 176, 268 (2009).

51 *See* Flynn et al, *supra* note 16.

52 *See* Bird, *supra* note 50.

53 *See* Lybecker & Fowler, *supra* note 36.

54 For a view consistent with that of the patent-based drug industry, *see* Patricia M. Danzon & Adrian Towse, *Differential Pricing for Pharmaceuticals: Reconciling Access, R&D and Patents*, 28–9 (AEI-Brookings Joint Ctr. for Reg. Studies, Working Paper No. 03-7, 2003), *available at* http://papers.ssrn.com/sol3/papers.cfm?abstract_id=422821. For a synthesis more attuned to the problems of access, *see* Kevin Outterson, *Pharmaceutical Arbitrage: Balancing Access and Innovation in International Prescription Drug Markets,* 5 YALE J. HEALTH POL'Y, LAW & ETHICS 193 (2005) [hereinafter Outterson, *Pharmaceutical Arbitrage*].

ways could be found to keep products sold at low prices to poor countries from being re-exported as parallel imports to rich countries, the originator suppliers could, in theory, price-discriminate their products on the basis of per capita GDP. They would thus obtain a large volume of sales at low profit margins in the poorest countries, offset by higher-priced sales in middle-income countries, and purely monopoly-priced revenues in countries that decline to institute price controls, such as Medicare and private insurance markets in the United States.

Price discrimination would, in turn, reduce the deadweight loss – that is, losses that occur when consumers who would like to buy the products cannot afford to do so – without causing the originator companies to sell below cost. Assuming that the originator company expects to recoup its R&D costs and make the bulk of its profits in rich OECD (Organisation for Economic Co-operation and Development) countries,[55] selling the same products to large numbers of poor people at very low prices (but still above the marginal cost of production) should nonetheless yield profits at least comparable to those of generic producers, who are not charitable institutions and who profitably market off-patent medicines in poor countries. Economist F.M. Scherer made this point clearly when he established that global welfare would be improved if the poorest countries were permitted to free ride on pharmaceutical innovation.[56]

So why do the pharmaceutical companies – with possibly one recent but clamorous exception[57] – decline to escape the heat by overtly adopting an optimal price discrimination strategy (coupled with binding agreements to limit parallel exports, which otherwise remain perfectly legal under article 6 of the TRIPS Agreement[58])? One authoritative answer, provided by Patricia Danzon and Adrian Towse, is that the originator companies are wary of so-called 'reference pricing' in rich OECD countries that maintain price control regimes for pharmaceuticals.[59] If the originator company

---

55 Kevin Outterson & Aaron Kesselheim, *Market-based Licenses for HPV Vaccines in Developing Countries,* 27 HEALTH AFFAIRS 130, 136–7 (2008).

56 F.M. Scherer, *A Note on Global Welfare in Pharmaceutical Patenting*, 27 WORLD ECON. 1127, 1141 (2004).

57 Gilead has announced a policy of price discrimination for major AIDS products that has elicited complaints from other companies. DAVID P. BARON, KEITH KREHBIEL & BRIAN TAYAN, THE GILEAD ACCESS PROGRAM FOR HIV DRUGS (2007). More recently, GlaxoSmithKline has announced steps in a similar direction, based on a proposed strategy of tiered pricing. See GSK Press Release, *Corporate Responsibility Report 2008 – Preferential Pricing*, *available at* http://www.gsk.com/responsibility/preferential_pricing. htm.

58 *See* TRIPS, *supra* note 4, art. 6; Declaration on TRIPS, *supra* note 5, para. 4.

59 Patricia M. Danzon & Adrian Towse, *Theory and Implementation of*

profitably sold its drug in Ruritania for a penny a pill, regulators in Occitania might balk at allowing it to charge 50 or 100 dollars for the same pill, even if those regulators understood perfectly that the company must recoup the often cited (but still controversial) billion dollar cost of R&D that each new FDA-approved molecule allegedly incurs.[60] Hence, Danzon and Towse propose a system of secret rebates that might promote greater price discrimination by limiting the foreign regulators' ability to discover the prices actually charged to distributors in poor countries for use as reference prices in rich countries.[61] One of Danzon's colleagues recently proposed a similar scheme of pricing opacity and secret discounts for the global vaccine procurement system.[62]

2.1.1 The Convex Demand Curve Problem

While this thesis undoubtedly identifies one relevant factor, an article by Sean Flynn, Aidan Hollis and Mike Palmedo[63] provides a more compelling explanation for originator companies' resistance to price discrimination in poor countries. These authors show that, in very poor countries characterized by great disparities of income, the rational-acting originator company seeking to maximize profits will logically charge high prices to the affluent sector of the society, because it will earn much greater profits than if it had distributed the same drug to poverty-stricken masses at prices they could afford.

Calling this the problem of 'highly convex demand curves'[64] for essential goods in countries with large disparities of income, Flynn et al. show, for

---

Differential Pricing for Pharmaceuticals, in International Public Goods and Transfer of Technology under a Globalized Intellectual Property Regime 425 (K.E. Maskus & J.H. Reichman, eds., Cambridge Univ. Press, 2005). *See also* Graham Dutfield, *Delivering Drugs to the Poor: Will the TRIPS Amendment Help?*, 34 Am. J.L. & Med. 107, 114 (2008) (citing authorities). The term 'reference pricing' is somewhat confusing as it also applies to pricing mechanisms within wealthy countries. An alternative term is 'virtual arbitrage'. Outterson, *Pharmaceutical Arbitrage, supra* note 54, at 283.

[60] Joseph A. DiMasi, Ronald W. Hansen, & Henry G. Grabowski, *The Price of Innovation: New Estimates of Drug Development Costs*, 22 J. Health Econ. 151, 151–85 (2003); *see also* Jerome H. Reichman, *Rethinking the Role of Clinical Trial Data in International Intellectual Property Law: The Case for a Public Goods Approach*, 13 Marq. Intell. Prop. L. Rev. 1, 9–11 (2009) (citing authorities with different estimates).

[61] Danzon & Towse, *supra* note 59, at 445.

[62] Sean McElligott, *Addressing Supply Side Barriers to Introduction of New Vaccines to the Developing World*, 35 Am. J.L. & Med. 415 (2009).

[63] Flynn et al., *supra* note 16.

[64] *Id.*, at 189.

example, that the rational-acting firm operating in South Africa would maximize profits 'by selling at the price that only the top 10% can afford'.[65] In effect, 'the firm will maximize its profits by setting a price unaffordable for at least 90% of . . . [the] people'.[66] That finding translates to a deadweight loss of 90 per cent, in a pharmaceutical sector where, as James Love famously observed, deadweight loss tends over time to become dead bodies.

Flynn et al. contrast their figures on South Africa with conditions in Norway, where there is a high degree of income equality and the 'convex demand curve' problem largely disappears. They demonstrate that a rational-acting originator company that price-discriminated a patented medicine in Norway would accordingly make much greater profits than one who charged a high flat rate for a privileged few.[67] The former company will considerably reduce deadweight loss as well, in its own self-interest.

These authors thus answer the question that mystifies so many newcomers to this field: originator companies avoid price discrimination in poor countries because it is considerably more profitable for them to charge monopoly prices to affluent citizens, as their patents enable them to do. The government of a poor country that wants lower prices in order to supply the bulk of the population thus priced out of the market must accordingly force the company to act against its private self-interest in the larger interests of public health. And the most powerful tool for achieving this end remains that of a threat by the state to impose a compulsory license. As the Thai government explained in a White Paper, for example, the goal behind its recent barrage of compulsory licenses was to move the relevant pharmaceutical companies from a 'low volume-high margin' pricing strategy to a 'high volume-low margin' alternative approach.[68]

A complementary strategy might focus on building price discrimination tools into the developing countries' pharmaceutical distribution systems, with a view to enabling more rational policies. Most commentators neglect

---

[65] *Id.*, at 189.

[66] *Id.*, at 189. While relatively few countries may fit the 10–90 matrix of South Africa, the principle could apply equally to other countries where the relevant matrix was 20–80 or 30–70, rather than 10–90.

[67] *Id.*, at 189, 90.

[68] The Ministry of Public Health & The National Health Security Office Thailand, *Facts and Evidences on the 10 Burning Issues Related to the Government Use of Patents on Three Patented Essential Drugs in Thailand*, 14–15, *available at* www.moph.go.th/hot/White Paper CL-EN.pdf (accessed Mar. 3, 2009); Abbott & Reichman, *supra* note 22, at 953.

this question, but if the US can maintain many levels of pharmaceutical price discrimination, perhaps developing countries could achieve two or three.[69] In Mexico, for example, Professor Outterson suggests that three distinct markets could be segmented: the elite private insurance markets, the Seguridad Social system for those working in the formal economy, and the public health system for the remaining citizens.[70]

2.2.2 Using Compulsory Licenses to Remedy the Problem

Governments adopting the compulsory licensing strategy must exercise caution in choosing the legal instruments best suited to accomplishing their goals, in order both to withstand the political and economic pressures they are certain to elicit and to emerge unscathed from any legal action filed against them at the WTO. Here Flynn et al. cast a yearning glance back to the days before 1992, when Canadian law imposed a 'license of right' on all patented pharmaceutical products marketed in that country.[71] Any would-be generic distributor could apply for such a license and, if granted, could produce and market the patented medicine at competitive prices, in return for a 4 per cent royalty that the Commissioner of Patents typically imposed.[72]

The Canadian license of right, which lasted for more than 50 years, undoubtedly helped to establish that country's robust generic industry, although critics contend that it discouraged the establishment of a research-based pharmaceutical sector at the same time. Both the generic industry and any research-based companies must, of course, operate in the shadow of larger US competitors, and under the regulatory constraints of national and provincial public health programs. In the early 1990s, the Reagan Administration pressed the Canadian government to abandon its license of right scheme, in exchange for a commitment by US producers to contribute a share of their profits to support medical research in Canada.[73] The Canadian compulsory licensing approach was

---

69 Outterson, *Pharmaceutical Arbitrage, supra* note 54, at 203–16, 232–35.

70 Personal communications with Professor Outterson.

71 Flynn et al., *supra* note 16, at 191.

72 For details, *see* Jerome H. Reichman with Catherine Hasenzahl, *Non-Voluntary Licensing of Patented Inventions: The Canadian Experience*, UNCTAD/ICTSD Project on IPRs and Sustainable Development (October 2002) at 37–8; *see also* Donald G. McFetridge, *Intellectual Property, Technology, Diffusion and Growth in the Canadian Economy, in* Competition Policy and Intellectual Property Rights in the Knowledge Economy 65 (R.D. Anderson & N.T. Gallini, eds. 1998).

73 *See* Reichman with Hasenzahl, *The Canadian Experience*, *supra* note 72, at 38–44. Industry Canada has, at various times, expressed satisfaction with the results of this arrangement.

then formally prohibited by the intellectual property chapter in the North American Free Trade Agreement (NAFTA), whose provisions, in turn, became a blueprint for article 31 of the TRIPS Agreement.[74]

Under the latter provision, a WTO Member government cannot subject whole classes of pharmaceuticals – such as 'essential medicines' – to a pre-established compulsory licensing scheme. It must, instead, adopt a case-by-case approach and shape the compulsory license to meet the purpose for which each license was authorized.[75] Under ordinary circumstances, the license would issue only after a failed negotiation with the rights holder,[76] and – at least in principle – could be terminated 'if and when the circumstances which led to it cease to exist and are unlikely to recur'.[77] Any decision to grant such a license must be subject to judicial review (or comparable review by another higher authority),[78] and 'adequate remuneration in the circumstances of each case' must be paid.[79]

Given these legal obstacles to a pure 'open access' scheme, Flynn et al. stress the importance of competition law as a viable alternative in many cases.[80] While an action sounding in anticompetitive conduct under article 31(k) will require some judicial or administrative process,[81] a finding of such conduct exempts the government from any need to negotiate with the patent holder, and even from the obligation to confine a compulsory license predominantly for the supply of the domestic market.[82] The amount of remuneration may also become negligible in such cases, given the punitive aspects of remedying anticompetitive behavior.[83]

However, our authors make resort to competition law sound much easier than it has so far proved to be for most developing countries. Competition law, as practiced in developed countries, entails complex economic

---

[74] *Id.*, at 42–43; see North American Free Trade Agreement, Can.-U.S.-Mex., ch. 17, Dec. 17, 1992, 32 ILM 605 (1993) [hereinafter NAFTA].

[75] TRIPS, *supra* note 4, at arts. 31(a), (c).

[76] *Id.*, at art. 31(b). This provision is waived in the case of national emergency, other circumstances of extreme urgency or in cases of governmental use. *Id.*

[77] *Id.*, at art. 31(g). For example, an abusive use of a patent could be purged, allowing a claim to void such a license.

[78] *Id.*, at art. 31(j).

[79] *Id.* at art. 31(h). The remuneration must take 'into account the economic value of the authorization'. *Id. See also* James Love, Remunerations Guidelines for Non-voluntary Use of a Patent on Medical Technologies, WHO/TCM/2005.1 (2005) *available at* http://www.who.int/medicines/areas/technical_cooperation/WHOTCM2005.1_OMS.pdf (last visited Mar. 7, 2009); Taubman, *supra* note 26.

[80] Flynn et al., *supra* note 16, at 191–2.

[81] TRIPS, *supra* note 4, at art. 31(k).

[82] *See id.*

[83] *Id.*

analysis, high transaction costs, and skilled regulators.[84] Moreover, the EU practise, built around measures to prevent abuse of a dominant position, varies considerably from the much less aggressive stance of the US authorities,[85] which looks for evidence of actual monopolization or intent to achieve it.[86] Both regimes depend on a complex showing of market power, although long-standing (but increasingly disfavored) common law precedents sounding in patent law still allow US courts to impose compulsory licenses for 'misuse of patents' in the absence of market power.[87]

Besides these technical intricacies, there are high-level policy decisions that must be made about the goals of competition law in general, that is, efficiency or fairness, or some combination of both,[88] and then about the proper relationship to be struck between that version of competition law and the incentives to innovate that flow from the exclusive rights of intellectual property law.[89] Increasingly, competition law in developed countries is seen – rightly or wrongly – as providing a supportive and complementary role of promoting welfare, one that is consistent with the goals of intellectual property law, rather than a serious restraint upon it.[90] This

---

[84] *See, e.g.,* Herbert J. Hovenkamp, *The Intellectual Property-Antitrust Interface,* University of Iowa College of Law, Legal Studies Research Paper No 08-46 (2008), available at http://ssrn.com/abstract=1287628; Eleanor M. Fox, *Can Antitrust Policy Protect the Global Commons from the Excesses of IPRs? in* INT'L PUBLIC GOODS AND TRANSFER OF TECHNOLOGY UNDER A GLOBALIZED INTELLECTUAL PROPERTY REGIME 758, 758–69 (K.E. Maskus & J.H. Reichman, eds, Cambridge Univ. Press, 2005).

[85] *See, e.g.*, Emanuella Arezzo, *Intellectual Property Rights at the Crossroad between Monopolization and Abuse of a Dominant Position: American and European Approaches Compared,* 24 J. MARSHALL J. COMPUTER & INFO. L. 456 (2006).

[86] *See, e.g.* Fox, *supra.* note 84, at 759–64; Hanns Ullrich, *Expansionist Intellectual Property Protection and Reductionist Competition Rules: A TRIPS Perspective, in* INT'L PUBLIC GOODS AND TRANSFER OF TECHNOLOGY UNDER A GLOBALIZED INTELLECTUAL PROPERTY REGIME 726, 726–57 (K.E. Maskus & J.H. Reichman, eds, Cambridge Univ. Press, 2005).

[87] *See* Hovenkamp, *supra* note 84, at 1991; *Illinois Tool Works v. Indep. Ink*, 126 Sup. Ct. 1281 (2006); *see also* Thomas F. Cotter, *Misuse,* 44 HOUS. L. REV. 901 (2007); Mark D. Janis, *'Minimal' Standards for Patent-related Antitrust Law under TRIPS, in* INT'L PUBLIC GOODS AND TRANSFER OF TECHNOLOGY UNDER A GLOBALIZED INTELLECTUAL PROPERTY REGIME 774, 790–92 (K.E. Maskus & J.H. Reichman, eds, Cambridge Univ. Press, 2005).

[88] *See, e.g.*, Fox, *supra* note 84, at 758; Ullrich, *supra* note 86, at 726.

[89] *See, e.g.,* GUSTAVO GHIDINI, INTELLECTUAL PROPERTY AND COMPETITION LAW: THE INNOVATION NEXUS 103–11 (Edward Elgar, 2006).

[90] *See supra* note 84; Josef Drexl, *The Critical Role of Competition Law in Preserving Public Goods in Conflict with Intellectual Property Rights, in* INT'L PUBLIC GOODS AND TRANSFER OF TECHNOLOGY UNDER A GLOBALIZED

view makes doctrines that override intellectual property rights, such as the 'essential facility' doctrine recommended by Flynn et al.,[91] much harder to obtain in practise than may appear in theory.[92]

Developing countries have lagged behind in the field of competition law, and some – such as China – are just beginning to explore its possibilities. These countries would be well advised to track early US cases, emphasizing fairness over efficiency;[93] and to adopt both the 'abuse of a dominant position' theory of EU law and a flexible doctrine of 'patent misuse' historically rooted in US patent law, which could reach refusals to deal, excessive prices, and undersupply of the market, without a showing of market power.[94] But such measures must be applied equally to domestic firms as to foreign firms,[95] without discrimination, and therein lies a serious rub.

While competition law can provide useful tools in appropriate cases, developing countries envisioning a need for compulsory licensing of patented pharmaceuticals should look to other tools not explored by our authors that lie outside competition law. One is the Waiver (and, eventually, Amendment scheme under pending article 31*bis* of the TRIPS Agreement), which enables developing countries without manufacturing capacity to implement compulsory licenses with the aid of countries that do possess such capacity, a topic already mentioned above.[96] A second tool worth exploring is the Belgian model also identified above, which facilitates compulsory licensing in the interest of public health under

---

Footnote 90 (*cont.*)
INTELLECTUAL PROPERTY REGIME 709, 709–25 (K.E. Maskus & J.H. Reichman eds., Cambridge Univ. Press 2005).

91 Flynn et al., *supra* note 16, at 191–2.

92 *See, e.g.*, Rita Coco, *Antitrust Liability for Refusal to License Intellectual Property: A Comparative Analysis and the International Setting*, 12 MARQ. L. REV. 1, 10–21 (2008) (citing authorities). *But see* Brett Frischmann and Spencer Weber Waller, 'Revitalizing Essential Facilities', 75, *Antitrust* L.J.1 (defending a more optimistic view).

93 Fox, *supra* note 84, at 768.

94 *See* Paris Convention, *supra* note 1, at art. 5A; G.H.C. BODENHAUSEN, GUIDE TO THE APPLICATION OF THE PARIS CONVENTION FOR THE PROTECTION OF INDUSTRIAL PROPERTY, AS REVISED AT STOCKHOLM IN 1967, 71 (1968). However, current precedents governing misuse in the US may no longer support such outcomes. *See* Hovenkamp, *supra* note 84, at 1091-5; Reichman with Hasenzahl (2003), *supra* note 2; Cotter, *supra* note 87.

95 TRIPS, *supra* note 4, at art. 3, 8.2, 40; Paris Convention, *supra* note 1, at art. 2(1).

96 However, for the disappointing story of the first attempt to use the Waiver, *see* Goodwin, *supra* note 32.

articles 8 and 30 of the TRIPS Agreement, rather than article 31 as such. While the legality of this route has yet to be tested by WTO tribunals,[97] the modalities it offers arguably remain consistent with TRIPS, so long as the preconditions of article 31 are largely observed in practise.

2.2 A sympathetic skeptic

In his article,[98] Professor Robert Bird sympathizes with the more than 1.7 billion people who have little or no access to essential medicines.[99] He recognizes that, by their growing reliance on compulsory licensing, developing countries have begun to lower prices below those the patent owner would otherwise charge, thereby 'potentially saving millions of lives and improving the public health of dozens of nations'.[100] His skepticism stems from concerns that the social costs of such licenses – what he calls 'secondary effects' – may 'negate any benefits from increased access'.[101]

Chief among the social costs warranting such concern are:

- a risk of diminished direct investment in countries that resort to compulsory licensing because patent owners will seek out more business-friendly legal environments;
- a risk that those who obtain compulsory licenses will 'shadow price' the patentees and thus generate deadweight loss of their own in pursuit of profits:
- a risk that compulsory licensing will reduce the research-driven pharmaceutical sector's incentives to innovate; and
- a risk that the patentees' governments will retaliate with trade sanctions that could 'cripple the economy of the licensing nation'.[102]

Professor Bird proposes a number of strategies for improving consumer access to medicines at lower social costs, without necessarily relying on the

---

[97] For an existing WTO panel decision that casts doubt on efforts to use art. 8 of the TRIPS Agreement to expand the limited exceptions to a patentee's exclusive rights under art. 30 of that Agreement, *see Canada – Patent Protection of Pharmaceutical Products*, WT/DS114/R, Mar. 17, 2000.

[98] Robert C. Bird, *Developing Nations and the Compulsory License: Maximizing Access to Essential Medicines while Minimizing Investment Side Effects*, 37 J.L. Med. & Ethics 209 (2009).

[99] *Id.*, at 209 (citing World Health Organization, The World Medicines Situation 61 (2004)),

[100] *Id.*, at 209–11.

[101] *Id.*, at 211.

[102] *Id.*, at 211–18.

generosity of donors.[103] To this end, he espouses five strategies to alleviate the social costs of compulsory licensing in developing countries, namely:

- more consultation and collaboration with the originator companies, with a view to preserving an investor friendly climate where possible;[104]
- narrowly tailored licenses that focus on real public health needs and avoid the appearance of impropriety, and that also ensure consumers actually obtain lower prices;[105]
- the need to focus public opinion on the suffering avoided by those who benefit from lower priced pharmaceuticals;[106]
- the need to lower tariff barriers that still impede imports of patented pharmaceuticals into developing countries;[107] and
- the need to address social and cultural barriers that discourage the use of modern medicines in those countries.[108]

While it is hard to quarrel with Professor Bird's five-pronged strategy, or the empirical evidence on which it rests, a degree of caution remains nonetheless in order.

Consultation and collaboration with originator pharmaceutical companies only become feasible when the latter are willing to negotiate. The patent-holding drug companies lack an incentive to negotiate so long as there are no clear legal sanctions with which to threaten them in case of refusals to deal. Negotiations are likewise less likely if powerful governments, such as the United States, are prepared to retaliate with trade sanctions and other economic pressures (most of which are illegal under international law)[109] when developing countries actually utilize TRIPS flexibilities.

The climate for negotiations does seem more favorable now than in the recent past. But this greater willingness to negotiate is partly because the multilateral system has devised a set of legal tools that states can use to lower prices, beyond price controls, which though perfectly legal under TRIPS, are seldom employed by developing country governments. Professor Bird also recognizes that the new tools make pooled procure-

---

103 *Id.*, at 211–18.
104 *Id.*, at 211–13.
105 *Id.*, at 213–14
106 *Id.*, at 214–15.
107 *Id.*, at 215–16.
108 *Id.*, at 216–18.
109 *See infra* text accompanying notes 173–79.

ment strategies both feasible and desirable (as Fred Abbott and I have been at pains to show),[110] and I shall return to this theme later on.[111]

One must also be wary of criticizing governments for over-extending the range of their medical concerns, lest one fall into the trap of thinking that people in developing countries do not suffer from the same Type I diseases as those that burden developed countries. The opposite is true, as Professor Outterson points out,[112] because studies show just how heavy the incidence of such diseases, including heart disease, really is in many developing countries. The difference does not lie in the disease burden as such, but in the means available to cope with it.

As Outterson demonstrates, for example, high patent prices charged for Type I diseases in developed countries are ameliorated by 'private and social insurance mechanisms, relatively high per capita incomes, and (in some cases) government monopsony procurement'; whereas in low and middle income countries, '[p]atent-based pricing denies access to the majority of direct purchasers'.[113] Hence, the Thai government issued a compulsory license on Plavix when the manufacturer allegedly refused to deal, on the grounds that people in Thailand suffer from heart disease just as they do in the United States.[114] By the same token, one may ask why 90 per cent of Egyptian males should be denied access to life-improving drugs, such as Viagra, so that exorbitant profits can be extracted from the most affluent 10 per cent in that country.[115]

Professor Bird rightly argues that efforts to reduce the prices of any medicines in the interest of public health must be accompanied by a scrupulous 'clean hands' approach that ensures the drugs will actually be distributed at the lowest profitable price, with adequate compensation to the patentees. The level of compensation was questionable in the Thais' treatment of Plavix,[116] the compulsory license on Viagra in Egypt was tainted by the appearance of impropriety and self-dealing,[117] and complaints about 'shadow pricing' in some Latin American countries merit serious attention.[118]

While all developing countries would benefit from Professor Bird's

---

110 Abbott & Reichman, *supra* note 22, at 973–80; *see infra* text accompanying notes 166–9.

111 *See infra* text accompanying notes 164–7.

112 Outterson, *Access to Medicine and TRIPS, supra* note 24, at 289–91.

113 *Id.*, at 333.

114 Abbott & Reichman, *supra* note 22, at 952, 954–6.

115 *See* Flynn et al., *supra* note 16; Bird, *supra* note 98.

116 *See infra* note 142 and accompanying text.

117 Bird, *supra* note 98, at 213–4.

118 *Id.*, at 213–4.

five-pronged strategy when considering the use of compulsory licenses on patented medicines, his higher-level concerns about negative impacts on foreign direct investment, about diminished incentives to invest in innovation, and about the risks of retaliation all require a more nuanced response. Because the article by Kristina Lybecker and Elizabeth Fowler raises these same concerns more vigorously, I prefer to address them below in connection with comments on that study.

2.3 Views of the hostile sympathizers

Professors Lybecker and Fowler approve of compulsory licenses that are invaluable when used to address healthcare emergencies or remove technological supply bottlenecks in developing countries.[119] However, they devote most of their article to denigrating Thailand's use of compulsory licenses, which they deem ill considered and illegitimate, while faintly praising Canada's own admittedly contorted efforts to implement the Waiver provisions of the Doha Ministerial Declaration as at least maintaining a higher degree of legitimacy. In short, they are decidedly hostile to much current practise and to the legal reasoning that supports it.

At the outset, the basis for comparing Thailand's and Canada's use of compulsory licenses is open to question. Thailand acted to obtain lower-cost supplies of AIDS and cardiovascular medicines for its domestic markets. Canada used its compulsory license to meet Rwanda's need for AIDS drugs under the Waiver.[120]

In this scenario, Canada is at best a Good Samaritan *manqué*, whose actions have zero impact on the Canadian market for the goods in question. Its authorities remain free to allow Canada's generic industry to assist Rwanda or not, at some or no profit, as the participants deem fit, without incurring any of the pressures and costs that would derive from a need to address Canada's own public health problems. At most, one may observe that Canada's action to assist Rwanda will perhaps adversely affect the patentee's global market expectations for sales of its AIDS product,[121] and that this constitutes a common denominator underlying the two situations. All the same, Thailand's concerns to meet its own public health needs by such means do not strike me as truly parallel with Canada's concerns to be a Good Samaritan. One must accordingly remain wary of drawing conclusions from a comparison of these two scenarios, even if they were depicted in a factually accurate manner.

---

119 *Id.*, at 222–4.
120 Goodwin, *supra* note 32, at 2.
121 *Cf.* Abbott & Reichman, *supra* note 22, at 957.

Unfortunately, the authors tend to accept the pharmaceutical industries' views of both the facts and the law as they pertain to Thailand, without sufficient attention to contrary evidence. For example, more peer-reviewed evidence would be advisable to claim that Thailand's quality standards were so low that they endangered AIDS patients by exposing them to drug-resistant strains of the disease.[122] Without such evidence, one is left to wonder if the drug-resistance rates in Thailand were dissimilar from those in, say, Malawi, where FDA-approved drugs are available, or for that matter, in certain more developed countries, where resistance has been encountered despite the use of drugs meeting the highest quality standards.

The authors also question the sincerity of the Thai government's stated goal of reducing the costs of drugs supplied under its public health program and thereby to promote universal access to essential medicines. Echoing spokesmen for the industry, this criticism stems from the claim that the government-owned producer turned a 'profit' on the products it distributed.[123] Yet, as Abbott and Reichman reported, when the authorities issued a government use license for efavirenz, 'Merck's price was approximately double that of the Indian generic price', although Merck later offered a price about 20 per cent above the Indian generic.[124] The Thai government expected to reduce the price of Kaletra to about 20 per cent of Abbott Laboratories' current price, and it hoped 'to reduce its costs for clopidogrel (Plavix) by a factor of 10'.[125] These products are all distributed 'through publicly funded government organizations' (which aim to provide universal access to HIV-AIDS treatment in that country). Thailand's soaring expenditures on public health 'now constitute approximately 10% of the total government budget'.[126] In this context, claims of 'profit' appear tendentious without proof that the funds in question did not benefit the public health sector as a whole.

To their credit, Professors Lybecker and Fowler recognize some of the infirmities in Canada's Access to Medicines Regime (CAMR), which was enacted ostensibly to enable Canadian generic drug manufacturers to assist poor countries obtain medicines they could not manufacture, under authority of the Waiver to (and, eventually Amendment of) article 31 of the TRIPS Agreement. For example, they criticize 'the layers of bureaucracy and technicalities' (not required by TRIPS) 'that it takes to work

---

122 Lybecker & Fowler, *supra* note 36, at 222–3.
123 *Id.*, at 228–9.
124 Abbott & Reichman, *supra* note 22, at 953.
125 *Id.*
126 *Id.*, at 952.

through the legislation',[127] obstacles that took Apotex about three years to ship a modest supply of AIDS drugs to Rwanda and convinced the firm not to repeat the experience in the future.

Passed over in silence, however, is the fact that the Canadian Act limited would-be local suppliers of foreign needs to 57 drugs or vaccines, mostly concerning AIDS, and most of those already available in generic form. As Outterson elsewhere explains, '[a]lmost all of the other drugs on the list are off-patent or face legal generic competition in a similar form'.[128] The very narrow list of drugs available under the CAMR thus 'operates as a disease-specific limitation on compulsory licensure under Paragraph 6' of the Doha Declaration,[129] even though that Declaration clearly supports the use of compulsory licensing 'without regard to the type of disease'.[130] In contrast, the European Union, spurred by vigorous Parliamentary oversight, adopted a comprehensive implementing Regulation[131] that appears to successfully incorporate most of the flexibilities available to WTO Members in making use of the Waiver Decision.[132]

Professors Lybecker and Fowler nonetheless praise the Canadian regime for its legitimacy, while castigating Thailand's approach as a controversial and possibly abusive Thai regime, both of which operate under the same WTO rules.[133] In their eyes, 'CAMR can be viewed as a success in that safe, effective and less expensive medicines were eventually shipped to Rwanda',[134] whereas Thailand's regime (apart from questions of product quality) appropriates patented products, such as Plavix, and is more difficult to understand as the public health necessity the Thai government has described. Therefore, Thailand's expansion of the compulsory licensing program weakens the international health community's consensus on the policy and could strip Article 31 of all future legitimacy.[135] In promoting

---

[127] Lybecker & Fowler, *supra* note 36, at 226.

[128] Outterson, *Access to Medicine and TRIPS, supra* note 24, at 282.

[129] *Id.*

[130] *Id.* (citing Declaration on TRIPS, *supra* note 5, at paras. 4, 5(b), 5(c), 5(d); US Gen. Accounting Office, GAO Report 07-1198, US Trade Policy Guidance on WTO Declaration on Access to Medicines May Need Clarification 15, 19, 23 (Sept. 2007)); *accord* Abbott & Reichman, *supra* note 22, at 936–7(citing Paragraph 6 Decision, *supra* note 25; Amendment of TRIPS, *supra* note 25).

[131] Regulation (EC) No. 816/2006 of the European Parliament and of the Council of 17 May 2006 on compulsory licensing of patents relating to the manufacture of pharmaceutical products for export to countries with public health problems.

[132] Abbott & Reichman, *supra* note 22, at 947.

[133] Lybecker & Fowler, *supra* note 36.

[134] *Id.*, at 231.

[135] *Id.*, at 232–7.

'industrial policy' rather than access to medicines, they imply, this regime violates both the letter and spirit of WTO law.[136]

These assertions reflect the influence of industry propagandists, who relentlessly misinterpret the few TRIPS provisions that escaped their control while insisting on strict compliance with all the rest. In reality, there are no disease-specific restrictions under either Article 31 or the Doha Declaration and its implementing measures.[137] Nor is there any requirement of a 'national emergency' to justify recourse to a compulsory license. All that an emergency adds is the power of WTO Members to waive the duty to negotiate with the patentee under article 31(b),[138] which applies under ordinary circumstances. For that matter, article 31(b) also dispenses with the duty to negotiate with patentees in the event that the WTO Member issues a government use license, rather than a public-interest license open to the private sector,[139] which is exactly the path that Thailand chose to follow.[140] Indeed, a government use license is the route normally preferred by the pharmaceutical industry because it can avoid (and did avoid, according to Thai authorities) disrupting private-sector distribution channels not financed by the government.[141]

In short, the Thai approach was a perfectly 'legitimate' exercise of the State's powers under the TRIPS Agreement, with a possible caveat for the low royalty paid the patentees (not mentioned by Lybecker and Fowler), which the Thai authorities claim was left open for negotiations that the patentees declined to undertake.[142] No similar cloak of legitimacy can, however, be extended to the US reprisals against Thailand which – as we shall see in a moment – appear directly in conflict with both the letter of WTO foundational law and an actual decision against the US by a duly constituted WTO tribunal.[143]

2.4 The big picture items

Disregarding these legal inaccuracies, Professors Lybecker and Fowler raise a number of policy issues that overlap to some extent with Professor

---

136 *Id.*, at 229.

137 *See supra* note 130 and accompanying text; *see also* Outterson, *Access to Medicine and TRIPS, supra* note 24.

138 TRIPS, *supra* note 4, at art. 31(b).

139 *Id.*

140 Abbott & Reichman, *supra* note 22, at 952. The extent to which negotiations actually occurred is disputed by both sides.

141 *See id.,* at 953.

142 *Id.*, at 952–3 (noting compensation at 0.5 per cent).

143 *See infra* notes 170–79 and accompanying text.

Bird's own evaluation. Here the major concerns that merit a fuller appreciation are the potential loss of foreign direct investment (FDI) that compulsory licensing may engender; a corresponding reduction of incentives to invest in innovation; the need for cooperative rather than confrontational approaches to the public health problems at issue; and the risk of retaliation against developing countries that continue to implement these TRIPS flexibilities. Let me end this chapter by briefly considering these issues one by one.

2.4.1 Potential Loss of FDI and Investment Opportunities

Professors Bird, Lybecker, and Fowler all express concerns that, when faced with the risk of compulsory licensing, pharmaceutical companies may vote with their feet. For example, patent-holding drug companies may cancel or reduce planned investments in the area,[144] decline to bring new products to the country in question,[145] or even withdraw from the territory altogether, as was threatened in both South Africa[146] and Thailand.[147]

In approaching this issue, let us first note the evidence showing that there is no clearly defined or established relation between the level of intellectual property protection a developing country provides and FDI. Some countries, such as China, attracted massive amounts of FDI, despite woefully inadequate intellectual property protection, because the market opportunities and other conditions remained irresistible.[148] Other poor countries, with little to offer in the way of comparable economic opportunities, attract virtually no FDI despite patent laws that sometimes afford more protection than that of the United States.[149]

This said, there is something intriguing about these threats to withhold new pharmaceutical products, or to withdraw from the territory, that merits deeper reflection. Consider, for example, what might happen if similar threats were carried out against Ruritania, whose government is

---

[144] *See e.g.,* Bird, *supra* note 98, at 211–3 (case of Pfizer with respect to Viagra in Egypt).

[145] *See e.g.,* Lybecker & Fowler, *supra* note 36, at 233 (case of Abbott Laboratories in Thailand).

[146] *See* Bird, *supra* note 96, at 212–3.

[147] *See* Lybecker & Fowler, *supra* note 36 at 233.

[148] *See, e.g.*, Peter Yu, *Intellectual Property, Economic Development, and the China Puzzle, in* Intellectual Property, Trade and Development 173, 176–83 (D. Gervais, ed., Oxford Univ. Press, 2007).

[149] Keith E. Maskus, *The Role of Intellectual Property Rights in Encouraging Foreign Direct Investment and Technology Transfer*, 9 Duke. J. Comp. & Int'l L. 109, 129–30 (1998).

assumed to possess legal expertise and a measure of political independence for present purposes. First, the Ruritanian health authorities would immediately understand that all new pharmaceutical products not the subject of local patent applications had fallen into the public domain by definition.[150] The authorities would thus remain free to reverse-engineer the relevant molecular entities in private laboratories or at their universities, as supplemented where necessary by hiring outside technical experts in order to obtain the key active ingredients.[151]

Once the molecule was successfully reverse engineered, the Health Ministry could tender bids to generic producers anywhere in the world – including Brazil, India and China – to establish plants in Ruritania for production of the drug in question. These producers could arguably supply both the local population and, as exporters of legitimate parallel drugs unfettered by patents, any country in the rest of the world that had adopted a policy of international exhaustion (which remains perfectly consistent with article 6 of the TRIPS Agreement). More importantly, Ruritania could also export these drugs to any other country that, lacking manufacturing capacity of its own, had issued a compulsory license for them under the Waiver machinery of the Doha Declaration.[152]

Of course, the market in Ruritania might afford insufficient economies of scale to attract such investment, although that apparently was not the case in Egypt or Thailand, where disgruntled foreign pharmaceutical companies canceled similar investments.[153] In that event, Ruritania, as a WTO Member without manufacturing capacity, could appeal to any other Member having that capacity for assistance under the Waiver to article 31 of the TRIPS Agreement.[154] Such an appeal would be administratively simpler to handle than was the case with Rwanda, because it would require only one compulsory license – in the exporting country – rather than back-to-back compulsory licenses in two countries, as the Waiver would normally entail.

---

[150] *See* TRIPS Agreement, *supra* note 4, arts. 2.1 (incorporating Paris Convention arts. 1–12), 27 (novelty); Paris Convention, *supra* note 1, arts. 2(1) (national treatment), 4*bis*(1) (independence of patents).

[151] The task of reverse-engineering key active ingredients (APIs) nonetheless remains difficult and costly for most developing countries. *See, e.g.*, FREDERICK M. ABBOTT & GRAHAM DUKES, GLOBAL PHARMACEUTICAL POLICY: ENSURING MEDICINES FOR TOMORROW'S WORLD 123–4 (Edward Elgar, 2009).

[152] *See* TRIPS Agreement, *supra* note 4, art. 6; Waiver Decision, *supra* note 25; Abbott & Reichman, *supra* note 22, at 975–6.

[153] *See, e.g.,* Lybecker & Fowler, *supra* note 36, at 233; Bird, *supra* note 96, at 213–4.

[154] *See supra* note 25.

Either way, a determined Ruritania appears likely to obtain the drugs, and possibly the capacity to compete with the originator company in third markets as well, while the originator company would lose its foothold in Ruritania and, perhaps, tarnish its image there and throughout the developing world. All this because the originator company had been unwilling to supply the drug at profit-making prices that a large percentage of the population could afford instead of at monopoly prices that only the richest elite could afford.[155]

At this point, the reader may well begin to ask who is threatening whom? Let us return to this question when we discuss the advantages of a cooperative, rather than a confrontational, approach below.[156]

2.4.2 Reducing Incentives to Innovate

Most informed observers agree that investing in pharmaceutical R&D is a very risky business, which is the principal justification offered for strong pharmaceutical patents. So Bird, Lybecker and Fowler logically worry about lessening those incentives by exposing originator firms to the risk of compulsory licenses (that is, *ex post* liability rules, in the form of a reasonable royalty) in place of the *ex ante* exclusive rights they had initially planned to exploit.[157]

In reality, as Professor Outterson and others have demonstrated, investment in cures for Type I diseases are geared to developed country markets and not to potential returns from developing countries, at least at the present time. The value of markets for these drugs in most poor countries remains relatively so low, compared to conditions in, say, the US and EU, that Outterson envisions a 'buy out' scheme that would enable patent-free distribution in poor countries, side-by-side with monopoly pricing in OECD countries.[158] In short, and under present-day condi-

---

[155] *Cf.* Flynn et al., *supra* note 16.

[156] *See infra* text accompanying notes 166-68; *cf.* Jerome H. Reichman, *The TRIPS Agreement Comes of Age: Conflict or Cooperation with the Developing Countries?,* 32 Case W. Res. J. Int'l L. 441 (2000).

[157] *See* Lybecker & Fowler, *supra* note 36; Bird, *supra* note 96; Alan O. Sykes, *TRIPs, Pharmaceuticals, Developing Countries, and the Doha 'Solution',* 3 Chi. J. Int'l L. 47 (2002). *But see* Bird, *supra* note 96, at 211, noting contrary empirical studies.

[158] *See, e.g.,* Kevin Outterson, *Patent Buy-outs for Global Disease Innovations for Low- and Middle-Income Countries,* 32 Am. J. Law & Med. 159, 161 (2006); *see also* J.O. Lanjouw, *Beyond TRIPS: A New Global Patent Regime*, Brief No. 3, The Center for Global Development, July 2002 (market segmentation); James Love, *Proposal for Patent Pool for Essential Medicines* (PPEM), Addis Ababa (Mar. 13, 2005).

tions, the issuance of compulsory licenses on Type I medications in poor countries would have virtually no impact on incentives to innovate in rich countries.[159]

Over time, however, the emergence of major middle-income markets, such as those in India, China, and Brazil, could increasingly affect incentives to invest in such drugs by expanding the potential for long-term aggregate revenues.[160] That prospect is another reason why big originator companies will likely invest in local production in those countries anyway, despite policies to ensure broader access to medicines that their governments may pursue. One way forward is to permit the drug companies to retain the elite markets in these poor countries, and to focus access proposals on the public sectors. In Brazil, for example, branded AIDS drugs are sold to the privately insured, despite the fact that any Brazilian may receive them for free at public clinics. The wealthy seldom frequent public clinics, and are willing to pay more for the branded drugs.

Professors Lybecker and Fowler express concerns about R&D pertaining to tropical, neglected and other diseases prevalent in poor developing countries.[161] There is virtually no investment in cures for such diseases by the major research-driven companies that compulsory licensing could discourage.[162] On the contrary, the hope for treating these diseases rests on public-private collaborations, funded largely by donors, in which big pharmaceutical companies have laudably participated for humanitarian reasons, with mixed results thus far.[163] This collaborative process may benefit from compulsory licensing machinery when some particular

---

159 *See, e.g.,* Outterson & Kesselheim, *supra* note 55, at 136–7; Outterson, *Patent Buy-outs, supra* note 158.

160 *Cf.* Sykes, *supra* note 157.

161 Lybecker & Fowler, *supra* note 36.

162 *See* Outterson & Kesselheim, *supra* note 55, at 136–7; Outterson, *Patent Buy-outs, supra* note 156, at 159–73.

163 *See* Mary Moran, Anne-Laure Ropars, Javier Guzman, Jose Diaz & Christopher Garrison, *The New Landscape of Neglected Diseases Drug Development* (2005), *available at* www.thegeorgeinstitute.org/shadomx/apps/fms/fmsdownload.cfm?file_uuid=F2B06396-EEA0-851E-3049-C9A030AEDE0F&siteName=iih (last accessed Mar. 7, 2009); Drugs for Neglected Diseases Initiative (DNDi), New, Once-a-day Fixed-dose Combination Against Malaria Now Available (Mar. 1, 2007); Press Release, DNDi, MSF and DNDi Call For Scale-Up of R&D For Neglected Diseases (Feb. 23, 2009) *available at* http://www.msfaccess.org/media-room/press-releases/press-release-detail/?tx_ttnews%5Btt_news%5D=1535&cHash=86e19504b2 (last accessed Mar. 7, 2009); Jean-René Kiechel & Bernard Pecoul, Innovative Partnership Brings New ACT Free of Patents, Guest Blog, PLOS Feb. 26, 2007, *available at* http://www.plos.org/cms/node/208 (last accessed Mar. 7, 2009).

patented component blocks collective action, rather than the other way around.[164]

In the future, one may imagine private research-based pharmaceutical industries in certain developing countries turning their attention to tropical, neglected and poverty-related diseases, in the hopes of financial gain, and they may also seek to adapt cures for Type I and Type II diseases to developing world conditions. In that event, the use of compulsory licenses must be handled with care, to ensure that incentives are maintained by means of a suitable correlation between risk and profit. If and when that eventuality should materialize, one might also dare to hope that the very firm that had invested in such projects might be inclined to market the resulting medicines on a 'high-volume, low profit margin' basis, for the benefit of both private and public interests, in which case compulsory licensing would become superfluous.[165]

2.4.3 The Advantages of Collaborative Action

Professors Bird, Lybecker, and Fowler rightly emphasize the need for a more collaborative approach to the issues that surround compulsory licensing; and both articles point to the advantages of a pooled procurement strategy, which Professor Abbott and I have recently explored in depth.[166] Without delving deeply into this topic here, let me stress in passing that the legal machinery adopted under the aegis of the Doha Declaration serves to promote, rather than to hinder, this very sort of collaboration.

If a number of developing countries pooled their procurement needs by coordinating the potential use of compulsory licenses for selected medicines, they could generate economies of scale and scope to entice even the originator pharmaceutical companies to play ball with them, rather than against them. The carrot in such a scenario is the possibility for the originator company to exercise its exclusive rights – including trademarks – over a suitably large area that would make it worth their while to collaborate even at discounted prices. Ideally, incentives can be calibrated to provide still greater rewards to those originator companies willing to invest in local production facilities serving the areas or countries that had coordinated

---

164 *See, e.g.,* Anthony D. So, Enabling Conditions for the Scientific Commons, paper presented at the Conference on Technology Development in the Life Sciences, Program on Science, Technology and Global Development, The Earth Inst. at Columbia Univ. (May 20–21, 2004).

165 *See, e.g.,* Abbott & Reichman, *supra* note 22, at 981–2.

166 *See id.*, at 969–81 ('Making the Amendment System Work').

their procurement needs.[167] Local production, in turn, implants know-how into the local community, and it tends to stimulate both capacity for – and commercial interest in – conducting research on diseases of local importance, with the possible use of indigenous resources.[168]

By the same token, originator companies unwilling to cooperate in a pooled procurement strategy would run the risk that the potential market for the drugs in question could be handed over to investors from other developing countries. If that occurred, it would provide the coordinating countries with many of the same advantages that would otherwise accrue from cooperation with the originator companies. In other words, pooled procurement strategies under the aegis of the Doha Declaration could produce a win-win situation for all concerned, in which the overall goal was that envisioned by Flynn et al., namely, to make medicines available at prices most people in developing countries could afford, and not just a privileged few.[169]

2.4.4 The Risk of Retaliatory Action

Meanwhile, living as we do in a more confrontational climate, one must remain acutely aware of the risks that powerful governments may retaliate against developing countries that press their rights under the Doha Declaration by issuing compulsory licenses on patented medicines. Both Bird and Lybecker emphasize these risks,[170] with Thailand as a case in point. Not only did USTR place Thailand under the 2007 Special 301 'Priority Watch List Surveillance',[171] it threatened to terminate Thailand's Generalized System of Preferences (GSP) privileges to export certain products to the US at low or no tariffs, in retaliation for its resort to the compulsory licenses in question.[172]

---

167 *Id.*, at 973–4.

168 *Id.*, at 977–8. *See also* Jerome H. Reichman & Tracy Lewis, *Using Liability Rules to Stimulate Local Innovation in Developing Countries, in* Int'l Public Goods and Transfer of Technology under a Globalized Intellectual Property Regime 337, 337–66 (K.E. Maskus & J.H. Reichman, eds, Cambridge Univ. Press, 2005).

169 *See* Flynn et al., *supra* note 16; Abbott & Reichman, *supra* note 22, at 982 ('Changing the Marketing Model').

170 *See* Bird, *supra* note 96, at 213, 215, 17; Lybecker & Fowler, *supra* note 36, at 233.

171 Abbott & Reichman, *supra* note 22, at 954.

172 *Brazil, Thailand Lose Trading Privileges in Wake of IP Disputes*, Food & Drug Letter, Aug. 17, 2007. In 2006, Thailand had $4.2 billion in GSP qualified exports to the US Vivian C. Jones, CRS Report for Congress, Generalized System of Preferences: Background and Renewal Debate (Jan. 25, 2008)

At the outset, it is well to acknowledge that we cannot infuse public officials in developing countries with the courage to defend themselves if they are unwilling to do so. What can, and should be said, is that governments ought not to contemplate issuing compulsory licenses on patented pharmaceuticals unless they are prepared to stand up for their legal rights; and if they do stand up for those rights, it is the retaliating state – not the victims – who will most likely be found to violate WTO rules.

Article 23 of the WTO Dispute Settlement Understanding (DSU) obliges Members to seek redress for alleged violations of the WTO Agreement, including its TRIPS component, by means of specified multilateral venues and procedures.[173] Under this provision, if the US authorities believe that a developing country government has abusively issued a compulsory license, they may lawfully haul that country before a WTO dispute settlement panel and state their case, with a right of appeal to the WTO Appellate Body. What USTR cannot legally do is to unilaterally impose sanctions for the loss of expected trade benefits, as it appears to have done in the case of Thailand.[174] In fact, there is already a WTO panel

---

Footnote 172 (*cont.*)
(Table A2) *available at* http://www.nationalaglawcenter.org/assets/crs/RL33663.pdf (last accessed Mar. 7, 2009).

[173] The DSU, *supra* note 6, at art. 23 provides as follows:

> 1. When Members seek the redress of a violation of obligations or other nullification or impairment of benefits under the covered agreements or an impediment to the attainment of any objective of the covered agreements, they shall have recourse to, and abide by, the rules and procedures of this Understanding. 2. In such cases, Members shall: (a) not make a determination to the effect that a violation has occurred, that benefits have been nullified or impaired or that the attainment of any objective of the covered agreements has been impeded, except through recourse to dispute settlement in accordance with the rules and procedures of this Understanding, and shall make any such determination consistent with the findings contained in the panel or Appellate Body report adopted by the DSB or an arbitration award rendered under this Understanding; (b) follow the procedures set forth in Article 21 to determine the reasonable period of time for the Member concerned to implement the recommendations and rulings; and (c) follow the procedures set forth in Article 22 to determine the level of suspension of concessions or other obligations and obtain DSB authorization in accordance with those procedures before suspending concessions or other obligations under the covered agreements in response to the failure of the Member concerned to implement the recommendations and rulings within that reasonable period of time.

[174] Abbott & Reichman, *supra* note 22, at 980–81. Freedom from unilateral action was, indeed, a major reason developing countries signed onto the Agreement Establishing the WTO of 1994 in the first place.

decision criticizing USTR for past use of Section 301 listings for TRIPS-related matters, and that decision expressly warned that sanctions would likely be authorized if such violations continued in the future.[175]

From a legal rather than a political-economic perspective, there is accordingly a greater risk that unilateral retaliatory action will be held in violation of WTO law than that governments issuing compulsory licenses in conformity with the Doha Declarations will themselves incur sanctions under WTO rules. Moreover, if powerful states continue to engage in unilateral retaliations of this sort, they run still another set of legal risks that has thus far been under-appreciated. Because such action constitutes a violation of the DSU and of the framework Agreement Establishing the WTO,[176] it would entitle the aggrieved party to all the remedies that the Vienna Convention on the Law of Treaties provides for breach of the relevant agreements.[177] A primary remedy thus provided is the age-old right of self-help implicit in the power of an aggrieved party to suspend its obligations under the treaty in question, pending compensation for breach.[178]

In sum, if Occitania wrongfully retaliates against Ruritania for issuing a compulsory license, Ruritania may become entitled to suspend its obligations to protect patented pharmaceuticals under the TRIPS Agreement, with respect to Occitania, until the treaty violation was either purged or compensated. In that event, if Occitania sued Ruritania at the WTO for nullification or impairment of benefits under TRIPS,[179] the likely result would be a vindication of Ruritania's counterclaim that Occitania's unilateral retaliation had violated article 23.1 of the DSU and, thereby, justified Ruritania's own self-help defensive action.

There is little reason to suppose that the new Administration in Washington will change pre-existing intellectual property policies, given that it continues to draw considerable support from those industries that obtained such policies from the Clinton and Bush Administrations.

---

175 *See* Panel Report, *United States – Sections 301–310 of the Trade Act of 1974*, WT/DS152/R (Dec. 22, 1999); Abbott & Reichman, *supra* note 22, at 980–81. While GSP privileges are not bound by GATT, and therefore remain revocable, one may doubt that this revocation can be used as a unilateral sanction for some alleged violation of TRIPS.

176 Marrakesh Agreement Establishing the WTO, *supra* note 4, art. II(2) (DSU is 'binding on all Members'); DSU, *supra* note 6, art. 23 (*quoted supra* note 173).

177 Vienna Convention on the Law of Treaties, UN Doc. A/Conf.39/27; 1155 UNTS 331; 8 ILM 679, at art. 60 (1969), *available at* untreaty.un.org/ilc/texts/instruments/english/conventions/1_1_1969.pdf.

178 *Id.*, at art. 60.2.

179 TRIPS, *supra* note 4, at art. 64.

Nevertheless, the new Administration has expressed serious concern to promote the rule of law in international relations, unlike its immediate predecessor. If so, there is hope that it will take steps to avoid the dubious legal position and corresponding risk of sanctions to which unilateral retaliatory action necessarily exposes it.

18 The Doha Declaration and access to medicines by countries without manufacturing capacity

S.K. Verma

1. Introduction

Ever since the Agreement on Trade-related Intellectual Property Rights (TRIPS) came into force on 1 January 1995, it has not steered clear of controversies, which have become more frequent in the last few years. Developing countries and certain groups within the industrialized nations have argued that the rules needed reform. The Agreement, which sets out detailed international law on patent rights, has been criticized for making medicines and other essential products unnecessarily expensive in poor countries, thereby undermining the public health priorities and national development goals of these countries. Accessibility to essential drugs was an issue at the time of negotiation of the TRIPS Agreement as well. However, the access to patented medicines debate is part of a larger debate relating to the value of the entire intellectual property regime. The debate had commenced in the early stages of negotiation of the TRIPS Agreement. Its opponents treated it with concern, suspicion and scepticism; others approached it with anticipation and optimism. Opponents claimed that developing countries do not reap equal benefits from the regime and that they are harmed by the stringent system of intellectual property protection that is embodied in the TRIPS Agreement and the subsequent bilateral agreements comprising TRIPS-plus provisions.[1] In this endeavour, developing countries are viewed as consumers rather than partners, which is evident in the case of the big pharmaceutical corporations.[2]

---

1 Lee G. Branstetter, 'Do Stronger Patents Induce More Local Innovation?', in Keith E. Maskus & Jerome H. Reichman (eds), *International Public Goods and Transfer of Technology Under a Globalized Intellectual Property Regime* 309, Cambridge, UK: Cambridge University Press (2005).

2 Amir H. Khoury, 'The '"Public Health" or the Conventional International Patent Regime and the Ethics of "Ethical": Access to Patented Medicines', 26 *Cardozo Arts and Entertainment Journal* 25 (2008), available at <http://www.cardozoaelj.net/issues/08/khoury.pdf>.

The TRIPS Agreement transformed the international intellectual property system by creating a prescriptive regime in place of the permissive regime existing thus far. The result of the Agreement has been to bolster the international protection of patents in a way that has narrowed the scope for differentiation within national patent policies. It has been criticized for adversely impacting the attainment of social goals by sharply curtailing the traditional capacity of nations to supply public goods, such as health care and nutrition, and to address the priority needs of the poor, particularly in developing and least-developed countries (LDCs). Public benefit is stated to lie at the heart of patent protection because high levels of patent protection are usually associated with correspondingly high levels of development;[3] but the effect of strong patent protection on development is controversial.[4] The AIDS pandemic that plagued many countries in the developing world around the turn of the century has underscored the gaping hole in patent theory and practice. Given the necessary implications of TRIPS for access to essential medicines, its adoption and implementation seemed unlikely to advance the interests of developing countries. The early years of its existence provided this confirmation.

By strengthening the international level of patent protection, TRIPS has inevitably had a significant impact on access to life-saving pharmaceuticals in developing countries, especially on poor countries that have no pharmaceutical manufacturing capacities and are afflicted with pandemics, as well as on countries that up until now had been dependent on the importation of life-saving drugs at low prices from countries that provided no patent protection to pharmaceuticals. In other words, TRIPS intensified the problem of access to essential medicines at affordable prices in developing countries. According to the World Health Organization (WHO), 1.7 billion people, or one out of three on Earth, lack access to essential medicines.[5] Approximately 3 million people died from HIV/AIDS in 2001, 2.3 million of these deaths occurring in Sub-Saharan Africa. Nearly 1.7 million people worldwide died from tuberculosis in the same year and there have been as many as 10.2 million new cases in 2005.[6] Currently, 40 million people are infected with AIDS. About 6 million people in the

---

[3] See generally Richard T. Rapp & Richard P. Rozek, 'Benefits and Costs of Intellectual Property in Developing Countries', 24(5) *J. World T.* 75 (1990).

[4] J. Michael Finger, 'The WTO's Special Burden on Less Developed Countries', 19 *Cato J.* 425 (2000) at 430.

[5] WHO Bulletin (2004), p. 61, 'The World Medicines Situation', WHO/EDM/PAR/2004.5.

[6] WHO Commission on Macroeconomics and Health. See Integrating Intellectual Property Rights and Development Policy', Report of the Commission

developing world living with HIV/AIDS need access to treatment now.[7] Of these, less than 8 per cent (some half a million) currently have access to medication.[8] Within the developing world, this ranges from access as high as 84 per cent in Latin America to little more than 2 per cent in Africa. Since more than two-thirds of those with HIV or AIDS live in Africa,[9] this means that at this moment very close to 6 million poor people are dying of AIDS. It is common knowledge that most of these deaths are preventable, that life-saving drugs do exist, and the problem lies in the inaccessibility of these drugs primarily for patients in poor countries afflicted with these diseases.

The measures taken by some of the countries afflicted with these epidemics of resorting to compulsory licences to import generic copies of the patented drugs have met with strong opposition from developed countries and pharmaceutical companies. Somewhat ironically, US trade pressure on South Africa and Thailand in 1997 galvanized criticism of TRIPS.[10] This laid the basis for the developments that took place in Doha a few years later. Seeking to increase access to essential medicines through various TRIPS-compliant regulatory mechanisms, both Thailand and South Africa suddenly found their domestic laws under attack from the Pharmaceutical Research and Manufacturers of America (PhRMA) and the office of the US Trade Representative (USTR).[11]

Most of the disputes between developed and developing countries pertaining to intellectual property rights (IPRs) and public health have so far been dealt in the political realm as opposed to the legal realm. Except for the court case in South Africa and the US case at the WTO against Brazil[12]

---

on Intellectual Property (September 2002), available at http://www.iprcommission.org/documents/final_report.htm at 1.

[7] Of an estimated 40 million people living with HIV/AIDS globally, approximately 95 per cent live in developing countries ('Treating 3 million by 2005: Making it happen – the WHO strategy' (World Health Organization: Geneva, 2003) at 3), see also Edwin Cameron, 'Patents and Public Health: Principle, Politics and Paradox', Inaugural British Academy Law Lecture held at the University of Edinburgh, 19 October 2004, available at <http://www.law.ed.ac.uk/script/newscript/home.htm>.

[8] Another 500000 people, or 53 per cent of all people currently accessing ARVS internationally, live in the developed world, home to less than 5 per cent of the global HIV/AIDS pandemic.

[9] 'Treating 3 million by 2005', *supra* note 7.

[10] See Susan K. Sell, 'TRIPs and the Access to Medicines Campaign', 20 *Wis. Int'l L.J.* 498–509 (2002) at 500.

[11] *Ibid.*

[12] See WTO Doc. WT/DS199/1,G/L/385,IP/D/23, 8 June 2000; WT/DS199/39, January 2001.

on local working requirements – both of which were later withdrawn,[13] largely for political considerations – most of the controversies in the area have been resolved bilaterally at political level. Both Canada[14] and Brazil have also provided under their laws for the use of compulsory licences for the sake of medicines and public health.

In order to meet the health emergencies that existed in South Africa, Thailand and many Sub-Saharan countries, the WTO Ministerial Meeting at Doha in 2001 adopted the Doha Declaration on the TRIPS Agreement and Public Health[15] (adopted against strong opposition from developed countries under the intense pressure from the pharmaceutical industry of these countries). The Declaration emphasizes the importance of public health considerations in implementing the TRIPS Agreement. It affirms that the TRIPS Agreement can and should be interpreted and implemented in a manner supportive of WTO members' right to protect public health and, in particular, to promote access to medicines for all. The Declaration was followed by the Implementing Decision on its Paragraph

---

[13] See Joint Communication of Brazil–United States, 25 June 2001. Following notification of the US decision to withdraw its complaint, the Joint Communication of Brazil–United States, 25 June 2001 stated, 'the Brazilian Government will agree, in the event it deems necessary to apply Article 68 to grant a compulsory licence on a patent held by a U.S. company, to provide advance and adequate opportunity for prior talks on the matter with the United States. These talks would be held within the scope of the U.S.-Brazil Consultative Mechanism, in a special session scheduled to discuss the subject. Brazil and the United States consider that this agreement is an important step towards greater cooperation between the two countries regarding our shared goals of fighting AIDS and protecting intellectual property rights.' The declared intention of the Brazilian Government was to procure anti-retrovirals at prices lower than those charged by patent owners, in the framework of the government-supported programme against AIDS.

[14] See *Canada – Patent Protection of Pharmaceutical Products*, Report of the Panel, WT/DS114/R, 17 March 2000, available online at www.wto.org/english/tratop_e/dispu_e/distab_e.htm. This decision was not taken on appeal to the Appellate Body, and has found its way into Canadian domestic law (see Regulations Repealing the Manufacturing and Storage of Patented Medicines Regulations, SOR/00 – 373). In this case, a DSB panel had to deal with three issues. First, does TRIPS permit the production and stockpiling of pharmaceutical products prior to patent expiry? Second, does the agreement allow for generic manufacturers to start and complete the drug regulatory process prior to patent expiry? Third, can pharmaceutical products be treated differently from inventions in other fields of technology?

[15] Declaration on the TRIPS Agreement and Public Health, WTO Res. WT/MIN(01)/DEC/2, 4th Sess., Ministerial Conference, 20 November 2001, available at <www.wto.org/english/thewto_e/minist_e/min01_e/mindecl_TRIPs_e.doc>.

6 of 30 August 2003[16] and an accompanying Chairperson's statement at the General Council meeting on 30 August 2003. The Declaration and Decision are related to national health emergencies, namely, HIV/AIDS, TB, Malaria and other epidemics. To make this decision as a part of the TRIPS Agreement, the WTO members on 6 December 2005 approved changes to the TRIPS Agreement in the form of Article *31bis* making permanent the decision on intellectual property and public health.[17] This will be formally built into the TRIPS Agreement when two-thirds of WTO members have accepted the change. They originally set themselves until 1 December 2007 to do this.[18] The deadline has now been extended to 31 December 2009 under a decision by the General Council on 18 December 2007.[19]

The WTO's adoption of the Doha Declaration, the Waiver Decision of 30 August 2003[20] and the Article 31*bis* Protocol of amendment, reflects international consensus on the true balance TRIPS strikes in patent protection. Article 31*bis* has been adopted to address the problem with Article 31 (on compulsory licences) of the TRIPS, which allows a country to issue a compulsory licence that only covers drugs made – and predominantly used – within the country's borders. This is an insurmountable obstacle for many poor countries, which have no manufacturing capacity in the pharmaceutical sector and desperately need cheap medicines to combat epidemics such as HIV/AIDS, malaria and tuberculosis and which have little or no manufacturing capacity or insufficient market demand.

It is a generally held view that the result of implementing TRIPS will be to curtail the supply of generic copies of patented drugs, after the switchover to product patents by developing countries by January 2005, as has been done by countries like India. It will lead to sharp increases in the prices of drugs, since patented medicines are generally more expensive

---

16 Implementation of Paragraph 6 of the Doha declaration on the TRIPS Agreement and Public Health, WTO Doc. WT/L/540 and Corr.1, 1 Sep. 2003 available at <http://www.wto.org/english/tratop_e/trips_e/implem_para 6_e.htm>.

17 Implementation of paragraph 11 of the General Council Decision of 30 August 2003 on the implementation of paragraph 6 of the Doha Declaration on the TRIPS Agreement and Public Health [the 'Decision'], WTO Doc. IP/C/41, 6 December 2005. The Decision and Article 31*bis* give effect to paragraph 6 of the Doha Declaration (known as the paragraph 6 system).

18 Amendment of the TRIPS Agreement, WTO Doc. WT/L/641, 8 December 2005, available at <http://www.wto.org/english/tratop_e/trips_e/wtl641_.htm>.

19 See at http://www.wto.org/english/tratop_e/trips_e/pharmapatent_e.htm.

20 2003 Decision on patents and public health, sometimes referred to as the 'waiver' on public health.

than their generic counterparts, thereby making them even more inaccessible to a large proportion of the population of these countries.[21]

The new rules under the Declaration and Article 31*bis* (also known as the paragraph 6 system) have raised few pertinent questions, namely, what will become of nations with no or insufficient manufacturing capacity after the system has been put in place? Will they be able to rely on imports of needed drugs from other countries? These questions are particularly significant since most developing countries will be switching over to product patents from 1 January 2005, thereby reducing the scope for generics and making access to cheaper drugs more difficult. The problem has further been aggravated by TRIPS-plus agreements concluded by developed countries with developing countries seeking higher levels of IPR protection than that provided in the TRIPS Agreement and also imposing restrictions on the importation of generics or the issuance of compulsory licences. It is against this backdrop and to find the answers to the above questions that this chapter considers the context for the adoption of the Doha Declaration at the outset, including the efforts of human rights bodies and the TRIPS provisions on compulsory licensing, which ultimately led to the adoption of the amendment to the TRIPS (Article 31*bis*). An examination of the Doha Declaration follows thereafter. The chapter thus examines the Decision of 2003 and Article 31*bis*. This is followed by taking stock of the implementation of the Decision/Article 31*bis*, where the case of India is considered as a special case as India has remained a major supplier of generics in poor countries with no or insufficient manufacturing capacity in the pharmaceutical sector. In conclusion, it attempts to look for a viable solution to the paragraph 6 problem of the Doha Declaration in case the Decision and the TRIPS amendment do not work.

2. A run-up to the Doha Declaration – the context

At the turn of the century, the impact of TRIPS was beginning to be felt by developing countries, particularly in Africa and other less developed countries, just as the devastating effect of the HIV/AIDS pandemic deepened.

---

21 The estimated increase in prices has been stated as being between 12 and 200 per cent; even the lower estimates imply very substantive costs for consumers. See J. Watal, 'Pharmaceutical Patents, Prices and Welfare Losses: A Simulation Study of Policy Options for India under the WTO TRIPS Agreement', 23(5) *The World Economy* 733–52 (2000); C. Fink, *How Stronger Patent Protection in India Might Affect the Behaviour of Transnational Pharmaceutical Industries,* World Bank Policy Research Paper No. 2352, World Bank, Washington, DC; see also Oxfam, 'Generic Competition, Price and Access to Medicines' Oxfam Briefing Paper No. 26, Oxfam, Oxford (2002). See http://www.oxfam.org.uk/policy/paper/26generic.html.

Prices of life-saving medicines meant they were no longer within the reach of the people, even as they became more urgently indispensable to preserve lives. Efforts made by developing countries during this period to ensure access to medicines for their people by invoking the flexibility provisions of the TRIPS Agreement were opposed by pharmaceutical companies.[22] There had been a number of international events in 2001 with regard to compulsory licensing. Specific situations were related to Thailand, Brazil and South Africa. South Africa[23] and Brazil[24] had both come under pressure for introducing or maintaining legal provisions concerning compulsory licensing that were not considered WTO compatible by the USA and EU.

The Brazilian patent law under Article 68 permits the use of compulsory licensing.[25] A threat by the Brazilian government to invoke this law to ensure access to HIV/AIDS medications for her citizens led to the filing of a petition by the United States before the WTO panel opposing the action of the Brazilian government. This petition was later withdrawn, by which time the Brazilian government through its threat, had forced pharmaceutical companies to reduce prices of patented HIV/AIDS drugs in that country.[26]

Then after 11 September 2001, after a series of anthrax attacks in the United States, both Canada and United States threatened to issue a compulsory licence to ensure access to anthrax medicines.[27] Thus far, the lack

---

[22] It is, however, to be noted that less than 5 per cent of medicines on the WHO's essential drugs list are protected by patents; patent protection for HIV/AIDS exists in just over 20 per cent of 53 African nations, with no patents whatsoever in 13 countries.

[23] South Africa in 1997 amended its law to provide new rules regarding compulsory licensing, parallel imports and price regulations of medicines. The Pharmaceutical Manufacturers' Association of South Africa challenged the act and argued that it was against the South Africa's TRIPS obligations. The USA and EU supported their case. An international campaign in support of South Africa led to the withdrawal of the case in 2001.

[24] In June 2001, the USA requested consultations with Brazil under the WTO dispute settlement mechanism. The USA argued that allowing compulsory licences for failure to work locally is inconsistent with Article 27.1 of the TRIPS. The dispute was subsequently settled bilaterally. See *supra* note 13.

[25] Industrial Property Law Act No. 23 (1998), which provides: 'A patent owner shall be subject to the grant of compulsory licence of his patent if the rights resulting there from are exercised in an abusive manner or if the patent is used in abuse of economic power, as proven by an administrative or judicial decision pursuant to the provisions of the law'.

[26] *Supra* note 13 & 24.

[27] Canada issued a compulsory licence and ordered a million tablets of a

of access to medicines in Africa and other less developed countries and the resulting public health crises concerning HIV/AIDS, tuberculosis, and malaria had attracted widespread international attention.[28] In the case of South Africa, 39 pharmaceutical companies instituted a court case against the South African government for enacting a new patent law in 1997.[29] The court action, filed at the Pretoria High Court, challenged sections 15C and 22C of the law that permitted the South African government to use both parallel importation and compulsory licensing respectively in the wake of the HIV/AIDS pandemic in the country.[30] The pharmaceutical companies, backed by the United States, claimed that the new law contravened the TRIPS Agreement and the Constitution of South Africa 1996. However, a fierce campaign by civil society groups and non-governmental organizations (NGOs) across the globe led to the withdrawal of the suit by the pharmaceutical companies in 2001.

There were, however, two major consequences of this case. First, it provoked clarification of the so-called flexibility of the TRIPS Agreement, especially as regards public health. Second, it clearly brought to the fore the fact that developed countries that exerted trade pressure in order to safeguard the interests of pharmaceutical companies could no longer do so without some repercussions even within their own territory.[31]

Footnote 27 (*cont.*)
generic version from a Canadian company. Later Canada withdrew this decision and reached an agreement with the patent holder. The USA succeeded in winning a major price concession from Bayer.

[28] See Access to Medication in the Context of Pandemics Such as HIV/AIDS, Tuberculosis and Malaria, Comm'n on Human Rights Res. 2004/26, UN Doc. E/CN.4/2004/127 (16 April 2004), available at http://ap.ohchr.org/documents/E/CHR/resolutions/E-CN_4-RES-2004-26.doc. For discussions of TRIPS developments in relation to access to medicines, see generally UNCTAD-ICTSD, *Negotiation Health: Intellectual Property and Access to Medicines* (Pedro Roffe et al. (eds), 2006); Frederick M. Abbott, 'The WTO Medicines Decision: World Pharmaceutical Trade and the Protection of Public Health', 99 *Am. J. Int'l. L.* 317 (2005).

[29] See Medicines and Related Substances Control Amendment Act No. 90 (1997).

[30] *Pharmaceutical Manufacturers' Association of South Africa v. President of the Republic of South Africa*, Case No. 4183/98 (filed 18 February 1998) (HC), available at http://www.fordham.edu/law/faculty/patterson/tech&hr/materials/phamace.txt.

[31] E. 't Hoen, 'TRIPS, Pharmaceutical Patents and Access to Essential Medicines', 3 *Chicago JIL* 31 (2002). See also, Ebenezer Durojaye, 'Compulsory Licensing and Access to Medicines in Post Doha Era; What Hope for Africa?', *LV Netherlands Int'l Law Review (NILR)* 33–71 (2008), at 41 available at <http://journals.cambridge.org/download.php?file=%2FNLR55_01%50165070X08000338a.pdf>.

The HIV/AIDS crisis in Sub-Saharan African countries, the attempts by the pharmaceutical industry, backed by some governments to block TRIPS-compatible measures by the South African government, the complaint of the United States before the Dispute Settlement body (DSB) of the WTO against Brazil regarding compulsory licences, were the perceived manifestation of an apparent conflict between intellectual property rights and public health objectives. The problem of lack of access to essential and life-saving drugs came to the fore in the run-up to the Doha ministerial conference of the WTO in November 2001.

During this period two important meetings took place. One was the United Nations General Assembly Special Session on HIV/AIDS, known as the Declaration of Commitment.[32] The other was the Abuja Declaration on HIV/AIDS and other related diseases by African leaders.[33] The issue of access to medicines was also taken up by the World Health Organization, and in 2001 its Assembly addressed the need to evaluate the impact of TRIPS Agreement on access to drugs, local manufacturing capacity and development of new drugs.[34] In the run-up to the Doha Ministerial Meeting, upon the request of the African Group, the Council for TRIPS agreed to deal specifically with the relationship between the TRIPS Agreement and public health.[35]

TRIPS and human rights discussion

The globalization of IPRs and its impact on the realization of the right to health also simultaneously triggered a debate on the relationship between human rights and intellectual property, because many developing countries, particularly least-developed countries, are not in a position to implement the TRIPS standards in their jurisdiction without further compromising their development at the cost of human rights. The HIV/AIDS pandemic in Brazil and South Africa generated a fundamental debate on the relationship between patents and the right to health. The expanding

---

[32] UN Declaration of Commitment on HIV/AIDS, 25–7 June 2001, UN GAOR, 26th Special Session, Res. 33/2001.

[33] African Summit on HIV/AIDS, Tuberculosis and other Related Infectious Diseases, Abuja-Nigeria, 24–7 April 2001, OAU/SPS/ABUJA/3.

[34] Resolutions WHA54.10 and WHA54.11, WHO website: <C:/Documents and Settings/Owner/Desktop/WHO>. Doha Declaration on the TRIPS Agreement and Public Health.

[35] For the background on the adoption of the Doha Declaration, see Carlos M. Correa, *Implications of the Doha Declaration on the TRIPS Agreement and Public Health* (WHO, 2002). WHO Doc. WHO/EDM/PAR/2002.3, pp. 1–3, available at <http://www.who.int/medicines/areas/policy/WHO-EDM-PAR-2002.3.pdf>.

subject matters and 'universalization' of both human rights and intellectual property law have prompted negotiations in various UN bodies, and also in the WTO, on the clarification of the complex relationships between the TRIPS Agreement and human rights.[36]

In the case of health care, there seems to be a conflict between IPRs and human rights. The present IPR regime is not flexible and it contains a 'one-size-fits-all approach'. According to some critics, the minimum standards of intellectual property protection set by TRIPS Agreement are too high for most developing countries, thereby putting them under tremendous pressure to adopt legislation that is not adapted to their specific needs. It limits their right to follow their human rights agenda and a large segment of society remains deprived of basic human rights. As the governments' policies derive their legitimacy from their protection of human dignity, the IPR system needs to be conducive to human rights agenda. While shaping and implementing IPR laws and policies, governments must derive their legitimacy from human rights instruments. As Audrey Chapman stated, '[a] human rights approach to intellectual property takes what is often an implicit balance between the rights of inventors and creators and the interests of the wider society within intellectual property paradigms and makes it far more explicit and exacting'.[37] This requires the easy availability and accessibility of all essential necessities to everyone. Every country has its specific needs which require the proper balancing of human rights and intellectual property. The right to health is recognized in major international human rights instruments.[38] There continue to be tensions between

---

[36] United Nations High Commissioner for Human Rights, Sub-commission on Human Rights resolution 2001/21, 'Intellectual Property and Human Rights', Doc. E.CN.4.SUB.2.RES.2001.21.En?, available at http://www.unhchr.ch/huridoca.nsf.

[37] Audrey Chapman, 'A Human Rights Perspective on Intellectual Property, Scientific Progress, and Access to the Benefits of Science', in WIPO/United Nations High Commissioner for Human Rights, *Intellectual Property and Human Rights* 1 (WIPO, 1999).

[38] Article 25 of the Universal Declaration of Human Rights (UDRH) states: 'Everyone has the right to a standard of living adequate for . . . health and well-being of himself and his family, including food, clothing, medical care and the right to security in the event of . . . sickness, disability . . . . Motherhood and childhood are entitled to special care and assistance . . . '. Articles 7, 11 and 12 of the International Covenant on Economic, Social and Cultural Rights (ICESCR); Articles 10, 12 and 14 of the Convention on the Elimination of All Forms of Discrimination Against Women (CEDAW); Article 5 of the International Convention on the Elimination of All Forms of Racial Discrimination (CERD); and Article 24 of the Convention on the Rights of the Child (CRC) are related to health.

human rights protection and economic development, particularly in the case of least developed countries.[39]

In August 2000 the UN Commission on Human Rights adopted a resolution on 'intellectual property and human rights',[40] which noted that actual or potential conflict exists between the implementation of the TRIPS Agreement and the realization of economic, social and cultural rights. It also examined the implications of IPRs on the right to health, looking specifically at access to medication in the context of pandemics such as HIV/AIDS.

The UN Committee on Economic, Social and Cultural Rights (ESCRs) in its General Comment No. 14 (2000) expanded the ambit of the right to health. It noted that the basic elements of the right to health include availability, accessibility, acceptability and quality. Access to medicines requires that such medicines must be accessible and affordable.[41] The Committee also noted that economic accessibility or affordability presupposes that health facilities, goods and services must be affordable to all. Ensuring access to health facilities, especially for marginalized groups, constitutes one of the core obligations of the right to health.[42] It recognized that 'any person or group victim of a violation of the right to health should have access to effective judicial or appropriate remedies at both national and international levels'.[43] The Comment further confirmed the potentially transnational legal effect of the human right to health: 'States parties have to respect the enjoyment of the right to health in other countries'; depending on the availability of resources, 'States should facilitate access to essential health facilities, goods and services in other countries, wherever possible and provide necessary aid when required'.[44] Since patents are very relevant in the field of drugs and pharmaceutical products, the intellectual property regime becomes relevant in connection with the access to medicines and thereby in the protection and fulfilment of the human right to health.[45]

---

39 See Jack Donnelly, *Universal Human Rights in Theory and Practice* 109–10, 194–203 (2nd ed., Ithaca: Cornell University Press, 2003); Margaret Chon, 'Intellectual Property and the Development Divide', 27 *Cardozo L. Rev.* 2821 (2006).

40 *Supra* note 36.

41 UN Committee on ESCRs, 'The Rights to the Highest Attainable Standards of Health', General Comment No. 14, UN Doc. E/C.12/2000/4, para. 12; see also in Compilation of General Comments and General Recommendations adopted by Human Rights Treaty Bodies, UN Doc. HRI/GEN/1/Rev.5 of 26 April 2001, at 90.

42 *Ibid.*, para. 43.

43 *Ibid.*, paras 9, 36.

44 *Ibid.*, para. 39.

45 For a comprehensive survey of health-related WTO provisions and the

Right to health depends upon the availability, acceptability, quality and non-discriminatory, physical as well as economic, accessibility of health goods and health services, which are tradable, and subject to legal regulation and liberalization of WTO/TRIPS law.[46] Because human rights are 'universal, indivisible and interdependent and interrelated',[47] the right to health is dependent on other rights such as the right to life, food, housing etc. National governments and intergovernmental organizations, such as the WTO or the WIPO, are likely to refer to international human rights instruments, like the Universal Declaration of Human Rights (UDHR) and the International Covenant on Economic, Social and Cultural Rights (ICESCR), in their discussion of the tension and conflict between human rights and IPRs.[48]

The advantages of IP as the reward and incentive for research and development (for example, of new pharmaceuticals) are no longer contested.[49] The proper balancing between the rights of the IP owner and the social objectives of the TRIPS Agreement are evident from Articles 7 and 8 of the Agreement,[50] and its 'regulatory exceptions' (in Article 6,[51] Article

---

Footnote 45 (*cont.*)
Doha Declaration on the TRIPS Agreement and Public Health, see the joint study by the WHO and WTO secretariat on *WTO Agreements and Public Health* (2002).

46 *Supra* note 41, para. 39.

47 World Conference on Human Rights, 14–25 June 1993, *Vienna Declaration and Programme of Action,* UN Doc. A/CONF.157/23, 12 July 1993.

48 The WTO has emphasized the in-built flexibilities in existing trade agreements to accommodate human rights. See the WTO submission, 'Protection of Intellectual Property under the TRIPS Agreement', UN Doc. E/C. 12/2000/18, 27 November 2000 to the Sub-Comm'n on the Promotion and Protection of Human Rights. See Peter K. Yu, 'Ten Common Questions about Intellectual Property and Human Rights', 23(4) *Georgia State University Law Review* 709 at 715 (2007).

49 See ECOSOC, Comm'n on Economic., Social and Cultural Rights (CESCR), 'General Comment No. 17: The Right of Everyone to Benefit from the Protection of the Moral and Material Interests Resulting from any Scientific, Literary or Artistic Production of Which he is the Author (Article 15, Paragraph 1(C), of the Covenant', UN Doc. E/C.12GC/17, 12 January 2006.

50 Art. 7 of the TRIPS provides: 'The protection and enforcement of intellectual property rights should contribute to the promotion of technological innovation and to the transfer and dissemination of technology, to the mutual advantage of producers and users of technological knowledge and in a manner conducive to social and economic welfare, and to a balance of rights and obligations'. Article 8 reads: ' Members may, in formulating or amending their national laws and regulations, adopt measures necessary to protect public health and nutrition, and to promote the public interest in sectors of vital importance to their socio-economic and technological development, provided that such measures are consistent with the provisions of this Agreement'.

51 Article 6 of TRIPS relates to exhaustion of IP rights and provides: '. . . subject to the provisions of Articles 3 and 4 nothing in this Agreement shall be

31 for compulsory licensing, Article 40 concerning abuses of IPRs), and the appropriate scope of IP protection raise numerous issues. These provisions, however, provide sufficient flexibility to TRIPS Members to address the health needs. Article 6 relates to the exhaustion of IP rights and leaves the issue of parallel imports open for countries to decide for themselves. Under Article 31, members may grant compulsory licences for lack of or insufficiency of working of an invention, to remedy an anti-competitive practice, for cases of emergency, government use and for other public interest grounds. Article 40 aims at curtailing the abuses of IPRs in contractual licences. Article 30 empowers the members to curtail the exclusive rights of the patentee, including the right to produce and export a patented drug under compulsory licences issued in the importing country. In national emergencies, countries can adopt a range of other measures to improve access to medicines in line with Articles 7 and 8 of TRIPS.

The fact, however, remains that many developing countries lack even the capacity to produce formulations and only a few of these countries invest in R&D or have pliable R&D capabilities for new drugs or even to conduct research in the pharmaceutical sector. The only hope for these countries is to import generic drugs through compulsory licensing. Generic drugs can improve health care and reduce the monopoly of the patent holder, but the possibility of importing is remote and debatable under the WTO/TRIPS regime. Fear, however, has been expressed that the introduction of product patents for pharmaceuticals by developing countries after January 2005 will reduce the supply of generic drugs to a large number of developing countries and least-developed countries.

Compulsory licensing under the TRIPS Agreement

To protect against abuses such as excessive pricing and a failure to satisfy local demand, many patent systems have historically made provision for compulsory licences, which may allow for the introduction of generic competition even without the patent holder's consent. Even though there has been general use of compulsory licences by many countries in the past, systematic use of compulsory licences is said to adversely affect innovation and investments.[52] It has often been argued that compulsory licences reduce

---

used to address the issue of the exhaustion of intellectual property rights'. Thus, the exhaustion issue is entirely to be settled by the country concerned under its national law. It thus leaves open the issue of parallel imports.

[52] Kommerskollegium, 'The WTO Decision on Compulsory Licensing: Does it Enable Import of Medicines for Developing Countries with Grave Health Problems?', Report of the National Board of Trade Sweden, No. 2 (2008), available at www.kommers.se, p. 7.

incentives for developed countries' enterprises to engage in R&D and that reduced R&D diminishes global welfare by lowering the future stock of useful inventions. However, the benefit to developing countries of increased R&D in developed countries is often remote, and there is no evidence that the granting of compulsory licences has led to a reduction in R&D investment.[53] Compulsory licences may help exert downward pressure on prices in the short run, which is not always very significant. Compulsory licences are permitted under Article 5A(2) of the Paris Convention. They may constitute a strategic tool for improving the negotiating position of the government vis-à-vis the patent holder on accessing a particular invention.

The TRIPS Agreement allows a compulsory licence for domestic use under Article 31. However, Article 31 of the Agreement sets forth a number of terms and conditions for the granting of compulsory licences. These include a case-by-case determination of compulsory licence applications, the need to demonstrate prior (unsuccessful) negotiations with the patent owner for a voluntary licence, the limited scope and duration of use of licence, non-exclusivity and non-assignability of the licence, use predominantly for the supply of the domestic market (this condition is not applicable in case of remedy of an anti-competitive practice), the licence to be terminated after the circumstances for its issuance cease to exist, and adequate remuneration to be paid to the right holder. Where compulsory licences are granted to address a national emergency or other circumstances of extreme urgency, certain requirements are waived in order to obtain a voluntary licence from the patent holder. It leaves members full freedom to stipulate other grounds, such as those related to the non-working or failure to work of patents, public health or public interest as grounds for the issuance of a compulsory licence.

While countries may authorize, pursuant to Article 31 of the TRIPS Agreement,[54] the issuance of non-voluntary and non-exclusive uses of patents, paragraph (f) of Article 31 stipulates that 'any such use shall be authorized predominantly for the supply of the domestic market of the Member authorizing such use', subject to certain exceptions.[55] The import of the provision is unclear. It has been argued that compulsory licence,

---

[53] See S.K. Verma, 'TRIPS – Development and Transfer of Technology', 27 *International Review of Industrial Property and Copyright Law* 331 (1996); F.M. Scherer, 'Comments' in Robert Anderson and Nancy Gallini (eds), *Competition Policy and Intellectual Property Rights in the Knowledge-based Economy* (University of Calgary Press, Alberta, 1998).

[54] Article 31 deals with the conditions in case of grant of compulsory licences: 'Other use without Authorization of the Right Holder'.

[55] As an exception, Article 31(k) provides: 'Members are not obliged to [this

under this provision, can be used for local consumption and not for export. Thus, the provision is of no avail to developing countries and LDCs if they lack the technological capacity to manufacture generics locally.[56] However, the word 'predominantly' in Article 31(f) does not quantify the share of the domestic market of the licensee's supply of production under a compulsory licence, but it is certainly more than 50 per cent. It means that under Article 31(f), the government can authorize the licensee to produce for export, so long as the licensee predominantly produces for the domestic market and imports are not in competition with the patent holder in the importing country.[57] But it is debatable whether 'predominantly' will help in exporting generic drugs to countries in dire need of drugs for epidemics/pandemics, with no manufacturing capacity, nor would it allow the importing country to issue a licence to import generics of life-saving drugs. It will hamper the access to medicines of countries with no or insufficient capabilities in two ways: (i) by limiting availability of exported drugs made under compulsory licence, it invariably restricts countries that are unable to support manufacturing under compulsory licence (or where patent protection is not in force, in the availability of supply of imported generic drugs); and (ii) by requiring licensees to restrict the predominant part of their production to the domestic market, it limits the flexibility of countries to authorize the export of compulsory licensed drugs and thus to exploit economies of scale.[58] Apparently, Article 31(f) does not prohibit the issuance of a compulsory licence for export purposes with some restrictions on such exports, namely, safeguarding the rights of the patent holder.

In the case of a national emergency, other circumstances of extreme urgency and public non-commercial use, prior negotiation with the patent holder need not be pursued. The licence can be terminated as soon as the circumstances which led to its granting no longer exist (Article 31(g)). This provision is a big disincentive for applicants for a compulsory licence, since the licensee may be exposed to revocation at any time.[59] On the other hand,

---

condition] . . . where such use is permitted to remedy a practice determined after judicial or administrative process to be anti-competitive'.

56 Durojaye, *supra* note 31, at 50.

57 A.S. Lowenfeld, *International Economic Law,* 108 (Oxford University Press, Oxford 2002).

58 F.M. Abbott, *WTO TRIPS Agreement and its Implications for Access to Medicines in Developing Countries*, a report prepared for Intellectual Property Rights Commission, p. 17 (Intellectual Property Rights Commission, Washington, DC, 2002).

59 UNCTAD–ICTSD, *Resource Book on TRIPS and Development*, ch. 25: 'Patents: Non-voluntary Uses (Compulsory Licences)', 460, at p. 474 (Cambridge University Press, Cambridge, 2005).

for the granting of a compulsory licence, few policy considerations need to be established, that is, (a) the party being granted licence within the country has the capability to exploit it through manufacturing or import. This requires financial ability or technical capability on the part of the country concerned; (b) there must be evidence of an existing sound legal and political structure to permit the granting and monitoring of the licence.

Going by these preconditions for exploiting compulsory licences, only developed countries would be able to successfully use these exceptions. Countries without domestic production capacity could not use them, nor are countries with production capacity allowed to grant compulsory licence for export to countries without such capacity. Many LDCs lack the financial resources and technical expertise to meet these preconditions. Nevertheless, the issuance of a compulsory licence, especially in the case of imports, remains a viable tool in advancing access to medicines and the right to health in most of these countries. This is because it promotes competition and breaks the monopoly enjoyed by the patent holder and facilitates access to cheap drugs. [60]

In the recent past, both Brazil and Thailand have issued compulsory licences for *Efavirenz*, a drug used to treat people infected with HIV/AIDS. Thailand overrode Merck & Co.'s patent on *Efavirenz* in December 2006.[61] Brazil overrode it in May 2007.[62] Both countries justified their action under their national law.[63] The countries acted under Article 31

---

[60] The provisions for compulsory licences are provided in developed countries' legislations. Even Canada and the United States threatened to use compulsory licences over Bayer's *Ciprofloxacin*, which was useful for the treatment of anthrax after the events of 11 September. See D. Alexander, '"Duplicated" Drugs Life-line for Millions in Africa: US Anthrax Scare Renews Debate on Generic Drugs Law', *The Monitor* 15 (1 November 2001); Durojaye, *supra* note 31, at 49.

[61] On 29 November 2006, the Thai government issued a compulsory licence for *Efavirenz* (Stocrin), the HIV/AIDS drug, still under patent by Merck, details available at http://www.ip-watch.org/weblog/index-php?p=499 visited on 18 November 2008. While other developing countries such as Zambia and Indonesia have issued compulsory licences for HIV/AIDS drugs in the past, the Thai move is significant for its longer duration and the fact that it opens the door to competitive imports of generics from India. Both steps will mean increased downward pressure on drug prices, according to public health advocates, who praised the government's decision.

[62] Ministerial Ordinance No. 866, dated 24 April 2007, was issued. See TWN Third World Network, 3 May 2007, http://www. twnside.org.sg/title2/wto.info/twninfo05073.htm, visited 18 November 2007. Brazil also used the threat of compulsory licence against Abbott Laboratories over pricing of protease inhibitor Kaletra (lopinavir/ritonavir) for its STD/AIDS programme.

[63] Brazilian Industrial Property Law (Law 9279, 1997) permitted the issuance of compulsory licenses in cases where patent holders chose to supply the

of the TRIPS, which allows countries to issue compulsory licences under certain conditions, and critics say neither Thailand nor Brazil met them.[64] However, Article 31(b) of TRIPS explicitly states that governments do not need to consult with patent holders when issuing a compulsory licence for national emergencies or public non-commercial use.

However, to make compulsory licences workable, developing countries need to establish workable laws and procedures to give effect to compulsory licensing, and provide appropriate provisions for government use. Article 30 of the TRIPS Agreement is also helpful in this connection, as it authorizes members to provide limited exceptions to the exclusive rights conferred on the patentee under a patent, 'provided that such exceptions do not unreasonably conflict with a normal exploitation of the patent and do not unreasonably prejudice the legitimate interests of the patent owner . . . '.[65] This provision can be used to produce and export a patented drug to another member to meet public health needs if a compulsory licence has been issued in the importing country.[66]

---

market through imports (non-working of the patent) rather than through local production. The law aimed primarily at encouraging local production of AIDS drugs through local firms and government agencies in order to reduce their prices below those on the US and EU markets. This step by the government dramatically reduced prices and treatment costs in Brazil. Issuance of compulsory licence was preceded by negotiation with the patent holder. The Thai government referred to the Thai Patent Act, empowering it to use any patent rights 'for non-commercial public uses'. Both the Thai and Brazilian governments justified their action under TRIPS and 'member countries have a right to issue a safeguard measure to protect public health, especially for universal access to essential medicines using compulsory licensing on the patent of pharmaceutical products.' They maintained that where a compulsory licence is issued for 'public non-commercial use', there is no requirement to engage in prior negotiations with the patent holder. See *supra* notes 62 and 63.

64 In 2007, the USTR elevated Thailand to the priority watch list from the watch list, citing Thailand's issuance of three compulsory licences on two HIV/AIDS medicines and one on heart disease medicine to be provided to the poor through the public health system. Brazil was also criticized for issuance of a compulsory licence. See *supra* notes 62 and 63.

65 The use of this provision by Canada to speed up the introduction of generic drugs in Canada has already become controversial following the EU's complaint against Canada before the WTO dispute settlement body. See Panel Report in WT/DS114/R, *Canada – Patent Protection of Pharmaceutical Products,* adopted on 7 April 2000. The use of this provision in a public health crisis is a matter of interpretation.

66 The European Parliament had adopted an Amendment to the European Directive on 23 October 2002, which provides, 'Manufacturing shall be allowed if the medicinal product is intended for export to a third country that has issued a compulsory license for that product, or where a patent is not in force and if there

Compulsory licences have rarely been used by developing countries for a number of reasons, namely, they require an administrative and legal infrastructure that is absent in many developing countries; these developing countries fear that sanctions might be threatened against them; compulsory licensing, under the TRIPS scheme, has to be predominantly for the domestic market; and as they are non-exclusive and for a limited duration, they tend to be less attractive for the holder of a compulsory licence. In certain cases, unless these issues are addressed, a compulsory licence will remain only a paper-tiger, though aimed at preventing abuses of the IP system.

3. Doha Declaration on the TRIPS Agreement and public health

In 2001, the WTO Members adopted a special Ministerial Declaration at the WTO Ministerial Conference in Doha on 'The TRIPS Agreement and Public Health'[67] to clarify ambiguities between the need for governments to apply the principles of public health and the terms of the TRIPS Agreement. It was adopted in the midst of growing concerns that patent rules might restrict access to affordable medicines for populations in developing countries in their efforts to control diseases of public health importance, including HIV, tuberculosis and malaria. The Declaration has seven paragraphs. In the opening paragraph, the members recognized the gravity of the public health problems afflicting many developing and least-developed countries, especially those resulting from HIV/AIDS, tuberculosis, malaria and other epidemics, and recognized the need for national and international action to address the issue.

The Declaration affirms that 'the TRIPS Agreement does not and should not prevent Members from taking measures to protect public health' and the Agreement 'can and should be interpreted and implemented in a manner supportive of WTO members' right to protect public health and, in particular, to promote access to medicines for all'.[68] Paragraph 5 states in its relevant part:

> 5(b) Each Member has the right to grant compulsory licences and the freedom to determine the grounds upon which such licences are granted.
> (c) Each Member has the right to determine what constitutes national emergency or other circumstances of extreme urgency . . .

Footnote 66 (*cont.*)
is a request to that effect of the competent public health authorities of that third country.' Article 10(4), sub-para. 1a (new), Directive 2001/83/EC.

67 Declaration on the TRIPS Agreement and Public Health, adopted on 14 November 2001; see WTO Doc. WTO/MIN(01)/DEC/2, 20 November 2001 available at <www.wto.org/english/thewto_e/minist_e/min01_e/mindecl_TRIPs_e.doc>.

68 *Ibid.*, para. 4.

> (d) . . . each member [is] free to establish its own regime of [. . .] exhaustion of without challenge . . .

Thus, the use of exceptions such as compulsory licences and their grounds for invocation is left to the members to decide rather than being limited to emergency or urgent situations only (Article 31 of the TRIPS) as well as to determine their own regime for exhaustion of IPRs and may thereby decide to allow parallel imports (Article 6, TRIPS). From a legal perspective, these provisions do not add anything new to the TRIPS obligations. They merely clarify the extent of existing rights and obligations of members in TRIPS and reaffirm the right of WTO members to use, to the full, the provisions which provide flexibility for this purpose. While paragraph (b) relates to members' discretion with regard to the grounds upon which compulsory licences are granted, paragraph (c) refers to Article 31(b), making it clear that the definition of the term 'national emergency' and 'other circumstances of extreme urgency' is left to members' discretion. Paragraph (d) reiterates Article 6 of TRIPS Agreement. This leaves members considerable room for the pursuit of public policy objectives, especially those related to public health. There seems to be broad agreement that the TRIPS provisions are sufficiently flexible to permit the necessary health protection measures to ensure access to affordable medicines to treat HIV/AIDS and other pandemics as malaria, tuberculosis etc. The Declaration, however, was unable to find a solution to Article 31(f) of the TRIPS Agreement, which has been described as a stumbling block to the use of compulsory licensing by developing countries.

During the Ministerial Meeting of WTO members in Doha, the issue of the incapacity of WTO members with insufficient or no manufacturing capacities in the pharmaceutical sector came up. Such members could face difficulties in making effective use of compulsory licences under the TRIPS to meet a health crisis. Therefore, the Declaration recommended that an expeditious solution be found to this problem. Paragraph 6 of the Doha Declaration recognizes that members with no or insufficient manufacturing capacities in the pharmaceutical sector could face difficulties in making effective use of compulsory licensing under the TRIPS Agreement and instructs the TRIPS Council to find an expeditious solution to this problem. Paragraph 6 of the Declaration provides:

> We recognize that WTO members with insufficient or no manufacturing capacities in the pharmaceutical sector could face difficulties in making effective use of compulsory licensing under the TRIPS Agreement. We instruct the Council for TRIPS to find an expeditious solution to this problem and report to the General Council before the end of 2002.

Closely related to this, however, similar problems may also exist in case of health-care technologies, lack of know-how or trade secrets necessary for manufacturing medicines or medical devices. The Declaration also granted an extension of the transition period to least-developed countries under Article 65 of the TRIPS Agreement of up to 1 January 2016.[69] However, the extension is limited to obligations under the provisions in the TRIPS Agreement relating to patents and marketing rights, and data protection for pharmaceutical products.[70] From a public health perspective, this extension of the transition period for LDCs is of significance. It is recognition of the implications of patent protection for public health, and thus, it is expected that all LDCs adopt the necessary measures to use the 2016 transition period in relation to pharmaceutical patents and test data protection. However, most least-developed countries already grant patent protection to pharmaceuticals under different bilateral or regional FTAs, thus leaving practically very little effect for the apparent concession granted under the Declaration.

The Doha Declaration represents the first public acknowledgement by the WTO that all may not be well with TRIPS. In expressly identifying the paragraph 6 problem, it instructed 'the Council for TRIPS to find an expeditious solution to this problem'.[71] The Declaration responds to the concerns of developing countries about the obstacles they faced when seeking to implement measures to promote access to affordable medicines in the interests of public health in general, without limitation to certain diseases. While acknowledging the role of intellectual property protection 'for the development of new medicines',[72] the Declaration specifically recognizes concerns about its effects on prices.[73] By reiterating member states' right to invoke the exceptions provided under the TRIPS, particularly with regard to compulsory licensing, it has vindicated attempts by developing countries like Brazil

---

[69] Para. 7 of the Doha Declaration allowed the formal introduction of patent protection for pharmaceuticals and of the protection of undisclosed regulatory data in least-developed countries until 1 January 2016. Earlier it was up to January 2010. See para. 7 of the Doha Declaration.

[70] The Decision was taken on Article 70.9, adopted by the General Council on 8 July 2002, with a view to ensuring attainment of the objectives of para. 7 of the Doha Declaration on the TRIPS Agreement and Public Health. It says least-developed countries will not have to give exclusive marketing rights to pharmaceuticals that are the subject of a patent application until 1 January 2016. Thus, LDCs were still obliged to implement the rest of their obligations under the TRIPS Agreement as of 2006.

[71] *Supra* note 63, para 6.

[72] *Ibid,* para. 3.

[73] *Ibid,* para. 7.

and South Africa to invoke these exceptions prior to Doha. TRIPS, when taken together with the Declaration, does not say that a government has to declare a national or health emergency before issuing a compulsory licence. A national emergency can be an implicit reason, but this does not have to be stated, as it is covered in TRIPS Article 31. The Declaration clarifies that all member states have the right to grant a compulsory licence to protect public health and improve access to medicines. Under the Declaration, each member can determine what constitutes a national emergency or other circumstances of extreme urgency; and that a public health crisis, such as HIV/AIDS, tuberculosis, malaria and other epidemics can constitute such circumstances.

While some developed countries attempted to limit the scope of the Declaration to the HIV/AIDS crisis, the adopted text is without limitation to certain epidemics specified therein. The reference to some specific epidemics does not imply that the Declaration is limited to them. It covers any 'public health problem',[74] including those that may be derived from diseases that affect the population in developing as well as developed countries, such as cancer or diabetes. Thus, it may be invoked in all public health emergencies. Apparently, the Declaration covers not only medicines, but any product, method or technology for health care.[75]

The use of compulsory licensing in particular has remained very controversial, even in the post-Doha era. It has been widely agreed that many developing countries, especially those in Africa, lack the capacity to manufacture generics even if they decide to invoke compulsory licensing in line with the TRIPS Agreement, because the Declaration did not provide any mechanism, or exception to TRIPS obligations, under Article 31. The only alternative open to them is to import generics from other countries. In sum, the Declaration did not materially change the situation then in existence under the TRIPS Agreement. The Declaration nevertheless recognized differentiation in patent rules necessary to protect public health and it may be concluded that pharmaceutical patents stand on a different footing under the WTO/TRIPS dispensation. It singled out public health, which had been the controversial issue since the adoption of TRIPS Agreement, particularly pharmaceutical patents, as an issue needing special attention in TRIPS implementation.

---

[74] In para. 1 of the Declaration, members recognized, 'the gravity of the *public health problems* afflicting many developing and least developed countries, especially those resulting from HIV/AIDS, tuberculosis, malaria and other epidemics' (emphasis added).

[75] Carlos M. Correa, *supra* note 35, p. 5 The definition of 'pharmaceutical product' in the Decision covers active pharmaceutical ingredients (APIs) and diagnostic kits.

Though the Declaration has been hailed as a ground-breaking development in ensuring access to medicines for people in developing countries, its legal status remains a debatable issue, as it is not formally being incorporated into the TRIPS Agreement. Skyes observes that within the WTO system, ministerial declarations are not 'legally binding', but may serve as a persuasive authority in interpreting the TRIPS Agreement.[76] According to Abbott, the Declaration would be the substantive equivalent of an interpretation of the TRIPS Agreement.[77] Correa states that it is a Ministerial Decision with legal effects on the members and on the WTO bodies, particularly the Dispute Settlement Body (DSB) and the Council of TRIPS.[78] But it will certainly have persuasive value for the interpretation of the text of the Agreement.

4. Decision on paragraph 6 and Article 31*bis*

In furtherance of paragraph 6 of the Doha Declaration, which mandated the TRIPS Council to find an *expeditious solution* (before the end of 2002) to the problem of WTO members with little or no manufacturing capacities in the pharmaceutical sector, the TRIPS Council adopted a Decision (the Decision)[79] on 30 August 2003,[80] preceded by the reading of the Chairperson's statement, to make it easier for countries in need to import cheaper generic medicines made under compulsory licensing if they were unable to manufacture the medicines themselves in order to meet the health emergencies as outlined in paragraph 1 of the Declaration.

---

[76] A.O. Sykes, 'TRIPS, Pharmaceuticals, Developing Countries and the Doha "Solution"', 3 *Chicago JIL* 47–68 (2002).

[77] F.M. Abbott, *WTO TRIPS Agreement and its Implications for Access to Medicines in Developing Countries*, a report prepared for Intellectual Property Rights Commission, p. 10 (Intellectual Property Rights Commission, Washington, DC, 2002).

[78] Carlos M. Correa, *supra* note 35, pp. viii and 34.

[79] For an analytical account of the Decision, see generally, Paul Vandoren and Jean Charles van Eeckhaute, 'The WTO Decision on Paragraph 6 of the Doha Declaration on the TRIPS Agreement and Public Health', 6 *JWIP* 779 (2003); Frederick M. Abbott, *Compulsory Licensing for Public Health: Giving Effect to the Decision on Implementation of Paragraph 6 of the Doha Declaration on the TRIPS Agreement and Public Health, A Guide and Model Document* (with R. Van Puymbroeck, World Bank Working Paper No. 61 (2005), Washington, DC, World Bank (2004); Carlos Correa, *Implementation of the WTO General Council Decision on Paragraph 6 of the Doha Declaration on the TRIPS Agreement and Public Health* (Geneva, Switzerland: World Health Organization, 2004).

[80] See *supra* note 16. The 2003 Decision is often called the paragraph 6 system because it implements paragraph 6 of the 2001 Doha Declaration on TRIPS and Public Health.

The Decision lays down the grounds for the use of compulsory licence by the importing and exporting countries. It establishes a mechanism under which the restriction of Article 31(f),[81] which limits compulsory licensing *predominantly* to the supply of the domestic market, will be waived for an exporting member when it is requested by an eligible importing member to supply products under compulsory licence issued in the exporting country. Similarly, Article 31(h), which talks about the adequate remuneration to be paid to the right holder on compulsory licensing, is waived for the importing country.

The Decision in paragraph 1(a) defines 'Pharmaceutical product' as 'any patented product, or product manufactured through a patented process, of the pharmaceutical sector needed to address the public health problems as recognized in paragraph 1 of the Declaration. It is understood that active pharmaceutical ingredients (APIs) necessary for its manufacture and diagnostic kits needed for its use would be included.'[82] This definition is sufficiently broad, and requires members other than least-developed country members to submit a notification of their intention to use the system in whole or in part, which may be modified at any time.[83] The notification establishes a member as an 'eligible importing member'.[84]

The Decision sets out a detailed process whereby one country can issue a compulsory licence to import drugs and a second country can issue a compulsory licence to export the drugs to the needy country. Paragraph 2 of the Decision establishes conditions for use of the waiver. The importing member must notify the TRIPS Council of its needs and (except for LDC members) must indicate that it has determined that it has insufficient or no manufacturing capacity for the product(s) in question. The latter

---

81 TRIPS Article 31 – *Other Use Without Authorization of the Right Holder*. . . . (f) any such use shall be authorized predominantly for the supply of the domestic market of the member authorizing such use.

82 This subparagraph is without prejudice to sub paragraph 1(b), which defines an 'eligible importing country'.

83 Such a notification does not need to be approved by a WTO body in order to use the system set out in the Decision; see para. 1(b) of the Decision.

84 'Eligible importing Member' under the Decision is any least developed country member, and any other member that has made a notification to the Council for TRIPS of the intention to use the system as an importer, it being understood that a Member may notify at any time that it will use the system in whole or in a limited way, for example only in the case of national emergency or other circumstances of extreme urgency or in case of public non-commercial use. It is understood that some members will not use the system as importing members and it lists 23 countries in this category; see footnotes 2 and 3 to para. 1(b) of the Decision.

determination is made in accordance with the Annex to the Decision.[85] When there is a patent in the importing member, it must indicate that it has issued, or intends to issue, a compulsory licence (except for LDC members that elect not to enforce patents pursuant to paragraph 7 of the Doha Declaration). The exporting member must notify the TRIPS Council of the terms of the export licence it issues, including the destination, quantities to be supplied and the duration of the licence. The products supplied under the licence must be identified by special packaging and/or colouring/shaping. Before quantities are shipped, the licensee must post on a publicly accessible website the destination and means it has used to identify the products as supplied under the system.

Waiver from the remuneration requirement for the importing country under Article 31(h) is provided in paragraph 3, which provides that if adequate remuneration for the same product has been paid by the exporting country under a compulsory licence, the requirements of Article 31(h) shall be waived for the eligible importing member.

Paragraph 4 requires an importing member country to take reasonable measures within its means and proportionate to its administrative capacity to prevent diversion of products imported under the system. The Decision does not specify the nature of such means, but if an importing member experiences difficulty in taking measures to prevent diversion, developed member countries can, on request, provide technical and financial cooperation. Other members are required to prevent the importation of diverted products into their territories by using the means which are available under the TRIPS Agreement. If these measures prove to be insufficient, the TRIPS Council may review the matter at the request of that member (paragraph 5).

Paragraph 6 provides an additional waiver of Article 31(f) for regional trading arrangements in order to enhance the purchasing power and facilitating the local production of pharmaceutical products, where at least half are least developed countries, as in Africa. This waiver allows a member to export to countries throughout the region under a single compulsory licence issued under Article 31(f), although it does not expressly waive the requirement for licences to be issued by importing countries of the region. The main benefit of the waiver may be to allow the import of APIs, formulation into finished products and export throughout the region that

[85] The Annex established the criterion in either of the following two ways: (i) the member in question has established that it has no manufacturing capacity in the pharmaceutical sector; or (ii) where the member has some manufacturing capacity, it is currently insufficient for the purposes of meeting its needs.

share the health problem in question. It will also help in addressing the problem of the size of the market of importing country, which is a determinant factor for the licensee to export to make it financially viable. It is understood that this will be without prejudice to the territorial nature of the patent rights in question. The need for the grant of regional patents has also been recognized.

Paragraph 7 recognizes the desirability of promoting transfer of technology to least-developed countries and capacity building in the pharmaceutical sector in pursuance of Article 66.2 of the TRIPS Agreement and paragraph 7 of the Declaration. The annual review of the system by the TRIPS Council is considered as the renewal of the waiver (paragraph 8). This Decision is without prejudice to rights, obligations and flexibilities that Members have under the provisions of TRIPS Agreement (such as the potential for exports under Article 30 or Article 31(f) to export pharmaceutical products under a compulsory licence). Paragraph 10 precludes any nullification or impairment action under Article 23 of the GATT against any measures taken in conformity with the provisions of the waiver. The preceding Statement of the Chairman indicated, among other things, that the members will act in good faith in using the Decision, to protect pubic health and not to pursue industrial or commercial policy objectives by way of waiver. Any member with any concerns about the implementation of the Decision may utilize the good offices of the Director-General of the TRIPS Council, with a view to finding a mutually acceptable solution (paragraph 3 of the statement).

While the Decision was a consensus statement of the members of the WTO on protecting public health under the TRIPS Agreement, it has raised a fair amount of criticism. It has been criticized as administratively too complex and burdensome to be a truly effective means to remove obstacles to access to cheaper drugs. Among scholars, it is a common view that the Decision will create more hurdles than solutions to the paragraph 6 problem of the Doha Declaration. It is saddled with many administrative prerequisites, which will hamper the very purpose of the paragraph 6 system. A country in need of required drugs to meet the health emergency, and lacking manufacturing capacity, will have to go through many layers of procedure. It will have to invoke a compulsory licence to make a request to another government or suspend the rights of the patent holder and the other government will provide a licence to local firm(s) to produce and export the needed drugs. They have to notify the TRIPS Council about the intention to use this system and the country that has issued the compulsory licence has to meet many conditions and all these measures will not only delay the manufacture and supply but also increase the cost of the drugs.[86] According to Correa, the so-called Decision is merely symbolic in nature and falls short of what can be regarded as an 'expeditious solution'.[87] He further argues that the series of conditions that need to be satisfied to make use of this Decision will ultimately deprive poor countries of the world access to the life-saving drugs that they need. It is described as a temporary solution which is difficult to operate. The Decision is not faithful to the Doha Declaration on TRIPS and Public Health. [88]

Article 31bis

Two years after the adoption of the waiver, on 6 December 2005, the TRIPS Council adopted the Protocol amending the TRIPS Agreement, by inserting Article 31*bis* after Article 31 and an Annex after Article 73.[89] The Annex to the Protocol specifies the provisions of Article 31*bis*. The new Article reiterates the provisions of the Decision. The amendment, the first ever to the 1994 TRIPS Agreement, implements a waiver that was temporarily agreed on 30 August 2003, making it possible for countries to export medicines under compulsory licence to countries with no or inadequate production facilities. Article 31*bis* provides for limited exceptions to Article 31(f), by allowing members to issue compulsory licences for the production and export of pharmaceuticals to an eligible importing member.

The amendment is in no way substantially different in its elements from the Decision, save for some slight changes in structure. It is merely a 'technical exercise' with no change to the paragraph 6 system. The text of the Article contains the entire 30 August Decision barring the preamble and paragraph 11 of the Decision, which contained the mandate to find a permanent solution and established a waiver from the requirements of Article 31(f) of the Agreement. It is also to be noted that the Decision remains operative in a WTO member state until the amendment takes effect in that member state (paragraph 11 of the Decision). In other words, the amendment has in no way abolished the Decision. Since the effective date of the amendment is not clearly ascertained, the implication of this is that the Decision may still be binding on members of the WTO.

---

86 K.R. Srinivas, 'Interpreting Paragraph 6 Deal on Patents and Access to Treatment', *Eco. and Political Weekly* (20 September 2003).

87 Carlos Correa, 'Recent International Developments in the Area of Intellectual Property Rights', ICSTD-UNCTAD Dialogue, 2nd Bellagio Series on Development and Intellectual Property, 18–21 September 2003, available at <www.iprsonline.org/unctadictsd/bellagio/docs/Correa_Bellagio2.pdf>.

88 Durojaye, *supra* note 31, at 52.

89 *Supra* note 18. For the text of Article 31*bis*, see the WTO website <http://www.wto.org/english/tratop_e/trips_e/pharmapatent_e.htm>.

The Protocol amending the TRIP Agreement has three main parts. First, there is Article 31*bis* which contains five paragraphs that in substantive part reproduce the main text of paragraphs 2, 3, sub-paragraph 6(1), paragraphs 10 and 9 of the Decision respectively. Second, the other part of the amendment is the Annex to the TRIPS Agreement, which contains seven paragraphs corresponding in substance to paragraph 1, sub-paragraphs 2(a), 2(b) and 2(c), paragraphs 4 and 5, sub-paragraph 6(ii) and paragraphs 7 and 8 of the Decision respectively. Finally, there is the Appendix to the Annex to the TRIPS Agreement, which corresponds to the Annex to the Decision and deals with assessment of manufacturing capacities for the product in question to be imported by the least developed or developing country concerned (former Annex to the Decision).

In its five paragraphs, Article 31*bis* consists of three waiver provisions of the Decision: non-application of Article 31(f), non-violation complaints, and preservation of TRIPS flexibilities. The Annex sets out terms for using the paragraph 6 system. Paragraph 1 of Article 31*bis* restates paragraph 2 of the Decision; paragraph 2 of the Article reproduces paragraph 3 of the Decision; paragraph 3 incorporates Paragraph 6 of the Decision.[90] Paragraph 4 is paragraph 10 of the Decision and paragraph 5 is a reiteration of paragraph 9 of the Decision. The small changes in line with the language between the two are inserted to bring the Article in the format of the TRIPS.

The Annex to the TRIPS Agreement defines in paragraph 1 the 'pharmaceutical product', 'eligible importing Member' and 'exporting Member' in a similar way to the Decision. In order to give effect to paragraph 1 of Article 31*bis,* to export pharmaceutical product to an eligible importing member(s), the Annex outlines the terms and conditions to carry out the exports and import of the product(s). It sets the terms for exporting and importing members. The eligible importing member(s) needs to make a notification to the TRIPS Council, which should:

---

[90] In the case of a least-developed country which is a member of a regional trade agreement, exporting to the markets of other developing or least-developed country parties to the regional trade agreement facing the same health problem, the Annex clarifies that a joint notification providing information about the required quantities of the product(s), establishing the insufficient or no manufacturing capacities of the importing countries and confirming that it intends to or has granted compulsory licence (where the product is patented in its territory) in accordance with Articles 31 and 31*bis*, by the regional organization(s) on behalf of eligible importing countries, that are parties to the system, with the agreement of those parties; see footnote 4 to the Annex.

(i) specify the names and expected quantities of the product(s) needed;
(ii) confirm that the importing member (other than the least developed country member) has insufficient or no manufacturing capacity as established in accordance with the Appendix; and
(iii) confirm in case of a pharmaceutical product patented in its territory that it has granted or intends to grant a compulsory licence in accordance with Article 31 and 31*bis* and the provisions of the Annex.

On the other hand, the compulsory licence issued by the exporting Member, should contain the following details:

(i) the amount necessary to meet the needs of the eligible importing Member(s) that may be manufactured under the licence and exported to the eligible importing Member(s);
(ii) clearly identify products produced under the licence through specific labelling or marking. Suppliers should distinguish such products through special packaging and/or special colouring/shaping of the products, provided that such distinction is feasible and does not impact the prices significantly;
(iii) the licensee is required to post on the website[91] the following details before the shipment starts:
    a. quantities supplied to each destination; and
    b. the distinguishing features of the product(s)

In addition, the exporting member is required to notify the Council of TRIPS about the grant of the licence and the conditions attached to it. The information will relate to the details of the licensee, the product(s) and the quantity, the importing country(ies) and the duration of the licence. The notification to be issued by the eligible importing member(s) need not to be approved by a WTO body, but it will be made available publicly by the WTO Secretariat on its website.[92]

Reiterating paragraph 4 of the Decision, paragraph 3 of the Annex requires the importing country to take measures proportionate to its means to prevent diversion of products imported under the system. In the same vein, paragraph 4 requires other members to take effective measures

---

[91] Footnote 9 of the Annex provides that for this purpose, the licensee can use its own website or, with the assistance of the WTO secretariat, the page on the WTO website specified for the system.

[92] Cf. footnotes 2 and 5 of the Annex.

to prevent the importation of the products diverted into their territories. Paragraphs 5, 6 and 7 of the Annex restate paragraphs 6, 7 and 8 of the Decision related to exports under regional trading arrangements, transfer of technology and the annual review of the waiver by the Council of TRIPS.

In contrast to the controversy regarding the inclusion of the chairperson's statement preceding the Decision into the amendment, the content of Article 31*bis* does not make any mention of the statement as this would have amounted to providing legal status to the statement. In the adoption of Article 31*bis,* it was noted that certain members will not use the system as importing countries, and these have been specified in the footnote.[93] Moreover, a statement made by the TRIPS Council chairman on 30 August 2003 was also read out loud and adopted to ensure a match with the 2003 adoption procedure.[94]

The new rules of paragraph 6 system will be applicable where the product is patented in both the exporting and importing countries, both are required to grant compulsory licence, but if the product is not patented in the importing country but in the exporting country, only the exporting country would grant the licence. Where the product is not patented in the exporting country, but not in the importing country, new rules will not be used and the importing country will issue the 'regular' compulsory licence under Article 31.[95] Where the product is not patented in both the countries, the new rules are not used, and the product may be imported from any manufacturer. The system will not to be used if local production is feasible, or voluntary licences have been issued by the patent holder, or if no patent exists for the pharmaceutical product in the exporting country, or where the exporting country is not a member of the WTO.

Article 31*bis,* in accordance with Article X:3 of the WTO Agreement will be formally built into the TRIPS Agreement after two-thirds of WTO members have accepted the change. As of November 2008, 46 WTO members, including the 28 members of the EU, have accepted the Protocol. These members are: the United States, Switzerland, El Salvador, the Republic of Korea, Norway, India, the Philippines, Israel, Australia,

---

[93] Countries mentioned in footnote 3 of the Annex are: Australia, Canada, the European Communities with its member states, Iceland, Japan, New Zealand, Norway, Switzerland, and the United States.

[94] Intellectual Property Watch, <http://www.ip.watch.org/weblog/index.php?p=168>.

[95] Thailand and Brazil resorted to this option in 2006 and 2007 respectively to import a generic drug of patented product of Merck from India, where there was no patent on the product in question. See *supra* notes 61 and 62.

Singapore, Hong Kong-China, China, the European Communities, Mauritius, Egypt, Mexico, Jordan and Brazil. A number of other members, including Canada and Kenya, have begun their domestic processes for formal acceptance. The amendment will take effect in those members and will replace the 2003 waiver for them. This will, nevertheless, create an anomalous situation as the amendment will apply to certain members and the Decision to others, since the amendment has not come to abrogate the Decision instantly. Most of these countries have decided to amend their patents legislation prior to accepting the amendment. Originally the Protocol was open for acceptance until 1 December 2007, which has now been extended to 31 December 2009 under a decision by the General Council on 18 December 2007.[96] Meanwhile, the 2003 waiver remains in effect. Thus, the exact date of entry into force of the amendment is not yet clear.

This amendment of the TRIPS Agreement is aimed at making it easier for countries with insufficient or no manufacturing capacity for pharmaceuticals to gain access to essential pharmaceuticals at a price they can afford. It will be of particular value to least-developed and developing countries facing significant public health problems. But Article 31*bis* regrettably is saddled with unnecessary administrative hurdles,[97] as is the case with the Decision. This is evident from the cases of Médecins Sans Frontières (MSF) and Rwanda, the only least-developed country to put the new rules into operation.

The MSF was the first to take recourse to the new rules. In May 2004, the MSF placed an order under the new rules, outlined in the Decision, for its project in a developing country, which required the MSF to locate a local generic manufacturing company within Canada.[98] The MSF approached Apotex, one of the big generic pharmaceutical companies in Canada, which agreed to produce a three-in-one anti-retroviral combination of zidovudine, lamivudine and nevirapine (AZT+3TC+NVP) drugs, which represent one of the first-line treatment regimens for HIV recom-

---

[96] WTO Doc. WT/L/711, 21 December 2007 – Amendment of the TRIPS Agreement – extension of the period for the acceptance by members of the protocol amending the TRIPS Agreement, Decision of 18 December 2007. See at <http://www.wto.org/english/tratop_e/trips_e/pharmapatent_e.htm>.

[97] Frederick M. Abbott and Jerome H. Reichman, 'The Doha Round's Public Health Legacy: Strategies for the Production and Diffusion of Patented Medicines under the Amended TRIPS Provisions', 10(4) *Journal of Int'l Economic Law* 921–87 (2007).

[98] R. Elliot, 'Will They Deliver Treatment Access?: WTO Rules and Canada's Law on Generic Medicine Exports', 11 *Canadian HIV/AIDS Law Policy Review* 13 (2006).

mended by the WHO. Apotex had to develop a fixed-dose combination of these drugs to simplify treatment for those in need. As the new fixed-dose combination drug was not included in the schedule of drugs that qualified for export under the legislation, it required an amendment of Canadian law. After the required amendment was put in place, Apotex in 2006 negotiated with the company holding the patent over exporting the proposed drugs under compulsory licence. Apotex was only able to get the go-ahead from the patent holder sometime in August 2007. In the meantime, the MSF abandoned the attempt when two Indian generic drug companies started marketing copies of certified quality of the same drug at a lower price than Canada. The drug was not patented in India.[99] This case has clearly exemplified the difficulties that may be encountered in successfully invoking the use of compulsory licensing even in developed jurisdictions.

As of August 2007, Rwanda has been the first country to use the paragraph 6 system and notified the WTO on 19 July 2007 that it would import pharmaceuticals produced under a compulsory licence.[100] The product wanted by the MSF and Rwanda was not on the list under Canadian law and it took three months to put it on the schedule of Canadian law. The Canadian company applied for a compulsory licence to export to Rwanda. The licence was granted and the patent holders have agreed to forgo compensation on certain conditions. The medicine is the same as in the case of MSF, in which the Indian companies have an edge in terms of price.[101] These cases indicate the inadequacy of the new rules under Article 31*bis* and the August 2003 Decision of the Council for TRIPS devised to resolve the problem of inaccessibility to drugs faced by poor countries. The MSF has termed the Decision as unworkable and cumbersome.[102]

5. Implementation of the paragraph 6 system

The Doha Declaration has tried to resolve the pressing problem of access to medicines, which had remained a burning issue since the coming into force of TRIPS, which has provided space for national legislators to give

---

[99] See *supra* note 52, p. 9.

[100] See Notification dated 17 July 2007 (IP/N/RWA/1) by Rwanda under para. 2(a) on the Implementation of paragraph 6 of the Doha Declaration on the TRIPS Agreement and Public Health, available at http://www.wto.org/english/news_e/news07_e/trips_health_notif_oct07_e.htm.

[101] See Canadian Notification to the TRIPS Council by Canada dated 5 October 2005 (IP/N/10?CAN?1) under para. 2(c) on issuing first compulsory licence to export generic drug, available at http://www.wto.org/english/news_e/news07_e/trips_health_notif_oct07_e.htm. Canada sent 15.6 million pills to Rwanda.

[102] MSF, *Neither Expeditious, Nor a Solution: The WTO August 2003 Decision is Unworkable* (MSF, Geneva, 2006), p. 6.

proper effect to achieve the social goals. However, even seven years after its adoption and the subsequent adoption by the WTO General Council of the Decision on the Implementation of paragraph 6 of the Doha Declaration (the August 30 decision), and the adoption of the amendment of the TRIPS Agreement by way of Article 31*bis*, the international consensus has for the most part still not been translated into domestic policy and law. Legislative amendments will be required to enable a country to use the provisions of the paragraph 6 system as an importing or exporting member.[103]

Implementation of the new rules is, however, independent of whether or not a country has accepted Article 31*bis*. Implementation is fully voluntary. So far only a handful of countries have taken legislative measures. On the exporter side, only Canada,[104] Norway,[105] India[106] and the EU[107] have implemented the rules and have notified the WTO to this effect. China[108] and Korea[109] have also made the changes in their laws but have not notified their laws to the WTO. There is, however, little information on the legal action on the part of most of the potential importing countries. Many of them can probably use the new rules on the basis of existing laws and regulations on compulsory licences.[110] A plausible explanation for this inaction is that most of these countries are now parties to bilateral or regional free trade agree-

---

[103] See http://www.wto.org/english/tratop_e/trips_e/amendment_e.htm, last visited on 18 November 2008.

[104] Bill C-9, An Act to Amend the Patent Act and the Food and Drugs Act (The Jean Chrétien Pledge to Africa) assented on 14 May 2004; see WTO Doc. IP/C/W/464, 15 November 2005.

[105] Regulations amending the Patent Regulations of 20 December 1996, No. 1162, see. 107–109, WTO Doc. IP/C/W/427, 17 September 2004.

[106] India inserted a new sec. 92A and amended sec. 90(1) of the Patents (Amendment) Act, 2005. Published in the Gazette of India, 5 April 2005, and effective 1 January 2005. See also WTO Doc. IP/N/I1/IND/D/2–5.

[107] EC Regulation No. 816/2006 of the European Parliament and of the Council of 17 May 2006 on compulsory licensing of patents relating to the manufacture of pharmaceutical products for export to countries with public health problems. Official Journal of the EU L/157/1, 9 June 2006.

[108] China's State Intellectual Property Office Order 37. Adopted in November 2005, effective w.e.f. I January 2006. For an unofficial translation of the Order see <http://www.cptech.org/ip/wto/p6/China-order37.html>.

[109] An amendment incorporated in Articles 106–116 of the Patent Act, came into force on 1 December. See WTO Doc. IO/C/M/48. The amendment mandates a quicker process for issuing compulsory licence, setting a norm of maximum 6 months.

[110] See Sisule F. Musungu and Cecilia Oh, 'The Use of Flexibilities in TRIPS by Developing Countries: Can they Promote Access to Medicines?' published by the South Centre in collaboration with the WHO (Geneva, 2006).

ments (FTAs), which have curtailed their flexibility in utilizing the new paragraph 6 system rules. The other reasons for absence of notifications under the system so far are: the availability of generic drugs outside the patent system (about 60 per cent of drugs under patents had come out of that protection by 2006); legislative changes in many exporting countries, which were to switch over to product patents in pharmaceuticals, drugs and chemicals, namely, India under Article 65.4 of the TRIPS Agreement, are recent or they have not been implemented yet in some cases; and in many cases, there have been voluntary licences and reduction of prices offered by the patent owner.

As foreseen in the 2003 Decision, the WTO secretariat has established a page on the WTO website[111] dedicated to this Decision, notably to ensure the public availability of notifications made pursuant to it.

In October 2002, the European Parliament adopted an amendment to the European Medicines Directive which states that 'manufacturing shall be allowed if the medicinal product is intended for export to a third country that has issued a compulsory licence for that product, or where a patent is not in force and if there is a request to that effect of the competent public health authorities of that third country'.[112] In response to the August 2003 Decision, a 2006 Regulation of the European Parliament has permitted use of compulsory licensing in EU members for export to least-developed countries or other countries with incapacity to manufacture generic drugs and that have notified the Council for TRIPS.[113] The Regulation has created the legal basis for the granting of compulsory licences for export purposes, in line with the WTO General Council Decisions of 30 August 2003 and 6 December 2005 (Article 31*bis*).[114] Article 6 of the Regulation urges EU members not to adopt any law or policies that will render cumbersome or difficult the application of the use of compulsory licensing within their territories.

The Canadian government passed a law in 2004 which aims at facilitating the export of lower-cost generic drugs to developing countries that lack

---

[111] http://www.wto.org/English/tratop_e/public_health_e.htm.

[112] Council Directive 2001/83/EC. Amendment 196 to the European Medicines Directive, adopted 23 October 2002.

[113] Regulation (EC) No. 816/2006 of the European Parliament and of the Council of 17 May 2006 on compulsory licensing of patents relating to the manufacture of pharmaceutical products for export to countries with public health problems, published in the Official Journal of the European Union on 9 June 2006 and entered into force on 29 June 2006.

[114] For further details see the European Communities' notification pursuant to Article 63.2 of the TRIPS Agreement (IP/N/1/EEC/P/5).

the capacity to manufacture pharmaceutical products.[115] This law allows the issuance of compulsory licences for generic pharmaceutical manufacturers to make generic versions of patented pharmaceuticals for export to countries that lack their own manufacturing capacity. This law makes Canada the first country to export medicines under compulsory licence as envisaged under the Decision to combat HIV/AIDS, tuberculosis, malaria and other epidemics. Under this law, the amount to be paid as royalty for use of a patent will depend on the ranking of the importing country on the UN Development Programme's Human Development Index (HDI).[116] Under the law, non-WTO members will not qualify as importing countries for the purpose of exports. It has also been criticized for allowing patent holders to apply for a court order terminating a compulsory licensing or ordering a higher royalty in certain situations. Other flaws in the law include restriction on lists of drugs that may be subject to compulsory licensing for export, a two-year period for the production of the generic drugs and the need to seek permission from patent holders before exporting manufactured generic drugs.[117] These provisions may act as a damper on using the law for export of generic drugs.

The case of India

India is first among the developing countries, with proven manufacturing capacity in the pharmaceutical sector, to give effect to the 2003 Decision. It has been one of the largest producers of generic drugs and has the capacity to produce them at a very cheap price. As mandated by Article 65.4 of the TRIPS Agreement, India was required to introduce product patents for pharmaceuticals and drugs from 1 January 2005. In compliance with its TRIPS obligation, India amended its patent law in 2005.[118] Prior to the adoption of Patents (Amendment) Act, 2005, the Patent Act of 1970

---

115 *Supra* note 104. The Jean Chrétien Pledge to Africa Act, Bill C-9 (2004) amends the Patent Act and the Food and Drugs Act.

116 The Canadian Access to Medicine Regime came into effect on 14 May 2005. In August 2006, Canada's Minister of Health announced an immediate and comprehensive review of the Access to Medicine Regime in consultation with stakeholders. The review had been built into the legislation because Canada was one of the first WTO members to implement the August 2003 Decision and had to address many key legal and policy issues for the first time; see WTO Doc. IP/C/42, 2 November 2006 WTO.

117 R. Elliott, 'TRIPS from Doha to Cancun . . . to Ottawa: Global Development in Access to Treatment and Canada Bill C-56', 8 *Canadian HIV/AIDS Law Policy Review* 1 (2003). (Originally the new Bill C-9 was known as Bill C-56.)

118 The Patents (Amendment) Act, 2005 (No. 15 of 2005). The Act was

prohibited patent product for pharmaceuticals, drugs and chemicals. This has helped in the growth of a strong generic pharmaceutical industry in India.[119] The restriction on product patent, prices and foreign investment triggered a rapid development of the industry which now accounts for more than 70 per cent of the domestic market, meeting nearly all the demands for formulations.[120] A significant consequence of this development in the generic pharmaceutical industry is the lower prices of drugs in India compared to other countries of the world. While prices of drugs in India were among the highest in the world at an early stage of development after independence, they are today among the cheapest.[121] Up until now, India's generic drug industry has been very vibrant and India is a major source of low-priced quality medicines and active pharmaceutical ingredients (APIs) as well as a major supplier of vaccines.[122] Presently almost one-fourth of the global generics markets are serviced by the Indian pharmaceutical industry.[123] India supplies about half the generic drugs in Africa. Once the product patents are introduced, this may not be possible. The likely implication of this change remains uncertain so far. While it may affect the poor countries, particularly those which do not have manufacturing

---

adopted on 4 April 2005 but became operative from 1 January 2005. The Act amended the Patents Act, 1970.

119 J.O. Lanjouw, 'The Introduction of Pharmaceutical Patent in India: Heartless Exploitation of the Poor and Suffering?', NBER Working Paper (NBER, Cambridge, MA, 1998), p. 24; Janice M. Mueller, 'The Tiger Awakens: The Tumultuous Transformation of India's Patent System and the Rise of Indian Pharmaceutical Innovation', 68 *University of Pittsburgh Law Review* 491 at 515 (2007).

120 Government of India, Department of Chemicals and Petrochemicals, 'Annual Report (1999-2000)', available at <chemicals.nic.in/annrep99.htm>. By 2005, it has been stated that the market share of MNCs was below 23 per cent, see Yusuf K. Hamied, 'Indian Pharma Industry – Decades of Struggle and Achievements' (2 April 2005) cited in Mueller, *supra* note 119 at p. 515, note 124.

121 Sudip Chaudhuri, *The WTO and India's Pharmaceutical Industry: Patent Protection, TRIPS and Developing Countries* 59 (2005); Sudip Chaudhuri, 'The Evolution of Indian Pharmaceutical Industry', in G. Frelker et al. (eds), *The Pharmaceutical Industry in India and Hungary: Policies, Institutions and Technological Development* (World Bank, Washington, DC, 1997), p. 6.

122 Cheri Grace, 'The effect of Changing Intellectual Property on Pharmaceutical Industry Prospects in India and China', DFID Issues paper – Access to medicines, June 2004.

123 Indian firms supply 1.5 per cent of the value of the global pharmaceutical market, but 20 per cent of the global consumption. Indian firms also produce 22 per cent of all generic medicines worldwide. See Gehl Sampr ath, 'India's Product Patent Protection Regime: Less or more of "pills for the poor"', 9(6) *JWIP* 694–726 (2006).

capabilities, it will also affect the local population in India, for whom accessibility to public health services is still far from ideal.[124]

In the new amended TRIPS-compliant Act, while switching over to product patents in pharmaceuticals, drugs and chemicals, India has also used all the flexibilities as outlined in the Doha Declaration and the Decision to fulfil the health needs of its vast population and has given effect to the paragraph 6 system. It contains provisions on compulsory licences, parallel imports and exportation of drugs to countries with no or insufficient manufacturing capacity to manufacture drugs. Despite switching over to product patent, it is still possible that:

- all products, including those under patent elsewhere, which are currently manufactured and marketed in India; and
- those which are currently not manufactured in India but their patent applications were filed before 1 January 1995, or with a priority date before 1 January 2005

will continue to be available in generic form in/from India. Only new drugs, whose applications were filed in India on or after 1 January 1995, would be product patent protected. They cannot be manufactured, sold or exported without appropriate authorization.

In the case of 'mailbox' applications received by India under Chapter IVA (inserted in the Patents Act in 1999[125] and repealed by the 2005 amendment of the Patents Act), between 1 January and 31 December, the right of the patentee shall accrue from the date of grant of the patent. Enterprises which were producing and marketing that drug prior to 1

---

[124] Guardian Unlimited (Special Reports), 'Cheap AIDS Drugs under Threat', available at <www.guardian.co.uk/aids/story/07369.144387200.htm> (visited on 2 December 2008).

[125] The Patents (Amendment) Act, 1999, which became operative from 1 January 1995, formally gave effect to mailbox procedure and EMRs for patent applications related to pharmaceutical and agrochemical products under TRIPS Article 70.8 and Article 70.9 respectively. The amendment was the follow-up action after India lost the case filed by the USA before the WTO's Appellate Body for India's failure to provide a legal regime for mailbox and EMR applications. For the Appellate Body Report, see *India – Patent Protection for Pharmaceutical and Agricultural Chemical Products*, WT/DS50/AB/R (4 Dec. 1997), available at http://www.wto.org/english/tratop_e/dispu_e/cases_e/ds50_e.htm, upholding the WTO's panel conclusion that India has not complied with its obligations under Article 70.8(a) and 70.9. See Report of the Panel, WT/DS50/R, 5 September 1997, also available at www.wto.org/english/tratop_e/dispu_e/distabase_wto_members2_e.htm.

January 2005 and which continue to manufacture the product covered by the patent on the date of grant of the patent (ongoing generic production) will not be subjected to infringement action and the patent holder will get a reasonable royalty only (section 11A), provided the manufacturers have made a significant investment. The Act, however, does not quantify 'the significant investment' nor does it specify the parameters of 'reasonable royalty'. The Act has been criticized for being vague on the issue of royalties.[126]

In order to keep its generic drug industry functional and vibrant, and to meet its national and international obligations, the amended Act does not allow patents for relatively trivial changes, known as 'ever-greening' the patent, and clarifies the conditions for obtaining a compulsory licence. It allows patents only for new chemical entities, which will enable the generic firms to produce a wide range of affordable products. The amended section 3(d), reads as follows:

> the mere discovery of a new form of a known substance which does not result *in the enhancement of the known efficacy* of that substance or the mere discovery of any new property or new use for a known substance or of the mere use of a known process, machine or apparatus unless such known process results in a new product or employs at least one new reactant.
> *Explanation* – For the purposes of this clause, salts, esters, ethers, polymorphs, metabolites, pure form, particle size, isomers, mixtures of isomers, complexes, combinations and other derivatives of known substance shall be considered to be the same substance, unless they differ significantly in properties with regard to efficacy (*Emphasis added.*)

Though section 3(d) is applicable to all types of inventions, the Explanation has particular reference to pharmaceutical inventions. It means that only new chemical entities are entitled to patents. The underlying assumption behind section 3(d) is that derivatives, such as salt forms, polymorphs, isomers, etc., that are structurally similar to known pharmaceutical substances, are likely to be functionally equivalent as well, and if this is not the case and the new form of an existing substance works better than the old form, it is up to the patent applicant to demonstrate this and justify the claim. To this extent, section 3(d) draws a distinction between 'ever-greening' and incremental innovation. By making derivatives with

---

[126] G. Crues, 'India: New Patent Law May Restrict Access to HIV/AIDS Treatment', 10 *Canadian HIV/AIDS Legal Network Policy and Review* 28 (2005); MSF, 'The Beginning of the End of Affordable Generics', 22 March 2005, available at <www.accessmed.msf.org/prod/publications.asp?scntid=2232005174897&contenttype>.

enhanced efficacy patentable, section 3(d) encourages the sequential development of existing products or technologies to help bring in improved products that address unmet public health needs.

Given that the majority of patent claims made are for minor changes, often verging on discoveries rather than innovations, it is arguably unlikely that patents will be granted to a substantial number of applications which are currently being held under the 'mailbox' system.[127] In *Novartis AG & Anr. v. Union of India & Others,*[128] the provision was challenged for allegedly being in contravention of the TRIPS Agreement and in violation of the Constitution of India for being vague, when its application for the drug Glivec (which was the beta crystalline form of imatinib mesylate) was rejected by the Indian Patent Office.[129] Since then, this provision has been invoked in other patent applications as well.[130]

On the issuance of a compulsory licence to meet any shortfall in the supply of pharmaceuticals or a national emergency, the 2002 and 2005 amendments of the Patents Act have made the Patents Act TRIPS compliant (Chapter XVI). The grounds for granting compulsory licences are that the: reasonable requirements of the public with respect to the patented invention have not been satisfied; or the patented invention is not available to the public at a reasonable and affordable price; or the patented invention is not worked in the territory of India (section 84(1)). The reasonable requirements of the public shall be deemed to have not been met if due to the patentee's refusal: (i) the establishment of a new trade/industry in India has suffered, (ii) demand for the patented article has not been met, (iii) a market of export of the patented article manufactured in India has not been supplied, and (iv) development of commercial activities in India has been prejudiced (section 84(7)). Now the procedure for granting a compulsory licence has been made simpler. The Act states that where the applicant has made efforts to obtain a licence from the patentee on reasonable terms and conditions and such efforts have not been successful within

---

[127] A total of 8926 mailbox applications were filed with the Indian Patent Office prior to 1 January 2005.

[128] (2007) 4 MLJ 1153.

[129] The court decided against *Novartis*. The case is presently before the Intellectual Property Appellate Board. For more details on the case and section 3(d), see Shamnad Basheer & T. Prashant Reddy, 'The "Efficacy" of Indian Patent Law: Ironing out the Creases in Section 3(d)', *Scripted*, 5(2) (August 2005).

[130] The claim of *Boehringer Ingelheim Pharmaceuticals (USA)* for its invention relating to a paediatric suspension of Nevirapine Hemihydrate used for treating HIV was rejected by the Controller of Patents in August 2007 but in almost 12 cases, the provision was found to be not applicable and patents have been granted.

a reasonable period, the Controller of Patents can now interpret reasonable period to mean a period not ordinarily exceeding 6 months (section 84(6); the aim is to speed up the process of dealing with an application for a compulsory licence).

Compulsory licences can also be issued on notification by the central government in the Official Journal in circumstances of national emergency or in cases of extreme urgency or in case of public non-commercial use, which may be required in cases, including public health crises, relating to HIV/AIDS, tuberculosis, malaria or other epidemic (section 92). The Controller, while granting the compulsory licence, shall endeavour to secure that the articles manufactured under the patent shall be available to the public at the lowest prices consistent with the patentees deriving a reasonable advantage from their patent rights. In order to keep prices under control, under the Drugs Price Control Order (DPCO), 1995, the government sets a price ceiling on many drugs. Also, the National Pharmaceutical Pricing Authority (NPPA) decides which drugs should be subject to price control.[131]

In accordance with the Doha Declaration (paragraph 4), the Patents Act, 2005 also provides for parallel imports. Newly inserted section 107A allows parallel imports by incorporating the principle of 'international exhaustion'.[132] The provision is ambiguous in the context of section 48 (Rights of the Patentees), which guarantees the patentee the exclusive right to import the patented product.

India accepted Article 31*bis* on 26 March 2007, but in order to comply with the paragraph 6 system of the Doha Declaration and to give effect to the Decision of August 2003, the Patents Act, 2005 has made significant amendment to the provisions related to compulsory licences. A newly added section 92A provides:

1. Compulsory licence shall be available for manufacture and export of patented pharmaceutical products to any country having insufficient or no manufacturing capacity in the pharmaceutical sector for the concerned product to address public health problems, provided compulsory licence has been granted by such country or such country has, by notification or otherwise allowed importation of the patented pharmaceutical products from India.
2. The Controller shall, on receipt of an application in the prescribed manner, grant a compulsory licence solely for manufacture and export of the concerned

---

131 On the price increase of patented drugs, see *supra* note 21.

132 Sec. 107A provides – 'Certain acts not to be considered as infringement for the purposes of this Act – (b) importation of patented products by any person who is duly authorized under the law to produce and sell or distribute the product, shall not be considered as infringement of patent rights'.

pharmaceutical product to such country under such terms and conditions as may be specified and published by him.
3. The provisions of sub-sections (1) and (2) shall be without prejudice to the extent to which pharmaceutical products produced under a compulsory licence can be exported under any other provision of this Act.

Explanation – 'pharmaceutical products' means any patented product, or product manufactured through a patented process, of the pharmaceutical sector needed to address public health problems and shall be inclusive of ingredients necessary for the manufacture and diagnostic kits required for their use.

Under this provision, a compulsory licence can be issued to facilitate export of patented pharmaceutical products by Indian companies to countries that do not have adequate or have no manufacturing capacities in the pharmaceutical sector to address public health problems, provided a compulsory licence has been granted by such country or such country has, by notification or otherwise, allowed importation of the patented pharmaceutical products from India. Products manufactured under this provision will be intended for exports to meet the public health emergencies in the countries with no or insufficient manufacturing capacity in the pharmaceutical sector. The provision has not been effectively invoked so far and it is too early to judge its viability. It was recently invoked unsuccessfully by NATCO, an Indian generic drug manufacturing firm, to export generic copies of Pfizer's patented anti-cancer drug Sutent (and Roche's patented drug Tarceva) to Nepal in view of the public health problem in Nepal. NATCO's application was rejected by the Patent Office in September 2008 on the basis of certain drawbacks in its application.[133]

The countries with insufficient or no manufacturing capacities in the pharmaceutical sector (particularly LDCs) can continue to source their requirements of these products from India under a compulsory licence issued in terms of the paragraph 6 system. There are fears already being expressed in many African countries that this law may be likely to hinder access to cheaper drugs in future. In AIDS pandemic cases, presently there are five or six pending mailbox application before the Patents Office for

---

[133] Drawbacks identified were: the Nepal government had not issued any TRIPS notification on pressing public health problem in Nepal; the letter issued by the Nepal government was merely a permission to import fixed quantities of drugs; it was not clear whether Pfizer is also selling in Nepal; and the failure of the applicant to set out the terms and conditions of the licence which he is willing to accept under Rule 96 of the Patents Rules 2006, *NATCO v. Pfizer/Roche* Compulsory Licensing dispute, information gathered from the Official Journal of the Patent Office.

antiretroviral (ARVs) drugs. However, most of these are related to ARVs of pre-1995 patented medicines and India's current production of these will not be affected by what is in the mailbox, unless patents are sought and granted for improvements (for the remainder of the 20 years of the patent period). It is most likely that some existing ARVs will remain available and off-patent in India (in the light of sections 3(d) and 11A) even now. This is, for example, the situation with the medicines that MSF could buy from India without using the Decision as they would have had to do in Canada.

So far, switching over to product patent in pharmaceuticals has not significantly affected Indian production of existing drugs, but India or any other developing country with manufacturing capacity in the pharmaceutical sector henceforth will not be able to produce generics of new medicines, introduced and patented after 1 January 2005.[134] Now the manufacturing of the generic copies of the patented product will not be smooth and will be entangled in administrative procedures. It is also important to note that HIV is a highly changeable virus and patients need to switch and change their medicines regularly. India may not be able to provide generics of second and third line AIDS drugs without the consent of the patent holders. New second and third line AIDS medicines are much more expensive and would cost substantially more. Presently, India can supply generics of first line AIDS medicines only. On the other hand, given limited financial resources and the high cost of drugs for second and third line drugs for HIV/AIDS treatment, most LDCs or countries with no manufacturing capacity will not be able to import these drugs, just like the situation existing in Zimbabwe. This may pose a great threat to lives in Africa and Asia.

Developments in the use of compulsory licensing

Governments around the world are in the process of deciding whether to ratify and accept the Article 31*bis* and implement the paragraph 6 system. Despite significant positive developments, poor nations suffering from the ill effects of AIDS pandemic have been slow to act to expand access to medicines.[135] Few have made use of their existing laws to increase access to

---

[134] *Supra* note 52, pp. 42–3.

[135] So far Rwanda is the only country to make use of these rules. Ghana also in collaboration with two Canadian NGOs – Access to Drugs Initiative (ADI) and The AIDS in Africa Working Group – expressed its interest in using the Canadian law to import generics, both for itself and as a regional importer to the benefit of the ECOWAS (Economic Community of West African States) countries. Canada issued a regular compulsory licence in 2005. Ghana has entered into a partnership

essential medicines.[136] They have failed to take advantage of existing statutory powers to make it easier to import or produce locally cheaper generic alternatives under a compulsory licence. It is possible that the new rules, with the possibility of compulsory licences, may improve the importing countries' negotiating position and may help to lower prices. However, it is too early to predict with certainty the price effects of these rules. But by their inaction, states are ignoring their international human rights commitments.[137] In many cases they are also disregarding powerful domestic constitutional obligations regarding the right of access to health care services.[138] The lack of interest in using the new rules could be one explanation, but there could be certain subtle reasons, even though the negotiations had appeared to be so important to many of the least developing countries. It is likely that the need for new rules will increase as many of these countries, such as India, have recently accorded product patent protection to medicines. The other reasons why it had not been used so far were that it took time for countries to implement the necessary changes to national law, and that up to now it has been possible to import cheap medicines, or active substances, from India, which introduced product patents for pharmaceuticals only in 2005. Now the new drugs will be patented in India, there is a greater likelihood that importing countries will need to use the waiver.

So far only Rwanda and Canada have notified under paragraph 2(a)

Footnote 135 (*cont.*)
with the ADI, which provides drafts and comments to Ghana to implement the Decision. Ghana also revised its law, but there was never any notification to the WTO to this effect; information available on http://www.law.utoronto.ca/accesstodrugs/index.html; see Swedish Report, p. 29.

136 Brazil and Thailand made use of their existing laws to access the generic drugs. Zimbabwe, in 2002, before the Decision on para. 6 of the Doha Round was taken, issued a compulsory licence under its Patent Act (Chap 26:03), 1971, under sections 34 and 35 to import generics of an anti-retroviral drug from India which was substantially cheaper than the patented drug. See MSF, 'Zimbabwe Government Takes Emergency Action against HIV/AIDS Overriding Patents will Dramatically Cut Prices of Treatment for Patients', available at www.cptech.org/ip/health/c/zimbabwe/msf05292002.html; see also *supra* note 110.

137 The International Guidelines on HIV/AIDS and Human Rights, which states in Revised Guideline 6 as follows: 'States should enact legislation to provide for the regulation of HIV-related goods . . . so as to ensure . . . safe and effective medication at an affordable price . . . [and] should also take measures necessary to ensure for all persons, on a sustained and equal basis, the availability and accessibility of . . . safe and effective medicines . . ..', See OHCHR and UNAIDS, HIV/AIDS and Human Rights, International Guidelines (March 2003, Geneva, New York) available at <http://whqlbdoc.who.int/publications/2002/9291730254.pdf>.

138 See, for example, section 27 of the Constitution of the Republic of South Africa, 1996.

and 2(c) of the Decision of 30 August 2003 respectively for the importation/exportation of the required drugs.[139]

What might be the possible reasons for this inaction? What is required to make the system to work? Is there a possibility of its becoming a viable mode of meeting the needs of countries with no or insufficient manufacturing capacity in pharmaceuticals? While it is admitted that the new amendment to the TRIPS Agreement strives to resolve the paragraph 6 problem of the Doha Declaration, it is doubtful whether it will achieve this aim. This is because several hurdles need to be overcome before a developing country can invoke the use of compulsory licensing under the Decision. The use of compulsory licensing – whether for import or to manufacture drugs locally – requires essentially both technological capability and political commitment on the part of a government, which most of these countries do not possess. The administrative hurdles as mentioned in the case of MSF will not be a singular problem. The case of Zimbabwe points towards another pertinent problem, that is, where almost 350 000 people are afflicted with HIV/AIDS and the harsh economic realities have resulted in a critically low supply of ARVs in the country.[140] This is in contrast to the situation that existed in 2002, when Zimbabwe issued a compulsory licence to import the drug.[141] The present situation in Zimbabwe is an indication that the use of a compulsory licence, whether to import or to manufacture drugs, requires essentially both technological capability and political commitment/capability on the part of the importing government.[142] In the case of exports, the licensee would like to be assured of some financial returns for undertaking the task of manufacturing and exporting the required drugs. Such situations raise pertinent questions, namely,

---

[139] See Notification dated 17 July 2007 (IP/N/RWA/1) by Rwanda under Para. 2(a) on the Implementation of Para. 6 of the Doha Declaration on the TRIPS Agreement and Public Health, and Notification by Canada dated 5 October 2005 (IP/N/10? CAN? 1) under Para. 2(c) on issuing a first compulsory licence to export generic drug, available at http://www.wto.org/english/news_e/news07_e/trips_health_notif_oct07_e.htm.

[140] At the end of 2006, about 350 000 people in Zimbabwe were in need of ARVs. See WHO, 'Towards Universal Access: Scaling up Priority HIV/AIDS Interventions in the Health Sector', April 2007, available at <www.who.int/hiv/mediacentre/universal_access_progress_report_en.pdf>.

[141] In 2002, the Zimbabwe government declared a state of emergency in the country under sections 34 & 35 of the Patent Act, 1971. See MSF, 'Zimbabwe Government takes emergency action against HIV/AIDS Overriding patents will dramatically cut prices of treatment for patients', available at www.cptech.org/ip/health/c/zimbabwe/msf05292002.html, visited on 21 November 2008.

[142] Durojaye, *supra* note 31, pp. 59–60.

what will be the fate of these nations? Will they be able to rely on imports from other countries? In considering various approaches to the problem of compulsory licensing in countries with little or no manufacturing capacity or insufficient market demand, members must be mindful of choosing an approach that provides adequate incentives for the production and export of the medicines required. There needs to be an analysis of the determinants for making a compulsory licence work, along with parallel developments, like bilateral and regional trade agreements, impacting thereby the working of the paragraph 6 system.

In this context, it is also important to note that the mere issuance of a compulsory licence will not be a panacea for the problems of poor countries related to medicines. The provision related to the implementation of the paragraph 6 system (in the case of India, section 92A) may not work efficiently for many reasons. It will take time to develop new drugs and also to get necessary approvals/notifications as required under the paragraph 6 system and the national laws. These provisions may be useful to an extent, but not adequate to meet national health emergencies if the drug concerned is a new one and generic copies of it have to be developed. It would take at least 36–48 months, because the production of a new generic drug requires investment in plant and machinery, as well as bio-equivalence tests and regulatory approval. Initial costs will be high. This will make it difficult to access the competitive procurement of the drug under the Decision. Furthermore, not many persons would be interested in the compulsory licence unless they are assured of some reasonable duration and non-exclusive right to recoup the benefits of their investments. The new manufacturer has to be assured of some returns, which will greatly depend upon the size of the market. A big market will be an incentive to offset costs. A case like Zimbabwe may be resolved through access to donor money, otherwise small markets will be left high and dry, thus making the Decision totally unworkable. Hence, the economic difficulties of production costs and market potential would need to be addressed to make the system work.[143] Local firms may not indulge in generics production as long as the drug is under a patent. In brief, the new rules are totally inadequate to address the very problem for which they have been devised. In some cases, they are also unworkable as is evident in the MSF case discussed above. At most, the value of new rules lies in the improved negotiating strength of an importing country vis-à-vis the patent holder. They have been described as an albatross hanging around the necks of developing countries. It does not

---

143 *Integrating Intellectual Property Rights and Development Policy*, Commission on Intellectual Property Rights, 45 (UK, 2002).

serve the interests of countries afflicted with an epidemic, as in Africa, nor is it consistent with realizing the right to health of vulnerable and marginalized people worst affected by life-threatening diseases.[144] They have been termed a betrayal of the spirit of the Doha Declaration.

Free Trade Agreements (FTAs)

The main thrust of the paragraph 6 system revolves around the rights to issue compulsory licences to access essential drugs and to manufacture and export generic versions of brand-name patented drugs to expand access. However, it may become impossible to use new rules if the countries in question have implanted provisions that go beyond the TRIPS (TRIPS-plus). The USA and European Union have sought to limit the practical effects of the paragraph 6 system of the Doha consensus through bilateral and regional free trade agreements (FTAs) with many countries with TRIPS-plus provisions that will ensure access to their markets in exchange of regulatory frameworks.

Countries like Chile, Jordan, Morocco and Singapore have already signed TRIPS-plus FTAs in response to pressure from the United States. Others, such as Bangladesh, Nepal and Yemen, have committed to cooperation agreements with the European Union with similar restrictions. Two of the world's poorest nations, Laos and Cambodia, have concluded agreements with both.[145] These agreements have typically barred compulsory licences and protected data exclusivity for pharmaceuticals and chemicals with a view to delaying the entry of generics in the market. In order to protect their pharmaceutical industry, these agreements are aimed at slowing down the entry of generic competition into the market. They may create obstacles in using the Decision. In the case of the EU, these agreements are aimed at higher standards of enforcement of intellectual property rights.

The United States has been the first country to accept Article 31*bis* and join the consensus of Doha, but the FTAs have undermined this effort. The FTAs restrict the use of TRIPS flexibilities, and the United States

---

144 Durojaye, *supra* note 31, p. 58.

145 The USA has so far concluded 17 FTAs (agreements with Colombia, Panama and Republic of Korea are awaiting Congressional approval), two BITs and 47 TIFAs. It is in negotiation with many countries, including Malaysia. All these contain important provisions on intellectual property. See the USTR website, <http://www.ustr.gov/Trade_Agreements/Bilateral/Section_Index.html>. Similarly, the EU has concluded a number of regional and bilateral FTAs and is currently in negotiation with ASEAN, India and South Korea. See <http://www.bilaterals.org/rubrigue.php3?id_rubrique=76>.

threatens countries using the flexibilities by its '301' actions. Standards are common in bilateral and regional trade agreements. The common TRIPS-plus features in bilateral and regional trade agreements that the United States has entered into with developing countries include:

- provisions establishing a special 5–10 year exclusivity period over pharmaceutical test data. Data exclusivity may effectively bar compulsory licensing or generic competition for drugs that are not patent protected;
- measures prohibiting drug regulatory agencies from granting marketing approval to a generic version of a medicine if the product is covered by a patent;
- patent extensions beyond the 20 years of monopoly protection mandated by the WTO;
- restrictions on the ability of countries to undertake parallel importation;
- obligations to extend patent protection to minor improvements in, or new uses of, older products.

These provisions clearly undermine the Doha Declaration. The United States also uses its political clout to ensure TRIPS-plus standards through its 'Special 301' instrument, which requires the United States Trade Representative (USTR) to identify countries that deny 'adequate' and 'effective' protection for intellectual property to its goods. These countries could be put on the 'watch list' and 'priority watch list' and may be subject to withdrawal of trade concessions. Recently, this has occurred in the case of Thailand.[146] The EU also uses political pressure to achieve higher standards of enforcement of these rights.[147] Though the Thai case is not directly linked to the new rules under the Decision/Article 31*bis,* it has become a part of the political climate surrounding the new system.

This trend is clearly an indication of the asymmetrical power relations that continue to shape IP policy, reducing the amount of leeway that

---

[146] After Thailand issued a compulsory licence for the HIV/AIDS drug in 2006, it was threatened with the 'Special 301' action and put on the 'priority watch list'. See USTR, '2007 Special 301 Report', <http://www.ustr.gov/assets/Document_Library/Reports_Publicatios/2007/2007_Special_301_Review/asset_upload_file230_1122.pdf>.

[147] See letter from EU Commissioner Peter Mandelson to Thai Minister of Commerce H.E. Mr Krirk-krai Jirapet, 10 July 2007. 2007/CAB24/PM/PTH/cmp/D-900. Also available at <http:// www.actupparis.org/article3126.html>.

poorer and weaker states have in devising regulatory approaches that are most suitable for their individual needs and stages of development.[148]

6. Conclusion

The adoption of new rules under paragraph 6 of the Doha Declaration – the Decision/Article 31*bis* – has given the WTO a very human face, which can be used by any country. This has addressed the public health issue and crisis in poor countries. It has also worked to lower prices on medicines for diseases such as HIV/AIDS. However, the new rules touch on a small part between the interface of intellectual property and public health. They can be used when there is insufficient or no domestic production capacity in the importing country and where a patent on the medicine exists in the exporting country. The countries that can't make their own generic drugs can import them under a compulsory licence. Since January 2005, many developing countries have adapted their patent laws to be TRIPS compliant, which will make access to cheaper drugs more difficult. So far there has not been enough empirical data to assess the credibility of the new rules on compulsory licensing. The analysis above reviews the potential for new rules to enable import of patented medicines to developing countries. Pertinent questions still remain to be answered: are all the necessary prerequisites in place? Can the rules address the health concerns of LDCs and can countries with little or no capacity put a system in place that will effectively meet health emergencies? How to overcome the administrative obstacles to accessing the medicines within a reasonable time at affordable prices? How can cases like the MSF or Zimbabwe, discussed above, be met?

The above analysis shows that the potential of new rules to address these issues is limited. The market size for exports will be a decisive factor. Besides the legal regime of the TRIPS Agreement, the countries' other international commitments as well as political factors will also go a long way to making the new system work. The increasing use of FTAs by developed economies and their threats of unilateral action under national laws, such as 'Special 301' actions by the United States, are undermining the very object of the new rules.

Access to medicines by countries with insufficient or no manufacturing capacity in the pharmaceutical sector and with small markets will depend upon their financial and political capacities rather than merely issuing the compulsory licence to import drugs. As this is not going to happen soon,

---

148 Susan K. Sell, 'TRIPS-plus Free Trade Agreements and Access to Medicines', 28 *Liverpool Law Review* 41–75 (2007).

and developed countries are championing the cause of their pharmaceutical companies, there is very little hope that the system will be effectively implemented. In this context, the 'expeditious solution' to the problem of paragraph 6 of the Doha Declaration remains an unmet goal. In fact, the new rules are too harsh for poor countries, imposing upon them an expensive, cumbersome and time-consuming process. At most, they can be used as a negotiating tool by importing countries to put some pressure on pharmaceutical companies to lower prices under the threat of compulsory licensing. In considering various approaches to the problem of compulsory licensing in countries with little or no manufacturing capacity or insufficient market demand, members must be mindful of choosing an approach that provides adequate incentives for the production and export of medicines in need. When all the countries switch over to product patent, the space and means to manufacture generics will be reduced substantially, which again raises questions about the utility of the new rules.

The fact also remains that so far not many countries have put in place the required national measures to make the new system work. The fact remains that since its adoption in 2005, only 30 per cent of members have accepted Article 31*bis* and very few countries have taken the necessary legislative measures towards issuing compulsory licences. Fears have already being expressed that failure to bring the Amendment into force will open the door to a campaign to undermine the Waiver Decision. Recent events in Brazil and Thailand illustrate both the opportunities and risks associated with implementing TRIPS exception mechanisms, and help inform views on the negotiating environment.[149] This situation is turning Article 31*bis* into a 'highly political issue'. This will leave the present situation unchanged and poor countries will be left at the mercy of pharmaceutical firms, which will keep these countries as captive markets for their products. Donations and differential pricing can improve access to some patented medicines, but cannot be a full solution for each and every country or for every product. There are no specific proposals to deal with the problem and it is unlikely in this political situation for there to be an improved negotiated solution. Leaving it to market forces will also not resolve the problem. Regional cooperation to solve the problem may similarly not work, if the region has no manufacturing capacity or if the market is small or economically not an attractive destination for the big drug companies.

Thus, while examining the IPRs and public health issue, an important factor that has to be borne in mind is that the solutions may not

---

[149] Abbott and Reichman, *supra* note 97.

necessarily be based on legal correctness and public health soundness, but on the power of the pharmaceutical companies and a number of developed countries, as opposed to the power of world public opinion (which is predominantly in favour of the poor) and the economically weaker developing countries. If this situation persists and Article 31*bis* fails to materialize, this may require in some cases the comprehensive adoption and active use of the public health safeguards identified in the Doha Declaration. In others cases, and more effectively, it could entail a departure from certain forms of IP protection, whereby pharmaceuticals could be left out of patent protection or patents for pharmaceuticals may be treated differently. In case this does not meet with approval, the alternative lies in the in-built flexibilities of the TRIPS Agreement. These countries will be able to scale up treatment for their citizens if they are allowed effectively to invoke the flexibility provisions contained in the TRIPS Agreement, particularly on compulsory licences. The flexibilities which the Doha Declaration talks about can be resorted to by these countries, with the issuance of compulsory licences under Articles 30 and 31. Similarly, developed countries must help them to improve their manufacturing capacity through transfer of technology. A problem like that in Zimbabwe can be addressed by an improvement in their technological and financial capability and this could be done by taking appropriate action under Article 66.2 by developed countries.

Apart from compulsory licences, which can be granted in national emergencies, the countries need to adopt a range of policies to improve access to medicines. Some of them may be taken within the existing IP system as is clear from the objectives (Article 7) and principles (Article 8) of the TRIPS. The TRIPS Agreement contains some safeguard provisions, such as parallel imports, early working exceptions and compulsory licences to ensure access to life-saving medications for their citizens. But it was not easy to implement these provisions in the past in the light of pressure from developed countries and their pharmaceutical companies. Besides, these countries can import cheap or generic drugs by allowing parallel imports by making provision of international exhaustion in their patent laws under Article 6 of the TRIPS Agreement. On the other hand, in order to stop the entry of cheap drugs originating from the same source into high-priced areas, developed countries can resort to the 'national exhaustion' principle, stopping thereby parallel imports of those drugs coming from developing countries, where that product is being sold at a lower price.[150]

150 See Report of the Commission on Intellectual Property Rights, *Integrating Intellectual Property Rights and Development Policy* 41 (London, 2002).

David Vaver has suggested that the future challenge for IP may be 'to make it more coherent and persuasive, not only domestically but also internationally': 'To achieve that goal may mean a movement away from the present insistence on rigid standardised norms towards greater toleration of diversity and flexibility'.[151] This suggestion may help to empower those resource-poor countries that have feared the power of governments and corporations in exercising their entitlements to balance the rights of intellectual property holders with those of the sick and dying. It might also restore some faith in patents by ensuring that they are used appropriately.[152] This may also mean keeping pharmaceuticals out of the realm of patents. Developed countries should pursue the concrete transfer of technology measures in support of developing country pharmaceutical manufacturing.[153]

The overall trend, however, remains disturbing, but some evidence of greater unity behind health-based TRIPS flexibilities provides some grounds for cautious optimism in addressing the problem of access to medicines by countries with inadequate manufacturing capacity. To meet the demands of countries with no or insufficient capacities in pharmaceutical sector, it may be necessary to know about the drugs which are out of the patent protection so that generics can be produced without any delay in time. For this, a WHO or WIPO Help Desk can be of great use to ascertain the current patent status of a product so as to decide whether a compulsory licence is required to meet the need of national health emergencies.

---

[151] See David Vaver, 'Canada's Intellectual Property Framework: A Comparative Overview', 17 *Intellectual Property Journal* 125 at 188 (2004).

[152] Edwin Cameron, *supra* note 7.

[153] *Supra* note 97.

19 Disease-based limitations on compulsory licenses under Articles 31 and 31*bis*

*Kevin Outterson**

1. Disease-based limitations on compulsory licenses in TRIPS Article 31

Article 31 of the Agreement on Trade-related Aspects of Intellectual Property Rights (TRIPS) permits a World Trade Organization (WTO) Member country to issue a compulsory license of a patent under certain conditions.[1] Compulsory licenses are not limited to any category of diseases. The text of Article 31 never mentions any specific diseases, a deliberate decision by the negotiating group to avoid any disease-based limitation.[2]

This provision has been misunderstood – perhaps deliberately so – in the pages of the *Wall Street Journal* and the *Financial Times* to imply that Article 31 only applies to national public health emergencies like HIV/AIDS or only to the least-developed countries. When Thailand (a middle-income country) attempted to use TRIPS flexibilities guaranteed and encouraged by the Doha Declaration on drugs for cancer and heart disease, a backlash ensued from the conservative media, pharmaceutical manufacturers, patent blogs, and the governments of the United States and the European Union.[3] A *Wall Street Journal* editorial attacked the

* This chapter is a modified and expanded version of Should Access to Medicines And TRIPS Flexibilities Be Limited To Specific Diseases? 34 AM. J. L. & MED. 279 (2008), used by permission. An earlier version of this project was submitted to the WHO IGWG in 2007: A Request for Clarification Concerning the Proper Scope of the IGWG's Work to Improve Access to Patented Medicines, Submission to the WHO IGWG (September 30, 2007).

1 Section 31 of the TRIPS Agreement does not use the term 'compulsory licenses,' preferring the longer phrase 'other use without authorization of the rights holder'. Herein, I use the more traditional term 'compulsory license' or its variations.

2 *See infra* nn. 11–28 and text accompanying; Frederick M. Abbott & Jerome H. Reichman, *The Doha Round's Public Health Legacy: Strategies for the Production and Diffusion of Patented Medicines under the Amended TRIPS Provisions,* 10 J. INT'L ECON. L. 921, 936–7 (2007) (referring to the Doha Declaration).

3 See Editorial, *Bangkok's Drug War Goes Global*, WALL STREET JOURNAL, (March 7, 2007); M. Vaughan, *In Clash with Activists, Critics Charge Thailand Violation of Trade Rules*, INTELLECTUAL PROPERTY WATCH, (March 19, 2007);

Thai compulsory licenses as 'seizures' that cynically distorted WTO rules, while a property-rights activist group charged the Thai government with violating global trade rules.[4] The *Financial Times* also ran articles critical of Thailand's moves.[5] Abbott, the manufacturer of lopinavir/ritonavir, withdrew pending applications for drugs in Thailand, including a heat-stable version of an important fixed-dose combination drug for AIDS with particular usefulness in a tropical climate.[6] The Unites States Trade Representative (USTR) then placed Thailand on the special 301 'priority watch list', for alleged violations of intellectual property law, mentioning in particular the compulsory license.[7] Peter Mandelson, the EU Trade Commissioner at that time, also warned Thailand not to issue the compulsory licenses.[8] According to the *Financial Times*, his letter to Thailand

---

Footnote 3 (*cont.*)
Editorial, *Drugs in Thailand*, FINANCIAL TIMES (January 31, 2007) (acknowledging that Thailand's proposal was legal under WTO rules, but questioning the wisdom of issuing a compulsory license for a preventative heart disease drug); Amy Kazmin & Andrew Jack, *Thai Government to Break Drug Patents*, FINANCIAL TIMES (January 25, 2007) ('some diplomats questioned whether Bangkok's breaking the Plavix patent would be consistent with Doha's aim to support licensing as a response to extreme emergencies like the Aids epidemic'); Apiradee Treerutkuarkul, *Talks with Pharma-Giants Collapse*, BANGKOK POST (December 18, 2007); Brent Savoie, *Thailand's Test: Compulsory Licensing in an Era of Epidemiologic Transition*, 48 VA. J. INT'L L. 211 (2007); K. Noonan, *Worldwide Drug Pricing Regime in Chaos* (Patent Docs blog, May 9, 2007); K. Noonan, *The Law of Unintended Consequences Arises in Applying TRIPS to Patented Drug Protection in Developing Countries* (Patent Docs Blog, May 1, 2007); *see generally* K. Outterson & A. Kesselheim, *Market-based Licensing for HPV Vaccines in Developing Countries*, 27 HEALTH AFFAIRS (January/February 2008) 130–39, at 133–4 [hereinafter, OUTTERSON & KESSELHEIM].

4 Editorial, *Bangkok's Drug War Goes Global*, WALL STREET JOURNAL (March 7, 2007); M. Vaughan, *In Clash with Activists, Critics Charge Thailand Violation of Trade Rules*, INTELLECTUAL PROPERTY WATCH (March 19, 2007).

5 Editorial, *Drugs in Thailand*, FINANCIAL TIMES (January 31, 2007) (acknowledging that Thailand's proposal was legal under WTO rules, but questioning the wisdom of issuing a compulsory license for a preventative heart disease drug); Amy Kazmin & Andrew Jack, *Thai Government to Break Drug Patents*, FINANCIAL TIMES (January 25, 2007) ('some diplomats questioned whether Bangkok's breaking the Plavix patent would be consistent with Doha's aim to support licensing as a response to extreme emergencies like the Aids epidemic').

6 Médecins Sans Frontières, *Press Release: Abbott should Reconsider its Unacceptable Decision to Not Sell New Medicines in Thailand* (March 23, 2007).

7 Office of the United States Trade Representative, 2007 SPECIAL 301 REPORT 27 (2007) [hereinafter, SPECIAL 301 REPORT].

8 Andrew Boundsin, *Thais warned over drug pricing pressure*, FINANCIAL TIMES (August 10, 2007).

claimed that compulsory licenses 'allow countries to waive intellectual property rules to fight emergency health epidemics once all other avenues have been explored'.[9] This claim is clearly mistaken, and finds almost no textual basis in Article 31.[10] Nor does anything in Article 31 limit its application only to the least-developed countries. Compulsory licenses are permitted to all WTO Members, not just the poorest.

Those who would circumscribe compulsory licenses draw support from Article 31(b), which refers to 'situations of national emergency or other circumstances of extreme urgency or in cases of public non-commercial use'. But this language is not a general limitation on compulsory licenses. Article 31(b) is an exception to the requirement of prior negotiation on 'reasonable commercial terms'. The Member may waive the negotiation requirement of Article 31(b) if one of three conditions exist: (1) a national emergency; (2) other circumstances of extreme urgency; or (3) public noncommercial use. If none of these exceptions applies, the Member must negotiate on reasonable commercial terms before proceeding with the compulsory licensure process. In the case of Thailand, if the proposed use is limited to public noncommercial use, then the license satisfies the waiver in Article 31(b). In any event, Thailand does not rely on the waiver, since it also claims to have negotiated for two years in an attempt to reach an agreement with the patent holder. If either of these conditions are true, then Thailand need not prove the existence of 'national emergency' or 'other circumstances of extreme urgency' in order to issue a compulsory license.

In the negotiating history of Article 31, disease-specific limitations were discussed and rejected. The Secretariat of the Negotiating Group on TRIPS made notes of the TRIPS negotiating meetings that were restricted from public distribution, although copies circulated informally. These notes have now been publicly released on the WTO website. The earliest substantive discussion of the scope of compulsory licenses is recorded in paragraph 13 of the Notes of the Meetings May 16–19, 1988.[11] At that

---

9 Id.

10 Frederick M. Abbott & Jerome H. Reichman, *The Doha Round's Public Health Legacy: Strategies for the Production and Diffusion of Patented Medicines under the Amended TRIPS Provisions,* 10 J. Int'l Econ. L. 921, 949–56 (2007). Nor was any disease-specific limitation found in the relevant compulsory licensure provisions of the Paris Convention. Paris Convention for the Protection of Industrial Property, Art. 5 A(2) (1967) ('Each country of the Union shall have the right to take legislative measures providing for the grant of compulsory licenses to prevent the abuses which might result from the exercise of the exclusive rights conferred by the patent, for example, failure to work.').

11 MTN.GNG/NG11/7, par. 13 (June 21, 1988).

meeting, one participant suggested the complete elimination of compulsory licensing: 'the prohibition of the use of compulsory licenses would be the most trade promoting solution, [but] there were many safeguards to limit the possible abuse of compulsory licensing that could be considered . . .'.[12] Five safeguards were then discussed:

(1) non-exclusivity (now Article 31(d));
(2) limitation to the local market (now 'predominately for the supply of the domestic market' in Article 31(f), as modified by Article 31*bis*);
(3) judicial review (now Article 31(i) and (j));
(4) limiting compulsory licenses for nonworking to workings that are economically feasible in the country (not in Article 31); and
(5) patents cannot be revoked for nonworking (not in Article 31).[13]

If disease-specific limitations were discussed at this meeting, it was not reflected in the Notes. Subsequent TRIPS negotiation meetings focused on potential limitations on the purposes for which compulsory licenses could be issued, but again specific diseases were not mentioned.[14] The first recorded discussion of the special health needs of developing countries occurred in May 11–12, 1989:

> To address these concerns, a participant suggested . . . a balance between the rights of intellectual property owners and the obligations to be fulfilled by them; that technologies notably those required to meet basic nutritional and health needs were made available to developing countries on fair and reasonable terms; and that effective curbs were imposed on abuses of intellectual property rights by rights holders.[15]

More substantive discussions occurred in July 12–14, 1989, when some participants suggested special and differential treatment for developing countries regarding patents for public health.[16] Other participants (appar-

---

12 Id.
13 Id.
14 MTN.GNG/NG11/9, pars. 13, 14 (October 13, 1988).
15 MTN.GNG/NG11/12, par. 5 (June 13, 1989).
16 MTN.GNG/NG11/14, pars. 70, 77 (September 12, 1989). Substantive policy discussions relating to patents and access to medicines occurred in the April 1990 meeting, the 20th meeting of the TRIPS negotiating group. MTN.GNG/NG11/20, pars. 29–41 (April 24, 1990). Some of the arguments that are now familiar in the access to medicines literature were discussed here. For example, the history of patents in developed countries was noted as a recent development, with many developed countries having eschewed patents when they were at a 'comparable level of development, including patents on pharmaceuticals'. MTN.GNG/NG11/20, par.

ently the US) argued for additional limitations on compulsory licensing,[17] while India argued for allowing developing countries to exclude patenting on pharmaceutical products altogether, a point India eventually conceded in Article 27.[18] The European Communities supported a stripped-down version of Article 31, with fewer restrictions on compulsory licenses, but the United States strongly opposed that view and argued for additional restrictions on compulsory licensing.[19] None of these discussions focused on specific diseases.

By the October 1989 meeting, the European Communities had changed course to support the US position on compulsory licensing. This meeting marked the debut of the key language requiring 'serious efforts . . . by the applicant in line with normal commercial practices to obtain a voluntary license'.[20] This text is the genesis of Article 31(b).

The representative of the European Communities also proposed a 'positive list' of permitted compulsory license grounds, and others also suggested limiting compulsory licenses to specific grounds.[21] Within a few months, by the April 1990 meeting, the EC abandoned their 'positive list' proposal as not 'useful' and likewise agreed not to specify the grounds for a compulsory license.[22] The final text of Article 31 simply refers to the law of the Member for these issues and does not specify grounds.[23]

The representative of Japan in the December 1989 negotiations initiated

---

31 (April 24, 1990). Delegates argued for flexibilities for 'essential articles, such as medicine and food to be available to the public at reasonable prices', MTN.GNG/NG11/20, par. 33 (April 24, 1990). A developed country representative responded: 'most pharmaceuticals, including the overwhelming majority of those on the WHO list of essential drugs, were in the public domain and not under patent protection'. MTN.GNG/NG11/20, par. 33 (April 24, 1990). The low level of R&D into tropical diseases was blamed on the lack of patent protection in developing countries. MTN.GNG/NG11/20, par. 33 (April 24, 1990).

17 MTN.GNG/NG11/14, par. 75 (September 12, 1989).

18 MTN.GNG/NG11/14, par. 79.1 (September 12, 1989).

19 MTN.GNG/NG11/14, pars. 83.1–83.7 (September 12, 1989).

20 MTN.GNG/NG11/16, par. 22 (December 4, 1989); MTN.GNG/NG11/17 par. 39 (January 23, 1990).

21 MTN.GNG/NG11/16, pars. 22, 23, 33(5) (December 4, 1989).

22 MTN.GNG/NG11/20, pars. 4, 22 (April 24, 1990). Grounds for compulsory licensure were still being discussed as late as November 1990. MTN.GNG/NG11/27 par. 4 (1 Nov. 1990).

23 TRIPS Art. 31. Carlos M. Correa, Trade Related Aspects of Intellectual Property Rights: A Commentary on the TRIPS Agreement 314–15 (Oxford: Oxford Univ. Press, 2007) ('WTO Members can determine the *grounds* under which such licenses can be granted. Said Article [31], as discussed below, only stipulates the *conditions* that governments must comply with. Paragraph 5(b) of the Doha Declaration categorically confirmed this interpretation').

the first substantive discussion of a disease-specific limitation, namely an 'epidemic'.[24] The context was a discussion of the proper limitations on compulsory licensing in paragraph 2(1)(i) of the draft text. The proposal supported by Japan included a phrase 'actual peril to life of the general public or body thereof'. In response to questions, the representative of Japan said 'the proposal was meant to be illustrative of certain situations, including for example the actual occurrence of events, such as an epidemic, that were of sufficiently serious magnitude to warrant the grant of compulsory licenses'.[25] In the next meeting, Mexico also proposed grounds including a 'critical shortage of a product in the domestic market'.[26]

None of these ideas survived in the Dunkel Draft of December 1991,[27] or in the final text of Article 31. The last appearance of limited purposes in Article 31 may be the draft dated July 23, 1990, but that draft also included a broad provision permitting compulsory licenses for food and medicines.[28] The Japanese comment represents the high-water mark of discussion of disease-specific limitations in the public history of the TRIPS committee negotiation, and it was merely a comment in response to a question. The provision in question did not survive in Article 31. Even so, it was not a limitation to any specific disease, but at most a limitation specifying epidemics. More properly understood, the Japanese phrase was focused on events that were actually occurring, as opposed to theoretical events. An epidemic was merely one possible example.

In short, nothing in the negotiating committee history of TRIPS supports a disease-specific limitation in Article 31. In fact, the 'positive list' approach to the granting of compulsory licenses was discussed and rejected.

In addition to Article 31 itself, three other texts should be examined for disease-specific restrictions: the Doha Declaration, the WTO TRIPS Council Decision of August 30, 2003 (the Council Decision), and Article 31*bis*, a proposed amendment to the TRIPS Agreement.

2. Disease-based limitations in the Doha Declaration, the Council Decision, and Article 31*bis*

In the negotiations leading to the Doha Declaration, the US requested an explicit 'positive list' including only the 'Big 3' diseases (HIV/AIDS,

---

24 MTN.GNG/NG11/17 par. 39 (January 23, 1990).

25 MTN.GNG/NG11/17 par. 39 (January 23, 1990); MTN.GNG/NG11/21 par. 52 (June 22, 1990).

26 MTN.GNG/NG11/18 par. 5 (February 27, 1990).

27 MTN.TNC/W/FA (December 20, 1991).

28 W/76 Art. 1A.2, 1B (July 23, 1990).

tuberculosis, and malaria).[29] This early demand specifically excluded all other epidemics. After much opposition, in an attempt to get some positive list limitation, the US finally proposed a broader list of 23 covered diseases, including the additional catch-all category of 'other epidemics of comparable gravity'.[30] This proposal was also not accepted. The US was the last country to assent to the unanimous resolution without their sought-after provisions.[31] The ultimate language of the Doha Declaration should be understood as a defeat for the US positive list approach, and a broad re-affirmation that Article 31 is not limited to particular diseases.

The Doha Declaration extended the technical deadline for least-developed countries to fully comply with TRIPS, although many were compliant with the pharmaceutical patent provisions years in advance.[32] Thailand did not rely on this delayed implementation provision, as it is not a least-developed country. The *Doha Declaration* mentions specific diseases in two contexts; neither operates as a disease-based limitation on compulsory licensure:

> 1. We recognize the gravity of the public health problems afflicting many developing and least-developed countries, especially those resulting from HIV/AIDS, tuberculosis, malaria and other epidemics.[33]
>
> 5. c. Each member has the right to determine what constitutes a national emergency or other circumstances of extreme urgency, it being understood that public health crises, including those relating to HIV/AIDS, tuberculosis, malaria and other epidemics, can represent a national emergency or other circumstances of extreme urgency.[34]

---

[29] IP/C/W/340 (March 14, 2002). Drugs for the poor. WASHINGTON POST p. A32 (November 14, 2002).

[30] *See* Daniel Gervais, THE TRIPS AGREEMENT: DRAFTING HISTORY AND ANALYSIS, 3RD EDITION par. 1.64 (London: Sweet & Maxwell/Thomson Renters, 2008).

[31] GAO Report 07-1198, US TRADE POLICY GUIDANCE ON WTO DECLARATION ON ACCESS TO MEDICINES MAY NEED CLARIFICATION 23 (September 2007) [hereinafter, GAO TRADE POLICY REPORT]; Duncan Matthews, 'Lessons from Negotiating an Amendment to the TRIPS Agreement: Compulsory Licensing and Access to Medicines', in Guido Westkamp, ed., EMERGING ISSUES IN INTELLECTUAL PROPERTY – TRADE, TECHNOLOGY AND MARKET FREEDOM: ESSAYS IN HONOR OF HERCHEL SMITH 227 (Cheltenham, UK and Northampton, MA, USA: Edward Elgar, 2007). Holger Hestermeyer, HUMAN RIGHTS AND THE WTO: THE CASE OF PATENTS AND ACCESS TO MEDICINES 263 (Oxford Univ. Press, 2007).

[32] Phil Thorpe, Study on the Implementation of the TRIPS Agreement by Developing Countries 1 (Comm. on Intellectual Prop. Rights, Study Paper 7 (circa 2004)).

[33] Doha Declaration, at par. 1 WT/MIN(01)/DEC/2.

[34] Doha Declaration, at par. 5.c WT/MIN(01)/DEC/2.

The Doha Declaration does not limit compulsory licenses to specific diseases or epidemics. Any such interpretation would be odd, since the express purpose of the Doha Declaration was to promote access. Paragraph 1 of the Doha Declaration merely uses some diseases as illustrative examples of 'public health problems afflicting many developing countries'. Paragraph 1 does not purport to limit or interpret Article 31. The core provisions of the Doha Declaration, such as the language of paragraphs 4 and 5(b) clearly apply to all diseases:

> 4. We agree that the TRIPS Agreement does not and should not prevent members from taking measures to protect public health. Accordingly, while reiterating our commitment to the TRIPS Agreement, we affirm that the Agreement can and should be interpreted and implemented in a manner supportive of WTO members' right to protect public health and, in particular, to promote access to medicines for all.
>
> 5. b. Each member has the right to grant compulsory licenses and the freedom to determine the grounds upon which such licenses are granted.

The Doha Declaration clearly supports WTO Members' rights to utilize TRIPS flexibilities – including compulsory licensure and parallel trade – to 'protect public health' without regard to the type of disease or development level of the country.[35]

The second specific disease list in the Doha Declaration is found in paragraph 5(c). Likewise, it is not a disease-specific limitation on compulsory licenses. Rather, it interprets Article 31(b) to create a safe harbor for situations when the government can waive the requirement of advance negotiations on reasonable commercial terms:

> 5.c. Each member has the right to determine what constitutes a national emergency or other circumstances of extreme urgency, it being understood that public health crises, including those relating to HIV/AIDS, tuberculosis, malaria and other epidemics, can represent a national emergency or other circumstances of extreme urgency.[36]

The first part of paragraph 5(c) grants WTO members autonomy in determining the meaning of 'national emergency or other circumstances of extreme urgency'. That phrase includes two of the three alternative grounds for a waiver of the commercial negotiation requirement in Article

---

35 Doha Declaration, at pars. 4, 5(b), 5(c), 5(d); GAO Trade Policy Report, at 11–26. Paragraph 7 grants an additional flexibility to least-developed countries, but that doesn't constrain existing rights under TRIPS.

36 Doha Declaration, at par. 5(c).

31(b). (The third ground is 'public noncommercial use'). The disease list is essentially a safe harbor for national decision-making. Arguments that disease-specific limitations are found in paragraph 5(c) of the Doha Declaration misinterpret the waiver provisions of Article 31(b).

The well-regarded treatise by Daniel Gervais discusses these provisions of the *Doha Declaration*:

> The list contained in the Declaration is not exhaustive and its emphasis on diseases 'afflicting many developing and least-developed countries' affords some flexibility in relation to diseases that affect those Members particularly. By application of the *ejusdem generis* interpretation rule, the reference to HIV/AIDS, tuberculosis, malaria and other epidemics shows that Members envisaged the application of the Decision to serious diseases. This must be read in context, together with paras 5(b) and (c) of the 2001 Declaration on TRIPS and Public Health. . .[37]

Gervais is not asserting disease-specific limitations under Article 31 generally, nor is he claiming that the Doha Declaration is limited to specific diseases. The point is more nuanced: under the Council Decision and Article 31*bis*, when attempting to define the terms 'national emergency or other circumstances of extreme urgency', for the limited purpose of the new exception to Article 31(f), then public health crises relating to the HIV/AIDS, tuberculosis, malaria and other epidemics are generally understood to qualify.[38] The WTO has effectively agreed, in advance, that these epidemics will presumptively qualify for the new exception to Article 31(f).

His application of the *ejusdem generis* interpretation rule might also be proper in this very limited context ('other epidemics'), as examples of diseases that are understood to presumptively qualify under paragraph 5(c) of the Doha Declaration. In other words, Members gain additional flexibility with regard to epidemic diseases, without any limitation on the application of Article 31 to other diseases. Members remain free to claim other diseases as the basis for action under Article 31, the Council Decision, and Article 31*bis*, but they do so without the additional presumptions afforded these particular epidemic diseases.

Another possible source of confusion arises under paragraph 6 of the Doha Declaration, which subsequently led to the Council Decision and

---

37 Daniel Gervais, The TRIPS Agreement: Drafting History and Analysis, 3rd Edition par. 2.288 (2008). *See also* id. at par. 1.64.

38 Decision on the Implementation of para. 6 of the Doha Declaration on the TRIPS Agreement and Public Health, adopted by the General Council on August 30, 2003.

then to the proposed Article 31*bis*. Under these provisions, compulsory licenses could be issued for export to least-developed countries, suspending Article 31(f) of the TRIPS Agreement, which restricts compulsory licenses predominantly for domestic use. Paragraph 6 does not limit compulsory licenses to any specific diseases or types of countries. Gervais also comments on these provisions, suggesting 'that Members envisaged the application of the Decision to serious diseases'.[39] This 'serious diseases' position was discussed in the negotiating history of Article 31 when some participants voiced objections to compulsory licenses on 'lifestyle' medicines. But these provisions were not adopted in the text of Article 31*bis*, which argues against their inclusion through interpretive principles. Furthermore, the Article 31*bis* process is itself a suspension of Article 31(f). The provisions in the Council Decision and Article 31*bis* 1(b) are a safe harbor for exports that would otherwise violate Article 31(f) rather than a general limitation on compulsory licensing. The fact that some Members voluntarily waived application of Article 31*bis* to imports by their own countries isn't relevant to countries like Thailand, except to strongly establish that Thailand did not join in this voluntary action.

The TRIPS Agreement is subject to dispute resolution under the WTO Dispute Settlement Understanding, but the US government is unlikely to initiate a WTO panel against Thailand. The TRIPS Agreement authorizes members like Thailand to issue compulsory licenses for these drugs.[40] For all the bluster in the *Wall Street Journal*, it is clear that the controlling legal texts do not limit the use of TRIPS flexibilities to any particular set of diseases. Nor should they. From the perspective of public health, limiting access programs and TRIPS flexibilities to particular diseases would be quite dangerous and unnecessary. Dangerous because the diseases of the world's rich and poor countries are converging, including non-communicative diseases such as heart disease, stroke, diabetes, cancer and depression. Radically cheaper medicines for these conditions could significantly improve health in lower- and middle-income countries (LMICs). Limitation is also unnecessary because proven tools can be

---

[39] Daniel Gervais, The TRIPS Agreement: Drafting History and Analysis, 3rd Edition par. 2.288 (2008).

[40] Indeed, as the GAO reports, the USTR itself concedes the point. GAO Trade Policy Report, at 48-49. The USTR stated that the decision to place Thailand on the special 301 'priority watch list' was 'not solely on [Thailand's] compulsory license decision'. Id., at 49. *See also* Frederick M. Abbott & Jerome H. Reichman, *The Doha Round's Public Health Legacy: Strategies for the Production and Diffusion of Patented Medicines under the Amended TRIPS Provisions,* 10 J. Int'l Econ. L. 921, 949–56 (2007).

deployed to preserve high-income markets while LMICs pursue equitable flexibilities.[41]

Perhaps another factor is at work here as well. An implicit assumption is that the diseases of developing countries are *essentially different* from diseases in the United States or Europe. Paradigmatic cases include exotic tropical diseases such as Ebola Hemorrhagic Fever[42] and onchocerciasis (river blindness). These neglected diseases and their victims are so remote from the US experience that special charitable programs seem unobjectionable. But only a very small portion of the disease burden in developing countries comes from these exotic tropical neglected diseases. Drugs produced for high-income markets can treat most of the global disease burden, such as the pressing need for cancer therapies in LMICs, where cancer deaths outnumber AIDS deaths.[43] The number one cause of death in LMICs isn't a neglected tropical disease, but a familiar 'rich country' killer: heart disease.[44]

Finally, the implementation of the Council Decision and Article 31*bis* has introduced some disease-specific limitations under national law. When Canada enacted its Access to Medicines Regime to permit Paragraph 6 exports, the law limited compulsory licenses to specific listed medicines.[45] This list has been criticized for its excessive narrowness – only 57 drugs or vaccines were included.[46] The list is effectively limited to AIDS and

---

41 For my most recent defense of equitable access in the face of diversion, *see* OUTTERSON & KESSELHEIM, at 136–7. For an earlier defense set in a broader theoretical context, *see Pharmaceutical Arbitrage,* at 261–8. In the context of adaptive innovation leading to the creation of a distinctive product, diversion is much less likely.

42 The Centers for Disease Control and Prevention, *Special Pathogens Branch* (2007) *available at* http://www.cdc.gov/ncidod/dvrd/spb/mnpages/dispages/ebola.htm.

43 Institute of Medicine, CANCER CONTROL OPPORTUNITIES IN LOW- AND MIDDLE-INCOME COUNTRIES (National Academies Press, 2007).

44 Thomas A. Gaziano, *Reducing The Growing Burden of Cardiovascular Disease in the Developing World*, 26 HEALTH AFFAIRS 13 (2007); The Center for Global Health and Economic Development, A RACE AGAINST TIME: THE CHALLENGE OF CARDIOVASCULAR DISEASE IN DEVELOPING ECONOMIES (New York: Columbia University, 2004).

45 The Jean Chrétien Pledge to Africa Act, House of Commons, 3d Sess., 37th Parliament, 52–3 Eliz. II, 2004 (Bill C-9) (received Royal Assent on May 14, 2004) [hereinafter CANADIAN ACCESS TO MEDICINES REGIME OR CAMR]. The law created a positive list of drugs eligible for compulsory licensure, a procedural hurdle not required by the WTO. Id., Sched. 1, *available at* http://www.canlii.org/ca/as/2004/c23/part2620%2Ehtml (visited January 2, 2008).

46 Jillian C. Cohen-Kohler, Laura C. Esmail, & Andrea Perez Cosio, *Canada's Implementation of the Paragraph 6 Decision: Is It Sustainable Public*

off-patent medications. Why any off-patent drugs were included is a mystery. Many of the listed drugs treat AIDS; most of those AIDS drugs are available generically already. Almost all of the other drugs on the list are off patent or face legal generic competition in a similar form.[47] The only patented non-AIDS drugs on the list are eflornithine (for the treatment of African sleeping sickness) and levofloxacin (an important antibiotic). Others are just curious choices considering the global burden of disease (testosterone injection).[48] Ivermectin is also listed, despite Merck's promise to donate it in the river blindness campaign. The very narrow positive list in the Canadian Access to Medicines Regime operates as a disease-specific limitation on compulsory licensure for export under Canadian law.

3. The shifting global burden of disease

To date, the important global legal texts retain broad application to all relevant diseases, but the some parties continue to propose disease-specific limitations, most recently in the World Health Organization's Intergovernmental Working Group on Public Health, Innovation and Intellectual Property (the 'WHO IGWG').[49] The WHO IGWG's task is to distill the WHO CIPIH Report[50] into a global strategy and plan of action.

Footnote 46 (*cont.*)
Policy?, 3 GLOBALIZATION AND HEALTH (2007) *available at* http://www.globalizationandhealth.com/content/3/1/12 (visited December 17, 2007).

47 The off-patent drugs include: amphotericin B, azithromycin, beclomethasone/beclometasone, ceftazidime, ceftriaxone, ciclosporin(e), ciprofloxacin, daunorubicin, doxorubicin, enalapril, erythromycin, etoposide, ibuprofen, isoniazid + pyrazinamide, insulin, ivermectin, levodopa + carbidopa, lithium carbonate, metoclopramide, metronidazole, morphine, nifedipine, nitrofurantoin, ofloxacin, potassium chloride, rifampin, salbutamol/albuterol, timolol. Patent status was taken from the US FDA Orange Book, *available at* http://www.fda.gov/cder/ob/default.htm (visited January 2, 2008).

48 Even in the absence of a 'national emergency or other circumstances of extreme urgency' the importing country could use the process for 'public non-commercial use' (TRIPS Art. 31*bis*, sec. 1(b)). Presumably, Canadian testosterone injections could qualify for the Paragraph 6 process under the 'public non-commercial use' provision.

49 WHO Intergovernmental Working Group on Public Health, Innovation and Intellectual Property, A/PHI/IGWG/2/2 (31 July 2007) [hereinafter, the WHO IGWG]. An early form of this article was submitted to the WHO IGWG Public Hearing in September 2007, *available at* http://www.who.int/phi/public_hearings/second/contributions_section1/Section1_Kevin_Outterson_Boston_Uni_Full_Contribution.pdf (visited January 2, 2008).

50 WHO, REPORT OF THE COMMISSION ON INTELLECTUAL PROPERTY RIGHTS,

While pharmaceutical markets vary significantly with the wealth of customers and governments, variations in global disease burdens call for careful analysis. As described above, attempts have been made to limit access initiatives and TRIPS flexibilities to specific diseases or categories, such as the 'Big 3' infections diseases (AIDS/HIV, malaria and tuberculosis) or 'public health emergencies'. Similarly, global drug companies have generally limited their differential pricing policies in LMICs to drugs treating AIDS, malaria and a small number of other drugs.[51] An implicit assumption is that these conditions represent the greatest disease burdens in LMICs. In fact, these infectious diseases are not the most significant drivers of disease burden in LMICs, where noncommunicable or chronic diseases play an increasingly significant role.[52]

The Global Forum for Health Research categorizes diseases and disease burdens in LMICs. Their system focuses on medical categories:

> Group 1: communicable diseases, maternal and perinatal conditions and nutritional deficiencies
> Group 2: noncommunicable conditions (NCDs), including cardiovascular disease, diabetes, cancer and mental and neurological conditions
> Group 3: injuries, both intentional and unintentional[53]

In high-income countries, the great majority of burden of disease comes from Group 2; in LMICs, Groups 1 and 2 both account for large shares of the burden of disease.[54] Historically, some thought of Group 2 diseases such as heart disease as diseases of affluence and Group 1 diseases such as infant mortality and infections as diseases of poverty. But the diseases of affluence and poverty are converging. As the Global Forum for Health Research states:

INNOVATION AND PUBLIC HEALTH 13 (2006) [hereinafter, the WHO CIPIH REPORT].

[51] Oxfam, INVESTING FOR LIFE: MEETING POOR PEOPLE'S NEEDS FOR ACCESS TO MEDICINES THROUGH RESPONSIBLE BUSINESS PRACTICES 13–15 (November 2007) (Oxfam Briefing Paper 109).

[52] *See, e.g.*, Roger S. Magnusson, *Non-communicable Diseases and Global Health Governance: Enhancing Global Processes to Improve Health Development*, 3 GLOBALIZATION AND HEALTH (May 22, 2007) *available at* http://www.globalizationandhealth.com/content/3/1/2 (visited December 27, 2007).

[53] Global Forum for Health Research, 2 GLOBAL FORUM UPDATE ON RESEARCH FOR HEALTH 10–11 (2005) (verbatim); *see also* Alan Lopez & Colin Mathers, *Inequities in Health Status: Findings from the 2001 Global Burden of Disease Study*, 4 Global Forum Update on Research for Health 163, 164 (2007).

[54] Global Forum for Health Research, 2 GLOBAL FORUM UPDATE ON RESEARCH FOR HEALTH 11 (Figure 3) (2005).

> A long-standing stereotype has held that noncommunicable conditions are 'diseases of affluence' characteristic of developed countries, while developing countries mainly suffer from communicable diseases. It is clear that this no longer applies and that a major epidemiological transition has taken place: there is an almost equal level of BoD [Burden of Disease] due to Group 1 and Group 2 for LMICs and a significantly higher rate of DALYs [Disability-adjusted Life Years] in LMICs due to injuries.'[55]

The top ten causes of death and burden of disease in LMICs include several conditions that are also top killers in high-income countries, in addition to more 'traditional' diseases of poverty (see Table 19.1).

Noncommunicable diseases (NCDs) are an increasingly significant problem in the developing world.[56] As Lopez and Mathers note:

> Surprisingly, almost 50% of the adult disease burden in low- and medium-income countries is now attributable to noncommunicable disease. Population ageing and changes in the distribution of risk factors have accelerated the epidemic of noncommunicable disease in many developing countries.[57]

The WHO CIPIH Report took a different taxonomic path to describe the global burden of disease, following the terminology of the Commission on Macroeconomics and Health (CMH).[58] The CMH and the WHO CIPIH Report categorized diseases with a market-based approach, according to their intrinsic appeal to global capitalism, and in particular the markets for innovation and medicine.

---

[55] Global Forum for Health Research, 2 Global Forum Update on Research for Health 11 (2005).

[56] *See, e.g.* the special issue of The Lancet in December 2007 devoted to the burden of chronic diseases, with several articles focusing upon LMICs. Dele O. Abegunde et al., *The Burden and Costs of Chronic Diseases in Low-income and Middle-income Countries*, 370 The Lancet 1929–38 (2007); Stephen S. Lim et al., *Prevention of Cardiovascular Disease in High-risk Individuals in Low-income and Middle-income Countries: Health Effects and Costs*, 370 The Lancet 370(5604): 2054–62 (published online December 11, 2007); Robert Beaglehole, Shah Reddy, Janet Voûte, & Steve Leeder, *Prevention of Chronic Diseases: A Call To Action,* 370 The Lancet xxx (2007). For a somewhat contrarian view, *see* Shah Ebrahim & Liam Smeeth, *Non-communicable Diseases in Low and Middle-income Countries: A Priority or a Distraction?*, 34 Int'l. J. Epidemiology, at 961 (2005); *but see* Kathleen Strong, Colin Mathers, Joanne Epping-Jordan, & Robert Beaglehole, *Preventing Chronic Disease: A Priority for Global Health*, Int'l. J. Epidemiology 492 (2006) (letter responding to the Ebrahim & Smeeth article). The WHO CIPIH Report strongly noted the growing rate of noncommunicable disease. WHO CIPIH Report, at 2–5, 44.

[57] Alan Lopez & Colin Mathers, *Inequities in Health Status: Findings from the 2001 Global Burden of Disease Study*, 4 Global Forum Update on Research for Health at 172.

[58] WHO CIPIH Report, at 13.

Table 19.1 Burden of disease in LMICs

	Death (2001)[1]	Death (2020 est.)[2]	Burden of disease (2001, DALYs)[3]
1.	Ischaemic heart disease	Ischaemic heart disease	Perinatal conditions
2.	Cerebrovascular disease	Cerebrovascular disease	Lower respiratory infections
3.	Lower respiratory infection	Chronic obstructive pulmonary disease	Ischaemic heart disease
4.	HIV/AIDS	Tuberculosis	Cerebrovascular disease
5.	Perinatal conditions	Road traffic accidents	HIV/AIDS
6.	Chronic obstructive pulmonary disease	Lower respiratory infections	Diarrhoeal diseases
7.	Diarrhoeal diseases	Trachea, bronchus, and lung cancers	Unipolar depressive disorders
8.	Tuberculosis	Stomach cancer	Malaria
9.	Malaria	Diarrhoeal disease	Chronic obstructive pulmonary disease
10.	Road traffic accidents	HIV/AIDS	Tuberculosis

Notes:

1 Alan Lopez & Colin Mathers, *Inequities in Health Status: Findings From the 2001 Global Burden of Disease Study*, 4 GLOBAL FORUM UPDATE ON RESEARCH FOR HEALTH 169 (Table 2) (2007).

2 Shah Ebrahim & Liam Smeeth, *Non-Communicable Diseases in Low and Middle-income Countries: A Priority or a Distraction?*, 34 INT'L. J. EPIDEMIOLOGY 961, 962 (Table 2) (2005).

3 Alan Lopez & Colin Mathers, *Inequities in Health Status: Findings from the 2001 Global Burden of Disease Study*, 4 GLOBAL FORUM UPDATE ON RESEARCH FOR HEALTH 171–2 (Tables 7 & 8) (2007) (correcting numbering errors in original chart).

Type I disease innovations

Type I diseases occur in high-income countries. The purchasing power of the high-income countries drives innovation for Type I diseases. Examples include cardiovascular disease, stroke, cancer, depression, and diabetes. These diseases may also be prevalent in LMICs,[59] but the defining characteristic of Type I diseases is a strong market demand for treatment of high-income patients. SARS and pandemic influenza are also Type I

[59] *See* Bradly Condon & Tapen Sinha, *Global Diseases, Global Patents and Differential Treatment in WTO Law: Criteria for Suspending Patent Obligations in Developing Countries*, NW. J. INT'L L. & BUS. 1, 25–8 (2005).

disease markets. Innovation in Type I diseases can be sufficiently supported by high-income markets alone.

Some Type I diseases disproportionately affect people in LMICs. Take the example of cervical cancer. The WHO Commission listed cervical cancer as a Type I disease.[60] In high-income countries, deaths from cervical cancer are relatively rare due to expensive population screening and treatment. About 260 000 women in developing countries die from cervical cancer each year,[61] exceeding the deaths from all diseases in the tropical-disease cluster.[62] A highly effective vaccine is now available to prevent most cases of cervical cancer,[63] but the price – US$360 per person – exceeds the per capita annual health budgets for most of the women worldwide who need it.[64] A relatively small number of deaths in high-income countries led to these two HPV vaccines that hold great promise in LMICs as well. These vaccines could be provided generically to the poorest without undermining optimal innovation. The deaths of less than 17 000 women per year in wealthy countries offered sufficient financial rewards to prompt both Merck and GlaxoSmithKline to spend hundreds of millions of dollars to bring HPV vaccines to market. The deaths of more than 222 000 poor women per year may have provided moral, scientific or humanitarian incentives to create HPV vaccines, but the potential financial rewards were modest, since these women can't afford them.[65] Merck has announced an equitable access program,[66] and some limited donations, but the scope of the program remains unknown at the present.[67]

---

60 WHO CIPIH REPORT, at 14 (Table 1.3).

61 F. Kamangar, G.M. Dores, & W.F. Anderson, *Patterns of Cancer Incidence, Mortality, and Prevalence across Five Continents: Defining Priorities to Reduce Cancer Disparities in Different Geographic Regions of the World,* 24 J. CLIN. ONCOLOGY 2137–50 (2006).

62 C.D. Mathers, A.D. Lopez, & C.J.L. Murray, GLOBAL BURDEN OF DISEASE AND RISK FACTORS (Table 3B.1) (Oxford: World Bank, 2006).

63 D.M. Harper, E. L. Franco, C.M. Wheeler, A. B. Moscicki, B. Romanowski, et al., *Sustained Efficacy up to 4.5 Years of a Bivalent L1 Virus-like Particle Vaccine against Human Papillomavirus Types 16 and 18: Follow-up from a Randomised Control Trial*, 367 THE LANCET 1247–55 (2006).

64 OUTTERSON & KESSELHEIM, at 130 and ff.

65 Id.

66 Bill and Melinda Gates Foundation Press Release, *Cervical Cancer Vaccine Project* (2006), *available at* http://www.path.org/files/RH_cc_vacc_proj_fs_update.pdf (accessed August 16, 2007).

67 Merck Press Release, *Merck to Donate Three Million Doses of Gardasil, its Cervical Cancer Vaccine, to Support Vaccination Programs in Lowest Income Nations* (September 26, 2007). Three million doses will vaccinate 1 million women, a very small percentage of the need.

Type III disease innovations

Type III diseases occur overwhelmingly or exclusively incident in developing countries. Little or no global commercial market exists for Type III diseases. Examples include onchocerciasis (river blindness), leishmaniasis (kala-azar), Chagas disease, and African sleeping sickness.

Many have recognized the market failures inherent in Type III diseases.[68] For these diseases, normal market conditions will be inadequate to stimulate sufficient R&D. Impoverished sick people are not attractive markets for global for-profit R&D programs.[69] Type III disease innovation will require substantial non-market incentives, such as public private product development partnerships[70] and market-making devices such as Advanced Market Commitments[71] or patent prizes.[72] Others look to non-market incentives such as grants and government-sponsored research.[73] Occasionally proposals are coupled with an expansion of IP rights in poor countries,[74] or a choice between exercising IP rights in either developed or developing countries, but not both.[75] Expanded IP rights are

---

68 WHO CIPIH Report, at 22 ('as is the case for diseases affecting millions of poor people in developing countries, patents are not a relevant factor or effective in stimulating R&D and bringing new products to market.'); *see also* Carl Nathan, *Aligning Pharmaceutical Innovation with Medical Need*, 13 NATURE MEDICINE 304–08 (2007). For a review of the literature, *see Pharmaceutical Arbitrage*, at 244–50.

69 *See, e.g.,* Médicins Sans Frontières, FATAL IMBALANCE: THE CRISIS IN RESEARCH AND DEVELOPMENT FOR DRUGS FOR NEGLECTED DISEASES (September 2001).

70 Mary Moran et al., *The New Landscape of Neglected Disease Drug Development* (2005), *available at* www.wellcome.ac.uk.

71 Michael Kremer & R. Glennerster, STRONG MEDICINE: CREATING INCENTIVES FOR PHARMACEUTICAL RESEARCH ON NEGLECTED DISEASES (Princeton, NJ: Princeton University Press) 2004).

72 Aiden Hollis & Thomas Pogge, *The Health Impact Fund: Making New Medicines Accessible for All*, INCENTIVES FOR GLOBAL HEALTH (2008), available at http://www.Yale.edu/MAc,illan/igh/hif_book.pdf.

73 Tim Hubbard & James Love, *A New Trade Framework for Global Healthcare R&D*, 2 PLoS BIOLOGY 0147–50 (February 2004); *but see* Joseph DiMasi & Henry G. Grabowski, *Patents and R&D Incentives: Comments on the Hubbard and Love Trade Framework for Financing Pharmaceutical R&D* 2 (2003), *available at* http://www.who.int/intellectualproperty/news/en/Submission3.pdf.

74 Alan O. Sykes, *TRIPS, Pharmaceuticals, Developing Countries, and the Doha 'Solution,'* 3 CHI. J. INT'L. L. 47, 56 (2002); *Neglected Diseases: Towards Policies without Borders*, 262 OECD OBSERVER (July 2007).

75 Jean O. Lanjouw & William Jack, *Trading Up: How Much Should Poor Countries Pay to Support Pharmaceutical Innovation?*, 4 CTR. FOR GLOBAL DEVELOPMENT 1–8 (2004), *available at* http://www.cgdev.org/content/publications/detail/2842/.

an unnecessary and unwelcome addition for neglected disease research. Expansion of IP rights will not create incentives in the absence of money to buy the product. These diseases are neglected due to the poverty of the afflicted, not the lack of IP rights.[76]

While Type III diseases are significant, we should note that total global deaths from the tropical-disease cluster in 2001 were only 128 000 people.[77] Residents of LMICs suffer from higher infectious disease burdens, but much of the DALYs lost stems from noncommunicable diseases, injuries, and communicable diseases other than the tropical and neglected disease cluster.[78]

Type II disease innovations

Type II diseases occupy an intermediate category, sharing some characteristics of the other categories. LMICs suffer a disproportionately large burden from Type II diseases. Tuberculosis and malaria were once Type I diseases, but are now classified as Type II by the WHO after the virtual eradication of malaria in the US and Europe, and a significantly lower disease burden from tuberculosis in high-income countries. Malaria is classified as Type II rather than Type III because it retains a small but significant financial footprint in the high-income countries to meet the needs of military and international travelers. If multiple-drug resistant and extremely-drug resistant tuberculosis spread significantly in high-income countries, tuberculosis may regain Type I status.

Innovation in Type II diseases also occupies an intermediate category. In many cases, innovation for high-income markets will be sufficient to create the necessary drugs. Such was the case with AIDS and the existing treatments for malaria and tuberculosis. But the global medical burden of malaria and tuberculosis has outmatched the innovation spurred by relatively modest high-income country markets. Type II diseases will require additional non-market incentives to fully correlate global need with innovation incentives.[79]

The WHO Commission classified AIDS as a Type II disease,[80] but that appears to be a debatable choice. AIDS is perhaps better classified as a

---

[76] WHO CIPIH Report, at *Pharmaceutical Arbitrage*, at 22, 244-50; *Pharmaceutical Arbitrage*, at 244–60.

[77] Mathers, et al., Global Burden of Disease and Risk Factors, at Table 3B.1.

[78] WHO CIPIH Report, at 3–4, Table 1.1 & 1.2.

[79] *See, e.g.,* Carl Nathan, *Aligning Pharmaceutical Innovation With Medical Need*, 13 Nature Medicine 304–08 (2007).

[80] WHO CIPIH Report, at 14.

Type I disease. While the greatest burden of AIDS disease falls outside of high-income countries, more than 2 million people are living with HIV in high-income countries[81] and infection rates are rising.[82] This high-income patient base is more than sufficient to spur innovation. The AIDS cases in the US and Europe sparked an avalanche of research, even before the true scope of the global crisis was known. AIDS may be considered a Type I disease at present, with the exception of adaptive research.

Adaptive Innovations for Type I diseases

Additional incentives may be required to adapt Type I innovations to developing country conditions.[83] Heat-stable formulations and fixed-dose combinations[84] are examples of adaptive innovations for a Type I disease (AIDS). Simpler and cheaper diagnostics are required for resource-constrained settings. Geographic variations in Human Papillomavirus (HPV) subtype incidence might require additions to the cervical cancer vaccines.[85] All of these are examples of adaptive innovation for Type I diseases. In the language of the WHO DRAFT GLOBAL STRATEGY (2007), these are 'needs of developing countries in relation to Type I diseases'.[86] Some of this adaptive innovation may come from drug companies located in developing countries, where cost structures are lower and researchers may be closer to the ground.[87] Other adaptive innovations may require non-market incentives, similar to other neglected disease issues.

Important distinctions between markets for innovation and medicine

The WHO typology is helpful for analyzing differences in the markets for innovation and medicine between high-income countries and LMICs.

---

81 UNAIDS, FACT SHEET: KEY FACTS BY REGION – 2007 AIDS EPIDEMIC UPDATE (November 2007) (estimating that 2.1 million people are living with HIV in 2007 in North America, Western and Central Europe).

82 Gardiner Harris, *Figures on H.I.V. Rate Expected to Rise,* NY TIMES (December 2, 2007) (reporting that estimates on US infection rates may be 50 per cent higher than previously thought).

83 WHO CIPIH REPORT, at 16–19, 44.

84 *Pharmaceutical Arbitrage,* at 234.

85 N. Munoz N, et al., *Against Which Human Papillomavirus Types Shall We Vaccinate and Screen? The International Perspective,* 111 INT'L. J. CANCER 278–85 (2004).

86 WHO, DRAFT GLOBAL STRATEGY AND PLAN OF ACTION ON PUBLIC HEALTH, INNOVATION AND INTELLECTUAL PROPERTY: PROGRESS TO DATE IN DRAFTING GROUPS A AND B (December 14, 2007) (A/PI/IGWG/2/Conf.Paper No.1 Rev.1) [hereinafter, WHO DRAFT GLOBAL STRATEGY (2007)].

87 WHO CIPIH REPORT, at 45.

Disease-specific incentives are required for innovation market failures in Type II and III diseases, but limitations are not appropriate for access programs and TRIPS flexibilities. The relevant factors are summarized in Table 19.2.

4. Disease-specific limitations in the WHO IGWG

With this background, we now turn to the recent discussions within the WHO IGWG concerning disease-specific limitations. The December 14, 2007 draft of the WHO Draft Global Strategy (2007)[88] frequently uses the following disease-limiting phrase or its permutations: 'diseases which disproportionately affect developing countries'.[89] The phrase was prominently discussed in the WHO CIPIH REPORT,[90] and was mentioned in the World Health Assembly Resolution that established the IGWG.[91] The phrase is occasionally used as an apparent synonym for Type II and III diseases.

The US position

The United States government appears to consider the phrase as a limitation on access programs. In the US Comments to the WHO Elements of a Global Strategy (2006), the United States claimed that the IGWG's mandate was limited to Type II and III diseases:

> The IGWG should *not* consider Recommendation 2.4 as the focus of its work should be on diseases that disproportionately affect developing countries, more commonly referred to as Type II and Type III diseases.[92]

The United States was commenting on Recommendation 2.4 from the WHO CIPIH Report, which explicitly included Type I diseases in its ambit:

> When addressing the health needs of people in developing countries, it is important to seek innovative ways of combating Type I diseases, as well as Type II and Type III diseases. Governments and funders need to assign higher priority

---

88 WHO DRAFT GLOBAL STRATEGY (2007), at 3. An earlier draft is: WHO, ELEMENTS OF A GLOBAL STRATEGY AND PLAN OF ACTION, A/PHI/IGWG/1/5 (December 8, 2006) [hereinafter, WHO ELEMENTS OF A GLOBAL STRATEGY (2006)].

89 WHO DRAFT GLOBAL STRATEGY (2007), at 3, par. 3 (consensus text), par. 4 (bracketed text, consensus pending decision by USA), at 4, par. 13 (with bracketed text), par. 14 (a) (consensus text), par. 14 (b) (consensus text, except for omitted footnote).

90 WHO CIPIH REPORT.

91 WHA 59.24.

92 US COMMENTS, at 2.

Table 19.2 Markets for innovation and medicines, by disease type and income level

	Innovation Market	Medicine Market
Type I		
HICs	High-income country purchasing power drives the market (e.g. Lipitor for high cholesterol). Innovation follows purchasing power rather than medical need (e.g. additional life style and me-too drugs rather than a first-in-class Gram-negative antibiotic).	Patent protection and sophisticated branding and marketing yield high drug prices. The impact of high prices is ameliorated by private and social insurance mechanisms, relatively high per capita incomes, and (in some cases) government monopsony procurement.
LMICs	Adaptive R&D may be needed to account for resource-constrained settings (e.g. non-refrigerated vaccines, polyvalent HPV vaccines, fixed-dose combinations). Regional companies may be able to supply some adaptive R&D. The balance must be provided through non-market incentives.	Patent-based pricing denies access to the majority of direct purchasers. Robust generic competition would drive prices closer to marginal cost (e.g. unlicensed AIDS drugs). LMIC governments and donors have limited ability to subsidize access (cf. Thailand & Brazil's AIDS programs).
Type II		
HICs	Largely ignored by high-income markets, except by tourists, military and other modest markets (e.g. prophylaxis for malaria).	Patented Type II innovative medicines are generally limited to HIC citizens who are residents in LMICs (e.g. military, tourists, expats, wealthy local elites).
LMICs	Adequate levels of innovation require additional R&D support from non-market incentives (e.g. malaria vaccine).	LMIC governments and donors have limited ability to subsidize access. Best medical practice may require significant subsidies to prevent resistance to communicable diseases (e.g. subsidies for ACTs for malaria).
Type III		
HICs	No market in HICs.	No medical need in HICs.
LMICs	These very neglected diseases require non-market incentives to support innovation.	Significant unmet medical need in LMICs.

> to combating the rapidly growing impact of Type I diseases in developing countries, and, through innovation, to finding affordable and technologically appropriate means for their diagnosis, prevention and treatment.[93]

Other actions by the US government have attempted to limit IGWG consideration of TRIPs flexibilities, especially with regard to Type I diseases. For example, the WHO CIPIH Report[94] and the World Health Assembly Resolution 59.24[95] supported the use of TRIPS flexibilities by developing countries. The WHO Elements of a Global Strategy (2006) included the following 'areas for action':

> 6(a) enact legislation in developed and developing countries for application of the flexibilities provided for in TRIPS and other international agreements
> 6(f) assure that bilateral trade agreements do not seek to incorporate 'TRIPS-plus' protection in ways that might reduce access to medicines in developing countries
> 6(i) focus on specific aspects of the intellectual property system, such as test data exclusivity, 'me-too' patents, and patent linkages
> 7(i) take necessary legislative steps in developed countries, and other countries with manufacturing and export capacity, to allow compulsory licensing for export consistent with the flexibilities provided for in TRIPS
> 7(j) provide in national legislation for measures to encourage generic entry on patent expiry, such as the 'early working' exception, and more generally policies that support greater competition between generics, whether branded or not, as an effective way to enhance access by improving affordability; restrictions should not be placed on the use of generic names[96]

The US COMMENTS requested that these discussions of TRIPS flexibilities be excluded from the WHO IGWG process:[97]

> Accordingly, the IGWG should *not* consider Subsection (a) of Paragraph Six of the document. The WHO Secretariat should not expand its work on matters better addressed by another international organization. Therefore, the IGWG should not consider Subsections (f) and (i) of Paragraph Six of the document, because they more appropriately fit within the scope and mandate of the WTO and WIPO.[98]
> While Subparagraph (j) of Paragraph Seven is important when balanced with incentives to develop new drugs, neither subparagraph (i) or (j) are appropriate

---

93 WHO CIPIH REPORT, at 48 (Recommendation 2.4).

94 WHO CIPIH REPORT, at 22.

95 WHA 59.24, at par. 2(4).

96 WHO ELEMENTS OF A GLOBAL STRATEGY (2006), at 6–8.

97 US COMMENTS, at 4–6, pars. 7–8. The US COMMENTS suggest that the WTO and WIPO are the better fora.

98 US COMMENTS, at 5, par. 6.

areas of action for the WHO Secretariat; thus the IGWG should not consider them.[99]

The US Comments are thus making a narrow, technocratic argument that the WHO is an inappropriate forum for discussing the intellectual property rights issues relating to access to medicines. They are trying to prevent discussion in a forum that might actually give some weight to global health. This argument ignores the history of the IGWG process, which was designed to offer a balanced, integrated analysis of intellectual property rights, innovation and public health. Each step of this process has highlighted all three issues: the WHO Commission on Intellectual Property Rights, Innovation and Public Health; the WHO CIPIH Report entitled Public Health, Innovation & Intellectual Property Rights; and the WHO IGWG ON Public Health, Innovation and Intellectual Property. The WHO is not claiming exclusive jurisdiction over these issues, merely the opportunity to speak to issues which impact global public health.

Disease-specific limitations are not appropriate

Nothing in the TRIPs Agreement or the Doha Declaration limits access programs or TRIPS flexibilities to Type II and III diseases. Neither does the WHO CIPIH Report, which cannot be read as arguing for any such restriction.

The phrase 'diseases which disproportionately affect developing countries' is best understood as an explanation for why the market has failed to produce medicines for neglected (Type II) or very neglected (Type III) diseases: diseases which occur disproportionately in poor people in LMICs are not an attractive market for the patent-based drug industry. As the WHO CIPIH Report concluded:

> Too few R&D resources are directed to the health needs of developing countries. In the private sector, companies do not have the incentive to devote adequate resources to develop products specifically adapted to the needs of developing countries, because profitability is mainly to be found in rich country markets. The great majority of health research funded by the public sector, takes place in developed countries, and its priorities principally reflect their own disease burden, resource position and social and economic circumstances.[100]

Difficulties with the US position are made more evident when one attempts to construct a list of qualifying diseases. The adverb 'disproportionately' appears to require that incidence on a *per capita* basis be

---

99 US COMMENTS, at 5, par. 7.
100 WHO CIPIH REPORT, at 172.

significantly higher. Surely the list includes all Type III diseases, including the very neglected tropical diseases, for by definition the *per capita* incidence is almost exclusively in LMICs. Similarly, the largest Type II diseases, such as malaria and tuberculosis, appear to qualify. For all of these diseases, markets are unable to stimulate the R&D required for global health.

AIDS presents a more troublesome case. The incidence and burden of AIDS falls disproportionately on sub-Saharan Africa, but the same may not hold true for India or China. As discussed above, AIDS may not be properly classified as a Type II disease at all, and its incidence is rising in the United States.[101]

Other infectious diseases are quite common in LMICs, and result in a substantial burden of disease there. In general, the incidence of infectious diseases falls disproportionately in LMICs, but significant medical need exists also in high-income countries for many infectious diseases.[102]

Most noncommunicable or chronic diseases would probably not qualify. While heart disease, depression, stroke, and diabetes are certainly major contributors to the burden of disease in LMICs, they do not impose a disproportionately higher *per capita* burden. If the phrase 'diseases which disproportionately affect developing countries' is considered a limitation on access programs and TRIPS flexibilities, then almost all chronic and noncommunicable diseases must be excluded.

Clearly, this is not an acceptable result. This interpretation is without support in the WHO CIPIH Report, and is at odds with the mandate of the WHO IGWG. The Report does not limit access programs or TRIPs flexibilities to specific diseases. In fact, it recommended exactly the opposite. Recommendations 4.13 to 4.27 are primarily concerned with encouraging developing countries to take advantage of TRIPS flexibilities and other laws in order to protect public health, without any limitations as to disease.[103] Recommendation 4.7 specifically includes noncommunicable diseases:

> 4.7 For noncommunicable diseases, governments and companies should consider how treatments, which are widely available in developed countries, can be made more accessible for patients in developing countries.[104]

---

[101] *See supra*, nn. 80–82 and text accompanying.

[102] *See, e.g.,* E. Klein, D.L. Smith, R. Laxminarayan, *Hospitalizations and Deaths Caused by Methicillin-Resistant Staphylococcus aureus, United States, 1999–2005*, 13 Emerging Inf. Dis. 1840–46 (2007); RM Klevens et al., *Invasive Methicillin-resistant Staphylococcus aureus Infections in the United States,* 298 J. Am. Med. Assn. 1763–71 (2007).

[103] WHO CIPIH Report, at 180–82.

[104] WHO CIPIH Report, at 180.

The phrase is relevant only as a descriptive term, identifying innovation market failures: patent-based pharmaceutical innovation doesn't work for diseases which disproportionately affect developing countries. Global markets under-supply commercial research into Type II, Type III diseases and adaptive research for Type I innovations for resource-constrained settings. No substantial market in high-income countries exists for these disease conditions, necessitating various non-market mechanisms in order to facilitate innovation. By definition, these conditions disproportionately affect developing countries; otherwise they would be Type I innovations.

But the innovation gap is not the only problem facing the IGWG. Its terms of reference also include ensuring equitable access to patented innovations treating all diseases, including Type I, II and III diseases. The market for medicines and the market for innovation must both be valued. WHA 59.24 urges Member states:

> to work to ensure that progress in basic science and biomedicine is translated into improved, safe and affordable health products – drugs, vaccines and diagnostics – to respond to all patients' and clients' needs, especially those living in poverty, taking into account the critical role of gender, and to ensure that capacity is strengthened to support rapid delivery of essential medicines to people.[105]

5. Conclusion

The pharmaceutical IP system works well in high-income countries with social insurance. It does not work for the poor in low- and middle-income countries. Governments should be free to fully utilize all TRIPS flexibilities to protect the health of their citizens, without regard to the type of disease. In particular, WTO Members must be permitted to confront the growing burden of chronic diseases by using TRIPS flexibilities for any type of disease, including, without limitation, Type I conditions such as cancer and cardiovascular diseases.

From the initial negotiations that led to the TRIPS Agreement until today, some governments – particularly the US government – have attempted to limit the flexibilities afforded to WTO Members under Article 31. This activity continues today in the WHO IGWG process, now using the phrase 'diseases disproportionately affecting developing countries'. Limiting TRIPS flexibilities to specific diseases is not supported under Article 31, the Doha Declaration, the Council Decision, the WHO Commission Report, nor by the shifting global burden of disease.

---

105 WHA 59.24 par. 2(3).

20 The protection of semiconductor chip products in TRIPS

Thomas Hoeren

1. Introduction

In the second half of the 20th century, semiconductor technology as integrated circuits (ic), commonly known as microchips, became more and more dominating in our lives. Microchips are the control center of simple things like toasters as well as of complex high-tech machines for medical use. Of course, they also depict the heart of each computer. With the invention of semiconductor technology, a whole new economic sector began to grow and soon played a major role in the economies of the big industrial countries like the USA, Japan and the EC. Especially, it stands out for its innovational power and its readiness to invest. Microchips are a symbol of modern industrial society.

Inexplicably, this new economic sector was totally ignored by the legislators for a long time. The power of innovation mentioned earlier was not as well protected as it should have been. In particular, the danger of forging microchips did not occur to governments. It is technically very easy and rather cheap to copy these chips, while development causes high costs. So the producers of microchips were exposed to an increasing number of copyists. Existing national patent and trademark laws fail to give sufficient protection to this economic sector, because they require a very high standard of originality or inventiveness.

At the beginning of the 1980s, the governments of the developed countries eventually realized the risks this posed for their local microchip industry.

1.1 Technical function of microchips[1]

In order to illustrate the regulations of the protection of semiconductor chip products in TRIPS, a first short look at the technical devices is necessary. Microchips consist of silicon dies (wafers) on which integrated circuits are 'printed'. These integrated circuits are miniaturized electronic circuits and mainly consist of semiconductor devices. The circuits are put on a wafer through specially created patterns (masks) in a photolithogra-

---

[1] Cf. Hoeren, Thomas, *Der Schutz von Mikrochips in der Bundesrepublik Deutschland*, Münster and New York: Waxmann, 1988, p. 3.

phy process. They send electrical impulses which, for example, control a computer. The three-dimensional disposition of the pattern, which designates the structure of the circuit, is called layout design or topography.

1.2 First protection in the USA

The first country which developed a new kind of industrial property law in order to protect the chip industry was the USA. The local producers of microchips who were threatened by copyists located in Korea and Japan forced the US legislators to enact a sui generis system of chip protection. With the Semiconductor Chip Protection Act 1984 (SCPA),[2] a new kind of industrial property containing elements of patent, copyright and competition law was created.[3] The object of protection was the 'mask-work'. The 'mask' is the pattern used to set the circuits on the silicon wafer in order to create the integrated circuit.

Additionally, the SCPA provides a new way of imposing international pressure. All nations must adopt the main elements of the SCPA. Otherwise, topographies and mask works of a foreign chip producer would not be protected in the United States. Furthermore, the SCPA only grants interim protection where a State convinces the US Patent and Trademark Office that it is applying 'good faith and reasonable progress' towards providing protection on substantially the same basis.[4]

These provisions led to a legislative race against time in all parts of the world. In Europe, the EC member states tried to establish harmonized chip protection legislation that conformed with the SCPA. Other European states, however, resisted the exhortative behavior of the United States and created their own way to protect chips.

1.3 Protection in the EC

After interim protection in the United States[5] had been accorded to the EC Commission for nationals and domiciliaries of EC member states until

---

[2] Tide III of Public Law 98-620 of November 8, 1984, now 17. USC Section 901 et seq.; *Industrial Property Laws and Treaties,* United States of America – Text 1-001.

[3] Chip Topography protection in die USA; Richard H. Stern, *Semiconductor Chip Protection,* New York 1986; David Ladd, David E. Leibowitz, Bruce G. Joseph, *Protection for Semiconductor Chip Masks in the United States,* Munich 1986; Charles N. Quinn, 'Protecting Semiconductor Chips in U. S.', *La Nouvelles,* September 1987, p. 95; Wade Woodson and Douglas C. Safreno, 'The Semiconductor Chip Protection Act of 1984', *Computer & High Technology Law Journal (Comp. & High Techn. L. J.)* 7 (19, 85), 1996.

[4] Section 902(a)(l)(2).

[5] The first Interim Order was issued on September 12, 1985 (51 *Fed. Reg.* 30690).

November 8, 1987, the EC authorities hastily prepared a new Directive for chip protection. Soon the Directive on the Legal Protection of Semiconductor Products (87/54/EEC) was adopted by the EC Council on December 16, 1986[6] in order to harmonize the composition of legal protection for semiconductor technology. In the Directive, the EC authorities set some guidelines which have to be achieved by member states for its protection in Europe:

(1) Not the microchip itself but its 'topography' is to be protected, that is, 'the three-dimensional pattern of the layers of which a semiconductor product is composed'.[7] Unlike the SCPA, this definition does not use the term 'mask work' to describe the object of chip protection. A topography is capable of protection if it is 'the result of its creator's own intellectual effort and is not commonplace in the semiconductor industry' (Article 2 (2)).
(2) The right holder must be a national of an EC member state or has to start commercial exploitation within the EC. Otherwise, the protection depends on special declarations of the member states in agreement with the Commission (Article 3).
(3) Article 5 provides the right holder with the exclusive right to authorize or prohibit the reproduction, commercial exploitation.

The EC member states had to implement this Directive into national law by November 7, 1987. The Federal Republic of Germany, for example, issued the *Halbleiterschutzgesetz*[8] (Semiconductor Protection Act) on November 1, 1987. Essentially, this act includes the guidelines from the Directive.

1.4 Criticism of the reciprocity rule in the particular law

With the semiconductor protection acts of the USA and the EC in the 1980s, a totally new type of intellectual property right has been created. All these acts have a material reciprocity in common. This is a totally new way to force other nations not only into accepting but also into adopting this new right in their own legislation in case they want to get protection for their own semiconductor industries as well.

This new system of material reciprocity was harshly criticized in

---

[6] *OJ*, L 24/36 of January 27, 1987.

[7] Art. 1(i) Council Directive 87/54/EEC of December 16, 1986 on the legal protection of topographies of semiconductor products.

[8] BGBl. I S. 2294 ff.

subsequent publications[9]. It was said to contradict the principles of industrial property law. For centuries, the national treatment principle had been regarded as the cornerstone of international patent and copyright law.[10] Inventions and copyright works had been protected irrespective of the nationality of their creators. This concept of protection was based upon the idea that creativity and originality are essential elements of human nature and should therefore be protected like the fundamental rights of each individual.

1.5 IPIC Treaty

Mainly because of the pressure from the new reciprocity rule, an international agreement on the minimum standards for semiconductor protection became more and more necessary.

A first try was the Treaty on the Protection of Intellectual Property in Respect of Integrated Circuits (IPIC), which was passed at the diplomatic conference of the WIPO in Washington on May 26, 1989.[11] Though the treaty was accepted by the majority of participating countries, it was never ratified. The major reason for this treaty never coming to life was the disclaiming position of the USA and Japan, both of which are leading countries in microchip production. A strong aspect of criticism, especially from the USA, was Article 8 IPIC which limited the protection time to only eight years.[12] However, important semiconductors like computer chips (Intel) do in fact have a lifespan which is much longer than only eight years.

Another major point of criticism on the part of the USA was the compulsory license ruled in Article 6 (3) IPIC. The USA, and also Japan, were protesting heavily against this article. Finally, it can be assumed that the IPIC Treaty collapsed due to the refusal of the USA and Japan.[13]

1.6 TRIPS

After the failure of IPIC, the protection of semiconductor technology was regulated in Articles 35 to 38 of the Agreement on Trade-related Aspects

---

[9] *Cf.* e.g. Hoeren, *Das deutsche Halbleiterschutzgesetz vom 1.11.1987*, BB 1988, 1904 ff.

[10] *See* T. Dreier, 'National Treatment, Reciprocity and Retorsion – The Case of Computer Programs and Integrated circuits', in: Friedrich-Karl Beier and Gerhard Schricker (eds), *GATT or WIPO? New Ways in the International Property of Intellectual Property,* Weinheim 1989, 63, 70 et seq.

[11] WIPO Doc. IPIC/DC/46.

[12] *Cf.* Hoeren, Thomas, *Das Washingtoner Abkommen zum Schutz des geistigen Eigentums an integrierten Schaltkreisen,* NJW 1989, 2605, 2606.

[13] *Cf.* Staehelin, Alesch, *Das TRIPs-Abkommen: Immaterialgüterrechte im Licht der globalisierten Handelspolitik,* Bern 1997, p. 100.

of Intellectual Property Rights (TRIPS) in 1994. The main norms from IPIC were leading in the direction of the arrangements in TRIPS, so that Article 35 refers to them.

2 The organization of semiconductor protection in TRIPS

The protection of the layout designs (topographies) of integrated circuits, that is, microchips, is regulated in Articles 35 to 38 of the TRIPS Agreement. Article 35 refers back to the IPIC Treaty to describe the object of protection. Article 36 codifies the scope of protection, Article 37 mentions acts which do not require the authorization of the right holder, and finally, in Article 38, the term of protection is illustrated.

2.1 Relation to IPIC Treaty

The IPIC Treaty constitutes the basis for regulation in Articles 35 to 38 TRIPS. This refers to the elementary parts of chip protection in IPIC, that is, the definition of the protection object, the requirement and the scope of protection. Furthermore, the IPIC Treaty constitutes the way the member states have to implement the regulations in national law. Moreover, it makes obeying the national treatment principle obligatory. Secondary rules in IPIC, including innocent infringements, exhaustion of rights, local commercial exploitation and registration, are referred to.

Consequently, with its reference to the regulation of protection, TRIPS mainly adopts the regulation of the IPIC Treaty. With the regulation in the TRIPS Agreement, only contentious issues of chip protection in the IPIC Treaty should be cleared. Thus, in order to clarify the international protection of semiconductor products, a further look at the rules in IPIC (with the amendments and changes in TRIPS) is necessary.

Basically, there were two major points on which the regulations in TRIPS amended the IPIC Treaty: compulsory licensing and the term of protection. Both points were either ruled on differently (term of protection) or omitted (compulsory licensing). Article 35 TRIPS explicitly excepts the controversial Article 6 (3) IPIC, which defines the compulsory licensing of its enumeration.

Article 35 TRIPS applies to the indisputable parts of the IPIC Treaty (Articles 2 to 7, apart from Article 6 (3); Articles 12 and 16 (3)) which primarily serve to regulate the object of protection in Article 3 IPIC (see below).

Furthermore, Article 35 TRIPS hints at Article 5 IPIC, in which the provision of national treatment is restored. The provision of national treatment was given up with the American SCPA in 1984 and, after that, in the majority of subsequent national acts in the world (see above).

The provision of national treatment tells the participants to give foreign chip producers (from a participating state) the same protection as local producers. It was a huge achievement of IPIC at last to give this provision – a maxim of intellectual property law – to the settlement of semiconductor protection.[14] Yet, this achievement is realized in TRIPS.

In Article 6 of the IPIC Treaty, the scope of protection (amended by Article 36 TRIPS) and acts not requiring the authorization of the right holder (amended by Article 37 TRIPS) are defined. In this Article, an exception from protection is allowed 'for private purposes'.[15] It also applies to reverse engineering[16] and allows exceptions for innocent infringements.[17]

Article 7 IPIC Treaty allows participating states to require local commercial registration (in addition to Article 38 TRIPS). Article 12 IPIC Treaty safeguards rights under the Paris and Berne Conventions. Finally, Article 16(3) IPIC Treaty, as the final clause, allows member states to exclude layout designs, which have already been in existence at the time of entry into force.

Articles 36 to 38 TRIPS are appendices to those parts of IPIC for which no consensus could be found.[18] Besides the major points of criticism, this part concerns in particular the scope of the rights.[19] Apart from that, in its vocabulary the regulation in TRIPS is oriented towards the formulations in the IPIC Treaty.

The details of the protection are not applied in TRIPS and IPIC. Each member state is free to set the protection of semiconductor technology in their own legal system either as a sui generis law or in existing copyright or patent law.[20]

2.2 The object of protection

The core element of setting a useful parameter for the protection of microchips is to find a clear definition for the object of protection. Only if such a clear definition can be found, can the treaty guarantee protection to the creators of new products. Also, a definition had to be found which allows for technical developments in the unstable microchip sector. In that case, giving protection to a specific newly created chip cannot meet

---

14 *Cf.* Hoeren, NJW 1989, 2605, 2606.

15 Article 6 (2) lit. a IPIC Treaty.

16 Article 6 (2) lit. b IPIC Treaty.

17 Article 6 (4) IPIC Treaty.

18 Staehelin, Alesch, p. 100.

19 *See* Gervais, Daniel, *The TRIPS Agreement: Drafting History and Analysis*, London 1998, p. 174.

20 Article 4 of the IPIC Treaty, *cf.* Hoeren, NJW 1989, 2605, 2606.

these requirements. Otherwise, the definition of the protection-object has to be constituted as clearly as possible so as to avoid ambiguity in interpretation.

Finally, in Article 35 of the TRIPS Agreement it is not the semiconductor product itself (that is, the microchip) that is defined as the object of protection. The member states of TRIPS rather have to provide protection 'to the layout-designs (topographies) of integrated circuits'.[21] Furthermore, for example, in the American SCPA (see above) it is not only the method of bringing the circuits on to the die with a mask (that is to say, the ic 'mask-work') that is protected. Here, other possible methods of setting the circuits on the wafer do not fall under this protection. Thus, protecting the topography of the integrated circuit is broader and offers guidelines for the semiconductor protection of technical developments in the future.

To find out how far the protection lasts, consideration of the definitions of both terms 'layout-designs (topographies)' and 'integrated circuit' is needed. TRIPS adopted the definitions from the IPIC Treaty (see above). They can be found in Article 2 (1), (2), where the layout design (topography) is defined as

> the three-dimensional disposition, however expressed, of the elements, at least one of which is an active element, and of some or all of the interconnections of an integrated circuit, or such a three-dimensional disposition prepared for an integrated circuit intended for manufacture.[22]

The layout design of an integrated circuit is protectable, that is,

> a product, in its final form or an intermediate form, in which the elements, at least one of which is an active element, and some or all of the interconnections are integrally formed in and/or on a piece of material and which is intended to perform an electronic function.[23]

These are very explicit definitions. In sum, the three-dimensional structure of the circuit-elements on the silicon-wafer, which has a specific layout design, known as topography, is protected. Every integrated circuit functions according to a different 'diagram'. The structure of this 'diagram' is its topography. So, the topography defines whether the microchip controls an icebox, a computer or even a jumbo-jet: it is the 'heart' and also

---

21 Article 35 of the TRIPS Agreement.

22 Article 2 (2) of the IPIC Treaty; *see* http://www.wipo.int/clea/en/text_html.jsp?lang=en&id=4029.

23 Article 2 (1) of the IPIC Treaty.

the 'thinking brain' of the integrated circuit, whereas the silicon material on which it is incorporated is only the naked corpus. Consequently, it is inevitable that this 'heart', that is the topography, should be protected and not the chip itself. The actual creation of the chip producer is the new topography.

The topography of the circuits and the silicon wafer, on which the circuits are 'printed', are together the 'integrated circuit'.

In conclusion, in a comparison with the EC Directive on the Legal Protection of Semiconductor Products (87/54/EEC),[24] the regulation with regard to the object of protection in TRIPS and IPIC was mostly influenced by this Directive. In both settlements the protection object is the topography of the integrated circuit.

2.3 Requirement for protection

In TRIPS, there are basically two major requirements for protection: first, the topography that is to be protected must show some originality and, moreover, it has to resemble some degree of newness.

Article 35 TRIPS, referring to Article 3 (2) lit. a IPIC, makes only minimum demands: in order to get protection, a special kind of originality for the layout design is required. This 'originality' is the basic requirement for protection.[25] The layout designs are original 'in the sense that they are the result of their creators' own intellectual effort and are not commonplace among creators of layout-designs (topographies) and manufactures of integrated circuits at the time of their creation'.[26] So, the topography first has to show some creativity in its design. Here 'intellectual effort' can be spoken of. Furthermore, the topography has to show some degree of inventiveness. This inventiveness is not acquired if the topography turns out to be 'commonplace'. Some new features have to be designed for the existing topography. Only in that case, the already developed topography turns out to be a 'creation', that is, the work of the developer. The criterion 'commonplace' seems not to be easy to substantiate. In order to find out about the meaning of 'commonplace', clearly defined standards for the semiconductor industry are required. Especially because of rapid developments in this industry, such a standard is difficult to find. Even if it is possible for such a standard to exist, it seems very complicated to ascertain it reliably for any particular case.

On the other hand, topographies do not need to present such a very high

---

24 See above.

25 *See* Gervais, Daniel, p. 175.

26 Article 3 (2) lit. a of the IPIC Treaty.

degree of inventiveness as a product getting patent protection. Indeed, protection is also possible for layout designs which consist of commonplace interconnections if only the combination taken as a whole achieves the requirements of a 'solo' topography (Article 3 (2) lit. b of the IPIC Treaty).

Secondly, the topography has to be 'new' to get protection. At the time of the development of the chip, its topography needs to bring some aspects which are 'fresh' to the semiconductor technology.

With the requirements set out in TRIPS and IPIC, on the one hand, a sui generis system of protection has been created. This becomes especially clear with regard to the term 'commonplace' as a negative definition for the requirement of originality. This term is alien to the system and new to the field of intellectual property law.

On the other hand, with the set of requirements for protection of semiconductors in TRIPS, the well-known vocabulary of intellectual property law is used. Thus, the term 'intellectual effort' is similar to criteria used in copyright law.[27]

Evidently, the pattern of requirements in TRIPS and IPIC combine new and familiar vocabulary in order to create a sui generis right in intellectual property law. This has mostly been influenced by copyright law ('originality', 'intellectual effort'), but it brings its own parts as well.

All in all, the requirements for getting protection in TRIPS (referring to Article 3 (2) IPIC) are not extremely hard to achieve. They could not stand comparison with patent law. Requirements for this sui generis right are more similar to those in utility patent law.

2.4 Scope of protection

The scope of protection, first of all, is mostly described with the reference to Article 6 (1) in Article 35 of the IPIC Treaty. According to this article, the chip creator is the keeper of the exclusive rights to, first, reproducing and, secondly, selling integrated circuits in which the layout design (topography) is used. The participating nations, however, are free to protect other acts than those mentioned.[28] As just said (see last point), the protection in the WTO treaties is similar to the utility patent law, and so is the scope of protection:[29] it contains not only the exclusive right of the creator to reproduce the microchip but also the exclusive right to commercialize the integrated circuit created.

---

27 Gervais, Daniel, p. 175.
28 Article 6 (1) lit. b IPIC Treaty.
29 *Cf. also* Staehelin, Alesch, p. 101.

2.4.1 The Act of Reproducing

The first right of the protected chip generator is the exclusive act of reproducing. Article 6 (1) lit. a (i) IPIC mentions

> the act of reproducing, whether by incorporation in an integrated circuit or otherwise, a protected layout design (topography) in its entirety or any part thereof, except the act of reproducing any part that does not comply with the requirement of originality referred to in Article 3 (2).

Incorporating the topography in an integrated circuit means the production of a microchip using the protected topography. Consequently, the topography of the integrated circuits is incorporated. This exclusive right is reserved for the creator of the protected topography. It requires the act of reproducing by another manufacturer to be approved by the right holder; he could issue a license to the producer in order to have a share in his profit. This point leads to the next one, namely the acts of distributing for commercial purpose.

2.4.2. The Acts of Distributing for Commercial Purpose

Connected to the right to reproduce is the exclusive right to use the produced microchip with its protected topography for commercial purposes. This is the second right of the creator. It is also pointed out by the reference to the IPIC Treaty in Article 35 TRIPS. Here, Article 6 (1) lit. a (ii) talks about 'the act of importing, selling or otherwise distributing for commercial purpose a protected layout-design (topography) or an integrated circuit in which a protected layout-design (topography) is incorporated'.

In particular, the acts of importing and selling are pinpointed here. These acts seem to be the most influential imaginable aspects in commercializing the created topography. Importing and selling are examples of commercial purpose. In order to protect not only these two acts, an abstract definition of the right of commercial use is added by 'otherwise distributing for commercial purpose'. This formulation includes all possible ways of commercial use to the greatest possible extent. So, this formulation is a general clause. The right holder could rely on this general clause if his exclusive right is attacked by other acts than importing or selling.

2.4.3 Amendments in Article 36 TRIPS

First of all, Article 36 TRIPS takes its wording from Article 6 (1) (a) (ii) IPIC about commercial purposes. There is only the addition: 'or an article incorporated such an integrated circuit only in so far as it continues to contain an unlawfully reproduced layout-design'. This addition became necessary because of the fear of member states that the extension of rights for products incorporating protected topographies would give rights not to the circuits themselves, but to any product incorporating them.[30] The formulation in Article 36 TRIPS provides that the right holder can only take legal action against the distributor of products with unlawfully incorporated integrated circuits. So, a diffusion of the scope of protection is avoided.

2.5 Acts not requiring the authorization of the right holder

There are some exceptions to the protections of the topography-creator which limit his rights. Some of these exceptions are named in Article 6 of the IPIC Treaty, to which we have referred. Other exceptions follow from amendments to the IPIC regulation in Article 37 of TRIPS.

2.5.1 Acts for Private Purposes

First, an exception is made to the right of reproduction without the authorization of the right holder 'where the act is performed by a third party for private purposes or for the sole purpose of evaluation, analysis, research, or teaching'.[31] In this phrase, two exceptions are made. The first is an exception for private purposes, that is, acting without profit motive. The other exception is relevant for academic research. Here, the right holder also has no right to stop such research.

2.5.2 Reverse Engineering

'Reverse engineering' means to create a new topography by analyzing an existing one. This principle is taken from the American SCPA.[32] Article 6 (2) lit. b speaks about 'reverse engineering', if

> the third party [. . .], on the basis of evaluation or analysis of the protected layout-design (topography) [. . .] creates a layout design (topography) complying with the requirement of originality [. . .], that third party may incorporate the second layout-design in an integrated circuit [. . .]'

Thus, a third person is allowed to analyze the existing topography of a microchip from another producer in order to create his own, new one. To put it the other way around, simply rebuilding the same chip is not 'reverse engineering'. The topography of the new chip has to fulfill the requirement of originality. If it does not fulfill this requirement, a mere copy of the existing chip has been created. It is, in fact, problematic which criteria of originality have to be met in order for a new chip to be made by

---

30 Gervais, Daniel, p. 177.
31 Article 6 (2) lit. a of the IPIC Treaty.
32 *Cf.* 17 USC § 906 (a) (2).

'reverse engineering'. In that case, the same considerations as taken for the requirement of protection (see above) are to be taken into account because Article 6 (2) (b) IPIC refers to the definition of the requirement in Article 3 (2) IPIC. Nevertheless, the principle of 'reverse engineering' seems to be defined only imprecisely, so that some copyists could refer to this principle in order to defend themselves against the right holder.

2.5.3 Innocent Infringements

The second exception to the protection is the so-called 'innocent infringement'. This principle is constituted in Article 6 (4) of the IPIC Treaty, which is also referred to in Article 35 TRIPS. In short, it says that a third person who did not know that the product in question consists of copied chips is unaffected by the consequences of the exclusive rights from the right holder. Article 6 (4) IPIC speaks about

> the performance of any of the acts referred to [. . .] in respect of an integrated circuit incorporating an unlawfully reproduced layout-design (topography) where the person performing or ordering such acts did not know and had no reasonable ground to know, when acquiring the said integrated circuit, that it incorporates an unlawfully reproduced layout-design (topography).

With this regulation, the trusting person shall be protected from right holder benefits which that person could not imagine being confronted with. Therefore, the working of the exchange is guaranteed.

2.5.4 Amendments in Article 37 TRIPS

Article 37 (1) TRIPS differs extensively from the principle of 'innocent infringement' of Article 6 (4) of the IPIC Treaty just mentioned.[33] While in Article 6 (4) IPIC, the formulation 'no Contracting Party shall be obliged to consider unlawful [. . .]' is used, Article 37 (1) TRIPS provides 'that no member shall consider unlawful [. . .]'. Its formulation is stricter than that used in IPIC. Another important amendment dealing with 'innocent infringement' is that a person who did not know about the protected topography has to pay 'a reasonable royalty such as would be payable under a freely negotiated license' to the right holder if he get to know about the protected topography. This amendment is reasonable, especially, because the person who gets to know about the real facts cannot be trusted anymore. Thus, he is to be handled like any third party who sells such products: this person has to pay for a license.

Another amendment, made in Article 37 (2) TRIPS, deals with

---

33 *Cf*. Gervais, Daniel, p. 179.

'compulsory licensing'. This issue was a big point of contention with IPIC (see above). Now, in Article 37 (2) TRIPS, it refers to the regulation concerning patents in TRIPS. Otherwise, the cases of compulsory licensing seem to be very limited.[34]

2.6 Term of Protection, Article 38 TRIPS

As already mentioned (see above), the term of protection was a major point of criticism in the IPIC Treaty on the part of the USA and Japan. The term of protection in Article 8 IPIC was constituted as at least eight years. The criticism is only partly acceptable. Indeed, the lifespan of some microchips is much longer than eight years. But the majority of microchips are far from being used longer than eight years. This is because of the fast-moving chip industry and the fast development of new layouts.

Nevertheless, the term of protection in Article 38 TRIPS was extended to ten years. Here, the same formula is used as in patent section.[35] It specifies the earliest date on which the protection may end.[36] According to Article 38 TRIPS, there are two possible starting dates: first, 'the date of filing an application for registration' and, secondly, 'from the first commercial exploitation wherever in the world it occurs'. In case WTO member states decide to establish a registration of the topography in order to get protection, the date of the application for this registration is the decisive factor. Otherwise, the decisive factor would be the first commercial use. Noticeably, in contrast to Article 8 IPIC, the date of creation of the layout would not be taken into account.[37]

According to Article 38 (3) TRIPS, it is also possible for a member state to decide to accord a term of protection to the creator which lapses 15 years from the creation of the microchip.

3. Relevance of the protection for practice

The question of how to protect semiconductor technology was extensivly discussed between the mid-1980s and the early 1990s. It was a big issue at that time. Consequently, a large number of literary works from all over the world were published during that period. The leading chip industries of the developed countries (especially the USA) feared potential copyists from the Far East. Thus, this industry put the American government under pressure to create a new part of intellectual property law and to give

---

[34] Gervais, Daniel, p. 179.
[35] '(. . .) shall not end before the expiration of a period of (. . .)'; cf. Article 33 TRIPS.
[36] Gervais, Daniel, p. 180.
[37] Gervais, Daniel, p. 181.

protection to their semiconductor products. The American government finally passed the SCPA – the beginning of enacting laws to protect integrated circuits all over the world. Afterwards, the protection of semiconductor products found its way into the international WTO treaties IPIC and, finally, into TRIPS.

However, since the mid-1990s, precisely since semiconductor protection has been included into TRIPS, this subject seems to have disappeared totally. There is hardly any publication on the protection of semiconductor technology, except for reviews in standard works, for example, textbooks. Furthermore, jurisdictions are nowhere to be found, either in the USA or in the EC or Germany. After the discussion of how to protect microchips, the issue seems to have lost its practical relevance. Remarkably, only a very small number of chip inventions are registered.[38] Apparently, the original interest in protection on part of the semiconductor industries has ceased. Already, some authors talk about chip protection as a dead subject.[39]

There are various reasons for senior industry executives to turn their backs on the legal protection of semiconductor technologies.

First, it is problematic that only the layout design (topography) of microchips is the object of protection. For industry, it is more important to protect the function of an integrated circuit than the design.[40] Furthermore, layout designs are easily variable without loss of functionality. However, topographies are no longer protected once the design is altered ('reverse-engineering'). It is a condition of semiconductor protection that layout designs are based upon intellectual effort. These days, however, topographies are often designed by software. Thus, the object of protection becomes unattractive for the chip industries.

A second reason could be that microchips, that is, their layout designs, are highly complex, miniature entities which are hardly ever copied.[41] This fact makes protection against forgers superfluous.

In the end, the protection of semiconductor technology is uninteresting from an economic point of view. Because it is a fast-developing technological sector, microchips have a short lifespan, while the process of getting legal protection is rather time-consuming. Furthermore, there seems little

---

38 Only 15469 registrations in Germany in 2007. The reduction of this number continues. In 2001, there were still c. 18500 registrations. *Cf.* http://presse.dpma.de/docs/pdf/jahresberichte/jb2007_dt.pdf.

39 *Cf.* Karnell, Gunnar, 'Protection of Layout-designs (Topographies) of Integrated Circuits – R.I.P.?', *IIC* 2001, 648. He says, that the protection is 'not only a "lame" but rather "dead duck".'

40 Karnell, Gunnar, p. 652.

41 *Cf.* Karnell, Gunnar, p. 654.

reason to protect semiconductor technology because of the 'danger' of reverse-engineering. As already mentioned, microchips with different topographies can accomplish the same function.

All in all, the market for semiconductor products is tough. The decline in prices of microchips places an added burden on producers. Most recently, the German chip producer Qimonda went bankrupt, thus endangering Infineon, one of the leading chip manufacturers in the world.

21 Data exclusivity for pharmaceuticals: TRIPS standards and industry's demands in free trade agreements[1]

Carlos M. Correa

Introduction

In his paper 'Knowledge as a Global Public Good', Stiglitz recalls Jefferson's statement: 'He who receives an idea from me, receives instruction himself without lessening mine; as he who lights his taper at mine, receives light without darkening me' as an accurate and early mirror of the modern concept of public good (1999: 1).

Economists argue that knowledge can be categorized as a public good because it has the two basic and fundamental particularities that differentiate public goods from private goods: non-rivalry and non-excludability. Knowledge is non-rivalrous since it can be enjoyed by many people at the same time with no additional cost; and knowledge is also non-excludable because its enjoyment by one person does not exclude others from enjoying it too. As an example, once a particular scientific theory is created and divulged, it can be learned by many at a zero marginal cost and its 'consumption' does not mean the impossibility of another enjoying that knowledge as well.

In the last twenty years, however, an expansive wave of protectionism has dramatically changed the balance between public and private interests concerning knowledge. While initiated in developed countries, the protectionist wave has extended to developing countries through coercion (via mechanisms such as the Special Section 301 of the US Trade Act), multilateral agreements (notably the WTO TRIPS Agreement) and free trade agreements (FTAs) (Correa, 2006).

As a result, knowledge is increasingly subject to a tough protectionist regime in a world that, paradoxically, proclaims the benefits of free trade. The new intellectual property rights (IPRs) regimes have been shaped by narrow industry interests, with little or no consideration of their likely implications for development and, particularly, the poor (Sell, 2003).

[1] This chapter is partially based on a study prepared for *the Comité Nacional de Ética en la Ciencia y la Tecnologia* of Argentina.

Scientific knowledge and data are cornerstones of scientific advancement. Science has been based on the availability of information, on open access to that information, and on transparency. Such access results in the further growth of science as well as of technology and applications (Menon, 2004: 5).

What others have discovered and collected before, constitutes a significant and fundamental basis upon which contemporary researchers and scientists rest their inquiries and work. From this perspective, science is essentially a social endeavour that has been traditionally based on a collaborative basis. Since knowledge and data are the basic pillars of research and innovation, broad and affordable access to them by other researchers and users must be ensured.

A robust and vast public domain for scientific data has been the supporting pillar of science and innovations over the last centuries. This was largely due to the combination of several particular circumstances that Reichman and Uhlir clearly detailed referring to the US case. Some of these circumstances can be summarized as follows:

- the government itself has been an important producer of scientific information and data and has renounced its claim to proprietary rights over them, allowing broad public accessibility;
- the government has given funds to universities and other scientific research institutions provided that they follow an open access policy with the resulting information and data;
- data and facts as such were not protected under classical patent and copyright paradigms; and
- there was a strong collaborative and open attitude inside the scientific community regarding sharing of information and data (Reichman and Uhlir, 2005: 1–2)

Recent decades have seen different pressures on these conditions, as a generalized tendency towards the commodification of scientific information and data took place. As Reichman describes it, 'there has been a marked tendency to shift the production of science-relevant databases from the public to the private sector' (2004: 74). In part, this was due to governmental cuts in research expenditure, which affected not only its own production but also the amount of money given to non-governmental scientific institutions which have an open access policy (Reichman and Uhlir, 2005: 2–3).

Moreover, in 1980, the Bayh-Dole Act allowed US universities to exploit their research results from projects carried out with federal funds. The purpose of this legislation was to encourage the academic community to give licenses for their inventions to private companies, as a way to 'motivate private investors to pick up where government sponsors left off and transform new discoveries into commercial products' (Rai and Eisenberg, 2003: 1). Similar developments have taken place in other countries, often influenced by the US model.

As a result, intellectual property law has been steadily expanding and threatening the delicate balance between exclusive rights, exceptions and limitations, thereby dangerously diminishing the scope of the public domain. On the one hand, the term of protection has been extended once again. On the other, more and more types of information have become subject matter for protection, and the scope of exclusive rights has enlarged, covering new forms of communication and uses. As noted by Reichman and Uhlir,

> traditional intellectual property laws, especially copyright law, excluded facts and data as eligible subject matter. Even when facts and data were embodied in some copyrightable works of authorship, such as historical or scientific works, well-established limits and exceptions to copyright protection allowed researchers to access, use and extract data for personal use and for public research purposes. However, recent developments in intellectual property laws in most developed countries now make it possible to assert and enforce proprietarial claims to virtually all the factual matter that previously entered the public domain once it had been disclosed (2005: 3).

A telling example of this trend is the protection of test data required for the approval of pharmaceutical and agrochemical products.[2]

The case of test data

Access to and use of test data for pharmaceutical and agrochemical products provides a good example of the above-mentioned trend towards appropriation of scientific data.

The results of clinical studies constitute the 'test data' that are protected under article 39.3 of the TRIPS Agreement as follows:

> Members, when requiring as a condition of approving the marketing of pharmaceutical or of agricultural chemical products which utilize new chemical entities, the submission of undisclosed test or other data, the origination of which involves a considerable effort, shall protect such data against unfair commercial use. In addition, Members shall protect such data against disclosure, except where necessary to protect the public, or unless steps are taken to ensure that the data are protected against unfair commercial use.

---

2 The following analysis is partially based on Correa (2002).

Test data are important for health and environmental purposes, since they permit national authorities and users to evaluate the merits and risks of new drugs and agrochemicals. They are also important for commercial purposes, as the availability of the data is a condition for obtaining marketing approval of new products, modifications or new uses of existing products.[3]

The development of test data typically represents more than 60 percent of the R&D costs of new drugs (Grabowski, 2002).[4] Given their nature (they are *scientific* data obtained on the basis of standard protocols), they are outside patent protection.

According to IFPMA (2004), 'the development and bringing to market of a new drug requires the originator to conduct extensive chemical, pharmacological, toxicological and clinical research and testing, at an average cost of US $800 million, and taking 10 to 15 years to complete. The data generated by such work, while proprietary to the originator, must be submitted to the regulatory authorities of countries around the world in order to obtain approval to market the drug'.

Lewis, Reichman and So have drawn attention to the conflict of interest underlying the development of data concerning the efficacy and safety of drugs. They have observed that:

> so long as drug companies retain primary responsibility for conducting or funding clinical trials, they will be tempted to selectively disclose information and to avoid research programs that could reveal unfavorable outcomes. Nor would a disclosure requirement alone ensure that the stakeholding company will conduct all the tests deemed most beneficial to public safety . . . There are few incentives to undertake costly testing [phase IV clinical trials] if the results might only serve to narrow use of the drug to a smaller subgroup of patients or prove unfavourable to its continued use. (2006: 1)

For this reason, these authors suggest 'to establish an independent testing agency to conduct clinical trials under specified conditions of transparency. . . This separation of clinical trials from sponsorship could attenuate the conflict of interest problem' (Lewis et al., 2006: 1).

The figures for both the cost and duration of testing activities are highly contentious. However costly and long they are, the research-based

---

[3] In addition to test data, national authorities generally require information on the quantitative and qualitative composition and other attributes of the product, as well as on manufacturing methods.

[4] It is important to note that while private companies generally undertake the development of new drugs, basic research and discovery is overwhelmingly made by public institutions.

pharmaceutical industry, supported by the US and some European governments, actively seeks to ensure a period of exclusive use of the data after marketing approval. During this period, national authorities would be prevented from *using* or *relying* on the data for marketing approval of generic versions of already registered products, *even in cases where no patent protection over the product exists.*

The basic argument for this exclusivity model is to permit the originator of data to recover the investments made for their development. The underlying assumption is that, without such protection, private firms would have no incentive to bear the considerable costs of producing the required data.

In the USA, Europe, Japan and other countries, the data submitted for the registration of pharmaceutical and agrochemical products are subject to *sui generis* systems of protection, based on a temporary right to the exclusive use of such data by the first applicant (generally the company that has developed a new product). In such a system, generic manufacturers cannot rely on the data submitted by the first applicant for the purpose of registering a similar product for commercial use.[5]

In other countries,[6] national authorities rely on data submitted by the first applicant[7] to process and approve third parties' subsequent applications for a similar product, subject to evidence that its physico-chemical attributes are equivalent to those of the first applicant's product. This approach emphasizes that the registration of products should not erect barriers to otherwise legitimate competition.

The issue of data protection has become especially relevant in countries that until recently did not provide patent protection for pharmaceuticals and that applied the transitional period that the TRIPS Agreement allowed until January 1, 2005. In these countries, there is a large pool of pharmaceutical products in the public domain which are subject to patent protection in other countries. Exclusive rights over data could, if provided, become a substitute for patent protection on such products.

---

5 The conferred exclusivity, however, theoretically does not prevent generic firms to develop their *own* data in order to obtain marketing approval of a product (provided that it is off-patent).

6 In a document on the status of data protection in selected countries, IFPMA identifies countries where data protection is deemed to be conferred on the basis of exclusive rights, as well as many (such as Argentina, Brazil) that have refused to grant such rights. See IFPMA (2004).

7 In some cases, national authorities do not request the relevant test data and just rely on the approval granted in a foreign country.

The TRIPS standard on data protection

Before the entry into force of the TRIPS Agreement, countries had full latitude to determine whether or not to confer protection on test data. The Agreement introduced the first *international* standard on the subject, as contained in its Article 39.3. But the Agreement only established broad parameters for national rules, thereby allowing WTO Member countries freedom to apply different models for such protection (Arrivillaga, 2003).

Article 39.3 of the TRIPS Agreement requires Members to protect test data necessary for the marketing approval of pharmaceuticals and chemical products for agriculture. Test data must therefore be protected, if national authorities require its submission. If they only rely on an approval granted in a foreign country, the obligation does not apply. In addition, Article 39.3 does not require protection to be given to data that are already publicly available, but only to undisclosed data. Further, protection is mandated only for new chemical entities. Members have considerable discretion in defining this concept, which in any case excludes second indications, new formulations or dosage forms. Finally, in order to grant protection, national regulatory authorities may request the applicant to prove that the information for which protection is sought is the result of significant investment.

Article 39.3 requires countries to protect test data against 'unfair commercial use'. Protection is therefore to be conferred against dishonest commercial practices. Practises expressly required or permitted by the law (such as abbreviated or summary procedures of marketing approval) may not be deemed dishonest. Granting marketing approval to a second entrant, based on similarity with a previously approved product, is not a proscribed 'use' under Article 39.3.

Test data must be protected under the discipline of unfair competition, as established in the Paris Convention for the Protection of Industrial Property (article 10*bis*) and the TRIPS Agreement (article 39.1). Under such discipline, *no exclusive rights are granted*, but only the right to take legal action against whomsoever has obtained a commercial advantage by means of a dishonest practice.

The US government and industry and the European Commission have argued that article 39.3 of the TRIPS Agreement mandates the granting of exclusive rights. This argument does not find support, however, in the text of said article interpreted in accordance with articles 31 and 32 of the Vienna Convention on the Law of the Treaties, since

- the discipline of unfair competition, applicable in accordance with article 39.1 of the Agreement, does not create exclusive rights;
- the granting of exclusivity constitutes a drastic derogation to the

principle of free competition, which cannot be inferred from a text that does not provide for it;

- the definition of what an 'unfair' or 'dishonest' commercial practice is depends on social perceptions in a particular country at a given time;
- obtaining a commercial advantage, as such, is not condemnable under unfair competition rules (Kamperman Sanders, 1997);
- the history of negotiations over article 39.3 shows that the US proposal for exclusive rights over data was rejected;
- despite the fact that a large number of WTO Members do not provide for exclusive rights over data, there has been no WTO ruling on the meaning of article 39.3.

The US government initiated a case under WTO rules complaining about Argentina's alleged failure to appropriately protect test data. The dispute was settled at the consultation stage[8] after two years of discussions. Argentina did not accept the US claim that exclusive rights should be granted for test data and maintained its law unchanged. No further action in the framework of the WTO has been taken by the USA against Argentina, nor against any other country that does not recognize data exclusivity. However, the USTR has listed, under the Special Section 301 of the Trade Act, a large number of countries that, according to the USTR, do not confer adequate (that is, exclusive) protection for test data.[9]

The Indian government has recently considered what kind of protection should be conferred to test data for pharmaceuticals in order to comply with the TRIPS Agreement, taking national interests into account. The Report produced by a Commission set up for that purpose concluded that

> After detailed deliberations it was noted that there is enough flexibility in the provisions of the TRIPS Agreement for a country to determine the appropriate means of protecting test data. In terms of paragraph 4 of Doha Declaration, the provisions are to be '*interpreted and implemented in a manner supportive of WTO Members' right to protect public health and, in particular, to promote access to medicines for all*' (para. 1.11).
>
> Hence, the policy decision should be taken keeping in view the national

---

[8] See Notification of Mutually Agreed Solution According to the Conditions Set Forth in the Agreement (IP/D/18/Add.1, IP/D/22/Add.1), available at www.wto.org.

[9] See 2007 Special 301 Report, available at http://www.ustr.gov/assets/Document_Library/Reports_Publications/2007/2007_Special_301_Review/asset_upload_file230_11122.pdf.

> interest of the country by making use of the flexibilities in the TRIPS Agreement, in particular, the need to ensure rapid and timely response to public health needs by facilitating timely entry of generics and encouraging competition. The ethical issues of conducting repeated human trials when data on quality and efficacy already exists should also be kept in mind. At the same time, the need to adequately promote innovation and R&D in pharmaceuticals and agro-chemicals by utilizing the rich human capital and the infrastructure available in the country should also be considered. This will help build India's strength in these areas on a long term sustainable basis (para. 1.12) (Reddy and Sandhu, 2007).

Although the US has failed to make its case for data exclusivity in the WTO, it was successful in incorporating this TRIPS-plus standard in FTAs with at least one developed country (Australia) and many developing countries. These FTAs impose a number of obligations that dilute important flexibilities allowed by the TRIPS Agreement and increase the protection for agrochemical and, particularly, pharmaceutical products.[10] While with different formulations, all FTAs establish *sui generis* regimes for test data requiring exclusive rights for at least five years for pharmaceuticals and ten years for agrochemicals[11]. Table 21.1 summarizes the content of the data exclusivity provisions contained in some FTAs.

Public health and ethical implications

The public health implications of data protection for developing countries are significant. The financial resources and the long time required to replicate test data create a market barrier that is too high or insurmountable for generic companies, particularly small and medium-sized companies in developing countries. As noted by Weissman,

> Data exclusivity poses major barriers to generic entry. In general, if generic firms are not able to rely on originators' data, they will not enter the market until they are able to rely on the data. Re-doing the tests conducted by brand-name companies is not only wasteful, it is frequently too time-consuming and expensive for the relatively low-capitalized generic industry to manage. Thus

---

[10] The FTAs oblige the Parties, *inter alia*, to extend the term of patent protection to compensate for delays in patent examination and in the marketing approval of protected products, as well as to link drug registration to the status of patent protection.

[11] For instance, in a bilateral understanding between the USA and South Korea (exchange of letters of March 12, 2002), the latter accepted six years of data exclusivity for drugs and 16 years for agrochemicals. Guatemala adopted 15 years' data exclusivity for drugs in 2000. A turbulent legislative process subsequently led to the derogation of data exclusivity, its reinstatement for five years, and its derogation again in November 2004.

Table 21.1 Overview of data exclusivity provisions in some US FTAs

Exclusivity provisions are expanded to: Period	2000	April–June 2003			May–September 2004				Oct.–Dec. 2005	
Country	Vietnam	Laos	Chile	Singapore	Australia	Morocco	CAFTA	Bahrein	Oman	Peru
New chemical entities (NCEs)	(+)	+	+	+	+	+	+	+	+	+
New indications	(+)	(+)		(+)	+	+		+	+	
When relying on foreign registration				+	+	+	+	+	+	+
When relying on disclosed data				+		+		+	+	+
Exclusivity period can surpass patent term				+	+			+	+	+
'Local' definition of NCEs to be used					+	+	+	+	+	+
Imposing quick registration prohibited							+			+

Notes: + means the FTA imposes this particular requirement or condition; (+) means the language is ambiguous but could impose the requirement.
The dates refer to the periods within which the texts were finalized, not to the ratification or entry into force of the respective agreements.

Source: Timmerman (2007).

data exclusivity confers an effective marketing monopoly for the term of exclusivity provided. (Weissman, 2006: 114–15)

Several studies have confirmed that the costs of data exclusivity for developing countries will exceed any alleged benefits.[12] A study for Peru relating to 43 products that could have been subject to data exclusivity estimated, for instance, that the average price of such products would have been between 94.3 and 114.4 percent higher than they actually have been in the absence of such protection.[13]

The duplication of pre-clinical and/or clinical trials in order to develop anew the test data necessary for the approval of a drug also raises ethical concerns. Such tests may put human beings at risk to obtain results that are already known. They would be unethical under the principles of the Helsinki Declaration adopted by the World Medical Association on 'Ethical Principles for Medical Research Involving Human Subjects',[14] which is generally relied upon in ethical matters by health authorities and the medical profession.

Data exclusivity, as described above, does not prevent access to the data as information, but their use for generic competition, which is essential to drive prices down and improve access to drugs, especially by the poor. Developing countries should avoid the expansive interpretation of the

---

[12] See Organización Panamericana de la Salud – Colombia – Fundación IFARMA, 'Modelo prospectivo del impacto de la protección a la propiedad intelectual sobre el acceso a medicamentos en Colombia', 2004, www.col.ops-oms.org; INDECOPI, 'Serie estudios de investigación: Balance del conocimiento y propiedad intelectual en el comercio', Lima, May 2005, www.indecopi.gob.pe; INDECOPI, 'Serie estudios de investigación: Incidencia de los derechos de propiedad intelectual en el gasto de las familias en el marco del TLC', Lima, May 2005, www.indecopi.gob.pe; República del Perú, Ministerio de Salud; Gerardo Valladares et al., 'Evaluación de los potenciales efectos sobre el acceso a medicamentos del tratado de libre comercio que se negocia con los Estados Unidos de América', www.minsa.gob.pe. Fedesarrollo/Fundación Santa Fé de Bogotá; Emilio J. Archila et al., 'Estudio sobre la propiedad intelectual en el sector farmacéutico Colombiano', Bogotá. June 2005.

[13] See Apoyo Consultoria, 'Impacto de las negociaciones del TLC con Estados Unidos en materia de propiedad intelectual en los mercados de medicamentos y plaguicidas', Lima, April 2005.

[14] Adopted by the 18th WMA General Assembly, Helsinki, Finland, June 1964, and amended by the 29th WMA General Assembly, Tokyo, Japan, October 1975; 35th WMA General Assembly, Venice, Italy, October 1983; 41st WMA General Assembly, Hong Kong, September 1989; 48th WMA General Assembly, Somerset West, Republic of South Africa, October 1996; and the 52nd WMA General Assembly, Edinburgh, Scotland, October 2000.

TRIPS Agreement and the adoption of *sui generis* regimes that create costs without any tangible benefits.

In fact, most developing countries have followed the unfair competition approach with regard to pharmaceuticals,[15] despite the external pressures exerted for the recognition of a data exclusivity regime. In the case of Argentina, several legal actions were initiated by foreign companies arguing that test data is a constitutionally protected form of 'property'. Should these claims be accepted by courts, such data – which are in the public domain – would be subject to a *sine die* protection.

Data exclusivity in FTAs

Clearly, protection of data under unfair competition is the best option from the perspective of public health, as dishonest practises are forbidden, while the entry of legitimate generic competition is not unduly delayed. In the light of the US refusal to flexibilize its position in FTA negotiations, alternatives for the protection of test data have been explored. Weissman has elaborated on a 'cost-sharing approach' that would give generic firms an automatic right to use originators' data, while requiring them to pay a share of the documented costs of generating the data, proportionate to the size of the markets in which they are selling their product (Weissman, 2006).

An approach of this type may be applied in the context of some the trade agreements entered into between the European Free Trade Area (EFTA), which allow the parties to provide either exclusivity or payment of a compensation for the use of data by competitors.[16] The US, however, bluntly rejected a compensation-based approach in the FTA negotiations with the Andean countries.

Most US FTAs have included extreme forms of data exclusivity, including no reference to the undisclosed nature of the information (as required by the TRIPS Agreement) and a waiting period of five years during which no generic product could be approved in a Party without the consent of the originator of data, even if he had not requested approval of his product in that Party. The five-year term of protection, in addition, is to be counted from the date of the approval in the Party. In practise, this might lead to up to ten years of exclusivity.

Countries that have accepted these extreme modalities of data exclusivity

---

15 The same applies to agrochemicals in Argentina. In Brazil, Law 10.603 of 2002 introduced data exclusivity only with regard to veterinary and agrochemical products.

16 See, for example, the Free Trade Agreement between the EFTA States and the Republic of Lebanon, Annex V, Montreux: June 24, 2004.

have, however, some scope for to mitigating their negative effects on competition and public health (Correa, 2006). Strategies for damage control might include:[17]

- limiting the duration of data exclusivity, and/or specifying that data exclusivity cannot extend beyond the patent term. This limitation was, until recently, explicitly provided for under EU regulations and was implemented by for instance Greece, Portugal and Spain;[18]
- specifying that data exclusivity will only apply to narrowly defined new chemical entities and that it will not extend to new indications or different forms of existing medicines – as in Colombia and Egypt;
- providing protection only if the application for approval is filed within a term (for example, one year) from the date of the first approval in the world (as established in Chile);
- creating procedures for 'compulsory licensing' of the data;
- enabling the Ministry of Health or the Regulatory Authority to waive data exclusivity when it is deemed in the interest of public health or of specific patients (for example, Decree 2085 of Colombia).

A bipartisan agreement reached in June 2007 between the Republican administration and Democratic leaders in the US Congress made concrete suggestions to mitigate the effects of the data exclusivity provisions of the FTAs signed by the US government with Peru and Panama. It introduced the concept of 'concurrent' protection, that is, the term of data exclusivity protection is to be counted from the date of marketing approval in the United States and not in the Party where protection is sought. In addition, data exclusivity is mandated for a period that 'shall normally mean five years from the data on which the Party granted approval to the person that produced the data for approval to market its product, taking account of the nature of the data and the person's efforts and expenditures in producing them'. This means that the period of exclusivity could be less than five years, that a country may require disclosure of information about the cost of producing the data and establish the period of exclusivity on a case-by-case-basis.

The bipartisan agreement has already led to the revision of the US FTA with Peru. The revised text clarifies that data exclusivity only applies:

---

17 See Timmermans (2007).

18 Some US FTAs, however, explicitly rule out the possibility of establishing such a limitation.

- to 'new chemical entities', thereby clearly allowing the exclusion of new uses or different forms of known chemical entities;
- when it is necessary (and not merely permitted) to submit data to determine the safety and efficacy of a drug. As a result, if such information is not required, for instance, because the health authority relies on a foreign approval, data exclusivity does not arise;
- when the data are 'undisclosed'.

With regard to the extent of protection, an important change is the substitution of the words 'at least' five years by 'a reasonable period shall normally mean 5 years', thereby allowing Peru to eventually provide protection for less than five years. The revised text also:

- eliminates the words 'same and similar' which could have created a significant barrier to authorizing not only a therapeutic family of medicines but also biogeneric/biosimilar drugs;
- clarifies that data exclusivity will not limit the approval of generic drugs based on bioequivalence or bioavailability tests;
- states that data exclusivity protection may not be enforced where required to protect public health according to the Doha Declaration on the TRIPS Agreement and Public Health, TRIPS.[19]

Conclusions

From a public health perspective, it is important to ensure the availability of test data relating to the approval of pharmaceuticals and agrochemical products, so as to enhance competition and access to such products, especially by the poor. Data exclusivity regimes, which are not required by existing international norms may, in particular, significantly reduce access to medicines, even where no patent protection exists, and aggravate the serious public health problems existing in developing countries.

The US FTAs have shown how sensible the USTR has been to the incessant demands for higher IPRs protection of the US pharmaceutical industry. Ironically, the US Congress limited such demands in a way that the countries negotiating with the US were unable to do, given their weak bargaining position. The Congress's intervention creates the expectation that the USTR and the US industry will have to admit more moderate TRIPS-plus conditions in future negotiations on the matter.

Despite the improvements made from a public health perspective to

---

[19] The bipartisan agreement provided that the FTA 'side letter' on public health should be 'made a part of the *text* of the FTA (emphasis in the original).

the US FTAs with Peru and Panama, these agreements still contain conditions that may negatively affect access to medicines. In addition, the action by the US Congress does not benefit the countries that had previously negotiated FTAs, such as in the case of the Dominican Republic-Central American Free Trade Agreement (DR-CAFTA). This asymmetry introduces further unfairness into the IPRs regimes emerging from the US bilateral strategy for the expansion of IPRs protection in pharmaceuticals. It also increases the diversity in the scope of data protection across countries.

References

Arrivillaga L (2003), 'An International Standard of Protection for Test Data Submitted to Authorities to Obtain Marketing Authorization for Drugs', *Journal of World Intellectual Property*, 6(1), January.

Basheer, Shamnad (2006), 'Data Protection under Article 39.3 of TRIPs: A "Compensatory Liability" Model?', Oxford University.

Correa, Carlos (2002), 'Protection of Data Submitted for the Registration of Pharmaceuticals: Implementing the Standards of the TRIPS Agreement', South Centre/WHO, Geneva.

Correa, Carlos (2006), 'Implementación de la proteccion de datos de prueba de productos farmacéuticos y agroqu'micos en Dr-Cafta-Ley Modelo, ICTSD', Geneva, available at www.iprsonline.org/unctadictsd/docs/ICTSD%20CAFTA%20proteccion%20de%20datos_Carlos_C.America.pdf.

Grabowski, H (2002), 'Patents and New Product Development in the Pharnaceutical and Biotechnology Industries', paper presented at Duke University (mimeo).

IFPMA (2004), 'A Review of Existing Data Exclusivity Legislation in Selected Countries', 3rd revised version, January.

Kamperman Sanders, Anselm (1997), *Unfair Competition Law*, Clarendon Press, Oxford.

Lewis T., Reichman J. and So, A. (2006), 'Treating Clinical Trials as a Public Good: The Most Logical Reform', eScholarship Repository, University of California, http://repositories.cdlib.org/berkeley law econ/spring2006/11.

Menon, M. (2004) 'Introduction by Symposium Chair', in Julie M. Esanu and Paul F. Uhlir (eds), *Open Access and the Public Domain in Digital Data and Information for Science, Proceedings of an International Symposium*, The National Academies Press, Washington, DC, www.nap.edu.

Priapantja, Priapantja, (2000), 'Trade Secret: How does this Apply to Drug Registration Data?', paper presented at ASEAN Workshop on the TRIPS Agreement and its Impact on Pharmaceuticals, Department of Health and World Health Organization, 2–4 May.

Rai, A., and Eisenberg, R. (2003), 'Bayh-Dole Reform and the Progress of Biomedicine', *Law and Contemporary Problems*, 66, 289.

Reddy, S. and Sandhu, G. (2007), 'Report on Steps to be taken by Government of India in the context of Data Protection Provisions of Article 39.3 of TRIPS Agreement', Department of Chemicals & Petrochemicals, Ministry of Chemicals & Fertilizers, Government of India, New Delhi, 31 May.

Reichman, J. (2004), 'Pressures on the Public Domain: Discussion Framework', in Julie M. Esanu and Paul F. Uhlir (eds), *Open Access and the Public Domain in Digital Data and Information for Science: Proceedings of an International Symposium*, The National Academics Press, Washington DC, www.nap.Edu.

Reichman, J. and Uhlir, P. (2005), 'Global Trends to Restrict Access to Data from Government Funded Research', paper prepared for use at the Yale University Conference on Global Information Flows.

Sell, S. (2003), *Private Power, Public Law: The Globalization of Intellectual Property Rights*, Cambridge University Press, Cambridge.

Stiglitz, J. (1999), 'Knowledge as a Global Public Good', World Bank. See http://www.worldbank.org/knowledge/chiefecon/articles/undpk2/index.htm.

Timmermans, Karin (2007), 'Monopolizing Clinical Trial Data: Implications and Trends', PLoS Med 4(2): available at http://medicine.plosjournals.org/perlserv/?request=get-document&doi=10.1371/journal.pmed.0040002.

Weissman, Robert (2006), 'Public Health-friendly Options for Protecting Pharmaceutical Registration Data', *International Journal of Intellectual Property Management*, 1(1).

Index